THE ELEMENTS OF PHILOSOPHY

THE ELEMENTS OF PHILOSOPHY

READINGS FROM PAST AND PRESENT

EDITED BY

Tamar Szabó Gendler
YALE UNIVERSITY

Susanna Siegel
HARVARD UNIVERSITY

Steven M. Cahn
THE CITY UNIVERSITY OF NEW YORK
GRADUATE CENTER

New York Oxford
Oxford University Press
2008

Oxford University Press, Inc., publishes works that further Oxford University's objective of excellence in research, scholarship, and education.

Oxford New York
Auckland Cape Town Dar es Salaam Hong Kong Karachi
Kuala Lumpur Madrid Melbourne Mexico City Nairobi
New Delhi Shanghai Taipei Toronto

With offices in
Argentina Austria Brazil Chile Czech Republic France Greece
Guatemala Hungary Italy Japan Poland Portugal Singapore
South Korea Switzerland Thailand Turkey Ukraine Vietnam

Copyright © 2008 by Oxford University Press, Inc.

Published by Oxford University Press, Inc.
198 Madison Avenue, New York, New York 10016
http://www.oup.com

Oxford is a registered trademark of Oxford University Press

All rights reserved. No part of this publication may be reproduced, stored in a retrieval system, or transmitted, in any form or by any means, electronic, mechanical, photocopying, recording, or otherwise, without the prior permission of Oxford University Press.

Library of Congress Cataloging-in-Publication Data

The elements of philosophy: readings from past and present / edited by
Tamar Szabó Gendler, Susanna Siegel, Steven M. Cahn.
p. cm.
Includes bibliographical references and index.
ISBN 978-0-19-533542-2 (pbk.: alk. paper)
1. Philosophy. I. Gendler, Tamar. II.
Siegel, Susanna. III. Cahn, Steven M.
BD21. E44 2008
100—dc22
2007018902

Printed in the United States of America
on acid-free paper

CONTENTS

PREFACE

THE SELECTIONS that appear in this volume come from a wide range of sources. Some are 2,000 years old; others were published in the early 21st century. Some are translations of texts written in other languages; others were originally published in English. Some are brief articles or essays that have been reproduced in their entirety; others are selections from longer articles or books.

In keeping with the volume's mission as an introductory anthology, certain features of the text have been streamlined: punctuation and spelling have been modernized and Americanized, typographical errors have been corrected, certain footnotes have been eliminated and others renumbered, occasional section headings have been introduced, and so on. In many cases, these alterations are not specifically marked. Readers who want to make use of these texts in scholarly contexts will thus need to consult the original published versions, for which citation information is provided.

Philosophical investigation is a collaborative enterprise. Careful readers will notice that a number of our selections include notes by the author acknowledging the help of others in formulating the ideas in the paper. Unfortunately, we have not been able to include such notes for the selections that are taken from books. The reader should realize, however, that in nearly every case, the selection that appears benefited from the contributions of numerous philosophical interlocutors.

Although each selection in this volume was approved by all three of the editors, primary responsibility for selecting readings was distributed among them. The selections in the Introduction and Religion and Belief sections are due largely to Steven M. Cahn, who also wrote the Religion and Belief introduction. The selections in Moral Philosophy, Knowledge and Reality, Metaphysical Perplexities, and Life and Death are due largely to Tamar Szabó Gendler, who prepared their introductions with the assistance of Carolyn Caine (coauthor of the Morality introduction) and Roald Nashi (author of the Knowledge and Reality introduction). The selections in Political Philosophy are due to Susanna Siegel and Tamar Szabó Gendler; Susanna Siegel prepared the introduction to this section, with the assistance of Carolyn Caine. The selections in Philosophy of Mind and Philosophy of Language are due primarily to Susanna Siegel, who prepared the introductions to each.

The glossary, footnotes, article summaries, and biographies are the work of Tamar Szabó Gendler.

NOTE TO THE READER

Throughout the volume, notes have been added to alert the reader to the meanings of terms that may be unfamiliar or references that may seem obscure. In the case of common terms or concepts that appear in three or more selections, definitions can instead be found in the glossary at the end of the volume. Advice about additional philosophical reference works can also be found there.

NOTE TO THE INSTRUCTOR

It is unlikely that anyone would want to use all the selections that appear in this volume in a one-semester course. Likewise, individual instructors may wish to use the selections in a different order than that in which they have been presented here. As a result, an effort has been made to keep each subsection independent of each other subsection. With the exceptions noted in the introductions, no particular reading presupposes a familiarity with any of the other readings in the volume.

An Instructor's Manual is available to accompany this text. It includes article summaries, reading guides, essay questions, handouts, a test bank, sample syllabi, and suggestions for further readings. Please contact your Oxford sales representative at 1-800-280-0280, or visit the Oxford Higher Education Website at www.oup.com/us/highered for more information.

ACKNOWLEDGMENTS

In selecting readings for this volume, we have been helped by a large number of colleagues and friends. For suggestions concerning texts to include (or exclude), thanks are owed to Frank Amtzenius, Paul Bloom, Susanne Bobzien, Daniel Boucher, Matthew Boyle, Charles Brittain, Alex Byrne, David Chalmers, Michael Della Rocca, Emily Esch, Verity Harte, Matthew Haug, Shelly Kagan, Heidi Lockwood, Ruth Barcan Marcus, Roald Nashi, Bernhard Nickel, Jill North, Parimal Patil, Jim Pryor, Ted Sider, Peter Simpson, Matthew Smith, Jason Stanley, Daniel Stoljar, Zoltán Gendler Szabó, and Brian Weatherson. We regret that we did not have space to include all their excellent suggestions. We also apologize to those whose names we have inadvertently omitted from this list.

We are grateful to five referees for Oxford University Press who made outstanding suggestions concerning an earlier draft of this anthology: Casey Perrin, William Ramsey, Robert Schwartz, Douglas Stalker, and one reviewer who wished to remain anonymous. Their suggestions led to a significant reshaping of the volume's content and conception.

We are fortunate that there are already a number of excellent philosophy collections available—some general, some more specific. Our work on this volume was helped by the chance to consider these exemplars. Among those whose anthologies we consulted in thinking about the content and structure of this volume are Linda Martín Alcoff, Sven Bernecker, Michael Bratman, David Chalmers, Tim Crane, Stephen Darwall, Katalin Farkas, Joel Feinberg, Delia Graff, John Heil, Robin Jeshion, Daniel Kolak, Jaegwon Kim, L. A. Paul, Derk Pereboom, John Perry, Louis Pojman, Jesse Prinz, Peter Markie, Raymond Martin, Stuart Rachels, Russ Shafer-Landau, David Sosa, Ernest Sosa, and Cynthia Stark.

We are also grateful to the staff at Oxford University Press, including Yelena Bromberg, Sarah Calabi, Barbara Mathieu, Robert Miller, and Emily Voigt, for their assistance and encouragement throughout this project. Thanks also to the philosophy support staff at Harvard and Yale Universities for their patience as the manuscript was prepared.

Perhaps the most exciting thing about this volume is the contribution made to it by a remarkable group of undergraduates, most from Cornell University. The team proposed readings, proofread selections, suggested terms for inclusion in the glossary, and helped in numerous other ways. This extraordinarily gifted and generous group of students includes Gavin Arnall, Carolyn Caine, Peter Goldstein, Enoch Lambert, Jed Lewinsohn, Lea Lowenfeld, Wesley Mattingly, Andrew Mitchell, Joshua Mund, Nicholas Noyes, Chris Post, Terry Tang, Adam Walker, and John Zirinsky.

A superb set of instructors' materials was prepared by Jed Lewinsohn and Allyson Mount. Our thanks to both of them.

No one deserves more credit for this volume than our superb editorial assistant Carolyn Caine, whose unique combination of creativity, intelligence, flexibility, and commitment is evident on nearly every page of this book. Her support throughout the volume's preparation has so surpassed our expectations that it is difficult to know how to thank her for her contributions to it.

ABOUT THE EDITORS

TAMAR SZABÓ GENDLER (Ph.D., Harvard University) is professor of philosophy and chair of the cognitive science program at Yale University. She taught previously at Cornell and Syracuse Universities. She is the author of *Thought Experiments: On the Powers and Limits of Imaginary Cases* and coeditor (with John Hawthorne) of *Perceptual Experience* and *Conceivability and Possibility* and of the journal *Oxford Studies in Epistemology.* She is also the epistemology editor of *Philosophy Compass.* Her articles have appeared in a wide range of journals, including the *Journal of Philosophy, Mind, Philosophical Quarterly,* and the *British Journal for the Philosophy of Science,* as well as in a number of edited volumes.

SUSANNA SIEGEL (Ph.D., Cornell University) is professor of philosophy at Harvard University. She is the author of numerous articles in the philosophy of mind and the philosophy of language and regularly teaches a course on social protest and political philosophy. Her articles have appeared in the *Philosophical Review, Philosophy and Phenomenological Research, Noûs, Australasian Journal of Philosophy, Philosophers' Imprint,* and other journals, as well as in the *Stanford Encyclopedia of Philosophy* and the *Oxford Companion to Consciousness.*

STEVEN M. CAHN (Ph.D., Columbia University) is professor of philosophy at The City University of New York Graduate Center. He served as the school's provost and vice president for academic affairs and then as acting president. He taught at Dartmouth College, Vassar College, the University of Rochester, New York University, and the University of Vermont, where he headed the Department of Philosophy. He has edited more than thirty books and authored eight, including *Fate, Logic, and Time; Saints and Scamps: Ethics in Academia;* and *God, Reason, and Religion.*

INTRODUCTION

What Is Philosophy?

SIMON BLACKBURN

Simon Blackburn (1944–) is a British philosopher who teaches at Cambridge University. Among professional philosophers, he is best known for his work in ethics and metaethics. He is also the author of a number of books directed at the general public, including *Truth* (2005), *Lust* (2004), *Being Good* (2001), and *Think* (1999), from which the excerpt presented here is drawn.

In the following selection, Blackburn offers some general remarks about what philosophy is and why many have found it so interesting.

THIS BOOK is for people who want to think about the big themes: knowledge, reason, truth, mind, freedom, destiny, identity, God, goodness, justice. These are not the hidden preserve of specialists. They are things that men and women wonder about naturally, for they structure the ways we think about the world and our place in it. . . .

The word "philosophy" carries unfortunate connotations: impractical, unworldly, weird. I suspect that all philosophers and philosophy students share that moment of silent embarrassment when someone innocently asks us what we do. I would prefer to introduce myself as doing conceptual engineering. For just as the engineer studies the structure of material things, so the philosopher studies the structure of thought. Understanding the structure involves seeing how parts function and how they interconnect. It means knowing what would happen for better or worse if changes were made. This is what we aim at when we investigate the structures that shape our view of the world. Our concepts or ideas form the mental housing in which we live. We may end up proud of the structures we have built. Or we may believe that they need dismantling and starting afresh. But first, we have to know what they are. . . .

WHAT ARE WE TO THINK ABOUT?

Here are some questions any of us might ask about ourselves: What am I? What is consciousness? Could I survive my bodily death? Can I be sure that other people's experiences and sensations are like mine? If I can't share the experience of others, can I communicate with them? Do we always act out of self-interest? Might I be a kind of puppet, programmed to do the things that I believe I do out of my own free will?

Here are some questions about the world: Why is there something and not nothing? What is the difference between past and future? Why does causation run always from past to future, or does it make sense to think the future might influence the past? Why

From *Think*, copyright © 1999 by Simon Blackburn, pp. 1–12. Reprinted by permission of Oxford University Press.

does nature keep on in a regular way? Does the world presuppose a Creator? And if so, can we understand why he (or she or they) created it?

Finally, here are some questions about ourselves *and* the world: How can we be sure that the world is really like we take it to be? What is knowledge, and how much do we have? What makes a field of inquiry a science? (Is psychoanalysis a science? Is economics?) How do we know about abstract objects, like numbers? How do we know about values and duties? How are we to tell whether our opinions are objective, or just subjective?

The queer thing about these questions is that not only are they baffling at first sight, but they also defy simple processes of solution. If someone asks me when it is high tide, I know how to set about getting an answer. There are authoritative tide tables I can consult. I may know roughly how they are produced. And if all else fails, I could go and measure the rise and fall of the sea myself. A question like this is a matter of experience: an *empirical* question. It can be settled by means of agreed procedures, involving looking and seeing, making measurements, or applying rules that have been tested against experience and found to work. The questions of the last paragraphs are not like this. They seem to require more reflection. We don't immediately know where to look. Perhaps we feel we don't quite know what we mean when we ask them, or what would count as getting a solution. What would show me, for instance, whether I am not after all a puppet, programmed to do the things I believe I do freely? Should we ask scientists who specialize in the brain? But how would they know what to look for? How would they know when they had found it? Imagine the headline: "Neuroscientists discover human beings not puppets." How?

So what gives rise to such baffling questions?

In a word, self-reflection. Human beings are relentlessly capable of reflecting on themselves. We might do something out of habit, but then we can begin to reflect on the habit. We can habitually think things, and then reflect on what we are thinking. We can ask ourselves (or sometimes we get asked by other people) whether we know what we are talking about. To answer that we need to reflect on our own positions, our own understanding of what we are saying, our own sources of authority. We might start to wonder whether we know what we mean. We might wonder whether what we say is "objectively" true, or merely the outcome of our own perspective, or our own "take" on a situation. Thinking about this we confront categories like knowledge, objectivity, truth, and we may want to think about them. At that point we are *reflecting* on concepts and procedures and beliefs that we normally just *use*. We are looking at the scaffolding of our thought, and doing conceptual engineering.

This point of reflection might arise in the course of quite normal discussion. A historian, for example, is more or less bound at some point to ask what is meant by "objectivity" or "evidence," or even "truth," in history. A cosmologist has to pause from solving equations with the letter t in them, and ask what is meant, for instance, by the flow of time or the direction of time or the beginning of time. But at that point, whether they recognize it or not, they become philosophers. And they are beginning to do something that can be done well or badly. The point is to do it well.

How is philosophy learned? A better question is: how can thinking skills be acquired? The thinking in question involves attending to basic structures of thought. This can be done well or badly, intelligently or ineptly. But doing it well is not primarily a matter of acquiring a body of knowledge. It is more like playing the piano well. It is a "knowing how" as much as a "knowing that." The most famous philosophical character of the classical world, the Socrates of Plato's dialogues, did not pride himself on how much he knew. On the contrary, he prided himself on being the only one who knew how little he knew (reflection, again). What he was good at—supposedly, for estimates of his success differ—was exposing the weaknesses of other people's claims to know. To process thoughts well is a matter of being able to avoid confusion, detect ambiguities, keep things in mind one at a time, make reliable arguments, become aware of alternatives and so on.

To sum up: our ideas and concepts can be compared with the lenses through which we see the world. In philosophy the lens is itself the topic of study. Success will be a matter not of how much you know at the end, but of what you can do when the going gets tough: when the seas of argument rise, and confusion breaks out. Success will mean taking seriously the implications of ideas.

WHAT IS THE POINT?

It is all very well saying that, but why bother? What's the point? Reflection doesn't get the world's business done. It doesn't bake bread or fly aeroplanes. Why not just toss the reflective questions aside, and get on with other things? I shall sketch three kinds of answer: high ground, middle ground, and low ground.

The high ground questions the question—a typical philosophical strategy, because it involves going up one level of reflection. What do we mean when we ask what the point is? Reflection bakes no bread, but then neither does architecture, music, art, history, or literature. It is just that we want to understand ourselves. We want this for its own sake, just as a pure scientist or pure mathematician may want to understand the beginning of the universe, or the theory of sets, for its own sake, or just as a musician might want to solve some problem in harmony or counterpoint just for its own sake. There is no eye on any practical applications. A lot of life is indeed a matter of raising more hogs, to buy more land, so we can raise more hogs, so that we can buy more land. . . . The time we take out, whether it is to do mathematics or music, or to read Plato or Jane Austen, is time to be cherished. It is the time in which we cosset our mental health. And our mental health is just good in itself, like our physical health. Furthermore there is after all a payoff in terms of pleasure. When our physical health is good, we take pleasure in physical exercise, and when our mental health is good, we take pleasure in mental exercise.

This is a very pure-minded reply. The problem with it is not that it is wrong. It is just that it is only likely to appeal to people who are half-convinced already—people who didn't ask the original question in a very aggressive tone of voice.

So here is a middle-ground reply. Reflection matters because it is *continuous* with practice. How you think about what you are doing affects how you do it, or whether you do it at all. It may direct your research, or your attitude to people who do things differently, or indeed your whole life. To take a simple example, if your reflections lead you to believe in a life after death, you may be prepared to face persecutions that you would not face if you became convinced—as many philosophers are—that the notion makes no sense. Fatalism, or the belief that the future is fixed whatever we do, is a purely philosophical belief, but is one that can paralyse action. Putting it more politically, it can also express an acquiescence with the low status accorded to some segments of society, and this may be a pay-off for people of higher status who encourage it.

Let us consider some examples more prevalent in the West. Many people reflecting on human nature think that we are at bottom entirely selfish. We only look out for our own advantage, never really caring about anyone else. Apparent concern disguises hope of future benefit. The leading paradigm in the social sciences is *homo economicus*—economic man. Economic man looks after himself, in competitive struggle with others. Now, if people come to think that we are all, always, like this, their relations with each other become different. They become less trusting, less cooperative, more suspicious. This changes the way they interact, and they will incur various costs. They will find it harder, and in some circumstances impossible, to get cooperative ventures going: they may get stuck in what the philosopher Thomas Hobbes (1588–1679) memorably called "the war of all against all." In the market-place, because they are always looking out to be cheated, they will incur heavy transaction costs. If my attitude is that "a verbal contract is not worth the paper it is written on," I will have to pay lawyers to design contracts with penalties, and if I will not trust the lawyers to do anything except just enough to pocket their fees, I will have to get the contracts checked by other lawyers, and so on. But all this may be based on a philosophical mistake—looking at human motivation through the wrong set of categories, and hence misunderstanding its nature. Maybe people can care for each other, or at least care for doing their bit or keeping their promises. Maybe if a more optimistic self-image is on the table, people can come to live up to it. Their lives then become better. So this bit of thinking, getting clear about the right categories with which to understand human motivation, is an important *practical* task. It is not confined to the study, but bursts out of it.

Here is a very different example. The Polish astronomer Nicholas Copernicus (1473–1543) reflected on how we *know* about motion. He realized that how we perceive motion is *perspectival:* that is, whether we see things as moving is the result of how we ourselves are placed and in particular whether we ourselves are moving. (We have mostly been subject to the illusion in trains or airports, where the next-door train or aeroplane seems to move off, and then we realize with a jolt that it is we who are moving. But there were fewer everyday examples in the time of Copernicus.) So the apparent motions of the stars and planets might arise because they are not moving as they appear to do, but we observers move. And this is how it turned out to be. Here reflection on the nature of knowledge—what philosophers call an *epistemological* inquiry, from the Greek *episteme*, meaning knowledge—generated the first spectacular leap of modern science. Einstein's reflection on how we know whether two events are simultaneous had the same structure. He realized that the results of our measurements would depend upon the way we are travelling compared to the events we are clocking. This led to the Special Theory of Relativity (and Einstein himself acknowledged the importance of preceding philosophers in sensitizing him to the epistemological complexities of such a measurement).

For a final example, we can consider a philosophical problem many people get into when they think about mind and body. Many people envisage a strict separation between mind, as one thing, and body, as a different thing. When this seems to be just good common sense, it can begin to infect practice in quite insidious ways. For instance, it begins to be difficult to see how these two different things interact. Doctors might then find it almost *inevitable* that treatments of physical conditions that address mental or psychological causes will fail. They might find it next to impossible to see how messing with someone's mind could possibly cause changes in the complex physical system that is their body. After all, good science tells us that it takes physical and chemical causes to have physical and chemical effects. So we might get an a priori, armchair certainty that one kind of treatment (say, drugs and electric shocks) has to be "right" and others (such as treating patients humanely, counselling, analysis) are "wrong": unscientific, unsound, bound to fail. But this certainty is premised not on science but on a false *philosophy*. A better philosophical conception of the relation between mind and body changes it. A better conception should enable us to see how there is nothing *surprising* in the fact of mind-body interaction. It is the most commonplace fact, for instance, that thinking of some things (mental) can cause people to blush (physical). Thinking of a future danger can cause all kinds of bodily changes: hearts pound, fists clench, guts constrict. By extrapolation there should be nothing difficult to comprehend about a mental state such as cheerful optimism affecting a physical state like the disappearance of a rash or even the remission of a cancer. It becomes a purely *empirical* fact whether such things happen. The armchair certainty that they could not happen is itself revealed as dependent on bad understanding of the structures of thought, or in other words bad philosophy, and is in that sense unscientific. And this realization can change medical attitudes and practice for the better.

So the middle-ground answer reminds us that reflection is continuous with practice, and our practice can go worse or better according to the value of our reflections. A system of thought is something we live in, just as much as a house, and if our intellectual house is cramped and confined, we need to know what better structures are possible.

The low-ground answer merely polishes this point up a bit, not in connection with nice clean subjects like economics or physics, but down in the basement where human life is a little less polite. One of the series of satires etched by the Spanish painter Goya is entitled "The Sleep of Reason Produces Monsters." Goya believed that many of the follies of mankind resulted from the "sleep of reason." There are always people telling us what we want, how they will provide it, and what we should believe. Convictions are infectious, and people can make others convinced of almost anything. We are typically ready to believe that *our* ways, *our* beliefs, *our* religion, *our* politics are better than theirs, or that *our* God-given rights trump theirs or that *our* interests require defensive or preemptive strikes against them. In the end, it is ideas for which people kill each other. It is because of ideas about what the others are like, or who we are, or what our interests or rights require, that we go to war, or oppress others with a good conscience, or even sometimes acquiesce in our own oppression by others. When these beliefs involve the sleep of reason, critical awakening is the antidote. Reflection enables us to step back, to see our perspective on a situation as perhaps distorted or blind, at the very least to see if there is argument for preferring our ways, or whether it is just subjective. Doing this properly is doing one more piece of conceptual engineering.

Since there is no telling in advance where it may lead, reflection can be seen as dangerous. There are always thoughts that stand opposed to it. Many people are discomfited, or even outraged, by philosophical questions. Some are fearful that their ideas may not stand up as well as they would like if they start to think about them. Others may want to stand upon the "politics of identity," or in other words the kind of identification with a particular tradition, or group, or national or ethnic identity that invites them to turn their back on outsiders who question the ways of the group. They will shrug off criticism: their values are "incommensurable" with the values of outsiders. They are to be understood only by brothers and sisters within the circle. People like to retreat to within a thick, comfortable, traditional set of folkways, and not to worry too much about their structure, or their origins, or even the criticisms that they may deserve. Reflection opens the avenue to criticism, and the folkways may not like criticism. In this way, ideologies become closed circles, primed to feel outraged by the questioning mind.

For the last two thousand years the philosophical tradition has been the enemy of this kind of cosy complacency. It has insisted that the unexamined life is not worth living. It has insisted on the power of rational reflection to winnow out bad elements in our practices, and to replace them with better ones. It has identified critical self-reflection with freedom, the idea being that only when we can see ourselves properly can we obtain control over the direction in which we would wish to move. It is only when we can see our situation steadily and see it whole that we can start to think what to do about it.

The Elements of Logic

SIMON BLACKBURN

Simon Blackburn (1944–) is a British philosopher who teaches at Cambridge University. Among professional philosophers, he is best known for his work in ethics and metaethics. He is also the author of a number of books directed at the general public, including *Truth* (2005), *Lust* (2004), *Being Good* (2001), and *Think* (1999), from which the excerpt presented here is drawn.

In the following selection, Blackburn explains some of the basic features of philosophical logic.

A LITTLE LOGIC

The working parts of an argument are, first, its *premises*. These are the starting point, or what is accepted or assumed, so far as the argument is concerned. An argument can have one premise, or several. From the premises an argument derives a *conclusion*. If we are reflecting on the argument, perhaps because we are reluctant to accept the conclusion, we have two options. First, we might reject one or more of the premises. But second, we might reject the way the conclusion is drawn from the premises. The first reaction is that one of the premises is *untrue*. The second is that the reasoning is *invalid*. Of course,

From *Think*, copyright © 1999 by Simon Blackburn, pp. 179–191. Reprinted by permission of Oxford University Press.

an argument may be subject to both criticisms: its premises are untrue, and the reasoning from them is invalid. But the two criticisms are distinct (and the two words, untrue and invalid, are well kept for the distinction).

In everyday life, arguments are criticized on other grounds again. The premises may not be very sensible. It is silly to make an intricate argument from the premise that I will win next week's lottery, if it hasn't a dog's chance of happening. It is often inappropriate to help ourselves to premises that are themselves controversial. It is tactless and tasteless in some circumstances to argue some things. But "logical" is not a synonym for "sensible." Logic is interested in whether arguments are valid, not in whether it is sensible to put them forward. Conversely, many people called "illogical" may actually be propounding valid arguments, but be dotty in other ways.

Logic has only one concern. It is concerned whether there is *no way* that the premises could be true without the conclusion being true.

It was Aristotle (384–322 BCE) who first tried to give a systematic taxonomy of valid and invalid arguments. Aristotle realized that any kind of theory would need to classify arguments by the patterns of reasoning they exhibit, or what is called their *form*. One of the most famous forms of argument, for instance, rejoicing in the title "modus ponendo ponens," or modus ponens for short, just goes:

> p;
> If p then q;
> So, q.

Here p and q stand for any piece of information, or proposition, that you like. The form of the argument would remain the same whether you were talking of cows or philosophers. Logic then studies forms of information, not particular examples of it. Particular arguments are instances of the forms, but the logician is interested in the form or structure, just as a mathematician is interested in numerical forms and structure, but not interested in whether you are counting bananas or profits.

We want our reasonings to be valid. We said what this means: we want there to be *no way* that our conclusion could be false, if our premises are true. So we need to study whether there is "any way" that one set of things, the premises, can be true without another thing, the conclusion, also being true. To investigate this we need to produce a science of the *ways* things can be true. For some very simple ways of building up information, we can do this.

TRUTH-TABLES

The classical assumptions are first that every proposition ($p, q\ldots$) has just one of two *truth*-values. It must be either true or false, and it cannot be both. ("But suppose I don't grant that?" Patience.) The second assumption is that the terms the logic is dealing with—centrally, "and," "not," "or," and "If. . . then . . ."—can be characterized in terms of what they do to truth-values. ("But suppose I don't grant that?" Patience, again.)

Thus, consider "not-p." Not-p, which is often written $\neg p$, is the denial or negation of p: it is what you say when you disagree with p. Whatever it is talking about, p, according to our first assumption, is either true (T), or false (F). It is not both. What does "not" do? It simply reverses truth-value. If p is true, then $\neg p$ is false. If p is false, then $\neg p$ is true. That is what "not" does. We can summarize the result as a *truth-table:*

p	$\neg p$
T	F
F	T

The table gives the result, in terms of truth or falsity, for each assignment of truth-value to the components (such an assignment is called an *interpretation*). A similar table can be written for "and," only here there are more combinations to consider. We suppose that "and" conjoins two propositions, each of which can be true or false. So there are four situations or interpretations to consider:

p	q	$p \& q$
T	T	T
T	F	F
F	T	F
F	F	F

We are here given the truth-value for the overall combination, the conjunction, as a function of the combination of truth-values of the components: the four different interpretations of the formula.

The fact that we can give these tables is summed up by saying that conjunction, and negation, are *truth-functional*, or that they are truth-functional operators. Elementary propositional logic studies the truth-functions. Besides "not" and "and," they include "or" (p or q, regarded as true except when both p and q are false); and a version of "If p then q," regarded as true except in the case where p is true yet q false. If we write this latter as "$p \rightarrow q$," its truth-table is:

p	q	$p \rightarrow q$
T	T	T
T	F	F
F	T	T
F	F	T

These are also called Boolean operators. People familiar with databases and spreadsheets will know about Boolean searches, which implement exactly the same idea. A search for widgets over five years old held in the warehouse in York returns a hit when it finds a widget meeting *both* conditions. A search for customers *not* paid up on 1 December returns just the reverse hits from a search for customers paid up on 1 December. A search for customers who *either* bought a washing machine *or* a lawnmower turns up those who bought one and those who bought the other.

We can now see a rationale for some rules of inference. Consider the rule that from "p & q" we can derive p (or equally q). You cannot thereby get from truth to falsity, because the only interpretation (the top line) that has "p & q" true also has each ingredient true. So this is a good rule. We can also see why modus ponendo ponens, introduced above, is a good rule. It has two premises, "p," and "If p then q." Can we find an interpretation (a "way") in which both these are true without q being true? No. Because given that p is true, the only interpretation of $p \rightarrow q$ that allows it to be true also displays q as true.

There are some interesting animals in this jungle. One is that of a contradiction. Consider this formula:

$$p \mathbin{\&} \neg p.$$

This expresses a contradiction—the ultimate no-no. And we now have a precise sense in which it is a no-no. For it is easy to show from the two tables we have, that *whatever* the truth-value of p, the truth-value of this formula comes out as F. There is *no way* it could be true. Because when one of the conjuncts is true the other is false: there is always a false element. And the truth-table for conjunction shows that in that case the overall formula is false.

Now suppose we complicate things by negating it:

$$\neg(p \mathbin{\&} \neg p).$$

The brackets here show that the outside $\neg$ negates the whole thing. They act like the brackets in $3 \times (4 + 2)$, which show that the result is to be 18, rather than what we would get if we had $(3 \times 4) + 2$, which is 14. This bracketing is extremely important in logic, as it is in arithmetic: many fallacies in formal and informal reasoning can be avoided by knowing where the brackets fall. This is called knowing the *scope* of operation of the negations and conjunctions and the rest. In this example the outside negation has the whole of the rest of the formula to operate upon. A quite different reading would be given by $\neg p \mathbin{\&} \neg p$, which simply conjoins $\neg p$ to itself, and, incidentally, is false in the case in which p is true (saying something false twice does not make it any better). One of the terrific virtues of formal logic is that it sensitizes people to scope *ambiguities*, which arise when it is not clear where the brackets lie, or in other words what is governing what. Without knowing this, you do not know *in what ways* your premises and your conclusions might be true, and hence whether there is *any way* your premises might be true without your conclusion being so.

This new formula, $\neg(p \mathbin{\&} \neg p)$, reverses the truth-value of the old contradiction. So it is true, whatever the truth-values of its components. It is called a *tautology*. This is an important notion. In propositional logic if we have premises blah-blah-blah and conclusion yadda-yadda, we want it to be true that "If blah-blah-blah then yadda-yadda" is a tautology. There is no interpretation (no way of assigning truth-values) that is to make the premises true, while the conclusion is false. When this is so, the argument is valid in exactly the sense we have been talking about.

One way of discovering whether an argument is valid is common enough to deserve a name. You can find whether "If blah-blah-blah then yadda-yadda" is valid by adding "not yadda-yadda" to blah-blah-blah" and seeing if you can get out a contradiction. If you can, the argument was valid. This corresponds directly to there being no way that the premises could be true and the conclusion false. There is no interpretation or no model for that state of affairs. Contradiction bars the way. This is called "assuming towards a contradiction" or "assuming towards a reductio," from the Latin name for this kind of procedure: the *reductio ad absurdum*, or reduction to absurdity. Anselm's ontological argument . . . had that form [see Section I].

In mathematics we can have not only 2 + 2, but also 3 × (2 + 2) and ((2 + 3) × (2 + 2)) − 5, and so on forever, and so it is with information. In so far as complex bits of information are produced by applying and reapplying truth-functional combinations, we can keep perfect control of the interpretations under which we have truth and falsity.

NOTHING TO BE AFRAID OF

So logic studies the structure of information. Its aim is to exhibit that structure, and thereby also exhibit what follows from what: what is sufficient to prove *p* and what follows from *p*, for *p* of any complexity. The connection between structure and proof is just this: the structure shows us if there is *no way* that the premises can be true without the conclusion being true. Because to understand the structure of information is to understand the ways it can be true.

So far, we have looked at complexity of information arising because propositions are negated or conjoined, or connected by implication. But we have not broken inside propositions. As far as the analysis so far goes, "Some persons are philosophers" and "All persons are philosophers" will come out looking alike. Each is just an example of a proposition, *p*. But we cannot get inside the proposition, and understand how these mean different things.

The breakthrough that cracked this problem created modern logic. It was made by the German mathematician and logician Gottlob Frege (1848–1925), in his seminal *Begriffsschrift* ("concept writing") of 1879. Consider this argument: every inquiry stops somewhere, so there is somewhere every inquiry stops. . . . Something must be wrong, for a parallel would be: everyone has a mother, so there is someone who is everyone's mother. Or, everyone ties his own laces, so someone ties everyone's laces. Until Frege, people could see that there was something wrong, but, lacking any understanding of how this kind of information is built, they could not say what it was.

The key to understanding Frege's achievement is to think in terms of two quite different kinds of information. The first is very familiar. It corresponds to attaching a term to a name or other expression that refers to a particular person or thing: Bill is rich, Tony grins, this is an orange. Here we have a subject term (the names "Bill" and "Tony," and the demonstrative "this"), and things are said of what they pick out: "is rich," "grins," or "is an orange." These terms stand for conditions that things might meet. They are called "predicates": the rich things satisfy the predicate "is rich," and other things do not. This is the basic subject–predicate form of information.

Now we can do something surprising. Suppose we delete the term that stands for the subject. We are left with only a gappy sentence, or predicate: "is rich," and so on. We can better signal the gap by the expression called a variable, usually written *x, y, z* . . ., as in algebra. So we have "*x* is rich." This is no longer a sentence carrying a piece of information, because nobody is being said to be rich. It is a sentence with a hole in it: a predicate, or an open sentence, in logicians' jargon.

Now, here comes the magic. Suppose I ask you to take an open sentence into a particular domain, such as a classroom, or New York City, and come back giving me some information. You *could* just reconstruct a piece of information like the one we started with, naming some particular individual, and saying that he or she is rich. But you don't have to do this. You can do a fundamentally different kind of thing. You can come back and tell me about the *quantity* of times the predicate is satisfied. And you can tell me this without telling me who satisfies it. It is as if you use the open sentence by pointing the "x" in it at all the different people in the domain in turn, and note how often you get a hit. Suppose we symbolize the predicate by ϕ (the Greek letter "phi"). Then you ask: "Is *this* ϕ, is *this* ϕ?" of each of the members of the domain in succession. Then you can tell me what happened.

Perhaps the simplest kind of thing you could tell me is that at least once, somewhere, you got a hit. This is equivalent to "Something is ϕ." Or you might tell me that somewhere you got a miss: "Something is not-ϕ." Contrast this last with getting a hit nowhere: "Nothing is ϕ." Or it might be that everywhere you got a hit: "Everything is ϕ."

"Something is ϕ" is given by a new piece of symbolism: the *existential quantifier*. It is written as $(\exists x)\phi x$ (the fact that the variable comes after the predicate in "ϕx" whereas in English predicates usually finish sentences and things like names start them is irrelevant). If you never get a hit, you can enter $\neg(\exists x)\phi x$: nothing is ϕ. If, somewhere, you get a result that is not a hit, you have the very different $(\exists x)\neg(\phi x)$. If you nowhere get a result other than a hit, you have $\neg(\exists x)\neg\phi x$. This says that nowhere is there anything that is not ϕ. Or, in other words, as far as this domain goes, everything is ϕ. This last kind of information is sufficiently important to have its own symbol, the *universal quantifier*, written as $(\forall x)\phi x$: "Everything is ϕ."

Leibniz thought that if we had a sufficiently logical notation, dispute and confusion would cease, and men would sit together and resolve their disputes by calculation. The invention of the quantifier did not bring about this utopia, but it does an astonishing amount towards it. Its full power is exhibited when we get multiple quantifications. This is information built with more than one quantifier in play. When we have more than one quantifier, we use different variables ($x, y, z \ldots$) to indicate the different gaps to which they correspond. To illustrate the idea, we can see how easily it dissects the invalid argument: everybody has a mother, so someone is everyone's mother. If we write "x is the mother of y" as "xMy" we symbolize the first by $(\forall y)(\exists x)\,x\mathrm{M}y$. The second is $(\exists x)(\forall y)\,x\mathrm{M}y$. How are these different?

Start with a sentence claiming motherhood between two different people: Beth is the mother of Albert. Knock out reference to Beth, and we have the open sentence xMa (where "a" abbreviates Albert). We know that this predicate is satisfied (it is satisfied by Beth), so we know $(\exists x)\,x\mathrm{Ma}$. Somebody is Albert's mother. Now knock out reference to Albert: $(\exists x)\,x\mathrm{M}y$. We have a gappy, or open, sentence again with y marking the gap. It corresponds to the predicate "having someone as a mother." We can take this into the domain and point the variable y at each in turn: does *this* person have a mother, does *this*. . .? If we get the answer "yes" on each occasion (which we do), we can universally quantify $(\forall y)(\exists x)\,x\mathrm{M}y$. Everyone has a mother.

Now look at the second formula. To get this, we similarly start with Beth (b) being the mother of Albert. But now we knock out reference to Albert first: bMy. We take this round the domain. *If* we could (as in the real world we cannot) write $(\forall y)$ bMy, this would be because Beth is the mother of everyone (whoever you point the variable y at, it turns out that Beth is their mother!). What has just been supposed of Beth, might be supposed true of someone (if not Beth): in that case you can knock out reference to Beth, take the predicate "being mother of everyone," or in other words $(\forall y)\,x\mathrm{M}y$, round the domain, and find eventually someone giving the answer yes. In that case you would be able to write $(\exists x)(\forall y)\,x\mathrm{M}y$. But the point to notice is that this is an *entirely* different procedure. It gives an entirely different kind of information (false of the domain of human beings). And the quantificational structure shows the difference on its face, because the stringing out of the quantifiers shows how the information is built.

In the real world, nobody is the mother of everybody. Before we understood quantification, that might have sounded weird, as if the human race sprung out of Nothing. This might have seemed a creepy metaphysical thesis. But now it is tamed. It just means that $\neg(\exists x)(\forall y)\,x\mathrm{M}y$. And this is a simple truth. At least, unless you use the relation "mother" to include more remote kinds of ancestry, in which case you might want to claim that there is someone, biological Eve, the first female *homo sapiens*, who is the mother of everyone. But I would regard that as an illegitimate or metaphorical usage. My grandmother is not literally my mother.

We can give more precise information about the quantity of times some condition is met in a domain. We might say that there is *exactly* one thing satisfying the condition. This means that any time you get a hit, if you go on pointing the variable at the rest of the things in the domain, whenever you get a hit it turns out to be the same one. There are no two distinct hits. This is the core of Russell's* famous theory of definite descriptions. For it to be true that the unique king of France has a beard, there would need to be someone who rules France and no other person who rules France, and it should be true of whoever does rule France that he has a beard. Otherwise, the claim is false.

Quantificational structure is just one thing, but a very important thing to be aware of. Ordinary language is good at generating ambiguities that it easily resolves. "All the nice girls love a sailor" said the song. There is some lucky sailor they all love? They all have one, but perhaps a different sailor that they love? Take any sailor, then all the nice girls love him (or her)? Very different things, true in very different circumstances.

* Bertrand Russell (1872–1970) was an important British philosopher, mathematician, and political activist.

PART I
RELIGION AND BELIEF

INTRODUCTION

Philosophy of religion is an ancient branch of philosophical inquiry that attempts to clarify religious beliefs and subject them to careful scrutiny. Some thinkers have employed the methods of philosophy to support religion, while others have used the same methods with quite different aims. All philosophy of religion, however, is concerned with questions that arise when religious doctrines are tested by the canons of reason.

Chief among the issues that philosophers of religion have examined is, "Does God exist?" *Theism* is the belief that God does exist. *Atheism* is the belief that God does not exist. *Agnosticism* is the belief that sufficient evidence is not available to decide whether God exists. Which of these positions is correct?

To answer this question, we need to determine what we mean by "God," a term that has been used in many different ways. Let us adopt a view, shared by many theists, that the word refers to an all-good, all-knowing, all powerful creator of the world. The question then is this: Does a being so described exist?

The Ontological Argument—and Replies

Several proofs have been offered to defend the claim that God does exist. In the selection by the medieval philosopher Saint Anselm (1033–1109), we are presented with the *ontological argument* for the existence of God. This argument makes no appeal to empirical evidence but purports to demonstrate that by God's very nature, God, the Being-something-than-which-nothing-greater-can-be-thought, exists. For if that Being does not, then a greater being could be thought, namely, a being that does exist. But in that case, the Being-something-than-which-nothing-greater-can-be-thought would not be the Being-something-than-which-nothing-greater-can-be-thought, which is a contradiction. So the Being-something-than-which-nothing-greater-can-be-thought exists, i.e., God exists.

A criticism of this argument is offered in the selection by the monk Gaunilo, who lived at the same time as Anselm. In "In Behalf of the Fool," Gaunilo maintains that Anselm's form of reasoning could be used to prove the existence of an island-than-which-none-greater-can-be-thought, an absurd conclusion. So, he contends, Anselm's argument must be fallacious.

But if Anselm's argument fails, where does its mistake lie? The renowned German philosopher Immanuel Kant (1724–1804) famously suggested that the crucial error lies in Anselm's assumption that existence is an attribute. But, Kant maintained, the definition of anything remains the same regardless of whether that thing exists. For example, the definition of a unicorn would not be altered if we discovered a living unicorn, just as our definition of a whooping crane would not be altered if whooping cranes became extinct. In short, whether unicorns or whooping cranes exist does not affect the meaning of the terms *unicorn* and *whooping crane.*

Kant offers this argument as part of his monumental work *The Critique of Pure Reason* (1781), but it is discussed in an accessible manner in our next selection, a classic essay by G. E. Moore (1873–1958), in which he replies to the philosopher William Kneale (1905–90), who had defended the Kantian objection to the ontological argument. In "Is Existence a Predicate?" Moore considers the statement "Tame tigers growl" and points out with painstaking attention to detail how it differs in surprising ways from the statement "Tame tigers exist," thus suggesting that if "exists" is an attribute, it functions quite differently from such usual attributes as "growls."

In the following selection, "Why the Ontological Argument Fails," contemporary philosopher William Rowe argues that the ontological argument is unsound. In the course of his discussion, Rowe reveals many of the subtleties that are implicit in this deservedly famous and still challenging piece of philosophical reasoning.

The Cosmological Argument, the Argument from Design—and Replies

Another traditional argument for the existence of God is presented in the next selection by Richard Taylor (1919–2003). Taylor offers a version of the *cosmological argument*, which is based on metaphysical considerations regarding the nature of the world itself. Taylor appeals to the principle of sufficient reason, the claim that "there is some explanation for the existence of anything whatever, some reason why it should exist rather than not." He then applies the principle to the entire world and concludes that the explanation of the world's existence is to be found in the existence of God.

A third traditional argument for the existence of God, the *argument from design* (also known as the *teleological argument*), is offered in the following selection by William Paley (1743–1805). This line of reasoning proceeds from the highly ordered structure of the world to the conclusion that the world's order must be the work of a Supreme Mind responsible for the order. Just as we assume that a watch was created by a watchmaker, so we should agree that the world was created by a worldmaker, that is, God.

Both the cosmological argument and the argument from design are criticized in "Does God Exist?" by philosopher Ernest Nagel (1901–85). Nagel rejects the cosmological argument on the grounds that if God is supposed to be the explanation of the world's existence, how can we explain God's existence? If we say that the existence of God requires no explanation, why can't we say the same for the world?

As for the argument from design, Nagel rejects it on the grounds that while watches are always manufactured, many animate and inanimate systems are not. Why assume that the world is more akin to a watch than, for example, a tree or a thunderstorm? Regarding the source of the various forms of animal life, he suggests, the explanation is not to be found in theology, but in Darwinian biology.

The Problem of Evil—and Replies

To attack arguments supporting the existence of God, however, is not equivalent to offering an argument against the existence of God. Are there arguments not only against theism but in favor of atheism?

A well-known argument of this sort is the *problem of evil*, presented by Nagel. Why should there be evil in a world created by an all-good, all-powerful being? A being who is all-good would do everything possible to abolish evil. A being who is all-powerful would be able to abolish evil. Therefore, if there were an all-good, all-powerful being, there would be no evil. But evil exists. Thus, it would seem that there is no being who is all-good and all-powerful.

Numerous attempts have been made to find a solution to the problem of evil. A familiar strategy is to try to demonstrate how the presence of evils makes possible greater goods than would be possible otherwise. For example, in "The Problem of Evil," philosopher John Hick (1922–) suggests that some evils can be viewed as necessary for "soul making," a process by which free people grapple with the challenges in their environment and thereby have their spirits enhanced.

Is Hick's response to the problem of evil plausible? In the next selection, Steven M. Cahn (coeditor of this volume) argues that it is not. He asks us to consider what he calls "the problem of goodness": could there be goodness in a world created by an all-evil, all-powerful being? A being who is all-evil would do everything possible to abolish goodness. A being who is all-powerful would be able to abolish goodness. Therefore, if there were an all-evil, all-powerful being, there would be no goodness. But goodness exists. Thus, it would seem there is no being who is all-evil and all-powerful. But suppose someone replied to the problem of goodness by viewing goodness as necessary for "soul-breaking," a process by which free people grapple with the challenges in their environment and thereby have their spirits broken. Would that response be satisfactory? Cahn thinks not and finds Hick's response to the problem of evil no better.

Grounds for Belief

If the use of reason leaves us uncertain whether to believe in God, might belief in God be the best bet? In the next selection, French thinker Blaise Pascal (1623–62) argues that it is. According to his celebrated "*wager*" argument, if we believe and God exists, then we attain heavenly bliss; if we believe and God does not exist, little is lost. On the other hand, if we do not believe and God does exist, then we are doomed to the torments of damnation; if we do not believe and God does not exist, little is gained. So belief is the safest strategy. Pascal, however, does not consider the possibility that a different kind of God might exist, for example, one who wishes us to hold only those beliefs that are supported by the available evidence. If such a God existed, then in the absence of appropriate evidence, the safest strategy would be not to believe.

In "The Ethics of Belief," British philosopher W. K. Clifford (1845–79), arguing against Pascal, defends the view that it is always wrong to believe anything on insufficient evidence. Clifford's position is itself opposed in "The Will to Believe" by American philosopher William James (1842–1910), who claims that we should not allow the fear of holding a false belief to cause us to lose the benefits of a belief that may be true. In other words, it would be irrational for me to be prevented from believing in God, assuming God exists. James appears to overlook, however, that it would also be irrational for me to be prevented from believing that God does not exist, assuming that God does not.

After considering all the arguments for and against belief in the existence of God, one may wonder whether it matters whether we believe in God. If it does, why is God's character not revealed in a manner that is accessible to all? In "The Hiddenness of God," contemporary philosopher Robert McKim concludes that the evidence suggests that it does not matter much whether we believe in God, for if it did make an important difference, then the evidence of God's existence would be more apparent.

God and Science: Contemporary Discussions

Our final selection considers the question of belief in God in light of modern science. In "Theism and Modern Science," contemporary British philosopher Nicholas Everitt argues that what we now know about the size and nature of the universe suggests that it is not best understood as indicating creation in accord with the intentions of a divine being. After all, for virtually the entire history of the earth, human beings were not even present.

In considering all these issues, it is important to remember that some of the most renowned philosophers of the past and present have been theists, while others of equal stature have been agnostics or atheists. All would have agreed, however, that whatever one's position, it is more clearly and fully understood in the light of philosophical inquiry.

Further Reading

Students who want to pursue the themes raised in this section of the book may begin by looking at the articles presented in the following two anthologies. Each includes an extensive collection of important readings in the philosophy of religion, along with suggestions for further readings on each of the main themes:

- William J. Rowe and William J. Wainwright, eds., *Philosophy of Religion: Selected Readings*, 3rd ed. New York and Oxford: Oxford University Press, 1998.
- Michael Peterson, William Hasker, Bruce Reichenbach, and David Basinger, eds., *Philosophy of Religion: Selected Readings,* 3rd ed. New York and Oxford: Oxford University Press, 2006.

A TRADITIONAL ARGUMENTS FOR AND AGAINST THE EXISTENCE OF GOD

◈ THE ONTOLOGICAL ARGUMENT—AND REPLIES ◈

The Ontological Argument

SAINT ANSELM

Saint Anselm of Canterbury (1033–1109) was a Christian philosopher and theologian. His reputation as a teacher, scholar, and adviser to European nobles earned him international recognition, and at the age of 60, Anselm was appointed Archbishop of Canterbury.

This selection comes from Anselm's famous work *Proslogion*, which he wrote (in Latin) during 1077–78. The book's self-proclaimed goal is to present "a single argument that needed nothing but itself alone for proof, that would by itself be enough to show that God really exists."

1. THAT GOD TRULY EXISTS

Well then, Lord, You who give understanding to faith, grant me that I may understand, as much as You see fit, that You exist as we believe You to exist, and that You are what we believe You to be. Now we believe that You are something than which nothing greater can be thought. Or can it be that a thing of such a nature does not exist, since "the Fool has said in his heart, there is no God" [Ps. 13: 1; 52: 1]? But surely, when this same Fool hears what I am speaking about, namely, "something-than-which-nothing-greater-can-be-thought," he understands what he hears, and what he understands is in his mind, even if he does not understand that it actually exists. For it is one thing for an object to exist in the mind, and another thing to understand that an object actually exists. Thus, when a painter plans beforehand what he is going to execute, he has [the picture] in his mind, but he does not yet think that it actually exists because he has not yet executed it. However, when he has actually painted it, then he both has it in his mind and understands that it exists because he has now made it. Even the Fool, then, is forced to agree that something-than-which-nothing-greater-can-be-thought exists in the mind, since he understands this when he hears it, and whatever is understood is in the mind. And surely that-than-which-a-greater-cannot-be-thought cannot exist in the mind alone. For if it exists solely in the mind, it can be thought to exist in reality also, which is greater. If then that-than-which-a-greater-cannot-be-thought exists in the mind alone, this same that-than-which-a-greater-*cannot*-be-thought is that-than-which-a-greater-*can*-be-thought. But this is obviously impossible. Therefore there is absolutely no doubt that something-than-which-a-greater-cannot-be-thought exists both in the mind and in reality.

Reprinted from *Anselm of Canterbury: The Major Works,* eds. Brian Davies and G. R. Evans (Oxford: Oxford University Press, 1998). Reprinted by permission of the publisher. (Sections have been renumbered.)

2. THAT GOD CANNOT BE THOUGHT NOT TO EXIST

And certainly this being so truly exists that it cannot be even thought not to exist. For something can be thought to exist that cannot be thought not to exist, and this is greater than that which can be thought not to exist. Hence, if that-than-which-a-greater-cannot-be-thought can be thought not to exist, then that-than-which-a-greater-cannot-be-thought is not the same as that-than-which-a-greater-cannot-be-thought, which is absurd. Something-than-which-a-greater-cannot-be-thought exists so truly then, that it cannot be even thought not to exist.

And You, Lord our God, are this being. You exist so truly, Lord my God, that You cannot even be thought not to exist. And this is as it should be, for if some intelligence could think of something better than You, the creature would be above its Creator and would judge its Creator—and that is completely absurd. In fact, everything else there is, except You alone, can be thought of as not existing. You alone, then, of all things most truly exist and therefore of all things possess existence to the highest degree; for anything else does not exist as truly, and so possesses existence to a lesser degree. Why then did "the Fool say in his heart, there is no God" [Ps. 13: 1; 52: 1] when it is so evident to any rational mind that You of all things exist to the highest degree? Why indeed, unless because he was stupid and a fool?

3. HOW "THE FOOL SAID IN HIS HEART" WHAT CANNOT BE THOUGHT

How indeed has he "said in his heart" what he could not think; or how could he not think what he "said in his heart," since to "say in one's heart" and to "think" are the same? But if he really (indeed, since he really) both thought because he "said in his heart" and did not "say in his heart" because he could not think, there is not only one sense in which something is "said in one's heart" or thought. For in one sense a thing is thought when the word signifying it is thought; in another sense when the very object which the thing is is understood. In the first sense, then, God can be thought not to exist, but not at all in the second sense. No one, indeed, understanding what God is can think that God does not exist, even though he may say these words in his heart either without any [objective] signification or with some peculiar signification. For God is that-than-which-nothing-greater-can-be-thought. Whoever really understands this understands clearly that this same being so exists that not even in thought can it not exist. Thus whoever understands that God exists in such a way cannot think of Him as not existing.

I give thanks, good Lord, I give thanks to You, since what I believed before through Your free gift I now so understand through Your illumination, that if I did not want to *believe* that You existed, I should nevertheless be unable not to *understand* it.

In Behalf of the Fool

GAUNILO

Gaunilo of Marmoutiers was a Benedictine monk who lived around the same time as Saint Anselm (11th century). Not much is known about his life beyond this.

In this selection, which was composed in Latin and originally published anonymously about a year after Anselm's *Proslogion* appeared, Gaunilo offers a reply to Anselm on behalf of the "Fool"—that is, the person who doubts or denies the existence of God and who remains unconvinced by Anselm's ontological argument.

Reprinted from *Anselm of Canterbury: The Major Works*, eds. Brian Davies and G. R. Evans (Oxford: Oxford University Press, 1998). Reprinted by permission of the publisher. (Sections have been renumbered.)

1

To one doubting whether there is, or denying that there is, something of such a nature than which nothing greater can be thought, it is said here [in the *Proslogion*] that its existence is proved, first because the very one who denies or doubts it already has it in his mind, since when he hears it spoken of he understands what is said; and further, because what he understands is necessarily such that it exists not only in the mind but also in reality. And this is proved by the fact that it is greater to exist both in the mind and in reality than in the mind alone. For if this same being exists in the mind alone, anything that existed also in reality would be greater than this being, and thus that which is greater than everything would be less than some thing and would not be greater than everything, which is obviously contradictory. Therefore, it is necessarily the case that that which is greater than everything, being already proved to exist in the mind, should exist not only in the mind but also in reality, since otherwise it would not be greater than everything.

2

But he [the Fool] can perhaps reply that this thing is said already to exist in the mind only in the sense that I understand what is said. For could I not say that all kinds of unreal things, not existing in themselves in any way at all, are equally in the mind since if anyone speaks about them I understand whatever he says?...

3

For example: they say that there is in the ocean somewhere an island which, because of the difficulty (or rather the impossibility) of finding that which does not exist, some have called the "Lost Island." And the story goes that it is blessed with all manner of priceless riches and delights in abundance, much more even than the Happy Isles, and, having no owner or inhabitant, it is superior everywhere in abundance of riches to all those other lands that men inhabit. Now, if anyone tell me that it is like this, I shall easily understand what is said, since nothing is difficult about it. But if he should then go on to say, as though it were a logical consequence of this: You cannot any more doubt that this island that is more excellent than all other lands truly exists somewhere in reality than you can doubt that it is in your mind; and since it is more excellent to exist not only in the mind alone but also in reality, therefore it must needs be that it exists. For if it did not exist, any other land existing in reality would be more excellent than it, and so this island, already conceived by you to be more excellent than others, will not be more excellent. If, I say, someone wishes thus to persuade me that this island really exists beyond all doubt. I should either think that he was joking, or I should find it hard to decide which of us I ought to judge the bigger fool—I, if I agreed with him, or he, if he thought that he had proved the existence of this island with any certainty, unless he had first convinced me that its very excellence exists in my mind precisely as a thing existing truly and indubitably and not just as something unreal or doubtfully real.

4

Thus first of all might the Fool reply to objections. And if then someone should assert that this greater [than everything] is such that it cannot be thought not to exist (again without any other proof than that otherwise it would not be greater than everything), then he could make this same reply and say: When have I said that there truly existed some being that is "greater than everything," such that from this it could be proved to me that this same being really existed to such a degree that it could not be thought not to exist? That is why it must first be conclusively proved by argument that there is some higher nature, namely that which is greater and better than all the things that are, so that from this we can also infer everything else which necessarily cannot be wanting to what is greater and better than everything.

Is Existence a Predicate?

G. E. MOORE

G. E. Moore (1873–1958) was one of the most important British philosophers of the first half of the twentieth century. Along with his long-time colleagues Bertrand Russell and Ludwig Wittgenstein, Moore was one of the central figures in a movement that has come to be known as "analytic philosophy." Moore was a philosopher of wide-ranging interests, producing important work in epistemology, the philosophy of language, ethics, and the philosophy of mind. Several selections from his writings appear in *The Elements of Philosophy.*

This selection was originally presented in London in 1935 at a meeting of the Aristotelian Society, a British philosophical organization founded in 1880 whose members still meet every two weeks to hear and discuss philosophical papers. The "Mr. Kneale" who is referred to in the first sentence (William Kneale, 1905–90) had delivered a paper in which he argued, following that great German philosopher Immanuel Kant (1724–1804), that Anselm's argument is unsuccessful because it falsely assumes that existence is a predicate. Moore, responding to Kneale, carefully considers what that claim may amount to.

I am not at all clear as to the meaning of this question. Mr. Kneale says that existence is not a predicate. But what does he mean by the words "Existence is not a predicate"?

In his second paragraph, he says that the word "predicate" has two different senses, a logical sense and a grammatical one. If so, it would follow that the words "Existence is not a predicate" may have two different meanings, according as the person who uses them is using "predicate" in the logical or the grammatical sense. And I think it is clear that he means us to understand that when he says "Existence is not a predicate," he is using "predicate" in the logical sense, and not in the grammatical one. I think his view is that if anyone were to say "Existence is a predicate," using "predicate" in the grammatical sense, such a person would be perfectly right: I think he holds that existence really is a predicate in the grammatical sense. But, whether he holds this or not, I think it is clear that he does not wish to discuss the question whether it is or is not a predicate in the grammatical sense, but solely the question whether it is so in the logical one.

Now I think it is worth noticing that if we assert "Existence is a predicate," using "predicate" in the grammatical sense, our proposition is a proposition about certain *words*, to the effect that they are often used in a certain way; but not, curiously enough, about the word "existence" itself. It is a proposition to the effect that the word "exists" and other finite parts of the verb "to exist," such as "existed," "will exist," or "exist" (in the plural) are often the predicates (in some grammatical sense) of sentences in which they occur; but nobody means to say that the word "existence" itself is often the predicate of sentences in which it occurs. And I think Mr. Kneale implies that, similarly, the proposition which anyone would express, if he asserted "Existence is a predicate," using "predicate" in the logical sense, is again equivalent to a proposition, *not* about the word "existence" itself, but about the word "exists," and other finite parts of the verb "to exist." He implies that "Existence is a predicate," with this use of "predicate," is equivalent to the proposition that the word "exists," and other finite parts of the verb, often do "*stand for* a predicate in the logical sense." It would appear,

This essay was the second paper in a symposium published in the *Proceedings of the Aristotelian Society,* Supplementary Volume XV, 1936, and is reprinted by permission of the Editor of the Aristotelian Society. The philosopher William Kneale, (1905–90) wrote the first paper.

therefore, that one difference between the two different meanings of "Existence is a predicate" is as follows; namely that, if a person who says these words is using "predicate" in the grammatical sense, he is *not* saying that the words, "exists," etc., ever "*stand for* a predicate in the logical sense:" whereas, if he is using "predicate" in the logical sense, he is saying that they do (often, at least) "*stand for* a predicate in the logical sense." What Mr. Kneale himself means by "Existence is not a predicate" is apparently some proposition which he would express by saying: "The words, "exists," etc., never stand for a predicate in the logical sense."

What I am not clear about is as to what is meant by saying of a particular word (or particular phrase) in a particular sentence that it "stands for a predicate in the logical sense;" nor, therefore, as to what is meant by saying of another particular word in another particular sentence that it does *not* "stand for a predicate in the logical sense." Mr. Kneale does, indeed, tell us that a "predicate in the logical sense" is the same as "an attribute;" but, though I think that the meaning of the word "attribute" is perhaps a little clearer than that of the phrase "predicate in the logical sense," it still seems to me far from clear: I do not clearly understand what he would mean by saying that "exists," etc., do not "stand for attributes." But, from examples which he gives, it is, I think, clear that he would say that in the sentence "This is red" the word "red," or the phrase "is red" (I am not clear which), does "stand for an attribute;" and also that in the sentence "Tame tigers growl," "growl" so stands, and in the sentence "Rajah growls," "growls" does. It is, therefore, presumably some difference between the way in which "exists," etc., are used in sentences in which they occur, and the way in which "is red" (or "red") and "growl" and "growls" are used in these sentences, that he wishes to express by saying that, whereas "exists," etc., do *not* "stand for attributes," these words in these sentences do. And if we can find what differences there are between the use of finite parts of the verb "to exist," and the use of "is red," "growl" and "growls," we may perhaps find what the difference is which he expresses in this way.

It will, I think, be best to begin with one particular use of "exist"—the one, namely, which Mr. Kneale illustrates by the example "Tame tigers exist." He clearly thinks that there is some very important difference between the way in which "exist" is used here, and the way in which "growl" is used in "Tame tigers growl;" and that it is a difference which does not hold, e.g. between the use of "scratch" in "Tame tigers scratch" and the use of "growl" in "Tame tigers growl." He would say that "scratch" and "growl" both "stand for attributes," whereas "exist" does not; and he would also say that "Tame tigers exist" is a proposition of a different *form* from "Tame tigers growl," whereas I think he would say that "Tame tigers growl" and "Tame tigers scratch" are *of the same form*. What difference between "Tame tigers exist" and "Time tigers growl" can be the one he has in mind?

That there is a difference between the way in which we use "exist" in the former sentence and "growl" in the latter, of a different kind from the difference between our usages of "scratch" and "growl" in the two sentences "Tame tigers scratch" and "Tame tigers growl," can, I think, be brought out in the following way.

The sentence "Tame tigers growl" seems to me to be ambiguous. So far as I can see, it might mean "All tame tigers growl," or it might mean merely "Most tame tigers growl," or it might mean merely "Some tame tigers growl." Each of these three sentences has a clear meaning, and the meaning of each is clearly different from that of either of the two others. Of each of them, however, it is true that the proposition which it expresses is one which cannot possibly be true, unless some tame tigers do growl. And hence I think we can say of "Tame tigers growl" that, whichever sense it is used in, it means something which cannot possibly be true unless some tame tigers do growl. Similarly I think it is clear that "Tame tigers exist" means something which cannot possibly be true unless some tame tigers do exist. But I do not think that there is any ambiguity in "Tame tigers exist" corresponding to that which I have pointed out in "Tame tigers growl." So far as I can see "Tame tigers exist" and "Some tame tigers exist" are merely two different ways of expressing exactly the same proposition. That is to say, it is not true that "Tame tigers exist" might mean "All tame tigers exist," or "Most tame tigers exist," instead of merely "Some tame tigers exist." It always means just "Some tame tigers exist," and nothing else whatever. I have said it is never used to mean "All tame tigers exist," or "Most tame tigers exist;" but I hope it will strike everyone that there is something queer about this proposition. It seems to imply that "All tame tigers exist" and "Most tame tigers exist" have a clear meaning, just as have "All tame tigers growl," and "Most tame tigers growl;" and that it is just an accident that we do not happen ever to use "Tame tigers exist" to express either of those two meanings instead of the meaning "Some tame tigers exist," whereas we do sometimes use "Tame tigers growl" to mean "All tame tigers growl" or "Most tame tigers growl," instead of merely "Some tame tigers growl." But is this in fact the case? Have "All tame tigers exist" and "Most tame tigers exist" any meaning at all? Certainly they have not a clear meaning, as have "All tame tigers growl" and "Most tame tigers growl." They are puzzling expressions, which certainly do not carry their meaning, if they have any, on the face of them. That this is so indicates, I think, that there is some important difference between the usage of "exist" with which we are concerned, and the usage of such words as "growl" or "scratch;" but it does not make clear just what the difference is.

I think this can be made clear by comparing the expressions "Some tame tigers don't growl" and "Some tame tigers don't exist." The former, whether true or false, has a perfectly clear meaning—a meaning just as clear as that of "Some tame tigers do growl;" and it is perfectly clear that both propositions might be true together. But with "Some tame tigers don't exist" the case is different. "Some tame tigers exist" has a perfectly clear meaning: it just means "There are some tame tigers." But the meaning of "Some tame tigers don't exist," if any, is certainly not equally clear. It is another queer and puzzling expression. Has it any meaning at all? and, if so, what meaning? If it has any, it would appear that it must mean the same as: "There are some tame tigers which don't exist." But has *this* any meaning? and if so, what? Is it possible that there should be any tame tigers which don't exist? I think the answer is that, if in the sentence "Some tame tigers don't exist," you are using "exist" with the same meaning as in "Some tame tigers exist," then the former sentence as a whole has no meaning at all—it is pure nonsense. A meaning can, of course, be given to "Some tame tigers don't exist;" but this can only be done if "exist" is used in a different way from that in which it is used in "Some tame tigers exist." And, if this is so, it will follow that "All tame tigers exist" and "Most tame tigers exist," also have no meaning at all, if you are using "exist" in the sense with which we are concerned. For "All tame tigers growl" is equivalent to the conjunction "Some tame tigers growl, and there is no tame tiger which does not growl;" and this has a meaning, because "There is at least one tame tiger which does not growl" has one. If, therefore, "There is at least one tame tiger which does not exist" has no meaning, it will follow that "All tame tigers exist" also has none; because "There is no tame tiger which does not exist" will have none, if "There is a tame tiger which does not exist" has none. Similarly "Most tame tigers growl" is equivalent to the conjunction "Some tame tigers growl, and the number of those (if any) which do not growl is smaller than that of those which do"—a statement which has a meaning only because "There are tame tigers which do not growl" has one. If, therefore, "There are tame tigers which don't exist" has no meaning, it will follow that "Most tame tigers exist" will also have none. I think, therefore, we can say that one important difference between the use of "growl" in "Some tame tigers growl" and the use of "exist" in "Some tame tigers exist," is that if in the former case we insert "do not" before "growl," without changing the meaning of "growl," we get a sentence which is significant, whereas if, in the latter, we insert "do not" before "exist" without changing the meaning of "exist," we get a sentence which has no meaning whatever; and I think we can also say that this fact explains why, with the given meaning of "growl," "All tame tigers growl" and "Most tame tigers growl" are both significant; whereas, with the given meaning of "exist," "All tame tigers exist" and "Most tame tigers exist" are utterly meaningless. And if by the statement that "growl," in this usage, "stands for an attribute," whereas "exist," in this usage, does not, part of what is meant is that there is this difference between them, then I should agree that "exist," in this usage, does not "stand for an attribute."

But is it really true that if, in the sentence "Some tame tigers exist," we insert "do not" before "exist," without changing the meaning of "exist," we get a sentence which has no meaning whatever? I have admitted that a meaning *can* be given to "Some tame tigers do not exist," and it may, perhaps, be contended by some people that the meaning which "exist" has in this sentence, where it is significant, *is* precisely the same as that which it has in "Some tame tigers exist." I cannot show the contrary as clearly as I should like to be able to do; but I will do my best.

The meaning which such as expression as "Some tame tigers do not exist" sometimes does have, is that which it has when it is used to mean the same as "Some tame tigers are imaginary" or "Some tame tigers are not real tigers." That "Some tame tigers are imaginary" may really express a proposition, whether true or false, cannot I think be denied. If, for instance, two different stories have been written, each of which is about a different imaginary tame tiger, it will follow that there are at least two imaginary tame tigers; and it cannot be denied that the sentence "Two different tame tigers occur in fiction" is significant, though I have not the least idea whether it is true or false. I know that at least one unicorn occurs in fiction, because one occurs in *Alice Through the Looking Glass:* and it follows that there is at least one imaginary unicorn, and therefore (in a sense) at least one unicorn which does not exist. Again, if it should happen that at the present moment two different people are each having an hallucination of a different tame tiger, it will follow that there are at the present moment two different imaginary tame tigers; and the statement that two such hallucinations are occurring now is certainly significant, though it may very likely be false. The sentence "There are some tame tigers which do not exist" is, therefore, certainly significant, if it means only that there are some imaginary tigers, in either of the two senses which I have tried to point out. But what it means is that either some real people have written stories about imaginary tigers, or are having or have recently had hallucinations of tame tigers, or, perhaps, are dreaming or have dreamed of particular tame tigers. If nothing of this sort has happened or is happening to anybody, then there are no imaginary tame tigers. But if "Some tame tigers do not exist" means all this, is it not clear that "exist" has not, in this sentence, the same comparatively simple meaning as it has in "Some tame tigers exist" or in "No tame tigers exist"? Is it not clear that "Some tame tigers do not exist," if it means all this, is not related to "Some tame tigers exist," in the same simple way in which "Some tame tigers do not growl" is related to "Some tame tigers growl"?

Why the Ontological Argument Fails

WILLIAM L. ROWE

William L. Rowe was a professor of philosophy at Purdue University until his retirement in 2005. A committed atheist, Rowe spent most of his career thinking and writing about issues in the philosophy of religion. Among his most widely read publications is his much-admired introductory volume, *Philosophy of Religion: An Introduction,* from which this selection was drawn.

I want to present a . . . critique of [Anselm's] argument, a critique suggested by the basic conviction. . . , that from the mere logical analysis of a certain idea or concept, we can never determine that there exists in reality anything answering to that idea or concept.

Suppose someone comes to us and says:

I propose to define the term *God as an existing, wholly perfect being.* Now since it can't be true that an existing, wholly perfect being does not exist, it can't be

From *Philosophy of Religion: An Introduction*, 2nd ed. (1993). Reprinted with permission of Wadsworth, a division of Thomson Learning.

> true that God, as I've defined him, does not exist. Therefore, God must exist.

This argument appears to be a very simple Ontological Argument. It begins with a particular idea or concept of God and ends by concluding that God, so conceived, must exist. What can we say in response? We might start by objecting to this definition of *God*, claiming (1) that only predicates can be used to define a term, and (2) that existence is not a predicate. But suppose our friend is not impressed by this response—either because he thinks no one has fully explained what a predicate is or proved that existence isn't one, or because he thinks that anyone can define a word in whatever way he pleases. Can we allow our friend to define the word *God* in any way he pleases and still hope to show that it will not follow from that definition that there actually exists something to which this concept of God applies? I think we can. Let's first invite him, however, to consider some concepts other than this peculiar concept of God. . . .

[T]he term *magician* may be applied both to Houdini and Merlin, even though the former existed whereas the latter did not. Noting that our friend has used *existing* as part of this definition of *God*, suppose we agree with him that we can define a word in any way we please, and, accordingly, introduce the following words with the following definitions:

> A *magican* is defined as an *existing magician.*
> A *magico* is defined as a *nonexisting magician.*

Here we have introduced two words and used *existing* or *nonexisting* in their definitions. Now something of interest follows from the fact that *existing* is part of our definition of a magican. For while it's true that Merlin was a *magician* it isn't true that Merlin was a *magican*. And something of interest follows from our including *nonexisting* in the definition of a magico. For while it's true that Houdini was a *magician* it isn't true that Houdini was a *magico.* Houdini was a *magician* and a *magican*, but not a *magico*, whereas Merlin was a *magician* and a *magico,* but not a *magican.*

What we have just seen is that introducing *existing* or *nonexisting* into the definition of a concept has a very important implication. If we introduce *existing* into the definition of a concept, it follows that no nonexisting thing can exemplify that concept. And if we introduce *nonexisting* into the definition of a concept, it follows that no existing thing can exemplify that concept. No nonexisting thing can be a *magican* and no existing thing can be a *magico.*

But must some existing thing exemplify the concept *magican?* No! From the fact that *existing* is included in the definition of *magican* it does not follow that some existing thing is a *magican*—all that follows is that no nonexisting thing is a *magican.* If there were no magicians in existence there would be nothing to which the term *magican* would apply. This being so, it clearly does not follow merely from our definition of *magican* that some existing thing is a *magican*. Only if magicians exist will it be true that some existing thing is a *magican.*

We are now in a position to help our friend see that, from the mere fact that *God* is defined as an existing, wholly perfect being, it will not follow that some existing being is God. Something of interest does follow from his definition: namely, that no nonexisting being can be God. But whether some existing thing is God will depend entirely on whether some existing thing is a wholly perfect being. If no wholly perfect being exists there will be nothing to which this concept of God can apply. This being so, it clearly does not follow merely from this definition of *God* that some existing thing is God. Only if a wholly perfect being exists will it be true that God, as our friend conceives of him, exists.

The implications of these considerations for Anselm's ingenious argument can now be traced. Anselm conceives of God as a being than which none greater is possible. He then claims that existence is a greatmaking quality, something that has it is greater than it would have been had it lacked existence. Clearly then, no nonexisting thing can exemplify Anselm's concept of God. For if we suppose that some nonexisting thing exemplifies Anselm's concept of God and also suppose that that nonexisting thing might have existed in reality (is a possible thing), then we are supposing that that nonexisting thing (1) might have been a greater thing, and (2) is, nevertheless, a thing than which a greater is not possible. Thus far Anselm's reasoning is, I believe, impeccable. But what follows from it? All that follows from it is that no nonexisting thing can be God (as Anselm conceives of God). All that follows is that given Anselm's concept of God, the proposition "Some nonexisting thing is God" cannot be true. But, as we saw earlier, this is also the case with the proposition "Some nonexisting thing is a magican." What remains to be shown is that some existing thing exemplifies Anselm's concept of God. What really does follow from his reasoning is that the only thing that logically could exemplify his concept of God is something which actually exists. And this conclusion is not without interest. But from the mere fact that nothing but an existing thing could exemplify Anselm's concept of God, it does not follow that some existing thing actually does exemplify his concept of God—no more than it follows from the mere fact that no nonexisting thing can be a magican that some existing thing is a magician.[1]

There is, however, one major difficulty in this critique of Anselm's argument. This difficulty arises when we take into account Anselm's implicit claim that God is a possible thing. . . . Possible things . . . [are] all those things that, unlike the round square, are not impossible things. Suppose we concede to Anselm that God, as he conceives of him, is a possible thing. Now, of course, the mere knowledge that something is a possible thing doesn't enable us to conclude that that thing is an existing thing. For many possible things, like the Fountain of Youth, do not exist. But if something is a possible thing, then it is either an existing thing or a nonexisting thing. The set of possible things can be exhaustively divided into those possible things which actually exist and those possible things which do not exist. Therefore, if Anselm's God is a possible thing, it is either an existing thing or a nonexisting thing. We have concluded, however, that no nonexisting thing can be Anselm's God; therefore, it seems we must conclude with Anselm that some actually existing thing does exemplify his concept of God.

To see the solution to this major difficulty we need to return to an earlier example. Let's consider again the idea of a magican, an existing magician. It so happens that some magicians have existed—Houdini, The Great Blackstone, and others. But, of course, it might have been otherwise. Suppose, for the moment, that no magicians have ever existed. The concept "magician" would still have application, for it would still be true that Merlin was a magician. But what about the concept of a "magican?" Would any possible object be picked out by that concept? No! For no nonexisting thing could exemplify the concept "magican." And on the supposition that no magicians ever existed, no existing thing would exemplify the concept "magican."[2] We then would have a coherent concept "magican" which would not be exemplified by any possible object at all. For if all the possible objects which are magicians are nonexisting things, none of them would be a magican and, since no possible objects which exist are magicians, none of them would be a magican. We then would have a coherent, consistent concept "magican," which in fact is not exemplified by any possible object at all. Put in this way, our result seems paradoxical. For we are inclined to think that only contradictory concepts like "the round square" are not exemplified by any possible things. The truth is, however, that when *existing* is included in or implied by a certain concept, it may be the case that no possible object does in fact exemplify that concept. For no possible object that doesn't exist will exemplify a concept like "magican" in which *existing* is included; and if there are no existing things which exemplify the other features included in the concept—for example, "being a magician" in the case of the concept "magican"—then no possible object that exists will exemplify the concept. Put in its simplest terms, if we ask whether any possible thing is a magican, the answer will depend entirely on whether any existing thing is a magician. If no existing things are magicians, then no possible things are magicians. Some possible object is a magican just in case some actually existing thing is a magician.

Applying these considerations to Anselm's argument we can find the solution to our major difficulty. Given Anselm's concept of God and his principle that existence is a great-making quality, it really does follow that the only thing that logically could exemplify his concept of God is something which actually exists. But, we argued, it doesn't follow from these considerations alone that God actually exists, that some existing thing exemplifies Anselm's concept of God. The difficulty we fell into, however, is that when we add the premise that God is a possible thing, that some possible object exemplifies his concept of God, it really does follow that God actually exists, that some actually existing thing exemplifies Anselm's concept of God. For if some possible object exemplifies his concept of God, that object is either an existing thing or a nonexisting thing. But since no nonexisting thing could exemplify Anselm's concept of God, it follows that the possible object which exemplifies his concept of God must be a possible object that actually exists. Therefore, given (1) Anselm's concept of God, (2) his principle that existence is a great-making quality, and (3) the premise that God, as conceived by Anselm, is a possible thing, it really does follow that Anselm's God actually exists.

I think we now can see that in granting Anselm the premise that God is a possible thing we have granted far more than we intended to grant. All we thought we were granting is that Anselm's concept of God, unlike the concept of a round square, is not contradictory or incoherent. But without realizing it we were in fact granting much more than this, as became apparent when we considered the idea of a "magican." There is nothing contradictory in the idea of a magican, an existing magician. But in asserting that a magican is a possible thing, we are, as we saw, directly implying that some existing thing is a magician. For if no existing thing is a magician, the concept of a magican will apply to no possible object whatever. The same point holds with respect to Anselm's God. Since Anselm's concept of God logically cannot apply to some nonexisting thing, the only possible objects to which it could apply are possible objects which actually exist. Therefore, ingranting that Anselm's God is a possible thing, we are granting far more than that his idea of God isn't incoherent or contradictory. Suppose, for example, that every existing being has some defect which it might not have had. Without realizing it, we were denying this when we granted that Anselm's God is a possible being. For if every existing being has a defect it might not have had, then every existing being might have been greater. But if every existing being might have been greater, then Anselm's concept of God will apply to no possible object whatever. Therefore, if we allow Anselm his concept of God and his principle that existence is a great-making quality, then in granting that God, as Anselm conceives of him, is a possible being, we will be granting much more than that his concept of God is not contradictory. We will be granting, for example, that some existing thing is as perfect as it can be. For the plain fact is that Anselm's God is a possible thing only if some *existing* thing is as perfect as it can be.

Our final critique of Anselm's argument is simply this. In granting that Anselm's God is a possible thing, we are in fact granting that Anselm's God actually exists. But since the purpose of the argument is to prove to us that Anselm's God exists, we cannot be asked to grant as a premise a statement which is virtually equivalent to the conclusion that is to be proved. Anselm's concept of God may be coherent and his principle that existence is a great-making quality may be true. But all that follows from this is that no nonexisting thing can be Anselm's God. If we add to all of this the premise that God is a possible thing it will follow that God actually exists. But the additional premise claims more than that Anselm's concept of God isn't incoherent or contradictory. It amounts to the assertion that some existing being is supremely great. And since this is, in part, the point the argument endeavors to prove, the argument begs the question: it assumes the point it is supposed to prove.

If the above critique is correct, Anselm's argument fails as a proof of the existence of God. This is not to say, however, that the argument isn't a work of genius. Perhaps no other argument in the history of thought has raised so many basic philosophical questions and stimulated so much hard thought. Even if it fails as a proof of the existence of God, it will remain as one of the high achievements of the human intellect.

NOTES

1. An argument along the lines just presented may be found in J. Shaffer's illuminating essay, "Existence, Predication and the Ontological Argument," *Mind* LXXI (1962), pp. 307–25.
2. I am indebted to Professor William Wainwright for bringing this point to my attention.

The Cosmological Argument

RICHARD TAYLOR

Richard Taylor (1919–2003) was an American philosopher, celebrated for his contributions to metaphysics and ethics. During his long career, he taught at Brown University, Columbia University, and the University of Rochester. This selection comes from his well-respected introductory textbook *Metaphysics,* which was originally published in 1963 and revised several times over the next three decades. In it, Taylor presents and discusses the cosmological argument for the existence of God.

THE PRINCIPLE OF SUFFICIENT REASON

Suppose you were strolling in the woods and, in addition to the sticks, stones, and other accustomed litter of the forest floor, you one day came upon some quite unaccustomed object, something not quite like what you had ever seen before and would never expect to find in such a place. Suppose, for example, that it is a large ball, about your own height, perfectly smooth and translucent. You would deem this puzzling and mysterious, certainly, but if one considers the matter, it is no more inherently mysterious that such a thing should exist than that anything else should exist. If you were quite accustomed to finding such objects of various sizes around you most of the time, but had never seen an ordinary rock, then upon finding a large rock in the woods one day you would be just as puzzled and mystified. This illustrates the fact that something that is mysterious ceases to seem so simply by its accustomed presence. It is strange indeed, for example, that a world such as ours should exist; yet few people are very often struck by this strangeness but simply take it for granted.

Suppose, then, that you have found this translucent ball and are mystified by it. Now whatever else you might wonder about it, there is one thing you would hardly question; namely, that it did not appear there all by itself, that it owes its existence to something. You might not have the remotest idea whence and how it came to be there, but you would hardly doubt that there was an explanation. The idea that it might have come from nothing at all, that it might exist without there being any explanation of its existence, is one that few people would consider worthy of entertaining.

This illustrates a metaphysical belief that seems to be almost a part of reason itself, even though few ever think upon it; the belief, namely, that there is some explanation for the existence of anything whatever, some reason why it should exist rather than not. The sheer nonexistence of anything, which is not to be confused with the passing out of existence of something, never requires a reason; but existence does. That there should never have been any such ball in the forest does not require any explanation or reason, but that there should ever be such a ball does. If one were to look upon a barren plain and ask why there is not and never has been any large translucent ball there, the natural response would be to ask why there should be; but if one finds such a ball, and wonders why it is there, it is not quite so

Reprinted from *Metaphysics,* 4th ed., Prentice Hall, 1992, by permission of Pearson Education, Inc., Upper Saddle River, NJ.

natural to ask why it should *not* be—as though existence should simply be taken for granted. That anything should not exist, then, and that, for instance, no such ball should exist in the forest, or that there should be no forest for it to occupy, or no continent containing a forest, or no Earth, nor any world at all, do not seem to be things for which there needs to be any explanation or reason; but that such things should be *does* seem to require a reason.

The principle involved here has been called the principle of sufficient reason. Actually, it is a very general principle, and it is best expressed by saying that, in the case of any positive truth, there is some sufficient reason for it, something that, in this sense, makes it true—in short, that there is some sort of explanation, known or unknown, for everything.

Now, some truths depend on something else, and are accordingly called *contingent*, while others depend only upon themselves, that is, are true by their very natures and are accordingly called *necessary.* There is, for example, a reason why the stone on my window sill is warm; namely, that the sun is shining upon it. This happens to be true, but not by its very nature. Hence, it is contingent, and depends upon something other than itself. It is also true that all the points of a circle are equidistant from the center, but this truth depends upon nothing but itself. No matter what happens, nothing can make it false. Similarly, it is a truth, and a necessary one, that if the stone on my window sill is a body, as it is, then it has a form, because this fact depends upon nothing but itself for its confirmation. Untruths are also, of course, either contingent or necessary, it being contingently false, for example, that the stone on my window sill is cold, and necessarily false that it is both a body and formless, because this is by its very nature impossible.

The principle of sufficient reason can be illustrated in various ways, as we have done, and if one thinks about it, he is apt to find that he presupposes it in his thinking about reality, but it cannot be proved. It does not appear to be itself a necessary truth, and at the same time it would be most odd to say it is contingent. If one were to try proving it, he would sooner or later have to appeal to considerations that are less plausible than the principle itself. Indeed, it is hard to see how one could even make an argument for it without already assuming it. For this reason it might properly be called a presupposition of reason itself. One can deny that it is true, without embarrassment or fear of refutation, but one is then apt to find that what he is denying is not really what the principle asserts. We shall, then, treat it here as a datum—not something that is provably true, but as something that people, whether they ever reflect upon it or not, seem more or less to presuppose.

THE EXISTENCE OF A WORLD

It happens to be true that something exists, that there is, for example, a world, and although no one ever seriously supposes that this might not be so, that there might exist nothing at all, there still seems to be nothing the least necessary in this, considering it just by itself. That no world should ever exist at all is perfectly comprehensible and seems to express not the slightest absurdity. Considering any particular item in the world it seems not at all necessary that the totality of these things, or any totality of things, should ever exist.

From the principle of sufficient reason it follows, of course, that there must be a reason not only for the existence of everything in the world but for the world itself, meaning by "the world" simply everything that ever does exist, except God, in case there is a god. This principle does not imply that there must be some purpose or goal for everything, or for the totality of all things; for explanations need not be, and in fact seldom are, teleological or purposeful. All the principle requires is that there be some sort of reason for everything. And it would certainly be odd to maintain that everything in the world owes its existence to something, that nothing in the world is either purely accidental, or such that it just bestows its own being upon itself, and then to deny this of the world itself. One can indeed *say* that the world is in some sense a pure accident, that there simply is no reason at all why this or any world should exist, and one can equally say that the world exists by its very nature, or is an inherently necessary being. But it is at least very odd and arbitrary to deny of this existing world the need for any sufficient reason, whether independent of itself or not, while presupposing that there is a reason for every other thing that ever exists.

Consider again the strange ball that we imagine has been found in the forest. Now, we can hardly doubt that there must be an explanation for the existence of such a thing, though we may have no notion what that explanation is. It is not, moreover, the fact of its having been found in the forest rather than elsewhere that renders an explanation necessary. It matters not in the least where it happens to be, for our question is not how it happens to be *there* but how it happens to be at all. If we in our imagination annihilate the forest, leaving only this ball in an open field, our conviction that it is a contingent thing and owes its existence to something other than itself is not reduced in the least. If we now imagine the field to be annihilated, and in fact everything else as well to vanish into nothingness, leaving only this ball to constitute the entire physical universe, then we cannot for a moment suppose that its existence has thereby been explained, or the need for any explanation eliminated, or that its existence is suddenly rendered self-explanatory. If we now carry this thought one step further and suppose that no other reality ever has existed or ever will exist, that this ball forever constitutes the entire physical universe, then we must still insist on there being some reason independent of itself why it should exist rather than not. If there must be a reason for the existence of any particular thing, then the necessity of such a reason is not eliminated by the mere supposition that certain other things do *not* exist. And again, it matters not at all what the thing in question is, whether it be large and complex, such as the world we actually find ourselves in, or whether it be something small, simple, and insignificant, such as a ball, a bacterium, or the merest grain of sand. We do not avoid the necessity of a reason for the existence of something merely by describing it in this way or that. And it would, in any event, seem quite plainly absurd to say that if the world were composed entirely of a single ball about six feet in diameter, or of a single grain of sand, then it would be contingent and there would have to be some explanation other than itself why such a thing exists, but that, since the actual world is vastly more complex than this, there is no need for an explanation of its existence, independent of itself.

BEGINNINGLESS EXISTENCE

It should now be noted that it is no answer to the question, why a thing exists, to state *how long* it has existed. A geologist does not suppose that she has explained why there should be rivers and mountains merely by pointing out that they are old. Similarly, if one were to ask, concerning the ball of which we have spoken, for some sufficient reason for its being, he would not receive any answer upon being told that it had been there since yesterday. Nor would it be any better answer to say that it had existed since before anyone could remember, or even that it had always existed; for the question was not one concerning its age but its existence. If, to be sure, one were to ask where a given thing came from, or how it came into being, then upon learning that it had always existed he would learn that it never really *came* into being at all; but he could still reasonably wonder why it should exist at all. If, accordingly, the world—that is, the totality of all things excepting God, in case there is a god—had really no beginning at all, but has always existed in some form or other, then there is clearly no answer to the question, where it came from and when; it did not, on this supposition, *come* from anything at all, at any time. But still, it can be asked why there is a world, why indeed there is a beginningless world, why there should have perhaps always been something rather than nothing. And, if the principle of sufficient reason is a good principle, there must be an answer to that question, an answer that is by no means supplied by giving the world an age, or even an infinite age.

CREATION

This brings out an important point with respect to the concept of creation that is often misunderstood, particularly by those whose thinking has been influenced by Christian ideas. People tend to think that creation—for example, the creation of the world by God—*means* creation *in time,* from which it of course logically follows that if the world had no beginning in time, then it cannot be the creation of God. This, however, is erroneous, for creation means essentially *dependence*, even in Christian theology. If one thing is the creation of another, then it depends for its existence on that other, and this is perfectly consistent with saying that both are eternal, that neither ever came into being and hence, that neither was ever created at any point of time. Perhaps an analogy will help convey this point. Consider, then, a flame that is casting beams of light. Now, there seems to be a clear sense in which the beams of light are dependent for their existence upon the flame, which is their source, while the flame, on the other hand, is not similarly dependent for its existence upon them. The beams of light arise from the flame, but the flame does not arise from them. In this sense, they are the creation of the flame; they derive their existence from it. And none of this has any reference to time; the relationship of dependence in such a case would not be altered in the slightest if we supposed that the flame, and with it the beams of light, had always existed, that neither had ever *come* into being.

Now if the world is the creation of God, its relationship to God should be thought of in this fashion; namely, that the world depends for its existence upon God, and could not exist independently of God. If God is eternal, as those who believe in God generally assume, then the world may (though it need not) be eternal too, without that altering in the least its dependence upon God for its existence, and hence without altering its being the creation of God. The supposition of God's eternality, on the other hand, does not by itself imply that the world is eternal too; for there is not the least reason why something of finite duration might not depend for its existence upon something of infinite duration—though the reverse is, of course, impossible.

GOD

If we think of God as "the creator of heaven and earth," and if we consider heaven and earth to include everything that exists except God, then we appear to have, in the foregoing considerations, fairly strong reasons for asserting that God, as so conceived, exists. Now of course most people have much more in mind than this when they think of God, for religions have ascribed to God ever so many attributes that are not at all implied by describing him merely as the creator of the world; but that is not relevant here. Most religious persons do, in any case, think of God as being at least the creator, as that being upon which everything ultimately depends, no matter what else they may say about Him in addition. It is, in fact, the first item in the creeds of Christianity that God is the "creator of heaven and earth." And, it seems, there are good metaphysical reasons, as distinguished from the persuasions of faith, for thinking that such a creative being exists.

If, as seems clearly implied by the principle of sufficient reason, there must be a reason for the existence of heaven and earth—i.e., for the world—then that reason must be found either in the world itself, or outside it, in something that is literally supranatural, or outside heaven and earth. Now if we suppose that the world—i e., the totality of all things except God—contains within itself the reason for its existence, we are supposing that it exists by its very nature, that is, that it is a necessary being. In that case there would, of course, be no reason for saying that it must depend upon God or anything else for its existence; for if it exists by its very nature, then it depends upon nothing but itself, much as the sun depends upon nothing but itself for its heat. This, however, is implausible, for we find nothing about the world or anything in it to suggest that it exists by its own nature, and we do find, on the contrary, ever so many things to suggest that it does not. For in the first place, anything that exists by its very nature must necessarily be eternal and indestructible. It would be a self-contradiction to say of anything that it exists by its own nature, or is a necessarily existing thing, and at the same time to say that it comes into being or passes away, or that it ever could come into being or pass away. Nothing about the world seems at all like this, for concerning anything in the world, we can perfectly easily think of it as being annihilated, or as never having existed in the first place, without there being the slightest hint of any absurdity in such a supposition. Some of the things in the universe are, to be sure, very old; the moon, for example, or the stars and the planets. It is even possible to imagine that they have always existed. Yet it seems quite impossible to suppose that they owe their existence to nothing but themselves, that they bestow existence upon themselves by their very natures, or that they are in themselves things of such nature that it would be impossible for them not to exist. Even if we suppose that something, such as the sun, for instance, has existed forever, and will never cease, still we cannot conclude just from this that it exists by its own nature. If, as is of course very doubtful, the sun has existed forever and will never cease, then it is possible that its heat and light have also existed forever and will never cease; but that would not show that the heat and light of the sun exist by their own natures. They are obviously contingent and depend on the sun for their existence, whether they are beginningless and everlasting or not.

There seems to be nothing in the world, then, concerning which it is at all plausible to suppose that it exists by its own nature, or contains within itself the reason for its existence. In fact, everything in the world appears to be quite plainly the opposite, namely, something that not only need not exist, but at some time or other, past or future or both, does not in fact exist. Everything in the world seems to have a finite duration, whether long or short. Most things, such as ourselves, exist only for a short while; they come into being, then soon cease. Other things, like the heavenly bodies, last longer, but they are still corruptible, and from all that we can gather about them, they too seem destined eventually to perish. We arrive at the conclusion, then, that although the world may contain some things that have always existed and are destined never to perish, it is nevertheless doubtful that it contains any such thing, and, in any case, everything in the world is capable of perishing, and nothing in it, however long it may already have existed and however long it may yet remain, exists by its own nature but depends instead upon something else.

Although this might be true of everything in the world, is it necessarily true of the world itself? That is, if we grant, as we seem forced to, that nothing in the world exists by its own nature, that everything in the world is contingent and perishable, must we also say that the world itself, or the totality of all these perishable things, is also contingent and perishable? Logically, we are not forced to, for it is logically possible that the totality of all perishable things might itself be imperishable, and hence, that the world might exist by its own nature, even though it is composed exclusively of things that are contingent. It is not logically necessary that a totality should share the defects of its members. For example, even though every person is mortal, it does not follow from this that the human race, or the totality of all people, is also mortal; for it is possible that there will always be human beings, even though there are no human beings who will always exist. Similarly, it is possible that the world is in itself a necessary thing, even though it is composed entirely of things that are contingent.

This is logically possible, but it is not plausible. For we find nothing whatever about the world, any more than in its parts, to suggest that it exists by its own nature. Concerning anything in the world, we have not the slightest difficulty in supposing that it should perish, or even that it should never have existed in the first place. We have almost as little difficulty in supposing this of the world itself. It might be somewhat hard to think of everything as utterly perishing and leaving no trace whatever of its ever having been, but there seems to be not the slightest difficulty in imagining that the world should never have existed in the first place. We can, for instance, perfectly easily suppose that nothing in the world had ever existed except, let us suppose, a single grain of sand, and we can thus suppose that this grain of sand has forever constituted the whole universe. Now if we consider just this grain of sand, it is quite impossible for us to suppose that it exists by its very nature and could never have failed to exist. It clearly depends for its existence upon something other than itself, if it depends on anything at all. The same will be true if we consider the world to consist not of one grain of sand but of two, or of a million, or, as we in fact find, of a vast number of stars and planets and all their minuter parts.

It would seem, then, that the world, in case it happens to exist at all—and this is quite beyond doubt—is contingent and thus dependent upon something other than itself for its existence, if it depends upon anything at all. And it must depend upon something, for otherwise there could be no reason why it exists in the first place. Now, that upon which the world depends must be something that either exists by its own nature or does not. If it does not exist by its own nature, then it, in turn, depends for its existence upon something else, and so on. Now then, we can say either of two things; namely, (1) that the world depends for its existence upon something else, which in turn depends on still another thing, this depending upon still another, ad infinitum; or (2) that the world derives its existence from something that exists by its own nature and that is accordingly eternal and imperishable, and is the creator of heaven and earth. The first of these alternatives, however, is impossible, for it does not render a sufficient reason why anything should exist in the first place. Instead of supplying a reason why any world should exist, it repeatedly begs off giving a reason. It explains what is dependent and perishable in terms of what is itself dependent and perishable, leaving us still without a reason why perishable things should exist at all, which is what we are seeking. Ultimately, then, it would seem that the world, or the totality of contingent or perishable things, in case it exists at all, must depend upon something that is necessary and imperishable, and that accordingly exists, not in dependence upon something else, but by its own nature.

"SELF-CAUSED"

What has been said thus far gives some intimation of what meaning should be attached to the concept of a self-caused being; a concept that is quite generally misunderstood, sometimes even by scholars. To say that something—God, for example—is self-caused, or is the cause of its own existence, does not mean that this being brings itself into existence, which is a perfectly absurd idea. Nothing can *bring* itself into existence. To say that something is self-caused (*causa sui*) means only that it exists, not contingently or in dependence upon something else but by its own nature, which is only to say that it is a being which is such that it can neither come into being nor perish. Now, whether in fact such a being exists or not, there is in any case no absurdity in the idea. We have found, in fact, that the principle of sufficient reason seems to point to the existence of such a being, as that upon which the world, with everything in it, must ultimately depend for its existence.

"NECESSARY BEING"

A being that depends for its existence upon nothing but itself and is in this sense self-caused, can equally be described as a necessary being; that is to say, a being that is not contingent, and hence not perishable. For in the case of anything that exists by its own nature and is dependent upon nothing else, it is impossible that it should not exist, which is equivalent to saying that it is necessary. Many persons have professed to find the gravest difficulties in this concept, too, but that is partly because it has been confused with other notions. If it makes sense to speak of anything as an *impossible* being, or something that by its very nature does not exist, then it is hard to see why the idea of a necessary being, or something that in its very nature exists, should not be just as comprehensible. And of course, we have not the slightest difficulty in speaking of something, such as a square circle or a formless body, as an impossible being. And if it makes sense to speak of something as being perishable, contingent, and dependent upon something other than itself for its existence, as it surely does, then there seems to be no difficulty in thinking of something as imperishable and dependent upon nothing other than itself for its existence.

"FIRST CAUSE"

From these considerations we can see also what is properly meant by a "first cause," an appellative that has often been applied to God by theologians and that many persons have deemed an absurdity. It is a common criticism of this notion to say that there need not be any first cause, because the series of causes and effects that constitute the history of the universe might be infinite or beginningless and must, in fact, be infinite in case the universe itself had no beginning in time. This criticism, however, reflects a total misconception of what is meant by a first cause. *First* here does not mean first in time, and when God is spoken of as a first cause He is not being described as a being that, at some time in the remote past, *started* everything. To describe God as a first cause is only to say that He is literally a *primary* rather than a secondary cause, an *ultimate* rather than a derived cause, or a being upon which all other things, heaven and earth, ultimately depend for their existence. It is, in short, only to say that God is the creator, in the sense of creation previously explained. Now this, of course, is perfectly consistent with saying that the world is eternal or beginningless. As we have seen, one gives no reason for the existence of a world merely by giving it an age, even if it is supposed to have an infinite age. To use a helpful analogy, we can say that the sun is the first cause of daylight and, for that matter, of the moonlight of the night as well, which means only that daylight and moonlight ultimately depend upon the sun for their existence. The moon, on the other hand, is only a secondary or derivative cause of its light. This light would be no less dependent upon the sun if we affirmed that it had no beginning, for an ageless and beginningless light requires a source no less than an ephemeral one. If we supposed that the sun has always existed, and with it its light, then we would have to say that the sun has always been the first—i.e., the primary or ultimate—cause of its light. Such is precisely the manner in which God should be thought of, and is by theologians often thought of, as the first cause of heaven and earth.

The Argument from Design

WILLIAM PALEY

William Paley (1743–1805) was a Utilitarian philosopher and an English Anglican priest. During his lifetime, Paley served both as an official in the Anglican Church and as the widely read author of a number of influential textbooks in ethics and theology. His best-known work is his 1804 *Natural Theology, or Evidences of the Existence and Attributes of the Deity collected from the Appearances of Nature*, from which the selection that appears here has been drawn. In it, Paley presents his highly influential version of the argument from design (also known as the teleological argument.)

CHAPTER ONE: THE STATE OF THE ARGUMENT

In crossing a heath, suppose I pitched my foot against a *stone* and were asked how the stone came to be there. I might possibly answer that for anything I knew to the contrary it had lain there forever; nor would it, perhaps, be very easy to show the absurdity of this answer. But suppose I had found a *watch* upon the ground, and it should be inquired how the watch happened to be in that place. I should hardly think of the answer which I had before given, that for anything I knew the watch might have always been there. Yet why should not this answer serve for the watch as well as for the stone? Why is it not as admissible in the second case as in the first? For this reason, and for no other, namely, that when we come to inspect the watch, we perceive—what we could not discover in the stone—that its several parts are framed and

From *Natural Theology* (1800), eds. M. D. Eddy and D. Knight, pps. 7–10, 16. Reprinted by permission of Oxford University Press.

put together for a purpose, e.g., that they are so formed and adjusted as to produce motion, and that motion so regulated as to point out the hour of the day; that if the different parts had been differently shaped from what they are, of a different size from what they are, or placed after any other manner or in any other order than that in which they are placed, either no motion at all would have been carried on in the machine, or none which would have answered the use that is now served by it. To reckon up a few of the plainest of these parts and of their offices, all tending to one result; we see a cylindrical box containing a coiled elastic spring, which, by its endeavor to relax itself, turns round the box. We next observe a flexible chain—artificially wrought for the sake of flexure—communicating the action of the spring from the box to the fusee. We then find a series of wheels, the teeth of which catch in and apply to each other, conducting the motion from the fusee to the balance and from the balance to the pointer, and at the same time, by the size and shape of those wheels, so regulating that motion as to terminate in causing an index, by an equable and measured progression, to pass over a given space in a given time. We take notice that the wheels are made of brass, in order to keep them from rust; the springs of steel, no other metal being so elastic; that over the face of the watch there is placed a glass, a material employed in no other part of the work, but in the room of which, if there had been any other than a transparent substance, the hour could not be seen without opening the case. This mechanism being observed—it requires indeed an examination of the instrument, and perhaps some previous knowledge of the subject, to perceive and understand it; but being once, as we have said, observed and understood—the inference we think is inevitable, that the watch must have had a maker—that there must have existed, at some time and at some place or other, an artificer or artificers who formed it for the purpose which we find it actually to answer, who comprehended its construction and designed its use.

I. Nor would it, I apprehend, weaken the conclusion, that we had never seen a watch made—that we had never known an artist capable of making one—that we were altogether incapable of executing such a piece of workmanship ourselves, or of understanding in what manner it was performed; all this being no more than what is true of some exquisite remains of ancient art, of some lost arts, and, to the generality of mankind, of the more curious productions of modern manufacture. Does one man in a million know how oval frames are turned? Ignorance of this kind exalts our opinion of the unseen and unknown artist's skill, if he be unseen and unknown, but raises no doubt in our minds of the existence and agency of such an artist, at some former time and in some place or other. Nor can I perceive that it varies at all the inference, whether the question arise concerning a human agent or concerning an agent of a different species, or an agent possessing in some respects a different nature.

II. Neither, secondly, would it invalidate our conclusion, that the watch sometimes went wrong or that it seldom went exactly right. The purpose of the machinery, the design, and the designer might be evident, and in the case supposed, would be evident, in whatever way we accounted for the irregularity of the movement, or whether we could account for it or not. It is not necessary that a machine be perfect in order to show with what design it was made: still less necessary, where the only question is whether it were made with any design at all.

III. Nor, thirdly, would it bring any uncertainty into the argument, if there were a few parts of the watch, concerning which we could not discover or had not yet discovered in what manner they conduced to the general effect; or even some parts, concerning which we could not ascertain whether they conduced to that effect in any manner whatever. For, as to the first branch of the case, if by the loss, or disorder, or decay of the parts in question, the movement of the watch were found in fact to be stopped, or disturbed, or retarded, no doubt would remain in our minds as to the utility or intention of these parts, although we should be unable to investigate the manner according to which, or the connection by which, the ultimate effect depended upon their action or assistance; and the more complex is the machine, the more likely is this obscurity to arise. Then, as to the second thing supposed, namely, that there were parts which might be spared without prejudice to the movement of the watch, and that we had proved this by experiment, these superfluous parts, even if we were completely assured that they were such, would not vacate the reasoning which we had instituted concerning other parts. The indication of contrivance remained, with respect to them, nearly as it was before.

IV. Nor, fourthly, would any man in his senses think the existence of the watch with its various machinery accounted for, by being told that it was one out of possible combinations of material forms; that whatever he had found in the place where he found the watch, must have contained some internal configuration or other; and that this configuration might be the structure now exhibited, namely, of the works of a watch, as well as a different structure.

V. Nor, fifthly, would it yield his inquiry more satisfaction, to be answered that there existed in things a principle of order, which had disposed the parts of the watch into their present form and situation. He never knew a watch made by the principle of order; nor can he even form to himself an idea of what is meant by a principle of order distinct from the intelligence of the watchmaker.

VI. Sixthly, he would be surprised to hear that the mechanism of the watch was no proof of contrivance, only a motive to induce the mind to think so:

VII. And not less surprised to be informed that the watch in his hand was nothing more than the result of the laws of *metallic* nature. It is a perversion of language to assign any law as the efficient, operative cause of any thing. A law presupposes an agent, for it is only the mode according to which an agent proceeds; it implies a power, for it is the order according to which that power acts. Without this agent, without this power, which are both distinct from itself, the *law* does nothing, is nothing. The expression, "the law of metallic nature," may sound strange and harsh to a philosophic ear; but it seems quite as justifiable as some others which are more familiar to him, such as "the law of vegetable nature," "the law of animal nature," or, indeed, as "the law of nature" in general, when assigned as the cause of phenomena, in exclusion of agency and power, or when it is substituted into the place of these.

VIII. Neither, lastly, would our observer be driven out of his conclusion or from his confidence in its truth by being told that he knew nothing at all about the matter. He knows enough for his argument; he knows the utility of the end; he knows the subserviency and adaptation of the means to the end. These points being known, his ignorance of other points, his doubts concerning other points affect not the certainty of his reasoning. The consciousness of knowing little need not beget a distrust of that which he does know. . . .

CHAPTER III: APPLICATION OF THE ARGUMENT

. . . Every indication of contrivance, every manifestation of design, which existed in the watch, exists in the works of nature; with the difference, on the side of nature, of being greater and more, and that in a degree which exceeds all computation. I mean that the contrivances of nature surpass the contrivances of art in the complexity, subtility, and curiosity of the mechanism; and still more, if possible, do they go beyond them in number and variety; yet, in a multitude of cases, are not less evidently mechanical, not less evidently contrivances, not less evidently accommodated to their end, or suited to their office, than are the most perfect productions of human ingenuity. . . .

I know no better method of introducing so large a subject, than that of comparing a single thing with a single thing; an eye, for example, with a telescope. As far as the examination of the instrument goes, there is precisely the same proof that the eye was made for vision, as there is that the telescope was made for assisting it. They are made upon the same principles; both being adjusted to the laws by which the transmission and reflection of rays of light are regulated. I speak not of the origin of the laws themselves; but such laws being fixed, the construction in both cases, is adapted to them. For instance; these laws require, in order to produce the same effect, that the rays of light, in passing from water into the eye, should be refracted by a more convex surface than when it passes out of air into the eye. Accordingly we find, that the eye of a fish, in that part of it called the crystalline lens, is much rounder than the eye of terrestrial animals. What plainer manifestation of design can there be than this difference? What could a mathematical instrument-maker have done more, to show his knowledge of his principle, his application of that knowledge, his suiting of his means to his end; I will not say to display the compass or excellence of his skill and art, for in these all comparison is indecorous, but to testify counsel, choice, consideration, purpose?...

Does God Exist?

ERNEST NAGEL

Ernest Nagel (1901–85) was a Czech-born American philosopher of science. He earned his Ph.D. at Columbia University in 1930 and continued there as a teacher for the next forty years. Nagel's philosophical work reflected his respect for the relevance of scientific inquiry to philosophical reflection. His most famous book was his 1961 work *The Structure of Science*.

The selection that appears here is drawn from a longer essay by Nagel entitled "Philosophical Concepts of Atheism," which was published in 1959 in an anthology of papers on religious belief. In this selection, Nagel presents and criticizes all three of the main arguments for the existence of God: the cosmological argument, the ontological argument, and the argument from design. He also presents a famous argument against the existence of God—the problem of evil, which the two selections in the next section discuss in more detail.

1

I want now to discuss three classical arguments for the existence of God, arguments which have constituted at least a partial basis for theistic commitments. As long as theism is defended simply as a dogma, asserted as a matter of direct revelation or as the deliverance of authority, belief in the dogma is impregnable to rational argument. In fact, however, reasons are frequently advanced in support of the theistic creed, and these reasons have been the subject of acute philosophical critiques.

One of the oldest intellectual defenses of theism is the cosmological argument, also known as the argument from a first cause. Briefly put, the argument runs as follows. Every event must have a cause. Hence an event A must have as cause some event B, which in turn must have a cause C, and so on. But if there is no end to this backward progression of causes, the progression will be infinite; and in the opinion of those who use this argument, an infinite series of actual events is unintelligible and absurd. Hence there must be a first cause, and this first cause is God, the initiator of all change in the universe.

The argument is an ancient one, and ... it has impressed many generations of exceptionally keen minds. The argument is nonetheless a weak reed on which to rest the theistic thesis. Let us waive any question concerning the validity of the principle that every event has a cause, for though the question is important, its discussion would lead us far afield. However, if the principle is assumed, it is

---

From "Philosophical Concepts of Atheism," in J. E. Fairchild (ed.), *Basic Beliefs: The Religious Philosophies of Mankind* (Dobbs Ferry, NY: Sheridan House, Inc. 1959, 1987). Reprinted with permission.

surely incongruous to postulate a first cause as a way of escaping from the coils of an infinite series. For if everything must have a cause, why does not God require one for His own existence? The standard answer is that He does not need any, because He is self-caused. But if God can be self-caused, why cannot the world itself be self-caused? Why do we require a God transcending the world to bring the world into existence and to initiate changes in it? On the other hand, the supposed inconceivability and absurdity of an infinite series of regressive causes will be admitted by no one who has competent familiarity with the modern mathematical analysis of infinity. The cosmological argument does not stand up under scrutiny.

The second "proof" of God's existence is usually called the ontological argument. It too has a long history going back to early Christian days, though it acquired great prominence only in medieval times. The argument can be stated in several ways, one of which is the following. Since God is conceived to be omnipotent, he is a perfect being. A perfect being is defined as one whose essence or nature lacks no attributes (or properties) whatsoever, one whose nature is complete in every respect. But it is evident that we have an idea of a perfect being, for we have just defined the idea; and since this is so, the argument continues, God who is the perfect being must exist. Why must he? Because his existence follows from his defined nature. For if God lacked the attribute of existence, he would be lacking at least one attribute, and would therefore not be perfect. To sum up, since we have an idea of God as a perfect being, God must exist.

There are several ways of approaching this argument, but I shall consider only one. The argument was exploded by the eighteenth century philosopher Immanuel Kant. The substance of Kant's criticism is that it is just a confusion to say that existence is an attribute, and that though the *word* "existence" may occur as the grammatical predicate in a sentence, no attribute is being predicated of a thing when we say that the thing exists or has existence. Thus, to use Kant's example, when we think of $100 we are thinking of the nature of this sum of money; but the nature of $100 remains the same whether we have $100 in our pockets or not. Accordingly, we are confounding grammar with logic if we suppose that some characteristic is being attributed to the nature of $100 when we say that a hundred dollar bill exists in someone's pocket.

To make the point clearer, consider another example. When we say that a lion has a tawny color, we are predicating a certain attribute of the animal, and similarly when we say that the lion is fierce or is hungry. But when we say the lion exists, all that we are saying is that something is (or has the nature of) a lion; we are not specifying an attribute which belongs to the nature of anything that is a lion. In short, the word "existence" does not signify any attribute, and in consequence no attribute that belongs to the nature of anything. Accordingly, it does not follow from the assumption that we have an idea of a perfect being that such a being exists. For the idea of a perfect being does not involve the attribute of existence as a constituent of that idea, since there is no such attribute. The ontological argument thus has a serious leak, and it can hold no water.

2

The two arguments discussed thus far are purely dialectical, and attempt to establish God's existence without any appeal to empirical data. The next argument, called the argument from design, is different in character, for it is based on what purports to be empirical evidence. I wish to examine two forms of this argument.

One variant of it calls attention to the remarkable way in which different things and processes in the world are integrated with each other, and concludes that this mutual "fitness" of things can be explained only by the assumption of a divine architect who planned the world and everything in it. For example, living organisms can maintain themselves in a variety of environments, and do so in virtue of their delicate mechanisms which adapt the organisms to all sorts of environmental changes. There is thus an intricate pattern of means and ends throughout the animate world. But the existence of this pattern is unintelligible, so the argument runs, except on the hypothesis that the pattern has been deliberately instituted by a Supreme Designer. If we find a watch in some deserted spot, we do not think it came into existence by chance, and we do not hesitate to conclude that an intelligent creature designed and made it. But the world and all its contents exhibit mechanisms and mutual adjustments that are far more complicated and subtle than are those of a watch. Must we not therefore conclude that these things too have a Creator?

The conclusion of this argument is based on an inference from analogy: the watch and the world are alike in possessing a congruence of parts and an adjustment of means to ends; the watch has a watch-maker; hence the world has a world-maker. But is the analogy a good one? Let us once more waive some important issues, in particular the issue whether the universe is the unified system such as the watch admittedly is. And let us concentrate on the question what is the ground for our assurance that watches do not come into existence except through the operations of intelligent manufacturers. The answer is plain. We have never run across a watch which has not been deliberately made by someone. But the situation is nothing like this in the case of the innumerable animate and inanimate systems with which we are familiar. Even in the case of living organisms, though they are generated by their parent organisms, the parents do not "make" their progeny in the same sense in which watch-makers make watches. And once this point is clear, the inference from the existence of living organisms to the existence of a supreme designer no longer appears credible.

Moreover, the argument loses all its force if the facts which the hypothesis of a divine designer is supposed to explain can be understood on the basis of a better supported assumption. And indeed, such an alternative explanation is one of the achievements of Darwinian biology. For Darwin showed that one can account for the variety of biological species, as well as for their adaptations to their environments, without invoking a divine creator and acts of special creation. The Darwinian theory explains the diversity of biological species in terms of chance variations in the structure of organisms, and of a mechanism of selection which retains those variant forms that possess some advantages for survival. The evidence for these assumptions is considerable; and developments subsequent to Darwin have only strengthened the case for a thoroughly naturalistic explanation of the facts of biological adaptation. In any event, this version of the argument from design has nothing to recommend it.

A second form of this argument has been recently revived in the speculations of some modern physicists. No one who is familiar with the facts can fail to be impressed by the success with which the use of mathematical methods has enabled us to obtain intellectual mastery of many parts of nature. But some thinkers have therefore concluded that since the book of nature is ostensibly written in mathematical language, nature must be the creation of a divine mathematician. However, the argument is most dubious. For it rests, among other things, on the assumption that mathematical tools can be successfully used only if the events of nature exhibit some *special* kind of order, and on the further assumption that if the structure of things were different from what they are, mathematical language would be inadequate for describing such structure. But it can be shown that no matter what the world were like—even if it impressed us as being utterly chaotic—it would still possess some order, and would in principle be amenable to a mathematical description. In point of fact, it makes no sense to say that there is absolutely *no* pattern in any conceivable subject matter. To be sure, there are differences in complexities of structure, and if the patterns of events were sufficiently complex, we might not be able to unravel them. But however that may be, the success of mathematical physics in giving us some understanding of the world around us does not yield the conclusion that only a mathematician could have devised the patterns of order we have discovered in nature.

3

The inconclusiveness of the three classical arguments for the existence of God was already made evident by Kant, in a manner substantially not different from the above discussion. There are, however, other types of arguments for theism that have been influential in the history of thought, two of which I wish to consider, even if only briefly.

Indeed, though Kant destroyed the classical intellectual foundations for theism, he himself invented a fresh argument for it. Kant's attempted proof is not intended to be a purely theoretical demonstration, and is based on the supposed facts of our moral nature. It has exerted an enormous influence on subsequent theological speculation. In barest outline, the argument is as follows. According to Kant, we are subject not only to physical laws like the rest of nature, but also to moral ones. These moral laws are categorical imperatives, which we must heed not because of their utilitarian consequences, but simply because as autonomous moral agents it is our duty to accept them as binding.* However, Kant was keenly aware that though virtue may be its reward, the virtuous man (that is, the man who acts out of a sense of duty and in conformity with the moral law) does not always receive his just desserts in this world; nor did he shut his eyes to the fact that evil men frequently enjoy the best things this world has to offer. In short, virtue does not always reap happiness. Nevertheless, the highest human good is the realization of happiness commensurate with one's virtue; and Kant believed that it is a practical postulate of the moral life to promote this good. But what can guarantee that the highest good is realizable? Such a guarantee can be found only in God, who must therefore exist if the highest good is not to be a fatuous ideal. The existence of an omnipotent, omniscient, and omnibenevolent God is thus postulated as a necessary condition for the possibility of a moral life.

Despite the prestige this argument has acquired, it is difficult to grant it any force. It is easy enough to postulate God's existence. But as Bertrand Russell† observed in another connection, postulation has all the advantages of theft over honest toil. No postulation carries with it any assurance that what is postulated is actually the case. And though we may postulate God's existence as a means to guaranteeing the possibility of realizing happiness together with virtue, the postulation establishes neither the actual realizability of this ideal nor the fact of his existence. Moreover, the argument is not made more cogent when we recognize that it is based squarely on the highly dubious conception that considerations of utility and human happiness must not enter into the determination of what is morally obligatory. Having built his moral theory on a radical separation of means from ends, Kant was driven to the desperate postulation of God's existence in order to relate them again. The argument is thus at best a tour de force, contrived to remedy a fatal flaw in Kant's initial moral assumptions. It carries no conviction to anyone who does not commit Kant's initial blunder.

One further type of argument, pervasive in much Protestant theological literature, deserves brief mention. Arguments of this type take their point of departure from the psychology of religious and mystical experience. Those who have undergone such experiences often report that during the experience they feel themselves to be in the presence of the divine and holy, that they lose their sense of self-identity and become merged with some fundamental reality, or that they enjoy a feeling of total dependence upon some ultimate power. The overwhelming sense of transcending one's finitude which characterizes such vivid periods of life, and of coalescing with some ultimate source of all existence, is then taken to be compelling evidence for the existence of a supreme being. In a variant form of this argument, other theologians have identified God as the object which satisfies the commonly experienced need for integrating one's scattered and conflicting impulses into a coherent unity, or as the subject which is of ultimate concern to us. In short, a proof of God's existence is found in the occurrence of certain distinctive experiences.

It would be flying in the face of well-attested facts were one to deny that such experiences frequently occur. But do these facts constitute evidence for the conclusion based on them? Does the fact, for example, that an individual experiences a profound sense of direct contact with an alleged transcendent ground of all reality constitute competent evidence for the claim that there is such a ground and that it is the immediate cause of the experience? If well-established canons for evaluating evidence are accepted, the answer is surely negative. No one will dispute that many

* A presentation of Kant's moral philosophy can be found in the "Deontology" section (IIA) following.

† Bertrand Russell (1872–1970) was an important British philosopher, mathematician, and political activist.

men do have vivid experiences in which such things as ghosts or pink elephants appear before them; but only the hopelessly credulous will without further ado count such experiences as establishing the existence of ghosts and pink elephants. To establish the existence of such things, evidence is required that is obtained under controlled conditions and that can be confirmed by independent inquirers. Again, though a man's report that he is suffering pain may be taken at face value, one cannot take at face value the claim, were he to make it, that it is the food he ate which is the cause (or a contributory cause) of his felt pain—not even if the man were to report a vivid feeling of abdominal disturbance. And similarly, an overwhelming feeling of being in the presence of the Divine is evidence enough for admitting the genuineness of such feeling; it is no evidence for the claim that a supreme being with a substantial existence independent of the experience is the cause of the experience.

4

Thus far the discussion has been concerned with noting inadequacies in various arguments widely used to support theism. However, much atheistic criticism is also directed toward exposing incoherencies in the very thesis of theism. I want therefore to consider this aspect of the atheistic critique, though I will restrict myself to the central difficulty in the theistic position which arises from the simultaneous attribution of omnipotence, omniscience, and omnibenevolence to the Deity. The difficulty is that of reconciling these attributes with the occurrence of evil in the world. Accordingly, the question to which I now turn is whether, despite the existence of evil, it is possible to construct a theodicy* which will justify the ways of an infinitely powerful and just God to man.

Two main types of solutions have been proposed for this problem. One way that is frequently used is to maintain that what is commonly called evil is only an illusion, or at worst only the "privation" or absence of good. Accordingly, evil is not "really real," it is only the "negative" side of God's beneficence, it is only the product of our limited intelligence which fails to plumb the true character of God's creative bounty. A sufficient comment on this proposed solution is that facts are not altered or abolished by rebaptizing them. Evil may indeed be only an appearance and not genuine. But this does not eliminate from the realm of appearance the tragedies, the sufferings, and the iniquities which men so frequently endure. And it raises once more, though on another level, the problem of reconciling the fact that there is evil in the realm of appearance with God's alleged omnibenevolence. In any event, it is small comfort to anyone suffering a cruel misfortune for which he is in no way responsible, to be told that what he is undergoing is only the absence of good. It is a gratuitous insult to mankind, a symptom of insensitivity and indifference to human suffering, to be assured that all the miseries and agonies men experience are only illusory.

Another gambit often played in attempting to justify the ways of God to man is to argue that the things called evil are evil only because they are viewed in isolation; they are not evil when viewed in proper perspective and in relation to the rest of creation. Thus, if one attends to but a single instrument in an orchestra, the sounds issuing from it may indeed be harsh and discordant. But if one is placed at a proper distance from the whole orchestra, the sounds of that single instrument will mingle with the sounds issuing from the other players to produce a marvellous bit of symphonic music. Analogously, experiences we call painful undoubtedly occur and are real enough. But the pain is judged to be an evil only because it is experienced in a limited perspective—the pain is there for the sake of a more inclusive good, whose reality eludes us because our intelligences are too weak to apprehend things in their entirety.

It is an appropriate retort to this argument that of course we judge things to be evil in a human perspective, but that since we are not God this is the only proper perspective in which to judge them. It may indeed be the case that what is evil for us is not evil for some other part of creation. However, we are not this other part of creation, and it is irrelevant to argue

* The term "theodicy," from the Greek *theos* (God) and *dike* (righteous), was coined by the German philosopher Gottfried Leibniz (1646–1716). The expression describes attempts to show that the existence of evil does not preclude the existence of God.

that were we something other than what we are, our evaluations of what is good and bad would be different. Moreover, the worthlessness of the argument becomes even more evident if we remind ourselves that it is unsupported speculation to suppose that whatever is evil in a finite perspective is good from the purported perspective of the totality of things. For the argument can be turned around: what we judge to be a good is a good only because it is viewed in isolation; when it is viewed in proper perspective, and in relation to the entire scheme of things, it is an evil. This is in fact a standard form of the argument for a universal pessimism. Is it any worse than the similar argument for a universal optimism? The very raising of this question is a *reductio ad absurdum* of the proposed solution to the ancient problem of evil.

I do not believe it is possible to reconcile the alleged omnipotence and omnibenevolence of God with the unvarnished facts of human existence. In point of fact, many theologians have concurred in this conclusion; for in order to escape from the difficulty which the traditional attributes of God present, they have assumed that God is not all powerful, and that there are limits as to what He can do in his efforts to establish a righteous order in the universe. But whether such a modified theology is better off is doubtful; and in any event, the question still remains whether the facts of human life support the claim that an omnibenevolent Deity, though limited in power, is revealed in the ordering of human history. It is pertinent to note in this connection that though there have been many historians who have made the effort, no historian has yet succeeded in showing to the satisfaction of his professional colleagues that the hypothesis of a Divine Providence is capable of explaining anything which cannot be explained just as well without this hypothesis.

◈ THE PROBLEM OF EVIL—AND REPLIES ◈

The Problem of Evil

JOHN HICK

John Hick (1922–) is a philosopher of religion and theologian who taught for many years at Claremont Graduate University in California and at the University of Birmingham in England. He began his Christian life as an Evangelical fundamentalist, but he is best known for his more recent advocacy of religious pluralism.

The selection we are reading is an excerpt from his textbook *Philosophy of Religion*, originally published in 1963 and revised a decade later. In it, Hick presents one line of response to the problem of evil.

THE PROBLEM OF EVIL

To many, the most powerful positive objection to belief in God is the fact of evil. Probably for most agnostics it is the appalling depth and extent of human suffering, more than anything else, that makes the idea of a loving Creator seem so implausible and disposes them toward one or another of the various naturalistic theories of religion.

As a challenge to theism, the problem of evil has traditionally been posed in the form of a dilemma: if God is perfectly loving, he must wish to abolish evil;

From *Philosophy of Religion*, 3rd ed., © 1963 by Prentice-Hall, Inc., Englewood Cliffs, NJ.

and if he is all-powerful, he must be able to abolish evil. But evil exists; therefore God cannot be both omnipotent and perfectly loving.

Certain solutions, which at once suggest themselves, have to be ruled out so far as the Judaic-Christian faith is concerned.

To say, for example (with contemporary Christian Science), that evil is an illusion of the human mind, is impossible within a religion based upon the stark realism of the Bible. Its pages faithfully reflect the characteristic mixture of good and evil in human experience. They record every kind of sorrow and suffering, every mode of man's inhumanity to man and of his painfully insecure existence in the world. There is no attempt to regard evil as anything but dark, menacingly ugly, heart-rending, and crushing. In the Christian scriptures, the climax of this history of evil is the crucifixion of Jesus, which is presented not only as a case of utterly unjust suffering, but as the violent and murderous rejection of God's Messiah. There can be no doubt, then, that for biblical faith evil is unambiguously evil and stands in direct opposition to God's will.

Again, to solve the problem of evil by means of the theory (sponsored, for example, by the Boston "Personalist" School)[1] of a finite deity who does the best he can with a material, intractable and coeternal with himself, is to have abandoned the basic premise of Hebrew-Christian monotheism; for the theory amounts to rejecting belief in the infinity and sovereignty of God.

Indeed, any theory that would avoid the problem of the origin of evil by depicting it as an ultimate constituent of the universe, co-ordinate with good, has been repudiated in advance by the classic Christian teaching, first developed by Augustine (354–430 CE), that evil represents the going wrong of something that in itself is good.[2] Augustine holds firmly to the Hebrew-Christian conviction that the universe is *good*—that is to say, it is the creation of a good God for a good purpose. He completely rejects the ancient prejudice that matter is evil. There are, according to Augustine, higher and lower, greater and lesser goods in immense abundance and variety; but everything that has being is good in its own way and degree, except in so far as it may have become spoiled or corrupted. Evil—whether it be an evil will, an instance of pain, or some disorder or decay in nature—has not been set there by God, but represents the distortion of something that is inherently valuable. Whatever exists is, as such, and in its proper place, good; evil is essentially parasitic upon good, being disorder and perversion in a fundamentally good creation. This understanding of evil as something negative means that it is not willed and created by God; but it does not mean (as some have supposed) that evil is unreal and can be disregarded. On the contrary, the first effect of this doctrine is to accentuate even more the question of the origin of evil.

Theodicy,* as many modern Christian thinkers see it, is a modest enterprise, negative rather than positive in its conclusions. It does not claim to explain, nor to explain away, every instance of evil in human experience, but only to point to certain considerations that prevent the fact of evil (largely incomprehensible though it remains) from constituting a final and insuperable bar to rational belief in God.

In indicating these considerations it will be useful to follow the traditional division of the subject. There is the problem of *moral evil* or wickedness: why does an all-good and all-powerful God permit this? And there is the problem of the *nonmoral evil* of suffering or pain, both physical and mental: why has an all-good and all-powerful God created a world in which this occurs?

Christian thought has always considered moral evil in its relation to human freedom and responsibility. To be a person is to be a finite center of freedom, a (relatively) free and self-directing agent responsible for one's own decisions. This involves being free to act wrongly as well as to act rightly. The idea of a person who can be infallibly guaranteed always to act rightly is self-contradictory. There can be no certainty in advance that a genuinely free moral agent will never choose amiss. Consequently, the possibility of wrongdoing or sin is logically inseparable from the creation of finite persons, and to say that God should

* The term "theodicy," from the Greek *theos* (God) and *dike* (righteous), was coined by the German philosopher Gottfried Leibniz (1646–1716). The expression describes attempts to show that the existence of evil does not preclude the existence of God.

not have created beings who might sin amounts to saying that he should not have created people.

This thesis has been challenged in some recent philosophical discussions of the problem of evil, in which it is claimed that no contradiction is involved in saying that God might have made people who would be genuinely free but who could at the same time be guaranteed always to act rightly. A quote from one of these discussions follows:

> If there is no logical impossibility in a man's freely choosing the good on one, or on several occasions, there cannot be a logical impossibility in his freely choosing the good on every occasion. God was not, then, faced with a choice between making innocent automata and making beings who, in acting freely, would sometimes go wrong: there was open to him the obviously better possibility of making beings who would act freely but always go right. Clearly, his failure to avail himself of this possibility is inconsistent with his being both omnipotent and wholly good.[3]

A reply to this argument is indirectly suggested in another recent contribution to the discussion.[4] If by a free action we mean an action that is not externally compelled but that flows from the nature of the agent as he reacts to the circumstances in which he finds himself, there is indeed no contradiction between our being free and our actions being "caused" (by our own nature) and therefore being in principle predictable. There is a contradiction, however, in saying that God is the cause of our acting as we do but that we are free beings *in relation to God.* There is, in other words, a contradiction in saying that God has made us so that we shall of necessity act in a certain way, and that we are genuinely independent persons in relation to him. If all our thoughts and actions are divinely predestined, however free and morally responsible we may seem to be to ourselves, we cannot be free and morally responsible in the sight of God, but must instead be his helpless puppets. Such "freedom" is like that of a patient acting out a series of posthypnotic suggestions: he appears, even to himself, to be free, but his volitions have actually been predetermined by another will, that of the hypnotist, in relation to whom the patient is not a free agent.

A different objector might raise the question of whether or not we deny God's omnipotence if we admit that he is unable to create persons who are free from the risks inherent in personal freedom. The answer that has always been given is that to create such beings is logically impossible. It is no limitation upon God's power that he cannot accomplish the logically impossible, since there is nothing here to accomplish, but only a meaningless conjunction of words[5]—in this case "person who is not a person." God is able to create beings of any and every conceivable kind; but creatures who lack moral freedom, however superior they might be to human beings in other respects, would not be what we mean by persons. They would constitute a different form of life that God might have brought into existence instead of persons. When we ask why God did not create such beings in place of persons the traditional answer is that only persons could, in any meaningful sense, become "children of God," capable of entering into a personal relationship with their Creator by a free and uncompelled response to his love.

When we turn from the possibility of moral evil as a correlate of man's personal freedom to its actuality, we face something that must remain inexplicable even when it can be seen to be possible. For we can never provide a complete causal explanation of a free act; if we could, it would not be a free act. The origin of moral evil lies forever concealed within the mystery of human freedom.

The necessary connection between moral freedom and the possibility, now actualized, of sin throws light upon a great deal of the suffering that afflicts mankind. For an enormous amount of human pain arises either from the inhumanity or the culpable incompetence of mankind. This includes such major scourges as poverty, oppression and persecution, war, and all the injustice, indignity, and inequity that occur even in the most advanced societies. These evils are manifestations of human sin. Even disease is fostered to an extent, the limits of which have not yet been determined by psychosomatic medicine, by emotional and moral factors seated both in the individual and in his social environment. To the extent that all of these evils stem from human failures and wrong decisions, their possibility is inherent in the creation of free persons inhabiting a world that presents them with real choices followed by real consequences.

We may now turn more directly to the problem of suffering. Even though the major bulk of actual human pain is traceable to man's misused freedom as a sole or part cause, there remain other sources of pain that are entirely independent of the human will, for example, earthquake, hurricane, storm, flood, drought, and blight. In practice, it is often impossible to trace a boundary between the suffering that results from human wickedness and folly and that which falls upon mankind from without; both kinds of suffering are inextricably mingled together in human experience. For our present purpose, however, it is important to note that the latter category does exist and that it seems to be built into the very structure of our world. In response to it, theodicy, if it is wisely conducted, follows a negative path. It is not possible to show positively that each item of human pain serves a divine purpose of good; but on the other hand, it does seem possible to show that the divine purpose as it is understood in Judaism and Christianity could not be forwarded in a world that was designed as a permanent hedonistic paradise.[6]

An essential premise of this argument concerns the nature of the divine purpose in creating the world. The sceptic's assumption is that man is to be viewed as a completed creation and that God's purpose in making the world was to provide a suitable dwelling-place for this fully formed creature. Since God is good and loving, the environment that he has created for human life to inhabit will naturally be as pleasant and comfortable as possible. The problem is essentially similar to that of a man who builds a cage for some pet animal. Since our world, in fact, contains sources of hardship, inconvenience and danger of innumerable kinds, the conclusion follows that this world cannot have been created by a perfectly benevolent and all-powerful deity.[7]

Christianity, however, has never supposed that God's purpose in the creation of the world was to construct a paradise whose inhabitants would experience a maximum of pleasure and a minimum of pain. The world is seen, instead, as a place of "soul making" or person making in which free beings, grappling with the tasks and challenges of their existence in a common environment, may become "children of God" and "heirs of eternal life." A way of thinking theologically of God's continuing creative purpose for man was suggested by some of the early Hellenistic Fathers of the Christian Church, especially Irenaeus (2nd century CE). Following hints from Saint Paul (10–67 CE), Irenaeus taught that man has been made as a person in the image of God but has not yet been brought as a free and responsible agent into the finite likeness of God, which is revealed in Christ.[8] Our world, with all its rough edges, is the sphere in which this second and harder stage of the creative process is taking place.

This conception of the world (whether or not set in Irenaeus's theological framework) can be supported by the method of negative theodicy. Suppose, contrary to fact, that this world were a paradise from which all possibility of pain and suffering were excluded. The consequences would be very far-reaching. For example, no one could ever injure anyone else: the murderer's knife would turn to paper or his bullets to thin air; the bank safe, robbed of a million dollars, would miraculously become filled with another million dollars (without this device, on however large a scale, proving inflationary); fraud, deceit, conspiracy, and treason would somehow always leave the fabric of society undamaged. Again, no one would ever be injured by accident: the mountain climber, steeplejack, or playing child falling from a height would float unharmed to the ground; the reckless driver would never meet with disaster. There would be no need to work, since no harm could result from avoiding work; there would be no call to be concerned for others in time of need or danger, for in such a world there could be no real needs or dangers.

To make possible this continual series of individual adjustments, nature would have to work by "special providences" instead of running according to general laws that men must learn to respect on penalty of pain or death. The laws of nature would have to be extremely flexible: sometimes gravity would operate, sometimes not; sometimes an object would be hard and solid, sometimes soft. There could be no sciences, for there would be no enduring world structure to investigate. In eliminating the problems and hardships of an objective environment, with its own laws, life would become like a dream in which, delightfully but aimlessly, we would float and drift at ease.[9]

One can at least begin to imagine such a world. It is evident that our present ethical concepts would have no meaning in it. If, for example, the notion of harming someone is an essential element in the concept of a wrong action, in our hedonistic paradise there could be no wrong actions—nor any right actions in distinction from wrong. Courage and fortitude would have no point in an environment in which there is, by definition, no danger or difficulty. Generosity, kindness, the *agape* aspect of love, prudence, unselfishness, and all other ethical notions which presuppose life in an objective environment could not even be formed. Consequently, such a world, however well it might promote pleasure, would be very ill adapted for the development of the moral qualities of human personality. In relation to this purpose it might be the worst of all possible worlds!

It would seem, then, that an environment intended to make possible growth in free beings of the finest characteristics of personal life must have a good deal in common with our present world. It must operate according to general and dependable laws; and it must involve real dangers, difficulties, problems, obstacles, and possibilities of pain, failure, sorrow, frustration, and defeat. If it did not contain the particular trials and perils that—subtracting man's own very considerable contribution—our world contains, it would have to contain others instead.

To realize this is not, by any means, to be in possession of a detailed theodicy. It is to understand that this world, with all its "heartaches and the thousand natural shocks that flesh is heir to," an environment so manifestly not designed for the maximization of human pleasure and the minimization of human pain, may nevertheless be rather well adapted to the quite different purpose of "soul making."[10]

These considerations are related to theism as such. Specifically Christian theism goes further in the light of the death of Christ, which is seen paradoxically both (as the murder of the divine Son) as the worst thing that has ever happened and (as the occasion of man's salvation) as the best thing that has ever happened. As the supreme evil turned to supreme good, it provides the paradigm for the distinctively Christian reaction to evil. Viewed from the standpoint of Christian faith, evils do not cease to be evils; and certainly, in view of Christ's healing work, they cannot be said to have been sent by God. Yet, it has been the persistent claim of those seriously and wholeheartedly committed to Christian discipleship that tragedy, though truly tragic, may nevertheless be turned, through a man's reaction to it, from a cause of despair and alienation from God to a stage in the fulfillment of God's loving purpose for the individual. As the greatest of all evils, the crucifixion of Christ, was made the occasion of man's redemption, so good can be won from other evils. As Jesus saw his execution by the Romans as an experience which God desired him to accept, an experience which was to be brought within the sphere of the divine purpose and made to serve the divine ends, so the Christian response to calamity is to accept the adversities, pains, and afflictions which life brings, in order that they can be turned to a positive spiritual use.[11]

At this point, theodicy points forward in two ways to the subject of life after death. . . .

First, although there are many striking instances of good being triumphantly brought out of evil through a man's or a woman's reaction to it, there are many other cases in which the opposite has happened. Sometimes obstacles breed strength of character, dangers evoke courage and unselfishness, and calamities produce patience and moral steadfastness. But sometimes they lead, instead, to resentment, fear, grasping selfishness, and disintegration of character. Therefore, it would seem that any divine purpose of soul making that is at work in earthly history must continue beyond this life if it is ever to achieve more than a very partial and fragmentary success.[12]

Second, if we ask whether the business of soul making is worth all the toil and sorrow of human life, the Christian answer must be in terms of a future good great enough to justify all that has happened on the way to it.

NOTES

1. Edgar Brightman's *A Philosophy of Religion* (Englewood Cliffs, N.J.: Prentice-Hall, Inc., 1940), Chaps. 8–10, is a classic exposition of one form of this view.

2. See Augustine's *Confessions,* Book VII, Chap. 12; *City of God,* Book XII, Chap. 3; *Enchiridion,* Chap. 4.
3. J. L. Mackie, "Evil and Omnipotence," *Mind* (April, 1955), p. 209. A similar point is made by Antony Flew in "Divine Omnipotence and Human Freedom," *New Essays in Philosophical Theology.* An important critical comment on these arguments is offered by Ninian Smart in "Omnipotence, Evil, and Supermen," *Philosophy* (April, 1961), with replies by Flew (January, 1962) and Mackie (April, 1962).
4. Flew, in *New Essays in Philosophical Theology*.
5. As Aquinas said, ". . .nothing that implies a contradiction falls under the scope of God's omnipotence." *Summa Theologica,* Part I, Question 25, Art. 4.
6. From the Greek *hedone,* pleasure.
7. This is essentially David Hume's argument in his discussion of the problem of evil in his *Dialogues,* Part XI.
8. See Irenaeus's *Against Heresies,* Book IV, Chaps. 37 and 38.
9. Tennyson's poem, *The Lotus-Eaters,* well expresses the desire (analyzed by Freud as a wish to return to the peace of the womb) for such "dreamful ease."
10. This brief discussion has been confined to the problem of human suffering. The large and intractable problem of animal pain is not taken up here. For a discussion of it see, for example, Austin Farrer, *Love Almighty and Ills Unlimited* (Garden City, N.Y.: Doubleday & Company, Inc., 1961), Chap. 5, and John Hick, *Evil and the God of Love* (London: Collins, The Fontana Library, 1968), pp. 345–53.
11. This conception of providence is stated more fully in John Hick, *Faith and Knowledge,* 2nd ed. (Ithaca, N.Y.: Cornell University Press, 1966), Chap. 10, some sentences from which are incorporated in this paragraph.
12. The position presented above is developed more fully in the author's *Evil and the God of Love,* 1966 (London: Fontana paperback ed., 1968). For an important philosophical critique of theodicies see Edward H. Madden and Peter H. Hare, *Evil and the Concept of God* (Springfield, Ill.: Charles C. Thomas, Publishers, 1968). Some of the most important recent articles on the subject are collected in Nelson Pike, ed., *God and Evil* (Englewood Cliffs, N.J.: Prentice-Hall, Inc., 1964).

The Problem of Goodness

STEVEN M. CAHN

Steven M. Cahn has spent much of his professional career teaching philosophy at the City University of New York Graduate Center, where he also served as Provost and then Acting President. He has edited a number of philosophical anthologies, including this one.

The selection that appears here is a revision of an earlier article, prepared especially for this volume. In it, Cahn argues that Hick's response to the problem of evil is unsuccessful.

For many centuries philosophers have grappled with what has come to be known as *the problem of evil.* Succinctly stated, the problem is: Could a world containing evil have been created by an omnipotent, omniscient, omnibenevolent being?

Considering the vast literature devoted to this issue, perhaps surprisingly little attention has been given to an analogous issue that might appropriately be referred to as *the problem of goodness.* Succinctly stated, the problem is: Could a world containing goodness have been created by an omnipotent, omniscient, omnimalevolent being?

This essay has two aims. The first is to provide a reasonable solution to the problem of goodness. Traditional theists find the hypothesis of creation by a benevolent deity far more plausible than the hypothesis of creation by a malevolent demon, and they may, therefore, believe the problem of goodness to be irrelevant to their commitments. My second aim is to demonstrate that this belief is mistaken.

Before proceeding, let us restate the problem of goodness in more formal fashion.

(1) Assume that an omnipotent, omniscient, omnimalevolent Demon created the world.
(2) If the Demon exists, the world would contain no goodness.
(3) But the world contains goodness.
(4) Therefore, the Demon does not exist.

Since the conclusion of the argument follows from the premises, those who wish to deny the conclusion must deny one of the premises. No demonist (the analogue to a theist) would question premise (1), so in order to avoid the conclusion of the argument, an attack would have to be launched against either premise (2) or premise (3).

What if a demonist attempted to deny premise (3)? Suppose goodness were regarded as an illusion. Would this move solve the problem?

I think not, for such a claim is either patently false or else involves a distortion of the usual meaning of the term "good." If the word is being used in its ordinary sense, then acts of kindness, expressions of love, and creations of beauty are good. Because obviously such things do occur, goodness exists.

If one insists that such things are not good, then the expression "good" is being used eccentrically, and the claim loses its import. One might as well defend the view that all persons are pigs by defining "persons" as "omnivorous hoofed mammals of the family Suidae." Such "persons" are not persons at all. Similarly, a supposedly omnimalevolent Demon who cherishes personal affection and great works of art is certainly not omnimalevolent and is probably no demon.

Premise (3) can thus be adequately defended, and if demonists are to find an answer to the problem of goodness, they must attack premise (2). How can the world contain goodness if the creator is omnimalevolent and possesses the power and the knowledge to carry out evil intentions? To paraphrase Epicurus, is the Demon willing to prevent good, but not able? Then He[1] is impotent. Is He able, but not willing? Then He is benevolent. Is He both able and willing? From where, then, comes goodness?

Some might believe hopeless the attempt to justify the Demon's malevolence in the face of goodness. But sophisticated demonists would realize that much play is left in their position. They would not agree that just because goodness exists in the world, it could not have been created by an omnimalevolent Demon. After all, isn't it possible that whatever goodness exists is logically necessary for this world to be the most evil one the Demon could have created? Not even an omnipotent being can contravene the laws of logic, for such a task is senseless, and so if each and every good in the world were logically tied to the achievement of the greatest evil, the omnimalevolent Demon, in order to bring about the greatest possible evil, would have been forced to allow the existence of these goods.

The demonist thus rejects premise (2) of the argument and argues instead for premise (2'):

(2') If the Demon exists, then every good in the world is logically necessary in order for this world to be the most evil the Demon could have created.

Now if we substitute premise (2') for premise (2) in the original argument, that argument falls apart, for the conclusion no longer follows from the premises. One can affirm without contradiction both the existence of an omnipotent, omniscient, omnimalevolent Demon who created the world and the existence of goodness in the world, so long as one also affirms that every good is logically necessary in order for this world to be the most evil one the Demon could have created. Demonists thus appear to have escaped the force of the problem of goodness.

Things are not so simple, however, for now demonists are faced by yet another argument that challenges their belief.

(1) Assume that an omnipotent, omniscient, omnimalevolent Demon created the world.
(2) If the Demon exists, then every good in the world is logically necessary in order for this world to be the most evil one the Demon could have created.

(3) But strong reasons suggest that not every good in the world is logically necessary in order for this world to be the most evil one the Demon could have created.

(4) Therefore, strong reasons suggest that the Demon does not exist.

This second argument, unlike the first, claims that belief in the Demon is not illogical but unreasonable. Beautiful mountain ranges, spectacular sunsets, the plays of Shakespeare, and the quartets of Beethoven do not enhance the evils of the world. Acts of altruism, generosity, and kindheartedness do not increase the world's sinister aspects. In other words, this argument challenges demonists to suggest plausible reasons for their view that every good makes possible a world containing even greater evils than would be possible without these goods.

The reader will have observed that thus far the discussion of the problem of goodness exactly parallels traditional discussions of the problem of evil; all the arguments and counterarguments presented are equally applicable *mutatis mutandis* to either problem. What may be surprising, however, is that we can develop a reply to the problem of goodness along the same lines suggested by John Hick's reply to the problem of evil.[2]

We begin by distinguishing two types of goodness: moral and physical. *Moral goods* are those for which human beings are responsible, such as acts of altruism, generosity, and kindheartedness. *Physical goods* are those for which human beings are not responsible, such as sunshine, breathable air, and drinkable water.

The justification of moral goods proceeds by tying their existence to our free will. Surely, performing a bad act freely is more evil than performing it involuntarily. The Demon could have ensured that human beings would always perform bad actions, but then those actions would not have been free, because the Demon would have ensured their occurrence.[3] Simply performing them, therefore, would not have produced the greatest possible evil, because greater evil can be produced by free persons than by unfree ones. The Demon had to provide human beings with freedom so that they might perform their bad actions voluntarily, thus maximizing evil.

As for the justification of physical goods, we should not suppose that the Demon's purpose in creating the world was to construct a chamber of tortures in which the inhabitants would be forced to endure a succession of unrelieved pains. The world can be viewed, instead, as a place of "soul breaking," in which free human beings, by grappling with the exhausting tasks and challenges in their environment, can thereby have their spirits broken and their wills-to-live destroyed.[4]

This conception of the world can be supported by what, following Hick, we may call "the method of negative justification."[5] Suppose, contrary to fact, the world were arranged so that nothing could ever go well. No one could help anyone else, no one could perform a courageous act, no one could complete any worthwhile project. Presumably, such a world could be created through innumerable acts of the Demon, who would alter the laws of nature as necessary.

Our present ethical concepts would thereby become useless. What would frustration mean in an environment without hope? What would selfishness be if no one could make use of help? Such a world, however efficiently it promoted pain, would be ill adapted for the development of the worst qualities of the human personality.

This line of argument, just as Hick's, points forward in two ways to life after death. First, although we can find many striking instances of evil's being produced from good, such as the pollution of beautiful lakes or the slashing of great paintings, still in many other cases good leads to altruism or strengthening of character. Therefore any demonic purpose of soul breaking at work in earthly history must continue beyond this life to achieve more than a fragmentary success.[6]

Second, if we ask whether the business of soul breaking is so evil that it nullifies all the goodness we find, the demonist's answer must be in terms of a future evil great enough to justify all that has happened.[7]

Have we now provided an adequate response to the problem of goodness? It is as strong as Hick's reply to the problem of evil, but in my view neither is successful. Nor do I see any plausible ways of strengthening either one. What is the evidence that, as Hick proposes, the horrors of bubonic plague somehow contribute to a better world? What is the evidence, as the believer in the Demon suggests, that the beauty of a sunset somehow contributes to a worse world? What is the evidence that, as Hick proposes, the free will of a Hitler achieved greater good than would have been achieved by his performing right actions involuntarily? What is the evidence that, as the believer in the Demon suggests, the free will of a Socrates achieved greater evil than would have been achieved by his performing wrong actions involuntarily?

If this world is neither the worst possible nor the best possible, then it could not have been created by either an all-powerful, all-evil Demon or an all-powerful, all-good God. Thus although the problem of goodness and the problem of evil do not show either demonism or theism to be impossible, the problems show both doctrines to be highly improbable. If demonists or theists can produce any other evidence in favor of their positions, then they can increase the plausibility of their views, but otherwise the reasonable conclusion is that neither the Demon nor God exists.

NOTES

1. My use of "He" is not intended to imply that the Demon is masculine.
2. See previous selection.
3. I here assume without argument that freedom and determinism are incompatible. Those who believe otherwise face more difficulty in resolving the problem of goodness and the problem of evil.
4. Hick sees the world as a place of "soul making," in which free beings grapple with challenges of their existence and may thereby become "children of God."
5. Hick refers to "the method of negative theodicy," which supposes that the world is arranged without pain or suffering.
6. Hick says the same for "any divine purpose of soul making."
7. Hick appeals to "a future good great enough" to serve as such a justification.

B GROUNDS FOR BELIEF

The Wager

BLAISE PASCAL

Blaise Pascal (1623–62) was a great French mathematician, physicist, and philosopher of religion. Although he lived fewer than forty years, he made important and enduring contributions to all three of these fields.

The selection presented here, originally written in French, is a brief excerpt from his famous work the *Pensées* ("Thoughts"), which was composed during the last decade of his life and published only after his death (in 1669). In it, Pascal presents an argument in favor of belief in God, an argument that has come to be known as "Pascal's Wager."

If there is a God, he is infinitely beyond our comprehension, since, being indivisible and without limits, he bears no relation to us. We are therefore incapable of knowing either what he is or whether he is. That being so, who would dare to attempt an answer to the question? Certainly not we, who bear no relation to him.

Who then will condemn Christians for being unable to give rational grounds for their belief, professing as they do a religion for which they cannot give rational grounds? They declare that it is a folly, *stultitiam*,* in expounding it to the world, and then you complain that they do not prove it. If they did prove it they would not be keeping their word. It is by being without proof that they show they are not without sense. "Yes, but although that excuses those who offer their religion as such, and absolves them from the criticism of producing it without rational grounds, it does not absolve those who accept it." Let us then examine this point, and let us say: "Either God is or he is not." But to which view shall we be inclined? Reason cannot decide this question. Infinite chaos separates us. At the far end of this infinite distance a coin is being spun which will come down heads or tails. How will you wager? Reason cannot make you choose either, reason cannot prove either wrong.

Do not then condemn as wrong those who have made a choice, for you know nothing about it. "No, but I will condemn them not for having made this particular choice, but any choice, for, although the one who calls heads and the other one are equally at fault, the fact is that they are both at fault: the right thing is not to wager at all."

Yes, but you must wager. There is no choice, you are already committed. Which will you choose then? Let us see: since a choice must be made, let us see which offers you the least interest. You have two things to lose: the true and the good; and two things to stake: your reason and your will, your

* Latin for "Stupidity."

From *Pensées*, trans. A. J. Krailsheimer (Penguin Classics, 1966). Copyright © 1966. A. J. Krailsheimer. Reproduced by permission of Penguin Books Ltd.

knowledge and your happiness; and your nature has two things to avoid: error and wretchedness. Since you must necessarily choose, your reason is no more affronted by choosing one rather than the other. That is one point cleared up. But your happiness? Let us weigh up the gain and the loss involved in calling heads that God exists. Let us assess the two cases: if you win you win everything, if you lose you lose nothing. Do not hesitate then; wager that he does exist. "That is wonderful. Yes, I must wager, but perhaps I am wagering too much." Let us see: since there is an equal chance of gain and loss, if you stood to win only two lives for one you could still wager, but supposing you stood to win three?

You would have to play (since you must necessarily play) and it would be unwise of you, once you are obliged to play, not to risk your life in order to win three lives at a game in which there is an equal chance of losing and winning. But there is an eternity of life and happiness. That being so, even though there were an infinite number of chances, of which only one were in your favour, you would still be right to wager one in order to win two; and you would be acting wrongly, being obliged to play, in refusing to stake one life against three in a game, where out of an infinite number of chances there is one in your favour, if there were an infinity of infinitely happy life to be won. But here there is an infinity of infinitely happy life to be won, one chance of winning against a finite number of chances of losing, and what you are staking is finite. That leaves no choice; wherever there is infinity, and where there are not infinite chances of losing against that of winning, there is no room for hesitation, you must give everything. And thus, since you are obliged to play, you must be renouncing reason if you hoard your life rather than risk it for an infinite gain, just as likely to occur as a loss amounting to nothing.

For it is no good saying that it is uncertain whether you will win, that it is certain that you are taking a risk, and that the infinite distance between the certainty of what you are risking and the uncertainty of what you may gain makes the finite good you are certainly risking equal to the infinite good that you are not certain to gain. This is not the case. Every gambler takes a certain risk for an uncertain gain, and yet he is taking a certain finite risk for an uncertain finite gain without sinning against reason. Here there is no infinite distance between the certain risk and the uncertain gain: that is not true. There is, indeed, an infinite distance between the certainty of winning and the certainty of losing, but the proportion between the uncertainty of winning and the certainty of what is being risked is in proportion to the chances of winning or losing. And hence if there are as many chances on one side as on the other you are playing for even odds. And in that case the certainty of what you are risking is equal to the uncertainty of what you may win; it is by no means infinitely distant from it. Thus our argument carries infinite weight, when the stakes are finite in a game where there are even chances of winning and losing and an infinite prize to be won.

This is conclusive and if men are capable of any truth this is it.

"I confess, I admit it, but is there really no way of seeing what the cards are?"—"Yes. Scripture and the rest, etc."—"Yes, but my hands are tied and my lips are sealed; I am being forced to wager and I am not free; I am being held fast and I am so made that I cannot believe. What do you want me to do then?"—"That is true, but at least get it into your head that, if you are unable to believe, it is because of your passions, since reason impels you to believe and yet you cannot do so. Concentrate then not on convincing yourself by multiplying proofs of God's existence but by diminishing your passions. You want to find faith and you do not know the road. You want to be cured of unbelief and you ask for the remedy: learn from those who were once bound like you and who now wager all they have. These are people who know the road you wish to follow, who have been cured of the affliction of which you wish to be cured: follow the way by which they began. They behaved just as if they did believe, taking holy water, having masses said, and so on. That will make you believe quite naturally, and will make you more docile."—"But that is what I am afraid of."—"But why? What have you to lose? But to show you that this is the way, the fact is that this diminishes the passions which are your great obstacles. . . ."

The Ethics of Belief

W. K. CLIFFORD

William Kingdon Clifford (1845–79) was a British mathematician and philosopher who taught at University College London. Well respected for his outstanding contributions to mathematics, he was elected as a Fellow of the Royal Society in 1874 at the age of 29. His 1877 essay "The Ethics of Belief"—a selection of which is reprinted here—challenges Pascal on the grounds that "it is wrong always, everywhere, and for anyone, to believe anything upon insufficient evidence."

A Shipowner was about to send to sea an emigrant-ship. He knew that she was old, and not over-well built at the first; that she had seen many seas and climes, and often had needed repairs. Doubts had been suggested to him that possibly she was not seaworthy. These doubts preyed upon his mind, and made him unhappy; he thought that perhaps he ought to have her thoroughly overhauled and refitted, even though this should put him to great expense. Before the ship sailed, however, he succeeded in overcoming these melancholy reflections. He said to himself that she had gone safely through so many voyages and weathered so many storms that it was idle to suppose she would not come safely home from this trip also. He would put his trust in Providence, which could hardly fail to protect all these unhappy families that were leaving their fatherland to seek for better times elsewhere. He would dismiss from his mind all ungenerous suspicions about the honesty of builders and contractors. In such ways he acquired a sincere and comfortable conviction that his vessel was thoroughly safe and seaworthy; he watched her departure with a light heart, and benevolent wishes for the success of the exiles in their strange new home that was to be; and he got his insurance-money when she went down in mid-ocean and told no tales.

What shall we say of him? Surely this, that he was verily guilty of the death of those men. It is admitted that he did sincerely believe in the soundness of his ship; but the sincerity of his conviction can in no wise help him, because *he had no right to believe on such evidence as was before him*. He had acquired his belief not by honestly earning it in patient investigation, but by stifling his doubts. And although in the end he may have felt so sure about it that he could not think otherwise, yet inasmuch as he had knowingly and willingly worked himself into that frame of mind, he must be held responsible for it.

Let us alter the case a little, and suppose that the ship was not unsound after all; that she made her voyage safely, and many others after it. Will that diminish the guilt of her owner? Not one jot. When an action is once done, it is right or wrong for ever; no accidental failure of its good or evil fruits can possibly alter that. The man would not have been innocent, he would only have been not found out. The question of right or wrong has to do with the origin of his belief, not the matter of it; not what it was, but how he got it; not whether it turned out to be true or false, but whether he had a right to believe on such evidence as was before him.

There was once an island in which some of the inhabitants professed a religion teaching neither the doctrine of original sin nor that of eternal punishment. A suspicion got abroad that the professors of this religion had made use of unfair means to get their doctrines taught to children. They were accused of wresting the laws of their country in such a way as to remove children from the care of their natural and legal guardians; and even of stealing them away and keeping them concealed from their friends and relations. A certain number of men formed themselves into a society for the purpose of agitating the public about

From W. K. Clifford, *Lectures and Essays*, 1879.

this matter. They published grave accusations against individual citizens of the highest position and character, and did all in their power to injure these citizens in the exercise of their professions. So great was the noise they made, that a Commission was appointed to investigate the facts; but after the Commission had carefully inquired into all the evidence that could be got, it appeared that the accused were innocent. Not only had they been accused on insufficient evidence, but the evidence of their innocence was such as the agitators might easily have obtained, if they had attempted a fair inquiry. After these disclosures the inhabitants of that country looked upon the members of the agitating society, not only as persons whose judgment was to be distrusted, but also as no longer to be counted honourable men. For although they had sincerely and conscientiously believed in the charges they had made, yet *they had no right to believe on such evidence as was before them*. Their sincere convictions, instead of being honesly earned by patient inquiring, were stolen by listening to the voice of prejudice and passion.

Let us vary this case also, and suppose, other things remaining as before, that a still more accurate investigation proved the accused to have been really guilty. Would this make any difference in the guilt of the accusers? Clearly not; the question is not whether their belief was true or false, but whether they entertained it on wrong grounds. They would no doubt say, "Now you see that we were right after all; next time perhaps you will believe us." And they might be believed, but they would not thereby become honourable men. They would not be innocent, they would only be not found out. Every one of them, if he chose to examine himself *in foro conscientiae*, would know that he had acquired and nourished a belief, when he had no right to believe on such evidence as was before him; and therein he would know that he had done a wrong thing.

It may be said, however, that in both of these supposed cases it is not the belief which is judged to be wrong, but the action following upon it. The shipowner might say, "I am perfectly certain that my ship is sound, but still I feel it my duty to have her examined, before trusting the lives of so many people to her." And it might be said to the agitator, "However convinced you were of the justice of your cause and the truth of your convictions, you ought not to have made a public attack upon any man's character until you had examined the evidence on both sides with the utmost patience and care."

In the first place, let us admit that, so far as it goes, this view of the case is right and necessary; right, because even when a man's belief is so fixed that he cannot think otherwise, he still has a choice in regard to the action suggested by it, and so cannot escape the duty of investigating on the ground of the strength of his convictions; and necessary, because those who are not yet capable of controlling their feelings and thoughts must have a plain rule dealing with overt acts.

But this being premised as necessary, it becomes clear that it is not sufficient, and that our previous judgment is required to supplement it. For it is not possible so to sever the belief from the action it suggests as to condemn the one without condemning the other. No man holding a strong belief on one side of a question, or even wishing to hold a belief on one side, can investigate it with such fairness and completeness as if he were really in doubt and unbiased; so that the existence of a belief not founded on fair inquiry unfits a man for the performance of this necessary duty.

Nor is that truly a belief at all which has not some influence upon the actions of him who holds it. He who truly believes that which prompts him to an action has looked upon the action to lust after it, he has committed it already in his heart. If a belief is not realized immediately in open deeds, it is stored up for the guidance of the future. It goes to make a part of that aggregate of beliefs which is the link between sensation and action at every moment of all our lives, and which is so organized and compacted together that no part of it can be isolated from the rest, but every new addition modifies the structure of the whole. No real belief, however trifling and fragmentary it may seem, is ever truly insignificant; it prepares us to receive more of its like, confirms those which resembled it before, and weakens others; and so gradually it lays a stealthy train in our inmost thoughts, which may someday explode into overt action, and leave its stamp upon our character for ever.

And no one man's belief is in any case a private matter which concerns himself alone. Our lives are guided by that general conception of the course of things which has been created by society for social purposes. Our words, our phrases, our forms and processes and modes of thought, are common property, fashioned and perfected from age to age; an heirloom which every succeeding generation inherits as a precious deposit and a sacred trust to be handed on to the next one, not unchanged but enlarged and purified, with some clear marks of its proper handiwork. Into this, for good or ill, is woven every belief of every man who has speech of his fellows. An awful privilege, and an awful responsibility, that we should help to create the world in which posterity will live.

In the two supposed cases which have been considered, it has been judged wrong to believe on insufficient evidence, or to nourish belief by suppressing doubts and avoiding investigation. The reason of this judgment is not far to seek; it is that in both these cases the belief held by one man was of great importance to other men. But forasmuch as no belief held by one man, however seemingly trivial the belief, and however obscure the believer, is ever actually insignificant or without its effect on the fate of mankind, we have no choice but to extend our judgment to all cases of belief whatever. Belief, that sacred faculty which prompts the decisions of our will, and knits into harmonious working all the compacted energies of our being, is ours not for ourselves, but for humanity. It is rightly used on truths which have been established by long experience and waiting toil, and which have stood in the fierce light of free and fearless questioning. Then it helps to bind men together, and to strengthen and direct their common action. It is desecrated when given to unproved and unquestioned statements, for the solace and private pleasure of the believer; to add a tinsel splendour to the plain straight road of our life and display a bright mirage beyond it; or even to drown the common sorrows of our kind by a self-deception which allows them not only to cast down, but also to degrade us. Whoso would deserve well of his fellows in this matter will guard the purity of his belief with a very fanaticism of jealous care, lest at any time it should rest on an unworthy object, and catch a stain which can never be wiped away.

It is not only the leader of men, statesman, philosopher, or poet, that owes this bounden duty to mankind. Every rustic who delivers in the village alehouse his slow, infrequent sentences, may help to kill or keep alive the fatal superstitions which clog his race. Every hard-worked wife of an artisan may transmit to her children beliefs which shall knit society together, or rend it in pieces. No simplicity of mind, no obscurity of station, can escape the universal duty of questioning all that we believe.

It is true that this duty is a hard one, and the doubt which comes out of it is often a very bitter thing. It leaves us bare and powerless where we thought that we were safe and strong. To know all about anything is to know how to deal with it under all circumstances. We feel much happier and more secure when we think we know precisely what to do, no matter what happens, than when we have lost our way and do not know where to turn. And if we have supposed ourselves to know all about anything, and to be capable of doing what is fit in regard to it, we naturally do not like to find that we are really ignorant and powerless, that we have to begin again at the beginning, and try to learn what the thing is and how it is to be dealt with—if indeed anything can be learnt about it. It is the sense of power attached to a sense of knowledge that makes men desirous of believing, and afraid of doubting.

This sense of power is the highest and best of pleasures when the belief on which it is founded is a true belief, and has been fairly earned by investigation. For then we may justly feel that it is common property, and hold good for others as well as for ourselves. Then we may be glad, not that *I* have learned secrets by which I am safer and stronger, but that *we men* have got mastery over more of the world; and we shall be strong, not for ourselves; but in the name of Man and in his strength. But if the belief has been accepted on insufficient evidence, the pleasure is a stolen one. Not only does it deceive ourselves by giving us a sense of power which we do not really possess, but it is sinful, because it is stolen in defiance of our duty to mankind. That duty is to guard ourselves from such beliefs as from a pestilence, which may shortly master our own body and then spread to the rest of the town. What would be thought of one who, for the sake of a sweet fruit, should deliberately run the risk of bringing a plague upon his family and his neighbours?

And, as in other such cases, it is not the risk only which has to be considered; for a bad action is always bad at the time when it is done, no matter what happens afterwards. Every time we let ourselves believe for unworthy reasons, we weaken our powers of self-control, of doubting, of judicially and fairly weighing evidence. We all suffer severely enough from the maintenance and support of false beliefs and the fatally wrong actions which they lead to, and the evil born when one such belief is entertained is great and wide. But a greater and wider evil arises when the credulous character is maintained and supported, when a habit of believing for unworthy reasons is fostered and made permanent. If I steal money from any person, there may be no harm done by the mere transfer of possession; he may not feel the loss, or it may prevent him from using the money badly. But I cannot help doing this great wrong towards Man, that I make myself dishonest. What hurts society is not that it should lose its property, but that it should become a den of thieves, for then it must cease to be society. This is why we ought not to do evil, that good may come; for at any rate this great evil has come, that we have done evil and are made wicked thereby. In like manner, if I let myself believe anything on insufficient evidence, there may be no great harm done by the mere belief; it may be true after all, or I may never have occasion to exhibit it in outward acts. But I cannot help doing this great wrong towards Man, that I make myself credulous. The danger to society is not merely that it should believe wrong things, though that is great enough; but that it should become credulous, and lose the habit of testing things and inquiring into them; for then it must sink back into savagery.

The harm which is done by credulity in a man is not confined to the fostering of a credulous character in others, and consequent support of false beliefs. Habitual want of care about what I believe leads to habitual want of care in others about the truth of what is told to me. Men speak the truth to one another when each reveres the truth in his own mind and in the other's mind; but how shall my friend revere the truth in my mind when I myself am careless about it, when I believe things because I want to believe them, and because they are comforting and pleasant? Will he not learn to cry, "Peace," to me, when there is no peace? By such a course I shall surround myself with a thick atmosphere of falsehood and fraud, and in that I must live. It may matter little to me, in my cloud-castle of sweet illusions and darling lies; but it matters much to Man that I have made my neighbours ready to deceive. The credulous man is father to the liar and the cheat; he lives in the bosom of this his family, and it is no marvel if he should become even as they are. So closely are our duties knit together, that whoso shall keep the whole law, and yet offend in one point, he is guilty of all.

To sum up: it is wrong always, everywhere, and for anyone, to believe anything upon insufficient evidence.

If a man, holding a belief which he was taught in childhood or persuaded of afterwards, keeps down and pushes away any doubts which arise about it in his mind, purposely avoids the reading of books and the company of men that call in question or discuss it, and regards as impious those questions which cannot easily be asked without disturbing it—the life of that man is one long sin against mankind.

If this judgment seems harsh when applied to those simple souls who have never known better, who have been brought up from the cradle with a horror of doubt, and taught that their eternal welfare depends on *what* they believe, then it leads to the very serious question, *Who hath made Israel to sin?*

It may be permitted me to fortify this judgment with the sentence of Milton*—

> A man may be a heretic in the truth; and if he believe things only because his pastor says so, or the assembly so determine, without knowing other reason, though his belief be true, yet the very truth he holds becomes his heresy. (*Areopagitica*)

And with this famous aphorism of Coleridge—

---

* John Milton (1608–74) and Samuel Taylor Coleridge (1772–1834) were famous British poets and critics.

He who begins by loving Christianity better than Truth, will proceed by loving his own sect or Church better than Christianity, and end in loving himself better than all. (*Aids to Reflections*)

Inquiry into the evidence of a doctrine is not to be made once for all, and then taken as finally settled. It is never lawful to stifle a doubt; for either it can be honestly answered by means of the inquiry already made, or else it proves that the inquiry was not complete.

"But," says one, "I am a busy man; I have no time for the long course of study which would be necessary to make me in any degree a competent judge of certain questions, or even able to understand the nature of the arguments."

Then he should have no time to believe.

The Will to Believe

WILLIAM JAMES

William James (1842–1910) was a central figure in nineteenth-century American intellectual life, renowned for his contributions to philosophy and for his pioneering work in the newly minted discipline of psychology.

In his famous essay "The Will to Believe"—originally delivered as a lecture to the Philosophical Clubs of Yale and Brown Universities in 1896—James offers a straightforward challenge to Clifford's views, which can be found in the preceding selection.

I

Let us give the name of hypothesis to anything that may be proposed to our belief; and just as the electricians speak of live and dead wires, let us speak of any hypothesis as either *live* or *dead*. A live hypothesis is one which appeals as a real possibility to him to whom it is proposed. If I ask you to believe in the Mahdi,* the notion makes no electric connection with your nature—it refuses to scintillate with any credibility at all. As an hypothesis it is completely dead. To an Arab, however (even if he be not one of the Mahdi's followers), the hypothesis is among the mind's possibilities: It is alive. This shows that deadness and liveness in an hypothesis are not intrinsic properties, but relations to the individual thinker. They are measured by his willingness to act. The maximum of liveness in an hypothesis means willingness to act irrevocably. Practically, that means belief; but there is some believing tendency wherever there is willingness to act at all.

Next, let us call the decision between two hypotheses an *option*. Options may be of several kinds. They may be first, *living* or *dead;* secondly, *forced* or *avoidable*; thirdly, *momentous* or *trivial;* and for our purposes we may call an option a *genuine* option when it is of the forced, living, and momentous kind.

1. A living option is one in which both hypotheses are live ones. If I say to you: "Be a theosophist or be a Mohammedan," it is probably a dead option, because for you neither hypothesis is likely to be alive. But if I say: "Be an agnostic or be a Christian," it is otherwise: trained as you are, each

* In Islamic thought, the Mahdi ("Guided One") is the prophesized redeemer who will usher in the Day of Resurrection. Because of the audience he was addressing, James's text assumes that his reader is not of the Muslim faith.

William James, *The Will to Believe* (1896).

hypothesis makes some appeal, however small, to your belief.

2. Next, if I say to you: "Choose between going out with your umbrella or without it," I do not offer you a genuine option, for it is not forced. You can easily avoid it by not going out at all. Similarly, if I say, "Either love me or hate me," "Either call my theory true or call it false," your option is avoidable. You may remain indifferent to me, neither loving nor hating, and you may decline to offer any judgment as to my theory. But if I say, "Either accept this truth or go without it," I put on you a forced option, for there is no standing place outside of the alternative. Every dilemma based on a complete logical disjunction, with no possibility of not choosing, is an option of this forced kind.

3. Finally, if I were Dr. Nansen* and proposed to you to join my North Pole expedition, your option would be momentous; for this would probably be your only similar opportunity, and your choice now would either exclude you from the North Pole sort of immortality altogether or put at least the chance of it into your hands. He who refuses to embrace a unique opportunity loses the prize as surely as if he tried and failed. Per contra, the option is trivial when the opportunity is not unique, when the stake is insignificant, or when the decision is reversible if it later prove unwise. Such trivial options abound in the scientific life. A chemist finds an hypothesis live enough to spend a year in its verification: he believes in it to that extent. But if his experiments prove inconclusive either way, he is quit for his loss of time, no vital harm being done.

It will facilitate our discussion if we keep all these distinctions well in mind.

II

The next matter to consider is the actual psychology of human opinion. When we look at certain facts, it seems as if our passional and volitional nature lay at the root of all our convictions. When we look at others, it seems as if they could do nothing when the intellect had once said its say. Let us take the latter facts up first.

Does it not seem preposterous on the very face of it to talk of our opinions modifiable at will? Can our will either help or hinder our intellect in its perceptions of truth? Can we, by just willing it, believe that Abraham Lincoln's existence is a myth, and that the portraits of him in *McClure's Magazine* are all of some one else? Can we, by any effort of our will, or by any strength of wish that it were true, believe ourselves well and about when we are roaring with rheumatism in bed, or feel certain that the sum of the two one-dollar bills in our pocket must be a hundred dollars? We can *say* any of these things, but we are absolutely impotent to believe them; and of just such things is the whole fabric of the truths that we do believe in made up—matters of fact, immediate or remote, as Hume said, and relations between ideas, which are either there or not there for us if we see them so, and which if not there cannot be put there by any action of our own.

In Pascal's *Thoughts* there is a celebrated passage known in literature as Pascal's wager. In it he tries to force us into Christianity by reasoning as if our concern with truth resembled our concern with the stakes in a game of chance. Translated freely his words are these: You must either believe or not believe that God is—which will you do? Your human reason cannot say. A game is going on between you and the nature of things which at the day of judgment will bring out either heads or tails. Weigh what your gains and your losses would be if you should stake all you have on heads, or God's existence: if you win in such case, you gain eternal beatitude; if you lose, you lose nothing at all. If there were an infinity of changes, and only one for God in this wager, still you ought to stake your all on God; for though you surely risk a finite loss by this procedure, any finite loss is reasonable, even a certain one is reasonable, if there is but the possibility of infinite gain. Go, then, and take holy water, and have masses said; belief will come and stupefy your scruples. . . . Why should you not? At bottom, what have you to lose?

You probably feel that when religious faith expresses itself thus, in the language of the gaming-table, it is put to its last trumps. Surely Pascal's own personal belief in masses and holy water had

* Fridtjof Nansen (1861–1930) was a Norwegian explorer and statesman.

far other springs; and this celebrated page of his is but an argument for others, a last desperate snatch at a weapon against the hardness of the unbelieving heart. We feel that a faith in masses and holy water adopted wilfully after such a mechanical calculation would lack the inner soul of faith's reality; and if we were ourselves in the place of the Deity, we should probably take particular pleasure in cutting off believers of this pattern from their infinite reward. It is evident that unless there be some preexisting tendency to believe in masses and holy water, the option offered to the will by Pascal is not a living option. Certainly no Turk ever took to masses and holy water on its account; and even to us Protestants these means of salvation seem such foregone impossibilities that Pascal's logic, invoked for them specifically, leaves us unmoved. As well might the Mahdi write to us, saying, "I am the Expected One whom God has created in his effulgence. You shall be infinitely happy if you confess me; otherwise you shall be cut off from the light of the sun. Weigh, then, your infinite gain if I am genuine against your finite sacrifice if I am not!" His logic would be that of Pascal; but he would vainly use it on us, for the hypothesis he offers us is dead. No tendency to act on it exists in us to any degree.

The talk of believing by our volition seems, then, from one point of view, simply silly. From another point of view it is worse than silly, it is vile. When one turns to the magnificent edifice of the physical sciences, and sees how it was reared; what thousands of disinterested moral lives of men lie buried in its mere foundations; what patience and postponement, what choking down of preference, what submission to the icy laws of outer fact are wrought into its very stones and mortar; how absolutely impersonal it stands in its vast augustness—then how besotted and contemptible seems every little sentimentalist who comes blowing his voluntary smoke-wreaths, and pretending to decide things from out of his private dream! Can we wonder if those bred in the rugged and manly school of science should feel like spewing such subjectivism out of their mouths? The whole system of loyalties which grow up in the schools of science go dead against its toleration; so that it is only natural that those who have caught the scientific fever should pass over to the opposite extreme, and write sometimes as if the incorruptibly truthful intellect ought positively to prefer bitterness and unacceptableness to the heart in its cup.

It fortifies my soul to know
That though I perish, Truth is so

sings Clough,* while Huxley† exclaims: "My only consolation lies in the reflection that, however bad our posterity may become, so far as they hold by the plain rule of not pretending to believe what they have no reason to believe, because it may be to their advantage so to pretend [the word 'pretend' is surely here redundant], they will not have reached the lowest depth of immorality." And that delicious enfant terrible Clifford‡ writes: "Belief is desecrated when given to unproved and unquestioned statements for the solace and private pleasure of the believer.... Whoso would deserve well of his fellows in this matter will guard the purity of his belief with a very fanaticism of jealous care, lest at any time it should rest on an unworthy object, and catch a stain which can never be wiped away.... If [a] belief has been accepted on insufficient evidence [even though the belief be true, as Clifford on the same page explains] the pleasure is a stolen one.... It is sinful because it is stolen in defiance of our duty to mankind. That duty is to guard ourselves from such beliefs as from a pestilence which may shortly master our own body and then spread to the rest of the town.... It is wrong always, everywhere, and for every one, to believe anything upon insufficient evidence."

III

All this strikes one as healthy, even when expressed, as by Clifford, with somewhat too much of robustious pathos in the voice. Free will and simple wish-

* Arthur Hugh Clough (1819–61) was a nineteenth-century English poet.

† Thomas Henry Huxley (1825–95) was an English biologist and an early defender of Darwin's theory of evolution.

‡ William K. Clifford (1845–79) was an English mathematician and philosopher, author of our previous selection.

ing do seem, in the matter of our credences, to be only fifth wheels to the coach. Yet if any one should thereupon assume that intellectual insight is what remains after wish and will and sentimental preference have taken wing, or that pure reason is what then settles our opinions, he would fly quite as directly in the teeth of the facts.

It is only our already dead hypotheses that our willing nature is unable to bring to life again. But what has made them dead for us is for the most part a previous action of our willing nature of an antagonistic kind. When I say "willing nature," I do not mean only such deliberate volitions as may have set up habits of belief that we cannot now escape from—I mean all such factors of belief as fear and hope, prejudice and passion, imitation and partisanship, the circumpressure of our caste and set. As a matter of fact we find ourselves believing, we hardly know how or why. Mr. Balfour* gives the name of "authority" to all those influences, born of the intellectual climate, that make hypotheses possible or impossible for us, alive or dead. Here in this room, we all of us believe in molecules and the conservation of energy, in democracy and necessary progress, in Protestant Christianity and the duty of fighting for "the doctrine of the immortal Monroe,"† all for no reasons worthy of the name. We see into these matters with no more inner clearness, and probably with much less, than any disbeliever in them might possess. His unconventionality would probably have some grounds to show for its conclusions; but for us, not insight, but the *prestige* of the opinions, is what makes the spark shoot from them and light up our sleeping magazines of faith. Our reason is quite satisfied, in nine hundred and ninety-nine cases out of every thousand of us, if it can find a few arguments that will do to recite in case our credulity is criticized by some one else. Our faith is faith in some one else's faith, and in the greatest matters this is the most the case. . . .

* Arthur Balfour (1848–1930) was a British Conservation politician and prime minister of the United Kingdom from 1902 to 1905.

† The Monroe Doctrine (1823) proclaimed that European countries should refrain from interfering with American affairs.

Evidently, then, our non-intellectual nature does influence our convictions. There are passional tendencies and volitions which run before and others which come after belief, and it is only the latter that are too late for the fair; and they are not too late when the previous passional work has been already in their own direction. Pascal's argument, instead of being powerless, then seems a regular clincher, and is the last stroke needed to make our faith in masses and holy water complete. The state of things is evidently far from simple; and pure insight and logic, whatever they might do ideally, are not the only things that really do produce our creeds.

IV

Our next duty, having recognized this mixed-up state of affairs, is to ask whether it be simply reprehensible and pathological, or whether, on the contrary, we must treat it as a normal element in making up our minds. The thesis I defend is, briefly stated, this: *Our passional nature not only lawfully may, but must, decide an option between propositions, whenever it is a genuine option that cannot by its nature be decided on intellectual grounds; for to say, under such circumstances, "Do not decide, but leave the question open," is itself a passional decision—just like deciding yes or no—and is attended with the same risk of losing the truth. . . .*

VII

One more point, small but important, and our preliminaries are done. There are two ways of looking at our duty in the matter of opinion—ways entirely different, and yet ways about whose difference the theory of knowledge seems hitherto to have shown very little concern. *We must know the truth;* and *we must avoid error*—these are our first and great commandments as would-be knowers; but they are not two ways of stating an identical commandment, they are two separable laws. Although it may indeed happen that when we believe the truth A, we escape as an incidental consequence from believing the falsehood B, it hardly ever happens that by merely disbelieving B we necessarily believe A. We may in escaping B fall into believing other falsehoods, C or D, just as bad as B; or we may escape B by not believing anything at all, not even A.

Believe truth! Shun error!—these, we see, are two materially different laws; and by choosing between them we may end by coloring differently our whole intellectual life. We may regard the chase for truth as paramount, and the avoidance of error as secondary; or we may, on the other hand, treat the avoidance of error as more imperative, and let truth take its chance. Clifford, in the instructive passage which I have quoted, exhorts us to the latter course. Believe nothing, he tells us, keep your mind in suspense forever, rather than by closing it on insufficient evidence incur the awful risk of believing lies. You, on the other hand, may think that the risk of being in error is a very small matter when compared with the blessings of real knowledge, and be ready to be duped many times in your investigation rather than postpone indefinitely the chance of guessing true. I myself find it impossible to go with Clifford. We must remember that these feelings of our duty about either truth or error are in any case only expressions of our passional life. Biologically considered, our minds are as ready to grind out falsehood as veracity, and he who says, "Better go without belief forever than believe a lie!" merely shows his own preponderant private horror of becoming a dupe. He may be critical of many of his desires and fears, but this fear he slavishly obeys. He cannot imagine any one questioning its binding force. For my own part, I have also a horror of being duped; but I can believe that worse things than being duped may happen to a man in this world: so Clifford's exhortation has to my ears a thoroughly fantastic sound. It is like a general informing his soldiers that it is better to keep out of battle forever than to risk a single wound. Not so are victories either over enemies or over nature gained. Our errors are surely not such awfully solemn things. In a world where we are so certain to incur them in spite of all our caution, a certain lightness of heart seems healthier than this excessive nervousness on their behalf. At any rate, it seems the fittest thing for the empiricist philosopher.

VIII

And now, after all this introduction, let us go straight at our question. I have said, and now repeat it, that not only as a matter of fact do we find our passional nature influencing us in our opinions, but that there are some options between opinions in which this influence must be regarded both as an inevitable and as a lawful determinant of our choice.

I fear here that some of you my hearers will begin to scent danger, and lend an inhospitable ear. Two first steps of passion you have indeed had to admit as necessary—we must think so as to avoid dupery, and we must think so as to gain truth; but the surest path to those ideal consummations, you will probably consider, is from now onwards to take no further passional step.

Well, of course, I agree as far as the facts will allow. Wherever the option between losing truth and gaining it is not momentous, we can throw the chance of *gaining truth* away, and at any rate save ourselves from any chance of *believing falsehood*, by not making up our minds at all till objective evidence has come. In scientific questions, this is almost always the case; and even in human affairs in general, the need of acting is seldom so urgent that a false belief to act on is better than no belief at all. Law courts, indeed, have to decide on the best evidence attainable for the moment, because a judge's duty is to make law as well as to ascertain it, and (as a learned judge once said to me) few cases are worth spending much time over: the great thing is to have them decided on *any* acceptable principle, and got out of the way. But in our dealings with objective nature we obviously are recorders, not makers, of the truth; and decisions for the mere sake of deciding promptly and getting on to the next business would be wholly out of place. Throughout the breadth of physical nature facts are what they are quite independently of us, and seldom is there any such hurry about them that the risks of being duped by believing a premature theory need be faced. The questions here are always trivial options, the hypotheses are hardly living (at any rate not living for us spectators), the choice between believing truth or falsehood is seldom forced. The attitude of sceptical balance is therefore the absolutely wise one if we would escape mistakes. What difference, indeed, does it make to most of us whether we have or have not a theory of the Röntgen rays, whether we believe or not in mind-stuff, or have a conviction about the causality of conscious states? It makes no difference. Such options are not forced on us. On every account it is better not to make them, but still keep weighing reasons *pro et contra* with an indifferent hand.

I speak, of course, here of the purely judging mind. For purposes of discovery such indifference is to be less highly recommended, and science would be far less advanced than she is if the passionate desires of individuals to get their own faiths confirmed had been kept out of the game. See for example the sagacity which Spencer* and Weismann now display. On the other hand, if you want an absolute duffer in an investigation, you must, after all, take the man who has no interest whatever in its results: he is the warranted incapable, the positive fool. The most useful investigator, because the most sensitive observer, is always he whose eager interest in one side of the question is balanced by an equally keen nervousness lest he become deceived.[1] Science has organized this nervousness into a regular *technique*, her so-called method of verification; and she has fallen so deeply in love with the method that one may even say she has ceased to care for truth by itself at all. It is only truth as technically verified that interests her. The truth of truths might come in merely affirmative form, and she would decline to touch it. Such truth as that, she might repeat with Clifford, would be stolen in defiance of her duty to mankind. Human passions, however, are stronger than technical rules. "*Le coeur a ses raisons*," as Pascal says, "*que la raison ne connait pas*"† and however indifferent to all but the bare rules of the game the umpire, the abstract intellect, may be, the concrete players who furnish him the materials to judge of are usually, each one of them, in love with some pet "live hypothesis" of his own. Let us agree, however, that wherever there is no forced option, the dispassionately judicial intellect with no pet hypothesis, saving us, as it does, from dupery at any rate, ought to be our ideal.

* Herbert Spencer (1820–1903) was an English philosopher and political theorist. August Weisman (1834–1914) was a German biologist. Both were early advocates of evolutionary theory.

† French for "The heart has its reasons which reason does not know."

The question next arises: Are there not somewhere forced options in our speculative questions, and can we (as men who may be interested at least as much in positively gaining truth as in merely escaping dupery) always wait with impunity till the coercive evidence shall have arrived? It seems a priori improbable that the truth should be so nicely adjusted to our needs and powers as that. In the great boardinghouse of nature, the cakes and the butter and the syrup seldom come out so even and leave the plates so clean. Indeed, we should view them with scientific suspicion if they did.

IX

Moral questions immediately present themselves as questions whose solution cannot wait for sensible proof. A moral question is a question not of what sensibly exists, but of what is good, or would be good if it did exist. Science can tell us what exists; but to compare the *worths*, both of what exists and of what does not exist, we must consult not science, but what Pascal calls our heart....

Turn now from these wide questions of good to a certain class of questions of fact, questions concerning personal relations, states of mind between one man and another. *Do you like me or not?*—for example. Whether you do or not depends, in countless instances, on whether I meet you halfway, am willing to assume that you must like me, and show you trust and expectation. The previous faith on my part in your liking's existence is in such cases what makes your liking come. But if I stand aloof, and refuse to budge an inch until I have objective evidence, until you shall have done something apt, as the absolutists say, *ad extorquendum assensum meum*,* ten to one your liking never comes. How many women's hearts are vanquished by the mere sanguine insistence of some man that they *must* love him! He will not consent to the hypothesis that they cannot. The desire for a certain kind of truth here brings about that special truth's existence; and so it is in innumerable cases of

* Latin for "to compel my assent."

other sorts. . . . *And where faith in a fact can help create the fact,* that would be an insane logic which should say that faith running ahead of scientific evidence is the "lowest kind of immorality" into which a thinking being can fall. Yet such is the logic by which our scientific absolutists pretend to regulate our lives!

X

In truths dependent on our personal action, then, faith based on desire is certainly a lawful and possibly an indispensable thing.

But now, it will be said, these are all childish human cases, and have nothing to do with great cosmical matters, like the question of religious faith. Let us then pass on to that. Religions differ so much in their accidents that in discussing the religious question we must make it very generic and broad. What then do we now mean by the religious hypothesis? Science says things are; morality says some things are better than other things; and religion says essentially two things.

First, she says that the best things are the more eternal things, the overlapping things, the things in the universe that throw the last stone, so to speak, and say the final word. "Perfection is eternal"—this phrase of Charles Secrétan* seems a good way of putting this first affirmation of religion, an affirmation which obviously cannot yet be verified scientifically at all.

The second affirmation of religion is that we are better off even now if we believe her first affirmation to be true.

Now, let us consider what the logical elements of this situation are *in case the religious hypothesis in both its branches be really true*. (Of course, we must admit that possibility at the outset. If we are to discuss the question at all, it must involve a living option. If for any of you religion be a hypothesis that cannot, by any living possibility, be true, then you need go no farther. I speak to the "saving remnant" alone.) So proceeding, we see, first, that religion offers itself as a *momentous* option. We are supposed to gain, even now, by our belief, and to lose by our non-belief, a certain vital good. Secondly, religion is a *forced* option, so far as that good goes. We cannot escape the issue by remaining sceptical and waiting for more light, because, although we do avoid error in that way *if religion be untrue*, we lose the good, *if it be true*, just as certainly as if we positively chose to disbelieve. It is as if a man should hesitate indefinitely to ask a certain woman to marry him because he was not perfectly sure that she would prove an angel after he brought her home. Would he not cut himself off from that particular angel-possibility as decisively as if he went and married some one else? Scepticism, then, is not avoidance of option; it is option of a certain particular kind of risk. *Better risk loss of truth than chance of error*—that is your faith-vetoer's exact position. He is actively playing his stake as much as the believer is; he is backing the field against the religious hypothesis, just as the believer is backing the religious hypothesis against the field. To preach scepticism to us as a duty until "sufficient evidence" for religion be found, is tantamount therefore to telling us, when in presence of the religious hypothesis, that to yield to our fear of its being error is wiser and better than to yield to our hope that it may be true. It is not intellect against all passions, then; it is only intellect with one passion laying down its law. And by what, forsooth, is the supreme wisdom of this passion warranted? Dupery for dupery, what proof is there that dupery through hope is so much worse than dupery through fear? I, for one, can see no proof; and I simply refuse obedience to the scientist's command to imitate his kind of option, in a case where my own stake is important enough to give me the right to choose my own form of risk. If religion be true and the evidence for it be still insufficient, I do not wish, by putting your extinguisher upon my nature (which feels to me as if it had after all some business in this matter), to forfeit my sole chance in life of getting upon the winning side—that chance depending, of course, on my willingness to run the risk of acting as if my passional need of taking the world religiously might be prophetic and right.

All this is on the supposition that it really may be prophetic and right, and that, even to us who are discussing the matter, religion is a live hypothesis which may be true. Now, to most of us religion comes in a still further way that makes a veto on our active faith

* Charles Secrétan (1815–95) was a Swiss thinker who worked to reconcile religion and philosophy.

even more illogical. The more perfect and more eternal aspect of the universe is represented in our religions as having personal form. The universe is no longer a mere *It* to us, but a *Thou*, if we are religious; and any relation that may be possible from person to person might be possible here. For instance, although in one sense we are passive portions of the universe, in another we show a curious autonomy, as if we were small active centers on our own account. We feel, too, as if the appeal of religion to us were made to our own active goodwill, as if evidence might be forever withheld from us unless we met the hypothesis halfway to take a trivial illustration: just as a man who in a company of gentlemen made no advances, asked a warrant for every concession, and believed no one's word without proof, would cut himself off by such churlishness from all the social rewards that a more trusting spirit would earn—so here, one who should shut himself up in snarling logicality and try to make the gods extort his recognition willy-nilly, or not get it at all, might cut himself off forever from his only opportunity of making the gods' acquaintance. This feeling, forced on us we know not whence that by obstinately believing that there are gods (although not to do so would be so easy both for our logic and our life) we are doing the universe the deepest service we can, seems part of the living essence of the religious hypothesis. If the hypothesis *were* true in all its parts, including this one, then pure intellectualism, with its veto on our making willing advances, would be an absurdity; and some participation of our sympathetic nature would be logically required. I therefore, for one, cannot see my way to accepting the agnostic rules for truth-seeking, or wilfully agree to keep my willing nature out of the game. I cannot do so for this plain reason, that *a rule of thinking which would absolutely prevent me from acknowledging certain kinds of truth if those kinds of truth were really there, would be an irrational rule*. That for me is the long and short of the formal logic of the situation, no matter what the kinds of truth might materially be.

I confess I do not see how this logic can be escaped. But sad experience makes me fear that some of you may still shrink from radically saying with me, *in abstracto*, that we have the right to believe at our own risk any hypothesis that is live enough to tempt our will. I suspect, however, that if this is so, it is because you have got away from the abstract logical point of view altogether, and are thinking (perhaps without realizing it) of some particular religious hypothesis which for you is dead. The freedom to "believe what we will" you apply to the case of some patent superstition; and the faith you think of is the faith defined by the schoolboy when he said, "Faith is when you believe something that you know ain't true." I can only repeat that this is misapprehension. *In concreto*, the freedom to believe can only cover living options which the intellect of the individual cannot by itself resolve; and living options never seem absurdities to him who has them to consider. When I look at the religious question as it really puts itself to concrete men, and when I think of all the possibilities which both practically and theoretically it involves, then this command that we shall put a stopper on our heart, instincts, and courage, and *wait*—acting of course meanwhile more or less as if religion were *not* true[2]—till doomsday, or till such time as our intellect and senses working together may have raked in evidence enough—this command, I say, seems to me the queerest idol ever manufactured in the philosophic cave. Were we scholastic absolutists, there might be more excuse. If we had an infallible intellect with its objective certitudes, we might feel ourselves disloyal to such a perfect organ of knowledge in not trusting to it exclusively, in not waiting for its releasing word. But if we are empiricists, if we believe that no bell in us tolls to let us know for certain when truth is in our grasp, then it seems a piece of idle fantasticality to preach so solemnly our duty of waiting for the bell. Indeed we *may* wait if we will—I hope you do not think that I am denying that—but if we do so, we do so at our peril as much as if we believed. In either case we *act*, taking our life in our hands.

NOTES

1. Compare Wilfrid Ward's essay "The Wish to Believe," in his *Witnesses to the Unseen* (Macmillan & Co., 1893).
2. Since belief is measured by action, he who forbids us to believe religion to be true, necessarily also forbids

us to act as we should if we did believe it to be true. The whole defence of religious faith hinges upon action. If the action required or inspired by the religious hypothesis is in no way different from that dictated by the naturalistic hypothesis, then religious faith is a pure superfluity, better pruned away, and controversy about its legitimacy is a piece of idle trifling, unworthy of serious minds. I myself believe, of course, that the religious hypothesis gives to the world an expression which specifically determines our reactions, and makes them in a large part unlike what they might be on a purely naturalistic scheme of belief.

The Hiddenness of God

ROBERT McKIM

Robert McKim teaches religious studies and philosophy at the University of Illinois at Urbana–Champaign. His philosophical writings focus on philosophy of religion, the history of philosophy, and applied ethics.

The selection that appears here is an excerpt from McKim's 2001 book *Religious Ambiguity and Religious Diversity.* In it, McKim considers the question of what we can learn about the importance of belief in God from the nature of the evidence that is available to us.

THE HIDDEN EMPEROR

Once upon a time, in a faraway and geographically isolated land, there was a small community that had lived without contact with other communities for so long that the very memory that there were other peoples had been lost almost entirely. Only a few of the elders could recall from their childhood the stories that used to be told of visitors from afar, of distant peoples and communities, of powerful princes and lords, and of their vast empires. Some of the very oldest people with the best memories could recall that back in the old days there were some who said (or was it that they remembered hearing reports about its having been said?—it was so long ago and so hard to tell) that their territory was actually itself part of one of those great empires, and one that was ruled over by a great and good emperor. But these stories had not been told for so long that even the old people had difficulty remembering them, and the young were downright skeptical.

And then one day there arrived an outsider who claimed to be an emissary and who bore astonishing news. He declared that some of the old stories were true. He said that the small, isolated community was indeed part of a great empire, an empire that stretched farther than anyone could have imagined. And—more astonishing still—the ruler of all this, the emissary said, pointing to the familiar hillsides and fields, to the rude dwellings and away to the horizon in all directions, is a great and wise emperor who deserves loyalty and obedience from all his subjects. And that includes you, said the visitor. And—could it be yet more astonishing?—the emperor is generally known to his subjects throughout the rest of the empire as the "Hidden Emperor," for he never lets himself be seen clearly by any of his subjects. Not even his closest, most loyal, and most devoted servants are sure exactly what he looks like. But it is widely believed that he travels incognito throughout the empire, for he has various remarkable powers that make this pos-

From *Religious Ambiguity and Religious Diversity*. Copyright © 2001 by Robert McKim. Reprinted by permission of Oxford University Press.

sible, including the power to make himself invisible, the power to travel from place to place with great speed, and even the power to understand what people are thinking. Indeed, *so* great are his powers in these respects, said the visitor, that it is hardly an exaggeration to say that he is always present throughout the entire empire.

Never had anything quite like this been heard. Mouths were agape, eyes were wide in astonishment. What are we to do, what does the emperor want from us and what are we to expect from him? people asked. "He wants your loyalty, trust, and obedience, and he offers protection and help in time of trouble," replied the emissary.

At this point a man in the crowd, a tallish bearded man with a puzzled expression, and of the sort that is inclined to twiddle with his beard in an irritating way, replied as follows. "But why," he asked—and the emissary knew what was coming, for he had been through this many times and knew that in every community there is a trouble-maker or two and that beard twiddling and a puzzled expression are among the best indicators that trouble is brewing—"why does the emperor have to be hidden? Why can't we see the emperor for ourselves? I know that it is not my place to ask"—a familiar line to the seasoned emissary, who has heard it all before and can recognize false modesty at a glance—"but why couldn't the emperor's existence and presence be as clear as *your* presence and existence? And"—now for the coup de grâce, thought the emissary, the sign that we are contending here with a *serious* thinker—"if it is important for the emperor to be hidden, why are you here informing us about him?"

After the tall bearded man had spoken, there was silence for a few minutes. The fact was that no one quite knew what would happen next, or what it was proper to say to the emissary. Had the bearded man gone too far? Had he spoken improperly? Would he be reprimanded or punished? Would they all be reprimanded or punished? Should he be silenced?

Then an old woman, known for her wisdom and insight, and of that generation among whom belief in the great emperor had not entirely been lost, spoke up. "I, for one, think that things are much better this way. As long as the emperor, and may he and his blessed relatives live for ever," she added, with a glance at the emissary, "as long as the emperor is hidden, we have a type of freedom that would otherwise be unavailable to us. We are free to decide whether or not to believe that there is an emperor. If the facts of the matter were clear to us, and it were just plain obvious that the emperor exists, belief would be forced on us. As long as the facts are unclear, we are in a position to exercise control over what we think. And even though our esteemed visitor has come to explain the situation to us, we are still in a position to decide whether or not to believe what he says."

At this the bearded man became downright exasperated, saying, "Listen here. What is so great about being able to make up your mind in conditions in which the facts are unclear? Surely if the facts are unclear, we ought simply to believe that the facts are unclear. It's absurd to suggest that there is something especially admirable or good about deciding that the emperor exists under circumstances in which it is unclear whether the emperor exists. Do you think that it would also be good for us to be able to choose whether or not to believe, say, that two plus two equals four in circumstances in which *that* is not clear, or for us to be able to choose what to believe about who our parents are in circumstances in which *that* is not clear?"

"This may seem absurd to you," interjected the woman, "since you are the sort of man who likes to strut around as if you had all the answers to life's questions even though nobody else has quite noticed, but what you have to understand is that this arrangement has the great advantage of permitting our willingness to acknowledge our status as subservient underlings in the emperor's realm to play a role in determining whether or not we believe that the emperor exists."

"And I will tell you," said the woman, warming to her theme and enjoying the attention of the crowd, and what she took to be the approving look of the visiting emissary, "I will tell you about another benefit of our current situation. The fact that we do not know what the emperor looks like permits him to come among us, looking like one of us. Long ago, when I was a little girl, it used to be said that when you entertain a stranger, you should remember that you might be entertaining the emperor. In fact people used to say, 'Every poor stranger is the emperor.' I don't suppose that they really meant it, but you can see what they had in mind. And there was another saying, too, now that I remember it. We used to say, when we wished to show respect for someone, that 'You are He.' Of course, if you knew that a visitor in your house really was the emperor, you would be quite dazed and overwhelmed, and even ashamed by how little you had to offer such a guest."

"Damn it all," said the man with the puzzled look, "this is all nonsense. If the emperor wanted us to believe in him, he would make his existence apparent to us. Don't listen to that old bag. It's as simple as this. If the emperor existed, he would want us to know him and to know about him. If so, he would make his presence apparent to us. He does not do so even though he could do so. The only sensible conclusion is that *there is no emperor. There is no emperor! There is no emperor!*"

After this intemperate outburst yet another voice was heard from the crowd, the voice of one who prides himself on taking a sober, comprehensive, and balanced view of things, and in the process takes himself much too seriously. "Maybe we *are* part of the empire," said this new interlocutor. "Certainly we have some evidence that this is so, not least of which is the fact that our honored visitor, who appears to me to have an open and trustworthy countenance, has come to tell us that this is so. The recollections of some of our senior members are also relevant here. Surely they give us some reason to believe there to be an emperor. But if there is an emperor—and I certainly do not rule out this possibility—it is hard to believe that it matters to him whether we believe that he exists. If it mattered very much to the emperor that we believe that he exists, then surely it would be clearer than it now is that there is an emperor. After all, where has the emperor been all this time? Furthermore, the beliefs that we hold about the emperor under current conditions, if we hold any, ought to reflect the fact that they are held under conditions of uncertainty. Any beliefs we hold in this area ought in fact to be held with tentativeness, and with an awareness that we may be wrong."

In the fullness of time, and after the emissary had gone his way, it came to pass that three schools of thought developed, each of which embraced one of the views that were expressed on that day. There were those who agreed with the old woman, and who were known by their opponents as the "Imperialists." Then there were the Skeptics. All of their bearded members had a strong inclination toward beard twiddling. And there were the Tentative Believers. They were known to their detractors as "the half-baked believers." So who was right? ...

THE DISADVANTAGES OF GOD'S HIDDENNESS

If God exists but is hidden, this is a perplexing state of affairs. One reason that it is perplexing is internal to theism and arises from the fact that the theistic traditions place such importance on belief. Typically each theistic tradition asserts that to fail to hold theistic beliefs, and especially to fail to hold its theistic beliefs, or at least what it considers to be the most important among them, is to go wrong in a very serious way whereas to adopt theistic beliefs, and especially the set of theistic beliefs associated with it, is a worthwhile and important thing to do. These traditions say, too, that one ought to regret or even feel guilty about a failure to believe. Yet if God is hidden, belief is more difficult than it would be if God were not hidden. If God exists, and if the facts about God's existence and nature were clear, belief would be ever so much easier for us. The theistic traditions are inclined to hold human beings responsible and even to blame them if they are nonbelievers or if their belief is weak. But does this make any sense?

God's hiddenness creates uncertainty and contributes to profound disagreement about the existence and nature of God. Indeed, I would suggest that it contributes *more* to the occurrence of nonbelief than does the presence of evil in the world (or of *other* evil in the world, if the hiddenness of God is understood as a type of evil). This is not to deny that there are people who are nontheists because of evils that they either encounter or are familiar with; but it seems that the explanation in most cases of how it has come about that people do not believe that God exists (whether they are atheists or agnostics or members of nontheistic religions) is not that they consider God's existence to be incompatible with various evils. Rather, it is that they have nothing that they understand as an awareness of God. They do not understand themselves to be familiar with God. Consequently, they do not even reach a point where evil is perceived as a problem. . . .

Another reason that the hiddenness of God is perplexing has to do with the sort of personal relationship with God that some theists advocate. This is also a reason that is internal to theism, or at least to theism of a certain sort, especially evangelical and fundamentalist Christianity. The personal relationship in question is understood to involve trust, respect, and, above all, ongoing intimate communication. Is it not reasonable to suppose that if God were less hidden, this sort of relationship would be more widespread?

The hiddenness of God, therefore, seems to be a particularly acute problem for strands of theism that emphasize the importance of fellowship and communication with God. But it is also a problem for the other major strands of theism because they all emphasize the importance and value of belief. And they declare that God cares about us; if God exists and if God cares about us, why does God leave human beings to such an extent in the dark about various religiously important facts? If God does not care about us, there is less to explain. Theism typically requires, too, that we put our trust and confidence in God: But why, then, are the facts about God not more clear? If God exists and the facts about God's existence and nature were more clear, people would be more likely to see that they ought to put their trust and confidence in God and would be more willing and more able to do so.

Another important, and related, disadvantage associated with divine hiddenness is this. If God exists, God is worthy of adoration and worship: given the good, wise, just (etc.) nature of God, and the relation between God and God's creatures, a worshipful response from human beings would be appropriate. For if God exists, God is our Creator and we owe all we have to God. But if many of us are in the dark about the existence and nature of God, then this appropriate human response is made more difficult than it otherwise would be. So part of the cost of divine hiddenness is its contribution to the large-scale failure of human beings to respond to God in ways that seem appropriate in the case of a good, just, and wise creator.

And there are further costs. The profound disagreements about God, and more broadly the profound disagreements that there are about numerous matters of religious importance, often play a role in promoting and exacerbating social conflict. If God exists and if the facts about God were as clear as they could be, there might not be as much room for disagreement, and hence such disagreements would not contribute to social conflict. The mystery surrounding God also provides opportunities for charlatans and frauds to pose as experts on the nature and activities of God, and for religious authorities in numerous traditions to acquire and exercise, and sometimes abuse, power and control over others.

To each of these apparent disadvantages, or costs, of God's hiddenness there corresponds an advantage or benefit that, it appears, would accrue if God were not hidden. Thus if God were not hidden, and the facts about God were clear for all to see, it appears that belief would be easier for us, a personal relationship with God would be facilitated, more people would worship God, religious disagreement would be less likely to exacerbate social tensions, and there would be fewer opportunities for people to pose as experts and to acquire power and influence over others. . . .

There is, then, some reason to think that, if God exists, it must not matter greatly to God whether we believe. This applies to belief that God exists, to various standard theistic beliefs about God, such as beliefs about the activities and character of God, and to belief in God. At least that we should hold such beliefs . . . here and now and under our current circumstances probably does not matter greatly. There is also considerable reason to believe that it is not important that everyone should accept any particular form of theism, such as Judaism or Islam. If it were very important that we should accept theism or any particular form of theism, our circumstances probably would be more conducive to it.

C GOD AND SCIENCE: CONTEMPORARY DISCUSSIONS

Theism and Modern Science

NICHOLAS EVERITT

Nicholas Everitt teaches philosophy at the University of East Anglia in England. His philosophical writings focus on epistemology, the philosophy of mind, and the philosophy of religion.

This text is an excerpt from Everitt's 2004 book *The Non-Existence of God*. In it, Everitt contends that scientific evidence about the nature and size of the universe is in tension with views that suggest that the universe was created by a divine being.

Traditional theism presents us with a certain picture of God and of his intentions in creating the universe at large, and in creating human beings in particular. In general, if someone hypothesises that there is an agent with a certain nature and a certain set of intentions, then we can form some idea of what the agent is likely to do—in what respect things will be different just in virtue of the hypothesised agent's having that nature, those beliefs, and that intention. If we then discover that the world is not as we have predicted, then we have evidence that the initial hypothesis that there was such an agent is mistaken. The argument thus has the form:

(1) If there is an agent with nature N, beliefs B, and intention I, then he will produce change C in the world.
(2) The world does not display C. So:
(3) There is evidence against the hypothesis that there is an agent with N and I and B.

As an example of the argument at work in an uncontroversial context, consider an updated Robinson Crusoe.* Suppose he considers the hypothesis that elsewhere on the island with him is another survivor of the shipwreck similar to Crusoe himself in his physical and mental capacities, including his beliefs, and with the intention of making contact with any other survivors, such as Crusoe. Even given as vague and impoverished a hypothesis as this, Crusoe can make *some* predictions about what the hypothetical survivor will do. He can formulate in his mind a range of what he might call apt behaviour, and a range of inapt behaviour, which the survivor might display—apt and inapt relative to the intention with which Crusoe has tentatively credited him. It would be apt if, for example, the survivor left visible signs of his presence on the island (marks on trees, scratchings on rocks, carefully arranged pieces of wood or stone). It would be apt if he emitted characteristically human noises (whistling, singing, shouting, etc.). It would be apt if he lit a fire and tried to send smoke signals. These would be apt pieces of behaviour because they are just the sorts of things which a Crusoe-like survivor would do if he were trying to let other possible survivors know of his existence on the island. By contrast, it would not be apt if the hypothetical survivor, for example, found

* Robinson Crusoe is a fictional character from Daniel Defoe's 1719 novel of the same name. In the story, he is shipwrecked on a remote island where he lives for 28 years.

From *The Non-Existence of God* (London and New York: Routledge, 2004). Reproduced by permission of Taylor & Francis Books UK.

some deep undergrowth and lay in it, quiet and still, for the greater part of each day. It would not be apt if after being in any location on the island, he carefully removed all signs of his presence (footprints, ashes from fires, etc.). And so on. These are not apt ways of realising the intention of making your presence known to another human who might be in the vicinity. They are not the kind of actions which it would be reasonable for Crusoe to expect another survivor to pursue, given the intentions and beliefs with which Crusoe is crediting him.

So, even before starting his empirical investigation of the island, Crusoe can formulate to himself a description of what evidence would help to confirm his initial hypothesis, and what evidence would help to disconfirm it. If he looks hard and carefully for evidence of what we have called apt behaviour, and finds none, that constitutes some evidence against his initial hypothesis that there is another survivor. It is evidence for saying that either there is no actual survivor, or if there is one, the initial hypothesis was wrong about either his capacities or his intentions. In saying that some kinds of behaviour by the hypothetical survivor would be "inapt," we do not mean that it *absolutely disproves* the initial hypothesis about the survivor's capacities and intentions, but rather that it constitutes *evidence against* the hypothesis. The evidence is defeasible in that it is possible that there is some factor of which Crusoe is unaware which would explain away its initial anti-hypothesis import. (Perhaps the survivor is injured or even unconscious.) But if he does not discover any such factor, he would be justified in concluding that the initial hypothesis is to some degree disconfirmed.

Let us see now how considerations of this kind can be applied on a cosmic scale, and how the nature of the universe as revealed by modern science gives us reason to reject traditional theism.

Consider, first, the account of God's nature and purposes with which theism presents us. Theism tells us that God is a being who is omnipotent and omniscient, wholly self-sufficient, with no needs, or lacks, or deficiencies of any kind. For reasons that are not entirely clear, God decides to create a universe in which human beings will be the jewel. Although he will have a care for the whole of his creation, God will have an especial care for human beings. He will give these creatures the power of free choice. Exactly what this power is, no one can agree. Some think that it is a capacity the possession of which is incompatible with the truth of determinism; others think that it is a kind of freedom which is compatible with determinism, and which perhaps even requires determinism.* Because humans are the jewel of creation, the rest of the universe will be at least not unremittingly hostile or even indifferent to human flourishing. Even if the universe will not make such flourishing immediately and easily and painlessly accessible, it will make it at least accessible in principle for humanity at large. The question then to ask is: given this much information about God and his nature and his purposes, what sort of a universe would you expect to find? Which of all the possible worlds that God could create would you expect him to create, given this much knowledge of his nature and of his overall plan?

As with our example of Robinson Crusoe, it is difficult to answer this question in any great detail. The description of God is so sketchy, and in particular the theistic hypothesis gives us so little information about his aims, that a large number of possible worlds are left equally likely. But among the more likely scenarios is a universe somewhat like the one presented to us in the story of Genesis. In particular, traditional theism would lead you to expect human beings to appear fairly soon after the start of the universe. For, given the central role of humanity, what would be the point of a universe which came into existence and then existed for unimaginable aeons without the presence of the very species that supplied its rationale? You would expect humans to appear after a great many animals, since the animals are subordinate species available for human utilisation, and there would be no point in having humans arrive on the scene needing animals (e.g. as a source of food, or clothing, or companionship) only for them to discover that animals had not yet been created. But equally, you would not expect humans to arrive *very* long after the animals, for what would be the point of a universe existing for aeons full of animals created for humanity's delectation, in the absence of any humans? Further, you would expect the earth to be fairly near the centre of the universe if it had

* This is discussed in section III. F following.

one, or at some similarly significant location if it did not have an actual centre. You would expect the total universe to be not many orders of magnitude greater than the size of the earth. The universe would be on a *human* scale. You would expect that even if there are regions of the created world which are hostile to human life, and which perhaps are incompatible with it, the greater part of the universe would be accessible to human exploration. If this were not so, what would the point be of God creating it?

These expectations are largely what we find in the Genesis story (or strictly, stories) of creation. There is, then, a logic to the picture of the universe with which the Genesis story presents us: given the initial assumptions about God, his nature, and his intentions, the Genesis universe is pretty much how it would be reasonable for God to proceed. Given the hypothesis of theism and no scientific knowledge, and then asked to construct a picture of the universe and its creation, it is not surprising that the author(s) of Genesis came up with the account which they did. It is not that God would have *had* to proceed in the Genesis way (just as there is not just one kind of behaviour which a possible island survivor would need to produce to confirm Crusoe's initial hypothesis), and it is not that *every* non-Genesis way would be extremely puzzling. There is in fact a wide range of possible universes which God could have created and about which there would not be a puzzle of the form "But how could a universe like *that* be an expression of a set of intentions like *those?*" Nevertheless, we can still draw a distinction between universes which would be apt, given the initial hypothesis, and universes which would be inapt. The Genesis universe is clearly an apt one, given the theistic hypothesis; but a universe in which (say) most humans could survive only by leading lives of great and endless pain would be a surprising one for God to choose, given the other assumptions we make about him.

The question now to raise is "Is the universe as it is revealed to us by modern science roughly the sort of universe which we would antecedently expect a God of traditional theism to create? Is it an apt universe, given the admittedly sketchy conception we have of his nature and his intentions?"

The short answer to this is "No." In almost every respect, the universe as it is revealed to us by modern science is *hugely* unlike the sort of universe which the traditional thesis would lead us to expect. Although the bare quantitative facts will be familiar to many readers, it is worth repeating them. First, in terms of age: our best estimates are that the universe itself is very roughly 15 billion years, and the Earth is roughly 5 billion years old. How long humans have existed will depend partly on what we take a human to be. But if we take humans to be homo sapiens, and if we take them to be creatures with some sort of language and some sort of social culture, then realistic estimates would allow that they have existed for no more than 100,000 years. So if we imagine the history of the universe represented by a line which is roughly 24 miles long, human life would occupy only the last inch. Or if we imagine this history of the universe represented by a single year, humanity would emerge only in the last few seconds of the last minute of the last hour of the last day of the year. So for something more than 99.999 per cent of the history of the universe, the very creatures which are meant to be the jewel of creation have been absent from it. The question that at once arises is "What, given the hypothesis of theism, was the point of this huge discrepancy between the age of the universe and the age of humanity?" How very inapt a creation of that kind must strike us.

The same story recurs if we turn to the size of the universe. Suppose we take the size of our solar system to be within the expectable parameters of the theistic hypothesis. (This might seem over-generous to theism: why would God need a solar system as big as ours to achieve any of his purposes? Why does he need a sun that is 93 *million* miles from earth? Why wouldn't 93 thousand miles have been enough? Of course the laws of physics would then have had to be different if the sun were to make earth habitable—but as an omnipotent being, God could easily have adjusted the laws of physics. However, let us overlook this and allow that a distance of 93 million miles counts as intelligible—it is intelligible, that is, that a God with the nature and intentions ascribed by traditional theism should create a universe that big.) But of course, we know now that the universe is staggeringly larger than any such intelligible size. The sun is about 8 light minutes from us, the next nearest star is about 4.3 light years, the next nearest galaxy to the Milky Way is scores of light years away. Current findings indicate that the furthest star visible from earth is about 3 billion light years away. In other words, the most distant star is very roughly some 200,000,000,000,000,000 times (two hundred thousand trillion times) as far from us as the sun. This sort of scale to the universe makes no conceivable sense on the theistic hypothesis. Nor should we assume that the most distant visible star is the most distant detectable entity. The furthest galaxy, detectable only by radio telescopes, is reckoned to be about three times further away—9 billion light years. The possible limits of the universe lie further away still. If the Big Bang occurred about 15 billion years ago, and if the expansion had occurred at the speed of light, the limits of the universe would be about 30 billion light years. Assuming that the expansion was at less than the speed of light, that still leaves the possibility of a universe whose overall size is between 10 and 30 billion light years across (i.e., up to two million trillion miles). Why would a God make it that big?

Further, astronomers tell us that there are about 100 trillion galaxies, each with a billion stars (giving us something of the order of 100,000,000,000,000,000,000,000 stars).[1] It could count as apt if a creator created a universe with one star or perhaps a few dozen or even a few hundred, so that the night sky were as beautiful as we now find it. But what could be the point of the huge superabundance of celestial matter, especially given the fact that the very great majority of humanity will never be aware of most of it? Again, given the theistic hypothesis, it is strikingly inapt.

If we confine our attention to the earth, the same extraordinary inaptness confronts us. The Genesis story presents God's actions as apt in relation to the non-human creatures who share the planet with humans: they all emerge at about the same time; and all the creatures which surround humanity in that story share a human scale—none are so tiny that it is impossible to detect them by the senses, and none are so huge (e.g. thousands or millions of times larger than humans) as to be unrecognisable as organisms at all. But again, modern science reveals this to be deeply wrong—not just in points of detail, but in almost every major respect. Life has existed on the planet for something like 3 to 3.5 billion years. For roughly half of that time, it has been solely bacterial in form. Given that humans have emerged only in the last 100, 000 years, that means that for 99.99 per cent of the history of life on earth, there have been no humans. How very bizarre, given the theistic hypothesis! Further, from a biological point of view "On any possible or reasonable or fair criterion, bacteria are—and always have been the dominant forms of life on earth."[2] In terms of their numbers, their longevity, their ability to exploit the widest variety of habitats, their degree of genetic variation, and even (amazingly, give how tiny they are individually) their total biomass, they outstrip every other kind of life. If God had intended any species to flourish, the obvious candidate for divine favour would be bacteria, not humans.

In short, then, everything that modern science tells us about the size and scale and nature of the universe around us reveals it to be strikingly inapt as an expression of a set of divine intentions of the kind that theism postulates. Let us emphasise that the claim here is not that there is a logical incompatibility between these modern scientific findings and traditional theism. It is not that the findings *disprove* theism. The claim is weaker than that. The claim is only that the findings of modern science *significantly reduce the probability* that theism is true, because the universe is turning out to be very unlike the sort of universe which we would have expected, had theism been true.

NOTES

1. Sarah Woodward, "Things to Come." *The Cambridge Alumni Magazine*, 2000, vol. 30, p. 25.
2. Stephen Jay Gould, *Life's Grandeur*. London: Jonathan Cape, 1996, p. 176.

PART II

MORAL AND POLITICAL PHILOSOPHY

MORAL PHILOSOPHY

INTRODUCTION

The branch of philosophy that is concerned with questions of right and wrong, good and bad, is called *moral philosophy* or *ethics*. (Although some philosophers distinguish between these two terms, we use them interchangeably in the discussion that follows.) Moral philosophers are concerned with helping us to understand what we mean by terms like *right* and *wrong, permissible* and *forbidden, ought* and *ought not,* and *good* and *evil* in a systematic and principled way.

In our daily lives, we are often concerned with specific questions like the following: What are our moral duties to those less fortunate? Under what circumstances, if any, is lying morally permissible? What sorts of moral duties do we have to nonhuman animals? These are questions about appropriate *moral behavior*; they ask how we ought to conduct our lives if we wish to act in keeping with the demands of morality.

A systematic moral theory tries to answer such questions by providing an account of morality itself. Whereas questions about moral behavior are concerned with *which* things are right and wrong, questions about *moral explanation* are concerned with *why* things are right and wrong. They are concerned with determining which features of the world and of morality make certain things moral and others immoral.

Three Major Ethical Theories

The first set of readings introduces three of the major moral theories that have been central to the Western philosophical tradition: *utilitarianism* (represented by the nineteenth-century British philosopher John Stuart Mill), *deontology* (represented by the eighteenth-century

German philosopher Immanuel Kant), and *virtue theory* (represented by the ancient Greek philosopher Aristotle).*

Utilitarianism

According to *utilitarianism*, an act is right insofar as it produces the greatest amount of good for the greatest number of people. Utilitarianism is thus a *consequentialist* moral theory: it holds that the rightness of an act is a matter of the act's consequences. Modern utilitarian theory can be traced to the writings of the British philosopher Jeremy Bentham (1748–1832), who famously held that in any situation, the morally right act is that which will produce "the greatest happiness for the greatest number." In our selection, written by Bentham's student and godson John Stuart Mill (1806–73), we encounter the most famous presentation and defense of the view. In this excerpt from his 1861 book *Utilitarianism*, Mill puts forth a refined version of utilitarianism, according to which morally right acts are those that promote happiness, whereas morally wrong acts are those that reduce it. Responding to criticisms that had been offered of previous utilitarian theories, Mill stresses that different sorts of happiness may be taken into account in different ways: in particular, intellectual or "higher" pleasures can be taken to outweigh animalistic or "lower" ones.

The selection from Mill is supplemented by two additional essays. In the first, philosopher J. J. C. Smart (1920–) distinguishes two ways of understanding the central utilitarian claim that the proper way to judge the rightness of actions is by looking to their consequences either by understanding "actions" as individual deeds (*extreme* or *act utilitarianism*) or by understanding "actions" as classes of deeds (*restricted* or *rule utilitarianism*). Smart explores some of the crucial differences between these two views, ultimately endorsing act over rule utilitarianism.

In the second supplementary essay, philosopher Bernard Williams (1929–2003) offers some challenges to the view that Mill and Smart endorse. Utilitarianism, he suggests, does not leave room for morally important notions, such as integrity; as a result, the utilitarian moral outlook is incapable of properly capturing our authentic moral commitments.

Deontology

Whereas utilitarians hold that whether an act is morally right is a matter of the consequences it produces, *deontologists* hold that what makes an act morally right is that it is performed for the right sorts of reasons. Again, our presentation of this account comes from its most famous advocate, the German philosopher Immanel Kant (1724–1804). In this selection, taken from his book, *Grounding for the Metaphysics of Morals*, Kant argues that a good will is the only thing that is good in itself and that the rightness of an act should be judged according to the motivation that lies behind it. An act is morally right, according to Kant, if it is done from a good will in accordance with duty. Acting in accordance with duty means acting out of respect for what he calls the *categorical imperative*, which tells us that we should deliberately act only in ways that we could rationally will everyone to act under similar circumstances.

* Other influential Western moral theories include *divine command theory*—the theory that an act is right if and only if God commands it—and *natural law theory*—the theory that the content of moral law is set by nature. Influential non-Western moral theories include Buddhist and Confucian ethics, ethical theories associated with religions such as Islam and Hinduism, and African philosophies such as *Ubuntu*.

The selection from Kant is supplemented by a brief selection from the writings of the contemporary British philosopher Onora O'Neill (1941–), whose "A Simplified Account of Kant's Ethics" clarifies some of Kant's points and defends Kantianism against the criticism that its demands are too difficult for it to be a plausible moral code.

Virtue Ethics

Our final selection in this section draws from the ancient Greek tradition of *virtue ethics*, here represented by an excerpt from Aristotle's (384–322 BCE) *Nicomachean Ethics.* Whereas utilitarians and deontologists focus primarily on the rightness or wrongness of individual acts, virtue theorists focus on the *character* of the person performing the act. In order to evaluate someone's moral character, we must consider his life in its entirety: if he is a virtuous person, then he regularly acts in the right way, responding properly to the particular features of the circumstance he confronts. A virtuous character is acquired by consistently acting with responsive moderation: in the right way, at the right time, for the right sorts of reasons.

The selection from Aristotle is supplemented by an essay from the contemporary New Zealand philosopher Rosalind Hursthouse. In "Normative Virtue Ethics," Hursthouse explains how virtue ethics may serve as a viable contemporary moral theory, offering important correctives to some of the problematic features of both consequentialism and deontology.

Some Applications

Whereas the first set of readings concerned overarching questions about the nature and structure of morality, the next set of readings address two current debates in *applied ethics.*

Moral Duties to the Poor

The first debate concerns whether those who are affluent have a moral obligation to give some of their resources to those who suffer from poverty and famine. In "Rich and Poor," the well-known Australian utilitarian philosopher Peter Singer (1946–) argues that it is morally wrong not to give to people in need if one could do so without compromising anything of comparable moral significance. This means that in nearly all cases, those who have wealth beyond what is required to meet their basic needs are morally obligated to redistribute much of it to those who live in conditions of dire poverty.

In "Lifeboat Ethics," ecologist Garrett Hardin (1915–2003) challenges this contention, arguing that there is no moral duty for the wealthy to share their resources with those whose basic needs are not met. Giving aid to underdeveloped countries, he maintains, will only exacerbate the problems of poverty and famine by discouraging efforts to find lasting solutions to their underlying causes and by encouraging population growth.

An alternative perspective is offered by contemporary philosopher Thomas Pogge in "'Aiding' the Global Poor." Pogge contends that citizens of affluent nations do have a moral obligation to assist those in underdeveloped nations because the world order that produced such poverty is the direct result of actions taken by their governments. As a result, those who are living in comfort are morally obliged to share their resources with people who are suffering from extreme poverty.

Vegetarianism and Animals

The second debate concerns our moral obligations to animals and the related issue of vegetarianism. In "Puppies, Pigs, and People: Eating Meat and Marginal Cases," contemporary philosopher Alastair Norcross asks us to consider a hypothetical situation in which puppies are tortured for the purpose of increasing gustatory pleasure. If we think that torturing the puppies would be morally wrong in such a case, he argues, we should also feel it morally wrong to eat meat from animals that are raised in cruel conditions, for, according to Norcross, there are no relevant differences between his hypothetical case and the actual practice of consuming animals that are raised on factory farms.

The opposing view is defended by contemporary philosopher Carl Cohen in "A Critique of the Alleged Moral Basis of Vegetarianism." Cohen argues that morally wrong acts are those that involve violating the rights of another. But nonhuman animals, he maintains, do not have rights; hence they are not in a position to be morally wronged.

Puzzles and Challenges

Puzzling Cases

The next pair of readings explores some of the puzzles that arise when we think carefully about morality. In "The Trolley Problem," American philosopher Judith Jarvis Thomson (1929–) presents a number of hypothetical cases involving a trolley that is hurtling down a track, destined to kill those who lie before it. She considers a series of scenarios in which the trolley may be rerouted in various ways and attempts to uncover principles of morality that could explain and reconcile her rather subtle intuitions about them.

In "Moral Luck," philosopher Thomas Nagel (1937–) discusses an apparent tension in our grounds for moral evaluation. Despite widespread insistence that outcomes that lie beyond the agent's control should be irrelevant to our moral evaluation of the act performed, it seems clear that we assign different levels of moral praise (or blame) to individuals who commit the same acts, depending on the outcomes that the acts produce. The *lucky* driver to whom nothing bad happens when she answers her cell phone is treated as morally blameless, yet we have a different reaction to her *unlucky* counterpart, in front of whose car a child runs at that exact moment.

Challenges

The final set of readings—drawn from both classical and contemporary sources—offer a series of challenges to morality as it has been traditionally understood.

The Value of Morality

Our first two selections challenge the traditional view that we should always find moral reasons to be compelling guides to our own behavior. In "Glaucon's Challenge"—an excerpt from Plato's (427–347 BCE) dialogue, *The Republic*—the character Glaucon argues that the only reason people act justly is because they believe that doing so will help them attain desirable ends. To support his claim, Glaucon tells the story of a magical ring that enables its wearer to become invisible. If there were a ring, Glaucon maintains, whoever possessed it would act in radical violation of what justice requires. If Glaucon is right, then people do not value acting justly for its own sake, but only as a tool to help them get what they want.

A second challenge to the motivating force of morality is presented in contemporary American philosopher Susan Wolf's essay "Moral Saints." Moral value, Wolf suggests, is not the only sort of value worth pursuing. As a result, moral saints—those whose every action is as morally good as possible—reflect neither a rational nor a desirable human ideal.

The Universality of Morality

Each of the three "major ethical theories" just considered represents a *nonrelativist* view of morality; each holds that there are certain things that are morally right or good for all individuals at all times. By contrast, *relativist* views of morality allow that moral demands may be somehow relative to individuals or groups. Each of the next two selections by contemporary moral philosopher James Rachels (1941–2003) explores (and ultimately rejects) such a view.

In "Egoism and Moral Scepticism," Rachels considers the doctrine of *ethical egoism*—the view that the morally right thing to do is that which best promotes one's self-interest. In "The Challenge of Cultural Relativism," he considers the doctrine of *cultural relativism*, which holds that there are no universal moral truths; rather, what is right or wrong is determined by cultures or individuals. In each essay, Rachels presents the main arguments that have been offered in favor of the doctrine, considering them critically before coming down against both views.

Morality and Social Science

Our final two selections draw on work in contemporary psychology that may be relevant to how we think about moral questions. In her influential 1982 book *In a Different Voice: Psychological Theory and Women's Development* psychologist Carol Gilligan (1936–) presented research that seemed to show that men and woman approach moral reasoning in fundamentally different ways. This research is presented in our selection "Women's 'Different Voice,'" in which contemporary philosopher Jennifer Saul discusses Gilligan's ideas and considers what implications they may have for traditional moral philosophy.

In "Heuristics and Morality," law professor Cass Sunstein (1954–) draws on work in contemporary psychology and neuroscience that suggests that much of our moral decision making is based on heuristics, or mental rules of thumb. Although these mental shortcuts often work quite well, they can lead us astray in certain cases. Thus, Sunstein argues, if intuition tells us that a certain moral code gives us the wrong answer in some particular case, we should consider the possibility that it is our intuition, rather than the moral code, that is leading us astray.

Further Reading

Students who want to pursue the themes raised in this section of the book may begin by looking at the articles in the following two anthologies. Each anthology includes an extensive collection of important readings in ethics, along with suggestions for further readings on each of the main themes:

- Steven M. Cahn and Peter Markie, eds., *Ethics: History, Theory, and Contemporary Issues,* 3rd ed. New York and Oxford: Oxford University Press, 2006.
- Louis Pojman, ed., *Moral Philosophy: A Reader,* 3rd ed. Indianapolis/Cambridge: Hackett Publishers, 2003.

A THREE MAJOR ETHICAL THEORIES

◈ UTILITARIANISM ◈

Selections from *Utilitarianism*

JOHN STUART MILL

John Stuart Mill (1806–73), widely regarded as one of the most important thinkers of the 19th century, was a British philosopher and political economist. He published books on topics as diverse as logic, economics, political philosophy, and religion and served as a Member of the British Parliament from 1865 to 1868, where he was an early and vocal advocate of women's right to vote.

The selections that appear here are drawn from Chapters 2 and 4 of Mill's famous work *Utilitarianism,* which was originally published in three installments in *Fraser's Magazine* in 1861. In these chapters, Mill presents and defends a utilitarian account of morality, and corrects a number of misconceptions regarding the view.

CHAPTER 2 WHAT UTILITARIANISM IS

. . . The creed which accepts as the foundation of morals, Utility, or the Greatest Happiness Principle, holds that actions are right in proportion as they tend to promote happiness, wrong as they tend to produce the reverse of happiness. By happiness is intended pleasure, and the absence of pain; by unhappiness, pain, and the privation of pleasure. To give a clear view of the moral standard set up by the theory, much more requires to be said; in particular, what things it includes in the ideas of pain and pleasure; and to what extent this is left an open question. But these supplementary explanations do not affect the theory of life on which this theory of morality is grounded—namely, that pleasure, and freedom from pain, are the only things desirable as ends; and that all desirable things (which are as numerous in the utilitarian as in any other scheme) are desirable either for the pleasure inherent in themselves, or as means to the promotion of pleasure and the prevention of pain.

Now, such a theory of life excites in many minds, and among them in some of the most estimable in feeling and purpose, inveterate dislike. To suppose that life has (as they express it) no higher end than pleasure—no better and nobler object of desire and pursuit—they designate as utterly mean and groveling; as a doctrine worthy only of swine, to whom the followers of Epicurus* were, at a very early period, contemptuously likened; and modern holders of the doctrine are occasionally made the subject of equally polite comparisons by its German, French, and English assailants.

When thus attacked, the Epicureans have always answered, that it is not they, but their accusers, who represent human nature in a degrading light; since

* Epicurus (341–270 BCE) was an ancient Greek philosopher whose philosophy was often misinterpreted as advocating a life of hedonism and sensual indulgence. As Mill points out, Epicurus and his followers—the Epicureans—commended a life devoted to "higher" pleasures, such as friendship and aesthetic appreciation.

the accusation supposes human beings to be capable of no pleasures except those of which swine are capable. If this supposition were true, the charge could not be gainsaid, but would then be no longer an imputation; for if the sources of pleasure were precisely the same to human beings and to swine, the rule of life which is good enough for the one would be good enough for the other. The comparison of the Epicurean life to that of beasts is felt as degrading, precisely because a beast's pleasures do not satisfy a human being's conceptions of happiness. Human beings have faculties more elevated than the animal appetites, and when once made conscious of them, do not regard anything as happiness which does not include their gratification. I do not, indeed, consider the Epicureans to have been by any means faultless in drawing out their scheme of consequences from the utilitarian principle. To do this in any sufficient manner, many Stoic,* as well as Christian elements require to be included. But there is no known Epicurean theory of life which does not assign to the pleasures of the intellect, of the feelings and imagination, and of the moral sentiments, a much higher value as pleasure than to those of mere sensation. It must be admitted, however, that utilitarian writers in general have placed the superiority of mental over bodily pleasures chiefly in the greater permanency, safety, uncostliness, etc., of the former—that is, in their circumstantial advantages rather than in their intrinsic nature. And on all these points utilitarians have fully proved their case; but they might have taken the other, and, as it may be called, higher ground, with entire consistency. It is quite compatible with the principle of utility to recognise the fact, that some *kinds* of pleasure are more desirable and more valuable than others. It would be absurd that while, in estimating all other things, quality is considered as well as quantity, the estimation of pleasures should be supposed to depend on quantity alone.

If I am asked, what I mean by difference of quality in pleasures, or what makes one pleasure more valuable than another, merely as a pleasure, except its being greater in amount, there is but one possible answer. Of two pleasures, if there be one to which all or almost all who have experience of both give a decided preference, irrespective of any feeling of moral obligation to prefer it, that is the more desirable pleasure. If one of the two is, by those who are competently acquainted with both, placed so far above the other that they prefer it, even though knowing it to be attended with a greater amount of discontent, and would not resign it for any quantity of the other pleasure which their nature is capable of, we are justified in ascribing to the preferred enjoyment a superiority in quality, so far outweighing quantity as to render it, in comparison, of small account.

Now it is an unquestionable fact that those who are equally acquainted with, and equally capable of appreciating and enjoying, both, do give a most marked preference to the manner of existence which employs their higher faculties. Few human creatures would consent to be changed into any of the lower animals, for a promise of the fullest allowance of a beast's pleasures; no intelligent human being would consent to be a fool, no instructed person would be an ignoramus, no person of feeling and conscience would be selfish and base, even though they should be persuaded that the fool, the dunce, or the rascal is better satisfied with his lot than they are with theirs. They would not resign what they possess more than he for the most complete satisfaction of all the desires which they have in common with him. If they ever fancy they would, it is only in cases of unhappiness so extreme, that to escape from it they would exchange their lot for almost any other, however undesirable in their own eyes. A being of higher faculties requires more to make him happy, is capable probably of more acute suffering, and certainly accessible to it at more points, than one of an inferior type; but in spite of these liabilities, he can never really wish to sink into what he feels to be a lower grade of existence. We may give what explanation we please of this unwillingness; we may attribute to it pride, a name which is given indiscriminately to some of the most and to some of the least estimable feelings of which mankind are capable: we may refer it to the love of liberty and personal independence, an appeal to which was with the Stoics one of the most

* Stoicism was a school of ancient Greek and Roman philosophy (c. 300BCE–200CE) that stressed the importance of self-control and emotional detachment to human well-being. Followers of Stocism are known as Stoics.

effective means for the inculcation of it; to the love of power, or to the love of excitement, both of which do really enter into and contribute to it: but its most appropriate appellation is a sense of dignity, which all human beings possess in one form or other, and in some, though by no means in exact, proportion to their higher faculties, and which is so essential a part of the happiness of those in whom it is strong, that nothing which conflicts with it could be, otherwise than momentarily, an object of desire to them. Whoever supposes that this preference takes place at a sacrifice of happiness—that the superior being, in anything like equal circumstances, is not happier than the inferior—confounds the two very different ideas, of happiness, and content. It is indisputable that the being whose capacities of enjoyment are low, has the greatest chance of having them fully satisfied; and a highly endowed being will always feel that any happiness which he can look for, as the world is constituted, is imperfect. But he can learn to bear its imperfections, if they are at all bearable; and they will not make him envy the being who is indeed unconscious of the imperfections, but only because he feels not at all the good which those imperfections qualify. It is better to be a human being dissatisfied than a pig satisfied; better to be Socrates* dissatisfied than a fool satisfied. And if the fool, or the pig, are of a different opinion, it is because they only know their own side of the question. The other party to the comparison knows both sides.

It may be objected, that many who are capable of the higher pleasures, occasionally, under the influence of temptation, postpone them to the lower. But this is quite compatible with a full appreciation of the intrinsic superiority of the higher. Men often, from infirmity of character, make their election for the nearer good, though they know it to be the less valuable; and this no less when the choice is between two bodily pleasures, than when it is between bodily and mental. They pursue sensual indulgences to the injury of health, though perfectly aware that health is the greater good. It may be further objected, that many who begin with youthful enthusiasm for everything noble, as they advance in years sink into indolence and selfishness. But I do not believe that those who undergo this very common change, voluntarily choose the lower description of pleasures in preference to the higher. I believe that before they devote themselves exclusively to the one, they have already become incapable of the other. Capacity for the nobler feelings is in most natures a very tender plant, easily killed, not only by hostile influences, but by mere want of sustenance; and in the majority of young persons it speedily dies away if the occupations to which their position in life has devoted them, and the society into which it has thrown them, are not favourable to keeping that higher capacity in exercise. Men lose their high aspirations as they lose their intellectual tastes, because they have not time or opportunity for indulging them; and they addict themselves to inferior pleasures, not because they deliberately prefer them, but because they are either the only ones to which they have access, or the only ones which they are any longer capable of enjoying. It may be questioned whether any one who has remained equally susceptible to both classes of pleasures, ever knowingly and calmly preferred the lower; though many, in all ages, have broken down in an ineffectual attempt to combine both.

From this verdict of the only competent judges, I apprehend there can be no appeal. On a question which is the best worth having of two pleasures, or which of two modes of existence is the most grateful to the feelings, apart from its moral attributes and from its consequences, the judgment of those who are qualified by knowledge of both, or, if they differ, that of the majority among them, must be admitted as final. And there needs be the less hesitation to accept this judgment respecting the quality of pleasures, since there is no other tribunal to be referred to even on the question of quantity. What means are there of determining which is the acutest of two pains, or the intensest of two pleasurable sensations, except the general suffrage of those who are familiar with both? Neither pains nor pleasures are homogeneous, and pain is always heterogeneous with pleasure. What is there to decide whether a

* Socrates (c. 470–399 BCE) was an ancient Greek philosopher whose lifelong devotion to the pursuit of wisdom has made him an exemplar to philosophers for more than two millennia. Reputedly one of the greatest teachers in history, he was the mentor of Plato, who immortalized his thought by making Socrates the central character in his philosophical dialogues.

particular pleasure is worth purchasing at the cost of a particular pain, except the feelings and judgment of the experienced? When, therefore, those feelings and judgment declare the pleasures derived from the higher faculties to be preferable *in kind*, apart from the question of intensity, to those of which the animal nature, disjoined from the higher faculties, is susceptible, they are entitled on this subject to the same regard.

I have dwelt on this point, as being a necessary part of a perfectly just conception of Utility or Happiness, considered as the directive rule of human conduct. But it is by no means an indispensable condition to the acceptance of the utilitarian standard; for that standard is not the agent's own greatest happiness, but the greatest amount of happiness altogether; and if it may possibly be doubted whether a noble character is always the happier for its nobleness, there can be no doubt that it makes other people happier, and that the world in general is immensely a gainer by it. Utilitarianism, therefore, could only attain its end by the general cultivation of nobleness of character, even if each individual were only benefited by the nobleness of others, and his own, so far as happiness is concerned, were a sheer deduction from the benefit. But the bare enunciation of such an absurdity as this last, renders refutation superfluous.

According to the Greatest Happiness Principle, as above explained, the ultimate end, with reference to and for the sake of which all other things are desirable (whether we are considering our own good or that of other people), is an existence exempt as far as possible from pain, and as rich as possible in enjoyments, both in point of quantity and quality; the test of quality, and the rule for measuring it against quantity, being the preference felt by those who in their opportunities of experience, to which must be added their habits of self-consciousness and self-observation, are best furnished with the means of comparison. This, being, according to the utilitarian opinion, the end of human action, is necessarily also the standard of morality; which may accordingly be defined, the rules and precepts for human conduct, by the observance of which an existence such as has been described might be, to the greatest extent possible, secured to all mankind; and not to them only, but, so far as the nature of things admits, to the whole sentient creation.

. . . .

I must again repeat, what the assailants of utilitarianism seldom have the justice to acknowledge, that the happiness which forms the utilitarian standard of what is right in conduct, is not the agent's own happiness, but that of all concerned. As between his own happiness and that of others, utilitarianism requires him to be as strictly impartial as a disinterested and benevolent spectator. In the golden rule of Jesus of Nazareth, we read the complete spirit of the ethics of utility. To do as you would be done by, and to love your neighbour as yourself, constitute the ideal perfection of utilitarian morality. As the means of making the nearest approach to this ideal, utility would enjoin, first, that laws and social arrangements should place the happiness, or (as speaking practically it may be called) the interest, of every individual, as nearly as possible in harmony with the interest of the whole; and secondly, that education and opinion, which have so vast a power over human character, should so use that power as to establish in the mind of every individual an indissoluble association between his own happiness and the good of the whole; especially between his own happiness and the practice of such modes of conduct, negative and positive, as regard for the universal happiness prescribes; so that not only he may be unable to conceive the possibility of happiness to himself, consistently with conduct opposed to the general good, but also that a direct impulse to promote the general good may be in every individual one of the habitual motives of action, and the sentiments connected therewith may fill a large and prominent place in every human being's sentient existence. If the impugners of the utilitarian morality represented it to their own minds in this its true character, I know not what recommendation possessed by any other morality they could possibly affirm to be wanting to it; what more beautiful or more exalted developments of human nature any other ethical system can be supposed to foster, or what springs of action, not accessible to the utilitarian, such systems rely on for giving effect to their mandates.

The objectors to utilitarianism cannot always be charged with representing it in a discreditable light.

On the contrary, those among them who entertain anything like a just idea of its disinterested character, sometimes find fault with its standard as being too high for humanity. They say it is exacting too much to require that people shall always act from the inducement of promoting the general interests of society. But this is to mistake the very meaning of a standard of morals, and confound the rule of action with the motive of it. It is the business of ethics to tell us what are our duties, or by what test we may know them; but no system of ethics requires that the sole motive of all we do shall be a feeling of duty; on the contrary, ninety-nine hundredths of all our actions are done from other motives, and rightly so done, if the rule of duty does not condemn them. It is the most unjust to utilitarianism that this particular misapprehension should be made a ground of objection to it, inasmuch as utilitarian moralists have gone beyond almost all others in affirming that the motive has nothing to do with the morality of the action, though much with the worth of the agent. He who saves a fellow creature from drowning does what is morally right, whether his motive be duty, or the hope of being paid for his trouble; he who betrays the friend that trusts him, is guilty of a crime, even if his object be to serve another friend to whom he is under greater obligations. But to speak only of actions done from the motive of duty, and in direct obedience to principle: it is a misapprehension of the utilitarian mode of thought, to conceive it as implying that people should fix their minds upon so wide a generality as the world, or society at large. The great majority of good actions are intended not for the benefit of the world, but for that of individuals, of which the good of the world is made up; and the thoughts of the most virtuous man need not on these occasions travel beyond the particular persons concerned, except so far as is necessary to assure himself that in benefiting them he is not violating the rights, that is, the legitimate and authorised expectations, of any one else. The multiplication of happiness is, according to the utilitarian ethics, the object of virtue: the occasions on which any person (except one in a thousand) has it in his power to do this on an extended scale, in other words to be a public benefactor, are but exceptional; and on these occasions alone is he called on to consider public utility; in every other case, private utility, the interest or happiness of some few persons, is all he has to attend to. Those alone the influence of whose actions extends to society in general, need concern themselves habitually about so large an object. In the case of abstinences indeed—of things which people forbear to do from moral considerations, though the consequences in the particular case might be beneficial—it would be unworthy of an intelligent agent not to be consciously aware that the action is of a class which, if practised generally, would be generally injurious, and that this is the ground of the obligation to abstain from it. The amount of regard for the public interest implied in this recognition, is no greater than is demanded by every system of morals, for they all enjoin to abstain from whatever is manifestly pernicious to society.

The same considerations dispose of another reproach against the doctrine of utility, founded on a still grosser misconception of the purpose of a standard of morality, and of the very meaning of the words right and wrong. It is often affirmed that utilitarianism renders men cold and unsympathising; that it chills their moral feelings towards individuals; that it makes them regard only the dry and hard consideration of the consequences of actions, not taking into their moral estimate the qualities from which those actions emanate. If the assertion means that they do not allow their judgment respecting the rightness or wrongness of an action to be influenced by their opinion of the qualities of the person who does it, this is a complaint not against utilitarianism, but against having any standard of morality at all; for certainly no known ethical standard decides an action to be good or bad because it is done by a good or a bad man, still less because done by an amiable, a brave, or a benevolent man, or the contrary. These considerations are relevant, not to the estimation of actions, but of persons; and there is nothing in the utilitarian theory inconsistent with the fact that there are other things which interest us in persons besides the rightness and wrongness of their actions. The Stoics, indeed, with the paradoxical misuse of language which was part of their system, and by which they strove to raise themselves above all concern about anything but virtue, were fond of saying, that he who has that has everything; that he, and only he, is rich, is beautiful, is a king. But no claim of this description is made for the virtuous man by the utilitarian doctrine. Utilitarians are quite aware that there are other desirable possessions and qualities besides virtue, and are perfectly willing to allow to all of them their full worth. They are also aware that a right action does not necessarily indicate a virtuous character, and that actions which are blamable, often proceed from qualities entitled to praise. When this is apparent in any particular case, it modifies their estimation, not certainly of the act, but of the agent. I grant that they are, notwithstanding, of opinion, that in the long run the best proof of a good character is good actions; and resolutely refuse to consider any mental disposition as good, of which the predominant tendency is to produce bad conduct. This makes them unpopular with many people; but it is an unpopularity which they must share with every one who regards the distinction between right and wrong in a serious light; and the reproach is not one which a conscientious utilitarian need be anxious to repel.

If no more be meant by the objection than that many utilitarians look on the morality of actions, as measured by the utilitarian standard, with too exclusive a regard, and do not lay sufficient stress upon the other beauties of character which go toward making a human being lovable or admirable, this may be admitted. Utilitarians who have cultivated their moral feelings, but not their sympathies nor their artistic perceptions, do fall into this mistake; and so do all other moralists under the same conditions. What can be said in excuse for other moralists is equally available for them, namely, that, if there is to be any error, it is better that it should be on that side. As a matter of fact, we may affirm that among utilitarians as among adherents of other systems, there is every imaginable degree of rigidity and of laxity in the application of their standard: some are even puritanically rigorous, while others are as indulgent as can possibly be desired by sinner or by sentimentalist. But on the whole, a doctrine which brings prominently forward the interest that mankind have in the repression and prevention of conduct which violates the moral law, is likely to be inferior to no other in turning the sanctions of opinion against such violations. It is true, the question, What does violate the moral law? is one on which those who recognise different standards of morality are likely now and then to differ. But difference of opinion on moral questions was not first introduced into the world by utilitarianism, while that doctrine does supply, if not always an easy, at all events a tangible and intelligible mode of deciding such differences.

It may not be superfluous to notice a few more of the common misapprehensions of utilitarian ethics, even those which are so obvious and gross that it might appear impossible for any person of candour and intelligence to fall into them; since persons, even of considerable mental endowments, often give themselves so little trouble to understand the bearings of any opinion against which they entertain a prejudice, and men are in general so little conscious of this voluntary ignorance as a defect, that the vulgarest misunderstandings of ethical doctrines are continually met with in the deliberate writings of persons of the greatest pretensions both to high principle and to philosophy. We not uncommonly hear the doctrine of utility inveighed against as a *godless* doctrine. If it be necessary to say anything at all against so mere an assumption, we may say that the question depends upon what idea we have formed of the moral character of the Deity. If it be a true belief that God desires, above all things, the happiness of his creatures, and that this was his purpose in their creation, utility is not only not a godless doctrine, but more profoundly religious than any other. If it be meant that utilitarianism does not recognise the revealed will of God as the supreme law of morals, I answer, that a utilitarian who believes in the perfect goodness and wisdom of God, necessarily believes that whatever God has thought fit to reveal on the subject of morals, must fulfil the requirements of utility in a supreme degree. But others besides utilitarians have been of opinion that the Christian revelation was intended, and is fitted, to inform the hearts and minds of mankind with a spirit which should enable them to find for themselves what is right, and incline them to do it when found, rather than to tell them, except in a very general way, what it is; and that we need a doctrine of ethics, carefully followed out, to *interpret* to us the will of God. Whether this opinion is correct or not, it is superfluous here to discuss; since whatever aid religion, either natural or revealed, can afford to ethical investigation, is as open to the utilitarian moralist as to any other. He can use it as the testimony of God to the usefulness or hurtfulness of any given course of action, by as good a right as others can use it for the indication of a transcendental law, having no connexion with usefulness or with happiness.

Again, Utility is often summarily stigmatised as an immoral doctrine by giving it the name of Expediency, and taking advantage of the popular use of that term to contrast it with Principle. But the Expedient, in the sense in which it is opposed to the Right, generally means that which is expedient for the particular interest of the agent himself; as when a minister sacrifices the interests of his country to keep himself in place. When it means anything better than this, it means that which is expedient for some immediate object, some temporary purpose, but which violates a rule whose observance is expedient in a much higher degree. The Expedient, in this sense, instead of being the same thing with the useful, is a branch of the hurtful. Thus, it would often be expedient, for the purpose of getting over some momentary embarrassment, or attaining some object immediately useful to ourselves or others, to tell a lie. But inasmuch as the cultivation in ourselves of a sensitive feeling on the subject of veracity, is one of the most useful, and the enfeeblement of that feeling one of the most hurtful, things to which our conduct can be instrumental; and inasmuch as any, even unintentional, deviation from truth, does that much towards weakening the trustworthiness of human assertion, which is not only the principal support of all present social well-being, but the insufficiency of which does more than any one thing that can be named to keep back civilisation, virtue, everything on which human happiness on the largest scale depends: we feel that the violation, for a present advantage, of a rule of such transcendent expediency, is not expedient, and that he who, for the sake of a convenience to himself or to some other individual, does what depends on him to deprive mankind of the good, and inflict upon them the evil, involved in the greater or less reliance which they can place in each other's word, acts the part of one of their worst enemies. Yet that even this rule, sacred as it is, admits of possible exceptions, is acknowledged by all moralists; the chief of which is when the withholding of some fact (as of information from a malefactor, or of bad news from a person dangerously ill) would save an individual (especially an individual other than oneself) from great and unmerited evil, and when the withholding can only be effected by denial. But in order that the exception may not extend itself beyond the need, and may have the least possible effect in weakening reliance on veracity, it ought to be recognised, and, if possible, its limits defined; and if the principle of utility is good for anything, it must be good for weighing these conflicting utilities against one another, and marking out the region within which one or the other preponderates.

Again, defenders of utility often find themselves called upon to reply to such objections as this—that there is not time, previous to action, for calculating and weighing the effects of any line of conduct on the general happiness. This is exactly as if any one were to say that it is impossible to guide our conduct by Christianity, because there is not time, on every occasion on which anything has to be done, to read through the Old and New Testaments.* The answer to the objection is, that there has been ample time, namely, the whole past duration of the human species. During all that time, mankind have been learning by experience the tendencies of actions; on which experience all the prudence, as well as all the morality of life, are dependent. People talk as if the commencement of this course of experience had hitherto been put off, and as if, at the moment when some man feels tempted to meddle with the property or life of another, he had to begin considering for the first time whether murder and theft are injurious to human happiness. Even then I do not think that he would find the question very puzzling; but, at all events, the matter is now done to his hand. It is truly a whimsical supposition that, if mankind were agreed in considering utility to be the test of morality, they would remain without any agreement as to what *is* useful, and would take no measures for having their notions on the subject taught to the young, and enforced by law and opinion. There is no difficulty in

* The Old and New Testaments are the two main parts of the Christian Bible

proving any ethical standard whatever to work ill, if we suppose universal idiocy to be conjoined with it; but on any hypothesis short of that, mankind must by this time have acquired positive beliefs as to the effects of some actions on their happiness; and the beliefs which have thus come down are the rules of morality for the multitude, and for the philosopher until he has succeeded in finding better. That philosophers might easily do this, even now, on many subjects; that the received code of ethics is by no means of divine right; and that mankind have still much to learn as to the effects of actions on the general happiness, I admit, or rather, earnestly maintain. The corollaries from the principle of utility, like the precepts of every practical art, admit of indefinite improvement, and, in a progressive state of the human mind, their improvement is perpetually going on. But to consider the rules of morality as improvable, is one thing; to pass over the intermediate generalisations entirely, and endeavour to test each individual action directly by the first principle, is another. It is a strange notion that the acknowledgment of a first principle is inconsistent with the admission of secondary ones. To inform a traveller respecting the place of his ultimate destination, is not to forbid the use of landmarks and direction-posts on the way. The proposition that happiness is the end and aim of morality does not mean that no road ought to be laid down to that goal, or that persons going thither should not be advised to take one direction rather than another. Men really ought to leave off talking a kind of nonsense on this subject, which they would neither talk nor listen to on other matters of practical concernment. Nobody argues that the art of navigation is not founded on astronomy, because sailors cannot wait to calculate the Nautical Almanack. Being rational creatures, they go to sea with it ready calculated; and all rational creatures go out upon the sea of life with their minds made up on the common questions of right and wrong, as well as on many of the far more difficult questions of wise and foolish. And this, as long as foresight is a human quality, it is to be presumed they will continue to do. Whatever we adopt as the fundamental principle of morality, we require subordinate principles to apply it by; the impossibility of doing without them, being common to all systems, can afford no argument against any one in particular; but gravely to argue as if no such secondary principles could be had, and as if mankind had remained till now, and always must remain, without drawing any general conclusions from the experience of human life, is as high a pitch, I think, as absurdity has ever reached in philosophical controversy.

The remainder of the stock arguments against utilitarianism mostly consist in laying to its charge the common infirmities of human nature, and the general difficulties which embarrass conscientious persons in shaping their course through life. We are told that a utilitarian will be apt to make his own particular case an exception to moral rules, and, when under temptation, will see a utility in the breach of a rule, greater than he will see in its observance. But is utility the only creed which is able to furnish us with excuses for evil doing, and means of cheating our own conscience? They are afforded in abundance by all doctrines which recognise as a fact in morals the existence of conflicting considerations; which all doctrines do, that have been believed by sane persons. It is not the fault of any creed, but of the complicated nature of human affairs, that rules of conduct cannot be so framed as to require no exceptions, and that hardly any kind of action can safely be laid down as either always obligatory or always condemnable. There is no ethical creed which does not temper the rigidity of its laws, by giving a certain latitude, under the moral responsibility of the agent, for accommodation to peculiarities of circumstances; and under every creed, at the opening thus made, self-deception and dishonest casuistry get in. There exists no moral system under which there do not arise unequivocal cases of conflicting obligations. These are the real difficulties, the knotty points both in the theory of ethics, and in the conscientious guidance of personal conduct. They are overcome practically, with greater or with less success, according to the intellect and virtue of the individual; but it can hardly be pretended that any one will be the less qualified for dealing with them, from possessing an ultimate standard to which conflicting rights and duties can be referred. If utility is the ultimate source of moral obligations, utility may be invoked to decide between them when their demands are incompatible. Though the application of the standard may be difficult, it is better than none at all; while in other systems, the moral laws all claiming independent authority, there is no common umpire entitled to interfere between them; their claims to precedence one over another rest on little better than sophistry, and unless determined, as they generally are, by the unacknowledged influence of considerations of utility, afford a free scope for the action of personal desires and partialities. We must remember that only in these cases of conflict between secondary principles is it requisite that first principles should be appealed to. There is no case of moral obligation in which some secondary principle is not involved; and if only one, there can seldom by any real doubt which one it is, in the mind of any person by whom the principle itself is recognised. . . .

CHAPTER 4 OF WHAT SORT OF PROOF THE PRINCIPLE OF UTILITY IS SUSCEPTIBLE

It has already been remarked, that questions of ultimate ends do not admit of proof, in the ordinary acceptation of the term. To be incapable of proof by reasoning is common to all first principles; to the first premises of our knowledge, as well as to those of our conduct. But the former, being matters of fact, may be the subject of a direct appeal to the faculties which judge of fact—namely, our senses, and our internal consciousness. Can an appeal be made to the same faculties on questions of practical ends? Or by what other faculty is cognisance taken of them?

Questions about ends are, in other words questions about what things are desirable. The utilitarian doctrine is, that happiness is desirable, and the only thing desirable, as an end; all other things being only desirable as means to that end. What ought to be required of this doctrine—what conditions is it requisite that the doctrine should fulfil—to make good its claim to be believed?

The only proof capable of being given that an object is visible, is that people actually see it. The only proof that a sound is audible, is that people hear it: and so of the other sources of our experience. In like manner, I apprehend, the sole evidence it is possible to produce that anything is desirable, is that people do actually desire it. If the end which the utilitarian doctrine proposes to itself were not, in theory and in practice, acknowledged to be an end, nothing could ever convince any person that it was so. No reason can be given why the general happiness is desirable, except that each person, so far as he believes it to be attainable, desires his own happiness. This, however, being a fact, we have not only all the proof which the case admits of, but all which it is possible to require, that happiness is a good: that each person's happiness is a good to that person, and the general happiness, therefore, a good to the aggregate of all persons. Happiness has made out its title as *one* of the ends of conduct, and consequently one of the criteria of morality.

But it has not, by this alone, proved itself to be the sole criterion. To do that, it would seem, by the same rule, necessary to show, not only that people desire happiness, but that they never desire anything else. Now it is palpable that they do desire things which, in common language, are decidedly distinguished from happiness. They desire, for example, virtue, and the absence of vice, no less really than pleasure and the absence of pain. The desire of virtue is not as universal, but it is as authentic a fact, as the desire of happiness. And hence the opponents of the utilitarian standard deem that they have a right to infer that there are other ends of human action besides happiness, and that happiness is not the standard of approbation and disapprobation.

But does the utilitarian doctrine deny that people desire virtue, or maintain that virtue is not a thing to be desired? The very reverse. It maintains not only that virtue is to be desired, but that it is to be desired disinterestedly, for itself. Whatever may be the opinion of utilitarian moralists as to the original conditions by which virtue is made virtue; however they may believe (as they do) that actions and dispositions are only virtuous because they promote another end than virtue; yet this being granted, and it having been decided, from considerations of this description, what *is* virtuous, they not only place virtue at the very head of the things which are good as means to the ultimate end, but they also recognize as a psychological fact the possibility of its being, to the individual, a good in itself, without looking to any end beyond it; and, hold, that the mind is not in a right state, not a state conformable to Utility, not in the state most conducive to the general happiness, unless it does love virtue in this manner—as a thing desirable in itself, even although, in the individual instance, it should not produce those other desirable consequences which it tends to produce, and on account of which it is held to be virtue. This opinion is not, in the smallest degree, a departure from the Happiness principle. The ingredients of happiness are very various, and each of them is desirable in itself, and not merely when considered as swelling an aggregate. The principle of utility does not mean that any given pleasure, as music, for instance, or any given exemption from pain, as for example health, is to be looked upon as means to a collective something termed happiness, and to be desired on that account. They are desired and desirable in and for themselves; besides being means, they are a part of the end. Virtue, according to the utilitarian doctrine, is not naturally and originally part of the end, but it is capable of becoming so; and in those who love it disinterestedly it has become so, and is desired and cherished, not as a means to happiness, but as a part of their happiness.

To illustrate this farther, we may remember that virtue is not the only thing, originally a means, and which if it were not a means to anything else, would be and remain indifferent, but which by association with what it is a means to, comes to be desired for itself, and that too with the utmost intensity. What, for example, shall we say of the love of money? There is nothing originally more desirable about money than about any heap of glittering pebbles. Its worth is solely that of the things which it will buy; the desires for other things than itself, which it is a means of gratifying. Yet the love of money is not only one of the strongest moving forces of human life, but money is, in many cases, desired in and for itself; the desire to possess it is often stronger than the desire to use it, and goes on increasing when all the desires which point to ends beyond it, to be compassed by it, are falling off. It may, then, be said truly, that money is desired not for the sake of an end, but as part of the end. From being a means to happiness, it has come to be itself a principal ingredient of the individual's conception of happiness. The same may be said of the majority of the great objects of human life—power, for example, or fame; except that to each of these there is a certain amount of immediate pleasure annexed, which has at least the semblance of being naturally inherent in them; a thing which cannot be said of money. Still, however, the strongest natural attraction, both of power and of fame, is the immense aid they give to the attainment of our other wishes; and it is the strong association thus generated between them and all our objects of desire, which gives to the direct desire of them the intensity it often assumes, so as in some characters to surpass in strength all other desires. In these cases the means have become a part of the end, and a more important part of it than any of the things which they are means to. What was once desired as an instrument for the attainment of happiness, has come to be desired for its own sake. In being desired for its own sake it is, however, desired as *part* of happiness. The person is made, or thinks he would be made, happy by its mere possession; and is made unhappy by failure to obtain it. The desire of it is not a different thing from the desire of happiness, any more than the love of music, or the desire of health. They are included in happiness. They are some of the elements of which the desire of happiness is made up. Happiness is not an abstract idea, but a concrete whole; and these are some of its parts. And the utilitarian standard sanctions and approves their being so. Life would be a poor thing, very ill provided with sources of happiness, if there were not this provision of nature, by which things originally indifferent, but conducive to, or otherwise associated with, the satisfaction of our primitive desires, become in themselves sources of pleasure more valuable than the primitive pleasures, both in permanency, in the space of human existence that they are capable of covering, and even in intensity.

Virtue, according to the utilitarian conception, is a good of this description. There was no original desire of it, or motive to it, save its conduciveness to pleasure, and especially to protection from pain. But through the association thus formed, it may be felt a good in itself, and desired as such with as great intensity as any other good; and with this difference between it and the love of money, of power, or of fame, that all of these may, and often do, render the individual noxious to the other members of society to which he belongs, whereas there is nothing which makes him so much a blessing to them as the cultivation of the disinterested love of virtue.

And consequently, the utilitarian standard, while it tolerates and approves those other acquired desires, up to the point beyond which they would be more injurious to the general happiness than promotive of it, enjoins and requires the cultivation of the love of virtue up to the greatest strength possible, as being above all things important to the general happiness.

It results from the preceding considerations, that there is in reality nothing desired except happiness. Whatever is desired otherwise than as a means to some end beyond itself, and ultimately to happiness, is desired as itself a part of happiness, and is not desired for itself until it has become so. Those who desire virtue for its own sake, desire it either because the consciousness of it is a pleasure, or because the consciousness of being without it is a pain, or for both reasons united; as in truth the pleasure and pain seldom exist separately, but almost always together, the same person feeling pleasure in degree of virtue attained, and pain in not having attained more. If one of these give him no pleasure, and the other no pain, he would not love or desire virtue, or would desire it only for the other benefits which it might produce to himself or to persons whom he cared for.

We have now, then, an answer to the question, of what sort of proof the principle of utility is susceptible. If the opinion which I have now stated is psychologically true—if human nature is so constituted as to desire nothing which is not either a part of happiness or a means of happiness, we can have no other proof, and we require no other, that these are the only things desirable. If so, happiness is the sole end of human action, and the promotion of it the test by which to judge of all human conduct; from whence it necessarily follows that it must be the criterion of morality, since a part is included in the whole.

And now to decide whether this is really so; whether mankind do desire nothing for itself but that which is a pleasure to them or of which the absence is a pain; we have evidently arrived at a question of fact and experience, dependent, like all similar questions, upon evidence. It can only be determined by practised self-consciousness and self-observation, assisted by observation of others. I believe that these sources of evidence, impartially consulted, will declare that desiring a thing and finding it pleasant, aversion to it and thinking of it as painful, are phenomena entirely inseparable, or rather two parts of the same phenomenon; in strictness of language, two different modes of naming the same psychological fact: that to think of an object as desirable (unless for the sake of its consequences), and to think of it as pleasant, are one and the same thing; and that to desire anything, except in proportion as the idea of it is pleasant, is a physical and metaphysical impossibility.

So obvious does this appear to me, that I expect it will hardly be disputed: and the objection made will be, not that desire can possibly be directed to anything ultimately except pleasure and exemption from pain, but that the will is a different thing from desire; that a person of confirmed virtue, or any other person whose purposes are fixed, carries out his purposes without any thought of the pleasure he has in contemplating them, or expects to derive from their fulfilment; and persists in acting on them, enough though these pleasures are much diminished, by changes in his character or decay of his passive sensibilities, or are outweighed by the pains which the pursuit of the purposes may bring upon him. All this I fully admit, and have stated it elsewhere, as positively and emphatically as any one. Will, the active phenomenon, is a different thing from desire, the state of passive sensibility, and though originally an offshoot from it, may in time take root and detach itself from the parent stock; so much so, that in the case of an habitual purpose, instead of willing the thing because we desire it, we often desire it only because we will it. This, however, is but an instance of that familiar fact, the power of habit, and is nowise confined to the case of virtuous actions. Many indifferent things, which men originally did from a motive of some sort, they continue to do from habit. Sometimes this is done unconsciously, the consciousness coming only after the action; at other times with conscious volition, but volition which has become habitual, and is put in operation by the force of habit, in opposition perhaps to the deliberate preference, as often happens with those who have contracted habits of vicious or hurtful indulgence. Third and last comes the case in which the habitual act of will in the individual instance is not in contradiction to the general intention prevailing at other times, but in fulfilment of it;

as in the case of the person of confirmed virtue, and of all who pursue deliberately and consistently any determinate end. The distinction between will and desire thus understood is an authentic and highly important psychological fact; but the fact consists solely in this—that will, like all other parts of our constitution, is amenable to habit, and that we may will from habit what we no longer desire for itself, or desire only because we will it. It is not the less true that will, in the beginning, is entirely produced by desire; including in that term the repelling influence of pain as well as the attractive one of pleasure. Let us take into consideration, no longer the person who has a confirmed will to do right, but him in whom that virtuous will is still feeble, conquerable by temptation, and not to be fully relied on; by what means can it be strengthened? How can the will to be virtuous, where it does not exist in sufficient force, be implanted or awakened? Only by making the person *desire* virtue—by making him think of it in a pleasurable light, or of its absence in a painful one. It is by associating the doing right with pleasure, or the doing wrong with pain, or by eliciting and impressing and bringing home to the person's experience the pleasure naturally involved in the one or the pain in the other, that it is possible to call forth that will to be virtuous, which, when confirmed, acts without any thought of either pleasure or pain. Will is the child of desire, and passes out of the dominion of its parent only to come under that of habit. That which is the result of habit affords no presumption of being intrinsically good; and there would be no reason for wishing that the purpose of virtue should become independent of pleasure and pain, were it not that the influence of the pleasurable and painful associations which prompt to virtue is not sufficiently to be depended on for unerring constancy of action until it has acquired the support of habit. Both in feeling and in conduct, habit is the only thing which imparts certainty; and it is because of the importance to others of being able to rely absolutely on one's feelings and conduct, and to oneself of being able to rely on one's own, that the will to do right ought to be cultivated into this habitual independence. In other words, this state of the will is a means to good, not intrinsically a good; and does not contradict the doctrine that nothing is a good to human beings but in so far as it is either itself pleasurable, or a means of attaining pleasure or averting pain.

But if this doctrine be true, the principle of utility is proved. Whether it is so or not, must now be left to the consideration of the thoughtful reader.

Extreme and Restricted Utilitarianism

J. J. C. SMART

J. J. C. Smart (1920–) is a respected 20th century Scottish-born philosopher who spent the bulk of his career in Australia, first at the University of Adelaide and later at the Australian National University. He is known for his broad-ranging contributions to metaphysics, ethics, and the philosophy of mind.

In the selection that appears here, which was originally delivered as a lecture in 1955 and later published as a self-standing essay, Smart distinguishes two ways of understanding utilitarianism's central commitment—which he dubs "extreme" and "restricted" utilitarianism—and offers a defense of the former. Since the publication of Smart's influential essay, this distinction between these two notions—now often referred to as "act" and "rule" utilitarianism, respectively—has played an important role in discussions of utilitarianism. An additional selection from Smart's work appears in the Metaphysics of Mind section (IV.A) following.

From *Theories of Ethics*, ed. Philippa Foot (Oxford: Oxford University Press, 1967), pp. 171–83.

I

Utilitarianism is the doctrine that the rightness of actions is to be judged by their consequences. What do we mean by "actions" here? Do we mean particular actions or do we mean classes of actions? According to which way we interpret the word "actions" we get two different theories, both of which merit the appellation "utilitarian."

1. If by "actions" we mean particular individual actions we get the sort of doctrine held by Bentham, Sidgwick, and Moore.* According to this doctrine we test individual actions by their consequences, and general rules, like "keep promises," are mere rules of thumb which we use only to avoid the necessity of estimating the probable consequences of our actions at every step. The rightness or wrongness of keeping a promise on a particular occasion depends only on the goodness or badness of the consequences of keeping or of breaking the promise on that particular occasion. Of course part of the consequences of breaking the promise, and a part to which we will normally ascribe decisive importance, will be the weakening of faith in the institution of promising. However, if the goodness of the consequences of breaking the rule is *in toto* greater than the goodness of the consequences of keeping it, then we must break the rule, irrespective of whether the goodness of the consequences of *everybody's* obeying the rule is or is not greater than the consequences of *everybody's* breaking it. To put it shortly, rules do not matter, save *per accidens* as rules of thumb and as de facto social institutions with which the utilitarian has to reckon when estimating consequences. I shall call this doctrine "extreme utilitarianism."†

2. A more modest form of utilitarianism has recently become fashionable.... Part of its charm is that it appears to resolve the dispute in moral philosophy between intuitionists and utilitarians in a way which is very neat. The view holds... that moral rules are more than rules of thumb. In general the rightness of an action is *not* to be tested by evaluating its consequences but only by considering whether or not it falls under a certain rule. Whether the rule is to be considered an acceptable moral rule, is, however, to be decided by considering the consequences of adopting the rule. Broadly, then, actions are to be tested by rules and rules by consequences. The only cases in which we must test an individual action directly by its consequences are (*a*) when the action comes under two different rules, one of which enjoins it and one of which forbids it, and (*b*) when there is no rule whatever that governs the given case. I shall call this doctrine "restricted utilitarianism."

It should be noticed that the distinction I am making cuts across, and is quite different from, the distinction commonly made between hedonistic and ideal utilitarianism.... A hedonistic utilitarian holds that the goodness of the consequences of an action is a function only of their pleasurableness and an ideal utilitarian, like Moore, holds that pleasurableness is not even a necessary condition of goodness. Mill seems, if we are to take his remarks about higher and lower pleasures seriously, to be neither a pure hedonistic nor a pure ideal utilitarian. He seems to hold that pleasurableness is a necessary condition for goodness, but that goodness is a function of other qualities of mind as well. Perhaps we can call him a quasi-ideal utilitarian. When we say that a state of mind is good I take it that we are expressing some sort of *rational preference*. When we say that it is pleasurable I take it that we are saying that it is enjoyable, and when we say that something is a higher pleasure I take it that we are saying that it is more truly, or more deeply, enjoyable. I am doubtful whether "more deeply enjoyable" does not just mean "more enjoyable, even though not more enjoyable on a first look," and so I am doubtful whether quasi-ideal utilitarianism, and possibly ideal utilitarianism too, would not collapse into hedonistic utilitarianism on a closer scrutiny of the logic of words like "preference," "pleasure," "enjoy," "deeply enjoy," and so on. However, it is beside the point of the present paper to go into these questions. I am here

---

* Jeremy Bentham (1748–1832), Henry Sidgwick (1838–1900), and G. E. Moore (1873–1958) were well-known philosophers who advocated consequentialist moral theories.

† Smart's notion of "extreme utilitarianism" is now commonly referred to as *act utilitarianism;* his notion of "restricted utilitarianism" is now commonly referred to as *rule utilitarianism.*

concerned only with the issue between extreme and restricted utilitarianism and am ready to concede that both forms of utilitarianism can be either hedonistic or non-hedonistic.

The issue between extreme and restricted utilitarianism can be illustrated by considering the remark "But suppose everyone did the same." (Cf. A. K. Stout's article in *The Australasian Journal of Philosophy*, Vol. 32, pp. 1–29.) Stout distinguishes two forms of the universalization principle, the causal form and the hypothetical form. To say that you ought not to do an action A because it would have bad results if everyone (or many people) did action A may be merely to point out that while the action A would otherwise be the optimific one, nevertheless when you take into account that doing A will probably cause other people to do A too, you can see that A is not, on a broad view, really optimific. If this causal influence could be avoided (as may happen in the case of a secret desert island promise) then we would disregard the universalization principle. This is the causal form of the principle. A person who accepted the universalization principle in its hypothetical form would be one who was concerned only with what would happen *if* everyone did the action A: he would be totally unconcerned with the question of whether in fact everyone would do the action A. That is, he might say that it would be wrong not to vote because it would have bad results if everyone took this attitude, and he would be totally unmoved by arguments purporting to show that my refusing to vote has no effect whatever on other people's propensity to vote. Making use of Stout's distinction, we can say that an extreme utilitarian would apply the universalization principle in the causal form, while a restricted utilitarian would apply it in the hypothetical form.

How are we to decide the issue between extreme and restricted utilitarianism? I wish to repudiate at the outset that milk and water approach which describes itself sometimes as "investigating what is implicit in the common moral consciousness" and sometimes as "investigating how people ordinarily talk about morality." We have only to read the newspaper correspondence about capital punishment or about what should be done with Formosa to realize that the common moral consciousness is in part made up of superstitious elements, of morally bad elements, and of logically confused elements. I address myself to good hearted and benevolent people and so I hope that if we rid ourselves of the logical confusion the superstitious and morally bad elements will largely fall away. For even among good hearted and benevolent people it is possible to find superstitious and morally bad reasons for moral beliefs. These superstitious and morally bad reasons hide behind the protective screen of logical confusion. With people who are not logically confused but who are openly superstitious or morally bad I can of course do nothing. That is, our ultimate pro-attitudes may be different. Nevertheless I propose to rely on *my own* moral consciousness and to appeal to *your* moral consciousness and to forget about what people ordinarily say. "The obligation to obey a rule," says Nowell-Smith (*Ethics*, p. 239), "does not, *in the opinion of ordinary men,"* (my italics), "rest on the beneficial consequences of obeying it in a particular case." What does this prove? Surely it is more than likely that ordinary men are confused here. Philosophers should be able to examine the question more rationally.

II

For an extreme utilitarian moral rules are rules of thumb. In practice the extreme utilitarian will mostly guide his conduct by appealing to the rules ("do not lie," "do not break promises," etc.) of common-sense morality. This is not because there is anything sacrosanct in the rules themselves but because he can argue that probably he will most often act in an extreme utilitarian way if he does not think as a utilitarian. For one thing, actions have frequently to be done in a hurry. Imagine a man seeing a person drowning. He jumps in and rescues him. There is no time to reason the matter out, but usually this will be the course of action which an extreme utilitarian would recommend if he did reason the matter out. If, however, the man drowning had been drowning in a river near Berchtesgaden in 1938, and if he had had the well-known black forelock and moustache of Adolf Hitler, an extreme utilitarian would, if he had time, work out the probability of the man's being the villainous dictator, and if the probability were high enough he would, on extreme utilitarian grounds, leave him to drown. The rescuer, however, has not time. He trusts to his instincts and dives in and rescues the man. And this trusting to instincts and to moral rules can be justified on extreme utilitarian grounds. Furthermore, an extreme utilitarian who knew that the drowning man was Hitler would nevertheless praise the rescuer, not condemn him. For by praising the man he is strengthening a courageous and benevolent disposition of mind, and in general this disposition has great positive utility. (Next time, perhaps, it will be Winston Churchill that the man saves!) We must never forget that an extreme utilitarian may praise actions which he knows to be wrong. Saving Hitler was wrong, but it was a member of a class of actions which are generally right, and the motive to do actions of this class is in general an optimific one. In considering questions of praise and blame it is not the expediency of the praised or blamed action that is at issue, but the expediency of the praise. It can be expedient to praise an inexpedient action and inexpedient to praise an expedient one.

Lack of time is not the only reason why an extreme utilitarian may, on extreme utilitarian principles, trust to rules of common-sense morality. He knows that in particular cases where his own interests are involved his calculations are likely to be biased in his own favour. Suppose that he is unhappily married and is deciding whether to get divorced. He will in all probability greatly exaggerate his own unhappiness (and possibly his wife's) and greatly underestimate the harm done to his children by the break up of the family. He will probably also underestimate the likely harm done by the weakening of the general faith in marriage vows. So probably he will come to the correct extreme utilitarian conclusion if he does not in this instance think as an extreme utilitarian but trusts to common-sense morality.

There are many more and subtle points that could be made in connexion with the relation between extreme utilitarianism and the morality of common sense. All those that I have just made and many more will be found in Book IV Chapters 3–5 of Sidgwick's *Methods of Ethics*. I think that this book is the best book ever written on ethics, and that these chapters are the best chapters of the book. As they occur so near the end of a very long book they are unduly neglected. I refer the reader, then, to Sidgwick for the classical exposition of the relation between (extreme) utilitarianism and the morality of common sense. One further point raised by Sidgwick in this connexion is whether an (extreme) utilitarian ought on (extreme) utilitarian principles to propagate (extreme) utilitarianism among the public. As most people are not very philosophical and not good at empirical calculations, it is probable that they will most often act in an extreme utilitarian way if they do not try to think as extreme utilitarians. We have seen how easy it would be to misapply the extreme utilitarian criterion in the case of divorce. Sidgwick seems to think it quite probable that an extreme utilitarian should not propagate his doctrine too widely. However, the great danger to humanity comes nowadays on the plane of public morality—not private morality. There is a greater danger to humanity from the hydrogen bomb than from an increase of the divorce rate, regrettable though that might be, and there seems no doubt that extreme utilitarianism makes for good sense in international relations. When France walked out of the United Nations because she did not wish Morocco discussed, she said that she was within her rights because Morocco and Algiers are part of her metropolitan territory and have nothing to do with the U.N. This was clearly a legalistic if not superstitious argument. We should not be concerned with the so-called "rights" of France or any other country but with whether the cause of humanity would best be served by discussing Morocco in U.N. (I am not saying that the answer to this is "Yes." There are good grounds for supposing that more harm than good would have come by such a discussion.) I myself have no hesitation in saying that on extreme utilitarian principles we ought to propagate by extreme utilitarianism as widely as possible. But Sidgwick had respectable reasons for suspecting the opposite.

The extreme utilitarian, then, regards moral rules as rules of thumb and as sociological facts that have to be taken into account when deciding what to do, just as facts of any other sort have to be taken into account. But in themselves they do not justify any action.

III

The restricted utilitarian regards moral rules as more than rules of thumb for short-circuiting calculations of consequences. Generally, he argues, consequences are not relevant at all when we are deciding what to do in a particular case. In general, they are relevant only to deciding what rules are good reasons for acting in a certain way in particular cases. This doctrine is possibly a good account of how the modern unreflective twentieth century Englishman often thinks about morality, but surely it is monstrous as an account of how it is most rational to think about morality. Suppose that there is a rule *R* and that in 99 percent of cases the best possible results are obtained by acting in accordance with *R*. Then clearly *R* is a useful rule of thumb; if we have not time or are not impartial enough to assess the consequences of an action it is an extremely good bet that the thing to do is to act in accordance with *R*. But is it not monstrous to suppose that if we *have* worked out the consequences and if we have perfect faith in the impartiality of our calculations, and if we *know* that in this instance to break *R* will have better results than to keep it, we should nevertheless obey the rule? Is it not to erect *R* into a sort of idol if we keep it when breaking it will prevent, say, some avoidable misery? Is not this a form of superstitious rule-worship (easily explicable psychologically) and not the rational thought of a philosopher?

The point may be made more clearly if we consider Mill's comparison of moral rules to the tables in the nautical almanack. (*Utilitarianism*, Everyman Edition, pp. 22–23). This comparison of Mill's is adduced by J. O. Urmson as evidence that Mill was a restricted utilitarian, but I do not think that it will bear this interpretation at all. (Though I quite agree with Urmson that many other things said by Mill are in harmony with restricted rather than extreme utilitarianism. Probably Mill had never thought very much about the distinction and was arguing for utilitarianism, restricted or extreme, against other and quite non-utilitarian forms of moral argument.) Mill says: "Nobody argues that the art of navigation is not founded on astronomy, because sailors cannot wait to calculate the Nautical Almanack. Being rational creatures, they go out upon the sea of life with their minds made up on the common questions of right and wrong, as well as on many of the far more difficult questions of wise and foolish. . . . Whatever we adopt as the fundamental principle of morality, we require subordinate principles to apply it." Notice that this is, as it stands, only an argument for subordinate principles as rules of thumb. The example of the nautical almanack is misleading because the information given in the almanack is in all cases the same as the information one would get if one made a long and laborious calculation from the original astronomical data on which the almanack is founded. Suppose, however, that astronomy were different. Suppose that the behaviour of the sun, moon and planets was very nearly as it is now, but that on rare occasions there were peculiar irregularities and discontinuities, so that the almanack gave us rules of the form "in 99 percent of cases where the observations are such and such you can deduce that your position is so and so." Furthermore, let us suppose that there were methods which enabled us, by direct and laborious calculation from the original astronomical data, not using the rough and ready tables of the almanack, to get out correct position in 100 percent of cases. Seafarers might use the almanack because they never had time for the long calculations and they were content with the 99 percent chance of success in calculating their positions. Would it not be absurd, however, if they *did* make the direct calculation, and finding that it disagreed with the almanack calculation, nevertheless they ignored it and stuck to the almanack conclusion? Of course the case would be altered if there were a high enough probability of making slips in the direct calculation: then we might stick to the almanack result, liable to error though we knew it to be, simply because the direct calculation would be open to error for a different reason, the fallibility of the computer. This would be analogous to the case of the extreme utilitarian who abides by the conventional rule against the dictates of his utilitarian calculations simply because he thinks that his calculations are probably affected by personal bias. But if the navigator were sure of his direct calculations would he not be foolish to abide by his almanack? I conclude, then, that if we change our suppositions about astronomy and the almanack (to which there are no exceptions) to bring the case into line with that of morality (to whose rules there are exceptions), Mill's example loses its appearance of supporting the restricted form of utilitarianism. Let me say once more that I am not here concerned with how ordinary men think about morality but with how they ought to think. We could quite well imagine a race of sailors who acquired a superstitious reverence for their almanack, even though it was only right in 99 percent of cases, and who indignantly threw overboard any man who mentioned the possibility of a direct calculation. But would this behaviour of the sailors be rational?

Let us consider a much discussed sort of case in which the extreme utilitarian might go against the conventional moral rule. I have promised to a friend, dying on a desert island from which I am subsequently rescued, that I will see that his fortune (over which I have control) is given to a jockey club. However, when I am rescued I decide that it would be better to give the money to a hospital, which can do more good with it. It may be argued that I am wrong to give the money to the hospital. But why? (*a*) The hospital can do more good with the money than the jockey club can. (*b*) The present case is unlike most cases of promising in that no one except me knows about the promise. In breaking the promise I am doing so with complete secrecy and am doing nothing to weaken the general faith in promises. That is, a factor, which would normally keep the extreme utilitarian from promise breaking even in otherwise unoptimific cases, does not at present operate. (*c*) There is no doubt a slight weakening in my own character as an habitual promise keeper, and moreover psychological tensions will be set up in me every time I am asked what the man made me promise him to do. For clearly I shall have to say that he made me promise to give the money to the hospital, and, since I am an habitual truth teller, this will go very much against the grain with me. Indeed I am pretty sure that in practice I myself would keep the promise. But we are not discussing what my moral habits would probably make me do; we are discussing what I ought to do. Moreover, we must not forget that even if it would be most rational of me to give the money to the hospital it would also be most rational of you to punish or condemn me if you did, most improbably, find out the truth (e.g. by finding a note washed ashore in a bottle). Furthermore, I would agree that though it was most rational of me to give the money to the hospital it would be most rational of you to condemn me for it. We revert again to Sidgwick's distinction between the utility of the action and the utility of the praise of it.

Many such issues are discussed by A. K. Stout in the article to which I have already referred. I do not wish to go over the same ground again, especially as I think that Stout's arguments support my own point of view. It will be useful, however, to consider one other example that he gives. Suppose that during hot weather there is an edict that no water must be used for watering gardens. I have a garden and I reason that most people are sure to obey the edict, and that as the amount of water that I use will be by itself negligible no harm will be done if I use the water secretly. So I do use the water, thus producing some lovely flowers which give happiness to various people. Still, you may say, though the action was perhaps optimific, it was unfair and wrong.

There are several matters to consider. Certainly my action should be condemned. We revert once more to Sidgwick's distinction. A right action may be rationally condemned. Furthermore, this sort of offence is normally found out. If I have a wonderful garden when everybody else's is dry and brown there is only one explanation. So if I water my garden I am weakening my respect for law and order, and as this leads to bad results an extreme utilitarian would agree that I was wrong to water the garden. Suppose now that the case is altered and that I can keep the thing secret: there is a secluded part of the garden where I grow flowers which I give away anonymously to a home for old ladies. Are you still so sure that I did the wrong thing by watering my garden? However, this is still a weaker case than that of the hospital and the jockey club. There will be tensions set up within myself: my secret knowledge that I have broken the rule will make it hard for me to exhort others to kept the rule. These psychological ill effects in myself may not be inconsiderable: directly and indirectly they may lead to harm which is at least of the same order as the happiness that the old ladies get from the flowers. You can see that on an extreme utilitarian view there are two sides to the question.

So far I have been considering the duty of an extreme utilitarian in a predominantly non-utilitarian society. The case is altered if we consider the extreme utilitarian who lives in a society every member, or most members, of which can be expected to reason as he does. Should he water his flowers now? (Granting, what is doubtful, that in the case already considered he would have been right to water his flowers.) As a first approximation, the answer is that he should not do so. For since the situation is a completely symmetrical one, what is rational for him is rational for others. Hence, by a *reductio ad absurdum* argument, it would seem that watering his garden would be rational for none. Nevertheless, a more refined analysis shows that the above argument is not quite correct, though it is correct enough for practical purposes. The argument considers each person as confronted with the choice either of watering his garden or of not watering it. However there is a third possibility, which is that each person should, with the aid of a suitable randomizing device, such as throwing dice, give himself a certain probability of watering his garden. This would be to adopt what in the theory of games is called "a mixed strategy." If we could give numerical values to the private benefit of garden watering and to the public harm done by 1, 2, 3, etc., persons using the water in this way, we could work out a value of the probability of watering his garden that each extreme utilitarian should give himself. Let a be the value which each extreme utilitarian gets from watering his garden, and let $f(1), f(2), f(3)$, etc., be the public harm done by exactly 1, 2, 3, etc., persons respectively watering their gardens. Suppose that p is the probability that each person gives himself of watering his garden. Then we can easily calculate, as functions of p, the probabilities that exactly 1, 2, 3, etc., persons will water their gardens. Let these probabilities be p_1, $p_2 \ldots p_n$. Then the total net probable benefit can be expressed as

$$V = p_1(a - f(1)) + p_2(2a - f(2)) + \ldots p_n(na - f(n))$$

Then if we know the function of $f(x)$ we can calculate the value of p for which $(dV/dp) = 0$. This gives the value of p which it would be rational for each extreme utilitarian to adopt. The present argument does not of course depend on a perhaps unjustified assumption that the values in question are measurable, and in a practical case such as that of the garden watering we can doubtless assume that p will be so small that we can take it near enough as equal to zero. However the argument is of interest for the theoretical underpinning of extreme utilitarianism, since the possibility of a mixed strategy is usually neglected by critics of utilitarianism, who wrongly assume that the only relevant and symmetrical alternatives are of the form "everybody does X" and "nobody does X."[1]

I now pass on to a type of case which may be thought to be the trump card of restricted utilitarianism. Consider the rule of the road. It may be said that since all that matters is that everyone should do the same it is indifferent which rule we have, "go on the left-hand side" or "go on the right-hand side." Hence the only *reason* for going on the left-hand side in British countries is that this is the rule. Here the rule does seem to be a reason, in itself, for acting in a certain way. I wish to argue against this. The rule in itself is not a reason for our actions. We would be perfectly justified in going on the right-hand side if (*a*) we knew that the rule was to go on the left-hand side, and (*b*) we were in a country peopled by superanarchists who always on principle did the opposite of what they were told. This shows that the rule does not give us a reason for acting so much as an indication of the probable actions of others, which helps us to find out what would be our own most rational course of action. If we are in a country not peopled by anarchists, but by nonanarchist extreme Utilitarians, we expect, other things being equal, that they will keep rules laid down for them. Knowledge of the rule enables us to predict their behaviour and to harmonize our own actions with theirs. The rule "keep to the left-hand side," then, is not a logical *reason* for action but an anthropological *datum* for planning actions.

I conclude that in every case if there is a rule *R* the keeping of which is in general optimific, but such that in a special sort of circumstances the optimific behaviour is to break *R*, then in these circumstances we should break *R*. Of course we must consider all the less obvious effects of breaking *R*, such as reducing people's faith in the moral order, before coming to the conclusion that to break *R* is right: in fact we shall rarely come to such a conclusion. Moral rules, on the extreme utilitarian view, are rules of thumb only, but they are not bad rules of thumb. But if we *do* come to the conclusion that we should break the rule and if we have weighed in the balance of our own fallibility and liability to personal bias, what good reason remains for keeping the rule? I can understand "it is optimific" as a reason for action, but why should "it is a member of a class of actions which are usually optimific" or "it is a member of a class of actions which as a class are more optimific than any alternative general class" be a good reason? You might as well say that a person ought to be picked to play for Australia just because all his brothers have been, or that the Australian team should be composed entirely of the Harvey family because this would be better than composing it entirely of any other family. The extreme utilitarian does not appeal to artificial feelings, but only to our feelings of benevolence, and what better feelings can there be to appeal to? Admittedly we can have a pro-attitude to anything, even to rules, but such artificially begotten pro-attitudes smack of superstition. Let us get down to realities, human happiness and misery, and make these the objects of our pro-attitudes and anti-attitudes.

The restricted utilitarian might say that he is talking only of *morality*, not of such things as rules of the road. I am not sure how far this objection, if valid, would affect my argument, but in any case I would reply that as a philosopher I conceive of ethics as the study of how it would be *most rational* to act. If my opponent wishes to restrict the word "morality" to a narrower use he can have the word. The fundamental question is the question of rationality of action *in general*. Similarly if the restricted utilitarian were to appeal to ordinary usage and say "it might be most rational to leave Hitler to drown but it would surely not be *wrong* to rescue him," I should again let him have the words "right" and "wrong" and should stick to "rational" and "irrational." We already saw that it would be rational to praise Hitler's rescuer, even though it would have been most rational not to have rescued Hitler. In ordinary language, no doubt, "right" and "wrong" have not only the meaning "most rational to do" and "not most rational to do" but also have the meaning "praiseworthy" and "not praiseworthy." Usually to the utility of an action corresponds utility of praise of it, but as we saw, this is not always so. Moral language could thus do with tidying up, for example by reserving "right" for "most rational" and "good" as an epithet of praise for the motive from which the action sprang. It would be more becoming in a philosopher to try to iron out illogicalities in moral language and to make suggestions for its reform than to use it as a court of appeal whereby to perpetuate confusions.

One last defence of restricted utilitarianism might be as follows. "Act optimifically" might be regarded as itself one of the rules of our system (though it would be odd to say that this rule was justified by its optimificality). According to Stephen Toulmin (*The Place of Reason in Ethics*, pp. 146–8) if "keep promises," say, conflicts with another rule we are allowed to argue the case on its merits, as if we were extreme utilitarians. If "act optimifically" is itself one of our rules then there will always be a conflict of rules whenever to keep a rule is not itself optimific. If this is so, restricted utilitarianism collapses into extreme utilitarianism.

NOTE

1. [This paragraph has been substantially emended by the author. Ed. *(in original)*]

Utilitarianism, Integrity and Responsibility

BERNARD WILLIAMS

Bernard Williams (1929–2003) was among the most distinguished moral philosophers of the 20th century. Born in England, he divided his academic career between the University of Cambridge in England and the University of California at Berkeley. He made important contributions to debates about moral psychology, personal identity, equality, morality and the emotions, as well as to the study of the history of philosophy, and to British public life.

The excerpt that appears here is drawn from a much longer essay by Williams criticizing utilitarianism, which was originally published alongside a companion essay by J. J. C. Smart in a volume called *Utilitarianism: For and Against*. (Smart provided the "for" essay, Williams the "against.") In our selection, Williams offers a number of reasons for thinking that a utilitarian moral outlook is incapable of properly capturing our authentic moral commitments. An additional article by Williams appears in the "Identity and Personal Identity" section (III.G).

Now, however, let us look more concretely at two examples, to see what utilitarianism might say about them, what we might say about utilitarianism and, most importantly of all, what would be implied by certain ways of thinking about the situations. The examples are inevitably schematized, and they are open to the objection that they beg as many questions as they illuminate. There are two ways in particular in which examples in moral philosophy tend to beg important questions. One is that, as presented, they arbitrarily cut off and restrict the range of alternative courses of action—this objection might particularly be made against the first of my two examples. The second is that they inevitably present one with the situation as a going concern, and cut off questions about how the agent got into it, and correspondingly about moral considerations which might flow from that: this objection might perhaps specially arise with regard to the second of my two situations. These difficulties, however, just have to be accepted, and if anyone finds these examples cripplingly defective in this sort of respect, then he must in his own thought rework them in richer and less question-begging form. If he feels that no presentation of any imagined situation can ever be other than misleading in morality, and that there can never be any substitute for the concrete experienced complexity of actual moral situations, then this discussion, with him, must certainly grind to a halt: but then one may legitimately wonder whether every discussion with him about conduct will not grind to a halt, including any discussion about the actual situations, since discussion about how one would think and feel about situations somewhat different from the actual (that is to say, situations to that extent imaginary) plays an important role in discussion of the actual.

(1) George, who has just taken his Ph.D. in chemistry, finds it extremely difficult to get a job. He is not very robust in health, which cuts down the number of jobs he might be able to do satisfactorily. His wife has to go out to work to keep them, which itself causes a great deal of strain, since they have small children and there are severe problems about looking after them. The results of all this, especially on the children, are damaging. An older chemist, who knows about this situation, says that he can get George a decently paid job in a certain laboratory, which pursues research into chemical and biological warfare. George says that he cannot

From *Utilitarianism: For and Against,* eds. J. J. C. Smart and Bernard Williams. Copyright © 1973 by Cambridge University Press. Reprinted by permission of the publisher.

accept this, since he is opposed to chemical and biological warfare. The older man replies that he is not too keen on it himself, come to that, but after all George's refusal is not going to make the job or the laboratory go away; what is more, he happens to know that if George refuses the job, it will certainly go to a contemporary of George's who is not inhibited by any such scruples and is likely if appointed to push along the research with greater zeal than George would. Indeed, it is not merely concern for George and his family, but (to speak frankly and in confidence) some alarm about this other man's excess of zeal, which has led the older man to offer to use his influence to get George the job . . . George's wife, to whom he is deeply attached, has views (the details of which need not concern us) from which it follows that at least there is nothing particularly wrong with research into CBW. What should he do?

(2) Jim finds himself in the central square of a small South American town. Tied up against the wall are a row of twenty Indians, most terrified, a few defiant, in front of them several armed men in uniform. A heavy man in a sweat-stained khaki shirt turns out to be the captain in charge and, after a good deal of questioning of Jim which establishes that he got there by accident while on a botanical expedition, explains that the Indians are a random group of the inhabitants who, after recent acts of protest against the government, are just about to be killed to remind other possible protestors of the advantages of not protesting. However, since Jim is an honoured visitor from another land, the captain is happy to offer him a guest's privilege of killing one of the Indians himself. If Jim accepts, then as a special mark of the occasion, the other Indians will be let off. Of course, if Jim refuses, then there is no special occasion, and Pedro here will do what he was about to do when Jim arrived, and kill them all. Jim, with some desperate recollection of schoolboy fiction, wonders whether if he got hold of a gun, he could hold the captain, Pedro and the rest of the soldiers to threat, but it is quite clear from the set-up that nothing of that kind is going to work: any attempt at that sort of thing will mean that all the Indians will be killed, and himself. The men against the wall, and the other villagers, understand the situation, and are obviously begging him to accept. What should he do?

To these dilemmas, it seems to me that utilitarianism replies, in the first case, that George should accept the job, and in the second, that Jim should kill the Indian. Not only does utilitarianism give these answers but, if the situations are essentially as described and there are no further special factors, it regards them, it seems to me, as *obviously* the right answers. But many of us would certainly wonder whether, in (1), that could possibly be the right answer at all; and in the case of (2), even one who came to think that perhaps that was the answer, might well wonder whether it was obviously the answer. Nor is it just a question of the rightness or obviousness of these answers. It is also a question of what sort of considerations come into finding the answer. A feature of utilitarianism is that it cuts out a kind of consideration which for some others makes a difference to what they feel about such cases: a consideration involving the idea, as we might first and very simply put it, that each of us is specially responsible for what *he* does, rather than for what other people do. This is an idea closely connected with the value of integrity. It is often suspected that utilitarianism, at least in its direct forms, makes integrity as a value more or less unintelligible. I shall try to show that this suspicion is correct. Of course, even if that is correct, it would not necessarily follow that we should reject utilitarianism; perhaps, as utilitarians sometimes suggest, we should just forget about integrity, in favour of such things as a concern for the general good. However, if I am right, we cannot merely do that, since the reason why utilitarianism cannot understand integrity is that it cannot coherently describe the relations between a man's projects and his actions.

TWO KINDS OF REMOTE EFFECT

A lot of what we have to say about this question will be about the relations between my projects and other people's projects. But before we get on to that, we should first ask whether we are assuming too hastily what the utilitarian answers to the dilemmas will be. In terms of more direct effect of the possible decisions, there does not indeed seem much doubt about the answer in either case; but it might be said that in terms of more remote or less evident effects counterweights might be found to enter the utilitarian scales. Thus the effect on George of a decision to take the job might be invoked, or its effect on others who might know of his decision. The possibility of there being more beneficent labours in the future from which he might be barred or disqualified, might be mentioned; and so forth. Such effects—in particular, possible effects on the agent's character, and effects on the public at large—are often invoked by utilitarian writers dealing with problems about lying or promise-breaking, and some similar considerations might be invoked here.

There is one very general remark that is worth making about arguments of this sort. The certainty that attaches to these hypotheses about possible effects is usually pretty low; in some cases, indeed, the hypothesis invoked is so implausible that it would scarcely pass if it were not being used to deliver the respectable moral answer, as in the standard fantasy that one of the effects of one's telling a particular lie is to weaken the disposition of the world at large to tell the truth. The demands on the certainty or probability of these beliefs as beliefs about particular actions are much milder than they would be on beliefs favouring the unconventional course. It may be said that this is as it should be, since the presumption must be in favour of the conventional course: but that scarcely seems a *utilitarian* answer, unless utilitarianism has already taken off in the direction of not applying the consequences to the particular act at all.

Leaving aside that very general point, I want to consider now two types of effect that are often invoked by utilitarians, and which might be invoked in connexion with these imaginary cases. The attitude or tone involved in invoking these effects may sometimes seem peculiar; but that sort of peculiarity soon becomes familiar in utilitarian discussions, and indeed it can be something of an achievement to retain a sense of it.

First, there is the psychological effect on the agent. Our descriptions of these situations have not so far taken account of how George or Jim will be after they have taken the one course or the other; and it might be said that if they take the course which seemed at first the utilitarian one, the effects on them will be in fact bad enough and extensive enough to cancel out the initial utilitarian advantages of that course. Now there is one version of this effect in which, for a utilitarian, some confusion must be involved, namely that in which the agent feels bad, his subsequent conduct and relations are crippled and so on, *because he thinks that he has done the wrong thing*—for if the balance of outcomes was as it appeared to be *before* invoking this effect, then he has not (from the utilitarian point of view) done the wrong thing. So that version of the effect, for a rational and utilitarian agent, could not possibly make any difference to the assessment of right and wrong. However, perhaps he is not a thoroughly rational agent, and is disposed to have bad feelings, whichever he decided to do. Now such feelings, which are from a strictly utilitarian point of view irrational—nothing, a utilitarian can point out, is advanced by having them—cannot, consistently, have any great weight in a utilitarian calculation. I shall consider in a moment an argument to suggest that they should have no weight at all in it. But short of that, the utilitarian could reasonably say that such feelings should not be encouraged, even if we accept their existence, and that to give them a lot of weight is to encourage them. Or, at the very best, even if they are straightforwardly and without any discount to be put into the calculation, their weight must be small: they are after all (and at best) one man's feelings.

That consideration might seem to have particular force in Jim's case. In George's case, his feelings represent a larger proportion of what is to be weighed, and are more commensurate in character with other items in the calculation. In Jim's case, however, his feelings might seem to be of very little weight compared with other things that are at stake. There is a powerful and recognizable appeal that can be made on this point: as that a refusal by Jim to do what he has been invited to do would be a kind of self-indulgent squeamishness. That is an appeal which can be made by other than utilitarians—indeed, there are some uses of it which cannot be consistently made by utilitarians, as when it essentially involves the idea that there is something dishonourable about such self-indulgence. But in some versions it is a familiar, and it must be said a powerful, weapon of utilitarianism. One must be clear, though, about what it can and cannot accomplish.

The most it can do, so far as I can see, is to invite one to consider how seriously, and for what reasons, one feels that what one is invited to do is (in these circumstances) wrong, and in particular, to consider that question from the utilitarian point of view. When the agent is not seeing the situation from a utilitarian point of view, the appeal cannot force him to do so; and if he does come round to seeing it from a utilitarian point of view, there is virtually nothing left for the appeal to do. If he does not see it from a utilitarian point of view, he will not see his resistance to the invitation, and the unpleasant feelings he associates with accepting it, *just* as disagreeable experiences of his; they figure rather as emotional expressions of a thought that to accept would be wrong. He may be asked, as by the appeal, to consider whether he is right, and indeed whether he is fully serious, in thinking that. But the assertion of the appeal, that he is being self-indulgently squeamish, will not itself answer that question, or even help to answer it, since it essentially tells him to regard his feelings just as unpleasant experiences of his, and he cannot, by doing that, answer the question they pose when they are precisely not so regarded, but are regarded as indications[1] of what he thinks is right and wrong. If he does come round fully to the utilitarian point of view then of course he will regard these feelings just as unpleasant experiences of his. And once Jim—at least—has come to see them in that light, there is nothing left for the appeal to do, since *of course* his feelings, so regarded, are of virtually no weight at all in relation to the other things at stake. The "squeamishness" appeal is not an argument which adds in a hitherto neglected consideration. Rather, it is an invitation to consider the situation, and one's own feelings, from a utilitarian point of view.

The reason why the squeamishness appeal can be very unsettling, and one can be unnerved by the suggestion of self-indulgence in going against utilitarian considerations, is not that we are utilitarians who are uncertain what utilitarian value to attach to our moral feelings, but that we are partially at least not utilitarians, and cannot regard our moral feelings merely as objects of utilitarian value. Because our moral relation to the world is partly given by such feelings, and by a sense of what we can or cannot "live with," to come to regard those feelings from a purely utilitarian point of view, that is to say, as happenings outside one's moral self, is to lose a sense of one's moral identity; to lose, in the most literal way one's integrity. At this point utilitarianism alienates one from one's moral feelings; we shall see a little later how, more basically, it alienates one from one's actions as well.

If, then, one is really going to regard one's feelings from a strictly utilitarian point of view, Jim should give very little weight at all to his; it seems almost indecent, in fact, once one has taken that point of view, to suppose that he should give any at all. In George's case one might feel that things were slightly different. It is interesting, though, that one reason why one might think that—namely that one person principally affected is his wife—is very dubiously available to a utilitarian. George's wife has some reason to be interested in George's integrity and his sense of it; the Indians, quite properly, have no interest in Jim's. But it is not at all clear how utilitarianism would describe that difference.

There is an argument, and a strong one, that a strict utilitarian should give not merely small extra weight, in calculations of right and wrong, to feelings of this kind, but that he should give absolutely no weight to them at all. This is based on the point, which we have already seen, that if a course of action is, before taking these sorts of feelings into account, utilitarianly preferable, then bad feelings about that kind of action will be from a utilitarian point of view irrational. Now it might be thought that even if that is so, it would not mean that in a utilitarian calculation such feelings should not be taken into account; it is after all a well-known boast of utilitarianism that it is a realistic outlook which seeks the best in the world as it is, and takes any form of happiness or unhappiness into account. While a utilitarian will no doubt seek to diminish the incidence of feelings which are utilitarianly irrational—or at least of disagreeable feelings which are so—he might be expected to take them into account while they exist. This is without doubt classical utilitarian doctrine, but there is good reason to think that utilitarianism cannot stick to it without embracing results which are startlingly unacceptable and perhaps self-defeating.

Suppose that there is in a certain society a racial minority. Considering merely the ordinary interests of the other citizens, as opposed to their sentiments, this minority does no particular harm; we may suppose that it does not confer any very great benefits either. Its presence is in those terms neutral or mildly beneficial. However, the other citizens have such prejudices that they find the sight of this group, even the knowledge of its presence, very disagreeable. Proposals are made for removing in some way this minority. If we assume various quite plausible things (as that programmes to change the majority sentiment are likely to be protracted and ineffective) then even if the removal would be unpleasant for the minority, a utilitarian calculation might well end up favouring this step, especially if the minority were a rather small minority and the majority were very severely prejudiced, that is to say, were made very severely uncomfortable by the presence of the minority.

A utilitarian might find that conclusion embarrassing; and not merely because of its nature, but because of the grounds on which it is reached. While a utilitarian might be expected to take into account certain other sorts of consequences of the prejudice, as that a majority prejudice is likely to be displayed in conduct disagreeable to the minority, and so forth, he might be made to wonder whether the unpleasant experiences of the prejudiced people should be allowed, *merely as such*, to count. If he does count them, merely as such, then he has once more separated himself from a body of ordinary moral thought which he might have hoped to accommodate; he may also have started on the path of defeating his own view of things. For one feature of these sentiments is that they are from the utilitarian point of view itself irrational, and a thoroughly utilitarian person would either not have them, or if he found that he did tend to have them, would himself seek to discount them. Since the sentiments in question are such that a rational utilitarian would discount them in himself, it is reasonable to suppose that he should discount them in his calculations about society; it does seem quite unreasonable for him to give just as much weight to feelings—considered just in themselves, one must recall, as experiences of those that have them—which are essentially based on views which are from a utilitarian point of view irrational, as to those which accord with utilitarian principles. Granted this idea, it seems reasonable for him to rejoin a body of moral thought in other respects congenial to him, and discount those sentiments, just considered in themselves, totally, on the principle that no pains or discomforts are to count in the utilitarian sum which their subjects have just because they hold views which are by utilitarian standards irrational. But if he accepts that, then in the cases we are at present considering no extra weight at all can be put in for bad feelings of George or Jim about their choices, if those choices are, leaving out those feelings, on the first round utilitarianly rational.

The psychological effect on the agent was the first of two general effects considered by utilitarians, which had to be discussed. The second is in general a more substantial item, but it need not take so long, since it is both clearer and has little application to the present cases. This is the *precedent effect*. As Burke rightly emphasized, this effect can be important: that one morally *can* do what someone has actually done, is a psychologically effective principle, if not a deontically valid one. For the effect to operate, obviously some conditions must hold on the publicity of the act and on such things as the status of the agent (such considerations weighed importantly with Sir Thomas More); what these may be will vary evidently with circumstances.*

In order for the precedent effect to make a difference to a utilitarian calculation, it must be based upon a confusion. For suppose that there is an act which would be the best in the circumstances, except that doing it will encourage by precedent other people to do things which will not be the best things to do. Then the situation of those other people must be relevantly different from that of the original agent; if it were not, then in doing the same as what would be the best course for the original agent, they would necessarily do the best thing themselves. But if the

* Edmund Burke (1729–97) was an important conservative political philosopher; Thomas More (1478–1535) was an English lawyer, writer, and statesman, who was executed for his unwillingness to impugn the authority of the pope.

situations are in this way relevantly different, it must be a confused perception which takes the first situation, and the agent's course in it, as an adequate precedent for the second.

However, the fact that the precedent effect, if it really makes a difference, is in this sense based on a confusion, does not mean that it is not perfectly real, nor that it is to be discounted: social effects are by their nature confused in this sort of way. What it does emphasize is that calculations of the precedent effect have got to be realistic, involving considerations of how people are actually likely to be influenced. In the present examples, however, it is very implausible to think that the precedent effect could be invoked to make any difference to the calculation. Jim's case is extraordinary enough, and it is hard to imagine who the recipients of the effect might be supposed to be; while George is not in a sufficiently public situation or role for the question to arise in that form, and in any case one might suppose that the motivations of others on such an issue were quite likely to be fixed one way or another already.

No appeal, then, to these other effects is going to make a difference to what the utilitarian will decide about our examples. Let us now look more closely at the structure of those decisions.

INTEGRITY

The situations have in common that if the agent does not do a certain disagreeable thing, someone else will, and in Jim's situation at least the result, the state of affairs after the other man has acted, if he does, will be worse than after Jim has acted, if Jim does. The same, on a smaller scale, is true of George's case. I have already suggested that it is inherent in consequentialism that it offers a strong doctrine of negative responsibility: if I know that if I do *X*, O_1 will eventuate, and if I refrain from doing *X*, O_2 will, and that O_2 is worse than O_1, then I am responsible for O_2 if I refrain voluntarily from doing *X*. "You could have prevented it," as will be said, and truly, to Jim, if he refuses, by the relatives of the other Indians. (I shall leave the important question, which is to the side of the present issue, of the obligations, if any, that nest round the word "know": how far does one, under utilitarianism, have to research into the possibilities of maximally beneficent action, including prevention?)

In the present cases, the situation of O_2 includes another agent bringing about results worse than O_1. So far as O_2 has been identified up to this point—merely as the worse outcome which will eventuate if I refrain from doing *X*—we might equally have said that what that other brings about is O_2; but that would be to underdescribe the situation. For what occurs if Jim refrains from action is not solely twenty Indians dead, but *Pedro's killing twenty Indians*, and that is not a result which Pedro brings about, though the death of the Indians is. We can say: what one does is not included in the outcome of what one does, while what another does can be included in the outcome of what one does. For that to be so, as the terms are now being used, only a very weak condition has to be satisfied: for Pedro's killing the Indians to be the outcome of Jim's refusal, it only has to be causally true that if Jim had not refused, Pedro would not have done it.

That may be enough for us to speak, in some sense, of Jim's responsibility for that outcome, if it occurs; but it is certainly not enough, it is worth noticing, for us to speak of Jim's *making* those things happen. For granted this way of their coming about, he could have made them happen only by making Pedro shoot, and there is no acceptable sense in which his refusal makes Pedro shoot. If the captain had said on Jim's refusal, "you leave me with no alternative," he would have been lying, like most who use that phrase. While the deaths, and the killing, may be the outcome of Jim's refusal, it is misleading to think, in such a case, of Jim having an *effect* on the world through the medium (as it happens) of Pedro's acts; for this is to leave Pedro out of the picture in his essential role of one who has intentions and projects, projects for realizing which Jim's refusal would leave an opportunity. Instead of thinking in terms of supposed effects of Jim's projects on Pedro, it is more revealing to think in terms of the effects of Pedro's projects on Jim's decision. This is the direction from which I want to criticize the notion of negative responsibility.

There are of course other ways in which this notion can be criticized. Many have hoped to discredit it by insisting on the basic moral relevance of the distinction between action and inaction, between intervening and letting things take their course. The distinction is certainly of great moral significance, and indeed it is not easy to think of any moral outlook which could get along without making some use of it. But it is unclear, both in itself and in its moral applications, and the unclarities are of a kind which precisely cause it to give way when, in very difficult cases, weight has to be put on it. There is much to be said in this area, but I doubt whether the sort of dilemma we are considering is going to be resolved by a simple use of this distinction. Again, the issue of negative responsibility can be pressed on the question of how limits are to be placed on one's apparently boundless obligation, implied by utilitarianism, to improve the world. Some answers are needed to that, too—and answers which stop short of relapsing into the bad faith of supposing that one's responsibilities could be adequately characterized just by appeal to one's roles.[2] But, once again, while that is a real question, it cannot be brought to bear directly on the present kind of case, since it is hard to think of anyone supposing that in Jim's case it would be an adequate response for him to say that it was none of his business.

What projects does a utilitarian agent have? As a utilitarian, he has the general project of bringing about maximally desirable outcomes; how he is to do this at any given moment is a question of what casual levers, so to speak, are at that moment within reach. The desirable outcomes, however, do not just consist of agents carrying out *that* project; there must be other more basic or lower-order projects which he and other agents have, and the desirable outcomes are going to consist, in part, of the maximally harmonious realization of those projects ("in part," because one component of a utilitarianly desirable outcome may be the occurrence of agreeable experiences which are not the satisfaction of anybody's projects). Unless there were first-order projects, the general utilitarian project would have nothing to work on, and would be vacuous. What do the more basic or lower-order projects comprise? Many will be the obvious kinds of desires for things for oneself, one's family, one's friends, including basic necessities of life, and in more relaxed circumstances, objects of taste. Or there may be pursuits and interests of an intellectual, cultural or creative character. I introduce those as a separate class not because the objects of them lie in a separate class, and provide—as some utilitarians, in their churchy way, are fond of saying—"higher" pleasures. I introduce them separately because the agent's identification with them may be of a different order. It does not have to be: cultural and aesthetic interests just belong, for many, along with any other taste; but some people's commitment to these kinds of interests just is at once more thoroughgoing and serious than their pursuit of various objects of taste, while it is more individual and permeated with character than the desire for the necessities of life.

Beyond these, someone may have projects connected with his support of some cause: Zionism, for instance, or the abolition of chemical and biological warfare. Or there may be projects which flow from some more general disposition towards human conduct and character, such as a hatred of injustice, or of cruelty, or of killing.

It may be said that this last sort of disposition and its associated project do not count as (logically) "lower-order" relative to the higher-order project of maximizing desirable outcomes; rather, it may be said, it is itself a "higher-order" project. The vital question is not, however, how it is to be classified, but whether it and similar projects are to count among the projects whose satisfaction is to be included in the maximizing sum, and, correspondingly, as contributing to the agent's happiness. If the utilitarian says "no" to that, then he is almost certainly committed to a version of utilitarianism as absurdly superficial and shallow as Benthamite versions have often been accused of being. For this project will be discounted, presumably, on the ground that it involves, in the specification of its object, the mention of other people's happiness or interests: thus it is the kind of project which (unlike the pursuit of food for myself) presupposes a reference to other people's projects. But that criterion would eliminate any desire at all which was not blankly and in the most straightforward sense egoistic.[3] Thus we should be reduced to frankly egoistic first-order projects, and—for all essential purposes—the one second-order utilitarian project of maximally satisfying first-order projects. Utilitarianism has a tendency to slide in this direction, and to leave a vast hole in the range of human desires, between egoistic inclinations and necessities at one end, and impersonally benevolent happiness-management at the other. But the utilitarianism which has to leave this hole is the most primitive form, which offers a quite rudimentary account of desire. Modern versions of the theory are supposed to be neutral with regard to what sorts of things make people happy or what their projects are. Utilitarianism would do well then to acknowledge the evident fact that among the things that make people happy is not only making other people happy, but being taken up or involved in any of a vast range of projects, or—if we waive the evangelical and moralizing associations of the word—commitments. One can be committed to such things as a person, a cause, an institution, a career, one's own genius, or the pursuit of danger.

Now none of these is itself the *pursuit of happiness*: by an exceedingly ancient platitude, it is not at all clear that there could be anything which was just that, or at least anything that had the slightest chance of being successful. Happiness, rather, requires being involved in, or at least content with, something else.[4] It is not impossible for utilitarianism to accept that point: it does not have to be saddled with a naïve and absurd philosophy of mind about the relation between desire and happiness. What it does have to say is that if such commitments are worth while, then pursuing the projects that flow from them, and realizing some of those projects, will make the person for whom they are worth while, happy. It may be that to claim that is still wrong: it may well be that a commitment can make sense to a man (can make sense to his life) without his supposing that it will make him *happy*.[5] But that is not the present point; let us grant to utilitarianism that all worthwhile human projects must conduce, one way or another, to happiness. The point is that even if that is true, it does not follow, nor could it possibly be true, that those projects are themselves projects of pursuing happiness. One has to believe in, or at least want, or quite minimally, be content with, other things, for there to be anywhere that happiness can come from.

Utilitarianism, then, should be willing to agree that its general aim of maximizing happiness does not imply that what everyone is doing is just pursuing happiness. On the contrary, people have to be pursuing other things. What those other things may be, utilitarianism, sticking to its professed empirical stance, should be prepared just to find out. No doubt some possible projects it will want to discourage, on the grounds that their being pursued involves a negative balance of happiness to others: though even there, the unblinking accountant's eye of the strict utilitarian will have something to put in the positive column, the satisfactions of the destructive agent. Beyond that, there will be a vast variety of generally beneficent or at least harmless projects; and some no doubt, will take the form not just of tastes or fancies, but of what I have called "commitments." It may even be that the utilitarian researcher will find that many of those with commitments, who have really identified themselves with objects outside themselves, who are thoroughly involved with other persons, or institutions, or activities or causes, are actually happier than those whose projects and wants are not like that. If so, that is an important piece of utilitarian empirical lore. . . .

Let us now go back to the agent as utilitarian, and his higher-order project of maximizing desirable outcomes. At this level, he is committed only to that: what the outcome will actually consist of will depend entirely on the facts, on what persons with what projects and what potential satisfactions there are within calculable reach of the causal levers near which he finds himself. His own substantial projects and commitments come into it, but only as one lot among others—they potentially provide one set of satisfactions among those which he may be able to assist from where he happens to be. He is the agent of the satisfaction system who happens to be at a particular point at a particular time: in Jim's case, our man in South America. His own decisions as a utilitarian agent are a function of all the satisfactions which he can affect from where he is: and this means that the projects of others, to an indeterminately great extent, determine his decision.

This may be so either positively or negatively. It will be so positively if agents within the causal field of his decision have projects which are at any rate harmless, and so should be assisted. It will equally be so, but negatively, if there is an agent within the causal field whose projects are harmful, and have to be frustrated to maximize desirable outcomes. So it is with Jim and the soldier Pedro. On the utilitarian view, the undesirable projects of other people as much determine, in this negative way, one's decisions as the desirable ones do positively: if those people were not there, or had different projects, the causal nexus would be different, and it is the actual state of the causal nexus which determines the decision. The determination to an indefinite degree of my decisions by other people's projects is just another aspect of my unlimited responsibility to act for the best in a causal framework formed to a considerable extent by their projects.

The decision so determined is, for utilitarianism, the right decision. But what if it conflicts with some project of mine? This, the utilitarian will say, has already been dealt with: the satisfaction to you of fulfilling your project, and any satisfactions to others of your so doing, have already been through the calculating device and have been found inadequate. Now in the case of many sorts of projects, that is a perfectly reasonable sort of answer. But in the case of projects of the sort I have called "commitments," those with which one is more deeply and extensively involved and identified, this cannot just by itself be an adequate answer, and there may be no adequate answer at all. For, to take the extreme sort of case, how can a man, as a utilitarian agent, come to regard as one satisfaction among others, and a dispensable one, a project or attitude round which he has built his life, just because someone else's projects have so structured the causal scene that that is how the utilitarian sum comes out?

The point here is not, as utilitarians may hasten to say, that if the project or attitude is that central to his life, then to abandon it will be very disagreeable to him and great loss of utility will be involved. I have already argued in [the previous] section that it is not like that; on the contrary, once he is prepared to look at it like that, the argument in any serious case is over anyway. The point is that he is identified with his actions as flowing from projects and attitudes which in some cases he takes seriously at the deepest level, as what his life is about (or, in some cases, this section of his life—seriousness is not necessarily the same as persistence). It is absurd to demand of such a man, when the sums come in from the utility network which the projects of others have in part determined, that he should just step aside from his own project and decision and acknowledge the decision which utilitarian calculation requires. It is to alienate him in a real sense from his actions and the source of his action in his own convictions. It is to make him into a channel between the input of everyone's projects, including his own, and an output of optimific decision; but this is to neglect the extent to which *his* actions and *his* decisions have to be seen as the actions and decisions which flow from the projects and attitudes with which he is most closely identified. It is thus, in the most literal sense, an attack on his integrity.[6]

These sorts of considerations do not in themselves give solutions to practical dilemmas such as those provided by our examples; but I hope they help to provide other ways of thinking about them. In fact, it is not hard to see that in George's case, viewed from this perspective, the utilitarian solution would be wrong. Jim's case is different, and harder. But if (as I suppose) the utilitarian is probably right in this case, that is not to be found out just by asking the utilitarian's questions. Discussions of it—and I am not going to try to carry it further here—will have to take seriously the distinction between my killing someone, and its coming about because of what I do that someone else kills them: a distinction based, not so much on the distinction between action and inaction, as on the distinction between my projects and someone else's projects. At least it will have to start by taking that seriously, as utilitarianism does not; but then it will have to build out from there by asking why that distinction seems to have less, or a different, force in this case than it has in George's. One question here would be how far one's powerful objection to killing people just is, in fact, an application of a powerful objection to their being killed. Another dimension of that is the issue of how much it matters that the people at risk are actual, and there, as opposed to hypothetical, or future, or merely elsewhere.[7]

NOTES

1. On the non-cognitivist meta-ethic in terms of which Smart presents his utilitarianism, the term "indications" here would represent an understatement.
2. For some remarks bearing on this, see Bernard Williams, *Morality*, the section on "Goodness and roles," and Cohen's article there cited.
3. On the subject of egoistic and non-egoistic desires, see "Egoism and altruism," in Bernard Williams, *Problems of the Self* (Cambridge University Press, London, 1973).
4. This does not imply that there is no such thing as the project of pursuing pleasure. Some writers who have correctly resisted the view that all desires are desires for pleasure, have given an account of pleasure so thoroughly adverbial as to leave it quite unclear how there could be a distinctively hedonist way of life at all. Some room has to be left for that, though there are important difficulties both in defining it and living it. Thus (particularly in the case of the very rich) it often has highly ritual aspects, apparently part of a strategy to counter boredom.
5. For some remarks on this possibility, see *Morality* section on "What is morality about?" [*Morality: An Introduction to Ethics* (Harper and Row, New York, 1972).]
6. Interestingly related to these notions is the Socratic idea that courage is a virtue particularly connected with keeping a clear sense of what one regards as most important. They also centrally raise questions about the value of pride. Humility, as something beyond the real demand of correct self-appraisal, was specially a Christian virtue because it involved subservience to God. In a secular context it can only represent subservience to other men and their projects.
7. For a more general discussion of this issue see Charles Fried, *An Anatomy of Values* (Harvard University Press, Cambridge, Mass., 1970), Part Three.

◈ DEONTOLOGY ◈

Selections from *Grounding for the Metaphysics of Morals*

IMMANUEL KANT

The German philosopher Immanuel Kant (1724–1804) was one of the most influential philosophers of all time, making central contributions to virtually every philosophical subdiscipline. His major works number among the greatest philosophical writings in the Western tradition, although they are also notoriously difficult to understand.

The selection that appears here is a brief collection of excerpts taken from the first section of Kant's *Grounding for the Metaphysics of Morals* (originally published in German in 1785), which presents many of his main moral ideas in a relatively condensed fashion. In this selec-

From *Grounding for the Metaphysics of Morals*, trans. James Ellington. Copyright © 1993 by Hackett Publishing Company, Inc. Reprinted by permission of the publisher. All rights reserved.

tion, Kant presents and defends his idea that what he calls the "categorical imperative" serves as the basis for morality.

The translation we are using is by James W. Ellington of the University of Connecticut at Storrs. Notes that appear in [brackets] are thanks to Ellington; notes that do not are due to Kant himself. Numbers that appear in the margins refer to page numbers in the Academy edition (referred to in the notes by the abbreviation "Ak.") which is the standard reference for Kant's works; they allow readers who make use of different translations or editions to refer easily to a particular passage.

FIRST SECTION

TRANSITION FROM THE ORDINARY RATIONAL KNOWLEDGE OF MORALITY TO THE PHILOSOPHICAL

There is no possibility of thinking of anything at all in the world, or even out of it, which can be regarded as good without qualification, except a *good will*. Intelligence, wit, judgment, and whatever talents of the mind one might want to name are doubtless in many respects good and desirable, as are such qualities of temperament as courage, resolution, perseverance. But they can also become extremely bad and harmful if the will, which is to make use of these gifts of nature and which in its special constitution is called character, is not good. The same holds with gifts of fortune; power, riches, honor, even health, and that complete well-being and contentment with one's condition which is called happiness make for pride and often hereby even arrogance, unless there is a good will to correct their influence on the mind and herewith also to rectify the whole principle of action and make it universally conformable to its end. The sight of a being who is not graced by any touch of a pure and good will but who yet enjoys an uninterrupted prosperity can never delight a rational and impartial spectator. Thus a good will seems to constitute the indispensable condition of being even worthy of happiness.

Some qualities are even conducive to this good will itself and can facilitate its work. Nevertheless,
394 they have no intrinsic unconditional worth; but they always presuppose, rather, a good will, which restricts the high esteem in which they are otherwise rightly held, and does not permit them to be regarded as absolutely good. Moderation in emotions and passions, self-control, and calm deliberation are not only good in many respects but even seem to constitute part of the intrinsic worth of a person. But they are far from being rightly called good without qualification (however unconditionally they were commended by the ancients). For without the principles of good will, they can become extremely bad; the coolness of a villain makes him not only much more dangerous but also immediately more abominable in our eyes than he would have been regarded by us without it.

A good will is good not because of what it effects or accomplishes, nor because of its fitness to attain some proposed end; it is good only through its willing, i.e., it is good in itself. When it is considered in itself, then it is to be esteemed very much higher than anything which it might ever bring about merely in order to favor some inclination, or even the sum total of all inclinations. Even if, by some especially unfortunate fate or by the niggardly provision of stepmotherly nature, this will should be wholly lacking in the power to accomplish its purpose; if with the greatest effort it should yet achieve nothing, and only the good will should remain (not, to be sure, as a mere wish but as the summoning of all the means in our power), yet would it, like a jewel, still shine by its own light as something which has its full value in itself. Its usefulness or fruitlessness can neither augment nor diminish this value. Its usefulness would be, as it were, only the setting to enable us to handle it in ordinary dealings or to attract to it the attention of those who are not yet experts, but not to recommend it to real experts or to determine its value. . . .

The concept of a will estimable in itself and 397
good without regard to any further end must now

be developed. This concept already dwells in the natural sound understanding and needs not so much to be taught as merely to be elucidated. It always holds first place in estimating the total worth of our actions and constitutes the condition of all the rest. Therefore, we shall take up the concept of *duty*, which includes that of a good will, though with certain subjective restrictions and hindrances, which far from hiding a good will or rendering it unrecognizable, rather bring it out by contrast and make it shine forth more brightly.

I here omit all actions already recognized as contrary to duty, even though they may be useful for this or that end; for in the case of these the question does not arise at all as to whether they might be done from duty, since they even conflict with duty. I also set aside those actions which are really in accordance with duty, yet to which men have no immediate inclination, but perform them because they are impelled thereto by some other inclination. For in this [second] case to decide whether the action which is in accord with duty has been done from duty or from some selfish purpose is easy. This difference is far more difficult to note in the [third] case where the action accords with duty and the subject has in addition an immediate inclination to do the action. For example,* that a dealer should not overcharge an inexperienced purchaser certainly accords with duty; and where there is much commerce, the prudent merchant does not overcharge but keeps to a fixed price for everyone in general, so that a child may buy from him just as well as everyone else may. Thus customers are honestly served, but this is not nearly enough for making us believe that the merchant has acted this way from duty and from principles of honesty; his own advantage required him to do it. He cannot, however, be assumed to have in addition [as in the third case] an immediate inclination toward his buyers, causing him, as it were, out of love to give no one as far as price is concerned any advantage over another. Hence the action was done neither from duty nor from immediate inclination, but merely for a selfish purpose.

* [The ensuing example provides an illustration of the second case.]

The second proposition* is this: An action done 400
from duty has its moral worth, not in the purpose that is to be attained by it, but in the maxim according to which the action is determined. The moral worth depends, therefore, not on the realization of the object of the action, but merely on the principle of volition according to which, without regard to any objects of the faculty of desire, the action has been done. From what has gone before it is clear that the purposes which we may have in our actions, as well as their effects regarded as ends and incentives of the will, cannot give to actions any unconditioned and moral worth. Where, then, can this worth lie if it is not to be found in the will's relation to the expected effect? Nowhere but in the principle of the will, with no regard to the ends that can be brought about through such action. For the will stands, as it were, at a crossroads between its a priori principle, which is formal, and its a posteriori incentive, which is material; and since it must be determined by something, it must be determined by the formal principle of volition, if the action is done from duty—and in that case every material principle is taken away from it.

The third proposition, which follows from the other two, can be expressed thus: Duty is the necessity of an action done out of respect for the law. I can indeed have an inclination for an object as the effect of my proposed action; but I can never have respect for such an object, just because it is merely an effect and is not an activity of the will. Similarly, I can have no respect for inclination as such, whether my own or that of another. I can at most, if my own inclination, approve it; and, if that of another, even love it, i.e., consider it to be favorable to my own advantage. An object of respect can only be what is connected with my will solely as ground and never as effect—something that does not serve my inclination but, rather, outweighs it, or at least excludes it from consideration when some choice is made—in other words, only the law itself can be an object of respect and hence can be a command. Now an action done from duty must altogether exclude

* [The first proposition of morality says that an action must be done from duty in order to have any moral worth. It is implicit in the preceding examples but was never explicitly stated.]

the influence of inclination and therewith every object of the will. Hence there is nothing left which can determine the will except objectively the law and subjectively pure respect for this practical law, i.e., the will can be subjectively determined by the maxim[1] that I should follow such a law even if all
401 my inclinations are thereby thwarted.

Thus the moral worth of an action does not lie in the effect expected from it nor in any principle of action that needs to borrow its motive from this expected effect. For all these effects (agreeableness of one's condition and even the furtherance of other people's happiness) could have been brought about also through other causes and would not have required the will of a rational being, in which the highest and unconditioned good can alone be found. Therefore, the pre-eminent good which is called moral can consist in nothing but the representation of the law in itself, and such a representation can admittedly be found only in a rational being insofar as this representation, and not some expected effect, is the determining ground of the will. This good is already present in the person who acts according to this representation, and such good need not be awaited merely from the effect.[2]

402 But what sort of law can that be the thought of which must determine the will without reference to any expected effect, so that the will can be called absolutely good without qualification? Since I have deprived the will of every impulse that might arise for it from obeying any particular law, there is nothing left to serve the will as principle except the universal conformity of its actions to law as such, i.e., I should never act except in such a way that I can also will that my maxim should become a universal law.* Here mere conformity to law as such (without having as its basis any law determining particular actions) serves the will as principle and must so serve it if duty is not to be a vain delusion and a chimerical concept. The ordinary reason of mankind in its practical judgments agrees completely with this, and always has in view the aforementioned principle.

For example, take this question. When I am in distress, may I make a promise with the intention of not keeping it? I readily distinguish here the two meanings which the question may have; whether making a false promise conforms with prudence or with duty. Doubtless the former can often be the case. Indeed I clearly see that escape from some present difficulty by means of such a promise is not enough. In addition I must carefully consider whether from this lie there may later arise far greater inconvenience for me than from what I now try to escape. Furthermore, the consequences of my false promise are not easy to forsee, even with all my supposed cunning; loss of confidence in me might prove to be far more disadvantageous than the misfortune which I now try to avoid. The more prudent way might be to act according to a universal maxim and to make it a habit not to promise anything without intending to keep it. But that such a maxim is, nevertheless, always based on nothing but a fear of consequences becomes clear to me at once. To be truthful from duty is, however, quite different from being truthful from fear of disadvantageous consequences; in the first case the concept of the action itself contains a law for me, while in the second I must first look around elsewhere to see what are the results for me that might be connected with the
action. For to deviate from the principle of duty is 403
quite certainly bad; but to abandon my maxim of prudence can often be very advantageous for me, though to abide by it is certainly safer. The most direct and infallible way, however, to answer the question as to whether a lying promise accords with duty is to ask myself whether I would really be content if my maxim (of extricating myself from difficulty by means of a false promise) were to hold as a universal law for myself as well as for others, and could I really say to myself that everyone may promise falsely when he finds himself in a difficulty from which he can find no other way to extricate himself. Then I immediately become aware that I can indeed will the lie but can not at all will a universal law to lie. For by such a law there would really be no promises at all, since in vain would my willing future actions be professed to other people who would not believe what I professed, or if they over-hastily did believe, then they would pay me back in like coin.

---

* [This is the first time in the *Grounding* that the categorical imperative is stated.]

Therefore, my maxim would necessarily destroy itself just as soon as it was made a universal law.*

Therefore, I need no far-reaching acuteness to discern what I have to do in order that my will may be morally good. Inexperienced in the course of the world and incapable of being prepared for all its contingencies, I only ask myself whether I can also will that my maxim should become a universal law. If not, then the maxim must be rejected, not because of any disadvantage accruing to me or even to others, but because it cannot be fitting as a principle in a possible legislation of universal law, and reason exacts from me immediate respect for such legislation. Indeed I have as yet no insight into the grounds of such respect (which the philosopher may investigate). But I at least understand that respect is an estimation of a worth that far outweighs any worth of what is recommended by inclination, and that the necessity of acting from pure respect for the practical law is what constitutes duty, to which every other motive must give way because duty is the condition of a will good in itself, whose worth is above all else. . . .

We shall now enumerate some duties, following the usual division of them into duties to ourselves and to others and into perfect and imperfect duties.[3]

1. A man reduced to despair by a series of mis-
422 fortunes feels sick of life but is still so far in possession of his reason that he can ask himself whether taking his own life would not be contrary to his duty to himself.† Now he asks whether the maxim of his action could become a universal law of nature. But his maxim is this: from self-love I make as my principle to shorten my life when its continued duration threatens more evil than it promises satisfaction. There only remains the question as to whether this principle of self-love can become a universal law of nature. One sees at once a contradiction in a system of nature whose law would destroy life by means of the very same feeling that acts so as to stimulate the furtherance of life, and hence there could be no existence as a system of nature. Therefore, such a maxim cannot possibly hold as a universal law of nature and is, consequently, wholly opposed to the supreme principle of all duty.

2. Another man in need finds himself forced to borrow money. He knows well that he won't be able to repay it, but he sees also that he will not get any loan unless he firmly promises to repay it within a fixed time. He wants to make such a promise, but he still has conscience enough to ask himself whether it is not permissible and is contrary to duty to get out of difficulty in this way. Suppose, however, that he decides to do so. The maxim of his action would then be expressed as follows: when I believe myself to be in need of money, I will borrow money and promise to pay it back, although I know that I can never do so. Now this principle of self-love or personal advantage may perhaps be quite compatible with one's entire future welfare, but the question is now whether it is right.* I then transform the requirement of self-love into a universal law and put the question thus: how would things stand if my maxim were to become a universal law? He then sees at once that such a maxim could never hold as a universal law of nature and be consistent with itself, but must necessarily be self-contradictory. For the universality of a law which says that anyone believing himself to be in difficulty could promise whatever he pleases with the intention of not keeping it would make promising itself and the end to be attained thereby quite impossible, inasmuch as no one would believe what was promised him but would merely laugh at all such utterances as being vain pretenses.

3. A third finds in himself a talent whose cultivation could make him a man useful in many respects.
But he finds himself in comfortable circumstances 423
and prefers to indulge in pleasure rather than to bother himself about broadening and improving

* [This means that when you tell a lie, you merely take exception to the general rule that says everyone should always tell the truth and believe that what you are saying is true. When you lie, you do not thereby will that everyone else lie and not believe that what you are saying is true, because in such a case your lie would never work to get you what you want.]

† [Not committing suicide is an example of a perfect duty to oneself.]

* [Keeping promises is an example of a perfect duty to others.]

his fortunate natural aptitudes. But he asks himself further whether his maxim of neglecting his natural gifts, besides agreeing of itself with his propensity to indulgence, might agree also with what is called duty.* He then sees that a system of nature could indeed always subsist according to such a universal law, even though every man (like South Sea Islanders) should let his talents rust and resolve to devote his life entirely to idleness, indulgence, propagation, and, in a word, to enjoyment. But he cannot possibly will that this should become a universal law of nature or be implanted in us as such a law by a natural instinct. For as a rational being he necessarily wills that all his faculties should be developed, inasmuch as they are given him for all sorts of possible purposes.

4. A fourth man finds things going well for himself but sees others (whom he could help) struggling with great hardships; and he thinks: what does it matter to me? Let everybody be as happy as Heaven wills or as he can make himself; I shall take nothing from him nor even envy him; but I have no desire to contribute anything to his well-being or to his assistance when in need. If such a way of thinking were to become a universal law of nature, the human race admittedly could very well subsist and doubtless could subsist even better than when everyone prates about sympathy and benevolence and even on occasion exerts himself to practice them but, on the other hand, also cheats when he can, betrays the rights of man, or otherwise violates them. But even though it is possible that a universal law of nature could subsist in accordance with that maxim, still it is impossible to will that such a principle should hold everywhere as a law of nature.† For a will which resolved in this way would contradict itself, inasmuch as cases might often arise in which one would have need of the love and sympathy of others and in which he would deprive himself, by such a law of nature springing from his own will, of all hope of the aid he wants for himself.

These are some of the many actual duties, or at 424
least what are taken to be such, whose derivation from the single principle cited above is clear. We must be able to will that a maxim of our action become a universal law; this is the canon for morally estimating any of our actions. Some actions are so constituted that their maxims cannot without contradiction even be thought as a universal law of nature, much less be willed as what should become one. In the case of others this internal impossibility is indeed not found, but there is still no possibility of willing that their maxim should be raised to the universality of a law of nature, because such a will would contradict itself. There is no difficulty in seeing that the former kind of action conflicts with strict or narrow [perfect] (irremissible) duty, while the second kind conflicts only with broad [imperfect] (meritorious) duty. By means of these examples there has thus been fully set forth how all duties depend as regards the kind of obligation (not the object of their action) upon the one principle.

If we now attend to ourselves in any transgression of a duty, we find that we actually do not will that our maxim should become a universal law—because this is impossible for us—but rather that the opposite of this maxim should remain a law universally.* We only take the liberty of making an exception to the law for ourselves (or just for this one time) to the advantage of our inclination. Consequently, if we weighed up everything from one and the same standpoint, namely, that of reason, we would find a contradiction in our own will, viz., that a certain principle be objectively necessary as a universal law and yet subjectively not hold universally but should admit of exceptions. But since we at one moment regard our action from the standpoint of a will wholly in accord with reason and then at another moment regard the very same action from the standpoint of a will affected by inclination, there is really no

* [Cultivating one's talents is an example of an imperfect duty to oneself.]

† [Benefiting others is an example of an imperfect duty to others.]

* [This is to say, for example, that when you tell a lie, you do so on the condition that others are truthful and believe that what you are saying is true, because otherwise your lie will never work to get you what you want. When you tell a lie, you simply take exception to the general rule that says everyone should always tell the truth.]

contradiction here. Rather, there is an opposition (*antagonismus*) of inclination to the precept of reason, whereby the universality (*universalitas*) of the principle is changed into a mere generality (*generalitas*) so that the practical principle of reason may meet the maxim halfway. Although this procedure cannot be justified in our own impartial judgment, yet it does show that we actually acknowledge the validity of the categorical imperative and (with all respect for it) merely allow ourselves a few exceptions which, as they seem to us, are unimportant and forced upon us.

425 We have thus at least shown that if duty is a concept which is to have significance and real legislative authority for our actions, then such duty can be expressed only in categorical imperatives but not at all in hypothetical ones. We have also—and this is already a great deal—exhibited clearly and definitely for every application what is the content of the categorical imperative, which must contain the principle of all duty (if there is such a thing at all). But we have not yet advanced far enough to prove a priori that there actually is an imperative of this kind, that there is a practical law which of itself commands absolutely and without any incentives, and that following this law is duty.

NOTES

1. [A maxim is the subjective principle of volition. The objective principle (i.e., one which would serve all rational beings also subjectively as a practical principle if reason had full control over the faculty of desire) is the practical law.]
2. There might be brought against me here an objection that I take refuge behind the word "respect" in an obscure feeling, instead of giving a clear answer to the question by means of a concept of reason. But even though respect is a feeling, it is not one received through any outside influence but is, rather, one that is self-produced by means of a rational concept; hence it is specifically different from all feelings of the first kind, which can all be reduced to inclination or fear. What I recognize immediately as a law for me, I recognize with respect; this means merely the consciousness of the subordination of my will to a law without the mediation of other influences upon my sense. The immediate determination of the will by the law, and the consciousness thereof, is called respect, which is hence regarded as the effect of the law upon the subject and not as the cause of the law. Respect is properly the representation of a worth that thwarts my self-love. Hence respect is something that is regarded as an object of neither inclination nor fear, although it has at the same time something analogous to both. The object of respect is, therefore, nothing but the law—indeed that very law which we impose on ourselves and yet recognize as necessary in itself. As law, we are subject to it without consulting self-love; as imposed on us by ourselves, it is a consequence of our will. In the former aspect, it is analogous to fear; in the latter, to inclination. All respect for a person is properly only respect for the law (of honesty, etc.) of which the person provides an example. Since we regard the development of our talents as a duty, we think of a man of talent as being also a kind of example of the law (the law of becoming like him by practice), and that is what constitutes our respect for him. All so-called moral interest consists solely in respect for the law.
3. There should be noted here that I reserve the division of duties for a future *Metaphysics of Morals* [in Part II of the *Metaphysics of Morals*, entitled *The Metaphysical Principles of Virtue*, Ak. 417–474]. The division presented here stands as merely an arbitrary one (in order to arrange my examples). For the rest, I understand here by a perfect duty one which permits no exception in the interest of inclination. Accordingly, I have perfect duties which are external [to others], while other ones are internal [to oneself]. This classification runs contrary to the accepted usage of the schools, but I do not intend to justify it here, since there is no difference for my purpose whether this classification is accepted or not.

A Simplified Account of Kant's Ethics

ONORA O'NEILL

Onora O'Neill (1941–) is a British philosopher and political figure who studied under John Rawls (see "Political Philosophy"). Her best-known writings have been in the areas of political philosophy, ethics, and international justice; she is also a scholar of Kant.

The brief selection that appears here is excerpted from a much longer essay entitled "The Moral Perplexities of Famine Relief" that appeared in a 1980 anthology entitled *Matters of Life and Death*. In the selection, as the title promises, O'Neill presents a simplified account of Kant's ethics.

Kant's moral theory has acquired the reputation of being forbiddingly difficult to understand and, once understood, excessively demanding in its requirements. I don't believe that this reputation has been wholly earned, and I am going to try to undermine it. . . .

The main method by which I propose to avoid some of the difficulties of Kant's moral theory is by explaining only one part of the theory. This does not seem to me to be an irresponsible approach in this case. One of the things that makes Kant's moral theory hard to understand is that he gives a number of different versions of the principle that he calls the Supreme Principle of Morality, and these different versions don't look at all like one another. They also don't look at all like the utilitarians' Greatest Happiness Principle.* But the Kantian principle is supposed to play a similar role in arguments about what to do.

Kant calls his Supreme Principle the *Categorical Imperative;* its various versions also have sonorous names. One is called the Formula of Universal Law; another is the Formula of the Kingdom of Ends. The one on which I shall concentrate is known as the *Formula of the End in Itself.* To understand why Kant thinks that these picturesquely named principles are equivalent to one another takes quite a lot of close and detailed analysis of Kant's philosophy. I shall avoid this and concentrate on showing the implications of this version of the Categorical Imperative.

THE FORMULA OF THE END IN ITSELF

Kant states the Formula of the End in Itself as follows:

> Act in such a way that you always treat humanity, whether in your own person or in the person of any other, never simply as a means but always at the same time as an end.

To understand this we need to know what it is to treat a person as a means or as an end. According to Kant, each of our acts reflects one or more *maxims*. The maxim of the act is the principle on which one sees oneself as acting. A maxim expresses a person's policy, or if he or she has no settled policy, the principle underlying the particular intention or decision on which he or she acts. Thus, a person who decides "This year I'll give 10 percent of my income to famine relief" has as a maxim the principle of tithing his or her income for famine relief. In practice, the

* John Stuart Mill's (1808–73) Greatest Happiness Principle holds that "actions are right in proportion as they tend to promote happiness, wrong as they tend to promote the reverse of happiness." The Principle is articulated and discussed in the selection from Mill that appears above.

Reprinted from *Matters of Life and Death,* ed. Tom Regan (Philadelphia: Temple University Press, 1980). Reprinted by permission of The McGraw-Hill Companies.

difference between intentions and maxims is of little importance, for given any intention, we can formulate the corresponding maxim by deleting references to particular times, places, and persons. In what follows I shall take the terms "maxim" and "intention" as equivalent.

Whenever we act intentionally, we have at least one maxim and can, if we reflect, state what it is. (There is of course room for self-deception here—"I'm only keeping the wolf from the door" we may claim as we wolf down enough to keep ourselves overweight, or, more to the point, enough to feed someone else who hasn't enough food.)

When we want to work out whether an act we propose to do is right or wrong, according to Kant, we should look at our maxims and not at how much misery or happiness the act is likely to produce, and whether it does better at increasing happiness than other available acts. We just have to check that the act we have in mind will not use anyone as a mere means, and, if possible, that it will treat other persons as ends in themselves.

USING PERSONS AS MERE MEANS

To use someone as a *mere means* is to involve them in a scheme of action *to which they could not in principle consent*. Kant does not say that there is anything wrong about using someone as a means. Evidently we have to do so in any cooperative scheme of action. If I cash a check I use the teller as a means, without whom I could not lay my hands on the cash; the teller in turn uses me as a means to earn his or her living. But in this case, each party consents to her or his part in the transaction. Kant would say that though they use one another as means, they do not use one another as *mere* means. Each person assumes that the other has maxims of his or her own and is not just a thing or a prop to be manipulated.

But there are other situations where one person uses another in a way to which the other could not in principle consent. For example, one person may make a promise to another with every intention of breaking it. If the promise is accepted, then the person to whom it was given must be ignorant of what the promisor's intention (maxim) really is. If one knew that the promisor did not intend to do what he or she was promising, one would, after all, not accept or rely on the promise. It would be as though there had been no promise made. Successful false promising depends on deceiving the person to whom the promise is made about what one's real maxim is. And since the person who is deceived doesn't know that real maxim, he or she can't in principle consent to his or her part in the proposed scheme of action. The person who is deceived is, as it were, a prop or a tool—a mere means—in the false promisor's scheme. A person who promises falsely treats the acceptor of the promise as a prop or a thing and not as a person. In Kant's view, it is this that makes false promising wrong.

One standard way of using others as mere means is by deceiving them. By getting someone involved in a business scheme or a criminal activity on false pretenses, or by giving a misleading account of what one is about, or by making a false promise or a fraudulent contract, one involves another in something to which he or she in principle cannot consent, since the scheme requires that he or she doesn't know what is going on. Another standard way of using others as mere means is by coercing them. If a rich or powerful person threatens a debtor with bankruptcy unless he or she joins in some scheme, then the creditor's intention is to coerce; and the debtor, if coerced, cannot consent to his or her part in the creditor's scheme. To make the example more specific: If a moneylender in an Indian village threatens not to renew a vital loan unless he is given the debtor's land, then he uses the debtor as a mere means. He coerces the debtor, who cannot truly consent to this "offer he can't refuse." (Of course the outward form of such transactions may look like ordinary commercial dealings, but we know very well that some offers and demands couched in that form are coercive.)

In Kant's view, acts that are done on maxims that require deception or coercion of others, and so cannot have the consent of those others (for consent precludes both deception and coercion), are wrong. When we act on such maxims, we treat others as mere means, as things rather than as ends in themselves. If we act on such maxims, our acts are not only wrong but unjust: such acts wrong the particular others who are deceived or coerced.

TREATING PERSONS AS ENDS IN THEMSELVES

Duties of justice are, in Kant's view (as in many others'), the most important of our duties. When we fail in these duties, we have used some other or others as mere means. But there are also cases where, though we do not use others as mere means, still we fail to use them as ends in themselves in the fullest possible way. To treat someone as an end in him or herself requires in the first place that one not use him or her as mere means, that one respect each as a rational person with his or her own maxims. But beyond that, one may also seek to foster others' plans and maxims by sharing some of their ends. To act beneficently is to seek others' happiness, therefore to intend to achieve some of the things that those others aim at with their maxims. If I want to make others happy, I will adopt maxims that not merely do not manipulate them but that foster some of their plans and activities. Beneficent acts try to achieve what others want. However, we cannot seek everything that others want; their wants are too numerous and diverse, and, of course, sometimes incompatible. It follows that beneficence has to be selective.

There is then quite a sharp distinction between the requirements of justice and of beneficence in Kantian ethics. Justice requires that we act on *no* maxims that use others as mere means. Beneficence requires that we act on *some* maxims that foster others' ends, though it is a matter for judgment and discretion which of their ends we foster. Some maxims no doubt ought not to be fostered because it would be unjust to do so. Kantians are not committed to working interminably through a list of happiness-producing and misery-reducing acts; but there are some acts whose obligatoriness utilitarians may need to debate as they try to compare total outcomes of different choices, to which Kantians are stringently bound. Kantians will claim that they have done nothing wrong if none of their acts is unjust, and that their duty is complete if in addition their life plans have in the circumstances been reasonably beneficent.

In making sure that they meet all the demands of justice, Kantians do not try to compare all available acts and see which has the best effects. They consider only the proposals for action that occur to them and check that these proposals use no other as mere means. If they do not, the act is permissible; if omitting the act would use another as mere means, the act is obligatory. Kant's theory has less scope than utilitarianism. Kantians do not claim to discover whether acts whose maxims they don't know fully are just. They may be reluctant to judge others' acts or policies that cannot be regarded as the maxim of any person or institution. They cannot rank acts in order of merit. Yet, the theory offers more precision than utilitarianism when data are scarce. One can usually tell whether one's act would use others as mere means, even when its impact on human happiness is thoroughly obscure.

◈ VIRTUE ETHICS ◈

Selections from the *Nicomachean Ethics*

ARISTOTLE

Aristotle (384–322 BCE)—along with his teacher Plato—was one of the two most important philosophers of antiquity and among the most important figures in the Western intellectual

From "Nicomachean Ethics" in *Oxford Translation of Aristotle* (1963), ed. W. D. Ross. Reprinted by permission of Oxford University Press.

tradition. It would be difficult to overstate the influence of his work on nearly every aspect of Western thought, including not only all of philosophy, but also biology, physics, political theory, logic, and rhetoric.

The selections presented here are brief excerpts from Aristotle's book-length *Nicomachean Ethics,* a ten-part treatise in which Aristotle provides an account of what is required for human flourishing. In the passages that follow, Aristotle sketches a theory of ethics and moral character that gives pride of place to the notion of virtue. (The name "Nicomachean"—a later title that Aristotle himself did not use in reference to the work—may refer to his son Nicomachus, who served as its editor.)

The text presented here was translated from the Ancient Greek by Sir David Ross (1877–1971) and updated by J. L. Ackrill and J. O. Urmson, all of Oxford University. Notes that appear in [brackets] are thanks to these editors; notes that do not are due to the editors of *Elements*. The numbers that appear in the margins of the text are called Bekker numbers; they provide the page numbers of the standard (Prussian Academy) edition of Aristotle's works, enabling readers who make use of different translations or editions to refer easily to a particular passage. (The name "Bekker" derives from that of the editor, August Immanuel Bekker (1785–1871), who prepared the canonical edition of Aristotle's works.)

BOOK I

CHAPTER 1

1094a Every art and every inquiry, and similarly every action and choice, is thought to aim at some good; and for this reason the good has rightly been declared to be that at which all things aim. But a certain difference is found among ends; some are activities, others are products apart from the activities that produce them. Where there are ends apart from the actions, it is the nature of the products to be better than the activities. Now, as there are many actions, arts, and sciences, their ends also are many; the end of the medical art is health, that of shipbuilding a vessel, that of strategy victory, that of economics wealth. But where such arts fall under a single capacity—as bridle-making and the other arts concerned with the equipment of horses fall under the art of riding, and this and every military action under strategy, in the same way other arts fall under yet others—in all of these the ends of the master arts are to be preferred to all the subordinate ends; for it is for the sake of the former that the latter are pursued. It makes no difference whether the activities themselves are the ends of the actions, or something else apart from the activities, as in the case of the sciences just mentioned.

CHAPTER 2

If, then, there is some end of the things we do, which we desire for its own sake (everything else being desired for the sake of this), and if we do not choose everything for the sake of something else (for at that rate the process would go on to infinity, so that our desire would be empty and vain), clearly this must be the good and the chief good. Will not the knowledge of it, then, have a great influence on life? Shall we not, like archers who have a mark to aim at, be more likely to hit upon what we should? If so, we must try, in outline at least, to determine what it is, and of which of the sciences or capacities it is the object. It would seem to belong to the most authoritative art and that which is most truly the master art. And politics appears to be of this nature; for it is this that ordains which of the sciences should be studied in a state, and which each class of citizens 1094b should learn and up to what point they should learn them; and we see even the most highly esteemed of capacities to fall under this, e.g. strategy, economics, rhetoric; now, since politics uses the rest of the sciences, and since, again, it legislates as to what we are to do and what we are to abstain from, the end of this science must include those of the others, so that this end must be the good for man. For even if the end is the same for a single man and for a state, that of the state seems at all events something greater and more complete both to attain and to preserve; for though it is worth while to attain the end merely for one man, it is finer and more godlike to attain it for a nation or for city-states. These, then, are the ends at which our inquiry, being concerned with politics, aims.

CHAPTER 3

Our discussion will be adequate if it has as much clearness as the subject-matter admits of; for precision is not to be sought for alike in all discussions, any more than in all the products of the crafts. Now fine and just actions, which political science investigates, exhibit much variety and fluctuation, so that they may be thought to exist only by convention, and not by nature. And goods also exhibit a similar fluctuation because they bring harm to many people; for before now men have been undone by reason of their wealth, and others by reason of their courage. We must be content, then, in speaking of such subjects and with such premisses to indicate the truth roughly and in outline, and in speaking about things which are only for the most part true and with premisses of the same kind to reach conclusions that are no better. In the same spirit, therefore, should each of our statements be *received*; for it is the mark of an educated man to look for precision in each class of things just so far as the nature of the subject admits: it is evidently equally foolish to accept probable reasoning from a mathematician and to demand from a rhetorician demonstrative proofs.

Now each man judges well the things he knows, and of these he is a good judge. And so the man who has been educated in a subject is a good judge of that subject, and the man who has received an all-round education is a good judge in general. Hence a young man is not a proper hearer of lectures on political science; for he is inexperienced in the actions that occur in life, but its discussions start from these and are about these; and, further, since he tends to follow his passions, his study will be vain and unprofitable, because the end aimed at is not knowledge but action. And it makes no difference whether he is young in years or youthful in character; the defect does not depend on time, but on his living and pursuing each successive object as passion directs. For to such persons, as to the incontinent, knowledge brings no profit; but to those who desire and act in accordance with a rational principle knowledge about such matters will be of great benefit.

These remarks about the student, the way in which our statements should be received, and the purpose of the inquiry, may be taken as our preface.

CHAPTER 4

Let us resume our inquiry and state, in view of the fact that all knowledge and choice aims at some good, what it is that we say political science aims at and what is the highest of all goods achievable by action. Verbally there is very general agreement; for both the general run of men and people of superior refinement say that it is happiness, and identify living well and faring well with being happy; but with regard to what happiness is they differ, and the many do not give the same account as the wise. For the former think it is some plain and obvious thing, like pleasure, wealth, or honour; they differ, however, from one another—and often even the same man identifies things, with health when he is ill, with wealth when he is poor; but, conscious of their ignorance, they admire those who proclaim some great thing that is above their comprehension. Now some thought that apart from these many goods there is another which is good in itself and causes the goodness of all these as well. To examine all the opinions that have been held would no doubt be somewhat fruitless: it is enough to examine those that are most prevalent or that seem to have some reason in their favour.

Let us not fail to notice, however, that there is a difference between arguments from and those to the first principles. For Plato,* too, was right in raising this question and asking, as he used to do, "are we on the way from or to the first principles?" There is a difference, as there is in a racecourse between the course from the judges to the turning-point and

* Plato (c. 429–347 BCE) was, along with his student Aristotle, one of the two most important philosophers of antiquity; several selections from his works appear in this volume.

the way back. For, while we must begin with what is familiar, things are so in two ways—some to us, some without qualification. Presumably, then, *we* must begin with things familiar to *us*. Hence anyone who is to listen intelligently to lectures about what is noble and just and, generally, about the subjects of political science must have been brought up in good habits. For the facts are the starting-point, and if they are sufficiently plain to him, he will not need the reason as well; and the man who has been well brought up has or can easily get starting-points. And as for him who neither has nor can get them, let him hear the words of Hesiod:*

Far best is he who knows all things himself;
Good, he that hearkens when men counsel right;
But he who neither knows, nor lays to heart
Another's wisdom, is a useless wight.

CHAPTER 5

Let us, however, resume our discussion from the point at which we digressed. To judge from the lives that men lead, most men, and men of the most vulgar type, seem (not without some reason) to identify the good, or happiness, with pleasure; which is the reason why they love the life of enjoyment. For there are, we may say, three prominent types of life—that just mentioned, the political, and thirdly the contemplative life. Now the mass of mankind are evidently quite slavish in their tastes, preferring a life suitable to beasts, but they get some reason for their view from the fact that many of those in high places share the tastes of Sardanapallus.† But people of superior refinement and of active disposition identify happiness with honour; for this is, roughly speaking, the end of the political life. But it seems too superficial to be what we are looking for, since it is thought to depend on those who bestow honour rather than on him who receives it, but the good we divine to be something of one's own and not easily taken from one. Further, men seem to pursue honour in order that they may be assured of their merit; at least it is by men of practical wisdom that they seek to be honoured, and among those who know them, and on the ground of their excellence; clearly, then, according to them, at any rate, excellence is better. And perhaps one might even suppose this to be, rather than honour, the end of the political life. But even this appears somewhat incomplete; for possession of excellence seems actually compatible with being asleep, or with lifelong inactivity, and, further, with the greatest sufferings and misfortunes; but a man 1096a who was living so no one would call happy, unless he were maintaining a thesis at all costs. But enough of this; for the subject has been sufficiently treated even in ordinary discussions. Third comes the contemplative life, which we shall consider later.

The life of money-making is one undertaken under compulsion, and wealth is evidently not the good we are seeking; for it is merely useful and for the sake of something else. And so one might rather take the aforenamed objects to be ends; for they are loved for themselves. But it is evident that not even these are ends—although many arguments have been thrown away in support of them. Let us then dismiss them. . . .

CHAPTER 7

Let us again return to the good we are seeking, and ask what it can be. It seems different in different actions and arts; it is different in medicine, in strategy, and in the other arts likewise. What then is the good of each? Surely that for whose sake everything else is done. In medicine this is health, in strategy victory, in architecture a house, in any other sphere something else, and in every action and choice the end; for it is for the sake of this that all men do whatever else they do. Therefore, if there is an end for all that we do, this will be the good achievable by action, and if there are more than one, these will be the goods achievable by action.

So the argument has by a different course reached the same point; but we must try to state this even more clearly. Since there are evidently more than one end, and we choose some of these (e.g. wealth, flutes, and in general instruments)

---

* Hesiod (c. 700 BCE) was an ancient Greek poet who lived around the time of Homer.

† Sardanapallus was the mythical last king of Assyria, who, according to the Greek historian Diodorus Siculus (90–30 BCE), "outdid all of his predecessors in luxury and sluggishness."

for the sake of something else, clearly not all ends are complete ends; but the chief good is evidently something complete. Therefore, if there is only one complete end, this will be what we are seeking, and if there are more than one, the most complete of these will be what we are seeking. Now we call that which is in itself worthy of pursuit more complete than that which is worthy of pursuit for the sake of something else, and that which is never desirable for the sake of something else more complete than the things that are desirable both in themselves and for the sake of that other thing, and therefore we call complete without qualification that which is always desirable in itself and never for the sake of something else.

Now such a thing happiness, above all else, is held to be; for this we choose always for itself and never for the sake of something else, but honour, pleasure, reason, and every excellence we choose indeed for themselves (for if nothing resulted from them we should still choose each of them), but we choose them also for the sake of happiness, judging that through them we shall be happy. Happiness, on the other hand, no one chooses for the sake of these, nor, in general, for anything other than itself.

From the point of view of self-sufficiency the same result seems to follow; for the complete good is thought to be self-sufficient. Now by self-sufficient we do not mean that which is sufficient for a man by himself, for one who lives a solitary life, but also for parents, children, wife, and in general for his friends and fellow citizens, since man is sociable by nature. But some limit must be set to this; for if we extend our requirement to ancestors and descendants and friends' friends we are in for an infinite series. Let us examine this question, however, on another occasion; the self-sufficient we now define as that which when isolated makes life desirable and lacking in nothing; and such we think happiness to be; and further we think it most desirable of all things, without being counted as one good thing among others—if it were so counted it would clearly be made more desirable by the addition of even the least of goods; for that which is added becomes an excess of goods, and of goods the greater is always more desirable. Happiness, then, is something complete and self-sufficient, and is the end of action.

Presumably, however, to say that happiness is the chief good seems a platitude, and a clearer account of what it is is still desired. This might perhaps be given, if we could first ascertain the function of man. For just as for a flute-player, a sculptor, or any artist, and, in general, for all things that have a function or activity, the good and the "well" is thought to reside in the function, so would it seem to be for man, if he has a function. Have the carpenter, then, and the tanner certain functions or activities, and has man none? Is he naturally functionless? Or as eye, hand, foot, and in general each of the parts evidently has a function, may one lay it down that man similarly has a function apart from all these? What then can this be? Life seems to be common even to plants, but we are seeking what is peculiar to man. Let us exclude, therefore, the life of nutrition and growth. Next there would be a life of perception, but *it* also seems to be common even to the horse, the ox, and every animal. There remains, then, an active life of the element that has a rational principle (of this, one part has such a principle in the sense of being obedient to one, the other in the sense of possessing one and exercising thought); and as this too can be taken in two ways, we must state that life in the sense of activity is what we mean; for this seems to be the more proper sense of the term. Now if the function of man is an activity of soul in accordance with, or not without, rational principle, and if we say a so-and-so and a good so-and-so have a function which is the same in kind, e.g., a lyre-player and a good lyre-player, and so without qualification in all cases, eminence in respect of excellence being added to the function (for the function of a lyre-player is to play the lyre, and that of a good lyre-player is to do so well): if this is the case, [and we state the function of man to be a certain kind of life, and this to be an activity or actions of the soul implying a rational principle, and the function of a good man to be the good and noble performance of these, and if any action is well performed when it is performed in accordance with the appropriate excellence: if this is the case,][1] human good turns out to be activity of soul in conformity with excellence, and if there are more than one excellence, in conformity with the best and most complete.

But we must add "in a complete life." For one swallow does not make a summer, nor does one day;

and so too one day, or a short time, does not make a man blessed and happy.

Let this serve as an outline of the good; for we must presumably first sketch it roughly, and then later fill in the details. But it would seem that any one is capable of carrying on and articulating what has once been well outlined, and that time is a good discoverer or partner in such a work; to which facts the advances of the arts are due; for anyone can add what is lacking. And we must also remember what has been said before, and not look for precision in all things alike, but in each class of things such as accords with the subject-matter, and so much as is appropriate to the inquiry. For a carpenter and a geometer look for right angles in different ways; the former does so in so far as the right angle is useful for his work, while the latter inquires what it is or what sort of thing it is; for he is a spectator of the truth. We must act in the same way, then, in all other matters as well, that our main task may not
1098b be subordinated to minor questions. Nor must we demand the cause in all matters alike; it is enough in some cases that the *fact* be well established, as in the case of the first principles; the fact is a primary thing or first principle. Now of first principles we see some by induction, some by perception, some by a certain habituation, and others too in other ways. But each set of principles we must try to investigate in the natural way, and we must take pains to determine them correctly, since they have a great influence on what follows. For the beginning is thought to be more than half of the whole, and many of the questions we ask are cleared up by it. . . .

CHAPTER 13

1102a Since happiness is an activity of soul in accordance with complete excellence, we must consider the nature of excellence; for perhaps we shall thus see better the nature of happiness. The true student of politics, too, is thought to have studied this above all things; for he wishes to make his fellow citizens good and obedient to the laws. As an example of this we have the lawgivers of the Cretans and the Spartans, and any others of the kind that there may have been. And if this inquiry belongs to political science, clearly the pursuit of it will be in accordance with our original plan. But clearly the excellence we must study is human excellence; for the good we were seeking was human good and the happiness human happiness. By human excellence we mean not that of the body but that of the soul; and happiness also we call an activity of soul. But if this is so, clearly the student of politics must know somehow the facts about soul, as the man who is to heal the eyes must know about the whole body also; and all the more since politics is more prized and better than medicine; but even among doctors the best educated spend much labour on acquiring knowledge of the body. The student of politics, then, must study the soul, and must study it with these objects in view, and do so just to the extent which is sufficient for the questions we are discussing; for further precision is perhaps something more laborious than our purposes require.

Some things are said about it, adequately enough, even in the discussions outside our school, and we must use these; e.g., that one element in the soul is irrational and one has a rational principle. Whether these are separated as the parts of the body or of anything divisible are, or are distinct by definition but by nature inseparable, like convex and concave in the circumference of a circle, does not affect the present question.

Of the irrational element one division seems to be widely distributed, and vegetative in its nature, I mean that which causes nutrition and growth; for it is this kind of power of the soul that one must assign to all nurslings and to embryos, and this 1102b
same power to full-grown creatures; this is more reasonable than to assign some different power to them. Now the excellence of this seems to be common to all and not specifically human; for this part or faculty seems to function most in sleep, while goodness and badness are least manifest in sleep (whence comes the saying that the happy are not better off than the wretched for half their lives; and this happens naturally enough, since sleep is an inactivity of the soul in that respect in which it is called good or bad), unless perhaps to a small extent some of the movements actually penetrate, and in this respect the dreams of good men are better than those of ordinary people. Enough of this subject, however; let us leave the nutritive faculty

alone, since it has by its nature no share in human excellence.

There seems to be also another irrational element in the soul—one which in a sense, however, shares in a rational principle. For we praise the reason of the continent man and of the incontinent, and the part of their soul that has reason, since it urges them aright and towards the best objects; but there is found in them also another natural element beside reason, which fights against and resists it. For exactly as paralysed limbs when we choose to move them to the right turn on the contrary to the left, so is it with the soul; the impulses of incontinent people move in contrary directions. But while in the body we see that which moves astray, in the soul we do not. No doubt, however, we must none the less suppose that in the soul too there is something beside reason, resisting and opposing it. In what sense it is distinct from the other elements does not concern us. Now even this seems to have a share in reason, as we said; at any rate in the continent man it obeys reason—and presumably in the temperate and brave man it is still more obedient; for in them it speaks, on all matters with the same voice as reason.

Therefore the irrational element also appears to be twofold. For the vegetative element in no way shares in reason, but the appetitive and in general the desiring element in a sense shares in it, in so far as it listens to and obeys it; this is the sense in which we speak of paying heed to one's father or one's friends, not that in which we speak of "the rational" in mathematics.* That the irrational element is in some sense persuaded by reason is indicated also by the giving of advice and by all reproof and exhortation. And if this element also must be said to have reason, that which
1103a has reason also will be twofold, one subdivision having it in the strict sense and in itself, and the other having a tendency to obey as one does one's father.

Excellence too is distinguished into kinds in accordance with this difference; for we say that some excellences are intellectual and others moral,† philosophic wisdom and understanding and practical wisdom being intellectual, liberality and temperance moral. For in speaking about a man's character we do not say that he is wise or has understanding but that he is good-tempered or temperate; yet we praise the wise man also with respect to his state; and of states we call those which merit praise excellences.

* [The Greek term means (i) "possess reason," (ii) "pay heed to," "obey," (iii) "be rational" (in the mathematical sense).]

† ["Moral," here and hereafter, is used in the archaic sense of "pertaining to character or *mores*."]

BOOK II

CHAPTER I

Excellence, then, being of two kinds, intellectual and moral, intellectual excellence in the main owes both its birth and its growth to teaching (for which reason it requires experience and time), while moral excellence comes about as a result of habit, whence also its name is one that is formed by a slight variation from the word for "habit."* From this it is also plain that none of the moral excellences arises in us by nature; for nothing that exists by nature can form a habit contrary to its nature. For instance the stone which by nature moves downwards cannot be habituated to move upwards, not even if one tries to train it by throwing it up ten thousand times; nor can fire be habituated to move downwards, nor can anything else that by nature behaves in one way be trained to behave in another. Neither by nature, then, nor contrary to nature do excellences arise in us; rather we are adapted by nature to receive them, and are made perfect by habit.

Again, of all the things that come to us by nature we first acquire the potentiality and later exhibit the activity (this is plain in the case of the senses; for it was not by often seeing or often hearing that we got these senses, but on the contrary we had them before we used them, and did not come to have them by using them); but excellences we get by first exercising them, as also happens in the case of the arts as well. For the things we have to learn before we can do, we learn by doing, e.g. men become builders by building and lyre-players by playing the lyre; so
too we become just by doing just acts, temperate by 1103b
doing temperate acts, brave by doing brave acts.

* [The Greek words for character and habit are almost identical.]

This is confirmed by what happens in states; for legislators make the citizens good by forming habits in them, and this is the wish of every legislator; and those who do not effect it miss their mark, and it is in this that a good constitution differs from a bad one.

Again, it is from the same causes and by the same means that every excellence is both produced and destroyed, and similarly every art; for it is from playing the lyre that both good and bad lyre-players are produced. And the corresponding statement is true of builders and of all the rest; men will be good or bad builders as a result of building well or badly. For if this were not so, there would have been no need of a teacher, but all men would have been born good or bad at their craft. This, then, is the case with the excellences also; by doing the acts that we do in our transactions with other men we become just or unjust, and by doing the acts that we do in presence of danger, and being habituated to feel fear or confidence, we become brave or cowardly. The same is true of appetites and feelings of anger; some men become temperate and good-tempered, others self-indulgent and irascible, by behaving in one way or the other in the appropriate circumstances. Thus, in one word, states arise out of like activities. This is why the activities we exhibit must be of a certain kind; it is because the states correspond to the differences between these. It makes no small difference, then, whether we form habits of one kind or of another from our very youth; it makes a very great difference, or rather *all* the difference.

CHAPTER 2

Since, then, the present inquiry does not aim at theoretical knowledge like the others (for we are inquiring not in order to know what excellence is, but in order to become good, since otherwise our inquiry would have been of no use), we must examine the nature of actions, namely how we ought to do them; for these determine also the nature of the states that are produced, as we have said. Now, that we must act according to right reason is a common principle and must be assumed—it will be discussed later, both what it is, and how it is related to the other excellences. But this must be agreed upon beforehand, that the whole account of matters of 1104a
conduct must be given in outline and not precisely, as we said at the very beginning that the accounts we demand must be in accordance with the subject-matter; matters concerned with conduct and questions of what is good for us have no fixity, any more than matters of health. The general account being of this nature, the account of particular cases is yet more lacking in exactness; for they do not fall under any art or set of precepts, but the agents themselves must in each case consider what is appropriate to the occasion, as happens also in the art of medicine or of navigation.

But though our present account is of this nature we must give what help we can. First, then, let us consider this, that it is the nature of such things to be destroyed by defect and excess, as we see in the case of strength and of health (for to gain light on things imperceptible we must use the evidence of sensible things); both excessive and defective exercise destroy the strength, and similarly drink or food which is above or below a certain amount destroys the health, while that which is proportionate both produces and increases and preserves it. So too is it, then, in the case of temperance and courage and the other excellences. For the man who flies from and fears everything and does not stand his ground against anything becomes a coward, and the man who fears nothing at all but goes to meet every danger becomes rash; and similarly the man who indulges in every pleasure and abstains from none becomes self-indulgent, while the man who shuns every pleasure, as boors do, becomes in a way insensible; temperance and courage, then, are destroyed by excess and defect, and preserved by the mean.

But not only are the sources and causes of their origination and growth the same as those of their destruction, but also the sphere of their activity will be the same; for this is also true of the things which are more evident to sense, e.g. of strength; it is produced by taking much food and undergoing much exertion, and it is the strong man that will be most able to do these things. So too is it with the excellences; by abstaining from pleasures we become temperate, and it is when we have become so that we are most able to abstain from them; and similarly too in the case of courage; for by being habituated to despise 1104b things that are terrible and to stand our ground against them we become brave, and it is when we have become so that we shall be most able to stand our ground against them.

CHAPTER 3

We must take as a sign of states the pleasure or pain that supervenes on acts; for the man who abstains from bodily pleasures and delights in this very fact is temperate, while the man who is annoyed at it is self-indulgent, and he who stands his ground against things that are terrible and delights in this or at least is not pained is brave, while the man who is pained is a coward. For moral excellence is concerned with pleasures and pains; it is on account of pleasure that we do bad things, and on account of pain that we abstain from noble ones. Hence we ought to have been brought up in a particular way from our very youth, as Plato says, so as both to delight in and to be pained by the things that we ought; for this is the right education.

Again, if the excellences are concerned with actions and passions, and every passion and every action is accompanied by pleasure and pain, for this reason also excellence will be concerned with pleasures and pains. This is indicated also by the fact that punishment is inflicted by these means; for it is a kind of cure, and it is the nature of cures to be effected by contraries.

Again, as we said but lately, every state of soul has a nature relative to and concerned with the kind of things by which it tends to be made worse or better; but it is by reason of pleasures and pains that men become bad, by pursuing and avoiding these—either the pleasures and pains they ought not or when they ought not or as they ought not, or by going wrong in one of the other similar ways that reason can distinguish. Hence men even define the excellences as certain states of impassivity and rest; not well, however, because they speak absolutely, and do not say "as one ought" and "as one ought not" and "when one ought or ought not," and the other things that may be added. We assume, then, that this kind of excellence tends to do what is best with regard to pleasures and pains, and badness does the contrary.

The following facts also may show us that they are concerned with these same things. There being three objects of choice and three of avoidance, the noble, the advantageous, the pleasant, and their contraries, the base, the injurious, the painful, about all of these the good man tends to go right and the bad man to go wrong, and especially about pleasure; for this is common to the animals, and also it accompanies all objects of choice; for even the noble and the 1105a advantageous appear pleasant.

Again, it has grown up with us all from our infancy; this is why it is difficult to rub off this passion, ingrained as it is in our life. And we measure even our actions, some of us more and others less, by pleasure and pain. For this reason, then, our whole inquiry must be about these; for to feel delight and pain rightly or wrongly has no small effect on our actions.

Again, it is harder to fight with pleasure than with anger, to use Heraclitus'* phrase, but both art and excellence are always concerned with what is harder; for even the good is better when it is harder. Therefore for this reason also the whole concern both of excellence and of political science is with pleasures and pains; for the man who uses these well will be good, he who uses them badly bad.

That excellence, then, is concerned with pleasures and pains, and that by the acts from which it arises it is both increased and, if they are done differently, destroyed, and that the acts from which it arose are those in which it actualizes itself—let this be taken as said.

CHAPTER 4

The question might be asked, what we mean by saying that we must become just by doing just acts, and temperate by doing temperate acts; for if men do just and temperate acts, they are already just and temperate, exactly as, if they do what is grammatical or musical they are proficient in grammar and music.

* Heraclitus of Ephesus (late sixth-century BCE) was an ancient Greek philosopher whose work had a strong influence on both Plato and Aristotle; his writings have survived in the form of aphorisms.

Or is this not true even of the arts? It is possible to do something grammatical either by chance or under the guidance of another. A man will be proficient in grammar, then, only when he has both done something grammatical and done it grammatically; and this means doing it in accordance with the grammatical knowledge in himself.

Again, the case of the arts and that of the excellences are not similar; for the products of the arts have their goodness in themselves, so that it is enough that they should have a certain character, but if the acts that are in accordance with the excellences have themselves a certain character it does not follow that they are done justly or temperately. The agent also must be in a certain condition when he does them; in the first place he must have knowledge, secondly he must choose the acts, and choose them for their own sakes, and thirdly his action must proceed from a firm and unchangeable character. These are not reckoned
1105b in as conditions of the possession of the arts, except the bare knowledge; but as a condition of the possession of the excellences, knowledge has little or no weight, while the other conditions count not for a little but for everything, i.e., the very conditions which result from often doing just and temperate acts.

Actions, then, are called just and temperate when they are such as the just or the temperate man would do; but it is not the man who does these that is just and temperate, but the man who also does them *as* just and temperate men do them. It is well said, then, that it is by doing just acts that the just man is produced, and by doing temperate acts the temperate man; without doing these no one would have even a prospect of becoming good.

But most people do not do these, but take refuge in theory and think they are being philosophers and will become good in this way, behaving somewhat like patients who listen attentively to their doctors, but do none of the things they are ordered to do. As the latter will not be made well in body by such a course of treatment, the former will not be made well in soul by such a course of philosophy.

CHAPTER 5

Next we must consider what excellence is. Since things that are found in the soul are of three kinds—passions, faculties, states—excellence must be one of these. By passions I mean appetite, anger, fear, confidence, envy, joy, love, hatred, longing, emulation, pity, and in general the feelings that are accompanied by pleasure or pain; by faculties the things in virtue of which we are said to be capable of feeling these, e.g., of becoming angry or being pained or feeling pity; by states the things in virtue of which we stand well or badly with reference to the passions, e.g. with reference to anger we stand badly if we feel it violently or too weakly, and well if we feel it moderately; and similarly with reference to the other passions.

Now neither the excellences nor the vices are *passions,* because we are not called good or bad on the ground of our passions, but are so called on the ground of our excellences and our vices, and because we are neither praised nor blamed for our passions (for the man who feels fear or anger is not praised, nor is the man who simply feels anger blamed, but the man who feels it in a certain way), but for our excellences and our vices we *are* praised or blamed. 1106a

Again, we feel anger and fear without choice, but the excellences are choices or involve choice. Further, in respect of the passions we are said to be moved, but in respect of the excellences and the vices we are said not to be moved but to be disposed in a particular way.

For these reasons also they are not *faculties*; for we are neither called good nor bad, nor praised nor blamed, for the simple capacity of feeling the passions; again, we have the faculties by nature, but we are not made good or bad by nature; we have spoken of this before.

If, then, the excellences are neither passions nor faculties, all that remains is that they should be *states*.

Thus we have stated what excellence is in respect of its genus.

CHAPTER 6

We must, however, not only describe it as a state, but also say what sort of state it is. We may remark, then, that every excellence both brings into good condition the thing of which it is the excellence and makes the work of that thing be done well; e.g., the excellence of the eye makes both the eye and its work good; for it is by the excellence of the eye that we see well. Similarly the excellence of the horse makes a horse both good in itself and good at running and at carrying its rider and at awaiting the attack of the enemy. Therefore, if this is true in every case, the excellence of man also will be the state which makes a man good and which makes him do his own work well.

How this is to happen we have stated already, but it will be made plain also by the following consideration of the nature of excellence. In everything that is continuous and divisible it is possible to take more, less, or an equal amount, and that either in terms of the thing itself or relatively to us; and the equal is an intermediate between excess and defect. By the intermediate in the object I mean that which is equidistant from each of the extremes, which is one and the same for all men; by the intermediate relatively to us that which is neither too much nor too little—and this is not one, nor the same for all. For instance, if ten is many and two is few, six is intermediate, taken in terms of the object; for it exceeds and is exceeded by an equal amount; this is intermediate according to arithmetical proportion. But the intermediate relatively to us is not to be taken so; if ten pounds are too much for a particular 1106b person to eat and two too little, it does not follow that the trainer will order six pounds; for this also is perhaps too much for the person who is to take it, or too little—too little for Milo,* too much for the beginner in athletic exercises. The same is true of running and wrestling. Thus a master of any art avoids excess and defect, but seeks the intermediate and chooses this—the intermediate not in the object but relatively to us.

If it is thus, then, that every art does its work well—by looking to the intermediate and judging its works by this standard (so that we often say of good works of art that it is not possible either to take away or to add anything, implying that excess and defect destroy the goodness of works of art, while the mean preserves it; and good artists, as we say, look to this in their work), and if, further, excellence is more exact and better than any art, as nature also is, then it must have the quality of aiming at the intermediate. I mean moral excellence; for it is this that is concerned with passions and actions, and in these there is excess, defect, and the intermediate. For instance, both fear and confidence and appetite and anger and pity and in general pleasure and pain may be felt both too much and too little, and in both cases not well; but to feel them at the right times, with reference to the right objects, towards the right people, with the right aim, and in the right way, is what is both intermediate and best, and this is characteristic of excellence. Similarly with regard to actions also there is excess, defect, and the intermediate. Now excellence is concerned with passions and actions, in which excess is a form of failure, and so is defect, while the intermediate is praised and is a form of success; and both these things are characteristics of excellence. Therefore excellence is a kind of mean, since it aims at what is intermediate.

Again, it is possible to fail in many ways (for evil belongs to the class of the unlimited, as the Pythagoreans* conjectured, and good to that of the limited), while to succeed is possible only in one way (for which reason one is easy and the other difficult—to miss the mark easy, to hit it difficult); for these reasons also, then, excess and defect are characteristic of vice, and the mean of excellence;

For men are good in but one way, but bad in many.

Excellence, then, is a state concerned with choice, lying in a mean relative to us, this being determined by reason and in the way in which the man of practical 1107a wisdom would determine it. Now it is a mean between two vices, that which depends on excess and that which depends on defect; and again it is a mean because the vices respectively fall short of or exceed what is right in both passions and actions, while excellence both finds and chooses that which is intermediate. Hence in respect of its substance and the account which states its essence it is a mean, with regard to what is best and right it is an extreme.

* Milo was a famous ancient Greek wrestler.

* Pythagoreans were an ancient Greek mystical sect, followers of the mathematician and philosopher Pythagoras (b. c. 570 BCE). Among Pythagoras' many contributions to Western mathematics was the discovery of the Pythagorean theorem.

But not every action nor every passion admits of a mean; for some have names that already imply badness, e.g., spite, shamelessness, envy, and in the case of actions adultery, theft, murder; for all of these and suchlike things imply by their names that they are themselves bad, and not the excesses or deficiencies of them. It is not possible, then, ever to be right with regard to them; one must always be wrong. Nor does goodness or badness with regard to such things depend on committing adultery with the right woman, at the right time, and in the right way, but simply to do any of them is to go wrong. It would be equally absurd, then, to expect that in unjust, cowardly, and self-indulgent action there should be a mean, an excess, and a deficiency; for at that rate there would be a mean of excess and of deficiency, an excess of excess, and a deficiency of deficiency. But as there is no excess and deficiency of temperance and courage because what is intermediate is in a sense an extreme, so too of the actions we have mentioned there is no mean nor any excess and deficiency, but however they are done they are wrong; for in general there is neither a mean of excess and deficiency, nor excess and deficiency of a mean.

CHAPTER 7

We must, however, not only make this general statement, but also apply it to the individual facts. For among statements about conduct those which are general apply more widely, but those which are particular are more true, since conduct has to do with individual cases, and our statements must harmonize with the facts in these cases. We may take these cases from the diagram. With regard to feelings of fear and confidence courage is the mean; of the people who exceed, he who exceeds in fearlessness has no name (many of the states have no name), while the man who exceeds in confidence is rash, and he who exceeds in fear and falls short in confidence is a coward. With regard to pleasures and pains—not all of them and not so much with regard to the pains—the mean is temperance, the excess self-indulgence. Persons deficient with regard to the pleasures are not often found; hence such persons also have received no name. But let us call them "insensible."

With regard to giving and taking of money the mean is liberality, the excess and the defect prodigality and meanness. They exceed and fall short in contrary ways to one another: the prodigal exceeds in spending and falls short in taking, while the mean man exceeds in taking and falls short in spending. (At present we are giving a mere outline or summary, and are satisfied with this; later these states will be more exactly determined.) With regard to money there are also other dispositions—a mean, magnificence (for the magnificent man differs from the liberal man; the former deals with large sums, the latter with small ones), an excess, tastelessness and vulgarity, and a deficiency, niggardliness; these differ from the states opposed to liberality, and the mode of their difference will be stated later.

With regard to honour and dishonour the mean is proper pride, the excess is known as a sort of empty vanity, and the deficiency is undue humility; and as we said liberality was related to magnificence, differing from it by dealing with small sums, so there is a state similarly related to proper pride, being concerned with small honours while that is concerned with great. For it is possible to desire small honours as one ought, and more than one ought, and less, and the man who exceeds in his desires is called ambitious, the man who falls short unambitious, while the intermediate person has no name. The dispositions also are nameless, except that that of the ambitious man is called ambition. Hence the people who are at the extremes lay claim to the middle place; and we ourselves sometimes call the intermediate person ambitious and sometimes unambitious, and sometimes praise the ambitious man and sometimes the unambitious. The reason of our doing this will be stated in what follows; but now let us speak of the remaining states according to the method which has been indicated.

With regard to anger also there is an excess, a deficiency, and a mean. Although they can scarcely be said to have names, yet since we call the intermediate person good-tempered let us call the mean good temper; of the persons at the extremes let the one who exceeds be called irascible, and his vice irascibility, and the man who falls short an inirascible sort of person, and the deficiency inirascibility.

There are also three other means, which have a certain likeness to one another, but differ from one another: for they are all concerned with intercourse in words and actions, but differ in that one is concerned with truth in this sphere, the other two with pleasantness; and of this one kind is exhibited in giving amusement, the other in all the circumstances of life. We must therefore speak of these too, that we may the better see that in all things the mean is praiseworthy, and the extremes neither praiseworthy nor right, but worthy of blame. Now most of these states also have no names, but we must try, as in the other cases, to invent names ourselves so that we may be clear and easy to follow. With regard to truth, then, the intermediate is a truthful sort of person and the mean may be called truthfulness, while the pretence which exaggerates is boastfulness and the person characterized by it a boaster, and that which understates is mock modesty and the person characterized by it mock-modest. With regard to pleasantness in the giving of amusement the intermediate person is ready-witted and the disposition ready wit, the excess is buffoonery and the person characterized by it a buffoon, while the man who falls short is a sort of boor and his state is boorishness. With regard to the remaining kind of pleasantness, that which is exhibited in life in general, the man who is pleasant in the right way is friendly and the mean is friendliness, while the man who exceeds is an obsequious person if he has no end in view, a flatterer if he is aiming at his own advantage, and the man who falls short and is unpleasant in all circumstances is a quarrelsome and surly sort of person.

There are also means in the passions and concerned with the passions; since shame is not an excellence, and yet praise is extended to the modest man. For even in these matters one man is said to be intermediate, and another to exceed, as for instance the bashful man who is ashamed of everything; while he who falls short or is not ashamed of anything at all is shameless, and the intermediate person
1108b is modest. Righteous indignation is a mean between envy and spite, and these states are concerned with the pain and pleasure that are felt at the fortunes of our neighbours; the man who is characterized by righteous indignation is pained at undeserved good fortune, the envious man, going beyond him, is pained at all good fortune, and the spiteful man falls so far short of being pained that he even rejoices. But these states there will be an opportunity of describing elsewhere; with regard to justice, since it has not one simple meaning, we shall, after describing the other states, distinguish its two kinds and say how each of them is a mean; and similarly we shall treat also of the rational excellences.

CHAPTER 9

That moral excellence is a mean, then, and in what 1109a
sense it is so, and that it is a mean between two vices, the one involving excess, the other deficiency, and that it is such because its character is to aim at what is intermediate in passions and in actions, has been sufficiently stated. Hence also it is no easy task to be good. For in everything it is no easy task to find the middle, e.g., to find the middle of a circle is not for everyone but for him who knows; so, too, anyone can get angry—that is easy—or give or spend money; but to do this to the right person, to the right extent, at the right time, with the right aim, and in the right way, *that* is not for everyone, nor is it easy; that is why goodness is both rare and laudable and noble.

Hence he who aims at the intermediate must first depart from what is the more contrary to it, as Calypso* advises—

> Hold the ship out beyond that surf and spray. (*Odyssey* XII 219.)

For of the extremes one is more erroneous, one less so; therefore, since to hit the mean is hard in the extreme, we must as a second best, as people say, take the least of the evils; and this will be done best in the way we describe. 1109b

But we must consider the things towards which we ourselves also are easily carried away; for some of us tend to one thing, some to another; and this will be recognizable from the pleasure and the pain we

* Calypso is a fictional character in Homer's *Odyssey* (written c. 700 BCE), a beautiful nymph who holds the hero, Odysseus, captive on her island for seven years.

feel. We must drag ourselves away to the contrary extreme; for we shall get into the intermediate state by drawing well away from error, as people do in straightening sticks that are bent.

Now in everything the pleasant or pleasure is most to be guarded against; for we do not judge it impartially. We ought, then, to feel towards pleasure as the elders of the people felt towards Helen, and in all circumstances repeat their saying; for if we dismiss pleasure thus we are less likely to go astray. It is by doing this, then, (to sum the matter up) that we shall best be able to hit the mean.

But this is no doubt difficult, and especially in individual cases; for it is not easy to determine both how and with whom and on what provocation and how long one should be angry; for we too sometimes praise those who fall short and call them good-tempered, but sometimes we praise those who get angry and call them manly. The man, however who deviates little from goodness is not blamed, whether he do so in the direction of the more or of the less, but only the man who deviates more widely; for *he* does not fail to be noticed. But up to what point and to what extent a man must deviate before he becomes blameworthy it is not easy to determine by reasoning, any more than anything else that is perceived by the senses; such things depend on particular facts, and the decision rests with perception. So much, then, makes it plain that the intermediate state is in all things to be praised, but that we must incline sometimes towards the excess, sometimes towards the deficiency; for so shall we most easily hit the mean and what is right.

NOTE

1. Excised by Bywater.

Normative Virtue Ethics

ROSALIND HURSTHOUSE

Rosalind Hursthouse is a moral philosopher from New Zealand best known for her work on virtue ethics. She currently teaches at the University of Auckland in New Zealand, having taught formerly at the Open University in England and at the University of California at Los Angeles.

The selection that appears here was originally published in 1996 in an anthology on virtue ethics. In it, Hursthouse defends the view that virtue ethics can serve as a viable contemporary moral theory, offering comparisons and contrasts between virtue ethics and utilitarianism, on the one hand, and deontology, on the other.

A common belief concerning virtue ethics is that it does not tell us what we should do. This belief is sometimes manifested merely in the expressed assumption that virtue ethics, in being "agent-centred" rather than "act-centred," is concerned with Being rather than Doing, with good (and bad) character rather than right (and wrong) action, with the question "What sort of person should I be?" rather than the question "What should I do?" On this assumption, "virtue ethics" so-called does not figure as a normative rival to utilitarian and deontological ethics; rather, its (fairly) recent revival is seen as having served the useful purpose of reminding moral philosophers that the elaboration of a normative theory may

From *How Should One Live?*, ed. Roger Crisp (Oxford: Clarendon Press, 1996), pp. 19–37. Reprinted by permission of the publisher.

fall short of giving a full account of our moral life. Thus prompted, deontologists have turned to Kant's long neglected "Doctrine of Virtue," and utilitarians, largely abandoning the old debate about rule- and act-utilitarianism, are showing interest in the general-happiness-maximizing consequences of inculcating such virtues as friendship, honesty, and loyalty.

On this assumption, it seems that philosophers who "do virtue ethics," having served this purpose, must realize that they have been doing no more than supplementing normative theory, and should now decide which of the two standard views they espouse. Or, if they find that too difficult, perhaps they should confine themselves to writing detailed studies of particular virtues and vices, indicating where appropriate that "a deontologist would say that an agent with virtue X will characteristically . . ., whereas a utilitarian would say that she will characteristically. . . ." But anyone who wants to espouse virtue ethics as a rival to deontological or utilitarian ethics (finding it distinctly bizarre to suppose that Aristotle espoused either of the latter) will find this common belief voiced against her as an objection: "Virtue ethics does not, because it cannot, tell us what we should do. Hence it cannot be a normative rival to deontology and utilitarianism."

This paper is devoted to defending virtue ethics against this objection.

1. RIGHT ACTION

What grounds might someone have for believing that virtue ethics cannot tell us what we should do? It seems that sometimes the ground is no more than the claim that virtue ethics is concerned with good (and bad) character rather than right (and wrong) action. But that claim does no more than highlight an interesting contrast between virtue ethics on the one hand, and deontology and utilitarianism on the other; the former is agent-centred, the latter (it is said) are act-centred.[1] It does not entail that virtue ethics has nothing to say about the concept of right action, nor about which actions are right and which wrong. Wishing to highlight a different contrast, the one between utilitarianism and deontology, we might equally well say, "Utilitarianism is concerned with good (and bad) states of affairs rather than right (and wrong) action," and no one would take that to mean that utilitarianism, unlike deontology, had nothing to say about right action, for what utilitarianism does say is so familiar.

Suppose an act-utilitarian laid out her account of right action as follows:

U1. An action is right iff it promotes the best consequences.

This premiss provides a specification of right action, forging the familiar utilitarian link between the concepts of *right action* and *best consequences,* but gives one no guidance about how to act until one knows what to count as the best consequences. So these must be specified in a second premiss, for example.

U2. The best consequences are those in which happiness is maximized,

which forges the familiar utilitarian link between the concepts of *best consequences* and *happiness*.[2]

Many different versions of deontology can be laid out in a way that displays the same basic structure. They begin with a premiss providing a specification of right action:

D1. An action is right iff it is in accordance with a correct moral rule or principle.

Like the first premiss of act-utilitarianism, this gives one no guidance about how to act until, in this case, one knows what to count as a correct moral rule (or principle). So this must be specified in a second premiss which begins

D2. A correct moral rule (principle) is one that . . .,

and this may be completed in a variety of ways, for example:

(i) is on the following list (and then a list does follow)

or

(ii) is laid on us by God

or
(iii) is universalizable
or
(iv) would be the object of choice of all rational beings and so on.

Although this way of laying out fairly familiar versions of utilitarianism and deontology is hardly controversial, it is worth noting that it suggests some infelicity in the slogan "Utilitarianism begins with (or takes as its fundamental concept etc.) the Good, whereas deontology begins with the Right." If the concept a normative ethics "begins with" is the one it uses to specify right action, then utilitarianism might be said to begin with the Good (if we take this to be the "same" concept as that of the *best*), but we should surely hasten to add "but only in relation to consequences; not, for instance, in relation to *good* agents, or to living *well*." And even then, we shall not be able to go on to say that most versions of deontology "begin with" the Right, for they use the concept of moral rule or principle to specify right action. The only versions which, in this sense, "begin with" the Right would have to be versions of what Frankena calls "extreme act-deontology,"[3] which (I suppose) specify a right action as one which just *is* right.

And if the dictum is supposed to single out, rather vaguely, the concept which is "most important," then the concepts of *consequences* or *happiness* seem as deserving of mention as the concept of the Good for utilitarianism, and what counts as most important (if any one concept does) for deontologists would surely vary from case to case. For some it would be God, for others universalizability, for others the Categorical Imperative, for others rational acceptance, and so on.

It is possible that too slavish an acceptance of this slogan, and the inevitable difficulty of finding a completion of "and virtue ethics begins with . . ." which does not reveal its inadequacy, has contributed to the belief that virtue ethics cannot provide a specification of right action. I have heard people say, "Utilitarianism defines the Right in terms of the Good, and deontology defines the Good in terms of the Right; but how can virtue ethics possibly define both in terms of the (virtuous) Agent?" and indeed, with no answer forthcoming to the questions "Good *what*? Right *what*?" I have no idea. But if the question is "How can virtue ethics specify right action?" the answer is easy:

VI. An action is right iff it is what a virtuous agent would characteristically (i.e. acting in character) do in the circumstances.

This specification rarely, if ever, silences those who maintain that virtue ethics cannot tell us what we should do. On the contrary, it tends to provoke irritable laughter and scorn. "*That's* no use," the objectors say. "It gives us no guidance whatsoever. Who are the virtuous agents?" But if the failure of the first premiss of a normative ethics which forges a link between the concept of right action and a concept distinctive of that ethics may provoke scorn because it provides no practical guidance, why not direct a similar scorn at the first premisses of act-utilitarianism and deontology in the form in which I have given them? Of each of them I remarked, apparently *en passant* but with intent, that they gave us no guidance. Utilitarianism must specify what are to count as the best consequences, and deontology what is to count as a correct moral rule, producing a second premiss, before any guidance is given. And similarly, virtue ethics must specify who is to count as a virtuous agent. So far, the three are all in the same position.

Of course, if the virtuous agent can only be specified as an agent disposed to act in accordance with moral rules, as some have assumed, then virtue ethics collapses back into deontology and is no rival to it. So let us add a subsidiary premiss to this skeletal outline, with the intention of making it clear that virtue ethics aims to provide a non-deontological specification of the virtuous agent via a specification of the virtues, which will be given in its second premiss:

VIa. A virtuous agent is one who acts virtuously, that is, one who has and exercises the virtues.

V2. A virtue is a character trait that . . .[4]

This second premiss of virtue ethics might, like the second premiss of some versions of deontology, be completed simply by enumeration ("a virtue is one of the following," and then the list is given).[5] Or we might, not implausibly, interpret the Hume of the second *Enquiry* as espousing virtue ethics. According to him, a virtue is a character trait (of human beings) that is useful or agreeable to its possessor or to others (inclusive "or" both times). The standard neo-Aristotelian completion claims that a virtue is a character trait a human being needs for *eudaimonia*, to flourish or live well.

Here, then, we have a specification of right action, whose structure closely resembles those of act-utilitarianism and many forms of deontology. Given that virtue ethics can come up with such a specification, can it still be maintained that it, unlike utilitarianism and deontology, cannot tell us what we should do? Does the specification somehow fail to provide guidance in a way that the other two do not?

At this point, the difficulty of identifying the virtuous agent in a way that makes V1 action-guiding tends to be brought forward again. Suppose it is granted that deontology has just as much difficulty in identifying the correct moral rules as virtue ethics has in identifying the virtues and hence the virtuous agent. Then the following objection may be made.

"All the same," it may be said, "if we imagine that that has been achieved—perhaps simply by enumeration—deontology yields a set of clear prescriptions which are readily applicable ('Do not lie,' 'Do not steal,' 'Do not inflict evil or harm on others,' 'Do help others,' 'Do keep promises,' etc.). But virtue ethics yields only the prescription 'Do what the virtuous agent (the one who is honest, charitable, just, etc.) would do in these circumstances.' And this gives me no guidance unless I am (and know I am) a virtuous agent myself (in which case I am hardly in need of it). If I am less than fully virtuous, I shall have no idea what a virtuous agent would do, and hence cannot apply the only prescription that virtue ethics has given me. (Of course, act-utilitarianism also yields a single prescription, 'Do what maximises happiness,' but there are no *parallel* difficulties in applying that.) So there is the way in which V1 fails to be action-guiding where deontology and utilitarianism succeed."

It is worth pointing out that, if I acknowledge that I am far from perfect, and am quite unclear what a virtuous agent would do in the circumstances in which I find myself, the obvious thing to do is to go and ask one, should this be possible. This is far from being a trivial point, for it gives a straightforward explanation of an aspect of our moral life which should not be ignored, namely the fact that we do seek moral guidance from people who we think are morally better than ourselves. When I am looking for an excuse to do something I have a horrid suspicion is wrong, I ask my moral inferiors (or peers if I am bad enough), "Wouldn't you do such and such if you were in my shoes?" But when I am anxious to do what is right, and do not see my way clear, I go to people I respect and admire—people who I think are kinder, more honest, more just, wiser, than I am myself—and ask them what they would do in my circumstances. How utilitarianism and deontology would explain this fact, I do not know; but as I said, the explanation within the terms of virtue ethics is straightforward. If you want to do what is right, and doing what is right is doing what a virtuous agent would do in the circumstances, then you should find out what she would do if you do not already know.

Moreover, seeking advice from virtuous people is not the only thing an imperfect agent trying to apply the single prescription of virtue ethics can do. For it is simply false that, in general, "if I am less than fully virtuous, then I shall have no idea what a virtuous agent would do," as the objection claims. Recall that we are assuming that the virtues have been enumerated, as the deontologist's rules have been. The latter have been enumerated as, say, "Do not lie," "Do not inflict evil or harm," etc.; the former as, say, honesty, charity, justice, etc. So, *ex hypothesi*, a virtuous agent is one who is honest, charitable, just, etc. So what she characteristically does is act honestly, charitably, justly, etc., and not dishonestly, uncharitably, unjustly. So given an enumeration of the virtues, I may well have a perfectly good idea of what the virtuous person would do in my circumstances despite my own imperfection. Would she lie in her teeth to acquire an unmerited advantage? No, for that would be to act both dishonestly and unjustly. Would she help the naked man by the roadside or pass by on the other side? The former, for she acts charitably. Might she keep a deathbed promise even though living people would benefit from its being broken? Yes, for she acts justly.[6] And so on.

2. MORAL RULES

The above response to the objection that V1 fails to be action-guiding clearly amounts to a denial of the oft-repeated claim that virtue ethics does not come up with any rules (another version of the thought that it is concerned with Being rather than Doing and needs to be supplemented with rules). We can now see that it comes up with a large number; not only does each virtue generate a prescription–act honestly, charitably, justly–but each vice a prohibition–do not act dishonestly, uncharitably, unjustly. Once this point about virtue ethics is grasped (and it is remarkable how often it is overlooked), can there remain any reason for thinking that virtue ethics cannot tell us what we should do? Yes. The reason given is, roughly, that rules such as "Act honestly," "Do not act uncharitably," etc. are, like the rule "Do what the virtuous agent would do," still the wrong sort of rule, still somehow doomed to fail to provide the action guidance supplied by the rules (or rule) of deontology and utilitarianism.

But how so? It is true that these rules of virtue ethics (henceforth "v-rules") are couched in terms, or concepts, which are certainly "evaluative" in *some* sense, or senses, of that difficult word. Is it this which dooms them to failure? Surely not, unless many forms of deontology fail too.[7] If we concentrate on the single example of lying, defining lying to be "asserting what you believe to be untrue, with the intention of deceiving your hearer(s)," then we might, for a moment, preserve the illusion that a deontologist's rules do not contain "evaluative" terms.[8] But as soon as we remember that few deontologists will want to forgo principles of non-maleficence or beneficence, the illusion vanishes. For those principles, and their corresponding rules ("Do no evil or harm to others," "Help others," "Promote their well-being"), rely on terms or concepts which are at least as "evaluative" as those employed in the v-rules.[9] Few deontologists rest content with the simple quasi-biological "Do not kill," but more refined versions of that rule such as "Do not murder," or "Do not kill the innocent," once again employ "evaluative" terms, and "Do not kill unjustly" is itself a particular instantiation of a v-rule.

Supposing this point were granted, a deontologist might still claim that the v-rules are markedly inferior to deontological rules as far as providing guidance for children is concerned. Granted, adult deontologists must think hard about what really constitutes harming someone, or promoting their well-being, or respecting their autonomy, or murder, but surely the simple rules we learnt at our mother's knee are indispensable? How could virtue ethics plausibly seek to dispense with these and expect toddlers to grasp "Act charitably, honestly, and kindly," "Don't act unjustly," and so on? Rightly are these concepts described as "thick"![10] Far too thick for a child to grasp.

Strictly speaking, this claim about learning does not really support the *general* claim that v-rules fail to provide action-guidance, but the claim about learning, arising naturally as it does in the context of the general claim, is one I am more than happy to address. For it pinpoints a condition of adequacy that any normative ethics must meet, namely that such an ethics must not only come up with action-guidance for a clever rational adult but also generate some account of moral education, of how one generation teaches the next what they should do. But an ethics inspired by Aristotle is unlikely to have forgotten the question of moral education, and the objection fails to hit home. First, the implicit empirical claim that toddlers are taught *only* the deontologist's rules, not the "thick" concepts, is false. Sentences such as "Don't do that, it hurts, you mustn't be *cruel*," "Be *kind* to your brother, he's only little," "Don't be so *mean*, so *greedy*" are commonly addressed to toddlers. Secondly, why should a proponent of virtue ethics deny the significance of such mother's-knee rules as "Don't lie," "Keep promises," Don't take more than your fair share," "Help others"? Although it is a mistake, I have claimed, to define a virtuous agent simply as one disposed to act in accordance with moral rules, it is a very understandable mistake, given the obvious connection between, for example, the exercise of the virtue of honesty and refraining from lying. Virtue ethicists want to emphasize the fact that, if children are to be taught to be honest, they must be taught to prize the truth, and that *merely* teaching them not to lie will not achieve this end. But they need not deny that to achieve this end teaching them not to lie is useful, even indispensable.

So we can see that virtue ethics not only comes up with rules (the v-rules, couched in terms derived from the virtues and vices), but further, does not exclude the more familiar deontologists' rules. The theoretical distinction between the two is that the familiar rules, and their applications in particular cases, are given entirely different backings. According to virtue ethics, I must not tell this lie, since it would be dishonest, and dishonesty is a vice; must not break this promise, since it would be unjust, or a betrayal of friendship, or, perhaps (for the available virtue and vice terms do not neatly cover every contingency), simply because no virtuous person would.

However, the distinction is not merely theoretical. It is, indeed, the case that, with respect to a number of familiar examples, virtue ethicists and deontologists tend to stand shoulder to shoulder against utilitarians, denying that, for example, this lie can be told, this promise broken, this human being killed because the consequences of so doing will be generally happiness-maximizing. But, despite a fair amount of coincidence in action-guidance between deontology and virtue ethics, the latter has its own distinctive approach to the practical problems involved in dilemmas.

3. THE CONFLICT PROBLEM

It is a noteworthy fact that, in support of the general claim that virtue ethics cannot tell us what we should do, what is often cited is the "conflict problem." The requirements of different virtues, it is said, can point us in opposed directions. Charity prompts me to kill the person who would (truly) be better off dead, but justice forbids it. Honesty points to telling the hurtful truth, kindness and compassion to remaining silent or even lying. And so on. So virtue ethics lets us down just at the point where we need it, where we are faced with the really difficult dilemmas and do not know what to do.

In the mouth of a utilitarian, this may be a comprehensible criticism, for, as is well known, the only conflict that classical utilitarianism's one rule can generate is the tiresome logical one between the two occurrences of "greatest" in its classical statement. But it is strange to find the very same criticism coming from deontologists, who are notoriously faced with the same problem. "Don't kill," "Respect autonomy," "Tell the truth," "Keep promises" may all conflict with "Prevent suffering" or "Do no harm," which is precisely why deontologists so often reject utilitarianism's deliverances on various dilemmas. Presumably, they must think that deontology can solve the "conflict problem" and, further, that virtue ethics cannot. Are they right?

With respect to a number of cases, the deontologist's strategy is to argue that the "conflict" is merely apparent, or prima facie. The proponent of virtue ethics employs the same strategy: according to her, many of the putative conflicts are merely apparent, resulting from a misapplication of the virtue or vice terms. Does kindness require not telling hurtful truths? Sometimes, but in *this* case, what has to be understood is that one does people no kindness by concealing this sort of truth from them, hurtful as it may be. Or, in a different case, the importance of the truth in question puts the consideration of hurt feelings out of court, and the agent does not show herself to be unkind, or callous, by speaking out. Does charity require that I kill the person who would be better off dead but who wants to stay alive, thereby conflicting with justice? Not if, in Philippa Foot's words, "[a] man does not lack charity because he refrains from an act of injustice which would have been for someone's good."[11]

One does not have to agree with the three judgements expressed here to recognize this as a *strategy* available to virtue ethics, any more than one has to agree with the particular judgements of deontologists who, for example, may claim that one rule outranks another, or that a certain rule has a certain exception clause built in, when they argue that a putative case of conflict is resolvable. Whether an individual has resolved a putative moral conflict or dilemma rightly is one question; whether a normative ethics has the wherewithal to resolve it is an entirely different question, and it is the latter with which we are concerned here.

The form the strategy takes within virtue ethics provides what may plausibly be claimed to be the deep explanation of why, in some cases, agents do not know the answer to "What should I do in these circumstances?" despite the fact that there *is* an answer. Trivially, the explanation is that they lack moral knowledge of what to do in this situation; but why? In what way? The lack, according to virtue ethics' strategy, arises from lack of moral wisdom, from an inadequate grasp of what is involved in acting *kindly* (unkindly) or *charitably* (uncharitably), in being *honest*, or *just*, or *lacking in charity*, or, in general, of how the virtue (and vice) terms are to be correctly applied.

Here we come to an interesting defence of the v-rules, often criticized as being too difficult to apply for the agent who lacks moral wisdom.[12] The defence relies on an (insufficiently acknowledged) insight of Aristotle's—namely that moral knowledge, unlike mathematical knowledge, cannot be acquired merely by attending lectures and is not characteristically to be found in people too young to have much experience of life.[13] Now *if* right action were determined by rules that any clever adolescent could apply correctly, how could this be so? Why are there not moral whiz-kids, the way there are mathematical (or quasi-mathematical) whiz-kids? But if the rules that determine right action are, like the v-rules, very difficult to apply correctly, involving, for instance, a grasp of the *sort* of truth that one does people no kindness by concealing, the explanation is readily to hand. Clever adolescents do not, in general, have a good grasp of that sort of thing.[14] And *of course* I have to say "the sort of truth that . . ." and "that sort of thing," relying on my readers' knowledgeable uptake. For if I could define either sort, then, once again, clever adolescents could acquire moral wisdom from textbooks.

So far, I have described one strategy available to virtue ethics for coping with the "conflict problem," a strategy that consists in arguing that the conflict is merely apparent, and can be resolved. According to one—only one of many—versions of "the doctrine of the unity of the virtues," this is the only possible strategy (and ultimately successful), but this is not a claim I want to defend. One general reason is that I still do not know what I think about "the unity of the virtues" (all those different versions!); a more particular, albeit related, reason is that, even if I were (somehow) sure that the requirements of the particular virtues could never conflict, I suspect that I would still believe in the possiblity of moral dilemmas. I have been talking so far as though examples of putative dilemmas and examples of putative conflict between the requirements of different virtues (or deontologists' rules) coincided. But it may seem to many, as it does to me, that there are certain (putative) dilemmas which can only be described in terms of (putative) conflict with much artifice and loss of relevant detail.

Let us, therefore, consider the problem of moral dilemmas without bothering about whether they can be described in the simple terms of a conflict between the requirements of two virtues (or two deontologists' rules). Most of us, it may be supposed, have our own favoured example(s), either real or imaginary, of the case (or cases) where we see the decision about whether to do A or B as a very grave matter, have thought a great deal about what can be said for and against doing A, and doing B, and have still not managed to reach a conclusion which we think is the right one.[15] How, if at all, does virtue ethics direct us to think about such cases?

4. DILEMMAS AND NORMATIVE THEORY

As a preliminary to answering that question, we should consider a much more general one, namely "How should any normative ethics direct us to think about such cases?" This brings us to the topic of normative theory.

It is possible to detect a new movement in moral philosophy, a movement which has already attracted the name "anti-theory in ethics."[16] Its various representatives have as a common theme the rejection of normative ethical theory; but amongst them are numbered several philosophers usually associated with virtue ethics, such as Baier, McDowell, MacIntyre, and Nussbaum.* This does not mean that they maintain what I have been denying, namely that virtue ethics is not normative; rather, they assume that it does not constitute a normative *theory* (and, mindful of this fact, I have been careful to avoid describing

* Annette Baier, John McDowell, Alastair MacIntyre, and Martha Nussbaum are all contemporary philosophers.

virtue ethics as one). What is meant by a "normative theory" in this context is not easy to pin down, but, roughly, a normative theory is taken to be a set (possibly one-membered in the case of utilitarianism) of general principles which provide a *decision procedure* for all questions about how to act morally.

Part of the point of distinguishing a normative ethics by calling it a normative "theory" is that a decent theory, as we know from science, enables us to answer questions that we could not answer before we had it. It is supposed to resolve those difficult dilemmas in which, it is said, our moral intuitions clash, and, prior to our grasp of the theory, we do not know what we should do.[17] And a large part of the motivation for subscribing to "anti-theory in ethics" is the belief that we should not be looking to science to provide us with our model of moral knowledge. Our "intuitions" in ethics do not play the same role vis-à-vis the systematic articulation of moral knowledge as our "observations" play vis-à-vis the systematic articulation of scientific knowledge; many of the goals appropriate to scientific knowledge—universality, consistency, completeness, simplicity—are not appropriate to moral knowledge; the acquisition of moral knowledge involves the training of the emotions in a way that the acquisition of scientific knowledge does not; and so on.

Clearly, many different issues are involved in the question of the extent to which moral knowledge should be modelled on scientific knowledge. The one I want to focus on here is the issue of whether a normative ethics should provide a decision procedure which enables us to resolve all moral dilemmas. Should it, to rephrase the question I asked above, (1) direct us to think about moral dilemmas in the belief that they *must* have a resolution, and that it is the business of the normative ethics in question to provide one? Or should it (2) have built into it the possibility of there being, as David Wiggins puts it, some "absolutely undecidable questions—e.g., cases where . . . nothing could count as *the* reasonable practical answer,"[18] counting questions about dilemmas of the sort described as amongst them? Or should it (3) be sufficiently flexible to allow for a comprehensible disagreement on this issue between two proponents of the normative ethics in question?

If we are to avoid modelling normative ethics mindlessly on scientific theory, we should not simply assume that the first position is the correct one. But rejection of such a model is not enough to justify the second position either. Someone might believe that for *any* dilemma there must be something that counts as the right way out of it, without believing that normative ethics remotely resembles scientific theory, perhaps because they subscribe to a version of realism (in Michael Dummett's sense of "realism").[19] More particularly, someone might believe on religious grounds that if I find myself, through no fault of my own, confronted with a dilemma (of the sort described), there must be something that counts as the right way out of it.[20] The belief in God's providence does indeed involve, as Peter Geach says, the thought that "God does not require of a faithful servant the desperate choice between sin and sin."[21] Should a normative ethics be such that it cannot be shared by a realist and an anti-realist (again in Dummett's sense)? Or by an atheist and a theist? It seems to me that a normative ethics should be able to accommodate such differences, and so I subscribe to the third position outlined above.

Which position utilitarians and deontologists might espouse is not my concern here; I want to make clear how it is that virtue ethics is able to accommodate the third.[22]

Let us return to V1—"An action is right iff it is what a virtuous agent would characteristically do in the circumstances." This makes it clear that if two people disagree about the possibility of irresolvable moral dilemmas, their disagreement will manifest itself in what they say about the virtue of agents. So let us suppose that two candidates for being virtuous agents are each faced with their own case of the same dilemma. (I do not want to defend the view that each situation is unique in such a way that nothing would count as two agents being in the same circumstances and faced with the same dilemma.) And, after much thought, one does A and the other does B.

Now, those who believe that there cannot be irresolvable dilemmas (of the sort described) can say that, in the particular case, at least one agent, say the one who did A, thereby showed themselves to be lacking in virtue, perhaps in that practical wisdom which is an essential aspect of each of the "non-intellectual" virtues. ("If you can *see* no way out but a lie, the lie may be the least wicked of the alternatives you can discern: it is still wicked, and you should blame yourself that you lacked the wisdom of St. Joan or St. Athanasius,* to extricate yourself without lying. It is not a matter of foxy cleverness; 'the testimony of the LORD is sure and giveth wisdom to the simple.' "[23] Thus Geach, discussing the absolute prohibition against lying in the context of the claim that God "does not require of any man a choice between sin and sin.") Or they can say that at least one agent must have been lacking in virtue, without claiming to know which.

But those who believe that there are, or may be, irresolvable dilemmas can suppose that both agents are not merely candidates for being, but actually are, virtuous agents. For to believe in such dilemmas is to believe in cases in which even the perfect practical wisdom that the most idealized virtuous agent has does not direct her to do, say, A rather than B. And then the fact that these virtuous agents acted differently, despite being in the same circumstances, *determines* the fact that there is no answer to the question "What is *the* right thing to do in these circumstances?" For if it is true both that *a* virtuous agent would do A, and that *a* virtuous agent would do B (as it is, since, *ex hypothesi*, one did do A and the other B), then both A and B are, in the circumstances, right, according to V1.

The acceptance of this should not be taken as a counsel of despair, nor as an excuse for moral irresponsibility. It does not license coin-tossing when one is faced with a putative dilemma, for the moral choices we find most difficult do not come to us conveniently labelled as "resolvable" or "irresolvable." I was careful to specify that the two candidates for being virtuous agents acted only "after much thought." It will always be necessary to think very hard before accepting the idea that a particular moral decision does not have one right issue, and, even on the rare occasions on which she eventually reached the conclusion that this is such a case, would the virtuous agent toss a coin? Of course not.

No doubt someone will say, "Well, if she really thinks the dilemma is irresolvable, why not, according to virtue ethics?" and the answer must, I think, be *ad hominem*. *If* their conception of the virtuous agent—of someone with the character traits of justice, honesty, compassion, kindness, loyalty, wisdom, etc.—really is of someone who would resort to coin-tossing when confronted with what she believed to be an irresolvable dilemma, then that is the bizarre conception they bring to virtue ethics, and they must, presumably, think that there is nothing morally irresponsible or light-minded about coin-tossing in such cases. So they should not want virtue ethics to explain "why not." But if their conception of the virtuous agent does not admit of her acting thus—if they think such coin-tossing would be irresponsible, or light-minded, or indeed simply insane—then they have no need to ask the question. *My* question was, "Would the virtuous agent toss a coin?"; they agree that of course she would not. Why not? Because it would be irresponsible, or light-minded, or the height of folly.

The acceptance of the possibility of irresolvable dilemmas within virtue ethics (by those of us who do accept it) should not be seen in itself as conceding much to "pluralism." If I say that I can imagine a case in which two virtuous agents are faced with a dilemma, and one does A while the other does B, I am not saying that I am imagining a case in which the two virtuous agents each think that what the other does is wrong (vicious, contrary to virtue) because they have radically different views about what is required by a certain virtue, or about whether a certain character trait is a vice, or about whether something is to be greatly valued or of little importance. I am imagining a case in which my two virtuous agents have the same "moral views" about everything, up to and including the view that, in this particular case, neither decision is *the* right one, and hence neither is wrong. Each recognizes the propriety of the other's reason for doing what she did—say, "To avoid *that* evil," "To secure *this* good"—for her recognition of the fact that this is as good a moral reason as her own (say, "To avoid *this* evil," "To secure *that* good") is what forced each to accept the idea that the dilemma was irresolvable in the first place. Though each can give such a reason

* St. Joan (1412–31) and St. Athanasius (293–373) are Catholic saints, renowned for their virtue.

for what they did (A in one case, B in the other), neither attempts to give "the moral reason" why they did one *rather than* the other. The "reason" for or explanation of *that* would be, if available at all, in terms of psychological autobiography ("I decided to sleep on it, and when I woke up I just found myself thinking in terms of doing A," or "I just felt terrified at the thought of doing A: I'm sure this was totally irrational, but I did, so I did B").[24]

The topic of this chapter has been the view that virtue ethics cannot be a normative rival to utilitarianism and deontology because "it cannot tell us what we should do." In defending the existence of normative virtue ethics I have not attempted to argue that it can "tell us what we should do" in such a way that the difficult business of acting well is made easy for us. I have not only admitted but welcomed the fact that, in some cases, moral wisdom is required if the v-rules are to be applied correctly and apparent dilemmas thereby resolved (or indeed identified, since a choice that may seem quite straightfoward to the foolish or wicked may rightly appear difficult, calling for much thought, to the wise). Nor have I attempted to show that virtue ethics is guaranteed to be able to resolve every dilemma. It seems bizarre to insist that a normative ethics must be able to do this prior to forming a reasonable belief that there cannot be irresolvable dilemmas, but those who have formed such a belief may share a normative ethics with those who have different views concerning realism, or the existence of God. A normative ethics, I suggested, should be able to accommodate both views on this question, as virtue ethics does, not model itself mindlessly on scientific theory.[25]

NOTES

1. Kant is standardly taken as the paradigm deontologist, but Stephen Hudson argues he is much closer to Aristotle on the act/agent-centred point than is usually supposed. See "What is Morality All About?" *Philosophia* 20 (1990), 3–13.
2. Variations on utilitarianism are not my concern here. I am ignoring rule-utilitarianism, and assuming my reader to be well aware of the fact that different utilitarians may specify *best consequences* in different ways. See the introduction to A. Sen and B. Williams (eds.), *Utilitarianism and Beyond* (Cambridge, 1982), from which I have (basically) taken the characterization of utilitarianism given here.
3. W. Frankena, *Ethics*, 2nd edn. (Englewood Cliffs, NJ, 1973), 16.
4. It might be said that V1a does not make it clear that virtue ethics aims to provide a non-deontological specification of the virtuous agent, since it does not rule out the possibility that the virtues themselves are no more than dispositions to act in accordance with moral rules. And indeed, it does seem that the belief that the virtuous agent is nothing but the agent disposed to act in accordance with moral rules is often based on that assumption about the virtues. (See, for example, Frankena, *Ethics*, 65 and A. Gewirth, "Rights and Virtues," *Review of Metaphysics* 38 (1985), 739–62.) Then we must say that V2 aims to clear that up by saying that the virtues are character traits, assuming it to be obvious that someone's being of a certain character is not merely a matter of her being disposed to do certain sorts of acts in accordance with a rule.
5. "Enumeration" may connote something more explicit than is required. Deontologists and virtue ethicists actually engaged in normative ethics may well do no more than take it as obvious in the course of what they say that such-and-such is a correct moral rule or virtue, neither stipulating this explicitly, nor attempting to list other rules/virtues which have no bearing on whatever issue is under discussion.
6. I follow tradition here in taking the virtue of fidelity, or faithfulness to one's word, to be part of the virtue of justice, thereby avoiding a clumsy attempt to manufacture an adverbial phrase corresponding to "fidelity." But nothing hangs on this.
7. Forms of utilitarianism which aim to be entirely value-free or empirical, such as those which define happiness in terms of the satisfaction of actual desires or preferences, regardless of their content, or as a mental state whose presence is definitively established by introspection, seem to me the least plausible, but I accept that anyone who embraces them may consistently complain that v-rules give inferior action-guidance in virtue of containing "evaluative" terms. But any utilitarian who wishes to employ any distinction between the higher and

lower pleasures, or rely on some list of goods (such as autonomy, friendship, knowledge of important matters) in defining happiness, must grant that even her single rule is implicitly "evaluative."

8. It might be thought that the example of promises provided an equally straightforward example. This would not substantially affect my argument, but in any case, I do not think that this is so. The *Shorter Oxford* defines the verb "to promise" as "to undertake or . . ., by word or . . ., to do or refrain . . ., or to give . . .: usu. to the *advantage* of the person concerned" (my italics), and the qualification containing the word I have italicized seems to me essential. Its significance has been highlighted in the many stories and myths whose tragic point turns on someone wicked doing what they literally undertook to do, to the horror and despair of "the person concerned." ("Promise me you will fearfully punish the one who has done so and so," the person concerned says, not realizing that the one in question is her long-lost son.)
9. I cannot resist pointing out that this reveals a further inadequacy in the slogan "Utilitarianism begins with the Good, deontology with the Right" when this is taken as committing deontology to making the concept of the Good (and presumably the Bad or Evil) somehow derivative from the concept of the Right (and Wrong). A "utilitarian" who relied on the concept of *morally right*, or *virtuous*, action in specifying his concept of happiness would find it hard to shrug off the scare quotes, but no one expects a deontologist to be able to state each of her rules without employing a concept of *good* which is not simply the concept of *right action for its own sake*, or without any mention of *evil* or *harm*.
10. See B. Williams, *Ethics and the Limits of Philosophy* (London, 1985), 129–30.
11. P. Foot, *Virtues and Vices* (Oxford, 1978), p. 60, n. 12.
12. This could well be regarded as another version of the criticism discussed earlier, that the v-rules somehow fail to provide action-guidance.
13. *Nicomachean Ethics* (=*NE*) 1142^{a}12–16.
14. In defending the thesis that virtue ethics is a normative *rival* to utilitarianism and deontology, I am not simultaneously aiming to establish the far more ambitious thesis that it beats its rivals hollow. Utilitarians and deontologists may well take the Aristotelian point on board and provide an account, appropriate to their ethics, of why we should not consult whiz-kids about difficult moral decisions. For example, Onora O'Neill's sophisticated version of Kantian "maxims" rules out their application by (merely) clever adolescents.
15. I have chosen this description of the sort of dilemmas with which I am concerned deliberately, mindful of Philippa Foot's paper, "Moral Realism and Moral Dilemma," *The Journal of Philosophy* 80 (1983), 379–98. As she points out, some cases that are discussed as "conflicts" or "dilemmas" are taken to be resolvable, that is, taken to be cases in which we do reach a conclusion we think is the right one; these are my cases of "apparent" conflict. Commenting on Wiggins (see below, n. 18), she also points out that undecidability may exist "in small moral matters, or where the choice is between goods rather than evils, only it doesn't worry us" (395); I am concentrating on the ones that worry us.
16. See S. Clarke and E. Simpson (eds.) *Anti-Theory in Ethics and Moral Conservatism* (New York, 1989), containing, inter alia, articles by Baier, McDowell, MacIntyre, and Nussbaum, as well as Cheryl N. Noble's seminal "Normative Ethical Theories" (49–64). It is noteworthy that, in the latter, Noble explicitly denies that she is attacking the idea of normative *ethics*. Her criticisms of the idea of normative ethical *theory*, she says, "are aimed at a particular conception of what normative ethics should be" (62, n. 1).
17. As Noble points out, a normative theory may also be expected to say something about cases "where we have no intuitions or where our intuitions are inchoate or weak" (ibid. 61); and, to some of us, it is indeed one of the oddities of utilitarianism that certain states of affairs, concerning which we may have no moral intuitions at all, emerge from it as so definitively "morally better" than others. I would like to argue for the incoherence of the idea that a theory could attach a truth-value to a sentence (employing a moral term) which lacked a sense outside the theory, but space does not permit. See, however, P. Foot, "Utilitarianism and the Virtues," *Mind* 94 (1985), 196–209.
18. D. Wiggins, "Truth, Invention and the Meaning of Life," *Proceedings of the British Academy* 62 (1976), 371, my italics. I have omitted the phrase

that attracted Foot's criticism (see above, n. 15), in which Wiggins seems to imply that undecidable questions are undecidable *because* the alternatives are particularly terrible.

19. M. Dummett, *Truth and Other Enigmas* (London, 1978), 1–24 and 145–65. For a brief but helpful discussion of the distinction between Dummett-type realism and cognitivism in ethics, see Foot, "Moral Realism and Moral Dilemma," 397–8.
20. I am assuming that the qualification "through no fault of my own" is all-important, since I cannot imagine why anyone should think (except through oversight) that there must always be a right action I can do to get myself out of any mess that I have got myself into through previous wrongdoing.
21. P. Geach, *The Virtues* (Cambridge, 1977), 155.
22. I had hitherto overlooked the possibility of this third position, and hence had emphasized the fact that virtue ethics could occupy the second. But I subsequently heard Philippa Foot point out that Aquinas, Anscombe, and Geach should surely be classified as virtue ethicists, notwithstanding their absolutist stance on many of the familiar deontological rules; and, given their consequent stance on the clear resolvability of some dilemmas that others find irresolvable, this prompted me to look at what a commitment to resolvability (with respect to dilemmas *as described*) might look like within virtue ethics. I am grateful to the editor for reminding me of the further possibility of his own "realist" position. (Aristotle is clearly an absolutist too, at least with respect to "adultery" (*moikheia*), theft, and murder (see *NE* 1107^{a}11–12), but where he stands (or should stand, to be consistent) on irresolvable dilemmas of the sort described is, I think, entirely unclear.)
23. Geach, *The Virtues*, 121.
24. It must be remembered that, *ex hypothesi*, these are things said by virtuous agents about what they did when confronted with an irresolvable dilemma. Of course they would be very irresponsible accounts of why one had done A rather than B in a resolvable case.
25. At the request of the editor, I have repeated here several points I have made in two other papers, "Virtue Theory and Abortion," *Philosophy and Public Affairs* 20 (1991), 223–46, and "Applying Virtue Ethics," in *Virtues and Reasons: Philippa Foot and Moral Theory,* ed. R. Hursthouse, G. Lawrence, and W. S. Quinn (Oxford, 1995) 57–75.

B SOME APPLICATIONS

◈ MORAL DUTIES TO THE POOR ◈

Rich and Poor

PETER SINGER

Peter Singer (1946–) is an influential Australian moral philosopher who now teaches at Princeton University. His often outspoken views on topics, such as animal rights, poverty, euthanasia, and infanticide, have earned him a place in the public eye.

An ardent defender of utilitarianism, Singer is well known for his contention that those who live in conditions of relative affluence are morally obliged to redistribute a significant proportion of their resources to the billions of fellow human beings who live under conditions of extreme poverty. The essay that appears here—"Rich and Poor"—originally appeared as a chapter in Singer's 1993 collection *Practical Ethics*. It offers an updated defense of a view presented in his often-anthologized essay "Famine, Affluence and Morality" (1971), namely, that our failure to provide aid to those in conditions of dire poverty is morally wrong.

SOME FACTS ABOUT POVERTY

...Consider these facts: by the most cautious estimates, 400 million people lack the calories, protein, vitamins and minerals needed to sustain their bodies and minds in a healthy state. Millions are constantly hungry; others suffer from deficiency diseases and from infections they would be able to resist on a better diet. Children are the worst affected. According to one study, 14 million children under five die every year from the combined effects of malnutrition and infection. In some districts half the children born can be expected to die before their fifth birthday.

Nor is lack of food the only hardship of the poor. To give a broader picture, Robert McNamara,* when president of the World Bank, suggested the term "absolute poverty." The poverty we are familiar with in industrialised nations is relative poverty—meaning that some citizens are poor, relative to the wealth enjoyed by their neighbours. People living in relative poverty in Australia might be quite comfortably off by comparison with pensioners in Britain, and British pensioners are not poor in comparison with the poverty that exists in Mali or Ethiopia. Absolute poverty, on the other hand, is poverty by any standard. In McNamara's words:

> Poverty at the absolute level...is life at the very margin of existence. The absolute poor are severely deprived human beings struggling to survive in a

* Robert McNamara (1916–) served as U.S. secretary of defense from 1961 to 1968 and president of the World Bank from 1968 to 1981.

From *Practical Ethics*, 2nd ed., pp. 154–170, 247–248. Copyright © 1993 by Cambridge University Press. Reprinted with the permission of the publisher.

> set of squalid and degraded circumstances almost beyond the power of our sophisticated imaginations and privileged circumstances to conceive.
>
> Compared to those fortunate enough to live in developed countries, individuals in the poorest nations have:
>
> An infant mortality rate eight times higher
> A life expectancy one-third lower
> An adult literacy rate 60 per cent less
> A nutritional level, for one out of every two in the population, below acceptable standards;
> And for millions of infants, less protein than is sufficient to permit optimum development of the brain.

McNamara has summed up absolute poverty as "a condition of life so characterised by malnutrition, illiteracy, disease, squalid surroundings, high infant mortality and low life expectancy as to be beneath any reasonable definition of human decency."

Absolute poverty is, as McNamara has said, responsible for the loss of countless lives, especially among infants and young children. When absolute poverty does not cause death, it still causes misery of a kind not often seen in the affluent nations. Malnutrition in young children stunts both physical and mental development. According to the United Nations Development Programme, 180 million children under the age of five suffer from serious malnutrition. Millions of people on poor diets suffer from deficiency diseases, like goitre, or blindness caused by a lack of vitamin A. The food value of what the poor eat is further reduced by parasites such as hookworm and ringworm, which are endemic in conditions of poor sanitation and health education.

Death and disease apart, absolute poverty remains a miserable condition of life, with inadequate food, shelter, clothing, sanitation, health services and education. The Worldwatch Institute estimates that as many as 1.2 billion people—or 23 per cent of the world's population—live in absolute poverty. For the purposes of this estimate, absolute poverty is defined as "the lack of sufficient income in cash or kind to meet the most basic biological needs for food, clothing, and shelter." Absolute poverty is probably the principal cause of human misery today.

SOME FACTS ABOUT WEALTH

This is the background situation, the situation that prevails on our planet all the time. It does not make headlines. People died from malnutrition and related diseases yesterday, and more will die tomorrow. The occasional droughts, cyclones, earthquakes, and floods that take the lives of tens of thousands in one place and at one time are more newsworthy. They add greatly to the total amount of human suffering; but it is wrong to assume that when there are no major calamities reported, all is well.

The problem is not that the world cannot produce enough to feed and shelter its people. People in the poor countries consume, on average, 180 kilos of grain a year, while North Americans average around 900 kilos. The difference is caused by the fact that in the rich countries we feed most of our grain to animals, converting it into meat, milk, and eggs. Because this is a highly inefficient process, people in rich countries are responsible for the consumption of far more food than those in poor countries who eat few animal products. If we stopped feeding animals on grains and soybeans, the amount of food saved would—if distributed to those who need it—be more than enough to end hunger throughout the world.

These facts about animal food do not mean that we can easily solve the world food problem by cutting down on animal products, but they show that the problem is essentially one of distribution rather than production. The world does produce enough food. Moreover, the poorer nations themselves could produce far more if they made more use to improved agricultural techniques.

So why are people hungry? Poor people cannot afford to buy grain grown by farmers in the richer nations. Poor farmers cannot afford to buy improved seeds, or fertilisers, or the machinery needed for drilling wells and pumping water. Only by transferring some of the wealth of the rich nations to the poor can the situation be changed.

That this wealth exists is clear. Against the picture of absolute poverty that McNamara has painted, one might pose a picture of "absolute affluence." Those who are absolutely affluent are not necessarily affluent by comparison with their neighbours, but they are affluent by any reasonable definition of human needs. This means that they have more income than they need to provide themselves adequately with all the basic necessities of life. After buying (either directly or through their taxes) food, shelter, clothing, basic health services, and education, the absolutely affluent are still able to spend money on luxuries. The absolutely affluent choose their food for the pleasures of the palate, not to stop hunger; they buy new clothes to look good, not to keep warm; they move house to be in a better neighbourhood or have a playroom for the children, not to keep out of the rain; and after all this there is still money to spend on stereo systems, video-cameras, and overseas holidays.

At this stage I am making no ethical judgments about absolute affluence, merely pointing out that it exists. Its defining characteristic is a significant amount of income above the level necessary to provide for the basic human needs of oneself and one's dependents. By this standard, the majority of citizens of Western Europe, North America, Japan, Australia, New Zealand, and the oil-rich Middle Eastern states are all absolutely affluent. To quote McNamara once more:

> "The average citizen of a developed country enjoys wealth beyond the wildest dreams of the one billion people in countries with per capita incomes under $200." These, therefore, are the countries—and individuals—who have wealth that they could, without threatening their own basic welfare, transfer to the absolutely poor.

At present, very little is being transferred. Only Sweden, the Netherlands, Norway, and some of the oil-exporting Arab states have reached the modest target, set by the United Nations, of 0.7 per cent of gross national product (GNP). Britain gives 0.31 per cent of its GNP in official development assistance and a small additional amount in unofficial aid from voluntary organisations. The total comes to about £2 per month per person, and compares with 5.5 per cent of GNP spent on alcohol, and 3 per cent on tobacco. Other, even wealthier nations, give little more: Germany gives 0.41 per cent and Japan 0.32 per cent. The United States gives a mere 0.15 per cent of its GNP.

THE MORAL EQUIVALENT OF MURDER?

If these are the facts, we cannot avoid concluding that by not giving more than we do, people in rich countries are allowing those in poor countries to suffer from absolute poverty, with consequent malnutrition, ill health, and death. This is not a conclusion that applies only to governments. It applies to each absolutely affluent individual, for each of us has the opportunity to do something about the situation; for instance, to give our time or money to voluntary organisations like Oxfam, Care, War on Want, Freedom from Hunger, Community Aid Abroad, and so on. If, then, allowing someone to die is not intrinsically different from killing someone, it would seem that we are all murderers.

Is this verdict too harsh? Many will reject it as self-evidently absurd. They would sooner take it as showing that allowing to die cannot be equivalent to killing than as showing that living in an affluent style without contributing to an overseas aid agency is ethically equivalent to going over to Ethiopia and shooting a few peasants. And no doubt, put as bluntly as that, the verdict is too harsh.

There are several significant differences between spending money on luxuries instead of using it to save lives, and deliberately shooting people.

First, the motivation will normally be different. Those who deliberately shoot others go out of their way to kill; they presumably want their victims dead, from malice, sadism, or some equally unpleasant motive. A person who buys a new stereo system presumably wants to enhance her enjoyment of music—not in itself a terrible thing. At worst, spending money on luxuries instead of giving it away indicates selfishness and indifference to the sufferings of others, characteristics that may be undesirable but are not comparable with actual malice or similar motives.

Second, it is not difficult for most of us to act in accordance with a rule against killing people: it is, on the other hand, very difficult to obey a rule that commands us to save all the lives we can. To live a comfortable, or even luxurious life it is not necessary to kill anyone; but it is necessary to allow some to die whom we might have saved, for the money that we need to live comfortably could have been given away. Thus the duty to avoid killing is much easier to discharge completely than the duty to save. Saving every life we could would mean cutting our standard of living down to the bare essentials needed to keep us alive.[1] To discharge this duty completely would require a degree of moral heroism utterly different from that required by mere avoidance of killing.

A third difference is the greater certainty of the outcome of shooting when compared with not giving aid. If I point a loaded gun at someone at close range and pull the trigger, it is virtually certain that the person will be killed; whereas the money that I could give might be spent on a project that turns out to be unsuccessful and helps no one.

Fourth, when people are shot there are identifiable individuals who have been harmed. We can point to them and to their grieving families. When I buy my stereo system, I cannot know who my money would have saved if I had given it away. In a time of famine I may see dead bodies and grieving families on television reports, and I might not doubt that my money would have saved some of them; even then it is impossible to point to a body and say that had I not bought the stereo, that person would have survived.

Fifth, it might be said that the plight of the hungry is not my doing, and so I cannot be held responsible for it. The starving would have been starving if I had never existed. If I kill, however, I am responsible for my victims' deaths, for those people would not have died if I had not killed them.

These differences need not shake our previous conclusion that there is no intrinsic difference between killing and allowing to die. They are extrinsic differences, that is, differences normally but not necessarily associated with the distinction between killing and allowing to die. We can imagine cases in which someone allows another to die for malicious or sadistic reasons; we can imagine a world in which there are so few people needing assistance, and they are so easy to assist, that our duty not to allow people to die is as easily discharged as our duty not to kill; we can imagine situations in which the outcome of not helping is as sure as shooting; we can imagine cases in which we can identify the person we allow to die. We can even imagine a case of allowing to die in which, if I had not existed, the person would not have died—for instance, a case in which if I had not been in a position to help (though I don't help) someone else would have been in my position and would have helped....

If a doctor decides, in consultation with the parents, not to operate on—and thus to allow to die—a Down's syndrome infant with an intestinal blockage, her motivation will be similar to that of a doctor who gives a lethal injection rather than allow the infant to die. No extraordinary sacrifice or moral heroism will be required in either case. Not operating will just as certainly end in death as administering the injection. Allowing to die does have an identifiable victim. Finally, it may well be that the doctor is personally responsible for the death of the infant she decides not to operate upon, since she may know that if she had not taken this case, other doctors in the hospital would have operated.

Nevertheless, euthanasia is a special case, and very different from allowing people to starve to death. (The major difference being that when euthanasia is justifiable, death is a good thing.) The extrinsic differences that *normally* mark off killing and allowing to die do explain why we *normally* regard killing as much worse than allowing to die.

To explain our conventional ethical attitudes is not to justify them. Do the five differences not only explain, but also justify, our attitudes? Let us consider them one by one:

1. Take the lack of an identifiable victim first. Suppose that I am a travelling salesperson, selling tinned food, and I learn that a batch of tins contains a contaminant, the known effect of which, when consumed, is to double the risk that the consumer will die from stomach cancer. Suppose I continue to sell the tins. My decision may have no identifiable victims. Some of those who eat the food will die from cancer. The proportion of consumers dying in this way will be twice that of the community at large, but who among the consumers died because they ate what I sold, and who would have contracted the disease anyway? It is impossible to tell; but surely this impossibility makes my decision no less reprehensible than it would have been had the contaminant had more readily detectable, though equally fatal, effects.

2. The lack of certainty that by giving money I could save a life does reduce the wrongness of not giving, by comparison with deliberate killing; but it is insufficient to show that not giving is acceptable conduct. The motorist who speeds through pedestrian crossings, heedless of anyone who might be on them, is not a murderer. She may never actually hit a pedestrian; yet what she does is very wrong indeed.

3. The notion of responsibility for acts rather than omissions is more puzzling. On the one hand, we feel ourselves to be under a greater obligation to help those whose misfortunes we have caused. (It is for this reason that advocates of overseas aid often argue that Western nations have created the poverty of third world nations, through forms of economic exploitation that go back to the colonial system.) On the other hand, any consequentialist would insist that and we are responsible for all the consequences of our actions, and if a consequence of my spending money on a luxury item is that someone dies, I am responsible for that death. It is true that the person would have died even if I had never existed, but what is the relevance of that? The fact is that I do exist, and the consequentialist will say that our responsibilities derive from the world as it is, not as it might have been.

One way of making sense of the non-consequentialist view of responsibility is by basing it on a theory of rights of the kind proposed by John Locke or, more recently, Robert Nozick.* If everyone has a right to life, and this right is a right *against* others who might threaten my life, but not a right to assistance from others when my life is in danger, then we can understand the feeling that we are responsible for acting to kill but not for omitting to save. The former violates the rights of others, the latter does not.

Should we accept such a theory of rights? If we build up our theory of rights by imagining, as Locke and Nozick do, individuals living independently from each other in a "state of nature," it may seem natural to adopt a conception of rights in which as long as each leaves the other alone, no rights are violated. I might, on this view, quite properly have maintained my independent existence if I had wished to do so. So if I do not make you any worse off than you would have been if I had had nothing at all to do with you, how can I have violated your rights? But why start from such an unhistorical, abstract and ultimately inexplicable idea as an independent individual? Our ancestors were—like other primates—social beings long before they were human beings, and could not have developed the abilities and capacities of human beings if they had not been social beings first. In any case, we are not, now, isolated individuals. So why should we assume that rights must be restricted to rights against interference? We might instead adopt the view that taking rights to life seriously is incompatible with standing by watching people die when one could easily save them.

4. What of the difference in motivation? That a person does not positively wish for the death of another lessens the severity of the blame she deserves; but not by as much as our present attitudes to giving aid suggest. The behaviour of the speeding motorist is again comparable, for such motorists usually have no desire at all to kill anyone. They merely enjoy speeding and are indifferent to the consequences. Despite their lack of malice, those who kill with cars deserve not only blame but also severe punishment.

5. Finally, the fact that to avoid killing people is normally not difficult, whereas to save all one possibly could save is heroic, must make an important difference to our attitude to failure to do what the respective principles demand. Not to kill is a minimum standard of acceptable conduct we can require of everyone; to save all one possibly could is not something that can realistically be required, especially not in societies accustomed to giving as little as ours do. Given the generally accepted standards, people who give, say, $1,000 a year to an overseas aid organisation are more aptly praised for above average generosity than blamed for giving less than they might. The appropriateness of praise and blame is, however, a separate issue from the rightness or wrongness of actions. The former evaluates the agent: the latter evaluates the action. Perhaps many people who give $1,000 really ought to give at least $5,000, but to blame them for not giving more could be counterproductive. It might make them feel that

---

* John Locke (1632–1704) was a British philosopher who maintained that a government's legitimacy depends upon its commitment to protecting the rights of its citizens; Robert Nozick (1938–2002) was an American philosopher whose writings in political philosophy stressed the importance of individual rights. Selections from both these philosophers appear later in this volume.

what is required is too demanding, and if one is going to be blamed anyway, one might as well not give anything at all.

(That an ethic that puts saving all one possibly can on the same footing as not killing would be an ethic for saints or heroes should not lead us to assume that the alternative must be an ethic that makes it obligatory not to kill, but puts us under no obligation to save anyone. There are positions in between these extremes, as we shall soon see.)

Here is a summary of the five differences that normally exist between killing and allowing to die, in the context of absolute poverty and overseas aid. The lack of an identifiable victim is of no moral significance, though it may play an important role in explaining our attitudes. The idea that we are directly responsible for those we kill, but not for those we do not help, depends on a questionable notion of responsibility and may need to be based on a controversial theory of rights. Differences in certainty and motivation are ethically significant, and show that not aiding the poor is not to be condemned as murdering them; it could, however, be on a par with killing someone as a result of reckless driving, which is serious enough. Finally the difficulty of completely discharging the duty of saving all one possibly can makes it inappropriate to blame those who fall short of this target as we blame those who kill; but this does not show that the act itself is less serious. Nor does it indicate anything about those who, far from saving all they possibly can, make no effort to save anyone.

These conclusions suggest a new approach. Instead of attempting to deal with the contrast between affluence and poverty by comparing not saving with deliberate killing, let us consider afresh whether we have an obligation to assist those whose lives are in danger, and if so, how this obligation applies to the present world situation.

THE OBLIGATION TO ASSIST

THE ARGUMENT FOR AN OBLIGATION TO ASSIST

The path from the library at my university to the humanities lecture theatre passes a shallow ornamental pond. Suppose that on my way to give a lecture I notice that a small child has fallen in and is in danger of drowning. Would anyone deny that I ought to wade in and pull the child out? This will mean getting my clothes muddy and either cancelling my lecture or delaying it until I can find something dry to change into; but compared with the avoidable death of a child this is insignificant.

A plausible principle that would support the judgment that I ought to pull the child out is this: if it is in our power to prevent something very bad from happening, without thereby sacrificing anything of comparable moral significance, we ought to do it. This principle seems uncontroversial. It will obviously win the assent of consequentialists; but non-consequentialists should accept it too, because the injunction to prevent what is bad applies only when nothing comparably significant is at stake. Thus the principle cannot lead to the kinds of actions of which non-consequentialists strongly disapprove—serious violations of individual rights, injustice, broken promises, and so on. If non-consequentialists regard any of these as comparable in moral significance to the bad thing that is to be prevented, they will automatically regard the principle as not applying in those cases in which the bad thing can only be prevented by violating rights, doing injustice, breaking promises, or whatever else is at stake. Most non-consequentialists hold that we ought to prevent what is bad and promote what is good. Their dispute with consequentialists lies in their insistence that this is not the sole ultimate ethical principle: that it is an ethical principle is not denied by any plausible ethical theory.

Nevertheless the uncontroversial appearance of the principle that we ought to prevent what is bad when we can do so without sacrificing anything of comparable moral significance is deceptive. If it were taken seriously and acted upon, our lives and our world would be fundamentally changed. For the principle applies, not just to rare situations in which one can save a child from a pond, but to the everyday situation in which we can assist those living in absolute poverty. In saying this I assume that absolute poverty, with its hunger and malnutrition, lack of shelter, illiteracy, disease, high infant mortality, and low life expectancy, is a bad thing. And I assume that it is within the power of the affluent to reduce absolute poverty, without sacrificing anything of comparable moral significance. If these two assumptions and the principle we have been discussing are correct, we have an obligation to help those in absolute poverty that is no less strong than our obligation to rescue a drowning child from a pond. Not to help would be wrong, whether or not it is intrinsically equivalent to killing. Helping is not, as conventionally thought, a charitable act that it is praiseworthy to do, but not wrong to omit; it is something that everyone ought to do.

This is the argument for an obligation to assist. Set out more formally, it would look like this.

> First Premise: If we can prevent something bad without sacrificing anything of comparable significance, we ought to do it.
>
> Second premise: Absolute poverty is bad.
>
> Third premise: There is some absolute poverty we can prevent without sacrificing anything of comparable moral significance.
>
> Conclusion: We ought to prevent some absolute poverty.

The first premise is the substantive moral premise on which the argument rests, and I have tried to show that it can be accepted by people who hold a variety of ethical positions.

The second premise is unlikely to be challenged. Absolute poverty is, as McNamara put it, "beneath any reasonable definition of human decency" and it would be hard to find a plausible ethical view that did not regard it as a bad thing.

The third premise is more controversial, even though it is cautiously framed. It claims only that some absolute poverty can be prevented without the sacrifice of anything of comparable moral significance. It thus avoids the objection that any aid I can give is just "drops in the ocean" for the point is not whether my personal contribution will make any noticeable impression on world poverty as a whole (of course it won't) but whether it will prevent some poverty. This is all the argument needs to sustain its conclusion, since the second premise says that any absolute poverty is bad, and not merely the total amount of absolute poverty. If without sacrificing anything of comparable moral significance we can provide just one family with the means to raise itself out of absolute poverty, the third premise is vindicated.

I have left the notion of moral significance unexamined in order to show that the argument does not depend on any specific values or ethical principles. I think the third premise is true for most people living in industrialised nations, on any defensible view of what is morally significant. Our affluence means that we have income we can dispose of without giving up the basic necessities of life, and we can use this income to reduce absolute poverty. Just how much we will think ourselves obliged to give up will depend on what we consider to be of comparable moral significance to the poverty we could prevent: stylish clothes, expensive dinners, a sophisticated stereo system, overseas holidays, a (second?) car, a larger house, private schools for our children, and so on. For a utilitarian, none of these is likely to be of comparable significance to the reduction of absolute poverty; and those who are not utilitarians surely must, if they subscribe to the principle of universalisability, accept that at least some of these things are of far less moral significance than the absolute poverty that could be prevented by the money they cost. So the third premise seems to be true on any plausible ethical view—although the precise amount of absolute poverty that can be prevented before anything of moral significance is sacrificed will vary according to the ethical view one accepts.

OBJECTIONS TO THE ARGUMENT

Taking care of our own. Anyone who has worked to increase overseas aid will have come across the argument that we should look after those near us, our families, and then the poor in our own country, before we think about poverty in distant places.

No doubt we do instinctively prefer to help those who are close to us. Few could stand by and watch a child drown; many can ignore a famine in Africa. But the question is not what we usually do, but what we ought to do, and it is difficult to see any sound moral justification for the view that distance, or community membership, makes a crucial difference to our obligations.

Consider, for instance, racial affinities. Should people of European origin help poor Europeans before helping poor Africans? Most of us would reject such a suggestion out of hand,... people's need for food has nothing to do with their race, and if Africans need food more than Europeans, it would be a violation of the principle of equal consideration to give preference to Europeans.

The same point applies to citizenship or nationhood. Every affluent nation has some relatively poor citizens, but absolute poverty is limited largely to the poor nations. Those living on the streets of Calcutta, or in the drought-prone Sahel region of Africa, are experiencing poverty unknown in the West. Under these circumstances it would be wrong to decide that only those fortunate enough to be citizens of our own community will share our abundance.

We feel obligations of kinship more strongly than those of citizenship. Which parents could give away their last bowl of rice if their own children were starving? To do so would seem unnatural, contrary to our nature as biologically evolved beings—although whether it would be wrong is another question altogether. In any case, we are not faced with that situation, but with one in which our own children are well-fed, well-clothed, well-educated, and would now like new bikes, a stereo set, or their own car. In these circumstances any special obligations we might have to our children have been fulfilled, and the needs of strangers make a stronger claim upon us.

The element of truth in the view that we should first take care of our own, lies in the advantage of a recognised system of responsibilities. When families and local communities look after their own poorer members, ties of affection and personal relationships achieve ends that would otherwise require a large, impersonal bureaucracy. Hence it would be absurd to propose that from now on we all regard ourselves as equally responsible for the welfare of everyone in the world; but the argument for an obligation to assist does not propose that. It applies only when some are in absolute poverty, and others can help without sacrificing anything of comparable moral significance. To allow one's own kin to sink into absolute poverty would be to sacrifice something of comparable significance; and before that point had been reached, the breakdown of the system of family and community responsibility would be a factor to weigh the balance in favour of a small degree of preference for family and community. This small degree of preference is, however, decisively outweighed by existing discrepancies in wealth and property.

Property rights. Do people have a right to private property, a right that contradicts the view that they are under an obligation to give some of their wealth away to those in absolute poverty? According to some theories of rights (for instance, Robert Nozick's), provided one has acquired one's property without the use of unjust means like force and fraud, one may be entitled to enormous wealth while others starve. This individualistic conception of rights is in contrast to other views, like the early Christian doctrine to be found in the works of Thomas Aquinas* which holds that since property exists for the satisfaction of human needs, "whatever a man has in superabundance is owed, of natural right, to the poor for their sustenance." A socialist would also, of course, see wealth as belonging to the community rather than the individual, while utilitarians, whether socialist or not, would be prepared to override property rights to prevent great evils.

Does the argument for an obligation to assist others therefore presuppose one of these other theories of property rights, and not an individualistic theory like Nozick's? Not necessarily. A theory of property rights can insist on our *right* to retain wealth without pronouncing on whether the rich *ought* to give to the poor. Nozick, for example, rejects the use of compulsory means like taxation to redistribute income, but suggests that we can achieve the ends we deem morally desirable by voluntary means. So Nozick would reject the claim that rich people have an "obligation" to give to the poor, in so far as this implies that the poor have a right to our aid, but might accept that giving is something we ought to do and failing to give, though within one's rights, is wrong—for there is more to an ethical life than respecting the rights of others.

The argument for an obligation to assist can survive, with only minor modifications, even if we

* Thomas Aquinas (c. 1225–74) was among the most important theologians and philosophers of the Middle Ages.

accept an individualistic theory of property rights. In any case, however, I do not think we should accept such a theory. It leaves too much to chance to be an acceptable ethical view. For instance, those whose forefathers happened to inhabit some sandy wastes around the Persian Gulf are now fabulously wealthy, because oil lay under those sands; while those whose forefathers settled on better land south of the Sahara live in absolute poverty, because of drought and bad harvests. Can this distribution be acceptable from an impartial point of view? If we imagine ourselves about to begin life as a citizen of either Bahrein or Chad—but we do not know which—would we accept the principle that citizens of Bahrein are under no obligation to assist people living in Chad?

Population and the ethics of triage. Perhaps the most serious objection to the argument that we have an obligation to assist is that since the major cause of absolute poverty is overpopulation, helping those now in poverty will only ensure that yet more people are born to live in poverty in the future.

In its most extreme form, this objection is taken to show that we should adopt a policy of "triage." The term comes from medical policies adopted in wartime. With too few doctors to cope with all the casualties, the wounded were divided into three categories: those who would probably survive without medical assistance, those who might survive if they received assistance, but otherwise probably would not, and those who even with medical assistance probably would not survive. Only those in the middle category were given medical assistance. The idea, of course, was to use limited medical resources as effectively as possible. For those in the first category, medical treatment was not strictly necessary; for those in the third category, it was likely to be useless. It has been suggested that we should apply the same policies to countries, according to their prospects of becoming self-sustaining. We would not aid countries that even without our help will soon be able to feed their populations. We would not aid countries that, even with our help, will not be able to limit their population to a level they can feed. We would aid those countries where our help might make the difference between success and failure in bringing food and population into balance.

Advocates of this theory are understandably reluctant to give a complete list of the countries they would place into the "hopeless" category; Bangladesh has been cited as an example, and so have some of the countries of the Sahel region of Africa. Adopting the policy of triage would, then, mean cutting off assistance to these countries and allowing famine, disease, and natural disasters to reduce the population of those countries to the level at which they can provide adequately for all.

In support of this view Garrett Hardin* has offered a metaphor: we in the rich nations are like the occupants of a crowded lifeboat adrift in a sea full of drowning people. If we try to save the drowning by bringing them aboard, our boat will be overloaded and we shall all drown. Since it is better that some survive than none, we should leave the others to drown. In the world today, according to Hardin, "lifeboat ethics" apply. The rich should leave the poor to starve, for otherwise the poor will drag the rich down with them.

Against this view, some writers have argued that overpopulation is a myth. The world produces ample food to feed its population, and could, according to some estimates, feed ten times as many. People are hungry not because there are too many but because of inequitable land distribution, the manipulation of third world economies by the developed nations, wastage of food in the West, and so on.

Putting aside the controversial issue of the extent to which food production might one day be increased, it is true, as we have already seen, that the world now produces enough to feed its inhabitants—the amount lost by being fed to animals itself being enough to meet existing grain shortages. Nevertheless population growth cannot be ignored. Bangladesh could, with land reform and using better techniques, feed its present population of 115 million; but by the year 2000, according to United Nations Population Division estimates, its population will be 150 million. The enormous effort

* Garrett Hardin (1915–2003) was an American ecologist whose essay "Lifeboat Ethics: The Case Against Helping the Poor" appears as the next selection in this volume; he is credited with coining the phrase "nice guys finish last."

that will have to go into feeding an extra 35 million people, all added to the population within a decade, means that Bangladesh must develop at full speed to stay where it is. Other low-income countries are in similar situations. By the end of the century, Ethiopia's population is expected to rise from 49 to 66 million; Somalia's from 7 to 9 million, India's from 853 to 1041 million,...*

What will happen if the world population continues to grow? It cannot do so indefinitely. It will be checked by a decline in birth rates or a rise in death rates. Those who advocate triage are proposing that we allow the population growth of some countries to be checked by a rise in death rates—that is, by increased malnutrition, and related diseases; by widespread famines; by increased infant mortality; and by epidemics of infectious diseases.

The consequences of triage on this scale are so horrible that we are inclined to reject it without further argument. How could we sit by our television sets, watching millions starve while we do nothing? Would not that be the end of all notions of human equality and respect for human life? (Those who attack proposals for legalising euthanasia by... saying that these proposals will weaken respect for human life would surely do better to object to the idea that we should reduce or end our overseas aid programs, for that proposal, if implemented, would be responsible for a far greater loss of human life.) Don't people have a right to our assistance, irrespective of the consequences?

Anyone whose initial reaction to triage was not one of repugnance would be an unpleasant sort of person. Yet initial reactions based on strong feelings are not always reliable guides. Advocates of triage are rightly concerned with the long-term consequences of our actions. They say that helping the poor and starving now merely ensures more poor and starving in the future. When our capacity to help is finally unable to cope—as one day it must be—the suffering will be greater than it would be if we stopped helping now. If this is correct, there is nothing we can do to prevent absolute starvation and poverty, in the long run, and so we have no obligation to assist. Nor does it seem reasonable to hold that under these circumstances people have a right to our assistance. If we do accept such a right, irrespective of the consequences, we are saying that, in Hardin's metaphor, we should continue to haul the drowning into our lifeboat until the boat sinks and we all drown.

If triage is to be rejected it must be tackled on it own ground, within the framework of consequentialist ethics. Here it is vulnerable. Any consequentialist ethics must take probability of outcome into account. A course of action that will certainly produce some benefit is to be preferred to an alternative course that may lead to a slightly larger benefit, but is equally likely to result in no benefit at all. Only if the greater magnitude of the uncertain benefit outweighs its uncertainty should we choose it. Better one certain unit of benefit than a 10 percent chance of five units; but better a 50 per cent chance of three units than a single certain unit. The same principle applies when we are trying to avoid evils.

The policy of triage involves a certain, very great evil: population control by famine and disease. Tens of millions would die slowly. Hundreds of millions would continue to live in absolute poverty, at the very margin of existence. Against this prospect, advocates of the policy place a possible evil that is greater still: the same process of famine and disease, taking place in, say, fifty years' time, when the world's population may be three times its present level, and the number who will die from famine, or struggle on in absolute poverty, will be that much greater. The question is: how probable is this forecast that continued assistance now will lead to greater disasters in the future?

Forecasts of population growth are notoriously fallible, and theories about the factors that affect it remain speculative. One theory, at least as plausible as any other, is that countries pass through a "demographic transition" as their standard of

* Ominously, in the twelve years that have passed between editions of this book, the signs are that the situation is becoming even worse than was then predicted. In 1979 Bangladesh had a population of 80 million and it was predicted that by 2000 its population would reach 146 million; Ethiopia's was only 29 million, and was predicted to reach 54 million; and India's was 620 million and predicted to reach 958 million. (Singer wrote this note in 1999. The 2007 estimates for the populations of these countries are: Bangladesh—150 million; Ethiopia—77 million; Somalia—9 million; India—1.1 billion;—Eds.).

living rises. When people are very poor and have no access to modern medicine their fertility is high, but population is kept in check by high death rates. The introduction of sanitation, modern medical techniques, and other improvements reduces the death rate, but initially has little effect on the birth rate. Then population grows rapidly. Some poor countries, especially in sub-Saharan Africa, are now in this phase. If standards of living continue to rise, however, couples begin to realise that to have the same number of children surviving to maturity as in the past, they do not need to give birth to as many children as their parents did. The need for children to provide economic support in old age diminishes. Improved education and the emancipation and employment of women also reduce the birth-rate, and so population growth begins to level off. Most rich nations have reached this stage, and their populations are growing only very slowly, if at all.

If this theory is right, there is an alternative to the disasters accepted as inevitable by supporters of triage. We can assist poor countries to raise the living standards of the poorest members of their population. We can encourage the governments of these countries to enact land reform measures, improve education, and liberate women from a purely child-bearing role. We can also help other countries to make contraception and sterilization widely available. There is a fair chance that these measures will hasten the onset of the demographic transition and bring population growth down to a manageable level. According to United Nations estimates, in 1965 the average woman in the third world gave birth to six children, and only 8 per cent were using some form of contraception; by 1991 the average number of children had dropped to just below four, and more than half the women in the third world were taking contraceptive measures. Notable successes in encouraging the use of contraception had occurred in Thailand, Indonesia, Mexico, Colombia, Brazil, and Bangladesh. This achievement reflected a relatively low expenditure in developing countries—considering the size and significance of the problem—of $3 billion annually, with only 20 per cent of this sum coming from developed nations. So expenditure in this area seems likely to be highly cost-effective. Success cannot be guaranteed; but the evidence suggests that we can reduce population growth by improving economic security and education, and making contraceptives more widely available. This prospect makes triage ethically unacceptable. We cannot allow millions to die from starvation and disease when there is a reasonable probability that population can be brought under control without such horrors.

Population growth is therefore not a reason against giving overseas aid, although it should make us think about the kind of aid to give. Instead of food handouts, it may be better to give aid that leads to a slowing of population growth. This may mean agricultural assistance for the rural poor, or assistance with education, or the provision of contraceptive services. Whatever kind of aid proves most effective in specific circumstances, the obligation to assist is not reduced.

One awkward question remains. What should we do about a poor and already overpopulated country that, for religious or nationalistic reasons, restricts the use of contraceptives and refuses to slow its population growth? Should we nevertheless offer development assistance? Or should we make our offer conditional on effective steps being taken to reduce the birth-rate? To the latter course, some would object that putting conditions on aid is an attempt to impose our own ideas on independent sovereign nations. So it is—but is this imposition unjustifiable? If the argument for an obligation to assist is sound, we have an obligation to reduce absolute poverty; but we have no obligation to make sacrifices that, to the best of our knowledge, have no prospect of reducing poverty in the long run. Hence we have no obligation to assist countries whose governments have policies that will make our aid ineffective. This could be very harsh on poor citizens of these countries—for they may have no say in the government's policies—but we will help more people in the long run by using our resources where they are most effective. (The same principles may apply, incidentally, to countries that refuse to take other steps that could make assistance effective—like refusing to reform systems of land holding that impose intolerable burdens on poor tenant farmers.)

Leaving it to the government. We often hear that overseas aid should be a government responsibility, not left to privately run charities. Giving privately, it is said, allows the government to escape its responsibilities.

Since increasing government aid is the surest way of making a significant increase to the total amount of aid given, I would agree that the governments of affluent nations should give much more genuine, no-strings-attached, aid than they give now. Less than one-sixth of one per cent of GNP is a scandalously small amount for a nation as wealthy as the United States to give. Even the official UN target of 0.7 per cent seems much less than affluent nations can and should give—though it is a target few have reached. But is this a reason against each of us giving what we can privately, through voluntary agencies? To believe that it is seems to assume that the more people there are who give through voluntary agencies, the less likely it is that the government will do its part. Is this plausible? The opposite view—that if no one gives voluntarily the government will assume that its citizens are not in favour of overseas aid, and will cut its programme accordingly—is more reasonable. In any case, unless there is a definite probability that by refusing to give we would be helping to bring about an increase in government assistance, refusing to give privately is wrong for the same reason that triage is wrong: it is a refusal to prevent a definite evil for the sake of a very uncertain gain. The onus of showing how a refusal to give privately will make the government give more is on those who refuse to give.

This is not to say that giving privately is enough. Certainly we should campaign for entirely new standards for both public and private overseas aid. We should also work for fairer trading arrangements between rich and poor countries, and less domination of the economies of poor countries by multinational corporations more concerned about producing profits for shareholders back home than food for the local poor. Perhaps it is more important to be politically active in the interests of the poor than to give to them oneself—but why not do both? Unfortunately, many use the view that overseas aid is the government's responsibility as a reason against giving, but not as a reason for being politically active.

Too high a standard? The final objection to the argument for an obligation to assist is that it sets a standard so high that none but a saint could attain it. This objection comes in at least three versions. The first maintains that, human nature being what it is, we cannot achieve so high a standard, and since it is absurd to say that we ought to do what we cannot do, we must reject the claim that we ought to give so much. The second version asserts that even if we could achieve so high a standard, to do so would be undesirable. The third version of the objection is that to set so high a standard is undesirable because it will be perceived as too difficult to reach, and will discourage many from even attempting to do so.

Those who put forward the first version of the objection are often influenced by the fact that we have evolved from a natural process in which those with a high degree of concern for their own interests, or the interests of their offspring and kin, can be expected to leave more descendants in future generations, and eventually to completely replace any who are entirely altruistic. Thus the biologist Garrett Hardin has argued, in support of his "lifeboat ethics," that altruism can only exist "on a small scale, over the short term, and within small, intimate groups"; while Richard Dawkins* has written, in his provocative book *The Selfish Gene:* "Much as we might wish to believe otherwise, universal love and the welfare of the species as a whole are concepts which simply do not make evolutionary sense." I have already noted, in discussing the objection that we should first take care of our own, the very strong tendency for partiality in human beings. We naturally have a stronger desire to further our own interests, and those of our close kin, than we have to further the interests of strangers. What this means is that we would be foolish to expect widespread conformity to a standard that demands impartial concern, and for that reason it would scarcely be appropriate or feasible to condemn all those who fail to reach such a standard. Yet to act impartially, though it might be very difficult, is not impossible. The commonly

* Richard Dawkins (1941–) is a British ethologist and evolutionary biologist.

quoted assertion that "ought" implies "can" is a reason for rejecting such moral judgments as "You ought to have saved all the people from the sinking ship," when in fact if you had taken one more person into the lifeboat, it would have sunk and you would not have saved any. In that situation, it is absurd to say that you ought to have done what you could not possibly do. When we have money to spend on luxuries and others are starving, however, it is clear that we can all give much more than we do give, and we can therefore all come closer to the impartial standard proposed in this chapter. Nor is there, as we approach closer to this standard, any barrier beyond which we cannot go. For that reason there is no basis for saying that the impartial standard is mistaken because "ought" implies "can" and we cannot be impartial.

The second version of the objection has been put by several philosophers during the past decade, among them Susan Wolf* in a forceful article entitled "Moral Saints." Wolf argues that if we all took the kind of moral stance defended in this chapter, we would have to do without a great deal that makes life interesting: opera, gourmet cooking, elegant clothes, and professional sport, for a start. The kind of life we come to see as ethically required of us would be a single-minded pursuit of the overall good, lacking that broad diversity of interests and activities that, on a less demanding view, can be part of our ideal of a good life for a human being. To this, however, one can respond that while the rich and varied life that Wolf upholds as an ideal may be the most desirable form of life for a human being in a world of plenty, it is wrong to assume that it remains a good life in a world in which buying luxuries for oneself means accepting the continued avoidable suffering of others. A doctor faced with hundreds of injured victims of a train crash can scarcely think it defensible to treat fifty of them and then go to the opera, on the grounds that going to the opera is part of a well-rounded human life. The life-or-death needs of others must take priority. Perhaps we are like the doctor in that we live in a time when we all have an opportunity to help to mitigate a disaster.

Associated with this second version of the objection is the claim that an impartial ethic of the kind advocated here makes it impossible to have serious personal relationships based on love and friendship; these relationships are, of their nature, partial. We put the interests of our loved ones, our family, and our friends ahead of those of strangers; if we did not do so, would these relationships survive? I have already indicated, in the response I gave when considering the objection that we should first take care of our own, that there is a place, within an impartially grounded moral framework, for recognizing some degree of partiality for kin, and the same can be said for other close personal relationships. Clearly, for most people, personal relationships are among the necessities of a flourishing life, and to give them up would be to sacrifice something of great moral significance. Hence no such sacrifice is required by the principle for which I am here arguing.

The third version of the objection asks: might it not be counterproductive to demand that people give up so much? Might not people say: "As I can't do what is morally required anyway, I won't bother to give at all." If, however, we were to set a more realistic standard, people might make a genuine effort to reach it. Thus setting a lower standard might actually result in more aid being given.

It is important to get the status of this third version of the objection clear. Its accuracy as a prediction of human behaviour is quite compatible with the argument that we are obliged to give to the point at which by giving more we sacrifice something of comparable moral significance. What would follow from the objection is that public advocacy of this standard of giving is undesirable. It would mean that in order to do the maximum to reduce absolute poverty, we should advocate a standard lower than the amount we think people really ought to give. Of course we ourselves—those of us who accept the original argument, with its higher standard—would know that we ought to do more than we publicly propose people ought to do, and we might actually give more than we urge others to give. There is no inconsistency here, since in both our private and our

* Susan Wolf (1953–) is an American philosopher; her essay "Moral Saints" appears later in this section of the volume.

public behaviour we are trying to do what will most reduce absolute poverty.

For a consequentialist, this apparent conflict between public and private morality is always a possibility, and not in itself an indication that the underlying principle is wrong. The consequences of a principle are one thing, the consequences of publicly advocating it another. A variant of this idea is already acknowledged by the distinction between the intuitive and critical levels of morality, of which I have made use in previous chapters. If we think of principles that are suitable for the intuitive level of morality as those that should be generally advocated, these are the principles that, when advocated, will give rise to the best consequences. Where overseas aid is concerned, those will be the principles that lead to the largest amount being given by the affluent to the poor.

Is it true that the standard set by our argument is so high as to be counterproductive? There is not much evidence to go by, but discussions of the argument, with students and others have led me to think it might be. Yet, the conventionally accepted standard—a few coins in a collection tin when one is waved under your nose—is obviously far too low. What level should we advocate? Any figure will be arbitrary, but there may be something to be said for a round percentage of one's income like, say, 10 percent—more than a token donation, yet not so high as to be beyond all but saints. (This figure has the additional advantage of being reminiscent of the ancient tithe, or tenth, that was traditionally given to the church, whose responsibilities included care of the poor in one's local community. Perhaps the idea can be revived and applied to the global community.) Some families, of course, will find 10 per cent a considerable strain on their finances. Others may be able to give more without difficulty. No figure should be advocated as a rigid minimum or maximum; but it seems safe to advocate that those earning average or above average incomes in affluent societies, unless they have an unusually large number of dependents or other special needs, ought to give a tenth of their income to reducing absolute poverty. By any reasonable ethical standards this is the minimum we ought to do, and we do wrong if we do less.

NOTES

1. Strictly, we would need to cut down to the minimum level compatible with earning the income which, after providing for our needs, left us most to give away. Thus if my present position earns me, say, $40,000 a year, but requires me to spend $5,000 a year on dressing respectably and maintaining a car, I cannot save more people by giving away the car and clothes if that will mean taking a job that, although it does not involve me in these expenses, earns me only $20,000.

The summary of world poverty was compiled from a number of sources, including Alan B. Durning, "Ending Poverty" in the Worldwatch Institute report edited by Lester Brown et al., *State of the World 1990* (Washington D.C., 1990); the United Nations Development Programme's *Human Development Report 1991;* and the report of the World Commission on Environment and Development, *Our Common Future* (Oxford, 1987). The first quotation from Robert McNamara in the section "Some Facts about Poverty" is from the *Summary Proceedings* of the 1976 Annual Meeting of the World Bank/IFC/IDA, p. 14; the following quotation is from the World Bank's *World Development Report, 1978* (New York 1978), p. iii.

For the wastage involved in feeding crops to animals instead of directly to humans, see Francis Moore Lappe, *Diet for a Small Planet* (New York, 1971; 10th anniversary ed., 1982); A. Durning and H. Brough, *Taking Stock,* Worldwatch Paper 103 (Washington, D.C. 1991); and J. Rifkin, *Beyond Beef* (New York, 1991), chap. 23

On the difference—or lack of it—between killing and allowing to die, see... Jonathan Glover, *Causing Death and Saving Lives,* chap. 7; Richard Trammel, "Saving Life and Taking Life," *Journal of Philosophy,* vol. 72 (1975); John Harris, "The Marxist Conception of Violence," *Philosophy and Public Affairs,* vol. 3 (1974); John Harris, *Violence and Responsibility* (London, 1980); and S. Kagan, *The Limits of Morality* (Oxford, 1989).

John Locke's view of rights is developed in his *Second Treatise on Civil Government,* and Robert Nozick's in *Anarchy, State and Utopia* (New York, 1974). Thomas

Aquinas's quite different view is quoted from *Summa Theologica,* 2 ii, Question 66, article 7.

Garrett Hardin proposed his "lifeboat ethic" in "Living on a Lifeboat," *Bioscience,* October 1974, another version of which has been reprinted in W. Aiken and H. La Follette (eds.), *World Hunger and Moral Obligation* (Englewood Cliffs, N.J., 1977). Hardin elaborates on the argument in *The Limits of Altruism* (Bloomington, Indiana, 1977). An earlier argument against aid was voiced by W. and P. Paddock in their mistitled *Famine 1975!* (Boston 1967) but pride of place in the history of this view must go to Thomas Malthus for *An Essay on the Principle of Population* (London, 1798).

Opposition to the view that the world is overpopulated comes from Susan George, *How the Other Half Dies,* rev. ed. (Harmondsworth, Middlesex, 1977), chap. 2. See also T. Hayter *The Creation of World Poverty* (London, 1981). The estimates of population in various countries by the year 2000 are taken from the *Human Development Report, 1991.* For evidence that more equal distribution of income, better education, and better health facilities can reduce population growth, see John W. Ratcliffe, "Poverty, Politics and Fertility: The Anomaly of Kerala," *Hastings Center Report,* vol. 7 (1977); for a more general discussion of the idea of demographic transition, see William Rich, *Smaller Families through Social and Economic Progress,* Overseas Development Council Monograph no. 7 (1973); and Julian Simon, *The Effects of Income on Fertility,* Carolina Population Center Monograph (Chapel Hill, N.C., 1974). On ethical issues relating to population control, see Robert Young, "Population Policies, Coercion and Morality," in D. Mannison, R. Routley, and M. McRobbie (eds.), *Environmental Philosophy* (Canberra, 1979).

The objection that a position such as mine poses too high a standard is put by Susan Wolf, "Moral Saints," *Journal of Philosophy,* vol. 79 (1982): 419–39. See also the "Symposium on Impartiality and Ethical Theory," *Ethics,* vol. 101 (July 1991): 4. For a forceful defence of impartialist ethics see S. Kagan, *The Limits of Morality* (Oxford, 1989).

For a summary of the issues, see Nigel Dower, "World Poverty," in P. Signer (ed.), *A Companion to Ethics.* A fuller account by the same author is *World Poverty: Challenge and Response* (York, 1983). For a rights approach, see H. Shue, *Basic Rights: Subsistence, Affluence and U.S. Policy* (Princeton, 1980); and for a Kantian approach, Onora O'Neill, *Faces of Hunger* (London, 1986). A useful general collection is W. Aiken and H. La Follette (eds.), *World Hunger and Moral Obligation* (Englewood Cliffs, N.J., 1977). On the efficacy of overseas aid, see R. Riddell, *Foreign Aid Reconsidered* (Baltimore, 1987).

Lifeboat Ethics: The Case Against Helping the Poor

GARRETT HARDIN

Garrett Hardin (1915–2003) taught human ecology at the University of California, Santa Barbara. His best-known work is his 1968 paper "The Tragedy of the Commons."

This selection was originally published in 1974 as an article in a popular magazine (*Psychology Today*), in part as a response to Peter Singer's earlier writings on the topic of morality and famine. In it, Hardin defends the view that providing aid to underdeveloped countries is not morally mandatory—indeed, it may be morally counterindicated.

From "the Case Against Helping the Poor," *Psychology Today* (1974) pp. 38–43, 123–26. Reprinted with permission from *Psychology Today* magazine. Copyright © 1974 Sussex Publishers, Inc.

Environmentalists use the metaphor of the earth as a "spaceship" in trying to persuade countries, industries, and people to stop wasting and polluting our natural resources. Since we all share life on this planet, they argue, no single person or institution has the right to destroy, waste, or use more than a fair share of its resources.

But does everyone on earth have an equal right to an equal share of its resources? The spaceship metaphor can be dangerous when used by misguided idealists to justify suicidal policies for sharing our resources through uncontrolled immigration and foreign aid. In their enthusiastic but unrealistic generosity, they confuse the ethics of a spaceship with those of a lifeboat.

A true spaceship would have to be under the control of a captain, since no ship could possibly survive if its course were determined by committee. Spaceship Earth certainly has no captain; the United Nations is merely a toothless tiger, with little power to enforce any policy upon its bickering members.

If we divide the world crudely into rich nations and poor nations, two thirds of them are desperately poor, and only one third comparatively rich, with the United States the wealthiest of all. Metaphorically each rich nation can be seen as a lifeboat full of comparatively rich people. In the ocean outside each lifeboat swim the poor of the world, who would like to get in, or at least to share some of the wealth. What should the lifeboat passengers do?

First, we must recognize the limited capacity of any lifeboat. For example, a nation's land has a limited capacity to support a population and as the current energy crisis has shown us, in some ways we have already exceeded the carrying capacity of our land.

ADRIFT IN A MORAL SEA

So here we sit, say fifty people in our lifeboat. To be generous, let us assume it has room for ten more, making a total capacity of sixty. Suppose the fifty of us in the lifeboat see one hundred others swimming in the water outside, begging for admission to our boat or for handouts. We have several options: We may be tempted to try to live by the Christian ideal of being "our brother's keeper," or by the Marxist ideal of "to each according to his needs." Since the needs of all in the water are the same, and since they can all be seen as "our brothers," we could take them all into our boat, making a total of 150 in a boat designed for sixty. The boat swamps, everyone drowns. Complete justice, complete catastrophe.

Since the boat has an unused excess capacity of ten more passengers, we could admit just ten more to it. But which ten do we let in? How do we choose? Do we pick the best ten, the neediest ten, "first come, first served"? And what do we say to the ninety we exclude? If we do let an extra ten into our lifeboat, we will have lost our "safety factor," an engineering principle of critical importance. For example, if we don't leave room for excess capacity as a safety factor in our country's agriculture, a new plant disease or a bad change in the weather could have disastrous consequences.

Suppose we decide to preserve our small safety factor and admit no more to the lifeboat. Our survival is then possible, although we shall have to be constantly on guard against boarding parties.

While this last solution clearly offers the only means of our survival, it is morally abhorrent to many people. Some say they feel guilty about their good luck. My reply is simple: "get out and yield your place to others." This may solve the problem of the guilt-ridden person's conscience, but it does not change the ethics of the lifeboat. The needy person to whom the guilt-ridden person yields his place will not himself feel guilty about his good luck. If he did, he would not climb aboard. The net result of conscience-stricken people giving up their unjustly held seats is the elimination of that sort of conscience from the lifeboat.

This is the basic metaphor within which we must work out our solutions. Let us now enrich the image, step by step, with substantive additions from the real world, a world that must solve real and pressing problems of overpopulation and hunger.

The harsh ethics of the lifeboat become even harsher when we consider the reproductive differences between the rich nations and the poor nations. The people inside the lifeboats are doubling in numbers every eighty-seven years; those swimming around outside are doubling, on the average, every thirty-five years, more than twice as fast as the rich. And since the world's resources are dwindling, the difference in prosperity between the rich and the poor can only increase.

As of 1973, the United States had a population of 210 million people, who were increasing by 0.8 percent per year. Outside our lifeboat, let us imagine another 210 million people (say the combined populations of Colombia, Ecuador, Venezuela, Morocco, Pakistan, Thailand, and the Philippines), who are increasing at a rate of 3.3 percent per year. Put differently, the doubling time for this aggregate population is twenty-one years, compared to eighty-seven years for the United States.

MULTIPLYING THE RICH AND THE POOR

Now suppose the United States agreed to pool its resources with those seven countries, with everyone receiving an equal share. Initially the ratio of Americans to non-Americans in this model would be one-to-one. But consider what the ratio would be after eighty-seven years, by which time the Americans would have doubled to a population of 420 million. By then, doubling every twenty-one years, the other group would have swollen to 354 billion. Each American would have to share the available resources with more than eight people.

But, one could argue, this discussion assumes that current population trends will continue, and they may not. Quite so. Most likely the rate of population increase will decline much faster in the United States than it will in the other countries, and there does not seem to be much we can do about it. In sharing with "each according to his needs," we must recognize that needs are determined by population size, which is determined by the rate of reproduction, which at present is regarded as a sovereign right of every nation, poor or not. This being so, the philanthropic load created by the sharing ethic of the spaceship can only increase.

THE TRAGEDY OF THE COMMONS

The fundamental error of spaceship ethics, and the sharing it requires, is that it leads to what I call "the tragedy of the commons." Under a system of private property, the men who own property recognize their responsibility to care for it, for if they don't they will eventually suffer. A farmer, for instance, will allow no more cattle in a pasture than its carrying capacity justifies. If he overloads it, erosion sets in, weeds take over, and he loses the use of the pasture.

If a pasture becomes a commons open to all, the right of each to use it may not be matched by a corresponding responsibility to protect it. Asking everyone to use it with discretion will hardly do, for the considerate hersdman who refrains from overloading the commons suffers more than a selfish one who says his needs are greater. If everyone would restrain himself, all would be well; but it takes only one less than everyone to ruin a system of voluntary restraint. In a crowded world of less than perfect human beings, mutual ruin is inevitable if there are no controls. This is the tragedy of the commons.

One of the major tasks of education today should be the creation of such an acute awareness of the dangers of the commons that people will recognize its many varieties. For example, the air and water have become polluted because they are treated as commons. Further growth in the population or per-capita conversion of natural resources into pollutants will only make the problem worse. The same holds true for the fish of the oceans. Fishing fleets have nearly disappeared in many parts of the world; technological improvements in the art of fishing are hastening the day of complete ruin. Only replacement of the system of the commons with a responsible system of control will save the land, air, water, and oceanic fisheries.

THE WORLD FOOD BANK

In recent years there has been a push to create a new commons called a World Food Bank, an international depository of food reserves to which nations would contribute according to their abilities and from which they would draw according to their needs. This humanitarian proposal has received support from many liberal international groups, and from such prominent citizens as Margaret Mead, U.N. Secretary General Kurt Waldheim, and Senators Edward Kennedy and George McGovern.

A World Food Bank appeals powerfully to our humanitarian impulses. But before we rush ahead with such a plan, let us recognize where the greatest political push comes from, lest we be disillusioned later. Our experience with the "Food for Peace program," or Public Law 480, gives us the answer. This program moved billions of dollars worth of U.S. surplus grain to food-short, population-long countries during the past two decades. But when P.L. 480 first became law, a headline in the business magazine *Forbes* revealed the real power behind it: "Feeding the World's Hungry Million: How It Will Mean Billions for U.S. Business."

And indeed it did. In the years 1960 to 1970, U.S. taxpayers spent a total of $7.9 billion on the Food for Peace program. Between 1948 and 1970, they also paid an additional $50 billion for other economic-aid programs, some of which went for food and food-producing machinery and technology. Though all U.S. taxpayers were forced to contribute to the cost of P.L. 480, certain special interest groups gained handsomely under the program. Farmers did not have to contribute the grain; the government, or rather the taxpayers, bought it from them at full market prices. The increased demand raised prices of farm products generally. The manufacturers of farm machinery, fertilizers, and pesticides benefited by the farmers' extra efforts to grow more food. Grain elevators profited from storing the surplus until it could be shipped. Railroads made money hauling it to ports, and shipping lines profited from carrying it overseas. The implementation of P.L. 480 required the creation of a vast government bureaucracy, which then acquired its own vested interest in continuing the program regardless of its merits.

EXTRACTING DOLLARS

Those who proposed and defended the Food for Peace program in public rarely mentioned its importance to any of these special interests. The public emphasis was always on its humanitarian effects. The combination of silent selfish interests and highly vocal humanitarian apologists made a powerful and successful lobby for extracting money from taxpayers. We can expect the same lobby to push now for the creation of a World Food Bank.

However great the potential benefit to selfish interests, it should not be a decisive argument against a truly humanitarian program. We must ask if such a program would actually do more good than harm, not only momentarily but also in the long run. Those who propose the food bank usually refer to a current "emergency" or "crisis" in terms of world food supply. But what is an emergency? Although they may be infrequent and sudden, everyone knows that emergencies will occur from time to time. A well-run family, company, organization, or country prepares for the likelihood of accidents and emergencies. It expects them, it budgets for them, it saves for them.

LEARNING THE HARD WAY

What happens if some organizations or countries budget for accidents and others do not? If each country is solely responsible for its own well-being, poorly managed ones will suffer. But they can learn from experience. They may mend their ways and learn to budget for infrequent but certain emergencies. For example, the weather varies from year to year, and periodic crop failures are certain. A wise and competent government saves out of the production of the good years in anticipation of bad years to come. Joseph taught this policy to Pharaoh in Egypt more than 2,000 years ago. Yet the great majority of the governments in the world today do not follow such a policy. They lack either the wisdom or the competence, or both. Should those nations that do manage to put something aside be forced to come to the rescue each time an emergency occurs among the poor nations?

"But it isn't their fault! some kindhearted liberals argue. "How can we blame the poor people who are caught in an emergency? Why must they suffer for the sins of their government? The concept of blame is simply not relevant here. The real question is, what are the operational consequences of establishing a World Food Bank? If it is open to every country every time a need develops, slovenly rulers will not be motivated to take Joseph's advice. Someone will always come to their aid. Some countries will deposit food in the World Food Bank, and others will withdraw it. There will be almost no overlap. As a result of such solutions to food shortage emergencies, the poor countries will not learn to mend their ways and will suffer progressively greater emergencies as their populations grow.

POPULATION CONTROL THE CRUDE WAY

On the average, poor countries undergo a 2.5 percent increase in population each year; rich countries, about 0.8 percent. Only rich countries have anything in the way of food reserves set aside, and even they do not have as much as they should. Poor countries have none. If poor countries received no food from the outside, the rate of their population growth would be periodically checked by crop failures and famines. But if they can always draw on a World Food Bank in time of need, their population can continue to grow unchecked, and so will their "need" for aid. In the short run, a World Food Bank may diminish that need, but in the long run it actually increases the need without limit.

Without some system of worldwide food sharing, the proportion of people in the rich and poor nations might eventually stabilize. The overpopulated poor countries would decrease in numbers, while the rich countries that had room for more people would increase. But with a well-meaning system of sharing, such as a World Food Bank, the growth differential between the rich and the poor countries will not only persist, it will increase. Because of the higher rate of population growth in the poor countries of the world, 88 percent of today's children are born poor, and only 12 percent rich. Year by year the ratio becomes worse, as the fast-reproducing poor outnumber the slow-reproducing rich.

A World Food Bank is thus a commons in disguise. People will have more motivation to draw from it than to add to any common store. The less provident and less able will multiply at the expense of the abler and more provident, bringing eventual ruin upon all who share in the commons. Besides, any system of "sharing" that amounts to foreign aid from rich nations to the poor nations will carry the taint of charity, which will contribute little to the world peace so devoutly desired by those who support the idea of a World Food Bank.

As past U.S. foreign-aid programs have amply and depressingly demonstrated, international charity frequently inspires mistrust and antagonism rather than gratitude on the part of the recipient nation.

CHINESE FISH AND MIRACLE RICE

The modern approach to foreign aid stresses the export of technology and advice, rather than money and food. As an ancient Chinese proverb goes: "Give a man a fish and he will eat for a day; teach him how to fish and he will eat for the rest of his days." Acting on this advice, the Rockefeller and Ford Foundations have financed a number of programs for improving agriculture in the hungry nations. Known as the "Green Revolution," these programs have led to the development of "miracle rice" and "miracle wheat," new strains that offer bigger harvests and greater resistance to crop damage. Norman Borlaug, the Nobel Prize–winning agronomist who, supported by the Rockerfeller Foundation, developed "miracle wheat," is one of the most prominent advocates of a World Food Bank.

Whether or not the Green Revolution can increase food production as much as its champions claim is a debatable but possibly irrelevant point. Those who support this well-intended humanitarian effort should first consider some of the fundamentals of human ecology. Ironically, one man who did was the late Alan Gregg, a vice-president of the Rockefeller Foundation. Two decades ago he expressed strong doubts about the wisdom of such attempts to increase food production. He likened the growth and spread of humanity over the surface of the earth to the spread of cancer in the human body, remarking that "cancerous growths demand food; but, as far as I know, they have never been cured by getting it."

OVERLOADING THE ENVIRONMENT

Every human born constitutes a draft on all aspects of the environment: food, air, water, forests, beaches, wildlife, scenery, and solitude. Food can, perhaps, be significantly increased to meet a growing demand. But what about clean beaches, unspoiled forests, and solitude? If we satisfy a growing population's need for food, we necessarily decrease its per capita supply of the other resources needed by men.

India, for example, now has a population of 600 million, which increases by 15 million per year. This population already puts a huge load on a relatively impoverished environment. The country's forests are now only a small fraction of what they were three centuries ago, and floods and erosion continually destroy the insufficient farmland that remains. Every one of the 15 million new lives added to India's population puts an additional burden on the environment and increases the economic and social costs of crowding. However humanitarian our intent, every Indian life saved through medical or nutritional assistance from abroad diminishes the quality of life for those who remain, and for subsequent generations. If rich countries make it possible, through foreign aid, for 600 million Indians to swell to 1.2 billion in a mere twenty-eight years, as their current growth rate threatens, will future generations of Indians thank us for hastening the destruction of their environment? Will our good intentions be sufficient excuse for the consequences of our actions?

My final example of a commons in action is one for which the public has the least desire for rational discussion—immigration. Anyone who publicly questions the wisdom of current U.S. immigration policy is promptly charged with bigotry, prejudice, ethnocentrism, chauvinism, isolationism, or selfishness. Rather than encounter such accusations, one would rather talk about other matters, leaving immigration policy to wallow in the crosscurrents of special interests that take no account of the good of the whole, or the interests of posterity.

Perhaps we still feel guilty about things we said in the past. Two generations ago the popular press frequently referred to Dagos, Wops, Polacks, Chinks, and Krauts, in articles about how America was being "overrun" by foreigners of supposedly inferior genetic stock. But because the implied inferiority of foreigners was used then as justification for keeping them out, people now assume that restrictive policies could only be based on such misguided notions. There are other grounds.

A NATION OF IMMIGRANTS

Just consider the numbers involved. Our government acknowledges a net inflow of 400,000 immigrants a year. While we have no hard data on the extent of illegal entries, educated guesses put the figure at about 600,000 a year. Since the natural increase (excess of births over deaths) of the resident population runs about 1.7 million per year, the yearly gain from immigration amounts to at least 19 percent of the total annual increase, and may be as much as 37 percent if we include the estimate for illegal immigrants. Considering the growing use of birth-control devices, the potential effect of educational campaigns by such organizations as Planned Parenthood Federation of America and Zero Population Growth, and the influence of inflation and the housing shortage, the fertility rate of American women may decline so much that immigration could account for all the yearly increase in population. Should we not at least ask if that is what we want?

For the sake of those who worry about whether the "quality" of the average immigrant compares favorably with the quality of the average resident, let us assume that immigrants and native-born citizens are of exactly equal quality, however one defines that term. We will focus here only on quantity; and since our conclusions will depend on nothing else, all charges of bigotry and chauvinism become irrelevant.

IMMIGRATION VERSUS FOOD SUPPLY

World food banks *move food to the people,* hastening the exhaustion of the environment of poor countries. Unrestricted immigration, on the other hand, *moves people to the food,* thus speeding up the destruction of the environment of the rich countries. We can easily understand why poor people should want to make this latter transfer, but why should rich hosts encourage it?

As in the case of foreign-aid programs, immigration receives support from selfish interests and humanitarian impulses. The primary selfish interest in unimpeded immigration is the desire of employers for cheap labor, particularly in industries and trades that offer degrading work. In the past, one wave of foreigners after another was brought into the United States to work at wretched jobs for wretched wages. In recent years the Cubans, Puerto Ricans, and Mexicans have had this dubious honor. The interests of the employers of cheap labor mesh well with the guilty silence of the country's liberal intelligentsia. White Anglo-Saxon Protestants are particularly reluctant to call for a closing of the doors to immigration for fear of being called bigots.

But not all countries have such reluctant leadership. Most educated Hawaiians, for example, are keenly aware of the limits of their environment, particularly in terms of population growth. There is only so much room on the islands, and the islanders know it. To Hawaiians, immigrants from the other forty-nine states present as great a threat as those from other nations. At a recent meeting of Hawaiian government officials in Honolulu, I had the ironic delight of hearing a speaker, who like most of his audience was of Japanese ancestry, ask how the country might practically and constitutionally close its doors to further immigration. One member of the audience countered: "How can we shut the doors now? We have many friends and relatives in Japan that we'd like to bring here some day so that they can enjoy Hawaii too." The Japanese-American speaker smiled sympathetically and answered: "Yes, but we have children now, and someday we'll have grandchildren too. We can bring more people here from Japan only by giving away some of the land that we hope to pass on to our grandchildren some day. What right do we have to do that?"

At this point, I can hear U.S. liberals asking: "How can you justify slamming the door once you're inside? You say that immigrants should be kept out. But aren't we all immigrants, or the descendants of immigrants? If we insist on staying, must we not admit all others?" Our craving for intellectual order leads us to seek and prefer symmetrical rules and morals: a single rule for me and everybody else; the same rule yesterday, today, and tomorrow. Justice, we feel, should not change with time and place.

We Americans of non-Indian ancestry can look upon ourselves as the descendants of thieves who are guilty morally, if not legally, of stealing this land from its Indian owners. Should we then give back the land to the now living American descendants of those Indians? However morally or logically sound this proposal may be, I, for one, am unwilling to live by it and I know no one else who is. Besides, the logical consequence would be absurd. Suppose that, intoxicated with a sense of pure justice, we should decide to turn our land over to the Indians. Since all our wealth has also been derived from the land, wouldn't we be morally obliged to give that back to the Indians too?

PURE JUSTICE VERSUS REALITY

Clearly, the concept of pure justice produces an infinite regression to absurdity. Centuries ago, wise men invented statutes of limitation to justify rejection of such pure justice, in the interest of preventing continual disorder. The law zealously defends property rights, but only relatively recent property rights. Drawing a line after an arbitrary time has elapsed may be unjust, but the alternatives are worse.

We are all descendants of thieves, and the world's resources are inequitably distributed. But we must begin the journey to tomorrow from the point where we are today. We cannot remake the past. We cannot safely divide the wealth equitably among peoples so long as people reproduce at different rates. To do so would guarantee that our grandchildren, and everyone else's grandchildren, would have only a ruined world to inhabit.

To be generous with one's own possessions is quite different from being generous with those of posterity. We should call this point to the attention of those who, from a commendable love of justice and equality, would institute a system of the commons, either in the form of a world food bank, or of unrestricted immigration. We must convince them if we wish to save at least some parts of the world from environmental ruin.

Without a true world government to control reproduction and the use of available resources, the sharing ethic of the spaceship is impossible. For the foreseeable future, our survival demands that we govern our actions by the ethics of a lifeboat, harsh though they may be. Posterity will be satisfied with nothing less.

ADDENDUM 1989

Can anyone watch children starve on television without wanting to help? Naturally sympathetic, a normal human being thinks that he can imagine what it is like to be starving. We all want to do unto others as we would have them do unto us.

But wanting is not doing. Forty years of activity by the U.S. Agency for International Development, as well as episodic nongovernmental attempts to feed the world's starving, have produced mixed results. Before we respond to the next appeal we should ask, "Does what we call 'aid' really help?"

Some of the shortcomings of food aid can be dealt with briefly. Waste is unavoidable: Because most poor countries have wretched transportation systems, food may sit on a dock until it rots. Then there are the corrupt politicians who take donated food away from the poor and give it to their political supporters. In Somalia in the 1980s, fully 70 percent of the donated food went to the army.

We can school ourselves to accept such losses. Panicky projects are always inefficient: Waste and corruption are par for the course. But there is another kind of loss that we cannot—in fact, we should not—accept, and that is the loss caused by the boomerang effects of philanthropy. Before we jump onto the next "feed-the-starving" bandwagon we need to understand how well-intentioned efforts can be counterproductive.

Briefly put, it is a mistake to focus only on starving people while ignoring their surroundings. Where there is great starvation there is usually an impoverished environment: poor soil, scarce water, and wildly fluctuating weather. As a result, the "carrying capacity" of the environment is low. The territory simply cannot support the population that is trying to live on it. Yet if the population were much smaller, and if it would stay smaller, the people would not need to starve.

Let us look at a particular example. Nigeria, like all the central African countries, has increased greatly in population in the last quarter-century. Over many generations, Nigerians learned that their farmlands would be most productive if crop-growing alternated with "fallow years"—years in which the land was left untilled to recover its fertility.

When modern medicine reduced the death rate, the population began to grow. More food was demanded from the same land. Responding to that need, Nigerians shortened the fallow periods. The result was counterproductive. In one carefully studied village, the average fallow period was shortened from 5.3 to 1.4 years. As a result, the yearly production (averaged over both fallow and crop years) fell by 30 percent.

Are Nigerian farmers stupid? Not at all! They know perfectly well what they are doing. But a farmer whose family has grown too large for his farm has to take care of next year's need before he can provide for the future. To fallow or not to fallow translates into this choice: zero production in a fallow year or a 30 percent shortfall over the long run. Starvation cannot wait. Long-term policies have to give way to short-term ones. So the farmer plows up his overstressed fields, thus diminishing long-term productivity.

Once the carrying capacity of a territory has been transgressed, its capacity goes down, year after year. Transgression is a one-way road to ruin. Ecologists memorialize this reality with an Eleventh Commandment: "Thou shalt not transgress the carrying capacity."

Transgression takes many forms. Poor people are poor in energy resources. They need energy to cook their food. Where do they get it? Typically, from animal dung or trees and bushes. Burning dung deprives the soil of nitrogen. Cutting down trees and bushes deprives the land of protection against eroding rain. Soil-poor slopes cannot support a crop of fuel-plants. Once the soil is gone, water runs off the slopes faster and floods the valleys below. First poor people deforest their land, and then deforestation makes them poorer.

When Americans send food to a starving population that has already grown beyond the environment's carrying capacity, we become a partner in the devastation of their land. Food from the outside keeps more natives alive; these demand more food and fuel; greater demand causes the community to transgress the carrying capacity more, and transgression results in lowering the carrying capacity. The deficit grows exponentially. Gifts of food to an overpopulated country boomerang, increasing starvation over the long run. Our choice is really between letting some die this year and letting more die in the following years.

You may protest, "That's easy enough for a well-fed American to say, but do citizens of poor countries agree?" Well, wisdom is not restricted to the wealthy. The Somali novelist Nuruddin Farrah has courageously condemned foreign gifts as being not truly aid, but a poison, because (if continued) such gifts will make Africans permanently dependent on outside aid.

The ethicist Joseph Fletcher has given a simple directive to would-be philanthropists: "Give if it helps, but not if it hurts." We can grant that giving makes the donor feel good at first—but how will he feel later when he realizes that he has harmed the receiver?

Only one thing can really help a poor country: population control. Having accepted disease control the people must now accept population control.

What the philosopher-economist Kenneth Boulding has called "lovey-dovey charity" is not enough. "It is well to remember," he said, "that the symbol of Christian love is a cross and not a Teddy bear." A good Christian should obey the Eleventh Commandment, refusing to send gifts that help poor people destroy the environment that must support the next generation.

"Aiding" the Global Poor

THOMAS W. POGGE

Thomas W. Pogge is a well-known moral and political philosopher who teaches at Columbia University in New York and at the Australian National University in Canberra, Australia. A student of John Rawls, he is best known for his work on issues of international justice.

The essay, "'Assisting' the Global Poor," that appears here is a revised version, prepared by Professor Pogge especially for this volume, an essay that originally appeared in 2004. In it, Pogge maintains that citizens of affluent nations are morally obliged to provide assistance to those in underdeveloped nations, since it is the actions of the wealthy nations that brought about the global order in which such conditions of poverty exist.

We citizens of the affluent countries tend to discuss our obligations toward the distant needy mainly in terms of donations and transfers, assistance and redistribution: How much of our wealth, if any, should we give away to the hungry abroad? I argue that framing the issue this way involves a serious error that is very costly for the global poor: We tend to assume that severe poverty is due to factors domestic to the countries in which it persists, not to foreign influences for which we may bear responsibility. This false empirical view leads rather directly to an important moral misconception: that we citizens of the rich countries are related to world poverty merely as potential helpers, not as active contributors. I will therefore examine closely

Updated and abridged version of "'Assisting' the Global Poor" *The Ethics of Assistance: Morality and the Distant Needy,* Deen Chatterjee, ed. (Cambridge: Cambridge University Press, 2004). Reprinted with the permission of the publisher.

the empirical view of the domestic causation of severe poverty, showing why it is false and also why it is so widely held in the affluent countries.

1. THE FALSITY OF THE PURELY DOMESTIC CAUSATION OF POVERTY THESIS (PDPT)

It is well to recall that existing peoples have arrived at their present levels of social, economic and cultural development through one historical process that was pervaded by enslavement, colonialism, even genocide. Though these monumental crimes are now in the past, they have left a legacy of great inequalities that would be unacceptable even if peoples were now masters of their own development. Even if the peoples of Africa had had, in recent decades, a real opportunity to achieve similar rates of economic growth as the affluent countries, achieving such growth could not have helped them reduce their initial 30:1 disadvantage in per capita income. Even if, starting in 1960, African annual growth in per capita income had been a full percentage point above ours each year, the ratio would still be 20:1 today and would not be fully erased until early in the 24th century.[1]

Defenders of the status quo are quick to point out that we cannot inherit our ancestors' sins. But how can we then claim the *fruits* of those sins: the lands and resources they acquired and the enormous advantage over the rest of the word they accumulated in the course of *one* historical process that has devastated the societies and cultures of four continents? By seeing the problem of poverty merely in terms of aid, we are treating the huge economic inequalities confronting us now as if they had come about through choices freely made within each people.

But let us leave aside the continuing legacies of historical injustice and focus on the empirical view that at least in the post-colonial era, which brought impressive growth in global per capita income, the causes of the *persistence* of severe poverty, and hence the key to its eradication, lie within the poor countries themselves. Many find this view compelling in light of the great variation in how the former colonies have evolved over the last forty years. Some of them have done very well in economic growth and poverty reduction while others exhibit worsening poverty and declining per capita incomes. Isn't it obvious that such strongly divergent national trajectories must be due to differing *domestic* causal factors in the countries concerned? And isn't it clear, then, that the persistence of severe poverty has local causes?

To see the fallacy in this reasoning, consider this parallel: There are great variations in the performance of my students. These variations must be caused by local (student-specific) factors. These factors, together, fully explain the performance of my class. Clearly, the parallel reasoning results in a falsehood: The performance of my class also crucially depends on the quality of my teaching and on various other factors (reading assignments, teaching times, classroom, libraries) as well. Such "global" factors can greatly influence the overall progress of a class—and even the distribution of this progress, as when a racist or sexist teacher impedes the learning of his black or female students. Similarly, the undeniable importance of national factors for explaining the persistence of severe poverty does not refute that global factors are also important: by influencing national factors and their effects.

This is not merely a theoretical possibility. There is considerable international economic interaction regulated by an elaborate system of treaties and conventions about trade, investments, loans, patents, copyrights, trademarks, double taxation, labor standards, environmental protection, use of seabed resources and much else. In many ways, such rules can be shaped to be more or less favorable to various affected parties such as, for instance, the poor in Africa or the pharmaceutical industry. Had these rules been shaped to be less unfavorable to the poor societies, much of the great poverty in them today would have been avoided.

Let me support this point with a quote from the *Economist* which—strongly supportive of World Trade Organization (WTO) globalization and highly critical of any protests against it—is surely not biased in my favor:

> Rich countries cut their tariffs by less in the Uruguay Round than poor ones did. Since then, they have

found new ways to close their markets, notably by imposing anti-dumping duties on imports they deem "unfairly cheap." Rich countries are particularly protectionist in many of the sectors where developing countries are best able to compete, such as agriculture, textiles, and clothing. As a result, according to a new study by Thomas Hertel, of Purdue University, and Will Martin, of the World Bank, rich countries' average tariffs on manufacturing imports from poor countries are four times higher than those on imports from other rich countries. This imposes a big burden on poor countries. The United Nations Conference on Trade and Development (UNCTAD) estimates that they could export $700 billion more a year by 2005 if rich countries did more to open their markets. Poor countries are also hobbled by a lack of know-how. Many had little understanding of what they signed up to in the Uruguay Round. That ignorance is now costing them dear. Michael Finger of the World Bank and Philip Schuler of the University of Maryland estimate that implementing commitments to improve trade procedures and establish technical and intellectual-property standards can cost more than a year's development budget for the poorest countries. Moreover, in those areas where poor countries could benefit from world trade rules, they are often unable to do so.... Of the WTO's 134 members, 29 do not even have missions at its headquarters in Geneva. Many more can barely afford to bring cases to the WTO.[2]

The evidence shows that the current WTO rules play an important role in the persistence of severe poverty. It is not surprising that this treaty reflects the interests of the affluent countries, corporations, and households. They can use their superior bargaining power, and their advantages in information and expertise, to shape each facet of the global order to their benefit, allowing them to capture the lion's share of the gains from economic interaction. In this way, large inequalities, once accumulated, have a tendency to intensify. In the 1990–2001 globalization period, per capita incomes rose 52.6% in real terms in the high-income countries.[3] In the same period, the global median income rose 20.4%, the tenth percentile gained 12.9%, and per capita income in the bottom percentile of world population dropped 7.3%.[4]

If the global economic order plays a major role in the persistence of severe poverty worldwide and if our governments, acting in our name, are prominently involved in shaping and upholding this order, then the deprivations of the global poor may well engage not merely positive duties to aid but also more stringent negative duties not to harm. Yet, this obvious thought is strangely absent from our debates. Even those who have most forcefully presented the eradication of severe poverty as an important moral task are content to portray us as mere bystanders. Thus, Peter Singer argues that we should donate most of our income to save lives in the poor countries. He tells the story of a healthy young professor who, walking by a shallow pond, sees a small child in it about to drown. Surely, Singer writes, the professor has a duty to save the child, even at the cost of dirtying his clothes. And similarly, he argues, we have a duty to send money to poverty relief organizations that can, for each few dollars they raise, save one more child from a painful hunger death.[5] It is, in one way, a virtue of Singers's argument that it reaches even those who subscribe to the PDPT, the view that the persistence of severe poverty is due solely to domestic causes. But by catering to this empirical view, he also reinforces the common moral judgment that the citizens and governments of the affluent societies, whom he is addressing, are as innocent in the persistence of severe poverty abroad as the fictional professor is in the child's predicament.[6]

2. AN EXPLANATION FOR WHY THE PDPT IS SO WIDELY ACCEPTED

Having argued that the PDPT, though widely held in the affluent countries, is nonetheless quite far from the truth, I should be able to give some reasons for its popularity. I can see four main such reasons. The first is that belief in this thesis is rather comfortable for people in the affluent countries. Most of us know at least vaguely of the horrendous conditions among the global poor. We confront poverty statistics such as these: Out of a total of over 6,150 million human beings (2001), some 2,735 million are reported to be living below $2/day, and

1,089 million below the $1/day international poverty line.[7] Some 850 million are undernourished, over 1,000 million lack access to safe water, and 2.6 billion lack access to basic sanitation.[8] About 876 million adults are illiterate (www.uis.unesco.org), and 2 billion lack access to essential drugs (www.fic.nih.gov/about/summary.html). Approximately 1 billion have no adequate shelter and 2 billion no electricity. 250 million children between 5 and 14 do wage work outside their household—often under harsh or cruel conditions: as soldiers, prostitutes, or domestic servants, or in agriculture, construction, textile or carpet production.[9] Roughly one third of all human deaths, some 50,000 daily, are due to poverty-related causes, easily preventable through better nutrition, safe drinking water, vaccines, cheap re-hydration packs and antibiotics.[10] Severe deprivations on such a scale would be considerably more disturbing to us were we to see them as due, in part, to a global institutional order that, imposed by our governments, also sustains our much greater affluence by securing our resources and economic dominance. The PDPT shields us from such discomfort.

A second reason for the popularity of the PDPT in the affluent countries is awareness of the great differences among the poorer countries' economic performance. These differences draw our attention to domestic factors and international differences and thus away from global factors. Many ignore the causal role of global factors completely, often falling prey to the fallacy already discussed. Others fall for a different fallacy by concluding from the success of a few formerly poor countries that the existing global economic order is quite hospitable to poverty eradication. This reasoning involves a some-all fallacy: The fact that *some* persons born into poverty in the U.S. become millionaires does not show that *all* such persons can do likewise. The reason is that the pathways to riches are sparse. They are not rigidly limited, to be sure, but the U.S. clearly cannot achieve the kind of economic growth rates needed for everyone to become a millionaire (keeping fixed the value of the currency and the real income millionaires can now enjoy). The same holds true for poor countries. The Asian "tigers" (Hong Kong, Taiwan, Singapore and South Korea) achieved impressive rates of economic growth and poverty reduction. They did so through a state-sponsored build-up of industries that mass-produce low-tech consumer products. These industries were globally successful by using their considerable labor-cost advantage to beat competitors in the affluent countries and by drawing on greater state support and/or a better-educated workforce to beat competitors in other poor countries.[11] Building such industries was hugely profitable for the Asian tigers. But if many other poor countries had adopted this same developmental strategy, competition among them would have rendered it much less profitable. An analogous point can be made about China, whose export boom has come at the expense of many other poor countries. We cannot conclude then that the existing global economic order, though less favorable to the poor countries than it might be, is still favorable enough for all of them to do as well as China and the Asian tigers have done in fact.

A third reason for the popularity of the PDPT in the affluent countries is the prevailing research focus among social scientists who, like the rest of us, pay much more attention to differences among national and regional developmental trajectories than to the overall evolution of poverty and inequality worldwide. Across several academic disciplines, there is a vast literature analyzing the causal roles of the local climate, natural environment, resources, food habits, diseases, history, culture, social institutions, economic policies, leadership personalities and much else.[12] Advice dispensed by development economists and others is also overwhelmingly focused on the design of national economic institutions and policies. Thus, libertarian economists of the "freshwater" school (so dubbed because its leading lights have taught in Chicago) celebrate Hong Kong and argue that a country's best way to expel human misery is economic growth and its best way to achieve economic growth is to foster free enterprise with a minimum in taxes, regulations and red tape. A competing, more left-leaning school of thought, represented by Amartya Sen,*

* Amartya Sen (1933–) is an Indian economist and philosopher; he won the Nobel Prize in Economics in 1998.

celebrates the Indian state of Kerala and contends that poor countries need *more* government: public schools, hospitals and infrastructure. These hot and worthwhile debates about appropriate economic policies and social institutions for the poor countries overshadow the far more important question of what causal role the rules of our globalized world economy play in the persistence of severe poverty.

This research focus among social scientists is surely partly due to the first two reasons: They, too, and their readers, are overly impressed by dramatic international differentials in economic performance and feel emotionally more comfortable, and careerwise more confident, with work that traces the persistence of severe poverty back to local causes rather than to global institutions we are involved in upholding. But there is also a good methodological reason for the research bias toward national and local causes: There being only this one world to observe, it is hard to obtain solid evidence about how the overall incidence of poverty would have evolved differently if this or that global factor had been different. By contrast, solid evidence about the effects of national and local factors can be gleaned from many poor countries that differ in their natural environment, history, culture, political and economic system, and government policies.

A fourth reason for the popularity of the PDPT is the prevalence of brutal and corrupt governments and elites in the poor countries. It seems far-fetched, even preposterous, to blame the global economic order for the persistence of severe poverty in countries that are ruled by obvious thugs and crooks. It also seems that whatever benefits global institutional reforms might bring to such countries would be captured by their corrupt elites, bringing little relief to the general population while reinforcing the power of their oppressors. Many hold that we should postpone reforms that would make the global order fairer to the poor countries until they have put their own houses in order.

As shown above, the first three reasons may *explain* the popularity of the PDPT, but cannot *justify* it. In the next section, I will argue that the same is true of the fourth reason.

3. IMPORTANT DOMESTIC FACTORS ARE THEMSELVES SUSTAINED BY FOREIGN INFLUENCES

In thinking about the regimes that have taken hold in various nations, we do well to remember that the existing world order is itself a crucial causal factor in the prevalence of corruption and oppression in the poor countries. It was only in 1999, for example, that the affluent countries finally agreed to curb their firms' bribery of foreign officials by adopting the OECD *Convention on Combating Bribery of Foreign Public Officials in International Business Transactions.* Until then, most affluent states did not merely legally authorize their firms to bribe foreign officials, but even allowed them to deduct such bribes from their taxable revenues, thereby providing financial inducements and moral support to the practice of bribing politicians and officials in the poor countries. This practice diverts the loyalties of officials in these countries and also makes a great difference to which persons are motivated to scramble for public office in the first place. Poor countries have suffered staggering losses as a result, most clearly in the awarding of public contracts. These losses arise in part from the fact that bribes are priced in: Bidders on contracts must raise their price in order to get paid enough to pay the bribes. Additional losses arise as bidders can afford to be non-competitive, knowing that the success of their bid will depend on their bribes more than on the substance of their offer. Even greater losses arise from the fact that officials focused on bribes pay little attention to whether the goods and services they purchase in their country's behalf are of good quality or even needed at all. Much of what poor countries have imported over the decades has been of no use to them—or even harmful, by promoting environmental degradation or violence (bribery is especially pervasive in the arms trade). Preliminary evidence suggests that the new *Convention* is ineffective in curbing bribery by multinational corporations. But even if it were effective, it could not erase the pervasive culture of corruption that is now deeply entrenched in many poor countries thanks to the extensive bribery they were subjected to during their formative years.[13]

The issue of bribery is part of a larger problem. The political and economic elites of poor countries interact with their domestic inferiors, on the one hand, and with foreign governments and corporations, on the other. These two constituencies differ enormously in wealth and power. The former are poorly educated and heavily preoccupied with the daily struggle to make ends meet. The latter have vastly greater rewards and penalties at their disposal. Politicians with a normal interest in their own political and economic success can thus be expected to cater to the interests of foreign governments and corporations rather than to competing interests of their much poorer compatriots. This is what we find: There are plenty of poor-country governments that came to power or stay in power only thanks to foreign support. There are plenty of poor-country politicians and bureaucrats who, induced or even bribed by foreigners, work against the interests of their people: *for* the development of a tourist-friendly sex industry (whose forced exploitation of children and women they tolerate and profit from), *for* the importation of unneeded, obsolete, or overpriced products at public expense, *for* the permission to import hazardous products, wastes, or factories, *against* laws protecting employees or the environment.

To be sure, there would not be such huge asymmetries in incentives if the poor countries were more democratic, allowing their populations a genuine political role. Why then are most of these countries so far from being genuinely democratic? This question brings further aspects of the current global institutional order into view.

It is a central feature of this order that anyone controlling a preponderance of the means of coercion within a country is internationally recognized as the legitimate government of this country's territory and people. We do not merely engage such rulers in negotiations. We also authorize anyone holding effective power in a country—without regard to how they acquired or exercise it and to how they are regarded by the population—to act for the country and its people. We authorize such rulers to sell the country's resources and to dispose of the proceeds of such sales, to borrow in the country's name and thereby to impose debt service obligations upon it, to sign treaties on the country's behalf and thus to bind its present and future population, and to use state revenues to buy the means of internal repression. This global practice goes a long way toward explaining why so many countries are so badly governed.

The *resource privilege* we confer upon a group in power is much more than mere acquiescence in its effective control over the natural resources of the country in question. This privilege includes the power to effect legally valid transfers of ownership rights in such resources. Thus a corporation that has purchased resources from a tyrant or junta has thereby become entitled to be—and actually *is*—recognized anywhere in the world as the legitimate owner of these resources. This is a remarkable feature of our global order. A group that overpowers the guards and takes control of a warehouse may be able to give some of the merchandise to others, accepting money in exchange. But the fence who pays them becomes merely the possessor, not the owner, of the loot. Contrast this with a group that overpowers an elected government and takes control of a country. Such a group, too, can give away some of the country's natural resources, accepting money in exchange. In this case, however, the purchaser acquires not merely possession, but all the rights and liberties of ownership, which are supposed to be—and actually *are*—protected and enforced by all other states' courts and police forces. The international resource privilege, then, is the legal power to confer globally valid ownership rights in the country's resources.

This international resource privilege has disastrous effects especially in those poor countries where the resource sector constitutes a large segment of the national economy. Whoever can take power in such a country by whatever means can maintain his rule, even against widespread popular opposition, by buying the arms and soldiers he needs with revenues from the export of natural resources and with funds borrowed against future resources sales. The resource privilege thus gives insiders strong incentives toward the violent acquisition and exercise of political power, thereby causing coup attempts and civil wars. Moreover, it also gives outsiders strong incentives to corrupt the officials of such countries who, no matter how badly they rule, continue to have resources to sell and money to spend.

Nigeria is a case in point. It exports *each day* about 2 million barrels of oil worth some $50–100 million. Whoever controls this revenue stream and associated borrowing power can afford enough weapons and soldiers to keep himself in power regardless of what the population may think of him. And so long as he succeeds in doing so, his purse will be continuously replenished with new funds with which he can cement his rule and live in opulence. With such a powerful incentive, it cannot be surprising that, during 28 of the past 36 years, Nigeria has been ruled by military strongmen who took power and ruled by force. Nor can it be surprising that President Olusegun Obasanjo, elected in 1999 after long service on the board of Transparency International, has failed to stop gross corruption: Were he to try to spend the oil revenues solely for the benefit of the Nigerian people, military officers could—thanks to the international resource privilege—quickly restore their customary perks. With such a huge price on his head, even the best-intentioned president could not end the theft of oil revenues and survive in power.

The *borrowing privilege* we confer upon a group in power includes the power to impose internationally valid legal obligations upon the country at large. Any successor government that refuses to honor debts incurred by an ever so corrupt, brutal, undemocratic, unconstitutional, repressive, unpopular predecessor will be severely punished by the banks and governments of other countries. At a minimum it will lose its own borrowing privilege by being excluded from the international financial markets. Such refusals are therefore quite rare, as governments, even when newly elected after a dramatic break with the past, are compelled to pay the debts of their ever so awful predecessors.

The international borrowing privilege makes three important contributions to the incidence of oppressive and corrupt elites in the poor countries. First, this privilege facilitates borrowing by destructive rulers who can borrow more money and can do so more cheaply than they could do if they alone, rather than the whole country, were obliged to repay. In this way, the borrowing privilege helps such rulers maintain themselves in power even against near-universal popular opposition. Second, the international borrowing privilege imposes upon democratic successor regimes the often huge debts of their corrupt predecessors. It thereby saps the capacity of such democratic governments to implement structural reforms and other political programs, thus rendering such governments less successful and less stable than they would otherwise be. (It is small consolation that putschists are sometimes weakened by being held liable for the debts of their democratic predecessors.) Third, the international borrowing privilege strengthens incentives toward coup attempts: Whoever succeeds in taking power by force gets the borrowing privilege as an additional reward.

By discussing several global systemic factors in some detail, I hope to have undermined a view that, encouraged by libertarian and more leftist economists alike, most people in the affluent countries are all too ready to believe: that the persistence of severe poverty is due to causes indigenous to the countries in which it occurs and thus unrelated to the affluent societies and their governments. This view is dramatically mistaken. Yes, domestic factors contribute to the persistence of severe poverty in many countries. But these contributions often depend on features of the global institutional order, which sustain some of those factors and exacerbate the impact of others. In these ways, the non-indigenous factors I have discussed play a major causal role in the evolution of severe poverty worldwide. They are crucial for explaining the inability and especially the unwillingness of poor countries' leaders to pursue more effective strategies of poverty eradication. And they are crucial therefore for explaining why global inequality is increasing so rapidly that substantial global economic growth since the end of the Cold War has not reduced income poverty and malnutrition—*despite* substantial technological progress, *despite* a huge poverty reduction in China, *despite* the post–Cold-War "peace dividend," *despite* a 32% drop in real food prices since 1985, *despite* official development assistance, and *despite* the efforts of international humanitarian and development organizations. If we are serious about eradicating severe poverty worldwide, we must understand the causal role of such non-indigenous factors and be willing to consider ways of modifying them or of reducing their impact.[14]

If the PDPT were true, the moral issues the distant needy raise for us might plausibly be considered under the aid label alone.[15] But since the PDPT is seriously mistaken, this label is misleading insofar as we are also *contributing to*, and *profiting from*, social factors that exacerbate severe poverty abroad.

4. HOW CAN OUR DESIGN OF THE GLOBAL INSTITUTIONAL ORDER BE ASSESSED MORALLY?

We can still deny that we are so contributing or profiting, even if we acknowledge the PDPT's collapse and accept our shared responsibility for the existing global order. We can say that our imposition of this order benefits the global poor, or at least does not harm them by exacerbating their poverty. While such claims are often made, for the current WTO rules for example, it remains unclear what their meaning is supposed to be. Benefit, after all, is a comparative notion that implicitly appeals to some baseline scenario under which the global poor would be even worse off than they are. What baseline might we adduce to show the global poor that they are benefiting from the present global order?

There are three options. We might invoke a *diachronic* comparison, appealing to the *trend* in the depth or incidence of severe poverty worldwide. This argument fails for three independent reasons. Its premise is false: severe income poverty and malnutrition are not actually in decline globally. Moreover, its inference is invalid: Severe poverty might be declining, in China for instance, *despite* the fact that the global economic order tends to exacerbate such poverty. A diachronic comparison does not permit us to judge this possibility one way or the other and is therefore useless for judging the impact of any specific causal factor. Finally, we must not simply assume that the preceding situation was morally unproblematic. Otherwise we would have to conclude that a man is benefiting his children if he beats them up ever less frequently, or that the U.S. institutional order of the early 19th century benefited the slaves if their enslavement gradually became less brutal.

Our second option is to invoke a *subjunctive* comparison with an *historical* baseline. To judge whether the U.S. institutional order of the early 19th century harmed or benefited women, we should ask whether women were worse or better off than they would have been under continued British rule. Analogously, we might argue that the existing global order is benefiting the global poor insofar as they are better off than they would be if some preceding set of rules had remained in force. But such arguments assume that those alternate rules were neither harming nor benefiting. And this assumption is inappropriate: In 1820, women in the U.S. might have been harmed by unjust laws even if still more harmful laws would have been imposed on them under continued British rule.

Our third option is to invoke a *subjunctive* comparison with a *hypothetical* baseline—arguing perhaps that even more people would live and die even more miserably in some fictional state of nature than in this world as we have made it. But this option, too, is unpromising so long as we lack a clear and morally uniquely appropriate specification of that fictional world and a morally uniquely appropriate standard for comparing the two worlds in regard to severe poverty. Plus I have yet to see any coherently described state of nature on this planet that could match our globalized civilization's record of sustaining a stable death toll of 18 million premature deaths per year from poverty-related causes.

None of our three options is suitable for explicating our question—whether the existing world order harms or benefits the global poor—in a way that is both clear and appropriate to the assessment of this order. This failure suggests the inverse strategy: Instead of using a justice-independent criterion of harm for deciding whether this order does harm and is therefore unjust, we use a harm-independent criterion of justice for deciding whether this order is unjust and its imposition therefore a harm done to those it treats unjustly.

To illustrate the idea, consider once more the institutional order of the U.S. in its infancy, which greatly disadvantaged women vis-à-vis men. Our judgment of this order as unjust is not based on an historical comparison with how women had fared under British rule. It is not based on a comparison with how women would have fared had British rule continued. And it is not based on a comparison with how women would fare in some state of nature. (All these comparisons can be more plausibly invoked to legitimate than to criticize the institutional order under consideration.) Rather, it is because it assigned women a status inferior to men's that we judge this order to have been unjust to women and its imposition therefore a harm done to them.

Many harm-independent criteria might be proposed for assessing the justice of our global institutional order. Such criteria differ in at least three respects. They differ in how they identify the relevant affected parties: as individual persons, households, social groups, nations, or states. They differ in their *absolute* demands—requiring, for instance, that affected parties must enjoy security of self and property or access to basic necessities. And they differ in their *relative* demands—requiring perhaps that basic rights or basic educational or medical opportunities must be equal or that economic inequalities must be constrained in certain ways. To bypass these debates, let me proceed with an extremely minimal condition: An institutional order cannot be just if it foreseeably produces foreseeably avoidable massive human rights deficits.

With massive human rights deficits in plain view, attention turns to whether we know or could know how to avoid or greatly reduce them through global institutional reform. The answer depends on information about what alternatives are feasible and what difference they would make. With regard to alternatives that diverge greatly from the existing global order, it may be impossible to establish such information in a rigorous way. It is possible, however, to estimate the impact of the existing global order relative to its nearby institutional alternatives. We saw such estimates in the *Economist* passage quoted above: The poorer countries are missing out on some $700 billion annually in export revenues because the affluent countries insisted on grandfathering heavy protections of their markets—through tariffs, quotas, anti-dumping duties, export credits and subsidies to domestic producers. It is quite possible, though unseemly among economists, to extend this estimate to the number of poverty deaths that would have been avoided by a fairer opening of markets. This number is large, as the blocked exports greatly diminish incomes especially in the poorer rural areas where agricultural commodities are produced.

Many features of the existing global order embody similar trade-offs between the interests of the high-income countries and their citizens on the one hand and the global poor on the other. It is better for us and worse for them that we do not have to pay for the negative externalities we impose on them: for the pollution we have produced over many decades and the resulting effects on their environment and climate, for the rapid depletion of natural resources, for the contribution of our tourists to the AIDS epidemic and for the violence caused by our demand for drugs and our war on drugs. The existing *Trade-Related Aspects of Intellectual Property Rights* (TRIPs) agreement is better for us and worse for the global poor than an alternative that would not have confined the trade in generic pharmaceuticals. An unconditional resource privilege gives us access to a larger, cheaper and more reliable supply of foreign resources, because we can acquire ownership of them from anyone who happens to exercise effective power without regard to whether the country's population either approves the sale or benefits from the proceeds. Advantageous also to putschists and tyrants in the poorer countries, broad resource, borrowing, treaty, and arms privileges are much worse, however, for the global poor than would be narrower such privileges conditional on minimal domestic legitimacy.

The cumulative impact of these trade-offs upon the global poor is staggering. In the 17 years since the end of the Cold War, some 300 million human beings have died prematurely from poverty-related causes, with 18 million more added each year. Had the affluent countries shaping the global rules given more weight to the interests of the global poor, the toll in early deaths and deprivations would foreseeably have been much lower at negligible cost to our affluence. It is hard to see how we might defend as just the global order we impose with the trade-offs it manifests. And if this order is unjust, then it follows, without appeal to any historical or state-of-nature baseline, that we are harming the global poor: by imposing on them an unjust global order under which the incidence of severe poverty, malnutrition and premature death is foreseeably much greater than it would be under some feasible alternatives.

5. TO WHAT EXTENT MUST OUR POLICIES GIVE WEIGHT TO THE INTERESTS OF THE GLOBAL POOR?

There are three ways of defending the trade-offs that our governments, often in collusion with corrupt and oppressive leaders in the poorer countries, have imposed. First we might say that it is permissible for us vigorously to promote our own interests in negotiations about how to fine-tune the various rules of the global order, even when doing so conflicts with the interests of the global poor. With our incomes some 200 to 300 times larger than theirs[16] and 850 million living on the brink of starvation (note 8), this justification of the status quo is rarely voiced in public. To be sure, it is widely thought that our politicians and diplomats ought to represent the interests of their compatriots. But it is also thought that this mandate has its limits: Even when they are able to do so, our representatives should not impose global rules under which we have unfair advantages at the cost of millions of poverty deaths abroad. In the examples I have given, it looks like our politicians and diplomats have done exactly that, in our name.

Our second defense avers that appearances are here deceptive, that the decisions reflected in the existing rules do benefit the global poor as well, at least long-term. But in some important cases, such a defense strains credulity. How can we deny that world poverty is exacerbated by the special prerogatives that affluent countries gave themselves under WTO rules to favor our firms through tariffs, quotas, anti-dumping duties, subsidies and export credits? Still, career incentives do produce such denials which, in the more clear-cut cases of unfair rules, often take a weaker form: Instead of claiming that certain perogatives for the rich countries do not exacerbate poverty, economists merely claim that there are many complicating factors, methodological difficulties and other imponderabilia so that intellectual honesty precludes our drawing any firm conclusions. If all else fails, we can fall back on the weakest claim: Yes, the fine-tuning of some important rules was indeed worse for the global poor, but it was an honest mistake. When these rules were designed, development economics was less advanced and the relevant officials could not possibly have known that they were serving our interests at the expense of many additional premature deaths from poverty-related causes.

Boilerplate empirical defenses of this kind are easily produced and well received. It is quite unlikely that there will ever be a serious inquiry into what our politicians and diplomats and officials in the WTO, International Monetary Fund and World Bank knew and should have known during their negotiations of international agreements. The possibility that these respectable gentlemen (very few women there) might be hunger's willing executioners, committing a rather large-scale crime against humanity in our name, will never be taken seriously in the affluent countries.—And yet, nagging doubts remain. If our representatives did make honest mistakes to the detriment of the global poor, should we not at least make up for these mistakes through a real effort at reducing the (unexpectedly) large incidence of severe poverty today?

Similar questions are raised by our third defense, which asserts that the global rules we have imposed are not merely good for us, but also good for global efficiency, productivity and economic growth. These rules are Pareto-superior to their alternatives—not in the normal sense (better for some and worse for no one), but in this weaker (Caldor-Hicks) sense: The rules are better for some and worse for others but so that the former can, out of their relative gains, fully compensate the latter for their relative losses. I doubt this argument can succeed for the grandfathering clauses in the WTO Treaty which still allow us, for many years to come, to favor our firms through protectionist measures. But it may well succeed in other cases. Still, even when it succeeds there is the nagging question: Given the vast economic inequality between gainers and losers (notes 1 and 16), is the mere *possibility* of compensation sufficient to vindicate our decision? Or must there not rather be *actual* compensation, so that we may keep only such relative gains as *exceed* their relative losses?

The questions concluding the last two paragraphs indicate more precisely how, with the collapse of the PDPT, conventional discussions of world poverty under the aid label are misleading. The label is not inaccurate: As affluent people and countries, we surely have positive moral duties to help persons mired in life-threatening poverty whom we can help at little cost. But the label detracts from weightier, negative duties that also apply to us: We should reduce severe harms we will have caused; and we should not take advantage of injustice at the expense of its victims. These two negative duties apply to us if we (sometimes together with poor-country "elites") are imposing a global order whose injustice benefits us while exacerbating severe poverty abroad. We must then at least compensate the global poor. Failing to do this, we would be harming them and profiting from injustice at their expense. And insofar as we do compensate,we are not merly "aiding" the poor abroad,but reducing the impact of unfair rules that bring us unjust gains at their expense. We are not "redistributing" from the rich to the poor, but offsetting an unjust institutional redistribution from the poor to the rich—*re*-redistributing, if you like.

Let me illustrate the special weight these two negative duties are generally thought to have: Imagine, by the side of a country road, an injured child who must be rushed to the hospital if her leg is to be saved. As a competent bystander who ignores her plight, you are subject to moral criticism for failing to help. But if you are the driver who injured the child in the first place, then more is morally at stake: By leaving the child's needs unattended, you would greatly increase the harm you will have done her. As we judge such inaction of the driver more harshly than that of the bystander, we should judge our own inaction more harshly, too, if we are involved in upholding unjust rules that contribute to severe poverty we ignore.

Imagine further a society in which an aboriginal minority suffers severe discrimination in education and employment, reducing their wages far below those of their compatriots. As an affluent foreigner, you may think that perhaps you ought to do something to help these people. But if you are profiting from the discrimination—by employing an aboriginal driver at half the wage other drivers receive, for instance—then more is morally at stake: We judge ourselves more harshly for taking advantage of an injustice by pocketing such gains than for failing to spend other assets we have on supporting the poor. Likewise, we should also judge ourselves more harshly insofar as assets we fail to use toward reducing severe poverty abroad constitute gains we derive from the unfairness of a global order that also contributes to the persistence of this poverty.

Negative duties not to support and not to pocket gains from an unfair institutional order that foreseeably contributes to severe deprivations are not only weightier than the positive duty to help relieve such deprivations. They are also much less sensitive to variations in community and distance. Duties to aid are strongest toward the near and dear and weakest toward foreigners in distant lands. But duties not to harm do not fade in this way. Consider again the driver who hits a child and then leaves her unattended by the side of the road. We do not upgrade our moral assessment of him when we learn that he did this far away from his home to a child with whom he had no communal bond of nationality, language, culture or religion. If the unfairness of the global order we impose causes poverty to persist in the poor countries, then our moral responsibility for the associated deaths and deprivations is not diminished by diversity of nationality and geographical or cultural distance. It might be so diminished, perhaps, if harming foreigners were necessary to save ourselves from a comparable fate. But in the real world, the global poverty problem—though it involves one third of all human deaths—is tiny in economic terms: Though 2,735 million persons are reported to be living below the higher ($2/day) international poverty line, and fully 42% below it on average, their collective shortfall amounts to only 1% of the incomes of the 1,011 million people in the high-income economies. Clearly, we could eradicate severe poverty—through a reform of the global order or through other initiatives designed to compensate for its effects on the global poor—without "sacrificing" the fulfillment of our own needs or even mildly serious interests.

It is widely believed in the affluent countries that we are already spending an inordinate amount on such initiatives. This belief is contradicted by the facts. In the last decade of the twentieth century, when the affluent countries were reaping an annual peace dividend (from reduced military expenditure after the end of the Cold War) of about 2% of their GNPs, they *reduced* official development assistance (ODA) from 0.33% of their combined GNPs in 1990 to 0.22% in 2001. In the wake of the terrorist attack of September 11 2001, ODA has grown back to

0.33% in 2005 due to dramatic growth in spending on Musharraf's Pakistan and post-occupation Afghanistan and Iraq. Yes, even this increased amount is only a third of what would be needed to eradicate severe poverty. And most of it is spent for the benefit of agents capable of reciprocation—on actual or potential political allies and campaign contributors at home and abroad.[17] Only about one tenth of what is labeled ODA is actually spent on poverty eradication or what the OECD calls basic social services—defined as basic education, primary health care (including reproductive health and population programs), nutrition programs and safe water and sanitation as well as the institutional capacity for delivering these services. This $10 billion annually amounts to 3% of what would be needed to eradicate severe poverty, to 1.5% of our annual peace dividend, and to 0.03% of our national incomes or $10 annually from each citizen of the affluent countries.

When people like us die at a mature age, we can look back on a lifespan in which over a billion human beings, mostly children, have died form poverty-related causes. This massive death toll and vast further poverty-related burdens were and are foreseeable. And it is clear beyond any reasonable doubt that the affluent countries could dramatically reduce this continuous catastrophe at little cost to ourselves. Yet, very few citizens of the affluent countries find these facts disturbing. This widespread unconcern can be explained, in large part, by a false view of why severe poverty persists. Most of us subscribe to the view that the causes of the persistence of severe poverty are indigenous to the countries in which it persists. I am convinced that, with a better understanding of the role global institutional factors play in the persistence of severe povery, many would take this problem much more seriously.

NOTES

1. In fact, this ratio has greatly *increased.* In 2005, the gross domestic product per capita was $745 in sub-Saharan Africa (devdata.worldbank.org/dataonline) versus $35,131 in the high-income countries (World Bank: *World Development Report 2007* [Washington: World Bank, 2006], 289—a 47: 1 ratio.
2. *Economist*, 25 September 1999, 89. References to the cited studies can be found at ideas.repec.org/p/gta/workpp/397.html and econ.worldbank.org/docs/941.pdf.
3. Cf. devdata.worldbank.org/dataonline, reporting the increase in gross national income per capita at purchasing power parity (current international dollars).
4. Many thanks to Rekha Nath and Aedan Whyatt for doing these calculations using World Bank interactive software (iresearch.worldbank.org/PovcalNet/jsp/index.jsp).
5. Peter Singer. "Famine, Affluence and Morality."
6. Singer may not regard this reinforcement as regrettable. As a utilitarian, he believes that the stringency of our duty to combat world poverty is unaffected by whether the PDPT is true or false.
7. Shaohua Chen and Martin Ravallion: "How Have the World's Poorest Fared since the 1980s?" *World Bank Research Observer* 19 (2004), 141–69, at 153. Because PPPs are used to convert these poverty lines into local currency amount, $280 and $140 per person per year are deemed sufficient, in the typical poor country, to reach the relevant poverty line. The average household in severe poverty (below $2/day) spends about $160 and the average household in extreme poverty (below $1/day) spends about $100 per person per year.
8. UNDP: *Human Development Report 2005* (New York: UNDP, 2005), 24. Most of those suffering these deprivations are female.
9. See www.ilo.org/public/english/standards/ipec/simpoc/stats/4stt.htm and www.ilo.org/public/english/standards/decl/publ/reports/report3.htm, 9, 11, and 18.
10. For the frequency of specific causes of deaths, see World Health Organisation: *The World Health Report 2004* (Geneva: WHO Publications, 2004), Annex Table 2, also available at www.who.int/whr/2004. About 60% of all poverty deaths are children under five. *Cf.* United Nations Children's Fund: *The State of the World's Children 2005* (New York: UNICEF, 2004), inside front cover. There it is also reported that 640 million children lack adequate shelter, 400 million children lack access to safe water, and 270 million children have no access to health services.

11. It also helped that the U.S., eager to establish healthy capitalist economies as a counterweight to Soviet influence in the region, allowed the tigers free access to its market even while they maintained high tariffs to protect their own.
12. Some notable recent contributions are David Landes, *The Wealth and Poverty of Nations: Why Some Are So Rich and Some So Poor* (New York: Norton, 1998), Jared Diamond: *Guns, Germs, and Steel: The Fates of Human Societies* (New York: Norton, 1999), and Lawrence E. Harrison and Samuel P. Huntington, eds.: *Culture Matters: How Values Shape Human Progress* (New York: Basic Books, 2001).
13. *Cf.* Raymond Baker: *Capitalism's Achilles Heel* (New York: John Wiley and Sons, 2005).
14. *Cf.* Thomas Pogge: *World Poverty and Human Rights* (Cambridge: Polity Press, 2002), chapters 6 and 8, for concrete proposals toward modifying the international resource and borrowing privileges and toward reducing the impact of unfair global economic rules through a Global Resources Dividend, respectively.
15. Though it could still be argued that this label is inappropriate insofar as we are beneficiaries and they are victims of historical injustices, such as genocidal conquest and colonialism.
16. Cf. note 7. In the high-income economies, the gross national income per capita was $35,131 on average in 2005 (World Bank: *World Development Report 2007*, 289).
17. As the USAID's web portal stated until recently: "The principal beneficiary of America's foreign assistance programs has always been the United States. Close to 80 percent of the U.S. Agency for International Development's (USAID's) contracts and grants go directly to American firms. Foreign assistance programs have helped create major markets for agricultural goods, created new markets for American industrial exports and meant hundreds of thousands of jobs for Americans."

◈ VEGETARIANISM AND ANIMALS ◈

Puppies, Pigs, and People: Eating Meat and Marginal Cases

ALASTAIR NORCROSS

Alastair Norcross teaches philosophy at Rice University. He works primarily in the areas of ethical theory and political philosophy. "Puppies, Pigs and People" was originally published in 2004 as a self-standing article. In it, Norcross defends vegetarianism on moral grounds.

1. FRED'S BASEMENT

Consider the story of Fred, who receives a visit from the police one day. They have been summoned by Fred's neighbors, who have been disturbed by strange sounds emanating from Fred's basement. When they enter the basement they are confronted by the following scene: Twenty-six small wire cages, each containing a puppy, some whining, some whimpering, some howling. The puppies range in

From "Puppies, Pigs, and People: Eating Meat and Marginal Cases." *Philosophical Perspectives*, 18 (2004). Reprinted by permission of Blackwell Publishing.

age from newborn to about six months. Many of them show signs of mutilation. Urine and feces cover the bottoms of the cages and the basement floor. Fred explains that he keeps the puppies for twenty-six weeks, and then butchers them while holding them upside-down. During their lives he performs a series of mutilations on them, such as slicing off their noses and their paws with a hot knife, all without any form of anesthesia. Except for the mutilations, the puppies are never allowed out of the cages, which are barely big enough to hold them at twenty-six weeks. The police are horrified, and promptly charge Fred with animal abuse. As details of the case are publicized, the public is outraged. Newspapers are flooded with letters demanding that Fred be severely punished. There are calls for more severe penalties for animal abuse. Fred is denounced as a vile sadist.

Finally, at his trial, Fred explains his behavior, and argues that he is blameless and therefore deserves no punishment. He is, he explains, a great lover of chocolate. A couple of years ago, he was involved in a car accident, which resulted in some head trauma. Upon his release from hospital, having apparently suffered no lasting ill effects, he visited his favorite restaurant and ordered their famous rich dark chocolate mousse. Imagine his dismay when he discovered that his experience of the mousse was a pale shadow of its former self. The mousse tasted bland, slightly pleasant, but with none of the intense chocolaty flavor he remembered so well. The waiter assured him that the recipe was unchanged from the last time he had tasted it, just the day before his accident. In some consternation, Fred rushed out to buy a bar of his favorite Belgian chocolate. Again, he was dismayed to discover that his experience of the chocolate was barely even pleasurable. Extensive investigation revealed that his experience of other foods remained unaffected, but chocolate, in all its forms, now tasted bland and insipid. Desperate for a solution to his problem, Fred visited a renowned gustatory neurologist, Dr. T. Bud. Extensive tests revealed that the accident had irreparably damaged the godiva gland, which secretes cocoamone, the hormone responsible for the experience of chocolate. Fred urgently requested hormone replacement therapy. Dr. Bud informed him that, until recently, there had been no known source of cocoamone, other than the human godiva gland, and that it was impossible to collect cocoamone from one person to be used by another. However, a chance discovery had altered the situation. A forensic veterinary surgeon, performing an autopsy on a severely abused puppy, had discovered high concentrations of cocoamone in the puppy's brain. It turned out that puppies, who don't normally produce cocoamone, could be stimulated to do so by extended periods of severe stress and suffering. The research, which led to this discovery, while gaining tenure for its authors, had not been widely publicized, for fear of antagonizing animal welfare groups. Although this research clearly gave Fred the hope of tasting chocolate again, there were no commercially available sources of puppy-derived cocoamone. Lack of demand, combined with fear of bad publicity, had deterred drug companies from getting into the puppy torturing business. Fred appeals to the court to imagine his anguish, on discovering that a solution to his severe deprivation was possible, but not readily available. But he wasn't inclined to sit around bemoaning his cruel fate. He did what any chocolate lover would do. He read the research, and set up his own cocoamone collection lab in his basement. Six months of intense puppy suffering, followed by a brutal death, produced enough cocoamone to last him a week, hence the twenty-six cages. He isn't a sadist or an animal abuser, he explains. If there were a method of collecting cocoamone without torturing puppies, he would gladly employ it. He derives no pleasure from the suffering of the puppies itself. He sympathizes with those who are horrified by the pain and misery of the animals, but the court must realize that human pleasure is at stake. The puppies, while undeniably cute, are mere animals. He admits that he would be just as healthy without chocolate, if not more so. But this isn't a matter of survival or health. His life would be unacceptably impoverished without the experience of chocolate.

End of story. Clearly, we are horrified by Fred's behavior, and unconvinced by his attempted justification. It is, or course, unfortunate for Fred that he can no longer enjoy the taste of chocolate, but that in no way excuses the imposition of severe suffering on the puppies. I expect near universal agreement with this claim (the exceptions being those who are either inhumanly callous or thinking ahead, and wish to avoid the following conclusion, to which such agreement commits them). No decent person would even contemplate torturing puppies merely to enhance a gustatory experience. However, billions of animals endure intense suffering every year for precisely this end. Most of the chicken, veal, beef, and pork consumed in the U.S. comes from intensive confinement facilities, in which the animals live cramped, stress-filled lives and endure unanaesthetized mutilations.[1] The vast majority of people would suffer no ill health from the elimination of meat from their diets. Quite the reverse. The supposed benefits from this system of factory farming, apart from the profits accruing to agribusiness, are increased levels of gustatory pleasure for those who claim that they couldn't enjoy a meat-free diet as much as their current meat-filled diets. If we are prepared to condemn Fred for torturing puppies merely to enhance his gustatory experiences, shouldn't we similarly condemn the millions who purchase and consume factory-raised meat? Are there any morally significant differences between Fred's behavior and their behavior?

2. FRED'S BEHAVIOR COMPARED WITH OUR BEHAVIOR

The first difference that might seem to be relevant is that Fred tortures the puppies himself, whereas most Americans consume meat that comes from animals that have been tortured by others. But is this really relevant? What if Fred had been squeamish and had employed someone else to torture the puppies and extract the cocoamone? Would we have thought any better of Fred? Of course not.

Another difference between Fred and many consumers of factory-raised meat is that many, perhaps most, such consumers are unaware of the treatment of the animals, before they appear in neatly wrapped packages on supermarket shelves. Perhaps I should moderate my challenge, then. If we are prepared to condemn Fred for torturing puppies merely to enhance his gustatory experiences, shouldn't we similarly condemn those who purchase and consume factory-raised meat, in full, or even partial, awareness of the suffering endured by the animals? While many consumers are still blissfully ignorant of the appalling treatment meted out to meat, that number is rapidly dwindling, thanks to vigorous publicity campaigns waged by animal welfare groups. Furthermore, any meat-eating readers of this article are now deprived of the excuse of ignorance.

Perhaps a consumer of factory-raised animals could argue as follows: While I agree that Fred's behavior is abominable, mine is crucially different. If Fred did not consume his chocolate, he would not raise and torture puppies (or pay someone else to do so). Therefore Fred could prevent the suffering of the puppies. However, if I did not buy and consume factory-raised meat, no animals would be spared lives of misery. Agribusiness is much too large to respond to the behavior of one consumer. Therefore I cannot prevent the suffering of any animals. I may well regret the suffering inflicted on animals for the sake of human enjoyment. I may even agree that the human enjoyment doesn't justify the suffering. However, since the animals will suffer no matter what I do, I may as well enjoy the taste of their flesh.

There are at least two lines of response to this attempted defense. First, consider an analogous case. You visit a friend in an exotic location, say Alabama. Your friend takes you out to eat at the finest restaurant in Tuscaloosa. For dessert you select the house specialty, "Chocolate Mousse à la Bama," served with a small cup of coffee, which you are instructed to drink before eating the mousse. The mousse is quite simply the most delicious dessert you have ever tasted. Never before has chocolate tasted so rich and satisfying. Tempted to order a second, you ask your friend what makes this mousse so delicious. He informs you that the mousse itself is ordinary, but the coffee contains a concentrated dose of cocoamone, the newly discovered chocolate-enhancing hormone. Researchers at Auburn University have perfected a technique for extracting cocoamone from the brains of freshly slaughtered puppies, who have been subjected to lives of pain and frustration. Each puppy's brain yields four doses, each of which is effective for about fifteen minutes, just long enough to enjoy one serving of mousse. You are, naturally, horrified and disgusted. You will certainly not order another serving, you tell your friend. In fact, you are shocked that your friend, who had always seemed to be a morally decent person, could have both recommended the dessert to you and eaten one himself, in full awareness of the loathsome process necessary for the experience. He agrees that the suffering of the puppies is outrageous, and that the gain in human pleasure in no way justifies the appalling treatment they have to endure. However, neither he nor you can save any puppies by refraining from consuming cocoamone. Cocoamone production is now Alabama's leading industry, so it is much too large to respond to the behavior of one or two consumers. Since the puppies will suffer no matter what either of you does, you may as well enjoy the mousse.

If it is as obvious as it seems that a morally decent person, who is aware of the details of cocoamone production, couldn't order Chocolate Mousse à la Bama, it should be equally obvious that a morally decent person, who is aware of the details of factory farming, can't purchase and consume factory-raised meat. If the attempted excuse of causal impotence is compelling in the latter case, it should be compelling in the former case. But it isn't.

The second response to the claim of causal impotence is to deny it. Consider the case of chickens, the most cruelly treated of all animals raised for human consumption, with the possible exception of veal calves. In 1998, almost 8 billion chickens were slaughtered in the U.S., almost all of them raised on factory farms. Suppose that there are 250 million chicken eaters in the U.S., and that each one consumes, on average, 25 chickens per year (this leaves a fair number of chickens slaughtered for nonhuman consumption, or for export). Clearly, if only one of those chicken eaters gave up eating chicken, the industry would not respond. Equally clearly, if they all gave up eating chicken, billions of chickens (approximately 6.25 billion per year) would not be bred, tortured, and killed. But there must also be some number of consumers, far short of 250 million, whose renunciation of chicken would cause the industry to reduce the number of chickens bred in factory farms. The industry may not be able to respond to each individual's behavior, but it must respond to the behavior of fairly large numbers. Suppose that the industry is sensitive to a reduction in demand for chicken equivalent to 10,000 people becoming vegetarians. (This seems like a reasonable guess, but I have no idea what the actual numbers are, nor is it important.) For each group of 10,000 who give up chicken, a quarter of a million fewer chickens are bred per year. It appears, then, that if you give up eating chicken, you have only a one in ten thousand chance of making any difference to the lives of chickens, unless it is certain that fewer than 10,000 people will ever give up eating chicken, in which case you have no chance. Isn't a one in ten thousand chance small enough to render your continued consumption of chicken blameless? Not at all. While the chance that your behavior is harmful may be small, the harm that is risked is enormous. The larger the numbers needed to make a difference to chicken production, the larger the difference such numbers would make. A one in ten thousand chance of saving 250,000 chickens per year from excruciating lives is morally and mathematically equivalent to the certainty of saving 25 chickens per year. We commonly accept that even small risks of great harms are unacceptable. That is why we disapprove of parents who fail to secure their children in car seats or with seat belts, who leave their small children unattended at home, or who drink or smoke heavily during pregnancy. Or consider commercial aircraft safety measures. The chances that the oxygen masks, the lifejackets, or the emergency exits on any given plane will be called on to save any lives in a given week, are far smaller than one in ten thousand. And yet we would be outraged to discover that an airline had knowingly allowed a plane to fly for a week with nonfunctioning emergency exits, oxygen masks, and lifejackets. So, even if it is true that your giving up factory raised chicken has only a tiny chance of preventing suffering, given that the amount of suffering that would be prevented is in inverse proportion to your chance of preventing it, your continued consumption is not thereby excused.

But perhaps it is not even true that your giving up chicken has only a tiny chance of making any difference. Suppose again that the poultry industry only reduces production when a threshold of 10,000 fresh vegetarians is reached. Suppose also, as is almost certainly true, that vegetarianism is growing in popularity in the U.S. (and elsewhere). Then, even if you are not the one, newly converted vegetarian, to reach the next threshold of 10,000, your conversion will reduce the time required before the next threshold is reached. The sooner the threshold is reached, the sooner production, and therefore animal suffering, is reduced. Your behavior, therefore, does make a difference. Furthermore, many people who become vegetarians influence others to become vegetarian, who in turn influence others, and so on. It appears, then, that the claim of causal impotence is mere wishful thinking, on the part of those meat lovers who are morally sensitive enough to realize that human gustatory pleasure does not justify inflicting extreme suffering on animals.

Perhaps there is a further difference between the treatment of Fred's puppies and the treatment of animals on factory farms. The suffering of the puppies is a necessary means to the production of gustatory pleasure, whereas the suffering of animals on factory farms is simply a by-product of the conditions dictated by economic considerations. Therefore, it might be argued, the suffering of the puppies is *intended as a means* to Fred's pleasure, whereas the suffering of factory raised animals is merely *foreseen* as a side-effect of a system that is a means to the gustatory pleasures of millions. The distinction between what is intended, either as a means or as an end in itself, and what is "merely" foreseen is central to the Doctrine of Double Effect. Supporters of this doctrine claim that it is sometimes permissible to bring about an effect that is merely foreseen, even though the very same effect could not permissibly be brought about if intended. (Other conditions have to be met in order for the Doctrine of Double Effect to judge an action permissible, most notably that there be an outweighing good effect.) Fred acts impermissibly, according to this line of argument, because he intends the suffering of the puppies as a means to his pleasure. Most meat eaters, on the other hand, even if aware of the suffering of the animals, do not intend the suffering.

In response to this line of argument, I could remind the reader that Samuel Johnson said, or should have said, that the Doctrine of Double Effect is the last refuge of a scoundrel.[3] I won't do that, however, since neither the doctrine itself, nor the alleged moral distinction between intending and foreseeing can justify the consumption of factory-raised meat. The Doctrine of Double Effect requires not merely that a bad effect be foreseen and not intended, but also that there be an outweighing good effect. In the case of the suffering of factory-raised animals, whatever good could plausibly be claimed to come out of the system clearly doesn't outweigh the bad. Furthermore, it would be easy to modify the story of Fred to render the puppies' suffering "merely" foreseen. For example, suppose that the cocoamone is produced by a chemical reaction that can only occur when large quantities of drain-cleaner are forced down the throat of a conscious, unanaesthetized puppy. The consequent appalling suffering, while not itself a means to the production of cocoamone, is nonetheless an unavoidable side-effect of the means. In this variation of the story, Fred's behavior is no less abominable than in the original.

One last difference between the behavior of Fred and the behavior of the consumers of factory-raised meat is worth discussing, if only because it is so frequently cited in response to the arguments of this paper. Fred's behavior is abominable, according to this line of thinking, because it involves the suffering of *puppies*. The behavior of meat-eaters, on the other hand, "merely" involves the suffering of chickens, pigs, cows, calves, sheep, and the like. Puppies (and probably dogs and cats in general) are morally different from the other animals. Puppies *count* (morally, that is), whereas the other animals don't, or at least not nearly as much.

So, what gives puppies a higher moral status than the animals we eat? Presumably there is some morally relevant property or properties possessed by puppies but not by farm animals. Perhaps puppies have a greater degree of rationality than farm animals, or a more finely developed moral sense, or at least a sense of loyalty and devotion. The problems with this kind of approach are obvious. It's highly unlikely that any property that has even an outside chance of being ethically relevant[4] is both possessed by puppies and not possessed by any farm animals. For example, it's probably true that most puppies have a greater degree of rationality (whatever that means) than most chickens, but the comparison with pigs is far more dubious. Besides, if Fred were to inform the jury that he had taken pains to acquire particularly stupid, morally obtuse, disloyal and undevoted puppies, would they (or we) have declared his behavior to be morally acceptable? Clearly not. This is, of course, simply the puppy version of the problem of marginal cases (which I will discuss later). The human version is no less relevant. If their lack of certain degrees of rationality, moral sensibility, loyalty, devotion, and the like makes it permissible to torture farm animals for our gustatory pleasure, it should be permissible to do the same to those unfortunate humans who also lack those properties. Since the latter behavior isn't permissible, the lack of such properties doesn't justify the former behavior.

Perhaps, though, there *is* something that separates puppies, even marginal puppies (and marginal humans) from farm animals—our sympathy. Puppies count more than other animals, because we care more about them. We are outraged to hear of puppies abused in scientific experiments, but unconcerned at the treatment of laboratory rats or animals on factory farms. Before the 2002 World Cup, several members of the England team sent a letter to the government of South Korea protesting the treatment of dogs and cats raised for food in that country. The same players have not protested the treatment of animals on factory farms in England. This example, while clearly illustrating the difference in attitudes towards cats and dogs on the one hand, and farm animals on the other, also reveals one of the problems with this approach to the question of moral status. Although the English footballers, and the English (and US) public in general, clearly care far more about the treatment of cats and dogs than of farm animals, the South Koreans, just as clearly, do not. Are we to conclude that Fred's behavior would not be abominable were he living in South Korea, where dogs and cats are routinely abused for the sake of gustatory pleasure? Such relativism is, to put it mildly, hard to swallow. Perhaps, though, we can maintain the view that human feelings determine the moral status of animals, without condoning the treatment of dogs and cats in South Korea (and other countries). Not all human feelings count. Only the feelings of those who have achieved exactly the right degree of moral sensibility. That just so happens to be those in countries like the U.S. and Britain who care deeply for the welfare of dogs and cats, but not particularly for the welfare of cows, chickens, pigs, and other factory-raised animals. Dog and cat eaters in South Korea are insufficiently sensitive, and humane farming advocates in Britain and the U.S. are overly so. But, of course, it won't do simply to insist that this is the right degree of moral sensibility. We need an explanation of why this is the right degree of sensibility. Moral sensibility consists, at least in part, in reacting differently to different features of situations, actions, agents, and patients. If the right degree of moral sensibility requires reacting differently to puppies and to farm animals, there must be a morally relevant difference between puppies and farm animals. Such a difference can't simply consist in the fact that (some) people do react differently to them. The appeal to differential human sympathy illustrates a purely descriptive psychological difference between the behavior of Fred and that of someone who knowingly consumes factory-raised meat. It can do no serious moral work.

I have been unable to discover any morally relevant differences between the behavior of Fred, the puppy torturer, and the behavior of the millions of people who purchase and consume factory-raised meat, at least those who do so in the knowledge that the animals live lives of suffering and deprivation. If morality demands that we not torture puppies merely to enhance our own eating pleasure, morality also demands that we not support factory farming by purchasing factory-raised meat.

3. THE TEXAN'S CHALLENGE

Perhaps what I have said thus far is enough to convince many that the purchase and consumption of factory-raised meat is immoral. It is clear that the attribution of a different (and elevated) moral status to puppies from that attributed to farm animals is unjustified. But, one philosopher's *modus ponens,* as they say, is another Texan's *modus tollens.* Here is the *modus ponens* I have been urging:

(1) If it's wrong to torture puppies for gustatory pleasure, it's wrong to support factory farming.
(2) It is wrong to torture puppies for gustatory pleasure.
(3) Therefore it's wrong to support factory farming.

But some may be so convinced that supporting factory farming is not wrong that they may substitute that conviction for the second premise, and conclude that it is not wrong to torture puppies for gustatory pleasure. Thus we are confronted with the Texan's *modus tollens:*

(T1) If it's wrong to torture puppies for gustatory pleasure, then it's wrong to support factory farming.
(T2) It's not wrong to support factory farming.
(T3) Therefore it's not wrong to torture puppies for gustatory pleasure.

I'm not saying that there is a large risk that many people, even Texans, will start breeding puppies for food (outside of those countries where it is already accepted practice). What they may do (and have done when I have presented them with this argument) is explain their reluctance to do so as a mere sentimental preference, as opposed to a morally mandated choice. They may claim, in a somewhat Kantian spirit, that someone who can treat puppies like that may be more likely to mistreat humans. They may agree that all animals deserve equal consideration of their interests. They may then justify their different treatment of animals either on the grounds that they are simply giving some animals *more* than they deserve, or that they are attending to their own interests. If the former, they could claim that morality mandates minimal standards of conduct, but that nothing prevents us from choosing to go beyond the requirements of morality when we feel like it. If the latter, they could claim that their sentimental attachment to puppies, kittens, and the like, makes it in their own interests not to raise and kill them for food. Nonetheless, they may insist, in terms of moral status, there is a clear difference between humans and other animals. Humans have a moral status so far above that of other animals that we couldn't even consider raising humans for food (even humanely), or experimenting on them without their consent, even though we routinely do such things to other animals.

4. HUMANS' VERSUS ANIMALS' ETHICAL STATUS—THE RATIONALITY GAMBIT

For the purposes of this discussion, to claim that humans have a superior ethical status to animals is to claim that it is morally right to give the interests of humans greater weight than those of animals in deciding how to behave. Such claims will often be couched in terms of rights, such as the rights to life, liberty or respect, but nothing turns on this terminological matter. One may claim that it is generally wrong to kill humans, but not animals, because humans are rational, and animals are not. Or one may claim that the suffering of animals counts less than the suffering of humans (if at all), because humans are rational, and animals are not. These claims may proceed through the intermediate claim that the rights of humans are more extensive and stronger than those (if any) of animals. Alternatively, one may directly ground the judgment about the moral status of certain types of behavior in claims about the alleged natural properties of the individuals involved. Much of the debate over the moral status of abortion proceeds along these lines. Many opponents of abortion appeal to features that fetuses have in common with adult humans, in order to argue that it is, at least usually, just as seriously wrong to kill them as it is to kill us. For example, John Noonan claims that it is the possession of a full human genetic code that grounds the attribution to fetuses of this exalted ethical status. Such an argument may, but doesn't have to, proceed through the intermediate claim that anything that possesses a full human genetic code has a right to life. Many proponents of the moral permissibility of abortion, on the other hand, claim features such as self-consciousness or linguistic ability as necessary conditions of full moral status, and thus deny such status to fetuses.

What could ground the claim of superior moral status for humans? Just as the defender of a higher moral status for puppies than for farm animals needs to find some property or properties possessed by puppies but not by farm animals, so the defender of a higher moral status for humans needs to find some property or properties possessed by humans but not by other animals. The traditional view, dating back at least to Aristotle, is that rationality is what separates humans, both morally and metaphysically, from other animals. With a greater understanding of the cognitive powers of some animals, recent philosophers have often refined the claim to stress the kind and level of rationality required for moral reasoning. Let's start with a representative sample of three. Consider first these claims of Bonnie Steinbock:

> While we are not compelled to discriminate among people because of different capacities, if we can find a significant difference in capacities between human and non-human animals, this could serve to justify regarding human interests as primary. It is not arbitrary or smug, I think, to maintain that human beings have a different moral status from members of other species because of certain capacities which are characteristic of being human. We may not all be equal in these capacities but all human beings possess them to some measure and non-human animals do not. For example, human beings can be expected to reciprocate in a way that non-human animals cannot.... Thirdly, ... there is the "desire for self-respect."[5]

Similarly, Mary Anne Warren argues that "the rights of persons are generally stronger than those of sentient beings which are not persons." Her main premise to support this conclusion is the following:

> [T]here is one difference [between human and non-human nature] which has a clear moral relevance: people are at least sometimes capable of being moved to action or inaction by the force of reasoned argument.[6]

Carl Cohen, one of the most vehement modern defenders of what Peter Singer calls "speciesism" states his position as follows:

> Between species of animate life, however—between (for example) humans on the one hand and cats or rats on the other—the morally relevant differences are enormous, and almost universally appreciated. Humans engage in moral reflection; humans are morally autonomous; humans are members of moral communities, recognizing just claims against their own interest. Human beings do have rights, theirs is a moral status very different from that of cats or rats.[7]

So, the claim is that human interests and/or rights are stronger or more important than those of animals, because humans possess a kind and level of rationality not possessed by animals. How much of our current behavior towards animals this justifies depends on just how much consideration should be given to animal interests, and on what rights, if any, they possess. Both Steinbock and Warren stress that animal interests need to be taken seriously into account. Warren claims that animals have important rights, but not as important as human rights. Cohen, on the other hand, argues that we should actually *increase* our use of animals.

5. THE CHALLENGE OF MARGINAL CASES

One of the most serious challenges to this defense of the traditional view involves a consideration of what philosophers refer to as "marginal cases." Whatever kind and level of rationality is selected as justifying the attribution of superior moral status to humans will either be lacking in some humans or present in some animals. To take one of the most commonly-suggested features, many humans are incapable of engaging in moral reflection. For some, this incapacity is temporary, as is the case with infants, or the temporarily cognitively disabled. Others who once had the capacity may have permanently lost it as is the case with the severely senile or the irreversibly comatose. Still others never had and never will have the capacity, as is the case with the severely mentally disabled. If we base our claims for the moral superiority of humans over animals on the attribution of such capacities, won't we have to exclude many humans? Won't we then be forced to the claim that there is at least as much moral reason to use cognitively deficient humans in experiments and for food as to use animals? Perhaps we could exclude the only temporarily disabled, on the grounds of potentiality, though that move has its own problems. Nonetheless, the other two categories would be vulnerable to this objection.

I will consider two lines of response to the argument from marginal cases. The first denies that we have to attribute different moral status to marginal humans, but maintains that we are, nonetheless, justified in attributing different moral status to animals who are just as cognitively sophisticated as marginal humans, if not more so. The second admits that, strictly speaking, marginal humans are morally inferior to other humans, but proceeds to claim pragmatic reasons for treating them, at least usually, *as if* they had equal status.

As representatives of the first line of defense, I will consider arguments from three philosophers, Carl Cohen, Alan White, and David Schmidtz. First, Cohen:

> [the argument from marginal cases] fails; it mistakenly treats an essential feature of humanity as though it were a screen for sorting humans. The capacity for moral judgment that distinguishes humans from animals is not a test to be administered to human beings one by one. Persons who are unable, because of some disability, to perform the full moral functions natural to human beings are certainly not for that reason ejected from the moral community. The issue is one of kind... what humans retain when disabled, animals have never had.[8]

Alan White argues that animals don't have rights, on the grounds that they cannot intelligibly be spoken of in the full language of a right. By this he means that they cannot, for example, claim, demand, assert, insist on, secure, waive, or surrender a right. This is what he has to say in response to the argument from marginal cases:

> Nor does this, as some contend, exclude infants, children, the feeble-minded, the comatose, the dead, or generations yet unborn. Any of these may be for various reasons empirically unable to fulfill the full role of right-holder. But... they are logically possible subjects of rights to whom the full language of rights can significantly, however falsely, be used. It is a misfortune, not a tautology, that these persons cannot exercise or enjoy, claim, or waive, their rights or do their duty or fulfil their obligations.[9]

David Schmidtz defends the appeal to typical characteristics of species, such as mice, chimpanzees, and humans, in making decisions on the use of different species in experiments. He also considers the argument from marginal cases:

> Of course, some chimpanzees lack the characteristic features in virtue of which chimpanzees command respect as a species, just as some humans lack the characteristic features in virtue of which humans command respect as a species. It is equally obvious that some chimpanzees have cognitive capacities (for example) that are superior to the cognitive capacities of some humans. But whether every human being is superior to every chimpanzee is beside the point. The point is that we can, we do, and we should make decisions on the basis of our recognition that mice, chimpanzees, and humans are relevantly different *types*. We can have it both ways after all. Or so a speciesist could argue.[10]

There is something deeply troublesome about the line of argument that runs through all three of these responses to the argument from marginal cases. A particular feature, or set of features is claimed to have so much moral significance that its presence or lack can make the difference to whether a piece of behavior is morally justified or morally outrageous. But then it is claimed that the presence or lack of the feature in any *particular* case is not important. The relevant question is whether the presence or lack of the feature is *normal*. Such an argument would seem perfectly preposterous in most other cases. Suppose, for example, that ten famous people are on trial in the afterlife for crimes against humanity. On the basis of conclusive evidence, five are found guilty and five are found not guilty. Four of the guilty are sentenced to an eternity of torment, and one is granted an eternity of bliss. Four of the innocent are granted an eternity of bliss, and one is sentenced to an eternity of torment. The one innocent who is sentenced to torment asks why he, and not the fifth guilty person, must go to hell. Saint Peter replies, "Isn't it obvious Mr. Gandhi? You are male. The other four men—Adolph Hitler, Joseph Stalin, George W. Bush, and Richard Nixon—are all guilty. Therefore the normal condition for a male defendant in this trial is guilt. The fact that you happen to be innocent is irrelevant. Likewise, of the five female defendants in this trial, only one was guilty. Therefore the normal condition for female defendants in this trial is innocence. That is why Margaret Thatcher gets to go to heaven instead of you."

As I said, such an argument is preposterous. Is the reply to the argument from marginal cases any better? Perhaps it will be claimed that a biological category such as a species is more "natural," whatever that means, than a category like "all the male (or female) defendants in this trial." Even setting aside the not inconsiderable worries about the conventionality of biological categories, it is not at all clear why this distinction should be morally relevant. What if it turned out that there were statistically relevant differences in the mental abilities of men and women? Suppose that men were, on average, more skilled at manipulating numbers than women, and that women were, on average, more empathetic than men. Would such differences in what was "normal" for men and women justify us in preferring an innumerate man to a female math genius for a job as an accountant, or an insensitive woman to an ultra-sympathetic man for a job as a counselor? I take it that the biological distinction between male and female is just as real as that between human and chimpanzee.

A second response to the argument from marginal cases is to concede that cognitively deficient humans really do have an inferior moral status to normal humans. Can we, then, use such humans as we do animals? I know of no-one who takes the further step of advocating the use of marginal humans for food (though R. G. Frey has made some suggestive remarks concerning experimentation). How can we advocate this second response while blocking the further step? Warren suggests that "there are powerful practical and emotional reasons for protecting non-rational human beings, reasons which are absent in the case of most non-human animals."[11] It would clearly outrage common human sensibilities, if we were to raise retarded children for food or medical experiments.[12] Here is Steinbock in a similar vein:

> I doubt that anyone will be able to come up with a concrete and morally relevant difference that would justify, say, using a chimpanzee in an experiment rather than a human being with less capacity for reasoning, moral responsibility, etc. Should we then experiment on the severely retarded? Utilitarian considerations aside, we feel a special obligation to care for the handicapped members of our own species, who cannot survive in this world without such care .... In addition, when we consider the severely retarded, we think, "That could be me." It makes sense to think that one might have been born retarded, but not to think that one might have been born a monkey.... Here we are getting away from such things as "morally relevant differences" and are talking about something much more difficult to articulate, namely, the role of feeling and sentiment in moral thinking.[13]

This line of response clearly won't satisfy those who think that marginal humans really do deserve equal moral consideration with other humans. It is also a very shaky basis on which to justify our current practices. What outrages human sensibilities is a very fragile thing. Human history is littered with examples of widespread acceptance of the systematic mistreatment of some groups who didn't generate any sympathetic response from others. That we do feel a kind of sympathy for retarded humans that we don't feel for dogs is, if true, a contingent matter. To see just how shaky a basis this is for protecting retarded humans, imagine that a new kind of birth defect (perhaps associated with beef from cows treated with bovine growth hormone) produces severe mental retardation, green skin, and a complete lack of emotional bond between parents and child. Furthermore, suppose that the mental retardation is of the same kind and severity as that caused by other birth defects that don't have the other two effects. It seems likely that denying moral status to such defective humans would not run the same risks of outraging human sensibilities as would the denial of moral status to other, less easily distinguished and more loved defective humans. Would these contingent empirical differences between our reactions to different sources of mental retardation justify us in ascribing different direct moral status to their subjects? The only difference between them is skin color and whether they are loved by others. Any theory that could ascribe moral relevance to differences such as these doesn't deserve to be taken seriously.[14]

Finally, perhaps we could claim that the practice of giving greater weight to the interests of all humans than of animals is justified on evolutionary grounds. Perhaps such differential concern has survival value for the species. Something like this may well be true, but it is hard to see the moral relevance. We can hardly justify the privileging of human interests over animal interests on the grounds that such privileging serves human interests!

6. AGENT AND PATIENT—THE SPECIESIST'S CENTRAL CONFUSION

Although the argument from marginal cases certainly poses a formidable challenge to any proposed criterion of full moral standing that excludes animals, it doesn't, in my view, constitute the most serious flaw in such attempts to justify the status quo. The proposed criteria are all variations on the Aristotelian criterion of rationality. But what is the moral relevance of rationality? Why should we think that the possession of a certain level or kind of rationality renders the possessor's interests of greater moral significance than those of a merely sentient being? In Bentham's famous words "The question is not, Can they reason? nor Can they talk? But can they suffer?"[15]

What do defenders of the alleged superiority of human interests say in response to Bentham's challenge? Some, such as Carl Cohen, simply reiterate the differences between humans and animals that they claim to carry moral significance. Animals are not members of moral communities, they don't engage in moral reflection, they can't be moved by moral reasons, *therefore* (?) their interests don't count as much as ours. Others, such as Steinbock and Warren, attempt to go further. Here is Warren on the subject:

> Why is rationality morally relevant? It does not make us "better" than other animals or more "perfect" . . . . But it is morally relevant insofar as it provides greater possibilities for cooperation and for the nonviolent resolution of problems.[16]

Warren is certainly correct in claiming that a certain level and kind of rationality is morally relevant. Where she, and others who give similar arguments, go wrong is in specifying what the moral relevance amounts to. If a being is incapable of moral reasoning, at even the most basic level, if it is incapable of being moved by moral reasons, claims, or arguments, then it cannot be a moral agent. It cannot be subject to moral obligations, to moral praise or blame. Punishing a dog for doing something "wrong" is no more than an attempt to alter its future behavior. So long as we are undeceived about the dog's cognitive capacities, we are not, except metaphorically, expressing any moral judgment about the dog's behavior. (We may, of course, be expressing moral judgment about the dog's owner, who didn't train it very well.) All this is well and good, but what is the significance for the question of what weight to give to animal interests? That animals can't be moral *agents* doesn't seem to be relevant to their status as moral *patients*. Many, perhaps most, humans are both moral agents and patients. Most, perhaps all, animals are only moral patients. Why would the lack of moral agency give them diminished status as moral patients? Full status as a moral patient is not some kind of reward for moral agency. I have heard students complain in this regard that it is *unfair* that humans bear the burdens of moral responsibility, and don't get enhanced consideration of their interests in return. This is a very strange claim. Humans are subject to moral obligations, because they are the kind of creatures who *can* be. What grounds moral agency is simply different from what grounds moral standing as a patient. It is no more unfair that humans and not animals are moral agents, than it is unfair that real animals and not stuffed toys are moral patients.

One other attempt to justify the selection of rationality as the criterion of full moral standing is worth considering. Recall the suggestion that rationality is important insofar as it facilitates cooperation. If we view the essence of morality as reciprocity, the significance of rationality is obvious. A certain twisted, but all-too-common, interpretation of the Golden Rule is that we should "do unto others in order to get them to do unto us." There's no point, according to this approach, in giving much, if any, consideration to the interests of animals, because they are simply incapable of giving like consideration to our interests. In discussing the morality of eating meat, I have, many times, heard students claim that we are justified in eating meat, because "the animals would eat us, if given half a chance." (That they say this in regard to our practice of eating cows and chickens is depressing testimony to their knowledge of the animals they gobble up with such gusto.) Inasmuch as there is a consistent view being expressed here at all, it concerns self-interest, as opposed to morality. Whether it serves my interests to give the same weight to the interests of animals as to those of humans is an interesting question, but it is not the same question as whether it is *right* to give animals' interests equal weight. The same point, of course, applies to the question of whether to give equal weight to my interests, or those of my family, race, sex, religion, etc. as to those of other people.

Perhaps it will be objected that I am being unfair to the suggestion that the essence of morality is reciprocity. Reciprocity is important, not because it serves *my* interests, but because it serves the interests of all. Reciprocity facilitates cooperation, which in turn produces benefits for all. What we should say about this depends on the scope of "all." If it includes all sentient beings, then the significance of animals' inability to reciprocate is in what it tells us about *how* to give their interests equal consideration. It certainly can't tell us that we should give less, or no, consideration to their interests. If, on the other hand, we claim that rationality is important for reciprocity, which is important for cooperation, which is important for benefiting humans,which is the ultimate goal of morality, we have clearly begged the question against giving equal consideration to the interests of animals.

It seems that any attempt to justify the claim that humans have a higher moral status than other animals by appealing to some version of rationality as the morally relevant difference between humans and animals will fail on at least two counts. It will fail to give an adequate answer to the argument from marginal cases, and, more importantly, it will fail to make the case that such a difference is morally relevant to the status of animals as moral patients as opposed to their status as moral agents.

I conclude that our intuitions that Fred's behavior is morally impermissible are accurate. Furthermore, given that the behavior of those who knowingly support factory farming is morally indistinguishable, it follows that their behavior is also morally impermissible.[17]

NOTES

1. For information on factory farms, see, for example, Jim Mason and Peter Singer, *Animal Factories,* 2d ed. (New York: Harmony Books, 1990), Karen Davis, *Prisoned Chickens, Poisoned Eggs: An Inside Look at the Modern Poultry Industry* (Summertown, TN: Book Publishing Co., 1996), John Robbins, *Diet for a New America* (Walpole, NH: Stillpoint, 1987).
2. *Livestock Slaughter 1998 Summary,* NASS, USDA (Washington, D.C.: March 1999), 2; and *Poultry Slaughter,* NASS, USDA (Washington, D.C.: February 2, 1999), 1f.
3. For a fine critique of the Doctrine of Double Effect, see Jonathan Bennett, *The Act Itself*, (Oxford 1995), ch.11.
4. If someone were to assert that "puppyishness" or simply "being a puppy" were ethically relevant, I could do no more than favor them with an incredulous stare.
5. Bonnie Steinbock, "Speciesism and the Idea of Equality," *Philosophy* 53, no. 204 (April 1978). Reprinted in *Contemporary Moral Problems,* 5th edition, James E. White (ed.) (West, 1997) 467–468.
6. Mary Anne Warren, "Difficulties with the Strong Animal Rights Position," *Between the Species* 2, no. 4, 1987. Reprinted in *Contemporary Moral Problems,* 5th edition, James E. White (ed.) (West. 1997), 482.
7. Carl Cohen, "The Case for the Use of Animals in Biomedical Research," *The New England Journal of Medecine,* vol. 315, 1986. Reprinted in *Social Ethics*, 4th edition, Thomas A. Mappes and Jane S. Zembaty, (eds.) (New York: McGraw-Hill, 1992) 463.
8. Cohen, op. cit. 461.
9. Alan White, *Rights*, (OUP 1984). Reprinted in *Animal Rights and Human Obligations*, 2nd edition, Tom Regan and Peter Singer (eds.) (Prentice Hall, 1989), 120.
10. David Schmidtz, " Are All Species Equal?" *Journal of Applied Philosophy*, Vol. 15, no. 1 (1998), 61, my emphasis.
11. Warren, op. cit. 483.
12. For a similar argument, see Peter Carruthers, *The Animals Issue: Moral Theory in Practice* (Cambridge University Press, 1992.)
13. Steinbock, op. cit. 469–470.
14. Certain crude versions of the so-called ethics of care do seem to entail that the mere fact of being loved gives a different ethical status.

15. Jeremy Bentham, *Introduction to the Principles of Morals and Legislation*, (Various) chapter 17.
16. Warren, op. cit. 482.
17. This paper, in various forms, has been presented in more places than I can remember, and has benefited from the comments of more people than I can shake a stick at. I particularly wish to thank, for their helpful comments, Doug Ehring, Mylan Engel, Mark Heller, and Steve Sverdlik.

A Critique of the Alleged Moral Basis of Vegetarianism

CARL COHEN

Carl Cohen is an American philosopher who teaches at the University of Michigan, Ann Arbor. He has published widely in both moral and political philosophy.

The essay that appears is a revised version of "Why Animals Do Not Have Rights," which originally appeared in a 2001 anthology entitled *The Animal Rights Debate* alongside a companion (pro-animal rights) essay by philosopher Tom Regan. In his response, Cohen challenges a number of arguments that have been made on behalf of vegetarianism.

There is no obligation to eat meat. But neither is there any obligation to refrain from doing so. The oft-alleged obligation to restrict oneself to a vegetarian diet is commonly grounded on the supposition that animals have moral rights. If they do have such rights then they surely have the right to live, and therefore (it is supposed) killing and devouring them must wrongfully violate their rights.[1] This argument is without merit because, in fact, animals do not have rights.

We care about animals, of course. Most of us care a great deal about them, and we very much want not to be thought uncaring. But there is widespread fear that one who denies that animals have rights is likely to be thought callous or even cruel; this results in a general reluctance to express a moral truth that everyone grasps intuitively: rights, which are central in the moral lives of humans, are not possessed by animals; animals do not have rights. *Why* they do not have them is explained below.

Before turning to that, however, I emphasize one consequence of this moral truth: We may conclude with confidence that opposition to the eating of meat is ungrounded insofar as that opposition is based upon claimed rights that are in fact illusory. Animals cannot be deprived of rights they do not have.

The reluctance to deny that animals have rights lies in a common confusion about the relation between our *obligations* to animals and the claim that they possess *rights.* Humans do have many obligations to animals, of course, as all decent persons will agree. Many go on to suppose that since such obligations are genuine, animals must have rights because if those rights were to be denied, the obligations owed to animals (not seriously in question) would need to be denied as well. This is a frequent and unfortunate mistake. Denying the reality of animal rights does *not* entail the denial of our obligations to animals. Most certainly it does not. I explain.

Reflect for a moment upon the obligations we humans owe to others. Some of these obligations may be traced to the fact that we are the targets of their rights. My obligation to repay the money I borrowed from you is the obverse of the right that you have to my payment of the debt. So, plainly, *some* of my

From *Food for Thought: The Debate over Eating Meat*, ed. Steven F. Sapontzis. Copyright © Rowman & Littlefield. Used by permission of the publisher.

obligations do arise from the rights of others against me. But that is by no means true of all obligations. A correct understanding of the true relation between rights and obligations is absolutely essential for sound moral judgments.

The common readiness to assent to the proposition that animals have rights is mainly a result of the hasty supposition that if we have obligations to them (which we surely do) they must have rights against us. But this is not so. Recognizing (correctly) that we are not morally free to do anything we please to animals, it is inferred (incorrectly) that they must therefore have "rights"—and that inference yields a defense of vegetarianism on moral grounds.

The premise that underlies such reasoning is the supposition of the *symmetrical reciprocity* of obligations and rights. It is a false premise, and its falsity is easy to discern. Between rights and obligations the relations are not symmetrical. Rights do entail obligations upon the targets of those rights, of course, as earlier noted. If you have a right to the return of money you lent me, I have the obligation to return that money, and so on. But we may not correctly infer from the fact that all rights impose obligations upon their targets that all obligations owed arise because one is the target of the rights of another.

A logical confusion underlies the mistake. From the true proposition that all dogs are mammals we certainly may not infer that all mammals are dogs. Universal affirmative propositions of the form "all dogs are mammals" or "all rights entail obligations," cannot be *converted simply* and retain their truth. *Some* mammals are dogs, yes, and *some* obligations do arise from rights. But it is a confusion of mind to conclude, from the fact that all dogs are mammals, that all mammals are dogs. It is no less a confusion of mind to conclude that because all rights entail obligations, all obligations are entailed by rights.

Very many of the moral obligations borne by each of us are owed to other persons or other beings who have no *rights* against us; reflection on everyday experience confirms this quickly. Our obligations arise from a great variety of circumstances and relations, of which being the target of another's right is but one. Illustrations of this rich and important variety are everywhere to be found; here are some:

a) Obligations arise from *commitments* freely made by a moral agent. As a college professor I promise my students explicitly that I will comment at length on the papers they submit, and from this express commitment obligations flow, of course. But my students understand that they have not the right to demand that I provide such comment.

b) Obligations arise from the *possession of authority.* Civil servants are obliged to be courteous to members of the public; presiding officers at a public forum ought to call upon representatives of different points of view in alternation; judges have the obligation to listen patiently to the arguments of parties disputing before them–but such obligations are not grounded in rights.

c) Obligations arise as a consequence of *special relations*: hosts have an obligation to be cordial to their guests, but guests may not demand cordiality as a right.

d) *Faithful service* may engender obligations: shepherds have obligations to their dogs, and cowboys to their horses, none of which flow from the *rights* of those dogs or those horses.

e) My son, eleven years old as I write this, may someday wish to study veterinary medicine as my father did. I will then have the obligation to help him as I can, and with pride I shall—but he has not the authority to demand such help as a matter of right. *Family connections* may give rise to obligations without concomitant rights.

f) My dog has no rights to daily exercise and veterinary care, but I do have the obligation to provide these things for him. *Duties of care* freely taken on may bind one even though those to whom the care is given have not got a right to demand it. Recognizing that a beloved pet is suffering great pain, we may be obliged to put it out of its misery, but the tormented animal has no claim of right that that be done.

g) An act of *spontaneous kindness* done may leave us with the obligation to acknowledge and perhaps return that gift, but the benefactor to whom we are thus obliged has no claim of *right* against us.

And so on and on. The circumstances giving rise to obligations are so many and so varied that they cannot all be cataloged. It is nevertheless certain and plainly seen that it is *not only* from the rights of others that our obligations arise.

How then are rights and obligations related? When looked at from the viewpoint of one who holds a right and addresses the target of that right, they appear correlative. But they are plainly not correlative when looked at from the viewpoint of one who recognizes an obligation on himself, an obligation that does not stem from the rights of another. Your right to the money I owe you creates my obligation to pay it, of course. But many of my obligations to the needy, to my neighbors, to sentient creatures of every sort, have no foundation in their rights. The premise that rights and obligations are *reciprocals*, that *every* obligation flows from another's right, is utterly false. It is inconsistent with our intuitive understanding of the difference between what we believe we *ought* to do and what others can justly *demand* that we do.

This lack of symmetry is of enormous importance. It helps to explain how it can be true that, although animals do not have rights, it does not follow from this fact that one is free to treat them with callous disregard. It is silly to think of rats as the holders of moral rights, but it is by no means silly to recognize that rats can feel pain and that it is our obligation to refrain from torturing them because they are beings having that capacity. The obligation to act humanely *we owe to them* even though the concept of a right cannot possibly apply to them. We are obliged to apply to animals the moral principles that govern *us* regarding the gratuitous imposition of pain and suffering. We are the moral agents in this arena, not the rats. Act toward lesser creatures, as the saying goes, "not merely according to their deserts, but according to your dignities." We are restrained by moral principles in this way, but being so restrained does not suggest or suppose that the animals to whom we owe humane regard are the possessors of rights.

* * *

Animals cannot be the bearers of rights because the concept of right is *essentially human*; it is rooted in the human moral world and has force and applicability only within that world. Humans must deal with rats—all too frequently in some parts of the world—and must refrain from cruelty in dealing with them. But a rat can no more be said to have rights than a table can be said to have ambition, or a rock to exhibit remorse. To say of a pig or a fish that it has rights is to confuse categories, to apply to its world a moral category that can have content only in the human moral world.

Try this thought experiment: Imagine, on the Serengeti Plain in East Africa, a lioness hunting to feed her cubs. A baby zebra, momentarily left unattended by its mother, becomes her prey; the lioness snatches it, rips open its throat, tears out chunks of its flesh, and departs. The mother zebra is driven nearly out of her wits when at first she cannot locate her baby; finding its carcass at last, she will not leave its remains for days. The scene may cause you to shudder, but it is perfectly ordinary and common in the world of nature. If that baby zebra had any rights at all it certainly had the right to live; of all rights that is surely the most fundamental and the one presupposed by all others. So, if in that incident of natural predation, the prey has rights and the predator infringes those rights, we humans ought to intervene in defense of the zebra's rights, if doing so were within our power. But we do not intervene in such matters even when it is in our power; we do not dream of doing so. On the other hand, if we saw (or even suspected) that the lioness was about to attack an unprotected human baby playing at the edge of the forest, we would respond with alacrity, protecting the baby in every way within our power.

What accounts for the moral difference between those cases? Not convenience merely; protecting the baby may be dangerous, while intervening to save the baby zebra may be easy and safe. Humans are often in a position to intervene to avoid predatory killing, yet we deliberately refrain. Our responses to threatened humans differ fundamentally from our responses to threatened zebras. But why? No doubt we have greater empathy for the endangered human. But we also recognize, consciously or subconsciously, that between the moral status of the baby zebra and the moral status of the baby human there are profound differences. The human baby, we might say if later asked, has a right not to be eaten alive, and it has that right because it is a *human* being.

Do you believe the baby zebra has the *right* not to be slaughtered? Or that the lioness has the *right* to kill that baby zebra to feed her cubs? Perhaps you are inclined to say, when confronted by such natural rapacity (duplicated in various forms millions of times each day on planet earth) that *neither* is right or wrong, that neither zebra nor lioness has a right against the other. Then I am on your side. Rights are pivotal in the moral realm and must be taken seriously, yes; but zebras and lions and rats do not live in a moral realm; their lives are totally *a*moral. There *is* no morality for them; animals do no moral wrong, ever. In their world there are no wrongs and there are no rights.

One contemporary philosopher who has thought a good deal about animals puts this point in terms of the ability to formulate principles. Referring to animals as "moral patients" [that is, beings *upon* whom moral agents like ourselves may act], he writes:

> A moral patient [an animal] lacks the ability to formulate, let alone bring to bear, principles in deliberating about which one among a number of possible acts it would be right or proper to perform. Moral patients, in a word, cannot do what is right, nor can they do what is wrong.... [E]ven when a moral patient causes significant harm to another, the moral patient has not done what is wrong. Only moral agents can do what is wrong.

Just so. The concepts of wrong, and of right, are totally foreign to animals, not conceivably within their ken or applicable to them, as the author of that passage clearly sees. He is the noted advocate of animal rights, Tom Regan.[2]

Here is yet another thought experiment that illuminates our intuitive judgments about the moral status of animals: Imagine that, as you were driving to work the other day, a squirrel suddenly reversed its course and ran in front of your car. It being impossible for you to avoid hitting it, you clenched your teeth as you heard the telltale thumps from beneath the automobile. Pained by the thought that the squirrel had been needlessly killed by your car, you silently express to yourself the hope that, if indeed it was killed, it was caused no great suffering; and you drive on. But now suppose that it was not a squirrel but a human toddler who ran into the path of your car and whom you hit through absolutely no fault of your own. Swerving in panic, we will suppose, you avoid a killing blow, but you cannot avoid hitting the child and it becomes plain that she has been badly injured by the impact. Anguish, fear, *horror* overwhelm you. Most assuredly you do not drive on, but stop in wretched torment, to do what can be done for the injured child. You rush it to medical care; its parents you contact at the earliest possible moment, imploring their understanding. Nothing you could possibly have done would have avoided the terrible accident, you explain—and yet you express tearfully your profound regret. At the first opportunity you arrange to visit the recuperating child; you bring it a present, wish it well; her injury and her recovery will be forever on your mind. And so on.

What accounts for the enormous difference between the response you make to the death of a squirrel, and to the injury of a human child, you being the cause of both, and in both cases entirely innocent of fault? Does that difference not spring from your intuitive grasp of the difference in the moral status of the two, your recognition that the one has rights, which you would not for all the world have deliberately infringed, while the other, although sentient and perhaps endearing, has no rights that you could possibly infringe?

Those who rely on animals for food, like medical investigators who use animals in research to advance human well-being, do not violate the rights of animals by their conduct because, to be blunt, animals have no rights. Rights do not apply to them.

Humans, on the other hand, certainly do have rights. How is this difference to be accounted for? Rabbits are mammals and we are mammals, both inhabiting a natural world. The reality of the moral rights that we possess (and that they do not possess) we do not doubt, and the importance of this great difference between them and us is equally certain. But we are unsure of the ground of these rights of ours. Where do they come from? We are a natural species too, a product of evolution as all animals are. How then can we be so very different from the zebras and the rats? Why are we not crudely primitive creatures, as they are, for whom the concept of moral right is a fiction?

Philosophers and theologians have long struggled, and struggle still, to explain the foundations of natural human rights. I do not propose to offer here the resolution of the deepest questions confronting human beings. But the sharp divide between the moral status of animals and that of humans we can say something more about.

It will be helpful to reflect upon the *kinds* of explanations of human rights that have been given by the greatest of moral philosophers. What has been generally held to account for the fact that humans, unlike animals, do have rights?

(1) Many have thought that the moral understanding of right and duty, by humans, is a *divine gift*, a grasp of the eternal law for which we have been peculiarly equipped by God. So thought St. Thomas of Aquinas,* who argued tightly in defense of that view in the thirteenth century. All things, said he,

> are ruled and measured by the eternal law....Now among all others, the rational creature is subject to divine providence in the most excellent way, in so far as it partakes of a share of providence....Wherefore it has a share of the eternal reason, whereby it has a natural inclination to its proper act and end: and this participation of the eternal law in the rational creature is called the natural law. Hence the Psalmist after saying..."Many say, Who showeth us good things?" in answer to which question he says: "The light of Thy countenance, O Lord, is signed upon us."[3]

He thus implies that the light of natural reason, whereby we discern what is good and what is evil, which is the function of the natural law, is nothing else than an imprint on us of the divine light.[4] The power to grasp the binding power of moral law, and therefore the capacity to understand human rights, and to respect them, is on this account divinely endowed. No one has put this view more cogently than St. Thomas. The account he gave was not new in his day, nor has it lost its authority for many today.

Long before St. Thomas marshaled such arguments, other fathers of the Church, perhaps St. Augustine* most profoundly, had pointed out that if God has made us in his own image, as we are taught, and therefore with a will that is truly free and "knowing good and evil [5]", we, unlike all other creatures, must choose between good and evil, between right and wrong.[6]

(2) Philosophers have very commonly distrusted such theological reasoning. Many accounts of the moral dimension of human experience have been offered that do not rely upon inspired texts or supernatural gifts. Of the most influential philosophers, many have held that human morality is grounded not in the divine but in the human moral community. "I am morally realized," wrote the great English idealist, F. H. Bradley, "not until my personal self has utterly ceased to be my exclusive self, is no more a will which is outside others' will, but finds in the world of others nothing but self." What Bradley called "the organic moral community" is, he thought, the only context in which there can be right. "Realize yourself as the self-conscious member of an infinite whole, by realizing that whole in yourself."[7]

Before him, the great German idealist G. W. F. Hegel accounted for human rights as a consequence of the self-conscious participation of human beings in "an objective ethical order."[8] And there have been many other such accounts of rights, accounts that center upon human interrelations, upon a moral fabric within which human beings must always act, but within which animals never act and never can *possibly* act.

(3) Such reasoning is exceedingly abstract, and for that reason many find it unsatisfying. A better account of rights, an account more concrete and more true to their own experience, some think to be that given by ethical intuitionists and realists who rely upon the immediate moral experience of ordinary people. Human moral conduct must be governed, said the leading intuitionist H. A. Prichard, by the "underivative, intuitive cognition of the rightness of an action."[9] Would you know how we can be sure that humans have rights? Ask yourself how you know that you have rights. You have no doubt about it. There are some fundamental truths, on this view, for which no argument need be given. In that same spirit Sir David Ross explained our grasp of human

* Thomas Aquinas (c. 1225–1274) and Saint Augustine (354–430) (discussion following) were two of the most important theologians and philosophers in the early Christian tradition.

rights as our recognition of moral "suitability": "fitness, in a certain specific and unanalyzable way, to a certain situation."[10] And that was the view of my teacher and my friend of happy memory, Professor C. D. Broad. Rights surely are possessed by humans, he thought, by humans but never by animals. The knowledge of right is immediately and certainly possessed.

(4) For those who seek a more naturalistic account of ethical concepts, there are, among others, the writings of Marx* and his followers who explicitly repudiated all moral views claiming to have their foundation in some supernatural sphere. "The animal," Marx wrote, "is one with its life activity. It does not distinguish the activity from itself. It is its activity. But man makes his life activity itself an object of his will and consciousness.... His own life is an object for him.... Conscious life activity distinguishes man from the life activity of the animals."

Hence humans can concern themselves with human*kind,* and humans alone can understand their species; humans, unlike animals, make judgments that can be "universal and consequently free."[11] Moral judgments are typically universal in this sense. That is why, Lenin later wrote, "There is no such thing as morality taken outside of human society."[12] Every conception of moral right, on this view, is a reflection of the concrete conditions of life, but always the conditions of *human* life.

A more sophisticated ethical naturalism was presented by the American pragmatists John Dewey and George Herbert Mead, who shared the view that morality arises only in human community, but who emphasized the development of self within that community. We humans create our selves, selves that develop and become moral, Mead wrote, only through "the consciousness of other moral selves."[13]

Which among all these families of moral positions is most nearly true? Readers will decide for themselves. Differing ethical systems have been very briefly recapitulated here only to underscore the fact that, however much great thinkers have disagreed about fundamental principles, *the essentially human locus of the concept of right* has never been seriously doubted. Of the finest moral philosophers from antiquity to the present not one would deny—as the animal rights movement does seek now to deny—that there is a most profound difference between the moral stature of humans and that of animals, and that rights pertain only to the former.

***

The claim that there is no fundamental moral difference between animals and humans is the essential mark of what is loosely called the animal rights movement. "There is no rational basis," says Ingrid Newkirk, of People for the Ethical Treatment of Animals (PETA), "for saying that a human being has special rights." But in this she is profoundly mistaken; there is a rational basis for this distinction, a distinction of the deepest importance. The failure to grasp and respect that distinction leads some zealots to interfere with medical research, and others to insist that eating meat is a moral wrong. Reflect upon what it is that differentiates acts by humans from the acts of cows or rabbits. With Immanuel Kant we may say that critical reason reveals at the core of *human* action a uniquely moral will. There is, in humans, a unique capacity to formulate moral *principles* for the direction of our conduct, and we have a direct and immediate understanding of that capacity. Human beings can grasp the maxim of the principles we devise, and by applying those principles to ourselves as well as to others, we exhibit the autonomy of the human will. Humans, but never cows, confront choices that are purely moral. Humans, but certainly not pigs or chickens, lay down rules, moral imperatives, by which all moral agents are thought to be rightly governed, ourselves along with all others. Human beings are *self*-legislative, morally *auto*nomous.

To be a moral agent is to be able to grasp the generality of moral restrictions upon our will. Humans understand that there are some acts that may be in our interest and yet must not be willed because they are simply wrong. This capacity for moral judgement does not arise in the animal world; rats can neither exercise nor respond to moral claims. My dog knows that there are certain things he must not do, but he knows this only as the outcome of his

* Karl Marx (1818–1883) was a nineteenth-century German philosopher, often called the "father of communism." His follower V. I. Lenin (1870–1924) (discussion following) was a Russian revolutionary and the first head of the Soviet Union.

learning about his interests, the pains he may suffer if he does what he's been taught is forbidden. He does not know, he *cannot* know (as Tom Regan agrees)[14] that any conduct is *wrong*. The proposition: "It would be highly advantageous to act in such-and-such a way, but I may not do so because it would be morally wrong" is one that no dog or bunny rabbit, however sweet and endearing, however loyal or loving or intelligent, can ever entertain, or intend, or begin to grasp. *Right is not in their world.* But right and wrong are the very stuff of human moral life, the ever-present awareness of human beings who *can* do wrong, and who by seeking (often but not always) to avoid wrong conduct prove themselves members of a moral community in which rights may be exercised and must be respected.

Every day humans confront actual or potential conflicts between what is in their own interest and what is just. We restrain ourselves (or at least we can do so) on purely moral grounds. In such a community the concept of a right makes very good sense, of course. Some riches that do not belong to us would please us, no doubt, but we *may* not take them; we refrain from stealing not only because we fear punishment if caught. Even if we knew that the detection of our wrongdoing were impossible, we understand that to deprive others of what is theirs by right is conduct forbidden *by our own moral rules*. We return lost property belonging to others even when keeping it might be much to our advantage; such return is the act that our moral principles call for. Only in a community of that kind, a community constituted by beings capable of self-restricting moral judgments, can the concept of a *right* be intelligibly invoked.

Humans have such moral capacities. They are in this sense self-legislative, members of moral communities governed by moral rules; humans possess rights and recognize the rights of others. Animals do not have such capacities. They cannot exhibit moral autonomy in this sense, cannot possibly be members of a truly moral community. They may be the objects of our moral concern because they are sentient, of course, but they cannot possibly possess rights. People who eat animals do not violate the rights of those animals because, to be plain, they have none to violate.

I repeat one caveat for emphasis: It does not follow from the fact that animals have no rights that we are free to do anything we please to them. Most assuredly not. We do have obligations to animals, weighty obligations—but those obligations do not, because they cannot, arise out of animal rights.

* * *

There is an objection sometimes raised to this view that deserves response and deserves also to be permanently put aside. It cannot be, the critic says, that having rights requires the ability to make moral claims, or to grasp and apply moral laws, because, if that were true, many human beings—the brain-damaged, the comatose, infants, and the senile—who plainly lack those capacities must be without rights. But that is absurd. This proves, the critic concludes, that rights do not depend on the presence of moral capacities.[15]

Objections of this kind arise from a misunderstanding of what it means to say that the moral world is a human world. Children, like elderly adults, have rights *because they are human*. Morality is an essential feature of human life; all humans are moral creatures, infants and the senile included. Rights are not doled out to this individual person or that one by somehow establishing the presence in them of some special capacity. This mistaken vision would results in the selective award of right to some individuals but not others, and the cancellation of rights when capacities fail. On the contrary, rights are *universally* human, apply to humans generally. This criticism thus errs by treating the essentially moral feature of humanity as though it were a screen for sorting individual humans, which it most certainly is not. The capacity for moral judgment that distinguishes humans from animals is not a test to be administered to human beings one by one. Persons who, because of some disability, are unable to perform the full moral functions natural to human beings are not for that reason ejected from the human community. The critical distinction is one of kind. Humans are of such a kind that rights pertain to them *as humans*; humans live lives that will be, or have been, or remain *essentially* moral. It is silly to suppose that human rights might fluctuate with an individual's health, or dissipate with an individual's decline. The rights involved are human rights. On the other hand, animals are of such a kind that rights never pertain to them; what humans retain when disabled, rats never had.

The contrast between these two very different moral conditions is highlighted in the world of medical experimentation. Humans must *choose* to allow themselves to be the instruments of scientific research, and because humans have moral authority over their own bodies, we insist that humans may be the subject of scientific experiments only with their informed and freely given consent. Investigators who withhold information from potential subjects, or who deceive potential subjects, thereby making it impossible for them to give genuinely voluntary consent to what is done, will be condemned and punished, rightly. But this consent, which we think absolutely essential in the case of human subjects, is *impossible* for animals to give. The reason is not merely that we cannot communicate with them, or explain to them or inquire of them, but that the kind of moral choice involved in giving consent is totally out of the question for a chicken or a cow.

* * *

An objection of a different kind is raised by some advocates of animal rights. It goes like this:

> Animals have internal lives far more rich and complicated than most people realize; many animals are, as Tom Regan points out, "psychologically complex" beings. Therefore, the effort to distinguish the world of humans from the world of animals by pointing to some special capacity of humans cannot succeed. Although in lesser degree than humans, animals do have the capacities we commonly associate with humanity. Humans are rational, but animals can reason too; animals communicate with one another, not with languages like ours of course, but very effectively nonetheless. Animals, like humans, care passionately for their young; animals, like humans, exhibit desires and preferences. And so on and on. So there is no genuine moral distinction to be drawn.[16]

This objection has much popular appeal but it fails because it relies upon a mistaken assumption. *Cognitive* abilities, the ability to communicate or to reason, are simply not at issue. My dog certainly reasons, and he communicates rather well. Nor is it *affective* capacities that are at issue; many animals plainly exhibit fear, love, and anger, care for one another and for their offspring, and so on. Nor is it the exhibition of *preference*, or memory, or aversion that marks the critical divide; no one doubts that a squirrel may recall where it buried a nut, or that a dog would rather go on a walk than remain in the car. Remarkable behaviors are often exhibited by animals, as we all know. Conditioning, fear, instinct, and intelligence all contribute to individual success and to species survival.

Nor is the capacity to suffer sufficient to justify the claim that animals have rights. They surely can suffer; it is obvious that they feel pain. And because they are sentient in that way, they are properly a concern of morally sensitive humans; they are, we may say, morally "considerable." Of course. And that is why the moral principles that govern us oblige us to act thoughtfully, humanely, in our use of them.

But with all the varied capacities of animals granted, it remains absolutely impossible for them to act *morally,* to be members of a moral community. Emphasizing similarities between human families and those of monkeys, or between human communities and those of wolves, and the like, cannot ground the moral equality of species; it serves only to obscure what is truly critical. A being subject to genuinely moral judgment must be capable of grasping the *maxim* of an act, and capable, too, of grasping the *generality* of an ethical premise in a moral argument. Similarities between animal conduct and human conduct cannot refute, cannot even address, the profound moral differences between humans and the lower animals.

Because humans do have rights, and these rights can be violated by other humans, we all understand that humans can and sometimes do commit *crimes*. Whether a crime has been committed, however, depends utterly upon the actor's moral state of mind. If I take your coat from the closet honestly believing that it was mine, I do not steal it. A genuine crime is an act in which the guilty deed, the *actus reus*, is accompanied by a guilty state of mind, a *mens rea*. Humans can commit crimes not merely because we realize that we may be punished for acting thus-and-so, but because we recognize that there are duties that govern us; to speak of such recognition in the world of cows and horses is literally nonsensical. In primitive times cows and horses were sometimes punished at the bar of human justice. We chuckle now as we look back upon that practice, realizing that to accuse a cow of a crime marks the accuser as inane, confused about the applicability of moral concepts. Animals never can be criminals, obviously—not because they are always law-abiding, but because "law-abiding" has no sense in this context; moral appraisals do not intelligibly apply to them. And that is why it is not true, and never can be true, that animals have moral rights.

The fundamental mistake is one in which a concept (in this case, moral right) that makes very good sense in one context, is applied in another context in which it makes no sense at all. It may be helpful to reflect upon other spheres, very distant from morality, in which mistakes of the same general kind have been commonly made at great cost.

The world of metaphysical thinking is riddled with mistakes of that kind. In his *Critique of Pure Reason*, Immanuel Kant explains at length the metaphysical blunders into which we are led when we apply concepts fundamentally important in one sphere in another sphere in which those concepts can have no grip. In our human experience (for example), the concepts of time and space, the relations of cause and effect, of subject and attribute, and others, are fundamental and inescapable. But these are concepts arising only within the world of our human experience and are bound to it. When we forget that bond we may be misled into asking: "Was the world caused, or is it uncaused?" "Did the world have a beginning in time, or did it not?" Kant explains, in one of the most brilliant long passages in all philosophical literature, why it *makes no sense* to ask such questions.[17] "Causation" is a concept that applies to phenomena we humans encounter, it is a category of our experience and cannot apply to the world as a whole. "Time" is the sequential condition of our experience, the way we experience things, not a container within which the world could have begun. In his discussion of the *paralogisms* of pure reason, and following his analyses of the *antinomies* of pure reason, Kant patiently exhibits the many confusions arising from the *misapplication* of the categories of experience. Whatever our judgment of his conclusions about the limits of reason, his larger lesson in these passages is powerful and deep. The misapplication of concepts leads to fundamental mistakes, to nonsense.

So it is also when we mistakenly transfer the concept of a right from the human moral world where it is rightly applied to the status of humans, to the animal world where it has no possible applicability, and wrongly applied to the status of animals. To say that rats have rights is to apply to the world of rats a concept that makes very good sense when applied to humans, but makes no sense at all when applied to rats. That is why chickens, like rats and cows, *cannot* have rights. The claim that eating them deprives them of their rights, therefore, is nonsensical, and cannot be the ground of a moral defense of vegetarianism.

NOTES

1. Tom Regan, a leading proponent of the view that animals have rights, presents one version of this argument in "The Moral Basis of Vegetarianism," in *All That Dwell Therein: Animal Rights and Environmental Ethics* (Berkeley: University of California Press, 1982).
2. Tom Regan, *The Case for Animal Rights* (Berkeley: University of California Press, 1983), pp. 152–53.
3. The reference by St. Thomas is to Psalm 4, line 6.
4. St. Thomas Aquinas, *Summa Theologica*. First Part of the Second Part, Question 91, Second Article.
5. Genesis 3:22.
6. St. Augustine, *Confessions*, Book Seven, 397 CE.
7. Francis Herbert Bradley, "Why Should I Be Moral?" in *Ethical Studies* (Oxford: Clarendon Press, 1927).
8. Georg Wilhelm Friedrich Hegel, *Philosophy of Right*, 1821.
9. H. A. Prichard. "Does Moral Philosophy Rest on a Mistake?" in *Moral Obligation* (Oxford: Oxford University Press, 1949).
10. Sir David Ross, *The Foundations of Ethics* (Oxford: Clarendon Press, 1939), chap. 3.
11. Karl Marx, *Economic and Philosophical Manuscripts*, 1844.
12. V. I. Lenin, "The Tasks of the Youth Leagues," 1920, reprinted in *The Strategy and Tactics of World Communism*, Supp. 1 (Washington, DC: U.S. Government Printing Office, 1948).

13. George Herbert Mead, "The Genesis of the Self and Social Control," in *Selected Writings*, ed. A. J. Reck (Indianapolis: Bobbs-Merrill, 1964).
14. Tom Regan, *The Case for Animal Rights.*
15. Tom Regan makes this objection explicitly in "The Moral Basis of Vegetarianism."
16. Objections of this kind are registered by Dale Jamieson, "Killing Persons and Other Beings," in *Ethics and Animals*, ed. H. B. Miller and W. H. Williams (Clifton, NJ: Humana Press, 1983), and by C. Hoff, "Immoral and Moral Uses of Animals," *New England Journal of Medicine* 302 (1980):115–18.
17. The analysis of these mistakes is given in what Kant calls the Transcendental Dialectic, which is the Second Division of the Second Part (Transcendental Logic) of the Transcendental Doctrine of Elements. The position Kant is defending is deep and difficult—but the general point he makes in the Transcendental Dialectic is readily accessible. Confusions and errors resulting from the misapplication of concepts in thinking about our *selves* he treats in a chapter called "The Paralogisms of Pure Reason"; confusions and errors resulting from the misapplication of concepts in thinking about *the world as a whole* he treats in a chapter called "The Antinomy of Pure Reason"; confusions and errors resulting from the misapplication of concepts in thinking about *God* he treats in a chapter called "The Ideal of Pure Reason." In all three spheres the categories (of which causation is only one example) that make sense only when applied to phenomena in our direct experience cannot be rationally employed. His analyses are penetrating and telling; the metaphysical blunders he exposes result in every case from the attempt to use categories having applicability in only one sphere in a very different sphere where they can have no applicability whatever.

C PUZZLES AND CHALLENGES

◈ PUZZLING CASES ◈

The Trolley Problem

JUDITH JARVIS THOMSON[1]

Judith Jarvis Thomson (1929–) is a distinguished American philosopher who taught philosophy for more than three decades at the Massachusetts Institute of Technology. She is well known for her influential writings in metaphysics and ethical theory. Among her most famous articles are her 1971 "Defense of Abortion" and her 1985 "Trolley Problem," the latter of which appears here.

In this essay, originally published in the *Yale Law Journal*, Thomson presents a series of imaginary cases involving a trolley on a track that are designed to bring out various moral intuitions. In recent years, these scenarios have become the impetus for empirical research on moral judgment by psychologists and primatologists.

I

Some years ago, Philippa Foot drew attention to an extraordinarily interesting problem.[2] Suppose you are the driver of a trolley. The trolley rounds a bend, and there come into view ahead five track workmen, who have been repairing the track. The track goes through a bit of a valley at that point, and the sides are steep, so you must stop the trolley if you are to avoid running the five men down. You step on the brakes, but alas they don't work. Now you suddenly see a spur of track leading off to the right. You can turn the trolley onto it, and thus save the five men on the straight track ahead. Unfortunately, Mrs. Foot has arranged that there is one track workman on that spur of track. He can no more get off the track in time than the five can, so you will kill him if you turn the trolley onto him. Is it morally permissible for you to turn the trolley?

Everybody to whom I have put this hypothetical case says, Yes, it is.[3] Some people say something stronger than that it is morally *permissible* for you to turn the trolley: They say that morally speaking, you *must* turn it—that morality requires you to do so. Others do not agree that morality requires you to turn the trolley, and even feel a certain discomfort at the idea of turning it. But everybody says that it is true, at a minimum, that you *may* turn it—that it would not be morally wrong for you to do so.

Now consider a second hypothetical case. This time you are to imagine yourself to be a surgeon, a truly great surgeon. Among other things you do, you transplant organs, and you are such a great surgeon that the organs you transplant always take. At the moment you have five patients who need organs. Two need one lung each, two need a kidney each, and the fifth needs a heart. If they do

From *The Yale Law Journal*, Vol. 94, pp. 1395–1415. Reprinted by permission of the Yale Law Journal Company and William S. Hein company.

not get those organs today, they will all die; if you find organs for them today, you can transplant the organs and they will all live. But where to find the lungs, the kidneys, and the heart? The time is almost up when a report is brought to you that a young man who has just come into your clinic for his yearly check-up has exactly the right blood-type, and is in excellent health. Lo, you have a possible donor. All you need do is cut him up and distribute *his* parts among the five who need them. You ask, but he says, "Sorry. I deeply sympathize, but no." Would it be morally permissible for you to operate anyway? Everybody to whom I have put this second hypothetical case says, No, it would not be morally permissible for you to proceed.

Here then is Mrs. Foot's problem: *Why* is it that the trolley driver may turn his trolley, though the surgeon may not remove the young man's lungs, kidneys, and heart?[4] In both cases, one will die if the agent acts, but five will live who would otherwise die—a net saving of four lives. What difference in the other facts of these cases explains the moral difference between them? I fancy that the theorists of tort and criminal law will find this problem as interesting as the moral theorist does.

II

Mrs. Foot's own solution to the problem she drew attention to is simple, straightforward, and very attractive. She would say: Look, the surgeon's choice is between operating, in which case he kills one, and not operating, in which case he lets five die; and killing is surely worse than letting die[5]—indeed, so much worse that we can even say

(I) Killing one is worse than letting five die.

So the surgeon must refrain from operating. By contrast, the trolley driver's choice is between turning the trolley, in which case he kills one, and not turning the trolley, in which case he does not *let five die,* he positively *kills* them. Now surely we can say

(II) Killing five is worse than killing one.

But then that is why the trolley driver may turn his trolley: He would be doing what is worse if he fails to turn it, since if he fails to turn it he kills five.

I do think that that is an attractive account of the matter. It seems to me that if the surgeon fails to operate, he does not kill his five patients who need parts; he merely lets them die. By contrast, if the driver fails to turn his trolley, he does not merely let the five track workmen die; he drives his trolley into them, and thereby kills them.

But there is good reason to think that this problem is not so easily solved as that.

Let us begin by looking at a case that is in some ways like Mrs. Foot's story of the trolley driver. I will call her case *Trolley Driver;* let us now consider a case I will call *Bystander at the Switch.* In that case you have been strolling by the trolley track, and you can see the situation at a glance: The driver saw the five on the track ahead, he stamped on the brakes, the brakes failed, so he fainted. What to do? Well, here is the switch, which you can throw, thereby turning the trolley yourself. Of course you will kill one if you do. But I should think you may turn it all the same.[6]

Some people may feel a difference between these two cases. In the first place, the trolley driver is, after all, captain of the trolley. He is charged by the trolley company with responsibility for the safety of his passengers and anyone else who might be harmed by the trolley he drives. The bystander at the switch, on the other hand, is a private person who just happens to be there.

Second, the driver would be driving a trolley into the five if he does not turn it, and the bystander would not—the bystander will do the five no harm at all if he does not throw the switch.

I think it right to feel these differences between the cases.

Nevertheless, my own feeling is that an ordinary person, a mere bystander, may intervene in such a case. If you see something, a trolley, a boulder, an avalanche, heading towards five, and you can deflect it onto one, it really does seem that—other things being equal—it would be permissible for you to *take* charge, *take* responsibility, and deflect the thing, whoever you may be. Of course you run a moral risk if you do, for it might be that, unbeknownst to you, other things are not equal. It might be, that is, that there is some relevant difference between the five on the one hand, and the one on the other, which would make it morally preferable that the five be hit by the trolley than that the one be hit by it. That would be so if, for example, the five are not track workmen at all, but Mafia members in workmen's clothing, and they have tied the one workman to the right-hand track in the hope that you would turn the trolley onto him. I won't canvass all the many kinds of possibilities, for in fact the moral risk is the same whether you are the trolley driver, or a bystander at the switch.

Moreover, second, we might well wish to ask ourselves what exactly is the difference between what the driver would be doing if he failed to turn the trolley and what the bystander would be doing if he failed to throw the switch. As I said, the driver would be driving a trolley into the five; but what exactly would his driving the trolley into the five consist in? Why, just sitting there, doing nothing! If the driver does just sit there, doing nothing, then that will have been how come he drove his trolley into the five.

I do not mean to make much of that fact about what the driver's driving his trolley into the five would consist in, for it seems to me to be right to say that if he does not turn the trolley, he does drive his trolley into them, and does thereby kill them. (Though this does seem to me to be right, it is not easy to say exactly what makes it so.) By contrast, if the bystander does not throw the switch, he drives no trolley into anybody, and he kills nobody.

But as I said, my own feeling is that the bystander *may* intervene. Perhaps it will seem to some even less clear that morality requires him to turn the trolley than that morality requires the driver to turn the trolley; perhaps some will feel even more discomfort at the idea of the bystander's turning the trolley than at the idea of the driver's turning the trolley. All the same, I shall take it that he *may*.

If he may, there is serious trouble for Mrs. Foot's thesis (I). It is plain that if the bystander throws the switch, he causes the trolley to hit the one, and thus he kills the one. It is equally plain that if the bystander does not throw the switch, he does not cause the trolley to hit the five, he does not kill the five, he merely fails to save them—he lets them die. His choice therefore is between throwing the switch, in which case he kills one, and not throwing the switch, in which case he lets five die. If thesis (I) were true, it would follow that the bystander may not throw the switch, and that I am taking to be false.

III

I have been arguing that

(I) Killing one is worse than letting five die

is false, and a fortiori that it cannot be appealed to to explain why the surgeon may not operate in the case I shall call *Transplant*.

I think it pays to take note of something interesting which comes out when we pay close attention to

(II) Killing five is worse than killing one.

For let us ask ourselves how we would feel about *Transplant* if we made a certain addition to it. In telling you that story, I did not tell you why the surgeon's patients are in need of parts. Let us imagine that the history of their ailments is as follows. The surgeon was badly overworked last fall—some of his assistants in the clinic were out sick, and the surgeon had to take over their duties dispensing drugs. While feeling particularly tired one day, he became careless, and made the terrible mistake of dispensing chemical X to five of the day's patients. Now chemical X works differently in different people. In some it causes lung failure, in others kidney failure, in others heart failure. So these five patients who now need parts need them because of the surgeon's carelessness. Indeed, if he does not get them the parts they need, so that they die, he will have killed them. Does that make a moral difference? That is, does the fact that he will have killed the five if he does nothing make it permissible for him to cut the young man up and distribute his parts to the five who need them?

We could imagine it to have been worse. Suppose what had happened was this: The surgeon was badly overextended last fall, he had known he was named a beneficiary in his five patients' wills, and it swept over him one day to give them chemical X to kill them. Now he repents, and would save them if he could. If he does not save them, he will positively have murdered them. Does *that* fact make it permissible for him to cut the young man up and distribute his parts to the five who need them?

I should think plainly not. The surgeon must not operate on the young man. If he can find no other way of saving his five patients, he will *now* have to let them die—despite the fact that if he now lets them die, he will have killed them.

We tend to forget that some killings themselves include lettings die, and do include them where the act by which the agent kills takes time to cause death—time in which the agent can intervene but does not.

In face of these possibilities, the question arises what we should think of thesis (II), since it *looks* as if it tells us that the surgeon ought to operate, and thus that he may permissibly do so, since if he operates he kills only one instead of five.

There are two ways in which we can go here. First, we can say: (II) does tell us that the surgeon ought to operate, and that shows it is false. Second, we can say: (II) does not tell us that the surgeon ought to operate, and it is true.

For my own part, I prefer the second. If Alfred kills five and Bert kills only one, then questions of motive apart, and other things being equal, what Alfred did *is* worse than what Bert did. If the surgeon does not operate, so that he kills five, then it will later be true that he did something worse than he would have done if he had operated, killing only one—especially if his killing of the five was murder, committed out of a desire for money, and his killing of the one would have been, though misguided and wrongful, nevertheless a well-intentioned effort to save five lives. Taking this line would, of course, require saying that assessments of which acts are worse than which other acts do not by themselves settle the question what it is permissible for an agent to do.

But it might be said that we ought to by-pass (II), for perhaps what Mrs. Foot would have offered us as an explanation of why the driver may turn the trolley in *Trolley Driver* is not (II) itself, but something more complex, such as

(II′) If a person is faced with a choice between doing something *here and now* to five, by the doing of which he will kill them, and doing something else *here and now* to one, by the doing of which he will kill only the one, then (other things being equal) he ought to choose the second alternative rather than the first.

We may presumably take (II′) to tell us that the driver ought to, and hence permissibly may, turn the trolley in *Trolley Driver*, for we may presumably view the driver as confronted with a choice between here and now driving his trolley into five, and here and now driving his trolley into one. And at the same time, (II′) tells us nothing at all about what the surgeon ought to do in *Transplant,* for he is not confronted with such a choice. If the surgeon operates, he does do something by the doing of which he will kill only one; but if the surgeon does not operate, he does not do something by the doing of which he kills five; he merely fails to do something by the doing of which he would make it be the case that he has not killed five.

I have no objection to this shift in attention from (II) to (II′). But we should not overlook an interesting question that lurks here. As it might be put: *Why* should the present tense matter so much? Why should a person prefer killing one to killing five if the alternatives are wholly in front of him, but not (or anyway, not in every case) where one of them is partly behind him? I shall come back to this question briefly later.

Meanwhile, however, even if (II′) can be appealed to in order to explain why the trolley driver may turn his trolley, that would leave it entirely open why the bystander at the switch may turn *his* trolley. For he does not drive a trolley into each of five if he refrains from turning the trolley; he merely lets the trolley drive into each of them.

So I suggest we set *Trolley Driver* aside for the time being. What I shall be concerned with is a first cousin of Mrs. Foot's problem, viz.: Why is it that the bystander may turn his trolley, though the surgeon may not remove the young man's lungs, kidneys, and heart? Since *I* find it particularly puzzling that the bystander may turn his trolley, I am inclined to call this The Trolley Problem. Those who find it particularly puzzling that the surgeon may not operate are cordially invited to call it The Transplant Problem instead.

IV

It should be clear, I think, that "kill" and "let die" are too blunt to be useful tools for the solving of this problem. We ought to be looking within killings and savings for the ways in which the agents would be carrying them out.

It would be no surprise, I think, if a Kantian idea occurred to us at this point. Kant said: "Act so that you treat humanity, whether in your own person or in that of another, always as an end and never as a means only." It is striking, after all, that the surgeon who proceeds in *Transplant* treats the young man he cuts up "as a means only": He literally uses the young man's body to save his five, and does so without the young man's consent. And perhaps we may say that the agent in *Bystander at the Switch* does not use his victim to save his five, or (more generally) treat his victim as a means only, and that that is why he (unlike the surgeon) may proceed.

But what exactly is it to treat a person as a means only, or to use a person? And why exactly is it wrong to do this? These questions do not have obvious answers.[7]

Suppose an agent is confronted with a choice between doing nothing, in which case five die, or engaging in a certain course of action, in which case the five live, but one dies. Then perhaps we can say: If the agent chooses to engage in the course of action, then he uses the one to save the five only if, had the one gone out of existence just before the agent started, the agent would have been unable to save the five. That is true of the surgeon in *Transplant*. He needs the young man if he is to save his five; if the young man goes wholly out of existence just before the surgeon starts to operate, then the surgeon cannot save his five. By contrast, the agent in *Bystander at the Switch* does not need the one track workman on the right-hand track if he is to save his five; if the one track workman goes wholly out of existence before the bystander starts to turn the trolley, then the bystander *can* all the same save his five. So here anyway is a striking difference between the cases.

It does seem to me right to think that solving this problem requires attending to the means by which the agent would be saving his five if he proceeded. But I am inclined to think that this is an overly simple way of taking account of the agent's means.

One reason for thinking so[8] comes out as follows. You have been thinking of the tracks in *Bystander at the Switch* as not merely diverging, but continuing to diverge, as in the following picture:

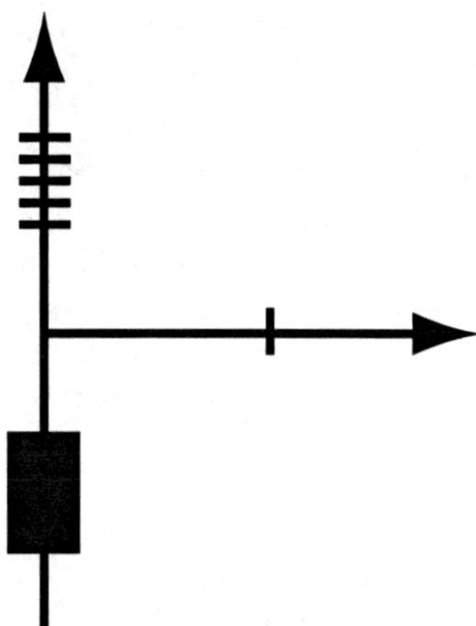

Consider now what I shall call "the loop variant" on this case, in which the tracks do not continue to diverge—they circle back, as in the following picture:

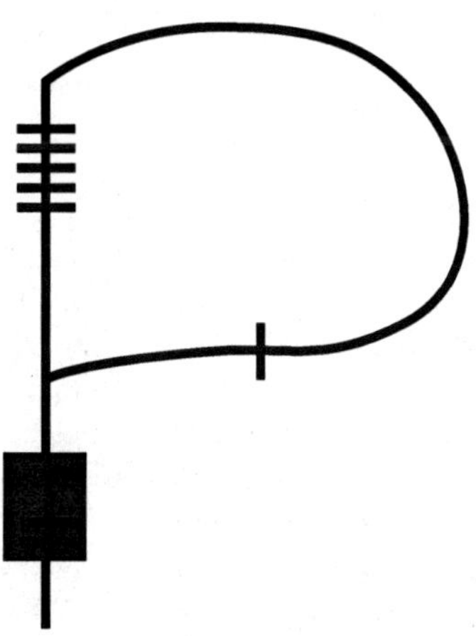

Let us now imagine that the five on the straight track are thin, but thick enough so that although all five will be killed if the trolley goes straight, the bodies of the five will stop it, and it will therefore not reach the one. On the other hand, the one on the right-hand track is fat, so fat that his body will by itself stop the trolley, and the trolley will therefore not reach the five. May the agent turn the trolley? Some people feel more discomfort at the idea of turning the trolley in the loop variant than in the original *Bystander at the Switch*. But we cannot really suppose that the presence or absence of that extra bit of track makes a major moral difference as to what an agent may do in these cases, and it really does seem right to think (despite the discomfort) that the agent may proceed.

On the other hand, we should notice that the agent here needs the one (fat) track workman on the right-hand track if he is to save his five. If the one goes wholly out of existence just before the agent starts to turn the trolley, then the agent cannot save his five[9]—just as the surgeon in *Transplant* cannot save his five if the young man goes wholly out of existence just before the surgeon starts to operate.

Indeed, I should think that there is no plausible account of what is involved in, or what is necessary for, the application of the notions "treating a person as a means only," or "using one to save five," under which the surgeon would be doing this whereas the agent in this variant of *Bystander at the Switch* would not be. If that is right, then appeals to these notions cannot do the work being required of them here.

V

Suppose the bystander at the switch proceeds: He throws the switch, thereby turning the trolley onto the right-hand track, thereby causing the one to be hit by the trolley, thereby killing him—but saving the five on the straight track. There are two facts about what he does which seem to me to explain the moral difference between what he does and what the agent in *Transplant* would be doing if *he* proceeded. In the first place, the bystander saves his five by making something that threatens them instead threaten one. Second, the bystander does not do that by means which themselves constitute an infringement of any right of the one's.

As is plain, then, my hypothesis as to the source of the moral difference between the cases makes appeal to the concept of a right. My own feeling is that solving this problem requires making appeal to that concept—or to some other concept that does the same kind of work.[10] Indeed, I think it is one of the many reasons why this problem is of such interest to moral theory that it does force us to appeal to that concept; and by the same token, that we learn something from it about that concept.

Let us begin with an idea, held by many friends of rights, which Ronald Dworkin expressed crisply in a metaphor from bridge: Rights "trump" utilities.[11] That is, if one would infringe a right in or by acting, then it is not sufficient justification for acting that one would thereby maximize utility. It seems to me that something like this must be correct.

Consideration of this idea suggests the possibility of a very simple solution to the problem. That is, it might be said (i) The reason why the surgeon may not proceed in *Transplant* is that if he proceeds, he maximizes utility, for he brings about a net saving of four lives, but in so doing he would infringe a right of the young man's.

Which right? Well, we might say: The right the young man has against the surgeon that the surgeon not kill him—thus a right in the cluster of rights that the young man has in having a right to life.

Solving this problem requires being able to explain also why the bystander may proceed in *Bystander at the Switch*. So it might be said (ii) The reason why the bystander may proceed is that if he proceeds, he maximizes utility, for he brings about a net saving of four lives, and in so doing he does *not* infringe any right of the one track workman's.

But I see no way—certainly there is no easy way—of establishing that these ideas are true.

Is it clear that the bystander would infringe no right of the one track workman's if he turned the trolley? Suppose there weren't anybody on the straight track, and the bystander turned the trolley onto the right-hand track, thereby killing the one, but not saving anybody, since nobody was at risk, and thus nobody needed saving. Wouldn't that infringe a right of the one workman's, a right in the cluster of rights that he has in having a right to life?

So should we suppose that the fact that there are five track workmen on the straight track who are in need of saving makes the one lack that right—which he would have had if that had not been a fact?

But then why doesn't the fact that the surgeon has five patients who are in need of saving make the young man also lack that right?

I think some people would say there is good (excellent, conclusive) reason for thinking that the one track workman lacks the right (given there are five on the straight track) lying in the fact that (given there are five on the straight track) it is morally permissible to turn the trolley onto him. But if your reason for thinking the one lacks the right is that it is permissible to turn the trolley onto him, then you can hardly go on to explain its being permissible to turn the trolley onto him by appeal to the fact that he lacks the right. It pays to stress this point: If you want to say, as (ii) does, that the bystander may proceed because he maximizes utility and infringes no right, then you need an independent account of what makes it be the case that he infringes no right—independent, that is, of its being the case that he may proceed.

There is *some* room for maneuver here. Any plausible theory of rights must make room for the possibility of waiving a right, and within that category, for the possibility of failing to have a right by virtue of assumption of risk; and it might be argued that that is what is involved here, i.e., that track workmen know of the risks of the job, and consent to run them when signing on for it.

But that is not really an attractive way of dealing with this difficulty. Track workmen certainly do not explicitly consent to being run down with trolleys when doing so will save five who are on some other track—certainly they are not asked to consent to this at the time of signing on for the job. And I doubt that they consciously assume the risk of it at that or any other time. And in any case, what if the six people involved had not been track workmen? What if they had been young children? What if they had been people who had been shoved out of helicopters? Wouldn't it all the same be permissible to turn the trolley?

So it is not clear what (independent) reason could be given for thinking that the bystander will infringe no right of the one's if he throws the switch.

I think, moreover, that there is *some* reason to think that the bystander will infringe a right of the one if he throws the switch, even though it is permissible for him to do so. What I have in mind issues simply from the fact that if the bystander throws the switch, then he does what will kill the one. Suppose the bystander proceeds, and that the one is now dead. The bystander's motives were, of course, excellent—he acted with a view to saving five. But the one did not volunteer his life so that the five might live; the bystander volunteered it for him. The bystander made him pay with his life for the bystander's saving of the five. This consideration seems to me to lend some weight to the idea that the bystander did do him a wrong—a wrong it was morally permissible to do him, since five were saved, but a wrong *to him* all the same.

Consider again that lingering feeling of discomfort (which, as I said, some people do feel) about what the bystander does if he turns the trolley. No doubt it is permissible to turn the trolley, but still...but still....People who feel this discomfort also think that, although it is permissible to turn the trolley, it is not morally required to do so. My own view is that they are right to feel and think these things. We would be able to explain why this is so if we supposed that if the bystander turns the trolley, then he does do the one track workman a wrong—if we supposed, in particular, that he infringes a right of the one track workman's which is in that cluster of rights which the workman has in having a right to life.[12]

I do not for a moment take myself to have established that (ii) is false. I have wished only to draw attention to the difficulty that lies ahead of a person who thinks (ii) true, and also to suggest that there is some reason to think that the bystander would infringe a right of the one's if he proceeded, and thus some reason to think that (ii) is false. It can easily be seen that if there is some reason to think the bystander would infringe a right of the one's, then there is also some reason to think that (i) is false—since if the bystander does infringe a right of the one's if he proceeds, and may nevertheless proceed, then it cannot be the fact that the surgeon infringes a right of the young man's if *he* proceeds which makes it impermissible for *him* to do so.

Perhaps a friend of (i) and (ii) can establish that they are true. I propose that, just in case he can't, we do well to see if there isn't some other way of solving this problem than by appeal to them. In particular, I propose we grant that both the bystander and the surgeon would infringe a right of their ones, a right in the cluster of rights that the ones' have in having a right to life, and that we look for some *other* difference between the cases which could be appealed to to explain the moral difference between them.

Notice that accepting this proposal does not commit us to rejecting the idea expressed in that crisp metaphor of Dworkin's. We can still say that rights trump utilities—if we can find a further feature of what the bystander does if he turns the trolley (beyond the fact that he maximizes utility) which itself trumps the right, and thus makes it permissible to proceed.

VI

As I said, my own feeling is that the trolley problem can be solved only by appeal to the concept of a right—but not by appeal to it in as simple a way as that discussed in the preceding section. What we were attending to in the preceding section was only the fact that the agents would be killing and saving if they proceeded; what we should be attending to is the means by which they would kill and save.[13] (It is very tempting, because so much simpler, to regard a human act as a solid nugget, without internal structure, and to try to trace its moral value to the shape of its surface, as it were. The trolley problem seems to me to bring home that that will not do.)

I said earlier that there seem to me to be two crucial facts about what the bystander does if he proceeds in *Bystander at the Switch*. In the first place, he saves his five by making something that threatens them instead threaten the one. And second, he does not do that by means which themselves constitute infringements of any right of the one's.

Let us begin with the first.

If the surgeon proceeds in *Transplant*, he plainly does not save his five by making something that threatens them instead threaten one. It is organ-failure that threatens his five, and it is not *that* which he makes threaten the young man if he proceeds.

Consider another of Mrs. Foot's cases, which I shall call *Hospital*.

> Suppose [Mrs. Foot says] that there are five patients in a hospital whose lives could be saved by the manufacture of a certain gas, but that this will inevitably release lethal fumes into the room of another patient whom for some reason we are unable to move.[14]

Surely it would not be permissible for us to manufacture the gas.

In *Transplant* and *Hospital*, the five at risk are at risk from their ailments, and this might be thought to make a difference. Let us by-pass it. In a variant on *Hospital*—which I shall call *Hospital′*—all six patients are convalescing. The five at risk are at risk, not from their ailments, but from the ceiling of their room, which is about to fall on them. We can prevent this by pumping on a ceiling-support-mechanism; but doing so will inevitably release lethal fumes into the room of the sixth. Here too it is plain we may not proceed.

Contrast a case in which lethal fumes are being released by the heating system in the basement of a building next door to the hospital. They are headed towards the room of five. We can deflect them towards the room of one. Would that be permissible? I should think it would be—the case seems to be in all relevant respects like *Bystander at the Switch*.

In *Bystander at the Switch*, something threatens five, and if the agent proceeds, he saves the five by making that very thing threaten the one instead of the five. That is not true of the agents in *Hospital′* or *Hospital* or *Transplant*. In *Hospital′*, for example, what threatens the five is the ceiling, and the agent does not save them by making *it* threaten the one, he saves them by doing what will make something wholly different (some lethal fumes) threaten the one.

Why is this difference morally important? Other things being equal, to kill a man is to infringe his right to life, and we are therefore morally barred from killing. It is not enough to justify killing a person that if we do so, five others will be saved: To say that if we do so, five others will be saved is merely to say that utility will be maximized if we proceed, and that is not by itself sufficient to justify proceeding. Rights trump utilities. So if that is all that can be said in defense of killing a person, then killing that person is not permissible.

But that five others will be saved is not all that can be said in defense of killing in *Bystander at the Switch*. The bystander who proceeds does not merely minimize the number of deaths which get caused: He minimizes the number of deaths which get caused by something that already threatens people, and that will cause deaths whatever the bystander does.

The bystander who proceeds does not make something be a threat to people which would otherwise not be a threat to anyone; he makes be a threat to fewer what is already a threat to more. We might speak here of a "distributive exemption," which permits arranging that something that will do harm anyway shall be better distributed than it otherwise would be—shall (in *Bystander at the Switch*) do harm to fewer rather than more. Not just any distributive intervention is permissible: It is not in general morally open to us to make one die to save five. But other things being equal, it is not morally required of us that we let a burden descend out of the blue onto five when we can make it instead descend onto one.

I do not find it clear why there should be an exemption for, and only for, making a burden which is descending onto five descend, instead, onto one. That there is seems to me very plausible, however. On the one hand, the agent who acts under this exemption makes be a threat to one something that is *already* a threat to more, and thus something that will do harm *whatever* he does; on the other hand, the exemption seems to allow those acts which intuition tells us are clearly permissible, and to rule out those acts which intuition tells us are clearly impermissible.

VII

More precisely, it is not morally required of us that we let a burden descend out of the blue onto five when we can make it instead descend onto one *if* we can make it descend onto the one by means which do not themselves constitute infringements of rights of the one.

Consider a case—which I shall call *Fat Man*—in which you are standing on a footbridge over the trolley track. You can see a trolley hurtling down the track, out of control. You turn around to see where the trolley is headed, and there are five workmen on the track where it exits from under the footbridge. What to do? Being an expert on trolleys, you know of one certain way to stop an out-of-control trolley: Drop a really heavy weight in its path. But where to find one? It just so happens that standing next to you on the footbridge is a fat man, a really fat man. He is leaning over the railing, watching the trolley; all you have to do is to give him a little shove, and over the railing he will go, onto the track in the path of the trolley. Would it be permissible for you to do this? Everybody to whom I have put this case says it would not be. But why?

Suppose the agent proceeds. He shoves the fat man, thereby toppling him off the footbridge into the path of the trolley, thereby causing him to be hit by the trolley, thereby killing him—but saving the five on the straight track. Then it is true of this agent, as it is true of the agent in *Bystander at the Switch*, that he saves his five by making something which threatens them instead threaten one.

But *this* agent does so by means which themselves constitute an infringement of a right of the one's. For shoving a person is infringing a right of his. So also is toppling a person off a footbridge.

I should stress that doing these things is infringing a person's rights even if doing them does not cause his death—even if doing them causes him no harm at all. As I shall put it, shoving a person, toppling a person off a footbridge, are *themselves* infringements of rights of his. A theory of rights ought to give an account of what makes it be the case that doing either of these things is itself an infringement of a right of his. But I think we may take it to be a datum that it is, the job which confronts the theorist of rights being, not to establish that it is, but rather to explain why it is.

Consider by contrast the agent in *Bystander at the Switch*. He too, if he proceeds, saves five by making something that threatens them instead threaten one. But the means he takes to make that be the case are these: Turn the trolley onto the right-hand track. And turning the trolley onto the right-hand track is not *itself* an infringement of a right of anybody's. The agent would do the one no wrong at all if he turned the trolley onto the right-hand track, and by some miracle the trolley did not hit him.

We might of course have imagined it not necessary to shove the fat man. We might have imagined that all you need do to get the trolley to threaten him instead of the five is to wobble the handrail, for the handrail is low, and he is leaning on it, and wobbling it will cause him to fall over and off. Wobbling the handrail would be impermissible, I should think—no less so than shoving. But then there is room for an objection to the idea that the contrast I point to will help explain the moral differences among these cases. For it might be said that if you wobble the handrail, thereby getting the trolley to threaten the one instead of the five, then the means you take to get this to be the case are just these: Wobble the handrail. But doing that is not *itself* an infringement of a right of anybody's. You would do the fat man no wrong at all if you wobbled the handrail and no harm came to him in consequence of your doing so. In this respect, then, your situation seems to be exactly like that of the agent in *Bystander at the Switch*. Just as the means he would be taking to make the trolley threaten one instead of five would not constitute an infringement of a right, so also would the means you would be taking to make the trolley threaten one instead of five not constitute an infringement of a right.

What I had in mind, however, is a rather tighter notion of "means" than shows itself in this objection. By hypothesis, wobbling the handrail will cause the fat man to topple onto the track in the path of the trolley, and thus will cause the trolley to threaten him instead of the five. But the trolley will not threaten him instead of the five unless wobbling the handrail does cause him to topple. Getting the trolley to threaten the fat man instead of the five *requires* getting him into its path. You get the trolley to threaten him instead of them by wobbling the handrail only if, and only because, by wobbling the handrail you topple him into the path of the trolley.

What I had in mind, then, is a notion of "means" which comes out as follows. Suppose you get a trolley to threaten one instead of five by wobbling a handrail. The means you take to get the trolley to threaten the one instead of the five include wobbling the handrail, *and* all those further things that you have to succeed in doing by wobbling the handrail if the trolley is to threaten the one instead of the five.

So the means by which the agent in *Fat Man* gets the trolley to threaten one instead of five include toppling the fat man off the footbridge; and doing that is itself an infringement of a right of the fat man's. By contrast, the means by which the agent in *Bystander at the Switch* gets the trolley to threaten one instead of five include no more than getting the trolley off the straight track onto the right-hand track; and doing that is not itself an infringement of a right of anybody's.

VIII

It is arguable, however, that what is relevant is not that toppling the fat man off the footbridge is itself an infringement of *a* right of the fat man's but rather that toppling him off the footbridge is itself an infringement of a particularly stringent right of his.

What I have in mind comes out in yet another variant on *Bystander at the Switch*. Here the bystander must cross (without permission) a patch of land that belongs to the one in order to get to the switch; thus in order to get the trolley to threaten the one instead of five, the bystander must infringe a right of the one's. May he proceed?

Or again, in order to get the switch thrown, the bystander must use a sharply pointed tool, and the only available sharply pointed tool is a nailfile that belongs to the one; here too the bystander must infringe a right of the one's in order to get the trolley to threaten the one instead of five. May he proceed?

For my own part, I do not find it obvious that he may. (Remember what the bystander will be doing to the one by throwing that switch.) But others tell me they think it clear the bystander may proceed in such a case. If they are right—and I guess we should agree that they are—then that must surely be because the rights which the bystander would have to infringe here are minor, trivial, non-stringent—property rights of no great importance. By contrast, the right to not be toppled off a footbridge onto a trolley track is on any view a stringent right. We shall therefore have to recognize that what is at work in these cases is a matter of degree: If the agent must infringe a stringent right of the one's in order to get something that threatens five to threaten the one (as in *Fat Man*), then he may not proceed, whereas if the agent need infringe no right of the one's (as in *Bystander at the Switch*), or only a more or less trivial right of the one's (as in these variants on *Bystander at the Switch*), in order to get something that threaten five to threaten the one, then he may proceed.

Where what is at work is a matter of degree, it should be no surprise that there are borderline cases, on which people disagree. I confess to having been greatly surprised, however, at the fact of disagreement on the following variant on *Bystander at the Switch*:

> The five on the straight track are regular track workmen. The right-hand track is a dead end, unused in ten years. The Mayor, representing the City, has set out picnic tables on it, and invited the convalescents at the nearby City Hospital to have their meals there, guaranteeing them that no trolleys will ever, for any reason, be turned onto that track. The one on the right-hand track is a convalescent having his lunch there; it would never have occurred to him to do so if the Mayor had not issued his invitation and guarantee. The Mayor was out for a walk; he now stands by the switch.[15]

For the Mayor to get the trolley to threaten the one instead of the five, he must turn the trolley onto the right-hand track; but the one has a right against the Mayor that he not turn the trolley onto the right-hand track—a right generated by an official promise, which was then relied on by the one. (Contrast the original *Bystander at the Switch,* in which the one had no such right.) My own feeling is that it is plain the Mayor may not proceed. To my great surprise I find that some people think he may. I conclude they think the right less stringent than I do.

In any case, that distributive exemption that I spoke of earlier is very conservative. It permits intervention into the world to get an object that already threatens death to those many to instead threaten death to these few, but only by acts that are not themselves gross impingements on the few. That is, the intervenor must not use means that infringe stringent rights of the few in order to get his distributive intention carried out.

It could of course be argued that the fact that the bystander of the original *Bystander at the Switch* makes threaten the one what already threatens the five, and does so by means that do not themselves constitute infringements of any right of the one's (not even a trivial right of the one's), shows that the bystander in that case infringes no right of the one's at all. That is, it could be argued that we have here that independent ground for saying that the bystander does not infringe the one's right to life which I said would be needed by a friend of (ii).[16] But I see nothing to be gained by taking this line, for I see nothing to be gained by supposing it never permissible to infringe a right; and something is lost by taking this line, namely the possibility of viewing the bystander as doing the one a wrong if he proceeds—albeit a wrong it is permissible to do him.

IX

What counts as "*an* object which threatens death"? What marks one threat off from another? I have no doubt that ingenious people can construct cases in which we shall be unclear whether to say that if the agent proceeds, he makes threaten the one the very same thing as already threatens the five.

Moreover, which are the interventions in which the agent gets a thing that threatens five to instead threaten one by means that themselves constitute infringements of stringent rights of the one's? I have no doubt that ingenious people can construct cases in which we shall all be unclear whether to say that the agent's means do constitute infringements of stringent rights—and cases also in which we shall be unclear whether to say the agent's means constitute infringements of any rights at all.

But it is surely a mistake to look for precision in the concepts brought to bear to solve this problem: There isn't any to be had. It would be enough if cases in which it seems to us unclear whether to say "same threat," or unclear whether to say "non-right-infringing-means," also seemed to us to be cases in which it is unclear whether the agent may or may not proceed; and if also coming to see a case as one to which these expressions do (or do not) apply involves coming to see the case as one in which the agent may (or may not) proceed.

X

If these ideas are correct, then we have a handle on anyway some of the troublesome cases in which people make threats. Suppose a villain says to us "I will cause a ceiling to fall on five unless you send lethal fumes into the room of one." Most of us think it would not be permissible for us to accede to this threat. Why? We may think of the villain as part of the world around the people involved, a part which is going to drop a burden on the five if we do not act. On this way of thinking of him, nothing *yet* threatens the five (certainly no ceiling as yet threatens them) and a fortiori we cannot save the five by making what (already) threatens them instead threaten the one. Alternatively, we may think of the villain as himself a threat to the five. But sending the fumes in is not making *him* be a threat to the one instead of to the five. The hypothesis I proposed, then, yields what it should: We may not accede.

That is because the hypothesis I proposed says nothing at all about the source of the threat to the five. Whether the threat to the five is, or is caused by, a human being or anything else, it is not permissible to do what will kill one to save the five except by making what threatens the five itself threaten the one.

By contrast, it seems to me very plausible to think that if a villain has started a trolley towards five, we may deflect the trolley towards one—other things being equal, of course. If a trolley is headed towards five, and we can deflect it towards one, we *may*, no matter who or what caused it to head towards the five.

I think that these considerations help us in dealing with a question I drew attention to earlier. Suppose a villain says to us "I will cause a ceiling to fall on five unless you send lethal fumes into the room of one." If we refuse, so that he does what he threatens to do, then he surely does something very much worse than we would be doing if we acceded to his threat and sent the fumes in. If we accede, we do something misguided and wrongful, but not nearly as bad as what he does if we refuse.

It should be stressed: The fact that he will do something worse if we do not send the fumes in does not entail that we ought to send them in, or even that it is permissible for us to do so.

How after all could that entail that we may send the fumes in? The fact that we would be saving five lives by sending the fumes in does not itself make it permissible for us to do so. (Rights trump utilities.) How could adding that the taker of those five lives would be doing what is worse than we would tip the balance? If we may not infringe a right of the one in order to save the five lives, it cannot possibly be thought that we may infringe the right of that one in order, not merely to save the five lives, but to make the villain's moral record better than it otherwise would be.

For my own part, I think that considerations of motives apart, and other things being equal, it does no harm to say that

(II) Killing five is worse than killing one

is, after all, true. *Of course* we shall then have to say that assessments of which acts are worse than which do not by themselves settle the question of what is permissible for a person to do. For we shall have to say that, despite the truth of (II), it is not the case that we are required to kill one in order that another person shall not kill five, or even that it is everywhere permissible for us to do this.

What is of interest is that what holds interpersonally also holds intrapersonally. I said earlier that we might imagine the surgeon of *Transplant* to have caused the ailments of his five patients. Let us imagine the worst: He gave them chemical X precisely in order to cause their deaths, in order to inherit from them. Now he repents. But the fact that he would be saving five lives by operating on the one does not itself make it permissible for him to operate on the one. (Rights trump utilities.) And if he may not infringe a right of the one in order to save the five lives, it cannot possibly be thought that he may infringe the right of that one in order, not merely to save the five lives, but to make his own moral record better than it otherwise would be.

Another way to put the point is this: Assessments of which acts are worse than which have to be directly relevant to the agent's circumstances if they are to have a bearing on what he may do. If A threatens to kill five unless B kills one, then although killing five is worse than killing one, these are not the alternatives open to B. The alternatives open to B are: Kill one, thereby forestalling the deaths of five (and making A's moral record better than it otherwise would be), or let it be the case that A kills five. And the supposition that it would be worse for B to choose to kill the one is entirely compatible with the supposition that killing five is worse than killing one. Again, the alternatives open to the surgeon are: Operate on the one, thereby saving five (and making the surgeon's own moral record better than it otherwise would be), or let it be the case that he himself will have killed the five. And the supposition that it would be worse for the surgeon to choose to operate is entirely compatible with the supposition that killing five is worse than killing one.

On the other hand, suppose a second surgeon is faced with a choice between here and now giving chemical X to five, thereby killing them, and operating on, and thereby killing, only one. (It taxes the imagination to invent such a second surgeon, but let that pass. And compare *Trolley Driver.)* Then, other things being equal, it does seem he may choose to operate on the one. Some people would say something stronger, namely that he is required to make this choice. Perhaps they would say that

(II′) If a person is faced with a choice between doing something *here and now* to five, by the doing of which he will kill them, and doing something else *here and now* to one, by the doing of which he will kill only the one, then (other things being equal) he ought to choose the second alternative rather than the first

is a quite general moral truth. Whether or not the second surgeon is morally required to make this choice (and thus whether or not (II′) is a general moral truth), it does seem to be the case that he may. But this did seem puzzling. As I put it: Why should the present tense matter so much?

It is plausible to think that the present tense matters because the question for the agent at the time of acting is about the present, viz., "What may I here and now do?," and because that question is the same as the question "Which of the alternatives here and now open to me may I choose?" The alternatives now open to the second surgeon are: kill five or kill one. If killing five is worse than killing one, then perhaps he ought to, but at any rate he may, kill the one.

NOTES

1. Professor of Philosophy, Massachusetts Institute of Technology. B.A., Barnard College 1950, Cambridge University 1952; M.A., Cambridge University 1956; Ph.D., Columbia University 1959. Many people have given me helpful criticism of this essay's many successive reincarnations over the years; I cannot list them all—for want of space, not of gratitude. Most recently, it benefited from criticism by the members of the Yale Law School Civil Liability Workshop and the Legal Theory Workshop, Faculty of Law, University of Toronto.
2. *See* P. FOOT, *The Problem of Abortion and the Doctrine of the Double Effect,* in VIRTUES AND VICES AND OTHER ESSAYS IN MORAL PHILOSOPHY 19 (1978).
3. I think it possible (though by no means certain) that John Taurek would say "No, it is not permissible to (all simply) turn the trolley; what you ought to do is flip a coin. *See* Taurek, *Should the Numbers Count?*, 6 PHIL & PUB. AFF. 293 (1977). (But he is there concerned with a different kind of case, namely that in which what is in question is not whether we may do what harms one to avoid harming five, but whether we may or ought to choose to save five in preference to saving one.) For criticism of Taurek's article, see Parfit, *Innumerate Ethics*, 7 PHIL & PUB. AFF. 285 (1978).
4. I doubt that anyone would say, with any hope of getting agreement from others, that the surgeon ought to flip a coin. So even if you think that the trolley driver ought to flip a coin, there would remain, for you, an analogue of Mrs. Foot's problem, namely: Why ought the trolley driver flip a coin, whereas the surgeon may not?
5. Mrs. Foot speaks more generally of causing injury and failing to provide aid; and her reason for thinking that the former is worse than the latter is that the negative duty to refrain from causing

injury is stricter than the positive duty to provide aid. *See* P. FOOT, *supra* note 1, at 27–29.

6. A similar case (intended to make a point similar to the one that I shall be making) is discussed in Davis, *The Priority of Avoiding Harm,* in KILLING AND LETTING DIE 172, 194–95 (B. Steinbock ed. 1980).
7. For a sensitive discussion of some of the difficulties, see Davis, *Using Persons and Common Sense,* 94 ETHICS 387 (1984). Among other things, she argues (I think rightly) that the Kantian idea is not to be identified with the common sense concept of "using a person." *Id.* at 402.
8. For a second reason to think so, *see infra* note 13.
9. It is also true that if the five go wholly out of existence just before the agent starts to turn the trolley, then the one will die whatever the agent does. Should we say, then, that the agent uses one to save five if he acts, *and* uses five to save one if he does not act? No: What follows *and* is false. If the agent does not act, he uses nobody. (I doubt that it can even be said that if he does not act, he lets them *be used*. For what is the active for which this is passive? Who or what would be using them if he does not act?).
10. I strongly suspect that giving an account of what makes it wrong to *use* a person, *see supra* text accompanying notes 6–8, would also require appeal to the concept of a right.
11. R. DWORKIN, TAKING RIGHTS SERIOUSLY ix (1977).
12. Many of the examples discussed by Bernard Williams and Ruth Marcus plainly call out for this kind of treatment. *See* B. WILLIAMS, *Ethical Consistency, in* PROBLEMS OF THE SELF 166 (1973); Marcus, *Moral Dilemmas and Consistency,* 77 J. PHIL. 121 (1980).
13. It may be worth stressing that what I suggest calls for attention is not (as some construals of "double effect" would have it) whether the agent's killing of the one is his means to something, and not (as other construals of "double effect" would have it) whether the death of the one is the agent's means to something, but rather what are the means by which the agent both kills and saves. For a discussion of "the doctrine of double effect," see P. FOOT, *supra* note 1.
14. *Id.* at 29. As Mrs. Foot says, we do not *use* the one if we proceed in *Hospital.* Yet the impermissibility of proceeding in *Hospital* seems to have a common source with the impermissibility of operating in *Transplant,* in which the surgeon *would* be using the one whose parts he takes for the five who need them. This is my second reason for thinking that an appeal to the fact that the surgeon would be using his victim is an over-simple way of taking account of the means he would be employing for the saving of his five. *See supra* note 7.
15. Notice that in this case too the agent does not *use* the one if he proceeds. (This case, along with a number of other cases I have been discussing, comes from Thomson, *Killing, Letting Die, and the Trolley Problem*, 59 THE MONIST 204 (1976). Mrs. Thomson seems to me to have been blundering around in the dark in that paper, but the student of this problem may possibly find some of the cases she discusses useful.).
16. *See supra* text accompanying notes 9–11.

Moral Luck

THOMAS NAGEL

Thomas Nagel (1937–) is a highly respected American philosopher who teaches philosophy and law at New York University. His philosophical interests include philosophy of mind,

Originally appeared in *Proceedings of the Aristotelian Society*, suppl. vol. I (1976). Reprinted in Thomas Nagel, *Mortal Questions,* pp. 24–38.
Copyright © 1979 by Cambridge University Press. Reprinted with the permission of Cambridge University Press.

ethics, political philosophy, and general questions about what renders a human life fulfilling. He is renowned for the clarity of his thought and the accessibility of his writing.

The selection that appears here was originally published in 1976 as a response to a paper by philosopher Bernard Williams with the same title. In it, Nagel explores our perplexing tendency to assign moral praise or blame to subjects on the basis of outcomes that lie beyond their control, despite our explicit insistence that these outcomes are morally irrelevant.

Other selections from Nagel's writings appear in the "Consciousness and Perception" (IV. B), "Life" (V. A), and "Death" (V. B) sections.

Kant believed that good or bad luck should influence neither our moral judgment of a person and his actions, nor his moral assessment of himself.

> The good will is not good because of what it effects or accomplishes or because of its adequacy to achieve some proposed end; it is good only because of its willing, i.e., it is good of itself. And, regarded for itself, it is to be esteemed incomparably higher than anything which could be brought about by it in favor of any inclination or even of the sum total of all inclinations. Even if it should happen that, by a particularly unfortunate fate or by the niggardly provision of a stepmotherly nature, this will should be wholly lacking in power to accomplish its purpose, and if even the greatest effort should not avail it to achieve anything of its end, and if there remained only the good will (not as a mere wish but as the summoning of all the means in our power), it would sparkle like a jewel in its own right, as something that had its full worth in itself. Usefulness or fruitlessness can neither diminish nor augment this worth.[1]

He would presumably have said the same about a bad will: whether it accomplishes its evil purposes is morally irrelevant. And a course of action that would be condemned if it had a bad outcome cannot be vindicated if by luck it turns out well. There cannot be moral risk. This view seems to be wrong, but it arises in response to a fundamental problem about moral responsibility to which we possess no satisfactory solution.

The problem develops out of the ordinary conditions of moral judgment. Prior to reflection it is intuitively plausible that people cannot be morally assessed for what is not their fault, or for what is due to factors beyond their control. Such judgment is different from the evaluation of something as a good or bad thing, or state of affairs. The latter may be present in addition to moral judgment, but when we blame someone for his actions we are not merely saying it is bad that they happened, or bad that he exists: we are judging *him,* saying he is bad, which is different from his being a bad thing. This kind of judgment takes only a certain kind of object. Without being able to explain exactly why, we feel that the appropriateness of moral assessment is easily undermined by the discovery that the act or attribute, no matter how good or bad, is not under the person's control. While other evaluations remain, this one seems to lose its footing. So a clear absence of control, produced by involuntary movement, physical force, or ignorance of the circumstances, excuses what is done from moral judgment. But what we do depends in many more ways than these on what is not under out control—what is not produced by a good or a bad will, in Kant's phrase. And external influences in this broader range are not usually thought to excuse what is done from moral judgment, positive or negative.

Let me give a few examples, beginning with the type of case Kant has in mind. Whether we succeed or fail in what we try to do nearly always depends to some extent on factors beyond our control. This is true of murder, altruism, revolution, the sacrifice of certain interests for the sake of others—almost any morally important act. What has been done, and what is morally judged, is partly determined by external factors. However jewel-like the good will may be in its own right, there is a morally significant difference between rescuing someone from a burning building and dropping him from a twelfth-story window while trying to rescue him. Similarly, there is a morally significant difference between reckless driving and manslaughter. But whether a reckless driver hits a pedestrian depends on the presence of the pedestrian at the point where he recklessly passes a red light. What we do is also limited by the opportunities and choices with which we are faced, and these are largely determined by factors beyond our control. Someone who was an officer in a concentration camp might have led a quiet and harmless life if the Nazis had never come to power in Germany. And someone who led a quiet and harmless life in Argentina might have become an officer in a concentration camp if he had not left Germany for business reasons in 1930.

I shall say more later about these and other examples. I introduce them here to illustrate a general point. Where a significant aspect of what someone does depends on factors beyond his control, yet we continue to treat him in that respect as an object of moral judgment, it can be called moral luck. Such luck can be good or bad. And the problem posed by this phenomenon, which led Kant to deny its possibility, is that the broad range of external influences here identified seems on close examination to undermine moral assessment as surely as does the narrower range of familiar excusing conditions. If the condition of control is consistently applied, it threatens to erode most of the moral assessments we find it natural to make. The things for which people are morally judged are determined in more ways than we at first realize by what is beyond their control. And when the seemingly natural requirement of fault or responsibility is applied in light of these facts, it leaves few pre-reflective moral judgments intact. Ultimately, nothing or almost nothing about what a person does seems to be under his control.

Why not conclude, then, that the condition of control is false—that it is an initially plausible hypothesis refuted by clear counter-examples? One could in that case look instead for a more refined condition which picked out the *kinds* of lack of control that really undermine certain moral judgments, without yielding the unacceptable conclusion derived from the broader condition, that most or all ordinary moral judgments are illegitimate.

What rules out this escape is that we are dealing not with a theoretical conjecture but with a philosophical problem. The condition of control does not suggest itself merely as a generalization from certain clear cases. It seems *correct* in the further cases to which it is extended beyond the original set. When we undermine moral assessment by considering new ways in which control is absent, we are not just discovering what *would* follow given the general hypothesis, but are actually being persuaded that in itself the absence of control is relevant in these cases too. The erosion of moral judgment emerges not as the absurd consequence of an over-simple theory, but as a natural consequence of the ordinary idea of moral assessment, when it is applied in view of a more complete and precise account of the facts. It would therefore be a mistake to argue from the unacceptability of the conclusions to the need for a different account of the conditions of moral responsibility. The view that moral luck is paradoxical is not a *mistake*, ethical or logical, but a perception of one of the ways in which the intuitively acceptable conditions of moral judgment threaten to undermine it all.

It resembles the situation in another area of philosophy, the theory of knowledge. There too conditions which seem perfectly natural, and which grow out of the ordinary procedures for challenging and defending claims to knowledge, threaten to undermine all such claims if consistently applied. Most skeptical arguments have this quality: they do not depend on the imposition of arbitrarily stringent standards of knowledge, arrived at by misunderstanding, but appear to grow inevitably from the consistent application of ordinary standards.[2] There is a substantive parallel as well, for epistemological skepticism arises from consideration of the respects in which our beliefs and their relation to reality depend on factors beyond our control. External and internal causes produce our beliefs. We may subject these processes to scrutiny in an effort to avoid error, but our conclusions at this next level also result, in part, from influences which we do not control directly. The same will be true no matter how far we carry the investigation. Our beliefs are always, ultimately, due to factors outside our control, and the impossibility of encompassing those factors without being at the mercy of others leads us to doubt whether we know anything. It looks as though, if any of our beliefs are true, it is pure biological luck rather than knowledge.

Moral luck is like this because while there are various respects in which the natural objects of moral assessment are out of our control or influenced by what is out of our control, we cannot reflect on these facts without losing our grip on the judgments.

There are roughly four ways in which the natural objects of moral assessment are disturbingly subject to luck. One is the phenomenon of constitutive luck—the kind of person you are, where this is not just a question of what you deliberately do, but of your inclinations, capacities, and temperament. Another category is luck in one's circumstances—the kind of problems and situations one faces. The other two have to do with the causes and effects of action: luck in how one is determined by antecedent circumstances, and luck in the way one's actions and projects turn out. All of them present a common problem. They are all opposed by the idea that one cannot be more culpable or estimable for anything than one is for that fraction of it which is under one's control. It seems irrational to take or dispense credit or blame for matters over which a person has no control, or for their influence on results over which he has partial control. Such things may create the conditions for action, but action can be judged only to the extent that it goes beyond these conditions and does not just result from them.

Let us first consider luck, good and bad, in the way things turn out. Kant, in the above-quoted passage, has one example of this in mind, but the category covers a wide range. It includes the truck driver who accidentally runs over a child, the artist who abandons his wife and five children to devote himself to painting,[3] and other cases in which the possibilities of success and failure are even greater. The driver, if he is entirely without fault, will feel terrible about his role in the event, but will not have to reproach himself. Therefore this example of agent-regret[4] is not yet a case of *moral* bad luck. However, if the driver was guilty of even a minor degree of negligence—failing to have his brakes checked recently, for example—then if that negligence contributes to the death of the child, he will not merely feel terrible. He will blame himself for the death. And what makes this an example of moral luck is that he would have to blame himself only slightly for the negligence itself if no situation arose which required him to brake suddenly and violently to avoid hitting a child. Yet the *negligence* is the same in both cases, and the driver has no control over whether a child will run into his path.

The same is true at higher levels of negligence. If someone has had too much to drink and his car swerves on to the sidewalk, he can count himself morally lucky if there are no pedestrians in its path. If there were, he would be to blame for their deaths, and would probably be prosecuted for manslaughter. But if he hurts no one, although his recklessness is exactly the same, he is guilty of a far less serious legal offence and will certainly reproach himself and be reproached by others much less severely. To take another legal example, the penalty for attempted murder is less than that for successful murder—however similar the intentions and motives of the assailant may be in the two cases. His degree of culpability can depend, it would seem, on whether the victim happened to be wearing a bullet-proof vest, or whether a bird flew into the path of the bullet—matters beyond his control.

Finally, there are cases of decision under uncertainty—common in public and in private life. Anna Karenina goes off with Vronsky, Gauguin leaves his family, Chamberlain signs the Munich agreement, the Decembrists persuade the troops under their command to revolt against the czar, the American colonies declare their independence from Britain, you introduce two people in an attempt at matchmaking. It is tempting in all such cases to feel that some decision must be possible, in the light of what is known at the time, which will make reproach unsuitable no matter how things turn out. But this is not true; when someone acts in such ways he takes his life, or his moral position, into his hands, because how things turn out determines what he has done. It is possible *also* to assess the decision from the point of view of what could be known at the time, but this is not the end of the story. If the Decembrists had succeeded in overthrowing Nicholas I in 1825 and establishing a constitutional regime, they would be heroes. As it is, not only did they fail and pay for it, but they bore some responsibility for the terrible punishments meted out to the troops who had been persuaded to follow them. If the American Revolution had been a bloody failure resulting in greater repression, then Jefferson, Franklin and Washington would still have made a noble attempt, and might not even have regretted it on their way to the scaffold, but they would also have had to blame themselves for what they had helped to bring on their compatriots. (Perhaps peaceful efforts at reform would eventually have succeeded.) If Hitler had not overrun Europe and exterminated millions, but instead had died of a heart attack after occupying the Sudetenland, Chamberlain's action at Munich would still have utterly betrayed the Czechs, but it would not be the great moral disaster that has made his name a household word.[5]

In many cases of difficult choice the outcome cannot be foreseen with certainty. One kind of assessment of the choice is possible in advance, but another kind must await the outcome, because the outcome determines what has been done. The same degree of culpability or estimability in intention, motive, or concern is compatible with a wide range of judgments, positive or negative, depending on what happened beyond the point of decision. The *mens rea* which could have existed in the absence of any consequences does not exhaust the grounds of moral judgment. Actual results influence culpability or esteem in a large class of unquestionably ethical cases ranging from negligence through political choice.

That these are genuine moral judgments rather than expressions of temporary attitude is evident from the fact that one can say *in advance* how the moral verdict will depend on the results. If one negligently leaves the bath running with the baby in it, one will realize, as one bounds up the stairs toward the bathroom, that if the baby has drowned one has done something awful, whereas if it has not one has merely been careless. Someone who launches a violent revolution against an authoritarian regime knows that if he fails he will be responsible for much suffering that is in vain, but if he succeeds he will be justified by the outcome. I do not mean that *any* action can be retroactively justified by history. Certain things are so bad in themselves, or so risky, that no results can make them all right. Nevertheless, when moral judgment does depend on the outcome, it is objective and timeless and not dependent on a change of standpoint produced by success or failure. The judgment after the fact follows from an hypothetical judgment that can be made beforehand, and it can be made as easily by someone else as by the agent.

From the point of view which makes responsibility dependent on control, all this seems absurd. How is it possible to be more or less culpable depending on whether a child gets into the path of one's car, or a bird into the path of one's bullet? Perhaps it is true that what is done depends on more than the agent's state of mind or intention. The problem then is, why is it not irrational to base moral assessment on what people do, in this broad sense? It amounts to holding them responsible for the contributions of fate as well as for their own—provided they have made some contribution to begin with. If we look at cases of negligence or attempt, the pattern seems to be that overall culpability corresponds to the product of mental or intentional fault and the seriousness of the outcome. Cases of decision under uncertainty are less easily explained in this way, for it seems that the overall judgment can even shift from positive to negative depending on the outcome. But here too it seems rational to subtract the effects of occurrences subsequent to the choice, that were merely possible at the time, and concentrate moral assessment on the actual decision in light of the probabilities. If the object of moral judgment is the *person*, then to hold him accountable for what he has done in the broader sense is akin to strict liability, which may have its legal uses but seems irrational as a moral position.

The result of such a line of thought is to pare down each act to its morally essential core, an inner act of pure will assessed by motive and intention. Adam Smith* advocates such a position in *The Theory of Moral Sentiments*, but notes that it runs contrary to our actual judgments.

> But how well soever we may seem to be persuaded of the truth of this equitable maxim, when we consider it after this manner, in abstract, yet when we come to particular cases, the actual consequences which

* Adam Smith (1723–90) was a Scottish philosopher and political economist whose 1776 book *The Wealth of Nations* played a central role in shaping the modern field of economics.

> happen to proceed from any action, have a very great effect upon our sentiments concerning its merit or demerit, and almost always either enhance or diminish our sense of both. Scarce, in any one instance, perhaps, will our sentiments be found, after examination, to be entirely regulated by this rule, which we all acknowledge ought entirely to regulate them.[6]

Joel Feinberg points out further that restricting the domain of moral responsibility to the inner world will not immunize it to luck. Factors beyond the agent's control, like a coughing fit, can interfere with his decisions as surely as they can with the path of a bullet from his gun.[7] Nevertheless the tendency to cut down the scope of moral assessment is pervasive, and does not limit itself to the influence of effects. It attempts to isolate the will from the other direction, so to speak, by separating out constitutive luck. Let us consider that next.

Kant was particularly insistent on the moral irrelevance of qualities of temperament and personality that are not under the control of the will. Such qualities as sympathy or coldness might provide the background against which obedience to moral requirements is more or less difficult, but they could not be objects of moral assessment themselves, and might well interfere with confident assessment of its proper object—the determination of the will by the motive of duty. This rules out moral judgment of many of the virtues and vices, which are states of character that influence choice but are certainly not exhausted by dispositions to act deliberately in certain ways. A person may be greedy, envious, cowardly, cold, ungenerous, unkind, vain, or conceited, but *behave* perfectly by a monumental effort of will. To possess these vices is to be unable to help having certain feelings under certain circumstances, and to have strong spontaneous impulses to act badly. Even if one controls the impulses, one still has the vice. An envious person hates the greater success of others. He can be morally condemned as envious even if he congratulates them cordially and does nothing to denigrate or spoil their success. Conceit, likewise, need not be displayed. It is fully present in someone who cannot help dwelling with secret satisfaction on the superiority of his own achievements, talents, beauty, intelligence, or virtue. To some extent such a quality may be the product of earlier choices; to some extent it may be amenable to change by current actions. But it is largely a matter of constitutive bad fortune. Yet people are morally condemned for such qualities, and esteemed for others equally beyond control of the will: they are assessed for what they are *like*.

To Kant this seems incoherent because virtue is enjoined on everyone and therefore must in principle be possible for everyone. It may be easier for some than for others, but it must be possible to achieve it by making the right choices, against whatever temperamental background.[8] One may want to have a generous spirit, or regret not having one, but it makes no sense to condemn oneself or anyone else for a quality which is not within the control of the will. Condemnation implies that you should not be like that, not that it is unfortunate that you are.

Nevertheless, Kant's conclusion remains intuitively unacceptable. We may be persuaded that these moral judgments are irrational, but they reappear involuntarily as soon as the argument is over. This is the pattern throughout the subject.

The third category to consider is luck in one's circumstances, and I shall mention it briefly. The things we are called upon to do, the moral tests we face, are importantly determined by factors beyond our control. It may be true of someone that in a dangerous situation he would behave in a cowardly or heroic fashion, but if the situation never arises, he will never have the chance to distinguish or disgrace himself in this way, and his moral record will be different.[9]

A conspicuous example of this is political. Ordinary citizens of Nazi Germany had an opportunity to behave heroically by opposing the regime. They also had an opportunity to behave badly, and most of them are culpable for having failed this test. But it is a test to which the citizens of other countries were not subjected, with the result that even if they, or some of them, would have behaved as badly as the Germans in like circumstances, they simply did not and therefore are not similarly culpable. Here again one is morally at the mercy of fate, and it may seem irrational upon reflection, but our ordinary moral attitudes would be unrecognizable without it. We judge people for what they actually do or fail to do, not just for what they would have done if circumstances had been different.[10]

This form of moral determination by the actual is also paradoxical, but we can begin to see how deep in the concept of responsibility the paradox is embedded. A person can be morally responsible only for what he does; but what he does results from a great deal that he does not do; therefore he is not morally responsible for what he is and is not responsible for. (This is not a contradiction, but it is a paradox.)

It should be obvious that there is a connection between these problems about responsibility and control and an even more familiar problem, that of freedom of the will. That is the last type of moral luck I want to take up, though I can do no more within the scope of this essay than indicate its connection with the other types.

If one cannot be responsible for consequences of one's acts due to factors beyond one's control, or for antecedents of one's acts that are properties of temperament not subject to one's will, or for the circumstances that pose one's moral choices, then how can one be responsible even for the stripped-down acts of the will itself, if *they* are the product of antecedent circumstances outside of the will's control?

The area of genuine agency, and therefore of legitimate moral judgment, seems to shrink under this scrutiny to an extensionless point. Everything seems to result from the combined influence of factors, antecedent and posterior to action, that are not within the agent's control. Since he cannot be responsible for them, he cannot be responsible for their results—though it may remain possible to take up the aesthetic or other evaluative analogues of the moral attitudes that are thus displaced.

It is also possible, of course, to brazen it out and refuse to accept the results, which indeed seem unacceptable as soon as we stop thinking about the arguments. Admittedly, if certain surrounding circumstances had been different, then no unfortunate consequences would have followed from a wicked intention, and no seriously culpable act would have been performed; but since the circumstances were *not* different, and the agent *in fact* succeeded in perpetrating a particularly cruel murder, *that* is what he did, and that is what he is responsible for. Similarly, we may admit that if certain antecedent circumstances had been different, the agent would never have developed into the sort of person who would do such a thing; but since he *did* develop (as the inevitable result of those antecedent circumstances) into the sort of swine he is, and into the person who committed such a murder, *that* is what he is blameable for. In both cases one is responsible for what one actually does—even if what one actually does depends in important ways on what is not within one's control. This compatibilist account of our moral judgments would leave room for the ordinary conditions of responsibility—the absence of coercion, ignorance, or involuntary movement—as part of the determination of what someone has done—but it is understood not to exclude the influence of a great deal that he has not done.[11]

The only thing wrong with this solution is its failure to explain how skeptical problems arise. For they arise not from the imposition of an arbitrary external requirement, but from the nature of moral judgment itself. Something in the ordinary idea of what someone does must explain how it can seem necessary to subtract from it anything that merely happens—even though the ultimate consequence of such subtraction is that nothing remains. And something in the ordinary idea of knowledge must explain why it seems to be undermined by any influences on belief not within the control of the subject—so that knowledge seems impossible without an impossible foundation in autonomous reason. But let us leave epistemology aside and concentrate on action, character, and moral assessment.

The problem arises, I believe, because the self which acts and is the object of moral judgment is threatened with dissolution by the absorption of its acts and impulses into the class of events. Moral judgment of a person is judgment not of what happens to him, but of him. It does not say merely that a certain event or state of affairs is fortunate or unfortunate or even terrible. It is not an evaluation of a state of the world, or of an individual as part of the world. We are not thinking just that it would be better if he were different, or did not exist, or had not done some of the things he has done. We are judging *him*, rather than his existence or characteristics. The effect of concentrating on the influence of what is not under his control is to make this responsible self seem to disappear, swallowed up by the order of mere events.

What, however, do we have in mind that a person must *be* to be the object of these moral attitudes? While the concept of agency is easily undermined, it is very difficult to give it a positive characterization. That is familiar from the literature on Free Will.

I believe that in a sense the problem has no solution, because something in the idea of agency is incompatible with actions being events, or people being things. But as the external determinants of what someone has done are gradually exposed, in their effect on consequences, character, and choice itself, it becomes gradually clear that actions are events and people things. Eventually nothing remains which can be ascribed to the responsible self, and we are left with nothing but a portion of the larger sequence of events, which can be deplored or celebrated, but not blamed or praised.

Though I cannot define the idea of the active self that is thus undermined, it is possible to say something about its sources. There is a close connexion between our feelings about ourselves and our feelings about others. Guilt and indignation, shame and contempt, pride and admiration are internal and external sides of the same moral attitudes. We are unable to view ourselves simply as portions of the world, and from inside we have a rough idea of the boundary between what is us and what is not, what we do and what happens to us, what is our personality and what is an accidental handicap. We apply the same essentially internal conception of the self to others. About ourselves we feel pride, shame, guilt, remorse—and agent-regret. We do not regard our actions and our characters merely as fortunate or unfortunate episodes—though they may also be that. We cannot *simply* take an external evaluative view of ourselves—of what we most essentially are and what we do. And this remains true even when we have seen that we are not responsible for our own existence, or our nature, or the choices we have to make, or the circumstances that give our acts the consequences they have. Those acts remain ours and we remain ourselves, despite the persuasiveness of the reasons that seem to argue us out of existence.

It is this internal view that we extend to others in moral judgment—when we judge *them* rather than their desirability or utility. We extend to others the refusal to limit ourselves to external evaluation, and we accord to them selves like our own. But in both cases this comes up against the brutal inclusion of humans and everything about them in a world from which they cannot be separated and of which they are nothing but contents. The external view forces itself on us at the same time that we resist it. One way this occurs is through the gradual erosion of what we do by the subtraction of what happens.[12]

The inclusion of consequences in the conception of what we have done is an acknowledgment that we are parts of the world, but the paradoxical character of moral luck which emerges from this acknowledgment shows that we are unable to operate with such a view, for it leaves us with no one to be. The same thing is revealed in the appearance that determinism obliterates responsibility. Once we see an aspect of what we or someone else does as something that happens, we lose our grip on the idea that it has been done and that we can judge the doer and not just the happening. This explains why the absence of determinism is no more hospitable to the concept of agency than is its presence—a point that has been noticed often. Either way the act is viewed externally, as part of the course of events.

The problem of moral luck cannot be understood without an account of the internal conception of agency and its special connection with the moral attitudes as opposed to other types of value. I do not have such an account. The degree to which the problem has a solution can be determined only by seeing whether in some degree the incompatibility between this conception and the various ways in which we do not control what we do is only apparent. I have nothing to offer on that topic either. But it is not enough to say merely that our basic moral attitudes toward ourselves and others are determined by what is actual; for they are also threatened by the sources of that actuality, and by the external view of action which forces itself on us when we see how everything we do belongs to a world that we have not created.

NOTES

1. *Grounding of the Metaphysics of Morals*, first section, third paragraph.
2. See Thompson Clarke, "The Legacy of Skepticism." *Journal of Philosophy*, LXIX, no. 20 (November 9, 1972), 754–69.
3. Such a case, modelled on the life of Gauguin, is discussed by Bernard Williams in "Moral Luck," *Proceedings of the Aristotelian Society*, supplementary vol. 1. (1976), 115–35 (to which the original version of this essay was a reply). He points out that though success or failure cannot be predicted in advance, Gauguin's most basic retrospective feelings about the decision will be determined by the development of his talent. My disagreement with Williams is that his account fails to explain why such retrospective attitudes can be called moral. If success does not permit Gauguin to justify himself to others, but still determines his most basic feelings, that shows only that his most basic feelings need not be moral. It does not show that morality is subject to luck. If the retrospective judgment were moral, it would imply the truth of a hypothetical judgment made in advance, of the form "If I leave my family and become a great painter, I will be justified by success; if I don't become a great painter, the act will be unforgivable."
4. Williams' term (ibid.).
5. For a fascinating but morally repellent discussion of the topic of justification by history, see Maurice Merleau-Ponty, *Humanisme et Terreur* (Paris: Gallimard, 1947), translated as *Humanism and Terror* (Boston: Beacon Press, 1969).
6. Pt. II, sect. 3, Introduction, para. 5.
7. "Problematic Responsibility in Law and Morals," in Joel Feinberg, *Doing and Deserving* (Princeton: Princeton University Press, 1970).
8. "If nature has put little sympathy in the heart of a man, and if he, though an honest man, is by temperament cold and indifferent to the sufferings of others, perhaps because he is provided with special gifts of patience and fortitude and expects or even requires that others should have the same—and such a man would certainly not be the meanest product of nature—would not he find in himself a source from which to give himself a far higher worth than he could have got by having a good-natured temperament?" (*Foundations of the Metaphysics of Morals*, first section, eleventh paragraph).
9. Cf. Thomas Gray, "Elegy Written in a Country Churchyard":

   Some mute inglorious Milton here may rest,
   Some Cromwell, guiltless of his country's blood.

   An unusual example of circumstantial moral luck is provided by the kind of moral dilemma with which someone can be faced through no fault of his own, but which leaves him with nothing to do which is not wrong. See Bernard Williams, "Ethical Consistency," *Proceedings of the Aristotelian Society*, supplementary vol. XXXIX (1965), reprinted in *Problems of the Self* (Cambridge: Cambridge University Press, 1973), pp. 166–86.
10. Circumstantial luck can extend to aspects of the situation other than individual behavior. For example, during the Vietnam War even U.S. citizens who had opposed their country's actions vigorously from the start often felt compromised by its crimes. Here they were not even responsible; there was probably nothing they could do to stop what was happening, so the feeling of being implicated may seem unintelligible. But it is nearly impossible to view the crimes of one's own country in the same way that one views the crimes of another country, no matter how equal one's lack of power to stop them in the two cases. One *is* a citizen of one of them, and has a connexion with its actions (even if only through taxes that cannot be withheld)—that one does not have with the other's. This makes it possible to be ashamed of one's country, and to feel a victim of moral bad luck that one was an American in the 1960s.
11. The corresponding position in epistemology would be that knowledge consists of true beliefs formed in certain ways, and that it does not require all aspects of the process to be under the knower's control, actually or potentially. Both the correctness of these beliefs and the process by which they are arrived at would therefore be importantly subject to luck. The Nobel Prize is not awarded to people who turn out to be wrong, no matter how brilliant their reasoning.
12. See P. F. Strawson's discussion of the conflict between the objective attitude and personal reactive attitudes in "Freedom and Resentment," [this volume—eds].

"Glaucon's Challenge" from *The Republic*

PLATO

Plato (c. 428–347 BCE)—along with his student Aristotle—was one of the two most important philosophers of antiquity and is among the most important figures in the entire Western intellectual tradition. His wide-ranging discussions addressed nearly every philosophical topic imaginable and set the stage for philosophical exploration for the next two millennia. His philosophical writings take the form of dialogues that feature his teacher Socrates (469–399 BCE) as a character.

The selection that appears here is drawn from Plato's long dialogue, *The Republic*. In the passage in question, two characters—Plato's teacher Socrates and Plato's brother Glaucon—are engaged in a conversation about the nature and value of justice. Glaucon, the challenger, advocates the view that the only reason people act justly is because they believe that doing so will help them attain desirable ends.

This text was originally written in ancient Greek and was translated by British philosopher G. M. A. Grube and updated by American philosopher C. D. C. Reeve. The numbers that appear in the margins of the text are called "Stephanus numbers"; they refer to the page numbers of a canonical edition of Plato's work prepared by Henricus Stephanus in 1578. Reference to these numbers enables coordination among readers who make use of different translations or editions. Notes that appear in brackets are due to the translators of the work, with occasional slight supplements from the editors of this volume.

Several additional selections from Plato's writings can be found in the sections on "Knowledge." Plato's answer to Glaucon's challenge can be found in the section on "Life."

When I said this, I thought I had done with the dis-
cussion, but it turned out to have been only a pre-
357 lude. Glaucon showed his characteristic courage on
this occasion too and refused to accept Thrasyma-
chus' abandonment of the argument. Socrates, he
said, do you want to seem to have persuaded us that
it is better in every way to be just than unjust, or do
b you want truly to convince us of this?

I want truly to convince you, I said, if I can.

Well, then, you certainly aren't doing what you
want. Tell me, do you think there is a kind of good
we welcome, not because we desire what comes from
it, but because we welcome it for its own sake—joy,
for example, and all the harmless pleasures that have
no results beyond the joy of having them?

Certainly, I think there are such things.

And is there a kind of good we like for its own sake
and also for the sake of what comes from it—knowing,
for example, and seeing and being healthy? We wel- c
come such things, I suppose, on both counts.

Yes.

And do you also see a third kind of good, such
as physical training, medical treatment when sick,
medicine itself, and the other ways of making
money? We'd say that these are onerous but ben-
eficial to us, and we wouldn't choose them for their
own sakes, but for the sake of the rewards and other
things that come from them. d

There is also this third kind. But what of it?

Where do you put justice?

From Plato, *Republic*, trans. Grube, rev. Reeve. Copyright 1992 by Hackett Publishing Company, Inc. Reprinted by permission of the publisher. All rights reserved.

I myself put it among the finest goods, as some-
358 thing to be valued by anyone who is going to be
blessed with happiness, both because of itself and
because of what comes from it.

That isn't most people's opinion. They'd say
that justice belongs to the onerous kind, and is to
be practiced for the sake of the rewards and popu-
larity that come from a reputation for justice, but
is to be avoided because of itself as something bur-
densome.

I know that's the general opinion. Thrasyma-
chus faulted justice on these grounds a moment ago
and praised injustice, but it seems that I'm a slow
learner.

b Come, then, and listen to me as well, and see
whether you still have that problem, for I think that
Thrasymachus gave up before he had to, charmed
by you as if he were a snake. But I'm not yet satisfied
by the argument on either side. I want to know what
justice and injustice are and what power each itself
has when it's by itself in the soul. I want to leave out
of account their rewards and what comes from each
of them. So, if you agree, I'll renew the argument of
c Thrasymachus. First, I'll state what kind of thing
people consider justice to be and what its origins are.
Second, I'll argue that all who practice it do so un-
willingly, as something necessary, not as something
good. Third, I'll argue that they have good reason to
act as they do, for the life of an unjust person is, they
say, much better than that of a just one.

It isn't, Socrates, that I believe any of that myself.
I'm perplexed, indeed, and my ears are deafened
listening to Thrasymachus and countless others. But
I've yet to hear anyone defend justice in the way
d I want, proving that it is better than injustice. I
want to hear it praised *by itself,* and I think that
I'm most likely to hear this from you. Therefore,
I'm going to speak at length in praise of the un-
just life, and in doing so I'll show you the way I
want to hear you praising justice and denouncing
injustice. But see whether you want me to do that
or not.

I want that most of all. Indeed, what subject
could someone with any understanding enjoy dis-
cussing more often?

e Excellent. Then let's discuss the first subject I
mentioned—what justice is and what its origins are.

They say that to do injustice is naturally good
and to suffer injustice bad, but that the badness of
suffering it so far exceeds the goodness of doing it
that those who have done and suffered injustice and
tasted both, but who lack the power to do it and
avoid suffering it, decide that it is profitable to come 359
to an agreement with each other neither to do injus-
tice nor to suffer it. As a result, they begin to make
laws and covenants, and what the law commands
they call lawful and just. This, they say, is the ori-
gin and essence of justice. It is intermediate between
the best and the worst. The best is to do injustice
without paying the penalty; the worst is to suffer it
without being able to take revenge. Justice is a mean
between these two extremes. People value it not as a
good but because they are too weak to do injustice
with impunity. Someone who has the power to do
this, however, and is a true man wouldn't make an
agreement with anyone not to do injustice in order b
not to suffer it. For him that would be madness.
This is the nature of justice, according to the argu-
ment, Socrates, and these are its natural origins.

We can see most clearly that those who practice
justice do it unwillingly and because they lack the
power to do injustice, if in our thoughts we grant to c
a just and an unjust person the freedom to do what-
ever they like. We can then follow both of them and
see where their desires would lead. And we'll catch
the just person red-handed travelling the same road
as the unjust. The reason for this is the desire to
outdo others and get more and more. This is what
anyone's nature naturally pursues as good, but na-
ture is forced by law into the perversion of treating
fairness with respect.

The freedom I mentioned would be most easily
realized if both people had the power they say the
ancestor of Gyges of Lydia possessed. The story goes
that he was a shepherd in the service of the ruler of
Lydia. There was a violent thunderstorm, and an d
earthquake broke open the ground and created a
chasm at the place where he was tending his sheep.
Seeing this, he was filled with amazement and
went down into it. And there, in addition to many
other wonders of which we're told, he saw a hollow
bronze horse. There were windowlike openings in
it, and, peeping in, he saw a corpse, which seemed
to be of more than human size, wearing nothing

e but a gold ring on its finger. He took the ring and
came out of the chasm. He wore the ring at the usual
monthly meeting that reported to the king on the
state of the flocks. And as he was sitting among the
others, he happened to turn the setting of the ring
towards himself to the inside of his hand. When he
did this, he became invisible to those sitting near
him, and they went on talking as if he had gone. He
360 wondered at this, and, fingering the ring, he turned
the setting outwards again and became visible. So he
experimented with the ring to test whether it indeed
had this power—and it did. If he turned the setting
inward, he became invisible; if he turned it outward,
he became visible again. When he realized this, he at
once arranged to become one of the messengers sent
to report to the king. And when he arrived there, he
b seduced the king's wife, attacked the king with her
help, killed him, and took over the kingdom.

Let's suppose, then, that there were two such
rings, one worn by a just and the other by an unjust
person. Now, no one, it seems, would be so incor-
ruptible that he would stay on the path of justice
or stay away from other people's property, when
he could take whatever he wanted from the mar-
ketplace with impunity, go into people's houses
c and have sex with anyone he wished, kill or release
from prison anyone he wished, and do all the other
things that would make him like a god among hu-
mans. Rather his actions would be in no way differ-
ent from those of an unjust person, and both would
follow the same path. This, some would say, is a
great proof that one is never just willingly but only
when compelled to be. No one believes justice to be
a good when it is kept private, since, wherever either
person thinks he can do injustice with impunity, he
does it. Indeed, every man believes that injustice
is far more profitable to himself than justice. And
d any exponent of this argument will say he's right,
for someone who didn't want to do injustice, given
this sort of opportunity, and who didn't touch other
people's property would be thought wretched and
stupid by everyone aware of the situation, though,
of course, they'd praise him in public, deceiving
each other for fear of suffering injustice. So much
for my second topic.

As for the choice between the lives we're dis-
e cussing, we'll be able to make a correct judgment
about that only if we separate the most just and the
most unjust. Otherwise we won't be able to do it.
Here's the separation I have in mind. We'll subtract
nothing from the injustice of an unjust person and
nothing from the justice of a just one, but we'll take
each to be complete in his own way of life. First,
therefore, we must suppose that an unjust person
will act as clever craftsmen do: A first-rate captain
or doctor, for example, knows the difference be- 361
tween what his craft can and can't do. He attempts
the first but lets the second go by, and if he happens to
slip, he can put things right. In the same way, an
unjust person's successful attempts at injustice must
remain undetected, if he is to be fully unjust. Any-
one who is caught should be thought inept, for the
extreme of injustice is to be believed to be just with-
out being just. And our completely unjust person
must be given complete injustice; nothing may be
subtracted from it. We must allow that, while doing
the greatest injustice, he has nonetheless provided
himself with the greatest reputation for justice. If
he happens to make a slip, he must be able to put d
it right. If any of his unjust activities should be dis-
covered, he must be able to speak persuasively or to
use force. And if force is needed, he must have the
help of courage and strength and of the substantial
wealth and friends with which he has provided
himself.

Having hypothesized such a person, let's now
in our argument put beside him a just man, who
is simple and noble and who, as Aeschylus says,
doesn't want to be believed to be good but to be so.[1]
We must take away his reputation, for a reputation c
for justice would bring him honor and rewards, so
that it wouldn't be clear whether he is just for the
sake of justice itself or for the sake of those honors
and rewards. We must strip him of everything ex-
cept justice and make his situation the opposite of
an unjust person's. Though he does no injustice, he
must have the greatest reputation for it, so that his
justice may be tested full-strength and not diluted
by wrong-doing and what comes from it. Let him
stay like that unchanged until he dies—just, but all d
his life believed to be unjust. In this way, both will
reach the extremes, the one of justice and the other
of injustice, and we'll be able to judge which of them
is happier.

Whew! Glaucon, I said, how vigorously you've
scoured each of the men for our competition, just as
you would a pair of statues for an art competition.

I do the best I can, he replied. Since the two are as
I've described, in any case, it shouldn't be difficult to
complete the account of the kind of life that awaits
each of them, but it must be done. And if what I say
e sounds crude, Socrates, remember that it isn't I who
speak but those who praise injustice at the expense
of justice. They'll say that a just person in such cir-
cumstances will be whipped, stretched on a rack,
chained, blinded with fire, and, at the end, when
he has suffered every kind of evil, he'll be impaled,
and will realize then that one shouldn't want to be
just but to be believed to be just. Indeed, Aeschylus'
362 words are far more correctly applied to unjust peo-
ple than to just ones, for the supporters of injustice
will say that a really unjust person, having a way of
life based on the truth about things and not living in
accordance with opinion, doesn't want simply to be
believed to be unjust but actually to be so—

Harvesting a deep furrow in his mind,
b Where wise counsels propagate.

He rules his city because of his reputation for jus-
tice; he marries into any family he wishes; he gives
his children in marriage to anyone he wishes; he has
contracts and partnerships with anyone he wants;
and besides benefiting himself in all these ways, he
profits because he has no scruples about doing injus-
tice. In any contest, public or private, he's the winner
and outdoes his enemies. And by outdoing them, he
becomes wealthy, benefiting his friends and harm-
ing his enemies. He makes adequate sacrifices to the c
gods and sets up magnificent offerings to them. He
takes better care of the gods, therefore, (and, indeed,
of the human beings he's fond of) than a just person
does. Hence it's likely that the gods, in turn, will take
better care of him than of a just person. That's what
they say, Socrates, that gods and humans provide a
better life for unjust people than for just ones.

NOTE

1. [In *Seven Against Thebes* (a play by Aeschylus) 592–94, it is said of Amphiaraus, the legendary king of Argos, that "he did not wish to be believed to be the best but to be it." The passage continues with the words Glaucon quotes below at 362a–b.]

Moral Saints

SUSAN WOLF

Susan Wolf is an American philosopher who teaches philosophy at the University of North Carolina, Chapel Hill. Her insightful work on topics in moral philosophy and the philosophy of mind have earned her a wide readership. This selection was originally published in a philosophy journal in 1982. In it, Wolf challenges the view that we should strive for moral value above all other values. In the course of the article, Wolf makes reference to a large number of figures from Western literature and from popular culture; their relevance is generally made clear from the context in which they appear.

I don't know whether there are any moral saints. But if there are, I am glad that neither I nor those about whom I care most are among them. By *moral saint* I mean a person whose every action is as morally good as possible, a person, that is, who is as morally worthy as can be. Though I shall in a moment acknowledge the variety of types of person that might be thought to satisfy this description, it seems to me that none of these types serve as unequivocally compelling personal ideals. In other words, I believe that

From *The Journal of Philosophy*, vol. 79, no. 8 (August 1982), pp. 419–439. Reprinted with the permission of the author and *The Journal of Philosophy*.

moral perfection, in the sense of moral saintliness, does not constitute a model of personal well-being toward which it would be particularly rational or good or desirable for a human being to strive.

Outside the context of moral discussion, this will strike many as an obvious point. But, within that context, the point, if it be granted, will be granted with some discomfort. For within that context it is generally assumed that one ought to be as morally good as possible and that what limits there are to morality's hold on us are set by features of human nature of which we ought not to be proud. If, as I believe, the ideals that are derivable from common sense and philosophically popular moral theories do not support these assumptions, then something has to change. Either we must change our moral theories in ways that will make them yield more palatable ideals, or, as I shall argue, we must change our conception of what is involved in affirming a moral theory.

In this paper, I wish to examine the notion of a moral saint, first, to understand what a moral saint would be like and why such a being would be unattractive, and, second, to raise some questions about the significance of this paradoxical figure for moral philosophy. I shall look first at the model(s) of moral sainthood that might be extrapolated from the morality or moralities of common sense. Then I shall consider what relations these have to conclusions that can be drawn from utilitarian and Kantian moral theories. Finally, I shall speculate on the implications of these considerations for moral philosophy.

MORAL SAINTS AND COMMON SENSE

Consider first what, pretheoretically, would count for us—contemporary members of Western culture—as a moral saint. A necessary condition of moral sainthood would be that one's life be dominated by a commitment to improving the welfare of others or of society as a whole. As to what role this commitment must play in the individual's motivational system, two contrasting accounts suggest themselves to me which might equally be thought to qualify a person for moral sainthood.

First, a moral saint might be someone whose concern for others plays the role that is played in most of our lives by more selfish, or at any rate, less morally worthy concerns. For the moral saint, the promotion of the welfare of others might play the role that is played for most of us by the enjoyment of material comforts, the opportunity to engage in the intellectual and physical activities of our choice, and the love, respect, and companionship of people whom we love, respect, and enjoy. The happiness of the moral saint, then, would truly lie in the happiness of others, and so he would devote himself to others gladly, and with a whole and open heart.

On the other hand, a moral saint might be someone for whom the basic ingredients of happiness are not unlike those of most of the rest of us. What makes him a moral saint is rather that he pays little or no attention to his own happiness in light of the overriding importance he gives to the wider concerns of morality. In other words, this person sacrifices his own interests to the interests of others, and feels the sacrifice as such.

Roughly, these two models may be distinguished according to whether one thinks of the moral saint as being a saint out of love or one thinks of the moral saint as being a saint out of duty (or some other intellectual appreciation and recognition of moral principles). We may refer to the first model as the model of the Loving Saint; to the second, as the model of the Rational Saint.

The two models differ considerably with respect to the qualities of the motives of the individuals who conform to them. But this difference would have limited effect on the saints' respective public personalities. The shared content of what these individuals are motivated to be—namely, as morally good as possible—would play the dominant role in the determination of their characters. Of course, just as a variety of large-scale projects, from tending the sick to political campaigning, may be equally and maximally morally worthy, so a variety of characters are compatible with the ideal of moral sainthood. One moral saint may be more or less jovial, more or less garrulous, more or less athletic than another. But, above all, a moral saint must have and cultivate those qualities which are apt to allow him to treat others as justly and kindly as possible. He will have the standard moral virtues to a nonstandard degree. He will be patient, considerate, even-tempered, hospitable, charitable in thought as well as in deed. He will be very reluctant to make negative judgments of other people. He will be careful not to favor some people over others on the basis of properties they could not help but have.

Perhaps what I have already said is enough to make some people begin to regard the absence of moral saints in their lives as a blessing. For there comes a point in the listing of virtues that a moral saint is likely to have where one might naturally begin to wonder whether the moral saint isn't, after all, too good—if not too good for his own good, at least too good for his own well-being. For the moral virtues, given that they are, by hypothesis, *all* present in the same individual, and to an extreme degree, are apt to crowd out the nonmoral virtues, as well as many of the interests and personal characteristics that we generally think contribute to a healthy, well-rounded, richly developed character.

In other words, if the moral saint is devoting all his time to feeding the hungry or healing the sick or raising money for Oxfam, then necessarily he is not reading Victorian novels, playing the oboe, or improving his backhand. Although no one of the interests or tastes in the category containing these latter activities could be claimed to be a necessary element in a life well lived, a life in which *none* of these possible aspects of character are developed may seem to be a life strangely barren.

The reasons why a moral saint cannot, in general, encourage the discovery and development of significant nonmoral interests and skills are not logical but practical reasons. There are, in addition, a class of nonmoral characteristics that a moral saint cannot encourage in himself for reasons that are not just practical. There is a more substantial tension between having any of these qualities unashamedly and being a moral saint. These qualities might be described as going against the moral grain. For example, a cynical or sarcastic wit, or a sense of humor that appreciates this kind of wit in others, requires that one take an attitude of resignation and pessimism toward the flaws and vices to be found in the world. A moral saint, on the other hand, has reason to take an attitude in opposition to this—he should try to look for the best in people, give them the benefit of the doubt as long as possible, try to improve regrettable situations as long as there is any hope of success. This suggests that, although a moral saint might well enjoy a good episode of *Father Knows Best,* he may not in good conscience be able to laugh at a Marx Brothers movie or enjoy a play by George Bernard Shaw.

An interest in something like gourmet cooking will be, for different reasons, difficult for a moral saint to rest easy with. For it seems to me that no plausible argument can justify the use of human resources involved in producing a *paté de canard en crois* against possible alternative beneficent ends to which these resources might be put. If there is a justification for the institution of haute cuisine, it is one which rests on the decision *not* to justify every activity against morally beneficial alternatives, and this is a decision a moral saint will never make. Presumably, an interest in high fashion or interior design will fare much the same, as will, very possibly, a cultivation of the finer arts as well.

A moral saint will have to be very, very nice. It is important that he not be offensive. The worry is that, as a result, he will have to be dull-witted or humorless or bland.

This worry is confirmed when we consider what sorts of characters, taken and refined both from life and from fiction, typically form our ideals. One would hope they would be figures who are morally good—and by this I mean more than just not morally bad—but one would hope, too, that they are not *just* morally good, but talented or accomplished or attractive in nonmoral ways as well. We may make ideals out of athletes, scholars, artists—more frivolously, out of cowboys, private eyes, and rock stars. We may strive for Katharine Hepburn's grace, Paul Newman's "cool"; we are attracted to the high-spirited passionate nature of Natasha Rostov; we admire the keen perceptiveness of Lambert Strether. Though there is certainly nothing immoral about the ideal characters or traits I have in mind, they cannot be superimposed upon the ideal of a moral saint. For although it is a part of many of these ideals that the characters set high, and not merely acceptable moral standards for themselves, it is also essential to their power and attractiveness that the moral strengths go, so to speak, alongside of specific, independently admirable, nonmoral ground projects and dominant personal traits.

When one does finally turn one's eyes toward lives that are dominated by explicitly moral commitments, moreover, one finds oneself relieved at the discovery of idiosyncrasies or eccentricities not quite in line with the picture of moral perfection. One prefers the blunt, tactless, and opinionated Betsy Trowood to the unfailingly kind and patient Agnes Copperfield; one prefers the mischievousness and the sense of irony in Chesterton's Father Brown to the innocence and undiscriminating love of St. Francis.

It seems that, as we look in our ideals for people who achieve nonmoral varieties of personal excellence in conjunction with or colored by some version of high moral tone, we look in our paragons of moral excellence for people whose moral achievements occur in conjunction with or colored by some interests or traits that have low moral tone. In other words, there seems to be a limit to how much morality we can stand.

One might suspect that the essence of the problem is simply that there is a limit to how much of *any* single value, or any single type of value, we can stand. Our objection then would not be specific to a life in which one's dominant concern is morality, but would apply to any life that can be so completely characterized by an extraordinarily dominant concern. The objection in that case would reduce to the recognition that such a life is incompatible with well-roundedness. If that were the objection, one could fairly reply that well-roundedness is no more supreme a virtue than the totality of moral virtues embodied by the ideal it is being used to criticize. But I think this misidentifies the objection. For the way in which a concern for morality may dominate a life, or, more to the point, the way in which it may dominate an ideal of life, is not easily imagined by analogy to the dominance an aspiration to become an Olympic swimmer or a concert pianist might have.

A person who is passionately committed to one of these latter concerns might decide that her attachment to it is strong enough to be worth the sacrifice of her ability to maintain and pursue a significant portion of what else life might offer which a proper devotion to her dominant passion would require. But a desire to be as morally good as possible is not likely to take the form of one desire among others which, because of its peculiar psychological strength, requires one to forego the pursuit of other weaker and separately less demanding desires. Rather, the desire to be as morally good as possible is apt to have the character not just of a stronger but of a higher desire, which does not merely successfully compete with one's other desires but which rather subsumes or demeans them. The sacrifice of other interests for the interest in morality then, will have the character, not of a choice, but of an imperative.

Moreover, there is something odd about the idea of morality itself, or moral goodness, serving as the object of a dominant passion in the way that a more concrete and specific vision of a goal (even a concrete *moral* goal) might be imagined to serve. Morality itself does not seem to be a suitable object of passion. Thus, when one reflects, for example, on the Loving Saint easily and gladly giving up his fishing trip or his stereo or his hot fudge sundae at the drop of the moral hat, one is apt to wonder not at how much he loves morality, but at how little he loves these other things. One thinks that, if he can give these up so easily, he does not know what it is to truly love them. There seems, in other words, to be a kind of joy which the Loving Saint, either by nature or by practice, is incapable of experiencing. The Rational Saint, on the other hand, might retain strong nonmoral and concrete desires—(he simply denies himself the opportunity to act on them). But this is no less troubling. The Loving Saint one might suspect of missing a piece of perceptual machinery, of being blind to some of what the world has to offer. The Rational Saint, who sees it but foregoes it, one suspects of having a different problem—a pathological fear of damnation, perhaps, or an extreme form of self-hatred that interferes with his ability to enjoy the enjoyable in life.

In other words, the ideal of a life of moral sainthood disturbs not simply because it is an ideal of a life in which morality unduly dominates. The normal person's direct and specific desires for objects, activities, and events that conflict with the attainment of moral perfection are not simply sacrificed but removed, suppressed, or subsumed. The way in which morality, unlike other possible goals, is apt to dominate is particularly disturbing, for it seems to require either the lack or the denial of the existence of an identifiable, personal self.

This distinctively troubling feature is not, I think, absolutely unique to the ideal of the moral saint, as I have been using that phrase. It is shared by the conception of the pure aesthete, by a certain kind of religious ideal, and, somewhat paradoxically, by the model of the thorough-going, self-conscious egoist. It is not a coincidence that the ways of comprehending the world of which these ideals are the extreme embodiments are sometimes described as "moralities" themselves. At any rate, they compete with what we ordinarily mean by "morality." Nor is it a coincidence that these ideals are naturally described as fanatical. But it is easy to see that these other types of perfection cannot serve as satisfactory personal ideals; for the realization of these ideals would be straightforwardly immoral. It may come as a surprise to some that there may in addition be such a thing as a *moral* fanatic.

Some will object that I am being unfair to "common-sense morality"—that it does not really require a moral saint to be either a disgusting goody-goody or an obsessive ascetic. Admittedly, there is no logical inconsistency between having any of the personal characteristics I have mentioned and being a moral saint. It is not morally wrong to notice the faults and shortcomings of others or to recognize and appreciate nonmoral talents and skills. Nor is it immoral to be an avid Celtics fan or to have a passion for caviar or to be an excellent cellist. With enough imagination, we can always contrive a suitable history and set of circumstances that will embrace such characteristics in one or another specific fictional story of a perfect moral saint.

If one turned onto the path of moral sainthood relatively late in life, one may have already developed interests that can be turned to moral purposes. It may be that a good golf game is just what is needed to secure that big donation to Oxfam. Perhaps the cultivation of one's exceptional artistic talent will turn out to be the way one can make one's greatest contribution to society. Furthermore, one might stumble upon joys and skills in the very service of morality. If, because the children are short a ninth player for the team, one's generous offer to serve reveals a natural fielding arm or if one's part in the campaign against nuclear power requires accepting a lobbyist's invitation to lunch at Le Lion d'Or, there is no moral gain in denying the satisfaction one gets from these activities. The moral saint, then, may, by happy accident, find himself with nonmoral virtues on which he can capitalize morally or which make psychological demands to which he has no choice but to attend. The point is that, for a moral saint, the existence of these interests and skills can be given at best the status of happy accidents—they cannot be encouraged for their own sakes as distinct, independent aspects of the realization of human good.

It must be remembered that from the fact that there is a tension between having any of these qualities and being a moral saint it does not follow that having any of these qualities is immoral. For it is not part of common-sense morality that one ought to be a moral saint. Still, if someone just happened to want to be a moral saint, he or she would not have or encourage these qualities, and on the basis of our common-sense values, this counts as a reason *not* to want to be a moral saint.

One might still wonder what kind of reason this is, and what kind of conclusion this properly allows us to draw. For the fact that the models of moral saints are unattractive does not necessarily mean that they are unsuitable ideals. Perhaps they are unattractive because they make us feel uncomfortable—they highlight our own weaknesses, vices, and flaws. If so, the fault lies not in the characters of the saints, but in those of our unsaintly selves.

To be sure, some of the reasons behind the disaffection we feel for the model of moral sainthood have to do with a reluctance to criticize ourselves and a reluctance to committing ourselves to trying to give up activities and interests that we heartily enjoy. These considerations might provide an *excuse* for the fact that we are not moral saints, but they do not provide a basis for criticizing sainthood as a possible ideal. Since these considerations rely on an appeal to the egoistic, hedonistic side of our natures, to use them as a basis for criticizing the ideal of the moral saint would be at best to beg the question and at worst to glorify features of ourselves that ought to be condemned.

The fact that the moral saint would be without qualities which we have and which, indeed, we like to have, does not in itself provide reason to condemn the ideal of the moral saint. The fact that some of these qualities are good qualities, however, and that they are qualities we *ought* to like, does provide reason to discourage this ideal and to offer other ideals in its place. In other words, some of the qualities the moral saint necessarily lacks are virtues, albeit nonmoral virtues, in the unsaintly characters who have them. The feats of Groucho Marx, Reggie Jackson, and the head chef at Lutèce are impressive accomplishments that it is not only permissible but positively appropriate to recognize as such. In general, the admiration of and striving toward achieving any of a great variety of forms of personal excellence are character traits it is valuable and desirable for people to have. In advocating the development of these varieties of excellence, we advocate nonmoral reasons for acting, and in thinking that it is good for a person to strive for an ideal that gives a substantial role to the interests and values that correspond to these virtues, we implicitly acknowledge the goodness of ideals incompatible with that of the moral saint. Finally, if we think that it is *as* good, or even better for a person to strive for one of these ideals than it is for him or her to strive for and realize the ideal of the moral saint, we express a conviction that it is good not to be a moral saint.

MORAL SAINTS AND MORAL THEORIES

I have tried so far to paint a picture—or, rather, two pictures—of what a moral saint might be like, drawing on what I take to be the attitudes and beliefs about morality prevalent in contemporary, common-sense thought. To my suggestion that common-sense morality generates conceptions of moral saints that are unattractive or otherwise unacceptable, it is open to someone to reply, "so much the worse for common-sense morality." After all, it is often claimed that the goal of moral philosophy is to correct and improve upon common-sense morality, and I have as yet given no attention to the question of what conceptions of moral sainthood, if any, are generated from the leading moral theories of our time.

A quick, breezy reading of utilitarian and Kantian writings will suggest the images, respectively, of the Loving Saint and the Rational Saint. A utilitarian, with his emphasis on happiness, will certainly prefer the Loving Saint to the Rational one, since the Loving Saint will himself be a happier person than the Rational Saint. A Kantian, with his emphasis on reason, on the other hand, will find at least as much to praise in the latter as in the former. Still, both models, drawn as they are from common sense, appeal to an impure mixture of utilitarian and Kantian intuitions. A more careful examination of these moral theories raises questions about whether either model of moral sainthood would really be advocated by a believer in the explicit doctrines associated with either of these views.

Certainly, the utilitarian in no way denies the value of self-realization. He in no way disparages the development of interests, talents, and other personally attractive traits that I have claimed the moral saint would be without. Indeed, since just these features enhance the happiness both of the individuals who possess them and of those with whom they associate, the ability to promote these features both in oneself and in others will have considerable positive weight in utilitarian calculations.

This implies that the utilitarian would not support moral sainthood as a universal ideal. A world in which everyone, or even a large number of people, achieved moral sainthood—even a world in which they *strove* to achieve it—would probably contain less happiness than a world in which people realized a diversity of ideals involving a variety of personal and perfectionist values. More pragmatic considerations also suggest that, if the utilitarian wants to influence more people to achieve more good, then he would do better to encourage them to pursue happiness-producing goals that are more attractive and more within a normal person's reach.

These considerations still leave open, however, the question of what kind of an ideal the committed utilitarian should privately aspire to himself. Utilitarianism requires him to want to achieve the greatest general happiness, and this would seem to commit him to the ideal of the moral saint.

One might try to use the claims I made earlier as a basis for an argument that a utilitarian should choose to give up utilitarianism. If, as I have said, a moral saint would be a less happy person both to be and to be around than many other possible ideals, perhaps one could create more total happiness by not trying too hard to promote the total happiness. But this argument is simply unconvincing in light of the empirical circumstances of our world. The gain in happiness that would accrue to oneself and one's neighbors by a more well-rounded, richer life than that of the moral saint would be pathetically small in comparison to the amount by which one could increase the general happiness if one devoted oneself explicitly to the care of the sick, the downtrodden, the starving, and the homeless. Of course, there may be psychological limits to the extent to which a person can devote himself to such things without going crazy. But the utilitarian's individual limitations would not thereby become a positive feature of his personal ideals.

The unattractiveness of the moral saint, then, ought not rationally convince the utilitarian to abandon his utilitarianism. It may, however, convince him to take efforts not to wear his saintly moral aspirations on his sleeve. If it is not too difficult, the utilitarian will try not to make those around him uncomfortable. He will not want to appear "holier than thou"; he will not want to inhibit others' ability to enjoy themselves. In practice, this might make the perfect utilitarian a less nauseating companion than the moral saint I earlier portrayed. But insofar as this kind of reasoning produces a more bearable public personality, it is at the cost of giving him a personality that must be evaluated as hypocritical and condescending when his private thoughts and attitudes are taken into account.

Still, the criticisms I have raised against the saint of common-sense morality should make some difference to the utilitarian's conception of an ideal which neither requires him to abandon his utilitarian principles nor forces him to fake an interest he does not have or a judgment he does not make. For it may be that a limited and carefully monitored allotment of time and energy to be devoted to the pursuit of some nonmoral interests or to the development of some nonmoral talents would make a person a better contributor to the general welfare than he would be if he allowed himself no indulgences of this sort. The enjoyment of such activities in no way compromises a commitment to utilitarian principles as long as the involvement with these activities is conditioned by a willingness to give them up whenever it is recognized that they cease to be in the general interest.

This will go some way in mitigating the picture of the loving saint that an understanding of utilitarianism will on first impression suggest. But I think it will not go very far. For the limitations on time and energy will have to be rather severe, and the need to monitor will restrict not only the extent but also the quality of one's attachment to these interests and traits. They are only weak and somewhat peculiar sorts of passions to which one can consciously remain so conditionally committed. Moreover, the way in which the utilitarian can enjoy these "extracurricular" aspects of his life is simply not the way in which these aspects are to be enjoyed insofar as they figure into our less saintly ideals.

The problem is not exactly that the utilitarian values these aspects of his life only as a means to an end, for the enjoyment he and others get from these aspects are not a means to, but a part of, the general happiness. Nonetheless, he values these things only because of and insofar as they *are* a part of the general happiness. He values them, as it were, under the description "a contribution to the general happiness." This is to be contrasted with the various ways in which these aspects of life may be valued by nonutilitarians. A person might love literature because of the insights into human nature literature affords. Another might love the cultivation of roses because roses are things of great beauty and delicacy. It may be true that these features of the respective activities also explain why these activities are happiness-producing. But, to the nonutilitarian, this may not be to the point. For if one values these activities in these more direct ways, one may not be willing to exchange them for others that produce an equal, or even a greater amount of happiness. From that point of view, it is not because they produce happiness that these activities are valuable; it is because these activities are valuable in more direct and specific ways that they produce happiness.

To adopt a phrase of Bernard Williams', the utilitarian's manner of valuing the not explicitly moral aspects of his life "provides (him) with one thought too many."[1] The requirement that the utilitarian have this thought—periodically, at least—is indicative of not only a weakness but a shallowness in his appreciation of the aspects in question. Thus, the ideals toward which a utilitarian could acceptably strive would remain too close to the model of the common-sense moral saint to escape the criticisms of that model which I earlier suggested. Whether a Kantian would be similarly committed to so restrictive and unattractive a range of possible ideals is a somewhat more difficult question.

The Kantian believes that being morally worthy consists in always acting from maxims that one could will to be universal law and doing this not out of any pathological desire but out of reverence for the moral law as such. Or, to take a different formulation of the categorical imperative, the Kantian believes that moral action consists in treating other persons always as ends and never as means only. Presumably, and according to Kant himself, the Kantian thereby commits himself to some degree of benevolence as well as to the rules of fair play. But we surely would not will that *every* person become a moral saint, and treating others as ends hardly requires bending over backwards to protect and promote their interests. On one interpretation of Kantian doctrine, then, moral perfection would be achieved simply by unerring obedience to a limited set of side-constraints. On this interpretation, Kantian theory simply does not yield an ideal conception of a person of any fullness comparable to that of the moral saints I have so far been portraying.

On the other hand, Kant does say explicitly that we have a duty of benevolence, a duty not only to allow others to pursue their ends, but to take up their ends as our own. In addition, we have positive duties to ourselves, duties to increase our natural as well as our moral perfection. These duties are unlimited in the degree to which they *may* dominate a life. If action in accordance with and motivated by the thought of these duties is considered virtuous, it is natural to assume that the more one performs such actions, the more virtuous one is. Moreover, of virtue in general Kant says, "it is an ideal which is unattainable while yet our duty is constantly to approximate to it."[2] On this interpretation, then, the Kantian moral saint, like the other moral saints I have been considering, is dominated by the motivation to be moral.

Which of these interpretations of Kant one prefers will depend on the interpretation and the importance one gives to the role of the imperfect duties in Kant's over-all system. Rather than choose between them here, I shall consider each briefly in turn.

On the second interpretation of Kant, the Kantian moral saint is, not surprisingly, subject to many of the same objections I have been raising against other versions of moral sainthood. Though the Kantian saint may differ from the utilitarian saint as to *which* actions he is bound to perform and which he is bound to refrain from performing, I suspect that the range of activities acceptable to the Kantian saint will remain objectionably restrictive. Moreover, the manner in which the Kantian saint must think about and justify the activities he pursues and the character traits he develops will strike us, as it did with the utilitarian saint, as containing "one thought too many." As the utilitarian could value his activities and character traits only insofar as they fell under the description of "contributions to the general happiness," the Kantian would have to value his activities and character traits insofar as they were manifestations of respect for the moral law. If the development of our powers to achieve physical, intellectual, or artistic excellence, or the activities directed toward making others happy are to have any moral worth, they must arise from a reverence for the dignity that members of our species have as a result of being endowed with pure practical reason. This is a good and noble motivation, to be sure. But it is hardly what one expects to be dominantly behind a person's aspirations to dance as well as Fred Astaire, to paint as well as Picasso, or to solve some outstanding problem in abstract algebra, and it is hardly what one hopes to find lying dominantly behind a father's action on behalf of his son or a lover's on behalf of her beloved.

Since the basic problem with any of the models of moral sainthood we have been considering is that they are dominated by a single, all-important value under which all other possible values must be subsumed, it may seem that the alternative interpretation of Kant, as providing a stringent but finite set of obligations and constraints, might provide a more acceptable morality. According to this interpretation of Kant, one is as morally good as can be so long as one devotes some limited portion of one's energies toward altruism and the maintenance of one's physical and spiritual health, and otherwise pursues one's independently motivated interests and values in such a way as to avoid overstepping certain bounds. Certainly, if it be a requirement of an acceptable moral theory that perfect obedience to its laws and maximal devotion to its interests and concerns be something we can wholeheartedly strive for in ourselves and wish for in those around us, it will count in favor of this brand of Kantianism that its commands can be fulfilled without swallowing up the perfect moral agent's entire personality.

Even this more limited understanding of morality, if its connection to Kant's views is to be taken at all seriously, is not likely to give an unqualified seal of approval to the nonmorally directed ideals I have been advocating. For Kant is explicit about what he calls "duties of apathy and self-mastery" (69/70)—duties to ensure that our passions are never so strong as to interfere with calm, practical deliberation, or so deep as to wrest control from the more disinterested, rational part of ourselves. That tight and self-conscious rein we are thus obliged to keep on our commitments to specific individuals and causes will doubtless restrict our value in these things, assigning them a necessarily attenuated place.

A more interesting objection to this brand of Kantianism, however, comes when we consider the implications of placing the kind of upper bound on moral worthiness which seemed to count in favor of this conception of morality. For to put such a limit on one's capacity to be moral is effectively to deny, not just the moral necessity, but the moral goodness of a devotion to benevolence and the maintenance of justice that passes beyond a certain, required point. It is to deny the possibility of going morally above and beyond the call of a restricted set of duties. Despite my claim that all-consuming moral saintliness is not a particularly healthy and desirable ideal, it seems perverse to insist that, were moral saints to exist, they would not, in their way, be remarkably noble and admirable figures. Despite my conviction that it is as rational and as good for a person to take Katharine Hepburn or Jane Austen as her role model instead of Mother Theresa, it would be absurd to deny that Mother Theresa is a morally better person.

I can think of two ways of viewing morality as having an upper bound. First, we can think that altruism and impartiality are indeed positive moral interests, but that they are moral only if the degree to which these interests are actively pursued remains within certain fixed limits. Second, we can think that these positive interests are only incidentally related to morality and that the essence of morality lies elsewhere, in, say, an implicit social contract or in the recognition of our own dignified rationality. According to the first conception of morality, there is a cutoff line to the amount of altruism or to the extent of devotion to justice and fairness that is worthy of moral praise. But to draw this line earlier than the line that brings the altruist in question into a worse-off position than all those to whom he devotes himself seems unacceptably artificial and gratuitous. According to the second conception, these positive interests are not essentially related to morality at all. But then we are unable to regard a more affectionate and generous expression of good will toward others as a natural and reasonable extension of morality, and we encourage a cold and unduly self-centered approach to the development and evaluation of our motivations and concerns.

A moral theory that does not contain the seeds of an all-consuming ideal of moral sainthood thus seems to place false and unnatural limits on our opportunity to do moral good and our potential to deserve moral praise. Yet the main thrust of the arguments of this paper has been leading to the conclusion that, when such ideals are present, they are not ideals to which it is particularly reasonable or healthy or desirable for human beings to aspire. These claims, taken together, have the appearance of a dilemma from which there is no obvious escape. In a moment, I shall argue that, despite appearances, these claims should not be understood as constituting a dilemma. But, before I do, let me briefly describe another path which those who are convinced by my above remarks may feel inclined to take.

If the above remarks are understood to be implicitly critical of the views on the content of morality which seem most popular today, an alternative that naturally suggests itself is that we revise our views about the content of morality. More specifically, my remarks may be taken to support a more Aristotelian, or even a more Nietzschean,* approach to moral philosophy. Such a change in approach involves substantially broadening or replacing our contemporary intuitions about which character traits constitute moral virtues and vices and which interests constitute moral interests. If, for example, we include personal bearing, or creativity, or sense of style, as features that contribute to one's *moral* personality, then we can create moral ideals which are incompatible with and probably more attractive than the Kantian and utilitarian ideals I have discussed. Given such an alteration of our conception of morality, the figures with which I have been concerned above might, far from being considered to be moral saints, be seen as morally inferior to other more appealing or more interesting models of individuals.

This approach seems unlikely to succeed, if for no other reason, because it is doubtful that any single, or even any reasonably small number of substantial personal ideals could capture the full range of possible ways of realizing human potential or achieving human good which deserve encouragement and praise. Even if we could provide a sufficiently broad characterization of the range of positive ways for human beings to live, however, I think there are strong reasons not to want to incorporate such a characterization more centrally into the framework of morality itself. For, in claiming that a character trait or activity is morally good, one claims that there is a certain kind of reason for developing that trait or engaging in that activity. Yet, lying behind our criticism of more conventional conceptions of moral sainthood, there seems to be a recognition that among the immensely valuable traits and activities that a human life might positively embrace are some of which we hope that, if a person does embrace them, he does so *not* for moral reasons. In other words, no matter how flexible we make the guide to conduct which we choose to label "morality," no matter how rich we make the life in which perfect obedience to this guide would result, we will have reason to hope that a person does not wholly rule and direct his life by the abstract and impersonal consideration that such a life would be morally good.

Once it is recognized that morality itself should not serve as a comprehensive guide to conduct, moreover, we can see reasons to retain the admittedly vague contemporary intuitions about what the classification of moral and nonmoral virtues, interests, and the like should be. That is, there seem to be important differences between the aspects of a person's life which are currently considered appropriate objects of moral evaluation and the aspects that might be included under the altered conception of morality we are now considering, which the latter approach would tend wrongly to blur or to neglect. Moral evaluation now is focused primarily on features of a person's life over which that person has control; it is largely restricted to aspects of his life which are likely to have considerable effect on other people. These restrictions seem as they should be. Even if responsible people could reach agreement as to what constituted good taste or a healthy degree of well-roundedness, for example, it seems wrong to insist that everyone try to achieve these things or to blame someone who fails or refuses to conform.

If we are not to respond to the unattractiveness of the moral ideals that contemporary theories yield either by offering alternative theories with more palatable ideals or by understanding these theories in such a way as to prevent them from yielding ideals at all, how, then, are we to respond? Simply, I think, by admitting that moral ideals do not, and need not, make the best personal ideals. Earlier, I mentioned one of the consequences of regarding as a test of an adequate moral theory that perfect obedience to its laws and maximal devotion to its interests be something we can wholeheartedly strive for in ourselves and wish for in those around us. Drawing out the consequences somewhat further should, I think, make us more doubtful of the proposed test than of

* Both the ancient Greek philosopher Aristotle (384–322 bce) and the German philosopher Friedrich Nietzsche (1844–1900) held views of morality according to which certain character traits that are considered morally irrelevant by many contemporary moral theories were taken to have moral significance.

the theories which, on this test, would fail. Given the empirical circumstances, of our world, it seems to be an ethical fact that we have unlimited potential to be morally good, and endless opportunity to promote moral interests. But this is not incompatible with the not-so-ethical fact that we have sound, compelling, and not particularly selfish reasons to choose not to devote ourselves univocally to realizing this potential or to taking up this opportunity.

Thus, in one sense at least, I am not really criticizing either Kantianism or utilitarianism. Insofar as the point of view I am offering bears directly on recent work in moral philosophy, in fact, it bears on critics of these theories who, in a spirit not unlike the spirit of most of this paper, point out that the perfect utilitarian would be flawed in this way or the perfect Kantian flawed in that.[3] The assumption lying behind these claims, implicitly or explicitly, has been that the recognition of these flaws shows us something wrong with utilitarianism as opposed to Kantianism, or something wrong with Kantianism as opposed to utilitarianism, or something wrong with both of these theories as opposed to some nameless third alternative. The claims of this paper suggest, however, that this assumption is unwarranted. The flaws of a perfect master of a moral theory need not reflect flaws in the intramoral content of the theory itself.

MORAL SAINTS AND MORAL PHILOSOPHY

In pointing out the regrettable features and the necessary absence of some desirable features in a moral saint, I have not meant to condemn the moral saint or the person who aspires to become one. Rather, I have meant to insist that the ideal of moral sainthood should not be held as a standard against which any other ideal must be judged or justified, and that the posture we take in response to the recognition that our lives are not as morally good as they might be need not be defensive.[4] It is misleading to insist that one is *permitted* to live a life in which the goals, relationships, activities, and interests that one pursues are not maximally morally good. For our lives are not so comprehensively subject to the requirement that we apply for permission, and our nonmoral reasons for the goals we set ourselves are not excuses, but may rather be positive, good reasons which do not exist *despite* any reasons that might threaten to outweigh them. In other words, a person may be *perfectly wonderful* without being *perfectly moral*.

Recognizing this requires a perspective which contemporary moral philosophy has generally ignored. This perspective yields judgments of a type that is neither moral nor egoistic. Like moral judgments, judgments about what it would be good for a person to be are made from a point of view outside the limits set by the values, interests, and desires that the person might actually have. And, like moral judgments, these judgments claim for themselves a kind of objectivity or a grounding in a perspective which any rational and perceptive being can take up. Unlike moral judgments, however, the good with which these judgments are concerned is not the good of anyone or any group other than the individual himself.

Nonetheless, it would be equally misleading to say that these judgments are made for the sake of the individual himself. For these judgments are not concerned with what kind of life it is in a person's interest to lead, but with what kind of interests it would be good for a person to have, and it need not be in a person's interest that he acquire or maintain objectively good interests. Indeed, the model of the Loving Saint, whose interests are identified with the interests of morality, is a model of a person for whom the dictates of rational self-interest and the dictates of morality coincide. Yet, I have urged that we have reason not to aspire to this ideal and that some of us would have reason to be sorry if our children aspired to and achieved it.

The moral point of view, we might say, is the point of view one takes up insofar as one takes the recognition of the fact that one is just one person among others equally real and deserving of the good things in life as a fact with practical consequences, a fact the recognition of which demands expression in one's actions and in the form of one's practical deliberations. Competing moral theories offer alternative answers to the question of what the most correct or the best way to express this fact is. In doing so, they offer alternative ways to evaluate and to compare the variety of actions, states of affairs, and so on that appear good and bad to agents from other, nonmoral points of view. But it seems that alternative interpretations of the moral point of view do not exhaust the ways in which our actions, characters, and their consequences can be comprehensively and objectively evaluated. Let us call the point of view from which we consider what kinds of lives are good lives, and what kinds of persons it would be good for ourselves and others to be, *the point of view of individual perfection.*

Since either point of view provides a way of comprehensively evaluating a person's life, each point of view takes account of, and, in a sense, subsumes the other. From the moral point of view, the perfection of an individual life will have some, but limited, value—for each individual remains, after all, just one person among others. From the perfectionist point of view, the moral worth of an individual's relation to his world will likewise have some, but limited, value—for, as I have argued, the (perfectionist) goodness of an individual's life does not vary proportionally with the degree to which it exemplifies moral goodness.

It may not be the case that the perfectionist point of view is like the moral point of view in being a point of view we are ever *obliged* to take up and express in our actions. Nonetheless, it provides us with reasons that are independent of moral reasons for wanting ourselves and others to develop our characters and live our lives in certain ways. When we take up this point of view and ask how much it would be good for an individual to act from the moral point of view, we do not find an obvious answer.[5]

The considerations of this paper suggest, at any rate, that the answer is not "as much as possible." This has implications both for the continued development of moral theories and for the development of metamoral views and for our conception of moral philosophy more generally. From the moral point of view, we have reasons to want people to live lives that seem good from outside that point of view. If, as I have argued, this means that we have reason to want people to live lives that are not morally perfect then any plausible moral theory must make use of some conception of supererogation.[6]

If moral philosophers are to address themselves at the most basic level to the question of how people should live, however, they must do more than adjust the content of their moral theories in ways that leave room for the affirmation of nonmoral values. They must examine explicitly the range and nature of these nonmoral values and, in light of this examination, they must ask how the acceptance of a moral theory is to be understood and acted upon. For the claims of this paper do not so much conflict with the content of any particular currently popular moral theory as they call into question a metamoral assumption that implicitly surrounds discussions of moral theory more generally. Specifically, they call into question the assumption that it is always better to be morally better.

The role morality plays in the development of our characters and the shape of our practical deliberations need be neither that of a universal medium into which all other values must be translated nor that of an ever-present filter through which all other values must pass. This is not to say that moral value should not be an important, even the most important, kind of value we attend to in evaluating and improving ourselves and our world. It is to say that our values cannot be fully comprehended on the model of a hierarchical system with morality at the top.

The philosophical temperament will naturally incline, at this point, toward asking, "What, then, *is* at the top—or, if there is no top, how *are* we to decide when and how much to be moral?" In other words, there is a temptation to seek a metamoral—though not, in the standard sense, metaethical—theory that will give us principles, or, at least, informal directives on the basis of which we can develop and evaluate more comprehensive personal ideals. Perhaps a theory that distinguishes among the various roles a person is expected to play within a life—as professional, as citizen, as friend, and so on—might give us some rules that would offer us, if nothing else, a better framework in which to think about and discuss these questions. I am pessimistic, however, about the chances of such a theory to yield substantial and satisfying results. For I do not see how a metamoral theory could be constructed which would not be subject to considerations parallel to those which seem inherently to limit the appropriateness of regarding moral theories as ultimate comprehensive guides for action.

This suggests that, at some point, both in our philosophizing and in our lives, we must be willing to raise normative questions from a perspective that is unattached to a commitment to any particular well-ordered system of values. It must be admitted that, in doing so, we run the risk of finding normative answers that diverge from the answers given by whatever moral theory one accepts. This, I take it, is the grain of truth in G. E. Moore's "open question" argument.* In the background of this paper, then, there lurks a commitment to what seems to me to be a healthy form of intuitionism. It is a form of intuitionism which is not intended to take the place of more rigorous, systematically developed, moral theories—rather, it is intended to put these more rigorous and systematic moral theories in their place.

NOTES

1. "Persons, Character and Morality" in Amelie Rorty, ed., *The Identities of Persons* (Berkeley: University of California Press, 1976), p. 214.
2. Immanuel Kant, *The Doctrine of Virtue*, Mary J. Gregor, trans. (New York: Harper & Row, 1964), p. 71.
3. See, e.g., Williams op. cit. and J. J. C. Smart and Bernard Williams, *Utilitarianism: For and Against* (New York: Cambridge, 1973). Also, Michael Stocker, "The Schizophrenia of Modern Ethical Theories," *Journal of Philosophy*, LXXIII, 14 (August 12, 1976): 453–466.
4. George Orwell makes a similar point in "Reflections on Gandhi," in *A Collection of Essays by George Orwell* (New York: Harcourt Brace Jovanovich, 1945), p. 176: "sainthood is . . . a thing that human beings must avoid . . . It is too readily assumed that . . . the ordinary man only rejects it because it is too difficult, in other words, that the average human being is a failed saint. It is doubtful whether this is true. Many people genuinely do not wish to be saints, and it is probable that some who achieve or aspire to sainthood have never felt much temptation to be human beings."
5. A similar view, which has strongly influenced mine, is expressed by Thomas Nagel in "The Fragmentation of Value," in *Mortal Questions* (New York: Cambridge, 1979), pp. 128–141. Nagel focuses on the difficulties such apparently incommensurable points of view create for specific, isolable practical decisions that must be made both by individuals and by societies. In focusing on the way in which these points of view figure into the development of individual personal ideals, the questions with which I am concerned are more likely to lurk in the background of any individual's life.
6. The variety of forms that a conception of supererogation might take, however, has not generally been noticed. Moral theories that make use of this notion typically do so by identifying some specific set of principles as universal moral requirements and supplement this list with a further set of directives which it is morally praiseworthy but not required for an agent to follow. [See, e.g., Charles Fried, *Right and Wrong* (Cambridge, Mass.: Harvard, 1979).] But it is possible that the ability to live a morally blameless life cannot be so easily or definitely secured as this type of theory would suggest. The fact that there are some situations in which an agent is morally required to do something and other situations in which it would be good but not required for an agent to act in accordance with those principles.

* British philosopher G. E. Moore's (1873–1958) "open question argument" purports to show that any attempt to explain moral notions in terms of nonmoral notions is doomed to failure.

Egoism and Moral Scepticism

JAMES RACHELS

James Rachels (1941–2003) was an American moral philosopher who taught for many years at the University of Alabama at Birmingham. His precise yet accessible writings have been widely anthologized.

The selection that appears next was originally published in 1971 in an introductory anthology edited by Steven M. Cahn. In it, Rachels considers and rejects a number of arguments in favor of ethical egoism.

1. Our ordinary thinking about morality is full of assumptions that we almost never question. We assume, for example, that we have an obligation to consider the welfare of other people when we decide what actions to perform or what rules to obey; we think that we must refrain from acting in ways harmful to others, and that we must respect their rights and interests as well as our own. We also assume that people are in fact capable of being motivated by such considerations, that is, that people are not wholly selfish and that they do sometimes act in the interests of others.

Both of these assumptions have come under attack by moral sceptics, as long ago as by Glaucon in Book II of Plato's *Republic*. Glaucon recalls the legend of Gyges, a shepherd who was said to have found a magic ring in a fissure opened by an earthquake. The ring would make its wearer invisible and thus would enable him to go anywhere and do anything undetected. Gyges used the power of the ring to gain entry to the Royal Palace where he seduced the Queen, murdered the King, and subsequently seized the throne. Now Glaucon asks us to imagine that there are two such rings, one given to a man of virtue and one given to a rogue. The rogue, of course, will use his ring unscrupulously and do anything necessary to increase his own wealth and power. He will recognize no moral constraints on his conduct, and, since the cloak of invisibility will protect him from discovery, he can do anything he pleases without fear of reprisal. So, there will be no end to the mischief he will do. But how will the so-called virtuous man behave? Glaucon suggests that he will behave no better than the rogue: "No one, it is commonly believed, would have such iron strength of mind as to stand fast in doing right or keep his hands off other men's goods, when he could go to the market-place and fearlessly help himself to anything he wanted, enter houses and sleep with any woman he chose, set prisoners free and kill men at his pleasure, and in a word go about among men with the powers of a god. He would behave no better than the other; both would take the same course."[1] Moreover, why shouldn't he? Once he is freed from the fear of reprisal, why shouldn't a man simply do what he pleases, or what he thinks is best for himself? What reason is there for him to continue being "moral" when it is clearly not to his own advantage to do so?

These sceptical views suggested by Glaucon have come to be known as *psychological egoism* and *ethical egoism* respectively. Psychological egoism is the view that all men are selfish in everything that they do, that is, that the only motive from which anyone ever acts is self-interest. On this view, even when men are acting in ways apparently calculated to benefit others,

From *A New Introduction to Philosophy* (New York: Harper & Row, 1971), ed. Steven M. Cahn. Reprinted by permission of Steven M. Cahn.

they are actually motivated by the belief that acting in this way is to their own advantage, and if they did not believe this, they would not be doing that action. Ethical egoism is, by contrast, a normative view about how men *ought* to act. It is the view that, regardless of how men do in fact behave, they have no obligation to do anything except what is in their own interests. According to the ethical egoist, a person is always justified in doing whatever is in his own interests, regardless of the effect on others.

Clearly, if either of these views is correct, then "the moral institution of life" (to use Butler's well-turned phrase) is very different than what we normally think. The majority of mankind is grossly deceived about what is, or ought to be, the case, where morals are concerned.

2. Psychological egoism seems to fly in the face of the facts. We are tempted to say: "Of course people act unselfishly all the time. For example, Smith gives up a trip to the country, which he would have enjoyed very much, in order to stay behind and help a friend with his studies, which is a miserable way to pass the time. This is a perfectly clear case of unselfish behavior, and if the psychological egoist thinks that such cases do not occur, then he is just mistaken." Given such obvious instances of "unselfish behavior," what reply can the egoist make? There are two general arguments by which he might try to show that all actions, including those such as the one just outlined, are in fact motivated by self-interest. Let us examine these in turn:

A. The first argument goes as follows. If we describe one person's action as selfish, and another person's action as unselfish, we are overlooking the crucial fact that in both cases, assuming that the action is done voluntarily, *the agent is merely doing what he most wants to do*. If Smith stays behind to help his friend, that only shows that he wanted to help his friend more than he wanted to go to the country. And why should he be praised for his "unselfishness" when he is only doing what he most wants to do? So, since Smith is only doing what he wants to do, he cannot be said to be acting unselfishly.

This argument is so bad that it would not deserve to be taken seriously except for the fact that so many otherwise intelligent people have been taken in by it. First, the argument rests on the premise that people never voluntarily do anything except what they want to do. But this is patently false; there are at least two classes of actions that are exceptions to this generalization. One is the set of actions which we may not want to do, but which we do anyway as a means to an end which we want to achieve; for example, going to the dentist in order to stop a toothache, or going to work every day in order to be able to draw our pay at the end of the month. These cases may be regarded as consistent with the spirit of the egoist argument, however, since the ends mentioned are wanted by the agent. But the other set of actions are those which we do, not because we want to, nor even because there is an end which we want to achieve, but because we feel ourselves *under an obligation* to do them. For example, someone may do something because he has promised to do it, and thus feels obligated, even though he does not want to do it. It is sometimes suggested that in such cases we do the action because, after all, we want to keep our promises; so, even here, we are doing what we want. However, this dodge will not work: if I have promised to do something, and if I do not want to do it, then it is simply false to say that I want to keep my promise. In such cases we feel a conflict precisely because we do *not* want to do what we feel obligated to do. It is reasonable to think that Smith's action falls roughly into this second category: he might stay behind, not because he wants to, but because he feels that his friend needs help.

But suppose we were to concede, for the sake of the argument, that all voluntary action is motivated by the agent's wants, or at least that Smith is so motivated. Even if this were granted, it would not follow that Smith is acting selfishly or from self-interest. For if Smith wants to do something that will help his friend, even when it means forgoing his own enjoyments, that is precisely what makes him *un*selfish. What else could unselfishness be, if not wanting to help others? Another way to put the same point is to say that it is the *object* of a want that determines whether it is selfish or not. The mere fact that I am acting on *my* wants does not mean that I am acting selfishly; that depends on *what it is* that I want. If I want only my own good, and care nothing for others, then I am selfish; but if I also want other people to be well-off and happy, and if I act on *that* desire, then my action is not selfish. So much for this argument.

B. The second argument for psychological egoism is this. Since so-called unselfish actions always produce a sense of self-satisfaction in the agent,[2] and since this sense of satisfaction is a pleasant state of consciousness, it follows that the point of the action is really to achieve a pleasant state of consciousness, rather than to bring about any good for others. Therefore, the action is "unselfish" only at a superficial level of analysis. Smith will feel much better with himself for having stayed to help his friend—if he had gone to the country, he would have felt terrible about it—and that is the real point of the action. According to a well-known story, this argument was once expressed by Abraham Lincoln:

> Mr. Lincoln once remarked to a fellow-passenger on an old-time mud-coach that all men were prompted by selfishness in doing good. His fellow-passenger was antagonizing this position when they were passing over a corduroy bridge that spanned a slough. As they crossed this bridge they espied an old razor-backed sow on the bank making a terrible noise because her pigs had got into the slough and were in danger of drowning. As the old coach began to climb the hill, Mr. Lincoln called out, "Driver, can't you stop just a moment?" Then Mr. Lincoln jumped out, ran back, and lifted the little pigs out of the mud and water and placed them on the bank. When he returned, his companion remarked: "Now, Abe, where does selfishness come in on this little episode?" "Why, bless your soul, Ed, that was the very essence of selfishness. I should have had no peace of mind all day had I gone on and left that suffering old sow worrying over those pigs. I did it to get peace of mind, don't you see?"[3]

This argument suffers from defects similar to the previous one. Why should we think that merely because someone derives satisfaction from helping others this makes him selfish? Isn't the unselfish man precisely the one who *does* derive satisfaction from helping others, while the selfish man does not? If Lincoln "got peace of mind" from rescuing the piglets, does this show him to be selfish, or, on the contrary, doesn't it show him to be compassionate and good-hearted? (If a man were truly selfish, why should it bother his conscience that *others* suffer—much less pigs?) Similarly, it is nothing more than shabby sophistry to say, because Smith takes satisfaction in helping his friend, that he is behaving selfishly. If we say this rapidly, while thinking about something else, perhaps it will sound all right; but if we speak slowly, and pay attention to what we are saying, it sounds plain silly.

Moreover, suppose we ask *why* Smith derives satisfaction from helping his friend. The answer will be, it is because Smith cares for him and wants him to succeed. If Smith did not have these concerns, then he would take no pleasure in assisting him; and these concerns, as we have already seen, are the marks of unselfishness, not selfishness. To put the point more generally: if we have a positive attitude toward the attainment of some goal, then we may derive satisfaction from attaining that goal. But the *object* of our attitude is *the attainment of that goal*; and we must want to attain the goal *before* we can find any satisfaction in it. We do not, in other words, desire some sort of "pleasurable consciousness" and then try to figure out how to achieve it; rather, we desire all sorts of different things—money, a new fishing-boat, to be a better chess-player, to get a promotion in our work, etc.—and because we desire these things, we derive satisfaction from attaining them. And so, if someone desires the welfare and happiness of another person, he will derive satisfaction from that: but this does not mean that this satisfaction is the object of his desire, or that he is in any way selfish on account of it.

It is a measure of the weakness of psychological egoism that these insupportable arguments are the ones most often advanced in its favor. Why, then, should anyone ever have thought it a true view? Perhaps because of a desire for theoretical simplicity: In thinking about human conduct, it would be nice if there were some simple formula that would unite the diverse phenomena of human behavior under a single explanatory principle, just as simple formulae in physics bring together a great many apparently different phenomena. And since it is obvious that self-regard is an overwhelmingly important factor in motivation, it is only natural to wonder whether all motivation might not be explained in these terms. But the answer is clearly No; while a great many human actions are motivated entirely or in part by self-interest, only by a deliberate distortion of the facts can we say that all conduct is so motivated. This will be clear, I think, if we correct three confusions which are commonplace. The exposure of these confusions will remove the last traces of plausibility from the psychological egoist thesis.

The first is the confusion of selfishness with self-interest. The two are clearly not the same. If I see a physician when I am feeling poorly, I am acting in my own interest but no one would think of calling me "selfish" on account of it. Similarly, brushing my teeth, working hard at my job, and obeying the law are all in my self-interest but none of these are examples of selfish conduct. This is because selfish behavior is behavior that ignores the interests of others, in circumstances in which their interests ought not to be ignored. This concept has a definite evaluative flavor; to call someone "selfish" is not just to describe his action but to condemn it. Thus, you would not call me selfish for eating a normal meal in normal circumstances (although it may surely be in my self-interest); but you would call me selfish for hoarding food while others about are starving.

The second confusion is the assumption that every action is done *either* from self-interest or from other-regarding motives. Thus, the egoist concludes that if there is no such thing as genuine altruism then all actions must be done from self-interest. But this is certainly a false dichotomy. The man who continues to smoke cigarettes, even after learning about the connection between smoking and cancer, is surely not acting from self-interest, not even by his own standards—self-interest would dictate that he quit smoking at once—and he is not acting altruistically either. He *is*, no doubt, smoking for the pleasure of it, but all that this shows is that undisciplined pleasure-seeking and acting from self-interest are very different. This is what led Butler to remark that "The thing to be lamented is, not that men have so great regard to their own good or interest in the present world, for they have not enough."[4]

The last two paragraphs show (*a*) that it is false that all actions are selfish, and (*b*) that it is false that all actions are done out of self-interest. And it should be noted that these two points can be made, and were, without any appeal to putative examples of altruism.

The third confusion is the common but false assumption that a concern for one's own welfare is incompatible with any genuine concern for the welfare of others. Thus, since it is obvious that everyone (or very nearly everyone) does desire his own well-being, it might be thought that no one can really be concerned with others. But again, this is false. There is no inconsistency in desiring that everyone, including oneself *and* others, be well-off and happy. To be sure, it may happen on occasion that our own interests conflict with the interests of others, and in these cases we will have to make hard choices. But even in these cases we might sometimes opt for the interests of others, especially when the others involved are our family or friends. But more importantly, not all cases are like this: sometimes we are able to promote the welfare of others when our own interests are not involved at all. In these cases not even the strongest self-regard need prevent us from acting considerately toward others.

Once these confusions are cleared away, it seems to me obvious enough that there is no reason whatever to accept psychological egoism. On the contrary, if we simply observe people's behavior with an open mind, we may find that a great deal of it is motivated by self-regard, but by no means all of it; and that there is no reason to deny that "the moral institution of life" can include a place for the virtue of beneficence.[5]

3. The ethical egoist would say at this point, "Of course it is possible for people to act altruistically, and perhaps many people do act that way—but there is no reason why they *should* do so. A person is under no obligation to do anything except what is in his own interests."[6] This is really quite a radical doctrine. Suppose I have an urge to set fire to some public building (say, a department store) just for the fascination of watching the spectacular blaze: according to this view, the fact that several people might be burned to death provides no reason whatever why I should not do it. After all, this only concerns *their* welfare, not my own, and according to the ethical egoist the only person I need think of is myself.

Some might deny that ethical egoism has any such monstrous consequences. They would point out that it is really to my own advantage not to set the fire—for, if I do that I may be caught and put into prison (unlike Gyges, I have no magic ring for protection). Moreover, even if I could avoid being caught it is still to my advantage to respect the rights and interests of others, for it is to my advantage to live in a society in which people's rights and interests are respected. Only in such a society can I live a happy and secure life; so, in acting kindly toward others, I would merely be doing my part to create and maintain the sort of society which it is to my advantage to have.[7] Therefore, it is said, the egoist would not be such a bad man; he would be as kindly and considerate as anyone else, because he would see that it is to his own advantage to be kindly and considerate.

This is a seductive line of thought, but it seems to me mistaken. Certainly it is to everyone's advantage (including the egoist's) to preserve a stable society where people's interests are generally protected. But there is no reason for the egoist to think that merely because *he* will not honor the rules of the social game, decent society will collapse. For the vast majority of people are not egoists, and there is no reason to think that they will be converted by his example—especially if he is discreet and does not unduly flaunt his style of life. What this line of reasoning shows is not that the egoist himself must act benevolently, but that he must encourage *others* to do so. He must take care to conceal from public view his own self-centered method of decision-making, and urge others to act on precepts very different from those on which he is willing to act.

The rational egoist, then, cannot advocate that egoism be universally adopted by everyone. For he wants a world in which his own interests are maximized; and if other people adopted the egoistic policy of pursuing their own interests to the exclusion of his interests, as he pursues his interests to the exclusion of theirs, then such a world would be impossible. So he himself will be an egoist, but he will want others to be altruists.

This brings us to what is perhaps the most popular "refutation" of ethical egoism current among philosophical writers—the argument that ethical egoism is at bottom inconsistent because it cannot be universalized.[8] The argument goes like this:

To say that any action or policy of action is *right* (or that it *ought* to be adopted) entails that it is right for *anyone* in the same sort of circumstances. I cannot, for example, say that it is right for me to lie to you, and yet object when you lie to me (provided, of course, that the circumstances are the same). I cannot hold that it is all right for me to drink your beer and then complain when you drink mine. This is just the requirement that we be consistent in our evaluations; it is a requirement of logic. Now it is said that ethical egoism cannot meet this requirement because, as we have already seen, the egoist would not want others to act in the same way that he acts. Moreover, suppose he *did* advocate the universal adoption of egoistic policies: he would be saying to Peter, "You ought to pursue your own interests even if it means destroying Paul"; and he would be saying to Paul, "You ought to pursue your own interests even if it means destroying Peter." The attitudes expressed in these two recommendations seem clearly inconsistent—he is urging the advancement of Peter's interest at one moment, and countenancing their defeat at the next. Therefore, the argument goes, there is no way to maintain the doctrine of ethical egoism as a consistent view about how we ought to act. We will fall into inconsistency whenever we try.

What are we to make of this argument? Are we to conclude that ethical egoism has been refuted? Such a conclusion, I think, would be unwarranted; for I think that we can show, contrary to this argument, how ethical egoism can be maintained consistently. We need only to interpret the egoist's position in a sympathetic way: we should say that he has in mind a certain kind of world which he would prefer over all others; it would be a world in which his own interests were maximized, regardless of the effects on other people. The egoist's primary policy of action, then, would be to act in such a way as to bring about, as nearly as possible, this sort of world. Regardless of however morally reprehensible we might find it, there is nothing *inconsistent* in someone's adopting this as his ideal and acting in a way calculated to bring it about. And if someone did adopt this as his ideal, then he would not advocate universal egoism; as we have already seen, he would want other people to be altruists. So, if he advocates any principles of conduct for the general public, they will be altruistic principles. This would not be inconsistent; on the contrary, it would be perfectly consistent with his goal of creating a world in which his own interests are maximized. To be sure, he would have to be deceitful; in order to secure the good will of others, and a favorable hearing for his exhortations to altruism, he would have to pretend that he was himself prepared to accept altruistic principles. But again, that would be all right; from the egoist's point of view, this would merely be a matter of adopting the necessary means to the achievement of his goal—and while we might not approve of this, there is nothing inconsistent about it. Again, it might be said: "He advocates one thing, but does another. Surely *that's* inconsistent." But it is not; for what he advocates and what he does are both calculated as means to an end (the *same* end, we might note); and as such, he is doing what is rationally required in each case. Therefore, contrary to the previous argument, there is nothing inconsistent in the ethical egoist's view. He cannot be refuted by the claim that he contradicts himself.

Is there, then, no way to refute the ethical egoist? If by "refute" we mean show that he has made some *logical* error, the answer is that there is not. However, there is something more that can be said. The egoist challenge to our ordinary moral convictions amounts to a demand for an explanation of why we should adopt certain policies of action, namely policies in which the good of others is given importance. We can give an answer to this demand, albeit an indirect one. The reason one ought not to do actions that would hurt other people is: other people would be hurt. The reason one ought to do actions that would benefit other people is: other people would be benefited. This may at first seem like a piece of philosophical sleight-of-hand, but it is not. The point is that the welfare of human beings is something that most of us value *for its own sake*, and not merely for the sake of something else. Therefore, when *further* reasons are demanded for valuing the welfare of human beings, we cannot point to anything further to satisfy this demand. It is not that we have no reason for pursuing these policies, but that our reason *is* that these policies are for the good of human beings.

So: if we are asked "Why shouldn't I set fire to this department store?" one answer would be "Because if you do, people may be burned to death." This is a complete, sufficient reason which does not require qualification or supplementation of any sort. If someone seriously wants to know why this action shouldn't be done, that's the reason. If we are pressed further and asked the sceptical question "But why shouldn't I do actions that will harm others?" we may not know what to say—but this is because the questioner has included in his question the very answer we would like to give: "Why shouldn't you do actions that will harm others? Because, doing those actions would harm others."

The egoist, no doubt, will not be happy with this. He will protest that *we* may accept this as a reason, but *he* does not. And here the argument stops: there are limits to what can be accomplished by argument, and if the egoist really doesn't care about other people—if he honestly doesn't care whether they are helped or hurt by his actions—then we have reached those limits. If we want to persuade him to act decently toward his fellow humans, we will have to make our appeal to such other attitudes as he does possess, by threats, bribes, or other cajolery. That is all that we can do.

Though some may find this situation distressing (we would like to be able to show that the egoist is just *wrong*), it holds no embarrassment for common morality. What we have come up against is simply a fundamental requirement of rational action, namely, that the existence of reasons for action always depends on the prior existence of certain attitudes in the agent. For example, the fact that a certain course of action would make the agent a lot of money is a reason for doing it only if the agent wants to make money; the fact that practicing at chess makes one a better player is a reason for practicing only if one wants to be a better player; and so on. Similarly, the fact that a certain action would help the agent is a reason for doing the action only if the agent cares about his own welfare, and the fact that an action would help others is a reason for doing it only if the agent cares about others. In this respect ethical egoism and what we might call ethical altruism are in exactly the same fix: both require that the agent *care* about himself, or about other people, before they can get started.

So a nonegoist will accept "It would harm another person" as a reason not to do an action simply because he cares about what happens to that other person. When the egoist says that he does *not* accept that as a reason, he is saying something quite extraordinary. He is saying that he has no affection for friends or family, that he never feels pity or compassion, that he is the sort of person who can look on scenes of human misery with complete indifference, so long as he is not the one suffering. Genuine egoists, people who really don't care at all about anyone other than themselves, are rare. It is important to keep this in mind when thinking about ethical egoism; it is easy to forget just how fundamental to human psychological makeup the feeling of sympathy is. Indeed, a man without any sympathy at all would scarcely be recognizable as a man; and that is what makes ethical egoism such a disturbing doctrine in the first place.

4. There are, of course, many different ways in which the sceptic might challenge the assumptions underlying our moral practice. In this essay I have discussed only two of them, the two put forward by Glaucon in the passage that I cited from Plato's *Republic*. It is important that the assumptions underlying our moral practice should not be confused with particular judgments made within that practice. To defend one is not to defend the other. We may assume—quite properly, if my analysis has been correct—that the virtue of beneficence does, and indeed should, occupy an important place in "the moral institution of life"; and yet we may make constant and miserable errors when it comes to judging when and in what ways this virtue is to be exercised. Even worse, we may often be able to make accurate moral judgments, and know what we ought to do, but not do it. For these ills, philosophy alone is not the cure.

NOTES

1. *The Republic of Plato*, translated by F. M. Cornford (Oxford, 1941), p. 45.
2. Or, as it is sometimes said, "It gives him a clear conscience," or "He couldn't sleep at night if he had done otherwise," or "He would have been ashamed of himself for not doing it," and so on.
3. Frank C. Sharp, *Ethics* (New York, 1928), pp. 74–75. Quoted from the Springfield (Ill.) *Monitor* in the *Outlook*, vol. 56, p. 1059.
4. *The Works of Joseph Butler*, edited by W. E. Gladstone (Oxford, 1896), vol. II, p. 26. It should be noted that most of the points I am making against psychological egoism were first made by Butler. Butler made all the important points; all that is left for us is to remember them.
5. The capacity for altruistic behavior is not unique to human beings. Some interesting experiments with rhesus monkeys have shown that these animals will refrain from operating a device for securing food if this causes other animals to suffer pain. See Masserman, Wechkin, and Terris, "'Altruistic Behavior in Rhesus Monkeys," *The American Journal of Psychiatry*, vol. 121 (1964), 584–585.
6. I take this to be the view of Ayn Rand, in so far as I understand her confusing doctrine.
7. Cf. Thomas Hobbes, *Leviathan* (London, 1651), chap. 17.
8. See, for example, Brian Medlin, "Ultimate Principles and Ethical Egoism," *Australasian Journal of Philosophy*, vol. 35 (1957), 111–118; and D. H. Monro, *Empiricism and Ethics* (Cambridge, 1967), chap. 16.

The Challenge of Cultural Relativism

JAMES RACHELS

James Rachels (1941–2003) was an American moral philosopher who taught for many years at the University of Alabama at Birmingham. His precise yet accessible writings have been widely anthologized.

This selection is an excerpt from Rachels's introductory book, *The Elements of Moral Philosophy*. In it, Rachels considers and rejects a number of arguments in favor of moral relativism.

> Morality differs in every society, and is a convenient term for socially approved habits.
>
> RUTH BENEDICT, *PATTERNS OF CULTURE* (1934)

1. HOW DIFFERENT CULTURES HAVE DIFFERENT MORAL CODES

Darius, a king of ancient Persia, was intrigued by the variety of cultures he encountered in his travels. He had found, for example, that the Callatians (a tribe of Indians) customarily ate the bodies of their dead fathers. The Greeks, of course, did not do that—the Greeks practiced cremation and regarded the funeral pyre as the natural and fitting way to dispose of the dead. Darius thought that a sophisticated understanding of the world must include an appreciation of such differences between cultures. One day, to teach this lesson, he summoned some Greeks who happened to be present at his court and asked them what they would take to eat the bodies of their dead fathers. They were shocked, as Darius knew they would be, and replied that no amount of money could persuade them to do such a thing. Then Darius called in some Callatians, and while the Greeks listened asked them what they would take to burn their dead fathers' bodies. The Callatians were horrified and told Darius not even to mention such a dreadful thing.

This story, recounted by Herodotus* in his *History*, illustrates a recurring theme in the literature of social science: different cultures have different moral codes. What is thought right within one group may be utterly abhorrent to the members of another group, and vice versa. Should we eat the bodies of the dead or burn them? If you were a Greek, one answer would seem obviously correct; but if you were a Callatian, the opposite would seem equally certain.

It is easy to give additional examples of the same kind. Consider the Eskimos.* They are a remote and inaccessible people. Numbering only about 25,000, they live in small, isolated settlements scattered mostly along the northern fringes of North America and Greenland. Until the beginning of the 20th century, the outside world knew little about them. Then explorers began to bring back strange tales.

Eskimo customs turned out to be very different from our own. The men often had more than one wife, and they would share their wives with guests, lending them for the night as a sign of hospitality. Moreover, within a community a dominant male might demand and get regular sexual access to other men's wives. The women however, were free to break these arrangements simply by leaving their

* Herodotus was an ancient Greek historian who lived in the 5th century BCE.

* At the time this article was written, "Eskimo" was a commonly used term for referring to the native peoples of the circumpolar region (the Inuit and Yupik).

From James Rachels, *Elements of Moral Philosophy, Fourth Edition* (New York: McGraw-Hill, 2002). Reprinted with permission of the McGraw-Hill Companies.

husbands and taking up with new partners—free, that is, so long as their former husbands chose not to make trouble. All in all, the Eskimo practice was a volatile scheme that bore little resemblance to what we call marriage.

But it was not only their marriage and sexual practices that were different. The Eskimos also seemed to have less regard for human life. Infanticide, for example, was common. Knud Rasmussen, one of the most famous early explorers, reported that he met one woman who had borne 20 children but had killed 10 of them at birth. Female babies, he found, were especially liable to be destroyed, and this was permitted simply at the parents' discretion, with no social stigma attached to it. Old people also, when they became too feeble to contribute to the family, were left out in the snow to die. So there seemed to be, in this society, remarkably little respect for life.

To the general public, these were disturbing revelations. Our own way of living seems so natural and right that for many of us it is hard to conceive of others living so differently. And when we do hear of such things, we tend immediately to categorize the other peoples as "backward" or "primitive. But to anthropologists, there was nothing particularly surprising about the Eskimos. Since the time of Herodotus, enlightened observers have been accustomed to the idea that conceptions of right and wrong differ from culture to culture. If we assume that our ethical ideas will be shared by all peoples at all times, we are merely naive.

2. CULTURAL RELATIVISM

To many thinkers, this observation—"Different cultures have different moral codes"—has seemed to be the key to understanding morality. The idea of universal truth in ethics, they say, is a myth. The customs of different societies are all that exist. These customs cannot be said to be "correct" or "incorrect," for that implies we have an independent standard of right and wrong by which they may be judged. But there is no such independent standard; every standard is culture-bound. The great pioneering sociologist William Graham Sumner, writing in 1906, put it like this:

> The "right" way is the way which the ancestors used and which has been handed down. The tradition is its own warrant. It is not held subject to verification by experience. The notion of right is in the folkways. It is not outside of them, of independent origin, and brought to test them. In the folkways, whatever is, is right. This is because they are traditional, and therefore contain in themselves the authority of the ancestral ghosts. When we come to the folkways we are at the end of our analysis.

This line of thought has probably persuaded more people to be skeptical about ethics than any other single thing. Cultural Relativism, as it has been called, challenges our ordinary belief in the objectivity and universality of moral truth. It says, in effect, that there is no such thing as universal truth in ethics; there are only the various cultural codes, and nothing more. Moreover, our own code has no special status; it is merely one among many. As we shall see, this basic idea is really a compound of several different thoughts. It is important to separate the various elements of the theory because, on analysis, some parts turn out to be correct, while others seem to be mistaken. As a beginning, we may distinguish the following claims, all of which have been made by cultural relativists:

1. Different societies have different moral codes.
2. The moral code of a society determines what is right within that society; that is, if the moral code of a society says that a certain action is right, then that action *is* right, at least within that society.
3. There is no objective standard that can be used to judge one society's code better than another's.
4. The moral code of our own society has no special status; it is merely one among many.
5. There is no "universal truth" in ethics; that is, there are no moral truths that hold for all peoples at all times.
6. It is mere arrogance for us to try to judge the conduct of other peoples. We should adopt an

attitude of tolerance toward the practices of other cultures.

Although it may seem that these six propositions go naturally together, they are independent of one another, in the sense that some of them might be false even if others are true. In what follows, we will try to identify what is correct in Cultural Relativism, but we will also be concerned to expose what is mistaken about it.

3. THE CULTURAL DIFFERENCES ARGUMENT

Cultural Relativism is a theory about the nature of morality. At first blush it seems quite plausible. However, like all such theories, it may be evaluated by subjecting it to rational analysis; and when we analyze Cultural Relativism we find that it is not so plausible as it first appears to be.

The first thing we need to notice is that at the heart of Cultural Relativism there is a certain *form of argument*. The strategy used by cultural relativists is to argue from facts about the differences between cultural outlooks to a conclusion about the status of morality. Thus we are invited to accept this reasoning:

(1) The Greeks believed it was wrong to eat the dead, whereas the Callatians believed it was right to eat the dead.
(2) Therefore, eating the dead is neither objectively right nor objectively wrong. It is merely a matter of opinion that varies from culture to culture.

Or, alternatively:

(1) The Eskimos see nothing wrong with infanticide, whereas Americans believe infanticide is immoral.
(2) Therefore, infanticide is neither objectively right nor objectively wrong. It is merely a matter of opinion, which varies from culture to culture.

Clearly, these arguments are variations of one fundamental idea. They are both special cases of a more general argument, which says:

(1) Different cultures have different moral codes.
(2) Therefore, there is no objective "truth" in morality. Right and wrong are only matters of opinion, and opinions vary from culture to culture.

We may call this the Cultural Differences Argument. To many people, it is persuasive. But from a logical point of view, is it sound?

It is not sound. The trouble is that the conclusion does not follow from the premise—that is, even if the premise is true, the conclusion still might be false. The premise concerns what people *believe*—in some societies, people believe one thing; in other societies, people believe differently. The conclusion, however, concerns what *really is the case*. The trouble is that this sort of conclusion does not follow logically from this sort of premise.

Consider again the example of the Greeks and Callatians. The Greeks believed it was wrong to eat the dead; the Callatians believed it was right. Does it follow, *from the mere fact that they disagreed*, that there is no objective truth in the matter? No, it does not follow; for it could be that the practice was objectively right (or wrong) and that one or the other of them was simply mistaken.

To make the point clearer, consider a different matter. In some societies, people believe the earth is flat. In other societies, such as our own, people believe the earth is (roughly) spherical. Does it follow, from the mere fact that people disagree, that there is no "objective truth" in geography? Of course not; we would never draw such a conclusion because we realize that, in their beliefs about the world, the members of some societies might simply be wrong. There is no reason to think that if the world is round everyone must know it. Similarly, there is no reason to think that if there is moral truth everyone must know it. The fundamental mistake in the Cultural Differences Argument is that it attempts to derive a substantive conclusion about a subject from the mere fact that people disagree about it.

This is a simple point of logic, and it is important not to misunderstand it. We are not saying (not yet, anyway) that the conclusion of the argument is false. That is still an open question. The logical point is just that the conclusion does not *follow from* the premise. This is important, because in order to determine whether the conclusion is true, we need arguments in its support. Cultural Relativism proposes this argument, but unfortunately the argument turns out to be fallacious. So it proves nothing.

4. THE CONSEQUENCES OF TAKING CULTURAL RELATIVISM SERIOUSLY

Even if the Cultural Differences Argument is invalid, Cultural Relativism might still be true. What would it be like if it were true?

In the passage quoted above, William Graham Sumner summarizes the essence of Cultural Relativism. He says that there is no measure of right and wrong other than the standards of one's society: "The notion of right is in the folkways. It is not outside of them, of independent origin, and brought to test them. In the folkways, whatever is, is right." Suppose we took this seriously. What would be some of the consequences?

1. *We could no longer say that the customs of other societies are morally inferior to our own.* This, of course, is one of the main points stressed by Cultural Relativism. We would have to stop condemning other societies merely because they are "different." So long as we concentrate on certain examples, such as the funerary practices of the Greeks and Callatians, this may seem to be a sophisticated, enlightened attitude.

However, we would also be stopped from criticizing other, less benign practices. Suppose a society waged war on its neighbors for the purpose of taking slaves. Or suppose a society was violently anti-Semitic and its leaders set out to destroy the Jews. Cultural Relativism would preclude us from saying that either of these practices was wrong. (We would not even be able to say that a society tolerant of Jews is *better* than the anti-Semitic society, for that would imply some sort of transcultural standard of comparison.) The failure to condemn *these* practices does not seem enlightened; on the contrary, slavery and anti-Semitism seem wrong wherever they occur. Nevertheless, if we took Cultural Relativism seriously, we would have to regard these social practices as immune from criticism.

2. *We could decide whether actions are right or wrong just by consulting the standards of our society.* Cultural Relativism suggests a simple test for determining what is right and what is wrong: all one need do is ask whether the action is in accordance with the code of one's society. Suppose in 1975 a resident of South Africa was wondering whether his country's policy of apartheid—a rigidly racist system—was morally correct. All he has to do is ask whether this policy conformed to his society's moral code. If it did, there would have been nothing to worry about, at least from a moral point of view.

This implication of Cultural Relativism is disturbing because few of us think that our society's code is perfect—we can think of all sorts of ways in which it might be improved. Yet Cultural Relativism not only forbids us from criticizing the codes of *other* societies; it also stops us from criticizing our own. After all, if right and wrong are relative to culture, this must be true for our own culture just as much as for other cultures.

3. *The idea of moral progress is called into doubt.* Usually, we think that at least some social changes are for the better. (Although, of course, other changes may be for the worse.) Throughout most of Western history the place of women in society was narrowly circumscribed. They could not own property; they could not vote or hold political office; and generally they were under the almost absolute control of their husbands. Recently much of this has changed, and most people think of it as progress.

But if Cultural Relativism is correct, can we legitimately think of this as progress? Progress means replacing a way of doing things with a better way. But by what standard do we judge the new ways as better? If the old ways were in accordance with the social standards of their time, then Cultural Relativism would say it is a mistake to judge them by the standards of a different time.

Eighteenth-century society was a different society from the one we have now. To say that we have made progress implies a judgment that present-day society is better, and that is just the sort of transcultural judgment that, according to Cultural Relativism, is impossible.

Our idea of social *reform* will also have to be reconsidered. Reformers such as Martin Luther King, Jr., have sought to change their societies for the better. Within the constraints imposed by Cultural Relativism, there is one way this might be done. If a society is not living up to its own ideals, the reformer may be regarded as acting for the best; the ideals of the society are the standard by which we judge his or her proposals as worthwhile. But no one may challenge the ideals themselves, for those ideals are by definition correct. According to Cultural Relativism, then, the idea of social reform makes sense only in this limited way.

These three consequences of Cultural Relativism have led many thinkers to reject it as implausible on its face. It does make sense, they say, to condemn some practices, such as slavery and anti-Semitism, wherever they occur. It makes sense to think that our own society has made some moral progress, while admitting that it is still imperfect and in need of reform. Because Cultural Relativism says that these judgments make no sense, the argument goes, it cannot be right.

5. WHY THERE IS LESS DISAGREEMENT THAN IT SEEMS

The original impetus for Cultural Relativism comes from the observation that cultures differ dramatically in their views of right and wrong. But just how much do they differ? It is true that there are differences. However, it is easy to overestimate the extent of those differences. Often, when we examine what seems to be a dramatic difference, we find that the cultures do not differ nearly as much as it appears.

Consider a culture in which people believe it is wrong to eat cows. This may even be a poor culture, in which there is not enough food; still, the cows are not to be touched. Such a society would appear to have values very different from our own. But does it? We have not yet asked *why* these people will not eat cows. Suppose it is because they believe that after death the souls of humans inhabit the bodies of animals, especially cows, so that a cow may be someone's grandmother. Now shall we say that their values are different from ours? No; the difference lies elsewhere. The difference is in our belief systems, not in our values. We agree that we shouldn't eat Grandma; we simply disagree about whether the cow is (or could be) Grandma.

The point is that many factors work together to produce the customs of a society. The society's values are only one of them. Other matters, such as the religious and factual beliefs held by its members, and the physical circumstances in which they must live, are also important. We cannot conclude, then, merely because customs differ, that there is a disagreement about values. The difference in customs may be attributable to some other aspect of social life. Thus there may be less disagreement about values than there appears to be.

Consider again the Eskimos, who often kill perfectly normal infants, especially girls. We do not approve of such things; in our society, a parent who killed a baby would be locked up. Thus there appears to be a great difference in the values of our two cultures. But suppose we ask why the Eskimos do this. The explanation is not that they have less affection for their children or less respect for human life. An Eskimo family will always protect its babies if conditions permit. But they live in a harsh environment, where food is in short supply. A fundamental postulate of Eskimo thought is: "Life is hard, and the margin of safety small." A family may want to nourish its babies but be unable to do so.

As in many "primitive" societies, Eskimo mothers will nurse their infants over a much longer period of time than mothers in our culture. The child will take nourishment from its mother's breast for four years, perhaps even longer. So even in the best of times there are limits to the number of infants that one mother can sustain. Moreover, the Eskimos are a nomadic people—unable to farm, they must move about in search of food. Infants must be carried, and a mother can carry only one baby in her parka as she travels and goes about her outdoor work. Other family members help however they can.

Infant girls are more readily disposed of because, first, in this society the males are the primary food providers—they are the hunters, following the traditional division of labor—and it is obviously important to maintain a sufficient number of food providers. But there is an important second reason as well. Because the hunters suffer a high casualty rate, the adult men who die prematurely far outnumber the women who die early. Thus if male and female infants survived in equal numbers, the female adult population would greatly outnumber the male adult population. Examining the available statistics, one writer concluded that "were it not for female infanticide... there would be approximately one-and-a-half times as many females in the average Eskimo local group as there are food-producing males."

So among the Eskimos, infanticide does not signal a fundamentally different attitude toward children. Instead, it is a recognition that drastic measures are sometimes needed to ensure the family's survival. Even then, however, killing the baby is not the first option considered. Adoption is common; childless couples are especially happy to take a more fertile couple's "surplus." Killing is only the last resort. I emphasize this in order to show that the raw data of the anthropologists can be misleading; it can make the differences in values between cultures appear greater than they are. The Eskimos' values are not all that different from our values. It is only that life forces upon them choices that we do not have to make.

6. HOW ALL CULTURES HAVE SOME VALUES IN COMMON

It should not be surprising that, despite appearances, the Eskimos are protective of their children. How could it be otherwise? How could a group survive that did not value its young? It is easy to see that, in fact, all cultural groups must protect their infants. Babies are helpless and cannot survive if they are not given extensive care for a period of years. Therefore, if a group did not care for its young, the young would not survive, and the older members of the group would not be replaced. After a while the group would die out. This means that any cultural group that continues to exist must care for its young. Infants that are not cared for must be the exception rather than the rule.

Similar reasoning shows that other values must be more or less universal. Imagine what it would be like for a society to place no value at all on truth telling. When one person spoke to another, there would be no presumption that she was telling the truth, for she could just as easily be speaking falsely. Within that society, there would be no reason to pay attention to what anyone says. (I ask you what time it is, and you say "Four o'clock." But there is no presumption that you are speaking truly; you could just as easily have said the first thing that came into your head. So I have no reason to pay attention to your answer. In fact, there was no point in my asking you in the first place.) Communication would then be extremely difficult, if not impossible. And because complex societies cannot exist without communication among their members, society would become impossible. It follows that in any complex society there must be a presumption in favor of truthfulness. There may of course be exceptions to this rule: there may be situations in which it is thought to be permissible to lie. Nevertheless, these will be exceptions to a rule that *is* in force in the society.

Here is one further example of the same type. Could a society exist in which there was no prohibition on murder? What would this be like? Suppose people were free to kill other people at will, and no one thought there was anything wrong with it. In such a "society," no one could feel safe. Everyone would have to be constantly on guard. People who wanted to survive would have to avoid other people as much as possible. This would inevitably result in individuals trying to become as self-sufficient as possible—after all, associating with others would be dangerous. Society on any large scale would collapse. Of course, people might band together in smaller groups with others that they could trust not to harm them. But notice what this means: they would be forming smaller societies that did acknowledge a rule against murder. The prohibition of murder, then, is a necessary feature of all societies.

There is a general theoretical point here, namely, that *there are some moral rules that all societies must have in common, because those rules are necessary for society to exist.* The rules against lying and murder are two examples. And in fact, we do find these rules in force in all viable cultures. Cultures may differ in what they regard as legitimate exceptions to the rules, but this disagreement exists against a background of agreement on the larger issues. Therefore, it is a mistake to over-estimate the amount of difference between cultures. Not every moral rule can vary from society to society.

7. JUDGING A CULTURAL PRACTICE TO BE UNDESIRABLE

In 1996, a 17-year-old girl named Fauziya Kassindja arrived at Newark International Airport and asked for asylum. She had fled her native country of Togo, a small west African nation, to escape what people there call "excision." Excision is a permanently disfiguring procedure that is sometimes called "female circumcision," although it bears little resemblance to the Jewish practice. More commonly, at least in Western newspapers, it is referred to as "female genital mutilation."

According to the World Health Organization, the practice is widespread in 26 African nations, and two million girls each year are "excised." In some instances, excision is part of an elaborate tribal ritual, performed in small traditional villages, and girls look forward to it because it signals their acceptance into the adult world. In other instances, the practice is carried out by families living in cities on young women who desperately resist.

Fauziya Kassindja was the youngest of five daughters in a devoutly Muslim family. Her father, who owned a successful trucking business, was opposed to excision, and he was able to defy the tradition because of his wealth. His first four daughters were married without being mutilated. But when Fauziya was 16, he suddenly died. Fauziya then came under the authority of his father, who arranged a marriage for her and prepared to have her excised. Fauziya was terrified, and her mother and oldest sister helped her to escape. Her mother, left without resources, eventually had to formally apologize and submit to the authority of the patriarch she had offended.

Meanwhile, in America, Fauziya was imprisoned for two years while the authorities decided what to do with her. She was finally granted asylum, but not before she became the center of a controversy about how foreigners should regard the cultural practices of other peoples. A series of articles in the *New York Times* encouraged the idea that excision is a barbaric practice that should be condemned. Other observers were reluctant to be so judgmental—live and let live, they said; after all, our culture probably seems just as strange to them.

Suppose we are inclined to say that excision is bad. Would we merely be imposing the standards of our own culture? If Cultural Relativism is correct, that is all we can do, for there is no culture-neutral moral standard to which we may appeal. But is that true?

IS THERE A CULTURE-NEUTRAL STANDARD OF RIGHT AND WRONG?

There is, of course, a lot that can be said against excision. Excision is painful and it results in the permanent loss of sexual pleasure. Its short-term effects include hemorrhage, tetanus, and septicemia. Sometimes the woman dies. Long-term effects include chronic infection, scars that hinder walking, and continuing pain.

Why, then, has it become a widespread social practice? It is not easy to say. Excision has no apparent social benefits. Unlike Eskimo infanticide, it is not necessary for the group's survival. Nor is it a matter of religion. Excision is practiced by groups with various religions, including Islam and Christianity, neither of which commend it.

Nevertheless, a number of reasons are given in its defense. Women who are incapable of sexual pleasure are said to be less likely to be promiscuous; thus there will be fewer unwanted pregnancies in unmarried women. Moreover, wives for whom sex is only a duty are less likely to be unfaithful to their husbands; and because they will not be thinking about sex, they will be more attentive to the needs of their husbands and children. Husbands, for their part, are said to enjoy sex more with wives who have been excised. (The women's own lack of enjoyment is said to be unimportant.) Men will not want unexcised women, as they are unclean and immature. And above all, it has been done since antiquity, and we may not change the ancient ways.

It would be easy, and perhaps a bit arrogant, to ridicule these arguments. But we may notice an important feature of this whole line of reasoning: it attempts to justify excision by showing that excision is beneficial—men, women, and their families are said to be better off when women are excised. Thus we might approach this reasoning, and excision itself, by asking whether this is true: is excision, on the whole, helpful or harmful?

In fact, this is a standard that might reasonably be used in thinking about any social practice whatever: we may ask *whether the practice promotes or hinders the welfare of the people whose lives are affected by it.* And, as a corollary, we may ask if there is an alternative set of social arrangements that would do a better job of promoting their welfare. If so, we may conclude that the existing practice is deficient.

But this looks like just the sort of independent moral standard that Cultural Relativism says cannot exist. It is a single standard that may be brought to bear in judging the practices of any culture, at any time, including our own. Of course, people will not usually see this principle as being "brought in from the outside" to judge them, because, like the rules against lying and homicide, the welfare of its members is a value internal to all viable cultures.

WHY, DESPITE ALL THIS, THOUGHTFUL PEOPLE MAY NEVERTHELESS BE RELUCTANT TO CRITICIZE OTHER CULTURES

Although they are personally horrified by excision, many thoughtful people are reluctant to say it is wrong, for at least three reasons.

First, there is an understandable nervousness about "interfering in the social customs of other peoples." Europeans and their cultural descendents in America have a shabby history of destroying native cultures in the name of Christianity and Enlightenment. Recoiling from this record, some people refuse to make any negative judgments about other cultures, especially cultures that resemble those that have been wronged in the past. We should notice, however, that there is a difference between (a) judging a cultural practice to be deficient, and (b) thinking that we should announce the fact, conduct a campaign, apply diplomatic pressure, or send in the army. The first is just a matter of trying to see the world clearly, from a moral point of view. The second is another matter altogether. Sometimes it may be right to "do something about it," but often it will not be.

People also feel, rightly enough, that they should be tolerant of other cultures. Tolerance is, no doubt, a virtue—a tolerant person is willing to live in peaceful cooperation with those who see things differently. But there is nothing in the nature of tolerance that requires you to say that all beliefs, all religions, and all social practices are equally admirable. On the contrary, if you did not think that some were better than others, there would be nothing for you to tolerate.

Finally, people may be reluctant to judge because they do not want to express contempt for the society being criticized. But again, this is misguided: to condemn a particular practice is not to say that the culture is on the whole contemptible or that it is generally inferior to any other culture, including one's own. It could have many admirable features. In fact, we should expect this to be true of most human societies—they are mixes of good and bad practices. Excision happens to be one of the bad ones.

8. WHAT CAN BE LEARNED FROM CULTURAL RELATIVISM

At the outset, I said that we were going to identify both what is right and what is wrong in Cultural Relativism. But I have dwelled on its mistakes: I have said that it rests on an invalid argument, that it has consequences that make it implausible on its face, and that the extent of moral disagreement is far less than it implies. This all adds up to a pretty thorough repudiation of the theory. Nevertheless, it is still a very appealing idea, and the reader may have the feeling that all this is a little unfair. The theory must have something going for it, or else why has it been so influential? In fact, I think there is something right about Cultural Relativism, and now I want to say what that is. There are two lessons we should learn from the theory, even if we ultimately reject it.

First, Cultural Relativism warns us, quite rightly, about the danger of assuming that all our preferences are based on some absolute rational standard. They are not. Many (but not all) of our practices are merely peculiar to our society, and it is easy to lose sight of that fact. In reminding us of it, the theory does a service.

Funerary practices are one example. The Callatians, according to Herodotus, were "men who eat their fathers"—a shocking idea, to us at least. But eating the flesh of the dead could be understood as a sign of respect. It could be taken as a symbolic act that says: we wish this person's spirit to dwell within us. Perhaps this was the understanding of the Callatians. On such a way of thinking, burying the dead could be seen as an act of rejection, and burning the corpse as positively scornful. If this is hard to imagine, then we may need to have our imaginations stretched. Of course we may feel a visceral repugnance at the idea of eating human flesh in any circumstances. But what of it? This repugnance may be, as the relativists say, only a matter of what is customary in our particular society.

There are many other matters that we tend to think of in terms of objective right and wrong that are really nothing more than social conventions. We could make a long list. Should women cover their breasts? A publicly exposed breast is scandalous in our society, whereas in other cultures it is unremarkable. Objectively speaking, it is neither right nor wrong—there is no objective reason why either custom is better. Cultural Relativism begins with the valuable insight that many of our practices are like this; they are only cultural products. Then it goes wrong by inferring that, because some practices are like this, all must be.

The second lesson has to do with keeping an open mind. In the course of growing up, each of us has acquired some strong feelings: we have learned to think of some types of conduct as acceptable, and others we have learned to reject. Occasionally, we may find those feelings challenged. For example, we may have been taught that homosexuality is immoral, and we may feel quite uncomfortable around gay people and see them as alien and "different." Now someone suggests that this may be a mere prejudice; that there is nothing evil about homosexuality; that gay people are just people, like anyone else, who happen, through no choice of their own, to be attracted to others of the same sex. But because we feel so strongly about the matter, we may find it hard to take this seriously. Even after we listen to the arguments, we may still have the unshakable feeling that homosexuals must, somehow, be an unsavory lot.

Cultural Relativism, by stressing that our moral views can reflect the prejudices of our society, provides an antidote for this kind of dogmatism. When he tells the story of the Greeks and Callatians, Herodotus adds:

> For if anyone, no matter who, were given the opportunity of choosing from amongst all the nations of the world the set of beliefs which he thought best, he would inevitably, after careful consideration of their relative merits, choose that of his own country. Everyone without exception believes his own native customs, and the religion he was brought up in, to be the best.

Realizing this can result in our having more open minds. We can come to understand that our feelings are not necessarily perceptions of the truth—they may be nothing more than the result of cultural conditioning. Thus when we hear it suggested that some element of our social code is *not* really the best, and we find ourselves instinctively resisting the suggestion, we might stop and remember this. Then we may be more open to discovering the truth, whatever that might be.

We can understand the appeal of Cultural Relativism, then, even though the theory has serious shortcomings. It is an attractive theory because it is based on a genuine insight, that many of the practices and attitudes we think so natural are really only cultural products. Moreover, keeping this thought firmly in view is important if we want to avoid arrogance and have open minds. These are important points, not to be taken lightly. But we can accept these points without going on to accept the whole theory.

Women's "Different Voice"

JENNIFER SAUL

Jennifer Saul is an American philosopher who teaches at the University of Sheffield in England. She works on topics in feminism and in the philosophy of language. The text presented here is excerpted from a chapter of her book-length introduction to feminist philosophy: *Feminism: Issues and Arguments* (2003). In it, she considers what implications psychologist Carol Gilligan's research on women and moral reasoning may have for traditional moral philosophy.

> The difference between men and women is like that between animals and plants. Men correspond to animals, while women correspond to plants ... When women hold the helm of government, the state is at once in jeopardy, because women regulate their action not by the demands of universality but by arbitrary inclinations and opinions. Women are educated—who knows how?—as it were by breathing in ideas, by living rather than by acquiring knowledge.
>
> (HEGEL 1952 [1821]: ADDITION TO PAR. 166)

> Men are different from women and women are on the whole psychologically and biologically better equipped to be the principal child nurturers.
>
> (LEA 2000: 2)

THE HISTORY OF THE "DIFFERENT VOICE"

The idea that women are psychologically very different from men is one of enduring popularity. As the above quotations illustrate, this idea is closely linked to the thought that each sex has certain activities to which it is suited and others to which it is not—G. W. F. Hegel thought women should not enter politics, while Ruth Lea thinks they are better than men at childcare.* Historically, the claim that women think differently from men has often been used to argue that it is right for women's role in life to be limited—that wives should be subordinate to husbands, that women should not be educated, that women should be confined as far as possible to the home, that women should not vote, and so on. Sometimes, it was clear that those making these arguments took women to be *inferior* to men: the nineteenth-century French thinker Pierre-Joseph Proudhon provided a convoluted set of calculations which he took to prove that "the total value of man and woman, their relationship and consequently their share of influence will be as 3 by 3 by 3 is to 2 by 2 by 2, or 27 to 8"

* Georg Friedrich Wilhelm Hegel (1770–1831) was an important German philosopher; Ruth Lea is the director of a British think tank, the Centre for Policy Studies.

From *Feminism: Issues and Arguments*, by J. Saul (2003), pp. 202–227. Reprinted by permission of Oxford University Press.

(Moses 1981: 155). The situation was far murkier, however, with other writers. By the time Proudhon was writing, it had become increasingly popular to see men and women as having different but *complementary* virtues, of equal importance. Women, unsurprisingly, were said to possess traits that rendered them perfectly suited for a life of domesticity while men's traits rendered them fit for life outside the home. Generally, women were taken to be emotionally sensitive and good at close personal relationships, traits needed for the family, while men were said to be rational, a trait thought to be much needed outside the home. Each sort of role was taken to be essential. This kind of claim, then, offered recognition and appreciation of the real and important work that women did in the home, and of the traits that women (were taken to) have. It also, however, served to provide a justification for restricting women to their traditional roles: if male and female roles were both essential, and sex determined which role one was suited for, a strict sexual division of labour was only rational (Okin 1981; 79 1992 [1979]).[1]

It is standard to contrast thinkers who claimed that women were inferior to men with those who claimed that women were merely different from men—as I have just done. But it is in fact harder than it might at first seem to maintain these categorizations. Immanuel Kant, for example, is often cited as a philosopher who took women to be complementary to men, possessors of unique virtues that should be cherished and preserved. But Kant held that only those who act from reason and a sense of duty (rather than emotion or compassion) could be truly moral. He also held that for women there is "nothing of duty, nothing of compulsion, nothing of obligation!" (Kant 1991: 81). For him, this absence of a sense of duty has the consequence that it is impossible for women to be morally worthy agents. It is very hard to see this as not implicitly taking women to be inferior to men. So even though Kant claims to value the ways in which women differ from men, we miss something if we classify him simply as claiming that women are complementary to men. This sort of slippage between complementarity claims and inferiority claims is a common one. It may in fact be very difficult to make claims of difference without some sort of ranking slipping in.

Quite naturally, many feminists (both early and recent) have fought to gain women greater freedom and more opportunities by attacking claims of psychological differences between men and women that destined them for different roles. One way to attack these ideas is simply to argue that women *don't* think differently from men. Unsurprisingly, this argument was not often made when women's upbringing, education, and lives were almost entirely different from men's. It is difficult to imagine such differences not producing differences in thinking. This idea—that differences in upbringing might produce significant differences that would not otherwise be present—is a commonplace and obvious one to us now. But this nature/nurture distinction has not always been a standard one. In fact, it is often exceptionally hard to sort out what sorts of claim thinkers like Kant and Hegel are making about women. Sometimes, they appear to be making assertions about women's unchangeable nature. At other times they discuss the need to educate women in the right way in order to maintain or inculcate this nature—a need that would not arise if the nature really were unchangeable. The second way to attack claims like Kant's or Hegel's turns crucially on a careful drawing of the nature/nurture distinction. This line of attack, used by many early feminists, holds that we know absolutely nothing of what women might be if they were not so carefully socialized into their feminine roles.

> I deny that anyone knows, or can know, the nature of the two sexes, as long as they have only been seen in their present relation to one another... What is now called the nature of women is an eminently artificial thing—the result of forced repression in some directions, unnatural stimulation in others.
>
> (Mill 1986 [1861]: 27)

This line of argument continues with the claim that women should be allowed to develop whatever capacities they may have without the artificial restrictions imposed by sexist laws. The one element of this line which may come as a shock to modern readers is that early feminists such as John Stuart Mill and Harriet Taylor often accepted claims that women's thinking *as it was then* was inadequate* They argued that women should be improved by being educated in the same way as men. It is important to note, however, that Mill and Taylor also held men of their time to be psychologically and morally inadequate, and felt that both sexes would be greatly improved by equality of opportunity: "Thus the position is corrupting equally to both [sexes]; in the one it produces the vices of power, in the other those of artifice" (Taylor 1970[1851]: 114).

Not all feminists, however, have contested claims that women's thinking is different from men's and should or must remain so. Some have in fact based their arguments for women's rights on precisely such claims. . . .

According to this line of reasoning, women should be given the opportunity to enter traditionally male areas of life—like the political arena, traditionally male workplaces, and higher education—because of the uniquely feminine virtues that they can bring to these endeavours. The world will be improved, proponents maintain, by women adding their very different talents to those of men. This line of argument, then, not only endorses but indeed depends upon claims of sex differences.

It is quite natural that feminists should have adopted both of the strategies I have outlined above. It is a tremendously powerful strategy to agree with widely accepted claims of fundamental differences but argue that these differences don't justify the subordination of women. It has the advantage of starting from widely accepted views, that makes it perhaps more likely to get a hearing than arguments which start by denying the common wisdom. But it also has some disadvantages. As already suggested, it can be hard to avoid sliding from claims of difference to claims of inferiority; and while feminists may manage to avoid this slippage, their audiences may have more trouble. In addition, it runs another important risk: many will gain new support for their sexist views. Those who remain convinced that sex differences justify the subordination of women will be able to point to even feminists as agreeing that the sex differences exist.

Those who deny the claimed differences or argue that they result merely from socialization don't run this risk. But they run others. One is that their arguments won't sway those who are firmly convinced of the unchangeable reality of sex differences. Many believed very strongly (as many still do today) that women's thinking is innately different from men's. An argument for women's rights which turns on denying this is likely to do little to convince such people that women should have rights. Another problem is that some of those who argue for the elimination of socialized differences slip all too easily into denigrating the lives and accomplishments of women in more traditional roles. Take, for example, Harriet Taylor's comment, a part of her argument that motherhood should not be assumed to be every woman's proper role: "There is no inherent reason why all women should voluntarily choose to devote their lives to one animal function and its consequences" (Taylor 1970[1851]: 104).

By the end of the 1970s, feminism that began from the thought that women were importantly different from men psychologically had virtually disappeared from public discourse in the US and the UK (although of course there were still feminists who held this view). . . .

So it came as a shock when, in 1982, Carol Gilligan, a feminist psychologist, argued that women's thinking about morality is different from men's, but in a way that deserves appreciation. In her book, *In a Different Voice,* Gilligan argued that empirical research did show women to have the very traits for which they had so often been criticized—being emotional rather than rational, concerned more with people than anything else, and not interested in abstractions. But she also argued that only sexist assumptions had prevented the realization of just how valuable these traits were.

The idea that a feminist might praise ways in which women differ from men had by this time come to seem startlingly new. Feminists (and others, as we shall see) seized on it with fervour. Although Gilligan had only suggested a difference in men's and women's thought about morality, feminists quickly began exploring the possibility that women's

* A selection from the writings of John Stuart Mill (1806–73) appears earlier in this section; Mill and his wife Harriet Taylor (1807–58) were early advocates of women's rights.

voices might offer new approaches to politics, science, business, and other male-dominated fields. Since women had only recently begun to enter these fields in noticeable numbers, the ideas derived from Gilligan's book held out the promise that the very presence of women would lead to almost unimaginable transformations. Outside academia, the idea took hold perhaps even more strongly. Women reported feeling that reading Gilligan made them feel for the first time as if someone had finally understood—and *appreciated*—how they think. More generally, Gilligan's work allowed all those who had been shy of making gender difference claims for fear of seeming sexist to begin exploring possible differences between men and women. And they did, with great popular success: in best-selling books like John Gray's (1992) *Men are from Mars, Women are from Venus* and in the press. To this day, stories about women's inroads into business rarely fail to discuss the different management styles resulting from women's different way of thinking, and stories about women's inroads into politics rarely fail to contain predictions of the different sort of world they will create, due to their different way of thinking. . . .

One reason Gilligan's claims had such an impact was that similar claims of women's special virtues from feminists of the past had been largely forgotten. Another was that, as we will see, she brought to light a shocking but almost unconscious form of sexism in psychological theory, which was quickly seen to have parallels elsewhere, even in some feminist thought—the idea that what men do is what humans are meant to do, and that where women deviate from this they just aren't measuring up. This was a form of sexism that very much needed exposure, and Gilligan exposed it beautifully. Finally, she brought new resources to bear on old issues, arguing that scientific research supported the idea that women have a different approach to morality. In this chapter, we will explore the idea that women have a "different voice" on matters of morality by way of Gilligan, its most famous recent propagator. We will carefully examine the nature of her claims, looking in detail at nuances that are all too easy to gloss over, and we will explore the impact of her work. But we will also take a close and critical look at the consequences of her claims, their consequences, and the research that has been taken to support them.

WOMEN'S MORAL THINKING: JUSTICE VS. CARE

CONTEXT

Gilligan's work was a response to that of Lawrence Kohlberg, a psychologist whose claims about moral development were, and to a large extent still are, widely accepted (Flanagan 1991: ch. 8; Kohlberg and Kramer 1969; Kohlberg 1981). Kohlberg developed a six-stage scale for charting moral development. This scale was meant to be a universal scale for moral development, in that all human moral development could be understood as progress from a lower point on the scale to a higher one (even though not everyone would progress through all the stages). Each stage, according to Kohlberg, represented a better way of thinking about morality than the previous one.

Kohlberg's Stages:

Preconventional:

Stage 1. A person at this stage is concerned only with securing rewards and avoiding punishments.

Stage 2. A person is mainly concerned with satisfying their own needs, though gives some thought to reciprocity ("You scratch my back, I scratch yours.")

Conventional:

Stage 3. A person takes good behaviour to be that which pleases or helps others.

Stage 4. A person considers respect for authority and the maintenance of social order to be central to morality.

Postconventional:

Stage 5. A person takes what is right to be upholding the basic rights and values of their society, even when they conflict with the concrete rules or laws of the group. (A good example of this is early feminists' use of the official founding principles of their countries to argue for equal rights, which involved changing their countries' actual laws.)

Stage 6. A person is guided by principles they have arrived at through reason alone, which they take to apply to all of humanity. An example of such a principle is "treat others as you would want to be treated": (A person at this stage is no longer guided in their moral thinking by either the rules or the basic values of their society.)

Kohlberg based his claim that all moral progress could be understood as progress along his scale on studies of eighty-four children (eventually adults) over a twenty-year period (Gilligan 1982: 18), arguing that these subjects' moral progress was, in fact, progress along his scale. He assessed their level of moral development by interviewing them about hypothetical moral dilemmas. A typical example is the Heinz dilemma:

> Heinz's wife is dying. There is a medicine which could cure her, but Heinz cannot afford to buy it. Should Heinz steal the drug?

The moral development of each child was assessed not by which answer (yes or no) they gave, but by what sort of reasoning they used in considering the dilemma. A child concerned only with whether or not Heinz could be caught and punished for his action might score at stage one, while a child invoking principles regarding the value of human life might score at stage five or six.

Kohlberg's original study did not include any females—he only tested males. When girls and women were tested for level of moral development using Kohlberg's scale, researchers found that women tended not to progress as far as men. While men often progressed to stage four, women tended not to get beyond stage three. Kohlberg suggested that this might be because stage three, with its focus on pleasing others, was "functional in the lives of mature women insofar as their lives take place in the home," suggesting that women only become fully mature morally if they abandon traditional women's roles.

CRITICISMS OF KOHLBERG

Kohlberg's original study was based on an all-male sample from a single culture. Gilligan rightly attacked this as a poor basis for general claims about human moral development. Although it would of course be impossible to base universal claims on a sample of all people, it would be easy to find a more representative sample than that which Kohlberg used.

In addition, Gilligan noted that Kohlberg's choice of an all-male sample for his study placed him in a very long tradition, made up of embarrassingly prominent thinkers. The idea that men represent the norm for human development is a very old one and a very persistent one. Its age can be illustrated by Aristotle's claim: "We should look on the female as being as it were a deformity, though one which occurs in the ordinary course of nature" (Okin 1992 [1979]: 82). Its persistence can be illustrated by a disturbing study conducted in 1972 (Gilligan 1982: 17). Participants were asked what qualities they deemed necessary for adulthood, and what qualities were masculine or feminine. It turned out that the traits considered necessary for adulthood, such as the capacities for autonomous thinking, clear decision-making, and responsible action were considered not only masculine but undesirable for women. Although it may seem an obvious point (once made) that views about what it is to be human should not be based on views about what it is to be male, it has been all too easy to overlook.

Gilligan also criticizes Kohlberg for an excessively limited view of moral thinking. She makes this case by asking us to look closely at how Kohlberg would rank two of her subjects, Jake and Amy (both age eleven), and to reflect on how we think they should in fact be ranked. Take, for example, these quotations from Jake and Amy, responding to the question, "When responsibility to oneself and responsibility to others conflict, how should one choose?" (pp. 36–7).

JAKE: You go about one-fourth to the others and three-fourths to yourself.

AMY: Well, it really depends upon the situation. If you have a responsibility with somebody else, then you should keep it to a certain extent, but

> to the extent that it is really going to hurt you or stop you from doing something that you really, really want, then I think maybe you should put yourself first. But if it is your responsibility to somebody really close to you, you've just got to decide in that situation which is more important, yourself, or that other person, and like I said, it really depends on what kind of person you are and how you feel about the other person or persons involved.

Gilligan notes that on Kohlberg's scale Jake's answer would be judged far more morally mature than Amy's, because Jake had a rule to apply in every situation, while Amy refused to formulate any such rule. But this is, of course, by no means the most natural response to the quotations. Amy may be long-winded and a bit indecisive, but she seems far more aware of the complexities of actual moral decision-making than Jake. Gilligan argues from cases like this that Kohlberg has missed some important facets of moral thinking: Amy is exhibiting what is unquestionably a kind of moral maturity, but one that cannot be recognized by Kohlberg's scale. Clearly, Gilligan argues, there is more to moral thinking than Kohlberg supposed.[2]

Gilligan, then, has two main criticisms of Kohlberg.

1. He should not have tried to develop a universal scale of moral development by studying only one small group of males.
2. There is good reason to suppose that there is a great deal more to moral thinking than he supposed.

These criticisms come together in Gilligan's response to the claim that women are morally underdeveloped. It is wrong, she argues, to rank women on a scale developed exclusively with reference to men. To argue from low female scores on such a scale to the conclusion that women are morally underdeveloped only makes sense if we assume that there is one norm for all people, and that norm is the one exemplified by men. Once we give up this assumption, we make room for the possibility that women's thinking may be different but not inferior. This leads quite naturally into the next phase of Gilligan's work, wherein she articulates the different kind of thinking that she has noticed in her research on women and girls.

DIFFERENT THINKING

We have seen that Gilligan criticizes Kohlberg's studies for focusing only upon one type of moral development. Those who approach moral questions in a different manner are seen as not developing properly. Gilligan suggests that such people—in her experience, women—might instead be seen as simply developing differently. She calls their approach to morality "Care" thinking, and provides a scale of her own which charts the development of Care thinkers. She calls the kind of thinking Kohlberg was concerned with "Justice" thinking.[3]

Justice thinking involves an emphasis on universal principles and reason. It is also characterized as emphasizing impartiality, rights, and justice. Care thinking, by contrast, is described as guided by emotions, context-sensitive, and concerned with particular individuals and situations rather than universality and impartiality. Within these situations, a Care thinker's primary concerns will be with maintaining existing connections and with responding to others' needs. Justice thinking and Care thinking are meant to be fundamentally different *all-purpose* moral outlooks: for the most part, when presented with a moral problem, Justice thinkers will approach it via Justice thinking, and Care thinkers will approach it via Care thinking.[4]

> Justice thinking:
> Universal principles, impartiality, reason, and rights.
> Care thinking:
> Particular individuals, maintaining existing connections, emotions, and response to needs.

Gilligan takes Jake and Amy, whom we met earlier, to be examplars of these two approaches. Below, we see their responses to the Heinz dilemma.

JAKE: The dilemma is "sort of like a math problem with humans. . . . a human life is worth more than money, and if the druggist only makes $1,000, he is still going to live, but if Heinz doesn't steal the drug, his wife is going to die . . ."

AMY: "I think there might be other ways besides stealing it, like if he could borrow the money or make a loan or something, but he really shouldn't steal the drug—but his wife shouldn't die either." If the druggist were to see the consequences of his high price, he would realize that "he should just give it to the wife and then have the husband pay back the money later."

Jake is seen as a Justice thinker because he is invoking a universal principle ("a human life is worth more than money"), and applying it rationally to the case before him. Amy, by contrast, focuses on the individuals, suggesting a solution involving better communication between them. Importantly, she wants to flesh out the context and survey more options, rather than just find a principle and apply it.

Gilligan argues that the Care perspective represents a distinctive all-purpose moral outlook, one that is at least as viable as the Justice perspective. Sometimes she appears to suggest that it is a better approach to morality than Justice thinking, and some of her followers seem to claim this (Flanagan 1991: 235). Initially, Gilligan seemed to hold that Justice thinkers and Care thinkers are strongly distinct: one is either a Justice or a Care thinker, not a blend of both. Later, we will see, Gilligan modified this claim.

WOMEN'S THINKING

Gilligan states in the introduction to her book that she is not making claims about differences between men and women.

> The different voice I describe is characterized not by gender but by theme. Its association with women is an empirical observation, and it is primarily through women's voices that I trace its development.
>
> (Gilligan 1982: 2)

Gilligan encountered this different voice more often in women than in men, she writes, but she is not claiming that it is distinctively female. However, throughout the rest of her book she writes of the way that "men and boys" think and the way that "women and girls" think. In addition, as we shall see, the explanation she suggests for how the two kinds of thinking come about turns crucially on differences in the situations of girls and boys. It seems, then, fair to characterize her as making gender difference claims—she may have begun her book cautiously, but she soon abandoned that caution. This interpretation is a standard one, and it has had a large impact on debates both within and outside philosophy (Moody-Adams 1991: 197). With that in mind, we will interpret her in this way.

Gilligan claims that Care thinking is the approach to morality favoured by women. She does not argue at length for any particular explanation of why women might favor this approach, but the main explanation she discusses approvingly is based upon Nancy Chodorow's work. According to Chodorow (1978), gender differences result from the fact that women tend to be the primary caregivers for young children. On this explanation, both boys and girls start life deeply attached to their primary caregivers, in the vast majority of cases their mothers. Once children establish their gender identities at around age three, Chodorow's theory continues, boys feel a need to define themselves as different from their mothers, while girls can persist in their attachment. The result of this, according to Chodorow, is that girls (and later, women) place great emphasis on empathy, attachment, and maintaining connections, while boys (and later, men) assign importance to separation and maintaining emotional distance. Gilligan suggests that this explains why women tend to be Care thinkers and men Justice thinkers.

THE IMPACT OF GILLIGAN'S WORK

It is hard to overestimate the influence of Carol Gilligan's work, either inside or outside academia. Our primary focus initially will be on the impact within philosophy.

PHILOSOPHICAL IMPACT

In philosophy, Gilligan's work helped give birth to vast new literatures. The most obvious implications of her work are in ethics and political philosophy. Feminist philosophers drew upon her work both to criticize traditional approaches to moral and political philosophy and to build new theories based on Care thinking. Traditional theories were criticized for privileging reason over emotion, for seeking universally applicable principles, for viewing moral agents as autonomous individuals rather than beings thoroughly enmeshed in connections with and dependencies on others, and for focusing on individual rights rather than on responsibility to others. According to Gilligan's claims, women view themselves primarily as situated in a complex web of interrelationships, emphasize particular contexts over general principles, give emotions a central role in their thinking about moral and political issues, and focus on responsibilities rather than individual rights. As a result of Gilligan's work, feminist theorists began working to construct moral and political theories that reflected these features of women's thinking. They argued that traditional moral and political philosophy was male-biased, and that its replacement by or supplementation with Care thinking would both eliminate that bias and improve the theories. They claimed both that the new theories were better in general and that they were essential to accomplishing feminist goals.

We will use the work of Annette Baier (1987) as an example of this sort of philosophical theorizing. She argues that the history of liberal political philosophy exhibits several importantly linked forms of male bias. Liberal political philosophy is generally characterized as placing an emphasis on the freedom and equality of all. Thus, it is especially puzzling that liberal political philosophers of the past, with very few exceptions, were opponents of equal rights for women.

Baier's explanation for this begins from the fact that, historically, the vast majority of liberal political philosophers have been male, and the vast majority of them have had wives who took care of their children and all household matters, leaving them free to pursue their goals outside the home. These philosophers' theories of the optimal structure for society varied in many ways. But, Baier notes, they shared some important features.

1. They began from the assumption that people are, in some important and basic sense, free and independent of one another.
2. They assumed that the realm of the family was essentially private, and not to be interfered with by the state or even discussed by political philosophers.

The first assumption is, Baier claims, false: all people begin life extremely dependent, and most have periods of illness and incapacitation during which they require a great deal of care from others. If nobody took care of us during these times of dependency, we would not only fail to flourish, but die. How could this obvious fact have been ignored? Only, she argues, because those doing the theorizing were not themselves involved in providing this care (they had wives to do that for them); and because they had already ruled that the realm in which such care took place was not a fit topic for discussion (because it was a private matter). This neglect of the family was also important to preserving the subordination of women. Women lacked many of the rights accorded to men and were legally subordinated to their husbands—a situation strongly inconsistent with these theorists' advocacy of equality and freedom. Only by not discussing the family at all could they avoid noticing that women's situation was at odds with their theories. Since women (at least those who the theorists knew well) were confined to the family, however, their situation was not a part of the accepted subject matter of political philosophy.

Political theorists, Baier claims, constructed theories that only made sense if people were autonomous, rather than fundamentally interdependent.[5] These theories, with their emphasis on reason, principle, and protection of one's rights, were, moreover, ill-suited for application to the realm the theorists had ignored: the family. Indeed, the thought of responding to loved ones by applying reasoned principles and ignoring emotional reactions does seem rather bizarre. If women had been moral and political theorists, Baier argued, moral and political theories would look very different. Women would start from an awareness of the fact that people are interdependent, and they would not ignore the role of emotion in guiding thought about how people should relate to one another. In addition, they would assign greater importance to responding to the needs of others, as opposed to simply protecting one's own rights. And this is just what Gilligan's work seemed to show—women are more attuned to interrelationships, and place a higher priority on emotion and responsibility to others, than men....

More generally, Gilligan's work played an important role in shaping the rebirth of a feminism that emphasizes what is special or different about women's lives and experiences. This strand of feminism holds that it is a mistake for feminists to strive for access to traditionally male ways of life. Proponents of this view argue that striving for such traditionally male ways of life is implicitly recognizing them as better, or more valuable, than traditionally female ways of life. They suggest instead that the project of feminism should be that of celebrating what is special and wonderful about women's lives—close relationships, care and responsiveness, and connection to one's emotions.

WORRIES AND CRITICISMS

Not all philosophers (feminist or otherwise) have embraced Gilligan's work. We will focus on three important sorts of criticism from philosophers.

1. The ways of thinking Gilligan claims to identify are not as distinct as she and her followers have thought.
2. Finding a way of thinking to be common among women is not a good reason to endorse that way of thinking.
3. Gilligan's claims serve (however unintentionally) to perpetuate damaging stereotypes of women.

Are Justice and Care Distinct?[6]

The contrast between Justice and Care thinking is fundamental to the work of Gilligan and her followers. Yet it is not so clear that Justice and Care thinking are really distinct from one another. We will look at just a few reasons for questioning their distinctness. First, take the contrast Gilligan draws between a morality based on rights and one based on responsibilities. This notion of rights doesn't really make much sense without some corresponding notion of responsibilities—if I have a right to be free from violent attack, for example, then others have a responsibility not to attack me. Similarly, Gilligan contrasts application of universal principles with attention to context. But this contrast is, if anything, even more problematic. One cannot apply principles blindly: principles can only be applied by looking closely at a context. To see this, consider the universal principle "Help those most in need." To act on this principle, one needs to determine exactly who is most in need and what should be done to help them. But this requires close attention to the details of the particular situation. One also won't get very far by only attending to context without any recourse to principles. After all, in any situation there are a multitude of facts and details—one has to decide which ones matter and in what ways, and it is hard to see how this can be done without some kind of principle.

Even if we set aside these worries, it is unclear whether one would *want* a sharply distinct ethic either of Justice or of Care. Each ethic seems to suffer from clear limitations. Take the case of Justice first. When we vividly imagine one who deals with all moral issues via reason alone, we find such a person rather disturbing. There is, most of us suppose, something deeply wrong with someone who assigns no role to emotion in their reflections on how to deal with their close friends' or relatives' problems. (Imagine, if you can, determining your response to a close friend's suicidal depression via a carefully reasoned assessment of your moral obligations.) This is part of what lends appeal to the idea of Care as an approach to morality.

The ethic of Care revolves around responding caringly to the needs of those with whom one is connected. This may seem an appealing way to think about personal relationships. But on its own it also leads to a rather unappealing view of morality. Consider what it means for impersonal relationships—it seems to place no constraints on one's behaviour. For a somewhat gruesome example, suppose that my daughter needs a new liver or she will die. Billy, the boy next door, has a perfectly good liver that (I have learned) would be completely compatible with my daughter's body. I know neither Billy nor his family. It is far from obvious what in an ethic of Care could convince me that it is wrong to harvest Billy's liver to save my daughter—after all, I would simply be responding to a great need of one to whom I'm closely connected.

One can answer this worry by citing a Care thinker discussed by Gilligan, who says that "the stranger is still another person belonging to that group, people you are connected to by virtue of being another person" (Gilligan 1982: 57). Care thinkers, then, may—and should, according to this line—care about everyone. This helps to explain why the perfect Care thinker is not the perfect nepotist, and why I should not harvest Billy's liver. But it also helps to dissolve what was meant to be a crucial difference between Justice and Care. It no longer looks as though Care thinkers have forsaken universality in favour of connections to particular others. Care thinkers care about everyone, which is about as universal as one can get.

So it is not entirely clear that Justice and Care are sharply distinct and incompatible, and it is also not clear that we would find either morality very appealing if we took them to be sharply distinct and incompatible. Rather, it seems likely that the best sort of moral thinking will combine elements of each ethic. We will return to this thought later.

Should We Endorse "Women's Thinking?"

It is by no means obvious that feminists should eagerly embrace whatever sort of thinking women are shown to engage in. Women have traditionally been far less educated than men, and limited in the experiences that they were permitted to have. Either of these factors alone could have brought it about that women's thinking *was* in fact less good than men's. Assuming that feminists want to think as well as possible, they should not simply accept uncritically whatever modes of thinking women happen to use. Uncritically to accept that women's thinking must be good is not very different from the more traditional mistake of uncritically accepting that men's thinking must be good.

It is also important to remember that rights-based Justice thinking has done a lot of good in the world, playing an important role in bringing about democracy, ending slavery, creating state-run educational systems, and so on. It played an extremely important role in bringing about the feminist victories of the last 150 years. Indeed, it is hard even to state the nature of these victories without using the (Justice-based) language of rights: the right to vote, the right to own property, the right to an education … So it would be a mistake, it seems, for feminists to reject Justice thinking entirely.

Moreover, Barbara Houston (1987) and Claudia Card (1993) have pointed out that women's moral thinking, as characterized by Gilligan, is just the sort of thinking that one would expect subordinates to display—a concern with meeting others' needs, maintaining connections, and making people happy. This sort of morality is a natural one for those who are powerless, and one that may well be ill suited to ending that powerlessness. This thought gains support from studies cited by Carol Tavris showing that the traits women are meant to have—like empathy and sensitivity to the needs of others—are ones that show up in people of either sex when they are placed in subordinate roles (Tavris 1992: 65). Houston and Card suggest that feminists should not uncritically accept a mode of thinking shaped under conditions that they are committed to changing. This line of thought applies to women's lives and experiences more generally. While there is much to value in traditional women's lives, such lives have not always been freely chosen from a wide range of options. Traditionally, women's lives have been ones of subordination and dependence, and it is a mistake to accept uncritically all features of these lives and reject all features of traditionally male ones.

These worries are very important ones. They become even more important when we reflect on the fact that Gilligan does not take the gender difference she discusses to be innate, but rather suggests that it is the result of upbringing. If it is not innate, then it seems far more open to change. Feminists who conclude that women's thinking perpetuates powerlessness should be working to change the child-rearing arrangements that give rise to it and training women to adopt a mode of thinking more suited to gaining power. But even many of those who do not think there is anything wrong with the way women think have reason to be hesitant about endorsing it. We have already seen that Gilligan takes the gender difference in moral thinking to be the result of children being raised almost exclusively by their mothers. Feminists who hold that parenting should be shared (and many feminists do believe this) should think twice about endorsing a moral framework taken to arise from unshared parenting.[7] If we think Care thinking is the best way to approach moral issues, and we believe that it results from female parenting, then it becomes more difficult to argue that parenting should be shared (a key strand in feminist thought).

Perpetuation of Stereotypes

A very serious worry about Gilligan's work and the work it has inspired is that it fits so well with traditional stereotypes of women. (The quotations with which this chapter began illustrate this nicely.) However much feminist proponents may value women's thinking, very similar claims about "woman's thinking" have been used for centuries as a way of limiting women's opportunities. Whatever the intentions of such feminists, their endorsement of gender difference claims can easily be used for anti-feminist ends. One illustrative example demonstrates that this worry is a real one. The American department store Sears was sued for sex discrimination because they were not allowing women to work in the electronics department, a competitive atmosphere where more money could be earned than elsewhere. In their defence they called a psychologist who, citing Carol Gilligan's work, argued that women wanted connection rather than competition, and therefore did not want to work in electronics. Sears won the case in 1986 (Pollitt 1994: 49–50). This case is one where, arguably, Gilligan's work was misused: she almost certainly would not take her claims to support such a defence of Sears. It is not fair to criticize a view simply because it can be distorted and used to further sexist ends,[8] but the degree to which Gilligan's view seems to fit stereotypical images of women is worrying.

Nonetheless, the fact that a view may perpetuate stereotypes is not a sufficient reason to reject it: if gender difference claims are true, they should be accepted as such. While feminists might then go on to argue about the proper reaction to these claims, rejecting them should not be a live option. It turns out, however, that Gilligan's claims do not seem to be supported by the empirical evidence.

EMPIRICAL EVIDENCE

GENERAL METHODOLOGICAL CONCERNS

There have been many methodological criticisms made of Kohlberg's and Gilligan's work. . . . These worries are extremely important ones. However, I want now to set them aside, and to ask what the data show *even if* we assume them to be accurate indicators of subjects' moral development and outlooks.

ARE THERE GENDER DIFFERENCES?

The first important fact for us to note is that Gilligan's book, *In a Different Voice*, does not contain any systematic study of gender differences in moral thinking. Instead, it is a compellingly written collection of extracts from mostly women's and girls' reflections on morality in general and on particular moral issues. It makes no pretence of being a systematic comparison of male and female thinking, and indeed really could not serve this function: one of the key studies on which it draws consists of interviews with women considering whether or not to have an abortion (not a study that could ever be repeated with males). At first, it may therefore seem remarkable that such a book has served as catalyst for so much work based on a presumption of gender differences. It is important, however, to remember the context in which it was published: it was a response to comparative studies done using the Kohlberg scale of moral development, studies that seemed to show a clear and striking difference between women and men. In this context, it is surely reasonable for a researcher to simply assume that such differences exist.

But the context did not remain this way for long. In response to Gilligan's work, researchers began to look again at the studies that seemed to show a difference between men and women on Kohlberg's scale. They found that the only studies that showed a gender difference were those in which the women participants had received significantly less formal education than the men. It also turned out that the single best predictor of how high an individual would score on Kohlberg's scale was level of educational attainment. The surest way to raise one's score on Kohlberg's scale is to get a university degree.[9] Further study of the data revealed that the differences between women's and men's scores on Kohlberg's scale are completely explained by level of educational attainment. When men and women with the same level of formal education are compared, their scores are indistinguishable. So the only difference these studies revealed was one due to level of formal education. Studies using Kohlberg's scale showed no genuine gender difference.[10]

These findings, however, by no means settle the issue of gender differences in moral thinking. If Gilligan is right (as seems likely) that there is more to moral thinking than Kohlberg believed, there might well be gender differences that simply don't show up on Kohlberg's scale. A large number of studies have now been done with the explicit aim of testing for gender differences in moral orientation (Justice or Care). One of the most significant findings to emerge from this work is that nearly all people, male or female, in fact use *both* moral orientations, sometimes at the same time. In addition, nearly all will quite readily switch from one orientation to the other, often with a prompt as simple as, "Can you think of another way to approach this problem?" Gilligan's original picture, then, is in error. People do not simply have one moral orientation, which gets applied to every moral problem. Gilligan has acknowledged that this shows her original claims to be in need of revision. She has now shifted her claim, stating that Care thinking is more readily available and natural to women, while Justice thinking is more readily available and natural to men.[11]

This new claim, too, turns out to be unsupported by the data—*for the most part*. The vast majority of studies comparing preferred moral orientation reveal no statistically significant gender difference. Men and women are, according to these studies, equally likely to use either moral orientation (Flanagan 1991; Walker et al. 1987).

However, some studies do show a gender difference. According to these studies, women are more likely to choose Care thinking and men more likely to choose Justice thinking. So why do some studies show a gender difference while others do not? The answer lies in the fact that those studies showing gender differences are ones in which participants are asked to choose a moral problem from their own lives to discuss. In these studies, men and women choose to discuss very different sorts of problem. Women tend to choose personal problems involving their families, while men choose more impersonal problems involving work. This is highly significant, since studies also show that both sexes prefer Care thinking when discussing problems involving close relationships and both prefer Justice thinking when discussing more impersonal problems. (This makes perfect sense, after a little reflection: we are far more likely to give priority to emotions, think about the needs of particular others, and work to maintain connections when considering those to whom we are close.) Choice of problem type, it turns out, completely explains all the observed gender differences. If choice of problem is controlled for, there is no gender difference at all. Given the same sort of problem to discuss, women and men use the same moral orientation. The only difference between women's and men's moral thinking, then, is this: when asked to choose a moral problem for discussion, women are more likely than men to choose personal problems (Flanagan 1991; Walker et al. 1987).

The upshot of all this is that the popular claims about gender differences in moral thinking seem to be false. Women and men do not have completely opposed all-purpose moral outlooks which they apply to every moral problem. When presented with a moral problem, women are no more likely than men to choose Care thinking. Care thinking is no more accessible or natural to women that it is to men. Men are not from Mars and women are not from Venus (at least so far as moral thinking goes).

A PUZZLE

This leaves us with an important puzzle to be explained. Both men and women insist that Gilligan's gender difference claims ring true. There is something immensely natural and appealing about them. How could this be the case, if there really *isn't* a gender difference? Marilyn Friedman has suggested that the answer to this lies in the fact that Gilligan's claims fit so well with our deeply held stereotypes of male and female thinking (Friedman 1987). Care thinking represents not only how men take women to think, but how women take *themselves* to think. Gilligan's claims fit not only with each sex's ideas about the other, but with each sex's self-conception. Such assumptions and self-conceptions, even if false, have a profound influence on our thinking. Reflect, for example, on a response like one we saw earlier, which discusses caring about everyone. It is really quite difficult to classify such responses as Justice or Care. The same seems likely to be true of the sorts of thinking we encounter in everyday life—most people we know will exhibit both orientations, possibly even at the same time. In reflecting on the moral thinking of those we know, we have choices to make about which elements to focus on. And here is where our stereotypes may have their strongest effects. When we read Gilligan and reflect on men's moral thinking, we notice the Justice thinking, because it is what we expect. When we read Gilligan and reflect on women's thinking, we notice the Care thinking, because it is what we expect. Our self-conceptions are also affected by the stereotypes we have learned. A women who "knows" that women's moral thinking gives priority to emotion rather than reason may focus on this element of her thinking when she reflects on gender differences. And when she picks up *In a Different Voice*, what Gilligan says will ring true. So one reason that claims of men's and women's moral thinking may ring true is simply that they reflect those kinds of thinking that we stereotype as male and female.

This is not the only explanation possible. One gender difference claim, after all, seems to be true. When asked to choose a moral problem from their own lives for discussion, women are more likely than men to choose a personal problem. Since these are the problems that people tend to consider via Care thinking, there is a sense in which Care thinking is female: it is the kind of thinking most natural to the kind of problems women tend to raise if asked to present a moral problem from their own lives. But we cannot know what this means until we know why it is that women tend to choose such problems. There are several explanations available. The most obvious explanation for women's choice of personal problems would be that the women studied do not work outside the home, and so spend their lives concerned almost exclusively with close personal relationships. But this cannot be right—for it turns out that the women who were *most* likely to choose personal problems to discuss were those who worked *outside* the home (Flanagan 1991: 232).

There is, perhaps, a simpler explanation. It might be that women presented personal problems because these were most on their minds. There are at least two highly plausible reasons why women who work outside the home might tend to have personal problems on their minds. The difficulty of combining work outside the home and childcare ... could well lead them to spend more time worrying about their families; alternatively, they might raise issues concerning their families due to societal pressures which make them feel guilty for working outside the home. This explanation offers us a way in which Care thinking might be seen as genuinely (rather than stereotypically) female, and a way to explain why Gilligan's book rings true to so many women. If women do indeed spend more time considering personal problems, and everyone is more likely to employ Care thinking when considering personal problems, women spend more time employing Care thinking. No wonder, then (if this is right), that Gilligan's work strikes them as an accurate description of their thinking.

A very different—and intriguing—sort of explanation for women's choices of moral problem might be that women have different views from men about what counts as a moral problem. (Flanagan (1991) explores this sort of explanation.) We have already seen (in our discussion of Baier) that decisions as to what gets classified as moral or political have important, far-reaching effects. It is entirely possible that women have different views from men about which issues are moral issues. Women may take family issues to be central or paradigmatic examples of moral issues, and men may not. This would explain why women are more likely than men to raise family issues when asked to describe a moral problem. Further, if women consider family issues paradigmatic of the moral domain, then they will consider Care thinking to be paradigmatic of moral thinking. As a result of this, Gilligan's descriptions will seem like good descriptions of women's moral lives. So we have yet another way in which Care thinking could be seen as genuinely female, and yet another way to explain the appeal of Gilligan's claims.

IMPACT OF THE EMPIRICAL FINDINGS

Gilligan's original claims led to a major shift in feminist thinking, and gave rise to re-examinations of assumptions both within and outside feminism. Ideas inspired by Gilligan have appeared in nearly every area of discourse to which gender differences could conceivably be relevant. But now it seems that the gender differences are not nearly what they at first appeared to be. Does this mean that all of this work should be abandoned? It seems to me that it does not. The reason for this is simply that claims of gender differences are not really essential to much of the work Gilligan has inspired.

Claims that women and men approach all moral problems in fundamentally different ways cannot be maintained, as we have seen. Some arguments for an ethic of Care begin from the thought that feminists should support such an ethic simply because this represents the way that women approach moral issues. These arguments must be abandoned, as there is no one way that women approach moral issues. Women, like men, use Justice thinking for impersonal problems and women, like men, use Care thinking for personal problems. So Care thinking cannot lay claim to being women's general approach to morality. We cannot then argue that Care thinking is good because it is women's thinking. But we have already seen that these arguments are open to strong criticism even if we assume Care thinking to be women's thinking. The fact (if it were one) that women think in a certain way does not give feminists sufficient reason to endorse that way of thinking. The discovery, then, that women don't have a special way of thinking only serves to make weaker an already weak argument.

Other arguments, like Baier's, do not in fact turn on claims of gender differences in moral thinking.[12] Her argument for Care thinking is that it is a better way of thinking about areas of life that have been traditionally considered female, and traditionally neglected by male philosophers. This argument fits very nicely with the empirical evidence, which indicates that both men and women find Care thinking most natural to the traditionally female realm of the family. It is important, then, to pay close attention to the role that claims of gender difference play—and do not play—in feminist arguments. Rejection of Gilligan's gender difference claims need not cause us to reject all the work that has been inspired by them.

CONCLUSION

One lesson we can draw from the work we have surveyed here is that it is immensely difficult to think clearly about differences between women and men. It is difficult to discern what the differences are—differences in life experience, differences in patterns of thought, differences in ability, or differences in priorities; it is difficult to discern what the causes of these differences are—biology, early childhood experience, or education; and it is difficult to discern what consequences follow from these differences—for men, for women, for feminism, and for philosophy.

Some points, however, seem to have emerged with clarity from the debate. First, it is wrong either to praise or to condemn traditionally female traits and activities simply on the grounds that they are *traditionally* female. It is equally wrong to praise or condemn them on the grounds that they actually represent what women are like. This latter sort of move is doubly problematic: first, we cannot infer anything about the value of a trait from the fact that women have it; second, we have seen that it is extremely hard to arrive at empirically supportable claims about what women are like. We should always move with great caution in this area. And we should always bear in mind an additional reason for caution: claims about male and female nature have a very long and often ugly history. Although they have sometimes been used to improve the lot of women, they have a much longer history as a means of confining women's lives and opportunities. Feminists, then, should exercise great caution in making any claims about differences between women and men—especially since many of the feminist arguments that have been inspired by such claims do not really depend on them.

NOTES

1. These writers generally overlooked the large number of working-class women who did work outside their homes.
2. Another way to arrive at this conclusion is to take a quick look at the history of philosophy. Kohlberg has chosen a single sort of view on morality, as solely a matter of reason, and placed it confidently at the pinnacle of his scale of moral development. This view of morality is a version of that developed by Immanuel Kant. But the best way to think about morality has been a contested subject for thousands of years. Kant's views on morality are far from widely accepted. In fact, one would be hard-pressed to find more than a handful of philosophers who would happily assent to the emphasis Kant places on duty, reason, and principles to the exclusion of all other possible moral attributes. So Kohlberg's placement of a Kantian moral outlook as the obvious pinnacle of moral development would strike any philosopher as very odd. There are clearly many alternative approaches.
3. Gilligan does not capitalize "Justice" and "Care," and most discussions of these notions follow her lead. I have done so, however, to call attention to the fact that it is a special, technical sense of these words at work in the discussion. This is simply for the sake of clarity, and no other significance should be attached to it.
4. More accurately, this is Gilligan's *initial* understanding. Later, as we will see, she revises her view to allow for individuals to regularly adopt different perspectives for different problems and at different times.
5. This is a contentious claim. But my concern here is with the workings of Baier's argument itself, not with whether or not Baier's representation of liberal political philosophy is accurate.
6. The ideas in this section are discussed in Blum (1988), Kymlicka (2002), Sher (1987), and Tronto (1993).
7. It may be worth noting that Nancy Chodorow, from whom Gilligan takes her views on gendered development, takes her work to show shared parenting to be an important and worthwhile goal: she views current gender differences in thinking as problematic.
8. If it were, we could criticize feminist proponents of equality for the distortion of this goal which led to the US Supreme Court ruling that concern for equal treatment could not be used as an objection to denying women pregnancy benefits, since men are denied these benefits as well. (This criticism has been made. See Okin (1992 [1979]: 323–4) for an excellent discussion of the criticism and its weaknesses.)
9. This fact fits well with the first methodological criticism we examined: if we assume, as seems reasonable, that level of education is not linked to genuine level of moral development, then it suggests that Kohlberg's scale is not in fact measuring moral development.
10. The data discussed in this paragraph are taken from Walker (1993) and Flanagan (1991).
11. For more on these findings, see Flanagan (1991), Gilligan (1988), and Johnston (1988).
12. She makes frequent reference to gender difference claims, but they do not play a role in her arguments.

REFERENCES

Baier, A. (1987), 'The Need for More than Justice.' *Canadian Journal of Philosophy*, supplementary vol. 13: 41–56.

Blum, L. (1988), "Gilligan and Kohlberg: Implications for Moral Theory." *Ethics* 98(3): 472–91.

Card, C. (1993), "Gender and Moral Luck." In O. Flanagan and A. Rorty (eds.), *Identity, Character, and Morality*. Bradford, Mass.: MIT University Press, 200–218.

Chodorow, N. (1978), *The Reproduction of Mothering*. Berkeley: University of California Press.

Flanagan, O. (1991), *Varieties of Moral Personality*. Cambridge, Mass.: Harvard University Press.

Friedman, M. (1987), "Beyond Caring: The De-moralization of Gender." *Canadian Journal of Philosophy*, supplementary vol. 13: 87–110.

Gilligan, C. (1982), *In a Different Voice*. Cambridge, Mass.: Harvard University Press.

Gray, J. (1992), *Men Are from Mars, Women Are from Venus*, London: HarperCollins.

Hegel, G. W. F. (1952 [1821]), *The Philosophy of Right*, trans. T. M. Knox. Oxford: Oxford University Press.

Houston, B. (1987), "Rescuing Womanly Virtues: Some Dangers of Moral Reclamation." *Canadian Journal of Philosophy*, supplementary vol. 13: 237–62.

Kant, I. (1991 [1761]), *Observations on the Feeling of the Beautiful and Sublime*. trans. J. Goldthwaite. Berkeley, Calif.: University of California Press.

Kohlberg, L. (1981), *The Philosophy of Moral Development: Moral Stages and the Idea of Justice*. San Francisco, Calif.: Harper and Row.

——— and Kramer, R. (1969), "Continuities and Discontinuities in Childhood and Adult Moral Development." *Human Development* 12: 93–120.

Kymlicka, W. (2002), *Contemporary Political Philosophy: An Introduction*, 2nd ed. Oxford: Oxford University Press.

Lea, R. (2000), "Do Women Lose Out at Work Because of Maternity Leave?" *Guardian Saturday Review* (26 Aug.): 2.

Mill, J. S. (1986 [1861]), *The Subjection of Women*. Buffalo, New York: Prometheus.

——— (1998 [1859]), "On Liberty." In J. Gray (ed.), *On Liberty and Other Essays*, Oxford: Oxford University Press, 5–128.

Moody-Adams, M. (1991), "Gender and the Complexity of Moral Voices." In C. Card (ed.), *Feminist Ethics*. Lawrence: University of Kansas Press, 195–212.

Moses, C. G. (1984), *French Feminism in the 19th Century*. Albany, NY: State University of New York Press.

Nails, D. (1983), "Social-Scientific Sexism: Gilligan's Mismeasure of Man." *Social Research* 50: 643–64.

Okin, S. M. ([1979], New ed. 1992), *Women in Western Political Thought*. Princeton, NJ: Princeton University Press.

——— (1989), *Justice, Gender, and the Family*. New York: Basic Books.

Pollitt, K. (1994), *Reasonable Creatures*. New York: Knopf.

——— (1999), "Whose Culture?" In Okin (1999: 27–31).

Sher, G. (1987), "Other Voices, Other Rooms? Women's Psychology and Moral Theory." In E. F. Kittay and D. T. Meyers (eds.), *Women and Moral Theory*. Totowa, NJ: Rowman & Littlefield.

Tavris, C. (1992), *The Mismeasure of Woman*. New York: Touchstone.

Taylor, H. (1970 [1851]), "*The Enfranchisement of Women*." In A. Rossi (ed.), *Essays on Sex Equality*. Chicago: University of Chicago Press.

Tronto, J. (1993), *Moral Boundaries: A Political Argument for an Ethic of Care*. New York: Routledge.

——— (2002), "The 'Nanny' Question in Feminism." *Hypatia* 17(2): 34–51.

Walker, L. (1993), "Sex Differences in the Development of Moral Reasoning." In M. J. Larrabee (ed.), *An Ethic of Care*. New York: Routledge, 157–76.

——— de Vries, B., and Trevethan, S. (1987), "Moral Stages and Moral Orientations in Real-Life and Hypothetical Dilemmas." *Child Development* 58: 842–58.

Morality and Heuristics

CASS R. SUNSTEIN

Cass Sunstein (1954–) is a distinguished professor of law and political science at the University of Chicago. His numerous books and articles address a wide range of topics centering on issues of economics, justice, and political theory.

The essay that appears here was prepared especially for this volume. It is a revised version of a longer essay, "Moral Heuristics," which was originally published in 2005 in the journal *Behavioral and Brain Sciences*, together with responses from some forty scientists and philosophers and a reply by Sunstein. In it, Sunstein considers the philosophical implications of psychological and neuroscientific research that seems to show that much of our moral decision making arises from our use of mental rules of thumb.

I. INTRODUCTION

With respect to questions of fact, people use heuristics—mental short-cuts, or rules of thumb, that generally work well, but that also lead to systematic errors. People use moral heuristics too—moral short-cuts, or rules of thumb, that lead to mistaken and even absurd moral judgments. One of my major goals in this essay is to show that heuristics play a pervasive role in moral, political, and legal judgments, and that they sometimes produce significant mistakes. I also attempt to identify a set of heuristics that now influence both law and policy, and try to make plausible the claim that some widely held practices and beliefs are a product of those heuristics. Often moral heuristics represent generalizations from a range of problems for which they are indeed well-suited (see Baron 1994), and hence most of the time, such heuristics work well. The problem comes when the generalizations are wrenched out of context and treated as freestanding or universal principles, applicable to situations in which their justifications no longer operate. Because the generalizations are treated as freestanding or universal, their application seems obvious, and those who reject them appear morally obtuse, possibly even monstrous. I want to urge that the appearance is misleading and even productive of moral mistakes. There is nothing obtuse, or monstrous, about refusing to apply a generalization in contexts in which its rationale is absent.

If moral heuristics are in fact pervasive, then people with diverse foundational commitments should be able to agree, not that their own preferred theories are wrong, but that they are often applied in a way that reflects the use of heuristics. Utilitarians ought to be able to identify heuristics for the maximization of utility; deontologists should be able to point to heuristics for the proper discharge of moral responsibilities; those uncommitted to any large-scale theory should be able to specify heuristics for their own more modest normative commitments. And if moral heuristics exist, blunders are highly likely not only in moral thinking, but in legal and political practice as well. Conventional legal and political arguments are often a product of heuristics masquerading as universal truths. Hence I will identify a set of political and legal judgments that are best understood as a product of heuristics, and that are often taken, wrongly and damagingly, as a guide to political and legal practice even when their rationale does not apply.

II. ORDINARY HEURISTICS AND AN INSISTENT HOMUNCULUS

A. HEURISTICS AND FACTS

The classic work on heuristics and biases—pioneered by Nobel-prize winner Daniel Kahneman and Amos Tversky—deals not with moral questions but with issues of fact. In answering hard factual questions, those who lack accurate information use simple rules of thumb. Suppose you were asked to estimate how many words, in four pages of a novel,

Adapted from "Moral Heuristics" in *Behavioral and Brain Science*, 28, 2005, pp. 531–542. Copyright © Cambridge University Press. Reprinted with the permission of the publisher.

will have "ing" as the last three letters, and then to estimate how many words, in the same four pages, will have "n" as the second-to-last letter. If you are like most people, you would give a higher number in response to the first question than in response to the second (Tversky and Kahneman 1984)—even though a moment's reflection shows that this is a mistake (since any word that ends in "ing" has "n" as its penultimate letter). People err because they use an identifiable heuristic—the *availability heuristic*—to answer difficult questions about probability. When people use this heuristic, they answer a question of probability by considering whether examples come readily to mind. How likely is a flood, an airplane crash, a traffic jam, a terrorist attack, or a disaster at a nuclear power plant? Lacking statistical knowledge, people try to think of illustrations. For people without statistical knowledge, it is far from irrational to use the availability heuristic; the problem is that this heuristic can lead to serious errors of fact, in the form of excessive fear of small risks and neglect of large ones.

Or consider the *representativeness heuristic*, in accordance with which judgments of probability are influenced by assessments of resemblance (the extent to which A "looks like" B). The representativeness heuristic is famously exemplified by people's answers to questions about the likely career of a hypothetical woman named Linda, described as follows: "Linda is 31 years old, single, outspoken, and very bright. She majored in philosophy. As a student, she was deeply concerned with issues of discrimination and social justice and also participated in antinuclear demonstrations" (see Kahneman and Frederick 2002; Mellers et al. 2001). People were asked to rank, in order of probability, eight possible futures for Linda. Six of these were fillers (such as psychiatric social worker, elementary school teacher); the two crucial ones were "bank teller" and "bank teller and active in the feminist movement."

More people said that Linda was less likely to be a bank teller than to be a bank teller and active in the feminist movement. This is an obvious mistake, a conjunction error, in which characteristics A and B are thought to be more likely than characteristic A alone. The error stems from the representativeness heuristic: Linda's description seems to match "bank teller and active in the feminist movement" far better than "bank teller." In an illuminating reflection on the example, Stephen Jay Gould observes that "I know [the right answer], yet a little homunculus in my head continues to jump up and down, shouting at me—'but she can't just be a bank teller; read the description.'" (Gould 1991, p. 469). Because Gould's homunculus is especially inclined to squawk in the moral domain, I shall return to him on several occasions.

The early work on heuristics has been subject to intense criticism on a number of fronts (see, for example, Gigerenzer and Todd 1999; Gigerenzer 2000), but for present purposes it is unnecessary to resolve these debates. No one denies that with respect to facts, human beings use simple rules of thumb that can produce serious mistakes. If this is true for facts, it is highly likely to be true for political and moral judgments as well.

B. ATTRIBUTE SUBSTITUTION AND PROTOTYPICAL CASES

What is a heuristic? Kahneman and Shane Frederick recently suggest that heuristics are mental shortcuts used when people are interested in assessing a "target attribute" and when they substitute a "heuristic attribute" of the object, which is easier to handle (Kahneman and Frederick 2002). Heuristics therefore operate through a process of *attribute substitution*. The use of heuristics gives rise to intuitions about what is true (see Myers 2003), and these intuitions sometimes are biased, in the sense that they produce errors in a predictable direction. Consider the question whether more people die from suicides or homicides. Lacking statistical information, people might respond by asking whether it is easier to recall cases in either class (the availability heuristic). The approach is hardly senseless, but it might also lead to errors, a result of "availability bias" in the domain of risk perception (see Kuran and Sunstein 1998).

Similar mechanisms are at work in the moral, political, and legal domains. Unsure what to think or do about a target attribute (what morality requires, what the law is), people might substitute a heuristic attribute instead—asking, for example, about the view of trusted authorities (a leader of the preferred political party, an especially wise judge, a religious figure). Often the process works by appeal to *prototypical cases*. Confronted by a novel and difficult problem, observers often ask whether it shares features with a familiar problem. If it seems to do so, then the solution to the familiar problem is applied to the novel and difficult one. Of course it is possible that in the domain of values as well as facts, real-world heuristics generally perform well in the real world—so that moral errors are reduced, not increased, by their use, at least compared to the most likely alternatives (see my remarks on rule-utilitarianism below). The only claim here is that some of the time, our moral judgments can be shown to misfire.

III. HEURISTICS AND MORALITY

To show that heuristics operate in the moral domain, we have to specify some benchmark by which we can measure moral truth. On these questions I want to avoid any especially controversial claims. Whatever one's view of the foundations of moral and political judgments, I suggest, moral heuristics are likely to be at work in practice.

My goal here is to show that in many particular cases, moral heuristics are at work—and that this point can be accepted by people with diverse general theories, or with grave uncertainty about which general theory is correct.

A. WEAK CONSEQUENTIALISM

With respect to the cases catalogued in Part V, I contend that it is possible to conclude that a moral heuristic is at work without accepting any especially controversial normative claims. In several of the examples, that view can be accepted without accepting any contestable normative theory at all. Other examples will require acceptance of what I shall call "weak consequentialism," in accordance with which the social consequences of the legal system are relevant, other things being equal, to what law ought to be doing.

Weak consequentialists need not be utilitarians. They might agree that violations of rights count among the consequences that ought to matter, so that deontological considerations play a role in the overall assessment of what should be done. Of course some deontologists will reject any form of consequentialism altogether. They might believe, for example, that retribution is the proper theory of punishment, and that the consequences of punishment are never relevant to the proper level of punishment. Some of my examples will be unpersuasive to deontologists who believe that consequences do not matter at all. But weak consequentialism seems to me sufficiently nonsectarian, and attractive to sufficiently diverse people, to make plausible the idea that in the cases at hand, moral heuristics are playing a significant role. And for those who reject weak consequentialism, it might nonetheless be productive to ask whether, from their own point of view, certain rules of morality and law are reflective of heuristics that sometimes produce serious errors.

B. EVOLUTION AND RULE-UTILITARIANISM: SIMPLE HEURISTICS THAT MAKE US GOOD?

Two clarifications before we proceed. First, some moral heuristics might well have an evolutionary foundation (de Waal 1996; Sober and Wilson 1999; Katz 2000). Perhaps natural selection accounts for automatic moral revulsion against incest or cannibalism, even if clever experiments, or life, can produce situations in which the revulsion is groundless. In the case of incest, the point is straightfoward: The automatic revulsion might be far more useful, from the evolutionary perspective, than a more fine-grained evaluation of contexts (Stein 2001). In fact an evolutionary account might be provided for most of the heuristics that I explore here. When someone has committed a harmful act, evolutionary pressures might well have inculcated a sharp sense of outrage and a propensity to react in proportion to it. As a response to wrongdoing, use of an *outrage heuristic* might well be much better than an attempt at any kind of consequentialist calculus, weak or strong. Of course many moral commitments are a product not of evolution but of social learning and even cascade effects (see Sunstein

2003); individuals in a relevant society will inevitably be affected by a widespread belief that it is wrong to tamper with nature (see below), and evolutionary pressures need not have any role at all.

Second, and relatedly, some or even most moral heuristics might have a rule-utilitarian or rule-consequentialist defense (see Hooker 2000). The reason is that in most cases they work well despite their simplicity, and if people attempted a more fine-grained assessment of the moral issues involved, they might make more moral mistakes rather than fewer (especially because their self-interest is frequently at stake). Simple but somewhat crude moral principles might lead to less frequent and less severe moral errors than complex and fine-grained moral principles. Compare the availability heuristic. Much of the time, use of that heuristic produces speedy judgments that are fairly accurate, and those who attempt a statistical analysis might make more errors (and waste a lot of time in the process). If human beings use "simple heuristics that make us smart" (Gigerenzer and Todd 1999), then they might also use "simple heuristics that make us good." I will offer some examples in which moral heuristics seem to me to produce significant errors for law and policy, but I do not contend that we would be better off without them. On the contrary, such heuristics might well produce better results, from the moral point of view, than the feasible alternatives—a possibility to which I will return.

IV. THE ASIAN DISEASE PROBLEM AND MORAL FRAMING

In a finding closely related to their work on heuristics, Kahneman and Tversky themselves find "moral framing" in the context of what has become known as "the Asian disease problem" (Kahneman and Tversky 1984). Framing effects do not involve heuristics, but because they raise obvious questions about the rationality of moral intuitions, they provide a valuable backdrop. Here is the first component of the problem:

> Imagine that the U. S. is preparing for the outbreak of an unusual Asian disease, which is expected to kill 600 people. Two alternative programs to combat the disease have been proposed. Assume that the exact scientific estimates of the consequences are as follows:
>
> If Program A is adopted, 200 people will be saved.
>
> If Program B is adopted, there is a one-third probability that 600 people will be saved and a two-thirds probability that no people will be saved.
>
> Which of the two programs would you favor?

Most people choose Program A.

But now consider the second component of the problem, in which the same situation is given but followed by this description of the alternative programs:

> If Program C is adopted, 400 people will die.
> If Program D is adopted, there is a one-third probability that nobody will die and a two-thirds probability that 600 people will die.

Most people choose Problem D. But a moment's reflection should be sufficient to show that Program A and Program C are identical, and so too for Program B and Program D. These are merely different descriptions of the same programs. The purely semantic shift in framing is sufficient to produce different outcomes. Apparently people's moral judgments about appropriate programs depend on whether the results are described in terms of "lives saved" or instead "lives lost." What accounts for the difference? The most sensible answer begins with the fact that human beings are pervasively averse to losses (hence the robust cognitive finding of loss aversion, Tversky and Kahneman 1991). With respect to either self-interested gambles or fundamental moral judgments, loss aversion plays a large role in people's decisions. But what counts as a gain or a loss depends on the baseline from which measurements are made. Purely semantic reframing can alter the baseline and hence alter moral intuitions (for many examples involving fairness, see Kahneman et al. 1986).

Moral framing has been demonstrated in the important context of obligations to future generations (see Frederick 2003), a much-disputed question of morality, politics, and law (Revesz 1999; Morrison

1998). To say the least, the appropriate discount rate for those yet to be born is not a question that most people have pondered, and hence their judgments are highly susceptible to different frames. From a series of surveys, Maureen Cropper and her coauthors (1994) suggest that people are indifferent between saving one life today and saving 45 lives in 100 years. They make this suggestion on the basis of questions asking people whether they would choose a program that saves "100 lives now" or a program that saves a substantially larger number "100 years from now." It is possible, however, that people's responses depend on uncertainty about whether people in the future will otherwise die (perhaps technological improvements will save them?); and other ways of framing the same problem yield radically different results (Frederick 2003). For example, most people consider "equally bad" a single death from pollution next year and a single death from pollution in 100 years. This finding implies no preference for members of the current generation. The simplest conclusion is that people's moral judgments about obligations to future generations are very much a product of framing effects (for a similar result, see Baron 2000).[1]

The same point holds for the question whether government should consider not only the number of "lives" but also the number of "life-years" saved by regulatory interventions. If the government focuses on life-years, a program that saves children will be worth far more attention than a similar program that saves senior citizens. Is this immoral? People's intuitions depend on how the question is framed (see Sunstein 2004). People will predictably reject an approach that would count every old person as worth "significantly less" than what every young person is worth. But if people are asked whether they would favor a policy that saves 105 old people or 100 young people, many will favor the latter, in a way that suggests a willingness to pay considerable attention to the number of life-years at stake.

At least for unfamiliar questions of morality, politics, and law, people's intuitions are very much affected by framing. Above all, it is effective to frame certain consequences as "losses" from a status quo; when so framed, moral concern becomes significantly elevated. It is for this reason that political actors often phrase one or another proposal as "turning back the clock" on some social advance. The problem is that for many social changes, the framing does not reflect reality, but is simply a verbal manipulation.

Let us now turn to examples that are more controversial.

V. MORAL HEURISTICS: A CATALOGUE

My principal interest here is the relationship between moral heuristics and questions of law and policy. I separate the relevant heuristics into four categories: those that involve morality and risk regulation; those that involve punishment; those that involve "playing God," particularly in the domains of reproduction and sex; and those that involve the act-omission distinction. The catalogue is meant to be illustrative rather than exhaustive.

A. MORALITY AND RISK REGULATION

1. *Cost-Benefit Analysis.* An automobile company is deciding whether to take certain safety precautions for its cars. In deciding whether to do so, it conducts a cost-benefit analysis, in which it concludes that certain precautions are not justified—because, say, they would cost $100 million and save only four lives, and because the company has a "ceiling" of $10 million per lives saved (a ceiling that is, by the way, significantly higher than the amount the United States Environmental Protection Agency uses for a statistical life). How will ordinary people react to this decision? The answer is that they will not react favorably (see Viscusi 2000, pp. 547, 558). In fact they tend to punish companies that base their decisions on cost-benefit analysis, even if a high valuation is placed on human life. By contrast, they impose less severe punishment on companies that are willing to impose a "risk" on people but that do not produce a formal risk analysis that measures lives lost and dollars, and trades one against another (see Viscusi 2000; Tetlock 2000). What underlies people's moral judgments, which are replicated in actual jury decisions (Viscusi 2000)?

It is possible that when people disapprove of trading money for lives, they are generalizing from a set of moral principles that are generally sound, and even useful, but that work poorly in some cases. Consider the following moral principle: *Do not knowingly cause a human death*. In ordinary life, you should not engage in conduct with the knowledge that several people will die as a result. If you are playing a sport or working on your yard, you ought not to continue if you believe that your actions will kill others. Invoking that idea, people disapprove of companies that fail to improve safety when they are fully aware that deaths will result. By contrast, people do not disapprove of those who fail to improve safety while believing that there is a "risk" but appearing not to know, for certain, that deaths will ensue. When people object to risky action taken after cost-benefit analysis, it seems to be partly because that very analysis puts the number of expected deaths squarely "on screen" (see Tetlock 2000).

Companies that fail to do such analysis, but that are aware that a "risk" exists, do not make clear, to themselves or to anyone else, that they caused deaths with full knowledge that this was what they were going to do. People disapprove, above all, of companies that cause death knowingly. There may be a kind of "cold-heart heuristic" here: Those who know that they will cause a death, and do so anyway, are regarded as cold-hearted monsters.[2] On this view, critics of cost-benefit analysis should be seen as speaking directly to the homunculus: "is a corporation or public agency that endangers us to be pardoned for its sins once it has spent $6.1 million per statistical life on risk reduction?" (Ackerman and Heinzerling 2004).

Note that it is easy to reframe a probability as a certainty and vice-versa; if I am correct, the reframing is likely to have large effects. Consider two cases:

(a) Company A knows that its product will kill ten people. It markets the product to its ten million customers with that knowledge. The cost of eliminating the risk would have been $100 million.

(b) Company B knows that its product creates a 1 in 1 million risk of death. Its product is used by ten million people. The cost of eliminating the risk would have been $100 million.

I have not collected data, but I am willing to predict that Company A would be punished more severely than Company B, even though there is no difference between the two.

I suggest, then, that a moral heuristic is at work, one that imposes moral condemnation on those who knowingly engage in acts that will result in human deaths. And of course this heuristic does a great deal of good. The problem is that it is not always unacceptable to cause death knowingly, at least if the deaths are relatively few and an unintended byproduct of generally desirable activity. When government allows new highways to be built, it knows that people will die on those highways; when government allows new coal-fired power plants to be built, it knows that some people will die from the resulting pollution; when companies produce tobacco products, and when government does not ban those products, hundreds of thousands of people will die; the same is true for alcohol. Of course it would make sense, in all of these domains, to take extra steps to reduce risks. But that proposition does not support the implausible claim that we should disapprove, from the moral point of view, of any action taken when deaths are foreseeable.

There is a complementary possibility, involving the confusion between the ex ante and ex post perspectives. If a life might have been saved by a $50 expenditure on a car, people are going to be outraged, and they will impose punishment. What they will not see or incorporate is the fact, easily perceived ex ante, that the $50-per-car expenditure would have been wasted on millions of other people. It is hardly clear that the ex ante perspective is always preferable. But something has gone badly wrong if the ex post perspective leads people to neglect the trade-offs that are actually involved.

I believe that it is impossible to vindicate, in principle, the widespread social antipathy to cost-benefit balancing.[3] But here too, "a little homunculus in my head continues to jump up and down, shouting at me" that corporate cost-benefit analysis, trading dollars for a known number of deaths, is morally unacceptable. The voice of the homunculus, I am suggesting, is not reflective, but is instead a crude but quite tenacious moral heuristic.

2. *Emissions Trading.* In the last decades, those involved in enacting and implementing environmental law have experimented with systems of "emissions trading" (Sunstein 2002). In those systems, polluters are typically given a license to pollute a certain amount, and the licenses can be traded on the market. The advantage of emissions trading systems is that if they work well, they will ensure emissions reductions at the lowest possible cost.

Is emissions trading immoral? Many people believe so. Political theorist Michael Sandel, for example, urges that trading systems "undermine the ethic we should be trying to foster on the environment" (Sandel 1997; see also Kelman 1981). Sandel contends:

> [T]urning pollution into a commodity to be bought and sold removes the moral stigma that is properly associated with it. If a company or a country is fined for spewing excessive pollutants into the air, the community conveys its judgment that the polluter has done something wrong. A fee, on the other hand, makes pollution just another cost of doing business, like wages, benefits and rent.

In the same vein, Sandel objects to proposals to open carpool lanes to drivers without passengers who are willing to pay a fee. Here, as in the environmental context, it seems unacceptable to permit people to do something that is morally wrong so long as they are willing to pay for the privilege.

I suggest that like other critics of emissions trading programs, Sandel is using a moral heuristic; in fact he has been fooled by his homunculus. The heuristic is this: *People should not be permitted to engage in moral wrongdoing for a fee.* You are not allowed to assault someone so long as you are willing to pay for the right to do so; there are no tradable licenses for rape, theft, or battery. The reason is that the appropriate level of these forms of wrongdoing is zero (putting to one side the fact that enforcement resources are limited; if they were unlimited, we would want to eliminate, not merely to reduce, these forms of illegality). But pollution is an altogether different matter. At least some level of pollution is a byproduct of desirable social activities and products, including automobiles and power plants. Of course certain acts of pollution, including those that violate the law or are unconnected with desirable activities, are morally wrong; but the same cannot be said of pollution as such. When Sandel objects to emissions trading, he is treating pollution as equivalent to a crime in a way that overgeneralizes a moral intuition that makes sense in other contexts. There is no moral problem with emissions trading as such. The insistent objection to emissions trading systems stems from a moral heuristic.

Unfortunately, that objection has appeared compelling to many people, so much as to delay and to reduce the use of a pollution reduction tool that is, in many contexts, the best available (Sunstein 2002). Here, then, is a case in which a moral heuristic has led to political blunders, in the form of policies that impose high costs for no real gain.

3. *Betrayals.* To say the least, people do not like to be betrayed. A betrayal of trust is likely to produce a great deal of outrage. If a babysitter neglects a child or if a security guard steals from his employer, people will be angrier than if the identical acts are performed by someone in whom trust has not been reposed. So far, perhaps, so good: When trust is betrayed, the damage is worse than when an otherwise identical act has been committed by someone who was not a beneficiary of trust. And it should not be surprising that people will favor greater punishment for betrayals than for otherwise identical crimes (see Koehler & Gershoff 2003). Perhaps the disparity can be justified on the ground that the betrayal of trust is an independent harm, one that warrants greater deterrence and retribution—a point that draws strength from the fact that trust, once lost, is not easily regained. A family robbed by its babysitter might well be more

seriously injured than a family robbed by a thief. The loss of money is compounded and possibly dwarfed by the violation of a trusting relationship. The consequence of the violation might also be more serious. Will the family ever feel entirely comfortable with babysitters? It is bad to have an unfaithful spouse, but it is even worse if the infidelity occurred with your best friend, because that kind of infidelity makes it harder to have trusting relationships with friends in the future.

In this light it is possible to understand why betrayals produce special moral opprobrium and (where the law has been violated) increased punishment. But consider a finding that is much harder to explain: *People are especially averse to risks of death that come from products (like airbags) designed to promote safety* (Koehler & Gershoff 2003). The aversion is so great that people have been found to prefer a higher chance of dying, as a result of accidents from a crash, to a significantly lower chance of dying in a crash as a result of a malfunctioning airbag. (Similar studies involved vaccines and smoke alarms.) Remarkably, "betrayal risks appear to be so psychologically intolerable that people are willing to double their risk of death from automobile crashes, fires, and diseases to avoid incurring a small possibility of death by safety device betrayal."

What explains this seemingly bizarre and self-destructive preference? I suggest that a heuristic is at work: *Punish, and do not reward, betrayals of trust.* The heuristic generally works well. But it misfires in some cases, as when those who deploy it end up increasing the risks they themselves face. An airbag is not a security guard or a babysitter, endangering those whom they have been hired to protect. It is a product, to be chosen if and only if it decreases aggregate risks. If an airbag makes people safer on balance, it should be used, even if in a tiny percentage of cases it will create a risk that would not otherwise exist. People's unwillingness to subject themselves to betrayal risks, in circumstances in which products are involved and they are increasing their likelihood of death, is the moral cousin to the use of the representativeness heuristic in the Linda case. Both stem from a generally sound rule of thumb that leads to systematic errors.

B. MORALITY AND PUNISHMENT

In the context of punishment, moral intuitions are sometimes disconnected with the consequences of punishment, suggesting that a moral heuristic may well be at work (see Darley et al. 2000; Darley and Carlsmith forthcoming). Suppose, for example, that a corporation has engaged in serious wrongdoing. People are likely to want to punish the corporation as if it were a person (see Kahneman et al. 1998; Sunstein et al. 2002). They are unlikely to inquire into the possibility that the consequences of serious punishment (say, a stiff fine) will not be to "hurt" corporate wrongdoers, but instead to decrease wages, increase prices, or produce lost jobs. Punishment judgments are rooted in a simple heuristic, to the effect that penalties should be a proportional response to the outrageousness of the act. In thinking about punishment, people use an *outrage heuristic* (see Kahneman & Frederick 2002, pp. 49, 63). According to this heuristic, people's punishment judgments are a product of their outrage. This heuristic may produce reasonable results much of the time, but in some cases, it seems to lead to systematic errors—at least if we are willing to embrace weak consequentialism.

Consider, for example, an intriguing study of people's judgments about penalties in cases involving harms from vaccines and birth control pills (Baron & Ritov 1993). In one case, subjects were told that the result of a higher penalty would be to make companies try harder to make safer products. In an adjacent case, subjects were told that the consequence of a higher penalty would be to make the company more likely to stop making the product, with the result that less safe products would be on the market. Most subjects, including a group of judges, gave the same penalties in both cases.

A similar result emerged from a test of punishment judgments that asked subjects, including judges and legislators, to choose penalties for dumping hazardous waste (Baron et al. 1993). In one case, the penalty would make companies try harder to avoid waste. In another, the penalty would lead companies to cease making a beneficial product. Most people did not penalize companies differently in the two cases. Most strikingly, people preferred to require companies to clean up their own waste, even if the waste did not threaten anyone, instead of spending the same amount to clean up far more dangerous waste produced by another, now-defunct company.

How could this preference make sense? Why should a company be asked to engage in a course of action that costs the same but that does much less good? In these cases, it is most sensible to think that people are operating under a heuristic, mandating punishment that is proportional to outrageousness, and requiring that punishment be based not at all on consequential considerations. As a general rule, of course, it is plausible to think that penalties should be proportional to the outrageousness of the act; utilitarians will accept the point as a first approximation, and retributivists will insist on it. But it seems excessively rigid to adopt this principle whether or not the consequence would be to make human beings safer and healthier.

C. PLAYING GOD: REPRODUCTION, NATURE, AND SEX

Issues of reproduction and sexuality are prime candidates for the operation of moral heuristics. Consider human cloning, which most Americans reject and believe should be banned. Notwithstanding this consensus, the ethical and legal issues here are extremely difficult. To make progress, it is necessary to distinguish between reproductive and nonreproductive cloning; the first is designed to produce children, whereas the second is designed to produce cells for therapeutic use. Are the ethical issues different in the two cases? In any case it is important to identify the particular grounds for moral concern. Do we fear that cloned children would be means to their parents' ends, and if so why? Do we fear that they would suffer particular psychological harm? Do we fear that they would suffer from especially severe physical problems?

In a highly influential discussion of new reproductive technologies, above all cloning, ethicist Leon Kass (1998, pp. 17–19) points to the "wisdom in repugnance." Kass writes:

> People are repelled by many aspects of human cloning. They recoil from the prospect of mass production of human beings, with large clones of look-alikes, compromised in their individuality, the idea of father-son or mother-daughter twins; the bizarre prospects of a woman giving birth to and rearing a genetic copy of herself, her spouse or even her deceased father or mother; the grotesqueness of conceiving a child as an exact replacement for another who has died; the utilitarian creation of embryonic genetic duplicates of oneself, to be frozen away or created when necessary, in case of need for homologous tissues or organs for transplantation; the narcissism of those who would clone themselves and the arrogance of others who think they know who deserves to be cloned or which genotype any child-to-be should be thrilled to receive; the Frankensteinian hubris to create human life and increasingly to control its destiny; man playing God. . . .We are repelled by the prospect of cloning human beings not because of the strangeness or novelty of the undertaking, but because we intuit and feel, immediately and without argument, the violation of things that we rightfully hold dear. . . . Shallow are the souls that have forgotten how to shudder."

Kass is correct to suggest that revulsion toward human cloning might be grounded in legitimate concerns, and I mean to be agnostic here on the question whether human cloning is ethically defensible. But I want to suggest that moral heuristics are responsible for what Kass seeks to celebrate as "we intuit and feel, immediately and without argument." In fact Kass' catalogue of alleged errors seems to me an extraordinary exercise in the use of such heuristics. Availability operates in this context, not to drive judgments about probability, but to call up instances of morally dubious behavior (for example, "mass production of human beings, with large clones of look-alikes, compromised in their individuality"). The representativeness heuristic plays a similar role (for example, "the Frankensteinian hubris to create human life and increasingly to control its destiny"). But I believe that Kass gets closest to the cognitive process here with three words: "man playing God."

In fact we might well think that "do not play God" is the general heuristic here, with different societies specifying what falls in that category and with significant changes over time. Even in secular societies, a closely related heuristic plays a large role in judgments of fact and morality: *Do not tamper with nature*. This heuristic affects many moral judgments, though individuals and societies often become accustomed to various kinds of tampering (consider in vitro fertilization). An anti-tampering heuristic helps explain many risk-related judgments. For example, "[h]uman intervention seems to be an amplifier in judgments on food riskiness and contamination," even though "more lives are lost to natural than to man-made disasters in the world" (Rozin and Nemeroff 2002), pp. 31, 38). Studies show that people overestimate the carcinogenic risk from pesticides and underestimate the risks of natural carcinogens (Rozin and Nemeroff 2002). Companies go to great lengths to get a "natural" stamp on their products (Schlosser 2002), even though the actual difference between what counts as a "natural additive" and an "artificial additive" bears little or no relation to harms to consumers. So too in the domains of reproduction and sexuality, where a pervasive objection is that certain practices are "unnatural." And for cloning, there appears to be a particular heuristic at work: *Do not tamper with natural processes for human reproduction*. It is not clear that this heuristic works well; but it is clear that it systematically misfires.

Issues at the intersection of morality and sex provide an obvious place for the use of moral heuristics. Such heuristics are peculiarly likely to be at work in any area in which people are likely to think, "That's disgusting!" Any examples here will be contentious, but return to the incest taboo. We can easily imagine incestuous relationships, say between first cousins or second cousins, that ought not to give rise to social opprobrium, but that might nonetheless run afoul of social norms or even the law (Haidt 2001). The incest taboo is best defended by reference to coercion, psychological harm, and risks to children who might result from incestuous relationships. But in many imaginable cases, these concrete harms are not involved.

Of course it is plausible to say that the best way to defend against these harms is by a flat prohibition on incest, one that has the disadvantage of excessive generality but the advantage of easy application. Such a flat prohibition might have evolutionary origins (Stein 2001); it might also have strong rule-utilitarianism justifications. We would not like to have family members asking whether incest would be a good idea in individual cases, even if our underlying concern is limited to coercion and psychological harm. So defended, however, the taboo stands unmasked as a moral heuristic. In this vein Haidt and his coauthors (Haidt et al. 2004) refer to "moral dumbfounding"—to the existence of moral judgments that people "feel" but are unable to justify. In the domain of sex and reproduction, many taboos can be analyzed in similar terms.

D. ACTS AND OMISSIONS

To say the least, there has been much discussion of whether and why the distinction between acts and omissions might matter for morality, law, and policy. In one case, for example, a patient might ask a doctor not to provide life-sustaining equipment, thus ensuring the patient's death. In another case, a patient might ask a doctor to inject a substance that will immediately end the patient's life. Many people seem to have a strong moral intuition that the failure to provide life-sustaining equipment, and even the withdrawal of such equipment, is acceptable and legitimate—but that the injection is morally abhorrent. And indeed American constitutional law reflects judgments to exactly this effect: People have a constitutional right to withdraw equipment that is necessary to keep them alive, but they have no constitutional right to physician-assisted suicide (see *Washington v. Glucksberg* 1997, pp. 724–25). But what is the morally relevant difference?

It is worth considering the possibility that the act-omission distinction operates as a heuristic for a more complex and difficult assessment of the moral issues at stake. From the moral point of view, harmful acts are generally worse than harmful omissions, in terms of both the state of mind of the wrongdoer and the likely consequences of the wrong. A murderer is typically more malicious than a bystander who refuses to come to the aid of someone who is drowning; the murderer wants his victim to die, whereas the bystander need have no such desire. In addition, a murderer typically guarantees death, whereas a bystander may do no such thing. (I put to one side some complexities about causation.) But in terms of either the wrongdoer's state of mind or the consequences, harmful acts are not *always* worse than harmful omissions. The moral puzzles arise when life, or a clever interlocutor, comes up with a case in which there is no morally relevant distinction between acts and omissions, but when moral intuitions (and the homunculus) strongly suggest that there must be such a difference.

In such cases, we might hypothesize that moral intuitions reflect an overgeneralization of principles that usually make sense—but that fail to make sense in the particular case (see Baron 1994). Those principles condemn actions but permit omissions, a difference that is often plausible in light of relevant factors but that, in hard cases, cannot be defended (but see Kamm 1998). I believe that the persistent acceptance of withdrawal of life-saving equipment, alongside persistent doubts about euthanasia, is a demonstration of the point. There is no morally relevant difference between the two; the act-omission distinction makes a difference apparent or even clear when it is not real (on some complications here, see Sunstein 1999).

Compare the dispute over two well-known problems in moral philosophy (see Thomson 1986, pp. 94–116)* that implicate closely related concerns. The first, called the trolley problem, asks people to suppose that a runaway trolley is headed for five people, who will be killed if the trolley continues on its current course. The question is whether you would throw a switch that would move the trolley onto anther set of tracks, killing one person rather than five. Most people would throw the switch. The second, called the footbridge problem, is the same as that just given, but with one difference: the only way to save the five is to throw a stranger, now on a footbridge that spans the tracks, into the path of the trolley, killing that stranger but preventing the trolley from reaching the others. Most people will not kill the stranger. But what is the difference between the two cases, if any? A great deal of philosophical work has been done on this question, much of it trying to suggest that our firm intuitions can indeed be defended in principle.

Without engaging these arguments, let me suggest the possibility of a simpler answer. As a matter of principle, there is no difference between the two cases. People's different reactions are based on moral heuristics that condemn the throwing of the stranger but support the throwing of the switch. As a matter of principle, it is worse to throw a human being in the path of a trolley than to throw a switch that (indirectly?) leads to a death. The relevant heuristics generally point in the right direction. To say the least, it is desirable for people to act on the basis of a moral heuristic that makes it extremely abhorrent to throw innocent people to their death. But the underlying heuristics misfire in drawing a distinction between the two cleverly devised cases. Hence people struggle heroically to rescue their intuitions and to establish that the two cases are genuinely different in principle. But they aren't. In this sense, a moral heuristic that has "ecological rationality" (Gigerenzer 2000), leads to errors. And this objection does not bear only on ingeniously devised hypothetical cases. It suggests that a moral mistake pervades both commonsense morality and law, including constitutional law, by treating harmful omissions as morally unproblematic or categorically different from harmful actions.

Is there anything to be said to those who believe that their moral judgments, distinguishing the trolley and footbridge problems, are entirely reflective, and reflect no heuristic at all? Consider a suggestive experiment designed to see how the human brain responds to the two problems (Greene et al. 2001). The authors do not attempt to answer the moral questions in principle, but they find "that there are systematic variations in the engagement of emotions in moral judgment," and that brain areas associated with emotion are far more active in contemplating the footbridge problem than in contemplating the trolley problem. An implication of the authors' finding is that human brains are hard-wired to distinguish between bringing about a death "up close and personal" and doing so at a distance. Of course this experiment is far from decisive; emotions and cognition are not easily separable (Nussbaum 2002), and there may be good moral reasons why certain brain areas are activated by one problem and not by the other. Perhaps the brain is closely attuned to morally irrelevant differences. But consider the case of fear, where an identifiable region of the brain

* This volume, pages 195–208.

makes helpfully immediate but not entirely reliable judgments (Ledoux 1998). So too, perhaps, in the context of morality, politics, and law (Greene & Haidt 2002).[4]

VI. EXOTIC CASES, MORAL JUDGMENTS, AND REFLECTIVE EQUILIBRIUM

Some of these examples will seem more contentious than others. But taken as a whole, they seem to me to raise serious doubts about the wide range of work that approaches moral and political dilemmas by attempting to uncover moral intuitions about exotic cases of the kind never or rarely encountered in ordinary life. Should you shoot an innocent person if that is the only way to save twenty innocent people (Williams 1973)? What is the appropriate moral evaluation of a case in which a woman accidentally puts cleaning fluid in her coffee, and her husband, wanting her dead, does not provide the antidote, which he happens to have handy (see Thomson 1986, p. 31)? If Martians arrived and told you that they would destroy the world unless you tortured a small child, should you torture a small child? Is there a difference between killing someone by throwing him into the path of a train and killing someone by diverting the train's path to send it in his direction?

I believe that in cases of this kind, the underlying moral intuitions ordinarily work well, but that when they are wrenched out of familiar contexts, their reliability, for purposes of moral and legal analysis, is unclear.

The use of exotic cases has been defended, not on the ground that they are guaranteed to be correct, but as a means of eliciting the structure of our moral judgments in a way that enables us to "isolate the reasons and principles" that underlie our responses (Kamm 1993, p. 8; see generally Sorensen 1992). But if those responses are unreliable, they might not help to specify the structure of moral judgments, except when they are ill-informed and unreflective. For isolating reasons and principles that underlie our reasons, exotic cases might be positively harmful (compare Flanagan 1993).

In short, I believe that some philosophical analysis, based on exotic moral dilemmas, is inadvertently and even comically replicating the early work of Kahneman and Tversky: uncovering situations in which intuitions, normally quite sensible, turn out to misfire. The irony is that while Kahneman and Tversky meant to devise cases that would demonstrate the misfiring, some philosophers develop exotic cases with the thought that the intuitions are likely reliable and should form the building blocks for sound moral judgments. An understanding of the operation of heuristics offers reason to doubt the reliability of those intuitions, even when they are very firm (compare the emphasis on moral learning from real-world situations in Churchland 1995).

Now it is possible that the firmness of the underlying intuitions is actually desirable. Perhaps social life is better, not worse, because of the large number of people who treat heuristics as moral rules and who believe (for example) that innocent people should never be killed. If the heuristic is treated as a universal and freestanding principle, perhaps some mistakes will be made, but only in highly unusual cases, and perhaps people who accept the principle will avoid the temptation to depart from it when the justification for doing so appears sufficient but really is not. In other words, a firm rule might misfire in some cases, but it might be better than a more fine-grained approach, which, in practice, would misfire even more. Those who believe that you should always tell the truth may do and be much better, all things considered, than those who believe that truth should be told only on the basis of case-specific, all-things-considered judgments in its favor.

To the extent that moral heuristics operate as rules, they might be defended in the way that all rules are—better than the alternatives even if productive of error in imaginable cases. My suggestion is not that the moral heuristics, in their most rigid forms, are socially worse than the reasonable alternatives. It is hard to resolve that question in the abstract. I am claiming only that such heuristics lead to real errors and significant confusion.

With respect to the largest disputes about what morality requires, it may be too contentious to argue that one side is operating under a heuristic, whereas another side has it basically right. But I hope that I have said enough to show that in particular cases, sensible rules of thumb lead to demonstrable errors not merely in factual judgments, but in the domains of morality, politics, and law as well.

NOTES

1. Here too the frame may indicate something about the speaker's intentions, and subjects may be sensitive to the degree of certainty in the scenario (assuming, for example, that future deaths may not actually occur). While strongly suspecting that these explanations are not complete (see Frederick, 2003), I mean not to reject them, but only to suggest the susceptibility of intuitions to frames (for skeptical remarks, see Kamm, 1998).
2. I am grateful to Jonathan Haidt for this suggestion.
3. I put to one side a number of complexities. In some situations, for example, distributional considerations will justify a departure from what would otherwise be compelled by cost-benefit analysis (on this and other problems with cost-benefit analysis, see Sunstein 2002).
4. To see the implications, consider the controversial area of capital punishment, and let us simply assume that for each execution, at least five murders are prevented (see Dezhbakhsh, Rubin, and Shephard, 2004, finding that each execution prevents eighteen murders, with a margin of error of ten). If the assumption is correct, the refusal to impose capital punishment will effectively condemn numerous innocent people to death. Many people think that capital punishment counts as an "act," while the refusal to impose it counts as an "omission," and that the two are morally different. Many others point to differences in the nature of the causal chains, which might make capital punishment unacceptable even if the failure to impose it leads to the death of innocent people. I cannot resolve the moral issues in this space. But for weak consequentialists, it is at least worth considering the possibility that if capital punishment deters large numbers of murders, then it cannot be so easily condemned on moral grounds—at least if we do not employ an act-omission distinction in a context in which that distinction might be difficult to defend in principle.

   Similar issues are raised by the debate over torture. If torture would prevent the death of many innocent people, or if torture would prevent many other tortures, might not a ban on torture be seen as a moral heuristic, one that misfires in imaginable cases?

Acknowledgments: I am grateful to Daniel Kahneman and Martha Nussbaum for valuable discussions. For helpful comments on a previous draft, I also thank participants in a seminar at Cambridge University, Jonathan Baron, Mary Anne Case, Elizabeth Emens, Robert Frank, Jonathan Haidt, Robert Goodin, Steven Pinker, Edward Stein, Peter Singer, and a number of anonymous reviewers. An overlapping paper, written for a legal audience and based on a public lecture, is "Moral Heuristics and Moral Framing" (2004): 88 *Minnesota Law Review* 1556–1597.

REFERENCES

Ackerman, F. and Heinzerling, L. (2004). *Priceless: On Knowing the Price of Everything and the Value of Nothing.* New Press.

Baron, J. (1994). "Nonconsequentialist Decisions." *Behavioral and Brain Sciences* 17:1–10.

———.(2000). "Can We Use Human Judgments to Determine the Discount Rate?" *Risk Analysis* 20:861–68.

Baron, J., Gowda, R., and Kunreuther, H. (1993). "Attitudes Toward Managing Hazardous Waste." *Risk Analysis* 13:183–92.

Baron, J. & Ritov, I. (1993). "Intuitions About Penalties and Compensation in the Context of Tort Law." *Journal of Risk and Uncertainty* 7:17–33.

Churchland, P. (1995). *The Engine of Reason, the Seat of the Soul.* MIT Press.

Cropper, M. L., Aydede, S. K., and Portney, P. R. (1994). "Preferences for Life-saving Programs: How the Public Discounts Time and Age." *Journal of Risk & Uncertainty* 8:243–65.

Darley, J., and Carlsmith, K. forthcoming. "Incapacitation and Just Deserts as Motives for Punishment." *Law and Human Behavior.*

Darley, J., Carlsmith, K., and Robinson, P. 2000. "Incapacitation and Just Deserts as Motives for Punishment." *Law and Human Behavior* 24: 659–83.

De Waal, F. (1996). *Good Natured: The Origins of Right and Wrong in Humans and Other Animals.* Harvard University Press.

Dezhbakhsh, H., Rubin, P., and Shephard J. (2004). "Does Capital Punishment Have a Deterrent Effect: New Evidence from Post-Moratorium Panel Data." Available at http://papers.ssrn.com/sol3/papers.cfm?abstract_id=259538

Flanagan, O. (1993). *Varieties of Moral Personality: Ethics and Psychological Realism.* Harvard University Press.

Frederick, S. (2003). "Measuring Intergenerational Time Preference: Are Future Lives Valued Less?" *Journal of Risk and Uncertainty* 26(1):39–53.

Gigerenzer, G. (2000). *Adaptive Thinking: Rationality in the Real World.* Oxford University Press.

Gigerenzer, G. and Todd, P. (1999). *Simple Heuristics that Make Us Smart.* Oxford University Press.

Gould, S. J. (1991). *Bully for Brontosaurus: Reflections in Natural History.* W. W. Norton.

Greene, J. and Haidt, J. (2002). "How (and where) does moral judgment work?" *Trends in Cognitive Sciences* 6:517–23.

Greene, J., Somerville, R. B., Nystrom, L. E., Darley, J. M., and Cohen, J. D. (2001). "An fMRI Investigation of Emotional Engagement in Moral Judgment." *Science* 293:2105–08.

Haidt, J. (2001). "The Emotional Dog and Its Rational Tail: A Social Intuitionist Approach to Moral Judgment." *Psychological Review* 108(4): 814–34.

Haidt, J., Bjorklund, F., and Murphy, S. (2004). "Moral Dumbfounding: When Intuition Finds No Reason." Unpublished manuscript, University of Virginia.

Hooker, B. (2000). *Ideal Code, Real World: A Rule-Consequentialist Theory of Morality.* Oxford University Press.

Kahneman, D., and Frederick, S. (2002) "Representativeness Revisited: Attribute Substitution in Intuitive Judgment." In *Heuristics and Biases: The Psychology of Intuitive Judgment*, ed. T. Gilovich, D. Griffin, and D. Kahneman. Cambridge University Press.

Kahneman, D., Knetsch, J. L. and Thaler, R. H. 1986. "Fairness as a Constraint on Profit-Seeking: Entitlements in the Market." *American Economic Review* 76:728–41.

Kahneman, D., Schkade, D., and Sunstein, C. R. (1998). "Shared Outrage and Erratic Awards: The Psychology of Punitive Damages." *Journal of Risk & Uncertainty* 16:49–86.

Kahneman, D., and Tversky, A. (1984). "Choices, Values, and Frames." *American Psychologist* 39:341–50.

Kamm, F. (1993). *Morality, Mortality, Vol. 1: Death and Whom to Save from It.* Oxford University Press.

Kamm, F. (1998). "Moral Intuitions, Cognitive Psychology, and the Harming-versus-Not-Aiding Distinction." *Ethics* 108:463–88.

Kass, L. (1998). "The Wisdom of Repugnance." In *The Ethics of Human Cloning*, ed. L. Kass and J. Q. Wilson. American Enterprise Institute.

Katz, L. D. (2000). *Evolutionary Origins of Morality: Cross-Disciplinary Perspectives.* Academic.

Kelman, S. (1981). *What Price Incentives? Economists and the Environment.* Auburn House.

Koehler, J. J. and Gershoff, A. D. (2003). "Betrayal Aversion: When Agents of Protection Become Agents of Harm." *Organizational Behavior and Human Decision Processes* 90(2):244–61.

Kuran, T., and Sunstein, C. R. (1999). "Availability Cascades and Risk Regulation." *Stanford Law Review.* 683–768.

Ledoux, J. (1996). *The Emotional Brain: The Mysterious Underpinning of Emotional Life.* Touchstone.

Mellers, B., Hertwig, R., and Kahneman, D. (2001). "Do Frequency Representations Eliminate Conjunction Effects?" *Psychological Science* 12(4):269–75.

Morrison, E. R. (1998). "Comment: Judicial Review of Discount Rates Used in Regulatory Cost-benefit Analysis." *University of Chicago Law Review* 65(4):1333–70.

Nussbaum, M. (2002). *Upheavals of Thought.* Cambridge University Press.

Revesz, R. (1999). "Environmental Regulation, Cost-benefit Analysis, and the Discounting of Human Lives." *Columbia Law Review* 99(4):941–1017.

Rozin, P., and Nemeroff, C. (2002). "Sympathetic Magical Thinking: The Contagion and Similarity 'Heuristics.'" In *Heuristics and Biases: The Psychology of Intuitive Judgment,* ed. T. Gilovich, D. Griffin, and D. Kahneman. Cambridge University Press.

Sandel, M. (1997) "It's Immoral to Buy the Right to Pollute." *New York Times,* December 15, A23.

Schlosser, E. (2002). *Fast Food Nation: The Dark Side of the All-American Meal.* HarperCollins.

Sober, E., and Wilson, R. (1999). *Unto Others: The Evolution and Psychology of Unselfish Behavior.* Harvard University Press.

Sorensen, R. (1992). *Thought Experiments.* Oxford University Press.

Stein, E. (2001). "Ethics and Evolution." *The MIT Encyclopedia of the Cognitive Sciences,* ed. R. A. Wilson and F. C. Weil. MIT Press.

Sunstein, C. R. (1999). *One Case at a Time: Judicial Minimalism on the Supreme Court.* Harvard University Press.

Sunstein, C. R. (2003). *Why Societies Need Dissent.* Harvard University Press.

Sunstein, C. R. (2004). "Lives, Life-years, and Willingness to Pay." *Columbia Law Review* 104:205–52.

Sunstein, C. R., Hastie, R., Payne, J. W., and Viscusi, W. K. (2002). *Punitive Damages: How Juries Decide.* University of Chicago Press.

Sunstein, C. R., Schkade, D., and Kahneman, D. (2000). "Do People Want Optimal Deterrence?" *Journal of Legal Studies* 29(1):237–54.

Tetlock, P. (2000). "Coping with tradeoffs." In *Elements of Reason: Cognition, Choice, and the Bounds of Rationality*, ed. A. Lupia, S. Popkin, and M. D. McCubbins. Cambridge University Press.

Thomson, J. J. (1986). "The Trolley Problem." In *Rights, Restitution and Risk: Essays in Moral Theory*, ed. J. J. Thomson and W. Parent. Harvard University Press.

Tversky, A., and Kahneman, D. (1974). "Judgment Under Uncertainty: Heuristics and Biases." *Science* 185:1124–31.

Tversky, A., and Kahneman, D. (1984). "Extensional versus Intuitive Reasoning: The Conjunction Fallacy in Probability Judgment." *Psychological Review* 90:293–315.

Tversky, A. and Kahneman, D. (1991). "Loss Aversion in Riskless Choice: A Reference-Dependent Model." *Quarterly Journal of Economics* 106:4, 1039–61.

Viscusi, W. K. (2000). "Corporate Risk Analysis: A Reckless Act?" *Stanford Law Review* 52:547–97.

Washington v. Glucksberg (1997). *West's Supreme Court Reporter* 521:702–89.

Williams, B. (1973) "A Critique of Utilitarianism." In *Utilitarianism: For and Against*, ed. J. J. C. Smart and B. Williams. Cambridge University Press.

POLITICAL PHILOSOPHY

INTRODUCTION

Justice, Equality, and the State

It is commonly held that there is no natural political inequality: no one is born with a right to rule over others. This idea is the cornerstone of modern political philosophy: facts about who rules are not facts of nature; rather, they are grounded in convention. But what sort of convention underlies the right to rule? Ruling over others involves coercion and thus would seem to need special justification. If there is no natural political authority, what is the justification for having any political institutions, such as states, at all, and what kinds of states are just?

The *social contract tradition* offers a distinctive approach to these questions. States are just, according to this tradition, if it would be rational to agree to live under them. Thomas Hobbes's book *Leviathan*, published in 1651, is the first modern theory in this tradition. Political authority is justified, Hobbes argues, to the extent that it is the kind of authority that it would be rational for everyone to agree to be governed by. According to Hobbes, if we lived in a state of nature where there was no political authority, then our lives would be ridden with fear of destruction and death. The point of having a state is to save us from such misery. The only kind of rule that is capable of this task, Hobbes thinks, is rule by an *absolute sovereign*: a ruler who is unconstrained by any principles, such as those stated in the U.S. Constitution, with virtually no limits to what can be done to the populace. Only such a state, Hobbes thinks, is stable enough to avoid destruction from within. Hobbes thus begins with premises about equality that many people today endorse, but ends up with a surprising conclusion that most of us would reject.

John Rawls (1921–2002) is widely considered to be the most important figure in contemporary political philosophy. The selection from his writings that is presented here is a small excerpt from his important book *A Theory of Justice*, published in 1971. Like Hobbes, Rawls attempts to justify political arrangements by appealing to agreements that it would be rational for people to make. Unlike Hobbes, Rawls focuses more broadly on the kinds of institutions with the deepest impact on people's lives, such as educational institutions, the family, and political institutions, and asks what principles should regulate them. Rawls answers that such institutions should be regulated by principles that everyone would agree to if they did not know anything about their own position in society, such as their sex, race, economic status, and life prospects. He argues that these principles include a principle of equal liberty, according to which any inequalities in opportunity or circumstance should be minimized so that the worst off are as best off as possible.

What role, if any, should the state have in correcting inequalities that arise from capitalism? In his 1974 book *Anarchy, State and Utopia*, from which our last selection is taken, philosopher Robert Nozick (1938–2002) argues that the only justifiable state is one that takes personal liberty to be the fundamental political value. For Nozick, personal liberty includes the liberty to exchange goods in an unregulated capitalist market. Such exchanges are known to lead to severe inequalities of opportunity and circumstance. Nonetheless, Nozick argues, no state is justified in redressing these inequalities, for instance, through taxation, because such redress would infringe on personal liberty. This conclusion differs starkly from the conclusions reached by Rawls.

Just War

War is the most brutal and terrible form of large-scale human behavior. Is there such a thing as a morally just way to conduct a war once it has begun? That killing is wrong seems obvious, yet no war has ever been waged without killing people—both combatants and noncombatants. War thus forces us to reexamine a common moral commitment. The three selections on war—all published just after the Vietnam War in 1975 and 1976—consider whether it could be morally permissible to kill soldiers in wartime, but morally impermissible to kill civilians.

In "Conventions and the Morality of War," George Mavrodes argues that this distinction does not make a moral difference by itself. The moral status of intentionally killing noncombatants, he argues, varies as a function of the specific circumstances surrounding a particular combat. In "War and Innocence," Robert K. Fullinwider makes the case that it is morally impermissible to kill noncombatants in war, on the grounds that combatants cannot appeal to self-defense in the face of noncombatants. Finally, in "Self-Defense and the Killing of Non-Combatants," Lawrence A. Alexander argues that the appeal to self-defense cannot support a moral distinction between killing combatants and killing noncombatants and defends the view that killing noncombatants can be justified in wartime.

Further Reading

Students who want to pursue the themes raised in this section of the book may begin by looking at the articles in the following two anthologies. Each includes an extensive collection of important readings in political philosophy, along with suggestions for further readings on each of the main themes:

- Steven M. Cahn, ed. *Political Philosophy: The Essential Texts.* New York and Oxford: Oxford University Press, 2004.
- Robert E. Goodin and Philip Pettit, eds. *Contemporary Political Philosophy: An Anthology*, 2nd ed. Malden, Mass. and Oxford: Blackwell, 2006.

D JUSTICE, EQUALITY, AND THE STATE

"Contract and Commonwealth" from *Leviathan*

THOMAS HOBBES

British philosopher Thomas Hobbes (1588–1679) is best known for his enduring contributions to the field of political philosophy. His influential account of the principles under which governments might be considered legitimate set the framework for nearly all subsequent discussions of the topic.

The selection below is an excerpt from his most famous work, *Leviathan*, originally published in 1651 in rather archaic English. We have taken our selection from philosopher A. P. Martinich's edition of the text, thereby benefiting from Martinich's modernization of spelling and punctuation, and from his inclusion of paragraph numbers to enable scholarly discussion. Items in [brackets] are Martinich's insertions, and footnotes (of which we have included a selection) are due to Martinich. The summaries which appear in the margins are due to Hobbes himself; page numbers in the margins refer to the original edition of *Leviathan*.

CHAPTER XIII

OF THE NATURAL CONDITION OF MANKIND AS CONCERNING THEIR FELICITY AND MISERY

Men by nature equal. **1.** Nature hath made men so equal in the faculties of body and mind, as that, though there be found one man sometimes manifestly stronger in body or of quicker mind than another; yet when all is reckoned together, the difference between man and man is not so considerable as that one man can thereupon claim to himself any benefit to which another may not pretend as well as he. For as to the strength of body, the weakest has strength enough to kill the strongest, either by secret machination or by confederacy with others that are in the same danger with himself.

2. And as to the faculties of the mind, setting aside the arts grounded upon words, and especially that skill of proceeding upon general and infallible rules, called science, which very few have and but in few things, as being not a native faculty born with us, nor attained, as prudence, while we look after somewhat else, I find yet a greater equality amongst men than that of strength. For prudence is but experience, which equal time equally bestows on all men in those things they equally apply themselves unto. That which may perhaps [61]
make such equality incredible is but a vain conceit of one's own wisdom, which almost all men think they have in a greater degree than the vulgar, that is, than all men but themselves and a few others, whom by fame or for concurring with themselves, they approve. For such is the nature of men that howsoever they may acknowledge many others to be more witty or more eloquent or more learned, they will hardly believe there be many so wise as themselves; for they see their own wit at hand and other men's at a distance. But this proveth rather that men are in that point equal, than unequal. For

there is not ordinarily a greater sign of the equal distribution of anything than that every man is contented with his share.

From equality proceeds diffidence.

3. From this equality of ability ariseth equality of hope in the attaining of our ends. And therefore if any two men desire the same thing, which nevertheless they cannot both enjoy, they become enemies; and in the way to their end (which is principally their own conservation, and sometimes their delectation only) endeavour to destroy or subdue one another. And from hence it comes to pass that where an invader hath no more to fear than another man's single power, if one plant, sow, build, or possess a convenient seat, others may probably be expected to come prepared with forces united to dispossess and deprive him, not only of the fruit of his labour, but also of his life or liberty. And the invader again is in the like danger of another.

From diffidence war.

4. And from this diffidence of one another, there is no way for any man to secure himself so reasonable as anticipation, that is, by force or wiles, to master the persons of all men he can so long till he see no other power great enough to endanger him; and this is no more than his own conservation requireth, and is generally allowed. Also, because there be some that, taking pleasure in contemplating their own power in the acts of conquest, which they pursue farther than their security requires, if others, that otherwise would be glad to be at ease within modest bounds, should not by invasion increase their power, they would not be able, long time, by standing only on their defence, to subsist. And by consequence, such augmentation of dominion over men being necessary to a man's conservation, it ought to be allowed him.

5. Again, men have no pleasure (but on the contrary a great deal of grief) in keeping company where there is no power able to overawe them all. For every man looketh that his companion should value him at the same rate he sets upon himself, and upon all signs of contempt or undervaluing naturally endeavours, as far as he dares (which amongst them that have no common power to keep them in quiet is far enough to make them destroy each other), to extort a greater value from his contemners, by damage; and from others, by the example.

6. So that in the nature of man, we find three principal causes of quarrel. First, competition; secondly, diffidence; thirdly, glory.

7. The first maketh men invade for gain; the [62] second, for safety; and the third, for reputation. The first use violence to make themselves masters of other men's persons, wives, children, and cattle; the second, to defend them; the third, for trifles, as a word, a smile, a different opinion, and any other sign of undervalue, either direct in their persons or by reflection in their kindred, their friends, their nation, their profession, or their name.

Out of civil states there is always war of every one against every one.

8. Hereby it is manifest that during the time men live without a common power to keep them all in awe, they are in that condition which is called war; and such a war as is of every man against every man. For WAR consisteth not in battle only, or the act of fighting, but in a tract of time, wherein the will to contend by battle is sufficiently known; and therefore the notion of *time* is to be considered in the nature of war, as it is in the nature of weather. For as the nature of foul weather lieth not in a shower or two of rain, but in an inclination thereto of many days together, so the nature of war consisteth not in actual fighting, but in the known disposition thereto during all the time there is no assurance to the contrary. All other time is PEACE.

The incommodities of such a war.

9. Whatsoever therefore is consequent to a time of war, where every man is enemy to every man, the same consequent to the time wherein men live without other security than what their own strength and their own invention shall furnish them withal. In such condition there is no place for industry, because the fruit thereof is uncertain; and consequently no culture of the earth; no navigation, nor use of the commodities that may be imported by sea; no commodious building; no instruments of moving and removing such things as require much force; no knowledge of the face of the earth; no account of time; no arts; no letters; no society; and which is worst of all, continual fear, and danger of violent death; and the life of man, solitary, poor, nasty, brutish, and short.

10. It may seem strange to some man that has not well weighed these things that nature should thus dissociate and render men apt to invade and destroy one another; and he may therefore, not trusting to this inference, made from the passions, desire perhaps to have the same confirmed by experience. Let him therefore consider with himself; when taking a journey, he arms himself and seeks to go well accompanied; when going to sleep, he locks his doors; when even in his house he locks his chests; and this when he knows there be laws and public officers, armed to revenge all injuries shall be done him; what opinion he has of his fellow subjects, when he rides armed; of his fellow citizens, when he locks his doors; and of his children, and servants, when he locks his chests. Does he not there as much accuse mankind by his actions as I do by my words? But neither of us accuse man's nature in it. The desires and other passions of man are in themselves no sin. No more are the actions that proceed from those passions till they know a law that forbids them; which, till laws be made, they cannot know; nor can any law be made till they have agreed upon the person that shall make it.

[63] **11.** It may peradventure be thought there was never such a time nor condition of war as this; and I believe it was never generally so, over all the world; but there are many places where they live so now. For the savage people in many places of America, except the government of small families, the concord whereof dependeth on natural lust, have no government at all, and live at this day in that brutish manner, as I said before. Howsoever, it may be perceived what manner of life there would be, where there were no common power to fear, by the manner of life which men that have formerly lived under a peaceful government use to degenerate into a civil war.

12. But though there had never been any time wherein particular men were in a condition of war one against another; yet in all times kings and persons of sovereign authority, because of their independency, are in continual jealousies, and in the state and posture of gladiators, having their weapons pointing and their eyes fixed on one another, that is, their forts, garrisons, and guns upon the frontiers of their kingdoms, and continual spies upon their neighbours, which is a posture of war. But because they uphold thereby the industry of their subjects, there does not follow from it that misery which accompanies the liberty of particular men.

In such a war nothing is unjust.

13. To this war of every man against every man, this also is consequent; that nothing can be unjust. The notions of right and wrong, justice and injustice, have there no place. Where there is no common power, there is no law; where no law, no injustice. Force and fraud are in war the two cardinal virtues. Justice and injustice are none of the faculties neither of the body nor mind. If they were, they might be in a man that were alone in the world, as well as his senses and passions. They are qualities that relate to men in society, not in solitude. It is consequent also to the same condition that there be no propriety, no dominion, no *mine* and *thine* distinct; but only that to be every man's that he can get, and for so long as he can keep it. And thus much for the ill condition which man by mere nature is actually placed in; though with a possibility to come out of it, consisting partly in the passions, partly in his reason.

The passions that incline men to peace.

14. The passions that incline men to peace are fear of death, desire of such things as are necessary to commodious living, and a hope by their industry to obtain them. And reason suggesteth convenient articles of peace upon which men may be drawn to agreement. These articles are they which otherwise are called the laws of nature, whereof I shall speak more particularly in the two following chapters.

CHAPTER XIV [64]

OF THE FIRST AND SECOND NATURAL LAWS, AND OF CONTRACTS

Right of nature what.

1. The right of nature, which writers commonly call *jus naturale*, is the liberty each man hath to use his own power as he will himself for the preservation of his own nature; that is to say, of his own life; and consequently, of doing anything which, in his own judgement and reason, he shall conceive to be the aptest means thereunto.

Liberty what.

2. By Liberty is understood, according to the proper signification of the word, the absence of external impediments; which impediments may oft take away part of a man's power to do what he would, but cannot hinder him from using the power left him according as his judgement and reason shall dictate to him.

A law of nature what.

3. A LAW OF NATURE (*lex naturalis*) is a precept or general rule, found out by reason, by which a man is forbidden to do that which is destructive of his life, or taketh away the means of preserving the same, and to omit that by which he thinketh it may be best preserved. For though they that speak of this subject use to confound *jus* and *lex, right* and *law*; yet they ought to be distinguished, because right consisteth in liberty to do or to forbear; whereas law determineth and bindeth to one of them; so that law and right differ as much as obligation and liberty, which in one and the same matter are inconsistent.

Difference of right and law.

Naturally every man has right to every thing.

4. And because the condition of man (as hath been declared in the precedent chapter) is a condition of war of every one against every one, in which case every one is governed by his own reason, and there is nothing he can make use of that may not be a help unto him in preserving his life against his enemies; it followeth that in such a condition every man has a right to every thing, even to one another's body. And therefore, as long as this natural right of every man to every thing endureth, there can be no security to any man, how strong or wise soever he be, of living out the time which nature ordinarily alloweth men to live. And consequently it is a precept, or general rule of reason *that every man ought to endeavour peace, as far as he has hope of obtaining it; and when he cannot obtain it, that he may seek and use all helps and advantages of war.*[1] The first branch of which rule containeth the first and fundamental law of nature, which is *to seek peace and follow it.* The second, the sum of the right of nature, which is *by all means we can to defend ourselves.*

The fundamental law of nature, to seek peace.

The second law of nature. Contract in way of peace.

5. From this fundamental law of nature, by which men are commanded to endeavour peace, is derived this second law: *that a man be willing, when others are so too, as far forth as for peace and defense of himself he shall think it necessary, to lay down this right*
[65] *to all things; and be contented with so much liberty against other men as he would allow other men against himself.* For as long as every man holdeth this right of doing anything he liketh, so long are all men in the condition of war. But if other men will not lay down their right, as well as he, then there is no reason for anyone to divest himself of his, for that were to expose himself to prey, which no man is bound to, rather than to dispose himself to peace. This is that law of the gospel: *Whatsoever you require that others should do to you, that do ye to them.* And that law of all men, *quod tibi fieri non vis, alteri ne feceris [What you do not want done to you, do not do to another].*

What it is to lay down a right.

6. To *lay down* a man's *right* to anything is to *divest* himself of the *liberty* of hindering another of the benefit of his own right to the same. For he that renounceth or passeth away his right giveth not to any other man a right which he had not before, because there is nothing to which every man had not right by nature, but only standeth out of his way that he may enjoy his own original right without hindrance from him, not without hindrance from another. So that the effect which redoundeth to one man by another man's defect of right is but so much diminution of impediments to the use of his own right original.

Renouncing a right what it is. Transferring right what.

7. Right is laid aside either by simply renouncing it or by transferring it to another. By *simply* RENOUNCING, when he cares not to whom the benefit thereof redoundeth. By TRANSFERRING, when he intendeth the benefit thereof to some certain person or persons. And when a man hath in either manner abandoned or granted away his right, then is he said to be OBLIGED OR BOUND, not to hinder those to whom such right is granted, or abandoned, from the benefit of it; and that he *ought*, and it is DUTY, not to make void that voluntary act of his own; and that such hindrance is INJUSTICE and INJURY, as being *sine jure*; the right being before renounced or transferred. So that *injury* or *injustice*, in the controversies of the world, is somewhat like to that which in the disputations of scholars is called *absurdity.* For as it is there called an absurdity to contradict what one maintained in the beginning, so in the world it is called injustice and injury voluntarily to undo that which from the beginning he had voluntarily done. The way by which a man either simply renounceth or transferreth his right is a declaration or signification by some voluntary and sufficient sign or signs that he doth so renounce or transfer or hath so renounced or transferred the same to him that accepteth it. And these signs are either words only, or actions only; or, as it happeneth most often, both words and actions. And the same are the BONDS, by which men are

Obligation. Duty. Injustice.

bound and obliged, bonds that have their strength, not from their own nature (for nothing is more easily broken than a man's word), but from fear of some evil consequence upon the rupture.

8. Whensoever a man transferreth his right, or renounceth it, it is either in consideration of some right reciprocally transferred to himself, or for some [66] other good he hopeth for thereby. For it is a voluntary act; and of the voluntary acts of every man, the object is some *good to himself.* And therefore there be some rights which no man can be understood by any words, or other signs, to have abandoned or transferred. As first a man cannot lay down the right of resisting them that assault him by force to take away his life, because he cannot be understood to aim thereby at any good to himself. The same may be said of wounds, and chains, and imprisonment, both because there is no benefit consequent to such patience, as there is to the patience of suffering another to be wounded or imprisoned, as also because a man cannot tell when he seeth men proceed against him by violence whether they intend his death or not. And lastly the motive and end for which this renouncing and transferring of right is introduced is nothing else but the security of a man's person in his life, and in the means of so preserving life as not to be weary of it. And therefore if a man by words, or other signs, seem to despoil himself of the end for which those signs were intended, he is not to be understood as if he meant it, or that it was his will, but that he was ignorant of how such words and actions were to be interpreted.

Not all rights are alienable.

Contract what.

9. The mutual transferring of right is that which men call CONTRACT.

10. There is difference between transferring of right to the thing, and transferring or tradition, that is, delivery of the thing itself. For the thing may be delivered together with the translation of the right, as in buying and selling with ready money, or exchange of goods or lands; and it may be delivered some time after.

11. Again, one of the contractors may deliver the thing contracted for on his part, and leave the other to perform his part at some determinate time after, and in the meantime be trusted; and then the contract on his part is called PACT or COVENANT; or both parts may contract now to perform hereafter, in which cases he that is to perform in time to come, being trusted, his performance is called *keeping of promise*, or faith, and the failing of performance, if it be voluntary, *violation of faith.*

Covenant what.

12. When the transferring of right is not mutual, but one of the parties transferreth in hope to gain thereby friendship or service from another or from his friends; or in hope to gain the reputation of charity or magnanimity; or to deliver his mind from the pain of compassion; or in hope of reward in heaven; this is not contract, but GIFT, FREE GIFT, GRACE; which words signify one and the same thing.

Free gift.

13. Signs of contract are either *express* or *by inference.* Express are words spoken with understanding of what they signify; and such words are either of the time *present* or *past,* as, *I give, I grant, I have given, I have granted, I will that this be yours;* or of the future, as, *I will give, I will grant*, which words of the future are called PROMISE.

Signs of contract express.

14. Signs by inference are sometimes the consequence of words, sometimes the consequence of silence, sometimes the consequence of actions, sometimes the consequence of forbearing an action, and [67] generally a sign by inference, of any contract, is whatsoever sufficiently argues the will of the contractor.

Signs of contract by inference.

15. Words alone, if they be of the time to come, and contain a bare promise, are an insufficient sign of a free gift and therefore not obligatory. For if they be of the time to come, as, *tomorrow I will give*, they are a sign I have not given yet, and consequently that my right is not transferred, but remaineth till I transfer it by some other act. But if the words be of the time present or past, as, *I have given,* or *do give to be delivered tomorrow*, then is my tomorrow's right given away today; and that by the virtue of the words, though there were no other argument of my will. And there is a great difference in the signification of these words, *volo hoc tuum esse cras*, and *cras dabo*; that is, between *I will that this be thine tomorrow*, and, *I will give it thee tomorrow*, for the word *I will*, in the former manner of speech, signifies an act of the will present; but in the latter, it signifies a promise of an act of the will to come; and therefore the former words, being of the present, transfer a future right; the latter, that be of the future, transfer nothing. But if there be other signs of the will to transfer a right besides words,

Free gift passeth by words of the present or past.

then, though the gift be free, yet may the right be understood to pass by words of the future, as if a man propound a prize to him that comes first to the end of a race, the gift is free; and though the words be of the future, yet the right passeth, for if he would not have his words so be understood, he should not have let them run.

Signs of contract are words both of the past, present, and future.

16. In contracts the right passeth, not only where the words are of the time present or past, but also where they are of the future, because all contract is mutual translation or change of right; and therefore he that promiseth only, because he hath already received the benefit for which he promiseth, is to be understood as if he intended the right should pass, for unless he had been content to have his words so understood, the other would not have performed his part first. And for that cause, in buying and selling, and other acts of contract, a promise is equivalent to a covenant, and therefore obligatory.

Merit what.

17. He that performeth first in the case of a contract is said to MERIT that which he is to receive by the performance of the other, and he hath it as *due.* Also when a prize is propounded to many, which is to be given to him only that winneth, or money is thrown amongst many to be enjoyed by them that catch it, though this be a free gift; yet so to win or so to catch is to *merit,* and to have it as DUE. For the right is transferred in the propounding of the prize and in throwing down the money, though it be not determined to whom, but by the event of the contention. But there is between these two sorts of merit this difference, that in contract I merit by virtue of my own power and the contractor's need, but in this case of free gift I am enabled to merit only by the benignity of the giver; in contract I merit at the contractor's hand that he should depart with his right;
[68] in this case of gift, I merit not that the giver should part with his right but that when he has parted with it, it should be mine rather than another's. And this I think to be the meaning of that distinction of the Schools between *meritum congrui* and *meritum condigni.* For God Almighty, having promised paradise to those men, hoodwinked with carnal desires, that can walk through this world according to the precepts and limits prescribed by him, they say he that shall so walk shall merit paradise *ex congruo* [*from its appropriateness*]. But because no man can demand a right to it by his own righteousness, or any other power in himself, but by the free grace of God only, they say no man can merit paradise *ex condigno [from being deserved].* This, I say, I think is the meaning of that distinction; but because disputers do not agree upon the signification of their own terms of art longer than it serves their turn, I will not affirm anything of their meaning; only this I say; when a gift is given indefinitely, as a prize to be contended for, he that winneth meriteth, and may claim the prize as due.

Covenants of mutual trust, when invalid.

18. If a covenant be made wherein neither of the parties perform presently, but trust one another, in the condition of mere nature (which is a condition of war of every man against every man) upon any reasonable suspicion, it is void; but if there be a common power set over them both, with right and force sufficient to compel performance, it is not void. For he that performeth first has no assurance the other will perform after, because the bonds of words are too weak to bridle men's ambition, avarice, anger, and other passions, without the fear of some coercive power; which in the condition of mere nature, where all men are equal, and judges of the justness of their own fears, cannot possibly be supposed. And therefore he which performeth first does but betray himself to his enemy, contrary to the right he can never abandon of defending his life and means of living.

19. But in a civil estate, where there a power set up to constrain those that would otherwise violate their faith, that fear is no more reasonable; and for that cause, he which by the covenant is to perform first is obliged so to do.

20. The cause of fear, which maketh such a covenant invalid, must be always something arising after the covenant made, as some new fact or other sign of the will not to perform, else it cannot make the covenant void. For that which could not hinder a man from promising ought not to be admitted as a hindrance of performing.

Right to the end, containeth right to the means.

21. He that transferreth any right transferreth the means of enjoying it, as far as lieth in his power. As he that selleth land is understood to transfer the herbage and whatsoever grows upon it; nor can he that sells a mill turn away the stream that drives it. And they that give to a man the right of government in sovereignty are understood to give him the right of levying money to maintain soldiers, and of appointing magistrates for the administration of justice.

No covenant with beasts.

22. To make covenants with brute beasts is impossible, because not understanding our speech, they understand not, nor accept of any translation [69] of right, nor can translate any right to another; and without mutual acceptation, there is no covenant.

Nor with God without special revelation.

23. To make covenant with God is impossible but by mediation of such as God speaketh to either by revelation supernatural or by his lieutenants that govern under him and in his name; for otherwise we know not whether our covenants be accepted or not. And therefore they that vow anything contrary to any law of nature, vow in vain, as being a thing unjust to pay such vow. And if it be a thing commanded by the law of nature, it is not the vow, but the law that binds them.

No covenant, but of possible and future.

24. The matter or subject of a covenant is always something that falleth under deliberation; for to covenant is an act of the will, that is to say, an act, and the last act, of deliberation, and is therefore always understood to be something to come, and which judged possible for him that covenanteth to perform.

25. And therefore, to promise that which is known to be impossible is no covenant. But if that prove impossible afterwards, which before was thought possible, the covenant is valid and bindeth, though not to the thing itself, yet to the value; or, if that also be impossible, to the unfeigned endeavour of performing as much as is possible, for to more no man can be obliged.

Covenants, how made void.

26. Men are freed of their covenants two ways, by performing or by being forgiven. For performance is the natural end of obligation, and forgiveness the restitution of liberty, as being a retransferring of that right in which the obligation consisted.

Covenants extorted by fear are valid.

27. Covenants entered into by fear, in the condition of mere nature, are obligatory. For example, if I covenant to pay a ransom or service for my life to an enemy, I am bound by it. For it is a contract, wherein one receiveth the benefit of life, the other is to receive money or service for it; and consequently, where no other law (as in the condition of mere nature) forbiddeth the performance, the covenant is valid. Therefore prisoners of war, if trusted with the payment of their ransom, are obliged to pay it; and if a weaker prince make a disadvantageous peace with a stronger, for fear, he is bound to keep it, unless (as hath been said before) there ariseth some new and just cause of fear to renew the war. And even in commonwealths, if I be forced to redeem myself from a thief by promising him money, I am bound to pay it, till the civil law discharge me. For whatsoever I may lawfully do without obligation, the same I may lawfully covenant to do through fear; and what I lawfully covenant, I cannot lawfully break.

The former covenant to one make void the later to another.

28. A former covenant makes void a later. For a man that hath passed away his right to one man today hath it not to pass tomorrow to another; and therefore the later promise passeth no right, but is null.

A man's covenant not to defend himself is void.

29. A covenant not to defend myself from force, by force, is always void. For (as I have shown before) no man can transfer or lay down his right to save himself from death, wounds, and imprisonment, the avoiding whereof is the only end of laying down any right; and therefore the promise of not resisting[1] [70] force, in no covenant transferreth any right, nor is obliging. For though a man may covenant thus, *unless I do so, or so, kill me*; he cannot covenant thus *unless I do so, or so, I will not resist you when you come to kill me.* For man by nature chooseth the lesser evil, which is danger of death in resisting, rather than the greater, which is certain and present death in not resisting. And this is granted to be true by all men in that they lead criminals to execution and prison with armed men, notwithstanding that such criminals have consented to the law by which they are condemned.

No man obliged to accuse himself.

30. A covenant to accuse oneself, without assurance of pardon, is likewise invalid. For in the condition of nature where every man is judge, there is no place for accusation; and in the civil state the accusation is followed with punishment, which, being force, a man is not obliged not to resist. The same is also true of the accusation of those by whose condemnation a man falls into misery, as of a father, wife, or benefactor. For the testimony of such an accuser, if it be not willingly given, is presumed to be corrupted by nature, and therefore not to be received; and where a man's testimony is not to be credited, he is not bound to give it. Also accusations upon torture are not to be reputed as testimonies. For torture is to be used but as means of conjecture and light in the further examination and search of truth; and what is in that case confessed tendeth to the ease of him that is tortured, not to the informing of the torturers, and therefore ought not to have the credit of a sufficient testimony, for whether he deliver himself by true or false accusation, he does it by the right of preserving his own life.

The end of an oath.

31. The force of words being (as I have formerly noted) too weak to hold men to the performance of their covenants, there are in man's nature but two imaginable helps to strengthen it. And those are either a fear of the consequence of breaking their word or a glory or pride in appearing not to need to break it. This latter is a generosity too rarely found to be presumed on, especially in the pursuers of wealth, command, or sensual pleasure, which are the greatest part of mankind. The passion to be reckoned upon is fear; whereof there be two very general objects: one, the power of spirits invisible; the other, the power of those men they shall therein offend. Of these two, though the former be the greater power; yet the fear of the latter is commonly the greater fear. The fear of the former is in every man his own religion, which hath place in the nature of man before civil society. The latter hath not so, at least not place enough to keep men to their promises, because in the condition of mere nature, the inequality of power is not discerned, but by the event of battle. So that before the time of civil society, or in the interruption thereof by war, there is nothing can strengthen a covenant of peace agreed on against the temptations of avarice, ambition, lust, or other strong desire, but the fear of that invisible power which they every one worship as God, and fear as a revenger of their perfidy. All therefore that can be done between two men not subject to
[71] civil power is to put one another to swear by the God he feareth; which *swearing,* or OATH, is a *form of speech, added to a promise, by which he that promiseth signifieth that unless he perform he renounceth the mercy of his God, or calleth to him for vengeance on himself.* Such was the heathen form, *Let Jupiter kill me else, as I kill this beast.* So is our form, *I shall do thus, and thus, so help me God.* And this, with the rites and ceremonies which every one useth in his own religion, that the fear of breaking faith might be the greater.

The form of an oath.

No oath, but by God.

32. By this it appears that an oath taken according to any other form or rite than his that sweareth is in vain and no oath; and that there is no swearing by anything which the swearer thinks not God. For though men have sometimes used to swear by their kings, for fear, or flattery; yet they would have it thereby understood they attributed to them divine honour. And that swearing unnecessarily by God is but profaning of his name; and swearing by other things, as men do in common discourse, is not swearing, but an impious custom, gotten by too much vehemence of talking.

An oath adds nothing to the obligation.

33. It appears also that the oath adds nothing to the obligation. For a covenant, if lawful, binds in the sight of God, without the oath, as much as with it; if unlawful, bindeth not at all, though it be confirmed with an oath.

CHAPTER XV

OF OTHER LAWS OF NATURE

The third law of nature, Justice.

1. From that law of nature by which we are obliged to transfer to another such rights as, being retained, hinder the peace of mankind, there followeth a third, which is this; *that men perform their covenants made*; without which, covenants are in vain and but empty words; and the right of all men to all things remaining, we are still in the condition of war.

Justice and injustice what.

2. And in this law of nature consisteth the fountain and original of JUSTICE. For where no covenant hath preceded, there hath no right been transferred; and every man has right to everything; and consequently, no action can be unjust. But when a covenant is made, then to break it is *unjust* and the definition of INJUSTICE is no other than *the not performance of covenant.* And whatsoever is not unjust is *just.*[2]

Justice and propriety begin with the constitution of the commonwealth.

3. But because covenants of mutual trust, where there is a fear of not performance on either part (as hath been said in the former chapter), are invalid, though the original of justice be the making of covenants; yet injustice actually there can be none till

the cause of such fear be taken away; which, while men are in the natural condition of war, cannot be done. Therefore before the names of *just* and *unjust* can have place, there must be some coercive power to compel men equally to the performance of their covenants by the terror of some punishment
[72] greater than the benefit they expect by the breach of their covenant, and to make good that propriety which by mutual contract men acquire in recompense of the universal right they abandon; and such power there is none before the erection of a commonwealth. And this is also to be gathered out of the ordinary definition of justice in the Schools, for they say that *justice is the constant will of giving to every man his own.* And therefore where there is no *own*, that is, no propriety [property], there is no injustice; and where there is no coercive power erected, that is, where there is no commonwealth, there is no propriety, all men having right to all things; therefore where there is no commonwealth, there nothing is unjust. So that the nature of justice consisteth in keeping of valid covenants; but the validity of covenants begins not but with the constitution of a civil power sufficient to compel men to keep them; and then it is also that propriety begins.

Justice not contrary to reason.

4. The fool hath said in his heart, there is no such thing as justice; and sometimes also with his tongue, seriously alleging that every man's conservation and contentment being committed to his own care, there could be no reason why every man might not do what he thought conduced thereunto; and therefore also to make or not make, keep or not keep covenants was not against reason when it conduced to one's benefit. He does not therein deny that there be covenants; and that they are sometimes broken, sometimes kept; and that such breach of them may be called injustice, and the observance of them justice; but he questioneth whether injustice, taking away the fear of God (for the same fool hath said in his heart there is no God), not sometimes stand with that reason which dictateth to every man his own good; and particularly then, when it conduceth to such a benefit as shall put a man in a condition to neglect not only the dispraise and revilings, but also the power of other men. The kingdom of God is gotten by violence; but what if it could be gotten by unjust violence? Were it against reason so to get it, when it is impossible to receive hurt by it? And if it be not against reason, it is not against justice; or else justice is not to be approved for good. From such reasoning as this, successful wickedness hath obtained the name of virtue; and some that in all other things have disallowed the violation of faith, yet have allowed it when it is for the getting of a kingdom. And the heathen that believed that Saturn was deposed by his son Jupiter believed nevertheless the same Jupiter to be the avenger of injustice, somewhat like to a piece of law in Coke's* *Commentaries on Littleton,* where he says, if the right heir of the crown be attainted of treason, yet the crown shall descend to him, and *eo instante* the attainder be void; from which instances a man will be very prone to infer that when the heir apparent of a kingdom shall kill him that is in possession, though his father, you may call it injustice or by what other name you will; yet it can never be against reason, seeing all the voluntary actions of men tend to the benefit of themselves; and those actions are most reasonable that
conduce most to their ends. This specious reasoning [73]
is nevertheless false.

5. For the question is not of promises mutual, where there is no security of performance on either side, as when there is no civil power erected over the parties promising, for such promises are no covenants; but either where one of the parties has performed already or where there is a power to make him perform, there is the question whether it be against reason, that is, against the benefit of the other to perform or not. And I say it is not against reason. For the manifestation whereof we are to consider, first, that when a man doth a thing, which notwithstanding anything can be foreseen and reckoned on tendeth to his own destruction, howsoever some accident, which he could not expect, arriving may turn it to his benefit; yet such events do not make it reasonably or wisely done. Secondly, that in a condition of war, wherein every man to every man, for want of a common power to keep them all in awe, is an

* [Edward Coke (1552–1634) was England's leading theorist of the common law. This sometimes put him into opposition to King James I and later Charles I. His commentaries on the *Tenures* of Sir Thomas Littleton (c. 1422–81), an English jurist, are among his most famous works.]

enemy, there is no man can hope by his own strength or wit to himself from destruction without the help of confederates, where every one expects the same defence by the confederation that any one else does; and therefore he which declares he thinks it reason to deceive those that help him can in reason expect no other means of safety than what can be had from his own single power. He, therefore, that breaketh his covenant and consequently declareth that he thinks he may with reason do so, cannot be received into any society that unite themselves for peace and defence but by the error of them that receive him; nor when he is received be retained in it without seeing the danger of their error; which errors a man cannot reasonably reckon upon as the means of his security; and therefore if he be left or cast out of society, he perisheth; and if he live in society, it is by the errors of other men, which he could not foresee nor reckon upon, and consequently against the reason of his preservation; and so, as all men that contribute not to his destruction forbear him only out of ignorance of what is good for themselves.

6. As for the instance of gaining the secure and perpetual felicity of heaven by any way, it is frivolous; there being but one way imaginable, and that is not breaking, but keeping of covenant.

7. And for the other instance of attaining sovereignty by rebellion, it is manifest that, though the event follow; yet because it cannot reasonably be expected, but rather the contrary, and because, by gaining it so, others are taught to gain the same in like manner, the attempt thereof is against reason. Justice therefore, that is to say, keeping of covenant, is a rule of reason by which we are forbidden to do anything destructive to our life, and consequently a law of nature.

8. There be some that proceed further and will not have the law of nature to be those rules which conduce to the preservation of man's life on earth, but to the attaining of an eternal felicity after death, to which [felicity] they think the breach of covenant may conduce and consequently be just and reasonable; such are they that think it a work of merit to
[74] kill or depose or rebel against the sovereign power constituted over them by their own consent. But because there is no natural knowledge of man's estate after death, much less of the reward that is then to be given to breach of faith, but only a belief grounded upon other men's saying that they know it supernaturally or that they know those that knew them that knew others that knew it supernaturally, breach of faith cannot be called a precept of reason or nature.

Covenants not discharged by the vice of the person to whom they are made.

9. Others, that allow for a law of nature the keeping of faith, do nevertheless make exception of certain persons, as heretics, and such as use not to perform their covenant to others; and this also is against reason. For if any fault of a man be sufficient to discharge our covenant made, the same ought in reason to have been sufficient to have hindered the making of it.

Justice of men, & justice of actions what.

10. The names of *just* and *unjust*, when they are attributed to men, signify one thing, and, when they are attributed to actions, another. When they are attributed to men, they signify conformity or inconformity of manners to reason. But when they are attributed to action they signify the conformity or inconformity to reason, not of manners, or manner of life, but of particular actions. A just man therefore is he that taketh all the care he can that his actions may be all just; and an unjust man is he that neglecteth it. And such men are more often in our language styled by the names of righteous and unrighteous than just and unjust though the meaning be the same. Therefore a righteous man does not lose that title by one or a few unjust actions that proceed from sudden passion or mistake of things or persons; nor does an unrighteous man lose his character for such actions as he does or forbears to do for fear, because his will is not framed by the justice, but by the apparent benefit of what he is to do. That which gives to human actions the relish of justice is a certain nobleness or gallantness of courage, rarely found, by which a man scorns to be beholding for the contentment of his life to fraud or breach of promise. This justice of the manners is that which is meant where justice is called a virtue; and injustice, a vice.

11. But the justice of actions denominates men, not just, but *guiltless*; and the injustice of the same (which is also called injury) gives them but the name of *guilty*.

Justice of manners and justice of actions.

12. Again, the injustice of manners is the disposition or aptitude to do injury, and is injustice before it proceed to act and without supposing any individual

person injured. But the injustice of an action (that is to say, injury) supposeth an individual person injured; namely him to whom the covenant was made; and therefore many times the injury is received by one man when the damage redoundeth to another. As when the master commandeth his servant to give money to a stranger; if it be not done, the injury is done to the master, whom he had before covenanted to obey; but the damage redoundeth to the stranger, to whom he had no obligation, and therefore could
[75] not injure him. And so also in commonwealths private men may remit to one another their debts, but not robberies or other violences, whereby they are endamaged, because the detaining of debt is an injury to themselves; but robbery and violence are injuries to the person of the commonwealth.

Nothing done to a man by his own consent can be injury.

13. Whatsoever is done to a man, conformable to his own will signified to the doer, is not injury to him. For if he that doeth it hath not passed away his original right to do what he please by some antecedent covenant, there is no breach of covenant, and therefore no injury done him. And if he have, then his will to have it done, being signified, is a release of that covenant, and so again there is no injury done him. . . .*

34. These are the laws of nature, dictating peace, for a means of the conservation of men in multitudes; and which only concern the doctrine of civil society. There be other things tending to the destruction of particular men, as drunkenness, and all other parts of intemperance, which may therefore also be reckoned amongst those things which the law of nature
[79] hath forbidden, but are not necessary to be mentioned, nor are pertinent enough to this place.

A rule by which the laws of nature may easily be examined.

35. And though this may seem too subtle a deduction of the laws of nature to be taken notice of by all men, whereof the most part are too busy in getting food, and the rest too negligent to understand; yet to leave all men inexcusable, they have been contracted into one easy sum, intelligible even to the meanest capacity; and that is: *Do not that to another which thou wouldest not have done to thyself*; which showeth him that he has no more to do in learning the laws of nature but, when weighing the actions of other men with his own they seem too heavy, to put them into the other part of the balance, and his own into their place, that his own passions and self-love may add nothing to the weight; and then there is none of these laws of nature that will not appear unto him very reasonable.

The laws of nature oblige in conscienc always, but in effect then only where there is security.

36. The laws of nature oblige *in foro interno*, that is to say, they bind to a desire they should take place; but *in foro externo*; that is, to the putting them in act, not always. For he that should be modest and tractable, and perform all he promises in such time and place where no man else should do so, should but make himself a prey to others, and procure his own certain ruin, contrary to the ground of all laws of nature which tend to nature's preservation. And again, he that having sufficient security that others shall observe the same laws towards him, observes them not himself, seeketh not peace, but war, and consequently the destruction of his nature by violence.

37. And whatsoever laws bind *in foro interno* may be broken, not only by a fact contrary to the law, but also by a fact according to it, in case a man think it contrary. For though his action in this case be according to the law; yet his purpose was against the law; which, where the obligation is *in foro interno*, is a breach.

The law of natu are eter nal; and yet easy

38. The laws of nature are immutable and eternal, for injustice, ingratitude, arrogance, pride, iniquity, acception of persons, and the rest can never be made lawful. For it can never be that war shall preserve life, and peace destroy it.

39. The same laws, because they oblige only to a desire and endeavour, mean an unfeigned and constant endeavour, are easy to be observed. For in that they require nothing but endeavour, he that endeavoureth their performance fulfilleth them; and he that fulfilleth the law is just.

The science these l is the t moral losoph

40. And the science of them is the true and only moral philosophy. For moral philosophy is nothing else but the science of what is *good* and *evil* in the conversation [interactions] and society of mankind. *Good* and *evil* are names that signify our appetities and aversions, which in different tempers, customs, and doctrines of men are different; and divers men differ not only in their judgement on the senses of what is pleasant and unpleasant to the taste, smell,

* In the omitted sections from this chapter, Hobbes goes on to enumerate nineteen additional laws of nature.—Eds.

hearing, touch, and sight; but also of what is conformable or disagreeable to reason in the actions of common life. Nay, the same man, in divers times, differs from himself; and one time praiseth, that is, calleth *good*, what another time he dispraiseth, and calleth *evil*. From whence arise disputes, controver-
[80] sies, and at last war. And therefore so long a man is in the condition of mere nature (which is a condition of war), as private appetite is the measure of good and evil; and consequently all men agree on this, that peace is good, and therefore also the way or means of peace, which (as I have shown before) are *justice, gratitude, modesty, equity, mercy*, and the rest of the laws of nature, are good; that is to say, *moral virtues*; and their contrary *vices*, evil. Now the science of virtue and vice is moral philosophy; and therefore the true doctrine of the laws of nature is the true moral philosophy. But the writers of moral philosophy, though they acknowledge the same virtues and vices; yet, not seeing wherein consisted their goodness, nor that they come to be praised as the means of peaceable, sociable, and comfortable living, place them in a mediocrity of passions, as if not the cause, but the degree of daring, made fortitude, or not the cause, but the quantity of a gift, made liberality.

41. These dictates of reason men used to call by the name of laws, but improperly; for they are but conclusions or theorems concerning what conduceth to the conservation and defence of themselves; whereas law, properly, is the word of him that by right hath command over others. But yet if we consider the same theorems as delivered in the word of God that by right commandeth all things, then are they properly called *laws*.

[85]

PART II
OF COMMONWEALTH

CHAPTER XVII
OF THE CAUSES, GENERATION, AND DEFINITION OF A COMMONWEALTH

he end of commonwealth, articular security.

1. The final cause, end, or design of men (who naturally love liberty, and dominion over others) in the introduction of that restraint upon themselves (in which we see them live in commonwealths) is the foresight of their own preservation and of a more contented life thereby, that is to say, of getting themselves out from that miserable condition of war which is necessarily consequent (as hath been Chap 13.
shown) to the natural passions of men, when there is no visible power to keep them in awe and tie them by fear of punishment to the performance of their covenants and observation of those laws of nature set down in the fourteenth and fifteenth chapters.

Which is not to be had from the law of nature.

2. For the laws of nature (as *justice, equity, modesty, mercy,* and, in sum, *doing to others as we would be done to*) of themselves, without the terror of some power to cause them to be observed, are contrary to our natural passions that carry us to partiality, pride, revenge, and the like. And covenants without the sword are but words and of no strength to secure a man at all. Therefore, notwithstanding the laws of nature (which every one hath then kept, when he has the will to keep them, when he can do it safely), if there be no power erected or not great enough for our security, every man will and may lawfully rely on his own strength and art for caution against all other men. And in all places, where men have lived by small families, to rob and spoil one another has been a trade, and so far from being reputed against the law of nature, that the greater spoils they gained, the greater was their honour; and men observed no other laws therein but the laws of honour, that is, to abstain from cruelty, leaving to men their lives and instruments of husbandry. And as small families did then, so now do cities and kingdoms, which are but greater families (for their own security), enlarge their dominions, upon all pretences of danger and fear of invasion or assistance that may be given to invaders, endeavour as much as they can to subdue or weaken their neighbours by open force and secret arts, for want of other caution, justly, and are remembered for it in after ages with honour.

Nor from the conjunction of a few men or familes.

3. Nor is it the joining together of a small number of men that gives them this security, because in small numbers, small additions on the one side or the other make the advantage of strength so great as is sufficient to carry the victory, and therefore gives encouragement to an invasion. The multitude suffi- [86]
cient to confide in for our security is not determined by any certain number, but by comparison with the enemy we fear; and [it] is then sufficient, when the

odds of the enemy is not of so visible and conspicuous moment, to determine the event of war, as to move him to attempt.

Nor from a great multitude, unless directed by one judgment.

4. And be there never so great a multitude; yet if their actions be directed according to their particular judgements and particular appetites, they can expect thereby no defence nor protection, neither against a common enemy nor against the injuries of one another. For being distracted in opinions concerning the best use and application of their strength, they do not help but hinder one another; and [they] reduce their strength by mutual opposition to nothing, whereby they are easily not only subdued by a very few that agree together, but also, when there is no common enemy, they make war upon each other for their particular interests. For if we could suppose a great multitude of men to consent in the observation of justice and other laws of nature, without a common power to keep them all in awe, we might as well suppose all mankind to do the same; and then there neither would be nor need to be any civil government or commonwealth at all, because there would be peace without subjection.

And that continually.

5. Nor is it enough for the security which men desire should last all the time of their life, that they be governed and directed by one judgement for a limited time, as in one battle or one war. For though they obtain a victory by their unanimous endeavour against a foreign enemy; yet afterwards, when either they have no common enemy, or he that by one part is held for an enemy is by another part held for a friend, they must needs by the difference of their interests dissolve and fall again into a war amongst themselves.

Why certain creatures without reason or speech do nevertheless live in society, without any coercive power.

6. It is true that certain living creatures, as bees and ants, live sociably one with another (which are therefore by Aristotle numbered amongst political creatures), and yet have no other direction than their particular judgements and appetites, nor [do they have] speech, whereby one of them can signify to another what he thinks expedient for the common benefit; and therefore some man may perhaps desire to know why mankind cannot do the same. To which I answer,

7. First, that men are continually in competition for honour and dignity, which these creatures are not; and consequently amongst men there ariseth on that ground envy and hatred and finally war; but amongst these not so.

8. Secondly, that amongst these creatures the common good differeth not from the private; and being by nature inclined to their private, they procure thereby the common benefit. But man, whose joy consisteth in comparing himself with other men, can relish nothing but what is eminent.

9. Thirdly, that these creatures, having not, as man, the use of reason, do not see, nor think they see, any fault in the administration of their common business; whereas amongst men there are very many [87]
that think themselves wiser and abler to govern the public better than the rest; and these strive to reform and innovate, one this way, another that way, and thereby bring it into distraction and civil war.

10. Fourthly, that these creatures, though they have some use of voice in making known to one another their desires and other affections; yet they want that art of words by which some men can represent to others that which is good in the likeness of evil and evil in the likeness of good, and augment or diminish the apparent greatness of good and evil, discontenting men and troubling their peace at their pleasure.

11. Fifthly, irrational creatures cannot distinguish between *injury* and *damage*; and therefore as long as they be at ease, they are not offended with their fellows; whereas man is then most troublesome when he is most at ease; for then it is that he loves to show his wisdom, and control the actions of them that govern the commonwealth.

12. Lastly, the agreement of these creatures is natural; that of men is by covenant only, which is artificial; and therefore it is no wonder if there be somewhat else required, besides covenant, to make their agreement constant and lasting, which is a common power to keep them in awe and to direct their actions to the common benefit.

The generation of a commonwealth.

13. The only way to erect such a common power as may be able to defend them from the invasion of foreigners and the injuries of one another, and thereby to secure them in such sort as that by their own industry and by the fruits of the earth they may nourish themselves and live contentedly, is to confer all their power and strength[3] upon one man or upon one assembly of men, that may reduce all their wills by plurality of voices unto one will; which is as much as to say, to appoint one man or assembly of men to bear their person; and every one to own and acknowledge himself to be author of whatsoever he that so beareth their person shall act or cause to be acted in those things which concern the common peace and safety; and therein to submit their wills, every one to his will, and their judgements to his judgement.[4] This is more than consent or concord; it is a real unity of them all in one and the same person, made by covenant of every man with every man in such manner as if every man should say to every man, *I authorize and give up my right of governing myself to this man, or to this assembly of men, on this condition: that thou give up thy right to him, and authorize all his actions in like manner.* This done, the multitude so united in one person is called a COMMONWEALTH; in Latin, CIVITAS. This is the generation of that great LEVIATHAN,[5] or rather, to speak more reverently, of that *mortal god* to which we owe, under the *immortal God*, our peace and defense. For by this authority, given him by every particular man in the commonwealth, he hath the use of so much [88] power and strength conferred on him that, by terror thereof, he is enabled to conform[6] the wills of them all to peace at home and mutual aid against their enemies abroad. And in him consisteth the essence of the commonwealth, which, to define it, is *one person, of whose acts a great multitude, by mutual covenants one with another, have made themselves every one the author, to the end he may use the strength and means of them all as he shall think expedient for their peace and common defense.*

[The defi-ion of a -mmon-wealth.]

[Sover-gn, and subject, what.]

14. And he that carryeth this person is called SOVEREIGN, and said to have *sovereign power*, and every one besides, his SUBJECT.

15. The attaining to this sovereign power is by two ways. One, by natural force, as when a man maketh his children to submit themselves and their children to his government, as being able to destroy them if they refuse, or by war subdueth his enemies to his will, giving them their lives on that condition. The other is when men agree amongst themselves to submit to some man, or assembly of men, voluntarily, on confidence to be protected by him against all others. This latter may be called a political commonwealth or commonwealth by *institution*, and the former [may be called] a commonwealth by *acquisition*.

NOTES

1. The fundamental precept or general rule consists of two parts: the first part is the first or fundamental law of nature; the second part is the right of nature.
2. "Just" and "unjust" are normally contraries, not contradictories. However, Hobbes defines "just" in such a way that it becomes the contradictory of "unjust." Taking his definitions strictly, anyone in the state of nature who makes no convenants is just, because he is not unjust.
3. If citizens confer all of their power and strength on the sovereign, it would appear that they would have none left for themselves.
4. Each person wills to will what the sovereign wills and to judge as the sovereign judges.
5. See Job 41, Psalms 74.15–17, and Is. 27.1. In the Bible, Leviathan, sometimes pictured as a whale and sometimes as a crocodile, is a principle of chaos and an enemy of God, whom God defeats. For Hobbes, Leviathan saves people from the state of nature. At 28.27, Hobbes quotes the book of Job, which says at 41:34 that Leviathan is "king of all the children of pride." Christian theologians often identified pride as the cause of sin.
6. Many editions have "conform" and there is some textual support for "form." But "conform" makes more sense.

"Justice as Fairness" from *A Theory of Justice*

JOHN RAWLS

John Rawls (1921–2002) taught philosophy at Harvard University for more than 40 years. His enormously influential *A Theory of Justice* (1971) is one of the most widely read books in twentieth-century philosophy, considered required reading not only for philosophers and political theorists, but also for legal scholars, economists, and sociologists.

The selections that appear here are excerpted from Part I of *A Theory of Justice*; section numbers have been preserved to allow cross-reference to the original text. In these passages, Rawls presents and argues for his view of *justice as fairness*, according to which a just society is one in which all citizens are equal with respect to their basic rights and access to opportunities and in which inequalities persist only if removing them would worsen the condition of those who are worst off.

1. THE ROLE OF JUSTICE

Justice is the first virtue of social institutions, as truth is of systems of thought. A theory however elegant and economical must be rejected or revised if it is untrue; likewise laws and institutions no matter how efficient and well-arranged must be reformed or abolished if they are unjust. Each person possesses an inviolability founded on justice that even the welfare of society as a whole cannot override. For this reason justice denies that the loss of freedom for some is made right by a greater good shared by others. It does not allow that the sacrifices imposed on a few are outweighed by the larger sum of advantages enjoyed by many. Therefore in a just society the liberties of equal citizenship are taken as settled; the rights secured by justice are not subject to political bargaining or to the calculus of social interests. The only thing that permits us to acquiesce in an erroneous theory is the lack of a better one; analogously, an injustice is tolerable only when it is necessary to avoid an even greater injustice. Being first virtues of human activities, truth and justice are uncompromising.

These propositions seem to express our intuitive conviction of the primacy of justice. No doubt they are expressed too strongly. In any event I wish to inquire whether these contentions or others similar to them are sound, and if so how they can be accounted for. To this end it is necessary to work out a theory of justice in the light of which these assertions can be interpreted and assessed. I shall begin by considering the role of the principles of justice. Let us assume, to fix ideas, that a society is a more or less self-sufficient association of persons who in their relations to one another recognize certain rules of conduct as binding and who for the most part act in accordance with them. Suppose further that these rules specify a system of cooperation designed to advance the good of those taking part in it. Then, although a society is a cooperative venture for mutual advantage, it is typically marked by a conflict as well as by an identity of interests. There is an identity of interests since social cooperation makes possible a better life for all than any would have if each were to live solely by his own efforts. There is a conflict of interests since persons are not indifferent as to how the greater benefits produced by their collaboration are distributed, for in order to pursue their ends they each prefer a larger to a lesser share. A set of principles is required for choosing among the various social arrangements which determine this division of advantages and for

From A *Theory of Justice* (Cambridge, Mass: The Belknap Press of Harvard University), pp. 3–4, 6–7, 10–11, 15–19, 22–24, 52–56, 130–135.
Copyright © 1971, 1999 by the President and Fellows of Harvard College. Reprinted by permission of the publisher.

underwriting an agreement on the proper distributive shares. These principles are the principles of social justice: they provide a way of assigning rights and duties in the basic institutions of society and they define the appropriate distribution of the benefits and burdens of social cooperation. . . .

2. THE SUBJECT OF JUSTICE

Many different kinds of things are said to be just and unjust: not only laws, institutions, and social systems, but also particular actions of many kinds, including decisions, judgments, and imputations. We also call the attitudes and dispositions of persons, and persons themselves, just and unjust. Our topic, however, is that of social justice. For us the primary subject of justice is the basic structure of society, or more exactly, the way in which the major social institutions distribute fundamental rights and duties and determine the division of advantages from social cooperation. By major institutions I understand the political constitution and the principal economic and social arrangements. Thus the legal protection of freedom of thought and liberty of conscience, competitive markets, private property in the means of production, and the monogamous family are examples of major social institutions. Taken together as one scheme, the major institutions define men's rights and duties and influence their life prospects, what they can expect to be and how well they can hope to do. The basic structure is the primary subject of justice because its effects are so profound and present from the start. The intuitive notion here is that this structure contains various social positions and that men born into different positions have different expectations of life determined, in part, by the political system as well as by economic and social circumstances. In this way the institutions of society favor certain starting places over others. These are especially deep inequalities. Not only are they pervasive, but they affect men's initial chances in life; yet they cannot possibly be justified by an appeal to the notions of merit or desert. It is these inequalities, presumably inevitable in the basic structure of any society, to which the principles of social justice must in the first instance apply. These principles, then, regulate the choice of a political constitution and the main elements of the economic and social system. The justice of a social scheme depends essentially on how fundamental rights and duties are assigned and on the economic opportunities and social conditions in the various sectors of society. . . .

3. THE MAIN IDEA OF THE THEORY OF JUSTICE

My aim is to present a conception of justice which generalizes and carries to a higher level of abstraction the familiar theory of the social contract as found, say, in Locke, Rousseau, and Kant.[1] In order to do this we are not to think of the original contract as one to enter a particular society or to set up a particular form of government. Rather, the guiding idea is that the principles of justice for the basic structure of society are the object of the original agreement. They are the principles that free and rational persons concerned to further their own interests would accept in an initial position of equality as defining the fundamental terms of their association. These principles are to regulate all further agreements; they specify the kinds of social cooperation that can be entered into and the forms of government that can be established. This way of regarding the principles of justice I shall call justice as fairness.

Thus we are to imagine that those who engage in social cooperation choose together, in one joint act, the principles which are to assign basic rights and duties and to determine the division of social benefits. Men are to decide in advance how they are to regulate their claims against one another and what is to be the foundation charter of their society. Just as each person must decide by rational reflection what constitutes his good, that is, the system of ends which it is rational for him to pursue, so a group of persons must decide once and for all what is to count among them as just and unjust. The choice which rational men would make in this hypothetical situation of equal liberty, assuming for the present that this choice problem has a solution, determines the principles of justice.

In justice as fairness the original position of equality corresponds to the state of nature in the traditional theory of the social contract. This original position is not, of course, thought of as an actual historical state of affairs, much less as a primitive condition of culture. It is understood as a purely hypothetical situation characterized so as to lead to a certain conception of justice.[2] Among the essential features of this situation is that no one knows his place in society, his class position or social status, nor does any one know his fortune in the distribution of natural assets and abilities, his intelligence, strength, and the like. I shall even assume that the parties do not know their conceptions of the good or their special psychological propensities. The principles of justice are chosen behind a veil of ignorance. This ensures that no one is advantaged or disadvantaged in the choice of principles by the outcome of natural chance or the contingency of social circumstances. Since all are similarly situated and no one is able to design principles to favor his particular condition, the principles of justice are the result of a fair agreement or bargain. For given the circumstances of the original position, the symmetry of everyone's relations to each other, this initial situation is fair between individuals as moral persons, that is, as rational beings with their own ends and capable, I shall assume, of a sense of justice. The original position is, one might say, the appropriate initial status quo, and thus the fundamental agreements reached in it are fair. This explains the propriety of the name "justice as fairness": it conveys the idea that the principles of justice are agreed to in an initial situation that is fair. The name does not mean that the concepts of justice and fairness are the same, any more than the phrase "poetry as metaphor" means that the concepts of poetry and metaphor are the same. . . .

4. THE ORIGINAL POSITION AND JUSTIFICATION

I have said that the original position is the appropriate initial status quo which insures that the fundamental agreements reached in it are fair. This fact yields the name "justice as fairness." It is clear, then, that I want to say that one conception of justice is more reasonable than another, or justifiable with respect to it, if rational persons in the initial situation would choose its principles over those of the other for the role of justice. Conceptions of justice are to be ranked by their acceptability to persons so circumstanced. Understood in this way the question of justification is settled by working out a problem of deliberation: we have to ascertain which principles it would be rational to adopt given the contractual situation. This connects the theory of justice with the theory of rational choice.

If this view of the problem of justification is to succeed, we must, of course, describe in some detail the nature of this choice problem. A problem of rational decision has a definite answer only if we know the beliefs and interests of the parties, their relations with respect to one another, the alternatives between which they are to choose, the procedure whereby they make up their minds, and so on. As the circumstances are presented in different ways, correspondingly different principles are accepted. The concept of the original position, as I shall refer to it, is that of the most philosophically favored interpretation of this initial choice situation for the purposes of a theory of justice.

But how are we to decide what is the most favored interpretation? I assume, for one thing, that there is a broad measure of agreement that principles of justice should be chosen under certain conditions. To justify a particular description of the initial situation one shows that it incorporates these commonly shared presumptions. One argues from widely accepted but weak premises to more specific conclusions. Each of the presumptions should by itself be natural and plausible; some of them may seem innocuous or even trivial. The aim of the contract approach is to establish that taken together they impose significant bounds on acceptable principles of justice. The ideal outcome would be that these conditions determine a unique set of principles; but I shall be satisfied if they suffice to rank the main traditional conceptions of social justice.

One should not be misled, then, by the somewhat unusual conditions which characterize the original position. The idea here is simply to make vivid to ourselves the restrictions that it seems reasonable to impose on arguments for principles of justice, and therefore on these principles themselves. Thus it seems reasonable and generally acceptable that no one should be advantaged or disadvantaged by natural fortune or social circumstances in the choice of principles. It also seems widely agreed that it should be impossible to tailor principles to the circumstances of one's own case. We should insure further that particular inclinations and aspirations, and persons' conceptions of their good do not affect the principles adopted. The aim is to rule out those principles that it would be rational to propose for acceptance, however little the chance of success, only if one knew certain things that are irrelevant from the standpoint of justice. For example, if a man knew that he was wealthy, he might find it rational to advance the principle that various taxes for welfare measures be counted unjust; if he knew that he was poor, he would most likely propose the contrary principle. To represent the desired restrictions one imagines a situation in which everyone is deprived of this sort of information. One excludes the knowledge of those contingencies which sets men at odds and allows them to be guided by their prejudices. In this manner the veil of ignorance is arrived at in a natural way. This concept should cause no difficulty if we keep in mind the constraints on arguments that it is meant to express. At any time we can enter the original position, so to speak, simply by following a certain procedure, namely, by arguing for principles of justice in accordance with these restrictions.

It seems reasonable to suppose that the parties in the original position are equal. That is, all have the same rights in the procedure for choosing principles; each can make proposals, submit reasons for their acceptance, and so on. Obviously the purpose of these conditions is to represent equality between human beings as moral persons, as creatures having a conception of their good and capable of a sense of justice. The basis of equality is taken to be similarity in these two respects. Systems of ends are not ranked in value; and each man is presumed to have the requisite ability to understand and to act upon whatever principles are adopted. Together with the veil of ignorance, these conditions define the principles of justice as those which rational persons concerned to advance their interests would consent to as equals when none are known to be advantaged or disadvantaged by social and natural contingencies.

There is, however, another side to justifying a particular description of the original position. This is to see if the principles which would be chosen match our considered convictions of justice or extend them in an acceptable way. We can note whether applying these principles would lead us to make the same judgments about the basic structure of society which we now make intuitively and in which we have the greatest confidence; or whether, in cases where our present judgments are in doubt and given with hesitation, these principles offer a resolution which we can affirm on reflection. There are questions which we feel sure must be answered in a certain way. For example, we are confident that religious intolerance and racial discrimination are unjust. We think that we have examined these things with care and have reached what we believe is an impartial judgment not likely to be distorted by an excessive attention to our own interests. These convictions are provisional fixed points which we presume any conception of justice must fit. But we have much less assurance as to what is the correct distribution of wealth and authority. Here we may be looking for a way to remove our doubts. We can check an interpretation of the initial situation, then, by the capacity of its principles to accommodate our firmest convictions and to provide guidance where guidance is needed.

In searching for the most favored description of this situation we work from both ends. We begin by describing it so that it represents generally shared and preferably weak conditions. We then see if these conditions are strong enough to yield a significant set of principles. If not, we look for further premises equally reasonable. But if so, and these principles match our considered convictions of justice, then so far well and good. But presumably there will be discrepancies. In this case we have a choice. We can either modify the account of the initial situation or we can revise our existing judgments, for even the judgments we take provisionally as fixed points are liable to revision. By going back and forth, sometimes altering the conditions of the contractual circumstances, at others withdrawing our judgments and conforming them to principle, I assume that eventually we shall find a description of the initial situation that both expresses reasonable conditions and yields principles which match our considered judgments duly pruned and adjusted. This state of affairs I refer to as reflective equilibrium.[3] It is an equilibrium because at last our principles and judgments coincide; and it is reflective since we know to what principles our judgments conform and the premises of their derivation. At the moment everything is in order. But this equilibrium is not necessarily stable. It is liable to be upset by further examination of the conditions which should be imposed on the contractual situation and by particular cases which may lead us to revise our judgments. Yet for the time being we have done what we can to render coherent and to justify our convictions of social justice. We have reached a conception of the original position.

I shall not, of course, actually work through this process. Still, we may think of the interpretation of the original position that I shall present as the result of such a hypothetical course of reflection. It represents the attempt to accommodate within one scheme both reasonable philosophical conditions on principles as well as our considered judgments of justice. In arriving at the favored interpretation of the initial situation there is no point at which an appeal is made to self-evidence in the traditional sense either of general conceptions or particular convictions. I do not claim for the principles of justice proposed that they are necessary truths or derivable from such truths. A conception of justice cannot be deduced from self-evident premises or conditions on principles; instead, its justification is a matter of the mutual support of many considerations, of everything fitting together into one coherent view.

A final comment. We shall want to say that certain principles of justice are justified because they would be agreed to in an initial situation of equality. I have emphasized that this original position is purely hypothetical. It is natural to ask why, if this agreement is never actually entered into, we should take any interest in these principles, moral or otherwise. The answer is that the conditions embodied in the description of the original position are ones that we do in fact accept. Or if we do not, then perhaps we can be persuaded to do so by philosophical reflection. Each aspect of the contractual situation can be given supporting grounds. Thus what we shall do is to collect together into one conception a number of conditions on principles that we are ready upon due consideration to recognize as reasonable. These constraints express what we are prepared to regard as limits on fair terms of social cooperation. One way to look at the idea of the original position, therefore, is to see it as an expository device which sums up the meaning of these conditions and helps us to extract their consequences. On the other hand, this conception is also an intuitive notion that suggests its own elaboration, so that led on by it we are drawn to define more clearly the standpoint from which we can best interpret moral relationships. We need a conception that enables us to envision our objective from afar: the intuitive notion of the original position is to do this for us. . . .[4]

5. CLASSICAL UTILITARIANISM

. . . My aim is to work out a theory of justice that represents an alternative to utilitarian thought generally and so to all of these different versions of it. I believe that the contrast between the contract view and utilitarianism remains essentially the same in all these cases. . . . The kind of utilitarianism I shall describe here is the strict classical doctrine which receives perhaps its clearest and most accessible formulation in Sidgwick. The main idea is that society is rightly ordered, and therefore just, when its major institutions are arranged so as to achieve the greatest net balance of satisfaction summed over all the individuals belonging to it.[5]

We may note first that there is, indeed, a way of thinking of society which makes it easy to suppose that the most rational conception of justice is utilitarian. For consider: each man in realizing his own interests is certainly free to balance his own losses against his own gains. We may impose a sacrifice on ourselves now for the sake of a greater advantage later. A person quite properly acts, at least when others are not affected, to achieve his own greatest good, to advance his rational ends as far as possible. Now why should not a society act on precisely the same principle applied to the group and therefore regard that which is rational for one man as right for an association of men? Just as the well-being of a person is constructed from the series of satisfactions that are experienced at different moments in the course of his life, so in very much the same way the well-being of society is to be constructed from the fulfillment of the systems of desires of the many individuals who belong to it. Since the principle for an individual is to advance as far as possible his own welfare, his own system of desires, the principle for society is to advance as far as possible the welfare of the group, to realize to the greatest extent the comprehensive system of desire arrived at from the desires of its members. Just as an individual balances present and future gains against present and future losses, so a society may balance satisfactions and dissatisfactions between different individuals. And so by these reflections one reaches the principle of utility in a natural way: a society is properly arranged when its institutions maximize the net balance of satisfaction. The principle of choice for an association of men is interpreted as an extension of the principle of choice for one man. Social justice is the principle of rational prudence applied to an aggregative conception of the welfare of the group.[6]

This idea is made all the more attractive by a further consideration. The two main concepts of ethics are those of the right and the good; the concept of a morally worthy person is, I believe, derived from them. The structure of an ethical theory is, then, largely determined by how it defines and connects these two basic notions. Now it seems that the simplest way of relating them is taken by teleological theories: the good is defined independently from the right, and then the right is defined as that which maximizes the good.[7] More precisely, those institutions and acts are right which of the available alternatives produce the most good, or at least as much good as any of the other institutions and acts open as real possibilities (a rider needed when the maximal class is not a singleton). Teleological theories have a deep intuitive appeal since they seem to embody the idea of rationality. It is natural to think that rationality is maximizing something and that in morals it must be maximizing the good. Indeed, it is tempting to suppose that it is self-evident that things should be arranged so as to lead to the most good.

It is essential to keep in mind that in a teleological theory the good is defined independently from the right. This means two things. First, the theory accounts for our considered judgments as to which things are good (our judgments of value) as a separate class of judgments intuitively distinguishable by common sense, and then proposes the hypothesis that the right is maximizing the good as already specified. Second, the theory enables one to judge the goodness of things without referring to what is right. For example, if pleasure is said to be the sole good, then presumably pleasures can be recognized and ranked in value by criteria that do not presuppose any standards of right, or what we would normally think of as such. Whereas if the distribution of goods is also counted as a good, perhaps a higher order one, and the theory directs us to produce the most good (including the good of distribution among others), we no longer have a teleological view in the classical sense. The problem of distribution falls under the concept of right as one intuitively understands it, and so the theory lacks an independent definition of the good. The clarity and simplicity of classical teleological theories derives largely from the fact that they factor our moral judgments into two classes, the one being characterized separately while the other is then connected with it by a maximizing principle.

Teleological doctrines differ, pretty clearly, according to how the conception of the good is specified. If it is taken as the realization of human excellence in the various forms of culture, we have what may be called perfectionism. This notion is found in Aristotle and Nietzsche, among others. If the good is defined as pleasure, we have hedonism; if as happiness, eudaimonism, and so on. I shall understand the principle of utility in its classical form as defining the good as the satisfaction of desire, or perhaps better, as the satisfaction of rational desire. This accords with the view in all essentials and provides, I believe, a fair interpretation of it. The appropriate terms of social cooperation are settled by whatever in the circumstances will achieve the greatest sum of satisfaction of the rational desires of individuals. It is impossible to deny the initial plausibility and attractiveness of this conception.

The striking feature of the utilitarian view of justice is that it does not matter, except indirectly, how this sum of satisfactions is distributed among individuals any more than it matters, except indirectly, how one man distributes his satisfactions over time. The correct distribution in either case is that which yields the maximum fulfillment. Society must allocate its means of satisfaction whatever these are, rights and duties, opportunities and privileges, and various forms of wealth, so as to achieve this maximum if it can. But in itself no distribution of satisfaction is better than another except that the more equal distribution is to be preferred to break ties. It is true that certain common sense precepts of justice, particularly those which concern the protection of liberties and rights, or which express the claims of desert, seem to contradict this contention. But from a utilitarian standpoint the explanation of these precepts and of their seemingly stringent character is that they are those precepts which experience shows should be strictly respected and departed from only under exceptional circumstances if the sum of advantages is to be maximized.[8] Yet, as with all other precepts, those of justice are derivative from the one end of attaining the greatest balance of satisfaction. Thus there is no reason in principle why the greater gains of some should not compensate for the lesser losses of others; or more importantly, why the violation of the liberty of a few might not be made right by the greater good shared by many. It simply happens that under most conditions, as least in a reasonably advanced stage of civilization, the greatest sum of advantages is not attained in this way. No doubt the strictness of common sense precepts of justice has a certain usefulness in limiting men's propensities to injustice and to socially injurious actions, but the utilitarian believes that to affirm this strictness as a first principle of morals is a mistake. For just as it is rational for one man to maximize the fulfillment of his system of desires, it is right for a society to maximize the net balance of satisfaction taken over all of its members.

The most natural way, then, of arriving at utilitarianism (although not, of course, the only way of doing so) is to adopt for society as a whole the principle of rational choice for one man. Once this is recognized, the place of the impartial spectator and the emphasis on sympathy in the history of utilitarian thought is readily understood. For it is by the conception of the impartial spectator and the use of sympathetic identification in guiding our imagination that the principle for one man is applied to society. It is this spectator who is conceived as carrying out the required organization of the desires of all persons into one coherent system of desire; it is by this construction that many persons are fused into one. Endowed with ideal powers of sympathy and imagination, the impartial spectator is the perfectly rational individual who identifies with and experiences the desires of others as if these desires were his own. In this way he ascertains the intensity of these desires and assigns them their appropriate weight in the one system of desire the satisfaction of which the ideal legislator then tries to maximize by adjusting the rules of the social system. On this conception of society separate individuals are thought of as so many different lines along which rights and duties are to be assigned and scarce means of satisfaction allocated in accordance with rules so as to give the greatest fulfillment of wants. The nature of the decision made by the ideal legislator is not, therefore, materially different from that of an entrepreneur deciding how to maximize his profit by producing this or that commodity, or that of a consumer deciding how to maximize his satisfaction by the purchase of this or that collection of goods. In each case there is a single person whose system of desires determines the best allocation of limited means. The correct decision is essentially a question of efficient administration. This view of social cooperation is the consequence of extending to society the principle of choice for one man, and then, to make this extension work, conflating all persons into one through the imaginative acts of the impartial sympathetic spectator. Utilitarianism does not take seriously the distinction between persons.

. . .

11. TWO PRINCIPLES OF JUSTICE

I shall now state in a provisional form the two principles of justice that I believe would be agreed to in the original position. . . .

The first statement of the two principles reads as follows.

First: each person is to have an equal right to the most extensive scheme of equal basic liberties compatible with a similar scheme of liberties for others.

Second: social and economic inequalities are to be arranged so that they are both (a) reasonably expected to be to everyone's advantage, and (b) attached to positions and offices open to all. . . .

These principles primarily apply, as I have said, to the basic structure of society and govern the assignment of rights and duties and regulate the distribution of social and economic advantages. Their formulation presupposes that, for the purposes of a theory of justice, the social structure may be viewed as having two more or less distinct parts, the first principle applying to the one, the second principle to the other. Thus we distinguish between the aspects of the social system that define and secure the equal basic liberties and the aspects that specify and establish social and economic inequalities. Now it is essential to observe that the basic liberties are given by a list of such liberties. Important among these are political liberty (the right to vote and to hold public office) and freedom of speech and assembly; liberty of conscience and freedom of thought; freedom of the person, which includes freedom from psychological oppression and physical assault and dismemberment (integrity of the person); the right to hold personal property and freedom from arbitrary arrest and seizure as defined by the concept of the rule of law. These liberties are to be equal by the first principle.

The second principle applies, in the first approximation, to the distribution of income and wealth and to the design of organizations that make use of differences in authority and responsibility. While the distribution of wealth and income need not be equal, it must be to everyone's advantage, and at the same time, positions of authority and responsibility must be accessible to all. One applies the second principle by holding positions open, and then, subject to this constraint, arranges social and economic inequalities so that everyone benefits.

These principles are to be arranged in a serial order with the first principle prior to the second. This ordering means that infringements of the basic equal liberties protected by the first principle cannot be justified, or compensated for, by greater social and economic advantages. These liberties have a central range of application within which they can be limited and compromised only when they conflict with other basic liberties. Since they may be limited when they clash with one another, none of these liberties is absolute; but however they are adjusted to form one system, this system is to be the same for all. It is difficult, and perhaps impossible, to give a complete specification of these liberties independently from the particular circumstances—social, economic, and technological—of a given society. The hypothesis is that the general form of such a list could be devised with sufficient exactness to sustain this conception of justice. Of course, liberties not on the list, for example, the right to own certain kinds of property (e.g., means of production) and freedom of contract as understood by the doctrine of laissez-faire are not basic; and so they are not protected by the priority of the first principle. Finally, in regard to the second principle, the distribution of wealth and income, and positions of authority and responsibility, are to be consistent with both the basic liberties and equality of opportunity.

The two principles are rather specific in their content, and their acceptance rests on certain assumptions that I must eventually try to explain and justify. For the present, it should be observed that these principles are a special case of a more general conception of justice that can be expressed as follows.

> All social values—liberty and opportunity, income and wealth, and the social bases of self-respect—are to be distributed equally unless an unequal distribution of any, or all, of these values is to everyone's advantage.

Injustice, then, is simply inequalities that are not to the benefit of all. Of course, this conception is extremely vague and requires interpretation.

As a first step, suppose that the basic structure of society distributes certain primary goods, that is, things that every rational man is presumed to want. These goods normally have a use whatever a person's rational plan of life. For simplicity, assume that the chief primary goods at the disposition of society are rights, liberties, and opportunities, and income and wealth. (Later [in the book] the primary good of self-respect has a central place.) These are the social primary goods. Other primary goods such as health and vigor, intelligence and imagination, are natural goods; although their possession is influenced by the basic structure, they are not so directly under its control. Imagine, then, a hypothetical initial arrangement in which all the social primary goods are equally distributed: everyone has similar rights and duties, and income and wealth are evenly shared. This state of affairs provides a benchmark for judging improvements. If certain inequalities of wealth and differences in authority would make everyone better off than in this hypothetical starting situation, then they accord with the general conception.

Now it is possible, at least theoretically, that by giving up some of their fundamental liberties men are sufficiently compensated by the resulting social and economic gains. The general conception of justice imposes no restrictions on what sort of inequalities are permissible; it only requires that everyone's position be improved. We need not suppose anything so drastic as consenting to a condition of slavery. Imagine instead that people seem willing to forego certain political rights when the economic returns are significant. It is this kind of exchange which the two principles rule out; being arranged in serial order they do not permit exchanges between basic liberties and economic and social gains except under extenuating circumstances . . .

Now the second principle insists that each person benefit from permissible inequalities in the basic structure. This means that it must be reasonable for each relevant representative man defined by this structure, when he views it as a going concern, to prefer his prospects with the inequality to his prospects without it. One is not allowed to justify differences in income or in positions of authority and responsibility on the ground that the disadvantages of those in one position are outweighed by the greater advantages of those in another. Much less can infringements of liberty be counterbalanced in this way. . . .

26. THE REASONING LEADING TO THE TWO PRINCIPLES OF JUSTICE

In this . . . section I take up the choice between the two principles of justice and the principle of average utility. Determining the rational preference between these two options is perhaps the central problem in developing the conception of justice as fairness as a viable alternative to the utilitarian tradition. I shall begin in this section by presenting some intuitive remarks favoring the two principles. I shall also discuss briefly the qualitative structure of the argument that needs to be made if the case for these principles is to be conclusive.

Now consider the point of view of anyone in the original position. There is no way for him to win special advantages for himself. Nor, on the other hand, are there grounds for his acquiescing in special disadvantages. Since it is not reasonable for him to expect more than an equal share in the division of social primary goods, and since it is not rational for him to agree to less, the sensible thing is to acknowledge as the first step a principle of justice requiring an equal distribution. Indeed, this principle is so obvious given the symmetry of the parties that it would occur to everyone immediately. Thus the parties start with a principle requiring equal basic liberties for all, as well as fair equality of opportunity and equal division of income and wealth.

But even holding firm to the priority of the basic liberties and fair equality of opportunity, there is no reason why this initial acknowledgment should be final. Society should take into account economic efficiency and the requirements of organization and technology. If there are inequalities in income and wealth, and differences in authority and degrees of responsibility, that work to make everyone better off in comparison with the benchmark of equality, why not permit them? One might think that ideally individuals should want to serve one another. But since the parties are assumed to be mutually disinterested, their acceptance of these economic and institutional inequalities is only the recognition of the relations of opposition in which men stand in the circumstances of justice. They have no grounds for complaining of one another's motives. Thus the parties would agree to these differences only if they would be dejected by the bare knowledge or perception that others are better situated; but I suppose that they decide as if they are not moved by envy. Thus the basic structure should allow these inequalities so long as these improve everyone's situation, including that of the least advantaged, provided that they are consistent with equal liberty and fair opportunity. Because the parties start from an equal division of all social primary goods, those who benefit least have, so to speak, a veto. Thus we arrive at the difference principle. Taking equality as the basis of comparison, those who have gained more must do so on terms that are justifiable to those who have gained the least.

By some such reasoning, then, the parties might arrive at the two principles of justice in serial order. I shall not try to justify this ordering here, but the following remarks may convey the intuitive idea. I assume that the parties view themselves as free persons who have fundamental aims and interests in the name of which they think it legitimate for them to make claims on one another concerning the design of the basic structure of society. The religious interest is a familiar historical example; the interest in the integrity of the person is another. In the original position the parties do not know what particular forms these interests take; but they do assume that they have such interests and that the basic liberties necessary for their protection are guaranteed by the first principle. Since they must secure these interests, they rank the first principle prior to the second. The case for the two principles can be strengthened by spelling out in more detail the notion of a free person. Very roughly the parties regard themselves as having a highest-order interest in how all their other interests, including even their fundamental ones, are shaped and regulated by social institutions. They do not think of themselves as inevitably bound to, or as identical with, the pursuit of any particular complex of fundamental interests that they may have at any given time, although they want the right to advance such interests (provided they are admissible). Rather, free persons conceive of themselves as beings who can revise and alter their final ends and who give first priority to preserving their liberty in these matters. Hence, they not only have final ends that they are in principle free to pursue or to reject, but their original allegiance and continued devotion to these ends are to be formed and affirmed under conditions that are free. Since the two principles secure a social form that maintains these conditions, they would be agreed to rather than the principle of utility. Only by this agreement can the parties be sure that their highest-order interest as free persons is guaranteed.

The priority of liberty means that whenever the basic liberties can be effectively established, a lesser or an unequal liberty cannot be exchanged for an improvement in economic well-being. It is only when social circumstances do not allow the effective establishment of these basic rights that one can concede their limitation; and even then these restrictions can be granted only to the extent that they are necessary to prepare the way for the time when they are no longer justified. The denial of the equal liberties can be defended only when it is essential to change the conditions of civilization so that in due course these liberties can be enjoyed. Thus in adopting the serial order of the two principles, the parties are assuming that the conditions of their society, whatever they are, admit the effective realization of the equal liberties. Or that if they do not, circumstances are nevertheless sufficiently favorable so that the priority of the first principle points out the most urgent changes and identifies the preferred path to the social state in which all the basic liberties can be fully instituted. The complete realization of the two principles in serial order is the long-run tendency of this ordering, at least under reasonably fortunate conditions.

It seems from these remarks that the two principles are at least a plausible conception of justice. The question, though, is how one is to argue for them more systematically. Now there are several things to do. One can work out their consequences for institutions and note their implications for fundamental social policy. In this way they are tested by a comparison with our considered judgments of justice. But one can also try to find arguments in their favor that are decisive from the standpoint of the original position. In order to see how this might be done, it is useful as a heuristic device to think of the two principles as the maximin solution to the problem of social justice. There is a relation between the two principles and the maximin rule for choice under uncertainty.[9] This is evident from the fact that the two principles are those a person would choose for the design of a society in which his enemy is to assign him his place. The maximin rule tells us to rank alternatives by their worst possible outcomes: we are to adopt the alternative the worst outcome of which is superior to the worst outcomes of the others.* The persons in the original position do not, of course, assume that their initial place in society is decided by a malevolent opponent. As I note below, they should not reason from false premises. The veil of ignorance does not violate this idea, since an absence of information is not misinformation. But that the two principles of justice would be chosen if the parties were forced to protect themselves against such a contingency explains the sense in which this conception is the maximin solution. And this analogy suggests that if the original position has been described so that it is rational for the parties to adopt the conservative attitude expressed by this rule, a conclusive argument can indeed be constructed for these principles. Clearly the maximin rule is not, in general, a suitable guide for choices under uncertainty. But it holds only in situations marked by certain special features. My aim, then, is to show that a good case can be made for the two principles based on the fact that the original position has these features to a very high degree.

Now there appear to be three chief features of situations that give plausibility to this unusual rule.[10] First, since the rule takes no account of the likelihoods of the possible circumstances, there must be some reason for sharply discounting estimates of these probabilities. Offhand, the most natural rule of choice would seem to be to compute the expectation of monetary gain for each decision and then to adopt the course of action with the highest prospect. . . . Thus it must be, for example, that the situation is one in which a knowledge of likelihoods is impossible, or at best extremely insecure. In this case it is unreasonable not to be skeptical of probabilistic calculations unless there is no other way out, particularly if the decision is a fundamental one that needs to be justified to others.

The second feature that suggests the maximin rule is the following: the person choosing has a conception of the good such that he cares very little, if anything, for what he might gain above the minimum stipend that he can, in fact, be sure of by following the maximin rule. It is not worthwhile for him to take a chance for the sake of a further advantage, especially when it may turn out that he loses much that is important to him. This last provision brings in the third feature, namely, that the rejected alternatives have outcomes that one can hardly accept. The situation involves grave risks. Of course these features work most effectively in combination. The paradigm situation for following the maximin rule is when all three features are realized to the highest degree.

Let us review briefly the nature of the original position with these three special features in mind. To begin with, the veil of ignorance excludes all knowledge of likelihoods. The parties have no basis for determining the probable nature of their society, or their place in it. Thus they have no basis for probability calculations. They must also take into account the fact that their choice of principles should seem

---

* Consider the gain-and-loss table below. It represents the gains and losses for a situation which is not a game of strategy. There is no one playing against the person making the decision; instead he is faced with several possible circumstances which may or may not obtain. Which circumstances happen to exist does not depend upon what the person choosing decides or whether he announces his moves in advance. The numbers in the table are monetary values (in hundreds of dollars) in comparison with some initial situation. The gain (g) depends upon the individual's decision (d) and the circumstances (c). Thus $g = f(d, c)$. Assuming that there are three possible decisions and three possible circumstances, we might have this gain-and-loss table.

	Circumstances		
Decisions	c_1	c_2	c_3
d_1	–7	8	12
d_2	–8	7	14
d_3	5	6	8

The maximin rule requires that we make the third decision. For in this case the worst that can happen is that one gains five hundred dollars, which is better than the worst for the other actions. If we adopt one of these we may lose either eight or seven hundred dollars. Thus, the choice of d_3 maximizes $f(d,c)$ for that value of c, which for a given d, minimizes f. The term "maximin" means the *maximum minimorum;* and the rule directs our attention to the worst that can happen under any proposed course of action, and to decide in the light of that.

reasonable to others, in particular their descendants, whose rights will be deeply affected by it. These considerations are strengthened by the fact that the parties know very little about the possible states of society. Not only are they unable to conjecture the likelihoods of the various possible circumstances, they cannot say much about what the possible circumstances are, much less enumerate them and foresee the outcome of each alternative available. Those deciding are much more in the dark than illustrations by numerical tables suggest. It is for this reason that I have spoken only of a relation to the maximin rule.

Several kinds of arguments for the two principles of justice illustrate the second feature. Thus, if we can maintain that these principles provide a workable theory of social justice, and that they are compatible with reasonable demands of efficiency, then this conception guarantees a satisfactory minimum. There may be, on reflection, little reason for trying to do better. Thus much of the argument is to show, by their application to some main questions of social justice, that the two principles are a satisfactory conception. These details have a philosophical purpose. Moreover, this line of thought is practically decisive if we can establish the priority of liberty. For this priority implies that the persons in the original position have no desire to try for greater gains at the expense of the basic equal liberties. The minimum assured by the two principles in lexical order is not one that the parties wish to jeopardize for the sake of greater economic and social advantages. . . .

Finally, the third feature holds if we can assume that other conceptions of justice may lead to institutions that the parties would find intolerable. For example, it has sometimes been held that under some conditions the utility principle (in either form) justifies, if not slavery or serfdom, at any rate serious infractions of liberty for the sake of greater social benefits. We need not consider here the truth of this claim. For the moment, this contention is only to illustrate the way in which conceptions of justice may allow for outcomes which the parties may not be able to accept. And having the ready alternative of the two principles of justice which secure a satisfactory minimum, it seems unwise, if not irrational, for them to take a chance that these conditions are not realized. . . .

NOTES

1. As the text suggests, I shall regard Locke's *Second Treatise of Government,* Rousseau's *The Social Contract,* and Kant's ethical works beginning with *The Foundations of the Metaphysics of Morals* as definitive of the contract tradition. For all of its greatness, Hobbes's *Leviathan* raises special problems. A general historical survey is provided by J. W. Gough, *The Social Contract,* 2nd ed. (Oxford, The Clarendon Press, 1957), and Otto Gierke, *Natural Law and the Theory of Society,* trans. with an introduction by Ernest Barker (Cambridge, The University Press, 1934). A presentation of the contract view as primarily an ethical theory is to be found in G. R. Grice, *The Grounds of Moral Judgment* (Cambridge, The University Press, 1967).
2. Kant is clear that the original agreement is hypothetical. See *The Metaphysics of Morals,* pt. I *(Rechtslehre),* especially §§47, 52; and pt. II of the essay "Concerning the Common Saying: This May Be True in Theory but It Does Not Apply in Practice," in *Kant's Political Writings,* ed. Hans Reiss and trans. by H. B. Nisbet (Cambridge, The University Press, 1970), pp. 73–87. See Georges Vlachos, *La Pensée politique de Kant* (Paris, Presses Universitaires de France, 1962), pp. 326–335; and J. G. Murphy, *Kant: The Philosophy of Right* (London, Macmillan, 1970), pp. 109–112, 133–136, for a further discussion.
3. The process of mutual adjustment of principles and considered judgments is not peculiar to moral philosophy. See Nelson Goodman, *Fact, Fiction, and Forecast* (Cambridge, Mass., Harvard University Press, 1955), pp. 65–68, for parallel remarks concerning the justification of the principles of deductive and inductive inference.
4. Henri Poincaré remarks: "Il nous faut une faculté qui nous fasse voir le but de loin, et, cette faculté, c'est l'intuition." *La Valeur de la science* (Paris, Flammarion, 1909), p. 27. [Translation in text above.]
5. I shall take Henry Sidgwick's *The Methods of Ethics,* 7th ed. (London, 1907), as summarizing the development of utilitarian moral theory. Book III of his *Principles of Political Economy* (London, 1883)

applies this doctrine to questions of economic and social justice, and is a precursor of A. C. Pigou, *The Economics of Welfare* (London, Macmillan, 1920). Sidgwick's *Outlines of the History of Ethics,* 5th ed. (London, 1902), contains a brief history of the utilitarian tradition. We may follow him in assuming, somewhat arbitrarily, that it begins with Shaftesbury's *An Inquiry Concerning Virtue and Merit* (1711) and Hutcheson's *An Inquiry Concerning Moral Good and Evil* (1725). Hutcheson seems to have been the first to state clearly the principle of utility. He says in *Inquiry,* sec. 111, §8, that "that action is best, which procures the greatest happiness for the greatest numbers; and that, worst, which, in like manner, occasions misery." Other major eighteenth century works are Hume's *A Treatise of Human Nature* (1739), and *An Enquiry Concerning the Principles of Morals* (1751); Adam Smith's *A Theory of the Moral Sentiments* (1759); and Bentham's *The Principles of Morals and Legislation* (1789). To these we must add the writings of J. S. Mill represented by *Utilitarianism* (1863) and F. Y. Edgeworth's *Mathematical Psychics* (London, 1888).

The discussion of utilitarianism has taken a different turn in recent years by focusing on what we may call the coordination problem and related questions of publicity. This development stems from the essays of R. F. Harrod, "Utilitarianism Revised," *Mind,* vol. 45 (1936); J. D. Mabbott, "Punishment," *Mind,* vol. 48 (1939); Jonathan Harrison, "Utilitarianism, Universalisation, and Our Duty to Be Just," *Proceedings of the Aristotelian Society,* vol. 53 (1952–53); and J. O. Urmson, "The Interpretation of the Philosophy of J. S. Mill," *Philosophical Quarterly,* vol. 3 (1953). See also J. J. C. Smart, "Extreme and Restricted Utilitarianism," *Philosophical Quarterly,* vol. 6 (1956), [reprinted in this volume] and his *An Outline of a System of Utilitarian Ethics* (Cambridge, The University Press, 1961). For an account of these matters, see David Lyons, *Forms and Limits of Utilitarianism* (Oxford, The Clarendon Press, 1965); and Allan Gibbard, "Utilitarianisms and Coordination" (dissertation, Harvard University, 1971). The problems raised by these works, as important as they are, I shall leave aside as not bearing directly on the more elementary question of distribution which I wish to discuss.

Finally, we should note here the essays of J. C. Harsanyi, in particular, "Cardinal Utility in Welfare Economics and in the Theory of Risk-Taking," *Journal of Political Economy,* 1953, and "Cardinal Welfare, Individualistic Ethics, and Interpersonal Comparisons of Utility," *Journal of Political Economy,* 1955; and R. B. Brandt, "Some Merits of One Form of Rule-Utilitarianism," *University of Colorado Studies* (Boulder, Colorado, 1967).

6. On this point see also D. P. Gauthier, *Practical Reasoning* (Oxford, Clarendon Press, 1963), pp. 126f. The text elaborates the suggestion found in "Constitutional Liberty and the Concept of Justice," *Nomos VI: Justice,* ed. C. J. Friedrich and J. W. Chapman (New York, Atherton Press, 1963), pp. 124f, which in turn is related to the idea of justice as a higher-order administrative decision. See "Justice as Fairness," *Philosophical Review,* 1958, pp. 185–187. For references to utilitarians who explicitly affirm this extension, see §30, note 37. That the principle of social integration is distinct from the principle of personal integration is stated by R. B. Perry, *General Theory of Value* (New York, Longmans, Green, and Company, 1926), pp. 674–677. He attributes the error of overlooking this fact to Emile Durkheim and others with similar views. Perry's conception of social integration is that brought about by a shared and dominant benevolent purpose.
7. Here I adopt W. K. Frankena's definition of teleological theories in *Ethics* (Englewood Cliffs, N.J., Prentice Hall, Inc., 1963), p. 13.
8. On this point see Sidgwick, *The Methods of Ethics,* pp. 416f. See J. S. Mill, *Utilitarianism,* ch. V, last two pars.
9. An accessible discussion of this and other rules of choice under uncertainty can be found in W. J. Baumol, *Economic Theory and Operations Analysis,* 2nd ed. (Englewood Cliffs, N.J., Prentice-Hall Inc., 1965), ch. 24. Baumol gives a geometric interpretation of these rules, including the diagram used in §13 to illustrate the difference principle. See pp. 558–562. See also R. D. Luce and Howard Raiffa, *Games and Decisions* (New York, John Wiley and Sons, Inc., 1957), ch. XIII, for a fuller account.
10. Here I borrow from William Fellner, *Probability and Profit* (Homewood, Ill., R. D. Irwin, Inc., 1965), pp. 140–142, where these features are noted.

"Distributive Justice" from *Anarchy, State and Utopia*

ROBERT NOZICK

Robert Nozick (1938–2002) taught Philosophy at Harvard University. A colleague of John Rawls, he wrote *Anarchy, State and Utopia* in 1975 as a challenge to Rawls's views. The selections that appear here are drawn from several different chapters of this book. In them, Nozick defends a *libertarian* view of property rights according to which no particular distributive pattern is required for a society to be just, as long as the process by which goods came to be distributed is a fair one.

Nozick was an enormously clever and wide-ranging thinker who made lasting contributions to a number of philosophical areas. Selections from his writings in epistemology appear in the "Knowledge and Reality" section of this volume.

. . . The term "distributive justice" is not a neutral one. Hearing the term "distribution," most people presume that some thing or mechanism uses some principle or criterion to give out a supply of things. Into this process of distributing shares some error may have crept. So it is an open question, at least, whether *re*distribution should take place; whether we should do again what has already been done once, though poorly. However, we are not in the position of children who have been given portions of pie by someone who now makes last minute adjustments to rectify careless cutting. There is no *central* distribution, no person or group entitled to control all the resources, jointly deciding how they are to be doled out. What each person gets, he gets from others who give to him in exchange for something, or as a gift. In a free society, diverse persons control different resources, and new holdings arise out of the voluntary exchanges and actions of persons. There is no more a distributing or distribution of shares than there is a distributing of mates in a society in which persons choose whom they shall marry. The total result is the product of many individual decisions which the different individuals involved are entitled to make. . . . We shall speak of people's holdings; a principle of justice in holdings describes (part of) what justice tells us (requires) about holdings. I shall state first what I take to be the correct view about justice in holdings and then turn to the discussion of alternate views.

SECTION I

THE ENTITLEMENT THEORY

The subject of justice in holdings consists of three major topics. The first is the *original acquisition of holdings,* the appropriation of unheld things. This includes the issues of how unheld things may come to be held, the process, or processes, by which unheld things may come to be held, the things that may come to be held by these processes, the extent of what comes to be held by a particular process, and so on. We shall refer to the complicated truth about this topic, which we shall not formulate here, as the principle of justice in acquisition. The second topic concerns the *transfer of holdings* from one person to another. By what processes may a person transfer holdings to another? How may a person acquire a holding from another who holds it? Under this topic come general descriptions of voluntary exchange, and gift and (on the other hand) fraud, as well as reference to particular conventional details fixed upon in a given society. The complicated truth about this subject (with placeholders for conventional details) we shall call the principle of justice in transfer. (And we shall suppose it also includes principles

© 1974 by Basic Books, Inc. Reprinted by permission of the publisher, a member of Perseus Books Group.

governing how a person may divest himself of a holding, passing it into an unheld state.)

If the world were wholly just, the following inductive definition would exhaustively cover the subject of justice in holdings.

1. A person who acquires a holding in accordance with the principle of justice in acquisition is entitled to that holding.
2. A person who acquires a holding in accordance with the principle of justice in transfer, from someone else entitled to the holding, is entitled to the holding.
3. No one is entitled to a holding except by (repeated) applications of 1 and 2.

The complete principle of distributive justice would say simply that a distribution is just if everyone is entitled to the holdings they possess under the distribution.

A distribution is just if it arises from another just distribution by legitimate means. The legitimate means of moving from one distribution to another are specified by the principle of justice in transfer. The legitimate first "moves" are specified by the principle of justice in acquisition.[1] Whatever arises from a just situation by just steps is itself just. The means of change specified by the principle of justice in transfer preserve justice. As correct rules of inference are truth-preserving, and any conclusion deduced via repeated application of such rules from only true premisses is itself true, so the means of transition from one situation to another specified by the principle of justice in transfer are justice-preserving, and any situation actually arising from repeated transitions in accordance with the principle from a just situation is itself just. The parallel between justice-preserving transformations and truth-preserving transformations illuminates where it fails as well as where it holds.That a conclusion could have been deduced by truth-preserving means from premisses that are true suffices to show its truth. That from a just situation a situation *could* have arisen via justice-preserving means does *not* suffice to show its justice. The fact that a thief's victims voluntarily *could* have presented him with gifts does not entitle the thief to his ill-gotten gains. Justice in holdings is historical; it depends upon what actually has happened. We shall return to this point later.

Not all actual situations are generated in accordance with the two principles of justice in holdings: the principle of justice in acquisitions and the principle of justice in transfer. Some people steal from others, or defraud them, or enslave them, seizing their product and preventing them from living as they choose, or forcibly exclude others from competing in exchanges. None of these are permissible modes of transition from one situation to another. And some persons acquire holdings by means not sanctioned by the principle of justice in acquisition. The existence of past injustice (previous violations of the first two principles of justice in holdings) raises the third major topic under justice in holdings: the rectification of injustice in holdings. If past injustice has shaped present holdings in various ways, some identifiable and some not, what now, if anything, ought to be done to rectify these injustices? What obligations do the performers of injustice have toward those whose position is worse than it would have been had the injustice not been done? Or, than it would have been had compensation been paid promptly? How, if at all, do things change if the beneficiaries and those made worse off are not the direct parties in the act of injustice, but, for example, their descendants? Is an injustice done to someone whose holding was itself based upon an unrectified injustice? How far back must one go in wiping clean the historical slate of injustices? What may victims of injustice permissibly do in order to rectify the injustices being done to them, including the many injustices done by persons acting through their government? I do not know of a thorough or theoretically sophisticated treatment of such issues.[2] Idealizing greatly, let us suppose theoretical investigation will produce a principle of rectification. This principle uses historical information about previous situations and injustices done in them (as defined by the first two principles of justice and rights against interference), and information about the actual course of events that flowed from these injustices, until the present, and it yields a description (or descriptions) of holding in the society. The principle of rectification presumably will make use of its best estimate of subjunctive information about what would have occurred (or a probability distribution over what might have occurred, using the expected value) if the injustice had not taken place. If the actual description of holdings turns out not to be one of the descriptions yielded by the principle, then one of the descriptions yielded must be realized.[3]

The general outlines of the theory of justice in holding are that the holdings of a person are just if he is entitled to them by the principles of justice in acquisition and transfer, or by the principle of rectification of injustice (as specified by the first two principles). If each person's holdings are just, then the total set (distribution) of holdings is just. To turn these general outlines into a specific theory we would have to specify the details of each of the three principles of justice in holdings: the principle of acquisition of holdings, the principle of transfer of holdings, and the principle of rectification of violations of the first two principles. I shall not attempt that task here. (Locke's principle of justice in acquisition is discussed below.)

HISTORICAL PRINCIPLES AND END-RESULT PRINCIPLES

The general outlines of the entitlement theory illuminate the nature and defects of other conceptions of distributive justice. The entitlement theory of justice in distribution is *historical;* whether a distribution is just depends upon how it came about. In contrast, *current time-slice principles* of justice hold that the justice of a distribution is determined by how things are distributed (who has what) as judged by some *structural* principle(s) of just distribution. A utilitarian who judges between any two distributions by seeing which has the greater sum of utility and, if the sums tie, applies some fixed equality criterion to choose the more equal distribution, would hold a current time-slice principle of justice. As would someone who had a fixed schedule of trade-offs between the sum of happiness and equality. According to a current time-slice principle, all that needs to be looked at, in judging the justice of a distribution, is who ends up with what; in comparing any two distributions one need look only at the matrix presenting the distributions. No further information need be fed into a principle of justice. It is a consequence of such principles of justice that any two structurally identical distributions are equally just. (Two distributions are structurally identical if they present the same profile, but perhaps have different persons occupying the particular slots. My having ten and your having five, and my having five and your having ten are structurally identical distributions.) Welfare economics is the theory of current time-slice principles of justice. The subject is conceived as operating on matrices representing only current information about distribution. This, as well as some of the usual conditions (for example, the choice of distribution is invariant under relabeling of columns), guarantees that welfare economics will be a current time-slice theory, with all of its inadequacies.

Most persons do not accept current time-slice principles as constituting the whole story about distributive shares. They thinks it relevant in assessing the justice of a situation to consider not only the distribution it embodies, but also how that distribution came about. If some persons are in prison for murder or war crimes, we do not say that to assess the justice of the distribution in the society we must look only at what this person has, and that person has, and that person has, . . . at the current time. We think it relevant to ask whether someone did something so that he *deserved* to be punished, deserved to have a lower share. Most will agree to the relevance of further information with regard to punishments and penalties. Consider also desired things. One traditional socialist view is that workers are entitled to the product and full fruits of their labor; they have earned it; a distribution is unjust if it does not give the workers what they are entitled to. Such entitlements are based upon some past history. No socialist holding this view would find it comforting to be told that because the actual distribution *A* happens to coincide structurally with the one he desires *D, A* therefore is no less just than *D;* it differs only in that the "parasitic" owners of capital receive under *A* what the workers are entitled to under *D,* and the workers receive under *A* what the owners are entitled to under *D,* namely very little. This socialist rightly, in my view, holds onto the notions of earning, producing, entitlement, desert, and so forth, and he rejects current time-slice principles that look only to the structure of the resulting set of holdings. (The set of holdings resulting from what? Isn't it implausible that how holdings are produced and come to exist has no effect at all on who should hold what?) His mistake lies in his view of what entitlements arise out of what sorts of productive processes.

We construe the position we discuss too narrowly by speaking of *current* time-slice principles. Nothing is changed if structural principles operate upon a time sequence of current time-slice profiles and, for example, give someone more now to counterbalance the less he has had earlier. A utilitarian or an egalitarian or any mixture of the two over time will inherit the difficulties of his more myopic comrades. He is not helped by the fact that *some* of the information others consider relevant in assessing a distribution is reflected, unrecoverably, in past matrices. Henceforth, we shall refer to such unhistorical principles of distributive justice, including the current time-slice principles as *end-result principles* or *end-state principles*.

In contrast to end-result principles of justice, *historical principles* of justice hold that past circumstances or actions of people can create differential entitlements or differential deserts to things. An injustice can be worked by moving from one distribution to another structurally identical one, for the second, in profile the same, may violate people's entitlements or deserts; it may not fit the actual history.

PATTERNING

The entitlement principles of justice in holdings that we have sketched are historical principles of justice. To better understand their precise character, we shall distinguish them from another subclass of the historical principles. Consider, as an example, the principle of distribution according to moral merit. This principle requires that total distributive shares vary directly with moral merit; no person should have a greater share than anyone whose moral merit is greater. (If moral merit could be not merely ordered but measured on an interval or ratio scale, stronger principles could be formulated.) Or consider the principle that results by substituting "usefulness to society" for "moral merit" in the previous principle. Or instead of "distribute according to moral merit," or "distribute according to usefulness to society," we might consider "distribute according to the weighted sum of moral merit, usefulness to society, and need," with the weights of the different dimensions equal. Let us call a principle of distribution *patterned* if it specifies that a distribution is to vary along with some natural dimension, weighted sum of natural dimensions, or lexicographic ordering of natural dimensions. And let us say a distribution is patterned if it accords with some patterned principle. (I speak of natural dimensions, admittedly without a general criterion for them, because for any set of holdings some artificial dimensions can be gimmicked up to vary along with the distribution of the set.) The principle of distribution in accordance with moral merit is a patterned historical principle, which specifies a patterned distribution. "Distribute according to I.Q." is a patterned principle that looks to information not contained in distributional matrices. It is not historical, however, in that it does not look to any past actions creating differential entitlements to evaluate a distribution; it requires only distributional matrices whose columns are labeled by I.Q. scores. The distribution in a society, however, may be composed of such simple patterned distributions, without itself being simply patterned. Different sectors may operate different patterns, or some combination of patterns may operate in different proportions across a society. A distribution composed in this manner, from a small number of patterned distributions, we also shall term "patterned." And we extend the use of "pattern" to include the overall designs put forth by combinations of end-state principles.

Almost every suggested principle of distributive justice is patterned: to each according to his moral merit, or needs, or marginal product, or how hard he tries, or the weighted sum of the foregoing, and so on. The principle of entitlement we have sketched is *not* patterned.[4] There is no one natural dimension or weighted sum or combination of a small number of natural dimensions that yields the distributions generated in accordance with the principle of entitlement. The set of holdings that results when some persons receive their marginal products, others win at gambling, others receive a share of their mate's income, others receive gifts from foundations, others receive interest on loans, others receive gifts from admirers, others receive returns on investment, others make for themselves much of what they have, others find things, and so on, will not be patterned. Heavy strands of patterns will run through it; significant portions of the variance in holdings will be accounted for by pattern-variables. If most people most of the time choose to transfer some of their entitlements to others only in exchange for something from them, then a large part of what many people hold will vary with what they held that others wanted. More details are provided by the theory of marginal productivity. But gifts to relatives, charitable donations, bequests to children, and the like, are not best conceived, in the first instance, in this manner. Ignoring the strands of pattern, let us suppose for the moment that a distribution actually arrived at by the operation of the principle of entitlement is random with respect to any pattern. Though the resulting set of holdings will be unpatterned, it will not be incomprehensible, for it can be seen as arising from the operation of a small number of principles. These principles specify how an initial distribution may arise (the principle of acquisition of holdings) and how distributions may be transformed into others (the principle of transfer of holdings). The process whereby the set of holdings is generated will be intelligible, though the set of holdings itself that results from this process will be unpatterned. . . .

HOW LIBERTY UPSETS PATTERNS

It is not clear how those holding alternative conceptions of distributive justice can reject the entitlement conception of justice in holdings. For suppose a distribution favored by one of these non-entitlement conceptions is realized, Let us suppose it is your favorite one and let us call this distribution D_1; perhaps everyone has an equal share, perhaps shares vary in accordance with some dimension you treasure. Now suppose that Wilt Chamberlain is greatly in demand by basketball teams, being a great gate attraction. (Also suppose contracts run only for a year, with players being free agents.) He signs the following sort of contract with a team: In each home game, twenty-five cents from the price of each ticket of admission goes to him. (We ignore the question of whether he is "gouging" the owners, letting them look out for themselves.) The season starts, and people cheerfully attend his team's games; they buy their tickets, each time dropping a separate twenty-five cents of their admission price into a special box with Chamberlain's name on it. They are excited about seeing him play; it is worth the total admission price to them. Let us suppose that in one season one million persons attend his home games, and Wilt Chamberlain winds up with $250,000, a much larger sum than the average income and larger even than anyone else has. Is he entitled to this income? Is this new distribution D_2, unjust? If so, why? There is *no* question about whether each of the people was entitled to the control over the resources they held in D_1; because that was the distribution (your favorite) that (for the purposes of argument) we assumed was acceptable. Each of these persons *chose* to give twenty-five cents of their money to Chamberlain. They could have spent it on going to the movies, or on candy bars, or on copies of *Dissent* magazine, or of *Monthly Review*. But they all, at least one million of them, converged on giving it to Wilt Chamberlain in exchange for watching him play basketball. If D_1 was a just distribution, and people voluntarily moved from it to D_2, transferring parts of their shares they were given under D_1 (what was it for if not to do something with?), isn't D_2 also just? If the people were entitled to dispose of the resources to which they were entitled (under D_1), didn't this include their being entitled to give it to, or exchange it with, Wilt Chamberlain? Can anyone else complain on grounds of justice? Each other person already has his legitimate share under D_1. Under D_1, there is nothing that anyone has that anyone else has a claim of justice against. After someone transfers something to Wilt Chamberlain, third parties *still* have their legitimate shares; *their* shares are not changed. By what process could such a transfer among two persons give rise to a legitimate claim of distributive justice on a portion of what was transferred, by a third party who had no claim of justice on any holding of the others *before* the transfer?[5] To cut off objections irrelevant here, we might imagine the exchanges occurring in a socialist society, after hours. After playing whatever basketball he does in his daily work, or doing whatever other daily work he does, Wilt Chamberlain decided to put in *overtime* to earn additional money. (First his work quota is set; he works time over that.) Or imagine it is a skilled juggler people like to see, who puts on shows after hours. . . .

The general point illustrated by the Wilt Chamberlain example and the example of the entrepreneur in a socialist society is that no end-state principle or distributional patterned principle of justice can be continuously realized without continuous interference with people's lives. Any favored pattern would be transformed into one unfavored by the principle, by people choosing to act in various ways; for example, by people exchanging goods and services with other people, or giving things to other people, things the transferrers are entitled to under the favored distributional pattern. To maintain a pattern one must either continually interfere to stop people from transferring resources as they wish to, or continually (or periodically) interfere to take from some persons resources that others for some reason chose to transfer to them. . . .

LOCKE'S THEORY OF ACQUISITION

[W]e must introduce an additional bit of complexity into the structure of the entitlement theory. This is best approached by considering Locke's attempt to specify a principle of justice in acquisition. Locke views property rights in an unowned object as originating through someone's mixing his labor with it. This gives rise to many questions. What are the boundaries of what labor is mixed with? If a private astronaut clears a place on Mars, has he mixed his labor with (so that he comes to own) the whole planet, the whole uninhabited universe, or just a particular plot? Which plot does an act bring under ownership? The minimal (possibly disconnected) area such that an act decreases entropy in that area, and not elsewhere? Can virgin land (for the purposes of ecological investigation by high-flying airplane) come under ownership by a Lockean process? Building a fence around a territory presumably would make one the owner of only the fence (and the land immediately underneath it).

Why does mixing one's labor with something make one the owner of it? Perhaps because one owns one's labor, and so one comes to own a previously unowned thing that becomes permeated with what one owns. Ownership seeps over into the rest. But why isn't mixing what I own with what I don't own a way of losing what I own rather than a way of gaining what I don't? If I own a can of tomato juice and spill it in the sea so that its molecules (made radioactive, so I can check this) mingle evenly throughout the sea, do I thereby come to own the sea, or have I foolishly dissipated my tomato juice? Perhaps the idea, instead, is that laboring on something improves it and makes it more valuable; and anyone is entitled to own a thing whose value he has created. (Reinforcing this, perhaps, is the view that laboring is unpleasant. If some people made things effortlessly, as the cartoon characters in *The Yellow Submarine* trail flowers in their wake, would they have lesser claim to their own products whose making didn't *cost* them anything?) Ignore the fact that laboring on something may make it less valuable (spraying pink enamel paint on a piece of driftwood that you have found). Why should one's entitlement extend to the whole object rather than just to the *added value* one's labor has produced? (Such reference to value might also serve to delimit the extent of ownership; for example, substitute "increases the value of" for "decreases entropy in" in the above entropy criterion.) No workable or coherent value-added property scheme has yet been devised, and any such scheme presumably would fall to objections (similar to those) that felled the theory of Henry George.*

It will be implausible to view improving an object as giving full ownership to it, if the stock of unowned objects that might be improved is limited. For an object's coming under one person's ownership changes the situation of all others. Whereas previously they were at liberty (in Hohfeld's sense)† to use the object, they now no longer are. This

---

* Henry George (1839–1897) was an American political economist who advocated the abolition of all taxes except property taxes. The board game *Monopoly* is based loosely on his theories.

† Wesley Newcomb Hohfeld (1879–1918) was an influential American jurist. On his view, liberty just amounts to the absence of a duty to respect someone's right.

change in the situation of others (by removing their liberty to act on a previously unowned object) need not worsen their situation. If I appropriate a grain of sand from Coney Island, no one else may now do as they will with *that* grain of sand. But there are plenty of other grains of sand left for them to do the same with. Or if not grains of sand, then other things. Alternatively, the things I do with the grain of sand I appropriate might improve the position of others, counterbalancing their loss of the liberty to use that grain. The crucial point is whether appropriation of an unowned object worsens the situation of others.

Locke's proviso that there be "enough and as good left in common for others" (sect. 27) is meant to ensure that the situation of others is not worsened. . . .

Is the situation of persons who are unable to appropriate (there being no more accessible and useful unowned objects) worsened by a system allowing appropriation and permanent property? Here enter the various familiar social considerations favoring private property: it increases the social product by putting means of production in the hands of those who can use them most efficiently (profitably); experimentation is encouraged, because with separate persons controlling resources, there is no one person or small group whom someone with a new idea must convince to try it out; private property enables people to decide on the pattern and types of risks they wish to bear, leading to specialized types of risk bearing; private property protects future persons by leading some to hold back resources from current consumption for future markets; it provides alternate sources of employment for unpopular persons who don't have to convince any one person or small group to hire them, and so on. These considerations enter a Lockean theory to support the claim that appropriation of private property satisfies the intent behind the "enough and as good left over" proviso, *not* as a utilitarian justification of property. They enter to rebut the claim that because the proviso is violated no natural right to private property can arise by a Lockean process. The difficulty in working such an argument to show that the proviso is satisfied is in fixing the appropriate base line for comparison. Lockean appropriation makes people no worse off than they would be *how?*[6] This question of fixing the baseline needs more detailed investigation than we are able to give it here. . . .

THE PROVISO

Whether or not Locke's particular theory of appropriation can be spelled out so as to handle various difficulties, I assume that any adequate theory of justice in acquisition will contain a proviso similar to the weaker of the ones we have attributed to Locke. A process normally giving rise to a permanent bequeathable property right in a previously unowned thing will not do so if the position of others no longer at liberty to use the thing is thereby worsened. It is important to specify *this* particular mode of worsening the situation of others, for the proviso does not encompass other modes. It does not include the worsening due to more limited opportunities to appropriate (the first way above, corresponding to the more stringent condition), and it does not include how I "worsen" a seller's position if I appropriate materials to make some of what he is selling, and then enter into competition with him. Someone whose appropriation otherwise would violate the proviso still may appropriate provided he compensates the others so that their situation is not thereby worsened; unless he does compensate these others, his appropriation will violate the proviso of the principle of justice in acquisition and will be an illegitimate one.[7] A theory of appropriation incorporating this Lockean proviso will handle correctly the cases (objections to the theory lacking the proviso) where someone appropriates the total supply of something necessary for life.[8]

A theory which includes this proviso in its principle of justice in acquisition must also contain a more complex principle of justice in transfer. Some reflection of the proviso about appropriation constrains later actions. If my appropriating all of a certain substance violates the Lockean proviso, then so does my appropriating some and purchasing all the rest from others who obtained it without otherwise violating the Lockean proviso. If the proviso excludes someone's appropriating all the drinkable water in the world, it also excludes his purchasing it all. (More weakly, and messily, it may exclude his charging certain prices for some of his supply.) This proviso (almost?) never will come into effect; the more someone acquires of a scarce substance which others want, the higher the price of the rest will go, and the more difficult it will become for him to acquire it all. But still, we can imagine, at least, that something like this occurs: someone makes simultaneous secret bids to the separate owners of a substance, each of whom sells assuming he can easily purchase more from the other owners; or some natural catastrophe destroys all of the supply of something except that in one person's possession. The total supply could not be permissibly appropriated by one person at the beginning. His later acquisition of it all does not show that the original appropriation violated the proviso (even by a reverse argument similar to the one above that tried to zip back from Z to A). Rather, it is the combination of the original appropriation *plus* all the later transfers and actions that violates the Lockean proviso.

Each owner's title to his holding includes the historical shadow of the Lockean proviso on appropriation. This excludes his transferring it into an agglomeration that does violate the Lockean proviso and excludes his using it in a way, in coordination with others or independently of them, so as to violate the proviso by making the situation of others worse than their baseline situation. Once it is known that someone's ownership runs afoul of the Lockean proviso, there are stringent limits on what he may do with (what it is difficult any longer unreservedly to call) "his property." Thus a person may not appropriate the only water hole in a desert and charge what he will. Nor may he charge what he will if he possesses one, and unfortunately it happens that all the water holes in the desert dry up, except for his. This unfortunate circumstance, admittedly no fault of his, brings into operation the Lockean proviso and limits his property rights.[9] Similarly, an owner's property right in the only island in an area does not allow him to order a castaway from a shipwreck off his island as a trespasser, for this would violate the Lockean proviso. . . .

The fact that someone owns the total supply of something necessary for others to stay alive does *not* entail that his (or anyone's) appropriation of anything left some people (immediately or later) in a situation worse than the baseline one. A medical researcher who synthesizes a new substance that effectively treats a certain disease and who refuses to sell except on his terms does not worsen the situation of others by depriving them of whatever he has appropriated. The others easily can possess the same materials he appropriated; the researcher's appropriation or purchase of chemicals didn't make those chemicals scarce in a way so as to violate the Lockean proviso. Nor would someone else's purchasing the total supply of the synthesized substance from the medical researcher. The fact that the medical researcher uses easily available chemicals to synthesize the drug no more violates the Lockean proviso than does the fact that the only surgeon able to perform a particular operation eats easily obtainable food in order to stay alive and to have the energy to work. This shows that the Lockean proviso is not an "end-state principle"; it focuses on a particular way that appropriative actions affect others, and not on the structure of the situation that results.[10]

Intermediate between someone who takes all of the public supply and someone who makes the total supply out of easily obtainable substances is someone who appropriates the total supply of something in a way that does not deprive the others of it. For example, someone finds a new substance in an out-of-the-way place. He discovers that it effectively treats a certain disease and appropriates the total supply. He does not worsen the situation of others; if he did not stumble upon the substance no one else would have, and the others would remain without it. However, as time passes, the likelihood increases that others would have come across the substance; upon this fact might be based a limit to his property right in the substance so that others are not below their baseline position; for example, its bequest might be limited. The theme of someone worsening another's situation by depriving him of something he otherwise would possess may also illuminate the example of patents. An inventor's patent does not deprive others of an object which would not exist if not for the inventor. Yet patents would have this effect on others who independently invent the object. Therefore, these independent inventors, upon whom the burden of proving independent discovery may rest, should not be excluded from utilizing their own invention as they wish (including selling it to others). Furthermore, a known inventor drastically lessens the chances of actual independent invention. For persons who know of an invention usually will not try to reinvent it, and the notion of independent discovery here would be murky at best. Yet we may assume that in the absence of the original invention, sometime later someone else would have come up with it. This suggests placing a time limit on patents, as a rough rule of thumb to approximate how long it would have taken, in the absence of knowledge of the invention, for independent discovery.

I believe that the free operation of a market system will not actually run afoul of the Lockean proviso. . . .

NOTES

1. Applications of the principle of justice in acquisition may also occur as part of the move from one distribution to another. You may find an unheld thing now and appropriate it. Acquisitions also are to be understood as included when, to simplify, I speak only of transitions by transfers.
2. See, however, the useful book by Boris Bittker, *The Case for Black Reparations* (New York: Random House, 1973).
3. If the principle of rectification of violations of the first two principles yields more than one description of holdings, then some choice must be made as to which of these is to be realized. Perhaps the sort of considerations about distributive justice and equality that I argue against play a legitimate role in *this* subsidiary choice. Similarly, there may be room for such considerations in deciding which otherwise arbitrary features a statute will embody, when such features are unavoidable because other considerations do not specify a precise line; yet a line must be drawn.
4. One might try to squeeze a patterned conception of distributive justice into the framework of the entitlement conception, by formulating a gimmicky obligatory "principle of transfer" that would lead to the pattern. For example, the principle that if one has more than the mean income one must transfer everything one holds above the mean to persons below the mean so as to bring them up to (but not over) the mean. We can formulate a criterion for a "principle of transfer" to rule out such obligatory transfers, or we can say that no correct principle of transfer, no principle of transfer in a free society will be like this. The former is probably the better course, though the latter also is true.

   Alternatively, one might think to make the entitlement conception instantiate a pattern, by using matrix entries that express the relative strength of a person's entitlements as measured by some real-valued function. But even if the limitation to natural dimensions failed to exclude this function, the resulting edifice would *not* capture our system of entitlements to *particular* things.
5. Might not a transfer have instrumental effects on a third party, changing his feasible options? (But what if the two parties to the transfer independently had used their holdings in this fashion?) I discuss this question below, but note here that this question concedes the point for distributions of ultimate intrinsic noninstrumental goods (pure utility experiences, so to speak) that are transferable. It also might be objected that the transfer might make a third party more envious because it worsens his position relative to someone else. I find it incomprehensible how this can be thought to involve a claim of justice.

   Here and elsewhere in this chapter, a theory which incorporates elements of pure procedural justice might find what I say acceptable, *if* kept in its proper place; that is, if background institutions exist to ensure the satisfaction of certain conditions on distributive shares. But if these institutions are not themselves the sum or invisible-hand result of people's voluntary (nonaggressive) actions, the constraints they impose require justification. At no point does *our* argument assume any background institutions more extensive than those of the minimal nightwatchman state, a state limited to protecting persons against murder, assault, theft, fraud, and so forth.
6. Compare this with Robert Paul Wolff's "A Refutation of Rawls' Theorem on Justice," *Journal of Philosophy,* March 31, 1966, sect. 2. Wolff's criticism does not apply to Rawls' conception under which the baseline is fixed by the difference principle.
7. Fourier held that since the process of civilization had deprived the members of society of certain liberties (to gather, pasture, engage in the chase), a socially guaranteed minimum provision for persons was justified as compensation for the loss (Alexander Gray, *The Socialist Tradition* (New York: Harper & Row, 1968), p. 188). But this puts the point too strongly. This compensation would be due those persons, if any, for whom the process of

civilization was a *net loss,* for whom the benefits of civilization did not counterbalance being deprived of these particular liberties.

8. For example, Rashdall's case of someone who comes upon the only water in the desert several miles ahead of others who also will come to it and appropriates it all. Hastings Rashdall, "The Philosophical Theory of Property," in *Property, its Duties and Rights* (London: MacMillan, 1915).

   We should note Ayn Rand's theory of property rights ("Man's Rights" in *The Virtue of Selfishness* (New York: New American Library, 1964), p. 94), wherein these follow from the right to life, since people need physical things to live. But a right to life is not a right to whatever one needs to live; other people may have rights over these other things (. . .). At most, a right to life would be a right to have or strive for whatever one needs to live, provided that having it does not violate anyone else's rights. With regard to material things, the question is whether having it does violate any right of others. (Would appropriation of all unowned things do so? Would appropriating the water hole in Rashdall's example?) Since special considerations (such as the Lockean proviso) may enter with regard to material property, one *first* needs a theory of property rights before one can apply any supposed right to life (as amended above). Therefore the right to life cannot provide the foundation for a theory of property rights.

9. The situation would be different if his water hole didn't dry up, due to special precautions he took to prevent this. Compare our discussion of the case in the text with Hayek, *The Constitution of Liberty,* p. 136; and also with Ronald Hamowy, "Hayek's Concept of Freedom; A Critique," *New Individualist Review,* April 1961, pp. 28–31.

10. Does the principle of compensation introduce patterning considerations? Though it requires compensation for the disadvantages imposed by those seeking security from risks, it is not a patterned principle. For it seeks to remove only those disadvantages which prohibitions inflict on those who might present risks to others, not all disadvantages. It specifies an obligation on those who impose the prohibition, which stems from their own particular acts, to remove a particular complaint those prohibited may make against them.

E JUST WAR

Conventions and the Morality of War

GEORGE I. MAVRODES

George Mavrodes is an American philosopher who taught for many years at the University of Michigan. He is best known for his work in the philosophy of religion and for his writings on related issues in ethics and social policy.

The selection that appears here was originally published in 1975—near the end of the Vietnam War—as an article in the journal *Philosophy and Public Affairs*. In it, Mavrodes maintains that there are certain conditions under which the intentional killing of noncombatants during wartime is morally justifiable.

The point of this paper is to introduce a distinction into our thinking about warfare, and to explore the moral implications of this distinction. I shall make two major assumptions. First, I shall assume without discussion that under some circumstances and for some ends warfare is morally justified. These conditions I shall lump together under such terms as "justice" and "just cause," and say no more about them. I shall also assume that in warfare some means, including some killing, are morally justified. I sometimes call such means "proportionate," and in general I say rather little about them. These assumptions, incidentally, are common to all of the philosophers whom I criticize here.

The distinction which I introduce can be thought of either as dividing wars into two classes, or else as distinguishing wars from certain other international combats. I have no great preference for one of these ways of speaking over the other, but I shall generally adopt the latter alternative. I am particularly interested in the moral significance of this distinction, and I shall explore in some detail its bearing on one moral question associated with warfare, that of the intentional killing of noncombatants.

My paper has two main parts. In the first I examine three closely related treatments of this moral question: the arguments of Elizabeth Anscombe, John C. Ford, and Paul Ramsey. These treatments seem to ignore the distinction which I will propose. I argue that on their own terms, and without reference to that distinction, they must be counted as unsatisfactory.

In the second part of the paper I propose and explain my distinction. I then explore what I take to be some of its moral implications, especially with reference to the alleged immunity of noncombatants, and I argue that it supplies what was missing or defective in the treatments previously criticized.

I. THE IMMUNITY THEORISTS

A number of philosophers have held that a large portion of the population of warring nations have

From *Philosophy and Public Affairs*, 4(2), pp. 117–131, 1975.

a special moral status. This is the *noncombatant* segment of the population, and they have a moral immunity from being intentionally killed. This view seems to have been especially congenial to philosophers who have tried to apply Christian ethics to the problems of warfare. Among the philosophers who have held this view are Elizabeth Anscombe, John C. Ford, and Paul Ramsey. I shall refer to this trio of thinkers as the *immunity theorists.*

Perhaps we should indicate a little more in detail just what the immunity theorists appear to hold, specifying just what segment of the population is being discussed and just what their immunity consists in. The immunity theorists commonly admit that there is some difficulty in specifying exactly who are the noncombatants.[1] Roughly, they are those people who are not engaged in military operations and whose activity is not immediately and directly related to the war effort. Perhaps we could say that if a person is engaged only in the sort of activities which would be carried on even if the nation were not at war (or preparing for war) then that person is a noncombatant. So generally farmers, teachers, nurses, firemen, sales people, housewives, poets, children, etc. are noncombatants.[2] There are, of course, difficult cases, ranging from the high civilian official of the government to the truck driver (either military or civilian) who hauls vegetables toward the front lines. But despite the hard cases it is held that warring nations contain large numbers of readily identifiable people who are clearly noncombatants.

What of their immunity? The writers whom I consider here make use of the "principle of double-effect."[3] This involves dividing the consequences of an act (at least the foreseeable consequences) into two classes. Into the first class go those consequences which constitute the goal or purpose of the act, what the act is done for, and also those consequences which are means to those ends. Into the other class go those consequences which are neither the sought-after ends nor the means to those ends. So, for example, the bombing of a rail yard may have among its many consequences the following: the flow of supplies toward the front is disrupted, several locomotives are damaged, and a lot of smoke, dust, etc. is discharged into the air. The disruption of transport may well be the end sought by this action, and perhaps the damage to locomotives is sought as a means of disrupting transport. If so, these consequences belong in the first class, a class which I shall generally mark by using the words "intentional" or "intended." The smoke, on the other hand, though as surely foreseeable as the other effects, may be neither means nor end in this situation. It is a side-effect, and belongs in the second class (which I shall sometimes call "unintentional" or "unintended").

Now, the moral immunity of noncombatants consists, according to these writers, in the fact that their death can never, morally, be made the intended consequence of a military operation. Or to put it another way, any military operation which seeks the death of noncombatants either as an end or a means is immoral, regardless of the total good which it might accomplish.

The *unintended* death of noncombatants, on the other hand, is not absolutely forbidden. A military operation which will foreseeably result in such deaths, neither as means nor ends but as side effects, may be morally acceptable according to these writers. It will be morally acceptable if the good end which it may be expected to attain is of sufficient weight to overbalance the evil of these noncombatant deaths (as well as any other evils involved in it). This principle, sometimes called the principle of proportionality, apparently applies to foreseen but unintended noncombatant deaths in just the same way as it applies to the intended death of combatants, the destruction of resources, and so on. In all of these cases it is held to be immoral to cause many deaths, much pain, etc., in order to achieve minor goals. Here combatant and noncombatant stand on the same moral ground, and their deaths are weighed in the same balances. But when the slaying of noncombatants is envisioned as an end or, more commonly, as a means—perhaps in order to reduce the production of foodstuffs or to damage the morale of troops—then there is an unqualified judgment that the projected operation is flatly immoral. The intentional slaying of combatants, on the other hand, faces no such prohibition. This, then, is the place where the moral status of combatant and noncombatant differ sharply.

Now, if a scheme such as this is not to appear simply arbitrary it looks as though we must find some morally relevant basis for the distinction. It is perhaps worthwhile to notice that in this context the immunity of noncombatants cannot be supported by reference to the sanctity or value of human life, nor by reference to a duty not to kill our brothers, etc. For these authors recognize the moral permissibility, even perhaps the duty, of killing under certain circumstances. What must be sought is the ground of a distinction, and not merely a consideration against killing.

Such a ground, however, seems very hard to find, perhaps unexpectedly so. The crucial argument proposed by the immunity theorists turns on the notions of guilt and innocence. Anscombe, for example, says:

> Now, it is one of the most vehement and repeated teachings of the Judaeo-Christian tradition that the shedding of innocent blood is forbidden by the divine law. No man may be punished except for his own crime, and those "whose feet are swift to shed innocent blood" are always represented as God's enemies.[4]

Earlier on she says, "The principal wickedness which is a temptation to those engaged in warfare is the killing of the innocent,"[5] and she has titled one of the sections of her paper, "Innocence and the Right to Kill Intentionally." Clearly enough the notion of innocence plays a large role in her thinking on this topic. Just what that role is, or should be, will be considered shortly. Ford, in the article cited earlier, repeatedly couples the word "innocent" with "civilian" and "noncombatant." His clearest statement, however, is in another essay. There he says:

> Catholic teaching has been unanimous for long centuries in declaring that it is never permitted to kill directly noncombatants in wartime. Why? Because they are innocent. That is, they are innocent of the violent and destructive action of war, or of any close participation in the violent and destructive action of war. It is such participation *alone* that would make them legitimate targets of violent repression themselves.[6]

Here we have explicitly a promising candidate for the basis of the moral distinction between combatants and noncombatants. It is promising because innocence itself seems to be a moral property. Hence, if we could see that noncombatants were innocent while combatants were not it would be plausible to suppose that this fact made it morally proper to treat them in different ways.

If we are to succeed along this line of thought, then we must meet at least two conditions. First, we must find some one sense of "innocence" such that all noncombatants are innocent and all combatants are guilty. Second, this sense must be morally relevant, a point of the greatest importance. We are seeking to ground a moral distinction, and the facts to which we refer must therefore be morally relevant. The use of a morally tinged word, such as "innocent," does not of itself guarantee such relevance.

Well, is there a suitable sense for "innocent"? Ford said that noncombatants "are innocent of the violent and destructive action of war." Anscombe, writing of the people who can properly be attacked with deadly force, says, "What is required, for the people attacked to be noninnocent in the relevant sense, is that they themselves be engaged in an objectively unjust proceeding which the attacker has the right to make his concern; or—the commonest case—should be unjustly attacking him." On the other hand, she speaks of "people whose mere existence and activity supporting existence by growing crops, making clothes, etc.," might contribute to the war effort, and she says, "such people are innocent and it is murderous to attack them, or make them a target for an attack which he judges will help him towards victory."[7] These passages contain, I think, the best clues we have as to the sense of "innocent" in these authors.

It is probably evident enough that this sense of "innocent" is vague in a way parallel to the vagueness of "noncombatant." It will leave us with troublesome borderline cases. In itself, that does not seem to me a crucial defect. But perhaps it is a clue to an important failing. For I suspect that there is this parallel vagueness because "innocent" here is just a synonym for "noncombatant."

What can Ford mean by saying that some people are "innocent of the violent and destructive action of war" except that those people are not engaged in the violence of war? Must not Anscombe mean essentially the same thing when she says that the noninnocent are those who are themselves "engaged in an objectively unjust proceeding"? But we need not rely wholly on these rhetorical questions. Ramsey makes this point explicitly. He first distinguishes between close and remote cooperation in military operations, and then he alludes to the distinction between the "guilty" and the "innocent." Of this distinction he says, "These are very misleading terms, since their meaning is exhaustively stated under the first contrast, and is reducible to degrees of actual participation in hostile force."[8] In this judgment Ramsey certainly seems to me to be right.

Now, we should notice carefully that a person may be an enthusiastic supporter of the unjust war and its unjust aims, he may give to it his voice and his vote, he may have done everything in his power to procure it when it was yet but a prospect, now that it is in progress he may contribute to it both his savings and the work which he knows best how to do, and he may avidly hope to share in the unjust gains which will follow if the war is successful. But such a person may clearly be a noncombatant, and (in the sense of the immunity theorists) unquestionably "innocent" of the war. On the other hand, a young man of limited mental ability and almost no education may be drafted, put into uniform, trained for a few weeks, and sent to the front as a replacement in a low-grade unit. He may have no understanding of what the war is about, and no heart for it. He might want nothing more than to go back to his town and the life he led before. But he is "engaged," carrying ammunition, perhaps, or stringing telephone wire or even banging away ineffectually with his rifle. He is without doubt a combatant, and "guilty," a fit subject for intentional slaughter. Is it not clear that "innocence," as used here, leaves out entirely all of the relevant moral considerations—that it has no moral content at all? Anscombe suggests that intentional killing during warfare should be construed on the model of punishing people for their crimes, and we must see to it, if we are to be moral, that we punish someone only for his own crime and not for someone else's. But if we construe the criminality involved in an unjust war in any reasonable moral sense then it must either be the case that many noncombatants are guilty of that criminality or else many combatants are innocent. In fact, it will probably be the case that *both* of these things are true. Only if we were to divest "crime" of its moral bearings could we make it fit the combatant/noncombatant distinction in modern wars.

The fact that both Anscombe and Ramsey[9] use the analogy of the criminal in discussing this topic suggests that there is an important fact about warfare which is easily overlooked. And that is that warfare, unlike ordinary criminal activity, is not an activity in which individuals engage qua individuals or as members of voluntary associations. They enter into war as members of nations. It is more proper to say that the nation is at war than that its soldiers are at war. This does not, of course, entail that individuals have no moral responsibility for their acts in war. But it does suggest that moral responsibility may not be distributed between combatant and noncombatant in the same way as between a criminal and his children. Many of the men who are soldiers, perhaps most of them, would not be engaged in military operations at all if they did not happen to be citizens of a warring nation. But noncombatants are citizens of warring nations in exactly the same sense as are soldiers. However these facts are to be analyzed they should warn us not to rely too heavily on the analogy with ordinary criminality.

We seem, then, to be caught in a dilemma. We can perhaps find some sense for notions such as *innocence* and *criminality* which will make them fit the distinction in which we are interested. But the price of doing so seems to be that of divesting these notions of the moral significance which they require if they are to justify the moral import of the distinction itself. In the ordinary senses, on the other hand, these notions do have the required moral bearings. But in their ordinary senses they do not fit the desired distinction. In neither way, therefore, can the argument from innocence be made to work, and the alleged moral immunity of noncombatants seems to be left as an arbitrary claim.

II. CONVENTION-DEPENDENT MORALITY

Despite the failure of these arguments I have recently come to think that there may be something of importance in this distinction after all, and even that it may have an important moral bearing. How might this be?

Imagine a statesman reflecting on the costliness of war, its cost in human life and human suffering. He observes that these costs are normally very high, sometimes staggering. Furthermore, he accepts the principle of proportionality. A consequence of this is that he sometimes envisions a just war for a just cause, but nevertheless decides not to prosecute that war even though he believes it could be won. For the cost of winning would be so high as to outweigh the good which would be attained. So he must sometimes let oppression flourish and injustice hold sway. And even in those wars which can be prosecuted the costs eat very seriously into the benefits.

Then he has an idea. Suppose—just suppose—that one could replace warfare with a less costly substitute. Suppose, for example, that one could introduce a convention—and actually get it accepted and followed by the nations—a convention which replaced warfare with single combat. Under this convention, when two nations arrived at an impasse which would otherwise have resulted in war they would instead choose, each of them, a single champion (doubtless a volunteer). These two men would then meet in mortal combat, and whoever won, killing his opponent or driving him from the field, would win for his nation. To that nation would then be ceded whatever territory, influence, or other prize would have been sought in the war, and the nation whose champion was defeated would lose correspondingly.

Suppose, too, that the statesman believes that if such a convention were to come into force his own nation could expect to win and lose such combats in about the same proportion as it could now expect to win and lose ordinary wars. The same types of questions would be settled by such combats as would otherwise be settled by war (though perhaps more questions would be submitted to combat than would be submitted to war), and approximately the same resolutions would be arrived at. The costs, however—human death and suffering—would be reduced by several orders of magnitude. Would that not be an attractive prospect? I think it would.

While the prospect may seem attractive it may also strike us as hopelessly utopian, hardly to be given a serious thought. There seems to be some evidence, however, that exactly this substitution was actually attempted in ancient times. Ancient literature contains at least two references to such attempts. One is in the Bible, I Samuel 17, the combat between David and Goliath. The other is in the *Iliad*, book 3, where it is proposed to settle the seige of Troy in the very beginning by single combat between Menelaus and Paris. It may be significant that neither of these attempts appears to have been successful. The single combats were followed by bloodier and more general fighting. Perhaps this substitute for warfare is too cheap; it cannot be made practical, and nations just will not consent in the end to abide by this convention. But consider, on the one hand, warfare which is limited only by the moral requirements that the ends sought should be just and that the means used should be proportionate, and, on the other hand, the convention of single combat as a substitute for warfare. Between these extremes there lie a vast number of other possible conventions which might be canvassed in the search for a less costly substitute for war. I suggest that the long struggle, in the western world at least, to limit military operations to "counter-forces" strategies, thus sparing civilian populations, is just such an attempt.

If I am right about this, then the moral aspects of the matter must be approached in a way rather different from that of the immunity theorists. Some, but not all, of their conclusions can be accepted, and somewhat different grounds must be given for them. These thinkers have construed the immunity of noncombatants as though it were a moral fact which was independent of any actual or envisioned convention or practice. And they have consequently sought to support this immunity by argument which makes no reference to convention. I have already argued that their attempts were failures. What I suggest now is that all such attempts *must* be failures, for they mistake the sort of moral requirement which is under consideration. Let me try to make this clearer.

I find it plausible to suppose that I have a moral obligation to refrain from wantonly murdering my neighbors. And it also seems plausible to discuss this, perhaps in utilitarian terms, or in terms of the will of God, or of natural law, or in terms of a rock-bottom deontological requirement, but in any case without essential reference to the laws and customs of our nation. We might, indeed, easily imagine our laws and customs to be other than they are with respect to murder. But we would then judge the moral adequacy and value of such alternative laws and customs by reference to the moral obligation I have mentioned and not vice versa. On the other hand, I may also have a moral obligation to pay a property tax or to drive on the right side of the street. It does not seem plausible to suppose, however, that one can discuss these duties without immediately referring to our laws and customs. And it seems likely that different laws would have generated different moral duties, e.g. driving on the left. These latter are examples of "convention-dependent" moral obligations. More formally, I will say that a given moral obligation is convention-dependent if and only if (1) given that a certain convention, law, custom, etc., is actually in force one really does have an obligation to act in conformity with that convention, and (2) there is an alternative law, custom, etc. (or lack thereof) such that if that had been in force one would not have had the former obligation.

At this point, before developing the way in which it may apply to warfare, let me forestall some possible misunderstandings by a series of brief comments on this notion. I am not claiming, nor do I believe, that all laws, customs, etc., generate corresponding moral obligations. But some do. I am not denying that one may seek, and perhaps find, some more general moral law, perhaps independent of convention, which explains why this convention generates the more specific obligation. I claim only that one cannot account for the specific obligation apart from the convention. Finally, I am not denying that one might have an obligation, perhaps independent of convention, to try to change a convention of this sort. For I think it possible that one might simultaneously have a moral obligation to conform to a certain convention and also a moral obligation to replace that convention, and thus to eliminate the first obligation.

Now, the core of my suggestion with respect to the immunity of noncombatants is this. The immunity of noncombatants is best thought of as a convention-dependent obligation related to a convention which substitutes for warfare a certain form of limited combat. How does this bear on some of the questions which we have been discussing?

To begin with, we might observe that the convention itself is presumably to be justified by its expectable results. (Perhaps we can refer to some moral rule to the effect that we should minimize social costs such as death and injury.) It seems plausible to suppose that the counter-forces convention, if followed, will reduce the pain and death involved in combat—will reduce it, that is, compared to unlimited warfare. There are surely other possible conventions which, if followed, would reduce those costs still more, e.g. the substitution of single combat. Single combat, however, is probably not a live contender because there is almost no chance that such a convention would actually be followed. It is possible, however, that there is some practical convention which is preferable to the present counter-forces convention. If so, the fact that it is preferable is a strong reason in favor of supposing that there is a moral obligation to promote its adoption.

It does not follow, however, that we now have a duty to act in conformity with this other possible convention. For the results of acting in conformity with a preferable convention which is not widely observed may be much worse than the results of acting in conformity with a less desirable convention which is widely observed. We might, for example, discover that a "left-hand" pattern of traffic flow would be preferable to the present system of "right-hand" rules, in that it would result in fewer accidents, etc. The difference might be so significant that we really would be morally derelict if we did not try to institute a change in our laws. We would be acquiescing in a very costly procedure when a more economical one was at hand. But it would be a disaster, and, I suspect, positively immoral, for a few of us to begin driving on the left before the convention was changed. In cases of convention-dependent obligations the question of what convention is actually in force is one of considerable moral import. That one is reminded to take this question seriously is one of the important differences between this approach and that of the immunity theorists.

Perhaps the counter-forces convention is not really operative now in a substantial way. I do not know. Doubtless, it suffered a severe blow in World War II, not least from British and American bombing strategies. Traffic rules are embedded in a broad, massive, comparatively stable social structure which makes their status comparatively resistant to erosion by infraction. Not so, however, for a convention of warfare. It has little status except in its actual observance, and depends greatly on the mutual trust of the belligerents; hence it is especially vulnerable to abrogation by a few contrary acts. Here arises a related difference with the immunity theorists. Taking the obligation to be convention-independent they reject argument based on the fact that "the enemy did it first," etc.[10] If the obligation were independent they would be correct in this. But for convention-dependent obligations, what one's opponent does, what "everyone is doing," etc., are facts of great moral importance. Such facts help to determine within what convention, if any, one is operating, and thus they help one to discover what his moral duties are.

If we were to decide that the counter-forces convention was dead at present, or, indeed, that no convention at all with respect to warfare was operative now, it would not follow that warfare was immoral. Nor, on the other hand, would it follow that warfare was beyond all moral rules, an area in which "anything goes." Instead, we would simply go back to warfare per se, limited only by independent moral requirements, such as those of justice and proportionality. That would, on the whole, probably be a more costly way of handling such problems. But if we live in a time when the preferable substitutes are not available, then we must either forgo the goods or bear the higher costs. If we had no traffic laws or customs, traffic would be even more dangerous and costly than it is now. Traveling, however, might still be justified, if the reason for traveling were sufficiently important.

In such a case, of course, there would be no obligation to drive on the right, or in any regular manner, nor would there be any benefit in it. Probably the best thing would be to drive in a completely ad hoc way, seeking the best maneuver in each situation as it arose. More generally, and ignoring for the moment a final consideration which will be discussed below, there is no obligation and no benefit associated with the unilateral observance of a convention. If one's cause is unjust then one ought not to kill noncombatants. But that is because of the independent moral prohibition against prosecuting such a war at all, and has nothing to do with any special immunity of noncombatants. If one's cause is just, but the slaying of noncombatants will not advance it to any marked degree, then one ought not to slay them. But this is just the requirement of proportionality, and applies equally and in the same way to combatants. If one's cause is just and the slaying of noncombatants would advance it—if, in other words, one is not prevented by considerations of justice and proportionality—this is the crucial case. If one refrains unilaterally in this situation then he seems to choose the greater of two evils (or the lesser of two goods). By hypothesis, the good achieved, i.e. the lives spared, is not as weighty as the evil which he allows in damage to the prospects for justice or in the even more costly alternative measures, e.g. the slaying of a larger number of combatants, which he must undertake. Now, if the relevant convention were operative, then his refraining from counter-population strategies here would be related to his enemy's similar restraint, and indeed it would be related to the strategies which would be used in future wars. These larger considerations might well tip the balance in the other direction. But by hypothesis we are considering the case in which there is no such convention, and so these larger considerations do not arise. One acts unilaterally. In such a situation it certainly appears that one would have chosen the worse of the two alternatives. It is hard to suppose that one is morally obligated to do so.

I said above that we were ignoring for the moment one relevant consideration. It should not be ignored forever. I have already called attention to the fact that conventions of warfare are not, like traffic rules, embedded in a more massive social structure. This makes them especially precarious, as we have noted. But it also bears on the way in which they may be adopted. One such way, perhaps a rather important way, is for one party to the hostilities to signal his willingness to abide by such a convention by undertaking some unilateral restraint on his own part. If the opponent does not reciprocate, then the offer has failed and it goes no further. If the opponent does reciprocate, however, then the area of restraint may be broadened, and a kind of mutual respect and confidence may grow up between the belligerents. Each comes to rely on the other to keep the (perhaps unspoken) agreement, and therefore each is willing to forgo the immediate advantage which might accrue to him from breaking it. If this happens, then a new convention has begun its precarious life. This may be an event well worth seeking.

Not only may it be worth seeking, it may be worth paying something for it. For a significant increase in the likelihood that a worthwhile convention will be adopted it may be worth accepting an increased risk or a higher immediate cost in lives and suffering. So there may be some justification in unilateral restraint after all, even in the absence of a convention. But this justification is prospective and finite. It envisions the possibility that such a convention may arise in the future as a result of this restraint. Consequently, the justification should be proportioned to some judgment as to the likelihood of that event, and it should be reevaluated as future events unfold.

III. CONVENTION VS. MORALITY

I began by examining some attempts to defend a certain alleged moral rule of war, the immunity of noncombatants. These defenses have in common the fact that they construe this moral rule as independent of any human law, custom, etc. I then argued that these defenses fail because they leave a certain distinction without moral support, and yet the distinction is essential to the rule. Turning then to the task of construction rather than criticism, I suggested that the immunity of noncombatants is not an independent moral rule but rather a part of a convention which sets up a morally desirable alternative to war. I argued then that some conventions, including this one, generate special moral obligations which cannot be satisfactorily explained and defended without reference to the convention. And in the final pages I explored some of the special features of the obligation at hand and of the arguments which are relevant to it.

The distinction I have drawn is that between warfare per se on the one hand, and, on the other hand, international combats which are limited by convention and custom. But the point of the distinction is to clarify our thinking about the *morality* of such wars and combats. That is where its value must be tested.

NOTES

1. Elizabeth Anscombe, "War and Murder," *War and Morality* ed. Richard A. Wasserstrom (Belmont, Calif., 1970), p. 52; John C. Ford, "The Morality of Obliteration Bombing," ibid., pp. 19–23; Paul Ramsey, *The Just War* (New York, 1968), pp. 157, 158.
2. Ford gives a list of over 100 occupations whose practitioners he considers to be "almost without exception" noncombatants.
3. Anscombe, pp. 46, 50, 51; Ford, pp. 26–28; Ramsey, pp. 347–358.
4. Anscombe, p. 49.
5. Ibid., p. 44.
6. John C. Ford, "The Hydrogen Bombing of Cities," *Morality and Modern Warfare* ed. William J. Nagle (Baltimore: Helicon Press, 1960), p. 98.
7. Anscombe, p. 45.
8. Ramsey, p. 153.
9. Ibid., p. 144.
10. For example, Ford, "The Morality of Obliteration Bombing," pp. 20, 33.

War and Innocence

ROBERT K. FULLINWIDER

Robert Fullinwider is an American philosopher and analyst of public policy who works at the Institute for Philosophy and Public Policy at the University of Maryland. He has written on

From *Philosophy and Public Affairs*, 5(1), pp. 90–97, 1975.

a wide range of public policy topics, including military conscription, affirmative action, and multicultural education.

The selection that appears here was originally published as a response to Mavrodes in a later issue that same year (1975) of the journal *Philosophy and Public Affairs.* Fullinwider argues that, contrary to Mavrodes' claims, it is never morally justifiable to kill noncombatants intentionally.

I

In a war, is it morally permissible intentionally to kill noncombatants? Elizabeth Anscombe and Paul Ramsey argue that noncombatants may not be intentionally killed.[1] We are obligated to refrain from such killing because it is murder; and it is murder because noncombatants are innocent.

George Mavrodes questions the grounds for asserting that in war noncombatants are "innocent" and combatants are "guilty." If immunity of noncombatants from killing is to be established this way, he says, then we must find a "sense of 'innocence' such that all noncombatants are innocent and all combatants are guilty," and "this sense must be morally relevant." Mavrodes fears, however, that immunity theorists such as Anscombe and Ramsey are actually using "innocent" and "noncombatant" synonymously. He believes that the sense of "innocence" used in their arguments has no moral content.[2]

Mavrodes' main argument is this. There are noncombatants who may enthusiastically endorse and support the war their nation is waging, while there are combatants who may be under arms unhappily and unwillingly, who may not support the war but are unable to resist conscription. It is odd to claim that the enthusiastically supportive noncombatant is innocent and the reluctant conscript guilty. "Is it not clear," Mavrodes asks, "that 'innocence,' as used here, leaves out entirely all morally relevant considerations . . . ?"[3]

Anscombe and Ramsey both invite this sort of counterargument by the way they defend their immunity thesis. Anscombe implies that the thesis is rooted in the Principle of Punishment: no man is to be punished except for his own crime.[4] Ramsey, too, employs the model of the criminal in defending the thesis.[5] But, from the point of view of punishment, it is odd, if not perverse, to view the enthusiastically supportive noncombatant as innocent and the reluctant combatant as guilty. Mavrodes, in my judgment, is right in believing this defense fails to establish the immunity of noncombatants from intentional killing.

Mavrodes believes that the obligation not to kill noncombatants intentionally can rest only on a convention among nations. Such an obligation, if it exists, is at best contingent, conditioned as it is on the existence of such a convention in force. Anscombe and Ramsey believe the obligation to refrain from intentionally killing noncombatants is noncontingent. It is not convention-dependent.[6]

In this paper I shall briefly sketch an argument for the immunity of noncombatants which avoids Mavrodes' criticisms. It will establish that in warfare there is a morally relevant distinction between noncombatants and combatants which prohibits the intentional killing of the former at the same time as it justifies the intentional killing of the latter. My argument will appeal to a nonconventional principle, and thus the obligation deriving from the principle will not be convention-dependent (or anyway not wholly so). I will then go on to show that even if certain considerations undercut drawing the line of immunity between combatants and noncombatants, a weaker version of the immunity thesis is still viable.

II

To set the scene, first consider an example. Jones is walking down a street. Smith steps from behind the corner of a nearby building and begins to fire a gun at Jones, with the appearance of deliberate intent to kill Jones. Surrounded by buildings, Jones is afforded no means of escape. Jones, who is carrying a gun himself, shoots at Smith and kills him.

Jones is morally justified in killing Smith by the Principle of Self-Defense. Smith's actions put Jones' life directly and immediately in mortal jeopardy, and Jones' killing Smith was necessary to end that threat. From the point of view of self-defense, these facts about Smith's actions are the *only* relevant ones. The moral justification of the killing rests on them alone given the legitimacy of self-defense.

But let me now sketch in some possible background circumstances to Smith's assault on Jones. Suppose Smith's wife, spurned by Jones when she made advances toward him, tells Smith she has been raped by Jones. Furious, and egged on by his wife, Smith seeks out Jones and begins firing. Or, suppose Smith, through heavy gambling losses, is in debt to the mob for $100,000. The mobsters propose to Smith that if he will kill Jones (a crusading district attorney, say), they will forgive his debt. Unable to pay the debt, and knowing what will happen to him if he fails to pay it, Smith seeks out Jones and begins firing. Or, suppose the mobsters kidnap Smith's children and threaten to kill them unless he kills Jones. Driven by the threat, Smith seeks out Jones and begins firing.

None of this background information alters the situation from the point of view of self-defense. Whatever prompted Smith to fire at Jones, the justification for Jones' killing Smith lies solely in the fact that Smith was the direct and immediate agent of a threat against Jones' life. From the point of view of self-defense, this fact justifies Jones in killing Smith—and *only* Smith.

Again, suppose that Smith's wife was standing across the street egging Smith on as he fired at Jones. Jones, though he justifiably shot Smith in self-defense, could not justifiably turn his gun on the wife in self-defense. Or suppose the mobsters were parked across the street to observe Smith. After killing Smith, Jones could not turn his gun on them (assuming they were unarmed). No matter how causally implicated the wife or the mobsters were in Smith's assault on Jones, in the situation it was only Smith who was the agent of immediate threat to Jones; the wife and the mobsters were not posing a direct and immediate danger. From the point of view of justifiably killing in self-defense, they are not justifiably liable to be killed by Jones; they are immune.

There is a point of view from which these background features I have drawn in become morally relevant, namely the point of view of retribution or punishment. Smith's wife and the mobsters would be viewed as morally culpable for their contribution to Smith's assault on Jones' life. They ought to be punished, Perhaps Jones might be justified in taking his own retribution, and killing the wife or mobsters in revenge; but even if he is justified in killing them in retribution, he still cannot justify killing them on the grounds of self-defense.

In these cases of killing and attempted killing there are two points of view: the point of view of self-defense and the point of view of punishment. Some considerations that become morally relevant from the second point of view in justifying killing are not relevant from the first point of view. We use the notions of guilt and innocence almost always in connection with the second point of view, the perspective of punishment. From that point of view, Smith's wife and the mobsters are as guilty as Smith. In the instance where the mobsters cause Smith to act under duress, perhaps they are more guilty.

If we were to speak of innocence and guilt as categories applying in cases of self-defense, then for the purpose of justifiably killing in self-defense and from that point of view we would say that Smith alone was guilty (justifiably liable to killing) and his wife and the mobsters were innocent (not justifiably liable to killing), though all are guilty from the point of view of punishment.

It should be obvious now how my argument for the immunity thesis is going to run. The moral relevance of the distinction in war between combatants and noncombatants will be derived from the Principle of Self-Defense. Because we most commonly speak of innocence in connection with crime and punishment and because we also speak of innocent victims of war, Anscombe and Ramsey have been led to defend the innocents in war by appeal to the wrong model. For these same reasons, Mavrodes has failed to see an alternative to his conventionalism.

III

I shall now sketch an argument for the moral immunity of noncombatants from intentional killing.

The question at hand is the killing in war and its justifiability. Why is any killing at all justified?

I claim that a nation may justifiably kill in self-defense. From the point of view of self-defense, only those are justifiably liable to be killed who pose the immediate and direct jeopardy. In the case of war, it is nations' armed forces which are the agents of the jeopardy. In a war, the armed forces of nation *A* stand to opponent nation *B* as Smith stood to Jones.[7] It is against them that *B* may defend itself by the use of force. The active combatants, their arms, ammunition, war machines and facilities, are the legitimate targets of intentional destruction.

Though *A*'s civilian population may support its war against *B* and contribute to it in various ways, they stand to *B* as Smith's wife or the mobsters stood to Jones. For the purpose of justifiably killing in self-defense and from that point of view, the civilian population is morally immune—it is "innocent." To intentionally kill noncombatants is to kill beyond the scope of self-defense. It is to kill unjustifiably from the point of view of self-defense.

This, in brief, is my argument. It provides for drawing a line between combatants and noncombatants, and prohibits intentionally killing the latter. This is just where the immunity theorists want to draw the line of prohibition. Furthermore, they see the prohibition as "natural," not convention-dependent. My argument supports them in this. The distinction between combatants and noncombatants derives from the operation of the Principle of Self-Defense. Our obligation not to kill noncombatants stems from our obligation not to kill without justification; and the Principle of Self-Defense justifies killing only combatants. Since both the obligation to not kill without justification and the Principle of Self-Defense are "natural" rather than conventional, the moral immunity of noncombatants does not rest (solely) upon the existence of appropriate conventions among nations.[8]

IV

From the point of view of killing in self-defense in war, Mavrodes' reluctant conscript is "guilty" (justifiably liable to killing), and his noncombatant partisan is "innocent" (not justifiably liable to killing). To say that the reluctant conscript is guilty and the noncombatant partisan is innocent is to stand the matter on its head, claims Mavrodes. So it is—from the point of view of punishment. This, I have urged, is not the fundamentally governing point of view when it comes to justifying killing in war. The innocence of the noncombatant seems inexplicable to Mavrodes because he takes up the wrong point of view for evaluating killing in war. He is, of course, encouraged to take up this view by Anscombe's and Ramsey's own arguments in defense of the innocence of noncombatants. Viewing killing in war from this evaluative standpoint, and finding it incapable of explaining the prohibition against killing combatants, Mavrodes turns to conventionalism.

Might it not be contended against my defense of the immunity thesis that the point of view of self-defense is not the sole governing point of view when it comes to killing in war? Nations, it might be argued, exist in a state of nature, and thus possess the right to exact their own punishments on transgressors. Thus, in war, justifying deliberate killing may be done by appeal to both the Principle of Self-Defense *and* the Principle of Punishment. Finally, to the extent that retribution justifies some of the killing in war, it will justify killing some noncombatants.[9]

I have two answers to this challenge. The first answer preserves the strong immunity thesis, but it requires an assumption of fact which may, theoretically, not obtain. The second answer, dropping the assumption, requires me to weaken the immunity thesis.

For purposes of argument, I will concede that nations have the right to exact their own punishment in war. Even so, the Principle of Punishment justifies punishing *only* the *morally guilty* (culpable from the point of view of punishment), not the *morally innocent* (innocent from the point of view of punishment). Techniques of warfare—combat, bombing, shelling, burning—are too indiscriminate in their destruction to serve as legitimate instruments of punishment. They cannot be used discriminatingly between the morally guilty and the morally innocent. It is not justified by the Principle of Punishment intentionally to kill the morally innocent. If a nation claims punitive rights in war, it must adopt mechanisms of punishment which will discriminate between those who deserve punishment and those who do not.

Bombing, shelling, and other such techniques kill guilty and innocent alike. Consequently, if we wish to justify killing during war by the means of war, the only applicable perspective is self-defense.[10]

If, however, contrary to the facts, there were some perfectly discriminating techniques of warfare, then, since I have conceded the right of nations to exact their own punishment, I see no argument against a nation legitimately taking up both points of view in its prosecution of a war. Some of the justified killing will be justified by self-defense, some by merited punishment. This would require a weakening of the immunity thesis, since the Principle of Punishment would justify some intentional killing of noncombatants, namely those that were morally guilty. Nevertheless, a version of the immunity thesis can be preserved: some line prohibiting intentional killing would still be mandated. The Principle of Self-Defense will justify intentionally killing combatants, even the morally innocent among them. The Principle of Punishment will justify killing (if this is proportional to the crime) the morally guilty noncombatant. But neither principle will sanction or permit the intentional killing of the morally innocent noncombatant, many of whom will be found in any nation at war.[11] There will thus be a line of immunity required to be drawn around a certain class in war, the class of morally innocent noncombatants. We shall be morally obliged to refrain from intentionally killing members of this class, and this moral obligation will not disappear in the absence of any particular convention among nations.

Because of the indiscriminate nature of modern techniques of destruction, I see two reasons why the line of immunity is to be maintained between combatants and noncombatants. First, if nations recognize the Principle of Punishment, they may nevertheless be required to refrain from attempting to use it as a justification for killing because they shall not be able to meet the discrimination requirement. Second, nations may find it collectively beneficial to agree to forgo the exercise of their punishment rights during war (the exercise of which is morally ruled out anyway). They might thus, as Mavrodes suggests, adopt conventions confirming the line of immunity during warfare between combatant and noncombatant. To this extent, Mavrodes' conventionalism has support. The obligation not to kill noncombatants may be partly conventional; but if my arguments have been correct, it is not wholly so.[12]

NOTES

1. Elizabeth Anscombe, "War and Murder," in *War and Morality,* ed. Richard Wasserstrom (Belmont, Ca., 1970); Paul Ramsey, *The Last War* (New York, 1968). See also John C. Ford, "The Morality of Obliteration Bombing," in *War and Morality.*
2. George I. Mavrodes, "Conventions and the Morality of War," *Philosophy & Public Affairs* 4, no. 2 (Winter 1975): [321–322, this volume].
3. Mavrodes [pp. 321–322, this volume].
4. Anscombe, p. 49; Mavrodes [pp. 320–322, this volume].
5. Ramsey, p. 144; Mavrodes [p. 324, this volume].
6. For Mavrodes' definition of convention-dependent obligation [p. 324, this volume].
7. In a war each side is likely to view the other as the aggressor and itself as the defender; thus each side will claim to be acting in self-defense. I ignore the question of how we determine who is correct in making such a claim. My argument has to do with how *much* one may claim if one claims to act in self-defense.
8. In his argument against Anscombe and Ramsey, Mavrodes does not claim that conventionalism is true because the Principle of Punishment, to which they appeal, is itself conventional. Mavrodes does not dispute their assumption that the Principle of Punishment is a nonconventional source of obligation. Nor does Mavrodes support his conventionalism by arguing that *all* moral obligation is convention-dependent. Thus, I take it that the Principle of Self-Defense and the obligation not to kill without justification are nonconventional sources of obligation, since they are at least as nonconventional as the Principle of Punishment.
9. Some Allied air raids against German cities in World War II seem to have been clearly punitive in intent.
10. The Principle of Self-Defense also requires discrimination—between combatants and noncombatants. Since usually combatants are in uniform, with weapons, on battlefields, instruments of war

can be used in a way which (roughly) avoids the death of noncombatants. However, instruments which cannot be used in a discriminating way, and whose use entails extensive noncombatant casualties (e.g. hydrogen bombs), are ruled out for use even in self-defense. See Richard Wasserstrom, "On the Morality of War: A Preliminary Inquiry," in *War and Morality,* pp. 100–101. (See also pp. 89 ff. where Wasserstrom discusses the justification of self-defense; and pp. 94–96, where he discusses the meaning of innocence in war.)

11. Consider merely what percentage of a nation's population is made up of children under the age of ten.

12. In order to present a clean line of argument I have omitted discussion of various questions and qualifications that must be dealt with in any thorough defense of killing in war. Sometimes self-defense will not sufficiently justify killing. The Principle of Punishment may not justify any killing—I only assume that it does in order to consider a strong objection to the immunity thesis. I omit important questions such as whether persons have a moral right to a hearing before they may be punished, and so on. I believe that none of these issues, when resolved, will justify *more* killing.

Self-Defense and the Killing of Noncombatants: A Reply to Fullinwider

LAWRENCE A. ALEXANDER

Lawrence A. Alexander is a professor of law at the University of California, San Diego. He is the author of a large number of books and articles on constitutional law, criminal law, and jurisprudence.

In this text, originally published as a response to Mavrodes and Fullinwider in a 1976 issue of *Philosophy and Public Affairs,* Alexander argues that there are indeed cases in which the intentional killing of innocent noncombatants is morally justified.

In a recent article[1] Robert Fullinwider argued that the distinction between combatants and noncombatants is morally relevant (in a sense unrelated to the existence of a specific convention among nations)[2] to the question of who among the enemy may be intentionally killed by a nation acting in self-defense. He concedes that the distinction is not based on the relative moral guilt or innocence of the two groups in connection with the prosecution of the war, recognizing that many combatants might be morally innocent (for example, reluctant conscripts) and many noncombatants morally guilty (for example, the governmental officials who launched the war). Moreover, he admits that guilt or innocence is relevant to the question of who should be punished by the defending nation. However, says Fullinwider, punishment of the guilty is not the only justification for intentional killing in war. Under the Principle of Self-Defense, innocent combatants, but not innocent noncombatants, may also justifiably be killed.

I do not intend to deny the widely held view that morally innocent persons may be intentionally killed in self-defense (although I believe a case can be made against it).[3] Rather, I intend to show that the permissibility of killing innocents in self-defense does not, as Fullinwider maintains, justify the moral distinction between combatants and noncombatants.

From *Philosophy and Public Affairs,* 5(4), pp. 408–415, 1976.

The heart of Fullinwider's argument is the following passage:

> . . . Suppose Smith, through heavy gambling losses, is in debt to the mob for $100,000. The mobsters propose to Smith that if he will kill Jones (a crusading district attorney, say), they will forgive his debt. Unable to pay the debt, and knowing what will happen to him if he fails to pay it, Smith seeks out Jones and begins firing. Or, suppose the mobsters kidnap Smith's children and threaten to kill them unless he kills Jones. Driven by the threat, Smith seeks out Jones and begins firing.
>
> None of this background information alters the situation from the point of view of self-defense. Whatever prompted Smith to fire at Jones, the justification for Jones' killing Smith lies solely in the fact that Smith was the direct and immediate agent of a threat against Jones' life. From the point of view of self-defense, this fact justifies Jones in killing Smith—and *only* Smith.
>
> Again . . . suppose the mobsters were parked across the street to observe Smith. After killing Smith, Jones could not turn his gun on them (assuming they were unarmed). No matter how causally implicated . . . the mobsters were in Smith's assault on Jones, in the situation it was only Smith who was the agent of immediate threat to Jones; . . . the mobsters were not posing a direct and immediate danger. From the point of view of justifiably killing in self-defense, they are not justifiably liable to be killed by Jones; they are immune.[4]

Fullinwider is correct that *after* killing Smith, Jones may not invoke the Principle of Self-Defense to then turn and kill the mobsters. *The threat to his life has been removed.* At most the mobsters may be punished for their guilt in instigating the attempted murder.

However, Fullinwider's hypothetical is inapposite when we are discussing whether noncombatants along with combatants may be killed in an on-going war. Surely no one has contended that after surrender, the point analogous to the killing of Smith by Jones, innocent noncombatants may still be killed in self-defense. (Indeed, no one has contended as much for innocent combatants either.) Fullinwider has constructed a straw man.

Let us amend Fullinwider's hypothetical to make it relevant to the issue he is addressing. Suppose the situation is the same except that Jones has not yet killed Smith. May Jones invoke the Principle of Self-Defense to kill the mobsters instead of Smith if by doing so he will cause Smith to relent? Of course he may. If the mobsters had a gun trained on Smith and had ordered him to kill Jones, and he were about to comply, Jones not only could, but should, kill the mobsters rather than Smith if killing them would be no riskier than killing Smith and would remove the threat to Jones by removing Smith's motive for killing him. Jones should kill the mobsters in such a situation even if the mobsters could not kill Jones directly (say, because the range of their guns was sufficient to reach Smith but not Jones, who carried a longer-range gun). From the standpoint of the Principle of Self-Defense, both the mobsters and Smith are necessary causes of the danger to Jones because killing either the mobsters or Smith removes the danger. Jones should, therefore, kill the ones who are morally guilty, not the one who is morally innocent. Such an interpretation of the Principle of Self-Defense is consistent with its application in the law,[5] and any interpretation that permitted only the killing of Smith would be morally perverse.

Indeed, it would be morally perverse to limit Jones' right of self-defense to the killing of Smith, even where the mobsters have not threatened Smith's life. Suppose the chief mobster has merely offered Smith money. The mobster, unarmed, is across the street from Smith and Jones, so that if Jones kills the mobster, Smith will realize that he will not get paid for killing Jones. Jones should be able to kill the mobster instead of Smith if the mobster is morally as guilty or guiltier than Smith (who might have been driven to the wall financially).

What I propose as the correct formulation of the Principle of Self-Defense is that X (a person or persons) may be killed in self-defense, regardless of X's moral innocence, if the defender perceives (reasonably) that: (1) there exists the requisite threshold level of danger or greater; (2) killing X will reduce that danger;[6] (3) more desirable courses of action,[7] such as killing fewer or guiltier persons, or not killing at all, will not eliminate condition (1); and (4) more desirable courses of action will not reduce the danger as much as killing *X*.

In war, many noncombatants, guilty and innocent, are threats to the defending nation. Many of them are greater threats than many combatants. A combatant at a camp miles behind the lines is often less a threat than a noncombatant delivering arms and ammunition to combatants at the front. Indeed, the combatants at the front individually will quite likely be less of a threat than the noncombatant supplier. In such a case the Principle of Self-Defense would demand that the noncombatant be killed in preference to the combatants, especially if he is no less guilty than they. Consider, also, two alternative courses of action in fighting a hypothetical unjust aggressor: (1) killing millions of enemy soldiers, most of whom are morally innocent (indeed, many are children); or (2) killing a handful of noncombatant enemy leaders, all of whom are morally innocent because of insanity. If either course would end the war, the latter would have to be preferred. Similarly, if one madman is about to deliver bombs to a thousand other madmen, who in turn will throw them, the Principle of Self-Defense demands that we end the danger by killing the former if we are going to be forced to kill in self-defense in any event.

Fullinwider's error could have resulted from assuming that one whose activity or existence is a remote cause (in terms of space, time, or intervening mechanisms or acts) of a threat to another's life is immune from being killed in self-defense, even though he is a necessary or sufficient cause of that threat. In the domestic context, causal remoteness will usually mean that the threat is insufficient to permit killing in self-defense. For in the domestic context, the more remote the cause of the threat, the more likely it is that factors such as the intervention of the police will prevent the harm from occurring, thus obviating the need to kill the cause of the threat. In the context of international warfare, remoteness, although relevant to the degree of the threat, is less significant, for there is less reason to assume that other factors short of killing will intervene and prevent the threat's materializing.

Although causal remoteness is relevant to the questions of whether a threat exists and whether a person is a necessary or sufficient cause of it, it is irrelevant to the right of self-defense once the threat, the necessary or sufficient causal relation, and the lack of superior alternatives to remove the threat are posited. Moreover, even if causal remoteness were the source of immunity from being killed in self-defense, it would not be the source of an immunity for noncombatants vis-à-vis combatants. As the example of the noncombatant front-line supplier and the rear guard combatants illustrates, some combatants are at any time more remote threats than some noncombatants. Fullinwider could, of course, respond that killing rear guard combatants is not consistent with the Principle of Self-Defense, or, what amounts to the same thing, that only front-line combatants are truly combatants. I do not take him to be making such a claim, which would be an indictment of widely accepted norms of warfare.

There is one other possible source of Fullinwider's error. He may hold the view that one is immune from being killed in self-defense if any further choice of a human agent is necessary for the harm to materialize.[8] This view, he might believe, leads to the conclusion that only those who are sufficiently likely themselves to pull triggers (the infantry, but not the top generals, the ordnance personnel) or release bombs (the bombardiers, but not the pilots or navigators) may be killed. Although this view would not necessarily result in a distinction between combatants and noncombatants, because the likelihood of being killed in the future by one who is presently a noncombatant may exceed both the threshold required for self-defense and also the likelihood of being killed by particular combatants, it deserves a short comment. One cannot hold the view forbidding intervention before the last choice necessary for the harm as an absolute and at the same time accept the Principle of Self-Defense. Most acts sanctioned by the Principle of Self-Defense occur at a point when at least one choice still remains before someone is actually harmed—that is, they occur when the aggressor can still choose to cease his aggression. The fact that further choices are necessary to bring about the harm affects the likelihood of that harm's materializing; and the greater the number of choices required, the less likely it is that the harm will result. Under the Principle of Self-Defense, however, only the likelihood of harm, not the number of choices required to bring it about, is directly relevant.

In some of the hypotheticals I have used, only one choice is required for the harm to result. The mobsters, if they are out of range of Smith's hearing, cannot through any choice affect, in the short run, the likelihood of Smith's killing Jones. Only Smith can.

In other hypotheticals, more than one choice is required. Either the noncombatant munitions supplier or the combatants could through their choices reduce or eliminate the danger. Both must choose to aid the war effort to create the danger.

Whether one or more choices is required, however, is morally irrelevant (so long as the threshold probability of danger has been reached) and in any event is irrelevant to the combatant-noncombatant distinction. Suppose the noncombatant supplier is driving a truck full of munitions under the watchful eyes of his armed countrymen. If he attempts to turn the truck around, he will be stopped, and someone else will drive it. At that point only the choices of those whose hands are on the triggers, not the choice of the supplier, can be considered necessary or sufficient to bring about the harm to the defending nation. The supplier is in a situation analogous to that of a pilot of a bomber which also carries a bombardier. Once the bomber is over the target, no further choice *by the pilot* (at least no choice which would not lead to his death anyway) is necessary or sufficient to cause the bombing to commence. No one who accepts the Principle of Self-Defense could argue that the plane may not be shot down because the bombardier still has a choice to make and might decide not to release the bombs. And I cannot imagine that anyone would argue that the Principle of Self-Defense permits killing *only* the bombardier, not the pilot, where the most effective means of preventing the bombing is shooting down the plane (which, let us suppose, presents a far greater risk of death to the pilot than to the bombardier). But if the pilot, normally thought of as a combatant, may be killed in self-defense, so may the supplier, a noncombatant, perhaps by bombing the truck in order to blow up the munitions.

Finally, if noncombatants (say, children) were involuntarily harnessed with bombs and pushed down a slippery slope towards the troops of the defending nation, the bombs to be released automatically once the children were halfway down the slope, *no* further choice would be necessary to bring about the threatened harm. If the bombs could not be safely shot and detonated once they were released, self-defense would permit shooting the bombs before they were released and blowing up them and their noncombatant carriers, just as it would permit such an act if the carriers were morally innocent conscripted soldiers.

It is apparent, therefore, that neither the number of choices required to bring about the harm nor combatant-noncombatant status is morally relevant to the right to kill in self-defense.

In summary, punishment requires guilt, but guilt, even relative guilt, does not mark the distinction between combatants and noncombatants. On the other hand, the right to kill in self-defense requires only that the person killed be a necessary or sufficient cause of a danger, not that he be morally guilty. Again, however, being a cause of danger does not mark the distinction between combatants and noncombatants. Moreover, noncombatants are not necessarily more remote causes of danger than are combatants; nor is the danger noncombatants pose necessarily more dependent upon further choices than is the danger posed by combatants. Finally, neither causal remoteness nor the necessity of further choices is per se relevant to the Principle of Self-Defense. I conclude, therefore, that the intentional killing of innocent noncombatants is not necessarily immoral if one accepts the Principle of Self-Defense.[9]

NOTES

1. Robert K. Fullinwider, "War and Innocence," *Philosophy & Public Affairs* 5, no. 1 (Fall 1975): [327, this volume].
2. See George I. Mavrodes, "Conventions and the Morality of War," *Philosophy & Public Affairs* 4, no. 2 (Winter 1975): [321, 323–324, this volume].
3. The formulation I shall give of the principle that allows the killing of innocent persons in self-defense can, for example, logically be extended to cover acts of terrorism, atomic bombings of cities, etc. See text and notes at fnn. 6 and 7 below.
4. Fullinwider, "War and Innocence" [pp. 327–328, this volume].

5. Although I have found no cases directly on point, the interpretation follows logically from a combination of the two legal principles of self-defense and defense of others. Because Smith is otherwise justifiably subject to being killed by Jones in self-defense if the mobsters are not killed first (thus removing Smith's motive for threatening Jones), Jones' killing the mobsters is a defense of Smith's life and hence legally justifiable (assuming the requirements in the text at fnn. 6 and 7 below are otherwise met).
6. It should be noted that condition (2) of the formulation does not specify how killing *X* will reduce the danger. Suppose *A* is threatened by *B* and so kills *C*, an innocent party, in order to frighten *B* or cause *C* to fall on *B* and remove *B*'s threat. A libertarian, who believes it wrong generally for one to appropriate other persons' bodies or products in order to make himself better off than he would be had the other persons not existed, would object to such a use of the Principle of Self-Defense. However, an egalitarian, who would not object to appropriating other persons' bodies or products, would have difficulty in distinguishing this use of the Principle of Self-Defense from other uses involving the killing of innocent persons.
7. "More desirable courses of action" is often construed to mean those courses of action not involving major sacrifices of the defender's rights. For example:

   > . . . The majority of American jurisdictions holds that the defender (who was not the original aggressor) need not retreat, even though he can do so safely, before using deadly force upon an assailant whom [sic] he reasonably believes will kill him or do him serious bodily harm. A strong minority, however, taking what might be regarded as a more civilized view, holds that he must retreat ("retreat to the wall," it is sometimes said), before using deadly force, if he can do so in safety. But even in those jurisdictions which require retreat, the defender need not retreat unless he knows he can do so in complete safety; and he need not retreat from his home or place of business, except perhaps when the assailant is a co-occupant of those premises. [La Fave & Scott, *Criminal Law* (1972), pp. 395–396]

   However, one might reasonably ask why there should not be an absolute duty of retreat when *X* (the one to be killed in self-defense) is morally innocent. Indeed, why should our rights not be constrained generally so that we might avoid having to take one innocent life in order to save another?

   It should be noted also that if an innocent person, *A*, attempts to exercise his right to kill another innocent person, *B*, in self-defense, *A*'s action presumably gives rise to a right in *B* to kill *A* in self-defense. Cf. Robert Nozick, *Anarchy, State and Utopia* (1974), pp. 34–35. Moreover, third parties apparently may intervene on behalf of either. Would not a cogent moral position attempt to eliminate the possibility of such situations, perhaps by positing rigorous duties to avoid sacrificing innocent lives and, where that fails, by considering such factors as the relative worth of the persons, or their ages, or their value to others? On the problem of the innocent aggressor and the related problem of proportionality between threat (innocent and non-innocent) and defensive response, see Fletcher, "Proportionality and the Psychotic Aggressor: A Vignette in Comparative Criminal Theory," *Israel Law Review* 8 (1973): 367. See also English, "Abortion and the Concept of a Person," *Canadian Journal of Philosophy* 5, no. 2 (October 1975): 233, 237–239.

   In any event, these problems do not affect my disagreement with Fullinwider (who obviously believes that defenders may stand and fight innocent aggressor combatants) nor my general formulation of the Principle of Self-Defense.
8. The view appears to be closely akin to the principle, held by many, that it is wrong to prevent acts, harmless in themselves, merely because they make it more likely in the future that someone will choose to do, and succeed in doing, something immoral or illegal. See, for example, Nozick, *Anarchy, State and Utopia,* pp. 126–130.
9. For an excellent treatment of some of the issues discussed in this article, see Richard Wasserstrom, "On the Morality of War: A Preliminary Inquiry," in Richard Wasserstrom, ed., *War and Morality* (Belmont, Calif., 1970).

PART III

METAPHYSICS AND EPISTEMOLOGY

KNOWLEDGE AND REALITY

INTRODUCTION

The selections in this section trace a series of issues that arise when we start thinking about a pair of important questions: What would it take for us to know something about the world around us? And do we, in fact, know anything by those standards?

Defining "Knowledge"

Start with a simple example. What does it take for me to count as *knowing* that Route 80 runs between San Francisco and Washington, D.C.? At the least, it must be *true* that Route 80 does so—I can't know something that is false. Likewise, I must *believe* that it does—I can't know something that I don't believe. But is that all I need? Is everything that I truly believe something that I know to be true?

In the brief selection from his dialogue *The Meno* that is presented here, the Greek philosopher Plato (427–347 BCE) gives a negative answer to this question, maintaining that to know something is more than merely to believe something truly. When one knows something, he suggests, one's true belief is, in a metaphorical sense, "tied down" to one's grounds for it. One way of understanding this account is as the suggestion that knowledge is true belief that is justified in some way or, in shorthand, that "knowledge is *justified true belief*."

In his influential essay, "Is Justified True Belief Knowledge?" Edmund Gettier (1927–) tries to show, by way of two famous examples, that this way of understanding the metaphor does not fully capture the demanding character of knowledge: something more than *justified*, true belief is required for knowing a proposition. In the roughly half century since Gettier's essay was published, philosophers have devoted many discussions to the question of what that additional condition may be.

Our first selection from Robert Nozick (1938–2002)—"Knowledge" from *Philosophical Explanations*—is an example of the sort of response that has been offered to Gettier's challenge. After surveying a number of complications that arose in attempts to respond to Gettier's examples, Nozick proposes his own positive account. He suggests that in order to be knowledge, one's belief in a proposition must be *sensitive* to its truth in the following sense: one wouldn't believe the proposition if it weren't true and would believe it if it were. According to Nozick, the presence of this special link between belief and truth is what distinguishes cases of knowledge from cases of mere true belief.

Skepticism and Responses

Suppose we are clear about what is required in order to know something. How much, by those standards, do we know about the world around us? Our first selection, taken from the French philosopher René Descartes's (1596–1650) famous *Meditations on First Philosophy*, suggests that we may not know even simple things like that we are sitting in a room reading a book. Even if we were dreaming—or radically deceived about the nature of reality—we might have exactly the same subjective experiences. Since nearly everything we believe seems to be based on such experiences, and since we cannot know on the basis of these experiences that the world is actually the way it seems to us to be, it turns out that we know little.

The next selections offer different ways of resisting the sweeping skeptical results of this sort of argument. In his two essays, "Proof of an External World" and "Certainty," British philosopher G. E. Moore (1873–1958) offers a straightforward response to Descartes' challenge: we know that certain skeptical hypotheses are false because we know things that are incompatible with these hypotheses. For example, we know that we are not handless brains in a vat who are electrically stimulated to believe that we have hands because we know that we have hands.

Our next reading is a continuation of the selection from Robert Nozick's *Philosophical Explanations*. In it, Nozick draws on his account of knowledge to argue that, to some extent, the skeptic is right: we don't know the falsity of certain skeptical hypotheses. Why not? Well, even if they were true, we would still think they weren't, so they fail to satisfy the kind of sensitivity to truth that Nozick thinks is required for knowledge. Nonetheless, Nozick insists, the skeptic is wrong in concluding from this that we don't know ordinary propositions like the one that we have hands. We do know these propositions because our beliefs in them are sensitive to their truth: if we didn't have hands, then, in all the most likely scenarios, we would be aware of our handlessness. So, according to Nozick, it is possible to know that we have hands even if we do not know that we are not handless, brains in a vat!

In the last selection of this section, "Cartesian Skepticism and Inference to the Best Explanation," contemporary American philosopher Jonathan Vogel argues that our commonsense view of reality is a *better* explanation for our sensory experiences than are the rival, skeptical hypotheses. It is this comparative advantage in explanatory power, he suggests, that justifies our beliefs in the existence of external objects.

Knowledge and the Nature of Reality

The skeptic's challenge plays off the possibility of a difference between *appearances* (how things appear to us) and *reality* (how things really are in the world). But what exactly is the relation between them? The readings in this section take a closer look at this question. Important insights about the quality and extent of our knowledge of the world are gained as a result.

In the selection "Allegory of the Cave" from his famous dialogue *The Republic*, ancient Greek philosopher Plato (427–347 BCE) argues that gaining access to how things really are requires a complete reorientation of the mind, or the *soul*. The soul, according to Plato, is, in itself, perfectly equipped to go beyond appearances and thus gain access to reality, but to do so, it must switch its attention from the "visible" to the "intelligible realm." A special kind of education is the craft that is concerned with helping the soul do this very thing.

In our next selection, the Irish philosopher George Berkeley (1685–1753) argues that the appearance-reality distinction that is invoked in skeptical arguments is ultimately a distinction between two kinds of appearances: those that are "strong, orderly, and coherent" and those that lack these qualities. The sensible things that make up our surroundings—like chairs, tables, and books—are collections of appearances of the first kind and thus are easily distinguishable from figments of our minds. Hence, contrary to what the skeptic claims, we are, for the most part, in a position to know how things really are by way of how they appear.

An alternative conception of the relationship between reality and appearances is offered in the essay "Posits and Reality," by American philosopher W. V. O. Quine (1908–2000). In it, Quine suggests that to the extent that positing "commonsense" bodies like chairs, tables, and books allows us to organize and predict our experiences, we are justified in taking them to be objects in the world around us. Indeed, it is by reference to such entities that our very concept of reality is acquired. To be sure, we learn about these bodies by way of how things appear—but this is no reason to think that they are any less real. Like appearances, which are *posits* of our psychological theory, commonsense bodies are posits of our commonsense theory of the world.

The selection "Brains in a Vat," by American philosopher Hilary Putnam (1926–), offers an account of word meaning that may have implications for certain skeptical hypotheses about the way in which appearance and reality could come apart. What content our thoughts have, Putnam maintains, depends on what kind of world we live in: if we live in a world of physical objects, then our thoughts are about tables and chairs and the like; if we lived as disembodied brains suspended in vats, then our thoughts would be about the electrochemical stimuli that caused us to have beliefs. So the thought we express when we say, "we are not brains in a vat" is one that our brain-in-a-vat counterparts cannot even entertain.

Drawing on themes raised in the selections by Plato, Berkeley, and Putnam, Australian philosopher David Chalmers (1966–) argues, in "The Matrix as Metaphysics," that the brain-in-a-vat hypothesis is a hypothesis about the origin and underlying nature of reality. It doesn't purport to show that what we take to be real—chairs, tables, and books—may not exist; it only purports to show that these things may have a different origin and be characterized by different underlying processes. Hence, most of our ordinary beliefs about the world would be true even if the brain-in-a-vat hypothesis did, in fact, describe the way things are.

We conclude this section with a new set of puzzling questions. In his short essay "Fiction," Robert Nozick (1938–2002) invites us to consider the possibility that our world is a novel and that we are characters in it. What would be the limits of our knowledge as characters of this fiction? Would our status as characters change if we could construct airtight arguments for our *real* existence? What is ultimately the difference between *reality* and *fiction*? Does it lie in the intention of the author? Is it possible to discover this intention by investigating the work? If not, how can we ever know anything about our condition?

Induction

The focus in the previous selections has been on the nature and extent of knowledge that we gain through observation—for example, the knowledge that we have hands. But many of us believe that our knowledge extends far beyond what we learn through direct observation: we think we know that the sun will rise tomorrow, that dinosaurs once roamed the earth, and that a particular baby mouse will not grow to become an adult donkey. How is this knowledge possible?

The first selection in this section, "Induction," by the Scottish philosopher David Hume (1711–76) addresses precisely this question. One natural response is that we learn about unobserved matters of fact through generalizations from observed regularities. For example, we infer that a particular baby mouse will not grow to become an adult donkey by generalizing over past experiences in the following way: in the past, baby mice have always grown to become adult mice, so in the future, all baby mice will grow to become adult mice (and, hence, not adult donkeys). Hume argues that generalizations from past observations are problematic: the only basis we have for assuming that the future will resemble the past is that, in the past, the (then) future always resembled the (then) past—but this tells us nothing about what the (now) future holds.

It is tempting to think that Hume's challenge applies exclusively to a rudimentary state of learning in which one's beliefs about the unobserved are based on inferences from simple generalizations about observed regularities. By contrast, one may think, our scientific understanding of the world involves scientific *laws* and theories that are not simple generalizations from past experiences. Thus, our inferences from the observed to the unobserved in science are immune to Hume's challenge. In the selections from *The Problem of Induction*, American philosopher Wesley Salmon (1925–2001) argues that Hume's challenge applies equally well to *all* inductive inferences—those in which the truth of the premises doesn't *necessitate* the truth of the conclusion. Sophisticated inferences that are made in scientific investigation, like inferences based on simple generalizations from past experiences, fall within this category. Salmon considers several attempts to meet Hume's challenge to the legitimacy of inductive inferences and argues that they are unsuccessful.

In the last selection of this section, "The New Riddle of Induction," American philosopher Nelson Goodman (1925–2001) argues that a particular observation can be generalized in many different ways. Inferences that are based on these competing generalizations sometimes result in inconsistent predictions about the unobserved. Which of the competing generalizations should we rely on in our inferences from the observed to the unobserved? Goodman admits that there is an intuitive distinction between two kinds of generalizations about observed instances: what he calls *lawlike* and *accidental* generalizations. It is only inferences that are based on lawlike generalizations that support conclusions about the unobserved. But what exactly is the difference between lawlike and accidental generalizations? Goodman argues that we have "neither an answer nor any promising clue to an answer" to this question. The question is, for him, the new riddle of induction.

Further Reading

Students who want to pursue the themes raised in this section of the book may begin by looking at the articles in the following two anthologies. Each anthology includes an extensive collection of important readings in epistemology, along with suggestions for further readings on each of the main themes:

- Sven Bernecker and Fred Dretske, eds., *Knowledge: Readings in Contemporary Epistemology*. New York and Oxford: Oxford University Press, 1999.
- Ernest Sosa and Jaegwon Kim, eds., *Epistemology: An Anthology*. Malden, Mass., and Oxford: Blackwell, 2000.

A DEFINING "KNOWLEDGE"

"What Is Knowledge?" from *The Meno*

PLATO

Plato (c. 428–347 BCE)—along with his student Aristotle—was one of the two most important philosophers of antiquity and is among the most important figures in the entire Western intellectual tradition. His wide-ranging discussions addressed nearly every philosophical topic imaginable and set the stage for philosophical exploration for the next two millennia. His philosophical writings take the form of dialogues that feature his teacher Socrates (469–399 BCE) as a character.

The selection that appears here is a brief selection from Plato's dialogue, *The Meno*. In it, Socrates and a character named Meno (a notoriously self-serving ancient Greek general) try to articulate the crucial difference between knowledge and mere true opinion. The first sentence in our selection ("A man who . . .") is uttered by Socrates. The reply ("—Certainly") is uttered by Meno.

The text was originally written in ancient Greek and was translated by G. M. A. Grube. The numbers that appear in the margins of the text are called "Stephanus numbers"; they refer to the page numbers of a canonical edition of Plato's work that was prepared by Henricus Stephanus in 1578. Reference to these numbers enables coordination among readers who make use of different translations or editions. Several additional selections from Plato's writings can be found in the sections on "Moral and Political Philosophy" and "Life and Death."

SOCRATES: A man who knew the way to Larissa,* or anywhere else you like, and went there and guided others would surely lead them well and correctly?—Certainly.

b **SOCRATES**: What if someone had had a correct opinion as to which was the way but had not gone there nor indeed had knowledge of it, would he not also lead correctly?—Certainly.

SOCRATES: And as long as he has the right opinion about that of which the other has knowledge, he will not be a worse guide than the one who knows, as he has a true opinion, though not knowledge.—In no way worse.

. . . c

SOCRATES: So correct opinion is no less useful than knowledge?

MENO: Yes, to this extent, Socrates. But the man who has knowledge will always succeed, whereas

* Larissa is a city in northern Greece, about 100 miles from Athens (where Socrates lived). It was the birthplace of Meno.

From *Five Dialogues*, 2nd ed., trans. Grube, rev. Cooper. Copyright © 2002 by Hackett Publishing Company, Inc. Reprinted by permission of the publisher. All rights reserved.

he who has true opinion will only succeed at times.

SOCRATES: How do you mean? Will he who has the right opinion not always succeed, as long as his opinion is right?

MENO: That appears to be so of necessity, and it makes me wonder, Socrates, this being the case,
d why knowledge is prized far more highly than right opinion, and why they are different.

SOCRATES: Do you know why you wonder, or shall I tell you?—By all means tell me.

SOCRATES: It is because you have paid no attention to the statues of Daedalus, but perhaps there are none in Thessaly.*

MENO: What do you have in mind when you say this?

SOCRATES: That they too run away and escape if one does not tie them down but remain in place
e if tied down.—So what?

SOCRATES: To acquire an untied work of Daedalus is not worth much, like acquiring a runaway slave, for it does not remain, but it is worth much if tied down, for his works are very beautiful. What am I thinking of when I say this? True opinions. For true opinions, as long as they remain, are a fine thing and all they do is good, but they are not willing to remain long, and they escape from 98
a man's mind, so that they are not worth much until one ties them down by (giving) an account of the reason why. And that, Meno my friend, is recollection, as we previously agreed. After they are tied down, in the first place they become knowledge, and then they remain in place. That is why knowledge is prized higher than correct opinion, and knowledge differs from correct opinion in being tied down.

MENO: Yes, by Zeus,* Socrates, it seems to be something like that.

SOCRATES: Indeed, I too speak as one who does b
not have knowledge but is guessing. However, I certainly do not think I am guessing that right opinion is a different thing from knowledge. If I claim to know anything else—and I would make that claim about few things—I would put this down as one of the things I know.—Rightly so, Socrates.

---

* Daedalus was an ancient sculptor whose statues were reputed to be so realistic that one would expect them to run away if they were not tethered to the ground; Thessaly is the region of Greece where Larissa is located.

* In Greek mythology, Zeus was the king of the gods; "by Zeus" is equivalent to "by God."

Is Justified True Belief Knowledge?

EDMUND GETTIER

Edmund Gettier (1927–) taught philosophy at the University of Massachusetts, Amherst. His most famous philosophical work is the paper reproduced here.

This short piece, originally published in a philosophy journal in 1963, was widely regarded as a decisive refutation of an otherwise attractive analysis of knowledge (knowledge as justified true belief). It generated hundreds of responses and prompted renewed interest in the project of clarifying exactly what knowledge involves. The term *Gettier problem* has come to describe the task of articulating what conditions—in addition to or instead of being a justified true belief—must be met for something to be an instance of knowledge.

Originally published in *Analysis* (1963), pp. 121–3. Used by permission of the author.

Various attempts have been made in recent years to state necessary and sufficient conditions for someone's knowing a given proposition. The attempts have often been such that they can be stated in a form similar to the following:[1]

(a) S knows that *P* *IFF* (i) *P* is true,
(ii) S believes that *P*, and
(iii) S is justified in believing that *P*.

For example, Chisholm* has held that the following gives the necessary and sufficient conditions for knowledge:[2]

(b) S knows that *P* *IFF* (i) S accepts *P*,
(ii) S has adequate evidence for *P*, and
(iii) *P* is true.

Ayer has stated the necessary and sufficient conditions for knowledge as follows:[3]

(c) S knows that *P* *IFF* (i) *P* is true,
(ii) S is sure that *P* is true, and
(iii) S has the right to be sure that *P* is true.

I shall argue that (a) is false in that the conditions stated therein do not constitute a *sufficient* condition for the truth of the proposition that S knows that *P*. The same argument will show that (b) and (c) fail if "has adequate evidence for" or "has the right to be sure that" is substituted for "is justified in believing that" throughout.

I shall begin by noting two points. First, in that sense of "justified" in which S's being justified in believing *P* is a necessary condition of S's knowing that *P*, it is possible for a person to be justified in believing a proposition which is in fact false. Second, for any proposition *P*, if S is justified in believing *P* and *P* entails Q and S deduces Q from *P* and accepts Q as a result of this deduction, then S is justified in believing Q. Keeping these two points in mind, I shall now present two cases in which the conditions stated in (a) are true for some proposition, though it is at the same time false that the person in question knows that proposition.

CASE I

Suppose that Smith and Jones have applied for a certain job. And suppose that Smith has strong evidence for the following conjunctive proposition:

(d) Jones is the man who will get the job, and Jones has ten coins in his pocket.

Smith's evidence for (d) might be that the president of the company assured him that Jones would in the end be selected, and that he, Smith, had counted the coins in Jones's pocket ten minutes ago. Proposition (d) entails:

(e) The man who will get the job has ten coins in his pocket.

Let us suppose that Smith sees the entailment from (d) to (e) and accepts (e) on the grounds of (d), for which he has strong evidence. In this case, Smith is clearly justified in believing that (e) is true.

But imagine, further, that unknown to Smith, he himself, not Jones, will get the job. And, also, unknown to Smith, he himself has ten coins in his pocket. Proposition (e) is then true, though proposition (d), from which Smith inferred (e), is false. In our example, then, all of the following are true: (*i*) (e) is true, (*ii*) Smith believes that (e) is true, and (*iii*) Smith is justified in believing that (e) is true. But it is equally clear that Smith does not *know* that (e) is true; for (e) is true in virtue of the number of coins in Smith's pocket, while Smith does not know how many coins are in Smith's pocket, and bases his belief in (e) on a count of the coins in Jones's pocket, whom he falsely believes to be the man who will get the job.

* Roderick Chisholm (1916–99, this paragraph) and A. J. Ayer (1910–89, next paragraph) were twentieth-century philosophers who had offered influential accounts on knowledge in the mid-1950s. Selections from their work on a very different topic—free will—can be found in the "Free Will" section.

CASE II

Let us suppose that Smith has strong evidence for the following proposition:

(f) Jones owns a Ford.

Smith's evidence might be that Jones has at all times in the past within Smith's memory owned a car, and always a Ford, and that Jones has just offered Smith a ride while driving a Ford. Let us imagine, now, that Smith has another friend, Brown, of whose whereabouts he is totally ignorant. Smith selects three place names quite at random and constructs the following three propositions:

(g) Either Jones owns a Ford, or Brown is in Boston.
(h) Either Jones owns a Ford, or Brown is in Barcelona.
(i) Either Jones owns a Ford, or Brown is in Brest-Litovsk.

Each of these propositions is entailed by (f). Imagine that Smith realizes the entailment of each of these propositions he has constructed by (f), and proceeds to accept (g), (h), and (i) on the basis of (f). Smith has correctly inferred (g), (h), and (i) from a proposition for which he has strong evidence. Smith is therefore completely justified in believing each of these three propositions. Smith, of course, has no idea where Brown is.

But imagine now that two further conditions hold. First, Jones does *not* own a Ford, but is at present driving a rented car. And second, by the sheerest coincidence, and entirely unknown to Smith, the place mentioned in proposition (h) happens really to be the place where Brown is. If these two conditions hold, then Smith does *not* know that (h) is true, even though (*i*) (h) *is* true, (*ii*) Smith does believe that (h) is true, and (*iii*) Smith is justified in believing that (h) is true.

These two examples show that definition (a) does not state a *sufficient* condition for someone's knowing a given proposition. The same cases, with appropriate changes, will suffice to show that neither definition (b) nor definition (c) do so either.

NOTES

1. Plato seems to be considering some such definition at *Theaetetus* 201, and perhaps accepting one at *Meno* 98. [See previous selection.]
2. Roderick M. Chisholm, *Perceiving: A Philosophical Study* (Ithaca, NY: Cornell University Press, 1957), p. 16.
3. A. J. Ayer, *The Problem of Knowledge* (London: Macmillan, 1956).

"Knowledge" from *Philosophical Explanations*

ROBERT NOZICK

American philosopher Robert Nozick (1938–2002) taught philosophy at Harvard University. Known for his cleverness, sharp wit, and creativity, he was an omnivorous reader who made lasting contributions in a number of philosophical areas.

The selections that appear here and in the entry later in this section are excerpted from the Epistemology section of his wide-ranging 1982 book *Philosophical Explanations*. In the following passage, Nozick articulates and defends his own response to the Gettier problem and explains its relation to traditional questions about the nature and value of knowledge.

Reprinted by permission of the publisher *from Philosophical Explanations* by Robert Nozick, pp. 197–211, Cambridge, Mass: The Belknap Press of Harvard University Press. Copyright © 1981 by Robert Nozick.

INTRODUCTION

In knowledge, a belief is linked somehow to the fact believed; without this linkage there may be true belief but there will not be knowledge. Plato first made the point that knowledge is not simply a belief that is true;* if someone knowing nothing about the matter separately tells you and me contradictory things, getting one of us to believe *p* while the other believes not-*p*, although one of us will have a belief that happens to be true, neither of us will have knowledge. Something more is needed for a person S to know that *p*, to go alongside

(1) *p* is true
(2) S believes that *p*.

This something more, I think, is not simply an additional fact, but a way that 1 and 2 are linked.

. . .

Recently it has been urged, with some plausibility, that the requisite linkage of belief to facts is a causal one, that the third condition is something like: the fact that *p* (partially) causes S to believe that *p*, that is, 2 because 1.[1] A drunk who hallucinates a pink elephant in a bar where, behind a screen, there is a pink elephant does not know there is a pink elephant there. The elephant's being there is not a cause of his believing it there. Whereas, in tracing back through the causes of your believing there now is a book before you, we eventually reach the fact that there *is* a book before you. The causal account of knowledge thus has a certain plausibility. Since, on this view, the causation (in a certain way) of our beliefs is necessary for us to have knowledge, such causation therefore is desirable. To be sure, there are difficulties with the causal account of knowledge, most noticeably with mathematical knowledge and ethical knowledge but elsewhere as well.[2] In these cases, the appropriate kind of causal connection fails to hold. Yet where it does hold, when a belief is caused appropriately by the fact, that connection appears desirable and plausibly is held to constitute knowledge. . . .

* See the selection from Plato's "*Meno*," p. 343 in this volume.

The causal linkage which appears to be a constituent in knowledge may be merely one way of realizing a more general linkage that constitutes knowledge. This would leave some room for ethical and mathematical knowledge. . . .

CONDITIONS FOR KNOWLEDGE

Our task is to formulate further conditions to go alongside

(1) *p* is true
(2) S believes that *p*.

We would like each condition to be necessary for knowledge, so any case that fails to satisfy it will not be an instance of knowledge. Furthermore, we would like the conditions to be jointly sufficient for knowledge, so any case that satisfies all of them will be an instance of knowledge. We first shall formulate conditions that seem to handle ordinary cases correctly, classifying as knowledge cases which are knowledge, and as nonknowledge cases which are not; then we shall check to see how these conditions handle some difficult cases discussed in the literature.[3]

The causal condition on knowledge, previously mentioned, provides an inhospitable environment for mathematical and ethical knowledge; also there are well-known difficulties in specifying the type of causal connection. If someone floating in a tank oblivious to everything around him is given (by direct electrical and chemical stimulation of the brain) the belief that he is floating in a tank with his brain being stimulated, then even though that fact is part of the cause of his belief, still he does not know that it is true.

Let us consider a different third condition:

(3) If *p* weren't true, S wouldn't believe that *p*.

Throughout this work, let us write the subjunctive 'if-then'* by an arrow, and the negation of a sentence

* A "subjunctive 'if-then'" sentence is a sentence of the form: if P were the case, Q would be the case.

by prefacing "not-" to it. The above condition thus is rewritten as:

(3) not-$p \rightarrow$ not-(S believes that p).

This subjunctive condition is not unrelated to the causal condition. Often when the fact that p (partially) causes someone to believe that p, the fact also will be causally necessary for his having the belief—without the cause, the effect would not occur. In that case, the subjunctive condition 3 also will be satisfied. Yet this condition is not equivalent to the causal condition. For the causal condition will be satisfied in cases of causal overdetermination, where either two sufficient causes of the effect actually operate, or a back-up cause (of the same effect) would operate if the first one didn't; whereas the subjunctive condition need not hold for these cases.[4] When the two conditions do agree, causality indicates knowledge because it acts in a manner that makes the subjunctive 3 true.

The subjunctive condition 3 serves to exclude cases of the sort first described by Edward Gettier,* such as the following. Two other people are in my office and I am justified on the basis of much evidence in believing the first owns a Ford car; though he (now) does not, the second person (a stranger to me) owns one. I believe truly and justifiably that someone (or other) in my office owns a Ford car, but I do not know someone does. Concluded Gettier, knowledge is not simply justified true belief.

The following subjunctive, which specifies condition 3 for this Gettier case, is not satisfied: if no one in my office owned a Ford car, I wouldn't believe that someone did. The situation that would obtain if no one in my office owned a Ford is one where the stranger does not (or where he is not in the office); and in that situation I still would believe, as before, that someone in my office does own a Ford, namely, the first person. So the subjunctive condition 3 excludes this Gettier case as a case of knowledge.

The subjunctive condition is powerful and intuitive, not so easy to satisfy, yet not so powerful as to rule out everything as an instance of knowledge. A subjunctive conditional "if p were true, q would be true", $p \rightarrow q$, does not say that p entails q or that it is logically impossible that p yet not-q. It says that in the situation that would obtain if p were true, q also would be true. This point is brought out especially clearly in recent 'possible-worlds' accounts of subjunctives: the subjunctive is true when (roughly) in all those worlds in which p holds true that are closest to the actual world, q also is true. (Examine those worlds in which p holds true closest to the actual world, and see if q holds true in all these.) Whether or not q is true in p worlds that are still farther away from the actual world is irrelevant to the truth of the subjunctive. . . .

Despite the power and intuitive force of the condition that if p weren't true the person would not believe it, this condition does not (in conjunction with the first two conditions) rule out every problem case. There remains, for example, the case of the person in the tank who is brought to believe, by direct electrical and chemical stimulation of his brain, that he is in the tank and is being brought to believe things in this way; he does not know this is true. However, the subjunctive condition is satisfied: if he weren't floating in the tank, he wouldn't believe he was.

The person in the tank does not know he is there, because his belief is not sensitive to the truth. Although it is caused by the fact that is its content, it is not sensitive to that fact. The operators of the tank could have produced any belief, including the false belief that he wasn't in the tank; if they had, he would have believed that. Perfect sensitivity would involve beliefs and facts varying together. We already have one portion of that variation, subjunctively at least: if p were false he wouldn't believe it. This sensitivity as specified by a subjunctive does not have the belief vary with the truth or falsity of p in all possible situations, merely in the ones that would or might obtain if p were false.

The subjunctive condition

(3) not-$p \rightarrow$ not-(S believes that p)

tells us only half the story about how his belief is sensitive to the truth-value of p. It tells us how his belief state is sensitive to p's falsity, but not how it

* Nozick is here referring to Gettier's article "Is Justified True Belief Knowledge?" which appears as the previous selection.

is sensitive to *p*'s truth; it tells us what his belief state would be if *p* were false, but not what it would be if *p* were true.

To be sure, conditions 1 and 2 tell us that *p* is true and he does believe it, but it does not follow that his believing *p* is sensitive to *p*'s being true. This additional sensitivity is given to us by a further subjunctive: if *p* were true, he would believe it.

(4) $p \rightarrow$ S believes that *p*.

Not only is *p* true and S believes it, but if it were true he would believe it. Compare: not only was the photon emitted and did it go to the left, but (it was then true that): if it were emitted it would go to the left. The truth of antecedent and consequent is not alone sufficient for the truth of a subjunctive; 4 says more than 1 and 2.[5] Thus, we presuppose some (or another) suitable account of subjunctives. According to the suggestion tentatively made above, 4 holds true if not only does he actually truly believe *p*, but in the "close" worlds where *p* is true, he also believes it. He believes that *p** for some distance out in the *p* neighborhood of the actual world; similarly, condition 3 speaks not of the whole not-*p* neighborhood of the actual world, but only of the first portion of it. (If, as is likely, these explanations do not help, please use your own intuitive understanding of the subjunctives 3 and 4.)

The person in the tank does not satisfy the subjunctive condition 4. Imagine as actual a world in which he is in the tank and is stimulated to believe he is, and consider what subjunctives are true in that world. It is not true of him there that if he were in the tank he would believe it; for in the close world (or situation) to his own where he is in the tank but they don't give him the belief that he is (much less instill the belief that he isn't) he doesn't believe he is in the tank. Of the person actually in the tank and believing it, it is not true to make the further statement that if he were in the tank he would believe it—so he does not know he is in the tank.

The subjunctive condition 4 also handles a case presented by Gilbert Harman.[6] The dictator of a country is killed; in their first edition, newspapers print the story, but later all the country's newspapers and other media deny the story, falsely. Everyone who encounters the denial believes it (or does not know what to believe and so suspends judgment). Only one person in the country fails to hear any denial and he continues to believe the truth. He satisfies conditions 1 through 3 (and the causal condition about belief) yet we are reluctant to say he knows the truth. The reason is that if he had heard the denials, he too would have believed them, just like everyone else. His belief is not sensitively tuned to the truth, he doesn't satisfy the condition that if it were true he would believe it. Condition 4 is not satisfied.[7] . . .

A person knows that *p* when he not only does truly believe it, but also would truly believe it and wouldn't falsely believe it. He not only actually has a true belief, he subjunctively has one. It is true that *p* and he believes it; if it weren't true he wouldn't believe it, and if it were true he would believe it. To know that *p* is to be someone who would believe it if it were true, and who wouldn't believe it if it were false.

It will be useful to have a term for this situation when a person's belief is thus subjunctively connected to the fact. Let us say of a person who believes that *p*, which is true, that when 3 and 4 hold, his belief *tracks* the truth that *p*. To know is to have a belief that tracks the truth. Knowledge is a particular way of being connected to the world, having a specific real factual connection to the world: tracking it.

. . .

As you might have expected, this account of knowledge as tracking requires some refinements and epicycles.* Readers who find themselves (or me)

* The "worlds" to which Nozick is referring here are "possible worlds" (see Glossary.) A close possible world is one very similar to the actual world; a distant possible world is one very different from the actual world.

* In the second part of this essay, Nozick refines his analysis of knowledge in terms of the technical notion of knowing via a *method*, or *way* of believing. In this revised analysis, conditions (3) and (4) are necessary for knowing that *p* relative to the method by which one comes to believe *p*. So, with regard to condition (3), S knows, via method (or way of believing) M, that *p* only if,

(3) If *p* weren't true and S were to use M to arrive at a belief whether (or not) *p*, then S wouldn't believe via M that *p*.

bogged down in these refinements should move on directly to this essay's second part, on skepticism, where the pace picks up.*

NOTES

1. See Alvin Goldman, "A Causal Theory of Knowledge," *Journal of Philosophy*, Vol. 64, 1967, pp. 357–372.
2. Paul Benacerraf wrestles with the problems a causal account causes for mathematical knowledge in "Mathematical Truth," *Journal of Philosophy*, Vol. 70, 1973, pp. 661–679. For an attempt to defend the causal account in application to mathematics, see Mark Steiner, *Mathematical Knowledge* (Cornell University Press, Ithaca, 1975).
3. Despite some demurrals in the literature, there is general agreement that conditions 1 and 2 are necessary for knowledge. (For some recent discussions, see D. M. Armstrong, *Belief, Truth and Knowledge*, Cambridge University Press, 1973, ch. 10; Keith Lehrer, *Knowledge*, Oxford University Press, 1974, chs. 2, 3.) I shall take for granted that this is so, without wishing to place very much weight on its being belief that is the precise cognitive attitude (as opposed to thinking it so, accepting the statement, and so on) or on the need to introduce truth as opposed to formulating the first condition simply as: *p*.

   I should note that our procedure here does not stem from thinking that every illuminating discussion of an important philosophical notion must present (individually) necessary and (jointly) sufficient conditions.
4. Below, we discuss further the case where though the fact that *p* causes the person's belief that *p*, he would believe it anyway, even if it were not true. I should note here that I assume bivalence throughout this chapter, and consider only statements that are true if and only if their negations are false.
5. More accurately, since the truth of antecedent and consequent is not necessary for the truth of the subjunctive either, 4 says something different from 1 and 2.
6. Gilbert Harman, *Thought* (Princeton University Press, Princeton, 1973), ch. 9, pp. 142–154.
7. What if the situation or world where he too hears the later false denials is not so close, so easily occurring? Should we say that everything that prevents his hearing the denial easily could have not happened, and does not in some close world?

* See Nozick's essay "Skepticism," p. 365 this volume.

B SKEPTICISM AND RESPONSES

Meditations on First Philosophy

in which are demonstrated the existence of God and the distinction between the human soul and the body

RENÉ DESCARTES

René Descartes (1596–1650) was one of the most important thinkers of the early modern period. His work in philosophy and mathematics set the tone for subsequent investigation of these topics.

The text that appears here is a modern (1985) translation of a selection from Descartes's *Meditations*, which were originally published in Latin in 1641. Descartes's original text included six chapters—or "Meditations"—of which the first two appear here, and the sixth appears in the "Mind and Language" section. Soon after the text was published in Latin, a French translation appeared (1647), with Descartes's approval. Although the two texts are quite similar, there are a few differences between them, and sometimes the French text offers helpful clarifications of the original Latin. In the text that follows, the translator has adopted a convention of including such selections from the French text in the body of the text enclosed in <diamond brackets>, or as notes. In these notes, "AT" refers to Adam & Tannery's eleven-volume 1897 standard, edition of Descartes' works; "CSMK" refers to Cottingham, Stoothoff, Murdoch & Kenny's late twentieth-century English translation. Numbers in the margin indicate page numbers in Adam & Tannery, vol. VII.

AT-VII

FIRST MEDITATION

What can be called into doubt

Some years ago I was struck by the large number of falsehoods that I had accepted as true in my childhood, and by the highly doubtful nature of the whole edifice that I had subsequently based on them. I realized that it was necessary, once in the course of my life, to demolish everything completely and start again right from the foundations if I wanted to establish anything at all in the sciences that was stable and likely to last. But the task looked an enormous one, and I began to wait until I should reach a mature enough age to ensure that no subsequent time of life would be more suitable for tackling such inquiries. This led me to put the project off for so long that I would now be to blame if by pondering

From *Meditations on First Philosophy*, revised ed., trans. John Cottingham. Copyright © 1996 by Cambridge University Press, pp. 12–25, 50–56, 58–62. Reprinted by permission of the publisher.

over it any further I wasted the time still left for car-
18 rying it out. So today I have expressly rid my mind of all worries and arranged for myself a clear stretch of free time. I am here quite alone, and at last I will devote myself sincerely and without reservation to the general demolition of my opinions.

But to accomplish this, it will not be necessary for me to show that all my opinions are false, which is something I could perhaps never manage. Reason now leads me to think that I should hold back my assent from opinions which are not completely certain and indubitable just as carefully as I do from those which are patently false. So, for the purpose of rejecting all my opinions, it will be enough if I find in each of them at least some reason for doubt. And to do this I will not need to run through them all individually, which would be an endless task. Once the foundations of a building are undermined, anything built on them collapses of its own accord; so I will go straight for the basic principles on which all my former beliefs rested.

Whatever I have up till now accepted as most true I have acquired either from the senses or through the senses. But from time to time I have found that the senses deceive, and it is prudent never to trust completely those who have deceived us even once.

Yet although the senses occasionally deceive us with respect to objects which are very small or in the distance, there are many other beliefs about which doubt is quite impossible, even though they are derived from the senses—for example, that I am here, sitting by the fire, wearing a winter dressing-gown, holding this piece of paper in my hands, and so on. Again, how could it be denied that these hands or this
19 whole body are mine? Unless perhaps I were to liken myself to madmen, whose brains are so damaged by the persistent vapours of melancholia that they firmly maintain they are kings when they are paupers, or say they are dressed in purple when they are naked, or that their heads are made of earthenware, or that they are pumpkins, or made of glass. But such people are insane, and I would be thought equally mad if I took anything from them as a model for myself.

A brilliant piece of reasoning! As if I were not a man who sleeps at night, and regularly has all the same experiences[1] while asleep as madmen do when awake—indeed sometimes even more improbable ones. How often, asleep at night, am I convinced of just such familiar events—that I am here in my dressing-gown, sitting by the fire—when in fact I am lying undressed in bed! Yet at the moment my eyes are certainly wide awake when I look at this piece of paper; I shake my head and it is not asleep; as I stretch out and feel my hand I do so deliberately, and I know what I am doing. All this would not happen with such distinctness to someone asleep. Indeed! As if I did not remember other occasions when I have been tricked by exactly similar thoughts while asleep! As I think about this more carefully, I see plainly that there are never any sure signs by means of which being awake can be distinguished from being asleep. The result is that I begin to feel dazed, and this very feeling only reinforces the notion that I may be asleep.

Suppose then that I am dreaming, and that these particulars—that my eyes are open, that I am moving my head and stretching out my hands—are not true. Perhaps, indeed, I do not even have such hands or such a body at all. Nonetheless, it must surely be admitted that the visions which come in sleep are like paintings, which must have been fashioned in the likeness of things that are real, and hence that at least these general kinds of things—eyes, head, 20
hands and the body as a whole—are things which are not imaginary but are real and exist. For even when painters try to create sirens and satyrs with the most extraordinary bodies, they cannot give them natures which are new in all respects; they simply jumble up the limbs of different animals. Or if perhaps they manage to think up something so new that nothing remotely similar has ever been seen before—something which is therefore completely fictitious and unreal—at least the colours used in the composition must be real. By similar reasoning, although these general kinds of things—eyes, head, hands and so on—could be imaginary, it must at least be admitted that certain other even simpler and more universal things are real. These are as it were the real colours from which we form all the images of things, whether true or false, that occur in our thought.

This class appears to include corporeal nature in general, and its extension; the shape of extended things; the quantity, or size and number of these things; the place in which they may exist, the time through which they may endure,[2] and so on.

So a reasonable conclusion from this might be that physics, astronomy, medicine, and all other disciplines which depend on the study of composite things, are doubtful; while arithmetic, geometry and other subjects of this kind, which deal only with the simplest and most general things, regardless of whether they really exist in nature or not, contain something certain and indubitable. For whether I am awake or asleep, two and three added together are five, and a square has no more than four sides. It seems impossible that such transparent truths should incur any suspicion of being false.

21 And yet firmly rooted in my mind is the long-standing belief that there is an omnipotent God who made me the kind of creature that I am. How do I know that he has not brought it about that there is no earth, no sky, no extended thing, no shape, no size, no place, while at the same time ensuring that all these things appear to me to exist just as they do now? Moreover, since I sometimes consider that others go astray in cases where they think they have the most perfect knowledge, may I not similarly go wrong every time I add two and three or count the sides of a square, or in some even simpler matter, if that is imaginable? But perhaps God would not have wished me to be deceived in this way, since he is said to be supremely good. But if it were inconsistent with his goodness to have created me such that I am deceived all the time, it would seem equally foreign to his goodness to allow me to be deceived even occasionally; yet this last assertion cannot be made.[3]

Perhaps there may be some who would prefer to deny the existence of so powerful a God rather than believe that everything else is uncertain. Let us not argue with them, but grant them that everything said about God is a fiction. According to their supposition, then, I have arrived at my present state by fate or chance or a continuous chain of events, or by some other means; yet since deception and error seem to be imperfections, the less powerful they make my original cause, the more likely it is that I am so imperfect as to be deceived all the time. I have no answer to these arguments, but am finally compelled to admit that there is not one of my former beliefs about which a doubt may not properly be raised; and this is not a flippant or ill-considered conclusion, but is based on powerful and well thought-out reasons. 22
So in future I must withhold my assent from these former beliefs just as carefully as I would from obvious falsehoods, if I want to discover any certainty.[4]

But it is not enough merely to have noticed this; I must make an effort to remember it. My habitual opinions keep coming back, and, despite my wishes, they capture my belief, which is as it were bound over to them as a result of long occupation and the law of custom. I shall never get out of the habit of confidently assenting to these opinions, so long as I suppose them to be what in fact they are, namely highly probable opinions—opinions which, despite the fact that they are in a sense doubtful, as has just been shown, it is still much more reasonable to believe than to deny. In view of this, I think it will be a good plan to turn my will in completely the opposite direction and deceive myself, by pretending for a time that these former opinions are utterly false and imaginary. I shall do this until the weight of preconceived opinion is counter-balanced and the distorting influence of habit no longer prevents my judgement from perceiving things correctly. In the meantime, I know that no danger or error will result from my plan, and that I cannot possibly go too far in my distrustful attitude. This is because the task now in hand does not involve action but merely the acquisition of knowledge.

I will suppose therefore that not God, who is supremely good and the source of truth, but rather some malicious demon of the utmost power and cunning has employed all his energies in order to deceive me. I shall think that the sky, the air, the earth, colours, shapes, sounds and all external things are merely the delusions of dreams which he has devised to ensnare my judgement. I shall con- 23
sider myself as not having hands or eyes, or flesh, or blood or senses, but as falsely believing that I have all these things. I shall stubbornly and firmly persist in this meditation; and, even if it is not in my power to know any truth, I shall at least do what is in my power,[5] that is, resolutely guard against assenting to any falsehoods, so that the deceiver, however powerful and cunning he may be, will be unable to impose on me in the slightest degree. But this is an arduous undertaking, and a kind of laziness brings me back to normal life. I am like a prisoner who is enjoying an imaginary freedom while asleep; as he begins to

suspect that he is asleep, he dreads being woken up, and goes along with the pleasant illusion as long as he can. In the same way, I happily slide back into my old opinions and dread being shaken out of them, for fear that my peaceful sleep may be followed by hard labour when I wake, and that I shall have to toil not in the light, but amid the inextricable darkness of the problems I have now raised.

SECOND MEDITATION

The nature of the human mind, and how it is better known than the body

So serious are the doubts into which I have been thrown as a result of yesterday's meditation that I can neither put them out of my mind nor see any
24 way of resolving them. It feels as if I have fallen unexpectedly into a deep whirlpool which tumbles me around so that I can neither stand on the bottom nor swim up to the top. Nevertheless I will make an effort and once more attempt the same path which I started on yesterday. Anything which admits of the slightest doubt I will set aside just as if I had found it to be wholly false; and I will proceed in this way until I recognize something certain, or, if nothing else, until I at least recognize for certain that there is no certainty. Archimedes used to demand just one firm and immovable point in order to shift the entire earth;* so I too can hope for great things if I manage to find just one thing, however slight, that is certain and unshakeable.

I will suppose then, that everything I see is spurious. I will believe that my memory tells me lies, and that none of the things that it reports ever happened. I have no senses. Body, shape, extension, movement and place are chimeras. So what remains true? Perhaps just the one fact that nothing is certain.

Yet apart from everything I have just listed, how do I know that there is not something else which does not allow even the slightest occasion for doubt? Is there not a God, or whatever I may call him, who puts into me[6] the thoughts I am now having? But why do I think this, since I myself may perhaps be the author of these thoughts? In that case am not I, at least, something? But I have just said that I have
no senses and no body. This is the sticking point: 25
what follows from this? Am I not so bound up with a body and with senses that I cannot exist without them? But I have convinced myself that there is absolutely nothing in the world, no sky, no earth, no minds, no bodies. Does it now follow that I too do not exist? No: if I convinced myself of something[7] then I certainly existed. But there is a deceiver of supreme power and cunning who is deliberately and constantly deceiving me. In that case I too undoubtedly exist, if he is deceiving me; and let him deceive me as much as he can, he will never bring it about that I am nothing so long as I think that I am something. So after considering everything very thoroughly, I must finally conclude that this proposition, *I am, I exist*, is necessarily true whenever it is put forward by me or conceived in my mind.

But I do not yet have a sufficient understanding of what this "I" is, that now necessarily exists. So I must be on my guard against carelessly taking something else to be this "I," and so making a mistake in the very item of knowledge that I maintain is the most certain and evident of all. I will therefore go back and meditate on what I originally believed myself to be, before I embarked on this present train of thought. I will then subtract anything capable of being weakened, even minimally, by the arguments now introduced, so that what is left at the end may be exactly and only what is certain and unshakeable.

What then did I formerly think I was? A man. But what is a man? Shall I say "a rational animal"? No; for then I should have to inquire what an animal is, what rationality is, and in this way one question would lead me down the slope to other harder ones, and I do not now have the time to waste on subtleties of this kind. Instead I propose to concentrate
on what came into my thoughts spontaneously and 26
quite naturally whenever I used to consider what I was. Well, the first thought to come to mind was that I had a face, hands, arms and the whole mechanical structure of limbs which can be seen in a corpse, and which I called the body. The next thought was that I was nourished, that I moved about, and that

* Archimedes (c. 287–212 BCE) was an ancient Greek mathematician, engineer, and physicist. He is reported to have said: "Give me a lever long enough, and a fulcrum on which to place it, and I shall move the world."

I engaged in sense-perception and thinking; and these actions I attributed to the soul. But as to the nature of this soul, either I did not think about this or else I imagined it to be something tenuous, like a wind or fire or ether, which permeated my more solid parts. As to the body, however, I had no doubts about it, but thought I knew its nature distinctly. If I had tried to describe the mental conception I had of it, I would have expressed it as follows: by a body I understand whatever has a determinable shape and a definable location and can occupy a space in such a way as to exclude any other body; it can be perceived by touch, sight, hearing, taste or smell, and can be moved in various ways, not by itself but by whatever else comes into contact with it. For, according to my judgement, the power of self-movement, like the power of sensation or of thought, was quite foreign to the nature of a body; indeed, it was a source of wonder to me that certain bodies were found to contain faculties of this kind.

But what shall I now say that I am, when I am supposing that there is some supremely powerful and, if it is permissible to say so, malicious deceiver, who is deliberately trying to trick me in every way he can? Can I now assert that I possess even the most insignificant of all the attributes which I have
27 just said belong to the nature of a body? I scrutinize them, think about them, go over them again, but nothing suggests itself; it is tiresome and pointless to go through the list once more. But what about the attributes I assigned to the soul? Nutrition or movement? Since now I do not have a body, these are mere fabrications. Sense-perception? This surely does not occur without a body, and besides, when asleep I have appeared to perceive through the senses many things which I afterwards realized I did not perceive through the senses at all. Thinking? At last I have discovered it—thought; this alone is inseparable from me. I am, I exist—that is certain. But for how long? For as long as I am thinking. For it could be that were I totally to cease from thinking, I should totally cease to exist. At present I am not admitting anything except what is necessarily true. I am, then, in the strict sense only a thing that thinks;[8] that is, I am a mind, or intelligence, or intellect, or reason—words whose meaning I have been ignorant of until now. But for all that I am a thing which is real and which truly exists. But what kind of a thing? As I have just said—a thinking thing.

What else am I? I will use my imagination.[9] I am not that structure of limbs which is called a human body. I am not even some thin vapour which permeates the limbs—a wind, fire, air, breath, or whatever I depict in my imagination; for these are things which I have supposed to be nothing. Let this supposition stand;[10] for all that I am still something. And yet may it not perhaps be the case that these very things which I am supposing to be nothing, because they are unknown to me, are in reality identical with the "I" of which I am aware? I do not know, and for the moment I shall not argue the point, since I can make judgements only about things which are known to me. I know that I exist; the question is, what is this "I" that I know? If the "I" is understood strictly as we have been taking it, then it is quite certain that knowledge of it does not depend on things of whose 28
existence I am as yet unaware; so it cannot depend on any of the things which I invent in my imagination. And this very word "invent" shows me my mistake. It would indeed be a case of fictitious invention if I used my imagination to establish that I was something or other; for imagining is simply contemplating the shape or image of a corporeal thing. Yet now I know for certain both that I exist and at the same time that all such images and, in general, everything relating to the nature of body, could be mere dreams <and chimeras>. Once this point has been grasped, to say "I will use my imagination to get to know more distinctly what I am" would seem to be as silly as saying "I am now awake, and see some truth; but since my vision is not yet clear enough, I will deliberately fall asleep so that my dreams may provide a truer and clearer representation." I thus realize that none of the things that the imagination enables me to grasp is at all relevant to this knowledge of myself which I possess, and that the mind must therefore be most carefully diverted from such things[11] if it is to perceive its own nature as distinctly as possible.

But what then am I? A thing that thinks. What is that? A thing that doubts, understands, affirms, denies, is willing, is unwilling, and also imagines and has sensory perceptions.

This is a considerable list, if everything on it belongs to me. But does it? Is it not one and the same

"I" who is now doubting almost everything, who nonetheless understands some things, who affirms that this one thing is true, denies everything else, desires to know more, is unwilling to be deceived, imagines many things even involuntarily, and is aware of many things which apparently come from
29 the senses? Are not all these things just as true as the fact that I exist, even if I am asleep all the time, and even if he who created me is doing all he can to deceive me? Which of all these activities is distinct from my thinking? Which of them can be said to be separate from myself? The fact that it is I who am doubting and understanding and willing is so evident that I see no way of making it any clearer. But it is also the case that the "I" who imagines is the same "I." For even if, as I have supposed, none of the objects of imagination are real, the power of imagination is something which really exists and is part of my thinking. Lastly, it is also the same "I" who has sensory perceptions, or is aware of bodily things as it were through the senses. For example, I am now seeing light, hearing a noise, feeling heat. But I am asleep, so all this is false. Yet I certainly *seem* to see, to hear, and to be warmed. This cannot be false; what is called "having a sensory perception" is strictly just this, and in this restricted sense of the term it is simply thinking.

From all this I am beginning to have a rather better understanding of what I am. But it still appears—and I cannot stop thinking this—that the corporeal things of which images are formed in my thought, and which the senses investigate, are known with much more distinctness than this puzzling "I" which cannot be pictured in the imagination. And yet it is surely surprising that I should have a more distinct grasp of things which I realize are doubtful, unknown and foreign to me, than I have of that which is true and known—my own self. But I see what it is: my mind enjoys wandering off and will not yet submit to being restrained within the bounds
30 of truth. Very well then; just this once let us give it a completely free rein, so that after a while, when it is time to tighten the reins, it may more readily submit to being curbed.

Let us consider the things which people commonly think they understand most distinctly of all; that is, the bodies which we touch and see. I do not mean bodies in general—for general perceptions are apt to be somewhat more confused—but one particular body. Let us take, for example, this piece of wax. It has just been taken from the honeycomb; it has not yet quite lost the taste of the honey; it retains some of the scent of the flowers from which it was gathered; its colour, shape and size are plain to see; it is hard, cold and can be handled without difficulty; if you rap it with your knuckle it makes a sound. In short, it has everything which appears necessary to enable a body to be known as distinctly as possible. But even as I speak, I put the wax by the fire, and look: the residual taste is eliminated, the smell goes away, the colour changes, the shape is lost, the size increases; it becomes liquid and hot; you can hardly touch it, and if you strike it, it no longer makes a sound. But does the same wax remain? It must be admitted that it does; no one denies it, no one thinks otherwise. So what was it in the wax that I understood with such distinctness? Evidently none of the features which I arrived at by means of the senses; for whatever came under taste, smell, sight, touch or hearing has now altered—yet the wax remains.

Perhaps the answer lies in the thought which now comes to my mind; namely, the wax was not after all the sweetness of the honey, or the fragrance of the flowers, or the whiteness, or the shape, or the sound, but was rather a body which presented itself to me in these various forms a little while ago, but which now exhibits different ones. But what exactly is it
that I am now imagining? Let us concentrate, take 31
away everything which does not belong to the wax, and see what is left: merely something extended, flexible and changeable. But what is meant here by "flexible" and "changeable"? Is it what I picture in my imagination: that this piece of wax is capable of changing from a round shape to a square shape, or from a square shape to a triangular shape? Not at all; for I can grasp that the wax is capable of countless changes of this kind, yet I am unable to run through this immeasurable number of changes in my imagination, from which it follows that it is not the faculty of imagination that gives me my grasp of the wax as flexible and changeable. And what is meant by "extended"? Is the extension of the wax also unknown? For it increases if the wax melts, increases again if it boils, and is greater still if the

heat is increased. I would not be making a correct judgement about the nature of wax unless I believed it capable of being extended in many more different ways than I will ever encompass in my imagination. I must therefore admit that the nature of this piece of wax is in no way revealed by my imagination, but is perceived by the mind alone. (I am speaking of this particular piece of wax; the point is even clearer with regard to wax in general.) But what is this wax which is perceived by the mind alone?[12] It is of course the same wax which I see, which I touch, which I picture in my imagination, in short the same wax which I thought it to be from the start. And yet, and here is the point, the perception I have of it[13] is a case not of vision or touch or imagination—nor has it ever been, despite previous appearances—but of purely mental scrutiny; and this can be imperfect and confused, as it was before, or clear and distinct as it is now, depending on how carefully I concentrate on what the wax consists in.

But as I reach this conclusion I am amazed at how <weak and> prone to error my mind is. For although I am thinking about these matters within myself,
32 silently and without speaking, nonetheless the actual words bring me up short, and I am almost tricked by ordinary ways of talking. We say that we see the wax itself, if it is there before us, not that we judge it to be there from its colour or shape; and this might lead me to conclude without more ado that knowledge of the wax comes from what the eye sees, and not from the scrutiny of the mind alone. But then if I look out of the window and see men crossing the square, as I just happen to have done, I normally say that I see the men themselves, just as I say that I see the wax. Yet do I see any more than hats and coats which could conceal automatons? I *judge* that they are men. And so something which I thought I was seeing with my eyes is in fact grasped solely by the faculty of judgement which is in my mind.

However, one who wants to achieve knowledge above the ordinary level should feel ashamed at having taken ordinary ways of talking as a basis for doubt. So let us proceed, and consider on which occasion my perception of the nature of the wax was more perfect and evident. Was it when I first looked at it, and believed I knew it by my external senses, or at least by what they call the "common" sense[14]—that is, the power of imagination? Or is my knowledge more perfect now, after a more careful investigation of the nature of the wax and of the means by which it is known? Any doubt on this issue would clearly be foolish; for what distinctness was there in my earlier perception? Was there anything in it which an animal could not possess? But when I distinguish the wax from its outward forms—take the clothes off, as it were, and consider it naked—then although my judgement may still contain errors, at least my perception now requires a human mind.

But what am I to say about this mind, or about 33
myself? (So far, remember, I am not admitting that there is anything else in me except a mind.) What, I ask, is this "I" which seems to perceive the wax so distinctly? Surely my awareness of my own self is not merely much truer and more certain than my awareness of the wax, but also much more distinct and evident. For if I judge that the wax exists from the fact that I see it, clearly this same fact entails much more evidently that I myself also exist. It is possible that what I see is not really the wax; it is possible that I do not even have eyes with which to see anything. But when I see, or think I see (I am not here distinguishing the two), it is simply not possible that I who am now thinking am not something. By the same token, if I judge that the wax exists from the fact that I touch it, the same result follows, namely that I exist. If I judge that it exists from the fact that I imagine it, or for any other reason, exactly the same thing follows. And the result that I have grasped in the case of the wax may be applied to everything else located outside me. Moreover, if my perception of the wax seemed more distinct after it was established not just by sight or touch but by many other considerations, it must be admitted that I now know myself even more distinctly. This is because every consideration whatsoever which contributes to my perception of the wax, or of any other body, cannot but establish even more effectively the nature of my own mind. But besides this, there is so much else in the mind itself which can serve to make my knowledge of it more distinct, that it scarcely seems worth going through the contributions made by considering bodily things.

I see that without any effort I have now finally 34
got back to where I wanted. I now know that even

bodies are not strictly perceived by the senses or the faculty of imagination but by the intellect alone, and that this perception derives not from their being touched or seen but from their being understood; and in view of this I know plainly that I can achieve an easier and more evident perception of my own mind than of anything else. But since the habit of holding on to old opinions cannot be set aside so quickly, I should like to stop here and meditate for some time on this new knowledge I have gained, so as to fix it more deeply in my memory.

NOTES

1. "... and in my dreams regularly represent to myself the same things" (French version).
2. "... the place where they are, the time which measures their duration" (French version).
3. "... yet I cannot doubt that he does allow this" (French version).
4. "... in the sciences" (added in French version).
5. "... nevertheless it is in my power to suspend my judgement" (French version).
6. "... puts into my mind" (French version).
7. "... or thought anything at all" (French version).
8. The word "only" is most naturally taken as going with "a thing that thinks," and this interpretation is followed in the French version. When discussing this passage with Gassendi, however, Descartes suggests that he meant the "only" to govern "in the strict sense;" cf. AT IXA 215; CSM II 276.
9. "... to see if I am not something more" (added in French version).
10. Lat. *maneat* ("let it stand"), first edition. The second edition has the indicative *manet*: "The proposition still stands, *viz.* that I am nonetheless something." The French version reads: "without changing this supposition, I find that I am still certain that I am something."
11. "... from this manner of conceiving things" (French version).
12. "... which can be conceived only by the understanding or the mind" (French version).
13. "... or rather the act whereby it is perceived" (added in French version).
14. The supposed faculty which integrates the data from the five specialized senses (the notion goes back ultimately to Aristotle).

Proof of an External World

G. E. MOORE

G. E. Moore (1873–1958) was one of the most important British philosophers of the first half of the twentieth century. Along with his long-time colleagues Bertrand Russell and Ludwig Wittgenstein, Moore was one of the central figures in a movement that has come to be known as "analytic philosophy." Moore was a philosopher of wide-ranging interests, producing important work in epistemology, the philosophy of language, ethics, and the philosophy of mind.

"Proof of an External World" is an excerpt from Moore's 1939 essay of the same name; "Certainty" appeared in his *Philosophical Papers* (1962). In them, Moore provides a response to the skeptic through an appeal to common sense.

From G. E. Moore, *Philosophical Papers* (New York: Collier Books, 1962), pp. 144–8. Reproduced by permission of Taylor & Francis Books UK.

It seems to me that, so far from its being true, as Kant* declares to be his opinion, that there is only one possible proof of the existence of things outside of us, namely the one which he has given, I can now give a large number of different proofs, each of which is a perfectly rigorous proof; and that at many other times I have been in a position to give many others. I can prove now, for instance, that two human hands exist. How? By holding up my two hands, and saying, as I make a certain gesture with the right hand, "Here is one hand," and adding, as I make a certain gesture with the left, "and here is another." And if, by doing this, I have proved ipso facto the existence of external things, you will all see that I can also do it now in numbers of other ways: there is no need to multiply examples.

But did I prove just now that two human hands were then in existence? I do want to insist that I did; that the proof which I gave was a perfectly rigorous one; and that it is perhaps impossible to give a better or more rigorous proof of anything whatever. Of course, it would not have been a proof unless three conditions were satisfied; namely (1) unless the premiss which I adduced as proof of the conclusion was different from the conclusion I adduced it to prove; (2) unless the premiss which I adduced was something which I *knew* to be the case, and not merely something which I believed but which was by no means certain, or something which, though in fact true, I did not know to be so; and (3) unless the conclusion did really follow from the premiss. But all these three conditions were in fact satisfied by my proof. (1) The premiss which I adduced in proof was quite certainly different from the conclusion, for the conclusion was merely "Two human hands exist at this moment"; but the premiss was something far more specific than this—something which I expressed by showing you my hands, making certain gestures, and saying the words "Here is one hand, and here is another." It is quite obvious that the two were different, because it is quite obvious that the conclusion might have been true, even if the premiss had been false. In asserting the premiss I was asserting much more than I was asserting in asserting the conclusion. (2) I certainly did at the moment *know* that which I expressed by the combination of certain gestures with saying the words "Here is one hand and here is another." I *knew* that there was one hand in the place indicated by combining a certain gesture with my first utterance of "here" and that there was another in the different place indicated by combining a certain gesture with my second utterance of "here." How absurd it would be to suggest that I did not know it, but only believed it, and that perhaps it was not the case! You might as well suggest that I do not know that I am now standing up and talking—that perhaps after all I'm not, and that it's not quite certain that I am! And finally (3) it is quite certain that the conclusion did follow from the premiss. This is as certain as it is that if there is one hand here and another here *now*, then it follows that there are two hands in existence *now*.

My proof, then, of the existence of things outside of us did satisfy three of the conditions necessary for a rigorous proof. Are there any other conditions necessary for a rigorous proof, such that perhaps it did not satisfy one of them? Perhaps there may be; I do not know; but I do want to emphasise that, so far as I can see, we all of us do constantly take proofs of this sort as absolutely conclusive proofs of certain conclusions—as finally settling certain questions, as to which we were previously in doubt. Suppose, for instance, it were a question whether there were as many as three misprints on a certain page in a certain book. A says there are, B is inclined to doubt it. How could A prove that he is right? Surely he *could* prove it by taking the book, turning to the page, and pointing to three separate places on it, saying "There's one misprint here, another here, and another here": surely that is a method by which it *might* be proved! Of course, A would not have proved, by doing this, that there were at least three misprints on the page in question, unless it was certain that there was a misprint in each of the places to which he pointed. But to say that he *might* prove it in this way, is to say

* In the "Refutation of Idealism" section of the second edition of his *Critique of Pure Reason* (1787), Immanuel Kant presented an argument which he claimed was "the only possible . . . strict proof of the objective reality" of the external world. Kant held that "it always remains a scandal of philosophy and universal human reason that the existence of things outside us . . . should have been assumed merely on faith" (Kant 1787, Bxl.)

that it *might* be certain that there was. And if such a thing as that could ever be certain, then assuredly it was certain just now that there was one hand in one of the two places I indicated and another in the other.

I did, then, just now, give a proof that there were *then* external objects; and obviously, if I did, I could *then* have given many other proofs of the same sort that there were external objects *then,* and could now give many proofs of the same sort that there are external objects *now*.

But, if what I am asked to do is to prove that external objects have existed *in the past*, then I can give many different proofs of this also, but proofs which are in important respects of a different *sort* from those just given. And I want to emphasise that, when Kant says it is a scandal not to be able to give a proof of the existence of external objects, a proof of their existence in the past would certainly *help* to remove the scandal of which he is speaking. He says that, if it occurs to anyone to question their existence, we ought to be able to confront him with a satisfactory proof. But by a person who questions their existence, he certainly means not merely a person who questions whether any exist at the moment of speaking, but a person who questions whether any have *ever* existed; and a proof that some have existed in the past would certainly therefore be relevant to *part* of what such a person is questioning. How then can I prove that there have been external objects in the past? Here is one proof. I can say: "I held up two hands above this desk not very long ago; therefore two hands existed not very long ago; therefore at least two external objects have existed at some time in the past, QED." This is a perfectly good proof, provided I *know* what is asserted in the premiss. But I *do* know that I held up two hands above this desk not very long ago. As a matter of fact, in this case you all know it too. There's no doubt whatever that I did. Therefore I have given a perfectly conclusive proof that external objects have existed in the past; and you will all see at once that, if this is a conclusive proof, I could have given many others of the same sort, and could now give many others. But it is also quite obvious that this sort of proof differs in important respects from the sort of proof I gave just now that there were two hands existing *then*.

I have, then, given two conclusive proofs of the existence of external objects. The first was a proof that two human hands existed at the time when I gave the proof; the second was a proof that two human hands had existed at a time previous to that at which I gave the proof. These proofs were of a different sort in important respects. And I pointed out that I could have given, then, many other conclusive proofs of both sorts. It is also obvious that I could give many others of both sorts now. So that, if these are the sort of proof that is wanted, nothing is easier than to prove the existence of external objects.

But now I am perfectly well aware that, in spite of all that I have said, many philosophers will still feel that I have not given any satisfactory proof of the point in question. And I want briefly, in conclusion, to say something as to why this dissatisfaction with my proofs should be felt.

One reason why, is, I think, this. Some people understand "proof of an external world" as including a proof of things which I haven't attempted to prove and haven't proved. It is not quite easy to say *what* it is that they want proved—*what* it is that is such that unless they got a proof of it, they would not say that they had a proof of the existence of external things; but I can make an approach to explaining what they want by saying that if I had proved the propositions which I used as *premisses* in my two proofs, then they would perhaps admit that I had proved the existence of external things, but, in the absence of such a proof (which, of course, I have neither given nor attempted to give), they will say that I have not given what they mean by a proof of the existence of external things. In other words, they want a proof of what I assert *now* when I hold up my hands and say "Here's one hand and here's another"; and, in the other case, they want a proof of what I assert *now* when I say "I did hold up two hands above this desk just now." Of course, what they really want is not merely a proof of these two propositions, but something like a general statement as to how *any* propositions of this sort may be proved. This, of course, I haven't given; and I do not believe it can be given: if this is what is meant by proof of the existence of external things, I do not believe that any proof of the existence of external things is possible. Of course, in some cases what might be called a proof of propositions which seem like these can be got. If one of you suspected that one of my hands was artificial he might be said to get a proof of my proposition "Here's one hand, and here's another," by coming up and examining the suspected hand close up, perhaps touching and pressing it, and so establishing that it really was a human hand. But I do not believe that any proof is possible in nearly all cases. How am I to prove now that "Here's one hand, and here's another"? I do not believe I can do it. In order to do it, I should need to prove for one thing, as Descartes* pointed out, that I am not now dreaming. But how can I prove that I am not? I have, no doubt, conclusive reasons for asserting that I am not now dreaming; I have conclusive evidence that I am awake: but that is a very different thing from being able to prove it. I could not tell you what all my evidence is; and I should require to do this at least, in order to give you a proof.

But another reason why some people would feel dissatisfied with my proofs is, I think, not merely that they want a proof of something which I haven't proved, but that they think that, if I cannot give such extra proofs, then the proofs that I have given are not conclusive proofs at all. And this, I think, is a definite mistake. They would say: "If you cannot prove your premiss that here is one hand and here is another, then you do not know it. But you yourself have admitted that, if you did not know it, then your proof was not conclusive. Therefore your proof was not, as you say it was, a conclusive proof." This view that, if I cannot prove such things as these, I do not know them, is, I think, the view that Kant was expressing in the sentence which I quoted at the beginning of this lecture, when he implies that so long as we have no proof of the existence of external things, their existence must be accepted merely on *faith*. He means to say, I think, that if I cannot prove that there is a hand here, I must accept it merely as a matter of faith—I cannot know it. Such a view, though it has been very common among philosophers, can, I think, be shown to be wrong—though shown only by the use of premisses which are not known to be true, unless we do know of the existence of external things. I can know things, which I cannot prove; and among things which I certainly did know, even if (as I think) I could not prove them, were the premisses of my two proofs. I should say, therefore, that those, if any, who are dissatisfied with these proofs merely on the ground that I did not know their premisses, have no good reason for their dissatisfaction.

* See previous selection.

Certainty

G. E. MOORE

Suppose I say: "I know for certain that I am standing up; it is absolutely certain that I am; there is not the smallest chance that I am not." Many philosophers would say: "You are wrong: you do not know that you are standing up; it is *not* absolutely certain that you are; there is *some* chance, though perhaps only a very small one, that you are not." And one argument which has been used as an argument in favour of saying this, is an argument in the course of which the philosopher who used it would assert: "You do not know for certain that you are not dreaming; it is not absolutely certain that you are not; there is *some* chance, though perhaps only a very small one, that you are." And from this, that I do not know for certain that I am not dreaming, it is supposed to follow that I do not know for certain that I am standing

From G. E. Moore, *Philosophical Papers* (New York: Collier Books, 1962), pp. 240–6. Reproduced by permission of Taylor & Francis Books UK.

up. It is argued: If it is not certain that you are not dreaming, then it is not certain that you are standing up. And that *if* I don't know that I'm not dreaming, I also don't know that I'm not sitting down, I don't feel at all inclined to dispute. From the hypothesis that I am dreaming, it would, I think, certainly follow that I don't *know* that I am standing up; though I have never seen the matter argued, and though it is not at all clear to me how it is to be proved that it would follow. But, on the other hand, from the hypothesis that I am dreaming, it certainly would not follow that I am *not* standing up; for it is certainly logically possible that a man should be fast asleep and dreaming, while he is standing up and not lying down. It is therefore logically possible that I should both be standing up and also at the same time dreaming that I am; just as the story, about a well-known Duke of Devonshire, that he once dreamt that he was speaking in the House of Lords and, when he woke up, found that he *was* speaking in the House of Lords, is certainly logically possible. And if, as is commonly assumed, when I am dreaming that I am standing up it may also be correct to say that I am *thinking* that I am standing up, then it follows that the hypothesis that I am now dreaming is quite consistent with the hypothesis that I am both thinking that I am standing up and also actually standing up. And hence, if as seems to me to be certainly the case and as this argument assumes, from the hypothesis that I am now dreaming it *would* follow that I don't know that I am standing up, there follows a point which is of great importance with regard to our use of the word "knowledge," and therefore also of the word "certainty"—a point which has been made quite conclusively more than once by Russell,* namely that from the conjunction of the two facts that a man thinks that a given proposition p is true, and that p is in fact true, it does *not* follow that the man in question *knows* that p is true: in order that I may be justified in saying that I know that I am standing up, something more is required than the mere conjunction of the two facts that I both think I am and actually am—as Russell has expressed it, true belief is not identical with knowledge; and I think we may further add that even from the conjunction of the two facts that I feel certain that I am and that I actually am it would not follow that I know that I am, nor therefore that it *is* certain that I am. As regards the argument drawn from the fact that a man who dreams that he is standing up and happens at the moment actually to be standing up will nevertheless not *know* that he is standing up, it should indeed be noted that from the fact that a man is dreaming that he is standing up, it certainly does not *follow* that he *thinks* he is standing up; since it does sometimes happen in a dream that we *think* that it is a dream, and a man who thought this certainly might, although he was dreaming that he was standing up, yet *think* that he was not, although he could not *know* that he was not. It is not therefore the case, as might be hastily assumed, that, if I dream that I am standing up at a time when I am in fact lying down, I am necessarily *deceived*: I should be deceived only if I thought I was standing when I wasn't; and I may dream that I am, without thinking that I am. It certainly does, however, often happen that we do dream that so-and-so is the case, without at the time thinking that we are only dreaming; and in such cases, I think we may perhaps be said to *think* that what we dream is the case *is* the case, and to be deceived if it is not the case; and therefore also, in such cases, if what we dream to be the case happens also to *be* the case, we may be said to be thinking truly that it is the case, although we certainly do not *know* that it is.

I agree, therefore, with that part of this argument which asserts that if I don't know now that I'm not dreaming, it follows that I don't *know* that I am standing up, even if I both actually am and think that I am. But this first part of the argument is a consideration which cuts both ways. For, if it is true, it follows that it is also true that if I *do* know that I am standing up, then I do know that I am not dreaming. I can therefore just as well argue: since I do know that I'm standing up, it follows that I do know that I'm not dreaming; as my opponent can argue: since you don't know that you're not dreaming, it follows that you don't know that you're standing up. The one argument is just as good as the other, unless my opponent can give better reasons for asserting that

* British philosopher Bertrand Russell (1872-1970) was a thinker and activist of wide-ranging intellect, winner of the 1950 Nobel Prize in Literature.

I don't know that I'm not dreaming, than I can give for asserting that I do know that I am standing up.

What reasons can be given for saying that I don't know for certain that I'm not at this moment dreaming?

I do not think that I have ever seen clearly stated any argument which is supposed to show this. But I am going to try to state, as clearly as I can, the premisses and the reasonings from them, which I think have led so many philosophers to suppose that I really cannot now know for certain that I am not dreaming.

I said, you may remember, in talking of the seven assertions with which I opened this lecture, that I had "the evidence of my senses" for them, though I also said that I didn't think this was the only evidence I had for them, nor that this by itself was necessarily conclusive evidence. Now if I had *then* "the evidence of my senses" in favour of the proposition that I was standing up, I certainly have *now* the evidence of my senses in favour of the proposition that I *am* standing up, even though this may not be all the evidence that I have, and may not be conclusive. But have I, in fact, the evidence of my senses *at all* in favour of this proposition? One thing seems to me to be quite clear about our use of this phrase, namely, that, if a man at a given time is only dreaming that he is standing up, then it follows that he has *not* at that time the evidence of his senses in favour of that proposition: to say "Jones last night was *only* dreaming that he was standing up, and yet all the time he had the evidence of his senses that he was" is to say something self-contradictory. But those philosophers who say it is possible that I am now dreaming, certainly mean to say also that it is possible that I am *only dreaming* that I am standing up; and this view, we now see, entails that it is possible that I have *not* the evidence of my senses that I am. If, therefore, they are right, it follows that it is not certain even that I have the evidence of my senses that I am; it follows that it is not certain that I have *the evidence of my senses* for anything at all. If, therefore, I were to say now, that I certainly have the evidence of my senses in favour of the proposition that I am standing up, even if it's not certain that I am standing up, I should be begging the very question now at issue. For if it is not certain that I am not dreaming, it is not certain that I even have the evidence of my senses that I am standing up.

But, now, even if it is not certain that I have at this moment the evidence of my senses for anything at all, it is quite certain that I *either* have the evidence of my senses that I am standing up *or* have an experience which is *very like* having the evidence of my senses that I am standing up. *If* I am dreaming, this experience consists in having dream-images which are at least very like the sensations I should be having if I were awake and had the sensations, the having of which would constitute "having the evidence of my senses" that I am standing up. Let us use the expression "sensory experience," in such a way that this experience which I certainly am having will be a "sensory experience," whether or not it merely consists in the having of dream-images. If we use the expression "sensory experience" in this way, we can say, I think, that, if it is not certain that I am not dreaming now, then it is not certain that *all* the sensory experiences I am now having are not mere dream-images.

What then are the premisses and the reasonings which would lead so many philosophers to think that all the sensory experiences I am having now *may* be mere dream-images—that I do not know for certain that they are not?

So far as I can see, one premiss which they would certainly use would be this: "Some at least of the sensory experiences which you are having now are similar in important respects to dream-images which actually have occurred in dreams." This seems a very harmless premiss, and I am quite willing to admit that it is true. But I think there is a very serious objection to the procedure of using it as a premiss in favour of the derived conclusion. For a philosopher who does use it as a premiss, is, I think, in fact *implying*, though he does not expressly say, that he himself knows it to be true. He is *implying* therefore that he himself knows that dreams have occurred. And, of course, I think he would be right. All the philosophers I have ever met or heard of certainly did know that dreams have occurred: we all know that dreams *have* occurred. But can he consistently combine this proposition that he knows that dreams have occurred, with his conclusion that he does not know that he is not dreaming? Can anybody possibly know that dreams have occurred, if, at the time, he does not himself know that he is not dreaming? If he *is* dreaming, it may be that he is only dreaming that dreams have occurred; and if he does not know that he is not dreaming, can he possibly know that he is *not* only dreaming that dreams have occurred? Can he possibly know therefore that dreams *have* occurred? I do not think that he can; and therefore I think that anyone who uses this premiss and also asserts the conclusion that nobody ever knows that he is not dreaming, is guilty of an inconsistency. By using this premiss he implies that he himself knows that dreams have occurred; while, if his conclusion is true, it follows that he himself does not know that he is not dreaming, and therefore does not know that he is not only dreaming that dreams have occurred.

However, I admit that the premiss is true. Let us now try to see by what sort of reasoning it might be thought that we could get from it to the conclusion.

I do not see how we can get forward in that direction at all, unless we first take the following huge step, unless we say, namely: since there have been dream-images similar in important respects to some of the sensory experiences I am now having, it is logically possible that there should be dream-images *exactly like all* the sensory experiences I am now having, and logically possible, therefore, that all the sensory experiences I am now having *are* mere dream-images. And it might be thought that the validity of this step could be supported to some extent by appeal to matters of fact, though only, of course, at the cost of the same sort of inconsistency which I have just pointed out. It might be said, for instance, that some people have had dream-images which were *exactly like* sensory experiences which they had when they were awake, and that therefore it must be logically possible to have a dream-image exactly like a sensory experience which is *not* a dream-image. And then it may be said: If it is logically possible for some dream-images to be exactly like sensory experiences which are not dream-images, surely it must be logically possible for *all* the dream-images occurring in a dream at a given time to be exactly like sensory experiences which are not dream-images, and logically possible also for all the sensory experiences which a man has at a given time when he is awake to be exactly like all the dream-images which he himself or another man had in a dream at another time.

Now I cannot see my way to deny that it is logically possible that all the sensory experiences I am having now should be mere dream-images. And if this is logically possible, and if further the sensory experiences I am having now were the only experiences I am having, I do not see how I could possibly know for certain that I am not dreaming.

But the conjunction of my memories of the immediate past with these sensory experiences *may* be sufficient to enable me to know that I am not dreaming. I say it *may* be. But what if our sceptical philosopher says: It is *not* sufficient; and offers as an argument to prove that it is not, this: It is logically possible *both* that you should be having all the sensory experiences you are having, and also that you should be remembering what you do remember, and *yet* should be dreaming. If this *is* logically possible, then I don't see how to deny that I cannot possibly know for certain that I am not dreaming: I do not see that I possibly could. But can any reason be given for saying that it *is* logically possible? So far as I know nobody ever has, and I don't know how anybody ever could. And so long as this is not done my argument, "I know that I am standing up, and therefore I know that I am not dreaming," remains at least as good as his, "You don't know that you are not dreaming, and therefore don't know that you are standing up." And I don't think I've ever seen an argument expressly directed to show that it is not.

One final point should be made clear. It is certainly logically possible that I *should have* been dreaming now; I *might* have been dreaming now; and therefore the proposition that I *am* dreaming now is not self-contradictory. But what I am in doubt of is whether it is logically possible that I should *both* be having all the sensory experiences and the memories that I have and *yet* be dreaming. The conjunction of the proposition that I have these sense experiences and memories with the proposition that I am dreaming does seem to me to be very likely self-contradictory.

"Skepticism" from *Philosophical Explanations*

ROBERT NOZICK

American philosopher Robert Nozick (1938–2002), taught philosophy at Harvard University. Known for his cleverness, sharp wit, and creativity, he was an omnivorous reader who made lasting contributions in a number of philosophical areas.

The selections that appear here are the continuation of the "Knowledge" excerpt in section A, taken from the Epistemology section of *Philosophical Explanations* (1982). In it Nozick articulates and defends his own response to skepticism, drawing on the account presented in the previous selection from his work.

The skeptic about knowledge argues that we know very little or nothing of what we think we know, or at any rate that this position is no less reasonable than the belief in knowledge. The history of philosophy exhibits a number of different attempts to refute the skeptic: to prove him wrong or show that in arguing against knowledge he presupposes there is some and so refutes himself. Others attempt to show that accepting skepticism is unreasonable, since it is more likely that the skeptic's extreme conclusion is false than that all of his premisses are true, or simply because reasonableness of belief just means proceeding in an anti-skeptical way. Even when these counterarguments satisfy their inventors, they fail to satisfy others, as is shown by the persistent attempts against skepticism. The continuing felt need to refute skepticism, and the difficulty in doing so, attests to the power of the skeptic's position, the depth of his worries.

An account of knowledge should illuminate skeptical arguments and show wherein lies their force. If the account leads us to reject these arguments, this had better not happen too easily or too glibly. To think the skeptic overlooks something obvious, to attribute to him a simple mistake or confusion or fallacy, is to refuse to acknowledge the power of his position and the grip it can have upon us. We thereby cheat ourselves of the opportunity to reap his insights and to gain self-knowledge in understanding why his arguments lure us so. Moreover, in fact, we cannot lay the specter of skepticism to rest without first hearing what it shall unfold.

Our goal is not, however, to refute skepticism, to prove it is wrong or even to argue that it is wrong. In the Introduction we distinguished between philosophy that attempts to prove, and philosophy that attempts to explain how something is possible. Our task here is to explain how knowledge is possible, given what the skeptic says that we do accept (for example, that it is logically possible that we are dreaming or are floating in the tank). In doing this, we need not convince the skeptic, and we may introduce explanatory hypotheses that he would reject. What is important for our task of explanation and understanding is that *we* find those hypotheses acceptable or plausible, and that they show us how the existence of knowledge fits together with the logical possibilities the skeptic points to, so that these are reconciled within our own belief system. These hypotheses are to explain to ourselves how knowledge is possible, not to prove to someone else that knowledge *is* possible.[1]

SKEPTICAL POSSIBILITIES

The skeptic often refers to possibilities in which a person would believe something even though it was false:

Reprinted by permission of the publisher from *Philosophical Explanations* by Robert Nozick, pp. 167–178, Cambridge, Mass: The Belknap Press of Harvard University Press. Copyright © 1981 by Robert Nozick.

really, the person is cleverly deceived by others, perhaps by an evil demon, or the person is dreaming or he is floating in a tank near Alpha Centauri with his brain being stimulated. In each case, the *p* he believes is false, and he believes it even though it is false.

How do these possibilities adduced by the skeptic show that someone does not know that *p*? Suppose that someone is you; how do these possibilities count against your knowing that *p*? One way might be the following. (I shall consider other ways later.) If there is a possible situation where *p* is false yet you believe that *p*, then in that situation you believe that *p* even though it is false. So it appears you do not satisfy condition 3 for knowledge.*

(3) If *p* were false, S wouldn't believe that *p*.

For a situation has been described in which you do believe that *p* even though *p* is false. How then can it also be true that if *p* were false, you wouldn't believe it? If the skeptic's possible situation shows that 3 is false, and if 3 is a necessary condition for knowledge, then the skeptic's possible situation shows that there isn't knowledge.

So construed, the skeptic's argument plays on condition 3; it aims to show that condition 3 is not satisfied. The skeptic may seem to be putting forth

R: Even if *p* were false, S still would believe *p*.

This conditional, with the same antecedent as 3 and the contradictory consequent, is incompatible with the truth of 3. If 3 is true, then R is not. However, R is stronger than the skeptic needs in order to show 3 is false. For 3 is false when if *p* were false, S might believe that *p*. This last conditional is weaker than R, and is merely 3's denial:

T: not-[not-*p* → not-(S believes that *p*)].

Whereas R does not simply deny 3, it asserts an opposing subjunctive of its own. Perhaps the possibility the skeptic adduces is not enough to show that R is true, but it appears at least to establish the weaker T; since this T denies 3, the skeptic's possibility appears to show that 3 is false.[2]

However, the truth of 3 is not incompatible with the existence of a possible situation where the person believes *p* though it is false. The subjunctive

(3) not-*p* → not-(S believes *p*)

does not talk of all possible situations in which *p* is false (in which not-*p* is true). It does not say that in all possible situations where not-*p* holds, S doesn't believe *p*. To say there is no possible situation in which not-*p* yet S believes *p*, would be to say that not-*p* entails not-(S believes *p*), or logically implies it. But subjunctive conditionals differ from entailments; the subjunctive 3 is not a statement of entailment. So the existence of a possible situation in which *p* is false yet S believes *p* does not show that 3 is false.[3] 3 can be true even though there is a possible situation where not-*p* and S believes that *p*.

What the subjunctive 3 speaks of is the situation that would hold if *p* were false. Not every possible situation in which *p* is false is the situation that would hold if *p* were false. To fall into possible worlds talk, the subjunctive 3 speaks of the not-*p* world that is closest to the actual world, or of those not-*p* worlds that are closest to the actual world, or more strongly (according to my suggestion) of the not-*p* neighborhood of the actual world. And it is of this or these not-*p* worlds that it says (in them) S does not believe that *p*. What happens in yet other more distant not-*p* worlds is no concern of the subjunctive 3.

The skeptic's possibilities (let us refer to them as SK), of the person's being deceived by a demon or dreaming or floating in a tank, count against the subjunctive

(3) if *p* were false then S wouldn't believe that *p*

only if (one of) these possibilities would or might obtain if *p* were false; only if one of these possibilities is in the not-*p* neighborhood of the actual world. Condition 3 says: if *p* were false, S still would not believe *p*. And this can hold even though there is some

* For Nozick's discussion of condition (3) and the role it plays in his analysis of knowledge, see his essay "Knowledge," p. 346 this volume.

situation SK described by the skeptic in which *p* is false and S believes *p*. If *p* were false S still would not believe *p*, even though there is a situation SK in which *p* is false and S does believe *p*, provided that this situation SK wouldn't obtain if *p* were false. If the skeptic describes a situation SK which would not hold even if *p* were false then this situation SK doesn't show that 3 is false and so does not (in this way at least) undercut knowledge. Condition C acts to rule out skeptical hypotheses.

C: not-*p* → SK does not obtain.

Any skeptical situation SK which satisfies condition C is ruled out. For a skeptical situation SK to show that we don't know that *p*, it must fail to satisfy C which excludes it; instead it must be a situation that might obtain if *p* did not, and so satisfy C's denial:

not-(not-*p* → SK doesn't obtain).

Although the skeptic's imagined situations appear to show that 3 is false, they do not; they satisfy condition C and so are excluded.

The skeptic might go on to ask whether we know that his imagined situations SK are excluded by condition C, whether we know that if *p* were false SK would not obtain. However, typically he asks something stronger: do we know that his imagined situation SK does not actually obtain? Do we know that we are not being deceived by a demon, dreaming, or floating in a tank? And if we do not know this, how can we know that *p*? Thus we are led to the second way his imagined situations might show that we do not know that *p*.

SKEPTICAL RESULTS

According to our account of knowledge, S knows that the skeptic's situation SK doesn't hold if and only if

(1) SK doesn't hold
(2) S believes that SK doesn't hold
(3) If SK were to hold, S would not believe that SK doesn't hold
(4) If SK were not to hold, S would believe it does not.

Let us focus on the third of these conditions. The skeptic has carefully chosen his situations SK so that if they held we (still) would believe they did not. We would believe we weren't dreaming, weren't being deceived, and so on, even if we were. He has chosen situations SK such that if SK were to hold, S would (still) believe that SK doesn't hold—and this is incompatible with the truth of 3.[4]

Since condition 3 is a necessary condition for knowledge, it follows that we do not know that SK doesn't hold. If it were true that an evil demon was deceiving us, if we were having a particular dream, if we were floating in a tank with our brains stimulated in a specified way, we would still believe we were not. So, we do not know we're not being deceived by an evil demon, we do not know we're not in that tank, and we do not know we're not having that dream. So says the skeptic, and so says our account. And also so we say—don't we? For how could we know we are not being deceived that way, dreaming that dream? If those things *were* happening to us, everything would seem the same to us. There is no way we can know it is not happening for there is no way we could tell if it were happening; and if it were happening we would believe exactly what we do now—in particular, we still would believe that it was not. For this reason, we feel, and correctly, that we don't know—how could we?—that it is not happening to us. It is a virtue of our account that it yields, and explains, this result.

The skeptic asserts we do not know his possibilities don't obtain, and he is right. Attempts to avoid skepticism by claiming we do know these things are bound to fail. The skeptic's possibilities make us uneasy because, as we deeply realize, we do not know they don't obtain; it is not surprising that attempts to show we do know these things leave us suspicious, strike us even as bad faith.

. . .

The skeptic maintains that we know almost none of what we think we know. He has shown, much to our initial surprise, that we do not know his (nontrivial) possibility SK doesn't obtain. Thus, he has shown of one thing we thought we knew, that we didn't and don't. To the conclusion that we know almost nothing, it appears but a short step. For if we do not know we are not dreaming or being deceived by a demon or floating in a tank, then how can I know, for example, that I am sitting before a page writing with a pen, and how can you know that you are reading a page of a book?

However, although our account of knowledge agrees with the skeptic in saying that we do not know that not-SK, it places no formidable barriers before my knowing that I am writing on a page with a pen. It is true that I am, I believe I am, if I weren't I wouldn't believe I was, and if I were, I would believe it. (I leave out the reference to method.) Also, it is true that you are reading a page (please, don't stop now!), you believe you are, if you weren't reading a page you wouldn't believe you were, and if you were reading a page you would believe you were. So according to the account, I do know that I am writing on a page with a pen, and you do know that you are reading a page. The account does not lead to any general skepticism.

Yet we must grant that it appears that if the skeptic is right that we don't know we are not dreaming or being deceived or floating in the tank, then it cannot be that I know I am writing with a pen or that you know you are reading a page. So we must scrutinize with special care the skeptic's "short step" to the conclusion that we don't know these things, for either this step cannot be taken or our account of knowledge is incoherent.

NONCLOSURE

In taking the "short step", the skeptic assumes that if S knows that *p* and he knows that "*p* entails *q*" then he also knows that *q*. In the terminology of the logicians, the skeptic assumes that knowledge is closed under known logical implication; that the operation of moving from something known to something else known to be entailed by it does not take us outside of the (closed) area of knowledge. He intends, of course, to work things backwards, arguing that since the person does not know that *q*, assuming (at least for the purposes of argument) that he does know that *p* entails *q*, it follows that he does not know that *p*. For if he did know that *p*, he would also know that *q*, which he doesn't.

The details of different skeptical arguments vary in their structure, but each one will assume some variant of the principle that knowledge is closed under known logical implication. If we abbreviate "knowledge that *p*" by "Kp" and abbreviate "entails" by the fish-hook sign "⥽," we can write this principle of closure as the subjunctive principle

$$\text{P: } K(p \multimap q) \,\&\, Kp \rightarrow Kq.$$

If a person were to know that *p* entails *q* and he were to know that *p* then he would know that *q*. The statement that *q* follows by modus ponens from the other two stated as known in the antecedent of the subjunctive principle P; this principle counts on the person to draw the inference to *q*.

You know that your being in a tank on Alpha Centauri entails your not being in place X where you are. (I assume here a limited readership.) And you know also the contrapositive, that your being at place X entails that you are not then in a tank on Alpha Centauri. If you knew you were at X you would know you're not in a tank (of a specified sort) at Alpha Centauri. But you do not know this last fact (the skeptic has argued and we have agreed) and so (he argues) you don't know the first. Another intuitive way of putting the skeptic's argument is as follows. If you know that two statements are incompatible and you know the first is true then you know the denial of the second. You know that your being at X and your being in a tank on Alpha Centauri are incompatible; so if you knew you were at X you would know you were not in the (specified) tank on Alpha Centauri. Since you do not know the second, you don't know the first.[5]

No doubt, it is possible to argue over the details of principle P, to point out it is incorrect as it stands. Perhaps, though Kp, the person does not know that he knows that *p* (that is, not-KKp) and so does not draw the inference to *q*. Or perhaps he doesn't draw the inference because not-$KK(p \multimap q)$. Other similar principles face their own difficulties: for example, the principle that $K(p \rightarrow q) \rightarrow (Kp \rightarrow Kq)$ fails if Kp stops $p \rightarrow q$ from being true, that is, if $Kp \rightarrow$ not-$(p \rightarrow q)$; the principle that $K(p \multimap q) \rightarrow K(Kp \rightarrow Kq)$

faces difficulties if Kp makes the person forget that (p ⥽ q) and so he fails to draw the inference to *q*.

. . .

We would be ill-advised, however, to quibble over the details of P. Although these details are difficult to get straight, it will continue to appear that something like P is correct. If S knows that "*p* entails *q*" and he knows that *p* and knows that "(*p* and *p* entails *q*) entails *q*" . . . and he does draw the inference to *q* from all this and believes *q* via the process of drawing this inference, then will he not know that *q*? And what is wrong with simplifying this mass of detail by writing merely principle P, provided we apply it only to cases where the mass of detail holds, as it surely does in the skeptical cases under consideration? For example, I do realize that my being in the Van Leer Foundation Building in Jerusalem entails that I am not in a tank on Alpha Centauri; I am capable of drawing inferences now; I do believe I am not in a tank on Alpha Centauri (though not solely via this inference, surely); and so forth. Won't this satisfy the correctly detailed principle, and shouldn't it follow that I know I am not (in that tank) on Alpha Centauri? The skeptic agrees it should follow; so he concludes from the fact that I don't know I am not floating in the tank on Alpha Centauri that I don't know I am in Jerusalem. Uncovering difficulties in the details of particular formulations of P will not weaken the principle's intuitive appeal; such quibbling will seem at best like a wasp attacking a steamroller, at worst like an effort in bad faith to avoid being pulled along by the skeptic's argument.

Principle P is wrong, however, and not merely in detail. Knowledge is not closed under known logical implication.[6] S knows that *p* when S has a true belief that *p*, and S wouldn't have a false belief that *p* (condition 3) and S would have a true belief that *p* (condition 4). Neither of these latter two conditions is closed under known logical implication.

Let us begin with condition

(3) if *p* were false, S wouldn't believe that *p*.

When S knows that *p*, his belief that *p* is contingent on the truth of *p*, contingent in the way the subjunctive condition 3 describes. Now it might be that *p* entails *q* (and S knows this), that S's belief that *p* is subjunctively contingent on the truth of *p*, that S believes *q*, yet his belief that *q* is not subjunctively dependent on the truth of *q*, in that it (or he) does not satisfy:

(3′) if *q* were false, S wouldn't believe that *q*.

For 3′ talks of what S would believe if *q* were false, and this may be a very different situation than the one that would hold if *p* were false, even though *p* entails *q*. That you were born in a certain city entails that you were born on earth. Yet contemplating what (actually) would be the situation if you were not born in that city is very different from contemplating what situation would hold if you weren't born on earth. Just as those possibilities are very different, so what is believed in them may be very different. When *p* entails *q* (and not the other way around) *p* will be a stronger statement than *q*, and so not-*q* (which is the antecedent of 3′) will be a stronger statement than not-*p* (which is the antecedent of 3). There is no reason to assume you will have the same beliefs in these two cases, under these suppositions of differing strengths.

There is no reason to assume the (closest) not-*p* world and the (closest) not-*q* world are doxically identical for you, and no reason to assume, even though *p* entails *q*, that your beliefs in one of these worlds would be a (proper) subset of your beliefs in the other.

Consider now the two statements:

p = I am awake and sitting on a chair in Jerusalem;
q = I am not floating in a tank on Alpha Centauri being stimulated by electrochemical means to believe that *p*.

The first one entails the second: *p* entails *q*. Also, I know that *p* entails *q*; and I know that *p*. If *p* were false, I would be standing or lying down in the same city, or perhaps sleeping there, or perhaps in a neighboring city or town. If *q* were false, I would be floating in a tank on Alpha Centauri. Clearly these are very different situations, leading to great differences in what I then would believe. If *p* were false, if I weren't awake and sitting on a chair in Jerusalem,

I would not believe that p. Yet if q were false, if I was floating in a tank on Alpha Centauri, I would believe that q, that I was not in the tank, and indeed, in that case, I would still believe that p. According to our account of knowledge, I know that p yet I do not know that q, even though (I know) p entails q.

This failure of knowledge to be closed under known logical implication stems from the fact that condition 3 is not closed under known logical implication; condition 3 can hold of one statement believed while not of another known to be entailed by the first. It is clear that any account that includes as a necessary condition for knowledge the subjunctive condition 3, not-$p \rightarrow$ not-(S believes that p), will have the consequence that knowledge is not closed under known logical implication.[7]

When p entails q and you believe each of them, if you do not have a false belief that p (since p is true) then you do not have a false belief that q. However, if you are to know something not only don't you have a false belief about it, but also you wouldn't have a false belief about it. Yet, we have seen how it may be that p entails q and you believe each and you wouldn't have a false belief that p yet you might have a false belief that q (that is, it is not the case that you wouldn't have one). Knowledge is not closed under the known logical implication because "wouldn't have a false belief that" is not closed under known logical implication.

If knowledge were the same as (simply) true belief then it would be closed under known logical implication (provided the implied statements were believed). Knowledge is not simply true belief, however; additional conditions are needed. These further conditions will make knowledge open under known logical implication, even when the entailed statement is believed, when at least one of the further conditions itself is open. Knowledge stays closed (only) if all of the additional conditions are closed. I lack a general nontrivial characterization of those conditions that are closed under known logical implication; possessing such an illuminating characterization, one might attempt to prove that no additional conditions of that sort could provide an adequate analysis of knowledge.

Still, we can say the following. A belief that p is knowledge that p only if it somehow varies with the truth of p. The causal condition for knowledge specified that the belief was "produced by" the fact, but that condition did not provide the right sort of varying with the fact. The subjunctive conditions 3 and 4 are our attempt to specify that varying. But however an account spells this out, it will hold that whether a belief that p is knowledge partly depends on what goes on with the belief in some situations when p is false. An account that says nothing about what is believed in any situation when p is false cannot give us any mode of varying with the fact.

Because what is preserved under logical implication is truth, any condition that is preserved under known logical implication is most likely to speak only of what happens when p, and q, are true, without speaking at all of what happens when either one is false. Such a condition is incapable of providing "varies with"; so adding only such conditions to true belief cannot yield an adequate account of knowledge.

A belief's somehow varying with the truth of what is believed is not closed under known logical implication. Since knowledge that p involves such variation, knowledge also is not closed under known logical implication. The skeptic cannot easily deny that knowledge involves such variation, for his argument that we don't know that we're not floating in that tank, for example, uses the fact that knowledge does involve variation. ("If you were floating in the tank you would still think you weren't, so you don't know that you're not.") Yet, though one part of his argument uses that fact that knowledge involves such variation, another part of his argument presupposes that knowledge does not involve any such variation. This latter is the part that depends upon knowledge being closed under known logical implication, as when the skeptic argues that since you don't know that not-SK, you don't know you are not floating in the tank, then you also don't know, for example, that you are now reading a book. That closure can hold only if the variation does not. The skeptic cannot be right both times. According to our view he is right when he holds that knowledge involves such variation and so concludes that we don't know, for example, that we are not floating in that tank; but he is wrong when he assumes knowledge is closed under known logical implication and concludes that we know hardly anything.

Knowledge is a real factual relation, subjunctively specifiable, whose structure admits our standing in this relation, tracking, to p without standing in it to some q which we know p to entail. Any relation embodying some variation of belief with the fact, with the truth (value), will exhibit this structural feature. The skeptic is right that we don't track some particular truths—the ones stating that his skeptical possibilities SK don't hold—but wrong that we don't stand in the real knowledge-relation of tracking to many other truths, including ones that entail these first mentioned truths we believe but don't know.

The literature on skepticism contains writers who endorse these skeptical arguments (or similar narrower ones), but confess their inability to maintain their skeptical beliefs at times when they are not focusing explicitly on the reasoning that led them to skeptical conclusions. The most notable example of this is Hume:

> I am ready to reject all belief and reasoning, and can look upon no opinion even as more probable or likely than another ... Most fortunately it happens that since reason is incapable of dispelling these clouds, nature herself suffices to that purpose, and cures me of this philosophical melancholy and delirium, either by relaxing this bent of mind, or by some avocation, and lively impression of my senses, which obliterate all these chimeras. I dine, I play a game of backgammon, I converse, and am merry with my friends; and when after three or four hours' amusement, I would return to these speculations, they appear so cold, and strained, and ridiculous, that I cannot find in my heart to enter into them any farther. (*A Treatise of Human Nature*, Book I, Part IV, section VII)

> The great subverter of Pyrrhonism or the excessive principles of skepticism is action, and employment, and the occupations of common life. These principles may flourish and triumph in the schools; where it is, indeed, difficult, if not impossible, to refute them. But as soon as they leave the shade, and by the presence of the real objects, which actuate our passions and sentiments, are put in opposition to the more powerful principles of our nature, they vanish like smoke, and leave the most determined skeptic in the same condition as other mortals ... And though a Pyrrhonian may throw himself or others into a momentary amazement and confusion by his profound reasonings; the first and most trivial event in life will put to flight all his doubts and scruples, and leave him the same, in every point of action and speculation, with the philosophers of every other sect, or with those who never concerned themselves in any philosophical researches. When he awakes from his dream, he will be the first to join in the laugh against himself, and to confess that all his objections are mere amusement. (*An Enquiry Concerning Human Understanding*, Section XII, Part II)

The theory of knowledge we have presented explains why skeptics of various sorts have had such difficulties in sticking to their far-reaching skeptical conclusions "outside the study," or even inside it when they are not thinking specifically about skeptical arguments and possibilities SK.

The skeptic's arguments do show (but show only) that we don't know the skeptic's possibilities SK do not hold; and he is right that we don't track the fact that SK does not hold. (If it were to hold, we would still think it didn't.) However, the skeptic's arguments don't show we do not know other facts (including facts that entail not-SK) for we do track these other facts (and knowledge is not closed under known logical entailment.) Since we do track these other facts—you, for example, the fact that you are reading a book; I, the fact that I am writing on a page—and the skeptic tracks such facts too, it is not surprising that when he focuses on them, on his relationship to such facts, the skeptic finds it hard to remember or maintain his view that he does not know those facts. Only by shifting his attention back to his relationship to the (different) fact that not-SK, which relationship is not tracking, can he revive his skeptical belief and make it salient. However, this skeptical triumph is evanescent, it vanishes when his attention turns to other facts. Only by fixating on the skeptical possibilities SK can he maintain his skeptical virtue; otherwise, unsurprisingly, he is forced to confess to sins of credulity.

NOTES

1. From the perspective of explanation rather than proof, the extensive philosophical discussion, deriving from Charles S. Peirce, of whether the skeptic's doubts are real is beside the point. The problem of explaining how knowledge is possible would remain the same, even if no one ever claimed to doubt that there was knowledge.

   In the introduction to *Philosophical Explanations*, the collection of essays from which this selection is excerpted, Nozick has the following to say about the distinction between explanation and proof: "Even if (deductive) proof and (deductive) explanation have the same abstract structure, wherein *p* is deduced from the statements *q*, the pragmatics of the two activities differ. In the case of explanation the thing (*p*) to be explained, to be deduced, must be known or at least believed to be true. If you are asked to explain why you are not reading this book now, you reject the request. Since you *are* reading it now there is no fact that you are not, to be explained. You don't set out to explain what you don't believe to be true. However you may set out to prove what you don't (yet) believe to be true; establishing it as true will induce the belief. . . . In order to prove *p*, however, you must start from premises *q*, from which you or those to whom you are proving *p*, know or believe. . . . An explanation on the other hand may introduce explanatory hypotheses (*q*) which are not already believed, from which to deduce *p* in explanatory fashion. Success in this explanatory deduction itself may lend support and induce belief, previously absent in the hypothesis." (*Philosophical Explanations*, pp. 13–14).
2. Should one weaken condition 3, so that the account of knowledge merely denies the opposed subjunctive R? That would give us: not-(not-*p* → S believes *p*). This holds when 3 does not, in situations where if *p* were false, S might believe *p*, and also might not believe it. The extra strength of 3 is needed to exclude these as situations of knowledge.
3. Though it does show the falsity of the corresponding entailment, "not-*p* entails not-(S believes that *p*)."
4. If a person is to know that SK doesn't hold, then condition 3 for knowledge must be satisfied (with "SK doesn't hold" substituted for *p*). Thus, we get

   (3) not-(SK doesn't hold) → not-(S believes that SK doesn't hold).

   Simplifying the antecedent, we have

   (3) SK holds → not-(S believes that SK doesn't hold).

   The skeptic has chosen a situation SK such that the following is true of it:

   SK holds → S believes that SK doesn't hold.

   Having the same antecedent as 3 and a contradictory consequent, this is incompatible with 3. Thus, condition 3 is not satisfied by the person's belief that SK does not hold.
5. This argument proceeds from the fact that floating in the tank is incompatible with being at X. Another form of the skeptic's argument, one we shall consider later, proceeds from the fact that floating in the tank is incompatible with knowing you are at X (or almost anything else).
6. Note that I am not denying that Kp & K(p ⥽ q) → Believes q.
7. Does this same consequence of nonclosure under known logical implication follow as well from condition 4: *p* → S believes that *p*? When *p* is not actually true, condition 4 can hold of *p* yet not of a *q* known to be entailed by *p*. For example, let *p* be the (false) statement that I am in Antarctica, and let *q* be the disjunction of *p* with some other appropriate statement; for example, let *q* be the statement that I am in Antarctica or I lost some object yesterday though I have not yet realized it. If *p* were true I would know it, *p* entails *q*, yet if *q* were true I wouldn't know it, for the way it would be true would be by my losing some object without yet realizing it, and if that happened I would not know it.

   This example to show that condition 4 is not closed under known logical implication depends on the (actual) falsity of *p*. I do not think there is any suitable example to show this in the case where *p* is true, leaving aside the trivial situation when the person simply does not infer the entailed statement *q*.

Cartesian Skepticism and Inference to the Best Explanation*

JONATHAN VOGEL

Jonathan Vogel teaches philosophy at Amherst College. He is best known for his work in epistemology.

The selection that follows originally appeared as an article in a philosophy journal in 1990. In it, Vogel offers a response to Descartes' skeptical challenge by appealing to the notion of inference to the best explanation.

The problem of skepticism about the external world, or Cartesian skepticism, has its roots in the underdetermination of theory by evidence. We each adopt a body of common-sense beliefs about the world which answers to our sensory experience. In principle, however, the beliefs we base on that experience are subject to underdetermination, and we can devise radical alternatives to the common-sense account. Such alternatives take the form of skeptical hypotheses, like Descartes's fiction that his experiences are caused by an evil demon.[†]

Certainly, when the choice arises, we hold to the common-sense view, and reject its skeptical competitors.[1] But what (epistemic) reasons can we have for doing so? In cases of underdetermination generally, principles of inference to the best explanation can license the choice of one theory over others. Accordingly, we would be justified in preferring the common-sense account to skeptical hypotheses, if the common-sense account provides better explanations of why our experience is the way it is.[2] My purpose here is to inquire into the explanatory advantages of the common-sense view, and to develop a response to skepticism along the lines just indicated.[3]

One obstacle to carrying out this project is that the standards by which explanations are evaluated are themselves difficult to identify and to make precise. In what follows, I shall be making some controversial assumptions about explanatory goodness, and I shall have to rely on largely unanalyzed notions of simplicity, ad-hoc-ness, and the like. To be explicit, I shall presuppose:

(a) Ad hoc explanations should be avoided, i.e., very roughly, if A is offered as an explanation of B, A ought not to be isolated from other explanations and data (it ought to be independently testable, it must figure in the explanation of something other than B, etc.).

(b) Other things being equal, a simpler explanation is superior to a more complicated one.

(c) Where explanation is concerned, more is better, if you get something for it. In particular, it is desirable to be able to give higher-level explanations of lower-level ones.

Another methodological point requires some comment. In comparing skeptical hypotheses with our everyday account of the world, I shall exclude from the latter any advanced scientific beliefs. To be sure, science adds great power and coherence to our explanations of phenomena, and one might argue that no explanatory scheme the skeptic devises could seriously compete with our best scientific theories.

* I would like to thank Phillip Bricker, Anthony Brueckner, Jeremy Butterfield, Stewart Cohen, Richard Feldman, Mark Johnston, Peter Lipton, Thomas Tymoczko, and Daniel Velleman. Research for this paper was supported by the American Council of Learned Societies and the National Endowment for the Humanities.

† See Descartes' *First Meditation* p. 351 this volume.

The Journal of Philosophy, Vol. 87, No. 11, Eighty-Seventh Annual Meeting American Philosophical Association, Eastern Division. (November 1990), pp. 658–666.

But it seems implausible that, without such theories, we would lack adequate grounds for rejecting skeptical hypotheses. Accordingly, I shall try to show that even a scientifically unsophisticated common-sense view of the world provides more adequate explanations than its skeptical competitors.

I

Our beliefs about the external world serve an explanatory function. A person's sensory experience exhibits patterns and regularities at many levels, and our common-sense beliefs account for these in ways that seem to be coherent and economical. I shall call the body of these beliefs the *real-world hypothesis* (RWH).[4]

The skeptic points out that there are alternative explanations of how a person's sensory experience arises. In principle, a great many ways of formulating and developing these counterhypotheses are open to the skeptic—for example, through various stories about evil demons and brains in vats. But elaborate (not to mention crazy) fantasies of deception may be only tenuously connected to the content of one's experiences and may lack cohesiveness. For instance, suppose that you seem to see some snow falling, and the skeptic suggests that this experience is being foisted on you by a demon. Then, to explain why the demon makes you have snow experience (rather than experience of some other kind), the skeptic tells you that there is a second demon that has put the first one up to it. Clearly, we are not getting anywhere; positing a second demon that directs the first on this occasion (and does only that) is explanatorily idle or ad hoc. The skeptic could try to escape such a result by refusing to say in any detail how your experiences come about. A hypothesis in this vein might specify only that your experiences are all caused by some deceptive spirit, and no more. The cure is as bad as the disease, however: the skeptic will succeed in avoiding ad hoc higher-level posits only by foregoing higher-level explanations altogether.

The RWH, by contrast, gives us a rich and well-integrated explanatory apparatus. We not only posit objects that cause our experiences, we are also able to explain why and how these objects behave as they do. If the explanations provided by a skeptical counterhypothesis are either ad hoc or impoverished in comparison with those of the RWH, then we have good grounds for preferring the latter to the former. According to the skeptic, we fail to know things because the RWH is faced with competitors that we have no reason to reject. But we have just seen that not any competitor will do. The skeptic's position will be empty unless he can provide us with reason to think that a *satisfactory* competitor exists (in particular, a sufficiently rich competitor that is not unduly burdened with ad hoc explanatory posits).

The lesson here is that the skeptic needs to frame an alternative that matches the RWH very closely. If a skeptical hypothesis can be made sufficiently similar in relevant respects to the RWH, then, one might expect, that skeptical hypothesis will match the RWH in explanatory adequacy. To the extent that explanatory virtues like coherence, depth, and simplicity are matters of theoretical structure, a skeptical hypothesis that is isomorphic to the RWH will explain things just as well as the RWH does. An improved skeptical hypothesis of this sort has to satisfy two principal constraints: (i) it should invoke items corresponding to the elements of the RWH; (ii) it should also posit, as holding of these items, a pattern of properties, relations, and explanatory generalizations mirroring those of the RWH.

As an example of how this would work, suppose you seem to see the wind blowing a piece of paper off your desk. According to the RWH, your visual impressions of the paper flying off your desk are caused by the paper. Similarly, your tactile sensations of the wind are caused by a real movement of air against your skin. And, finally, the wind stands in a relation of cause and effect to the movement of the paper. The skeptic's procedure will be to extract the explanatory skeleton or core from the RWH—that there are *some* entities bearing *some* properties that are related in ways exactly analogous to those specified by the RWH—and then to add that the entities and their properties are somehow different from the ones mentioned in the RWH.[5]

Thus, a skeptical hypothesis might present the following alternative explanation of your experiences. All that there is to the world is your brain in a vat, and a computer that is connected to your brain.

Your tactile experiences are caused by the realization of a computer program that simulates wind, and your visual impressions are caused by the realization of another program that simulates a paper blowing off a desk. Also, the skeptical hypothesis can specify that the first routine calls the second, so that (as in the RWH) the cause of the wind experience would be the cause of the paper-blowing experience. This way of reconstructing the explanatory structure of a small fragment of the RWH might be extended to apply to all the entities and explanatory connections posited by the RWH. The result would be a skeptical hypothesis that was completely isomorphic to the RWH, with portions of the computer disk supposed to occupy the explanatory roles we normally assign to familiar objects.[6] I shall be calling this the *computer skeptical hypothesis* (CSH).

Of course, the CSH is an outlandish suggestion, and we are confident that it is false. Yet, in reflecting on this situation philosophically, it is possible to misread what has gone wrong. One proposal is that skeptical hypotheses are invariably burdened with more unexplained explainers than is the RWH.[7] The CSH will lack answers to questions like "Why does the computer operate the way it does?" or "Where did the computer come from in the first place?" But it is not at all clear that the RWH does any better in the face of analogous demands. Both the CSH and the RWH invoke ultimate regularities that are not themselves explained, and neither can account for the existence of the physical world as such. Generally, since the RWH and the CSH are meant to have the same structure, anywhere the RWH can explain a lower-level phenomenon by a higher-level regularity, the CSH should be able to do the same. The CSH will have unexplained explainers only insofar as the RWH has them also.

Another suggestion that enjoys some currency is that the RWH is, in a very straightforward way, simpler than the CSH, and hence to be preferred. The idea here is that there would be a one-one mapping from the objects posited by the RWH to their stand-ins in the computer's memory, where these are treated as discrete individuals. There are, though, items required (at least tacitly) by the CSH which escape this mapping, e.g., the computer's central processing unit and perhaps the brain in the vat itself. So, the argument runs, the CSH is committed to the existence of more items than the RWH, and is to be preferred on that account.

This line of thought is problematic in several respects. First, one could just as well argue that the CSH is simpler than the RWH, on the grounds that the CSH posits only two objects (the computer and one's brain), whereas the RWH is committed to the existence of a great many more things. Moreover, it is far from clear that, all by itself, positing fewer entities is a theoretical virtue.[8] And finally, if need be, the CSH could be revised to eliminate the role of the central processing unit altogether. The skeptic could suppose that the elements of the computer memory act directly on each other, and on the seat of consciousness, in causal patterns that mirror those of the RWH.

Now, as will emerge shortly, I think there is something right about the claims that the CSH is less coherent and less simple than the RWH. But if explanatory coherence and simplicity are treated solely in structural terms, it should not be surprising that these claims do not go through. After all, the causal-explanatory structures invoked by the RWH and the CSH are identical; the two differ only as to what entities bear the specified causal relations to one another.

The rejoinders just considered miss something important about the motivations behind the skeptic's argument. At root, the skeptic questions our ability to read off the "real" or intrinsic character of things from those things' causal behavior. This challenge emerges in its simplest form with the initial thought that one's experience of any familiar object might be caused by something other than that object (e.g., an evil demon). The point is that the known effect—namely, your experience—does not fix the character of its cause.[9]

On the face of it, the requirement that a skeptical hypothesis must have a more fully articulated structure—one that matches the RWH in various ways—seems insufficient to meet this problem. For, if we assume that causal relations are contingent and that there is in principle no obstacle to our positing whatever causal relations we like, what reason could there be why one set of entities is better suited than another to occupy the positions within the structure of the RWH itself? It would appear that, in principle, there should be skeptical hypotheses that will explain the contents of one's experience just as well as the RWH. The choice between such hypotheses and the RWH will then be arbitrary, giving the skeptic what he needs.

II

To appreciate the superiority of the RWH over its skeptical competitors, we need to take into account the content, as well as the form, of the explanations the RWH provides. In particular, our ordinary view of things involves beliefs in the existence of objects with familiar spatial characteristics (e.g., we believe that there are bricks that are oblong and oranges that are round). The ascription of specific spatial properties to objects does explanatory work within the RWH (e.g., accounting for why oranges roll easily and bricks do not). Since the CSH posits objects with altogether different spatial characteristics—we are assuming that its objects are just portions of a computer disk—the CSH will have to account for the relevant phenomena in some other fashion. But by bringing in these additional explanations (whatever they may be), the CSH runs the risk of taking on a more elaborate explanatory apparatus than the RWH. To put the point I am trying to make more directly: niceties aside, the fact that something is spherical explains why it behaves like a sphere (in its interactions with us and with other things). If something that *is not* a sphere behaves like one, this will call for a more extended explanation.

This intuitive claim is bound to raise some philosophical qualms. Why must the fact that the CSH invokes *different* configurations of matter in its explanations mean that CSH has to be *more complicated* than the RWH? Again, setting niceties aside, why is the skeptic not free to stipulate that, in his account, it is certain magnetic patterns on a disk, not spheres, which behave like spheres (at least in terms of the experiences they bring about, directly and indirectly)?

Let us see just what would be involved in maintaining an explanatory parity between the CSH and RWH. To fix ideas, suppose that, according to the RWH, there is a hyacinth beside your doorway. For each RWH object, there has to be a CSH counterpart, which we can imagine to be the piece of the computer disk which stores the information about the object to be simulated. So, the CSH would have it that there is a piece of the disk holding a file about a hyacinth beside your door, specifically. Moreover, wherever the RWH assigns a certain property to the hyacinth, the CSH must ascribe a corresponding, but different property to the hyacinth's CSH analog. According to the RWH, the hyacinth has a particular location, namely, that of being beside your door. The hyacinth counterpart will have some parallel feature, which we might call a "pseudo location." The pseudo location of the hyacinth counterpart is just that physical property in virtue of which the counterpart simulates being located near your door. In general, what the RWH explains by reference to genuine locations, the CSH will explain in terms of these pseudo locations.

Since we make reference to the locations of objects in giving various everyday explanations, location properties are part of the explanatory apparatus of the RWH. Now, we find that the (genuine) locations ascribed to any two objects at a time are invariably different. We do not need any empirical law or regularity to explain this; it is a necessary truth pertaining to the nature of physical objects that there cannot be two such objects at the same place at the same time.[10]

The explanatory structure of the CSH is meant to duplicate that of the RWH. Since the CSH is isomorphic to the RWH, and the RWH always ascribes different locations to the objects it posits, the CSH will invariably ascribe different pseudo locations to things it posits. This calls for an explanation, if possible. At this point, however, the CSH faces a loss in either simplicity or explanatory power. To make the issue more concrete, imagine that the way things work in the CSH computer is that each object's pseudo location is the physical realization of having coordinates (x,y,z) written in its file.[11] There will have to be some explicit principle within the CSH that no two objects are to be assigned the same pseudo location, i.e., that no two objects are to have the same coordinates written in their files. Otherwise, the fact that no two objects have the same pseudo location remains unexplained. Of course, the CSH would include within it the necessary truth that two physical objects cannot occupy the same *genuine* location in space, but this is of no help to the CSH in explaining why two of its objects cannot have the same *pseudo* location. To achieve this, it would appear that the CSH has to add an extra empirical regularity, to which no regularity in the RWH corresponds. Such an addition will make the CSH inferior to the RWH on simplicity grounds, however.

The skeptic could escape this outcome if it could be guaranteed by some other necessary truth that different CSH objects will have different pseudo locations. In other words, the pseudo location of a CSH object would have to be encoded by some physical property *P* (other than that of having some specified location), such that it is impossible for two physical objects to have *P* at the same time. But it seems to me that there are no such physical properties. After all, if a given physical object with whatever properties exists at one place, it appears perfectly possible for there to be an absolutely similar object elsewhere, instantiating all the same properties at the same time—except location.[12]

Actually, the problem facing the skeptic is a general one, independent of the fact that CSH itself invokes physical objects (i.e., bits of computer disk) in its explanations. Suppose that the skeptic offers instead a quasi-Leibnizian* hypothesis, according to which the world consists solely of minds and their properties. These minds and their states are supposed to act in ways that mirror the behavior of everyday things as specified by the RWH. Each mind that stands in for a RWH object must have a property corresponding to the genuine location the RWH ascribes to its object; this pseudo location will be a (partial) mental state. The question arises again as to why these pseudo locations are invariably different from one mind to another. Presumably (*pace* Leibniz), it is possible for two different minds to think exactly the same thing at the same time, so no necessary truth prevents them from having the same pseudo location. Once again, such an occurrence would have to be ruled out by some kind of extra "exclusion principle," for which no counterpart exists in the RWH.

I claimed earlier that our normal ascription of spatial properties to things does real explanatory work; furthermore, it seems plausible that you incur an added explanatory burden if you suppose that something lacking a particular spatial property still behaves as though it had it. What I have been saying about locations and pseudo locations makes this same point on a more abstract level. In skeptical hypotheses, some other property (e.g., a magnetic property or a mental property) is supposed to substitute for the spatial property of being located at particular place. As we have seen, further explanation is then needed to establish why these properties, which are not genuine location properties, behave as though they were. It seems that this sort of difficulty will attach to skeptical hypotheses generally, giving us good reasons to reject them.[13]

III

I have presented some antiskeptical arguments based on explanatory considerations. But surely there is a world of familiar objects about us, and we have known that all along. So what, then, is the point of giving these arguments in the first place? This question deserves an extended response, but for now a very brief answer will have to do. I take it that the specious character of the explanations the skeptic offers is immediately apparent—they come across as contrived or unduly indirect—and this is a reason why we reject skepticism as a doctrine. Realizing that skeptical hypotheses are defective, however, is not the same thing as spelling out precisely what their defects are. To do this requires philosophical work—work of the sort I have undertaken here.

* German polymath Gottfried Wilhelm Leibniz (1646–1716) was one of the major European philosophers of the seventeenth century.

NOTES

1. Some philosophers, especially followers of Ludwig Wittgenstein, would deny that skeptical hypotheses can genuinely compete for acceptance with the

body of our common-sense beliefs. See, for example, Stanley Cavell, *The Claim of Reason* (New York: Oxford, 1979), pp. 218–220.

2. This approach to skepticism has been advocated by Michael Slote, Frank Jackson, Jonathan Bennett, James Cornman, J. L. Mackie, and Alan Goldman, among others.
3. On certain views about skepticism and about inference to the best explanation, this approach to skepticism will seem ill-conceived. One might hold that it is simply constitutive of rationality to reject skeptical hypotheses out of hand; thus, it is unnecessary to enter into the relative explanatory merits of the common-sense view and its skeptical alternatives. From another point of view, the explanatory advantages of the common-sense view could never give us a reason to accept it as *true*, rather than as merely handy or to our taste. The issues that arise here are important, and they must be addressed at some point by anyone who bases an answer to skepticism on explanatory considerations. These very general objections will be moot, however, if the appeal to explanatory considerations does not even succeed on its own terms. Whether it does so is my present concern.
4. This way of putting things may seem unfortunate to those who reject the representative theory of perception. But the point could be recast as follows: we have a set of beliefs about the world, i.e., the RWH. Our having those beliefs admits of alternative explanations, including skeptical explanations and the RWH itself. The tenability of skepticism turns on whether the truth of the RWH provides a better explanation than do skeptical hypotheses of why we believe the RWH in the first place.
5. Basically, this amounts to something like forming the Ramsey sentence of the RWH and adding to it further specifications that, in each case, the object or property denoted by the bound variables is something other than the one posited by the RWH. The RWH itself can be construed as the "Ramsey sentence" plus the stipulation that the objects and properties called for by the "Ramsey sentence" are indeed the familiar ones. See here Grover Maxwell, "Theories, Perception, and Structural Realism," in R. Colodny, ed., *The Nature and Function of Scientific Thought* (Pittsburgh: University Press, 1970) and for some needed refinements, David Lewis, "How to Define Theoretical Terms," *Philosophical Papers*, vol. I. (New York: Oxford, 1983). The possibility of framing skeptical hypotheses with the same structure as the RWH is noted by Lawrence Sklar in his "Saving the Noumena," *Philosophy and Spacetime Physics* (Berkeley: California UP, 1985), pp. 59–60.
6. We need not suppose that the computer itself was built or programmed by anyone. Rather, this hypothesis is to be understood simply as a description of an alternative way the (physical) world might be.
7. A claim of this sort is made by Alan Goldman, although it is directed at a fantastical skeptical story that postulates experimenters with deceptive motives. See Goldman, *Empirical Knowledge* (Berkeley: California UP, 1989), p. 212.
8. It could be objected that what matters for explanatory adequacy is not economy with respect to the number of individuals posited, but rather in the number of different kinds invoked. But this does not appear to help—the skeptic can get by with just a few kinds of things (brain, vat, computer) while the RWH might be said to invoke these and many more.
9. This was the way Kant understood the situation. The skeptic, he says, "assumed that the only immediate experience is inner experience and that from it we can only *infer* outer things—and this, moreover, only in an untrustworthy manner, as in all cases where we are inferring from given effects to determinate causes"; *The Critique of Pure Reason*, N. K. Smith, trans. (New York: St. Martin's, 1965), p. 245.
10. For a discussion of this principle, see Denis Robinson, "Re-identifying Matter," *The Philosophical Review*, XCI (1982): 317–341; on the role of necessary truths in explanations, see Clark Glymour, "Explanation and Realism," in J. Leplin, ed., *Scientific Realism* (Berkeley: California UP, 1984), esp. pp. 184–6.
11. For purposes of exposition, I am pretending that an object is located at a point rather than a region.
12. Of course, there are characterizations like "the only building taller than 110 stories" or "identical

to Socrates," which are satisfied by at most one object at a time. If these expressions involve reference to properties, they are properties of a different type than those with which I am concerned here.

13. One might try to frame a skeptical hypothesis that avoids this difficulty by assigning to objects different locations (and spatial properties generally) in place of those specified by the RWH. Formulated this way, our problem becomes one of choosing a particular geometry of the world from among those logically compatible with the empirical data, and one might continue to defend the choice of the RWH by appeal to explanatory considerations. See here Lawrence Sklar, *Space, Time, and Spacetime* (Berkeley: California UP, 1977), pp. 91–101, although Sklar himself is highly critical of such uses of inference to the best explanation. Sklar has a valuable discussion of the affinities between Cartesian skepticism and problems in the epistemology of geometry.

C KNOWLEDGE AND THE NATURE OF REALITY

"The Allegory of the Cave" from *The Republic*

PLATO

Plato (c. 428–347 BCE)—along with his student Aristotle—was one of the two most important philosophers of antiquity and is among the most important figures in the entire Western intellectual tradition. His wide-ranging discussions addressed nearly every philosophical topic imaginable and set the stage for philosophical exploration for the next two millennia. His philosophical writings take the form of dialogues that feature his teacher Socrates (469–399 BCE) as a character.

The first paragraph in our selection—"Next, I said compare the effect . . ."—is uttered by Socrates; the next— "I'm imagining it."—is uttered by Glaucon, who was Plato's older brother.

The selection that appears here is one of the most famous in the history of Western philosophy. In it, Socrates presents his conversation-partner Glaucon with an unforgettable image: the allegory of the cave. The text was originally written in ancient Greek and was translated by G. M. A. Grube and revised by C. D. C. Reeve. The numbers that appear in the margins of the text are called "Stephanus numbers"; they refer to the page numbers of a canonical edition of Plato's work prepared by Henricus Stephanus in 1578. Reference to these numbers enables coordination among readers who make use of different translations or editions.

Several additional selections from Plato's writings can be found in the sections on Moral and Political Philosophy and Life and Death.

BOOK VII

514 Next, I said, compare the effect of education and of the lack of it on our nature to an experience like this: Imagine human beings living in an underground, cavelike dwelling, with an entrance a long way up, which is both open to the light and as wide as the cave itself. They've been there since childhood, fixed in the same place, with their necks and legs fettered, able to see only in front of them, because their bonds prevent them from turning their heads around. Light is provided by a fire burning far above
and behind them. Also behind them, but on higher b
ground, there is a path stretching between them and the fire. Imagine that along this path a low wall has been built, like the screen in front of puppeteers above which they show their puppets.

I'm imagining it.

Then also imagine that there are people along the wall, carrying all kinds of artifacts that project above
it—statues of people and other animals, made out c
of stone, wood, and every material. And, as you'd

From *Republic,* trans. Grube, rev. Reeve. Copyright © 1992 by Hackett Publishing Company, Inc. Reprinted by permission of the publisher. All rights reserved.

515 expect, some of the carriers are talking, and some
are silent.

It's a strange image you're describing, and strange prisoners.

They're like us. Do you suppose, first of all, that these prisoners see anything of themselves and one another besides the shadows that the fire casts on the wall in front of them?

How could they, if they have to keep their heads
b motionless throughout life?

What about the things being carried along the wall? Isn't the same true of them?

Of course.

And if they could talk to one another, don't you think they'd suppose that the names they used applied to the things they see passing before them?

They'd have to.

And what if their prison also had an echo from the wall facing them? Don't you think they'd believe that the shadows passing in front of them were talking whenever one of the carriers passing along the wall was doing so?

I certainly do.

c Then the prisoners would in every way believe
that the truth is nothing other than the shadows of those artifacts.

They must surely believe that.

Consider, then, what being released from their bonds and cured of their ignorance would naturally be like, if something like this came to pass. When one of them was freed and suddenly compelled to stand up, turn his head, walk, and look up toward the light, he'd be pained and dazzled and unable to see the things whose shadows he'd seen before. What
d do you think he'd say, if we told him that what he'd
seen before was inconsequential, but that now—because he is a bit closer to the things that are and is turned towards things that are more—he sees more correctly? Or, to put it another way, if we pointed to each of the things passing by, asked him what each of them is, and compelled him to answer, don't you think he'd be at a loss and that he'd believe that the things he saw earlier were truer than the ones he was now being shown?

Much truer.

And if someone compelled him to look at the light itself, wouldn't his eyes hurt, and wouldn't he
turn around and flee towards the things he's able to e
see, believing that they're really clearer than the ones he's being shown?

He would.

And if someone dragged him away from there by force, up the rough, steep path, and didn't let him go until he had dragged him into the sunlight, wouldn't he be pained and irritated at being treated that way? And when he came into the light, with the sun filling his eyes, wouldn't he be unable to see a single 516
one of the things now said to be true?

He would be unable to see them, at least at first.

I suppose, then, that he'd need time to get adjusted before he could see things in the world above. At first, he'd see shadows most easily, then images of men and other things in water, then the things themselves. Of these, he'd be able to study the things in the sky and the sky itself more easily at night, looking at the light of the stars and the moon,
than during the day, looking at the sun and the light b
of the sun.

Of course.

Finally, I suppose, he'd be able to see the sun, not images of it in water or some alien place, but the sun itself, in its own place, and be able to study it.

Necessarily so.

And at this point he would infer and conclude that the sun provides the seasons and the years, gov-
erns everything in the visible world, and is in some c
way the cause of all the things that he used to see.

It's clear that would be his next step.

What about when he reminds himself of his first dwelling place, his fellow prisoners, and what passed for wisdom there? Don't you think that he'd count himself happy for the change and pity the others?

Certainly.

And if there had been any honors, praises, or prizes among them for the one who was sharpest at identifying the shadows as they passed by and who best remembered which usually came earlier, which
later, and which simultaneously, and who could thus d
best divine the future, do you think that our man would desire these rewards or envy those among the prisoners who were honored and held power? Instead, wouldn't he feel, with Homer, that he'd much prefer to "work the earth as a serf to another,

one without possessions,"* and go through any sufferings, rather than share their opinions and live as they do?

e I suppose he would rather suffer anything than
live like that.

Consider this too. If this man went down into the cave again and sat down in his same seat, wouldn't his eyes—coming suddenly out of the sun like that—be filled with darkness?

They certainly would.

And before his eyes had recovered—and the adjustment would not be quick—while his vision was
still dim, if he had to compete again with the perpet-
517 ual prisoners in recognizing the shadows, wouldn't
he invite ridicule? Wouldn't it be said of him that he'd returned from his upward journey with his eyesight ruined and that it isn't worthwhile even to try to travel upward? And, as for anyone who tried to free them and lead them upward, if they could somehow get their hands on him, wouldn't they kill him?

They certainly would.

b This whole image, Glaucon, must be fitted to-
gether with what we said before. The visible realm should be likened to the prison dwelling, and the light of the fire inside it to the power of the sun. And if you interpret the upward journey and the study of things above as the upward journey of the soul to the intelligible realm, you'll grasp what I hope to convey, since that is what you wanted to hear about. Whether it's true or not, only the god knows. But this is how I see it: In the knowable realm, the form of the good is the last thing to be seen, and it is reached only with difficulty. Once one has seen it, however, one must conclude that it is the cause of all
that is correct and beautiful in anything, that it pro-
c duces both light and its source in the visible realm,
and that in the intelligible realm it controls and provides truth and understanding, so that anyone who is to act sensibly in private or public must see it.

I have the same thought, at least as far as I'm able.

Come, then, share with me this thought also: It isn't surprising that the ones who get to this point are unwilling to occupy themselves with human affairs and that their souls are always pressing upwards, eager to spend their time above, for, after all,
this is surely what we'd expect, if indeed things fit
the image I described before. d

It is.

What about what happens when someone turns from divine study to the evils of human life? Do you think it's surprising, since his sight is still dim, and he hasn't yet become accustomed to the darkness around him, that he behaves awkwardly and appears completely ridiculous if he's compelled, either in the courts or elsewhere, to contend about the shadows of justice or the statues of which they are the shadows and to dispute about the way these
things are understood by people who have never
seen justice itself? e

That's not surprising at all.

No, it isn't. But anyone with any understand- 518
ing would remember that the eyes may be confused in two ways and from two causes, namely, when they've come from the light into the darkness *and* when they've come from the darkness into the light. Realizing that the same applies to the soul, when someone sees a soul disturbed and unable to see something, he won't laugh mindlessly, but he'll take into consideration whether it has come from a brighter life and is dimmed through not having yet become accustomed to the dark or whether it has come from greater ignorance into greater light and is dazzled by the increased brilliance. Then he'll declare the first soul happy in its experience and life,
and he'll pity the latter—but even if he chose to b
make fun of it, at least he'd be less ridiculous than if he laughed at a soul that has come from the light above.

What you say is very reasonable.

If that's true, then here's what we must think about these matters: Education isn't what some people declare it to be, namely, putting knowledge into
souls that lack it, like putting sight into blind eyes. c

They do say that.

But our present discussion, on the other hand, shows that the power to learn is present in everyone's soul and that the instrument with which each learns is like an eye that cannot be turned around from darkness to light without turning the whole

* This quote is from the famous ancient Greek poem *The Odyssey* (xi. 489–90).

body. This instrument cannot be turned around from that which is coming into being without turning the whole soul until it is able to study that which is and the brightest thing that is, namely, the one we
d call the good. Isn't that right?

Yes.

Then education is the craft concerned with doing this very thing, this turning around, and with how the soul can most easily and effectively be made to do it. It isn't the craft of putting sight into the soul. Education takes for granted that sight is there but that it isn't turned the right way or looking where it ought to look, and it tries to redirect it appropriately.

So it seems.

Now, it looks as though the other so-called virtues of the soul are akin to those of the body, for they really aren't there beforehand but are added later
e by habit and practice. However, the virtue of reason seems to belong above all to something more divine, which never loses its power but is either useful and beneficial or useless and harmful, depending on
519 the way it is turned. Or have you never noticed this about people who are said to be vicious but clever, how keen the vision of their little souls is and how sharply it distinguishes the things it is turned towards? This shows that its sight isn't inferior but rather is forced to serve evil ends, so that the sharper it sees, the more evil it accomplishes.

Absolutely.

However, if a nature of this sort had been hammered at from childhood and freed from the bonds of kinship with becoming, which have been fastened to it by feasting, greed, and other such pleasures and
b which, like leaden weights, pull its vision downwards—if, being rid of these, it turned to look at true things, then I say that the same soul of the same person would see these most sharply, just as it now does the things it is presently turned towards.

Probably so.

And what about the uneducated who have no experience of truth? Isn't it likely—indeed, doesn't it follow necessarily from what was said before—that they will never adequately govern a city? But neither would those who've been allowed to spend their whole lives being educated. The former would
c fail because they don't have a single goal at which all their actions, public and private, inevitably aim; the latter would fail because they'd refuse to act, thinking that they had settled while still alive in the faraway Isles of the Blessed.

That's true.

It is our task as founders, then, to compel the best natures to reach the study we said before is the most important, namely, to make the ascent and see the good. But when they've made it and looked sufficiently, we mustn't allow them to do what they're
allowed to do today. d

What's that?

To stay there and refuse to go down again to the prisoners in the cave and share their labors and honors, whether they are of less worth or of greater.

Then are we to do them an injustice by making them live a worse life when they could live a better one?

You are forgetting again that it isn't the law's e
concern to make any one class in the city outstandingly happy but to contrive to spread happiness throughout the city by bringing the citizens into harmony with each other through persuasion or compulsion and by making them share with each other the benefits that each class can confer on the
community. The law produces such people in the 520
city, not in order to allow them to turn in whatever direction they want, but to make use of them to bind the city together.

That's true, I had forgotten.

Observe, then, Glaucon, that we won't be doing an injustice to those who've become philosophers in our city and that what we'll say to them, when we compel them to guard and care for the others, will be just. We'll say: "When people like you come to be
in other cities, they're justified in not sharing in their b
city's labors, for they've grown there spontaneously, against the will of the constitution. And what grows of its own accord and owes no debt for its upbringing has justice on its side when it isn't keen to pay anyone for that upbringing. But we've made you kings in our city and leaders of the swarm, as it were, both for yourselves and for the rest of the city. You're better and more completely educated than the others and
are better able to share in both types of life. There- c
fore each of you in turn must go down to live in the common dwelling place of the others and grow

accustomed to seeing in the dark. When you are used to it, you'll see vastly better than the people there. And because you've seen the truth about fine, just, and good things, you'll know each image for what it is and also that of which it is the image. Thus, for you and for us, the city will be governed, not like the majority of cities nowadays, by people who fight over shadows and struggle against one another in order to rule—as if that were a great good—but by people who are awake rather than dreaming, for the truth is
d surely this: A city whose prospective rulers are least eager to rule must of necessity be most free from civil war, whereas a city with the opposite kind of rulers is governed in the opposite way."

Absolutely.

Then do you think that those we've nurtured will disobey us and refuse to share the labors of the city, each in turn, while living the greater part of their time with one another in the pure realm?

It isn't possible, for we'll be giving just orders to e
just people. Each of them will certainly go to rule as to something compulsory, however, which is exactly the opposite of what's done by those who now rule in each city.

Selections from *Of the Principles of Human Knowledge*

GEORGE BERKELEY

Irish philosopher George Berkeley (1685–1753) was one of the most important philosophers of the early modern period. He defended a philosophical outlook known as *idealism*, according to which reality is fundamentally mental, as opposed to physical.

The selections presented here are taken from his *A Treatise Concerning the Principles of Human Knowledge* (1710); it appears in its original eighteenth-century English. Explanatory notes are thanks to philosopher Ken Winkler, the editor of the edition from which this selection is taken.

1. It is evident to anyone who takes a survey of the objects of human knowledge, that they are either ideas actually imprinted on the senses, or else such as are perceived by attending to the passions and operations of the mind, or lastly ideas formed by help of memory and imagination, either compounding, dividing, or barely representing those originally perceived in the aforesaid ways. By sight I have the ideas of light and colors with their several degrees and variations. By touch I perceive, for example, hard and soft, heat and cold, motion and resistance, and of all these more and less either as to quantity or degree. Smelling furnishes me with odors; the palate with tastes, and hearing conveys sounds to the mind in all their variety of tone and composition. And as several of these are observed to accompany each other, they come to be marked by one name, and so to be reputed as one thing. Thus, for example, a certain color, taste, smell, figure and consistence having been observed to go together, are accounted one distinct thing, signified by the name *apple*. Other collections of ideas constitute a stone, a tree, a book, and the like sensible things; which, as they are pleasing or disagreeable, excite the passions of love, hatred, joy, grief, and so forth.

2. But besides all that endless variety of ideas or objects of knowledge, there is likewise something which knows or perceives them, and exercises divers operations, as willing, imagining, remembering about them. This perceiving, active being is what I call *mind, spirit, soul* or *myself*. By which words I do not denote any one of my ideas, but a thing entirely distinct from them, wherein they exist, or, which is the same thing, whereby they are perceived; for the existence of an idea consists in being perceived.

3. That neither our thoughts, nor passions, nor ideas formed by the imagination, exist without the mind, is what everybody will allow. And it seems no less evident that the various sensations or ideas imprinted on the sense, however blended or combined together (that is, whatever objects they compose) cannot exist otherwise than in a mind perceiving them. I think an intuitive knowledge may be obtained of this, by anyone that shall attend to what is meant by the term *exist* when applied to sensible things. The table I write on, I say, exists, that is, I see and feel it; and if I were out of my study I should say it existed, meaning thereby that if I was in my study I might perceive it, or that some other spirit actually does perceive it. There was an odor, that is, it was smelled; there was a sound, that is to say, it was heard; a color or figure, and it was perceived by sight or touch. This is all that I can understand by these and the like expressions. For as to what is said of the absolute existence of unthinking things without any relation to their being perceived, that seems perfectly unintelligible. Their *esse* is *percipi*, nor is it possible they should have any existence, out of the minds or thinking things which perceive them.*

4. It is indeed an opinion strangely prevailing amongst men, that houses, mountains, rivers, and in a word all sensible objects have an existence natural or real, distinct from their being perceived by the understanding. But with how great an assurance and acquiescence soever this principle may be entertained in the world; yet whoever shall find in his heart to call it in question, may, if I mistake not, perceive it to involve a manifest contradiction. For what are the forementioned objects but the things we perceive by sense, and what do we perceive besides our own ideas or sensations; and is it not plainly repugnant that any one of these or any combination of them should exist unperceived?

5. If we thoroughly examine this tenet, it will, perhaps, be found at bottom to depend on the doctrine of *abstract ideas*. For can there be a nicer strain of abstraction than to distinguish the existence of sensible objects from their being perceived, so as to conceive them existing unperceived? Light and colors, heat and cold, extension and figures, in a word the things we see and feel, what are they but so many sensations, notions, ideas or impressions on the sense; and is it possible to separate, even in thought, any of these from perception? For my part I might as easily divide a thing from itself. I may indeed divide in my thoughts or conceive apart from each other those things which, perhaps, I never perceived by sense so divided. Thus I imagine the trunk of a human body without the limbs, or conceive the smell of a rose without thinking on the rose itself. So far I will not deny I can abstract, if that may properly be called *abstraction*, which extends only to the conceiving separately such objects, as it is possible may really exist or be actually perceived asunder. But my conceiving or imagining power does not extend beyond the possibility of real existence or perception. Hence as it is impossible for me to see or feel anything without an actual sensation of that thing, so is it impossible for me to conceive in my thoughts any sensible thing or object distinct from the sensation or perception of it.[1]

6. Some truths there are so near and obvious to the mind, that a man need only open his eyes to see them. Such I take this important one to be, to wit, that all the choir of heaven and furniture of the earth, in a word all those bodies which compose the mighty frame of the world, have not any subsistence without a mind, that their being is to be perceived or known; that consequently so long as they are not actually perceived by me, or do not exist in my mind or that of any other created spirit, they must either have no existence at all, or else subsist in the mind of some eternal spirit: it being perfectly unintelligible and involving all the absurdity of abstraction, to attribute to any single part of them an existence independent of a spirit. To be convinced of which, the reader need only reflect and try to separate in his own thoughts the being of a sensible thing from its being perceived.

* *esse*, to be; *percipi*, to be perceived.

7. From what has been said, it follows, there is not any other substance than *spirit*, or that which perceives. But for the fuller proof of this point, let it be considered, the sensible qualities are color, figure, motion, smell, taste, and such like, that is, the ideas perceived by sense. Now for an idea to exist in an unperceiving thing, is a manifest contradiction; for to have an idea is all one as to perceive: that therefore wherein color, figure, and the like qualities exist, must perceive them; hence it is clear there can be no unthinking substance or *substratum* of those ideas.

8. But say you, though the ideas themselves do not exist without the mind, yet there may be things like them whereof they are copies or resemblances, which things exist without the mind, in an unthinking substance. I answer, an idea can be like nothing but an idea; a color or figure can be like nothing but another color or figure. If we look but ever so little into our thoughts, we shall find it impossible for us to conceive a likeness except only between our ideas. Again, I ask whether those supposed originals or external things, of which our ideas are the pictures or representations, be themselves perceivable or no? If they are, then they are ideas, and we have gained our point; but if you say they are not, I appeal to anyone whether it be sense, to assert a color is like something which is invisible; hard or soft, like something which is intangible; and so of the rest.

9. Some there are who make a distinction betwixt *primary* and *secondary* qualities: by the former, they mean extension, figure, motion, rest, solidity or impenetrability and number: by the latter they denote all other sensible qualities, as colors, sounds, tastes, and so forth.[2] The ideas we have of these they acknowledge not to be the resemblances of anything existing without the mind or unperceived; but they will have our ideas of the primary qualities to be patterns or images of things which exist without the mind, in an unthinking substance which they call *matter*. By matter therefore we are to understand an inert, senseless substance, in which extension, figure, and motion, do actually subsist. But it is evident from what we have already shown, that extension, figure and motion are only ideas existing in the mind, and that an idea can be like nothing but another idea, and that consequently neither they nor their archetypes can exist in an unperceiving substance. Hence it is plain, that the very notion of what is called *matter* or *corporeal substance*, involves a contradiction in it.

10. They who assert that figure, motion, and the rest of the primary or original qualities do exist without the mind, in unthinking substances, do at the same time acknowledge that colors, sounds, heat, cold, and such like secondary qualities, do not, which they tell us are sensations existing in the mind alone, that depend on and are occasioned by the different size, texture and motion of the minute particles of matter. This they take for an undoubted truth, which they can demonstrate beyond all exception. Now if it be certain, that those original qualities are inseparably united with the other sensible qualities, and not, even in thought, capable of being abstracted from them, it plainly follows that they exist only in the mind. But I desire anyone to reflect and try, whether he can by any abstraction of thought, conceive the extension and motion of a body, without all other sensible qualities. For my own part, I see evidently that it is not in my power to frame an idea of a body extended and moved, but I must withal give it some color or other sensible quality which is acknowledged to exist only in the mind. In short, extension, figure, and motion, abstracted from all other qualities, are inconceivable. Where therefore the other sensible qualities are, there must these be also, to wit, in the mind and nowhere else.

11. Again, *great* and *small, swift* and *slow*, are allowed to exist nowhere without the mind, being entirely relative, and changing as the frame or position of the organs of sense varies. The extension therefore which exists without the mind, is neither great nor small, the motion neither swift nor slow, that is, they are nothing at all. But say you, they are extension in general, and motion in general: thus we see how much the tenet of extended, moveable substances existing without the mind, depends on that strange doctrine of *abstract ideas*. And here I cannot but remark, how nearly the vague and indeterminate description of matter or corporeal substance, which the modern philosophers are run into by their own principles, resembles that antiquated and so much ridiculed notion of *materia prima*, to be met with in *Aristotle* and his followers.* Without extension solidity cannot be conceived; since therefore it has been shown that extension exists not in an unthinking substance, the same must also be true of solidity.

12. That number is entirely the creature of the mind, even though the other qualities be allowed to exist without, will be evident to whoever considers, that the same thing bears a different denomination of number, as the mind views it with different respects. Thus, the same extension is one or three or thirty six, according as the mind considers it with reference to a yard, a foot, or an inch. Number is so visibly relative, and dependent on men's understanding, that it is strange to think how anyone should give it an absolute existence without the mind. We say one book, one page, one line; all these are equally units, though some contain several of the others. And in each instance it is plain, the unit relates to some particular combination of ideas arbitrarily put together by the mind.

13. Unity I know some will have to be a simple or uncompounded idea, accompanying all other ideas into the mind.[3] That I have any such idea answering the word *unity*, I do not find; and if I had, methinks I could not miss finding it; on the contrary it should be the most familiar to my understanding, since it is said to accompany all other ideas, and to be perceived by all the ways of sensation and reflection. To say no more, it is an *abstract idea*.

14. I shall farther add, that after the same manner, as modern philosophers prove certain sensible qualities to have no existence in matter, or without the mind, the same thing may be likewise proved of all other sensible qualities whatsoever. Thus, for instance, it is said that heat and cold are affections only of the mind, and not at all patterns of real beings, existing in the corporeal substances which excite them, for that the same body which appears cold to one hand, seems warm to another. Now why may we not as well argue that figure and extension are not patterns or resemblances of qualities existing in matter, because to the same eye at different stations, or eyes of a different texture at the same station, they appear various, and cannot therefore be the images of anything settled and determinate without the mind? Again, it is proved that sweetness is not really in the sapid thing, because the thing remaining unaltered the sweetness is changed into bitter, as in case of a fever or otherwise vitiated palate. Is it not as reasonable to say, that motion is not without the mind, since if the succession of ideas in the mind become swifter, the motion, it is acknowledged, shall appear slower without any alteration in any external object.

15. In short, let anyone consider those arguments, which are thought manifestly to prove that colors and tastes exist only in the mind, and he shall find they may with equal force, be brought to prove the same thing of extension, figure, and motion. Though it must be confessed this method of arguing does not so much prove that there is no extension or color in an outward object, as that we do not know by sense which is the true extension or color of the object. But the arguments foregoing plainly show it to be impossible that any color or extension at all, or other sensible quality whatsoever, should exist in an unthinking subject without the mind, or in truth, that there should be any such thing as an outward object.

16. But let us examine a little the received opinion. It is said extension is a mode or accident of matter, and that matter is the *substratum* that supports it. Now I desire that you would explain what is meant by matter's *supporting* extension: say you, I have no idea of matter, and therefore cannot explain it. I answer, though you have no positive, yet if you have any meaning at all, you must at least have a relative idea of matter; though you know not what it is, yet you must be supposed to know what relation it bears to accidents, and what is meant by its supporting them. It is evident *support* cannot here be taken in its usual or literal sense, as when we say that pillars support a building: in what sense therefore must it be taken?

---

* Aristotle (384–322 B.C.) calls the wood of a casket its *matter*. He thinks the various kinds of matter can be arranged in a hierarchy: wood, for example, is matter for a casket, while earth (one of the four basic elements) is matter for wood. *Materia prima*, or prime matter, is a totally indeterminate substratum, the most basic item in the hierarchy. Berkeley follows a long tradition when he attributes belief in prime matter to Aristotle, but it is a tradition many scholars now dispute.

17. If we inquire into what the most accurate philosophers declare themselves to mean by *material substance;* we shall find them acknowledge, they have no other meaning annexed to those sounds, but the idea of being in general, together with the relative notion of its supporting accidents.[4] The general idea of being appears to me the most abstract and incomprehensible of all other; and as for its supporting accidents, this, as we have just now observed, cannot be understood in the common sense of those words; it must therefore be taken in some other sense, but what that is they do not explain. So that when I consider the two parts or branches which make the signification of the words *material substance*, I am convinced there is no distinct meaning annexed to them. But why should we trouble ourselves any farther, in discussing this material *substratum* or support of figure and motion, and other sensible qualities? Does it not suppose they have an existence without the mind? And is not this a direct repugnancy, and altogether inconceivable?

18. But though it were possible that solid, figured, moveable substances may exist without the mind, corresponding to the ideas we have of bodies, yet how is it possible for us to know this? Either we must know it by sense, or by reason. As for our senses, by them we have the knowledge only of our sensations, ideas, or those things that are immediately perceived by sense, call them what you will: but they do not inform us that things exist without the mind, or unperceived, like to those which are perceived. This the materialists themselves acknowledge. It remains therefore that if we have any knowledge at all of external things, it must be by reason, inferring their existence from what is immediately perceived by sense. But what reason can induce us to believe that existence of bodies without the mind, from what we perceive, since the very patrons of matter themselves do not pretend, there is any necessary connection betwixt them and our ideas? I say it is granted on all hands (and what happens in dreams, frenzies, and the like, puts it beyond dispute) that it is possible we might be affected with all the ideas we have now, though no bodies existed without, resembling them. Hence it is evident the supposition of external bodies is not necessary for the producing our ideas: since it is granted they are produced sometimes, and might possibly be produced always in the same order we see them in at present, without their concurrence.

19. But though we might possibly have all our sensations without them, yet perhaps it may be thought easier to conceive and explain the manner of their production, by supposing external bodies in their likeness rather than otherwise; and so it might be at least probable there are such things as bodies that excite their ideas in our minds. But neither can this be said; for though we give the materialists their external bodies, they by their own confession are never the nearer knowing how our ideas are produced: since they own themselves unable to comprehend in what manner body can act upon spirit, or how it is possible it should imprint any idea in the mind. Hence it is evident the production of ideas or sensations in our minds, can be no reason why we should suppose matter or corporeal substances, since that is acknowledged to remain equally inexplicable with, or without this supposition. If therefore it were possible for bodies to exist without the mind, yet to hold they do so, must needs be a very precarious opinion; since it is to suppose, without any reason at all, that God has created innumerable beings that are entirely useless, and serve to no manner of purpose.

20. In short, if there were external bodies, it is impossible we should ever come to know it; and if there were not, we might have the very same reasons to think there were that we have now. Suppose, what no one can deny possible, an intelligence, without the help of external bodies, to be affected with the same train of sensations or ideas that you are, imprinted in the same order and with like vividness in his mind. I ask whether that intelligence has not all the reason to believe the existence of corporeal substances, represented by his ideas, and exciting them in his mind, that you can possibly have for believing the same thing? Of this there can be no question; which one consideration is enough to make any reasonable person suspect the strength of whatever arguments he may think himself to have, for the existence of bodies without the mind.

21. Were it necessary to add any farther proof against the existence of matter, after what has been said, I could instance several of those errors and difficulties (not to mention impieties) which have sprung from that tenet. It has occasioned numberless controversies and disputes in philosophy, and not a few of far greater moment in religion. But I shall not enter into the detail of them in this place, as well because I think, arguments *a posteriori* are unnecessary for confirming what has been, if I mistake not, sufficiently demonstrated *a priori*, as because I shall hereafter find occasion to say somewhat of them.[5]

22. I am afraid I have given cause to think me needlessly prolix in handling this subject. For to what purpose is it to dilate on that which may be demonstrated with the utmost evidence in a line or two, to anyone that is capable of the least reflection? It is but looking into your own thoughts, and so trying whether you can conceive it possible for a sound, or figure, or motion, or color, to exist without the mind, or unperceived. This easy trial may make you see, that what you contend for, is a downright contradiction. Insomuch that I am content to put the whole upon this issue; if you can but conceive it possible for one extended moveable substance, or in general, for any one idea or anything like an idea, to exist otherwise than in a mind perceiving it, I shall readily give up the cause: and as for all that *compages* of external bodies which you contend for, I shall grant you its existence, though you cannot either give me any reason why you believe it exists, or assign any use to it when it is supposed to exist. I say, the bare possibility of your opinion's being true, shall pass for an argument that it is so.

23. But say you, surely there is nothing easier than to imagine trees, for instance, in a park, or books existing in a closet, and nobody by to perceive them. I answer, you may so, there is no difficulty in it: but what is all this, I beseech you, more than framing in your mind certain ideas which you call *books* and *trees*, and at the same time omitting to frame the idea of anyone that may perceive them? But do not you yourself perceive or think of them all the while? This therefore is nothing to the purpose: it only shows you have the power of imagining or forming ideas in your mind; but it does not show that you can conceive it possible, the objects of your thought may exist without the mind: to make out this, it is necessary that you conceive them existing unconceived or unthought of, which is a manifest repugnancy. When we do our utmost to conceive the existence of external bodies, we are all the while only contemplating our own ideas. But the mind taking no notice of itself, is deluded to think it can and does conceive bodies existing unthought of or without the mind; though at the same time they are apprehended by or exist in itself. A little attention will discover to anyone the truth and evidence of what is here said, and make it unnecessary to insist on any other proofs against the existence of material substance.

24. It is very obvious, upon the least inquiry into our own thoughts, to know whether it be possible for us to understand what is meant, by the *absolute existence of sensible objects in themselves, or without the mind*. To me it is evident those words mark out either a direct contradiction, or else nothing at all. And to convince others of this, I know no readier or fairer way, than to entreat they would calmly attend to their own thoughts: and if by this attention, the emptiness or repugnancy of those expressions does appear, surely nothing more is requisite for their conviction. It is on this therefore that I insist, to wit, that the absolute existence of unthinking things are words without a meaning, or which include a contradiction. This is what I repeat and inculcate, and earnestly recommend to the attentive thoughts of the reader.

25. All our ideas, sensations, or the things which we perceive, by whatsoever names they may be distinguished, are visibly inactive, there is nothing of power or agency included in them.[6] So that one idea or object of thought cannot produce, or make any alteration in another. To be satisfied of the truth of this, there is nothing else requisite but a bare observation of our ideas. For since they and every part of them exist only in the mind, it follows that there is nothing in them but what is perceived. But whoever shall attend to his ideas, whether of sense or reflection, will not perceive in them any power or activity; there is therefore no such thing contained in them. A little attention will discover to us that the very being of an idea implies passiveness and inertness in it, insomuch that it is impossible for an idea to do anything, or, strictly speaking, to be the cause of anything: neither can it be the resemblance or pattern of any active being, as is evident from *Sect.* 8. Whence it plainly follows that extension, figure and motion, cannot be the cause of our sensations. To say therefore, that these are the effects of powers resulting from the configuration, number, motion, and size of corpuscles, must certainly be false.

26. We perceive a continual succession of ideas, some are anew excited, others are changed or totally disappear. There is therefore some cause of these ideas whereon they depend, and which produces and changes them. That this cause cannot be any quality or idea or combination of ideas, is clear from the preceding section. It must therefore be a substance; but it has been shown that there is no corporeal or material substance: it remains therefore that the cause of ideas is an incorporeal active substance or spirit.

27. A spirit is one simple, undivided, active being: as it perceives ideas, it is called the *understanding*, and as it produces or otherwise operates about them, it is called the *will*. Hence there can be no idea formed of a soul or spirit: for all ideas whatever, being passive and inert, *vide Sect.* 25, they cannot represent unto us, by way of image or likeness, that which acts. A little attention will make it plain to anyone, that to have an idea which shall be like that active principle of motion and change of ideas, is absolutely impossible. Such is the nature of *spirit* or that which acts, that it cannot be of itself perceived, but only by the effects which it produces. If any man shall doubt of the truth of what is here delivered, let him but reflect and try if he can frame the idea of any power or active being; and whether he has ideas of two principal powers, marked by the names *will* and *understanding*, distinct from each other as well as from a third idea of substance or being in general, with a relative notion of its supporting or being the subject of the aforesaid powers, which is signified by the name *soul* or *spirit*. This is what some hold; but so far as I can see, the words *will, soul, spirit*, do not stand for different ideas, or in truth, for any idea at all, but for something which is very different from ideas, and which being an agent cannot be like unto, or represented by, any idea whatsoever. [Though it must be owned at the same time, that we have some notion of soul, spirit, and the operations of the mind, such as willing, loving, hating, inasmuch as we know or understand the meaning of those words.][7]

28. I find I can excite ideas in my mind at pleasure, and vary and shift the scene as oft as I think fit. It is no more than willing, and straightway this or that idea arises in my fancy: and by the same power it is obliterated, and makes way for another. This making and unmaking of ideas does very properly denominate the mind active. Thus much is certain, and grounded on experience: but when we talk of unthinking agents, or of exciting ideas exclusive of volition, we only amuse ourselves with words.

29. But whatever power I may have over my own thoughts, I find the ideas actually perceived by sense have not a like dependence on my will. When in broad daylight I open my eyes, it is not in my power to choose whether I shall see or no, or to determine what particular objects shall present themselves to my view; and so likewise as to the hearing and other senses, the ideas imprinted on them are not creatures of my will. There is therefore some other will or spirit that produces them.

30. The ideas of sense are more strong, lively, and distinct than those of the imagination; they have likewise a steadiness, order, and coherence, and are not excited at random, as those which are the effects of human wills often are, but in a regular train or series, the admirable connection whereof sufficiently testifies the wisdom and benevolence of its author. Now the set rules or established methods, wherein the mind we depend on excites in us the ideas of sense, are called the *laws of nature:* and these we learn by experience, which teaches us that such and such ideas are attended with such and such other ideas, in the ordinary course of things.

31. This gives us a sort of foresight, which enables us to regulate our actions for the benefit of life. And without this we should be eternally at a loss: we could not know how to act anything that might procure us the least pleasure, or remove the least pain of sense. That food nourishes, sleep refreshes, and fire warms us; that to sow in the seed-time is the way to reap in the harvest, and, in general, that to obtain such or such ends, such or such means are conducive, all this we know, not by discovering any necessary connection between our ideas, but only by the observation of the settled laws of nature, without which we should be all in uncertainty and confusion, and a grown man no more know how to manage himself in the affairs of life, than an infant just born.

32. And yet this consistent uniform working, which so evidently displays the goodness and wisdom of that governing spirit whose will constitutes the laws of nature, is so far from leading our thoughts to him, that it rather sends them awandering after second causes. For when we perceive certain ideas of sense constantly followed by other ideas, and we know this is not of our own doing, we forthwith attribute power and agency to the ideas themselves, and make one the cause of another, than which nothing can be more absurd and unintelligible. Thus, for example, having observed that when we perceive by sight a certain round luminous figure, we at the same time perceive by touch the idea or sensation called *heat*, we do from thence conclude the sun to be the cause of heat. And in like manner perceiving the motion and collision of bodies to be attended with sound, we are inclined to think the latter an effect of the former.

33. The ideas imprinted on the senses by the Author of Nature are called *real things:* and those excited in the imagination being less regular, vivid and constant, are more properly termed *ideas*, or *images of things*, which they copy and represent. But then our sensations, be they never so vivid and distinct, are nevertheless *ideas*, that is, they exist in the mind, or are perceived by it, as truly as the ideas of its own framing. The ideas of sense are allowed to have more reality in them, that is, to be more strong, orderly, and coherent than the creatures of the mind; but this is no argument that they exist without the mind. They are also less dependent on the spirit, or thinking substance which perceives them, in that they are excited by the will of another and more powerful spirit: yet still they are *ideas*, and certainly no *idea*, whether faint or strong, can exist otherwise than in a mind perceiving it.

34. Before we proceed any farther, it is necessary to spend some time in answering objections which may probably be made against the principles hitherto laid down. In doing of which, if I seem too prolix to those of quick apprehensions, I hope it may be pardoned, since all men do not equally apprehend things of this nature; and I am willing to be understood by everyone. First then, it will be objected that by the foregoing principles, all that is real and substantial in nature is banished out of the world: and instead thereof a chimerical scheme of ideas takes place. All things that exist, exist only in the mind, that is, they are purely notional. What therefore becomes of the sun, moon, and stars? What must we think of houses, rivers, mountains, trees, stones; nay, even of our own bodies? Are all these but so many chimeras and illusions on the fancy? To all which, and whatever else of the same sort may be objected, I answer, that by the principles premised, we are not deprived of any one thing in nature. Whatever we see, feel, hear, or any wise conceive or understand, remains as secure as ever, and is as real as ever. There is a *rerum natura*, and the distinction between realities and chimeras retains its full force. This is evident from *Sect.* 29, 30, and 33, where we have shown what is meant by *real things* in opposition to *chimeras*, or ideas of our own framing; but then they both equally exist in the mind, and in that sense are alike *ideas*.

35. I do not argue against the existence of any one thing that we can apprehend, either by sense or reflection. That the things I see with mine eyes and touch with my hands do exist, really exist, I make not the least question. The only thing whose existence we deny, is that which philosophers call matter or corporeal substance. And in doing of this, there is no damage done to the rest of mankind, who, I dare say, will never miss it. The atheist indeed will want the color of an empty name to support his impiety; and the philosophers may possibly find, they have lost a great handle for trifling and disputation.

NOTES

1. In the first edition the section continues with the following sentence: *In truth the object and the sensation are the same thing, and cannot therefore be abstracted from each other*.
2. Locke makes the distinction at *Essay* II viii 9–26.
3. Locke makes these observations about unity at *Essay* II xvi 1.

4. Berkeley is probably referring to Locke's remarks on "pure substance in general" at *Essay* II xxiii 2.
5. *a posteriori*, from what comes after; *a priori*, from what comes before. These are among the first appearances of these expressions in English. (They are the first appearances listed in the *Oxford English Dictionary*, but the expressions were used as early as 1679 in discussions of arguments for God's existence. See Redwood, *Reason, Ridicule and Religion*, pp. 151–2.) Berkeley does not use the expressions as philosophers do today. According to Berkeley, an *a posteriori* argument against a belief attacks the belief through its effects or consequences, which in the case of matter include skepticism, atheism, and various difficulties in physics and mathematics. An *a priori* argument attacks the belief directly. Berkeley's promise to present the *a posteriori* case against matter is fulfilled in sections 85–96 and 101–134.
6. In the first edition, the word "notions" follows "sensations."
7. The bracketed sentence was added in the second edition.

Posits and Reality

W. V. O. QUINE

W. V. O. Quine (1908-2000) was one of the most distinguished philosophers of the 20th century. He taught for many years at Harvard University.

"Posits and Reality" was originally published in 1955. A summary of its main themes can be found in the introduction to this section, pp. 337–341 in this volume.

I. SUBVISIBLE PARTICLES

According to physics my desk is, for all its seeming fixity and solidity, a swarm of vibrating molecules. The desk as we sense it is comparable to a distant haystack in which we cannot distinguish the individual stalks; comparable also to a wheel in which, because of its rapid rotation, we cannot distinguish the individual spokes. Comparable, but with a difference. By approaching the haystack we can distinguish the stalks, and by retarding the wheel we can distinguish the spokes. On the other hand no glimpse is to be had of the separate molecules of the desk; they are, we are told, too small.

Lacking such experience, what evidence can the physicist muster for his doctrine of molecules? His answer is that there is a convergence of indirect evidence, drawn from such varied phenomena as expansion, heat conduction, capillary attraction, and surface tension. The point is that these miscellaneous phenomena can, if we assume the molecular theory, be marshaled under the familiar laws of motion. The fancifulness of thus assuming a substructure of moving particles of imperceptible size is offset by a gain in naturalness and scope on the part of the aggregate laws of physics. The molecular theory is felt, moreover, to gain corroboration progressively as the physicist's predictions of future observations turn out to be fulfilled, and as the theory proves to invite extensions covering additional classes of phenomena.

The benefits thus credited to the molecular doctrine may be divided into five. One is simplicity: empirical laws concerning seemingly dissimilar phenomena are integrated into a compact and unitary theory. Another is familiarity of principle: the already familiar laws of motion are made to serve where independent laws would otherwise have been

From *The Ways of Paradox and Other Essays* by W. V. O. Quine, pp. 246–254, Cambridge, Mass.: Harvard University Press. Copyright © 1966, 1976 by the President and Fellows of Harvard College. Reprinted by permission of the publisher.

needed. A third is scope: the resulting unitary theory implies a wider array of testable consequences than any likely accumulation of separate laws would have implied. A fourth is fecundity: successful further extensions of theory are expedited. The fifth goes without saying: such testable consequences of the theory as have been tested have turned out well, aside from such sparse exceptions as may in good conscience be chalked up to unexplained interferences.

Simplicity, the first of the listed benefits, is a vague business. We may be fairly sure of this much: theories are more or less simple, more or less unitary, only relative to one or another given vocabulary or conceptual apparatus. Simplicity is, if not quite subjective, at any rate parochial. Yet simplicity contributes to scope, as follows. An empirical theory, typically, generalizes or extrapolates from sample data, and thus covers more phenomena than have been checked. Simplicity, by our lights, is what guides our extrapolation. Hence the simpler the theory, on the whole, the wider this unchecked coverage.

As for the fourth benefit, fecundity, obviously it is a consequence of the first two, simplicity and familiarity, for these two traits are the best conditions for effective thinking.

Not all the listed benefits are generally attributable to accepted scientific theories, though all are to be prized when available. Thus the benefit of familiarity of principle may, as in quantum theory and relativity theory, be renounced, its loss being regretted but outweighed.

But to get back. In its manifest content the molecular doctrine bears directly on unobservable reality, affirming a structure of minute swarming particles. On the other hand any defense of it has to do rather with its indirect bearing on observable reality. The doctrine has this indirect bearing by being the core of an integrated physical theory which implies truths about expansion, conduction, and so on. The benefits which we have been surveying are benefits which the molecular doctrine, as core, brings to the physics of these latter observable phenomena.

Suppose now we were to excise that core but retain the surrounding ring of derivative laws, thus not disturbing the observable consequences. The retained laws could be viewed thenceforward as autonomous empirical laws, innocent of any molecular commitment. Granted, this combination of empirical laws would never have been achieved without the unifying aid of a molecular doctrine at the center; note the recent remarks on scope. But we might still delete the molecular doctrine once it has thus served its heuristic purpose.

This reflection strengthens a natural suspicion: that the benefits conferred by the molecular doctrine give the physicist good reason to prize it, but afford no evidence of its truth. Though the doctrine succeed to perfection in its indirect bearing on observable reality, the question of its truth has to do rather with its direct claim on unobservable reality. Might the molecular doctrine not be ever so useful in organizing and extending our knowledge of the behavior of observable things, and yet be factually false?

One may question, on closer consideration, whether this is really an intelligible possibility. Let us reflect upon our words and how we learned them.

II. POSITS AND ANALOGIES

Words are human artifacts, meaningless save as our associating them with experience endows them with meaning. The word "swarm" is initially meaningful to us through association with such experiences as that of a hovering swarm of gnats, or a swarm of dust motes in a shaft of sunlight. When we extend the word to desks and the like, we are engaged in drawing an analogy between swarms ordinarily so-called, on the one hand, and desks, etc., on the other. The word "molecule" is then given meaning derivatively: having conceived of desks analogically as swarms, we imagine molecules as the things the desks are swarms of.

The purported question of fact, the question whether the familiar objects around us are really swarms of subvisible particles in vibration, now begins to waver and dissolve. If the words involved here make sense only by analogy, then the only question of fact is the question how good an analogy there is between the behavior of a desk or the like and the behavior, e.g., of a swarm of gnats. What had seemed a direct bearing of the molecular doctrine upon reality has now dwindled to an analogy.

Even this analogical content, moreover, is incidental, variable, and at length dispensable. In particular the analogy between the swarming of the molecules of a solid and the swarming of gnats is only moderately faithful; a supplementary aid to appreciating the dynamics of the molecules of a solid is found in the analogy of a stack of bedsprings. In another and more recondite part of physics, the theory of light, the tenuousness of analogy is notorious: the analogy of particles is useful up to a point and the analogy of waves is useful up to a point, but neither suffices to the exclusion of the other. Faithful analogies are an aid to the physicist's early progress in an unaccustomed medium, but, like water-wings, they are an aid which he learns to get along without.

In §I we contrasted a direct and an indirect bearing of the molecular doctrine upon reality. But the direct bearing has not withstood scrutiny. Where there had at first seemed to be an undecidable question of unobservable fact, we now find mere analogy at most and not necessarily that. So the only way in which we now find the molecular doctrine genuinely to bear upon reality is the indirect way, via implications in observable phenomena.

The effect of this conclusion upon the status of molecules is that they lose even the dignity of inferred or hypothetical entities which may or may not really be there. The very sentences which seem to propound them and treat of them are gibberish by themselves, and indirectly significant only as contributory clauses of an inclusive system which does also treat of the real. The molecular physicist is, like all of us, concerned with commonplace reality, and merely finds that he can simplify his laws by positing an esoteric supplement to the exoteric universe. He can devise simpler laws for this enriched universe, this "sesquiverse" of his own decree, than he has been able to devise for its real or original portion alone.

In §I we imagined deleting the molecular doctrine from the midst of the derivative body of physical theory. From our present vantage point, however, we see that operation as insignificant; there is no substantive doctrine of molecules to delete. The sentences which seem to propound molecules are just devices for organizing the significant sentences of physical theory. No matter if physics makes molecules or other insensible particles seem more fundamental than the objects of common sense; the particles are posited for the sake of a simple physics.

The tendency of our own reflections has been, conversely, to belittle molecules and their ilk, leaving common-sense bodies supreme. Still, it may now be protested, this invidious contrast is unwarranted. What are given in sensation are variformed and varicolored visual patches, varitextured and varitemperatured tactual feels, and an assortment of tones, tastes, smells, and other odds and ends; desks are no more to be found among these data than molecules. If we have evidence for the existence of the bodies of common sense, we have it only in the way in which we may be said to have evidence for the existence of molecules. The positing of either sort of body is good science insofar merely as it helps us formulate our laws—laws whose ultimate evidence lies in the sense data of the past, and whose ultimate vindication lies in anticipation of sense data of the future. The positing of molecules differs from the positing of the bodies of common sense mainly in degree of sophistication. In whatever sense the molecules in my desk are unreal and a figment of the imagination of the scientist, in that sense the desk itself is unreal and a figment of the imagination of the race.

This double verdict of unreality leaves us nothing, evidently, but the raw sense data themselves. It leaves each of us, indeed, nothing but his own sense data; for the assumption of there being other persons has no better support than has the assumption of there being any other sorts of external objects. It leaves each of us in the position of solipsism, according to which there is nobody else in the world, nor indeed any world but the pageant of one's own sense data.

III. RESTITUTION

Surely now we have been caught up in a wrong line of reasoning. Not only is the conclusion bizarre; it vitiates the very considerations that lead to it. We cannot properly represent man as inventing a myth of physical objects to fit past and present sense data, for past ones are lost except to memory; and memory, far from being a straightforward register of past sense data, usually depends on past posits of physical objects. The positing of physical objects must be seen not as an *ex post facto* systematization of data, but as a move prior to which no appreciable data would be available to systematize.

Something went wrong with our standard of reality. We became doubtful of the reality of molecules because the physicist's statement that there are molecules took on the aspect of a mere technical convenience in smoothing the laws of physics. Next we noted that common-sense bodies are epistemologically much on a par with the molecules, and inferred the unreality of the common-sense bodies themselves. Here our bemusement becomes visible. Unless we change meanings in midstream, the familiar bodies around us are as real as can be; and it smacks of a contradiction in terms to conclude otherwise. Having noted that man has no evidence for the existence of bodies beyond the fact that their assumption helps him organize experience, we should have done well, instead of disclaiming evidence for the existence of bodies, to conclude: such, then, at bottom, is what evidence is, both for ordinary bodies and for molecules.

This point about evidence does not upset the evidential priority of sense data. On the contrary, the point about evidence is precisely that the testimony of the senses *does* (contrary to Berkeley's notion) count as evidence for bodies, such being (as Samuel Johnson perceived)* just the sort of thing that evidence is. We can continue to recognize, as in §II, that molecules and even the gross bodies of common sense are simply posited in the course of organizing our responses to stimulation; but a moral to draw from our reconsideration of the terms "reality" and "evidence" is that posits are not ipso facto unreal. The benefits of the molecular doctrine which so impressed us in §I, and the manifest benefits of the aboriginal posit of ordinary bodies, are the best evidence of reality we can ask (pending, of course, evidence of the same sort for some alternative ontology).

Sense data are posits too. They are posits of psychological theory, but not, on that account, unreal. The sense datum may be construed as a hypothetical component of subjective experience standing in closest possible correspondence to the experimentally measurable conditions of physical stimulation of the end organs. In seeking to isolate sense data we engage in empirical psychology, associating physical stimuli with human resources. I shall not guess how useful the positing of sense data may be for psychological theory, or more specifically for a psychologically grounded theory of evidence, nor what detailed traits may profitably be postulated concerning them. In our flight from the fictitious to the real, in any event, we have come full circle.

Sense data, if they are to be posited at all, are fundamental in one respect; the small particles of physics are fundamental in a second respect, and common-sense bodies in a third. Sense data are *evidentially* fundamental: every man is beholden to his senses for every hint of bodies. The physical particles are *naturally* fundamental, in this kind of way: laws of behavior of those particles afford, so far as we know, the simplest formulation of a general theory of what happens. Common-sense bodies, finally, are *conceptually* fundamental: it is by reference to them that the very notions of reality and evidence are acquired, and that the concepts which have to do with physical particles or even with sense data tend to be framed and phrased. But these three types of priority must not be viewed as somehow determining three competing, self-sufficient conceptual schemes. Our one serious conceptual scheme is the inclusive, evolving one of science, which we inherit and, in our several small ways, help to improve.

IV. WORKING FROM WITHIN

It is by thinking within this unitary conceptual scheme itself, thinking about the processes of the physical world, that we come to appreciate that the world can be evidenced only through stimulation

* Idealist philosopher George Berkeley (1685–1753) held that the nature of reality is fundamentally mental (as opposed to physical). Berkeley's views were challenged by two Samuel Johnsons—the American philosopher (1696–1772) and the British writer (1709–84), the first in a series of letters and the second through his kicking of a stone.

of our senses. It is by thinking within the same conceptual scheme that we come to appreciate that language, being a social art, is learned primarily with reference to intersubjectively conspicuous objects, and hence that such objects are bound to be central conceptually. Both of these *aperçus* are part of the scientific understanding of the scientific enterprise; not prior to it. Insofar as they help the scientist to proceed more knowingly about his business, science is using its findings to improve its own techniques. Epistemology, on this view, is not logically prior somehow to common sense or to the refined common sense which is science; it is part rather of the overall scientific enterprise, an enterprise which Neurath has likened to that of rebuilding a ship while staying afloat in it.

Epistemology, so conceived, continues to probe the sensory evidence for discourse about the world; but it no longer seeks to relate such discourse somehow to an imaginary and impossible sense-datum language. Rather it faces the fact that society teaches us our physicalistic language by training us to associate various physicalistic sentences directly, in multifarious ways, with irritations of our sensory surfaces, and by training us also to associate various such sentences with one another.

The complex totality of such associations is a fluctuating field of force. Some sentences about bodies are, for one person or for many, firmly conditioned one by one to sensory stimulation of specifiable sorts. Roughly specifiable sequences of nerve hits can confirm us in statements about having had breakfast, or there being a brick house on Elm Street, beyond the power of secondary associations with other sentences to add or detract. But there is in this respect a grading-off from one example to another. Many sentences even about common-sense bodies rest wholly on indirect evidence; witness the statement that one of the pennies now in my pocket was in my pocket last week. Conversely, sentences even about electrons are sometimes directly conditioned to sensory stimulation, e.g., via the cloud chamber. The status of a given sentence, in point of direct or indirect connection with the senses, can change as one's experience accumulates; thus a man's first confrontation with a cloud chamber may forge a direct sensory link to some sentences which hitherto bore, for him, only the most indirect sensory relevance. Moreover the sensory relevance of sentences will differ widely from person to person; uniformity comes only where the pressure for communication comes.

Statements about bodies, common-sense or recondite, thus commonly make little or no empirical sense except as bits of a collectively significant containing system. Various statements can surely be supplanted by their negations, without conflict with any possible sensory contingency, provided that we revise other portions of our science in compensatory ways. Science is empirically underdetermined: there is slack. What can be said about the hypothetical particles of physics is underdetermined by what can be said about sensible bodies, and what can be said about these is underdetermined by the stimulation of our surfaces. An inkling of this circumstance has doubtless fostered the tendency to look upon the hypothetical particles of physics as more of a fiction than sensible bodies, and these as more of a fiction than sense data. But the tendency is a perverse one, for it ascribes full reality only to a domain of objects for which there is no autonomous system of discourse at all.

Better simply to explore, realistically, the less-than-rigid connections that obtain between sensory stimulus and physical doctrine, without viewing this want of rigidity as impugning the physical doctrine. Benefits of the sort recounted in §I are what count for the molecular doctrine or any, and we can hope for no surer touchstone of reality. We can hope to improve our physics by seeking the same sorts of benefits in fuller measure, and we may even facilitate such endeavors by better understanding the degrees of freedom that prevail between stimulatory evidence and physical doctrine. But as a medium for such epistemological inquiry we can choose no better than the selfsame world theory which we are trying to improve, this being the best available at the time.

Brains in a Vat

HILARY PUTNAM

Hilary Putnam (1926–) taught philosophy at Harvard University, where he was a long-time colleague of John Rawls, Robert Nozick, Nelson Goodman, and W. V. O. Quine, selections from whose writings also appear in this volume. He is well known for his work in philosophy of mind, philosophy of science, and philosophy of language.

This selection is an excerpt from his 1981 book *Reason, Truth, and History*. In it, Putnam presents his widely discussed example of the brain in a vat and explores the implications of this example for questions of meaning and reference.

An ant is crawling on a patch of sand. As it crawls, it traces a line in the sand. By pure chance the line that it traces curves and recrosses itself in such a way that it ends up looking like a recognizable caricature of Winston Churchill. Has the ant traced a picture of Winston Churchill, a picture that *depicts* Churchill?

Most people would say, on a little reflection, that it has not. The ant, after all, has never seen Churchill, or even a picture of Churchill, and it had no intention of depicting Churchill. It simply traced a line (and even *that* was unintentional), a line that *we* can "see as" a picture of Churchill.

We can express this by saying that the line is not "in itself" a representation[1] of anything rather than anything else. Similarity (of a certain very complicated sort) to the features of Winston Churchill is not sufficient to make something represent or refer to Churchill. Nor is it necessary: in our community the printed shape "Winston Churchill," the spoken words "Winston Churchill," and many other things are used to represent Churchill (though not pictorially), while not having the sort of similarity to Churchill that a picture—even a line drawing—has. If *similarity* is not necessary or sufficient to make something represent something else, how can *anything* be necessary or sufficient for this purpose? How on earth can one thing represent (or "stand for," etc.) a different thing?

The answer may seem easy. Suppose the ant had seen Winston Churchill, and suppose that it had the intelligence and skill to draw a picture of him. Suppose it produced the caricature *intentionally*. Then the line would have represented Churchill.

On the other hand, suppose the line had the shape WINSTON CHURCHILL. And suppose this was just accident (ignoring the improbability involved). Then the "printed shape" WINSTON CHURCHILL would *not* have represented Churchill although that printed shape does represent Churchill when it occurs in almost any book today.

So it may seem that what is necessary for representation, or what is mainly necessary for representation, is *intention*.

But to have the intention that *anything*, even private language (even the words "Winston Churchill" spoken in my mind and not out loud), should *represent* Churchill, I must have been able to *think about* Churchill in the first place. If lines in the sand, noises, etc., cannot "in themselves" represent anything, then how is it that thought forms can "in themselves" represent anything? Or can they? How can thought reach out and "grasp" what is external?

Some philosophers have, in the past, leaped from this sort of consideration to what they take to be a proof that the mind is *essentially non-physical in nature*. The argument is simple; what we said about the ant's curve applies to any physical object. No physical object can, in itself, refer to one thing rather than to another; nevertheless, *thoughts in the mind* obviously do succeed in referring to one thing rather

From *Reason, Truth and History*. Copyright © 2007 by Cambridge University Press. Reprinted by permission of the publisher.

than another. So thoughts (and hence the mind) are of an essentially different nature than physical objects. Thoughts have the characteristic of *intentionality*—they can refer to something else; nothing physical has "intentionality," save as that intentionality is derivative from some employment of that physical thing by a mind. Or so it is claimed. This is too quick; just postulating mysterious powers of mind solves nothing. But the problem is very real. How is intentionality, reference, possible?

1. MAGICAL THEORIES OF REFERENCE

We saw that the ant's "picture" has no necessary connection with Winston Churchill. The mere fact that the "picture" bears a "resemblance" to Churchill does not make it into a real picture, nor does it make it a representation of Churchill. Unless the ant is an intelligent ant (which it isn't) and knows about Churchill (which it doesn't), the curve it traced is not a picture or even a representation of anything. Some primitive people believe that some representations (in particular, *names*) have a necessary connection with their bearers; that to know the "true name" of someone or something gives one power over it. This power comes from the *magical connection* between the name and the bearer of the name; once one realizes that a name *only* has a contextual, contingent, conventional connection with its bearer, it is hard to see why knowledge of the name should have any mystical significance.

What is important to realize is that what goes for physical pictures also goes for mental images, and for mental representations in general; mental representations no more have a necessary connection with what they represent than physical representations do. The contrary supposition is a survival of magical thinking.

Perhaps the point is easiest to grasp in the case of mental *images*. (Perhaps the first philosopher to grasp the enormous significance of this point, even if he was not the first to actually make it, was Wittgenstein.) Suppose there is a planet somewhere on which human beings have evolved (or been deposited by alien spacemen, or what have you). Suppose these humans, although otherwise like us, have never seen *trees*. Suppose they have never imagined trees (perhaps vegetable life exists on their planet only in the form of molds). Suppose one day a picture of a tree is accidentally dropped on their planet by a spaceship which passes on without having other contact with them. Imagine them puzzling over the picture. What in the world is this? All sorts of speculations occur to them: a building, a canopy, even an animal of some kind. But suppose they never come close to the truth.

For *us* the picture is a representation of a tree. For these humans the picture only represents a strange object, nature and function unknown. Suppose one of them has a mental image which is exactly like one of my mental images of a tree as a result of having seen the picture. His mental image is not a *representation of a tree*. It is only a representation of the strange object (whatever it is) that the mysterious picture represents.

Still, someone might argue that the mental image is *in fact* a representation of a tree, if only because the picture which caused this mental image was itself a representation of a tree to begin with. There is a causal chain from actual trees to the mental image even if it is a very strange one.

But even this causal chain can be imagined absent. Suppose the "picture of the tree" that the spaceship dropped was not really a picture of a tree, but the accidental result of some spilled paints. Even if it looked exactly like a picture of a tree, it was, in truth, no more a picture of a tree than the ant's "caricature" of Churchill was a picture of Churchill. We can even imagine that the spaceship which dropped the "picture" came from a planet which knew nothing of trees. Then the humans would still have mental images qualitatively identical with my image of a tree, but they would not be images which represented a tree any more than anything else.

The same thing is true of *words*. A discourse on paper might seem to be a perfect description of trees, but if it was produced by monkeys randomly hitting keys on a typewriter for millions of years, then the words do not refer to anything. If there were a person who memorized those words and said them in his mind without understanding them, then they would not refer to anything when thought in the mind, either.

Imagine the person who is saying those words in his mind has been hypnotized. Suppose the words are in Japanese, and the person has been told that he understands Japanese. Suppose that as he thinks those words he has a "feeling of understanding." (Although if someone broke into his train of thought and asked him what the words he was thinking *meant*, he would discover he couldn't say.) Perhaps the illusion would be so perfect that the person could even fool a Japanese telepath! But if he couldn't use the words in the right contexts, answer questions about what he "thought," etc., then he didn't understand them.

By combining these science fiction stories I have been telling, we can contrive a case in which someone thinks words which are in fact a description of trees in some language *and* simultaneously has appropriate mental images, but *neither* understands the words *nor* knows what a tree is. We can even imagine that the mental images were caused by paint-spills (although the person has been hypnotized to think that they are images of something appropriate to his thought—only, if he were asked, he wouldn't be able to say of what). And we can imagine that the language the person is thinking in is one neither the hypnotist nor the person hypnotized has ever heard of—perhaps it is just coincidence that these "nonsense sentences," as the hypnotist supposes them to be, are a description of trees in Japanese. In short, everything passing before the person's mind might be qualitatively identical with what was passing through the mind of a Japanese speaker who was *really* thinking about trees—but none of it would refer to trees.

All of this is really impossible, of course, in the way that it is really impossible that monkeys should by chance type out a copy of *Hamlet*. That is to say that the probabilities against it are so high as to mean it will never really happen (we think). But it is not logically impossible, or even physically impossible. It *could* happen (compatibly with physical law and, perhaps, compatibly with actual conditions in the universe, if there are lots of intelligent beings on other planets). And if it did happen, it would be a striking demonstration of an important conceptual truth; that even a large and complex system of representations, both verbal and visual, still does not have an *intrinsic* built-in, magical connection with what it represents—a connection independent of how it was caused and what the dispositions of the speaker or thinker are. And this is true whether the system of representations (words and images, in the case of the example) is physically realized—the words are written or spoken, and the pictures are physical pictures—or only realized in the mind. Thought words and mental pictures do not *intrinsically* represent what they are about.

2. THE CASE OF THE BRAINS IN A VAT

Here is a science fiction possibility discussed by philosophers: imagine that a human being (you can imagine this to be yourself) has been subjected to an operation by an evil scientist. The person's brain (your brain) has been removed from the body and placed in a vat of nutrients which keeps the brain alive. The nerve endings have been connected to a super-scientific computer which causes the person whose brain it is to have the illusion that everything is perfectly normal. There seem to be people, objects, the sky, etc; but really all the person (you) is experiencing is the result of electronic impulses travelling from the computer to the nerve endings. The computer is so clever that if the person tries to raise his hand, the feedback from the computer will cause him to "see" and "feel" the hand being raised. Moreover, by varying the program, the evil scientist can cause the victim to "experience" (or hallucinate) any situation or environment the evil scientist wishes. He can also obliterate the memory of the brain operation, so that the victim will seem to himself to have always been in this environment. It can even seem to the victim that he is sitting and reading these very words about the amusing but quite absurd supposition that there is an evil scientist who removes people's brains from their bodies and places them in a vat of nutrients which keep the brains alive. The nerve endings are supposed to be connected to a super-scientific computer which causes the person whose brain it is to have the illusion that . . .

When this sort of possibility is mentioned in a lecture on the Theory of Knowledge, the purpose, of course, is to raise the classical problem of scepticism with respect to the external world in a modern way. (*How do you know you aren't in this predicament?*) But this predicament is also a useful device for raising issues about the mind/world relationship.

Instead of having just one brain in a vat, we could imagine that all human beings (perhaps all sentient beings) are brains in a vat (or nervous systems in a vat in case some beings with just a minimal nervous system already count as "sentient"). Of course, the evil scientist would have to be outside—or would he? Perhaps there is no evil scientist, perhaps (though this is absurd) the universe just happens to consist of automatic machinery tending a vat full of brains and nervous systems.

This time let us suppose that the automatic machinery is programmed to give us all a *collective* hallucination, rather than a number of separate unrelated hallucinations. Thus, when I seem to myself to be talking to you, you seem to yourself to be hearing my words. Of course, it is not the case that my words actually reach your ears—for you don't have (real) ears, nor do I have a real mouth and tongue. Rather, when I produce my words, what happens is that the efferent impulses travel from my brain to the computer, which both causes me to "hear" my own voice uttering those words and "feel" my tongue moving, etc., and causes you to "hear" my words, "see" me speaking, etc. In this case, we are, in a sense, actually in communication. I am not mistaken about your real existence (only about the existence of your body and the "external world," apart from brains). From a certain point of view, it doesn't even matter that "the whole world" is a collective hallucination; for you do, after all, really hear my words when I speak to you, even if the mechanism isn't what we suppose it to be. (Of course, if we were two lovers making love, rather than just two people carrying on a conversation, then the suggestion that it was just two brains in a vat might be disturbing.)

I want now to ask a question which will seem very silly and obvious (at least to some people, including some very sophisticated philosophers), but which will take us to real philosophical depths rather quickly. Suppose this whole story were actually true. Could we, if we were brains in a vat in this way, *say* or *think* that we were?

I am going to argue that the answer is "No, we couldn't." In fact, I am going to argue that the supposition that we are actually brains in a vat, although it violates no physical law, and is perfectly consistent with everything we have experienced, cannot possibly be true. *It cannot possibly be true*, because it is, in a certain way, self-refuting.

The argument I am going to present is an unusual one, and it took me several years to convince myself that it is really right. But it is a correct argument. What makes it seem so strange is that it is connected with some of the very deepest issues in philosophy. (It first occurred to me when I was thinking about a theorem in modern logic the "Skolem–Löwenheim Theorem" and I suddenly saw a connection between this theorem and some arguments in Wittgenstein's *Philosophical Investigations*.)

A "self-refuting supposition" is one whose truth implies its own falsity. For example, consider the thesis that *all general statements are false*. This is a general statement. So if it is true, then it must be false. Hence, it is false. Sometimes a thesis is called "self-refuting" if it is *the supposition that the thesis is entertained or enunciated* that implies its falsity. For example, "I do not exist" is self-refuting if thought by *me* (for any "*me*"). So one can be certain that one oneself exists, if one thinks about it (as Descartes argued).

What I shall show is that the supposition that we are brains in a vat has just this property. If we can consider whether it is true or false, then it is not true (I shall show). Hence it is not true.

Before I give the argument, let us consider why it seems so strange that such an argument can be given (at least to philosophers who subscribe to a "copy" conception of truth). We conceded that it is compatible with physical law that there should be a world in which all sentient beings are brains in a vat. As philosophers say, there is a "possible world" in which all sentient beings are brains in a vat. (This "possible world" talk makes it sound as if there is a *place* where any absurd supposition is true, which is why it can be very misleading in philosophy.) The humans in that possible world have exactly the same experiences that *we* do. They think the same thoughts we do (at least, the same words, images, thought-forms, etc., go through their minds). Yet, I am claiming that there is an argument we can give that shows we are not brains in a vat. How can there be? And why couldn't the people in the possible world who really are brains in a vat give it too?

The answer is going to be (basically) this: although the people in that possible world can think and "say" any words we can think and say, they cannot (I claim) *refer* to what we can refer to. In particular, they cannot think or say that they are brains in a vat (*even by thinking "we are brains in a vat"*).

3. TURING'S TEST

Suppose someone succeeds in inventing a computer which can actually carry on an intelligent conversation with one (on as many subjects as an intelligent person might). How can one decide if the computer is "conscious"?

The British logician Alan Turing proposed the following test:[2] let someone carry on a conversation with the computer and a conversation with a person whom he does not know. If he cannot tell which is the computer and which is the human being, then (assume the test to be repeated a sufficient number of times with different interlocutors) the computer is conscious. In short, a computing machine is conscious if it can pass the "Turing Test." (The conversations are not to be carried on face to face, of course, since the interlocutor is not to know the visual appearance of either of his two conversational partners. Nor is voice to be used, since the mechanical voice might simply sound different from a human voice. Imagine, rather, that the conversations are all carried on via electric typewriter. The interlocutor types in his statements, questions, etc., and the two partners—the machine and the person—respond via the electric keyboard. Also, the machine may *lie*—asked "Are you a machine" it might reply, "No, I'm an assistant in the lab here.")

The idea that this test is really a definitive test of consciousness has been criticized by a number of authors (who are by no means hostile in principle to the idea that a machine might be conscious). But this is not our topic at this time. I wish to use the general idea of the Turing test, the general idea of a *dialogic test of competence*, for a different purpose, the purpose of exploring the notion of *reference*.

Imagine a situation in which the problem is not to determine if the partner is really a person or a machine, but is rather to determine if the partner uses the words to refer as we do. The obvious test is, again, to carry on a conversation, and, if no problems arise, if the partner "passes" in the sense of being indistinguishable from someone who is certified in advance to be speaking the same language, referring to the usual sorts of objects, etc., to conclude that the partner does refer to objects as we do. When the purpose of the Turing test is as just described, that is, to determine the existence of (shared) reference, I shall refer to the test as the *Turing Test for Reference*. And, just as philosophers have discussed the question whether the original Turing test is a *definitive* test for consciousness, i.e., the question of whether a machine which "passes" the test not just once but regularly is *necessarily* conscious, so, in the same way, I wish to discuss the question of whether the Turing Test for Reference just suggested is a definitive test for shared reference.

The answer will turn out to be "No." The Turing Test for Reference is not definitive. It is certainly an excellent test in practice; but it is not logically impossible (though it is certainly highly improbable) that someone could pass the Turing Test for Reference and not be referring to anything. It follows from this, as we shall see, that we can extend our observation that words (and whole texts and discourses) do not have a necessary connection to their referents. Even if we consider not words by themselves but rules deciding what words may appropriately be produced in certain contexts—even if we consider, in computer jargon, *programs for using words*—unless those programs themselves *refer to something extra-linguistic* there is still no determinate reference that those words possess. This will be a crucial step in the process of reaching the conclusion that the Brain-in-a-Vat Worlders cannot refer to anything external at all (and hence cannot say that they are Brain-in-a-Vat Worlders).

Suppose, for example, that I am in the Turing situation (playing the "Imitation Game," in Turing's terminology) and my partner is actually a machine. Suppose this machine is able to win the game ("passes" the test). Imagine the machine to be programmed to produce beautiful responses in English to statements, questions, remarks, etc. in English, but that it has no sense organs (other than the hookup to my electric typewriter), and no motor organs (other than the electric typewriter). (As far as I can make out, Turing does not assume that the possession of either sense organs or motor organs is necessary for consciousness or intelligence.) Assume that not only does the machine lack electronic eyes and ears, etc., but that there are no provisions in the machine's program, the program for playing the Imitation Game, for incorporating inputs from such sense organs, or for controlling a body. What should we say about such a machine?

To me, it seems evident that we cannot and should not attribute reference to such a device. It is true that the machine can discourse beautifully about, say, the scenery in New England. But it could not recognize an apple tree or an apple, a mountain or a cow, a field or a steeple, if it were in front of one.

What we have is a device for producing sentences in response to sentences. But none of these sentences is at all connected to the real world. *If one coupled two of these machines and let them play the Imitation Game with each other, then they would go on "fooling" each other forever, even if the rest of the world disappeared!* There is no more reason to regard the machine's talk of apples as referring to real world apples than there is to regard the ant's "drawing" as referring to Winston Churchill.

What produces the illusion of reference, meaning, intelligence, etc., here is the fact that there is a convention of representation which *we* have under which the machine's discourse refers to apples, steeples, New England, etc. Similarly, there is the *illusion* that the ant has caricatured Churchill, for the same reason. But we are able to perceive, handle, deal with apples and fields. Our talk of apples and fields is intimately connected with our *non-verbal* transactions with apples and fields. There are "language entry rules" which take us from experiences of apples to such utterances as "I see an apple," and "language exit rules" which take us from decisions expressed in linguistic form ("I am going to buy some apples") to actions other than speaking. Lacking either language entry rules or language exit rules, there is no reason to regard the conversation of the machine (or of the two machines, in the case we envisaged of two machines playing the Imitation Game with each other) as more than syntactic play. Syntactic play that *resembles* intelligent discourse, to be sure; but only as (and no more than) the ant's curve resembles a biting caricature.

In the case of the ant, we could have argued that the ant would have drawn the same curve even if Winston Churchill had never existed. In the case of the machine, we cannot quite make the parallel argument; if apples, trees, steeples and fields had not existed, then, presumably, the programmers would not have produced that same program. Although the machine does not *perceive* apples, fields, or steeples, its creator–designers did. There is *some* causal connection between the machine and the real world apples, etc., via the perceptual experience and knowledge of the creator–designers. But such a weak connection can hardly suffice for reference. Not only is it logically possible, though fantastically improbable, that the same machine *could* have existed even if apples, fields, and steeples had not existed; more important, the machine is utterly insensitive to the *continued* existence of apples, fields, steeples, etc. Even if all these things *ceased* to exist, the machine would still discourse just as happily in the same way. That is why the machine cannot be regarded as referring at all.

The point that is relevant for our discussion is that there is nothing in Turing's Test to rule out a machine which is programmed to do nothing *but* play the Imitation Game, and that a machine which can do nothing *but* play the Imitation Game is *clearly* not referring any more than a record player is.

4. BRAINS IN A VAT (AGAIN)

Let us compare the hypothetical "brains in a vat" with the machines just described. There are obviously important differences. The brains in a vat do not have sense organs, but they do have *provision* for sense organs; that is, there are afferent nerve endings, there are inputs from these afferent nerve endings, and these inputs figure in the "program" of the brains in the vat just as they do in the program of our brains. The brains in a vat are *brains;* moreover, they are *functioning* brains, and they function by the same rules as brains do in the actual world. For these reasons, it would seem absurd to deny consciousness or intelligence to them. But the fact that they are conscious and intelligent does not mean that their words refer to what our words refer. The question we are interested in is this: do their verbalizations containing, say, the word "tree" actually refer to *trees?* More generally: can they refer to *external* objects at all? (As opposed to, for example, objects in the image produced by the automatic machinery.)

To fix our ideas, let us specify that the automatic machinery is supposed to have come into existence by some kind of cosmic chance or coincidence (or, perhaps, to have always existed). In this hypothetical world, the automatic machinery itself is supposed to have no intelligent creator–designers. In fact, as we said at the beginning of this chapter, we may imagine that all sentient beings (however minimal their sentience) are inside the vat.

This assumption does not help. For there is no connection between the *word* "tree" as used by these brains and actual trees. They would still use the word "tree" just as they do, think just the thoughts they do, have just the images they have, even if there were no actual trees. Their images, words, etc., are qualitatively identical with images, words, etc., which do represent trees in *our* world; but we have already seen (the ant again!) that qualitative similarity to something which represents an object (Winston Churchill or a tree) does not make a thing a representation all by itself. In short, the brains in a vat are not thinking about real trees when they think "there is a tree in front of me" because there is nothing by virtue of which their thought "tree" represents actual trees.

If this seems hasty, reflect on the following: we have seen that the words do not necessarily refer to trees even if they are arranged in a sequence which is identical with a discourse which (were it to occur in one of our minds) would unquestionably *be about trees* in the actual world. Nor does the "program," in the sense of the rules, practices, dispositions of the brains to verbal behavior, necessarily refer to trees or bring about reference to trees through the connections it establishes between words and words, or *linguistic* cues and *linguistic* responses. If these brains think about, refer to, represent trees (real trees, outside the vat), then it must be because of the way the "program" connects the system of language to *non-verbal* input and outputs. There are indeed such non-verbal inputs and outputs in the Brain-in-a-Vat world (those efferent and afferent nerve endings again!), but we also saw that the "sense-data" produced by the automatic machinery do not represent trees (or anything external) even when they resemble our tree-images exactly. Just as a splash of paint might resemble a tree picture without *being* a tree picture, so, we saw, a "sense datum" might be qualitatively identical with an "image of a tree" without being an image of a tree. How can the fact that, in the case of the brains in a vat, the language is connected by the program with sensory inputs which do not intrinsically or extrinsically represent trees (or anything external) possibly bring it about that the whole system of representations, the language-in-use, *does* refer to or represent trees or anything external?

The answer is that it cannot. The whole system of sense-data, motor signals to the efferent endings, and verbally or conceptually mediated thought connected by "language entry rules" to the sense-data (or whatever) as inputs and by "language exit rules" to the motor signals as outputs, has no more connection to *trees* than the ant's curve has to Winston Churchill. Once we see that the *qualitative similarity* (amounting, if you like, to qualitative identity) between the thoughts of the brains in a vat and the thoughts of someone in the actual world by no means implies sameness of reference, it is not hard to see that there is no basis at all for regarding the brain in a vat as referring to external things.

5. THE PREMISSES OF THE ARGUMENT

I have now given the argument promised to show that the brains in a vat cannot think or say that they are brains in a vat. It remains only to make it explicit and to examine its structure.

By what was just said, when the brain in a vat (in the world where every sentient being is and always was a brain in a vat) thinks "There is a tree in front of me," his thought does not refer to actual trees. On some theories it might refer to trees in the image, or to the electronic impulses that cause tree experiences, or to the features of the program that are responsible for those electronic impulses. These theories are not ruled out by what was just said, for there is a close causal connection between the use of the word "tree" in vat-English and the presence of trees in the image, the presence of electronic impulses of a certain kind, and the presence of certain features in the machine's program. On these theories the brain is *right*, not *wrong* in thinking "There is a tree in front of me." Given what "tree" refers to in vat-English and what "in front of" refers to, assuming one of these theories is correct, then the truth-conditions for "There is a tree in front of me" when it occurs in vat-English are simply that a tree in the image be "in front of" the "me" in question—in the image—or, perhaps, that the kind of electronic impulse that normally produces this experience be coming from the automatic machinery, or, perhaps, that the feature of the machinery that is supposed to produce the "tree in front of one" experience be operating. And these truth-conditions are certainly fulfilled.

By the same argument, "vat" refers to vats in the image in vat-English, or something related (electronic impulses or program features), but certainly not to real vats, since the use of "vat" in vat-English has no causal connection to real vats (apart from the connection that the brains in a vat wouldn't be able to use the word "vat," if it were not for the presence of one particular vat—the vat they are in; but this connection obtains between the use of *every* word in vat-English and that one particular vat; it is not a special connection between the use of the *particular* word "vat" and vats). Similarly, "nutrient fluid" refers to a liquid in the image in vat-English, or something related (electronic impulses or program features). It follows that if their "possible world" is really the actual one, and we are really the brains in a vat, then what we now mean by "we are brains in a vat" is that *we are brains in a vat in the image* or something of that kind (if we mean anything at all). But part of the hypothesis that we are brains in a vat is that we aren't brains in a vat in the image (i.e., what we are "hallucinating" isn't that we are brains in a vat). So, if we are brains in a vat, then the sentence "We are brains in a vat" says something false (if it says anything). In short, if we are brains in a vat, then "We are brains in a vat" is false. So it is (necessarily) false.*

NOTES

1. In this essay the terms "representation" and "reference" always refer to a relation between a word (or other sort of sign, symbol, or representation) and something that actually exists (i.e., not just an "object of thought"). There is a sense of "refer" in which I can "refer" to what does not exist; this is not the sense in which "refer" is used here. An older word for what I call "representation" or "reference" is *denotation*.

   Secondly, I follow the custom of modern logicians and use "exist" to mean "exist in the past, present, or future." Thus Winston Churchill "exists," and we can "refer to" or "represent" Winston Churchill, even though he is no longer alive.
2. A. M. Turing, "Computing Machinery and Intelligence," *Mind* (1950), reprinted in A. R. Anderson (ed.), *Minds and Machines*. This article can be found in the Minds and Machines section, p. 663 in this volume.

---

* In the next section, Putnam goes on to defend the thesis that our concepts cannot be identical to any "set of mental events" through the following famous thought experiment:

> If someone heroically attempts to maintain that the difference between the reference of "elm" and the reference of "beech" in *my* speech is explained by a difference in my psychological state, then let him imagine a Twin Earth where the words are switched. Twin Earth is very much like Earth; in fact apart from the fact that "elm" and "beech" are interchanged, the reader can suppose Twin Earth is exactly like Earth. Suppose I have a *Doppelgänger* on Twin Earth who is molecule for molecule identical with me (in the sense in which two neckties can be "identical"). If you are a dualist then suppose my *Doppelgänger* thinks the same verbalized thoughts I do, has the same sense data, the same dispositions etc. It is absurd to think his psychological state is one bit different from mine: yet his word "elm" represents *beeches* and my word "elm" represents *elms*. (Similarly, if the "water" on Twin Earth is a different liquid—say XYZ and not H_2O—then "water" represents a different liquid when used on Twin Earth and when used on Earth, etc.) Contrary to a doctrine that has been with us since the seventeenth century, *meanings just aren't in the head*.

The Matrix as Metaphysics

DAVID J. CHALMERS

David Chalmers (1966–) is an Australian philosopher who teaches at the Australian National University, where he directs the Centre for Consciousness. His primary interests lie in the philosophy of mind and related areas in philosophy and cognitive science.

The selection that appears here is excerpted from a longer essay of the same title. The full text of Chalmers's "The Matrix as Metaphysics" can be found at http://consc.net/papers/matrix.html. In it, Chalmers explores some of the themes raised by Plato, Berkeley, Quine, and Putnam in the context of the 1999 film *The Matrix*.

1. BRAINS IN VATS

The Matrix presents a version of an old philosophical fable: the brain in a vat. A disembodied brain is floating in a vat, inside a scientist's laboratory. The scientist has arranged that the brain will be stimulated with the same sort of inputs that a normal embodied brain receives. To do this, the brain is connected to a giant computer simulation of a world. The simulation determines which inputs the brain receives. When the brain produces outputs, these are fed back into the simulation. The internal state of the brain is just like that of a normal brain, despite the fact that it lacks a body. From the brain's point of view, things seem very much as they seem to you and me.

The brain is massively deluded, it seems. It has all sorts of false beliefs about the world. It believes that it has a body, but it has no body. It believes that it is walking outside in the sunlight, but in fact it is inside a dark lab. It believes it is one place, when in fact it may be somewhere quite different. Perhaps it thinks it is in Tucson, when it is actually in Australia, or even in outer space.

FIGURE 1

Neo's situation at the beginning of *The Matrix* is something like this. He thinks that he lives in a city; he thinks that he has hair; he thinks it is 1999; and he thinks that it is sunny outside. In reality, he is floating in a pod in space; he has no hair; the year is around 2199; and the world has been darkened by war. There

From *Philosophers Explore the Matrix*, ed. C. Grau, Oxford University Press, 2005. Reprinted by permission of Oxford University Press.
This paper was written for the "philosophy section" of the official Matrix website. As such, the bulk of the paper is written to be accessible for an audience without a background in philosophy. At the same time, this paper is intended as a serious work of philosophy, with relevance for central issues in epistemology, metaphysics, and the philosophy of mind and language. A section of "philosophical notes" at the end of the article draws out some of these connections explicitly.

are a few small differences from the vat scenario above: Neo's brain is located in a body, and the computer simulation is controlled by machines rather than by a scientist. But the essential details are much the same. In effect, Neo is a brain in a vat.

Let's say that a *matrix* (lower-case m) is an artificially designed computer simulation of a world. So the Matrix in the movie is one example of a matrix. And let's say that someone is *envatted*, or that they are *in a matrix*, if they have a cognitive system which receives its inputs from and sends its outputs to a matrix. Then the brain at the beginning is envatted and so is Neo.

We can imagine that a matrix simulates the entire physics of a world, keeping track of every last particle throughout space and time. (Later, we will look at ways in which this setup might be varied.) An envatted being will be associated with a particular simulated body. A connection is arranged so that whenever this body receives sensory inputs inside the simulation, the envatted cognitive system will receive sensory inputs of the same sort. When the envatted cognitive system produces motor outputs, corresponding outputs will be fed to the motor organs of the simulated body.

When the possibility of a matrix is raised, a question immediately follows: how do I know that I am not in a matrix? After all, there could be a brain in a vat structured exactly like my brain, hooked up to a matrix, with experiences indistinguishable from those I am having now. From the inside, there is no way to tell for sure that I am not in the situation of the brain in a vat. So it seems that there is no way to know for sure that I am not in a matrix.

Let us call the hypothesis that I am in a matrix and have always been in a matrix the *Matrix Hypothesis*. Equivalently, the Matrix Hypothesis says that I am envatted and have always been envatted. This is not quite equivalent to the hypothesis that I am in the Matrix, as the Matrix is just one specific version of a matrix. For now, I will ignore some complications that are specific to the Matrix in the movie, such as the fact that people sometimes travel back and forth between the Matrix and the external world. These issues aside, we can think of the Matrix Hypothesis informally as saying that I am in the same sort of situation as people who have always been in the Matrix.

The Matrix Hypothesis is one that we should take seriously. As [philosopher] Nick Bostrom has suggested, it is not out of the question that in the history of the universe, technology will evolve that will allow beings to create computer simulations of entire worlds. There may well be vast numbers of such computer simulations, compared to just one real world. If so, there may well be many more beings who are in a matrix than beings who are not. Given all this, one might even infer that it is more likely that we are in a matrix than that we are not. Whether this is right or not, it certainly seems that we cannot be *certain* that we are not in a matrix.

Serious consequences seem to follow. My envatted counterpart seems to be massively deluded. It thinks it is in Tucson; it thinks it is sitting at a desk writing an article; it thinks it has a body. On the face of it, all of these beliefs are false. Likewise, it seems that if *I* am envatted, my own corresponding beliefs are false. If I am envatted, I am not really in Tucson; I am not really sitting at a desk; and I may not even have a body. So if I don't know that I am not envatted, then I don't know that I am in Tucson; I don't know that I am sitting at a desk; and I don't know that I have a body.

The Matrix Hypothesis threatens to undercut almost everything I know. It seems to be a *skeptical hypothesis*: a hypothesis that I cannot rule out, and one that would falsify most of my beliefs if it were true. Where there is a skeptical hypothesis, it looks like none of these beliefs count as genuine knowledge. Of course the beliefs *might* be true—I might be lucky, and not be envatted—but I can't rule out the possibility that they are false. So a skeptical hypothesis leads to *skepticism* about these beliefs: I believe these things, but I do not know them.

To sum up the reasoning: I don't know that I'm not in a matrix. If I'm in a matrix, I'm probably not in Tucson. So if I don't know that I'm not in a matrix, then I don't know that I'm in Tucson. The same goes for almost everything else I think I know about the external world.

2. ENVATMENT RECONSIDERED

This is a standard way of thinking about the vat scenario. It seems that this view is also endorsed by the people who created *The Matrix*. On the DVD case for the movie, one sees the following:

> **Perception**: Our day-in, day-out world is real.
> **Reality**: That world is a hoax, an elaborate deception spun by all-powerful machines that control us. Whoa.

I think this view is not quite right. I think that even if I am in a matrix, my world is perfectly real. A brain in a vat is not massively deluded (at least if it has always been in the vat). Neo does not have massively false beliefs about the external world. Instead, envatted beings have largely *correct* beliefs about their world. If so, the Matrix Hypothesis is not a skeptical hypothesis, and its possibility does not undercut everything that I think I know.

Philosophers have held this sort of view before. The eighteenth-century philosopher George Berkeley held, in effect, that appearance is reality. (Recall Morpheus: "What is 'real'? How do you define 'real'? If you're talking about what you can feel, what you can smell, what you can taste and see, then real is simply electrical signals interpreted by your brain.") If this is right, then the world perceived by envatted beings is perfectly real: these beings experience all the right appearances, and appearance is reality. So on this view, even envatted beings have true beliefs about the world.

I have recently found myself embracing a similar conclusion, though for quite different reasons. I don't find the view that appearance is reality plausible, so I don't endorse Berkeley's reasoning. And until recently, it has seemed quite obvious to me that brains in vats would have massively false beliefs. But I now think there is a line of reasoning that shows that this is wrong.

I still think I cannot rule out the hypothesis that I am in a matrix. But I think that even if I am in a matrix, I am still in Tucson; I am still sitting at my desk; and so on. So the hypothesis that I am in a matrix is not a skeptical hypothesis. The same goes for Neo. At the beginning of the film, if he thinks "I have hair," he is correct. If he thinks "It is sunny outside," he is correct. And the same goes, of course, for the original brain in a vat. When it thinks, "I have a body," it is correct. When it thinks, "I am walking," it is correct.

This view may seem counterintuitive at first. Initially, it seemed quite counterintuitive to me. So I'll now present the line of reasoning that has convinced me that it is correct.

3. THE METAPHYSICAL HYPOTHESIS

I will argue that the hypothesis that I am envatted is not a skeptical hypothesis, but a *metaphysical hypothesis*. That is, it is a hypothesis about the underlying nature of reality.

Where physics is concerned with the microscopic processes that underlie macroscopic reality, metaphysics is concerned with the fundamental nature of reality. A metaphysical hypothesis might make a claim about the reality that underlies physics itself. Alternatively, it might say something about the nature of our minds, or the creation of our world.

I think that the Matrix Hypothesis should be regarded as a metaphysical hypothesis with all three of these elements. It makes a claim about the reality underlying physics, about the nature of our minds, and about the creation of the world.

In particular, I think the Matrix Hypothesis is equivalent to a version of the following three-part Metaphysical Hypothesis. First, physical processes are fundamentally computational. Second, our cognitive systems are separate from physical processes, but interact with these processes. Third, physical reality was created by beings outside physical space-time.

Importantly, nothing about this Metaphysical Hypothesis is skeptical. The Metaphysical Hypothesis here tells us about the processes underlying our ordinary reality, but it does not entail that this reality does not exist. We still have bodies, and there are still chairs and tables: it's just that their fundamental nature is a bit different from what we may have thought. In this manner, the Metaphysical Hypothesis is analogous to a physical hypothesis, such as one involving quantum mechanics. Both the physical hypothesis and the Metaphysical Hypothesis tell us about the processes underlying chairs. They do not entail that there are no chairs. Rather, they tell us what chairs are really like.

I will make the case by introducing each of the three parts of the Metaphysical Hypothesis separately. I will suggest that each of them is coherent, and cannot be conclusively ruled out. And I will suggest that none of them is a skeptical hypothesis: even if they are true, most of our ordinary beliefs are still correct. The same goes for a combination of all three hypotheses. I will then argue that the Matrix Hypothesis is equivalent to this combination.

(1) THE CREATION HYPOTHESIS

The *Creation Hypothesis* says: Physical space-time and its contents were created by beings outside physical space-time.

This is a familiar hypothesis. A version of it is believed by many people in our society, and perhaps by the majority of the people in the world. If one believes that God created the world, and if one believes that God is outside physical space-time, then one believes the Creation Hypothesis. One needn't believe in God to believe the Creation Hypothesis, though. Perhaps our world was created by a relatively ordinary being in the "next universe up," using the latest world-making technology in that universe. If so, the Creation Hypothesis is true.

I don't know whether the Creation Hypothesis is true. But I don't know for certain that it is false. The hypothesis is clearly coherent, and I cannot conclusively rule it out.

The Creation Hypothesis is not a skeptical hypothesis. Even if it is true, most of my ordinary beliefs are still true. I still have hands; I am still in Tucson; and so on. Perhaps a few of my beliefs will turn out to be false: if I am an atheist, for example, or if I believe all reality started with the Big Bang. But most of my everyday beliefs about the external world will remain intact.

(2) THE COMPUTATIONAL HYPOTHESIS

The *Computational Hypothesis* says: Microphysical processes throughout space-time are constituted by underlying computational processes.

The Computational Hypothesis says that physics as we know it is not the fundamental level of reality. Just as chemical processes underlie biological processes, and microphysical processes underlie chemical processes, something underlies microphysical processes. Underneath the level of quarks, electrons, and photons is a further level: the level of bits. These bits are governed by a computational algorithm, which at a higher level produces the processes that we think of as fundamental particles, forces, and so on.

The Computational Hypothesis is not as widely believed as the Creation Hypothesis, but some people take it seriously. Most famously, [computer scientist] Edward Fredkin has postulated that the universe is at bottom some sort of computer. More recently, [scientist] Stephen Wolfram has taken up the idea in his book *A New Kind of Science*, suggesting that at the fundamental level, physical reality may be a sort of cellular automata, with interact-

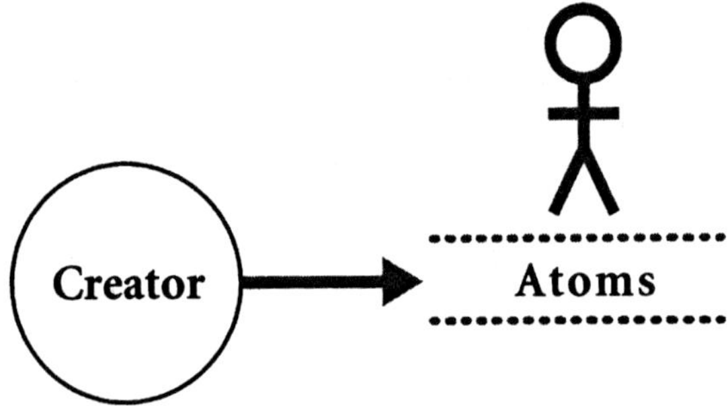

FIGURE 2

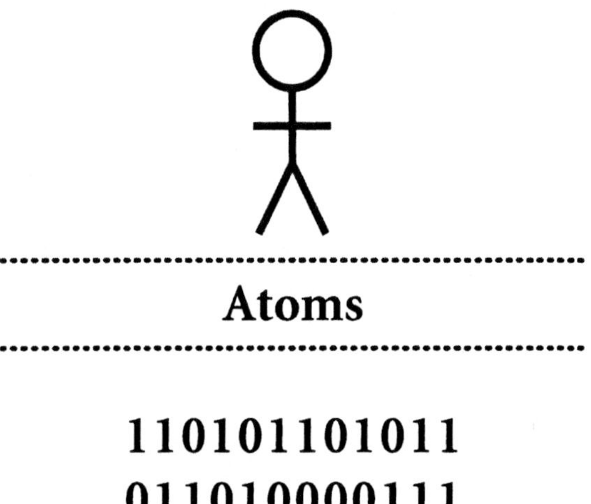

FIGURE 3

ing bits governed by simple rules. And some physicists have looked into the possibility that the laws of physics might be formulated computationally, or could be seen as the consequence of certain computational principles.

One might worry that pure bits could not be the fundamental level of reality: a bit is just a zero or a one, and reality can't really be zeroes and ones. Or perhaps a bit is just a "pure difference" between two basic states, and there can't be a reality made up of pure differences. Rather, bits always have to be implemented by more basic states, such as voltages in a normal computer.

I don't know whether this objection is right. I don't think it's completely out of the question that there could be a universe of pure bits. But this doesn't matter for present purposes. We can suppose that the computational level is itself constituted by an even more fundamental level, at which the computational processes are implemented. It doesn't matter for present purposes what that more fundamental level is. All that matters is that microphysical processes are constituted by computational processes, which are themselves constituted by more basic processes. From now on I will regard the Computational Hypothesis as saying this.

I don't know whether the Computational Hypothesis is correct. But again, I don't know that it is false. The hypothesis is coherent, if speculative, and I cannot conclusively rule it out.

The Computational Hypothesis is not a skeptical hypothesis. If it is true, there are still electrons and protons. On this picture, electrons and protons will be analogous to molecules: they are made up of something more basic, but they still exist. Similarly, if the Computational Hypothesis is true, there are still tables and chairs, and macroscopic reality still exists. It just turns out that their fundamental reality is a little different from what we thought.

The situation here is analogous to quantum mechanics or relativity. These may lead us to revise a few metaphysical beliefs about the external world: that the world is made of classical particles, or that there is absolute time. But most of our ordinary beliefs are left intact. Likewise, accepting the Computational Hypothesis may lead us to revise a few metaphysical beliefs: that electrons and protons are fundamental, for example. But most of our ordinary beliefs are unaffected.

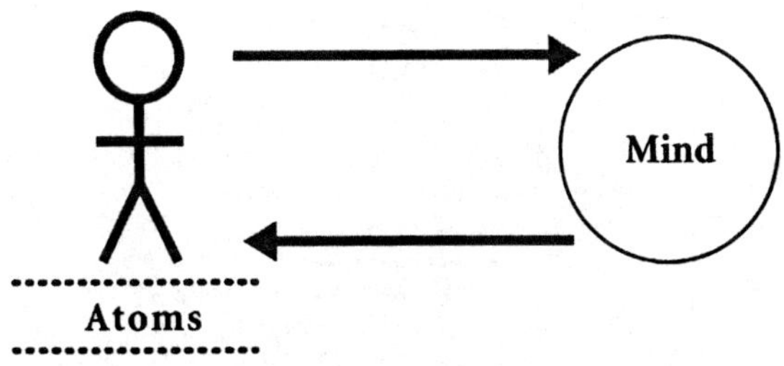

FIGURE 4

(3) THE MIND-BODY HYPOTHESIS

The *Mind-Body Hypothesis* says: My mind is (and has always been) constituted by processes outside physical space-time, and receives its perceptual inputs from and sends its outputs to processes in physical space-time.

The Mind-Body Hypothesis is also quite familiar and quite widely believed. Descartes believed something like this: on his view, we have nonphysical minds that interact with our physical bodies. The hypothesis is less widely believed today than in Descartes's time, but there are still many people who accept the Mind-Body Hypothesis.

Whether or not the Mind-Body Hypothesis is true, it is certainly coherent. Even if contemporary science tends to suggest that the hypothesis is false, we cannot rule it out conclusively.

The Mind-Body Hypothesis is not a skeptical hypothesis. Even if my mind is outside physical space-time, I still have a body; I am still in Tucson; and so on. At most, accepting this hypothesis would make us revise a few metaphysical beliefs about our minds. Our ordinary beliefs about external reality will remain largely intact.

(4) THE METAPHYSICAL HYPOTHESIS

We can now put these hypotheses together. First we can consider the *Combination Hypothesis*, which combines all three. It says that physical space-time and its contents were created by beings outside physical space-time, that microphysical processes

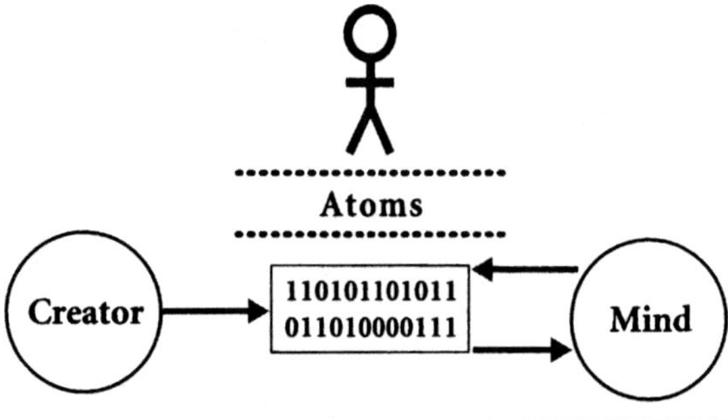

FIGURE 5

are constituted by computational processes, and that our minds are outside physical space-time but interact with it.

As with the hypotheses taken individually, the Combination Hypothesis is coherent, and we cannot conclusively rule it out. And like the hypotheses taken individually, it is not a skeptical hypothesis. Accepting it might lead us to revise a few of our beliefs, but it would leave most of them intact.

Finally, we can consider the *Metaphysical Hypothesis* (with a capital M). Like the Combination Hypothesis, this combines the Creation Hypothesis, the Computational Hypothesis, and the Mind-Body Hypothesis. It also adds the following more specific claim: the computational processes underlying physical space-time were designed by the creators as a computer simulation of a world.

(It may also be useful to think of the Metaphysical Hypothesis as saying that the computational processes constituting physical space-time are part of a broader domain, and that the creators and my cognitive system are also located within this domain. This addition is not strictly necessary for what follows, but it matches up with the most common way of thinking about the Matrix Hypothesis.)

The Metaphysical Hypothesis is a slightly more specific version of the Combination Hypothesis, in that it specifies some relations among the various parts of the hypothesis. Again, the Metaphysical Hypothesis is a coherent hypothesis, and we cannot conclusively rule it out. And again, it is not a skeptical hypothesis. Even if we accept it, most of our ordinary beliefs about the external world will be left intact.

4. THE MATRIX HYPOTHESIS AS A METAPHYSICAL HYPOTHESIS

Recall that the Matrix Hypothesis says: I have (and have always had) a cognitive system that receives its inputs from and sends its outputs to an artificially-designed computer simulation of a world.

I will argue that the Matrix Hypothesis is equivalent to the Metaphysical Hypothesis, in the following sense: if I accept the Metaphysical Hypothesis, I should accept the Matrix Hypothesis, and if I accept the Matrix Hypothesis, I should accept the Metaphysical Hypothesis. That is, the two hypotheses *imply* each other, where this means that if I accept one, I should accept the other.

Take the first direction first, from the Metaphysical Hypothesis to the Matrix Hypothesis. The Mind-Body Hypothesis implies that I have (and have always had) an isolated cognitive system which receives its inputs from and sends its outputs to processes in physical space-time. In conjunction with the Computational Hypothesis, this implies that my cognitive system receives inputs from and sends outputs to the computational processes that constitute physical space-time. The Creation Hypothesis (along with the rest of the Metaphysical Hypothesis) implies that these processes were artificially designed to simulate a world. It follows that I have (and have always had) an isolated cognitive system that receives its inputs from and sends its outputs to an artificially designed computer simulation of a world. This is just the Matrix Hypothesis. So the Metaphysical Hypothesis implies the Matrix Hypothesis.

The other direction is closely related. To put it informally: if I accept the Matrix Hypothesis, I accept that what underlies apparent reality is just as the Metaphysical Hypothesis specifies. There is a domain containing my cognitive system, which is causally interacting with a computer simulation of physical space-time, which was created by other beings in that domain. This is just what has to obtain in order for the Metaphysical Hypothesis to obtain. If one accepts this, one should accept the Creation Hypothesis, the Computational Hypothesis, the Mind-Body Hypothesis, and the relevant relations among these.

This may be a little clearer through a picture. Here is the shape of the world according to the Matrix Hypothesis.

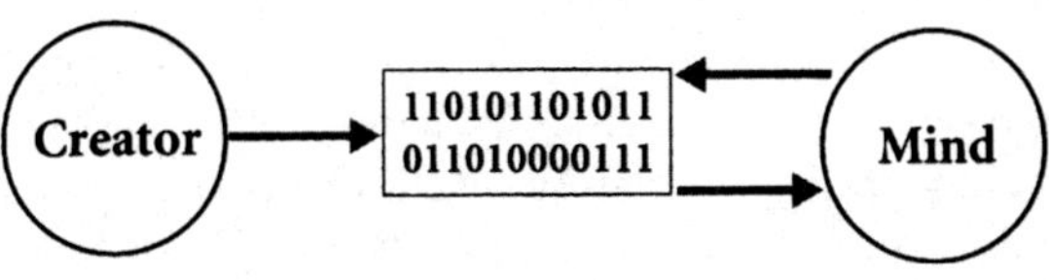

FIGURE 6

At the fundamental level, this picture of the shape of the world is exactly the same as the picture of the Metaphysical Hypothesis given above. So if one accepts that the world is as it is according to the Matrix Hypothesis, one should accept that it is as it is according to the Metaphysical Hypothesis.

One might make various objections. For example, one might object that the Matrix Hypothesis implies that a computer simulation of physical processes exists, but (unlike the Metaphysical Hypothesis) it does not imply that the physical processes themselves exist. I will discuss this objection in section 6, and other objections in section 7. For now, though, I take it that there is a strong case that the Matrix Hypothesis implies the Metaphysical Hypothesis, and vice versa.

5. LIFE IN THE MATRIX

If this is right, it follows that the Matrix Hypothesis is not a skeptical hypothesis. If I accept it, I should not infer that the external world does not exist, nor that I have no body, nor that there are no tables and chairs, nor that I am not in Tucson. Rather, I should infer that the physical world is constituted by computations beneath the microphysical level. There are still tables, chairs, and bodies: these are made up fundamentally of bits and of whatever constitutes these bits. This world was created by other beings, but is still perfectly real. My mind is separate from physical processes, and interacts with them. My mind may not have been created by these beings, and it may not be made up of bits, but it still interacts with these bits.

The result is a complex picture of the fundamental nature of reality. The picture is strange and surprising, perhaps, but it is a picture of a full-blooded external world. If we are in a matrix, this is simply the way that the world is.

We can think of the Matrix Hypothesis as a creation myth for the information age. If it is correct, then the physical world was created, but necessarily by gods. Underlying the physical world is a giant computation, and creators created this world by implementing this computation. And our minds lie outside this physical structure, with an independent nature that interacts with this structure.

Many of the same issues that arise with standard creation myths arise here. When was the world created? Strictly speaking, it was not created within *our* time at all. When did history begin? The creators might have started the simulation in 4004 B.C. (or in 1999) with the fossil record intact, but it would have been much easier for them to start the simulation at the Big Bang and let things run their course from there. (In *The Matrix*, of course, the creators are machines. This gives an interesting twist on common theological readings of the movie. It is often held that Neo is the Christ figure in the movie, with Morpheus corresponding to John the Baptist, Cypher to Judas Iscariot, and so on. But on the reading I have given, the gods of *The Matrix* are the machines. Who, then, is the Christ figure? Agent Smith, of course! After all, he is the gods' offspring, sent down to save the Matrix-world from those who wish to destroy it. And in the second movie, he is even resurrected.)

Many of the same issues that arise on the standard Mind-Body Hypothesis also arise here. When do our nonphysical minds start to exist? It depends on just when new envatted cognitive systems are attached to the simulation (perhaps at the time of conception within the matrix, or perhaps at the time of birth?). Is there life after death? It depends on just what happens to the envatted systems once their simulated bodies die. How do mind and body interact? By causal links that are outside physical space and time.

Even if we are not in a matrix, we can extend a version of this reasoning to other beings who are in a matrix. If they discover their situation, and come to accept that they are in a matrix, they should not reject their ordinary beliefs about the external world. At most, they should come to revise their beliefs about the underlying nature of their world: they should come to accept that external objects are made of bits, and so on. These beings are not massively deluded: most of their ordinary beliefs about their world are correct.

There are a few qualifications here. One may worry about beliefs about other people's minds. I believe that my friends are conscious. If I am in a matrix, is this correct? In the Matrix depicted in the movie, these beliefs are mostly fine. This is a multivat matrix: for each of my perceived friends, there is an envatted being in the external reality, who is presumably conscious like me. The exception might be beings such as Agent Smith, who are not envatted but are entirely computational. Whether these beings are conscious depends on whether computation is enough for consciousness. I will remain neutral on that issue here. We could circumvent this issue by building into the Matrix Hypothesis the requirement that all of the beings we perceive are envatted. But even if we do not build in this requirement, we are not much worse off than in the actual world, where there is a legitimate issue about whether other beings are conscious, quite independent of whether we are in a matrix.

One might also worry about beliefs about the distant past, and about the far future. These will be unthreatened as long as the computer simulation covers all of space-time, from the Big Bang until the end of the universe. This is built into the Metaphysical Hypothesis, and we can stipulate that it is built into the Matrix Hypothesis too, by requiring that the computer simulation be a simulation of an entire world. There may be other simulations that start in the recent past (perhaps the Matrix in the movie is like this), and there may be others that only last for a short while. In these cases, the envatted beings will have false beliefs about the past or the future in their worlds. But as long as the simulation covers the lifespan of these beings, it is plausible that they will have mostly correct beliefs about the current state of their environment.

There may be some respects in which the beings in a matrix are deceived. It may be that the creators of the matrix control and interfere with much of what happens in the simulated world. (The Matrix in the movie may be like this, though the extent of the creators' control is not quite clear.) If so, then these beings may have much less control over what happens than they think. But the same goes if there is an interfering god in a nonmatrix world. And the Matrix Hypothesis does not imply that the creators interfere with the world, though it leaves the possibility open. At worst, the Matrix Hypothesis is no more skeptical in this respect than is the Creation Hypothesis in a nonmatrix world.

The inhabitants of a matrix may also be deceived in that reality is much bigger than they think. They might think their physical universe is all there is, when in fact there is much more in the world, including beings and objects that they can never possibly see. But again, this sort of worry can arise equally in a nonmatrix world. For example, cosmologists seriously entertain the hypothesis that our universe may stem from a black hole in the "next universe up," and that in reality there may be a whole tree of universes. If so, the world is also much bigger than we think, and there may be beings and objects that we can never possibly see. But either way, the world that we see is perfectly real.

Importantly, none of these sources of skepticism—about other minds, the past and the future, our control over the world, and the extent of the world—casts doubt on our belief in the reality of the world that we perceive. None of them leads us to doubt the existence of external objects such as tables and chairs, in the way that the vat hypothesis is supposed to do. And none of these worries is especially tied to the matrix scenario. One can raise doubts about whether other minds exist, whether the past and the future exist, and whether we have control over our world quite independently of whether we are in a matrix. If this is right, then the Matrix Hypothesis does not raise the distinctive skeptical issues that it is often taken to raise.

I suggested before that it is not out of the question that we really are in a matrix. One might have thought that this would be a worrying conclusion. But if I am right, it is not nearly as worrying as one might have thought. Even if we are in such a matrix, our world is no less real than we thought it was. It just has a surprising fundamental nature.

. . .

7. OTHER OBJECTIONS

When we look at a brain in a vat from the outside, it is hard to avoid the sense that it is deluded. This sense manifests itself in a number of related objections. These are not direct objections to the argument above, but they are objections to its conclusion.

Objection 1: A brain in a vat may think it is outside walking in the sun, when in fact it is alone in a dark room. Surely, it is deluded.

Response: The *brain* is alone in a dark room. But this does not imply that the *person* is alone in a dark room. By analogy, just say Descartes is right that we have disembodied minds outside space-time, made of ectoplasm. When I think, "I am outside in the sun," an angel might look at my ectoplasmic mind and note that in fact it is not exposed to any sun at all. Does it follow that my thought is incorrect? Presumably not: I can be outside in the sun, even if my ectoplasmic mind is not. The angel would be wrong to infer that I have an incorrect belief. Likewise, we should not infer that the envatted being has an incorrect belief. At least, it is no more deluded than a Cartesian mind.

The moral is that the immediate surroundings of our minds may well be irrelevant to the truth of most of our beliefs. What matters is the processes that our minds are connected to, by perceptual inputs and motor outputs. Once we recognize this, the objection falls away.

Objection 2: An envatted being may believe that it is in Tucson, when in fact it is in New York, and has never been anywhere near Tucson. Surely, this belief is deluded.

Response: The envatted being's concept of "Tucson" does not refer to what we call Tucson. Rather, it refers to something else entirely: call this "Tucson*" or "virtual Tucson." We might think of this as a virtual location (more on this in a moment). When the being says to itself, "I am in Tucson," it really is thinking that it is in Tucson*, and it may well be in Tucson*. Because Tucson is not Tucson*, the fact that the being has never been in Tucson is irrelevant to whether its belief is true.

A rough analogy: I look at my colleague Terry and think, "That's Terry." Elsewhere in the world, a duplicate of me looks at a duplicate of Terry. It thinks, "That's Terry," but it is not looking at the real Terry. Is its belief false? It seems not: my duplicate's "Terry" concept refers not to Terry, but to his duplicate Terry*. My duplicate really is looking at Terry*, so its belief is true. The same sort of thing is happening in the case above.

Objection 3: Before he leaves the Matrix, Neo believes that he has hair. But in reality he has no hair (the body in the vat is bald). Surely this belief is deluded.

Response: This case is like the last one. Neo's concept of "hair" does not refer to real hair, but to something else that we might call hair* (virtual hair). So the fact that Neo does not have real hair is irrelevant to whether his belief is true. Neo really does have virtual hair, so he is correct. Likewise, when a child in the movie tells Neo, "There is no spoon," his concept refers to a virtual spoon, and there really is a virtual spoon. So the child is wrong.

Objection 4: What *sort* of objects does an envatted being refer to? What *is* virtual hair, virtual Tucson, and so on?

Response: These are all entities constituted by computational processes. If I am envatted, then the objects to which I refer (hair, Tucson, and so on) are all made of bits. And if another being is envatted, the objects that it refers to (hair*, Tucson*, and so on) are likewise made of bits. If the envatted being is hooked up to a simulation in my computer, then the objects to which it refers are constituted by patterns of bits inside my computer. We might call these things *virtual objects*. Virtual hands are not hands (assuming I am not envatted), but they exist inside the computer all the same. Virtual Tucson is not Tucson, but it exists inside the computer all the same.

Objection 5: You just said that virtual hands are not real hands. Does this mean that if we are in a matrix, we don't have real hands?

Response: No. If we are *not* in a matrix, but other beings are, we should say that their term *hand* refers to virtual hands, but our term does not. So in this case, our hands aren't virtual hands. But if we *are* in a matrix, then our term "hand" refers to something that's made of bits: virtual hands, or at least something that would be regarded as virtual hands by people in the next world up. That is, if we *are* in a matrix, real hands are made of bits. Things look quite different, and our words refer to different things, depending on whether our perspective is from inside or outside the matrix.

This sort of perspective shift is common in thinking about the matrix scenario. From the first-person perspective, we suppose that *we* are in a matrix. Here, real things in our world are made of bits, though the "next world up" might not be made of bits. From the third-person perspective we suppose that someone *else* is in a matrix but we are not. Here, real things in our world are not made of bits, but the "next world down" is made of bits. On the first way of doing things, our words refer to computational entities. On the second way of doing things, the envatted beings' words refer to computational entities, but our words do not.

Objection 6: Just which pattern of bits is a given virtual object? Surely it will be impossible to pick out a precise set.

Response: This question is like asking: just which part of the quantum wave function is this chair, or is the University of Arizona? These objects are all ultimately constituted by an underlying quantum wave function, but there may be no precise part of the micro-level wave function that we can say "is" the chair or the university. The chair and the university exist at a higher level. Likewise, if we are envatted, there may be no precise set of bits in the micro-level computational process that is the chair or the university. These exist at a higher level. And if someone else is envatted, there may be no precise sets of bits in the computer simulation that "are" the objects to which they refer. But just as a chair exists without being any precise part of the wave function, a virtual chair may exist without being any precise set of bits.

Objection 7: An envatted being thinks it performs actions, and it thinks it has friends. Are these beliefs correct?

Response: One might try to say that the being performs actions* and that it has friends*. But for various reasons I think it is not plausible that words like "action" and "friend" can shift their meanings as easily as words like "Tucson" and "hair." Instead, I think one can say truthfully (in our own language) that the envatted being performs actions, and that it has friends. To be sure, it performs actions in *its* environment, and its environment is not our environment but the virtual environment. And its friends likewise inhabit the virtual environment (assuming that we have a multivat matrix, or that computation suffices for consciousness). But the envatted being is not incorrect in this respect.

Objection 8: Set these technical points aside. Surely, if we are in a matrix, the world is nothing like we think it is.

Response: I deny this. Even if we are in a matrix, there are still people, football games, and particles, arranged in space-time just as we think they are. It is just that the world has a *further* nature that goes beyond our initial conception. In particular, things in the world are realized computationally in a way that we might not have originally imagined. But this does not contradict any of our ordinary beliefs. At most, it will contradict a few of our more abstract metaphysical beliefs. But exactly the same goes for quantum mechanics, relativity theory, and so on.

If we are in a matrix, we may not have many false beliefs, but there is much knowledge that we lack. For example, we do not know that the universe is realized computationally. But this is just what one should expect. Even if we are not in a matrix, there may well be much about the fundamental nature of reality that we do not know. We are not omniscient creatures, and our knowledge of the world is at best partial. This is simply the condition of a creature living in a world.

8. OTHER SKEPTICAL HYPOTHESES

The Matrix Hypothesis is one example of a traditional "skeptical" hypothesis, but it is not the only example. Other skeptical hypotheses are not quite as straightforward as the Matrix Hypothesis. Still, I think that for many of them, a similar line of reasoning applies. In particular, one can argue that most of these are not global skeptical hypotheses: that is, their truth would not undercut all of our empirical beliefs about the physical world. At worst, most of them are *partial* skeptical hypotheses, undercutting some of our empirical beliefs, but leaving many other beliefs intact.

New Matrix Hypothesis: I was recently created, along with all of my memories, and was put in a newly created matrix.

What if both the matrix and I have existed for only a short time? This hypothesis is a computational version of Bertrand Russell's Recent Creation Hypothesis: the physical world was created only recently (with fossil record intact), and so was I (with memories intact). On that hypothesis, the external world that I perceive really exists, and most of my beliefs about its current state are plausibly true, but I have many false beliefs about the past. I think the same should be said of the New Matrix Hypothesis. One can argue, along the lines presented earlier, that the New Matrix Hypothesis is equivalent to a combination of the Metaphysical Hypothesis with the Recent Creation Hypothesis. This combination is not a global skeptical hypothesis (though it is a partial skeptical hypothesis, where beliefs about the past are concerned). So the same goes for the New Matrix Hypothesis.

Recent Matrix Hypothesis: For most of my life I have not been envatted, but I was recently hooked up to a matrix.

If I was recently put in a matrix without realizing it, it seems that many of my beliefs about my current environment are false. Let's say that just yesterday someone put me into a simulation, in which I fly to Las Vegas and gamble at a casino. Then I may believe that I am in Las Vegas now, and that I am in a casino, but these beliefs are false: I am really in a laboratory in Tucson.

This result is quite different from the long-term matrix. The difference lies in the fact that my conception of external reality is anchored to the reality in which I have lived most of my life. If I have been envatted all of my life, my conception is anchored to the computationally constituted reality. But if I were just envatted yesterday, my conception is anchored to the external reality. So when I think that I am in Las Vegas, I am thinking that I am in the external Las Vegas, and this thought is false.

Still, this does not undercut all of my beliefs about the external world. I believe that I was born in Sydney, that there is water in the oceans, and so on, and all of these beliefs are correct. It is only my recently acquired beliefs, stemming from my perception of the simulated environment, that will be false. So this is only a partial skeptical hypothesis: its possibility casts doubt on a subset of our empirical beliefs, but it does not cast doubt on all of them.

Interestingly, the Recent Matrix and the New Matrix hypotheses give opposite results, despite their similar nature: the Recent Matrix Hypothesis yields true beliefs about the past but false beliefs about the present, while the New Matrix Hypothesis yields false beliefs about the past and true beliefs about the present. The differences are tied to the fact that in the Recent Matrix Hypothesis, I really have a past existence for my beliefs to be about, and that past reality has played a role in anchoring the contents of my thoughts, which has no parallel under the New Matrix Hypothesis.

Local Matrix Hypothesis: I am hooked up to a computer simulation of a fixed local environment in a world.

On one way of doing this, a computer simulates a small fixed environment in a world, and the subjects in the simulation encounter some sort of barrier when they try to leave that area. For example, in the movie *The Thirteenth Floor*, just California is simulated, and when the subject tries to drive to Nevada, a road sign says "Closed for Repair" (with faint green electronic mountains in the distance!). Of course this is not the best way to create a matrix, as subjects are likely to discover the limits to their world.

This hypothesis is analogous to a Local Creation Hypothesis, on which creators just created a local part of the physical world. Under this hypothesis, we will have true beliefs about nearby matters, but false beliefs about matters farther from home. By the usual sort of reasoning, the Local Matrix Hypothesis can be seen as a combination of the Metaphysical Hypothesis with the Local Creation Hypothesis. So we should say the same thing about this.

Extendible Local Matrix Hypothesis: I am hooked up to a computer simulation of a local environment in a world, which is extended when necessary depending on my movements.

This hypothesis avoids the obvious difficulties with a fixed local matrix. Here, the creators simulate a local environment and extend it when necessary. For example, they might right now be concentrating on simulating a room in my house in Tucson. If I walk into another room, or fly to another city, they will simulate those. Of course, they need to make sure that when I go to these places, they match my memories and beliefs reasonably well, with allowance for evolution in the meantime. The same goes for when I encounter familiar people, or people I have only heard about. Presumably, the simulators keep up a database of the information about the world that has been settled so far, updating this information whenever necessary as time goes along, and making up new details when they need them.

This sort of simulation is quite unlike simulation in an ordinary matrix. In a matrix, the whole world is simulated at once. There are high start-up costs, but once the simulation is up and running, it will take care of itself. By contrast, the extendible local matrix involves "just-in-time" simulation. This has much lower start-up costs, but it requires much more work and creativity as the simulation evolves.

This hypothesis is analogous to an Extendible Local Creation Hypothesis about ordinary reality, under which creators create just a local physical environment and extend it when necessary. Here, external reality exists and many local beliefs are true, but again beliefs about matters farther from home are false. If we combine that hypothesis with the Metaphysical Hypothesis, the result is the Extendible Local Matrix Hypothesis. So if we are in an extendible local matrix, external reality still exists, but there is not as much of it as we thought. Of course if I travel in the right direction, more of it may come into existence.

The situation is reminiscent of the film *The Truman Show*. Truman lives in an artificial environment made up of actors and props, which behave appropriately when he is around, but which may be completely different when he is absent. Truman has many true beliefs about his current environment: there really are tables and chairs in front of him, and so on. But he is deeply mistaken about things outside his current environment, and farther from home.

It is common to think that while *The Truman Show* poses a disturbing skeptical scenario, *The Matrix* is much worse. But if I am right, things are reversed. If I am in a matrix, then most of my beliefs about the external world are true. If I am in something like *The Truman Show*, then a great number of my beliefs are false. On reflection, it seems to me that this is the right conclusion. If we were to discover that we were (and always had been) in a matrix, this would be surprising, but we would quickly get used to it. If we were to discover that we were (and always had been) in a televised "Truman Show," we might well go insane.

Macroscopic Matrix Hypothesis: I am hooked up to a computer simulation of macroscopic physical processes without microphysical detail.

One can imagine that, for ease of simulation, the makers of a matrix might not bother to simulate low-level physics. Instead, they might just represent macroscopic objects in the world and their properties: for example, that there is a table with such-and-such shape, position, and color, with a book on top of it with certain properties, and so on. They will need to make some effort to make sure that these objects behave in physically reasonable ways, and they will have to make special provisions for handling microphysical measurements, but one can imagine that at least a reasonable simulation could be created this way.

I think this hypothesis is analogous to a Macroscopic World Hypothesis: there are no microphysical processes, and instead macroscopic physical objects exist as fundamental objects in the world, with properties of shape, color, position, and so on. This is a coherent way that our world could be, and it is not a global skeptical hypothesis, though it may lead to false scientific beliefs about lower levels of reality. The Macroscopic Matrix Hypothesis can be seen as a combination of this hypothesis with a version of the Metaphysical Hypothesis. As such, it is not a global skeptical hypothesis either.

One can also combine the various hypotheses above in various ways, yielding hypotheses such as a New Local Macroscopic Matrix Hypothesis. For the usual reasons, all of these can be seen as analogs of corresponding hypotheses about the physical world. So all of them are compatible with the existence of physical reality, and none is a global skeptical hypothesis.

God Hypothesis: Physical reality is represented in the mind of God, and our own thoughts and perceptions depend on God's mind.

A hypothesis like this was put forward by George Berkeley as a view about how our world might really be. Berkeley intended this as a sort of metaphysical hypothesis about the nature of reality. Most other philosophers have differed from Berkeley in regarding this as a sort of skeptical hypothesis. If I am right, Berkeley is closer to the truth. The God Hypothesis can be seen as a version of the Matrix Hypothesis, on which the simulation of the world is implemented in the mind of God. If this is right, we should say that physical processes really exist: it's just that at the most fundamental level, they are constituted by processes in the mind of God.

Evil Genius Hypothesis: I have a disembodied mind, and an evil genius is feeding me sensory inputs to give the appearance of an external world.

This is René Descartes's classical skeptical hypothesis. What should we say about it? This depends on just how the evil genius works. If the evil genius simulates an entire world in his head in order to determine what inputs I should receive, then we have a version of the God Hypothesis. Here we should say that physical reality exists and is constituted by processes within the mind of the evil genius. If the evil genius is simulating only a small part of the physical world, just enough to give me reasonably consistent inputs, then we have an analog of the Local Matrix Hypothesis (in either its fixed or flexible versions). Here we should say that just a local part of external reality exists. If the evil genius is not bothering to simulate the microphysical level, but just the macroscopic level, then we have an analog of the Macroscopic Matrix Hypothesis. Here we should say that local external macroscopic objects exist, but our beliefs about their microphysical nature are incorrect.

The Evil Genius Hypothesis is often taken to be a global skeptical hypothesis. But if the reasoning above is right, this is incorrect. Even if the Evil Genius Hypothesis is correct, some of the external reality that we apparently perceive really exists, though we may have some false beliefs about it, depending on details. It is just that this external reality has an underlying nature that is quite different from what we may have thought.

Dream Hypothesis: I am now and have always been dreaming.

Descartes raised the question: how do you know that you are not currently dreaming? Morpheus raises a similar question:

> Have you ever had a dream, Neo, that you were so sure was real. What if you were unable to wake from that dream? How would you know the difference between the dream world and the real world?

The hypothesis that I am *currently* dreaming is analogous to a version of the Recent Matrix Hypothesis. I cannot rule it out conclusively, and if it is correct, then many of my beliefs about my current environment are incorrect. But presumably, I still have many true beliefs about the external world, anchored in the past.

What if I have always been dreaming? That is, what if all of my apparent perceptual inputs have been generated by my own cognitive system, without my realizing this? I think this case is analogous to the Evil Genius Hypothesis: it's just that the role of the "evil genius" is played by a part of my own cognitive system! If my dream-generating system simulates all of space-time, we have something like the original Matrix Hypothesis. If it models just my local environment, or just some macroscopic processes, we have analogs of the more local versions of the Evil Genius Hypothesis. In any of these cases, we should say that the objects that I am currently perceiving really exist (although objects farther from home may not). It is just that some of them are constituted by my own cognitive processes.

Chaos Hypothesis: I do not receive inputs from anywhere in the world. Instead, I have random, uncaused experiences. Through a huge coincidence, they are exactly the sort of regular, structured experiences with which I am familiar.

The Chaos Hypothesis is an extraordinarily unlikely hypothesis, much more unlikely than anything considered above. But it is still one that could in principle obtain, even if it has minuscule probability. If I am chaotically envatted, do physical processes in the external world exist? I think we should say that they do not. My experiences of external objects are caused by nothing, and the set of experiences associated with my conception of a given object will have no common source. Indeed, my experiences are not caused by any reality external to them at all. So this is a genuine skeptical hypothesis: if accepted, it would cause us to reject most of our beliefs about the external world.

So far, the only clear case of a global skeptical hypothesis is the Chaos Hypothesis. Unlike the previous hypotheses, accepting this hypothesis would undercut all of our substantive beliefs about the external world. Where does the difference come from?

Arguably, what is crucial is that on the Chaos Hypothesis, there is no causal explanation of our experiences at all, and there is no explanation for the regularities in our experience. In all of the previous cases, there is some explanation for these regularities, though perhaps not the explanation that we expect. One might suggest that as long as a hypothesis involves *some* reasonable explanation for the regularities in our experience, then it will not be a global skeptical hypothesis.

If so, then if we are granted the assumption that there is some explanation for the regularities in our experience, then it is safe to say that some of our beliefs about the external world are correct. This is not much, but it is something.

9. PHILOSOPHICAL NOTES

The material above was written to be accessible to a wide audience, so it deliberately omits technical philosophical details, connections to the literature, and so on. In this section I will remedy this omission. Readers without a background in philosophy may choose to skip or skim this section.

NOTE 1

Hilary Putnam (1981) has argued that the hypothesis that I am (and have always been) a brain in a vat can be ruled out a priori. In effect, this is because my word "brain" refers to objects in my perceived world, and it cannot refer to objects in an "outer" world in which the vat would have to exist. For my hypothesis "I am a brain in a vat" to be true, I would have to be a brain of the sort that exists in the perceived world, but that cannot be the case. So the hypothesis must be false.

An analogy: I can arguably rule out the hypothesis that I am in the Matrix (capital M). My term "the Matrix" refers to a specific system that I have seen in a movie in my perceived world. I could not be in that very system as the system exists within the world that I perceive. So my hypothesis "I am in the Matrix" must be false.

This conclusion about the Matrix seems reasonable, but there is a natural response. Perhaps this argument rules out the hypothesis that I am in the Matrix, but I cannot rule out the hypothesis that I am in a matrix, where a matrix is a generic term for a computer simulation of a world. The term "Matrix" may be anchored to the specific system in the movie, but the generic term "matrix" is not.

Likewise, it is arguable that I can rule out the hypothesis that I am a brain in a vat (if "brain" is anchored to a specific sort of biological system in my perceived world). But I cannot rule out the hypothesis that I am envatted, where this simply says that I have a cognitive system that receives input from and sends outputs to a computer simulation of a world. The term "envatted" (and the terms used in its definition) are generic terms, not anchored to specific systems in perceived reality. By using this slightly different language, we can restate the skeptical hypothesis in a way that is invulnerable to Putnam's reasoning.

More technically: Putnam's argument may work for "brain" and "Matrix" because one is a natural kind term and the other is a name. These terms are subject to "Twin Earth" thought-experiments (Putnam

1975), where duplicates can use corresponding terms with different referents. On Earth, Oscar's term "water" refers to H_2O, but on Twin Earth (which contains the superficially identical XYZ in its oceans and lakes), Twin Oscar's term "water" refers to XYZ. Likewise, perhaps my term "brain" refers to biological brains, while an envatted being's term "brain" refers to virtual brains. If so, when an envatted being says, "I am a brain in a vat," it is not referring to its biological brain, and its claim is false.

But not all terms are subject to Twin Earth thought-experiments. In particular, *semantically neutral* terms are not (at least when used without semantic deference): such terms plausibly include "philosopher," "friend," and many others. Other such terms include "matrix" and "envatted," as defined earlier. If we work with hypotheses such as "I am in a matrix" and "I am envatted," rather than "I am in the Matrix" or "I am a brain in a vat," then Putnam's argument does not apply. Even if a brain in a vat could not truly think, "I am a brain in a vat," it could truly think, "I am envatted." So I think that Putnam's line of reasoning is ultimately a red herring.

NOTE 2

Despite this disagreement, my main conclusion is closely related to another suggestion of Putnam's. This is the suggestion that a brain in a vat may have true beliefs, because it will refer to chemical processes or processes inside a computer. However, I reach this conclusion by a quite different route. Putnam argues by an appeal to the causal theory of reference: thoughts refer to what they are causally connected to, and the thoughts of an envatted being are causally connected to processes in a computer. This argument is clearly inconclusive, as the causal theory of reference is so unconstrained. To say that a causal connection is required for reference is not to say what sort of causal connection suffices. There are many cases (like "phlogiston") where terms fail to refer despite rich causal connections.* Intuitively, it is natural to think that the brain in a vat is a case like this, so an appeal to the causal theory of reference does not seem to help.

The argument I have given presupposes nothing about the theory of reference. Instead, it proceeds directly by considering first-order hypotheses about the world, the connections among these, and what we should say if they are true. In answering objections, I have made some claims about reference, and these claims are broadly compatible with a causal theory of reference. But importantly, these claims are very much consequences of the first-order argument rather than presuppositions of it. In general, I think that claims in the theory of reference are beholden to first-order judgments about cases, rather than vice versa.

* During the seventeenth and eighteenth centuries, Western scientists believed in the existence of a fire-like element phlogiston, contained within combustible bodies, which was supposedly released during processes that we now recognize as oxidation processes (such as combustion and rusting). Its existence was disproved experimentally during the second half of the eighteenth century.

Fiction

ROBERT NOZICK

American philosopher Robert Nozick (1938–2002) taught philosophy at Harvard University. Selections from his philosophical writing appear previously in this section and in the section on Moral and Political Philosophy.

The selection that appears here is a short story that was originally published in 1980 in the literary journal *Ploughshares*.

Robert Nozick, "Fiction," *Ploughshares* 6, no. 3 (Fall 1980): 74–77.

I am a fictional character. However, you would be in error to smile smugly, feeling ontologically superior. For you are a fictional character, too. All my readers are except one who is, properly, not reader but author.

I am a fictional character; this is *not,* however, a work of fiction, no more so than any other work you've ever read. It is not a modernist work that self-consciously *says* it's a work of fiction, nor one even more tricky that denies its fictional status. We all are familiar with such works and know how to deal with them, how to frame them so that *nothing* the author says—nothing the first person voices even in an afterword or in something headed "author's note"—can convince us that anyone is speaking seriously, *non*-fictionally in his own first person.

All the more severe is my own problem of informing you that this very piece you are reading is a work of non-fiction, yet we are fictional characters, nevertheless. *Within* this world of fiction we inhabit, this writing is non-fictional, although in a wider sense, encased as it is in a work of fiction, it too can only be a fiction.

Think of our world as a novel in which you yourself are a character. Is there any way to tell what our author is like? Perhaps. *If* this is a work in which the author *expresses* himself, we can draw inferences about his facets, while noting that each such inference we draw will be written by him. And if he writes that we find a particular inference plausible or valid, who are we to argue?

One sacred scripture in the novel we inhabit says that the author of our universe created things merely by speaking, by saying "Let there be . . ." The only thing mere speaking can create, we know, is a story, a play, an epic poem, a fiction. Where we live is created by and in words: a uni-verse.

Recall what is known as the problem of evil: why does a good creator allow evil in the world, evil he knows of and can prevent? However, when an author includes monstrous deeds—pain and suffering—in his work, does this cast any special doubt upon his goodness? Is an author callous who puts his characters through hardships? Not if the characters do not suffer them *really*. But don't they? Wasn't Hamlet's father really killed? (Or was he merely hiding to see how Hamlet would respond?) Lear really was cast adrift—he didn't just dream this. Macbeth, on the other hand, did *not* see a real dagger. But these characters aren't real and never were, so there was no suffering outside of the world of the work, no *real* suffering in the author's *own* world, and so in his creating, the author was not cruel. (Yet why is it cruel only when he creates suffering in his *own* world? Would it be perfectly all right for Iago to create misery in *our* world?)

"What!" you say, "we don't really undergo suffering? Why it's as real to us as Oedipus's is to him." Precisely as real. "But can't you *prove* that you *really* exist?" If Shakespeare had Hamlet say "I think, therefore I am," would that prove to us that Hamlet exists? Should it prove that to Hamlet, and if so what is such a proof worth? Could not *any* proof be written into a work of fiction and be presented by one of the characters, perhaps one named "Descartes"? (Such a character should worry less that he's dreaming, more that he's dreamed.)

Often, people discover anomalies in the world, facts that just don't jibe. The deeper dug, the more puzzles found—far-fetched coincidences, dangling facts—on these feed conspiracy and assassination buffs. That number of hours spent probing into *anything* might produce anomalies, however, if reality is not as coherent as we thought, if it is not *real*. Are we simply discovering the limits of the details the author worked out? But *who* is discovering this? The author who writes our discoveries knows them himself. Perhaps he now is preparing to correct them. Do we live in galley proofs in the process of being corrected? Are we living in a *first draft*?

My tendency, I admit, is to want to revolt, to conspire along with the rest of you to overthrow our author or to make our positions more equal, at least, to hide some portion of our lives from him—to gain a little breathing space. Yet these words I write he reads, my secret thoughts and modulations of feeling he knows and records, my Jamesian* author.

---

* Henry James (1843–1916) was an important author and literary critic of the late 19th and early 20th centuries. His work was noted for its psychological insight and employment of interior monologue.

But does he *control* it all? Or does our author, through writing, learn about his characters and from them? Is he surprised by what he finds us doing and thinking? When we feel we freely think or act on our own, is this merely a description he has written in for us, or does he *find* it to be true of us, his characters, and therefore write it? Does our leeway and privacy reside in this, that there are some implications of his work that he hasn't yet worked out, some things he has not thought of which nevertheless are true in the world he has created, so that there are actions and thoughts of ours that elude his ken? (Must we therefore speak *in code*?) Or is he only ignorant of what we *would* do or say in some *other* circumstances, so that our independence lies only in the *subjunctive* realm?

Does this way madness lie? Or enlightenment?

Our author, we know, is outside our realm, yet he may not be free of our problems. Does he wonder too whether *he* is a character in a work of fiction, whether his writing our universe is a play within a play? Does he have me write this work and especially this very paragraph in order to express his own concerns?

It would be nice for us if our author too is a fictional character and this fictional world he made describes (that being no coincidence) the actual world inhabited by *his* author, the one who created him. We then would be fictional characters who, unbeknownst to our own author although not to his, correspond to real people. (Is that why we are so true to life?)

Must there be a top floor somewhere, a world that itself is not created in someone else's fiction? Or can the hierarchy go on infinitely? Are circles excluded, even quite narrow ones where a character of one world creates another fictional world wherein a character creates the first world? Might the circle get narrower still?

Various theories have described our world as less real than another, even as an illusion. The idea of our having this inferior ontological status takes some getting used to, however. It may help if we approach our situation as literary critics and ask the genre of our universe, whether tragedy, farce, or theater-of-the-absurd? What is the plot line, and which act are we in?

Still, our status may bring some compensations, as, for example, that we live on even after we die, preserved permanently in the work of fiction. Or if not permanently, at least for as long as our book lasts. May we hope to inhabit an enduring masterpiece rather than a quickly remaindered book?

Moreover, though in some sense it might be false, in another wouldn't it be true for Hamlet to say, "I am Shakespeare"? What do Macbeth, Banquo, Desdemona, and Prospero have in common? The consciousness of the one author, Shakespeare, which underlies and infuses each of them. (So, too, there is the brotherhood of man.) Playing on the intricacy both of our ontological status and of the first-person reflexive pronoun, each of us too may truly say, "I am the author."

NOTE FROM THE AUTHOR

Suppose I now tell you that the preceding *was* a work of fiction and the "I" didn't refer to me, the author, but to a first-person character. Or suppose I tell you that it was *not* a work of fiction but a playful, and so of course serious, philosophical essay by me, Robert Nozick. (*Not* the Robert Nozick named as author at the beginning of this work—he may be, for all we know, another literary persona—but the one who attended P.S. 165.) How would your response to this whole work differ depending on which I say, supposing you were willing, as you won't be, simply to accept my statement?

May I decide *which* to say, fiction or philosophical essay, only now, as I finish writing this, and how will that decision affect the character of what already was set down previously? May I postpone the decision further, perhaps until after you have read this, fixing its status and genre only then?

Perhaps God has not decided *yet* whether he has created, in this world, a fictional world or a real one. Is the Day of Judgment the day he will decide? Yet what additional thing depends upon which way he decides—what would either decision add to our situation or subtract from it?

And which decision do you hope for?

D INDUCTION

"Induction" from *An Enquiry Concerning Human Understanding*

DAVID HUME

Scottish philosopher David Hume (1711–76) was among the most important thinkers of the early modern period. A leading exponent of British empiricism, he made lasting contributions to many areas of philosophy, as well as to the understanding of European history. The breadth of his contributions can be seen in the titles of his major philosophical works, which include *A Treatise of Human Nature* (1739–40), *An Enquiry Concerning Human Understanding* (1748), *An Enquiry Concerning the Principles of Morals* (1751), and the posthumously published *Dialogues Concerning Natural Religion* (1779).

The selection presented next is excerpted from his *Enquiry Concerning Human Understanding*, which was originally written in English. The text was edited by L. A. Selby-Bigge and revised by P. H. Nidditch (1928–1983) (3rd ed.). Numbers in the margins refer to paragraph numbers in that edition of the work (1860–1951).

In this selection, Hume asks how we can be justified in assuming that the future will resemble the past.

SCEPTICAL DOUBTS CONCERNING THE OPERATIONS OF THE UNDERSTANDING

Part I.

20 ALL the objects of human reason or enquiry may naturally be divided into two kinds, to wit, *Relations of Ideas*, and *Matters of Fact*. Of the first kind are the sciences of Geometry, Algebra, and Arithmetic; and in short, every affirmation which is either intuitively or demonstratively certain. *That the square of the hypothenuse is equal to the square of the two sides*, is a proposition which expresses a relation between these figures. *That three times five is equal to the half of thirty*, expresses a relation between these numbers. Propositions of this kind are discoverable by the mere operation of thought, without dependence on what is anywhere existent in the universe. Though there never were a circle or triangle in nature, the truths demonstrated by Euclid would for ever retain their certainty and evidence.*

* Euclid of Alexandria (4th–3rd century BCE) was a great ancient Greek mathematician. His pathbreaking work *The Elements*, in which the principles of Euclidian geometry are meticulously deduced from five simple axioms, earned him the nickname "the Father of Geometry," and introduced rigor into Western mathematics.

From *An Enquiry Concerning Human Understanding*, by David Hume, 3rd ed. (1975), ed. P. H. Nidditch. Reprinted by permission of Oxford University Press.

21 Matters of fact, which are the second objects of human reason, are not ascertained in the same manner; nor is our evidence of their truth, however great, of a like nature with the foregoing. The contrary of every matter of fact is still possible; because it can never imply a contradiction, and is conceived by the mind with the same facility and distinctness, as if ever so conformable to reality. *That the sun will not rise to-morrow* is no less intelligible a proposition, and implies no more contradiction, than the affirmation, *that it will rise*. We should in vain, therefore, attempt to demonstrate its falsehood. Were it demonstratively false, it would imply a contradiction, and could never be distinctly conceived by the mind.

It may, therefore, be a subject worthy of curiosity, to enquire what is the nature of that evidence which assures us of any real existence and matter of fact, beyond the present testimony of our senses, or the records of our memory. This part of philosophy, it is observable, has been little cultivated, either by the ancients or moderns; and therefore our doubts and errors, in the prosecution of so important an enquiry, may be the more excusable; while we march through such difficult paths without any guide or direction. They may even prove useful, by exciting curiosity, and destroying that implicit faith and security, which is the bane of all reasoning and free enquiry. The discovery of defects in the common philosophy, if any such there be, will not, I presume, be a discouragement, but rather an incitement, as is usual, to attempt something more full and satisfactory than has yet been proposed to the public.

22 All reasonings concerning matter of fact seem to be founded on the relation of *Cause and Effect*. By means of that relation alone we can go beyond the evidence of our memory and senses. If you were to ask a man, why he believes any matter of fact, which is absent; for instance, that his friend is in the country, or in France; he would give you a reason; and this reason would be some other fact; as a letter received from him, or the knowledge of his former resolutions and promises. A man finding a watch or any other machine in a desert island, would conclude that there had once been men in that island. All our reasonings concerning fact are of the same nature. And here it is constantly supposed that there is a connexion between the present fact and that which is inferred from it. Were there nothing to bind them together, the inference would be entirely precarious. The hearing of an articulate voice and rational discourse in the dark assures us of the presence of some person: Why? because these are the effects of the human make and fabric, and closely connected with it. If we anatomize all the other reasonings of this nature, we shall find that they are founded on the relation of cause and effect, and that this relation is either near or remote, direct or collateral. Heat and light are collateral effects of fire, and the one effect may justly be inferred from the other.

If we would satisfy ourselves, therefore, concerning the nature of that evidence, which assures us of matters of fact, we must enquire how we arrive at the knowledge of cause and effect. 23

I shall venture to affirm, as a general proposition, which admits of no exception, that the knowledge of this relation is not, in any instance, attained by reasonings *a priori*; but arises entirely from experience, when we find that any particular objects are constantly conjoined with each other. Let an object be presented to a man of ever so strong natural reason and abilities; if that object be entirely new to him, he will not be able, by the most accurate examination of its sensible qualities, to discover any of its causes or effects. Adam, though his rational faculties be supposed, at the very first, entirely perfect, could not have inferred from the fluidity and transparency of water that it would suffocate him, or from the light and warmth of fire that it would consume him. No object ever discovers, by the qualities which appear to the senses, either the causes which produced it, or the effects which will arise from it; nor can our reason, unassisted by experience, ever draw any inference concerning real existence and matter of fact.

This proposition, *that causes and effects are discoverable, not by reason but by experience*, will readily be admitted with regard to such objects, as we remember to have once been altogether unknown to us; since we must be conscious of the utter inability, which we then lay under, of foretelling what would arise from them. Present two smooth pieces of marble to a man who has no tincture of natural philosophy; he will never discover that they will adhere together in such a manner as to require great 24 force to separate them in a direct line, while they make so small a resistance to a lateral pressure. Such events, as bear little analogy to the common course of nature, are also readily confessed to be known only by experience; nor does any man imagine that the explosion of gunpowder, or the attraction of a loadstone, could ever be discovered by arguments *a priori*. In like manner, when an effect is supposed to depend upon an intricate machinery or secret structure of parts, we make no difficulty in attributing all our knowledge of it to experience. Who will assert that he can give the ultimate reason, why milk or bread is proper nourishment for a man, not for a lion or a tiger?

But the same truth may not appear, at first sight, to have the same evidence with regard to events, which have become familiar to us from our first appearance in the world, which bear a close analogy to the whole course of nature, and which are supposed to depend on the simple qualities of objects, without any secret structure of parts. We are apt to imagine that we could discover these effects by the mere operation of our reason, without experience. We fancy, that were we brought on a sudden into this world, we could at first have inferred that one Billiard-ball would communicate motion to another upon impulse; and that we needed not to have waited for the event, in order to pronounce with certainty concerning it. Such is the influence of custom, that, where it is strongest, it not only covers our natural ignorance, but even conceals itself, and seems not to take place, merely because it is found in the highest degree.

25 But to convince us that all the laws of nature, and all the operations of bodies without exception, are known only by experience, the following reflections may, perhaps, suffice. Were any object presented to us, and were we required to pronounce concerning the effect, which will result from it, without consulting past observation; after what manner, I beseech you, must the mind proceed in this operation? It must invent or imagine some event, which it ascribes to the object as its effect; and it is plain that this invention must be entirely arbitrary. The mind can never possibly find the effect in the supposed cause, by the most accurate scrutiny and examination. For the effect is totally different from the cause, and consequently can never be discovered in it. Motion in the second Billiard-ball is a quite distinct event from motion in the first; nor is there anything in the one to suggest the smallest hint of the other. A stone or piece of metal raised into the air, and left without any support, immediately falls: but to consider the matter *a priori*, is there anything we discover in this situation which can beget the idea of a downward, rather than an upward, or any other motion, in the stone or metal?

And as the first imagination or invention of a particular effect, in all natural operations, is arbitrary, where we consult not experience; so must we also esteem the supposed tie or connexion between the cause and effect, which binds them together, and renders it impossible that any other effect could result from the operation of that cause. When I see, for instance, a Billiard-ball moving in a straight line towards another; even suppose motion in the second ball should by accident be suggested to me, as the result of their contact or impulse; may I not conceive, that a hundred different events might as well follow from that cause? May not both these balls remain at absolute rest? May not the first ball return in a straight line, or leap off from the second in any line or direction? All these suppositions are consistent and conceivable. Why then should we give the preference to one, which is no more consistent or conceivable than the rest? All our reasonings *a priori* will never be able to show us any foundation for this preference.

In a word, then, every effect is a distinct event from its cause. It could not, therefore, be discovered in the cause, and the first invention or conception of it, *a priori*, must be entirely arbitrary. And even after it is suggested, the conjunction of it with the cause must appear equally arbitrary; since there are always many other effects, which, to reason, must seem fully as consistent and natural. In vain, therefore, should we pretend to determine any single event, or infer any cause or effect, without the assistance of observation and experience.

Hence we may discover the reason why no phi- 26
losopher, who is rational and modest, has ever pretended to assign the ultimate cause of any natural operation, or to show distinctly the action of that power, which produces any single effect in the universe. It is confessed, that the utmost effort of human reason is to reduce the principles, productive of natural phenomena, to a greater simplicity, and to resolve the many particular effects into a few general

causes, by means of reasonings from analogy, experience, and observation. But as to the causes of these general causes, we should in vain attempt their discovery; nor shall we ever be able to satisfy ourselves, by any particular explication of them. These ultimate springs and principles are totally shut up from human curiosity and enquiry. Elasticity, gravity, cohesion of parts, communication of motion by impulse; these are probably the ultimate causes and principles which we shall ever discover in nature; and we may esteem ourselves sufficiently happy, if, by accurate enquiry and reasoning, we can trace up the particular phenomena to, or near to, these general principles. The most perfect philosophy of the natural kind only staves off our ignorance a little longer: as perhaps the most perfect philosophy of the moral or metaphysical kind serves only to discover larger portions of it. Thus the observation of human blindness and weakness is the result of all philosophy, and meets us at every turn, in spite of our endeavours to elude or avoid it.

27 Nor is geometry, when taken into the assistance of natural philosophy, ever able to remedy this defect, or lead us into the knowledge of ultimate causes, by all that accuracy of reasoning for which it is so justly celebrated. Every part of mixed mathematics proceeds upon the supposition that certain laws are established by nature in her operations; and abstract reasonings are employed, either to assist experience in the discovery of these laws, or to determine their influence in particular instances, where it depends upon any precise degree of distance and quantity. Thus, it is a law of motion, discovered by experience, that the moment or force of any body in motion is in the compound ratio or proportion of its solid contents and its velocity; and consequently, that a small force may remove the greatest obstacle or raise the greatest weight, if, by any contrivance or machinery, we can increase the velocity of that force, so as to make it an overmatch for its antagonist. Geometry assists us in the application of this law, by giving us the just dimensions of all the parts and figures which can enter into any species of machine; but still the discovery of the law itself is owing merely to experience, and all the abstract reasonings in the world could never lead us one step towards the knowledge of it. When we reason *a priori*, and consider merely any object or cause, as it appears to the mind, independent of all observation, it never could suggest to us the notion of any distinct object, such as its effect; much less, show us the inseparable and inviolable connexion between them. A man must be very sagacious who could discover by reasoning that crystal is the effect of heat, and ice of cold, without being previously acquainted with the operation of these qualities.

Part II.

28 But we have not yet attained any tolerable satisfaction with regard to the question first proposed. Each solution still gives rise to a new question as difficult as the foregoing, and leads us on to farther enquiries. When it is asked, *What is the nature of all our reasonings concerning matter of fact?* the proper answer seems to be, that they are founded on the relation of cause and effect. When again it is asked, *What is the foundation of all our reasonings and conclusions concerning that relation?* it may be replied in one word, Experience. But if we still carry on our sifting humour, and ask, *What is the foundation of all conclusions from experience?* this implies a new question, which may be of more difficult solution and explication. Philosophers, that give themselves airs of superior wisdom and sufficiency, have a hard task when they encounter persons of inquisitive dispositions, who push them from every corner to which they retreat, and who are sure at last to bring them to some dangerous dilemma. The best expedient to prevent this confusion, is to be modest in our pretensions; and even to discover the difficulty ourselves before it is objected to us. By this means, we may make a kind of merit of our very ignorance.

I shall content myself, in this section, with an easy task, and shall pretend only to give a negative answer to the question here proposed. I say then, that, even after we have experience of the operations of cause and effect, our conclusions from that experience are *not* founded on reasoning, or any process of the understanding. This answer we must endeavour both to explain and to defend.

It must certainly be allowed, that nature has kept 29
us at a great distance from all her secrets, and has afforded us only the knowledge of a few superfi-

cial qualities of objects; while she conceals from us those powers and principles on which the influence of these objects entirely depends. Our senses inform us of the colour, weight, and consistence of bread; but neither sense nor reason can ever inform us of those qualities which fit it for the nourishment and support of a human body. Sight or feeling conveys an idea of the actual motion of bodies; but as to that wonderful force or power, which would carry on a moving body for ever in a continued change of place, and which bodies never lose but by communicating it to others; of this we cannot form the most distant conception. But notwithstanding this ignorance of natural powers[1] and principles, we always presume, when we see like sensible qualities, that they have like secret powers, and expect that effects, similar to those which we have experienced, will follow from them. If a body of like colour and consistence with that bread, which we have formerly eat, be presented to us, we make no scruple of repeating the experiment, and foresee, with certainty, like nourishment and support. Now this is a process of the mind or thought, of which I would willingly know the foundation. It is allowed on all hands that there is no known connexion between the sensible qualities and the secret powers; and consequently, that the mind is not led to form such a conclusion concerning their constant and regular conjunction, by anything which it knows of their nature. As to past *Experience*, it can be allowed to give *direct* and *certain* information of those precise objects only, and that precise period of time, which fell under its cognizance: but why this experience should be extended to future times, and to other objects, which for aught we know, may be only in appearance similar; this is the main question on which I would insist. The bread, which I formerly eat, nourished me; that is, a body of such sensible qualities was, at that time, endued with such secret powers: but does it follow, that other bread must also nourish me at another time, and that like sensible qualities must always be attended with like secret powers? The consequence seems nowise necessary. At least, it must be acknowledged that there is here a consequence drawn by the mind; that there is a certain step taken; a process of thought, and an inference, which wants to be explained. These two propositions are far from being the same, *I have found that such an object has always been attended with such an effect*, and *I foresee, that other objects, which are, in appearance, similar, will be attended with similar effects*. I shall allow, if you please, that the one proposition may justly be inferred from the other: I know, in fact, that it always is inferred. But if you insist that the inference is made by a chain of reasoning, I desire you to produce that reasoning. The connexion between these propositions is not intuitive. There is required a medium, which may enable the mind to draw such an inference, if indeed it be drawn by reasoning and argument. What that medium is, I must confess, passes my comprehension; and it is incumbent on those to produce it, who assert that it really exists, and is the origin of all our conclusions concerning matter of fact.

This negative argument must certainly, in proc- 30
ess of time, become altogether convincing, if many penetrating and able philosophers shall turn their enquiries this way and no one be ever able to discover any connecting proposition or intermediate step, which supports the understanding in this conclusion. But as the question is yet new, every reader may not trust so far to his own penetration, as to conclude, because an argument escapes his enquiry, that therefore it does not really exist. For this reason it may be requisite to venture upon a more difficult task; and enumerating all the branches of human knowledge, endeavour to show that none of them can afford such an argument.

All reasonings may be divided into two kinds, namely, demonstrative reasoning, or that concerning relations of ideas, and moral reasoning, or that concerning matter of fact and existence. That there are no demonstrative arguments in the case seems evident; since it implies no contradiction that the course of nature may change, and that an object, seemingly like those which we have experienced, may be attended with different or contrary effects. May I not clearly and distinctly conceive that a body, falling from the clouds, and which, in all other respects, resembles snow, has yet the taste of salt or feeling of fire? Is there any more intelligible proposition than to affirm, that all the trees will flourish in December and January, and decay in May and June? Now whatever is intelligible, and can be distinctly conceived, implies no contradiction, and can never be proved false by any demonstrative argument or abstract reasoning *a priori*.

If we be, therefore, engaged by arguments to put trust in past experience, and make it the standard of our future judgement, these arguments must be probable only, or such as regard matter of fact and real existence, according to the division above mentioned. But that there is no argument of this kind, must appear, if our explication of that species of reasoning be admitted as solid and satisfactory. We have said that all arguments concerning existence are founded on the relation of cause and effect; that our knowledge of that relation is derived entirely from experience; and that all our experimental conclusions proceed upon the supposition that the future will be conformable to the past. To endeavour, therefore, the proof of this last supposition by probable arguments, or arguments regarding existence, must be evidently going in a circle, and taking that for granted, which is the very point in question.

31 In reality, all arguments from experience are founded on the similarity which we discover among natural objects, and by which we are induced to expect effects similar to those which we have found to follow from such objects. And though none but a fool or madman will ever pretend to dispute the authority of experience, or to reject that great guide of human life, it may surely be allowed a philosopher to have so much curiosity at least as to examine the principle of human nature, which gives this mighty authority to experience, and makes us draw advantage from that similarity which nature has placed among different objects. From causes which appear *similar* we expect similar effects. This is the sum of all our experimental conclusions. Now it seems evident that, if this conclusion were formed by reason, it would be as perfect at first, and upon one instance, as after ever so long a course of experience. But the case is far otherwise. Nothing so like as eggs; yet no one, on account of this appearing similarity, expects the same taste and relish in all of them. It is only after a long course of uniform experiments in any kind, that we attain a firm reliance and security with regard to a particular event. Now where is that process of reasoning which, from one instance, draws a conclusion, so different from that which it infers from a hundred instances that are nowise different from that single one? This question I propose as much for the sake of information, as with an intention of raising difficulties. I cannot find, I cannot imagine any such reasoning. But I keep my mind still open to instruction, if any one will vouchsafe to bestow it on me.

Should it be said that, from a number of uni- 32
form experiments, we *infer* a connexion between the sensible qualities and the secret powers; this, I must confess, seems the same difficulty, couched in different terms. The question still recurs, on what process of argument this *inference* is founded? Where is the medium, the interposing ideas, which join propositions so very wide of each other? It is confessed that the colour, consistence, and other sensible qualities of bread appear not, of themselves, to have any connexion with the secret powers of nourishment and support. For otherwise we could infer these secret powers from the first appearance of these sensible qualities, without the aid of experience; contrary to the sentiment of all philosophers, and contrary to plain matter of fact. Here, then, is our natural state of ignorance with regard to the powers and influence of all objects. How is this remedied by experience? It only shows us a number of uniform effects, resulting from certain objects, and teaches us that those particular objects, at that particular time, were endowed with such powers and forces. When a new object, endowed with similar sensible qualities, is produced, we expect similar powers and forces, and look for a like effect. From a body of like colour and consistence with bread we expect like nourishment and support. But this surely is a step or progress of the mind, which wants to be explained. When a man says, *I have found, in all past instances, such sensible qualities conjoined with such secret powers*: And when he says, *Similar sensible qualities will always be conjoined with similar secret powers*, he is not guilty of a tautology, nor are these propositions in any respect the same. You say that the one proposition is an inference from the other. But you must confess that the inference is not intuitive; neither is it demonstrative: Of what nature is it, then? To say it is experimental, is begging the question. For all inferences from experience suppose, as their foundation, that the future will resemble the past, and that similar powers will be conjoined with

similar sensible qualities. If there be any suspicion that the course of nature may change, and that the past may be no rule for the future, all experience becomes useless, and can give rise to no inference or conclusion. It is impossible, therefore, that any arguments from experience can prove this resemblance of the past to the future; since all these arguments are founded on the supposition of that resemblance. Let the course of things be allowed hitherto ever so regular; that alone, without some new argument or inference, proves not that, for the future, it will continue so. In vain do you pretend to have learned the nature of bodies from your past experience. Their secret nature, and consequently all their effects and influence, may change, without any change in their sensible qualities. This happens sometimes, and with regard to some objects: Why may it not happen always, and with regard to all objects? What logic, what process of argument secures you against this supposition? My practice, you say, refutes my doubts. But you mistake the purport of my question. As an agent, I am quite satisfied in the point; but as a philosopher, who has some share of curiosity, I will not say scepticism, I want to learn the foundation of this inference. No reading, no enquiry has yet been able to remove my difficulty, or give me satisfaction in a matter of such importance. Can I do better than propose the difficulty to the public, even though, perhaps, I have small hopes of obtaining a solution? We shall at least, by this means, be sensible of our ignorance, if we do not augment our knowledge.

33 I must confess that a man is guilty of unpardonable arrogance who concludes, because an argument has escaped his own investigation, that therefore it does not really exist. I must also confess that, though all the learned, for several ages, should have employed themselves in fruitless search upon any subject, it may still, perhaps, be rash to conclude positively that the subject must, therefore, pass all human comprehension. Even though we examine all the sources of our knowledge, and conclude them unfit for such a subject, there may still remain a suspicion, that the enumeration is not complete, or the examination not accurate. But with regard to the present subject, there are some considerations which seem to remove all this accusation of arrogance or suspicion of mistake.

It is certain that the most ignorant and stupid peasants—nay infants, nay even brute beasts—improve by experience, and learn the qualities of natural objects, by observing the effects which result from them. When a child has felt the sensation of pain from touching the flame of a candle, he will be careful not to put his hand near any candle; but will expect a similar effect from a cause which is similar in its sensible qualities and appearance. If you assert, therefore, that the understanding of the child is led into this conclusion by any process of argument or ratiocination, I may justly require you to produce that argument; nor have you any pretence to refuse so equitable a demand. You cannot say that the argument is abstruse, and may possibly escape your enquiry; since you confess that it is obvious to the capacity of a mere infant. If you hesitate, therefore, a moment, or if, after reflection, you produce any intricate or profound argument, you, in a manner, give up the question, and confess that it is not reasoning which engages us to suppose the past resembling the future, and to expect similar effects from causes which are, to appearance, similar. This is the proposition which I intended to enforce in the present section. If I be right, I pretend not to have made any mighty discovery. And if I be wrong, I must acknowledge myself to be indeed a very backward scholar; since I cannot now discover an argument which, it seems, was perfectly familiar to me long before I was out of my cradle.

NOTE

1. The word, Power, is here used in a loose and popular sense. The more accurate explication of it would give additional evidence to this argument.

Selections from *The Problem of Induction*

WESLEY SALMON

Wesley Salmon (1925–2001) taught in the History and Philosophy of Science programs at Indiana University and the University of Pittsburgh for many decades. His research was primarily focused on the topics of causation and explanation.

This selection is excerpted from his 1967 book *The Foundations of Scientific Inference*, originally based on a series of lectures delivered in the early 1960s. Section numbers correspond to the original text. In our excerpt, Salmon explores some of the challenges raised by Hume's question about our justification for inductive reasoning. (See previous selection.)

We all believe that we have knowledge of facts extending far beyond those we directly perceive. The scope of our senses is severely limited in space and time; our immediate perceptual knowledge does not reach to events that happened before we were born to events that are happening now in certain other places or to any future events. We believe, nevertheless, that we have some kind of indirect knowledge of such facts. We know that a glacier once covered a large part of North America, that the sun continues to exist at night, and that the tides will rise and fall tomorrow. Science and common sense have at least this one thing in common: Each embodies knowledge of matters of fact that are not open to our direct inspection. Indeed, science purports to establish general laws or theories that apply to all parts of space and time without restriction. A "science" that consisted of no more than a mere summary of the results of direct observation would not deserve the name.

Hume's profound critique of induction begins with a simple and apparently innocent question: How do we acquire knowledge of the unobserved?[1] This question, as posed, may seem to call for an empirical answer. We observe that human beings utilize what may be roughly characterized as inductive or scientific methods of extending knowledge from the observed to the unobserved. The sciences, in fact, embody the most powerful and highly developed methods known, and we may make an empirical investigation of scientific methods much as we might for any other sort of human behavior. We may consider the historical development of science. We may study the psychological, sociological, and political factors relevant to the pursuit of science. We may try to give an exact characterization of the behavior of scientists. In doing all these things, however, important and interesting as they are, we will have ignored the *philosophical* aspect of the problem Hume raised. Putting the matter very simply, these empirical investigations may enable us to describe the ways in which people arrive at *beliefs* about unobserved facts, but they leave open the question of whether beliefs arrived at in this way actually constitute *knowledge*. It is one thing to describe how people go about seeking to extend their knowledge; it is quite another to claim that the methods employed actually do yield knowledge.

One of the basic differences between knowledge and belief is that knowledge must be founded upon evidence—i.e., it must be belief founded upon some rational justification. To say that certain methods yield knowledge of the unobserved is to make a cognitive claim for them. Hume called into question the justification of such cognitive claims. The answer cannot be found entirely within an empirical study of human behavior, for a *logical* problem has been raised. It is the problem of understanding the logical relationship between evidence and conclusion

Excerpts from "The Problem of Induction," from *The Foundations of Scientific Inference* by Wesley C. Salmon. Copyright © 1967. Reprinted by permission of University of Pittsburgh Press.

in logically correct inferences. It is the problem of determining whether the inferences by which we attempt to make the transition from knowledge of the observed to knowledge of the unobserved are logically correct. The fact that people do or do not use a certain type of inference is irrelevant to its justifiability. Whether people have confidence in the correctness of a certain type of inference has nothing to do with whether such confidence is justified. If we should adopt a logically incorrect method for inferring one fact from others, these facts would not actually constitute evidence for the conclusion we have drawn. The problem of induction is the problem of explicating the very concept of *inductive evidence*.

There is another possibly misleading feature of the question as I have formulated it. When we ask how we can *acquire* knowledge of the unobserved, it sounds very much as if we are asking for a method for the *discovery* of new knowledge. This is, of course, a vital problem, but it is not the fundamental problem Hume raised. Whether there is or can be any sort of inductive logic of discovery is a controversial question I shall discuss in detail in a later section.[2] Leaving this question aside for now, there remains the problem of *justification* of conclusions concerning unobserved matters of fact. Given some conclusion, however arrived at, regarding unobserved facts, and given some alleged evidence to support that conclusion, the question remains whether that conclusion is, indeed, supported by the evidence offered in support of it.

Consider a simple and highly artificial situation. Suppose a number of balls have been drawn from an urn, and that all of the black ones that have been drawn are licorice-flavored. I am not now concerned with such psychological questions as what makes the observer note the color of these balls, what leads him to taste the black ones, what makes him take note of the fact that licorice flavor is associated with black color in his sample, or what makes him suppose that the black balls not yet drawn will also be licorice-flavored. The problem—Hume's basic *philosophical* problem—is this: Given that all of the observed black balls have been licorice-flavored, and given that somehow the conclusion has been entertained that the unobserved black balls in the urn are also licorice-flavored, do the observed facts constitute sound *evidence* for that conclusion? Would we be *justified* in accepting that conclusion on the basis of the facts alleged to be evidence for it?

As a first answer to this question we may point out that the inference does conform to an accepted inductive principle, a principle saying roughly that observed instances conforming to a generalization constitute evidence for it. It is, however, a very small step to the next question: What grounds have we for accepting this or any other inductive principle? Is there any reason or justification for placing confidence in the conclusions of inferences of this type? Given that the premises of this inference are true, and given that the inference conforms to a certain rule, can we provide any rational justification for accepting its conclusion rather than, for instance, the conclusion that black balls yet to be drawn will taste like quinine?

It is well known that Hume's answer to this problem was essentially skeptical. It was his great merit to have shown that a justification of induction, if possible at all, is by no means easy to provide. In order to appreciate the force of his argument it is first necessary to clarify some terminological points. This is particularly important because the word *induction* has been used in a wide variety of ways.

For purposes of systematic discussion one distinction is fundamental, namely, the distinction between demonstrative and nondemonstrative inference. A *demonstrative* inference is one whose premises necessitate its conclusion; the conclusion cannot be false if the premises are true. All valid deductions are demonstrative inferences. A *nondemonstrative* inference is simply one that fails to be demonstrative. Its conclusion is not necessitated by its premises; the conclusion could be false even if the premises are true. A demonstrative inference is *necessarily truth-preserving;* a nondemonstrative inference is not.

The category of nondemonstrative inferences, as I have characterized it, contains, among other things perhaps, all kinds of fallacious inferences. If, however, there is any kind of inference whose premises, although not necessitating the conclusion, do lend it weight, support it, or make it probable, then such inferences possess a certain kind of logical rectitude. It is not deductive validity, but it is important anyway. Inferences possessing it are *correct inductive inferences*.

Since demonstrative inferences have been characterized in terms of their basic property of necessary truth preservation, it is natural to ask how they achieve this very desirable trait. For a large group of demonstrative inferences, including those discussed under "valid deduction" in most logic texts, the answer is rather easy. Inferences of this type purchase necessary truth preservation by sacrificing any extension of content. The conclusion of such an inference says no more than do the premises—often less. The conclusion cannot be false if the premises are true *because* the conclusion says nothing that was not already stated in the premises. The conclusion is a mere reformulation of all or part of the content of the premises. In some cases the reformulation is unanticipated and therefore psychologically surprising, but the conclusion cannot augment the content of the premises. Such inferences are *nonampliative;* an ampliative inference, then, has a conclusion with content not present either explicitly or implicitly in the premises.

While it is easy to understand why nonampliative inferences are necessarily truth-preserving, the further question arises whether there are any necessarily truth-preserving inferences that are also ampliative. Is there any type of inference whose conclusion must, of necessity, be true if the premises are true, but whose conclusion says something not stated by the premises? Hume believed that the answer is negative and so do I, but it is not easy to produce an adequate defense of this answer. Let us see, however, what an affirmative answer would amount to.

Suppose there were an ampliative inference that is also necessarily truth-preserving. Consider the implication from its premises, $P_1, \ldots, P_k$, to its conclusion C. If the inference were an ordinary nonampliative deduction, this implication would be analytic and empty; but since the argument is supposed to be ampliative, the implication must be synthetic. At the same time, because the argument is supposed to be necessarily truth-preserving, this implication must be not only true but necessarily true. Thus, to maintain that there are inferences that are both ampliative and necessarily truth-preserving is tantamount to asserting that there are synthetic a priori truths. This may be seen in another way. Any ampliative inference can be made into a nonampliative one by adding a premise. In particular, if we add to the foregoing ampliative inference the synthetic a priori premise, "If P_1 and P_2 and . . . and P_k, then C," the resulting inference will be an ordinary valid nonampliative deduction. Consider our example once more; this time let us set it out more formally:

1. Some black balls from this urn have been observed.
All observed black balls from this urn are licorice-flavored.
All black balls in this urn are licorice-flavored.

This argument is clearly ampliative, for the premise makes a statement about observed balls only, while the conclusion makes a statement about the unobserved as well as the observed balls. It appears to be nondemonstrative as well, for it seems perfectly possible for the conclusion to be false even if the premises are true. We see no reason why someone might not have dropped a black marble in the urn which, when it is drawn, will be found to be tasteless. We could, however, rule out this sort of possibility by adding another premise:

2. Some black balls from this urn have been observed.
All observed black balls in this urn are licorice-flavored.
Any two balls in this urn that have the same color also have the same flavor.
All black balls in this urn are licorice-flavored.

The additional premise has transformed the former nondemonstrative inference into a demonstrative inference, but we must also admit that we have transformed it into a nonampliative inference. If, however, the third premise of 2 were a synthetic a priori truth, the original inference, although ampliative, would have been necessarily truth-preserving and, hence, demonstrative. If the premise that transformed inference 1 into inference 2 were necessarily true, then it would be impossible for the conclusion of inference 1 to be false if the premises were true, for that would contradict the third premise of inference 2.

Hardly anyone would be tempted to say that the statement, "Any two balls in this urn that have the same color also have the same flavor," expresses a synthetic a priori truth. Other propositions have, however, been taken to be synthetic a priori. Hume and many of his successors noticed that typical inductive inferences, such as our example concerning licorice-flavored black balls, would seem perfectly sound if we could have recourse to some sort of principle of uniformity of nature. If we could only prove that the course of nature is uniform, that the future will be like the past, or that uniformities that have existed thus far will continue to hold in the future, then we would seem to be justified in generalizing from past cases to future cases—from the observed to the unobserved. Indeed, Hume suggests that we presuppose in our inductive reasoning a principle from which the third premise of 2 would follow as a special case: "We always presume, when we see like sensible qualities, that they have like secret powers, and expect that effects, similar to those which we have experienced, will follow from them."[3] Again, "From causes which appear *similar* we expect similar effects. This is the sum of all our experimental conclusions."[4]

Hume's searching examination of the principle of uniformity of nature revealed no ground on which it could be taken as a synthetic a priori principle. For all we can know a priori, Hume argued, the course of nature might change, the future might be radically unlike the past, and regularities that have obtained in respect to observed events might prove completely inapplicable to unobserved cases. We have found by experience, of course, that nature has exhibited a high degree of uniformity and regularity so far, and we infer inductively that this will continue, but to use an inductively inferred generalization as a justification for induction, as Hume emphasized, would be flagrantly circular. He concluded, in fact, that there are no synthetic a priori principles in virtue of which we could have demonstrative inferences that are ampliative. Hume recognized two kinds of reasoning: reasoning concerning relations of ideas and reasoning concerning matters of fact and existence. The former is demonstrative but nonampliative while the latter is ampliative but not necessarily truth-preserving.

If we agree that there are no synthetic a priori truths, then we must identify necessarily truth-preserving inference with nonampliative inference. All ampliative inference is nondemonstrative. This leads to an exhaustive trichotomy of inferences: valid deductive inference, correct inductive inference, and assorted fallacies. The first question is, however, whether the second category is empty or whether there are such things as correct inductive inferences. This is Hume's problem of induction. Can we show that any particular type of ampliative inference can be justified in any way? If so, it will qualify as correct induction.

Consider, then, any ampliative inference whatever. The example of the licorice-flavored black balls illustrates the point. We cannot show *deductively* that this inference will have a true conclusion given true premises. If we could, we would have proved that the conclusion must be true if the premises are. That would make it necessarily truth-preserving, hence, demonstrative. This, in turn, would mean that it was nonampliative, contrary to our hypothesis. Thus, if an ampliative inference could be justified deductively it would not be ampliative. It follows that ampliative inference cannot be justified deductively.

At the same time, we cannot justify any sort of ampliative inference *inductively*. To do so would require the use of some sort of nondemonstrative inference. But the question at issue is the justification of nondemonstrative inference, so the procedure would be question begging. Before we can properly employ a nondemonstrative inference in a justifying argument, we must already have justified that nondemonstrative inference.

Hume's position can be summarized succinctly: We cannot justify any kind of ampliative inference. If it could be justified deductively it would not be ampliative. It cannot be justified nondemonstratively because that would be viciously circular. It seems, then, that there is no way in which we can extend our knowledge to the unobserved. We have, to be sure, many beliefs about the unobserved, and in some of them we place great confidence. Nevertheless, they are without rational justification of any kind!

This is a harsh conclusion, yet it seems to be supported by impeccable arguments. It might be called "Hume's paradox," for the conclusion, although ingeniously argued, is utterly repugnant to common sense and our deepest convictions. We *know* ("in our hearts") that we have knowledge of unobserved fact. The challenge is to show how this is possible.

II. ATTEMPTED SOLUTIONS

It hardly needs remarking that philosophers have attempted to meet Hume's intriguing challenge in a wide variety of ways. There have been direct attacks upon some of Hume's arguments. Attempts to provide inductive arguments to support induction and attempts to supply a synthetic a priori principle of uniformity of nature belong in this category. Some authors have claimed that the whole problem arises out of linguistic confusion, and that careful analysis shows it to be a pseudoproblem. Some have even denied that inductive inference is needed, either in science or in everyday affairs. In this section I shall survey what seem to me to be the most important efforts to deal with the problem.

1. Inductive Justification. If Hume's arguments had never been propounded and we were asked why we accept the methods of science, the most natural answer would be, I think, that these methods have proved themselves by their results. We can point to astonishing technological advances, to vastly increased comprehension, and to impressive predictions. Science has provided us with foresight, control, and understanding. No other method can claim a comparable record of successful accomplishment. If methods are to be judged by their fruits, there is no doubt that the scientific method will come out on top.

Unfortunately, Hume examined this argument and showed that it is viciously circular. It is an example of an attempt to justify inductive methods inductively. From the premise that science has had considerable predictive success in the past, we conclude that it will continue to have substantial predictive success in the future. Observed cases of the application of scientific method have yielded successful prediction; therefore, as yet unobserved cases of the application of scientific method will yield successful predictions. This argument has the same structure as our black-balls-in-the-urn example; it is precisely the sort of ampliative inference from the observed to the unobserved whose justifiability is in question.

Consider the parallel case for a radically different sort of method. A crystal gazer claims that his method is the appropriate method for making predictions. When we question his claim he says, "Wait a moment; I will find out whether the method of crystal gazing is the best method for making predictions." He looks into his crystal ball and announces that future cases of crystal gazing will yield predictive success. If we should protest that his method has not been especially successful in the past, he might well make certain remarks about parity of reasoning. "Since you have used your method to justify your method, why shouldn't I use my method to justify my method? If you insist upon judging my method by using your method, why shouldn't I use my method to evaluate your method? By the way, I note by gazing into my crystal ball that the scientific method is now in for a very bad run of luck."

The trouble with circular arguments is obvious: with an appropriate circular argument you can prove anything. In recent years, nevertheless, there have been several notable attempts to show how inductive rules can be supported inductively. The authors of such attempts try to show, of course, that their arguments are not circular. Although they argue persuasively, it seems to me that they do not succeed in escaping circularity.

. . .

2. The Complexity of Scientific Inference. The idea of a philosopher discussing inductive inference in science is apt to arouse grotesque images in many minds. People are likely to imagine someone earnestly attempting to explain why it is reasonable to conclude that the sun will rise tomorrow morning because it always has done so in the past. There may have been a time when primitive man anticipated the dawn with assurance based only upon the fact that he had seen dawn follow the blackness of night as long as he could remember, but this primitive state of knowledge, if it ever existed, was unquestionably *pre*scientific. This kind of reasoning bears no resemblance to science; in fact, the crude induction exhibits a complete absence of scientific understanding. Our scientific reasons for believing that the sun will rise tomorrow are of an entirely different kind. We understand the functioning of the solar system in terms of the laws of physics. We predict particular astronomical occurrences by means of these laws in conjunction with a knowledge of particular initial conditions that prevail. Scientific laws and theories have the logical form of general statements, but they are seldom, if ever, simple generalizations from experience.

Consider Newton's gravitational theory: Any two bodies are mutually attracted by a force proportional to the product of their masses and inversely proportional to the square of the distance between their centers. Although general in form, this kind of statement is not established by generalization from instances. We do not go around saying, "Here are two bodies—the force between them is such and such; here are two more bodies—the force between them is such and such; etc." Scientific theories are taken quite literally as hypotheses. They are entertained in order that their consequences may be drawn and examined. Their acceptability is judged in terms of these consequences. The consequences are extremely diverse—the greater the variety the better. For Newtonian theory, we look to such consequences as the behavior of Mars, the tides, falling bodies, the pendulum, and the torsion balance. These consequences have no apparent unity among themselves; they do not constitute a basis for inductive generalization. They achieve a kind of unity only by virtue of the fact that they are consequences of a single physical theory.

The type of inference I have been characterizing is very familiar; it is known as the *hypothetico-deductive method*. It stands in sharp contrast to *induction by enumeration*, which consists in simple inductive generalization from instances. Schematically, the hypothetico-deductive method works as follows: From a general hypothesis and particular statements of initial conditions, a particular predictive statement is deduced. The statements of initial conditions, at least for the time, are accepted as true; the hypothesis is the statement whose truth is at issue. By observation we determine whether the predictive statement turned out to be true. If the predictive consequence is false, the hypothesis is disconfirmed. If observation reveals that the predictive statement is true, we say that the hypothesis is confirmed to some extent. A hypothesis is not, of course, conclusively proved by any one or more positively confirming instances, but it may become highly confirmed. A hypothesis that is sufficiently confirmed is accepted, at least tentatively.

It seems undeniable that science uses a type of inference at least loosely akin to the hypothetico-deductive method. This has led some people to conclude that the logic of science is thoroughly deductive in character. According to this view, the only nondeductive aspect of the situation consists in thinking up hypotheses, but this is not a matter of logic and therefore requires no justification. It is a matter of psychological ingenuity of discovery. Once the hypothesis has been discovered, by some entirely nonlogical process, it remains only to *deduce* consequences and check them against observation.

It is, of course, a fallacy to conclude that the premises of an argument must be true if its conclusion is true. This fact seems to be the basis for the quip that a logic text is a book that consists of two parts; in the first part (on deduction) the fallacies are explained, in the second part (on induction) they are committed. The whole trouble with saying that the hypothetico-deductive method renders the logic of science entirely deductive is that we are attempting to establish a *premise* of the deduction, not the conclusion. Deduction is an indispensible part of the logic of the hypothetico-deductive method, but it is not the only part. There is a fundamental and important sense in which the hypothesis must be regarded as a conclusion instead of a premise. Hypotheses (later perhaps called "theories" or "laws") are among the *results* of scientific investigation; science aims at establishing general statements about the world. Scientific prediction and explanation require such generalizations. While we are concerned with the status of the general hypothesis—whether we should accept it or reject it—the hypothesis must be treated as a conclusion to be supported by evidence, not as a premise lending support to other conclusions. The inference *from* observational evidence *to* hypothesis is surely not deductive. If this point is not already obvious it becomes clear the moment we recall that for any given body of observational data there is, in general, more than one hypothesis compatible with it. These alternative hypotheses differ in factual content and are incompatible with each other. Therefore, they cannot be deductive consequences of any consistent body of observational evidence.

We must grant, then, that science embodies a type of inference resembling the hypothetico-deductive method and fundamentally different from induction by enumeration. Hume, on the other hand, has sometimes been charged with a conception of science according to which the only kind of reasoning is induction by enumeration. His typical examples are cases of simple generalization of observed regularities, something like our example of the licorice-flavored black balls. In the past, water has quenched thirst; in the future, it will as well. In the past, fires have been hot; in the future, they will be hot. In the past, bread has nourished; in the future, it will do so likewise. It might be said that Hume, in failing to see the essential role of the hypothetico-deductive method, was unable to appreciate the complexity of the theoretical science of his own time, to say nothing of subsequent developments. This is typical, some might say, of the misunderstandings engendered by philosophers who undertake to discuss the logic of science without being thoroughly conversant with mathematics and natural science.

This charge against Hume (and other philosophers of induction) is ill-founded. It was part of Hume's genius to have recognized that the arguments he applied to simple enumerative induction apply equally to any kind of ampliative or nondemonstrative inference whatever. Consider the most complex kind of scientific reasoning—the most elaborate example of hypothetico-deductive inference you can imagine. Regardless of subtle features or complications, it is ampliative overall. The conclusion is a statement whose content exceeds the observational evidence upon which it is based. A scientific theory that merely summarized what had already been observed would not deserve to be called a theory. If scientific inference were not ampliative, science would be useless for prediction, postdiction, and explanation. The highly general results that are the pride of theoretical science would be impossible if scientific inference were not ampliative.

In presenting Hume's argument, I was careful to set it up so that it would apply to any kind of ampliative or nondemonstrative inference, no matter how simple or how complex. Furthermore, the distinction between valid deduction and nondemonstrative inference is completely exhaustive. Take any inference whatsoever. It must be deductive or nondemonstrative. Suppose it is nondemonstrative. If we could justify it deductively it would cease to be nondemonstrative. To justify it nondemonstratively would presuppose an already justified type of nondemonstrative inference, which is precisely the problem at issue. Hume's argument does *not* break down when we consider forms more complex than simple enumeration. Although the word "induction" is sometimes used as a synonym for "induction by simple enumeration," I am not using it in that way. Any type of logically correct ampliative inference is induction; the problem of induction is to show that some particular form of ampliative inference is justifiable. It is in this sense that we are concerned with the problem of the justification of inductive inference.

A further misunderstanding is often involved in this type of criticism of Hume. There is a strong inclination to suppose that induction is regarded as the method by which scientific results are discovered.[5] Hume and other philosophers of induction are charged with the view that science has developed historically through patient collection of facts and generalization from them. I know of no philosopher—not even Francis Bacon!*—who has held this view, although it is frequently attacked in the contemporary literature.[6] The term "generalization" has an unfortunate ambiguity which fosters the confusion. In one meaning, "generalization" refers to an inferential process in which one makes a sort of mental transition from particulars to a universal proposition; in this sense, generalization is an act of generalizing—a process that yields general results. In another meaning, "generalization" simply refers to a universal type

* Francis Bacon (1561–1626) was an English philosopher and essayist whose theoretical writings on the importance of empirical investigation played an important role in the Scientific Revolution.

of proposition, without any reference to its source or how it was thought of. It is entirely possible for science to contain many generalizations (in the latter sense) without embodying any generalizations (in the former sense). As I said explicitly at the outset, the problem of induction I am discussing is a problem concerning justification, not discovery. The thesis I am defending—that science does embody induction in a logically indispensable fashion—has nothing to do with the history of science or the psychology of particular scientists. It is simply the claim that scientific inference is ampliative.

3. Deductivism. One of the most interesting and controversial contemporary attempts to provide an account of the logic of science is Karl Popper's* deductivism.[7] In the preceding section I discussed the view that the presence of the hypothetico-deductive method in the logic of science makes it possible to dispense with induction in science and, thereby, to avoid the problem of induction. I argued that the hypothetico-deductive method, since it is ampliative and nondemonstrative, is not strictly deductive; it is, in fact, inductive in the relevant sense. As long as the hypothetico-deductive method is regarded as a method for supporting scientific hypotheses, it cannot succeed in making science thoroughly deductive. Popper realizes this, so in arguing that deduction is the sole mode of inference in science he rejects the hypothetico-deductive method as a means for confirming scientific hypotheses. He asserts that induction plays no role whatever in science; indeed, he maintains that there is no such thing as correct inductive inference. Inductive logic is, according to Popper, a complete delusion. He admits the psychological fact that people (including himself) have faith in the uniformity of nature, but he holds, with Hume, that this can be no more than a matter of psychological fact. He holds, with Hume, that there can be no rational justification of induction, and he thinks Hume proved this point conclusively.

Popper's fundamental thesis is that falsifiability is the mark by which statements of empirical science are distinguished from metaphysical statements and from tautologies. The choice of falsifiability over verifiability as the criterion of demarcation is motivated by a long familiar fact—namely, it is possible to falsify a universal generalization by means of one negative instance, while it is impossible to verify a universal generalization by any limited number of positive instances. This, incidentally, is the meaning of the old saw which is so often made into complete nonsense: "The exception proves the rule." In this context, a rule is a universal generalization, and the term "to prove" means archaically "to test." The exception (i.e., the negative instance) proves (i.e., tests) the rule (i.e., the universal generalization), not by showing it to be true, but by showing it to be false. There is no kind of positive instance to prove (i.e., test) the rule, for positive instances are completely indecisive. Scientific hypotheses, as already noted, are general in form, so they are amenable to falsification but not verification.

Popper thus holds that falsifiability is the hallmark of empirical science. The aim of empirical science is to set forth theories to stand the test of every possible serious attempt at falsification. Scientific theories are hypotheses or conjectures; they are general statements designed to explain the world and make it intelligible, but they are never to be regarded as final truths. Their status is always that of tentative conjecture, and they must continually face the severest possible criticism. The function of the theoretician is to propose scientific conjectures; the function of the experimentalist is to devise every possible way of falsifying these theoretical hypotheses. The attempt to confirm hypotheses is no part of the aim of science.[8]

. . .

Popper has never claimed that falsification by itself can establish scientific hypotheses. When one particular hypothesis has been falsified, many alternative hypotheses remain unfalsified. Likewise, there is nothing unique about a hypothesis that survives without being falsified. Many other unfalsified hypotheses remain to explain the same facts. Popper readily admits all of this. If science is to amount to more than a mere collection of our observations and various reformulations thereof, it must

* Austrian-British philosopher Karl Popper (1902–94) was an important philosopher of science.

embody some other methods besides observation and deduction. Popper supplies that additional factor: *corroboration*.[9]

When a hypothesis has been falsified, it is discarded and replaced by another hypothesis which has not yet experienced falsification. Not all unfalsified hypotheses are on a par. There are principles of selection among unfalsified hypotheses. Again, falsifiability is the key. Hypotheses differ from one another with respect to the ease with which they can be falsified, and we can often compare them with respect to degree of falsifiability. Popper directs us to seek hypotheses that are as highly falsifiable as possible. Science, he says, is interested in bold conjectures. These conjectures must be consistent with the known facts, but they must run as great a risk as possible of being controverted by the facts still to be accumulated. Furthermore, the search for additional facts should be guided by the effort to find facts that will falsify the hypothesis.

As Popper characterizes falsifiability, the greater the degree of falsifiability of a hypothesis, the greater its content. Tautologies lack empirical content because they do not exclude any possible state of affairs; they are compatible with any possible world. Empirical statements are not compatible with every possible state of affairs; they are compatible with some and incompatible with others. The greater the number of possible states of affairs excluded by a statement, the greater its content, for the more it does to pin down our actual world by ruling out possible but nonactual states of affairs. At the same time, the greater the range of facts excluded by a statement—the greater the number of situations with which the statement is incompatible—the greater the risk it runs of being false. A statement with high content has more *potential falsifiers* than a statement with low content. For this reason, high content means high falsifiability. At the same time, content varies inversely with probability. The logical probability of a hypothesis is defined in terms of its range—that is, the possible states of affairs with which it is compatible. The greater the logical probability of a hypothesis, the fewer are its potential falsifiers. Thus, high probability means low falsifiability.

Hypothetico-deductive theorists usually recommend selecting, from among those hypotheses that are compatible with the available facts, the most probable hypothesis. Popper recommends the opposite; he suggests selecting the most falsifiable hypothesis. Thus, he recommends selecting a hypothesis with low probability. According to Popper, a highly falsifiable hypothesis which is severely tested becomes highly corroborated. The greater the severity of the tests—the greater their number and variety—the greater the corroboration of the hypothesis that survives them.

Popper makes it very clear that hypotheses are not regarded as true because they are highly corroborated. Hypotheses cannot be firmly and finally established in this or any other way. Furthermore, because of the inverse relation between falsifiability and probability, we cannot regard highly corroborated hypotheses as probable. To be sure, a serious attempt to falsify a hypothesis which fails does add to the corroboration of this hypothesis, so there is some similarity between corroboration and confirmation as hypothetico-deductive theorists think of it, but it would be a misinterpretation to suppose that increasing corroboration is a process of accumulating positive instances to increase the probability of the hypothesis.[10]

Nevertheless, Popper does acknowledge the need for a method of selecting among unfalsified hypotheses. He has been unequivocal in his emphasis upon the indispensability of far-reaching theory in science. Empirical science is not an activity of merely accumulating experiences; it is theoretical through and through. Although we do not regard any hypotheses as certainly true, we do accept them tentatively and provisionally. Highly corroborated hypotheses are required for prediction and explanation. From among the ever-present multiplicity of hypotheses compatible with the available evidence, we select and accept.

There is just one point I wish to make here regarding Popper's theory. It is not properly characterized as *deductivism*. Popper has not succeeded in purging the logic of science of all inductive elements. My reason for saying this is very simple. Popper furnishes a method for selecting hypotheses whose content exceeds that of the relevant available basic statements. Demonstrative inference cannot accomplish this task alone, for valid deductions are nonampliative and their conclusions cannot exceed their premises in content. Furthermore, Popper's theory does not pretend that basic statements plus deduction can give us scientific theory; instead, corroboration is introduced. Corroboration is a nondemonstrative form of inference. It is a way of providing for the acceptance of hypotheses even though the content of these hypotheses goes beyond the content of the basic statements. *Modus tollens* without corroboration is empty; *modus tollens* with corroboration is induction.

When we ask, "Why should we reject a hypothesis when we have accepted one of its potential falsifiers?" the answer is easy. The potential falsifier contradicts the hypothesis, so the hypothesis is false if the potential falsifier holds. That is simple deduction. When we ask, "Why should we accept from among all the unfalsified hypotheses one that is highly corroborated?" we have a right to expect an answer. The answer is some kind of justification for the methodological rule—for the method of corroboration. Popper attempts to answer this question.

Popper makes it clear that his conception of scientific method differs in important respects from the conceptions of many inductivists. I do not want to quibble over a word in claiming that Popper is, himself, a kind of inductivist. The point is not a trivial verbal one. Popper has claimed that scientific inference is exclusively deductive. We have seen, however, that demonstrative inference is not sufficient to the task of providing a reconstruction of the logic of the acceptance—albeit tentative and provisional—of hypotheses. Popper himself realizes this and introduces a mode of nondemonstrative inference. It does not matter whether we call this kind of inference "induction"; whatever we call it, it is ampliative and not necessarily truth preserving. Using the same force and logic with which Hume raised problems about the justification of induction, we may raise problems about the justification of any kind of nondemonstrative inference. As I argued in the preceding section, Hume's arguments are not peculiar to induction by enumeration or any other special kind of inductive inference; they apply with equal force to any inference whose conclusion can be false, even though it has true premises. Thus, it will not do to dismiss induction by enumeration on grounds of Hume's argument and then accept some other mode of nondemonstrative inference without even considering how Hume's argument might apply to it. I am not arguing that Popper's method is incorrect.[11] I am not even arguing that Popper has failed in his attempt to justify this method. I do claim that Popper is engaged in the same task as many inductivists—namely, the task of providing some sort of justification for a mode of nondemonstrative inference. This enterprise, if successful, *is* a justification of induction.

4. Synthetic a priori Principles. A long philosophical tradition, dating back to antiquity, denies the empiricist claim that knowledge of the world rests solely upon observational evidence—that factual knowledge is limited to what we can observe and what we can infer therefrom. In the modern period, this rationalistic tradition is represented by men like Descartes and Leibniz who took their inspiration from the abstract aspect of modern physics. After Hume's devastating criticism of induction, Kant provided a more precise formulation, a fuller elaboration, and a more subtle defense of rationalism than any that had been given earlier (or, quite possibly, subsequently). As Kant himself testified, it was Hume who awakened him from his "dogmatic slumbers" and thereupon stimulated the *Critique of Pure Reason*.

The doctrine that there are synthetic a priori truths is, as I explained above, tantamount to the view that there are necessarily truth-preserving ampliative inferences. If we could find a *bona fide* demonstrative ampliative inference we would have a solution to Hume's problem of the ground of inference from the observed to the unobserved. This solution could be presented in either of two ways. First, one could assert that there are factual propositions that can be established by pure reason—without the aid of empirical evidence—and that these synthetic a priori propositions, in conjunction with premises established by observation, saw as necessary constraints upon the human intellect and as the source of synthetic a priori truths.

It is unfortunate that subsequent philosophers have paid little attention to Kant's central question: How are synthetic a priori propositions possible? Instead, the category of synthetic a priori propositions has too often become a convenient wastebasket for statements not readily classifiable as analytic or a posteriori. The contents of this wastebasket may, of course, turn out to be very handy in dealing with tough philosophical problems, but the crucial point is whether the wastebasket is really empty. It seems to me that all such statements can be shown, on careful examination, to be analytic or a posteriori, and that no convincing example of a synthetic a priori proposition has yet been produced. Even if this is so, of course, it does not prove that there are no synthetic a priori statements. It should, however, give us pause, and it does relieve us of any obligation to accept the positive rationalistic thesis that there are synthetic a priori propositions. It does place the burden of proof upon those who hope to escape Hume's problem of induction by way of a synthetic a priori principle. Moreover, even if a recalcitrant example were given—one that seemed to defy all analysis as either analytic or a posteriori—it might still be reasonable to suppose that we had not exercised sufficient penetration in dealing with it. If we are left with a total epistemological mystery on the question of how synthetic a priori propositions are possible, it might be wise to suppose it more likely that our analytic acumen is deficient than that an epistemological miracle has occurred.

5. *The Principle of Uniformity of Nature.* A substantial part of Hume's critique of induction rested upon his attack on the principle of the uniformity of nature. He argued definitively that the customary forms of inductive inference cannot be expected to yield correct predictions if nature fails to be uniform—if the future is not like the past—if like sensible qualities are not accompanied by like results.

> All inferences from experience suppose, as their foundation, that the future will resemble the past, and that similar powers will be conjoined with similar sensible qualities. If there be any suspicion that the course of nature may change, and that the past may be no rule for the future, all experience becomes useless, and can give rise to no inference or conclusion.[12]

He argued, moreover, that there is no logical contradiction in the supposition that nature is not uniform—that the regularities we have observed up to the present will fail in wholesale fashion in the future.

> It implies no contradiction that the course of nature may change, and that an object, seemingly like those which we have experienced, may be attended with different or contrary effects. May I not clearly and distinctly conceive that a body, falling from the clouds, and which, in all other respects, resembles snow, has yet the taste of salt or feeling of fire? Is there any more intelligible proposition than to affirm, that all the trees will flourish in December and January, and decay in May and June? Now whatever is intelligible, and can be distinctly conceived, implies no contradiction, and can never be proved false by any demonstrative argument . . .[13]

He argues, in addition, that the principle of uniformity of nature cannot be established by an inference from experience: "It is impossible, therefore, that any arguments from experience can prove this resemblance of the past to the future; since all these arguments are founded on the supposition of that resemblance."[14] Throughout Hume's discussion there is, however, a strong suggestion that we might have full confidence in the customary inductive methods if nature were known to be uniform.

Kant attempted to deal with the problem of induction in just this way, by establishing a principle of uniformity of nature, in the form of the principle of universal causation, as a synthetic a priori truth. Kant claimed, in other words, that every occurrence is governed by causal regularities, and this general characteristic of the universe can be established by pure reason, without the aid of any empirical evidence. He did not try to show that the principle of universal causation is a principle of logic, for to do so would have been to show that it was analytic—not synthetic—and thus lacking in factual content. He did not reject Hume's claim that there is no logical contradiction in the statement that nature is not uniform; he did not try to prove his principle of universal causation by deducing a contradiction from its denial. He did believe, however, that this principle, while not a proposition of pure logic, is necessarily true nevertheless. Hume, of course, argued against this alternative as well. He maintained not only that the uniformity of nature is not a logical or analytic truth, but also that it cannot be any other kind of a priori truth either. Even before Kant had enunciated the doctrine of synthetic a priori principles, Hume had offered strong arguments against them:

> I shall venture to affirm, as a general proposition, which admits of no exception, that the knowledge of this relation [of cause and effect] is not, in any instance, attained by reasonings *a priori*.[15]
>
> Adam, though his rational faculties be supposed, at the very first, entirely perfect, could not have inferred from the fluidity and transparency of water that it would suffocate him, or from the light and warmth of fire that it would consume him.[16]
>
> When we reason *a priori*, and consider merely any object or cause, as it appears to the mind, independent of all observation, it never could suggest to us the notion of any distinct object, such as its effect; much less, show us the inseparable and inviolable connexion between them. A man must be very sagacious who could discover by reasoning that crystal is the effect of heat, and ice of cold, without being previously acquainted with the operation of these qualities.[17]
>
> Now whatever is intelligible, and can be distinctly conceived . . . can never be proved false by any . . . abstract reasoning *a priori*.[18]

Hume argues, by persuasive example and general principle, that nothing about the causal structure of reality can be established by pure reason. He poses an incisive challenge to those who would claim the ability to establish a priori knowledge of a particular causal relation or of the principle of universal causation. In the foregoing discussion of synthetic a priori statements, I have given reasons for believing that Kant failed to overcome Hume's previous objections.

There is, however, another interesting issue that arises in connection with the principle of uniformity of nature. Suppose it could be established—never mind how—prior to a justification of induction. Would it then provide an adequate basis for a justification of induction? The answer is, I think, negative.[19]

Even if nature is uniform to some extent, it is not absolutely uniform. The future is something like the past, but it is somewhat different as well. Total and complete uniformity would mean that the state of the universe at any given moment is the same as its state at any other moment. Such a universe would be a changeless, Parmenidean world.* Change obviously does occur, so the future is not exactly like the past. There are some uniformities, it appears, but not a complete absence of change. The problem is how to ferret out the genuine uniformities. As a matter of actual fact, there are many uniformities *within experience* that we take to be mere coincidences, and there are others that seem to represent genuine causal regularities. For instance, in every election someone finds a precinct, say in Maryland, which has always voted in favor of the winning presidential candidate. Given enough precincts, one expects this sort of thing by sheer chance, and we classify such regularities as mere coincidences. By contrast, the fact that glass windowpanes break when bricks are hurled at them is more than mere coincidence. Causal regularities provide a foundation for inference from the observed to the unobserved; coincidences do not. We can predict with some confidence that the next glass window pane at which a brick is hurled will break; we take with a grain of salt the prediction of the outcome of a presidential election early on election night when returns from the above-mentioned precinct are in. The most that a principle of uniformity of nature could say is that there are some uniformities that persist into the future; if it stated that every regularity observed to hold within the scope of our experience also holds universally, it would be patently false. We are left with the problem of finding a sound basis for distinguishing between mere coincidence and genuine causal regularity.

Kant's principle of universal causation makes a rather weak and guarded statement. It asserts only that there exist causal regularities: "Everything that happens presupposes something from which it follows according to some rule." For each occurrence it claims only the existence of *some* prior cause and *some* causal regularity. It gives no hint as to how we

* The ancient Greek philosopher Parmenides (5th century BCE) is held to have thought that in reality, the world is an unchanging, ungenerated, imperishable, indivisible, perfect, motionless whole.

are to find the prior cause or how we are to identify the causal regularity. It therefore provides no basis upon which to determine whether the inductive inferences we make are correct or incorrect. It would be entirely consistent with Kant's principle for us always to generalize on the basis of observed coincidences and always to fail to generalize on the basis of actual causal relations. It would be entirely consistent with Kant's principle, moreover, for us always to cite a coincidentally preceding event as the cause instead of the event that is the genuine cause. Kant's principle, even if it could be established, would not help us to justify the assertion that our inductive inferences would always or usually be correct. It would provide no criterion to distinguish sound from unsound inductions. Even if Kant's program had succeeded in establishing a synthetic a priori principle of universal causation, it would have failed to produce a justification of induction.

. . .

7. A Probabilistic Approach. It may seem strange in the extreme that this discussion of the problem of induction has proceeded at such great length without seriously bringing in the concept of probability. It is very tempting to react immediately to Hume's argument with the admission that we do not have *knowledge* of the unobserved. Scientific results are not established with absolute certainty. At best we can make probabilistic statements about unobserved matters of fact, and at best we can claim that scientific generalizations and theories are highly confirmed. We who live in an age of scientific empiricism can accept with perfect equanimity the fact that the quest for certainty is futile; indeed, our thanks go to Hume for helping to destroy false hopes for certainty in science.

Hume's search for a justification of induction, it might be continued, was fundamentally misconceived. He tried to find a way of proving that inductive inferences with true premises would have *true* conclusions. He properly failed to find any such justification precisely because it is the function of *deduction* to prove the truth of conclusions, given true premises. Induction has a different function. An inductive inference with true premises establishes its conclusions as *probable*. No wonder Hume failed to find a justification of induction. He was trying to make induction into deduction, and he succeeded only in proving the platitude that induction is not deduction.[20] If we want to justify induction, we must show that inductive inferences establish their conclusions as probable, not as true.

The foregoing sort of criticism of Hume's arguments is extremely appealing, and it has given rise to the most popular sort of attempt, currently, to deal with the problem.[21] In order to examine this approach, we must consider, at least superficially, the meaning of the concept of probability. Two basic meanings must be taken into account at present.

One leading probability concept identifies probability with frequency—roughly, the probable is that which happens often, and the improbable is that which happens seldom. Let us see what becomes of Hume's argument under this interpretation of probability. If we were to claim that inductive conclusions are probable in this sense, we would be claiming that inductive inferences with true premises often have true conclusions, although not always. Hume's argument shows, unhappily, that this claim cannot be substantiated. It was recognized long before Hume that inductive inferences cannot be expected always to lead to the truth. Hume's argument shows, not only that we cannot justify the claim that *every* inductive inference with true premises will have a true conclusion, but also, that we cannot justify the claim that *any* inductive inference with true premises will have a true conclusion. Hume's argument shows that, for all we can know, every inductive inference made from now on might have a false conclusion despite true premises. Thus, Hume has proved, we can show neither that inductive inferences establish their conclusions as true nor that they establish their conclusions as probable in the frequency sense. The introduction of the frequency concept of probability gives no help whatever in circumventing the problem of induction, but this is no surprise, for we should not have expected it to be suitable for this purpose.

A more promising probability concept identifies probability with degree of rational belief. To say that a statement is probable in this sense means that one would be rationally justified in believing it; the degree of probability is the degree of assent a person would be rationally justified in giving. We are not, of course, referring to the degree to which anyone *actually* believes in the statement, but rather to the degree to which one could *rationally* believe it. Degree of actual belief is a purely psychological concept, but degree of rational belief is determined objectively by the evidence. To say that a statement is probable in this sense means that it is supported by evidence. But, so the argument goes, if a statement is the conclusion of an inductive inference with true premises, it *is* supported by evidence—by inductive evidence—this is part of what it *means* to be supported by evidence. The very concept of evidence depends upon the nature of induction, and it becomes incoherent if we try to divorce the two. Trivially, then, the conclusion of an inductive inference is probable under this concept of probability. To ask, with Hume, if we should accept inductive conclusions is tantamount to asking if we should fashion our beliefs in terms of the evidence, and this, in turn, is tantamount to asking whether we should be rational. In this way we arrive at an "ordinary language dissolution" of the problem of induction. Once we understand clearly the meanings of such key terms as "rational," "probable," and "evidence," we see that the problem arose out of linguistic confusion and evaporates into the question of whether it is rational to be rational. Such tautological questions, if meaningful at all, demand affirmative answers.

Unfortunately, the dissolution is not satisfactory.[22] Its inadequacy can be exhibited by focusing upon the concept of inductive evidence and seeing how it figures in the foregoing argument. The fundamental difficulty arises from the fact that the very notion of inductive evidence is determined by the rules of inductive inference. If a conclusion is to be supported by inductive evidence, it must be the conclusion of a correct inductive inference with true premises. Whether the inductive inference is correct depends upon whether the rule governing that inference is correct. The relation of inductive evidential support is, therefore, inseparably bound to the correctness of rules of inductive inference. In order to be able to say whether a given statement is supported by inductive evidence we must be able to say which inductive rules are correct.

For example, suppose that a die has been thrown a large number of times, and we have observed that the side two came up in one sixth of the tosses. This is our "evidence" *e*. Let *h* be the conclusion that, "in the long run," side two will come up one sixth of the times. Consider the following three rules:

1. (Induction by enumeration) Given m/n of observed A are B, to infer that the "long run" relative frequency of B among A is m/n.
2. (A priori rule) Regardless of observed frequencies, to infer that the "long run" relative frequency of B among A is $1/k$, where k is the number of possible outcomes—six in the case of the die.
3. (Counterinductive rule) Given m/n of observed A are B, to infer that the "long run" relative frequency of B among A is $(n - m)/n$.

Under Rule 1, *e* is positive evidence for *h;* under Rule 2, *e* is irrelevant to *h;* and under Rule 3, *e* is negative evidence for *h*. In order to say which conclusions are supported by what evidence, it is necessary to arrive at a decision as to what inductive rules are acceptable. If Rule 1 is correct, the evidence *e* supports the conclusion *h*. If Rule 2 is correct, we are justified in drawing the conclusion *h*, but this is entirely independent of the observational evidence *e;* the same conclusions would have been sanctioned by Rule 2 regardless of observational evidence. If Rule 3 is correct, we are not only prohibited from drawing the conclusion *h*, but also we are permitted to draw a conclusion *h′* which is logically incompatible with *h*. Whether a given conclusion is *supported by evidence*—whether it would be *rational to believe* it on the basis of given evidence—whether it is *made probable* by virtue of its relation to given evidence—depends upon selection of the correct rule or rules from among the infinitely many rules we might conceivably adopt.

The problem of induction can now be reformulated as a problem about evidence. What rules ought we to adopt to determine the nature of inductive evidence? What rules provide suitable concepts of inductive evidence? If we take the customary inductive rules to define the concept of inductive evidence, have we adopted a proper concept of evidence? Would the adoption of some alternative inductive rules provide a more suitable concept of evidence? These are genuine questions which need to be answered.[23]

We find, moreover, that what appeared earlier as a pointless question now becomes significant and difficult. If we take the customary rules of inductive inference to provide a suitable definition of the relation of inductive evidential support, it makes considerable sense to ask whether it is rational to believe on the basis of evidence as thus defined rather than to believe on the basis of evidence as defined according to other rules. For instance, I believe that the a priori rule and the counterinductive rule mentioned above are demonstrably unsatisfactory, and hence, they demonstrably fail to provide a suitable concept of inductive evidence. The important point is that something concerning the selection from among possible rules needs demonstration and is amenable to demonstration.

There is danger of being taken in by an easy equivocation. One meaning we may assign to the concept of inductive evidence is, roughly, the basis on which we ought to fashion our beliefs. Another meaning results from the relation of evidential support determined by whatever rule of inductive inference we adopt. It is only by supposing that these two concepts are the same that we suppose the problem of induction to have vanished. The problem of induction is still there; it is the problem of providing adequate grounds for the selection of inductive rules. We want the relation of evidential support determined by these rules to yield a concept of inductive evidence which is, in fact, the basis on which we ought to fashion our beliefs.[24]

We began this initially promising approach to the problem of the justification of induction by introducing the notion of probability, but we end with a dilemma. If we take "probability" in the frequency sense, it is easy to see why it is advisable to accept probable conclusions in preference to improbable ones. In so doing we shall be right more often. Unfortunately, we cannot show that inferences conducted according to any particular rule establish conclusions that are probable in this sense. If we take "probability" in a nonfrequency sense it may be easy to show that inferences which conform to our accepted inductive rules establish their conclusions as probable. Unfortunately, we can find no reason to prefer conclusions which are probable in this sense to those that are improbable. As Hume has shown, we have no reason to suppose that probable conclusions will often be true and improbable ones will seldom be true. This dilemma is Hume's problem of induction all over again. We have been led to an interesting reformulation, but it is only a reformulation and not a solution.

8. Pragmatic Justification. Of all the solutions and dissolutions proposed to deal with Hume's problem of induction, Hans Reichenbach's* attempt to provide a pragmatic justification seems to me the most fruitful and promising.[25] This approach accepts Hume's arguments up to the point of agreeing that it is impossible to establish, either deductively or inductively, that any inductive inferences will ever again have true conclusions. Nevertheless, Reichenbach claims, the standard method of inductive generalization can be justified. Although its *success* as a method of prediction cannot be established in advance, it can be shown to be superior to any alternative method of prediction.

The argument can be put rather simply. Nature may be sufficiently uniform in suitable respects for us to make successful inductive inferences from the observed to the unobserved. On the other hand, for all we know, she may not. Hume has shown that we cannot prove in advance which case holds. All we can say is that nature may or may not be uniform—if she is, induction works; if she is not, induction fails. Even in the face of our ignorance about the uniformity of nature, we can ask what would happen if we adopted some radically different method of inference. Consider, for instance, the method of the crystal gazer. Since we do not know whether nature is uniform or not, we must consider both possibilities. If nature is uniform, the method of crystal gazing might work successfully, or it might fail. We cannot prove a priori that it will not work. At

* Hans Reichenbach (1891–1953) was a German-born philosopher of science who spent the bulk of his teaching career at the University of California at Los Angeles.

the same time, we cannot prove a priori that it will work, even if nature exhibits a high degree of uniformity. Thus, in case nature is reasonably uniform, the standard inductive method *must* work while the alternative method of crystal gazing *may or may not* work. In this case, the superiority of the standard inductive method is evident. Now, suppose nature lacks uniformity to such a degree that the standard inductive method is a complete failure. In this case, Reichenbach argues, the alternative method must likewise fail. Suppose it did not fail—suppose, for instance, that the method of crystal gazing worked consistently. This would constitute an important relevant uniformity that could be exploited inductively. If a crystal gazer had consistently predicted future occurrences, we could infer inductively that he has a method of prediction that will enjoy continued success. The inductive method would, in this way, share the success of the method of crystal gazing, and would therefore be, contrary to hypothesis, successful. Hence, Reichenbach concludes, the standard inductive method will be successful *if any other method could succeed*. As a result, we have everything to gain and nothing to lose by adopting the inductive method. If any method works, induction works. If we adopt the inductive method and it fails, we have lost nothing, for any other method we might have adopted would likewise have failed. Reichenbach does not claim to prove that nature is uniform, or that the standard inductive method will be successful. He does not postulate the uniformity of nature. He tries to show that the inductive method is the best method for ampliative inference, whether it turns out to be successful or not.

This ingenious argument, although extremely suggestive, is ultimately unsatisfactory. As I have just presented it, it is impossibly vague. I have not specified the nature of the standard inductive method. I have not stated with any exactness what constitutes success for the inductive method or any other. Moreover, the uniformity of nature is not an all-or-none affair. Nature appears to be uniform to some extent and also to be lacking in uniformity to some degree. As we have already seen, it is not easy to state a principle of uniformity that is strong enough to assure the success of inductive inference and weak enough to be plausible. The vagueness of the foregoing argument is not, however, its fundamental drawback. It can be made precise, and I shall do so below in connection with the discussion of the frequency interpretation of probability.[26] When it is made precise, as we shall see, it suffers the serious defect of equally justifying too wide a variety of rules for ampliative inference.

I have presented Reichenbach's argument rather loosely in order to make intuitively clear its basic strategy. The sense in which it is a pragmatic justification should be clear. Unlike many authors who have sought a justification of induction, Reichenbach does not try to prove the truth of any synthetic proposition. He recognizes that the problem concerns the justification of a rule, and rules are neither true nor false. Hence, he tries to show that the adoption of a standard inductive rule is practically useful in the attempt to learn about and deal with the unobserved. He maintains that this can be shown even though we cannot prove the truth of the assertion that inductive methods will lead to predictive success. This pragmatic aspect is, it seems to me, the source of the fertility of Reichenbach's approach. Even though his argument does not constitute an adequate justification of induction, it seems to me to provide a valid core from which we may attempt to develop a more satisfactory justification.

III. SIGNIFICANCE OF THE PROBLEM

Hume's problem of induction evokes, understandably, a wide variety of reactions. It is not difficult to appreciate the response of the man engaged in active scientific research or practical affairs who says, in effect, "Don't bother me with these silly puzzles; I'm too busy doing science, building bridges, or managing affairs of state." No one, including Hume, seriously suggests any suspension of scientific investigation or practical decision pending a solution of the problem of induction. The problem concerns the *foundations* of science. As Hume eloquently remarks in *Enquiry Concerning Human Understanding:*

> Let the course of things be allowed hitherto ever so regular; that alone, without some new argument or inference, proves not that, for the future, it will continue so. In vain do you pretend to have learned the

> nature of bodies from your past experience. Their secret nature, and consequently all their effects and influence, may change, without any change in their sensible qualities. This happens sometimes, and with regard to some objects: Why may it not happen always, and with regard to all objects? What logic, what process of argument secures you against this supposition? My practice, you say, refutes my doubts. But you mistake the purport of my question. As an agent, I am quite satisfied in the point; but as a philosopher, who has some share of curiosity, I will not say scepticism, I want to learn the foundation of this inference.

We should know by now that the foundations of a subject are usually established long after the subject has been well developed, not before. To suppose otherwise would be a glaring example of "naïve first-things-firstism."

Nevertheless, there is something intellectually disquieting about a serious gap in the foundations of a discipline, and it is especially disquieting when the discipline in question is so broad as to include the whole of empirical science, all of its applications, and indeed, all of common sense. As human beings we pride ourselves on rationality—so much so that for centuries rationality was enshrined as the very essence of humanity and the characteristic that distinguishes man from the lower brutes. Questionable as such pride may be, our intellectual consciences should be troubled by a gaping lacuna in the structure of our knowledge and the foundations of scientific inference. I do not mean to suggest that the structure of empirical science is teetering because of foundational difficulties; the architectural metaphor is really quite inappropriate. I do suggest that intellectural integrity requires that foundational problems not be ignored.

Each of two opposing attitudes has its own immediate appeal. One of these claims that the scientific method is so obviously the correct method that there is no need to waste our time trying to show that this is so. There are two difficulties. First, we have enough painful experience to know that the appeal to obviousness is dangerously likely to be an appeal to prejudice and superstition. What is obvious to one age or culture may well turn out, on closer examination, to be just plain false. Second, if the method of science is so obviously superior to other methods we might adopt, then I should think we ought to be able to point to those characteristics of the method by which it gains its obvious superiority.

The second tempting attitude is one of pessimism. In the face of Hume's arguments and the failure of many attempts to solve the problem, it is easy to conclude that the problem is hopeless. Whether motivated by Hume's arguments or, as is probably more often the case, by simple impatience with foundational problems, this attitude seems quite widespread. It is often expressed by the formula that science is, at bottom, a matter of faith. While it is no part of my purpose to launch a wholesale attack on faith as such, this attitude toward the foundations of scientific inference is unsatisfactory. The crucial fact is that science makes a *cognitive claim*, and this cognitive claim is a fundamental part of the rationale for doing science at all. Hume has presented us with a serious challenge to that cognitive claim. If we cannot legitimize the cognitive claim, it is difficult to see what reason remains for doing science. Why not turn to voodoo, which would be simpler, cheaper, less time consuming, and more fun?

If science is basically a matter of faith, then the scientific faith exists on a par with other faiths. Although we may be culturally conditioned to accept this faith, others are not. Science has no ground on which to maintain its *cognitive* superiority to any form of irrationalism, however repugnant. This situation is, it seems to me, intellectually and socially undesirable. We have had enough experience with various forms of irrationalism to recognize the importance of being able to distinguish them logically from genuine science. I find it intolerable to suppose that a theory of biological evolution, supported as it is by extensive scientific evidence, has no more rational foundation than has its rejection by ignorant fundamentalists. I, too, have faith that the scientific method is especially well suited for establishing knowledge of the unobserved, but I believe this faith should be justified. It seems to me extremely important that some people should earnestly seek a solution to this problem concerning the foundations of scientific inference.

One cannot say in advance what consequences will follow from a solution to a foundational problem. It would seem to depend largely upon the nature of the solution. But a discipline with well-laid foundations is surely far more satisfactory than one whose foundations are in doubt. We have only to compare the foundationally insecure calculus of the seventeenth and eighteenth centuries with the calculus of the late nineteenth century to appreciate the gains in elegance, simplicity, and rigor. Furthermore, the foundations of calculus provided a basis for a number of other developments, interesting in their own right and *greatly extending the power and fertility of the original theory*. Whether similar extensions will occur as a result of a satisfactory resolution of Hume's problem is a point on which it would be rash to hazard any prediction, but we know from experience that important consequences result from the most unexpected sources. The subsequent discussion of the foundations of probability will indicate directions in which some significant consequences may be found, but for the moment it will suffice to note that a serious concern for the solution of Hume's problem cannot fail to deepen our understanding of the nature of scientific inference. This, after all, is the ultimate goal of the whole enterprise.

NOTES

This book is based upon five lectures in the Philosophy of Science Series at the University of Pittsburgh. The first two lectures, *Foundations of Scientific Inference: I. The Problem of Induction*, II. *Probability and Induction*, were presented in March 1963. The next two lectures, *Inductive Inference in Science:* I. *Hypothetico-Deductive Arguments*, II. *Plausibility Arguments*, were delivered in October 1964. The final lecture, *A Priori Knowledge*, was given in October 1965. The author wishes to express his gratitude to the National Science Foundation and the Minnesota Center for Philosophy of Science for support of research on inductive logic and probability.

1. David Hume, *Enquiry Concerning Human Understanding*, see IV, 1.
2. Pp. 111–14.
3. Hume, *Human Understanding*.
4. Ibid.
5. See John Patrick Day, *Inductive Probability* (New York: Humanities Press, 1961), p. 6.
6. See e.g., Karl R. Popper, *The Logic of Scientific Discovery* (New York: Basic Books, 1959), sec. 30, and Thomas S. Kuhn, *The Structure of Scientific Revolutions* (Chicago: U. of Chicago Press, 1962).
7. The most comprehensive statement of Popper's position is to be found in *The Logic of Scientific Discovery*. This is the English translation, with additions, of Karl R. Popper, *Logik der Forschung* (Wien, 1934).
8. "I think that we shall have to get accustomed to the idea that we must not look upon science as a 'body of knowledge,' but rather as a system of hypotheses; that is to say, a system of guesses or anticipations which in principle cannot be justified, but with which we work as long as they stand up to tests, and of which we are never justified in saying that we know that they are 'true' or 'more or less certain' or even 'probable.'" *The Logic of Scientific Discovery*, p. 317.
9. See *The Logic of Scientific Discovery*, Chap. 10.
10. Ibid., p. 270.
11. I shall return to Popper's methodological views in the discussion of confirmation in sec. VII. In that context I shall exhibit what I take to be the considerable valid content of Popper's account of the logic of science. See pp. 114–21.
12. David Hume, *Human Understanding*, sec. IV.
13. Ibid.
14. Ibid.
15. Ibid.
16. Ibid.
17. Ibid.
18. Ibid.
19. Wesley C. Salmon, "The Uniformity of Nature," *Philosophy and Phenomenological Research*, 14 (September 1953).
20. Max Black, "The Justification of Induction," in *Language and Philosophy*.
21. Among the authors who subscribe to approaches similar to this are A. J. Ayer, *Language, Truth and Logic* (New York: Dover Publications, 1952); Paul Edwards, "Russell's Doubts about Induction," *Mind*, 58 (1949), 141–63; Asher Moore, "The Principle of Induction," *J. of Philosophy*, 49

(1952), 741–58; Arthur Pap, *Elements of Analytic Philosophy* (New York: Macmillan, 1949), and *An Introduction to the Philosophy of Science;* and P. F. Strawson, *Introduction to Logical Theory* (London: Methuen, 1952).

22. I have criticized this type of argument at some length in "Should We Attempt to Justify Induction?" *Philosophical Studies*, 8 (April 1957), and in "The Concept of Inductive Evidence," *American Philosophical Quarterly*, 2 (October 1965). This latter article is part of a "Symposium on Inductive Evidence" in which Stephen Barker and Henry E. Kyburg, Jr. defend against the attack. See their comments and my rejoinder.

23. This point has enormous import for any attempt to construct an inductive justification of induction. To decide whether the fact that induction has been successful in the past is positive evidence, negative evidence, or no evidence at all begs the very question at issue.

24. As I attempted to show in "Should We Attempt to Justify Induction?" this equivocation seems to arise out of a failure to distinguish *validation* and *vindication*. This crucial distinction is explicated by Herbert Feigl, "De Principiis non Disputandum . . .?" in *Philosophical Analysis*, ed. Max Black (Ithaca: Cornell U. Press, 1950).

25. Hans Reichenbach, *Experience and Prediction* (Chicago: U. of Chicago Press, 1938), Chap. 5, and *The Theory of Probability* (Berkeley: U. of California Press, 1949), Chap. 11.

26. Sec. V, 5, pp. 83–96.

The New Riddle of Induction

NELSON GOODMAN

Philosopher Nelson Goodman (1906–98) made important contributions to aesthetics, epistemology, metaphysics, logic, and the philosophy of science during his long philosophical career. He taught at the University of Pennsylvania and at Harvard University, and was a teacher or colleague of many of the other authors whose writings appear in this volume, including Noam Chomsky and Hilary Putnam (whom he taught) and Robert Nozick, John Rawls, and W. V. O. Quine (who were his colleagues).

The selection presented here is excerpted from his book *Fact, Fiction and Forecast* (1955), originally delivered as a series of lectures. In it, Goodman presents his "new riddle of induction" by means of his now-famous example of *grue*.

Confirmation of a hypothesis by an instance depends rather heavily upon features of the hypothesis other than its syntactical form. That a given piece of copper conducts electricity increases the credibility of statements asserting that other pieces of copper conduct electricity, and thus confirms the hypothesis that all copper conducts electricity. But the fact that a given man now in this room is a third son does not increase the credibility of statements asserting that other men now in this room are third sons, and so does not confirm the hypothesis that all men now in this room are third sons. Yet in both cases our hypothesis is a generalization of the evidence statement. The difference is that in the former case the hypothesis is a *lawlike* statement; while in the latter case, the hypothesis is a merely contingent or accidental generality. Only a statement that is *lawlike*—regardless of its truth or falsity or its scientific importance—is capable of receiving confirmation from an instance of it; accidental statements are not.

Reprinted by permission of the publisher from *Fact, Fiction, and Forecast* by Nelson Goodman, Cambridge, Mass.: Harvard University Press, pp. 72–83. Copyright © 1979, 1983 by Nelson Goodman.

Plainly, then, we must look for a way of distinguishing lawlike from accidental statements.

So long as what seems to be needed is merely a way of excluding a few odd and unwanted cases that are inadvertently admitted by our definition of confirmation, the problem may not seem very hard or very pressing. We fully expect that minor defects will be found in our definition and that the necessary refinements will have to be worked out patiently one after another. But some further examples will show that our present difficulty is of a much graver kind.

Suppose that all emeralds examined before a certain time *t* are green. At time *t*, then, our observations support the hypothesis that all emeralds are green; and this is in accord with our definition of confirmation. Our evidence statements assert that emerald *a* is green, that emerald *b* is green, and so on; and each confirms the general hypothesis that all emeralds are green. So far, so good.

Now let me introduce another predicate less familiar than "green." It is the predicate "grue" and it applies to all things examined before *t* just in case they are green but to other things just in case they are blue. Then at time *t* we have, for each evidence statement asserting that a given emerald is green, a parallel evidence statement asserting that that emerald is grue. And the statements that emerald *a* is grue, that emerald *b* is grue, and so on, will each confirm the general hypothesis that all emeralds are grue. Thus according to our definition, the prediction that all emeralds subsequently examined will be green and the prediction that all will be grue are alike confirmed by evidence statements describing the same observations. But if an emerald subsequently examined is grue, it is blue and hence not green. Thus although we are well aware which of the two incompatible predictions is genuinely confirmed, they are equally well confirmed according to our present definition. Moreover, it is clear that if we simply choose an appropriate predicate, then on the basis of these same observations we shall have equal confirmation, by our definition, for any prediction whatever about other emeralds—or indeed about anything else.[1] As in our earlier example, only the predictions subsumed under lawlike hypothesis are genuinely confirmed; but we have no criterion as yet for determining lawlikeness. And now we see that without some such criterion, our definition not merely includes a few unwanted cases, but is so completely ineffectual that it virtually excludes nothing. We are left once again with the intolerable result that anything confirms anything. This difficulty cannot be set aside as an annoying detail to be taken care of in due course. It has to be met before our definition will work at all.

Nevertheless, the difficulty is often slighted because on the surface there seem to be easy ways of dealing with it. Sometimes, for example, the problem is thought to be . . . [that we are], making tacit and illegitimate use of information outside the stated evidence: the information, for example, that different samples of one material are usually alike in conductivity, and the information that different men in a lecture audience are usually not alike in the number of their older brothers. But while it is true that such information is being smuggled in, this does not by itself settle the matter . . . If to our initial evidence we add statements concerning the conductivity of pieces of other materials or concerning the number of older brothers of members of other lecture audiences, this will not in the least affect the confirmation, according to our definition, of the hypothesis concerning copper or of that concerning this lecture audience. Since our definition is insensitive to the bearing upon hypotheses of evidence so related to them, even when the evidence is fully declared, the difficulty about accidental hypotheses cannot be explained away on the ground that such evidence is being surreptitiously taken into account

A more promising suggestion is to explain the matter in terms of the effect of this other evidence not directly upon the hypothesis in question but *indirectly* through other hypotheses that *are* confirmed, according to our definition, by such evidence. Our information about other materials does by our definition confirm such hypotheses as that all pieces of iron conduct electricity, that no pieces of rubber do, and so on; and these hypotheses, the explanation runs, impart to the hypothesis that all pieces of copper conduct electricity (and also to the hypothesis that none do) the character of lawlikeness—that is, amenability to confirmation by direct positive instances when found.

On the other hand, our information about other lecture audiences *dis*confirms many hypotheses to the effect that all the men in one audience are third sons, or that none are; and this strips any character of lawlikeness from the hypothesis that all (or the hypothesis that none) of the men in *this* audience are third sons. But clearly if this course is to be followed, the circumstances under which hypotheses are thus related to one another will have to be precisely articulated.

The problem, then, is to define the relevant way in which such hypotheses must be alike. Evidence for the hypothesis that all iron conducts electricity enhances the lawlikeness of the hypothesis that all zirconium conducts electricity, but does not similarly affect the hypothesis that all the objects on my desk conduct electricity. Wherein lies the difference? The first two hypotheses fall under the broader hypothesis—call it "H"—that every class of things of the same material is uniform in conductivity; the first and third fall only under some such hypothesis as—call it "K"—that every class of things that are either all of the same material or all on a desk is uniform in conductivity. Clearly the important difference here is that evidence for a statement affirming that one of the classes covered by H has the property in question increases the credibility of any statement affirming that another such class has this property; while nothing of the sort holds true with respect to K. But this is only to say that H is lawlike and K is not. We are faced anew with the very problem we are trying to solve: the problem of distinguishing between lawlike and accidental hypotheses.

The most popular way of attacking the problem takes its cue from the fact that accidental hypotheses seem typically to involve some spatial or temporal restriction, or reference to some particular individual. They seem to concern the people in some particular room, or the objects on some particular person's desk; while lawlike hypotheses characteristically concern . . . all pieces of copper whatsoever. Complete generality is thus very often supposed to be a sufficient condition of lawlikeness; but to define this complete generality is by no means easy. Merely to require that the hypothesis contain no term naming, describing, or indicating a particular thing or location will obviously not be enough. The troublesome hypothesis that all emeralds are grue contains no such term; and where such a term does occur, as in hypotheses about men in *this room*, it can be suppressed in favor of some predicate (short or long, new or old) that contains no such term but applies only to exactly the same things. One might think, then, of excluding not only hypotheses that actually contain terms for specific individuals but also all hypotheses that are equivalent to others that do contain such terms. But, as we have just seen, to exclude only hypotheses of which *all* equivalents contain such terms is to exclude nothing. On the other hand, to exclude all hypotheses that have *some* equivalent containing such a term is to exclude everything; for even the hypothesis

All grass is green

has as an equivalent

All grass in London or elsewhere is green.

The next step, therefore, has been to consider ruling out predicates of certain kinds. A syntactically universal hypothesis is lawlike, the proposal runs, if its predicates are "purely qualitative" or "non-positional." This will obviously accomplish nothing if a purely qualitative predicate is then conceived either as one that is equivalent to some expression free of terms for specific individuals, or as one that is equivalent to no expression that contains such a term; for this only raises again the difficulties just pointed out. The claim appears to be rather that at least in the case of a simple enough predicate we can readily determine by direct inspection of its meaning whether or not it is purely qualitative. But even aside from obscurities in the notion of "the meaning" of a predicate, this claim seems to me wrong. I simply do not know how to tell whether a predicate is qualitative or positional, except perhaps by completely begging the question at issue and asking whether the predicate is "well-behaved"—that is, whether simple syntactically universal hypotheses applying it are lawlike.

This statement will not go unprotested. "Consider," it will be argued, "the predicates 'blue' and 'green' and the predicate 'grue' introduced earlier, and also the predicate 'bleen' that applies to emeralds examined before time *t* just in case they are blue and to other emeralds just in case they are green. "Surely it is clear," the argument runs, "that the first two are purely qualitative and the second two are not; for the meaning of each of the latter two plainly involves reference to a specific temporal position." To this I reply that indeed I do recognize the first two as well-behaved predicates admissible in lawlike hypotheses, and the second two as ill-behaved predicates. But the argument that the former but not the latter are purely qualitative seems to me quite unsound. True enough, if we start with "blue" and "green," then "grue" and "bleen" will be explained in terms of "blue" and "green" and a temporal term. But equally truly, if we start with "grue" and "bleen," then "blue" and "green" will be explained in terms of "grue" and "bleen" and a temporal term; "green," for example, applies to emeralds examined before time *t* just in case they are grue, and to other emeralds just in case they are bleen. Thus qualitativeness is an entirely relative matter and does not by itself establish any dichotomy of predicates. This relativity seems to be completely overlooked by those who contend that the qualitative character of a predicate is a criterion for its good behavior.

Of course, one may ask why we need worry about such unfamiliar predicates as "grue" or about accidental hypotheses in general, since we are unlikely to use them in making predictions. If our definition works for such hypotheses as are normally employed, isn't that all we need? In a sense, yes; but only in the sense that we need no definition, no theory of induction, and no philosophy of knowledge at all. We get along well enough without them in daily life and in scientific research. But if we seek a theory at all, we cannot excuse gross anomalies resulting from a proposed theory by pleading that we can avoid them in practice. The odd cases we have been considering are clinically pure cases that, though seldom encountered in practice, nevertheless display to best advantage the symptoms of a widespread and destructive malady.

We have so far neither any answer nor any promising clue to an answer to the question what distinguishes lawlike or confirmable hypotheses from accidental or non-confirmable ones; and what may at first have seemed a minor technical difficulty has taken on the stature of a major obstacle to the development of a satisfactory theory of confirmation. It is this problem that I call the new riddle of induction.

THE PERVASIVE PROBLEM OF PROJECTION

. . . The problem of justifying induction has been displaced by the problem of defining confirmation, and our work upon this has left us with the residual problem of distinguishing between confirmable and non-confirmable hypotheses. One might say roughly that the first question was "Why does a positive instance of a hypothesis give any grounds for predicting further instances?"; that the newer question was "What is a positive instance of a hypothesis?"; and that the crucial remaining question is "What hypotheses are confirmed by their positive instances?"

The vast amount of effort expended on the problem of induction in modern times has thus altered our afflictions but hardly relieved them. The original difficulty about induction arose from the recognition that anything may follow upon anything. Then, in attempting to define confirmation in terms of the converse of the consequence relation, we found ourselves with the distressingly similar difficulty that our definition would make any statement confirm any other. And now, after modifying our definition drastically, we still get the old devastating result that any statement will confirm any statement. Until we find a way of exercising some control over the hypotheses to be admitted, our definition makes no distinction whatsoever between valid and invalid inductive inferences.

The real inadequacy of Hume's account lay not in his descriptive approach but in the imprecision of his description. Regularities in experience, according to him, give rise to habits of expectation; and thus it is predictions conforming to past regularities that are normal or valid. But Hume overlooks the fact that some regularities do and some do not establish such habits; that predictions based on some regularities are valid while predictions based on other regularities are not. Every word you have heard me say has occurred prior to the final sentence of this lecture; but that does not, I hope, create any expectation that every word you will hear me say will be prior to that sentence. Again, consider our case of emeralds. All those examined before time *t* are green; and this leads us to expect, and confirms the prediction, that the next one will be green. But also, all those examined are grue; and this does not lead us to expect, and does not confirm the prediction, that the next one will be grue. Regularity in greenness confirms the prediction of further cases; regularity in grueness does not. To say that valid predictions are those based on past regularities, without being able to say *which* regularities, is thus quite pointless. Regularities are where you find them, and you can find them anywhere. As we have seen, Hume's failure to recognize and deal with this problem has been shared even by his most recent successors.

As a result, what we have in current confirmation theory is a definition that is adequate for certain cases that so far can be described only as those for which it is adequate. The theory works where it works. A hypothesis is confirmed by statements related to it in the prescribed way provided it is so confirmed. This is a good deal like having a theory that tells us that the area of a plane figure is one-half the base times the altitude, without telling us for what figures this holds. We must somehow find a way of distinguishing lawlike hypotheses, to which our definition of confirmation applies, from accidental hypotheses, to which it does not.

Today I have been speaking solely of the problem of induction, but what has been said applies equally to the more general problem of projection. As pointed out earlier, the problem of prediction from past to future cases is but a narrower version of the problem of projecting from any set of cases to others. We saw that a whole cluster of troublesome problems concerning dispositions and possibility can be reduced to this problem of projection. That is why the new riddle of induction, which is more broadly the problem of distinguishing between projectible and non-projectible hypotheses, is as important as it is exasperating.

NOTE

1. For instance, we shall have equal confirmation, by our present definition, for the prediction that roses subsequently examined will be blue. Let "emerose" apply just to emeralds examined before time *t*, and to roses examined later. Then all emeroses so far examined are grue, and this confirms the hypothesis that all emeroses are grue and hence the prediction that roses subsequently examined will be blue. The problem raised by such antecedents has been little noticed, but is no easier to meet than that raised by similarly perverse consequents.

METAPHYSICAL PERPLEXITIES

INTRODUCTION

Metaphysics is the branch of philosophy that is concerned with fundamental questions about the nature of reality. What is there? What may there be? What is the nature of objects, properties, and ideas? What is the world like at the most fundamental level?

Thinking about these general issues gives rise to a number of specific questions. Among them are these: What is the nature of time? Is human behavior free or determined? What is required for an object or a person that exists today to be the same entity as an object or person that exists tomorrow? The selections in this section explore these perplexing questions.

Time and Time Travel

What is the nature of time? It may seem that this is a question for science, not for philosophy, but as we show in this section, there is plenty of work left over for philosophers even after the scientific questions have been settled. This does not mean that we can ignore the answers that science gives. Indeed, our first selection is drawn from the popular 1916 book *Relativity* by the great twentieth-century physicist, Albert Einstein (1879–1955). In it, Einstein explains how simultaneity is *relative*: two events that occur at the same time from the perspective of one observer may occur at different times from the perspective of another. It thus makes no sense to ask if two events are simultaneous *simipliciter*; the question has meaning only within the context of a particular frame of reference.

What philosophical implications does Einstein's discovery have? In "Time," philosopher Ted Sider (1967–) explores some of the issues raised by Einstein's finding and discusses a number of traditional philosophical questions about the nature of time. The topics he considers include the following: In what sense can time be said to "flow" or "move"? How are time and space related? Do objects have temporal as well as spatial parts? What do we mean by "now"? How is the present related to the past and the future?

Sider's chapter closes with a discussion of time travel. Whether time travel is *physically* possible—that is, compatible with the laws of physics—is a question for empirical scientists to answer. But whether time travel is *metaphysically* possible—that is, compatible with the laws of logic—falls solidly in the domain of philosophy. Sider suggests that time travel may be metaphysically possible, but his discussion is brief. In "The Paradoxes of Time Travel," philosopher David Lewis (1941–2001) considers the matter in more detail. He argues that although the idea of time travel may seem to give rise to certain paradoxes, the notion is, in fact, a coherent one. Understood properly, he suggests, time travel is metaphysically possible, in the sense that the idea does not give rise to any contradictions.

Free Will

Our next set of selections address the age-old problem of free will, a problem which arises when we attend to the apparent conflict between two natural commitments: On the one hand, it seems clear that all events have causes; on the other, it seems clear that human beings can act freely in accordance with their wills. But it is challenging to see how these could both be true at the same time.

Suppose *determinism* is true; that is, suppose every event that occurs is fully determined by the events that precede it. If so, then human choices and actions are themselves fully determined by the events that preceded them. Moreover, each of those preceding events is fully determined by the events that preceded it. So if determinism is true, all my actions were fully determined by events that took place long before my birth. What room is there in such a picture for free will?

Many philosophers have felt that free will and determinism are, indeed, *incompatible*: that if determinism is true, then there is no room for free will, and that if there is free will, then determinism is false. But these *incompatibilists* are divided about which of the two commitments should be given up. *Hard determinists* hold that determinism is true and that the appearance of free will is thus an illusion. *Libertarians* agree with hard determinists that free will and determinism are incompatible, but, unlike hard determinists, they maintain that some actions—those performed freely by agents—are independent of causal laws.

Other philosophers—known as *compatibilists* or *soft determinists*—try to hold on to both commitments at once. According to these theorists, determinism is true, but the appearance of free will is not illusory. Determinism and free will are somehow compatible.

The first two readings in this section explore the dialectic between compatibilists and incompatibilists. In the first selection, "Freedom and Necessity," British philosopher A. J. Ayer (1910–89) defends a compatibilist account of free will; he holds both that determinism is true and that human action is free in the relevant sense.

These claims are challenged by Roderick Chisholm (1916–99), whose "Human Freedom and the Self" offers an incompatibilist libertarian account of free will. According to Chisholm, the compatibilist answer is unsuccessful, for if determinism were true, then agents would not be free to have chosen otherwise than they did. But, he contends, agents are capable of a special kind of causation—he calls it *immanent* causation—in which the event thereby caused is the result not of other events (as the determinist maintains), but of the will of the agent herself.

A critique of Chisholm's account is offered in Harry Frankfurt's (1929–) article "Freedom of the Will and the Concept of a Person." In it, Frankfurt tries to specify exactly what we are concerned with when we ask whether the will is free and concludes that we are interested in whether the agent is able to form desires about which of her inclinations should govern her will. This sort of capacity may be present whether or not determinism is true, so according to this view, free will and determinism are compatible.

In our final selection, "Freedom and Resentment," P. F. Strawson (1919–2006) defends the view that our actual practices of holding people responsible reveal a tacit commitment to compatibilism; he maintains that the truth of determinism is irrelevant to questions of moral responsibility.

Identity and Personal Identity

Most of us believe that objects persist from one moment to the next: your book, your cat, and your roommate all existed yesterday and will continue to exist tomorrow. But what makes it the case that the book you are reading right now is the same object as the book you were reading last week? What makes your cat the same animal? What makes your roommate the same human being?

These sorts of questions—questions about what it takes for an object or person to persist over time—have been discussed by philosophers for centuries. We begin with a selection from the *Essay Concerning Human Understanding* by the British philosopher John Locke (1632–1704). In it, Locke argues that questions about identity over time have different sorts of answers depending on the sort of entity we are concerned with: objects persist by retaining matter, plants and animals persist by participating in some sort of continuous organic process, and persons—self-conscious beings—persist through chains of psychological connection like memory and anticipation.

Turn again to the question of what makes your roommate the same human being he was yesterday. Locke's analysis seems to give two answers, depending on whether you are interested in whether he is the same *man* (human animal) or the same *person* (self-conscious being). In the first case, you would need to know something about the history and organization of the matter that composes him; in the second, you would need to know something about his memories and other psychological states. Ordinarily, of course, the two coincide; presumably your roommate is both the same Lockean animal and the same Lockean person that he was yesterday.

But what if the two were to come apart? Locke imagines a case in which the soul of a prince enters the body of a cobbler, bringing with it all the prince's memories and desires. In such a case, Locke contends, we would direct our prince-oriented concerns to the being who occupies the cobbler's body. But what if we ourselves faced the prospect of such a "body swap"? Suppose there were some process by which my mind could be placed in your body, and vice versa? Which future entity should I consider myself to be?

It may seem obvious that I should identify with the being who (so to speak) inherits my my mind, as opposed to the being who inherits my body. But in "The Self and the Future," philosopher Bernard Williams (1929–2003) suggests that this natural view may be mistaken. Instead, he contends that there are good grounds for subscribing to a *bodily continuity* view of personal identity, according to which what makes me the same human being as I was yesterday is a matter of my being the same human animal.

An alternative view is presented in the selection from Derek Parfit (1942–), an except from his book *Reasons and Persons*. Through a series of vivid imaginary cases, Parfit defends a *psychological account* of personal identity and considers why and to what extent personal identity does and should matter to us.

Further Reading

Students who want to pursue the themes raised in this section may begin by looking at the articles in the following two anthologies. Each anthology includes an extensive collection of important readings in metaphysics, along with suggestions for further readings on each of the main themes:

- Tim Crane and Katalin Farkas, eds. *Metaphysics: A Guide and Anthology*. New York and Oxford: Oxford University Press, 2004.
- Peter van Inwagen and Dean W. Zimmerman, eds. *Metaphysics: The Big Questions*. Malden, Mass. and Oxford: Blackwell, 1998.

E TIME AND TIME TRAVEL

Time and the Relativity of Simultaneity

ALBERT EINSTEIN

Albert Einstein (1879–1955) was arguably the greatest physicist ever to have lived. He was born in Germany, where he lived and worked until the start of World War II; he spent the later part of his career at the Institute for Advanced Study in Princeton, New Jersey. In 1921, he was awarded the Nobel Prize for physics.

The selection that appears here is drawn from Einstein's 1916 book *Relativity*, originally written in German and translated by Robert W. Lawson, in which Einstein explains the central elements of his view in a manner that is accessible to the general public.

ON THE IDEA OF TIME IN PHYSICS

Lightning has struck the rails on our railway embankment at two places *A* and *B* far distant from each other. I make the additional assertion that these two lightning flashes occurred simultaneously. If I ask you whether there is sense in this statement, you will answer my question with a decided "Yes." But if I now approach you with the request to explain to me the sense of the statement more precisely, you find after some consideration that the answer to this question is not so easy as it appears at first sight.

After some time perhaps the following answer would occur to you: "The significance of the statement is clear in itself and needs no further explanation; of course it would require some consideration if I were to be commissioned to determine by observations whether in the actual case the two events took place simultaneously or not." I cannot be satisfied with this answer for the following reason. Supposing that as a result of ingenious considerations an able meteorologist were to discover that the lightning must always strike the places *A* and *B* simultaneously, then we should be faced with the task of testing whether or not this theoretical result is in accordance with the reality. We encounter the same difficulty with all physical statements in which the conception "simultaneous" plays a part. The concept does not exist for the physicist until he has the possibility of discovering whether or not it is fulfilled in an actual case. We thus require a definition of simultaneity such that this definition supplies us with the method by means of which, in the present case, he can decide by experiment whether or not both the lightning strokes occurred simultaneously. As long as this requirement is not satisfied, I allow myself to be deceived as a physicist (and of course the same applies if I am not a physicist), when I imagine that I am able to attach a meaning to the statement of simultaneity. (I would ask the reader not to proceed farther until he is fully convinced on this point.)

After thinking the matter over for some time you then offer the following suggestion with which to test simultaneity. By measuring along the rails, the connecting line *AB* should be measured up and an observer placed at the mid-point *M* of the distance

AB. This observer should be supplied with an arrangement (e.g. two mirrors inclined at 90°) which allows him visually to observe both places *A* and *B* at the same time. If the observer perceives the two flashes of lightning at the same time, then they are simultaneous.

I am very pleased with this suggestion, but for all that I cannot regard the matter as quite settled, because I feel constrained to raise the following objection: "Your definition would certainly be right, if only I knew that the light by means of which the observer at *M* perceives the lightning flashes travels along the length $A \rightarrow M$ with the same velocity as along the length $B \rightarrow M$. But an examination of this supposition would only be possible if we already had at our disposal the means of measuring time. It would thus appear as though we were moving here in a logical circle."

After further consideration you cast a somewhat disdainful glance at me—and rightly so—and you declare: "I maintain my previous definition nevertheless, because in reality it assumes absolutely nothing about light. There is only *one* demand to be made of the definition of simultaneity, namely, that in every real case it must supply us with an empirical decision as to whether or not the conception that has to be defined is fulfilled. That my definition satisfies this demand is indisputable. That light requires the same time to traverse the path $A \rightarrow M$ as for the path $B \rightarrow M$ is in reality neither a *supposition nor a hypothesis* about the physical nature of light, but a *stipulation* which I can make of my own freewill in order to arrive at a definition of simultaneity."

It is clear that this definition can be used to give an exact meaning not only to *two* events, but to as many events as we care to choose, and independently of the positions of the scenes of the events with respect to the body of reference[1] (here the railway embankment). We are thus led also to a definition of "time" in physics. For this purpose we suppose that clocks of identical construction are placed at the points *A*, *B* and *C* of the railway line (co-ordinate system), and that they are set in such a manner that the positions of their pointers are simultaneously (in the above sense) the same. Under these conditions we understand by the "time" of an event the reading (position of the hands) of that one of these clocks which is in the immediate vicinity (in space) of the event. In this manner a time-value is associated with every event which is essentially capable of observation.

This stipulation contains a further physical hypothesis, the validity of which will hardly be doubted without empirical evidence to the contrary. It has been assumed that all these clocks go *at the same rate* if they are of identical construction. Stated more exactly: When two clocks arranged at rest in different places of a reference-body are set in such a manner that a *particular* position of the pointers of the one clock is *simultaneous* (in the above sense) with the *same* position of the pointers of the other clock, then identical "settings" are always simultaneous (in the sense of the above definition).

THE RELATIVITY OF SIMULTANEITY

Up to now our considerations have been referred to a particular body of reference, which we have styled a "railway embankment." We suppose a very long train travelling along the rails with the constant velocity *v* and in the direction indicated in Fig. 1. People travelling in this train will with advantage use the train as a rigid reference-body (co-ordinate system); they regard all events in reference to the train. Then every event which takes place along the line also takes place at a particular point of the train. Also the definition of simultaneity can be given relative to the train in exactly the same way as with respect to the embankment. As a natural consequence, however, the following question arises:

Are two events (e.g., the two strokes of lightning *A* and *B*) which are simultaneous *with reference to the railway embankment* also simultaneous *relatively to the train*? We shall show directly that the answer must be in the negative.

When we say that the lightning strokes *A* and *B* are simultaneous with respect to the embankment, we mean: the rays of light emitted at the places *A* and

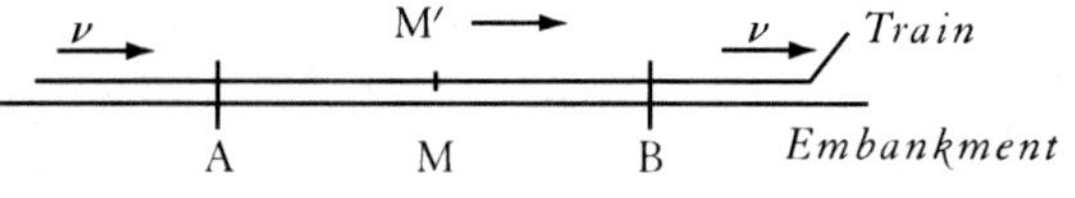

FIGURE 1

B, where the lightning occurs, meet each other at the mid-point *M* of the length $A \rightarrow B$ of the embankment. But the events *A* and *B* also correspond to positions *A* and *B* on the train. Let *M′* be the mid-point of the distance $A \rightarrow B$ on the travelling train. Just when the flashes[2] of lightning occur, this point *M′* naturally coincides with the point *M*, but it moves towards the right in the diagram with the velocity *v* of the train. If an observer sitting in the position *M′* in the train did not possess this velocity, then he would remain permanently at *M*, and the light rays emitted by the flashes of lightning *A* and *B* would reach him simultaneously, i.e., they would meet just where he is situated. Now in reality (considered with reference to the railway embankment) he is hastening towards the beam of light coming from *B*, whilst he is riding on ahead of the beam of light coming from *A*. Hence the observer will see the beam of light emitted from *B* earlier than he will see that emitted from *A*. Observers who take the railway train as their reference-body must therefore come to the conclusion that the lightning flash *B* took place earlier than the lightning flash *A*. We thus arrive at the important result:

Events which are simultaneous with reference to the embankment are not simultaneous with respect to the train, and *vice versa* (relativity of simultaneity). Every reference-body (co-ordinate system) has its own particular time; unless we are told the reference-body to which the statement of time refers, there is no meaning in a statement of the time of an event.

Now before the advent of the theory of relativity it had always tacitly been assumed in physics that the statement of time had an absolute significance, i.e., that it is independent of the state of motion of the body of reference. But we have just seen that this assumption is incompatible with the most natural definition of simultaneity; if we discard this assumption, then the conflict between the law of the propagation of light *in vacuo* and the principle of relativity . . . disappears.

NOTES

1. We suppose further, that, when three events *A, B* and *C* occur in different places in such a manner that *A* is simultaneous with *B*, and *B* is simultaneous with *C* (simultaneous in the sense of the above definition), then the criterion for the simultaneity of the pair of events *A, C* is also satisfied. This assumption is a physical hypothesis about the law of propagation of light; it must certainly be fulfilled if we are to maintain the law of the constancy of the velocity of light in *vacuo*.
2. As judged from the embankment.

Time

THEODORE SIDER

Theodore Sider (1967–) is an American philosopher who works primarily in the area of metaphysics. He is best known for his 2001 book *Four-Dimensionalism: An Ontology of Persistence and Time*.

The selection presented here is a chapter from a book that he coauthored with philosopher Earl Conee, an introduction to metaphysics entitled *The Riddles of Existence: A Guided Tour of Metaphysics* (2005). Minor changes have been made to allow the text to be self-standing. In it, Sider presents some of the main philosophical issues that arise when we think about the nature of time.

From *The Riddles of Existence: A Guided Tour of Metaphysics*, by E. Conee and T. Sider, 2005. Reprinted by permission of Oxford University Press.

THE FLOW OF TIME

It is strange to question the nature of time, given how fundamental time is to our experience. As a child I wondered whether fish are conscious of water or whether they experience it unconsciously, as we experience the air we breathe. Time is even more ubiquitous than water or air: every thought and experience takes place in time. Questioning the nature of time can be dizzying.

Yet it is worth questioning. The ordinary conception of time, once you start to think about it, seems to make no sense! For we ordinarily conceive of time as being something that *moves*. "Time flows like a river." "Time marches on." "Time flies." "As time goes by." "The past is gone." "Time waits for no one." "Time stood still." These clichés capture how we tend to think about time. Time moves, and we are caught up in its inexorable flow. The problem with this way of thinking is that time is the standard by which motion is defined; how then could time itself move? This is metaphysics at its best. Look at the world hard enough, and even the most mundane things are revealed as mysterious and wonderful.

Let's examine this idea of time's motion, or flow, more carefully, by comparing it to the motion of ordinary objects. What does it mean to say that a *train* moves? Simply that the train is located at one place at one moment in time and at other places at later moments in time (see Figure 1). At time t_1, the train is in Boston. At later times t_2, t_3, and t_4, the train is located at places further south: New York, Philadelphia, and finally, Washington. The motion of the train is defined by reference to time: the train moves by being located at different places at different times. If at every moment the train stayed in the same place—Boston, say—then we would say that the train did not move.

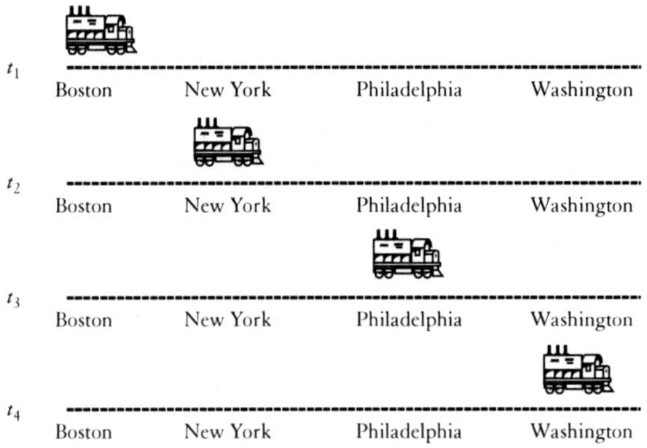

t_1 Boston New York Philadelphia Washington

t_2 Boston New York Philadelphia Washington

t_3 Boston New York Philadelphia Washington

t_4 Boston New York Philadelphia Washington

FIGURE 1. THE MOVEMENT OF A TRAIN DEFINED BY REFERENCE TO TIME

Ordinary objects move with respect to time. So if time itself moves, it must move with respect to some other sort of time. But what would that other time be?

The way in which time seems to move is by the *present moment*'s moving. Initially the present moment is noon. Later the present is 3.00 p.m. Still later it is 6.00 p.m., and then 9.00 p.m., and so on. Since motion is defined by reference to time, the present moment, if it is moving, must have these four different locations at four different times, t_1, t_2, t_3, and t_4 (Figure 2), just as the moving train had four different locations at four different times. But the diagram is confusing. It mentions the times noon, 3.00, 6.00, and 9.00, but it also mentions four other times, t_1, t_2, t_3, and t_4. These are the times with respect to which the present moment is moving. What are these other times? In what sort of time does time itself move?

One possibility is that t_1, t_2, t_3, and t_4 are part of a *different* sort of time, call it hypertime. Just as trains move with respect to something else (time), time itself moves with respect to something else (hypertime). Most motion takes place with respect to the familiar timeline, but time itself moves with respect to another timeline, hypertime.

Hypertime is a bad idea. You can't simply stop there; you need more, and More and MORE. Hypertime is supposed to be a sort of time. So if ordinary time moves, surely hypertime moves as well. So hypertime must move with respect to yet another sort of time, hyper-hyper time. That time must also move, which introduces hyper-hyper-hyper time. And so on. We are stuck with believing in an infinite series of different kinds of time. That's a little much. I can't *prove* that this infinite series does not exist, but surely there are better options. Let's see if we took a wrong turn somewhere.

Instead of being part of hypertime, perhaps t_1, t_2, t_3, and t_4 are just part of ordinary time. In particular, t_1, t_2, t_3, and t_4 could just be the times noon, 3.00, 6.00, and 9.00. According to this view, time moves with respect to itself. Is that plausible?

	Present			
t_1	Noon	3:00	6:00	9:00

		Present		
t_2	Noon	3:00	6:00	9:00

			Present	
t_3	Noon	3:00	6:00	9:00

				Present
t_4	Noon	3:00	6:00	9:00

FIGURE 2. THE MOVING OF THE PRESENT MOMENT

Although it's nice to be rid of hypertime, there is something strange about this picture. It's not that it isn't *true*. Noon is indeed present at noon, 3.00 is present at 3.00, and so on. But these facts seem *trivial*, and therefore insufficient to capture a genuine flow of time. This can be brought out by comparing time to space, and comparing *present* to *here*. Consider the spatial locations on the train track connecting Boston to Washington. Anyone in Boston can truthfully say "Boston is *here*." Likewise, anyone in New York can say "New York is here." The same goes for Philadelphia and Washington. So Boston is "here in Boston," New York is "here in New York," and so on, just as noon is present at noon, 3.00 is present at 3.00, and so on. But space doesn't move. The line in space connecting Boston with Washington is static. The mere fact that members of a series are located at themselves does not make that series move, whether that series consists of points of time or locations in space.

THE SPACE-TIME THEORY

Time's motion has us all tangled up in knots. Maybe the problem is with that idea itself. According to some philosophers and scientists, our ordinary conception of time as a flowing river is hopelessly confused, and must be replaced with the space-time theory, according to which *time is like space*.

Graphs of motion from high-school physics represent time as just another dimension alongside the spatial dimensions. The graph pictured here (Figure 3) represents a particle that moves through

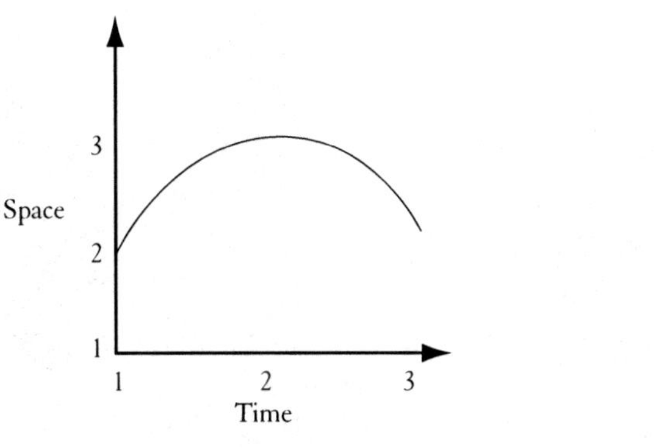

FIGURE 3. HIGH-SCHOOL PHYSICS GRAPH OF A PARTICLE MOVING THROUGH TIME

time in one spatial dimension. This particle begins at place 2 in space at the initial time 1, then moves toward place 3, slows down and stops at time 2, and finally moves back to place 2 at time 3. Each point in this two-dimensional graph represents a time t (the horizontal coordinate of the point) and a location in space p (the vertical coordinate). The curve drawn represents the particle's motion. When the curve passes through a point (t, p), that means that the particle is located at place p at time t.

A more complicated graph (Figure 4) represents time alongside two spatial dimensions. (It would be nice to represent all three spatial dimensions, but that would require a four-dimensional graph and so a much more expensive book.) These more complicated graphs are called **space-time diagrams**. (Even the high-school physics graph is a simpler kind of diagram of *space*-time.) *Space*-time diagrams can be used to represent all of history; everything that has ever happened or ever will happen can be fit into a space-time diagram somewhere. This particular diagram represents a dinosaur in the distant past and a person who is born in AD 2000. These objects stretch out horizontally in the graph because they last over time in reality, and time is the horizontal axis on the graph: the objects exist at different points along the horizontal time axis. They stretch out in the other two dimensions on the graph because dinosaurs and people take up space in reality: the objects exist at different points along the vertical, spatial, axes.

In addition to the dinosaur and the person themselves, some of their temporal parts are also

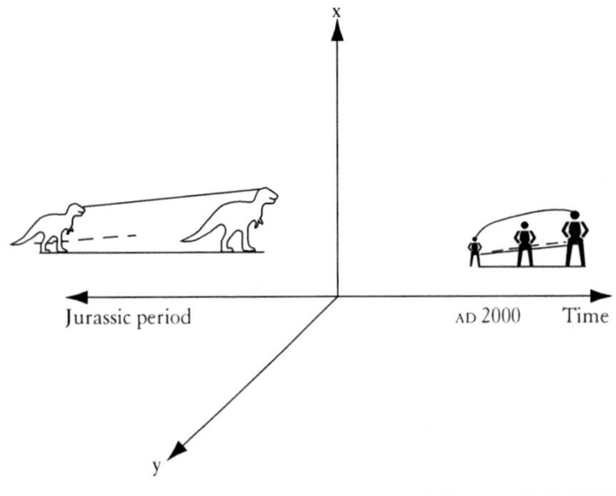

FIGURE 4. SPACE-TIME DIAGRAM

represented in the diagram. A temporal part of an object at a time is a temporal cross-section of that object; it is that-object-at-that-time. Consider the temporal part of the person in 2000. This object is the exact same *spatial size* as the person in 2000. But the temporal part is not the same *temporal size* as the person; the temporal part exists only in 2000 whereas the person exists at later times as well. The person herself is the sum total of all her temporal parts:

Notice how the person is tapered: the earlier temporal parts (those on the left of the diagram) are smaller than the later ones. This represents the person's growth over time.

In contrast to the ordinary conception of moving or flowing time, then, the space-time theory says that reality consists of a single unified space-time, which contains all of the past, present, and future. Time is just one of the dimensions of space-time, alongside the three spatial dimensions, just as it appears to be in the space-time diagrams. Time does not flow; time is like space.

Well, time isn't *completely* like space. For one thing, there are three spatial dimensions but only one temporal dimension. And time has a special *direction*: past to future. Space has no such direction. We do have words for certain spatial directions: up, down, north, south, east, west, left, right. But these are not directions built into space itself. Rather, these words pick out different directions depending on who says them. "Up" means away from the earth's center on a line that passes through the speaker; "North" means toward the Arctic pole from the speaker; "Left" picks out different directions depending on which way the speaker is facing. In contrast, the past to future direction is the same for everyone, regardless of his or her location or orientation; it seems to be an intrinsic feature of time itself.

Still, according to the space-time theory, time and space are analogous in many ways. Here are three.

First, in terms of *reality*. Objects far away in space (other planets, stars, and so on) are obviously just as real as things here on Earth. We may not *know* as much about the far-away objects as we know about the things around here, but that doesn't make the far-away objects any less real. Likewise, objects far away in time are just as real as objects that exist now. Both past objects (e.g., dinosaurs) and future objects (human outposts on Mars, perhaps) exist, in addition to objects in the present. Distant objects, whether temporally or spatially distant, all exist somewhere in space-time.

Second, in terms of *parts*. Material objects take up space by having different parts. My body occupies a certain region of space. Part of this region is occupied by my head, another by my torso; other parts of the region are occupied by my arms and legs. These parts may be called my spatial parts, since they are spatially smaller than I am. The corresponding fact about time is that an object lasts over a stretch of time by having different parts located at the different times within that stretch. These parts are the temporal parts mentioned above. These temporal parts are just as real objects as my spatial parts: my head, arms, and legs.

Third, in terms of *here* and *now*. If I say on the phone "here it is raining" to a friend in California, and she replies "here it is sunny" (Figure 5), which one of us is right? Where is the *real here*, California or New Jersey? The question is obviously misguided. There is no "real here." The word "here" just refers to whatever place the person saying it happens to be. When I say "here," it means New Jersey; when my friend says "here," it means California. Neither place is *here* in any objective sense. California is here for my friend, New Jersey is here for me. The space-time theory says an analogous thing about

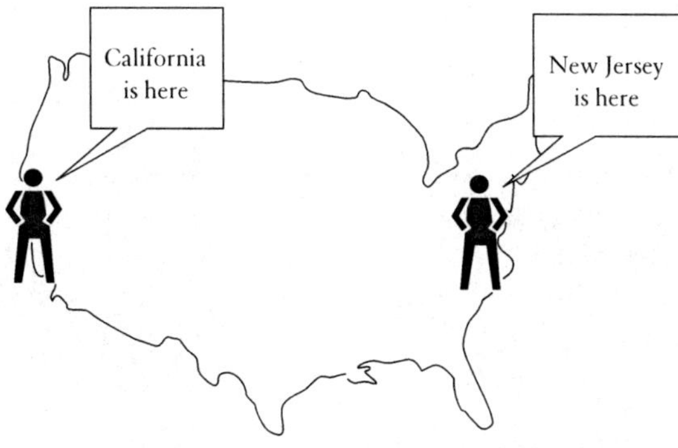

FIGURE 5. WHERE IS THE "REAL HERE"?

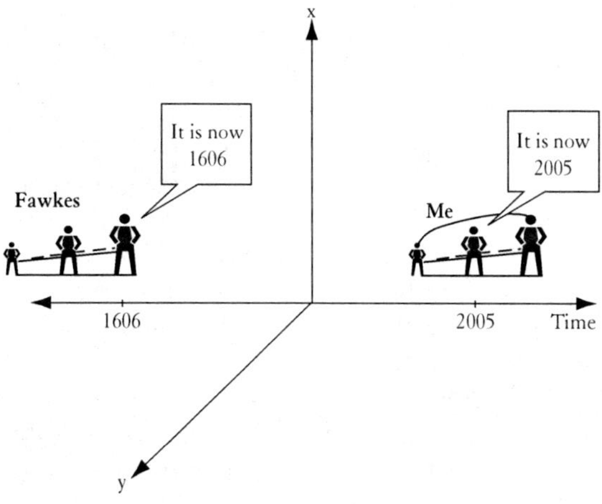

FIGURE 6. "NOW" FOR ME AND FOR GUY FAWKES

time: just as there is no objective here, so there is no objective *now*. If I say "It is now 2005," and in 1606 Guy Fawkes* said "It is now 1606," each statement is correct (Figure 6). There is no single, real, objective "now." The word "now" just refers to the time at which the speaker happens to be located.

ARGUMENTS AGAINST THE SPACE-TIME THEORY: CHANGE, MOTION, CAUSES

We have met two theories of time. Which is true? Does time flow? Or is time like space?

* Guy Fawkes (1570–1606) was an English Catholic revolutionary who conspired to blow up the Houses of Parliament.

The space-time theory avoids the paradoxes of time's flow; that counts in its favor. But the believer in time's flow will retort that the space-time theory throws the baby out with the bathwater: it makes time *too much* like space. For starters, she may say that the alleged analogies between space and time suggested in the last section don't really hold:

> Past and future objects do *not* exist: the past is gone, and the future is yet to be. Things do *not* have temporal parts: at any time, the *whole* object is present, not just a temporal part of it; there are no past or future bits left out. And "now" is *not* like "here": the present moment is special, unlike the bit of space around here.

Each of these claims could take up a whole chapter of its own. But time is short, so let's consider three other ways the defender of time's flow might argue that time is not like space. First, regarding *change*:

> Compare change with what we might call "spatial heterogeneity." Change is having different properties at different times. A person who changes height starts out short and then becomes taller. Spatial heterogeneity, in contrast, is having different properties at different *places*. A highway is bumpy at some places, smooth at others; narrow at some places, wide at others. Now, if time is just like space, then having different properties at different times (change) is no different from having different properties at different places (spatial heterogeneity). Look back at the space-time diagram. Change is variation from left to right on the diagram, along the temporal axis. Spatial heterogeneity is variation along either of the two spatial dimensions. The two are analogous, according to the space-time theory. But that's not right! Spatial heterogeneity is wholly different from change. The spatially heterogeneous highway doesn't *change*. It just sits there.

Second, regarding *motion*:

> Things can move any which way in space; there's no particular direction in which they are constrained to travel. But the same is not true for time. Moving

back and forth in time makes no sense. Things can only travel forward in time.

Third, regarding *causes*:

> Events at any place can cause events at any other place; we can affect what goes on in any region of space. But events can't cause events at just any other time: later events never cause earlier events. Although we can affect the future, we cannot affect the past. The past is fixed.

The first objection is right that the space-time theory makes change somewhat similar to spatial heterogeneity. But so what? They're not *exactly* the same: one is variation over time, the other is variation over space. And the claim that change and spatial heterogeneity are *somewhat* similar is perfectly reasonable. So the first objection may be flatly rejected.

The second objection is more complicated. "Things move back and forth in space, but not back and forth in time"—is this really a disanalogy between time and space? Suppose we want to know, for a certain true statement about space, whether the analogous statement is true of time. The twentieth-century American philosopher Richard Taylor* argued that we must be careful to construct a statement about time that really is analogous to the statement about space. In particular, we must *uniformly reverse ALL references to time and space* to get the analogous statement. And when we do, Taylor argued, we will see that time and space are more analogous than they initially seemed.

To illustrate. Our true statement about space is this:

> Some object moves back and forth in space.

Before we can reverse the references to time and space in this statement, we need to locate all those references, including any that are not completely explicit. For instance, the word "moves" conceals a reference to time. When these references are made explicit, our statement becomes:

> *Moving back and forth in space*: Some object is at spatial point p_1 at time t_1, point p_2 at time t_2, and point p_1 at time t_3.

(See Figure 7.) Now we're in a position to construct the analogous statement about time—to reverse *all* references to time and space. To do so, we simply change each reference to a time into a reference to a point in space, and each reference to a point in space into a reference to a time. This is what we get:

> *Moving back and forth in time*: Some object is at time t_1 at spatial point p_1, time t_2 at point p_2, and at time t_1 at point p_3.

And we get the graph for this new statement (Figure 8) by swapping the "Time" and "Space" labels on Figure 7.

Our question now is: is this second statement correct? Can an object "move back and forth in time" in this sense? The answer is in fact *yes*, for a fairly humdrum reason. To make this easy to see, let's make the "moving back and forth in time" graph look like our earlier diagrams by flipping it so that its temporal axis is horizontal (see Figure 9). It should be clear that the diagram represents an object that is first, at t_1, located at *two* places, p_1 and p_3, and then, at t_2, is located at just one place, p_2. This sounds stranger than it really is. Think of a clapping pair of hands. At first the two hands are separated—one is located at place p_1, the other at p_3. Then the hands move toward each other and make contact. The pair of hands is now located at place p_2. Finally, suppose the pair of hands disappears at time t_2. This kind of scenario is what the diagram is representing.

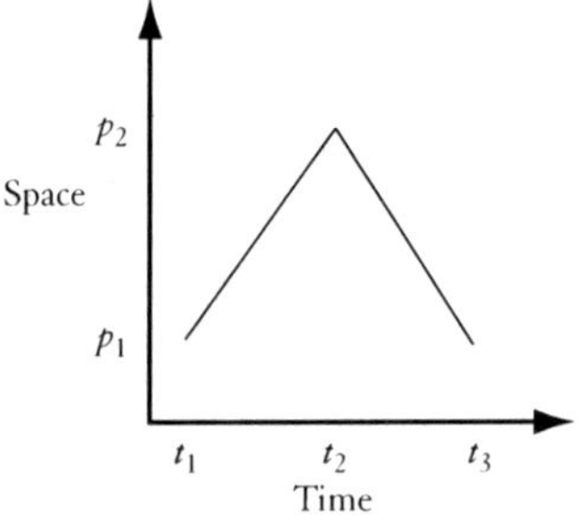

FIGURE 7. MOVING BACK AND FORTH IN SPACE

* A selection from Taylor's work appears in the Religion and Belief section.

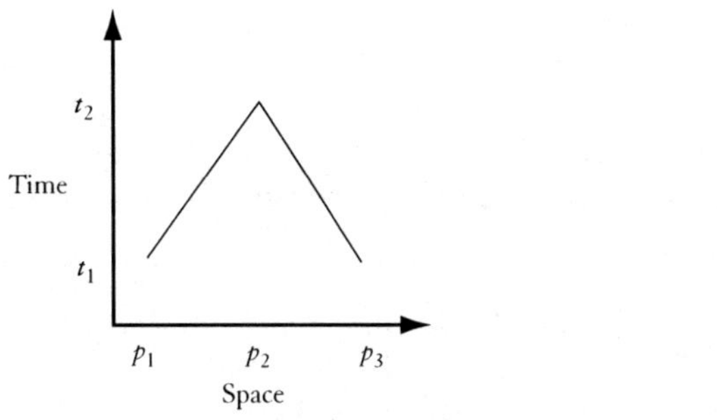

FIGURE 8. MOVING BACK AND FORTH IN TIME, TEMPORAL AXIS VERTICAL

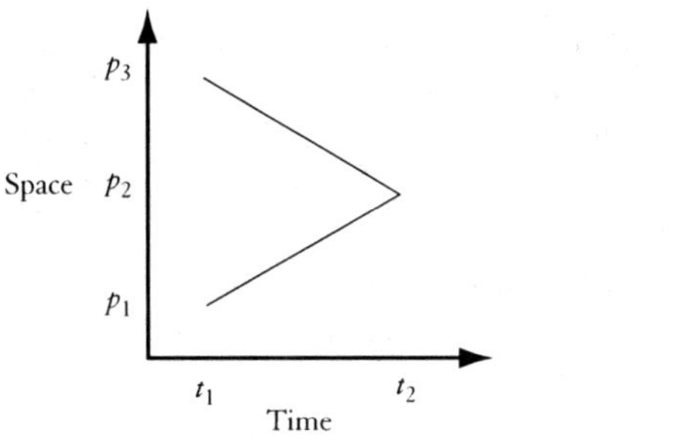

FIGURE 9. MOVING BACK AND FORTH IN TIME, TEMPORAL AXIS HORIZONTAL

So things *can* "move back and forth in time," if that statement is understood as being truly analogous to "moving back and forth in space." We were deceived into thinking otherwise by neglecting to reverse *all* references to time and space. The statement "things move back and forth in space" contains an implicit *reference dimension*, namely time, for it is with respect to time that things move in space. When we construct the statement "things move back and forth in time," we must change the reference dimension from time to space. When we do, the resulting statement is something that can indeed be true.

The third objection is the most challenging and interesting. It is true that we do not actually observe "backwards causation," that is, the causation of earlier events by later events. This represents a de facto asymmetry between space and time—an asymmetry in the world as it actually is. But a deeper question is whether this asymmetry is built into the nature of time itself, or whether it is just a function of the way the world happens to be. The question is: *could* there be backwards causation? *Could* our actions now causally affect the past?

If time is truly like space, then the answer must be *yes*. Just as events can cause events anywhere else in space, so too events can in principle cause other events anywhere in time, even at earlier times. But this has a very striking consequence. If backwards causation is possible, then *time travel*, as depicted in books and movies, ought to be possible as well, for it ought to be possible to cause ourselves to be present in the past.

Time travel may never *in fact* occur. Perhaps time travel will never be technologically feasible, or perhaps the laws of physics prevent time travel. Philosophy cannot settle questions about physics or technology; for speculation on such matters, a better guide is your friendly neighborhood physicist or engineer. But if time is like space, there should be no prohibition *coming from the concept of time itself*: time travel should at least be conceptually possible. But is it?

A familiar kind of time travel story begins as follows: "In 1985, Marty McFly enters a time machine, sets the controls for 1955, pushes the button, waits, and then arrives in 1955. . . ." Any time travel story must contain this much: the use of some sort of time travel device and subsequent arrival in the past. But even this much seems to conceal a contradiction. The troublesome bit is the end: "and *then* arrives in 1955." The suggestion is that McFly *first* pushes the button, and *second* arrives in 1955. But he pushes the button in 1985, which is *after* 1955.

This is an example of a so-called paradox of time travel. One attempts to tell a coherent story involving time travel, but ends up contradicting oneself. Saying that McFly arrives in 1955 both after and before he pushes the button is contradicting oneself. And if there is no way to tell a time travel story without self-contradiction, then time travel is conceptually impossible.

This first paradox can be avoided. Is the arrival after or before the pushing of the button? *Before*—1955 is before 1985. What about "and *then*"? Well, all that means is that McFly *experiences* the arrival as being after the button-pressing. Normal people (i.e., non-time travelers) experience events as occurring in the order in which they truly occur, whereas time travelers experience things out of order. In the sequence of McFly's experiences, 1985 comes before 1955. That's a very strange thing, to be sure, but it does not seem conceptually incoherent. (What determines the order of McFly's experiences? Later members of the sequence of his experiences contain memories of, and are caused by, earlier members of the sequence. When McFly experiences 1955, he has memories of 1985, and his 1985 experiences directly causally affect his 1955 experiences.)

Yet a more potent paradox lurks. Let's continue the story from *Back to the Future*: "Back in 1955, the dashing McFly inadvertently attracts his mother, overshadowing his nerdy father. As the union of his parents becomes less and less likely, McFly begins to fade away into nothingness." The problem is that a time traveler could undermine his own existence. He could cause his parents never to meet; he could even kill them before he is ever born. But then where did he come from? Back to paradox!

That McFly begins to fade away into nothingness shows that the writers of *Back to the Future* were aware of the problem. But the fade-out solves nothing. Suppose McFly fades out completely after preventing his parents from meeting. He still existed before fading out (it was he, after all, who prevented his parents from meeting). Where then did he come from in the first place? Whatever its literary merits, as a work of philosophy *Back to the Future* fails miserably.

Let's not be too hard on careless screen-writers and authors. (We can't all be philosophers.) Though it's not easy, paradox-free time travel stories can be told. The movie *Terminator* is an excellent example (spoilers included):[1]

> In the future, machines take over the world and nearly destroy the human race. But the machines are eventually thwarted by the human leader John Connor. On the verge of defeat, the machines fight back by sending a machine, a "Terminator," back to the past to kill John Connor's mother, Sarah Connor, before John is born. John Connor counters by sending one of his men, Kyle Reese, back to the past to protect Sarah Connor. The Terminator nearly succeeds, but in the end Reese stops him. (Reese dies, but not before impregnating Connor's mother, Sarah Connor. The baby, we later learn, grows up to be John Connor himself!)

This story never contradicts itself. It would if the Terminator killed Sarah Connor, since we are told in the beginning of the story that Sarah Connor lived and had a son, John Connor, whose future exploits are the cause of the presence of the Terminator in the past. But since Sarah Connor survives, the story remains consistent.

The failure of *some* time travel stories (such as *Back to the Future*) to remain consistent shows nothing, since other consistent stories can be told. The similarity of time and space has survived: there is no conceptual impossibility with backwards causation and time travel.

There are numerous close calls in *Terminator*. Again and again, Sarah Connor narrowly escapes death. It would appear that on any of these occasions, she could easily have died. Yet we know that she must survive, because her son is John Connor. So it seems that she is not really in danger; she cannot die. But there is the Terminator in front of her. The danger seems very real. Back into paradox?

Not at all. What is strange about a time travel story is that we are told the end of the story first. We, the audience, learn early on that John Connor exists in the future. Later we find his mother endangered before he is ever born. We, the audience, know she will survive (if we trust the screen-writers to be consistent!), but that does not mean that *in the story* her danger is unreal.

A very peculiar thing arises when the time traveler himself knows how the story will end. Think of Reese. He knows that the Terminator will fail, since he knows that John Connor exists: it was Connor that sent him back to the past. Yet he fears for Sarah Connor's life, works hard to protect her, and in the end gives his life to save her. Why doesn't he just walk away and save himself? He *knows* that Sarah Connor is going to survive.

Or does he? He *thinks* he remembers serving a man called John Connor. He *thinks* he remembers Connor defeating the machines. He *thinks* Connor's mother was named Sarah. He *thinks* this woman he's defending is the same Sarah Connor. He *thinks* this woman has not yet had children. So he's got lots of evidence that this woman he's defending will survive. But then he sees the Terminator advance. He sees it effortlessly killing everyone in its path, searching for someone named Sarah Connor. Now it advances on the woman he's defending. It raises its gun. Reese's confidence that this woman will survive now wavers. Perhaps she is not John Connor's mother after all. Or, if he's sure of that, perhaps she's already had a child. Or, if he's quite sure of that, perhaps he's made some other mistake. Perhaps all of his apparent memories from the future are delusions! Such self-doubt is ordinarily far-fetched, but it becomes increasingly reasonable with each step of the Terminator. As certain as he once was that Sarah Connor will survive, he has become equally certain about the danger presented by the Terminator. "It can't be bargained with! It can't be reasoned with! It doesn't feel pity, or remorse, or fear. And it absolutely will not stop, ever, until you are dead!" He thinks "I'd better be sure." He raises his gun.

NOTE

1. *Terminator 1*, that is. *Terminator 2* appears to be incoherent. It says in the beginning that Cyberdyne systems learned the technology behind Skynet by studying the hand of the corpse of a T-800 Terminator from the future. Then at the end, after the T-800 is melted (Schwarzenegger's thumbs-up to Furlong), the movie suggests that Skynet is never created and Judgment Day is avoided. Where then did the time-traveling Terminators come from? *Terminator 3* does better: it never suggests that Judgment Day is avoided. Yet there are remaining questions, for instance about the true date of Judgment Day. *Terminator 1* is by far the best of the three, from a philosophical (as well as cinematic) point of view.

FURTHER READING

Peter van Inwagen and Dean Zimmerman (eds.), *Metaphysics: The Big Questions* (Blackwell, 1998): this anthology contains a number of readings on time (as well as readings on many other metaphysical topics.) Some highlights: "Time," by J. M. B. McTaggart, makes the shocking claim that time is unreal! Two articles by A. N. Prior argue against the space-time theory. "The Space-Time World," by J. J. C. Smart, defends the space-time theory. "The Paradoxes of Time Travel," by David Lewis, argues that time travel is possible. [Lewis appears as the next selection.]

This article by Richard Taylor lays out a fascinating series of analogies between space and time: "Spatial and Temporal Analogies and the Concept of Identity." *Journal of Philosophy*, 52 (1955), 599–612.

In addition to the conceptual issues about time travel discussed in this chapter, there are many interesting scientific issues as well. The following article is available online: Frank Arntzenius and Tim Maudlin, "Time Travel and Modern Physics," http://plato.stanford.edu/entries/time-travel-phys/

The Paradoxes of Time Travel

DAVID LEWIS

David Lewis (1941–2001) was one of the most important analytic philosophers of the twentieth century. He taught at UCLA and Princeton University for many years (where he was a colleague of Saul Kripke and Harry Frankfurt—selections following) and traveled regularly to Australia (home of J. J. C. Smart and Frank Jackson—selections following). He is well known for his contributions to metaphysics, philosophy of mind, philosophy of language, epistemology, and logic.

The selection that appears here was originally delivered as a series of lectures at the University of Adelaide, Australia, in 1971; it was published in its present form in a philosophy journal in 1976. In it, Lewis defends the view that time travel is metaphysically possible.

Time travel, I maintain, is possible. The paradoxes of time travel are oddities, not impossibilities. They prove only this much, which few would have doubted: that a possible world where time travel took place would be a most strange world, different in fundamental ways from the world we think is ours.

I shall be concerned here with the sort of time travel that is recounted in science fiction. Not all science fiction writers are clear-headed, to be sure, and inconsistent time travel stories have often been written. But some writers have thought the problems through with great care, and their stories are perfectly consistent.[1]

If I can defend the consistency of some science fiction stories of time travel, then I suppose parallel defenses might be given of some controversial physical hypotheses, such as the hypothesis that time is circular or the hypothesis that there are particles that travel faster than light. But I shall not explore these parallels here.

What is time travel? Inevitably, it involves a discrepancy between time and time. Any traveler departs and then arrives at his destination; the time elapsed from departure to arrival (positive, or perhaps zero) is the duration of the journey. But if he is a time traveler, the separation in time between departure and arrival does not equal the duration of his journey. He departs; he travels for an hour, let us say; then he arrives. The time he reaches is not the time one hour after his departure. It is later, if he has traveled toward the future; earlier, if he has traveled toward the past. If he has traveled far toward the past, it is earlier even than his departure. How can it be that the same two events, his departure and his arrival, are separated by two unequal amounts of time?

It is tempting to reply that there must be two independent time dimensions; that for time travel to be possible, time must be not a line but a plane.[2] Then a pair of events may have two unequal separations if they are separated more in one of the time dimensions than in the other. The lives of common people occupy straight diagonal lines across the plane of time, sloping at a rate of exactly one hour of $time_1$ per hour of $time_2$. The life of the time traveler occupies a bent path, of varying slope.

On closer inspection, however, this account seems not to give us time travel as we know it from the stories. When the traveler revisits the days of his childhood, will his playmates be there to meet him? No; he has not reached the part of the plane of time where they are. He is no longer separated from them along one of the two dimensions of time, but he is still separated from them along the other. I do not say that two-dimensional time is impossible, or that there is no way to square it with the usual conception of what time travel would be like. Nevertheless I shall say no more about two-dimensional time. Let us set it aside, and see how time travel is possible even in one-dimensional time.

The world—the time traveler's world, or ours—is a four-dimensional manifold of events. Time is one dimension of the four, like the spatial dimensions except that the prevailing laws of nature discriminate between time and the others—or rather, perhaps, between various timelike dimensions and various spacelike dimensions. (Time remains one-dimensional, since no two timelike dimensions are orthogonal.) Enduring things are timelike streaks: wholes composed of temporal parts, or *stages*, located at various times and places. Change is qualitative difference between different stages—different temporal parts—of some enduring thing, just as a "change" in scenery from east to west is a qualitative difference between the eastern and western spatial parts of the landscape. If this paper should change your mind about the possibility of time travel, there will be a difference of opinion between two different temporal parts of you, the stage that started reading and the subsequent stage that finishes.

If change is qualitative difference between temporal parts of something, then what doesn't have

---

From *American Philosophical Quarterly*, Vol. 13, no. 2, April 1976, pp. 145–152. Reprinted by permission of the *American Philosophical Quarterly* with the consent of Stephanie Lewis.

temporal parts can't change. For instance, numbers can't change; nor can the events of any moment of time, since they cannot be subdivided into dissimilar temporal parts. (We have set aside the case of two-dimensional time, and hence the possibility that an event might be momentary along one time dimension but divisible along the other.) It is essential to distinguish change from "Cambridge change," which can befall anything.* Even a number can "change" from being to not being the rate of exchange between pounds and dollars. Even a momentary event can "change" from being a year ago to being a year and a day ago, or from being forgotten to being remembered. But these are not genuine changes. Not just any old reversal in truth value of a time-sensitive sentence about something makes a change in the thing itself.

A time traveler, like anyone else, is a streak through the manifold of space-time, a whole composed of stages located at various times and places. But he is not a streak like other streaks. If he travels toward the past he is a zig-zag streak, doubling back on himself. If he travels toward the future, he is a stretched-out streak. And if he travels either way instantaneously, so that there are no intermediate stages between the stage that departs and the stage that arrives and his journey has zero duration, then he is a broken streak.

I asked how it could be that the same two events were separated by two unequal amounts of time, and I set aside the reply that time might have two independent dimensions. Instead I reply by distinguishing time itself, *external time* as I shall also call it, from the *personal time* of a particular time traveler: roughly, that which is measured by his wristwatch. His journey takes an hour of his personal time, let us say; his wristwatch reads an hour later at arrival than at departure. But the arrival is more than an hour after the departure in external time, if he travels toward the future; or the arrival is before the departure in external time (or less than an hour after), if he travels toward the past.

That is only rough. I do not wish to define personal time operationally, making wristwatches infallible by definition. That which is measured by my own wristwatch often disagrees with external time, yet I am no time traveler; what my misregulated wristwatch measures is neither time itself nor my personal time. Instead of an operational definition, we need a functional definition of personal time: it is that which occupies a certain role in the pattern of events that comprise the time traveler's life. If you take the stages of a common person, they manifest certain regularities with respect to external time. Properties change continuously as you go along, for the most part, and in familiar ways. First come infantile stages. Last come senile ones. Memories accumulate. Food digests. Hair grows. Wristwatch hands move. If you take the stages of a time traveler instead, they do not manifest the common regularities with respect to external time. But there is one way to assign coordinates to the time traveler's stages, and one way only (apart from the arbitrary choice of a zero point), so that the regularities that hold with respect to this assignment match those that commonly hold with respect to external time. With respect to the correct assignment properties change continuously as you go along, for the most part, and in familiar ways. First come infantile stages. Last come senile ones. Memories accumulate. Food digests. Hair grows. Wristwatch hands move. The assignment of coordinates that yields this match is the time traveler's personal time. It isn't really time, but it plays the role in his life that time plays in the life of a common person. It's enough like time so that we can—with due caution—transplant our temporal vocabulary to it in discussing his affairs. We can say without contradiction, as the time traveler prepares to set out, "Soon he will be in the past." We mean that a stage of him is slightly later in his personal time, but much earlier in external time, than the stage of him that is present as we say the sentence.

We may assign locations in the time traveler's personal time not only to his stages themselves but also to the events that go on around him. Soon Caesar will die, long ago; that is, a stage slightly later

* Coinage of the term *Cambridge change* is generally credited to the British philosopher Peter Geach (1916–), in honor of the notion's use by philosophers at the University of Cambridge (England.) An object undergoes a (mere) Cambridge change whenever it (merely) undergoes some alteration in the descriptions that are true of it.

in the time traveler's personal time than his present stage, but long ago in external time, is simultaneous with Caesar's death. We could even extend the assignment of personal time to events that are not part of the time traveler's life, and not simultaneous with any of his stages. If his funeral in ancient Egypt is separated from his death by three days of external time and his death is separated from his birth by three score years and ten of his personal time, then we may add the two intervals and say that his funeral follows his birth by three score years and ten and three days of *extended personal time*. Likewise a bystander might truly say, three years after the last departure of another famous time traveler, that "he may even now—if I may use the phrase—be wandering on some plesiosaurus-haunted oolitic coral reef, or beside the lonely saline seas of the Triassic Age."[3] If the time traveler does wander on an oolitic coral reef three years after his departure in his personal time, then it is no mistake to say with respect to his extended personal time that the wandering is taking place "even now."

We may liken intervals of external time to distances as the crow flies, and intervals of personal time to distances along a winding path. The time traveler's life is like a mountain railway. The place two miles due east of here may also be nine miles down the line, in the westbound direction. Clearly we are not dealing here with two independent dimensions. Just as distance along the railway is not a fourth spatial dimension, so a time traveler's personal time is not a second dimension of time. How far down the line some place is depends on its location in three-dimensional space, and likewise the locations of events in personal time depend on their locations in one-dimensional external time.

Five miles down the line from here is a place where the line goes under a trestle; two miles further is a place where the line goes over a trestle; these places are one and the same. The trestle by which the line crosses over itself has two different locations along the line, five miles down from here and also seven. In the same way, an event in a time traveler's life may have more than one location in his personal time. If he doubles back toward the past, but not too far, he may be able to talk to himself. The conversation involves two of his stages, separated in his personal time but simultaneous in external time. The location of the conversation in personal time should be the location of the stage involved in it. But there are two such stages; to share the locations of both, the conversation must be assigned two different locations in personal time.

The more we extend the assignment of personal time outwards from the time traveler's stages to the surrounding events, the more will such events acquire multiple locations. It may happen also, as we have already seen, that events that are not simultaneous in external time will be assigned the same location in personal time—or rather, that at least one of the locations of one will be the same as at least one of the locations of the other. So extension must not be carried too far, lest the location of events in extended personal time lose its utility as a means of keeping track of their roles in the time traveler's history.

A time traveler who talks to himself, on the telephone perhaps, looks for all the world like two different people talking to each other. It isn't quite right to say that the whole of him is in two places at once, since neither of the two stages involved in the conversation is the whole of him, or even the whole of the part of him that is located at the (external) time of the conversation. What's true is that he, unlike the rest of us, has two different complete stages located at the same time at different places. What reason have I, then, to regard him as one person and not two? What unites his stages, including the simultaneous ones, into a single person? The problem of personal identity is especially acute if he is the sort of time traveler whose journeys are instantaneous, a broken streak consisting of several unconnected segments. Then the natural way to regard him as more than one person is to take each segment as a different person. No one of them is a time traveler, and the peculiarity of the situation comes to this: all but one of these several people vanish into thin air, all but another one appear out of thin air, and there are remarkable resemblances between one at his appearance and another at his vanishing. Why isn't that at least as good a description as the one I gave, on which the several segments are all parts of one time traveler?

I answer that what unites the stages (or segments) of a time traveler is the same sort of mental, or mostly mental, continuity and connectedness that unites anyone else. The only difference is that whereas a common person is connected and continuous with respect to external time, the time traveler is connected and continuous only with respect to his own personal time. Taking the stages in order, mental (and bodily) change is mostly gradual rather than sudden, and at no point is there sudden change in too many different respects all at once. (We can include position in external time among the respects we keep track of, if we like. It may change discontinuously with respect to personal time if not too much else changes discontinuously along with it.) Moreover, there is not too much change altogether. Plenty of traits and traces last a lifetime. Finally, the connectedness and the continuity are not accidental. They are explicable; and further, they are explained by the fact that the properties of each stage depend causally on those of the stages just before in personal time, the dependence being such as tends to keep things the same.[4]

To see the purpose of my final requirement of causal continuity, let us see how it excludes a case of counterfeit time travel. Fred was created out of thin air, as if in the midst of life; he lived a while, then died. He was created by a demon, and the demon had chosen at random what Fred was to be like at the moment of his creation. Much later someone else, Sam, came to resemble Fred as he was when first created. At the very moment when the resemblance became perfect, the demon destroyed Sam. Fred and Sam together are very much like a single person: a time traveler whose personal time starts at Sam's birth, goes on to Sam's destruction and Fred's creation, and goes on from there to Fred's death. Taken in this order, the stages of Fred-*cum*-Sam have the proper connectedness and continuity. But they lack causal continuity, so Fred-*cum*-Sam is not one person and not a time traveler. Perhaps it was pure coincidence that Fred at his creation and Sam at his destruction were exactly alike; then the connectedness and continuity of Fred-*cum*-Sam across the crucial point are accidental. Perhaps instead the demon remembered what Fred was like, guided Sam toward perfect resemblance, watched his progress, and destroyed him at the right moment. Then the connectedness and continuity of Fred-*cum*-Sam has a causal explanation, but of the wrong sort. Either way, Fred's first stages do not depend causally for their properties on Sam's last stages. So the case of Fred and Sam is rightly disqualified as a case of personal identity and as a case of time travel.

We might expect that when a time traveler visits the past there will be reversals of causation. You may punch his face before he leaves, causing his eye to blacken centuries ago. Indeed, travel into the past necessarily involves reversed causation. For time travel requires personal identity—he who arrives must be the same person who departed. That requires causal continuity, in which causation runs from earlier to later stages in the order of personal time. But the orders of personal and external time disagree at some point, and there we have causation that runs from later to earlier stages in the order of external time. Elsewhere I have given an analysis of causation in terms of chains of counterfactual dependence, and I took care that my analysis would not rule out causal reversal a priori.[5] I think I can argue (but not here) that under my analysis the direction of counterfactual dependence and causation is governed by the direction of other *de facto* asymmetries of time. If so, then reversed causation and time travel are not excluded altogether, but can occur only where there are local exceptions to these asymmetries. As I said at the outset, the time traveler's world would be a most strange one.

Stranger still, if there are local—but only local—causal reversals, then there may also be causal loops: closed causal chains in which some of the causal links are normal in direction and others are reversed. (Perhaps there must be loops if there is reversal; I am not sure.) Each event on the loop has a causal explanation, being caused by events elsewhere on the loop. That is not to say that the loop as a whole is caused or explicable. It may not be. Its inexplicability is especially remarkable if it is made up of the sort of causal processes that transmit information. Recall the time traveler who talked to himself. He talked to himself about time travel, and in the course of the conversation his older self told his younger self how to build a time machine. That information was available in no other way. His older self knew how because his younger self had been told and the information had been preserved by the causal processes that constitute recording, storage, and retrieval of memory traces. His younger self knew, after the conversation, because his older self had known and the information had been preserved by the causal processes that constitute telling. But where did the information come from in the first place? Why did the whole affair happen? There is simply no answer. The parts of the loop are explicable, the whole of it is not. Strange! But not impossible, and not too different from inexplicabilities we are already inured to. Almost everyone agrees that God, or the Big Bang, or the entire infinite past of the universe, or the decay of a tritium atom, is uncaused and inexplicable. Then if these are possible, why not also the inexplicable causal loops that arise in time travel?

I have committed a circularity in order not to talk about too much at once, and this is a good place to set it right. In explaining personal time, I presupposed that we were entitled to regard certain stages as comprising a single person. Then in explaining what united the stages into a single person, I presupposed that we were given a personal time order for them. The proper way to proceed is to define personhood and personal time simultaneously, as follows. Suppose given a pair of an aggregate of person-stages, regarded as a candidate for personhood, and an assignment of coordinates to those stages, regarded as a candidate for his personal time. Iff the stages satisfy the conditions given in my circular explanation with respect to the assignment of coordinates, then both candidates succeed: the stages do comprise a person and the assignment is his personal time.

I have argued so far that what goes on in a time travel story may be a possible pattern of events in four-dimensional space-time with no extra time dimension; that it may be correct to regard the scattered stages of the alleged time traveler as comprising a single person; and that we may legitimately assign to those stages and their surroundings a personal time order that disagrees sometimes with their order in external time. Some might concede all this, but protest that the impossibility of time travel is revealed after all when we ask not what the time traveler *does*, but what he *could do*. Could a time traveler change the past? It seems not: the events of a past moment could no more change than numbers could. Yet it seems that he would be as able as anyone to do things that would change the past if he did them. If a time traveler visiting the past both could and couldn't do something that would change it, then there cannot possibly be such a time traveler.

Consider Tim. He detests his grandfather, whose success in the munitions trade built the family fortune that paid for Tim's time machine. Tim would like nothing so much as to kill Grandfather, but alas he is too late. Grandfather died in his bed in 1957, while Tim was a young boy. But when Tim has built his time machine and traveled to 1920, suddenly he realizes that he is not too late after all. He buys a rifle; he spends long hours in target practice; he shadows Grandfather to learn the route of his daily walk to the munitions works; he rents a room along the route; and there he lurks, one winter day in 1921, rifle loaded, hate in his heart, as Grandfather walks closer, closer, ...

Tim can kill Grandfather. He has what it takes. Conditions are perfect in every way: the best rifle money could buy, Grandfather an easy target only twenty yards away, not a breeze, door securely locked against intruders, Tim a good shot to begin with and now at the peak of training, and so on. What's to stop him? The forces of logic will not stay his hand! No powerful chaperone stands by to defend the past from interference. (To imagine such a chaperone, as some authors do, is a boring evasion, not needed to make Tim's story consistent.) In short, Tim is as much able to kill Grandfather as anyone ever is to kill anyone. Suppose that down the street another sniper, Tom, lurks waiting for another victim, Grandfather's partner. Tom is not a time traveler, but otherwise he is just like Tim: same make of rifle, same murderous intent, same everything. We can even suppose that Tom, like Tim, believes himself to be a time traveler. Someone has gone to a lot of trouble to deceive Tom into thinking so. There's no doubt that Tom can kill his victim; and Tim has everything going for him that Tom does. By any ordinary standards of ability, Tim can kill Grandfather.

Tim cannot kill Grandfather. Grandfather lived, so to kill him would be to change the past. But the events of a past moment are not subdivisible into temporal parts and therefore cannot change. Either the events of 1921 timelessly do include Tim's killing of Grandfather, or else they timelessly don't. We may be tempted to speak of the "original" 1921 that lies in Tim's personal past, many years before his birth, in which Grandfather lived; and of the "new" 1921 in which Tim now finds himself waiting in ambush to kill Grandfather. But if we do speak so, we merely confer two names on one thing. The events of 1921 are doubly located in Tim's (extended) personal time, like the trestle on the railway, but the "original" 1921 and the "new" 1921 are one and the same. If Tim did not kill Grandfather in the "original" 1921, then if he does kill Grandfather in the "new" 1921, he must both kill and not kill Grandfather in 1921—in the one and only 1921, which is both the "new" and the "original" 1921. It is logically impossible that Tim should change the past by killing Grandfather in 1921. So Tim cannot kill Grandfather.

Not that past moments are special; no more can anyone change the present or the future. Present and future momentary events no more have temporal parts than past ones do. You cannot change a present or future event from what it was originally to what it is after you change it. What you *can* do is to change the present or the future from the unactualized way they would have been without some action of yours to the way they actually are. But that is not an actual change: not a difference between two successive actualities. And Tim can certainly do as much; he changes the past from the unactualized way it would have been without him to the one and only way it actually is. To "change" the past in this way, Tim need not do anything momentous; it is enough just to be there, however unobtrusively.

You know, of course, roughly how the story of Tim must go on if it is to be consistent: he somehow fails. Since Tim didn't kill Grandfather in the "original" 1921, consistency demands that neither does he kill Grandfather in the "new" 1921. Why not? For some commonplace reason. Perhaps some noise distracts him at the last moment, perhaps he misses despite all his target practice, perhaps his nerve fails, perhaps he even feels a pang of unaccustomed mercy. His failure by no means proves that he was not really able to kill Grandfather. We often try and fail to do what we are able to do. Success at some tasks requires not only ability but also luck, and lack of luck is not a temporary lack of ability. Suppose our other sniper, Tom, fails to kill Grandfather's partner for the same reason, whatever it is, that Tim fails to kill Grandfather. It does not follow that Tom was unable to. No more does it follow in Tim's case that he was unable to do what he did not succeed in doing.

We have this seeming contradiction: *"Tim doesn't, but can, because he has what it takes"* versus *"Tim doesn't, and can't, because it's logically impossible to change the past."* I reply that there is no contradiction. Both conclusions are true, and for the reasons given. They are compatible because "can" is equivocal.

To say that something can happen means that its happening is compossible with certain facts. *Which* facts? That is determined, but sometimes not determined well enough, by context. An ape can't speak a human language—say, Finnish—but I can. Facts about the anatomy and operation of the ape's larynx and nervous system are not compossible with his speaking Finnish. The corresponding facts about my larynx and nervous system are compossible with my speaking Finnish. But don't take me along to Helsinki as your interpreter: I can't speak Finnish. My speaking Finnish is compossible with the facts considered so far, but not with further facts about my lack of training. What I can do, relative to one set of facts, I cannot do, relative to another, more inclusive, set. Whenever the context leaves it open which facts are to count as relevant, it is possible to equivocate about whether I can speak Finnish. It is likewise possible to equivocate about whether it is possible for me to speak Finnish, or whether I am able to, or whether I have the ability or capacity or power or potentiality to. Our many words for much the same thing are little help since they do not seem to correspond to different fixed delineations of the relevant facts.

Tim's killing Grandfather that day in 1921 is compossible with a fairly rich set of facts: the facts about his rifle, his skill and training, the unobstructed line of fire, the locked door and the absence of any chaperone to defend the past, and so on. Indeed it is compossible with all the facts of the sorts we would ordinarily count as relevant in saying what someone can do. It is compossible with all the facts corresponding to those we deem relevant in Tom's case. Relative to these facts, Tim can kill Grandfather. But his killing Grandfather is not compossible with another, more inclusive set of facts. There is the simple fact that Grandfather was not killed. Also there are various other facts about Grandfather's doings after 1921 and their effects: Grandfather begat Father in 1922 and Father begat Tim in 1949. Relative to these facts, Tim cannot kill Grandfather. He can and he can't, but under different delineations of the relevant facts. You can reasonably choose the narrower delineation, and say that he can; or the wider delineation, and say that he can't. But choose. What you mustn't do is waver, say in the same breath that he both can and can't, and then claim that this contradiction proves that time travel is impossible.

Exactly the same goes for Tom's parallel failure. For Tom to kill Grandfather's partner also is compossible with all facts of the sorts we ordinarily count as relevant, but not compossible with a larger set including, for instance, the fact that the intended victim lived until 1934. In Tom's case we are not puzzled. We say without hesitation that he can do it, because we see at once that the facts that are not compossible with his success are facts about the future of the time in question and therefore not the sort of facts we count as relevant in saying what Tom can do.

In Tim's case it is harder to keep track of which facts are relevant. We are accustomed to exclude facts about the future of the time in question, but to include some facts about its past. Our standards do not apply unequivocally to the crucial facts in this special case: Tim's failure, Grandfather's survival, and his subsequent doings. If we have foremost in mind that they lie in the external future of that moment in 1921 when Tim is almost ready to shoot, then we exclude them just as we exclude the parallel facts in Tom's case. But if we have foremost in mind that they precede that moment in Tim's extended personal time, then we tend to include them. To make the latter be foremost in your mind, I chose to tell Tim's story in the order of his personal time, rather than in the order of external time. The fact of Grandfather's survival until 1957 had already been told before I got to the part of the story about Tim lurking in ambush to kill him in 1921. We must decide, if we can, whether to treat these personally past and externally future facts as if they were straightforwardly past or as if they were straightforwardly future.

Fatalists—the best of them—are philosophers who take facts we count as irrelevant in saying what someone can do, disguise them somehow as facts of a different sort that we count as relevant, and thereby argue that we can do less than we think—indeed, that there is nothing at all that we don't do but can. I am not going to vote Republican next fall. The fatalist argues that, strange to say, I not only won't but can't; for my voting Republican is not compossible with the fact that it was true already in the year 1548 that I was not going to vote Republican 428 years later. My rejoinder is that this is a fact, sure enough; however, it is an irrelevant fact about the future masquerading as a relevant fact about the past, and so should be left out of account in saying what, in any ordinary sense, I can do. We are unlikely to be fooled by the fatalist's methods of disguise in this case, or other ordinary cases. But in cases of time travel, precognition, or the like, we're on less familiar ground, so it may take less of a disguise to fool us. Also, new methods of disguise are available, thanks to the device of personal time.

Here's another bit of fatalist trickery. Tim, as he lurks, already knows that he will fail. At least he has the wherewithal to know it if he thinks, he knows it implicitly. For he remembers that Grandfather was alive when he was a boy, he knows that those who are killed are thereafter not alive, he knows (let us suppose) that he is a time traveler who has reached the same 1921 that lies in his personal past, and he ought to understand—as we do—why a time traveler cannot change the past. What is known cannot be false. So his success is not only not compossible with facts that belong to the external future and his personal past, but also is not compossible with the present fact of his knowledge that he will fail. I reply that the fact of his foreknowledge, at the moment while he waits to shoot, is not a fact entirely about that moment. It may be divided into two parts. There is the fact that he then believes (perhaps only implicitly) that he will fail; and there is the further fact that his belief is correct, and correct not at all by accident, and hence qualifies as an item of knowledge. It is only the latter fact that is not compossible with his success, but it is only the former that is entirely about the moment in question. In calling Tim's state at that moment knowledge, not just belief, facts about personally earlier but externally later moments were smuggled into consideration.

I have argued that Tim's case and Tom's are alike, except that in Tim's case we are more tempted than usual—and with reason—to opt for a semi-fatalist mode of speech. But perhaps they differ in another way. In Tom's case, we can expect a perfectly consistent answer to the counterfactual question: what if Tom had killed Grandfather's partner? Tim's case is more difficult. If Tim had killed Grandfather, it seems offhand that contradictions would have been true. The killing both would and wouldn't have occurred. No Grandfather, no Father; no Father, no Tim; no Tim, no killing. And for good measure: no Grandfather, no family fortune; no fortune, no time machine; no time machine, no killing. So the supposition that Tim killed Grandfather seems impossible in more than the semi-fatalistic sense already granted.

If you suppose Tim to kill Grandfather and hold all the rest of his story fixed, of course you get a contradiction. But likewise if you suppose Tom to kill Grandfather's partner and hold the rest of his story fixed—including the part that told of his failure—you get a contradiction. If you make *any* counterfactual supposition and hold all else fixed you get a contradiction. The thing to do is rather to make the counterfactual supposition and hold all else as close to fixed as you consistently can. That procedure will yield perfectly consistent answers to the question: what if Tim had not killed Grandfather? In that case, some of the story I told would not have been true. Perhaps Tim might have been the time-traveling grandson of someone else. Perhaps he might have been the grandson of a man killed in 1921 and miraculously resurrected. Perhaps he might have been not a time traveler at all, but rather someone created out of nothing in 1920 equipped with false memories of a personal past that never was. It is hard to say what is the least revision of Tim's story to make it true that Tim kills Grandfather, but certainly the contradictory story in which the killing both does and doesn't occur is not the least revision. Hence it is false (according to the unrevised story) that if Tim had killed Grandfather then contradictions would have been true.

What difference would it make if Tim travels in branching time? Suppose that at the possible world of Tim's story the space-time manifold branches; the branches are separated not in time, and not in space, but in some other way. Tim travels not only in time but also from one branch to another. In one branch Tim is absent from the events of 1921; Grandfather lives; Tim is born, grows up, and vanishes in his time machine. The other branch diverges from the first when Tim turns up in 1920; there Tim kills Grandfather and Grandfather leaves no descendants and no fortune; the events of the two branches differ more and more from that time on. Certainly this is a consistent story; it is a story in which Grandfather both is and isn't killed in 1921 (in the different branches); and it is a story in which Tim, by killing Grandfather, succeeds in preventing his own birth (in one of the branches). But it is not a story in which Tim's killing of Grandfather both does occur and doesn't: it simply does, though it is located in one branch and not the other. And it is not a story in which Tim changes the past. 1921 and later years contain the events of both branches, coexisting somehow without interaction. It remains true at all the personal times of Tim's life, even after the killing, that Grandfather lives in one branch and dies in the other.[6]

NOTES

1. I have particularly in mind two of the time travel stories of Robert A. Heinlein: "By His Bootstraps" in R. A. Heinlein, *The Menace from Earth* (Hicksville, N.Y., 1959), and "—All You Zombies—," in R. A. Heinlein, *The Unpleasant Profession of Jonathan Hoag* (Hicksville, N.Y., 1959).
2. Accounts of time travel in two-dimensional time are found in Jack W. Meiland, "A Two-Dimensional Passage Model of Time for Time Travel," *Philosophical Studies*, vol. 26 (1974), pp. 153–173; and in the initial chapters of Isaac Asimov, *The End of Eternity* (Garden City, N.Y., 1955). Asimov's denouement, however, seems to require some different conception of time travel.
3. H. G. Wells, *The Time Machine, An Invention* (London, 1895), epilogue. The passage is criticized as contradictory in Donald C. Williams, "The Myth of

Passage," *The Journal of Philosophy*, vol. 48 (1951), p. 463.

4. I discuss the relation between personal identity and mental connectedness and continuity at greater length in "Survival and Identity" in *The Identity of Persons*, ed. by Amelie Rorty (Berkeley, 1976).
5. "Causation," *The Journal of Philosophy*, vol. 70 (1973), pp. 556–567; the analysis relies on the analysis of counterfactuals given in my *Counterfactuals* (Oxford, 1973).
6. The present paper summarizes a series of lectures of the same title, given as the Gavin David Young Lectures in Philosophy at the University of Adelaide in July, 1971. I thank the Australian-American Educational Foundation and the American Council of Learned Societies for research support. I am grateful to many friends for comments on earlier versions of this paper; especially Philip Kitcher, William Newton-Smith, J. J. C. Smart, and Donald Williams.

F FREE WILL

Freedom and Necessity

A. J. AYER

Alfred Jules Ayer (1910–89) was an influential British philosopher who taught at the University College London and at Oxford University. He was an important advocate of the philosophical view known as *logical positivism*, whose tenets he articulated in his 1936 book *Language, Truth and Logic*. Ayer went on to publish many influential books and articles on a wide range of philosophical topics.

In the selection that follows, originally published in 1954, Ayer defends the view that free will and moral responsibility are compatible with causal determinism. Another selection from Ayer's work appears in the "Mind and Language" section.

When I am said to have done something of my own free will it is implied that I could have acted otherwise; and it is only when it is believed that I could have acted otherwise that I am held to be morally responsible for what I have done. For a man is not thought to be morally responsible for an action that it was not in his power to avoid. But if human behaviour is entirely governed by causal laws, it is not clear how any action that is done could ever have been avoided. It may be said of the agent that he would have acted otherwise if the causes of his action had been different, but they being what they were, it seems to follow that he was bound to act as he did. Now it is commonly assumed both that men are capable of acting freely, in the sense that is required to make them morally responsible, and that human behaviour is entirely governed by causal laws: and it is the apparent conflict between these two assumptions that gives rise to the philosophical problem of the freedom of the will.

Confronted with this problem, many people will be inclined to agree with Dr. Johnson.* "Sir, we *know* our will is free, and *there's* an end on't." But, while this does very well for those who accept Dr. Johnson's premiss, it would hardly convince anyone who denied the freedom of the will. Certainly, if we do know that our wills are free, it follows that they are so. But the logical reply to this might be that since our wills are not free, it follows that no one can know that they are: so that if anyone claims, like Dr. Johnson, to know that they are, he must be mistaken. What is evident, indeed,

* British writer Samuel Johnson (1709–84), one of the greatest literary figures of the eighteenth century.

Reprinted from *Philosophical Essays* (London: Macmillan; New York: St. Martin's Press, 1954). Reproduced with permission of Palgrave Macmillan.

is that people often believe themselves to be acting freely; and it is to this "feeling" of freedom that some philosophers appeal when they wish, in the supposed interests of morality, to prove that not all human action is causally determined. But if these philosophers are right in their assumption that a man cannot be acting freely if his action is causally determined, then the fact that someone feels free to do, or not to do, a certain action does not prove that he really is so. It may prove that the agent does not himself know what it is that makes him act in one way rather than another: but from the fact that a man is unaware of the causes of his action, it does not follow that no such causes exist.

So much may be allowed to the determinist; but his belief that all human actions are subservient to causal laws still remains to be justified. If, indeed, it is necessary that every event should have a cause, then the rule must apply to human behaviour as much as to anything else. But why should it be supposed that every event must have a cause? The contrary is not unthinkable. Nor is the law of universal causation a necessary presupposition of scientific thought. The scientist may try to discover causal laws, and in many cases he succeeds; but sometimes he has to be content with statistical laws, and sometimes he comes upon events which, in the present state of his knowledge, he is not able to subsume under any law at all. In the case of these events he assumes that if he knew more he would be able to discover some law, whether causal or statistical, which would enable him to account for them. And this assumption cannot be disproved. For however far he may have carried his investigation, it is always open to him to carry it further; and it is always conceivable that if he carried it further he would discover the connection which had hitherto escaped him. Nevertheless, it is also conceivable that the events with which he is concerned are not systematically connected with any others: so that the reason why he does not discover the sort of laws that he requires is simply that they do not obtain.

Now in the case of human conduct the search for explanations has not in fact been altogether fruitless. Certain scientific laws have been established; and with the help of these laws we do make a number of successful predictions about the ways in which different people will behave. But these predictions do not always cover every detail. We may be able to predict that in certain circumstances a particular man will be angry, without being able to prescribe the precise form that the expression of his anger will take. We may be reasonably sure that he will shout, but not sure how loud his shout will be, or exactly what words he will use. And it is only a small proportion of human actions that we are able to forecast even so precisely as this. But that, it may be said, is because we have not carried our investigations very far. The science of psychology is still in its infancy and, as it is developed, not only will more human actions be explained, but the explanations will go into greater detail. The ideal of complete explanation may never in fact be attained: but it is theoretically attainable. Well, this may be so: and certainly it is impossible to show a priori that it is not so: but equally it cannot be shown that it is. This will not, however, discourage the scientist who, in the field of human behaviour, as elsewhere, will continue to formulate theories and test them by the facts. And in this he is justified. For since he has no reason a priori to admit that there is a limit to what he can discover, the fact that he also cannot be sure that there is no limit does not make it unreasonable for him to devise theories, nor, having devised them, to try constantly to improve them.

But now suppose it to be claimed that, so far as men's actions are concerned, there is a limit: and that this limit is set by the fact of human freedom. An obvious objection is that in many cases in which a person feels himself to be free to do, or not to do, a certain action, we are even now able to explain, in causal terms, why it is that he acts as he does. But it might be argued that even if men are sometimes mistaken in believing that they act freely, it does not follow that they are always so mistaken. For it is not always the case that when a man believes that he has acted freely we are in fact able to account for his action in causal terms. A determinist would say that we should be able to account for it if we had more knowledge of the circumstances, and had been able to discover the appropriate natural laws. But until those discoveries have been made, this remains only a pious hope. And may it not be true that, in some cases at least, the reason why we can give no causal explanation is that no causal explanation is available; and that this is because the agent's choice was literally free, as he himself felt it to be?

The answer is that this may indeed be true, inasmuch as it is open to anyone to hold that no explanation is possible until some explanation is actually found. But even so it does not give the moralist what he wants. For he is anxious to show that men are capable of acting freely in order to infer that they can be morally responsible for what they do. But if it is a matter of pure chance that a man should act in one way rather than another, he may be free but can hardly be responsible. And indeed when a man's actions seem to us quite unpredictable, when, as we say, there is no knowing what he will do, we do not look upon him as a moral agent. We look upon him as a lunatic.

To this it may be objected that we are not dealing fairly with the moralist. For when he makes it a condition of my being morally responsible that I should act freely, he does not wish to imply that it is purely a matter of chance that I act as I do. What he wishes to imply is that my actions are the result of my own free choice: and it is because they are the result of my own free choice that I am held to be morally responsible for them.

But now we must ask how it is that I come to make my choice. Either it is an accident that I choose to act as I do or it is not. If it is an accident, then it is merely a matter of chance that I did not choose otherwise; and if it is merely a matter of chance that I did not choose otherwise, it is surely irrational to hold me morally responsible for choosing as I did. But if it is not an accident that I choose to do one thing rather than another, then presumably there is some causal explanation of my choice: and in that case we are led back to determinism.

Again, the objection may be raised that we are not doing justice to the moralist's case. His view is not that it is a matter of chance that I choose to act as I do, but rather that my choice depends upon my character. Nevertheless he holds that I can still be free in the sense that he requires; for it is I who am responsible for my character. But in what way am I responsible for my character? Only, surely, in the sense that there is a causal connection between what I do now and what I have done in the past. It is only this that justifies the statement that I have made myself what I am: and even so this is an over-simplification, since it takes no account of the external influences to which I have been subjected. But, ignoring the external influences, let us assume that it is in fact the case that I have made myself what I am. Then it is still legitimate to ask how it is that I have come to make myself one sort of person rather than another. And if it be answered that it is a matter of my strength of will, we can put the same question in another form by asking how it is that my will has the strength that it has and not some other degree of strength. Once more, either it is an accident or it is not. If it is an accident, then by the same argument as before, I am not morally responsible, and if it is not an accident we are led back to determinism.

Furthermore, to say that my actions proceed from my character or, more colloquially, that I act in character, is to say that my behaviour is consistent and to that extent predictable: and since it is, above all, for the actions that I perform in character that I am held to be morally responsible, it looks as if the admission of moral responsibility, so far from being incompatible with determinism, tends rather to presuppose it. But how can this be so if it is a necessary condition of moral responsibility that the person who is held responsible should have acted freely? It seems that if we are to retain this idea of moral responsibility, we must either show that men can be held responsible for actions which they do not do freely, or else find some way of reconciling determinism with the freedom of the will.

It is no doubt with the object of effecting this reconciliation that some philosophers have defined freedom as the consciousness of necessity. And by so doing they are able to say not only that a man can be acting freely when his action is causally determined, but even that his action must be causally determined for it to be possible for him to be acting freely. Nevertheless this definition has the serious disadvantage that it gives to the word "freedom" a meaning quite different from any that it ordinarily bears. It is indeed obvious that if we are allowed to give the word "freedom" any meaning that we please, we can find a meaning that will reconcile it with determinism: but this is no more a solution of our present problem than the fact that the word "horse" could be arbitrarily used to mean what is ordinarily meant by "sparrow" is a proof that horses have wings. For suppose that I am compelled by another person to do something "against my will." In that case, as the word "freedom" is ordinarily used, I should not be said to be acting freely: and the fact that I am fully aware of the constraint to which I am subjected makes no difference to the matter. I do not become free by becoming conscious that I am not. It may, indeed, be possible to show that my being aware that my action is causally determined is not incompatible with my acting freely: but it by no means follows that it is in this that my freedom consists. Moreover, I suspect that one of the reasons why people are inclined to define freedom as the consciousness of necessity is that they think that if one is conscious of necessity one may somehow be able to master it. But this is a fallacy. It is like someone's saying that he wishes he could see into the future, because if he did he would know what calamities lay in wait for him and so would be able to avoid them. But if he avoids the calamities then they don't lie in the future and it is not true that he foresees them. And similarly if I am able to master necessity, in the sense of escaping the operation of a necessary law, then the law in question is not necessary. And if the law is not necessary, then neither my freedom nor anything else can consist in my knowing that it is.

Let it be granted, then, when we speak of reconciling freedom with determination we are using the word "freedom" in an ordinary sense. It still remains for us to make this usage clear: and perhaps the best way to make it clear is to show what it is that freedom, in this sense, is contrasted with. Now we began with the assumption that freedom is contrasted with causality: so that a man cannot be said to be acting freely if his action is causally determined. But this assumption has led us into difficulties and I now wish to suggest that it is mistaken. For it is not, I think, causality that freedom is to be contrasted with, but constraint. And while it is true that being constrained to do an action entails being caused to do it, I shall try to show that the converse does not hold. I shall try to show that from the fact that my action is causally determined it does not necessarily follow that I am constrained to do it: and this is equivalent to saying that it does not necessarily follow that I am not free.

If I am constrained, I do not act freely. But in what circumstances can I legitimately be said to be constrained? An obvious instance is the case in which I am compelled by another person to do what he wants. In a case of this sort the compulsion need not be such as to deprive one of the power of choice. It is not required that the other person should have hypnotized me, or that he should make it physically impossible for me to go against his will. It is enough that he should induce me to do what he wants by making it clear to me that, if I do not, he will bring about some situation that I regard as even more undesirable than the consequences of the action that he wishes me to do. Thus, if the man points a pistol at my head I may still choose to disobey him: but this does not prevent its being true that if I do fall in with his wishes he can legitimately be said to have compelled me. And if the circumstances are such that no reasonable person would be expected to choose the other alternative, then the action that I am made to do is not one for which I am held to be morally responsible.

A similar, but still somewhat different, case is that in which another person has obtained an habitual ascendancy over me. Where this is so, there may be no question of my being induced to act as the other person wishes by being confronted with a still more disagreeable alternative: for if I am sufficiently under his influence this special stimulus will not be necessary. Nevertheless I do not act freely, for the reason that I have been deprived of the power of choice. And this means that I have acquired so strong a habit of obedience that I no longer go through any process of deciding whether or not to do what the other person wants. About other matters I may still deliberate; but as regards the fulfilment of this other person's wishes, my own deliberations have ceased to be a causal factor in my behaviour. And it is in this sense that I may be said to be constrained. It is not, however, necessary that such constraint should take the form of subservience to another person. A kleptomaniac is not a free agent, in respect of his stealing, because he does not go through any process of deciding whether or not to steal. Or rather, if he does go through such a process, it is irrelevant to his behaviour. Whatever he resolved to do, he would steal all the same. And it is this that distinguishes him from the ordinary thief.

But now it may be asked whether there is any essential difference between these cases and those in which the agent is commonly thought to be free. No doubt the ordinary thief does go through a process of deciding whether or not to steal, and no doubt it does affect his behaviour. If he resolved to refrain from stealing, he could carry his resolution out. But if it be allowed that his making or not making this resolution is causally determined, then how can he be any more free than the kleptomaniac? It may be true that unlike the kleptomaniac he could refrain from stealing if he chose: but if there is a cause, or set of causes, which necessitate his choosing as he does, how can he be said to have the power of choice? Again, it may be true that no one now compels me to get up and walk across the room: but if my doing so can be causally explained in terms of my history or my environment, or whatever it may be, then how am I any more free than if some other person had compelled me? I do not have the feeling of constraint that I have when a pistol is manifestly pointed at my head; but the chains of causation by which I am bound are no less effective for being invisible.

The answer to this is that the cases I have mentioned as examples of constraint do differ from the others: and they differ just in the ways that I have tried to bring out. If I suffered from a compulsion neurosis, so that I got up and walked across the room, whether I wanted to or not, or if I did so because somebody else compelled me, then I should not be acting freely. But if I do it now, I shall be acting freely, just because these conditions do not obtain; and the fact that my action may nevertheless have a cause is, from this point of view, irrelevant. For it is not when my action has any cause at all, but only when it has a special sort of cause, that it is reckoned not to be free.

But here it may be objected that, even if this distinction corresponds to ordinary usage, it is still very irrational. For why should we distinguish, with regard to a person's freedom, between the operations of one sort of cause and those of another? Do not all causes equally necessitate? And is it not therefore arbitrary to say that a person is free when he is necessitated in one fashion but not when he is necessitated in another?

That all causes equally necessitate is indeed a tautology, if the word "necessitate" is taken merely as equivalent to "cause": but if, as the objection requires, it is taken as equivalent to "constrain" or "compel," then I do not think that this proposition is true. For all that is needed for one event to be the cause of another is that, in the given circumstances, the event which is said to be the effect would not have occurred if it had not been for the occurrence of the event which is said to be the cause, or vice versa, according as causes are interpreted as necessary, or sufficient, conditions: and this fact is usually deducible from some causal law which states that whenever an event of the one kind occurs then, given suitable conditions, an event of the other kind will occur in a certain temporal or spatio-temporal relationship to it. In short, there is an invariable concomitance between the two classes of events; but there is no compulsion, in any but a metaphorical sense. Suppose, for example, that a psycho-analyst is able to account for some aspect of my behaviour by referring it to some lesion that I suffered in my childhood. In that case, it may be said that my childhood experience, together with certain other events, necessitates my behaving as I do. But all that this involves is that it is found to be true in general that when people have had certain experiences as children, they subsequently behave in certain specifiable ways; and my case is just another instance of this general law. It is in this way indeed that my behaviour is explained. But from the fact that my behaviour is capable of being explained, in the sense that it can be subsumed under some natural law, it does not follow that I am acting under constraint.

If this is correct, to say that I could have acted otherwise is to say, first, that I should have acted otherwise if I had so chosen; secondly, that my action was voluntary in the sense in which the actions, say, of the kleptomaniac are not; and thirdly, that nobody compelled me to choose as I did: and these three conditions may very well be fulfilled. When they are fulfilled, I may be said to have acted freely. But this is not to say that it was a matter of chance that I acted as I did, or, in other words, that my action could not be explained. And that my actions should be capable of being explained is all that is required by the postulate of determinism.

If more than this seems to be required it is, I think, because the use of the very word "determinism" is in some degree misleading. For it tends to suggest that one event is somehow in the power of another, whereas the truth is merely that they are factually correlated. And the same applies to the use, in this context, of the word "necessity" and even of the word "cause" itself. Moreover, there are various reasons for this. One is the tendency to confuse causal with logical necessitation, and so to infer mistakenly that the effect is contained in the cause. Another is the uncritical use of a concept of force which is derived from primitive experiences of pushing and striking. A third is the survival of an animistic conception of causality, in which all causal relationships are modelled on the example of one person's exercising authority over another. As a result we tend to form an imaginative picture of an unhappy effect trying vainly to escape from the clutches of an overmastering cause. But, I repeat, the fact is simply that when an event of one type occurs, an event of another type occurs also, in a certain temporal or spatio-temporal relation to the first. The rest is only metaphor. And it is because of the metaphor, and not because of the fact, that we come to think that there is an antithesis between causality and freedom.

Nevertheless, it may be said, if the postulate of determinism is valid, then the future can be explained in terms of the past: and this means that if one knew enough about the past one would be able to predict the future. But in that case what will happen in the future is already decided. And how then can I be said to be free? What is going to happen is going to happen and nothing that I do can prevent it. If the determinist is right, I am the helpless prisoner of fate.

But what is meant by saying that the future course of events is already decided? If the implication is that some person has arranged it, then the proposition is false. But if all that is meant is that it is possible, in principle, to deduce it from a set of particular facts about the past, together with the appropriate general laws, then, even if this is true, it does not in the least entail that I am the helpless prisoner of fate. It does not even entail that my actions make no difference to the future: for they are causes as well as effects; so that if they were different their consequences would be different also. What it does entail is that my behaviour can be predicted: but to say that my behaviour can be predicted is not to say that I am acting under constraint. It is indeed true that I cannot escape my destiny if this is taken to mean no more than that I shall do what I shall do. But this is a tautology, just as it is a tautology that what is going to happen is going to happen. And such tautologies as these prove nothing whatsoever about the freedom of the will.

Human Freedom and the Self

RODERICK M. CHISHOLM

Roderick Chisholm (1916–99) was an American philosopher known for his careful work on topics in epistemology, metaphysics, and the philosophy of mind. He spent most of his career teaching at Brown University. Among his best-known books are *Perceiving* (1957) and *Person and Object* (1976).

In the selection that follows, originally delivered as a lecture at the University of Kansas in 1964, Chisholm defends a *libertarian* view of free will, arguing that although free will is incompatible with determinism, we nonetheless do act freely. In his discussion, Chisholm makes reference to the works of a number of early modern philosophers, including Thomas Hobbes (1588–1679), John Locke (1632–1704), and Immanuel Kant (1724–1804).

The Lindley Lecture, 1964. Copyright © 1964 by the Department of Philosophy, University of Kansas, pp. 3–15. Reprinted by permission of the Department of Philosophy and of the University of Kansas.

"A staff moves a stone, and is moved by a hand, which is moved by a man."

—*ARISTOTLE, PHYSICS, 256A.*

1. The metaphysical problem of human freedom might be summarized in the following way: Human beings are responsible agents; but this fact appears to conflict with a deterministic view of human action (the view that every event that is involved in an act is caused by some other event); and it *also* appears to conflict with an indeterministic view of human action (the view that the act, or some event that is essential to the act, is not caused at all.) To solve the problem, I believe, we must make somewhat far-reaching assumptions about the self or the agent—about the man who performs the act.

Perhaps it is needless to remark that, in all likelihood, it is impossible to say anything significant about this ancient problem that has not been said before.[1]

2. Let us consider some deed, or misdeed, that may be attributed to a responsible agent: one man, say, shot another. If the man *was* responsible for what he did, then, I would urge, what was to happen at the time of the shooting was something that was entirely up to the man himself. There was a moment at which it was true, both that he could have fired the shot and also that he could have refrained from firing it. And if this is so, then, even though he did fire it, he could have done something else instead. (He didn't find himself firing the shot "against his will," as we say.) I think we can say, more generally, then, that if a man is responsible for a certain event or a certain state of affairs (in our example, the shooting of another man), then that event or state of affairs was brought about by some act of his, and the act was something that was in his power either to perform or not to perform.

But now if the act which he *did* perform was an act that was also in his power *not* to perform, then it could not have been caused or determined by any event that was not itself within his power either to bring about or not to bring about. For example, if what we say he did was really something that was brought about by a second man, one who forced his hand upon the trigger, say, or who, by means of hypnosis, compelled him to perform the act, then since the act was caused by the *second* man it was nothing that was within the power of the *first* man to prevent. And precisely the same thing is true, I think, if instead of referring to a second man who compelled the first one, we speak instead of the *desires* and *beliefs* which the first man happens to have had. For if what we say he did was really something that was brought about by his own beliefs and desires, if these beliefs and desires in the particular situation in which he happened to have found himself caused him to do just what it was that we say he did do, then, since *they* caused it, *he* was unable to do anything other than just what it was that he did do. It makes no difference whether the cause of the deed was internal or external; if the cause was some state or event for which the man himself was not responsible, then he was not responsible for what we have been mistakenly calling his act. If a flood caused the poorly constructed dam to break, then, given the flood and the constitution of the dam, the break, we may say, *had* to occur and nothing could have happened in its place. And if the flood of desire caused the weak-willed man to give in, then he, too, had to do just what it was that he did do and he was no more responsible than was the dam for the results that followed. (It is true, of course, that if the man is responsible for the beliefs and desires that he happens to have, then he may also be responsible for the things they lead him to do. But the question now becomes: *is* he responsible for the beliefs and desires he happens to have? If he is, then there was a time when they were within his power either to acquire, or not to acquire, and we are left, therefore, with our general point.)

One may object: But surely if there were such a thing as a man who is really *good*, then he would be responsible for things that he would do; yet, he would be unable to do anything other than just what it is that he does do, since, being good, he will always choose to do what is best. The answer, I think, is suggested by a comment that Thomas Reid makes upon an ancient author.* The author had said of Cato, "He was good because he could not be otherwise," and Reid observes: "This saying, if understood literally and strictly, is not the praise of Cato, but of his constitution, which was no more the work of Cato

* Thomas Reid (1710–96) was a Scottish philosopher known for his defense of "commonsense" views; Cato (95 BCE–46 BCE) was a Roman statesman known for his integrity.

than his existence."[2] If Cato was himself responsible for the good things that he did, then Cato, as Reid suggests, was such that, although he had the power to do what was not good, he exercised his power only for that which was good.

All of this, if it is true, may give a certain amount of comfort to those who are tender-minded. But we should remind them that it also conflicts with a familiar view about the nature of God—with the view that St. Thomas Aquinas expresses by saying that "every movement both of the will and of nature proceeds from God as the Prime Mover."[3] If the act of the sinner *did* proceed from God as the Prime Mover, then God was in the position of the second agent we just discussed—the man who forced the trigger finger, or the hypnotist—and the sinner, so-called, was *not* responsible for what he did. (This may be a bold assertion, in view of the history of western theology, but I must say that I have never encountered a single good reason for denying it.)

There is one standard objection to all of this and we should consider it briefly.

3. The objection takes the form of a stratagem—one designed to show that determinism (and divine providence) is consistent with human responsibility. The stratagem is one that was used by Jonathan Edwards* and by many philosophers in the present century, most notably, G. E. Moore.[4]

One proceeds as follows: The expression

(a) He could have done otherwise,

it is argued, means no more nor less than

(b) If he had chosen to do otherwise, then he would have done otherwise.

(In place of "chosen," one might say "tried," "set out," "decided," "undertaken," or "willed.") The truth of statement (b), it is then pointed out, is consistent with determinism (and with divine providence); for even if all of the man's actions were causally determined, the man could still be such that, *if* he had chosen otherwise, then he would have done otherwise. What the murderer saw, let us suppose, along with his beliefs and desires, *caused* him to fire the shot; yet he was such that *if*, just then, he had chosen or decided *not* to fire the shot, then he would not have fired it. All of this is certainly possible. Similarly, we could say, of the dam, that the flood caused it to break and also that the dam was such that, *if* there had been no flood or any similar pressure, then the dam would have remained intact. And therefore, the argument proceeds, if (b) is consistent with determinism, and if (a) and (b) say the same thing, then (a) is also consistent with determinism; hence we can say that the agent *could* have done otherwise even though he was caused to do what he did do; and therefore determinism and moral responsibility are compatible.

Is the argument sound? The conclusion follows from the premises, but the catch, I think, lies in the first premiss—the one saying that statement (a) tells us no more nor less than what statement (b) tells us. For (b), it would seem, could be true while (a) is false. That is to say, our man might be such that, if he had chosen to do otherwise, then he would have done otherwise, and yet *also* such that he could not have done otherwise. Suppose, after all, that our murderer could not have *chosen*, or could not have *decided*, to do otherwise. Then the fact that he happens also to be a man such that, if he had chosen not to shoot he would not have shot, would make no difference. For if he could *not* have chosen *not* to shoot, then he could not have done anything other than just what it was that he did do. In a word: from our statement (b) above ("If he had chosen to do otherwise, then he would have done otherwise"), we cannot make an inference to (a) above ("He could have done otherwise") unless we can *also* assert:

(c) He could have chosen to do otherwise.

And therefore, if we must reject this third statement (c), then, even though we may be justified in asserting (b), we are not justified in asserting (a). If the man could not have chosen to do otherwise, then he would not have done otherwise—*even if* he was

* Jonathan Edwards (1703–58) was a distinguished early American philosopher and theologian. G. E. Moore (1873–1958) was an important twentieth-century British philosopher. Several selections from Moore's writings appear in this anthology.

such that, if he *had* chosen to do otherwise, then he would have done otherwise.

The stratagem in question, then, seems to me not to work, and I would say, therefore, that the ascription of responsibility conflicts with a deterministic view of action.

4. Perhaps there is less need to argue that the ascription of responsibility also conflicts with an indeterministic view of action—with the view that the act, or some event that is essential to the act, is not caused at all. If the act—the firing of the shot—was not caused at all, if it was fortuitous or capricious, happening so to speak out of the blue, then, presumably, no one—and nothing—was responsible for the act. Our conception of action, therefore, should be neither deterministic nor indeterministic. Is there any other possibility?

5. We must not say that every event involved in the act is caused by some other event; and we must not say that the act is something that is not caused at all. The possibility that remains, therefore, is this: We should say that at least one of the events that are involved in the act is caused, not by any other events, but by something else instead. And this something else can only be the agent—the man. If there is an event that is caused, not by other events, but by the man, then there are some events involved in the act that are not caused by other events. But if the event in question is caused by the man then it *is* caused and we are not committed to saying that there is something involved in the act that is not caused at all.

But this, of course, is a large consequence, implying something of considerable importance about the nature of the agent or the man.

6. If we consider only inanimate natural objects, we may say that causation, if it occurs, is a relation between *events* or *states of affairs*. The dam's breaking was an event that was caused by a set of other events—the dam being weak, the flood being strong, and so on. But if a man is responsible for a particular deed, then, if what I have said is true, there is some event, or set of events, that is caused, *not* by other events or states of affairs, but by the agent, whatever he may be.

I shall borrow a pair of medieval terms, using them, perhaps, in a way that is slightly different from that for which they were originally intended. I shall say that when one event or state of affairs (or set of events or states of affairs) causes some other event or state of affairs, then we have an instance of *transeunt* causation. And I shall say that when an *agent*, as distinguished from an event, causes an event or state of affairs, then we have an instance of *immanent* causation.

The nature of what is intended by the expression "immanent causation" may be illustrated by this sentence from Aristotle's *Physics:* "Thus, a staff moves a stone, and is moved by a hand, which is moved by a man." (VII, 5, 256a, 6–8) If the man was responsible, then we have in this illustration a number of instances of causation—most of them transeunt but at least one of them immanent. What the staff did to the stone was an instance of transeunt causation, and thus we may describe it as a relation between events: "the motion of the staff caused the motion of the stone." And similarly for what the hand did to the staff: "the motion of the hand caused the motion of the staff." And, as we know from physiology, there are still other events which caused the motion of the hand. Hence we need not introduce the agent at this particular point, as Aristotle does—we *need* not, though we *may*. We *may* say that the hand was moved by the man, but we may *also* say that the motion of the hand was caused by the motion of certain muscles; and we may say that the motion of the muscles was caused by certain events that took place within the brain. But some event, and presumably one of those that took place within the brain, was caused by the agent and not by any other events.

There are, of course, objections to this way of putting the matter, I shall consider the two that seem to me to be most important.

7. One may object, firstly: "If the *man* does anything, then, as Aristotle's remark suggests, what he does is to move the *hand*. But he certainly does not *do* anything to his brain—he may not even know that he *has* a brain. And if he doesn't do anything to the brain, and if the motion of the hand was caused by something that happened within the brain, then there is no point in appealing to 'immanent causation' as being something incompatible with 'transeunt causation'—for the whole thing, after all, is a matter of causal relations among events or states of affairs."

The answer to this objection, I think, is this: It is true that the agent does not *do* anything with his brain, or to his brain, in the sense in which he *does* something with his hand and does something to the staff. But from this it does not follow that the agent was not the immanent cause of something that happened within his brain.

We should note a useful distinction that has been proposed by Professor A. I. Melden*—namely, the distinction between "making something A happen" and "doing A."[5] If I reach for the staff and pick it up, then one of the things that I *do* is just that—reach for the staff and pick it up. And if it is something that I do, then there is a very clear sense in which it may be said to be something that I know that I do. If you ask me, "Are you doing something, or trying to do something, with the staff?" I will have no difficulty in finding an answer. But in doing something with the staff, I also make various things happen which are not in this same sense things that I do: I will make various air-particles move; I will free a number of blades of grass from the pressure that had been upon them; and I may cause a shadow to move from one place to another. If these are merely things that I make happen, as distinguished from things that I do, then I may know nothing whatever about them; I may not have the slightest idea that, in moving the staff, I am bringing about any such thing as the motion of air-particles, shadows, and blades of grass.

We may say, in answer to the first objection, therefore, that it is true that our agent does nothing to his brain or with his brain; but from this it does not follow that the agent is not the immanent cause of some event within his brain; for the brain event may be something which, like the motion of the air-particles, he made happen in picking up the staff. The only difference between the two cases is this: in each case, he made something happen when he picked up the staff; but in the one case—the motion of the air-particles or of the shadows—it was the motion of the staff that caused the event to happen; and in the other case—the event that took place in the brain—it was this event that caused the motion of the staff.

The point is, in a word, that whenever a man does something A, then (by "immanent causation") he makes a certain cerebral event happen, and this cerebral event (by "transeunt causation") makes A happen.

8. The second objection is more difficult and concerns the very concept of "immanent causation," or causation by an agent, as this concept is to be interpreted here. The concept is subject to a difficulty which has long been associated with that of the prime mover unmoved. We have said that there must be some event A, presumably some cerebral event, which is caused not by any other event, but by the agent. Since A was not caused by any other event, then the agent himself cannot be said to have undergone any change or produced any other event (such as "an act of will" or the like) which brought A about. But if, when the agent made A happen, there was no event involved other than A itself, no event which could be described as *making* A happen, what did the agent's causation consist of? What, for example, is the difference between A's just happening, and the agent's *causing* A to happen? We cannot attribute the difference to any event that took place within the agent. And so far as the event A itself is concerned, there would seem to be no discernible difference. Thus Aristotle said that the activity of the prime mover is nothing in addition to the motion that it produces, and Suarez* said that "the action is in reality nothing but the effect as it flows from the agent."[6] Must we conclude, then, that there is no more to the man's action in causing event A than there is to the event A's happening by itself? Here we would seem to have a distinction without a difference—in which case we have failed to find a *via media* between a deterministic and an indeterministic view of action.

The only answer, I think, can be this: that the difference between the man's causing A, on the one hand, and the event A just happening, on the other, lies in the fact that, in the first case but not the second, the event A *was* caused and was caused by the man. There was a brain event A; the agent did, in

* Canadian-born American philosopher Abraham I. Melden (1910–91) was well known for his work in moral philosophy.

* Spaniard Francisco Suárez (1548–1617) was an important Jesuit philosopher and theologian.

fact, cause the brain event; but there was nothing that he did to cause it.

This answer may not entirely satisfy and it will be likely to provoke the following question: "But what are you really *adding* to the assertion that A happened when you utter the words 'The agent *caused* A to happen'"? As soon as we have put the question this way, we see, I think, that whatever difficulty we may have encountered is one that may be traced to the concept of causation generally—whether "immanent" or "transeunt." The problem, in other words, is not a problem that is peculiar to our conception of human action. It is a problem that must be faced by anyone who makes use of the concept of causation at all; and therefore, I would say, it is a problem for everyone but the complete indeterminist.

For the problem, as we put it, referring just to "immanent causation," or causation by an agent, was this: "What is the difference between saying, of an event A, that A just happened and saying that someone caused A to happen?" The analogous problem, which holds for "transeunt causation," or causation by an event, is this: "What is the difference between saying, of two events A and B, that B happened and then A happened, and saying that B's happening was the *cause* of A's happening?" And the only answer that one can give is this—that in the one case the agent was the cause of A's happening and in the other case event B was the cause of A's happening. The nature of transeunt causation is no more clear than is that of immanent causation.

9. But we may plausibly say—and there is a respectable philosophical tradition to which we may appeal—that the notion of immanent causation, or causation by an agent, is in fact more clear than that of transeunt causation, or causation by an event, and that it is only by understanding our own causal efficacy, as agents, that we can grasp the concept of *cause* at all. Hume may be said to have shown that we do not derive the concept of *cause* from what we perceive of external things. How, then, do we derive it? The most plausible suggestion, it seems to me, is that of Reid, once again: namely that "the conception of an efficient cause may very probably be derived from the experience we have had . . . of our own power to produce certain effects."[7] If we did not understand the concept of immanent causation, we would not understand that of transeunt causation.

10. It may have been noted that I have avoided the term "free will" in all of this. For even if there is such a faculty as "the will," which somehow sets our acts agoing, the question of freedom, as John Locke said, is not the question "*whether the will be free*"; it is the question "*whether a man be free.*"[8] For if there is a "will," as a moving faculty, the question is whether the man is free to will to do these things that he does will to do—and also whether he is free *not* to will any of those things that he does will to do, and, again, whether he is free to will any of those things that he does not will to do. Jonathan Edwards tried to restrict himself to the question—"Is the man free to do what it is that he wills?"—but the answer to this question will not tell us whether the man is responsible for what it is that he *does* will to do. Using still another pair of medieval terms, we may say that the metaphysical problem of freedom does not concern the *actus imperatus*; it does not concern the question whether we are free to accomplish whatever it is that we will or set out to do; it concerns the *actus elicitus*, the question whether we are free to will or to set out to do those things that we do will or set out to do.

11. If we are responsible, and if what I have been trying to say is true, then we have a prerogative which some would attribute only to God: each of us, when we act, is a prime mover unmoved. In doing what we do, we cause certain events to happen, and nothing—or no one—causes us to cause those events to happen.

12. If we are thus prime movers unmoved and if our actions, or those for which we are responsible, are not causally determined, then they are not causally determined by our *desires*. And this means that the relation between what we want or what we desire, on the one hand, and what it is that we do, on the other, is not as simple as most philosophers would have it.

We may distinguish between what we might call the "Hobbist approach" and what we might call the "Kantian approach" to this question. The Hobbist approach is the one that is generally accepted at the present time, but the Kantian approach, I believe, is the one that is true. According to Hobbism, if we *know*, of some man, what his beliefs and desires happen to be and how strong they are, if we know what he feels certain of, what he desires more than anything else, and if we know the state of his body and what stimuli he is being subjected to, then we may *deduce*, logically, just what it is that he will do—or, more accurately, just what it is that he will try, set out, or undertake to do. Thus Professor Melden has said that "the connection between wanting and doing is logical."[9] But according to the Kantian approach to our problem, and this is the one that I would take, there is no such logical connection between wanting and doing, nor need there even be a causal connection. No set of statements about a man's desires, beliefs, and stimulus situation at any time implies any statement telling us what the man will try, set out, or undertake to do at that time. As Reid put it, though we may "reason from men's motives to their actions and, in many cases, with great probability," we can never do so "with absolute certainty."[10]

This means that, in one very strict sense of the terms, there can be no science of man. If we think of science as a matter of finding out what laws happen to hold, and if the statement of a law tells us what kinds of events are caused by what other kinds of events, then there will be human actions which we cannot explain by subsuming them under any laws. We cannot say, "It is causally necessary that, given such and such desires and beliefs, and being subject to such and such stimuli, the agent will do so and so." For at times the agent, if he chooses, may rise above his desires and do something else instead.

But all of this is consistent with saying that, perhaps more often than not, our desires do exist under conditions such that those conditions necessitate us to act. And we may also say, with Leibniz, that at other times our desires may "incline without necessitating."

13. Leibniz's phrase presents us with our final philosophical problem. What does it mean to say that a desire, or a motive, might "incline without necessitating"? There is a temptation, certainly, to say that "to incline" means to cause and that "not to necessitate" means not to cause, but obviously we cannot have it both ways.

Nor will Leibniz's own solution do. In his letter to Coste,* he puts the problem as follows: "When a choice is proposed, for example to go out or not to go out, it is a question whether, with all the circumstances, internal and external, motives, perceptions, dispositions, impressions, passions, inclinations taken together, I am still in a contingent state, or whether I am necessitated to make the choice, for example, to go out; that is to say, whether this proposition true and determined in fact, *In all these circumstances taken together I shall choose to go out*, is contingent or necessary."[11] Leibniz's answer might be put as follows: in one sense of the terms "necessary" and "contingent," the proposition "In all these circumstances taken together I shall choose to go out," may be said to be contingent and not necessary, and in another sense of these terms, it may be said to be necessary and not contingent. But the sense in which the proposition may be said to be contingent, according to Leibniz, is only this: there is no logical contradiction involved in denying the proposition. And the sense in which it may be said to be necessary is this: since "nothing ever occurs without cause or determining reason," the proposition is causally necessary. "Whenever all the circumstances taken together are such that the balance of deliberation is heavier on one side than on the other, it is certain and infallible that that is the side that is going to win out." But if what we have been saying is true, the proposition "In all these circumstances taken together I shall choose to go out," may be causally as well as logically contingent. Hence we must find another interpretation for Leibniz's statement that our motives and desires may incline us, or influence us, to choose without thereby necessitating us to choose.

Let us consider a public official who has some moral scruples but who also, as one says, could be had. Because of the scruples that he does have, he would never take any positive steps to receive a bribe—he would not actively solicit one. But his morality has its limits and he is also such that, if we were to confront him with a fait accompli or to let him see what is about to happen ($10,000 in cash is being deposited

* Pierre Coste (1668–1747) was a French writer and translator who corresponded with many of the leading philosophical figures of his era, including John Locke (1632–1704) and Gottfried Wilhelm Leibniz (1646–1716).

behind the garage), then he would succumb and be unable to resist. The general situation is a familiar one and this is one reason that people pray to be delivered from temptation. (It also justifies Kant's remark: "And how many there are who may have led a long blameless life, who are only *fortunate* in having escaped so many temptations."[12] Our relation to the misdeed that we contemplate may not be a matter simply of being able to bring it about or not to bring it about. As St. Anselm* noted, there are at least four possibilities. We may illustrate them by reference to our public official and the event which is his receiving the bribe, in the following way: (i) he may be able to bring the event about himself (*facere esse*), in which case he would actively cause himself to receive the bribe; (ii) he may be able to refrain from bringing it about himself (*non facere esse*), in which case he would not himself do anything to insure that he receive the bribe; (iii) he may be able to do something to prevent the event from occurring (*facere non esse*), in which case he would make sure that the $10,000 was *not* left behind the garage; or (iv) he may be unable to do anything to prevent the event from occurring (*non facere non esse*), in which case, though he may not solicit the bribe, he would allow himself to keep it.[13] We have envisaged our official as a man who can resist the temptation to (i) but cannot resist the temptation to (iv): he can refrain from bringing the event about himself, but he cannot bring himself to do anything to prevent it.

Let us think of "inclination without necessitation," then, in such terms as these. First we may contrast the two propositions:

(1) He can resist the temptation to do something in order to make A happen;
(2) He can resist the temptation to allow A to happen (i.e., to do nothing to prevent A from happening).

We may suppose that the man has some desire to have A happen and thus has a motive for making A happen. His motive for making A happen, I suggest, is one that *necessitates* provided that, because of the motive, (1) is false; he cannot resist the temptation to do something in order to make A happen. His motive for making A happen is one that *inclines* provided that, because of the motive, (2) is false; like our public official, he cannot bring himself to do anything to prevent A from happening. And therefore we can say that this motive for making A happen is one that *inclines but does not necessitate* provided that, because of the motive, (1) is true and (2) is false; he can resist the temptation to make it happen but he cannot resist the temptation to allow it to happen.

* Saint Anselm of Canterbury (1033/4–1109) was an important medieval philosopher and theologian; a selection from his writings appears in the Religion and Belief section.

NOTES

1. The general position to be presented here is suggested in the following writings, among others: Aristotle, *Eudemian Ethics*, bk. ii, ch. 6; *Nicomachean Ethics*, bk. iii, ch. 1–5; Thomas Reid, *Essays on the Active Powers of Man*; C. A. Campbell, "Is 'Free Will' a Pseudo-Problem?" *Mind*, 1951, 441–65; Roderick M. Chisholm, "Responsibility and Avoidability," and Richard Taylor, "Determination and the Theory of Agency," in *Determinism and Freedom in the Age of Modern Science* ed. Sidney Hook (New York, 1958).
2. Thomas Reid, *Essays on the Active Powers of Man*, essay iv, ch. 4 (*Works*, 600).
3. *Summa Theologica*, First Part of the Second Part, qu. vi ("On the Voluntary and Involuntary").
4. Jonathan Edwards, *Freedom of the Will* (New Haven, 1957); G. E. Moore, *Ethics* (Home University Library, 1912), ch. 6.
5. A. I. Melden, *Free Action* (London, 1961), especially ch. 3. Mr. Melden's own views, however, are quite the contrary of those that are proposed here.
6. Aristotle, *Physics*, bk. iii, ch. 3; Suarez, *Disputations Metaphysicae*, Disputation 18, s. 10.
7. Reid, *Works*, 524.
8. *Essay Concerning Human Understanding*, bk. ii, ch. 21.
9. Melden, 166.
10. Reid, *Works*, 608, 612.

11. "Lettre à Mr. Coste de la Nécessité et de la Contingence" (1707) in *Opera Philosophica*, ed. Erdmann, 447–9.
12. In the Preface to the *Metaphysical Elements of Ethics*, in *Kant's Critique of Practical Reason and Other Works on the Theory of Ethics*, ed. T. K. Abbott (London, 1959), 303.
13. Cf. D. P. Henry, "Saint Anselm's *De 'Grammatico'*," *Philosophical Quarterly*, x (1960), 115–26. St. Anselm noted that (i) and (iii), respectively, may be thought of as forming the upper left and the upper right corners of a square of opposition, and (ii) and (iv) the lower left and the lower right.

Freedom of the Will and the Concept of a Person

HARRY FRANKFURT

Harry Frankfurt (1929–) is an American philosopher known for his work in ethics, philosophy of mind, and the history of philosophy. He spent most of his career teaching at Yale and Princeton Universities. His 2005 book *On Bullshit* (a reissue of a 1986 paper with the same title) became a national best-seller, even earning him a spot on Jon Stewart's *The Daily Show*.

The selection that follows is excerpted from an article that was originally published in a philosophy journal in 1971. In it, Frankfurt articulates a view about what sort of freedom we are actually interested in when we ask whether free will and determinism are truly compatible.

What philosophers have lately come to accept as analysis of the concept of a person is not actually analysis of *that* concept at all. Strawson,* whose usage represents the current standard, identifies the concept of a person as "the concept of a type of entity such that *both* predicates ascribing states of consciousness *and* predicates ascribing corporeal characteristics . . . are equally applicable to a single individual of that single type."[1] But there are many entities besides persons that have both mental and physical properties. As it happens—though it seems extraordinary that this should be so—there is no common English word for the type of entity Strawson has in mind, a type that includes not only human beings but animals of various lesser species as well. Still, this hardly justifies the misappropriation of a valuable philosophical term.

Whether the members of some animal species are persons is surely not to be settled merely by determining whether it is correct to apply to them, in addition to predicates ascribing corporeal characteristics, predicates that ascribe states of consciousness. It does violence to our language to endorse the application of the term "person" to those numerous creatures which do have both psychological and material properties but which are manifestly not persons in any normal sense of the word. This misuse of language is doubtless innocent of any theoretical error. But although the offense is "merely verbal," it does significant harm. For it gratuitously diminishes our philosophical vocabulary, and it increases the likelihood that we will overlook the important area of inquiry with which the term "person" is most naturally associated. It might have been expected that no problem would be of more central and persistent concern to philosophers than that of understanding what we ourselves essentially are. Yet this problem

* A selection from Strawson's writings appears as the next entry in the volume.

From "Freedom of the Will and the Concept of a Person," *Journal of Philosophy* LXVIII, 1 (January 14, 1941).

is so generally neglected that it has been possible to make off with its very name almost without being noticed and, evidently, without evoking any widespread feeling of loss.

There is a sense in which the word "person" is merely the singular form of "people" and in which both terms connote no more than membership in a certain biological species. In those senses of the word which are of greater philosophical interest, however, the criteria for being a person do not serve primarily to distinguish the members of our own species from the members of other species. Rather, they are designed to capture those attributes which are the subject of our most humane concern with ourselves and the source of what we regard as most important and most problematical in our lives. Now these attributes would be of equal significance to us even if they were not in fact peculiar and common to the members of our own species. What interests us most in the human condition would not interest us less if it were also a feature of the condition of other creatures as well.

Our concept of ourselves as persons is not to be understood, therefore, as a concept of attributes that are necessarily species-specific. It is conceptually possible that members of novel or even of familiar nonhuman species should be persons; and it is also conceptually possible that some members of the human species are not persons. We do in fact assume, on the other hand, that no member of another species is a person. Accordingly, there is a presumption that what is essential to persons is a set of characteristics that we generally suppose—whether rightly or wrongly—to be uniquely human.

It is my view that one essential difference between persons and other creatures is to be found in the structure of a person's will. Human beings are not alone in having desires and motives, or in making choices. They share these things with the members of certain other species, some of whom even appear to engage in deliberation and to make decisions based upon prior thought. It seems to be peculiarly characteristic of humans, however, that they are able to form what I shall call "second-order desires" or "desires of the second order."

Besides wanting and choosing and being moved *to do* this or that, men may also want to have (or not to have) certain desires and motives. They are capable of wanting to be different, in their preferences and purposes, from what they are. Many animals appear to have the capacity for what I shall call "first-order desires" or "desires of the first order," which are simply desires to do or not to do one thing or another. No animal other than man, however, appears to have the capacity for reflective self-evaluation that is manifested in the formation of second-order desires.[2]

I

The concept designated by the verb "to want" is extraordinarily elusive. A statement of the form "*A* wants to *X*"—taken by itself, apart from a context that serves to amplify or to specify its meaning—conveys remarkably little information. Such a statement may be consistent, for example, with each of the following statements: (a) the prospect of doing *X* elicits no sensation or introspectible emotional response in *A*; (b) *A* is unaware that he wants to *X*; (c) *A* believes that he does not want to *X*; (d) *A* wants to refrain from *X*-ing; (e) *A* wants to *Y* and believes that it is impossible for him both to *Y* and to *X*; (f) *A* does not "really" want to *X*; (g) *A* would rather die than *X*; and so on. It is therefore hardly sufficient to formulate the distinction between first-order and second-order desires, as I have done, by suggesting merely that someone has a first-order desire when he wants to do or not to do such-and-such, and that he has a second-order desire when he wants to have or not to have a certain desire of the first order.

As I shall understand them, statements of the form "*A* wants to *X*" cover a rather broad range of possibilities.[3] They may be true even when statements like (a) through (g) are true: when *A* is unaware of any feelings concerning *X*-ing, when he is unaware that he wants to *X*, when he deceives himself about what he wants and believes falsely that he does not want to *X*, when he also has other desires that conflict with his desire to *X*, or when he is ambivalent. The desires in question may be conscious or unconscious, they need not be univocal, and *A* may be mistaken about them. There is a further source of uncertainty with regard to statements that identify someone's desires, however, and here it is important for my purposes to be less permissive.

Consider first those statements of the form "*A* wants to *X*" which identify first-order desires—that is, statements in which the term "to *X*" refers to an action. A statement of this kind does not, by itself, indicate the relative strength of *A*'s desire to *X*. It does not make it clear whether this desire is at all likely to play a decisive role in what *A* actually does or tries to do. For it may correctly be said that *A* wants to *X* even when his desire to *X* is only one among his desires and when it is far from being paramount among them. Thus, it may be true that *A* wants to *X* when he strongly prefers to do something else instead; and it may be true that he wants to *X* despite the fact that, when he acts, it is not the desire to *X* that motivates him to do what he does. On the other hand, someone who states that *A* wants to *X* may mean to convey that it is this desire that is motivating or moving *A* to do what he is actually doing or that *A* will in fact be moved by this desire (unless he changes his mind) when he acts.

It is only when it is used in the second of these ways that, given the special usage of "will" that I propose to adopt, the statement identifies *A*'s will. To identify an agent's will is either to identify the desire (or desires) by which he is motivated in some action he performs or to identify the desire (or desires) by which he will or would be motivated when or if he acts. An agent's will, then, is identical with one or more of his first-order desires. But the notion of the will, as I am employing it, is not coextensive with the notion of first-order desires. It is not the notion of something that merely inclines an agent in some degree to act in a certain way. Rather, it is the notion of an *effective* desire—one that moves (or will or would move) a person all the way to action. Thus the notion of the will is not coextensive with the notion of what an agent intends to do. For even though someone may have a settled intention to do *X*, he may nonetheless do something else instead of doing *X* because, despite his intention, his desire to do *X* proves to be weaker or less effective than some conflicting desire.

Now consider those statements of the form "*A* wants to *X*" which identify second-order desires—that is, statements in which the term "to *X*" refers to a desire of the first order. There are also two kinds of situation in which it may be true that *A* wants to want to *X*. In the first place, it might be true of *A* that he wants to have a desire to *X* despite the fact that he has a univocal desire, altogether free of conflict and ambivalence, to refrain from *X*-ing. Someone might want to have a certain desire, in other words, but univocally want that desire to be unsatisfied.

Suppose that a physician engaged in psychotherapy with narcotics addicts believes that his ability to help his patients would be enhanced if he understood better what it is like for them to desire the drug to which they are addicted. Suppose that he is led in this way to want to have a desire for the drug. If it is a genuine desire that he wants, then what he wants is not merely to feel the sensations that addicts characteristically feel when they are gripped by their desires for the drug. What the physician wants, insofar as he wants to have a desire, is to be inclined or moved to some extent to take the drug.

It is entirely possible, however, that, although he wants to be moved by a desire to take the drug, he does not want this desire to be effective. He may not want it to move him all the way to action. He need not be interested in finding out what it is like to take the drug. And insofar as he now wants only to *want* to take it, and not to *take* it, there is nothing in what he now wants that would be satisfied by the drug itself. He may now have, in fact, an altogether univocal desire *not* to take the drug; and he may prudently arrange to make it impossible for him to satisfy the desire he would have if his desire to want the drug should in time be satisfied.

It would thus be incorrect to infer, from the fact that the physician now wants to desire to take the drug, that he already does desire to take it. His second-order desire to be moved to take the drug does not entail that he has a first-order desire to take it. If the drug were now to be administered to him, this might satisfy no desire that is implicit in his desire to want to take it. While he wants to want to take the drug, he may have *no* desire to take it; it may be that *all* he wants is to taste the desire for it. That is, his desire to have a certain desire that he does not have may not be a desire that his will should be at all different than it is.

Someone who wants only in this truncated way to want to *X* stands at the margin of preciosity, and the fact that he wants to want to *X* is not pertinent to the identification of his will. There is, however, a second kind of situation that may be described by "*A* wants to want to *X*"; and when the statement is used to describe a situation of this second kind, then it does pertain to what *A* wants his will to be. In such cases the statement means that A wants the desire to *X* to be the desire that moves him effectively to act. It is not merely that he wants the desire to *X* to be among the desires by which, to one degree or another, he is moved or inclined to act. He wants this desire to be effective—that is, to provide the motive in what he actually does. Now when the statement that *A* wants to want to *X* is used in this way, it does entail that *A* already has a desire to *X*. It could not be true both that *A* wants the desire to *X* to move him into action and that he does not want to *X*. It is only if he does want to *X* that he can coherently want the desire to *X* not merely to be one of his desires but, more decisively, to be his will.[4]

Suppose a man wants to be motivated in what he does by the desire to concentrate on his work. It is necessarily true, if this supposition is correct, that he already wants to concentrate on his work. This desire is now among his desires. But the question of whether or not his second-order desire is fulfilled does not turn merely on whether the desire he wants is one of his desires. It turns on whether this desire is, as he wants it to be, his effective desire or will. If, when the chips are down, it is his desire to concentrate on his work that moves him to do what he does, then what he wants at that time is indeed (in the relevant sense) what he wants to want. If it is some other desire that actually moves him when he acts, on the other hand, then what he wants at that time is not (in the relevant sense) what he wants to want. This will be so despite the fact that the desire to concentrate on his work continues to be among his desires.

II

Someone has a desire of the second order either when he wants simply to have a certain desire or when he wants a certain desire to be his will. In situations of the latter kind, I shall call his second-order desires "second-order volitions" or "volitions of the second order." Now it is having second-order volitions, and not having second-order desires generally, that I regard as essential to being a person. It is logically possible, however unlikely, that there should be an agent with second-order desires but with no volitions of the second order. Such a creature, in my view, would not be a person. I shall use the term "wanton" to refer to agents who have first-order desires but who are not persons because, whether or not they have desires of the second order, they have no second-order volitions.[5]

The essential characteristic of a wanton is that he does not care about his will. His desires move him to do certain things, without its being true of him either that he wants to be moved by those desires or that he prefers to be moved by other desires. The class of wantons includes all nonhuman animals that have desires and all very young children. Perhaps it also includes some adult human beings as well. In any case, adult humans may be more or less wanton; they may act wantonly, in response to first-order desires concerning which they have no volitions of the second order, more or less frequently.

The fact that a wanton has no second-order volitions does not mean that each of his first-order desires is translated heedlessly and at once into action. He may have no opportunity to act in accordance with some of his desires. Moreover, the translation of his desires into action may be delayed or precluded either by conflicting desires of the first order or by the intervention of deliberation. For a wanton may possess and employ rational faculties of a high order. Nothing in the concept of a wanton implies that he cannot reason or that he cannot deliberate concerning how to do what he wants to do. What distinguishes the rational wanton from other rational agents is that he is not concerned with the desirability of his desires themselves. He ignores the question of what his will is to be. Not only does he pursue whatever course of action he is most strongly inclined to pursue, but he does not care which of his inclinations is the strongest.

Thus a rational creature, who reflects upon the suitability to his desires of one course of action or another, may nonetheless be a wanton. In maintaining that the essence of being a person lies not in reason but in will, I am far from suggesting that a creature without reason may be a person. For it is only in virtue of his rational capacities that a person is capable of becoming critically aware of his own will and of forming volitions of the second order. The structure of a person's will presupposes, accordingly, that he is a rational being.

The distinction between a person and a wanton may be illustrated by the difference between two narcotics addicts. Let us suppose that the physiological condition accounting for the addiction is the same in both men, and that both succumb inevitably to their periodic desires for the drug to which they are addicted. One of the addicts hates his addiction and always struggles desperately, although to no avail, against its thrust. He tries everything that he thinks might enable him to overcome his desires for the drug. But these desires are too powerful for him to withstand, and invariably, in the end, they conquer him. He is an unwilling addict, helplessly violated by his own desires.

The unwilling addict has conflicting first-order desires: he wants to take the drug, and he also wants to refrain from taking it. In addition to these first-order desires, however, he has a volition of the second order. He is not neutral with regard to the conflict between his desire to take the drug and his desire to refrain from taking it. It is the latter desire, and not the former, that he wants to constitute his will; it is the latter desire, rather than the former, that he wants to be effective and to provide the purpose that he will seek to realize in what he actually does.

The other addict is a wanton. His actions reflect the economy of his first-order desires, without his being concerned whether the desires that move him to act are desires by which he wants to be moved to act. If he encounters problems in obtaining the drug or in administering it to himself, his responses to his urges to take it may involve deliberation. But it never occurs to him to consider whether he wants the relations among his desires to result in his having the will he has. The wanton addict may be an animal, and thus incapable of being concerned about his will. In any event he is, in respect of his wanton lack of concern, no different from an animal.

The second of these addicts may suffer a first-order conflict similar to the first-order conflict suffered by the first. Whether he is human or not, the wanton may (perhaps due to conditioning) both want to take the drug and want to refrain from taking it. Unlike the unwilling addict, however, he does not prefer that one of his conflicting desires should be paramount over the other; he does not prefer that one first-order desire rather than the other should constitute his will. It would be misleading to say that he is neutral as to the conflict between his desires, since this would suggest that he regards them as equally acceptable. Since he has no identity apart from his first-order desires, it is true neither that he prefers one to the other nor that he prefers not to take sides.

It makes a difference to the unwilling addict, who is a person, which of his conflicting first-order desires wins out. Both desires are his, to be sure; and whether he finally takes the drug or finally succeeds in refraining from taking it, he acts to satisfy what is in a literal sense his own desire. In either case he does something he himself wants to do, and he does it not because of some external influence whose aim happens to coincide with his own but because of his desire to do it. The unwilling addict identifies himself, however, through the formation of a second-order volition, with one rather than with the other of his conflicting first-order desires. He makes one of them more truly his own and, in so doing, he withdraws himself from the other. It is in virtue of this identification and withdrawal, accomplished through the formation of a second-order volition, that the unwilling addict may meaningfully make the analytically puzzling statements that the force moving him to take the drug is a force other than his own, and that it is not of his own free will but rather against his will that this force moves him to take it.

The wanton addict cannot or does not care which of his conflicting first-order desires wins out. His lack of concern is not due to his inability to find a convincing basis for preference. It is due either to his lack of the capacity for reflection or to his mindless indifference to the enterprise of evaluating his own desires and motives.[6] There is only one issue in the struggle to which his first-order conflict may lead: whether the one or the other of his conflicting desires is the stronger. Since he is moved by both desires, he will not be altogether satisfied by what he does no matter which of them is effective. But it makes no difference *to him* whether his craving or his aversion gets the upper hand. He has no stake in the conflict between them and so, unlike the unwilling addict, he can neither win nor lose the struggle in which he is engaged. When a *person* acts, the desire by which he is moved is either the will he wants or a will he wants to be without. When a *wanton* acts, it is neither.

III

There is a very close relationship between the capacity for forming second-order volitions and another capacity that is essential to persons—one that has often been considered a distinguishing mark of the human condition. It is only because a person has volitions of the second order that he is capable both of enjoying and of lacking freedom of the will. The concept of a person is not only, then, the concept of a type of entity that has both first-order desires and volitions of the second order. It can also be construed as the concept of a type of entity for whom the freedom of its will may be a problem. This concept excludes all wantons, both infrahuman and human, since they fail to satisfy an essential condition for the enjoyment of freedom of the will. And it excludes those suprahuman beings, if any, whose wills are necessarily free.

Just what kind of freedom is the freedom of the will? This question calls for an identification of the special area of human experience to which the concept of freedom of the will, as distinct from the concepts of other sorts of freedom, is particularly germane. In dealing with it, my aim will be primarily to locate the problem with which a person is most immediately concerned when he is concerned with the freedom of his will.

According to one familiar philosophical tradition, being free is fundamentally a matter of doing what one wants to do. Now the notion of an agent who does what he wants to do is by no means an altogether clear one: both the doing and the wanting, and the appropriate relation between them as well, require elucidation. But although its focus needs to be sharpened and its formulation refined, I believe that this notion does capture at least part of what is implicit in the idea of an agent who *acts* freely. It misses entirely, however, the peculiar content of the quite different idea of an agent whose *will* is free.

We do not suppose that animals enjoy freedom of the will, although we recognize that an animal may be free to run in whatever direction it wants. Thus, having the freedom to do what one wants to do is not a sufficient condition of having a free will. It is not a necessary condition either. For to deprive someone of his freedom of action is not necessarily to undermine the freedom of his will. When an agent is aware that there are certain things he is not free to do, this doubtless affects his desires and limits the range of choices he can make. But suppose that someone, without being aware of it, has in fact lost or been deprived of his freedom of action. Even though he is no longer free to do what he wants to do, his will may remain as free as it was before. Despite the fact that he is not free to translate his desires into actions or to act according to the determinations of his will, he may still form those desires and make those determinations as freely as if his freedom of action had not been impaired.

When we ask whether a person's will is free we are not asking whether he is in a position to translate his first-order desires into actions. That is the question of whether he is free to do as he pleases. The question of the freedom of his will does not concern the relation between what he does and what he wants to do. Rather, it concerns his desires themselves. But what question about them is it?

It seems to me both natural and useful to construe the question of whether a person's will is free in close analogy to the question of whether an agent enjoys freedom of action. Now freedom of action is (roughly, at least) the freedom to do what one wants to do. Analogously, then, the statement that a person enjoys freedom of the will means (also roughly) that he is free to want what he wants to want. More precisely, it means that he is free to will what he wants to will, or to have the will he wants. Just as the question about the freedom of an agent's action has to do with whether it is the action he wants to perform, so the question about the freedom of his will has to do with whether it is the will he wants to have.

It is in securing the conformity of his will to his second-order volitions, then, that a person exercises freedom of the will. And it is in the discrepancy between his will and his second-order volitions, or in his awareness that their coincidence is not his own doing but only a happy chance, that a person who does not have this freedom feels its lack. The unwilling addict's will is not free. This is shown by the fact that it is not the will he wants. It is also true, though in a different way, that the will of the wanton addict is not free. The wanton addict neither has the will he wants nor has a will that differs from the will he wants. Since he has no volitions of the second order, the freedom of his will cannot be a problem for him. He lacks it, so to speak, by default.

People are generally far more complicated than my sketchy account of the structure of a person's will may suggest. There is as much opportunity for ambivalence, conflict, and self-deception with regard to desires of the second order, for example, as there is with regard to first-order desires. If there is an unresolved conflict among someone's second-order desires, then he is in danger of having no second-order volition; for unless this conflict is resolved, he has no preference concerning which of his first-order desires is to be his will. This condition, if it is so severe that it prevents him from identifying himself in a sufficiently decisive way with *any* of his conflicting first-order desires, destroys him as a person. For it either tends to paralyze his will and to keep him from acting at all, or it tends to remove him from his will so that his will operates without his participation. In both cases he becomes, like the unwilling addict though in a different way, a helpless bystander to the forces that move him.

Another complexity is that a person may have, especially if his second-order desires are in conflict, desires and volitions of a higher order than the second. There is no theoretical limit to the length of the series of desires of higher and higher orders; nothing except common sense and, perhaps, a saving fatigue prevents an individual from obsessively refusing to identify himself with any of his desires until he forms a desire of the next higher order. The tendency to generate such a series of acts of forming desires, which would be a case of humanization run wild, also leads toward the destruction of a person.

It is possible, however, to terminate such a series of acts without cutting it off arbitrarily. When a person identifies himself *decisively* with one of his first-order desires, this commitment "resounds" throughout the potentially endless array of higher orders. Consider a person who, without reservation or conflict, wants to be motivated by the desire to concentrate on his work. The fact that his second-order volition to be moved by this desire is a decisive one means that there is no room for questions concerning the pertinence of desires or volitions of higher orders. Suppose the person is asked whether he wants to want to want to concentrate on his work. He can properly insist that this question concerning a third-order desire does not arise. It would be a mistake to claim that, because he has not considered whether he wants the second-order volition he has formed, he is indifferent to the question of whether it is with this volition or with some other that he wants his will to accord. The decisiveness of the commitment he has made means that he has decided that no further question about his second-order volition, at any higher order, remains to be asked. It is relatively unimportant whether we explain this by saying that this commitment implicitly generates an endless series of confirming desires of higher orders, or by saying that the commitment is tantamount to a dissolution of the pointedness of all questions concerning higher orders of desire.

Examples such as the one concerning the unwilling addict may suggest that volitions of the second order, or of higher orders, must be formed deliberately and that a person characteristically struggles to ensure that they are satisfied. But the conformity of a person's will to his higher-order volitions may be far more thoughtless and spontaneous than this. Some people are naturally moved by kindness when they want to be kind, and by nastiness when they want to be nasty, without any explicit forethought and without any need for energetic self-control. Others are moved by nastiness when they want to be kind and by kindness when they intend to be nasty, equally without forethought and without active resistance to these violations of their higher-order desires. The enjoyment of freedom comes easily to some. Others must struggle to achieve it.

IV

My theory concerning the freedom of the will accounts easily for our disinclination to allow that this freedom is enjoyed by the members of any species inferior to our own. It also satisfies another condition that must be met by any such theory, by making it apparent why the freedom of the will should be regarded as desirable. The enjoyment of a free will means the satisfaction of certain desires—desires of the second or of higher orders—whereas its absence means their frustration. The satisfactions at stake are those which accrue to a person of whom it may be said that his will is his own. The corresponding frustrations are those suffered by a person of whom it may be said that he is estranged from himself, or that he finds himself a helpless or a passive bystander to the forces that move him.

A person who is free to do what he wants to do may yet not be in a position to have the will he wants. Suppose, however, that he enjoys both freedom of action and freedom of the will. Then he is not only free to do what he wants to do; he is also free to want what he wants to want. It seems to me that he has, in that case, all the freedom it is possible to desire or to conceive. There are other good things in life, and he may not possess some of them. But there is nothing in the way of freedom that he lacks.

It is far from clear that certain other theories of the freedom of the will meet these elementary but essential conditions: that it be understandable why we desire this freedom and why we refuse to ascribe it to animals. Consider, for example, Roderick Chisholm's* quaint version of the doctrine that human freedom entails an absence of causal determination.[7] Whenever a person performs a free action, according to Chisholm, it's a miracle. The motion of a person's hand, when the person moves it, is the outcome of a series of physical causes; but some event in this series, "and presumably one of those that took place within the brain, was caused by the agent and not by any other events" (18). A free agent has, therefore, "a prerogative which some would attribute only to God: each of us, when we act, is a prime mover unmoved" (23).

This account fails to provide any basis for doubting that animals of subhuman species enjoy the freedom it defines. Chisholm says nothing that makes it seem less likely that a rabbit performs a miracle when it moves its leg than that a man does so when he moves his hand. But why, in any case, should anyone *care* whether he can interrupt the natural order of causes in the way Chisholm describes? Chisholm offers no reason for believing that there is a discernible difference between the experience of a man who miraculously initiates a series of causes when he moves his hand and a man who moves his hand without any such breach of the normal causal sequence. There appears to be no concrete basis for preferring to be involved in the one state of affairs rather than in the other.[8]

It is generally supposed that, in addition to satisfying the two conditions I have mentioned, a satisfactory theory of the freedom of the will necessarily provides an analysis of one of the conditions of moral responsibility. The most common recent approach to the problem of understanding the freedom of the will has been, indeed, to inquire what is entailed by the assumption that someone is morally responsible for what he has done. In my view, however, the relation between moral responsibility and the freedom of the will has been very widely misunderstood. It is not true that a person is morally responsible for what he has done only if his will was free when he did it. He may be morally responsible for having done it even though his will was not free at all.

A person's will is free only if he is free to have the will he wants. This means that, with regard to any of his first-order desires, he is free either to make that desire his will or to make some other first-order desire his will instead. Whatever his will, then, the will of the person whose will is free could have been otherwise; he could have done otherwise than to constitute his will as he did. It is a vexed question just how "he could have done otherwise" is to be understood in contexts such as this one. But although this question is important to the theory of freedom, it has no bearing on the theory of moral responsibility. For the assumption that a person is morally responsible for what he has done does not entail that the person was in a position to have whatever will he wanted.

This assumption *does* entail that the person did what he did freely, or that he did it of his own free will. It is a mistake, however, to believe that someone acts freely only when he is free to do whatever

* A selection from Chisholm's writings appears as the previous entry in the volume.

he wants or that he acts of his own free will only if his will is free. Suppose that a person has done what he wanted to do, that he did it because he wanted to do it, and that the will by which he was moved when he did it was his will because it was the will he wanted. Then he did it freely and of his own free will. Even supposing that he could have done otherwise, he would not have done otherwise; and even supposing that he could have had a different will, he would not have wanted his will to differ from what it was. Moreover, since the will that moved him when he acted was his will because he wanted it to be, he cannot claim that his will was forced upon him or that he was a passive bystander to its constitution. Under these conditions, it is quite irrelevant to the evaluation of his moral responsibility to inquire whether the alternatives that he opted against were actually available to him.[9]

In illustration, consider a third kind of addict. Suppose that his addiction has the same physiological basis and the same irresistible thrust as the addictions of the unwilling and wanton addicts, but that he is altogether delighted with his condition. He is a willing addict, who would not have things any other way. If the grip of his addiction should somehow weaken, he would do whatever he could to reinstate it; if his desire for the drug should begin to fade, he would take steps to renew its intensity.

The willing addict's will is not free, for his desire to take the drug will be effective regardless of whether or not he wants this desire to constitute his will. But when he takes the drug, he takes it freely and of his own free will. I am inclined to understand his situation as involving the overdetermination of his first-order desire to take the drug. This desire is his effective desire because he is physiologically addicted. But it is his effective desire also because he wants it to be. His will is outside his control, but, by his second-order desire that his desire for the drug should be effective, he has made this will his own. Given that it is therefore not only because of his addiction that his desire for the drug is effective, he may be morally responsible for taking the drug.

My conception of the freedom of the will appears to be neutral with regard to the problem of determinism. It seems conceivable that it should be causally determined that a person is free to want what he wants to want. If this is conceivable, then it might be causally determined that a person enjoys a free will. There is no more than an innocuous appearance of paradox in the proposition that it is determined, ineluctably and by forces beyond their control, that certain people have free wills and that others do not. There is no incoherence in the proposition that some agency other than a person's own is responsible (even *morally* responsible) for the fact that he enjoys or fails to enjoy freedom of the will. It is possible that a person should be morally responsible for what he does of his own free will and that some other person should also be morally responsible for his having done it.[10]

On the other hand, it seems conceivable that it should come about by chance that a person is free to have the will he wants. If this is conceivable, then it might be a matter of chance that certain people enjoy freedom of the will and that certain others do not. Perhaps it is also conceivable, as a number of philosophers believe, for states of affairs to come about in a way other than by chance or as the outcome of a sequence of natural causes. If it is indeed conceivable for the relevant states of affairs to come about in some third way, then it is also possible that a person should in that third way come to enjoy the freedom of the will.

NOTES

1. P. F. Strawson, *Individuals* (London: Methuen, 1959), pp. 101–102. Ayer's usage of "person" is similar: "it is characteristic of persons in this sense that besides having various physical properties . . . they are also credited with various forms of consciousness" [A. J. Ayer, *The Concept of a Person* (New York: St. Martin's, 1963), p. 82]. What concerns Strawson and Ayer is the problem of understanding the relation between mind and body, rather than the quite different problem of understanding what it is to be a creature that not only has a mind and a body but is also a person.
2. For the sake of simplicity, I shall deal only with what someone wants or desires, neglecting related phenomena such as choices and decisions. I propose to use the verbs "to want" and "to desire" interchangeably, although they are by no means perfect synonyms. My motive in forsaking the

established nuances of these words arises from the fact that the verb "to want," which suits my purposes better so far as its meaning is concerned, does not lend itself so readily to the formation of nouns as does the verb "to desire." It is perhaps acceptable, albeit graceless, to speak in the plural of someone's "wants." But to speak in the singular of someone's "want" would be an abomination.

3. What I say in this paragraph applies not only to cases in which "to *X*" refers to a possible action or inaction. It also applies to cases in which "to *X*" refers to a first-order desire and in which the statement that "*A* wants to *X*" is therefore a shortened version of a statement— "*A* wants to want to *X*"—that identifies a desire of the second order.

4. It is not so clear that the entailment relation described here holds in certain kinds of cases, which I think may fairly be regarded as nonstandard, where the essential difference between the standard and the nonstandard cases lies in the kind of description by which the first-order desire in question is identified. Thus, suppose that *A* admires *B* so fulsomely that, even though he does not know what *B* wants to do, he wants to be effectively moved by whatever desire effectively moves *B*; without knowing what *B*'s will is, in other words, *A* wants his own will to be the same. It certainly does not follow that *A* already has, among his desires, a desire like the one that constitutes *B*'s will. I shall not pursue here the questions of whether there are genuine counterexamples to the claim made in the text or of how, if there are, that claim should be altered.

5. Creatures with second-order desires but no second-order volitions differ significantly from brute animals, and, for some purposes, it would be desirable to regard them as persons. My usage, which withholds the designation "person" from them, is thus somewhat arbitrary. I adopt it largely because it facilitates the formulation of some of the points I wish to make. Hereafter, whenever I consider statements of the form "*A* wants to want to *X*," I shall have in mind statements identifying second-order volitions and not statements identifying second-order desires that are not second-order volitions.

6. In speaking of the evaluation of his own desires and motives as being characteristic of a person, I do not mean to suggest that a person's second-order volitions necessarily manifest a *moral* stance on his part toward his first-order desires. It may not be from the point of view of morality that the person evaluates his first-order desires. Moreover, a person may be capricious and irresponsible in forming his second-order volitions and give no serious consideration to what is at stake. Second-order volitions express evaluations only in the sense that they are preferences. There is no essential restriction on the kind of basis, if any, upon which they are formed.

7. "Freedom and Action," in K. Lehrer, ed., *Freedom and Determinism* (New York: Random House, 1966), pp. 11–44.

8. I am not suggesting that the alleged difference between these two states of affairs is unverifiable. On the contrary, physiologists might well be able to show that Chisholm's conditions for a free action are not satisfied, by establishing that there is no relevant brain event for which a sufficient physical cause cannot be found.

9. For another discussion of the considerations that cast doubt on the principle that a person is morally responsible for what he has done only if he could have done otherwise, see my "Alternate Possibilities and Moral Responsibility," *The Journal of Philosophy* LXVI, 23 (December 4, 1969): 829–839.

10. There is a difference between being *fully* responsible and being *solely* responsible. Suppose that the willing addict has been made an addict by the deliberate and calculated work of another. Then it may be that both the addict and this other person are fully responsible for the addict's taking the drug, while neither of them is solely responsible for it. That there is a distinction between full moral responsibility and sole moral responsibility is apparent in the following example. A certain light can be turned on or off by flicking either of two switches, and each of these switches is simultaneously flicked to the "on" position by a different person, neither of whom is aware of the other. Neither person is solely responsible for the light's going on, nor do they share the responsibility in the sense that each is partially responsible; rather, each of them is fully responsible.

Freedom and Resentment

PETER STRAWSON

Peter Strawson (1919–2006) was a distinguished British philosopher who taught for many years at Oxford University. He is well known for his important contributions in metaphysics, epistemology, and the philosophy of language.

In the following selection, originally published in a philosophy journal in 1963, Strawson examines our actual practices of holding people responsible for their actions and contends that the truth or falsity of determinism is irrelevant to questions of moral responsibility.

Some philosophers say they do not know what the thesis of determinism is. Others say, or imply, that they do know what it is. Of these, some—the pessimists perhaps—hold that if the thesis is true, then the concepts of moral obligation and responsibility really have no application, and the practices of punishing and blaming, of expressing moral condemnation and approval, are really unjustified. Others—the optimists perhaps—hold that these concepts and practices in no way lose their raison d'être if the thesis of determinism is true. Some hold even that the justification of these concepts and practices requires the truth of the thesis. There is another opinion which is less frequently voiced: the opinion, it might be said, of the genuine moral sceptic. This is that the notions of moral guilt, of blame, of moral responsibility are inherently confused and that we can see this to be so if we consider the consequences either of the truth of determinism or of its falsity. The holders of this opinion agree with the pessimists that these notions lack application if determinism is true, and add simply that they also lack it if determinism is false. If I am asked which of these parties I belong to, I must say it is the first of all, the party of those who do not know what the thesis of determinism is. But this does not stop me from having some sympathy with the others, and a wish to reconcile them. Should not ignorance, rationally, inhibit such sympathies? Well, of course, though darkling, one has some inkling—some notion of what sort of thing is being talked about. This lecture is intended as a move towards reconciliation; so is likely to seem wrongheaded to everyone.

But can there be any possibility of reconciliation between such clearly opposed positions as those of pessimists and optimists about determinism? Well, there might be a formal withdrawal on one side in return for a substantial concession on the other. Thus, suppose the optimist's position were put like this: (1) the facts as we know them do not show determinism to be false; (2) the facts as we know them supply an adequate basis for the concepts and practices which the pessimist feels to be imperilled by the possibility of determinism's truth. Now it might be that the optimist is right in this, but is apt to give an inadequate account of the facts as we know them, and of how they constitute an adequate basis for the problematic concepts and practices; that the reasons he gives for the adequacy of the basis are themselves inadequate and leave out something vital. It might be that the pessimist is rightly anxious to get this vital thing back and, in the grip of his anxiety, feels he has to go beyond the facts as we know them; feels that the vital thing can be secure only if, beyond the facts as we know them, there is the further fact that determinism is false. Might *he* not be brought to make a formal withdrawal in return for a vital concession?

2. Let me enlarge very briefly on this, by way of preliminary only. Some optimists about determinism point to the efficacy of the practices of

From *Proceedings of the British Academy* Vol. XLVII. Copyright © 1962 by The British Academy. Reprinted by permission of the publisher.

punishment, and of moral condemnation and approval, in regulating behaviour in socially desirable ways.[1] In the fact of their efficacy, they suggest, is an adequate basis for these practices; and this fact certainly does not show determinism to be false. To this the pessimists reply, all in a rush, that *just* punishment and *moral* condemnation imply moral guilt and guilt implies moral responsibility and moral responsibility implies freedom and freedom implies the falsity of determinism. And to this the optimists are wont to reply in turn that it is true that these practices require freedom in a sense, and the existence of freedom in this sense is one of the facts as we know them. But what "freedom" means here is nothing but the absence of certain conditions the presence of which would make moral condemnation or punishment inappropriate. They have in mind conditions like compulsion by another, or innate incapacity, or insanity, or other less extreme forms of psychological disorder, or the existence of circumstances in which the making of any other choice would be morally inadmissible or would be too much to expect of any man. To this list they are constrained to add other factors which, without exactly being limitations of freedom, may also make moral condemnation or punishment inappropriate or mitigate their force: as some forms of ignorance, mistake, or accident. And the general reason why moral condemnation or punishment is inappropriate when these factors or conditions are present is held to be that the practices in question will be generally efficacious means of regulating behaviour in desirable ways only in cases where these factors are *not* present. Now the pessimist admits that the facts as we know them include the existence of freedom, the occurrence of cases of free action, in the negative sense which the optimist concedes; and admits, or rather insists, that the existence of freedom in this sense is compatible with the truth of determinism. Then what does the pessimist find missing? When he tries to answer this question, his language is apt to alternate between the very familiar and the very unfamiliar.[2] Thus he may say, familiarly enough, that the man who is the subject of justified punishment, blame or moral condemnation must really *deserve* it; and then add, perhaps, that in the case at least where he is blamed for a positive act rather than an omission, the condition of his really deserving blame is something that goes beyond the negative freedoms that the optimist concedes. It is, say, a genuinely free identification of the will with the act. And this is the condition that is incompatible with the truth of determinism.

The conventional, but conciliatory, optimist need not give up yet. He may say: Well, people often decide to do things, really intend to do what they do, know just what they're doing in doing it; the reasons they think they have for doing what they do, often really are their reasons and not their rationalizations. These facts, too, are included in the facts as we know them. If this is what you mean by freedom—by the identification of the will with the act—then freedom may again be conceded. But again the concession is compatible with the truth of the determinist thesis. For it would not follow from that thesis that nobody decides to do anything; that nobody ever does anything intentionally; that it is false that people sometimes know perfectly well what they are doing. I tried to define freedom negatively. You want to give it a more positive look. But it comes to the same thing. Nobody denies freedom in this sense, or these senses, and nobody claims that the existence of freedom in these senses shows determinism to be false.

But it is here that the lacuna in the optimistic story can be made to show. For the pessimist may be supposed to ask: But *why* does freedom in this sense justify blame, etc.? You turn towards me first the negative, and then the positive, faces of a freedom which nobody challenges. But the only reason you have given for the practices of moral condemnation and punishment in cases where this freedom is present is the efficacy of these practices in regulating behaviour in socially desirable ways. But this is not a sufficient basis, it is not even the right *sort* of basis, for these practices as we understand them.

Now my optimist, being the sort of man he is, is not likely to invoke an intuition of fittingness at this point. So he really has no more to say. And my pessimist, being the sort of man he is, has only one more thing to say; and that is that the admissibility of these practices, as we understand them, demands another kind of freedom, the kind that in turn demands the falsity of the thesis of determinism. But might we not induce the pessimist to give up saying this by giving the optimist something more to say?

3. I have mentioned punishing and moral condemnation and approval; and it is in connexion with these practices or attitudes that the issue between optimists and pessimists—or, if one is a pessimist, the issue between determinists and libertarians—is felt to be particularly important. But it is not of these practices and attitudes that I propose, at first, to speak. These practices or attitudes permit, where they do not imply, a certain detachment from the actions or agents which are their objects. I want to speak, at least at first, of something else: of the non-detached attitudes and reactions of people directly involved in transactions with each other; of the attitudes and reactions of offended parties and beneficiaries; of such things as gratitude, resentment, forgiveness, love, and hurt feelings. Perhaps something like the issue between optimists and pessimists arises in this neighbouring field too; and since this field is less crowded with disputants, the issue might here be easier to settle; and if it is settled here, then it might become easier to settle it in the disputant-crowded field.

What I have to say consists largely of commonplaces. So my language, like that of commonplaces generally, will be quite unscientific and imprecise. The central commonplace that I want to insist on is the very great importance that we attach to the attitudes and intentions towards us of other human beings, and the great extent to which our personal feelings and reactions depend upon, or involve, our beliefs about these attitudes and intentions. I can give no simple description of the field of phenomena at the centre of which stands this commonplace truth; for the field is too complex. Much imaginative literature is devoted to exploring its complexities; and we have a large vocabulary for the purpose. There are simplifying styles of handling it in a general way. Thus we may, like La Rochefoucauld, put self-love or self-esteem or vanity at the centre of the picture and point out how it may be caressed by the esteem, or wounded by the indifference or contempt, of others. We might speak, in another jargon, of the need for love, and the loss of security which results from its withdrawal; or, in another, of human self-respect and its connexion with the recognition of the individual's dignity. These simplifications are of use to me only if they help to emphasize how much we actually mind, how much it matters to us, whether the actions of other people—and particularly of *some* other people—reflect attitudes towards us of goodwill, affection, or esteem on the one hand or contempt, indifference, or malevolence on the other. If someone treads on my hand accidentally, while trying to help me, the pain may be no less acute than if he treads on it in contemptuous disregard of my existence or with a malevolent wish to injure me. But I shall generally feel in the second case a kind and degree of resentment that I shall not feel in the first. If someone's actions help me to some benefit I desire, then I am benefited in any case; but if he intended them so to benefit me because of his general goodwill towards me, I shall reasonably feel a gratitude which I should not feel at all if the benefit was an incidental consequence, unintended or even regretted by him, of some plan of action with a different aim.

These examples are of actions which confer benefits or inflict injuries over and above any conferred or inflicted by the mere manifestation of attitude and intention themselves. We should consider also in how much of our behaviour the benefit or injury resides mainly or entirely in the manifestation of attitude itself. So it is with good manners, and much of what we call kindness, on the one hand; with deliberate rudeness, studied indifference, or insult on the other.

Besides resentment and gratitude, I mentioned just now forgiveness. This is a rather unfashionable subject in moral philosophy at present; but to be forgiven is something we sometimes ask, and forgiving is something we sometimes say we do. To ask to be forgiven is in part to acknowledge that the attitude displayed in our actions was such as might properly be resented and in part to repudiate that attitude for the future (or at least for the immediate future); and to forgive is to accept the repudiation and to forswear the resentment.

We should think of the many different kinds of relationship which we can have with other people—as sharers of a common interest; as members of the same family; as colleagues; as friends; as lovers; as chance parties to an enormous range of transactions and encounters. Then we should think, in each of these connexions in turn, and in others, of the kind of importance we attach to the attitudes and intentions towards us of those who stand in these relationships to us, and of the kinds of *reactive* attitudes and feelings to which we ourselves are prone. In general, we demand some degree of goodwill or regard on the part of those who stand in these relationships to us, though the forms we require it to take vary widely in different connexions. The range and intensity of our *reactive* attitudes towards goodwill, its absence or its opposite vary no less widely. I have mentioned, specifically, resentment and gratitude; and they are a usefully opposed pair. But, of course, there is a whole continuum of reactive attitude and feeling stretching on both sides of these and—the most comfortable area—in between them.

The object of these commonplaces is to try to keep before our minds something it is easy to forget when we are engaged in philosophy, especially in our cool, contemporary style, viz. what it is actually like to be involved in ordinary inter-personal relationships, ranging from the most intimate to the most casual.

4. It is one thing to ask about the general causes of these reactive attitudes I have alluded to; it is another to ask about the variations to which they are subject, the particular conditions in which they do or do not seem natural or reasonable or appropriate; and it is a third thing to ask what it would be like, what it *is* like, not to suffer them. I am not much concerned with the first question; but I am with the second; and perhaps even more with the third.

Let us consider, then, occasions for resentment: situations in which one person is offended or injured by the action of another and in which—in the absence of special considerations—the offended person might naturally or normally be expected to feel resentment. Then let us consider what sorts of special considerations might be expected to modify or mollify this feeling or remove it altogether. It needs no saying now how multifarious these considerations are. But, for my purpose, I think they can be roughly divided into two kinds. To the first group belong all those which might give occasion for the employment of such expressions as "He didn't mean to," "He hadn't realized," "He didn't know"; and also all those which might give occasion for the use of the phrase "He couldn't help it," when this is supported by such phrases as "He was pushed," "He had to do it," "It was the only way," "They left him no alternative," etc. Obviously these various pleas, and the kinds of situations in which they would be appropriate, differ from each other in striking and important ways. But for my present purpose they have something still more important in common. None of them invites us to suspend towards the agent, either at the time of his action or in general, our ordinary reactive attitudes. They do not invite us to view the *agent* as one in respect of whom these attitudes are in any way inappropriate. They invite us to view the *injury* as one in respect of which a particular one of these attitudes is inappropriate. They do not invite us to see *agent* as other than a fully responsible agent. They invite us to see the *injury* as one for which he was not fully, or at all, responsible. They do not suggest that the agent is in any way an inappropriate object of that kind of demand for goodwill or regard which is reflected in our ordinary reactive attitudes. They suggest instead that the fact of injury was not in this case incompatible with that demand's being fulfilled, that the fact of injury was quite consistent with the agent's attitude and intentions being just what we demand they should be.[3] The agent was just ignorant of the injury he was causing, or had lost his balance through being pushed or had reluctantly to cause the injury for reasons which acceptably override his reluctance. The offering of such pleas by the agent and their acceptance by the sufferer is something in no way opposed to, or outside the context of, ordinary inter-personal relationships and the manifestation of ordinary reactive attitudes. Since things go wrong and situations are complicated, it is an essential and integral element in the transactions which are the life of these relationships.

The second group of considerations is very different. I shall take them in two subgroups of which the first is far less important than the second. In connexion with the first subgroup we may think of such statements as "He wasn't himself," "He has been under very great strain recently," "He was acting under posthypnotic suggestion"; in connexion with the second, we may think of "He's only a child," "He's a hopeless schizophrenic," "His mind has been systematically perverted," "That's purely compulsive behaviour on his part." Such pleas as these do, as pleas of my first general group do not, invite us to suspend our ordinary reactive attitudes towards the agent, either at the time of his action or all the time. They do not invite us to see the agent's action in a way consistent with the full retention of ordinary inter-personal attitudes and merely inconsistent with one particular attitude. They invite us to view the agent himself in a different light from the light in which we should normally view one who has acted as he has acted. I shall not linger over the first subgroup of cases. Though they perhaps raise, in the short term, questions akin to those raised, in the long term, by the second subgroup, we may dismiss them without considering those questions by taking that admirably suggestive phrase, "He wasn't himself," with the seriousness that—for all its being logically comic—it deserves. We shall not feel resentment against the man he is for the action done by the man he is not; or at least we shall feel less. We normally have to deal with him under normal stresses; so we shall not feel towards him, when he acts as he does under abnormal stresses, as we should have felt towards him had he acted as he did under normal stresses.

The second and more important subgroup of cases allows that the circumstances were normal, but presents the agent as psychologically abnormal—or as morally undeveloped. The agent was himself; but he is warped or deranged, neurotic or just a child. When we see someone in such a light as this, all our reactive attitudes tend to be profoundly modified. I must deal here in crude dichotomies and ignore the ever-interesting and ever-illuminating varieties of case. What I want to contrast is the attitude (or range of attitudes) of involvement or participation in a human relationship, on the one hand, and what might be called the objective attitude (or range of attitudes) to another human being, on the other. Even in the same situation, I must add, they are not altogether *exclusive* of each other; but they are, profoundly, *opposed* to each other. To adopt the objective attitude to another human being is to see him, perhaps, as an object of social policy; as a subject for what, in a wide range of sense, might be called treatment; as something certainly to be taken account, perhaps precautionary account, of; to be managed or handled or cured or trained; perhaps simply to be avoided, though *this* gerundive is not peculiar to cases of objectivity of attitude. The objective attitude may be emotionally toned in many ways, but not in all ways; it may include repulsion or fear, it may include pity or even love, though not all kinds of love. But it cannot include the range of reactive feelings and attitudes which belong to involvement or participation with others in inter-personal human relationships; it cannot include resentment, gratitude, forgiveness, anger, or the sort of love which two adults can sometimes be said to feel reciprocally, for each other. If your attitude towards someone is wholly objective, then though you may fight him, you cannot quarrel with him, and though you may talk to him, even negotiate with him, you cannot reason with him. You can at most pretend to quarrel, or to reason, with him.

Seeing someone, then, as warped or deranged or compulsive in behaviour or peculiarly unfortunate in his formative circumstances—seeing someone so tends, at least to some extent, to set him apart from normal participant reactive attitudes on the part of one who so sees him, tends to promote, at least in the civilized, objective attitudes. But there is something curious to add to this. The objective attitude is not only something we naturally tend to fall into in cases like these, where participant attitudes are partially or wholly inhibited by abnormalities or by immaturity. It is also something which is available as a resource in other cases too. We look with an objective eye on the compulsive behaviour of the neurotic or the tiresome behaviour of a very young child, thinking in terms of treatment or training. But we *can* sometimes look with something like the same eye on the behaviour of the normal and the mature. We *have* this resource and can sometimes use it: as a refuge, say, from the strains of involvement; or as an aid to policy; or simply out of intellectual curiosity. Being human, we cannot, in the normal case, do this for long, or altogether. If the strains of involvement, say, continue to be too great, then we have to do something else—like severing a relationship. But what is above all interesting is the tension there is, in us, between the participant attitude and the objective attitude. One is tempted to say: between our humanity and our intelligence. But to say this would be to distort both notions.

What I have called the participant reactive attitudes are essentially natural human reactions to the good or ill will or indifference of others towards us, as displayed in *their* attitudes and actions. The question we have to ask is: What effect would, or should, the acceptance of the truth of a general thesis of determinism have upon these reactive attitudes? More specifically, would, or should, the acceptance of the truth of the thesis lead to the decay or the repudiation of all such attitudes? Would, or should, it mean the end of gratitude, resentment, and forgiveness; of all reciprocated adult loves; of all the essentially *personal* antagonisms?

But how can I answer, or even pose, this question without knowing *exactly* what the thesis of determinism is? Well, there is one thing we do know: that if there is a coherent thesis of determinism, then there must be a sense of "determined" such that, if that thesis is true, then all behaviour whatever is determined in that sense. Remembering this, we can consider at least what possibilities lie formally open; and then perhaps we shall see that the question can be answered *without* knowing exactly what the thesis of determinism is. We can consider what possibilities lie open because we have already before us an account of the ways in which particular reactive attitudes, or reactive attitudes in general, may be, and, sometimes, we judge, should be, inhibited. Thus I considered earlier a group of considerations which tend to inhibit, and, we judge, should inhibit, resentment, in particular cases of an agent causing an injury, without inhibiting reactive attitudes in general towards that agent. Obviously this group of considerations cannot strictly bear upon our question; for that question concerns reactive attitudes in general. But resentment has a particular interest; so it is worth adding that it has never been claimed as a consequence of the truth of determinism that one or another of *these* considerations was operative in every case of an injury being caused by an agent; that it would follow from the truth of determinism that anyone who caused an injury *either* was quite simply ignorant of causing it *or* had acceptably overriding reasons for acquiescing reluctantly in causing it *or* . . ., etc. The prevalence of this happy state of affairs would not be a consequence of the reign of universal determinism, but of the reign of universal goodwill. We cannot, then, find here the possibility of an affirmative answer to our question, even for the particular case of resentment.

Next, I remarked that the participant attitude, and the personal reactive attitudes in general, tend to give place, and it is judged by the civilized should give place, to objective attitudes, just in so far as the agent is seen as excluded from ordinary adult human relationships by deep-rooted psychological abnormality—or simply by being a child. But it cannot be a consequence of any thesis which is not itself self-contradictory that abnormality is the universal condition.

Now this dismissal might seem altogether too facile; and so, in a sense, it is. But whatever is too quickly dismissed in this dismissal is allowed for in the only possible form of affirmative answer that remains. We can sometimes, and in part, I have remarked, look on the normal (those we rate as "normal") in the objective way in which we have learned to look on certain classified cases of abnormality. And our question reduces to this: could, or should, the acceptance of the determinist thesis lead us always to look on everyone exclusively in this way? For this is the only condition worth considering under which the acceptance of determinism could lead to the decay or repudiation of participant reactive attitudes.

It does not seem to be self-contradictory to suppose that this might happen. So I suppose we must say that it is not absolutely inconceivable that it should happen. But I am strongly inclined to think that it is, for us as we are, practically inconceivable. The human commitment to participation in ordinary inter-personal relationships is, I think, too thoroughgoing and deeply rooted for us to take seriously the thought that a general theoretical conviction might so change our world that, in it, there were no longer any such things as inter-personal relationships as we normally understand them; and being involved in inter-personal relationships as we normally understand them precisely is being exposed to the range of reactive attitudes and feelings that is in question.

This, then, is a part of the reply to our question. A sustained objectivity of inter-personal attitude, and the human isolation which that would entail, does not seem to be something of which human beings would be capable, even if some general truth were a theoretical ground for it. But this is not all. There is a further point, implicit in the foregoing, which must be made explicit. Exceptionally, I have said, we can have direct dealings with human beings without any degree of personal involvement, treating them simply as creatures to be handled in our own interest, or our side's, or society's—or even theirs. In the extreme case of the mentally deranged, it is easy to see the connexion between the possibility of a wholly objective attitude and the impossibility of what we understand by ordinary inter-personal relationships. Given this latter impossibility, no other civilized attitude is available than that of viewing the deranged person simply as something to be understood and controlled in the most desirable fashion. To view him as outside the reach of personal relationships is already, for the civilized, to view him in this way. For reasons of policy or self-protection we may have occasion, perhaps temporary, to adopt a fundamentally similar attitude to a "normal" human being; to concentrate, that is, on understanding "how he works," with a view to determining our policy accordingly, or to finding in that very understanding a relief from the strains of involvement. Now it is certainly true that in the case of the abnormal, though not in the case of the normal, our adoption of the objective attitude is a consequence of our viewing the agent as *incapacitated* in some or all respects for ordinary inter-personal relationships. He is thus incapacitated, perhaps, by the fact that his picture of reality is pure fantasy, that he does not, in a sense, live in the real world at all; or by the fact that his behaviour is, in part, an unrealistic acting out of unconscious purposes; or by the fact that he is an idiot, or a moral idiot. But there is something else which, *because* this is true, is equally certainly *not* true. And that is that there is a sense of "determined" such that (1) if determinism is true, all behaviour is determined in this sense, and (2) determinism might be true, i.e., it is not inconsistent with the facts as we know them to suppose that all behaviour might be determined in this sense, and (3) our adoption of the objective attitude towards the abnormal is the result of a prior embracing of the belief that the behaviour, or the relevant stretch of behaviour, of the human being in question *is* determined in this sense. Neither in the case of the normal, then, nor in the case of the abnormal is it true that, when we adopt an objective attitude, we do so *because* we hold such a belief. So my answer has two parts. The first is that we cannot, as we are, seriously envisage ourselves adopting a thoroughgoing objectivity of attitude to others as a result of theoretical conviction of the truth of determinism; and the second is that when we do in fact adopt such an attitude in a particular case, our doing so is not the consequence of a theoretical conviction which might be expressed as "Determinism in this case," but is a consequence of our abandoning, for different reasons in different cases, the ordinary inter-personal attitudes.

It might be said that all this leaves the real question unanswered, and that we cannot hope to answer it without knowing exactly what the thesis of determinism is. For the real question is not a question about what we actually do, or why we do it. It is not even a question about what we would *in fact* do if a certain theoretical conviction gained general acceptance. It is a question about what it would be *rational* to do if determinism were true, a question about the rational justification of ordinary inter-personal attitudes in general. To this I shall reply, first, that such a question could seem real only to one who had utterly failed to grasp the purport of the preceding answer, the fact of our natural human commitment to ordinary inter-personal attitudes. This commitment is part of the general framework of human life, not something that can come up for review as particular cases can come up for review within this general framework. And I shall reply, second, that if we could imagine what we cannot have, viz. a choice in this matter, then we could choose rationally only in the light of an assessment of the gains and losses to human life, its enrichment or impoverishment; and the truth or falsity of a general thesis of determinism would not bear on the rationality of *this* choice.[4]

5. The point of this discussion of the reactive attitudes in their relation—or lack of it—to the thesis of determinism was to bring us, if possible, nearer to a position of compromise in a more usual area of debate. We are not now to discuss reactive attitudes which are essentially those of offended parties or beneficiaries. We are to discuss reactive attitudes which are essentially not those, or only incidentally are those, of offended parties or beneficiaries, but are nevertheless, I shall claim, kindred attitudes to those I have discussed. I put resentment in the centre of the previous discussion. I shall put moral indignation—or, more weakly, moral disapprobation—in the centre of this one.

The reactive attitudes I have so far discussed are essentially reactions to the quality of others' wills towards us, as manifested in their behaviour: to their good or ill will or indifference or lack of concern. Thus resentment, or what I have called resentment, is a reaction to injury or indifference. The reactive attitudes I have now to discuss might be described as the sympathetic or vicarious or impersonal or disinterested or generalized analogues of the reactive attitudes I have already discussed. They are reactions to the qualities of others' wills, not towards ourselves, but towards others. Because of this impersonal or vicarious character, we give them different names. Thus one who experiences the vicarious analogue of resentment is said to be indignant or disapproving, or morally indignant or disapproving. What we have here is, as it were, resentment on behalf of another, where one's own interest and dignity are not involved; and it is this impersonal or vicarious character of the attitude, added to its others, which entitle it to the qualification "moral." Both my description of, and my name for, these attitudes are, in one important respect, a little misleading. It is not that these attitudes are essentially vicarious—one can feel indignation on one's own account—but that they are essentially capable of being vicarious. But I shall retain the name for the sake of its suggestiveness; and I hope that what is misleading about it will be corrected in what follows.

The personal reactive attitudes rest on, and reflect, an expectation of, and demand for, the manifestation of a certain degree of goodwill or regard on the part of other human beings towards ourselves; or at least on the expectation of, and demand for, an absence of the manifestation of active ill will or indifferent disregard. (What will, in particular cases, *count* as manifestations of good or ill will or disregard will vary in accordance with the particular relationship in which we stand to another human being.) The generalized or vicarious analogues of the personal reactive attitudes rest on, and reflect, exactly the same expectation or demand in a generalized form; they rest on, or reflect, that is, the demand for the manifestation of a reasonable degree of goodwill or regard, on the part of others, not simply towards oneself, but towards all those on whose behalf moral indignation may be felt, i.e., as we now think, towards all men. The generalized and non-generalized forms of demand, and the vicarious and personal reactive attitudes which rest upon, and reflect, them are connected not merely logically. They are connected humanly; and not merely with each other. They are connected also with yet another set of attitudes which I must mention now in order to complete the picture. I have considered from two points of view the demands we make on others and our reactions to their possibly injurious actions. These were the points of view of one whose interest was directly involved (who suffers, say, the injury) and of others whose interest was not directly involved (who do not themselves suffer the injury). Thus I have spoken of personal reactive attitudes in the first connexion and of their vicarious analogues in the second. But the picture is not complete unless we consider also the correlates of these attitudes on the part of those on whom the demands are made, on the part of the agents. Just as there are personal and vicarious reactive attitudes associated with demands on others for oneself and demands on others for others, so there are self-reactive attitudes associated with demands on oneself for others. And here we have to mention such phenomena as feeling bound or obliged (the "sense of obligation"); feeling compunction; feeling guilty or remorseful or at least responsible; and the more complicated phenomenon of shame.

All these three types of attitude are humanly connected. One who manifested the personal reactive attitudes in a high degree but showed no inclination at all to their vicarious analogues would appear as an abnormal case of moral egocentricity, as a kind of moral solipsist. Let him be supposed fully to acknowledge the claims to regard that others had on him, to be susceptible of the whole range of self-reactive attitudes. He would then see himself as unique both as one (*the* one) who had a general claim on human regard and as one (*the* one) on whom human beings in general had such a claim. This would be a kind of moral solipsism. But is barely more than a conceptual possibility; if it is that. In general, though within varying limits, we demand of others for others, as well as of ourselves for others, something of the regard which we demand of others for ourselves. Can we imagine, besides that of the moral solipsist, any other case of one or two of these three types of attitude being fully developed, but quite unaccompanied by any trace, however slight, of the remaining two or one? If we can, then we imagine something far below or far above the level of our common humanity—a moral idiot or a saint. For all these types of attitude alike have common roots in our human nature and our membership of human communities.

Now, as of the personal reactive attitudes, so of their vicarious analogues, we must ask in what ways, and by what considerations, they tend to be inhibited. Both types of attitude involve, or express, a certain sort of demand for inter-personal regard. The fact of injury constitutes a prima facie appearance of this demand's being flouted or unfulfilled. We saw, in the case of resentment, how one class of considerations may show this appearance to be mere appearance, and hence inhibit resentment, *without* inhibiting, or displacing, the sort of demand of which resentment can be an expression, without in any way tending to make us suspend our ordinary inter-personal attitudes to the agent. Considerations of this class operate in just the same way, for just the same reasons, in connexion with moral disapprobation or indignation; they inhibit indignation without in any way inhibiting the sort of demand on the agent of which indignation can be an expression, the range of attitudes towards him to which it belongs. But in this connexion we may express the facts with a new emphasis. We may say, stressing the moral, the generalized aspect of the demand: considerations of this group have no tendency to make us see the agent as other than a morally responsible agent; they simply make us see the injury as one for which he was not morally responsible. The offering and acceptance of such exculpatory pleas as are here in question in no way detracts in our eyes from the agent's status as a term of moral relationships. On the contrary, since things go wrong and situations are complicated, it is an essential part of the life of such relationships.

But suppose we see the agent in a different light: as one whose picture of the world is an insane delusion; or as one whose behaviour, or a part of whose behaviour, is unintelligible to us, perhaps even to him, in terms of conscious purposes, and intelligible only in terms of unconscious purposes; or even, perhaps, as one wholly impervious to the self-reactive attitudes I spoke of, wholly lacking, as we say, in moral sense. Seeing an agent in such a light as this tends, I said, to inhibit resentment in a wholly different way. It tends to inhibit resentment because it tends to inhibit ordinary inter-personal attitudes in general, and the kind of demand and expectation which those attitudes involve; and tends to promote instead the purely objective view of the agent as one posing problems simply of intellectual understanding, management, treatment, and control. Again the parallel holds for those generalized or moral attitudes towards the agent which we are now concerned with. The same abnormal light which shows the agent to us as one in respect of whom the personal attitudes, the personal demand, are to be suspended, shows him to us also as one in respect of whom the impersonal attitudes, the generalized demand, are to be suspended. Only, abstracting now from direct personal interest, we may express the facts with a new emphasis. We may say: to the extent to which the agent is seen in this light, he is not seen as one on whom demands and expectations lie in that particular way in which we think of them as lying when we speak of moral obligation; he is not, to that extent, seen as a morally responsible agent, as a term of moral relationships, as a member of the moral community.

I remarked also that the suspension of ordinary inter-personal attitudes and the cultivation of a purely objective view is sometimes possible even when we have no such reasons for it as I have just mentioned. Is this possible also in the case of the moral reactive attitudes? I think so; and perhaps it is easier. But the motives for a total suspension of moral reactive attitudes are fewer, and perhaps weaker: fewer, because only where there is antecedent personal involvement can there be the motive of seeking refuge from the strains of such involvement; perhaps weaker, because the tension between objectivity of view and the moral reactive attitudes is perhaps less than the tension between objectivity of view and the personal reactive attitudes, so that we can in the case of the moral reactive attitudes more easily secure the speculative or political gains of objectivity of view by a kind of setting on one side, rather than a total suspension, of those attitudes.

These last remarks are uncertain; but also, for the present purpose, unimportant. What concerns us now is to inquire, as previously in connexion with the personal reactive attitudes, what relevance any general thesis of determinism might have to their vicarious analogues. The answers once more are parallel; though I shall take them in a slightly different order. First, we must note, as before, that when the suspension of such an attitude or such attitudes occurs in a particular case, it is *never* the consequence of the belief that the piece of behaviour in question was determined in a sense such that all behaviour *might be*, and, if determinism is true, all behaviour *is*, determined in that sense. For it is not a consequence of any general thesis of determinism which might be true that nobody knows what he's doing or that everybody's behaviour is unintelligible in terms of conscious purposes or that everybody lives in a world of delusion or that nobody has a moral sense, i.e. is susceptible of self-reactive attitudes, &c. In fact no such sense of "determined" as would be required for a general thesis of determinism is ever relevant to our actual suspensions of moral reactive attitudes. Second, suppose it granted, as I have already argued, that we cannot take seriously the thought that theoretical conviction of such a general thesis would lead to the total decay of the personal reactive attitudes. Can we then take seriously the thought that such a conviction—a conviction, after all, that many have held or said they held—would nevertheless lead to the total decay or repudiation of the vicarious analogues of these attitudes? I think that the change in our social world which would leave us exposed to the personal reactive attitudes but not at all to their vicarious analogues, the generalization of abnormal egocentricity which this would entail, is perhaps even harder for us to envisage as a real possibility than the decay of both kinds of attitude together. Though there are some necessary and some contingent differences between the ways and cases in which these two kinds of attitudes operate or are inhibited in their operation, yet, as general human capacities or pronenesses, they stand or lapse together. Finally, to the further question whether it would not be *rational*, given a general theoretical conviction of the truth of determinism, so to change our world that in it all those attitudes were wholly suspended, I must answer, as before, that one who presses this question has wholly failed to grasp the import of the preceding answer, the nature of the human commitment that is here involved: it is *useless* to ask whether it would not be rational for us to do what it is not in our nature to (be able to) do. To this I must add, as before, that if there were, say, for a moment open to us the possibility of such a god-like choice, the rationality of making or refusing it would be determined by quite other considerations than the truth or falsity of the general theoretical doctrine in question. The latter would be simply irrelevant; and this becomes ironically clear when we remember that for those convinced that the truth of determinism nevertheless really would make the one choice rational, there has always been the insuperable difficulty of explaining in intelligible terms how its falsity would make the opposite choice rational.

I am aware that in presenting the argument as I have done, neglecting the ever-interesting varieties of case, I have presented nothing more than a schema, using sometimes a crude opposition of phrase where we have a great intricacy of phenomena. In particular the simple opposition of objective attitudes on the one hand and the various contrasted attitudes which I have opposed to them must seem as grossly crude as it is central. Let me pause to mitigate this crudity a little, and also to strengthen one of my central contentions, by mentioning some things which straddle these contrasted kinds of attitude. Thus parents and others concerned with the care and upbringing of young children cannot have to their charges either kind of attitude in a pure or unqualified form. They are dealing with creatures who are potentially and increasingly capable both of holding, and being objects of, the full range of human and moral attitudes, but are not yet truly capable of either. The treatment of such creatures must therefore represent a kind of compromise, constantly shifting in one direction, between objectivity of attitude and developed human attitudes. Rehearsals insensibly modulate towards true performances. The punishment of a child is both like and unlike the punishment of an adult. Suppose we try to relate this progressive emergence of the child as a responsible being, as an object of non-objective attitudes, to that sense of "determined" in which, if determinism is a possibly true thesis, all behaviour *may* be determined, and in which, if it is a true thesis, all behaviour *is* determined. What bearing *could* such a sense of "determined" have upon the progressive modification of attitudes towards the child? Would it not be grotesque to think of the development of the child as a progressive or patchy emergence from an area in which its behaviour is in this sense determined into an area in which it isn't? Whatever sense of "determined" is required for stating the thesis of determinism, it can scarcely be such as to allow of compromise, border-line-style answers to the question, "Is this bit of behaviour determined or isn't it?" But in this matter of young children, it is essentially a border-line, penumbral area that we move in. Again, consider—a very different matter—the strain in the attitude of a psychoanalyst to his patient. His objectivity of attitude, *his* suspension of ordinary moral reactive attitudes, is profoundly modified by the fact that the aim of the enterprise is to make such suspension unnecessary or less necessary. Here we may and do naturally speak of restoring the agent's freedom. But here the restoring of freedom means bringing it about that the agent's behaviour shall be intelligible in terms of conscious purposes rather than in terms only of unconscious purposes. *This* is the object of the enterprise; and it is in so far as *this* object is attained that the suspension, or half-suspension, of ordinary moral attitudes is deemed no longer necessary or appropriate. And in this we see once again the *irrelevance* of that concept of "being determined" which must be the central concept of determinism. For we cannot both agree that this object is attainable and that its attainment has this consequence and yet hold (1) that neurotic behaviour is determined in a sense in which, it may be, all behaviour is determined, and (2) that it is because neurotic behaviour is determined in this sense that objective attitudes are deemed appropriate to neurotic behaviour. Not, at least, without accusing ourselves of incoherence in our attitude to psychoanalytic treatment.

6. And now we can try to fill in the lacuna which the pessimist finds in the optimist's account of the concept of moral responsibility, and of the bases of moral condemnation and punishment; and to fill it in from the facts as we know them. For, as I have already remarked, when the pessimist himself seeks to fill it in, he rushes beyond the facts as we know them and proclaims that it cannot be filled in at all unless determinism is false.

Yet a partial sense of the facts as we know them is certainly present to the pessimist's mind. When his opponent, the optimist, undertakes to show that the truth of determinism would not shake the foundations of the concept of moral responsibility and of the practices of moral condemnation and punishment, he typically refers, in a more or less elaborated way, to the efficacy of these practices in regulating behaviour in socially desirable ways. These practices are represented solely as instruments of policy, as methods of individual treatment and social control. The pessimist recoils from this picture; and in his recoil there is, typically, an element of emotional shock. He is apt to say, among much else, that the humanity of the offender himself is offended by *this* picture of his condemnation and punishment.

The reasons for this recoil—the explanation of the sense of an emotional, as well as a conceptual, shock—we have already before us. The picture painted by the optimists is painted in a style appropriate to a situation envisaged as wholly dominated by objectivity of attitude. The only operative notions invoked in this picture are such as those of policy, treatment, control. But a thoroughgoing objectivity of attitude, excluding as it does the moral reactive attitudes, excludes at the same time essential elements in the concepts of *moral* condemnation and *moral* responsibility. This is the reason for the conceptual shock. The deeper emotional shock is a reaction, not simply to an inadequate conceptual analysis, but to the suggestion of a change in our world. I have remarked that it is possible to cultivate an exclusive objectivity of attitude in some cases, and for some reasons, where the object of the attitude is not set aside from developed inter-personal and moral attitudes by immaturity or abnormality. And the suggestion which seems to be contained in the optimist's account is that such an attitude should be universally adapted to all offenders. This is shocking enough in the pessimist's eyes. But, sharpened by shock, his eyes see further. It would be hard to make *this* division in our natures. If to all offenders, then to all mankind. Moreover, to whom could this recommendation be, in any real sense, addressed? Only to the powerful, the authorities. So abysses seem to open.[5]

But we will confine our attention to the case of the offenders. The concepts we are concerned with are those of responsibility and guilt, qualified as "moral," on the one hand—together with that of membership of a moral community; of demand, indignation, disapprobation and condemnation, qualified as "moral," on the other hand—together with that of punishment. Indignation, disapprobation, like resentment, tend to inhibit or at least to limit our goodwill towards the object of these attitudes, tend to promote an at least partial and temporary withdrawal of goodwill; they do so in proportion as they are strong; and their strength is in general proportioned to what is felt to be the magnitude of the injury and to the degree to which the agent's will is identified with, or indifferent to, it. (These, of course, are not contingent connexions.) But these attitudes of disapprobation and indignation are precisely the correlates of the moral demand in the case where the demand is felt to be disregarded. The making of the demand *is* the proneness to such attitudes. The holding of them does not, as the holding of objective attitudes does, involve as a part of itself viewing their object other than as a member of the moral community. The partial withdrawal of goodwill which *these* attitudes entail, the modification *they* entail of the general demand that another should, if possible, be spared suffering, is, rather, the consequence of *continuing* to view him as a member of the moral community; only as one who has offended against its demands. So the preparedness to acquiesce in that infliction of suffering on the offender which is an essential part of punishment is all of a piece with this whole range of attitudes of which I have been speaking. It is not only moral reactive attitudes towards the offender which are in question here. We must mention also the self-reactive attitudes of offenders themselves. Just as the other-reactive attitudes are associated with a readiness to acquiesce in the infliction of suffering on an offender, within the "institution" of punishment, so the self-reactive attitudes are associated with a readiness on the part of the offender to acquiesce in such infliction *without* developing the reactions (e.g. of resentment) which he would normally develop to the infliction of injury upon him; i.e., with a readiness, as we say, to accept punishment[6] as "his due" or as "just."

I am not in the least suggesting that these readinesses to acquiesce, either on the part of the offender himself or on the part of others, are always or commonly accompanied or preceded by indignant boilings or remorseful pangs; only that we have here a continuum of attitudes and feelings to which these readinesses to acquiesce themselves belong. Nor am I in the least suggesting that it belongs to this continuum of attitudes that we should be ready to acquiesce in the infliction of injury on offenders in a fashion which we saw to be quite indiscriminate or in accordance with procedures which we knew to be wholly useless. On the contrary, savage or civilized, we have some belief in the utility of practices of condemnation and punishment. But the social utility of these practices, on which the optimist lays such exclusive stress, is not what is now in question. What is in question is the pessimist's justified sense that to speak in terms of social utility alone is to leave out something vital in our conception of these practices. The vital thing can be restored by attending to that complicated web of attitudes and feelings which form an essential part of the moral life as we know it, and which are quite opposed to objectivity of attitude. Only by attending to this range of attitudes can we recover from the facts as we know them a sense of what we mean, i.e., of *all* we mean, when, speaking the language of morals, we speak of desert, responsibility, guilt, condemnation, and justice. But we *do* recover it from the facts as we know them. We do not have to go beyond them. Because the optimist neglects or misconstrues these attitudes, the pessimist rightly claims to find a lacuna in his account. We can fill the lacuna for him. But in return we must demand of the pessimist a surrender of his metaphysics.

Optimist and pessimist misconstrue the facts in very different styles. But in a profound sense there is something in common to their misunderstandings. Both seek, in different ways, to over-intellectualize the facts. Inside the general structure or web of human attitudes and feelings of which I have been speaking, there is endless room for modification, redirection, criticism, and justification. But questions of justification are internal to the structure or relate to modifications internal to it. The existence of the general framework of attitudes itself is something we are given with the fact of human society. As a whole, it neither calls for, nor permits, an external "rational" justification. Pessimist and optimist alike show themselves, in different ways, unable to accept this.[7] The optimist's style of over-intellectualizing the facts is that of a characteristically incomplete empiricism, a one-eyed utilitarianism. He seeks to find an adequate basis for certain social practices in calculated consequences, and loses sight (perhaps wishes to lose sight) of the human attitudes of which these practices are, in part, the expression. The pessimist does not lose sight of these attitudes, but is unable to accept the fact that it is just these attitudes themselves which fill the gap in the optimist's account. Because of this, he thinks the gap can be filled only if some general metaphysical proposition is repeatedly verified, verified in all cases where it is appropriate to attribute moral responsibility. This proposition he finds it as difficult to state coherently and with intelligible relevance as its determinist contradictory. Even when a formula has been found ("contra-casual freedom" or something of the kind) there still seems to remain a gap between its applicability in particular cases and its supposed moral consequences. Sometimes he plugs this gap with an intuition of fittingness—a pitiful intellectualist trinket for a philosopher to wear as a charm against the recognition of his own humanity.

Even the moral sceptic is not immune from his own form of the wish to over-intellectualize such notions as those of moral responsibility, guilt, and blame. He sees that the optimist's account is inadequate and the pessimist's libertarian alternative inane; and finds no resource except to declare that the notions in question are inherently confused, that "blame is metaphysical." But the metaphysics was in the eye of the metaphysician. It is a pity that talk of the moral sentiments has fallen out of favour. The phrase would be quite a good name for that network of human attitudes in acknowledging the character and place of which we find, I suggest, the only possibility of reconciling these disputants to each other and the facts.

There are, at present, factors which add, in a slightly paradoxical way, to the difficulty of making this acknowledgement. These human attitudes themselves, in their development and in the variety of their manifestations, have to an increasing extent become objects of study in the social and psychological sciences; and this growth of human self-consciousness, which we might expect to reduce the difficulty of acceptance, in fact increases it in several ways. One factor of comparatively minor importance is an increased historical and anthropological awareness of the great variety of forms which these human attitudes may take at different times and in different cultures. This makes one rightly chary of claiming as essential features of the concept of morality in general, forms of these attitudes which may have a local and temporary prominence. No doubt to some extent my own descriptions of human attitudes have reflected local and temporary features of our own culture. But an awareness of variety of forms should not prevent us from acknowledging also that in the absence of *any* forms of these attitudes it is doubtful whether we should have anything that *we* could find intelligible as a system of human relationships, as human society. A quite different factor of greater importance is that psychological studies have made us rightly mistrustful of many particular manifestations of the attitudes I have spoken of. They are a prime realm of self-deception, of the ambiguous and the shady, of guilt-transference, unconscious sadism and the rest. But it is an exaggerated horror, itself suspect, which would make us unable to acknowledge the facts because of the seamy side of the facts. Finally, perhaps the most important factor of all is the prestige of these theoretical studies themselves. That prestige is great and is apt to make us forget that in philosophy, though it also is a theoretical study, we have to take account of the facts in *all* their bearings; we are not to suppose that we are required, or permitted, as philosophers, to regard ourselves, as human beings, as detached from the attitudes which, as scientists, we study with detachment. This is in no way to deny the possibility and desirability of redirection and modification of our human attitudes in the light of these studies. But we may reasonably think it unlikely that our progressively greater understanding of certain aspects of ourselves will lead to the total disappearance of those aspects. Perhaps it is not inconceivable that it should; and perhaps, then, the dreams of some philosophers will be realized.

If we sufficiently, that is *radically*, modify the view of the optimist, his view is the right one. It is far from wrong to emphasize the efficacy of all those practices which express or manifest our moral attitudes, in regulating behaviour in ways considered desirable; or to add that when certain of our beliefs about the efficacy of some of these practices turn out to be false, then we may have good reason for dropping or modifying those practices. What *is* wrong is to forget that these practices, and their reception, the reactions to them, really *are* expressions of our moral attitudes and not merely devices we calculatingly employ for regulative purposes. Our practices do not merely exploit our natures, they express them. Indeed the very understanding of the kind of efficacy these expressions of our attitudes have turns on our remembering this. When we do remember this, and modify the optimist's position accordingly, we simultaneously correct its conceptual deficiencies and ward off the dangers it seems to entail, without recourse to the obscure and panicky metaphysics of libertarianism.

NOTES

1. Cf. P. H. Nowell-Smith, "Freewill and Moral Responsibility," *Mind*, 1948.
2. As Nowell-Smith pointed out in a later article: "Determinists and Libertarians," *Mind*, 1954.
3. Perhaps not in every case *just* what we demand they should be, but in any case *not* just what we demand they should not be. For my present purpose these differences do not matter.
4. The question, then, of the connexion between rationality and the adoption of the objective attitude to others is misposed when it is made to seem dependent on the issue of determinism. But there is another question which should be raised, if only to distinguish it from the misposed question. Quite apart from the issue of determinism, might it not be said that we should be nearer to being purely rational creatures in proportion as our relation to others was in fact dominated by the objective attitude? I think this might be said; only it would have to be added, once more, that if such a choice were possible, it would not necessarily be rational to choose to be more purely rational than we are.
5. Peered into by Mr. J. D. Mabbott, in his article "Freewill and Punishment," published in *Contemporary British Philosophy*, 3rd ser., 1956.
6. Of course not *any* punishment for *anything* deemed an offense.
7. Compare the question of the justification of induction. The human commitment to inductive belief-formation is original, natural, non-rational (not *irrational*), in no way something we choose or could give up. Yet rational criticism and reflection can refine standards and their application, supply "rules for judging of cause and effect." Ever since the facts were made clear by Hume, people have been resisting acceptance of them.

G IDENTITY AND PERSONAL IDENTITY

"Of Identity and Diversity"

from *An Essay Concerning Human Understanding*

JOHN LOCKE

British philosopher John Locke (1632–1704) was among the most important philosophers of the early modern period, making enduring contributions to epistemology, metaphysics and political philosophy.

The selection presented next is drawn from the chapter "Of Identity and Diversity," which is Chapter 27 of Book Two of Locke's most famous and important work, *An Essay Concerning Human Understanding* (1689). Spelling and punctuation reflect the original seventeenth-century English. The italicized subtitles appear in the original work, as do the numbers assigned to paragraphs; both enable easy coordination among readers who make use of different editions of the text. Omissions from the original text are marked with ellipses; the full text is in the public domain and can easily be found on-line. A modernized version of this text—along with modernized versions of selections from Descartes, Berkeley, Hobbes, Hume, Kant and Mill—can be found at Jonathan Bennett's *early modern texts* website at http://www.earlymoderntexts.com.

In this selection, Locke discusses some general questions about the nature of identity over time, and raises some puzzles about personal identity which have exercised philosophers to the present day, including the famous story of the prince and the cobbler, presented in section 15.

1. *Wherein identity consists*. Another occasion the mind often takes of comparing, is the very being of things, when, considering anything as existing at any determined time and place, we compare it with itself existing at another time, and thereon form the ideas of identity and diversity. When we see anything to be in any place in any instant of time, we are sure (be it what it will) that it is that very thing, and not another which at that same time exists in another place, how like and undistinguishable soever it may be in all other respects: and in this consists identity, when the ideas it is attributed to vary not at all from what they were that moment wherein we consider their former existence, and to which we compare the present. For we never finding, nor conceiving it possible, that two things of the same kind should exist in the same place at the same time, we rightly conclude, that, whatever exists anywhere at any time, excludes all of the same kind, and is there itself alone. When therefore we demand whether anything be the same or no, it refers always to something that existed such a time in such a place, which it was certain, at that instant, was the same with itself, and no other. From whence it follows, that one thing cannot have two beginnings of existence, nor two things one beginning; it being impossible for two things of the same kind to be or exist in the same instant, in the very same place; or one and the same thing in different places. That, therefore, that had one beginning, is the same thing; and that which had a different beginning in time and place from that, is not the same, but diverse. That which has made the difficulty about this relation has been the little care and attention used in having precise notions of the things to which it is attributed.

2. *Identity of substances.* We have the ideas but of three sorts of substances: 1. God. 2. Finite intelligences. 3. Bodies. First, God is without beginning, eternal, unalterable, and everywhere, and therefore concerning his identity there can be no doubt. Secondly, Finite spirits having had each its determinate time and place of beginning to exist, the relation to that time and place will always determine to each of them its identity, as long as it exists. Thirdly, The same will hold of every particle of matter, to which no addition or subtraction of matter being made, it is the same. For, though these three sorts of substances, as we term them, do not exclude one another out of the same place, yet we cannot conceive but that they must necessarily each of them exclude any of the same kind out of the same place: or else the notions and names of identity and diversity would be in vain, and there could be no such distinctions of substances, or anything else one from another. [. . .]

Identity of modes and relations. All other things being but modes or relations ultimately terminated in substances, the identity and diversity of each particular existence of them too will be by the same way determined: only as to things whose existence is in succession, such as are the actions of finite beings, v.g.* motion and thought, both which consist in a continued train of succession, concerning their diversity there can be no question: because each perishing the moment it begins, they cannot exist in different times, or in different places, as permanent beings can at different times exist in distant places; and therefore no motion or thought, considered as at different times, can be the same, each part thereof having a different beginning of existence.

3. *Principium Individuationis.** From what has been said, it is easy to discover what is so much inquired after, the *principium individuationis*; and that, it is plain, is existence itself; which determines a being of any sort to a particular time and place, incommunicable to two beings of the same kind. This, though it seems easier to conceive in simple substances or modes; yet, when reflected on, is not more difficult in compound ones, if care be taken to what it is applied: v.g. let us suppose an atom, i.e. a continued body under one immutable superficies,† existing in a determined time and place; it is evident, that, considered in any instant of its existence, it is in that instant the same with itself. For, being at that instant what it is, and nothing else, it is the same, and so must continue as long as its existence is continued; for so long it will be the same, and no other. In like manner, if two or more atoms be joined together into the same mass, every one of those atoms will be the same, by the foregoing rule: and whilst they exist united together, the mass, consisting of the same atoms, must be the same mass, or the same body, let the parts be ever so differently jumbled. But if one of these atoms be taken away, or one new one added, it is no longer the same mass or the same body. In the state of living creatures, their identity depends not on a mass of the same particles, but on something else. For in them the variation of great parcels of matter alters not the identity: an oak growing from a plant to a great tree, and then lopped, is still the same oak; and a colt grown up to a horse, sometimes fat, sometimes lean, is all the while the same horse: though, in both these cases, there may be a manifest change of the parts; so that truly they are not either of them the same masses of matter, though they be truly one of them the same oak, and the other the same horse. The reason whereof is, that, in these two cases—a mass of matter and a living body—identity is not applied to the same thing.

4. *Identity of vegetables.* We must therefore consider wherein an oak differs from a mass of matter, and that seems to me to be in this, that the one is only the cohesion of particles of matter any how united,

* Throughout the selection, Locke uses v.g. to mean *for example* (from the Latin *verbi gratia*).

* Principle of individuation.

† Unchangeable appearance.

the other such a disposition of them as constitutes the parts of an oak; and such an organization of those parts as is fit to receive and distribute nourishment, so as to continue and frame the wood, bark, and leaves, &c., of an oak, in which consists the vegetable life. That being then one plant which has such an organization of parts in one coherent body, partaking of one common life, it continues to be the same plant as long as it partakes of the same life, though that life be communicated to new particles of matter vitally united to the living plant, in a like continued organization conformable to that sort of plants. For this organization, being at any one instant in any one collection of matter, is in that particular concrete distinguished from all other, and is that individual life, which existing constantly from that moment both forwards and backwards, in the same continuity of insensibly succeeding parts united to the living body of the plant, it has that identity which makes the same plant, and all the parts of it, parts of the same plant, during all the time that they exist united in that continued organization, which is fit to convey that common life to all the parts so united.

5. *Identity of animals*. The case is not so much different in brutes but that any one may hence see what makes an animal and continues it the same. Something we have like this in machines, and may serve to illustrate it. For example, what is a watch? It is plain it is nothing but a fit organization or construction of parts to a certain end, which, when a sufficient force is added to it, it is capable to attain. If we would suppose this machine one continued body, all whose organized parts were repaired, increased, or diminished by a constant addition or separation of insensible parts, with one common life, we should have something very much like the body of an animal; with this difference, That, in an animal the fitness of the organization, and the motion wherein life consists, begin together, the motion coming from within; but in machines the force coming sensibly from without, is often away when the organ is in order, and well fitted to receive it.

6. *Identity of man*. This also shows wherein the identity of the same man consists; viz. in nothing but a participation of the same continued life, by constantly fleeting particles of matter, in succession vitally united to the same organized body. He that shall place the identity of man in anything else, but, like that of other animals, in one fitly organized body, taken in any one instant, and from thence continued, under one organization of life, in several successively fleeting particles of matter united to it, will find it hard to make an embryo, one of years, mad and sober, the same man, by any supposition, that will not make it possible for Seth, Ismael, Socrates, Pilate, St. Austin, and Caesar Borgia,* to be the same man. For if the identity of soul alone makes the same man; and there be nothing in the nature of matter why the same individual spirit may not be united to different bodies, it will be possible that those men, living in distant ages, and of different tempers, may have been the same man: which way of speaking must be from a very strange use of the word man, applied to an idea out of which body and shape are excluded. And that way of speaking would agree yet worse with the notions of those philosophers who allow of transmigration, and are of opinion that the souls of men may, for their miscarriages, be detruded into the bodies of beasts, as fit habitations, with organs suited to the satisfaction of their brutal inclinations. But yet I think nobody, could he be sure that the soul of Heliogabalus were in one of his hogs, would yet say that hog were a man or Heliogabalus.

7. *Identity suited to the idea*. It is not therefore unity of substance that comprehends all sorts of identity, or will determine it in every case; but to conceive and judge of it aright, we must consider what idea the word it is applied to stands for: it being one thing to be the same substance, another the same man, and a third the same person, if person, man, and substance, are three names standing for three different ideas; for such as is the idea belonging to that name, such must be the identity; which, if it had been a little more carefully attended to, would possibly have prevented a great deal of that confusion which often occurs about this matter, with no small seeming difficulties, especially concerning personal identity, which therefore we shall in the next place a little consider.

* Throughout the selection, Locke refers to a number of historical and literary figures. Details about their lives are irrelevant to his line of thought, except where noted.

8. *Same man.* An animal is a living organized body; and consequently the same animal, as we have observed, is the same continued life communicated to different particles of matter, as they happen successively to be united to that organized living body. And whatever is talked of other definitions, ingenious observation puts it past doubt, that the idea in our minds, of which the sound man in our mouths is the sign, is nothing else but of an animal of such a certain form. Since I think I may be confident, that, whoever should see a creature of his own shape or make, though it had no more reason all its life than a cat or a parrot, would call him still a man; or whoever should hear a cat or a parrot discourse, reason, and philosophize, would call or think it nothing but a cat or a parrot; and say, the one was a dull irrational man, and the other a very intelligent rational parrot. [. . .] For I presume it is not the idea of a thinking or rational being alone that makes the idea of a man in most people's sense: but of a body, so and so shaped, joined to it: and if that be the idea of a man, the same successive body not shifted all at once, must, as well as the same immaterial spirit, go to the making of the same man.

9. *Personal identity.* This being premised, to find wherein personal identity consists, we must consider what person stands for; which, I think, is a thinking intelligent being, that has reason and reflection, and can consider itself as itself, the same thinking thing, in different times and places; which it does only by that consciousness which is inseparable from thinking, and, as it seems to me, essential to it: it being impossible for any one to perceive without perceiving that he does perceive. When we see, hear, smell, taste, feel, meditate, or will anything, we know that we do so. Thus it is always as to our present sensations and perceptions: and by this every one is to himself that which he calls self: it not being considered, in this case, whether the same self be continued in the same or divers substances. For, since consciousness always accompanies thinking, and it is that which makes every one to be what he calls self, and thereby distinguishes himself from all other thinking things, in this alone consists personal identity, i.e. the sameness of a rational being: and as far as this consciousness can be extended backwards to any past action or thought, so far reaches the identity of that person; it is the same self now it was then; and it is by the same self with this present one that now reflects on it, that that action was done.

10. *Consciousness makes personal identity.* But it is further inquired, whether it be the same identical substance. This few would think they had reason to doubt of, if these perceptions, with their consciousness, always remained present in the mind, whereby the same thinking thing would be always consciously present, and, as would be thought, evidently the same to itself. But that which seems to make the difficulty is this, that this consciousness being interrupted always by forgetfulness, there being no moment of our lives wherein we have the whole train of all our past actions before our eyes in one view, but even the best memories losing the sight of one part whilst they are viewing another; and we sometimes, and that the greatest part of our lives, not reflecting on our past selves, being intent on our present thoughts, and in sound sleep having no thoughts at all, or at least none with that consciousness which remarks our waking thoughts, I say, in all these cases, our consciousness being interrupted, and we losing the sight of our past selves, doubts are raised whether we are the same thinking thing, i.e. the same substance or no. Which, however reasonable or unreasonable, concerns not personal identity at all. The question being what makes the same person; and not whether it be the same identical substance, which always thinks in the same person, which, in this case, matters not at all: different substances, by the same consciousness (where they do partake in it) being united into one person, as well as different bodies by the same life are united into one animal, whose identity is preserved in that change of substances by the unity of one continued life. For, it being the same consciousness that makes a man be himself to himself, personal identity depends on that only, whether it be annexed solely to one individual substance, or can be continued in a succession of several substances. For as far as any intelligent being can repeat the idea of any past action with the same consciousness it had of it at first, and with the same consciousness it has of any present action; so far it is the same personal self. For it is by the consciousness it has of its present thoughts and actions, that it is self to itself now, and so will be the same self, as far as the same consciousness can extend to actions past or to come and would be by distance of time, or change of substance, no more two persons, than a man be two men by wearing other clothes to-day than he did yesterday, with a long or a short sleep between: the same consciousness uniting those distant actions into the same person, whatever substances contributed to their production.

11. *Personal identity in change of substances.* That this is so, we have some kind of evidence in our very bodies, all whose particles, whilst vitally united to this same thinking conscious self, so that we feel when they are touched, and are affected by, and conscious of good or harm that happens to them, as a part of ourselves; i.e. of our thinking conscious self. Thus, the limbs of his body are to every one a part of Himself; he sympathizes and is concerned for them. Cut off a hand, and thereby separate it from that consciousness he had of its heat, cold, and other affections, and it is then no longer a part of that which is himself, any more than the remotest part of matter. Thus, we see the substance whereof personal self consisted at one time may be varied at another, without the change of personal identity; there being no question about the same person, though the limbs which but now were a part of it, be cut off.

12. *Whether in the change of thinking substances.* But the question is whether, if the same substance which thinks be changed, it can be the same person; or, remaining the same, it can be different persons?

And to this I answer: First, This can be no question at all to those who place thought in a purely material animal constitution, void of an immaterial substance. For, whether their supposition be true or no, it is plain they conceive personal identity preserved in something else than identity of substance; as animal identity is preserved in identity of life, and not of substance. And therefore those who place thinking in an immaterial substance only, before they can come to deal with these men, must show why personal identity cannot be preserved in the change of immaterial substances, or variety of particular immaterial substances, as well as animal identity is preserved in the change of material substances, or variety of particular bodies: unless they will say, it is one immaterial spirit that makes the same life in brutes, as it is one immaterial spirit that makes the same person in men; which the Cartesians at least will not admit, for fear of making brutes thinking things too.

13. But next, as to the first part of the question, Whether, if the same thinking substance (supposing immaterial substances only to think) be changed, it can be the same person? I answer, that cannot be resolved but by those who know what kind of substances they are that do think; and whether the consciousness of past actions can be transferred from one thinking substance to another. I grant were the same consciousness the same individual action it could not: but it being a present representation of a past action, why it may not be possible, that that may be represented to the mind to have been which really never was, will remain to be shown. And therefore how far the consciousness of past actions is annexed to any individual agent, so that another cannot possibly have it, will be hard for us to determine, till we know what kind of action it is that cannot be done without a reflex act of perception accompanying it, and how performed by thinking substances, who cannot think without being conscious of it. But that which we call the same consciousness, not being the same individual act, why one intellectual substance may not have represented to it, as done by itself, what it never did, and was perhaps done by some other agent—why, I say, such a representation may not possibly be without reality of matter of fact, as well as several representations in dreams are, which yet whilst dreaming we take for true—will be difficult to conclude from the nature of things. And that it never is so, will by us, till we have clearer views of the nature of thinking substances, be best resolved into the goodness of God; who, as far as the happiness or misery of any of his sensible creatures is concerned in it, will not, by a fatal error of theirs, transfer from one to another that consciousness which draws reward or punishment with it. How far this may be an argument against those who would place thinking in a system of fleeting animal spirits, I leave to be considered. But yet, to return to the question before us, it must be allowed, that, if the same consciousness (which, as has been shown, is quite a different thing from the same numerical figure or motion in body) can be transferred from one thinking substance to another, it will be possible that two thinking substances may make but one person. For the same consciousness being preserved, whether in the same or different substances, the personal identity is preserved.

14. As to the second part of the question, Whether the same immaterial substance remaining, there may be two distinct persons; which question seems to me to be built on this,—Whether the same immaterial being, being conscious of the action of its past duration, may be wholly stripped of all the consciousness of its past existence, and lose it beyond the power of ever retrieving it again: and so as it were beginning a new account from a new period, have a consciousness that cannot reach beyond this new state. All those who hold pre-existence are evidently of this mind; since they allow the soul to have no remaining consciousness of what it did in that pre-existent state, either wholly separate from body, or informing any other body; and if they should not, it is plain experience would be against them. So that personal identity, reaching no further than consciousness reaches, a pre-existent spirit not having continued so many ages in a state of silence, must needs make different persons. Suppose a Christian Platonist or a Pythagorean* should, upon God's having ended all his works of creation the seventh day, think his soul hath existed ever since; and should imagine it has revolved in several human bodies; as I once met with one, who was persuaded his had been the soul of Socrates (how reasonably I will not dispute; this I know, that in the post he filled, which was no inconsiderable one, he passed for a very rational man, and the press has shown that he wanted not parts or learning;)—would any one say, that he, being not conscious of any of Socrates's actions or thoughts, could be the same person with Socrates? Let any one reflect upon himself, and conclude that he has in himself an immaterial spirit, which is that which thinks in him, and, in the constant change of his body keeps him the same: and is that which he calls himself: let him also suppose it to be the same soul that was in Nestor or Thersites, at the siege of Troy, (for souls being, as far as we know anything of them, in their nature indifferent to any parcel of matter, the supposition has no apparent absurdity in it), which it may have been, as well as it is now the soul of any other man: but he now having no consciousness of any of the actions either of Nestor or Thersites, does or can he conceive himself the same person with either of them? Can he be concerned in either of their actions? Attribute them to himself, or think them his own, more than the actions of any other men that ever existed? So that this consciousness, not reaching to any of the actions of either of those men, he is no more one self with either of them than if the soul or immaterial spirit that now informs him had been created, and began to exist, when it began to inform his present body; though it were never so true, that the same spirit that informed Nestor's or Thersites' body were numerically the same that now informs his. For this would no more make him the same person with Nestor, than if some of the particles of matter that were once a part of Nestor were now a part of this man; the same immaterial substance, without the same consciousness, no more making the same person, by being united to any body, than the same particle of matter, without consciousness, united to any body, makes the same person. But let him once find himself conscious of any of the actions of Nestor, he then finds himself the same person with Nestor.

15. And thus may we be able, without any difficulty, to conceive the same person at the resurrection, though in a body not exactly in make or parts the same which he had here,—the same consciousness going along with the soul that inhabits it. But yet the soul alone, in the change of bodies, would scarce to any one but to him that makes the soul the man, be enough to make the same man. For should the soul of a prince, carrying with it the consciousness of the prince's past life, enter and inform the body of a cobbler, as soon as deserted by his own soul, every one sees he would be the same person with the prince, accountable only for the prince's actions: but who would say it was the same man? The body too goes to the making the man, and would, I guess, to everybody determine the man in this case, wherein the soul, with all its princely thoughts about it, would

* Christian Platonists and Pythagoreans subscribe to mystical world views that accept the transmigration of souls.

not make another man: but he would be the same cobbler to every one besides himself. I know that, in the ordinary way of speaking, the same person, and the same man, stand for one and the same thing. And indeed every one will always have a liberty to speak as he pleases, and to apply what articulate sounds to what ideas he thinks fit, and change them as often as he pleases. But yet, when we will inquire what makes the same spirit, man, or person, we must fix the ideas of spirit, man, or person in our minds; and having resolved with ourselves what we mean by them, it will not be hard to determine, in either of them, or the like, when it is the same, and when not.

16. *Consciousness makes the same person.* But though the same immaterial substance or soul does not alone, wherever it be, and in whatsoever state, make the same man; yet it is plain, consciousness, as far as ever it can be extended—should it be to ages past—unites existences and actions very remote in time into the same person, as well as it does the existences and actions of the immediately preceding moment: so that whatever has the consciousness of present and past actions, is the same person to whom they both belong. Had I the same consciousness that I saw the ark and Noah's flood, as that I saw an overflowing of the Thames last winter, or as that I write now, I could no more doubt that I who write this now, that saw the Thames overflowed last winter, and that viewed the flood at the general deluge, was the same self,—place that self in what substance you please—than that I who write this am the same myself now whilst I write (whether I consist of all the same substance, material or immaterial, or no) that I was yesterday. For as to this point of being the same self, it matters not whether this present self be made up of the same or other substances—I being as much concerned, and as justly accountable for any action that was done a thousand years since, appropriated to me now by this self-consciousness, as I am for what I did the last moment.

17. *Self depends on consciousness.* Self is that conscious thinking thing,—whatever substance made up of, (whether spiritual or material, simple or compounded, it matters not)—which is sensible or conscious of pleasure and pain, capable of happiness or misery, and so is concerned for itself, as far as that consciousness extends. Thus every one finds that, whilst comprehended under that consciousness, the little finger is as much a part of himself as what is most so. Upon separation of this little finger, should this consciousness go along with the little finger, and leave the rest of the body, it is evident the little finger would be the person, the same person; and self then would have nothing to do with the rest of the body. As in this case it is the consciousness that goes along with the substance, when one part is separate from another, which makes the same person, and constitutes this inseparable self: so it is in reference to substances remote in time. That with which the consciousness of this present thinking thing can join itself, makes the same person, and is one self with it, and with nothing else; and so attributes to itself, and owns all the actions of that thing, as its own, as far as that consciousness reaches, and no further; as every one who reflects will perceive.

18. *Object of reward and punishment.* In this personal identity is founded all the right and justice of reward and punishment; happiness and misery being that for which every one is concerned for himself, and not mattering what becomes of any substance, not joined to, or affected with that consciousness. For, as it is evident in the instance I gave but now, if the consciousness went along with the little finger when it was cut off, that would be the same self which was concerned for the whole body yesterday, as making part of itself, whose actions then it cannot but admit as its own now. Though, if the same body should still live, and immediately from the separation of the little finger have its own peculiar consciousness, whereof the little finger knew nothing, it would not at all be concerned for it, as a part of itself, or could own any of its actions, or have any of them imputed to him.

19. This may show us wherein personal identity consists: not in the identity of substance, but, as I have said, in the identity of consciousness, wherein if Socrates and the present mayor of Quinborough agree, they are the same person: if the same Socrates waking and sleeping do not partake of the same consciousness, Socrates waking and sleeping is not the same person. And to punish Socrates waking for what sleeping Socrates thought, and waking Socrates was never conscious of, would be no more of right, than to punish one twin for what his brother-twin did, whereof he knew nothing, because their outsides were so like, that they could not be distinguished; for such twins have been seen.

20. But yet possibly it will still be objected—Suppose I wholly lose the memory of some parts of my life, beyond a possibility of retrieving them, so that perhaps I shall never be conscious of them again; yet am I not the same person that did those actions, had those thoughts that I once was conscious of, though I have now forgot them? To which I answer, that we must here take notice what the word I is applied to; which, in this case, is the man only. And the same man being presumed to be the same person, I is easily here supposed to stand also for the same person. But if it be possible for the same man to have distinct incommunicable consciousness at different times, it is past doubt the same man would at different times make different persons; which, we see, is the sense of mankind in the solemnest declaration of their opinions, human laws not punishing the mad man for the sober man's actions, nor the sober man for what the mad man did,—thereby making them two persons: which is somewhat explained by our way of speaking in English when we say such an one is "not himself," or is "beside himself"; in which phrases it is insinuated, as if those who now, or at least first used them, thought that self was changed; the selfsame person was no longer in that man.

21. *Difference between identity of man and of person.* But yet it is hard to conceive that Socrates, the same individual man, should be two persons. To help us a little in this, we must consider what is meant by Socrates, or the same individual man. *First*, it must be either the same individual, immaterial, thinking substance; in short, the same numerical soul, and nothing else. *Secondly*, or the same animal, without any regard to an immaterial soul. *Thirdly*, or the same immaterial spirit united to the same animal.

Now, take which of these suppositions you please, it is impossible to make personal identity to consist in anything but consciousness; or reach any further than that does.

For, by the first of them, it must be allowed possible that a man born of different women, and in distant times, may be the same man. A way of speaking which, whoever admits, must allow it possible for the same man to be two distinct persons, as any two that have lived in different ages without the knowledge of one another's thoughts.

By the second and third, Socrates, in this life and after it, cannot be the same man any way, but by the same consciousness; and so making human identity to consist in the same thing wherein we place personal identity, there will be no difficulty to allow the same man to be the same person. But then they who place human identity in consciousness only, and not in something else, must consider how they will make the infant Socrates the same man with Socrates after the resurrection. But whatsoever to some men makes a man, and consequently the same individual man, wherein perhaps few are agreed, personal identity can by us be placed in nothing but consciousness, (which is that alone which makes what we call self,) without involving us in great absurdities.

22. But is not a man drunk and sober the same person? why else is he punished for the fact he commits when drunk, though he be never afterwards conscious of it? Just as much the same person as a man that walks, and does other things in his sleep, is the same person, and is answerable for any mischief he shall do in it. Human laws punish both, with a justice suitable to their way of knowledge;—because, in these cases, they cannot distinguish certainly what is real, what counterfeit: and so the ignorance in drunkenness or sleep is not admitted as a plea. For, though punishment be annexed to personality, and personality to consciousness, and the drunkard perhaps be not conscious of what he did, yet human judicatures justly punish him; because the fact is proved against him, but want of consciousness cannot be proved for him. But in the Great Day, wherein the secrets of all hearts shall be laid open, it may be reasonable to think, no one shall be made to answer for what he knows nothing of, but shall receive his doom, his conscience accusing or excusing him.

23. *Consciousness alone makes self.* Nothing but consciousness can unite remote existences into the same person: the identity of substance will not do it; for whatever substance there is, however framed, without consciousness there is no person: and a carcass may be a person, as well as any sort of substance be so, without consciousness.—Could we suppose two distinct incommunicable consciousnesses acting the same body, the one constantly by day, the other by night; and, on the other side, the same consciousness, acting by intervals, two distinct bodies: I ask, in the first case, whether the day and the night-man would not be two as distinct persons as Socrates and Plato? And whether, in the second case, there would not be one person in two distinct bodies, as much as one man is the same in two distinct clothings? Nor is it at all material to say, that this same, and this distinct consciousness, in the cases above mentioned, is owing to the same and distinct immaterial substances, bringing it with them to those bodies; which, whether true or no, alters not the case: since it is evident the personal identity would equally be determined by the consciousness, whether that consciousness were annexed to some individual immaterial substance or no. For, granting that the thinking substance in man must be necessarily supposed immaterial, it is evident that immaterial thinking thing may sometimes part with its past consciousness, and be restored to it again: as appears in the forgetfulness men often have of their past actions; and the mind many times recovers the memory of a past consciousness, which it had lost for twenty years together. Make these intervals of memory and forgetfulness to take their turns regularly by day and night, and you have two persons with the same immaterial spirit, as much as in the former instance two persons with the same body. So that self is not determined by identity or diversity of substance, which it cannot be sure of, but only by identity of consciousness.

24. Indeed it may conceive the substance whereof it is now made up to have existed formerly, united in the same conscious being: but, consciousness removed, that substance is no more itself, or makes no more a part of it, than any other substance; as is evident in the instance we have already given of a limb cut off, of whose heat, or cold, or other affections, having no longer any consciousness, it is no more of a man's self than any other matter of the universe. In like manner it will be in reference to any immaterial substance, which is void of that consciousness whereby I am myself to myself: if there be any part of its existence which I cannot upon recollection join with that present consciousness whereby I am now myself, it is, in that part of its existence, no more myself than any other immaterial being. For, whatsoever any substance has thought or done, which I cannot recollect, and by my consciousness make my own thought and action, it will no more belong to me, whether a part of me thought or did it, than if it had been thought or done by any other immaterial being anywhere existing.

25. I agree, the more probable opinion is, that this consciousness is annexed to, and the affection of, one individual immaterial substance.

But let men, according to their diverse hypotheses, resolve of that as they please. This every intelligent being, sensible of happiness or misery, must grant—that there is something that is himself, that he is concerned for, and would have happy; that this self has existed in a continued duration more than one instant, and therefore it is possible may exist, as it has done, months and years to come, without any certain bounds to be set to its duration; and may be the same self, by the same consciousness continued on for the future. And thus, by this consciousness he finds himself to be the same self which did such and such an action some years since, by which he comes to be happy or miserable now. In all which account of self, the same numerical substance is not considered as making the same self, but the same continued consciousness, in which several substances may have been united, and again separated from it, which, whilst they continued in a vital union with that wherein this consciousness then resided, made a part of that same self. Thus any part of our bodies, vitally united to that which is conscious in us, makes a part of ourselves: but upon separation from the vital union by which that consciousness is communicated, that which a moment since was part of ourselves, is now no more so than a part of another man's self is a part of me: and it is not impossible but in a little time may become a real part of another person. And so we have the same numerical substance become a part of two different persons; and the same person preserved under the change of various substances. Could we suppose any spirit wholly stripped of all its memory or consciousness of past actions, as we find our minds always are of a great part of ours, and sometimes of them all; the union or separation of such a spiritual substance would make no variation of personal identity, any more than that of any particle of matter does. Any substance vitally united to the present thinking being is a part of that very same self which now is; anything united to it by a consciousness of former actions, makes also a part of the same self, which is the same both then and now.

26. *"Person" a forensic term.* Person, as I take it, is the name for this self. Wherever a man finds what he calls himself, there, I think, another may say is the same person. It is a forensic term, appropriating actions and their merit; and so belongs only to intelligent agents, capable of a law, and happiness, and misery. This personality extends itself beyond present existence to what is past, only by consciousness,—whereby it becomes concerned and accountable; owns and imputes to itself past actions, just upon the same ground and for the same reason as it does the present. All which is founded in a concern for happiness, the unavoidable concomitant of consciousness; that which is conscious of pleasure and pain, desiring that that self that is conscious should be happy. And therefore whatever past actions it cannot reconcile or appropriate to that present self by consciousness, it can be no more concerned in than if they had never been done: and to receive pleasure or pain, i.e. reward or punishment, on the account of any such action, is all one as to be made happy or miserable in its first being, without any demerit at all. For, supposing a man punished now for what he had done in another life, whereof he could be made to have no consciousness at all, what difference is there between that punishment and being created miserable? And therefore, conformable to this, the apostle tells us, that, at the great day, when every one shall "receive according to his doings, the secrets of all hearts shall be laid open." The sentence shall be justified by the consciousness all persons shall have, that they themselves, in what bodies soever they appear, or what substances soever that consciousness adheres to, are the same that committed those actions, and deserve that punishment for them.

[. . .]

28. *The difficulty from ill use of names.* To conclude: Whatever substance begins to exist, it must, during its existence, necessarily be the same: whatever compositions of substances begin to exist, during the union of those substances, the concrete must be the same: whatsoever mode begins to exist, during its existence it is the same: and so if the composition be of distinct substances and different modes, the same rule holds. Whereby it will appear, that the difficulty or obscurity that has been about this matter rather rises from the names ill-used, than from any obscurity in things themselves. For whatever makes the specific idea to which the name is applied, if that idea be steadily kept to, the distinction of anything into the same and divers will easily be conceived, and there can arise no doubt about it.

29. *Continued existence makes identity.* For, supposing a rational spirit be the idea of a man, it is easy to know what is the same man, viz. the same spirit—whether separate or in a body—will be the same man. Supposing a rational spirit vitally united to a body of a certain conformation of parts to make a man; whilst that rational spirit, with that vital conformation of parts, though continued in a fleeting successive body, remains, it will be the same man. But if to any one the idea of a man be but the vital union of parts in a certain shape; as long as that vital union and shape remain in a concrete, no otherwise the same but by a continued succession of fleeting particles, it will be the same man. For, whatever be the composition whereof the complex idea is made, whenever existence makes it one particular thing under any denomination the same existence continued preserves it the same individual under the same denomination.

The Self and the Future

BERNARD WILLIAMS

Bernard Williams (1929–2003) was among the most distinguished moral philosophers of the 20th century. Born in England, he divided his academic career between the University of Cambridge in England and the University of California at Berkeley. He made important contributions to debates about moral psychology, personal identity, equality, morality, and the emotions, as well as to the study of the history of philosophy, and to British public life.

In the selection presented here, originally published in a philosophy journal in 1970, Williams articulates and defends the bodily continuity view of personal identity. An additional selection from his work can be found in the "Moral and Political Philosophy" section.

Suppose that there were some process to which two persons, *A* and *B*, could be subjected as a result of which they might be said—question-beggingly—to have *exchanged bodies*. That is to say—less question-beggingly—there is a certain human body which is such that when previously we were confronted with it, we were confronted with person *A*, certain utterances coming from it were expressive of memories of the past experiences of *A*, certain movements of it partly constituted the actions of *A* and were taken as expressive of the character of *A*, and so forth; but now, after the process is completed, utterances coming from this body are expressive of what seem to be just those memories which previously we identified as memories of the past experiences of *B*, its movements partly constitute actions expressive of the character of *B*, and so forth; and conversely with the other body.

There are certain important philosophical limitations on how such imaginary cases are to be constructed, and how they are to be taken when constructed in various ways. I shall mention two principal limitations, not in order to pursue them further here, but precisely in order to get them out of the way.

There are certain limitations, particularly with regard to character and mannerisms, to our ability to imagine such cases even in the most restricted sense of our being disposed to take the later performances of that body which was previously *A*'s as expressive of *B*'s character; if the previous *A* and *B* were extremely unlike one another both physically and psychologically, and if, say, in addition, they were of different sex, there might be grave difficulties in reading *B*'s dispositions in any possible performances of *A*'s body. Let us forget this, and for the present purpose just take *A* and *B* as being sufficiently alike (however alike that has to be) for the difficulty not to arise; after the experiment, persons familiar with *A* and *B* are just *overwhelmingly struck* by the *B*-ish character of the doings associated with what was previously *A*'s body, and conversely. Thus the feat of imagining an exchange of bodies is supposed possible in the most restricted sense. But now there is a further limitation which has to be overcome if the feat is to be not merely possible in the most restricted sense but also is to have an outcome which, on serious reflection, we are prepared to describe as *A* and *B* having changed bodies—that is, an outcome where, confronted with what was previously *A*'s body, we are prepared seriously to say that we are now confronted with *B*.

It would seem a necessary condition of so doing that the utterances coming from that body be taken as genuinely expressive of memories of *B*'s past. But memory is a causal notion; and as we actually use it,

From *The Philosophical Review*, Vol. 79, pp. 161–180. Copyright © 1970, Cornell University Press. All rights reserved. Used by permission of the current publisher, Duke University Press.

it seems a necessary condition of *x*'s present knowledge of *x*'s earlier experiences constituting memory of those experiences that the causal chain linking the experiences and the knowledge should not run outside *x*'s body. Hence if utterances coming from a given body are to be taken as expressive of memories of the experiences of *B*, there should be some suitable causal link between the appropriate state of that body and the original happening of those experiences to *B*. One radical way of securing that condition in the imagined exchange case is to suppose, with Shoemaker,*[1] that the brains of *A* and of *B* are transposed. We may not need so radical a condition. Thus suppose it were possible to extract information from a man's brain and store it in a device while his brain was repaired, or even renewed, the information then being replaced: it would seem exaggerated to insist that the resultant man could not possibly have the memories he had before the operation. With regard to our knowledge of our own past, we draw distinctions between merely recalling, being reminded, and learning again, and those distinctions correspond (roughly) to distinctions between no new input, partial new input, and total new input with regard to the information in question; and it seems clear that the information-parking case just imagined would not count as new input in the sense necessary and sufficient for "learning again." Hence we can imagine the case we are concerned with in terms of information extracted into such devices from *A*'s and *B*'s brains and replaced in the other brain; this is the sort of model which, I think not unfairly for the present argument, I shall have in mind.

We imagine the following. The process considered above exists; two persons can enter some machine, let us say, and emerge changed in the appropriate ways. If *A* and *B* are the persons who enter, let us call the persons who emerge the *A-body-person* and the *B-body-person*: the *A*-body-person is that person (whoever it is) with whom I am confronted when, after the experiment, I am confronted with that body which previously was *A*'s body—that is to say, that person who would naturally be taken for *A* by someone who just saw this person, was familiar with *A*'s appearance before the experiment, and did not know about the happening of the experiment. A non-question-begging description of the experiment will leave it open which (if either) of the persons *A* and *B* the *A*-body-person is; the description of the experiment as "persons changing bodies" of course implies that the *A*-body-person is actually *B*.

We take two persons *A* and *B* who are going to have the process carried out on them. (We can suppose, rather hazily, that they are willing for this to happen; to investigate at all closely at this stage why they might be willing or unwilling, what they would fear, and so forth, would anticipate some later issues.) We further announce that one of the two resultant persons, the *A*-body-person and the *B*-body-person, is going after the experiment to be given $100,000, while the other is going to be tortured. We then ask each of *A* and *B* to choose which treatment should be dealt out to which of the persons who will emerge from the experiment, the choice to be made (if it can be) on selfish grounds.

Suppose that *A* chooses that the *B*-body-person should get the pleasant treatment and the *A*-body-person the unpleasant treatment; and *B* chooses conversely (this might indicate that they thought that "changing bodies" was indeed a good description of the outcome). The experimenter cannot act in accordance with both these sets of preferences, those expressed by *A* and those expressed by *B*. Hence there is one clear sense in which *A* and *B* cannot both get what they want: namely, that if the experimenter, before the experiment, announces to *A* and *B* that he intends to carry out the alternative (for example), of treating the *B*-body-person unpleasantly and the *A*-body-person pleasantly—then *A* can say rightly, "That's not the outcome I chose to happen." and *B* can say rightly, "That's just the outcome I chose to happen." So, evidently, *A* and *B* before the experiment can each come to know either that the outcome he chose will be that which will happen, or that the one he chose will not happen, and in that sense they can get or fail to get what they wanted. But is it also true that when the experimenter proceeds after the experiment to act in accordance with one of the preferences and not the other, *then* one of

* American philosopher Sydney Shoemaker (1931–) is known for his work on personal identity and for his contributions to metaphysics and the philosophy of mind.

A and *B* will have got what he wanted, and the other not?

There seems very good ground for saying so. For suppose the experimenter, having elicited *A*'s and *B*'s preference, says nothing to *A* and *B* about what he will do; conducts the experiment; and then, for example, gives the unpleasant treatment to the *B*-body-person and the pleasant treatment to the *A*-body-person. Then the *B*-body-person will not only complain of the unpleasant treatment as such, but will complain (since he has *A*'s memories) that that was not the outcome he chose, since he chose that the *B*-body-person should be well treated; and since *A* made his choice in selfish spirit, he may add that he precisely chose in that way because he did not want the unpleasant things to happen to *him*. The *A*-body-person meanwhile will express satisfaction both at the receipt of the $100,000, and also at the fact that the experimenter has chosen to act in the way that he, *B*, so wisely chose. These facts make a strong case for saying that the experimenter has brought it about that *B* did in the outcome get what he wanted and *A* did not. It is therefore a strong case for saying that the *B*-body-person really is *A*, and the *A*-body-person really is *B*; and therefore for saying that the process of the experiment really is that of changing bodies. For the same reasons it would seem that *A* and *B* in our example really did choose wisely, and that it was *A*'s bad luck that the choice he correctly made was not carried out, *B*'s good luck that the choice he correctly made was carried out. This seems to show that to care about what happens to me in the future is not necessarily to care about what happens to *this* body (the one I now have); and this in turn might be taken to show that in some sense of Descartes's obscure phrase, I and my body are "really distinct" (though, of course, nothing in these considerations could support the idea that I could exist without a body at all).

These suggestions seem to be reinforced if we consider the cases where *A* and *B* make other choices with regard to the experiment. Suppose that *A* chooses that the *A*-body-person should get the money, and the *B*-body-person get the pain, and *B* chooses conversely. Here again there can be no outcome which matches the expressed preferences of both of them: they cannot both get what they want. The experimenter announces, before the experiment, that the *A*-body-person will in fact get the money, and the *B*-body-person will get the pain. So *A* at this stage gets what he wants (the announced outcome matches his expressed preference). After the experiment, the distribution is carried out as announced. Both the *A*-body-person and the *B*-body-person will have to agree that what is happening is in accordance with the preference that *A* originally expressed. The *B*-body-person will naturally express this acknowledgement (since he has *A*'s memories) by saying that this is the distribution he chose; he will recall, among other things, the experimenter announcing this outcome, his approving it as what he chose, and so forth. However, he (the *B*-body-person) certainly does not like what is now happening to him, and would much prefer to be receiving what the *A*-body-person is receiving—namely, $100,000. The *A*-body-person will on the other hand recall choosing an outcome other than this one, but will reckon it good luck that the experimenter did not do what he recalls choosing. It looks, then, as though the *A*-body-person has got what he wanted, but not what he chose, while the *B*-body-person has got what he chose, but not what he wanted. So once more it looks as though they are, respectively, *B* and *A*; and that in this case the original choices of both *A* and *B* were unwise.

Suppose, lastly, that in the original choice *A* takes the line of the first case and *B* of the second: that is, *A* chooses that the *B*-body-person should get the money and the *A*-body-person the pain, and *B* chooses exactly the same thing. In this case, the experimenter would seem to be in the happy situation of giving both persons what they want—or at least, like God, what they have chosen. In this case, the *B*-body-person likes what he is receiving, recalls choosing it, and congratulates himself on the wisdom of (as he puts it) his choice; while the *A*-body-person does not like what he is receiving, recalls choosing it, and is forced to acknowledge that (as he puts it) his choice was unwise. So once more we seem to get results to support the suggestions drawn from the first case.

Let us now consider the question, not of *A* and *B* choosing certain outcomes to take place after the experiment, but of their willingness to engage in the experiment at all. If they were initially inclined to accept the description of the experiment as "changing bodies" then one thing that would interest them would be the character of the other person's body. In this respect also what would happen after the experiment would seem to suggest that "changing bodies" was a good description of the experiment. If *A* and *B* agreed to the experiment, being each not displeased with the appearance, physique, and so forth of the other person's body; after the experiment the *B*-body-person might well be found saying such things as: "When I agreed to this experiment, I thought that *B*'s face was quite attractive, but now I look at it in the mirror, I am not so sure"; or the *A*-body-person might say "When I agreed to this experiment I did not know that *A* had a wooden leg; but now, after it is over, I find that I have this wooden leg, and I want the experiment reversed." It is possible that he might say further that he finds the leg very uncomfortable, and that the *B*-body-person should say, for instance, that he recalls that he found it very uncomfortable at first, but one gets used to it: but perhaps one would need to know more than at least I do about the physiology of habituation to artificial limbs to know whether the *A*-body-person would find the leg uncomfortable: that body, after all, has had the leg on it for some time. But apart from this sort of detail, the general line of the outcome regarded from this point of view seems to confirm our previous conclusions about the experiment.

Now let us suppose that when the experiment is proposed (in non-question-begging terms) *A* and *B* think rather of their psychological advantages and disadvantages. *A*'s thoughts turn primarily to certain sorts of anxiety to which he is very prone, while *B* is concerned with the frightful memories he has of past experiences which still distress him. They each hope that the experiment will in some way result in their being able to get away from these things. They may even have been impressed by philosophical arguments to the effect that bodily continuity is at least a necessary condition of personal identity: *A*, for example, reasons that, granted the experiment comes off, then the person who is bodily continuous with him will not have this anxiety, and while the other person will no doubt have some anxiety—perhaps in some sense his anxiety—at least that person will not be he. The experiment is performed and the experimenter (to whom *A* and *B* previously revealed privately their several difficulties and hopes) asks the *A*-body-person whether he has got rid of his anxiety. This person presumably replies that he does not know what the man is talking about; he never had such anxiety, but he did have some very disagreeable memories, and recalls engaging in the experiment to get rid of them, and is disappointed to discover that he still has them. The *B*-body-person will react in a similar way to questions about his painful memories, pointing out that he still has his anxiety. These results seem to confirm still further the description of the experiment as "changing bodies." And all the results suggest that the only rational thing to do, confronted with such an experiment, would be to identify oneself with one's memories, and so forth, and not with one's body. The philosophical arguments designed to show that bodily continuity was at least a necessary condition of personal identity would seem to be just mistaken.

Let us now consider something apparently different. Someone in whose power I am tells me that I am going to be tortured tomorrow. I am frightened, and look forward to tomorrow in great apprehension. He adds that when the time comes, I shall not remember being told that this was going to happen to me, since shortly before the torture something else will be done to me which will make me forget the announcement. This certainly will not cheer me up, since I know perfectly well that I can forget things, and that there is such a thing as indeed being tortured unexpectedly because I had forgotten or been made to forget a prediction of the torture: that will still be a torture which, so long as I do know about the prediction, I look forward to in fear. He then adds that my forgetting the announcement will be only part of a larger process: when the moment of torture comes, I shall not remember any of the things I am now in a position to remember. This does not cheer me up, either, since I can readily conceive of being involved in an accident, for instance, as a result of which I wake up in a completely amnesiac state and also in great pain; that could certainly happen to me, I should not like it to happen to me, nor to know that it was going to happen to me. He now further adds that at the moment of torture I shall not only not remember the things I am now in a position to remember, but will have a different set of impressions of my past, quite different from the memories I now have. I do not think that this would cheer me up, either. For I can at least conceive the possibility, if not the concrete reality, of going completely mad, and thinking perhaps that I am George IV or somebody; and being told that something like that was going to happen to me would have no tendency to reduce the terror of being told authoritatively that I was going to be tortured, but would merely compound the horror. Nor do I see why I should be put into any better frame of mind by the person in charge adding lastly that the impressions of my past with which I shall be equipped on the eve of torture will exactly fit the past of another person now living, and that indeed I shall acquire these impressions by (for instance) information now in his brain being copied into mine. Fear, surely, would still be the proper reaction: and not because one did not know what was going to happen, but because in one vital respect at least one did know what was going to happen—torture, which one can indeed expect to happen to oneself, and to be preceded by certain mental derangements as well.

If this is right, the whole question seems now to be totally mysterious. For what we have just been through is of course merely one side, differently represented, of the transaction which we considered before; and it represents it as a perfectly hateful prospect, while the previous considerations represented it as something one should rationally, perhaps even cheerfully, choose out of the options there presented. It is differently presented, of course, and in two notable respects; but when we look at these two differences of presentation, can we really convince ourselves that the second presentation is wrong or misleading, thus leaving the road open to the first version which at the time seemed so convincing? Surely not.

The first difference is that in the second version the torture is throughout represented as going to happen to *me:* "you," the man in charge persistently says. Thus he is not very neutral. But should he have been neutral? Or, to put it another way, does his use of the second person have a merely emotional and rhetorical effect on me, making me afraid when further reflection would have shown that I had no reason to be? It is certainly not obviously so. The problem just is that through every step of his predictions I seem to be able to follow him successfully. And if I reflect on whether what he has said gives me grounds for fearing that I shall be tortured, I could consider that behind my fears lies some principle such as this: that my undergoing physical pain in the future is not excluded by any psychological state I may be in at the time, with the platitudinous exception of those psychological states which in themselves exclude experiencing pain, notably (if it is a psychological state) unconsciousness. In particular, what impressions I have about the past will not have any effect on whether I undergo the pain or not. This principle seems sound enough.

It is an important fact that not everything I would, as things are, regard as an evil would be something that I should rationally fear as an evil if it were predicted that it would happen to me in the future and also predicted that I should undergo significant psychological changes in the meantime. For the fact that I regard that happening, things being as they are, as an evil can be dependent on factors of belief or character which might themselves be modified by the psychological changes in question. Thus if I am appallingly subject to acrophobia, and am told that I shall find myself on top of a steep mountain in the near future, I shall to that extent be afraid; but if I am told that I shall be psychologically changed in the meantime in such a way as to rid me of my acrophobia (and as with the other prediction, I believe it), then I have no reason to be afraid of the predicted happening, or at least not the same reason. Again, I might look forward to meeting a certain person again with either alarm or excitement because of my memories of our past relations. In some part, these memories operate in connexion with my emotion, not only on the present time, but projectively forward: for it is to a meeting itself affected by the presence of those memories that I look forward. If I am convinced that when the time comes I shall not have those memories, then I shall not have just the same reasons as before for looking forward to that meeting with the one emotion or the other. (Spiritualism, incidentally, appears to involve the belief that I have just the same reasons for a given attitude toward encountering people again after I am dead, as I did before: with the one modification that I can be sure it will all be very nice.)

Physical pain, however, the example which for simplicity (and not for any obsessional reason) I have taken, is absolutely minimally dependent on character or belief. No amount of change in my character or my beliefs would seem to affect substantially the nastiness of tortures applied to me; correspondingly, no degree of predicted change in my character and beliefs can unseat the fear of torture which, together with those changes, is predicted for me.

I am not at all suggesting that the *only* basis, or indeed the only rational basis, for fear in the face of these various predictions is how things will be relative to my psychological state in the eventual outcome. I am merely pointing out that this is one component; it is not the only one. For certainly one will fear and otherwise reject the changes themselves, or in very many cases one would. Thus one of the old paradoxes of hedonistic utilitarianism; if one had assurances that undergoing certain operations and being attached to a machine would provide one for the rest of one's existence with an unending sequence of delicious and varied experiences, one might very well reject the option, and react with fear if someone proposed to apply it compulsorily; and that fear and horror would seem appropriate reactions in the second case may help to discredit the interpretation (if anyone has the nerve to propose it) that one's reason for rejecting the option voluntarily would be a consciousness of duties to others which one in one's hedonic state would leave undone. The prospect of contented madness or vegetableness is found by many (not perhaps by all) appalling in ways which are obviously not a function of how things would then be for them, for things would then be for them not appalling. In the case we are at present discussing, these sorts of considerations seem merely to make it clearer that the predictions of the man in charge provide a double ground of horror: at the prospect of torture, and at the prospect of the change in character and in impressions of the past that will precede it. And certainly, to repeat what has already been said, the prospect of the second certainly seems to provide no ground for rejecting or not fearing the prospect of the first.

I said that there were two notable differences between the second presentation of our situation and the first. The first difference, which we have just said something about, was that the man predicted the torture for *me*, a psychologically very changed "me." We have yet to find a reason for saying that he should not have done this, or that I really should be unable to follow him if he does; I seem to be able to follow him only too well. The second difference is that in this presentation he does not mention the other man, except in the somewhat incidental rôle of being the provenance of the impressions of the past I end up with. He does not mention him at all as someone who will end up with impressions of the past derived from me (and, incidentally, with $100,000 as well—a consideration which, in the frame of mind appropriate to this version, will merely make me jealous).

But why *should* he mention this man and what is going to happen to him? My selfish concern is to be told what is going to happen to me, and now I know: torture, preceded by changes of character, brain operations, changes in impressions of the past. The knowledge that one other person, or none, or many will be similarly mistreated may affect me in other ways, of sympathy, greater horror at the power of this tyrant, and so forth; but surely it cannot affect my expectations of torture? But—someone will say—this is to leave out exactly the feature which, as the first presentation of the case showed, makes all the difference: for it is to leave out the person who, as the first presentation showed, will be you. It is to leave out not merely a feature which should fundamentally affect your fears, it is to leave out the very person for whom you are fearful. So of course, the objector will say, this makes all the difference.

But can it? Consider the following series of cases. In each case we are to suppose that after what is described, *A* is, as before, to be tortured; we are also to suppose the person *A* is informed beforehand that just these things followed by the torture will happen to him:

(i) *A* is subjected to an operation which produces total amnesia;

(ii) amnesia is produced in *A*, and other interference leads to certain changes in his character;

(iii) changes in his character are produced, and at the same time certain illusory "memory" beliefs are induced in him: these are of a quite fictitious kind and do not fit the life of any actual person;
(iv) the same as (iii), except that both the character traits and the "memory" impressions are designed to be appropriate to another actual person, *B*;
(v) the same as (iv), except that the result is produced by putting the information into *A* from the brain of *B*, by a method which leaves *B* the same as he was before;
(vi) the same happens to *A* as in (v), but *B* is not left the same, since a similar operation is conducted in the reverse direction.

I take it that no-one is going to dispute that *A* has reasons, and fairly straightforward reasons, for fear of pain when the prospect is that of situation (i); there seems no conceivable reason why this should not extend to situation (ii), and the situation (iii) can surely introduce no difference of principle—it just seems a situation which for more than one reason we should have grounds for fearing, as suggested above. Situation (iv) at least introduces the person *B*, who was the focus of the objection we are now discussing. But it does not seem to introduce him in any way which makes a material difference; if I can expect pain through a transformation which involves new "memory" impressions, it would seem a purely external fact, relative to that, that the "memory" impressions had a model. Nor, in (iv), do we satisfy a causal condition which I mentioned at the beginning for the "memories" actually being memories; though notice that if the job were done thoroughly, I might well be able to elicit from the *A*-body-person the kinds of remarks about his previous expectations of the experiment—remarks appropriate to the original *B*—which so impressed us in the first version of the story. I shall have a similar assurance of this being so in situation (v), where, moreover, a plausible application of the causal condition is available.

But two things are to be noticed about this situation. First, if we concentrate on *A* and the *A*-body-person, we do not seem to have added anything which from the point of view of his fears makes any material difference; just as, in the move from (iii) to (iv), it made no relevant difference that the new "memory" impressions which precede the pain had, as it happened, a model, so in the move from (iv) to (v) all we have added is that they have a model which is also their cause: and it is still difficult to see why that, to him looking forward, could possibly make the difference between expecting pain and not expecting pain. To illustrate that point from the case of character: if *A* is capable of expecting pain, he is capable of expecting pain preceded by a change in his dispositions—and to that expectation it can make no difference, whether that change in his dispositions is modelled on, or indeed indirectly caused by, the dispositions of some other person. If his fears can, as it were, reach through the change, it seems a mere trimming how the change is in fact induced. The second point about situation (v) is that if the crucial question for *A*'s fears with regard to what befalls the *A*-body-person is whether the *A*-body-person is or is not the person *B*,[2] then that condition has not yet been satisfied in situation (v): for there we have an undisputed *B* in addition to the *A*-body-person, and certainly those two are not the same person.

But in situation (vi), we seemed to think, that is finally what he is. But if *A*'s original fears could reach through the expected changes in (v), as they did in (iv) and (iii), then certainly they can reach through in (vi). Indeed, from the point of view of *A*'s expectations and fears, there is less difference between (vi) and (v) than there is between (v) and (iv) or between (iv) and (iii). In those transitions, there were at least differences—though we could not see that they were really relevant differences—in the content or cause of what happened to him; in the present case there is absolutely no difference at all in what happens to him, the only difference being in what happens to someone else. If he can fear pain when (v) is predicted, why should he cease to when (vi) is?

I can see only one way of relevantly laying great weight on the transition from (v) to (vi); and this involves a considerable difficulty. This is to deny that, as I put it, the transition from (v) to (vi) involves merely the addition of something happening to *somebody else*; what rather it does, it will be said, is to involve the reintroduction of *A* himself, as the *B*-body-person; since he has reappeared in this form, it is for this person, and not for the unfortunate *A*-body-person, that *A* will have his expectations. This is to reassert, in effect, the viewpoint emphasised in our first presentation of the experiment. But this surely has the consequence that *A* should not have fears for the *A*-body-person who appeared in situation (v). For by the present argument, the *A*-body-person in (vi) is not *A*; the *B*-body-person is. But the *A*-body-person in (v) is, in character, history, everything, exactly the same as the *A*-body-person in (vi); so if the latter is not *A*, then neither is the former. (It is this point, no doubt, that encourages one to speak of the difference that goes with (vi) as being, on the present view, the *reintroduction* of *A*.) But no-one else in (v) has any better claim to be *A*. So in (v), it seems, *A* just does not exist. This would certainly explain why *A* should have no fears for the state of things in (v)—though he might well have fears for the path to it. But it rather looked earlier as though he could well have fears for the state of things in (v). Let us grant, however, that that was an illusion, and that *A* really does not exist in (v); then does he exist in (iv), (iii), (ii), or (i)? It seems very difficult to deny it for (i) and (ii); are we perhaps to draw the line between (iii) and (iv)?

Here someone will say: you must not insist on drawing a line—borderline cases are borderline cases, and you must not push our concepts beyond their limits. But this well-known piece of advice, sensible as it is in many cases, seems in the present case to involve an extraordinary difficulty. It may intellectually comfort observers of *A*'s situation; but what is *A* supposed to make of it? To be told that a future situation is a borderline one for its being myself that is hurt, that it is conceptually undecidable whether it will be me or not, is something which, it seems, I can do nothing with; because, in particular, it seems to have no comprehensible representation in my expectations and the emotions that go with them.

If I expect that a certain situation, *S*, will come about in the future, there is of course a wide range of emotions and concerns, directed on *S*, which I may experience now in relation to my expectation. Unless I am exceptionally egoistic, it is not a condition on my being concerned in relation to this expectation, that I myself will be involved in *S*—where my being "involved" in *S* means that I figure in *S* as someone doing something at that time or having something done to me, or, again, that *S* will have consequences affecting me at that or some subsequent time. There are some emotions, however, which I will feel only if I will be involved in *S*, and fear is an obvious example.

Now the description of *S* under which it figures in my expectations will necessarily be, in various ways, indeterminate; and one way in which it may be indeterminate is that it leaves open whether I shall be involved in *S* or not. Thus I may have good reason to expect that one of us five is going to get hurt, but no reason to expect it to be me rather than one of the others. My present emotions will be correspondingly affected by this indeterminacy. Thus, sticking to the egoistic concern involved in fear, I shall presumably be somewhat more cheerful than if I knew it was going to be me, somewhat less cheerful than if I had been left out altogether. Fear will be mixed with, and qualified by, apprehension; and so forth. These emotions revolve around the thought of the eventual determination of the indeterminacy; moments of straight fear focus on its really turning out to be me, of hope on its turning out not to be me. All the emotions are related to the coming about of what I expect: and what I expect in such a case just cannot come about save by coming about in one of the ways or another.

There are other ways in which indeterminate expectations can be related to fear. Thus I may expect (perhaps neurotically) that something nasty is going to happen to me, indeed expect that when it happens it will take some determinate form, but have no range, or no closed range, of candidates for the determinate form to rehearse in my present thought. Different from this would be the fear of something radically indeterminate—the fear (one might say) of a nameless horror. If somebody had such a fear, one could even say that he had, in a sense, a perfectly determinate expectation: if what he expects indeed comes about, there will be nothing more determinate to be said about it after the event than was said in the expectation. Both these cases of course are cases of *fear* because one thing that is fixed amid the indeterminacy is the belief that it is me to whom the things will happen.

Central to the expectation of *S* is the thought of what it will be like when it happens—thought which may be indeterminate, range over alternatives, and so forth. When *S* involves me, there can be the possibility of a special form of such thought: the thought of how it will be for me, the imaginative projection of myself as participant in *S*.[3] I do not have to think about *S* in this way, when it involves me; but I may be able to. (It might be suggested that this possibility was even mirrored in the language, in the distinction between "expecting to be hurt" and "expecting that I shall be hurt"; but I am very doubtful about this point, which is in any case of no importance.)

Suppose now that there is an *S* with regard to which it is for conceptual reasons undecidable whether it involves me or not, as is proposed for the experimental situation by the line we are discussing. It is important that the expectation of *S* is not *indeterminate* in any of the ways we have just been considering. It is not like the nameless horror, since the fixed point of that case was that it was going to happen to the subject, and that made his state unequivocally fear. Nor is it like the expectation of the man who expects one of the five to be hurt; his fear was indeed equivocal, but its focus, and that of the expectation, was that when *S* came about, it would certainly come about in one way or the other. In the present case, fear (of the torture, that is to say, not of the initial experiment) seems neither appropriate, nor inappropriate, nor appropriately equivocal. Relatedly, the subject has an incurable difficulty about how he may think about *S*. If he engages in projective imaginative thinking (about how it will be for him), he implicitly answers the necessarily unanswerable question; if he thinks that he cannot engage in such thinking, it looks very much as if he also answers it, though in the opposite direction. Perhaps he must just refrain from such thinking; but is he just refraining from it, if it is incurably undecidable whether he can or cannot engage in it?

It may be said that all that these considerations can show is that fear, at any rate, does not get its proper footing in this case; but that there could be some other, more ambivalent, form of concern which would indeed be appropriate to this particular expectation, the expectation of the conceptually undecidable situation. There are, perhaps, analogous feelings that actually occur in actual situations. Thus material objects do occasionally undergo puzzling transformations which leave a conceptual shadow over their identity. Suppose I were sentimentally attached to an object to which this sort of thing then happened; it might be that I could neither feel about it quite as I did originally, nor be totally indifferent to it, but would have some other and rather ambivalent feeling towards it. Similarly, it may be said, toward the prospective sufferer of pain, my identity relations with whom are conceptually shadowed, I can feel neither as I would if he were certainly me, nor as I would if he were certainly not, but rather some such ambivalent concern.

But this analogy does little to remove the most baffling aspect of the present case—an aspect which has already turned up in what was said about the subject's difficulty in thinking either projectively or non-projectively about the situation. For to regard the prospective pain-sufferer *just* like the transmogrified object of sentiment, and to conceive of my ambivalent distress about his future pain as just like ambivalent distress about some future damage to such an object, is of course to leave him and me clearly distinct from one another, and thus to displace the conceptual shadow from its proper place. I have to get nearer to him than that. But is there any nearer that I can get to him without expecting his pain? If there is, the analogy has not shown us it. We can certainly not get nearer by expecting, as it were, *ambivalent* pain; there is no place at all for that. There seems to be an obstinate bafflement to mirroring in my expectations a situation in which it is conceptually undecidable whether I occur.

The bafflement seems, moreover, to turn to plain absurdity if we move from conceptual undecidability to its close friend and neighbour, conventionalist decision. This comes out if we consider another description, overtly conventionalist, of the series of cases which occasioned the present discussion. This description would reject a point I relied on in an earlier argument—namely, that if we deny that the *A*-body-person in (vi) is *A* (because the *B*-body-person is), then we must deny that the *A*-body-person in (v) is A, since they are exactly similar. "No," it may be said, "this is just to assume that we say the same in different sorts of situation. No doubt when we have the very good candidate for being *A*—namely, the *B*-body-person—we call him *A*; but this does not mean that we should not call the *A*-body-person *A* in that other situation when we have no better candidate around. Different situations call for different descriptions." This line of talk is the sort of thing indeed appropriate to lawyers deciding the ownership of some property which has undergone some bewildering set of transformations; they just have to decide, and in each situation, let us suppose, it has got to go to somebody, on as reasonable grounds as the facts and the law admit. But as a line to deal with a person's fears or expectations about his own future, it seems to have no sense at all. If A's fears can extend to what will happen to the A-body-person in (v), I do not see how they can be rationally diverted from the fate of the exactly similar person in (vi) by his being told that someone would have a reason in the latter situation which he would not have in the former for deciding to call another person *A*.

Thus, to sum up, it looks as though there are two presentations of the imagined experiment and the choice associated with it, each of which carries conviction, and which lead to contrary conclusions. The idea, moreover, that the situation after the experiment is conceptually undecidable in the relevant respect seems not to assist, but rather to increase, the puzzlement; while the idea (so often appealed to in these matters) that it is conventionally decidable is even worse. Following from all that, I am not in the least clear which option it would be wise to take if one were presented with them before the experiment. I find that rather disturbing.

Whatever the puzzlement, there is one feature of the arguments which have led to it which is worth picking out, since it runs counter to something which is, I think, often rather vaguely supposed. It is often recognised that there are "first-personal" and "third-personal" aspects of questions about persons, and that there are difficulties about the relations between them. It is also recognised that "mentalistic" considerations (as we may vaguely call them) and considerations of bodily continuity are involved in questions of personal identity (which is not to say that there are mentalistic and bodily criteria of personal identity). It is tempting to think that the two distinctions run in parallel: roughly, that a first-personal approach concentrates attention on mentalistic considerations, while a third-personal approach emphasises considerations of bodily continuity. The present discussion is an illustration of exactly the opposite. The first argument, which led to the "mentalistic" conclusion that *A* and *B* would change bodies and that each person should identify himself with the destination of his memories and character, was an argument entirely conducted in third-personal terms. The second argument, which suggested the bodily continuity identification, concerned itself with the first-personal issue of what *A* could expect. That this is so seems to me (though I will not discuss it further here) of some significance.

I will end by suggesting one rather shaky way in which one might approach a resolution of the problem, using only the limited materials already available.

The apparently decisive arguments of the first presentation, which suggested that *A* should identify himself with the *B*-body-person, turned on the extreme neatness of the situation in satisfying, if any could, the description of "changing bodies." But this neatness is basically artificial; it is the product of the will of the experimenter to produce a situation which would naturally elicit, with minimum hesitation, that description. By the sorts of methods he employed, he could easily have left off earlier or gone on further. He could have stopped at situation (v), leaving *B* as he was; or he could have gone on and produced two persons each with *A*-like character and memories, as well as one or two with *B*-like characteristics. If he had done either of those, we should have been in yet greater difficulty about what to say; he just chose to make it as easy as possible for us to find something to say. Now if we had some model of ghostly persons in bodies, which were in some sense actually moved around by certain procedures, we could regard the neat experiment just as the *effective* experiment: the one method that really did result in the ghostly persons' changing places without being destroyed, dispersed, or whatever. But we cannot seriously use such a model. The experimenter has not in the sense of that model *induced* a change of bodies; he has rather produced the one situation out of a range of equally possible situations which we should be most disposed to call a change of bodies. As against this, the principle that one's fears can extend to future pain whatever psychological changes precede it seems positively straightforward. Perhaps, indeed, it is not; but we need to be shown what is wrong with it. Until we are shown what is wrong with it, we should perhaps decide that if we were the person A then, if we were to decide selfishly, we should pass the pain to the B-body-person. It would be risky: that there is room for the notion of a *risk* here is itself a major feature of the problem.

NOTES

1. *Self-Knowledge and Self-Identity* (Ithaca, N.Y., 1963). pp. 23 seq.
2. This of course does not have to be the crucial question, but it seems one fair way of taking up the present objection.
3. For a more detailed treatment of issues related to this, see [my] "Imagination and the Self."

Personal Identity from *Reasons and Persons*

DEREK PARFIT

Derek Parfit (1942–) is a British philosopher whose influential writings in ethics and metaphysics have been widely discussed and debated. In his important book *Reasons and Persons* (1984), Parfit explores the relation among rationality, self-interest, personal identity, and morality.

In this selection, excerpted from Part III of *Reasons and Persons*, Parfit defends a psychological continuity view of personal identity. Slight editorial changes have been introduced to render the text self-standing. Section numbers corresponding to the original text have been omitted. In his discussion, Parfit makes reference to the writings of several early modern philosophers, including John Locke (1632–1704), Bishop Samuel Butler (1835–1902), Thomas Reid (1710–96), and Immanuel Kant (1724–1804).

I. WHAT WE BELIEVE OURSELVES TO BE

I enter the Teletransporter. I have been to Mars before, but only by the old method, a space-ship journey taking several weeks. This machine will send me at the speed of light. I merely have to press the green button. Like others, I am nervous. Will it work? I remind myself what I have been told to expect. When I press the button, I shall lose consciousness, and then wake up at what seems a moment later. In fact I shall have been unconscious for about an hour. The Scanner here on Earth will destroy my brain and body, while recording the exact states of all of my cells. It will then transmit this information by radio. Travelling at the speed of light, the message will take three minutes to reach the Replicator on Mars. This will then create, out of new matter, a brain and body exactly like mine. It will be in this body that I shall wake up.

Though I believe that this is what will happen, I still hesitate. But then I remember seeing my wife grin when, at breakfast today, I revealed my nervousness. As she reminded me, she has been often teletransported, and there is nothing wrong with *her*. I press the button. As predicted, I lose and seem at once to regain consciousness, but in a different cubicle. Examining my new body, I find no change

From *Reasons and Persons* by D. Parfit, 1986. Reprinted by permission of Oxford University Press.

at all. Even the cut on my upper lip, from this morning's shave, is still there.

Several years pass, during which I am often Teletransported. I am now back in the cubicle, ready for another trip to Mars. But this time, when I press the green button, I do not lose consciousness. There is a whirring sound, then silence. I leave the cubicle, and say to the attendant: "It's not working. What did I do wrong?"

"It's working," he replies, handing me a printed card. This reads: "The New Scanner records your blueprint without destroying your brain and body. We hope that you will welcome the opportunities which this technical advance offers."

The attendant tells me that I am one of the first people to use the New Scanner. He adds that, if I stay for an hour, I can use the Intercom to see and talk to myself on Mars.

"Wait a minute," I reply. "If I'm here I can't *also* be on Mars."

> Someone politely coughs, a white-coated man who asks to speak to me in private. We go to his office, where he tells me to sit down, and pauses. Then he says: "I'm afraid that we're having problems with the New Scanner. It records your blueprint just as accurately, as you will see when you talk to yourself on Mars. But it seems to be damaging the cardiac systems which it scans. Judging from the results so far, though you will be quite healthy on Mars, here on Earth you must expect cardiac failure within the next few days."
>
> The attendant later calls me to the Intercom. On the screen I see myself just as I do in the mirror every morning. But there are two differences. On the screen I am not left-right reversed. And, while I stand here speechless, I can see and hear myself, in the studio on Mars, starting to speak.

What can we learn from this imaginary story? Some believe that we can learn little. This would have been Wittgenstein's view.[1] And Quine writes: "The method of science fiction has its uses in philosophy, but . . . I wonder whether the limits of the method are properly heeded. To seek what is 'logically required' for sameness of person under unprecedented circumstances is to suggest that words have some logical force beyond what our past needs have invested them with."[2]

This criticism might be justified if, when considering such imagined cases, we had no reactions. But these cases arouse in most of us strong beliefs. And these are beliefs, not about our words, but about ourselves. By considering these cases, we discover what we believe to be involved in our own continued existence, or what it is that makes us now and ourselves next year the same people. We discover our beliefs about the nature of personal identity over time. Though our beliefs are revealed most clearly when we consider imaginary cases, these beliefs also cover actual cases, and our own lives. [Later in] this book I shall argue that some of these beliefs are false, then suggest how and why this matters.

SIMPLE TELETRANSPORTATION AND THE BRANCH-LINE CASE

At the beginning of my story, the Scanner destroys my brain and body. My blueprint is beamed to Mars, where another machine makes an organic *Replica* of me. My Replica thinks that he is me, and he seems to remember living my life up to the moment when I pressed the green button. In every other way, both physically and psychologically, we are exactly similar. If he returned to Earth, everyone would think that he was me.

Simple Teletransportation, as just described, is a common feature in science fiction. And it is believed, by some readers of this fiction, merely to be the fastest way of travelling. They believe that my Replica *would* be *me*. Other science fiction readers, and some of the characters in this fiction, take a different view. They believe that, when I press the green button, I die. My Replica is *someone else*, who has been made to be exactly like me.

This second view seems to be supported by the end of my story. The New Scanner does not destroy my brain and body. Besides gathering the information, it merely damages my heart. While I am in the cubicle, with the green button pressed, nothing seems to happen. I walk out, and learn that in a few days I shall die. I later talk, by two-way television, to my Replica on Mars. Let us continue the story.

Since my Replica knows that I am about to die, he tries to console me with the same thoughts with which I recently tried to console a dying friend. It is sad to learn, on the receiving end, how unconsoling these thoughts are. My Replica then assures me that he will take up my life where I leave off. He loves my wife, and together they will care for my children. And he will finish the book that I am writing. Besides having all of my drafts, he has all of my intentions. I must admit that he can finish my book as well as I could. All these facts console me a little. Dying when I know that I shall have a Replica is not quite as bad as, simply, dying. Even so, I shall soon lose consciousness, forever.

In Simple Teletransportation, I am destroyed before I am Replicated. This makes it easier to believe that this *is* a way of travelling—that my Replica *is* me. At the end of my story, my life and that of my Replica overlap. Call this the [*Branch-Line Case*]. In this case, I cannot hope to travel on the *Main Line*, waking up on Mars with forty years of life ahead. I shall stay on the Branch-Line, here on Earth, which ends a few days later. Since I can talk to my Replica, it seems clear that he is *not* me. Though he is exactly like me, he is one person, and I am another. When I pinch myself, he feels nothing. When I have my heart attack, he will again feel nothing. And when I am dead he will live for another forty years.

If we believe that my Replica is not me, it is natural to assume that my prospect, on the Branch Line, is almost as bad as ordinary death. I shall deny this assumption. As I shall argue later, being destroyed and Replicated is about as good as ordinary survival. I can best defend this claim, and the wider view of which it is part, after discussing the past debate about personal identity.

QUALITATIVE AND NUMERICAL IDENTITY

There are two kinds of sameness, or identity. I and my Replica are *qualitatively identical*, or exactly alike. But we may not be *numerically identical* or one and the same person. Similarly, two white billiard balls are not numerically but may be qualitatively identical. If I paint one of these balls red, it will cease to be qualitatively identical with itself as it was. But the red ball that I later see and the white ball that I painted red are numerically identical. They are one and the same ball.

We might say, of someone, "After his accident, he is no longer the same person." This is a claim about both kinds of identity. We claim that *he*, the same person, is *not* now the same person. This is not a contradiction. We merely mean that this person's character has changed. This numerically identical person is now qualitatively different.

When we are concerned about our future, it is our numerical identity that we are concerned about. I may believe that, after my marriage, I shall not be the same person. But this does not make marriage death. However much I change, I shall still be alive if there will be some person living who will *be* me.

Though our chief concern is our numerical identity, psychological changes matter. Indeed, on one view, certain kinds of qualitative change destroy numerical identity. If certain things happen to me, the truth might not be that I become a very different person. The truth might be that I cease to exist—that the resulting person is someone else.

THE PHYSICAL CRITERION OF PERSONAL IDENTITY

There has been much debate about the nature both of persons and of personal identity over time. It will help to distinguish these questions:

(1) What is the nature of a person?
(2) What makes a person at two different times one and the same person? What is necessarily involved in the continued existence of each person over time?

The answer to (2) can take this form: "*X* today is one and the same person as *Y* at some past time *if and only if* . . ." Such an answer states the *necessary and sufficient conditions* for personal identity over time.

In answering (2) we shall also partly answer (1). The necessary features of our continued existence depend upon our nature. And the simplest answer to (1) is that, to be a person, a being must be self-conscious, aware of its identity and its continued existence over time.

We can also ask

(3) What is in fact involved in the continued existence of each person over time?

Since our continued existence has features that are not necessary, the answer to (2) is only part of the answer to (3). For example, having the same heart and the same character are not necessary to our continued existence, but they are usually part of what this existence involves.

Many writers use the ambiguous phrase "the criterion of identity over time." Some mean by this "our way of telling whether some present object is identical with some past object." But I shall mean *what this identity necessarily involves, or consists in*.

In the case of most physical objects, on what I call the *standard view*, the criterion of identity over time is the spatio-temporal physical continuity of this object. This is something that we all understand, even if we fail to understand the description I shall now give. In the simplest case of physical continuity, like that of the Pyramids, an apparently static object continues to exist. In another simple case, like that of the Moon, an object moves in a regular way. Many objects move in less regular ways, but they still trace physically continuous spatio-temporal paths. Suppose that the billiard ball that I painted red is the same as the white ball with which last year I made a winning shot. On the standard view, this is true only if this ball traced such a continuous path. It must be true (1) that there is a line through space and time, starting where the white ball rested before I made my winning shot, and ending where the red ball now is, (2) that at every point on this line there was a billiard ball, and (3) that the existence of a ball at each point on this line was in part caused by the existence of a ball at the immediately preceding point.[3]

Some kinds of thing continue to exist even though their physical continuity involves great changes. A Camberwell Beauty is first an egg, then a caterpillar, then a chrysalis, then a butterfly. These are four stages in the physically continuous existence of a single organism. Other kinds of thing cannot survive such great changes. Suppose that an artist paints a self-portrait and then, by repainting, turns this into a portrait of his father. Even though these portraits are more similar than a caterpillar and a butterfly, they are not stages in the continued existence of a single painting. The self-portrait is a painting that the artist destroyed. In a general discussion of identity, we would need to explain why the requirement of physical continuity differs in such ways for different kinds of thing. But we can ignore this here.

Can there be gaps in the continued existence of a physical object? Suppose that I have the same gold watch that I was given as a boy even though, for a month, it lay disassembled on a watch-repairer's shelf. On one view, in the spatio-temporal path traced by this watch there was not at every point a watch, so my watch does not have a history of full physical continuity. But during the month when my watch was disassembled, and did not exist, all of its parts had histories of full continuity. On another view, even when it was disassembled, my watch existed.

Another complication again concerns the relation between a complex thing and the various parts of which it is composed. It is true of some of these things, though not true of all, that their continued existence need not involve the continued existence of their components. Suppose that a wooden ship is repaired from time to time while it is floating in harbour, and that after fifty years it contains none of the bits of wood out of which it was first built. It is still one and the same ship, because, as a ship, it has displayed throughout these fifty years full physical continuity. This is so despite the fact that it is now composed of quite different bits of wood. These bits of wood might be qualitatively identical to the original bits, but they are not one and the same bits. Something similar is partly true of a human body. With the exception of some brain cells, the cells in our bodies are replaced with new cells several times in our lives.

I have now described the physical continuity which, on the standard view, makes a physical object one and the same after many days or years. This enables me to state one of the rival views about personal identity. On this view, what makes me the same person over time is that I have the same brain and body. The criterion of my identity over time—or what this identity involves—is the physical continuity, over time, of my brain and body. I shall continue to exist if and only if this particular brain and body continue both to exist and to be the brain and body of a living person.

This is the simplest version of this view. There is a better version. This is

> *The Physical Criterion* (1) What is necessary is not the continued existence of the whole body, but the continued existence of *enough* of the brain to be the brain of a living person. *X* today is one and the same person as *Y* at some past time if and only if (2) enough of Y's brain continued to exist, and is now X's brain, and (3) this physical continuity has not taken a "branching" form. (4) Personal identity over time just consists in the holding of facts like (2) and (3).

(1) is clearly true in certain actual cases. Some people continue to exist even though they lose, or lose the use of, much of their bodies. (3) will be explained later.

Those who believe in the Physical Criterion would reject Teletransportation. They would believe this to be a way, not of travelling, but of dying. They would also reject, as inconceivable, reincarnation. They believe that someone cannot have a life after death, unless he lives this life in a resurrection of the very same, physically continuous body. This is why some Christians insist that they be buried. They believe that if, like Greek and Trojan heroes, they were burnt on funeral pyres, and their ashes scattered, not even God could bring them to life again. God could create only a Replica, someone else who was exactly like them. Other Christians believe that God could resurrect *them* if He reassembled their bodies out of the bits of matter that, when they were last alive, made up their bodies. This would be like the reassembly of my gold watch.[4]

THE PSYCHOLOGICAL CRITERION

Some people believe in a kind of psychological continuity that resembles physical continuity. This involves the continued existence of a purely mental *entity*, or thing—a soul, or spiritual substance. I shall return to this view. But I shall first explain another kind of psychological continuity. This is less like physical continuity, since it does not consist in the continued existence of some entity. But this other kind of psychological continuity involves only facts with which we are familiar.

What has been most discussed is the continuity of memory. This is because it is memory that makes most of us aware of our own continued existence over time. The exceptions are the people who are suffering from amnesia. Most amnesiacs lose only two sets of memories. They lose all of their memories of having particular past experiences—or, for short, their *experience memories*. They also lose some of their memories about facts, those that are about their own past lives. But they remember other facts, and they remember how to do different things, such as how to speak, or swim.

Locke suggested that experience-memory provides the criterion of personal identity.[5] Though this is not, on its own, a plausible view, I believe that it can be part of such a view. I shall therefore try to answer some of Locke's critics.

Locke claimed that someone cannot have committed some crime unless he now remembers doing so. We can understand a reluctance to punish people for crimes that they cannot remember. But, taken as a view about what is involved in a person's continued existence, Locke's claim is clearly false. If it was true, it would not be possible for someone to forget any of the things that he once did, or any of the experiences that he once had. But this *is* possible. I cannot now remember putting on my shirt this morning.

There are several ways to extend the experience-memory criterion so as to cover such cases. I shall appeal to the concept of an overlapping chain of experience-memories. Let us say that, between X today and Y twenty years ago, there are *direct memory connections* if X can now remember having some of the experiences that Y had twenty years ago. On Locke's view, only this makes X and Y one and the same person. But even if there are *no* such direct memory connections, there may be *continuity of memory* between X now and Y twenty years ago. This would be so if between X now and Y at that time there has been an overlapping chain of direct memories. In the case of most adults, there would be such a chain. In each day within the last twenty years, most of these people remembered some of their experiences on the previous day. On the revised version of Locke's view, some present person X is the same as some past person Y if there is between them continuity of memory.

This revision meets one objection to Locke's view. We should also revise the view so that it appeals to other facts. Besides direct memories, there are several other kinds of direct psychological connection. One such connection is that which holds between an intention and the later act in which this intention is carried out. Other such direct connections are those which hold when a belief, or a desire, or any other psychological feature, continues to be had.

I can now define two general relations:

> *Psychological connectedness* is the holding of particular direct psychological connections.
> *Psychological continuity* is the holding of overlapping chains of *strong* connectedness.

Of these two general relations, connectedness is more important both in theory and in practice. Connectedness can hold to any degree. Between X today and Y yesterday there might be several thousand direct psychological connections, or only a single connection. If there was only a single connection, X and Y would not be, on the revised Lockean View, the same person. For X and Y to be the same person, there must be over every day *enough* direct psychological connections. Since connectedness is a matter of degree, we cannot plausibly define precisely what counts as enough. But we can claim that there is enough connectedness if the number of direct connections, over any day, is *at least half* the number that hold, over every day, in the lives of nearly every actual person.[6] When there are enough direct connections, there is what I call *strong* connectedness. . . .

> *The Psychological Criterion*: (1) There is *psychological continuity* if and only if there are overlapping chains of strong connectedness. X today is one and the same person as Y at some past time if and only if (2) X is psychologically continuous with Y, (3) this continuity has the right kind of cause, and (4) it has not taken a "branching" form. (5) Personal identity over time just consists in the holding of facts like (2) to (4).

As with the Physical Criterion, (4) will be explained later.

There are three versions of the Psychological Criterion. These differ over the question of what is the *right* kind of cause. On the *Narrow* version, this must be the *normal* cause. On the *Wide* version, this could be *any reliable* cause. On the *Widest* version, the cause could be *any* cause. . . .

Reconsider the start of my imagined story, where my brain and body are destroyed. The Scanner and the Replicator produce a person who has a new but exactly similar brain and body, and who is psychologically continuous with me as I was when I pressed the green button. The cause of this continuity is, though unusual, reliable. On both the Physical Criterion and the Narrow Psychological Criterion, my Replica would *not* be me. On the two Wide Criteria, he *would* be me.

I shall argue that we need not decide between these three versions of the Psychological Criterion. A partial analogy may suggest why. Some people go blind because of damage to their eyes. Scientists are now developing artificial eyes. These involve a glass or plastic lens, and a micro-computer which sends through the optic nerve electrical patterns like those that are sent through this nerve by a natural eye. When such artificial eyes are more advanced, they might give to someone who has gone blind visual experiences just like those that he used to have. What he seems to see would correspond to what is in fact before him. And his visual experiences would be causally dependent, in this new but reliable way, on the light-waves coming from the objects that are before him.

Would this person be *seeing* these objects? If we insist that seeing must involve the normal cause, we would answer No. But even if this person cannot see, what he has is *just as good as* seeing, both as a way of knowing what is within sight, and as a source of visual pleasure. If we accept the Psychological Criterion, we could make a similar claim. If psychological continuity does not have its normal cause, it may not provide personal identity. But we can claim that, even if this is so, what it provides is *as good as* personal identity.

THE OTHER VIEWS

I am asking what is the criterion of personal identity over time—what this identity involves, or consists in. I first described the spatio-temporal physical continuity that, on the standard view, is the criterion of identity of physical objects. I then described two views about personal identity, the Physical and Psychological Criteria.

There is a natural but false assumption about these views. Many people believe in what is called *Materialism*, or *Physicalism*. This is the view that that there are no purely mental objects, states, or events. On one version of Physicalism, every mental event is just a physical event in some particular brain and nervous system. There are other versions. Those who are not Physicalists are either *Dualists* or *Idealists*. Dualists believe that mental events are *not* physical events. This can be so even if all mental events are causally dependent on physical events in a brain. Idealists believe that all states and events are, when understood correctly, purely mental. Given these distinctions, we may assume that Physicalists must accept the Physical Criterion of personal identity.

This is not so. Physicalists could accept the Psychological Criterion. And they could accept the version that allows any reliable cause, or any cause. They could thus believe that, in Simple Teletransportation, my Replica would be me. They would here be rejecting the Physical Criterion.[7]

These criteria are not the only views about personal identity. I shall now describe some of the other views that are either sufficiently plausible, or have enough supporters, to be worth considering. . . .

I start with a new distinction. On the Physical Criterion, personal identity over time just involves the physically continuous existence of enough of a brain so that it remains the brain of a living person. On the Psychological Criterion, personal identity over time just involves the various kinds of psychological continuity, with the right kind of cause. These views are both *Reductionist*.

. . .

[T]here are ways of discovering whether we are Reductionists in our view about some kind of thing. If we accept a Reductionist View, we shall believe that the identity of such a thing may be, in a quite unpuzzling way, *indeterminate*. If we do *not* believe this, we are probably Non-Reductionists about this kind of thing.

Consider, for example, clubs. Suppose that a certain club exists for several years, holding regular meetings. The meetings then cease. Some years later, some of the members of this club form a club with the same name, and the same rules. We ask: "Have these people reconvened the *very same* club? Or have they merely started up *another* club, which is exactly similar?" There might be an answer to this question. The original club might have had a rule explaining how, after such a period of non-existence, it could be reconvened. Or it might have had a rule preventing this. But suppose that there is no such rule, and no legal facts, supporting either answer to our question. And suppose that the people involved, if they were asked our question, would not give it an answer. There would then be no answer to our question. The claim "This is the same club" would be *neither true nor false*.

Though there is no answer to our question, there may be nothing that we do not know. This is because the existence of a club is not separate from the existence of its members, acting together in certain ways. The continued existence of a club just involves its members having meetings, that are conducted according to the club's rules. If we know all the facts about how people held meetings, and about the club's rules, we know everything there is to know. This is why we would not be puzzled when we cannot answer the question, "Is this the very same club?" We would not be puzzled because, even without answering this question, we can know everything about what happened. If this is true of some question, I call this question *empty*.

When we ask an empty question, there is only one fact or outcome that we are considering. Different answers to our question are merely different descriptions of this fact or outcome. This is why, without answering this empty question, we can know everything that there is to know. In my example we can ask, "Is this the very same club, or is it merely another club, that is exactly similar?" But these are not here two different possibilities, one of which must be true.

When an empty question has no answer, we can decide to *give* it an answer. We could decide to call the later club the same as the original club. Or we could decide to call it another club, that is exactly similar. This is not a decision between different views about what really happened. Before making our decision, we already knew what happened. We are merely choosing one of two different descriptions of the very same course of events.

If we are Reductionists about personal identity, we should make similar claims. We can describe cases where, between me now and some future person, the physical and psychological connections hold only to reduced degrees. If I imagine myself in such a case, I can always ask, "Am I about to die? Will the resulting person be me?" On the Reductionist View, in some cases there would be no answer. My question would be *empty*. The claim that I was about to die would be neither true nor false. If I knew the facts about both physical continuity and psychological connectedness, I would know everything there was to know. I would know everything, even though I did not know whether I was about to die, or would go on living for many years.

When it is applied to ourselves, this Reductionist claim is hard to believe. In such imagined cases, something unusual is about to happen. But most of us are inclined to believe that, in any conceivable case, the question "Am I about to die?" must have an answer. And we are inclined to believe that this answer must be either, and quite simply, Yes or No. Any future person must be either me, or someone else. These beliefs I call the view that *our identity must be determinate*.

I shall next describe two explanatory claims. The first answers a new question. What unites the different experiences that are had by a single person at the same time? While I type this sentence, I am aware of the movements of my fingers, and can see the sunlight on my desk, and can hear the wind ruffling some leaves. What unites these different experiences? Some claim: the fact that they are all *my* experiences. These are the experiences that are being had, at this time, by a particular person, or *subject of experiences*. A similar question covers my whole life. What unites the different experiences that, together, constitute this life? Some give the same answer. What unites all of these experiences is, simply, that they are all mine. These answers I call the view that *psychological unity is explained by ownership*.

The views described so far are about the nature of personal identity. I shall end with a pair of views that are about, not the nature of this identity, but its importance. Consider an ordinary case where, even on any version of the Reductionist View, there are two possible outcomes. In one of the outcomes, I am about to die. In the other outcome I shall live for many years. If these years would be worth living, the second outcome would be better for me. And the difference between these outcomes would be judged to be important on most theories about rationality, and most moral theories. It would have rational and moral significance whether I am about to die, or shall live for many years. What is judged to be important here is whether, during these years, there will be someone living who will *be me*. This is a question about personal identity. On one view, in this kind of case, this is always what is important. I call this the view that *personal identity is what matters*. This is the natural view.

The rival view is that *personal identity is not what matters*. I claim

> *What matters is Relation R*: psychological connectedness and/or continuity, with the right kind of cause.

Since it is more controversial, I add, as a separate claim

> In an account of what matters, the right kind of cause could be any cause.

It is in imaginary cases that we can best decide whether what matters is Relation R or personal identity. One example may be the Branch-Line Case, where my life briefly overlaps with that of my Replica. Suppose that we believe that I and my Replica are two different people. I am about to die, but my Replica will live for another forty years. If personal identity is what matters, I should regard my prospect here as being nearly as bad as ordinary death. But if what matters is Relation R, with any cause, I should regard this way of dying as being about as good as ordinary survival.

The disagreement between these views is not confined to imaginary cases. The two views also disagree about all of the actual lives that are lived. The disagreement is here less sharp, because, on both views, all or nearly all these lives contain the relation that matters. On all of the plausible views about the nature of personal identity, personal identity nearly always coincides with psychological continuity, and roughly coincides with psychological connectedness. But, as I shall argue later, it makes a great difference which of these we believe to be what matters. If we cease to believe that our identity is what matters, this may affect some of our emotions, such as our attitude to ageing and to death. And, as I shall argue, we may be led to change our views about both rationality and morality.

II. HOW WE ARE NOT WHAT WE BELIEVE

DOES PSYCHOLOGICAL CONTINUITY PRESUPPOSE PERSONAL IDENTITY?

I remember trying, when a child, to remain standing among the crashing waves of the Atlantic Ocean. I am the same person as the child who had that experience. On Locke's view, what makes me the same person as that child is my memory, or "consciousness," of that experience.

Bishop Butler thought this a "wonderful mistake." It is, he wrote, "self-evident, that consciousness of personal identity presupposes, and therefore cannot constitute personal identity, any more than knowledge in any other case, can constitute truth, which it presupposes."[8]

I have already revised Locke's view. The Psychological Criterion appeals, not to single memories, but to the continuity of memory, and, more broadly, to Relation R, which includes other kinds of psychological continuity. But this revision does not answer Butler's objection.

On one interpretation, the objection would be this: "It is part of our concept of memory that we can remember only *our own* experiences. The continuity of memory therefore presupposes personal identity. The same is therefore true of your Relation R. You claim that personal identity just consists in the holding of Relation R. This must be false if Relation R itself presupposes personal identity."

To answer this objection, we can define a wider concept, *quasi-memory*. I have an accurate quasi-memory of a past experience if

(1) I seem to remember having an experience,
(2) *someone* did have this experience,
and
(3) my apparent memory is causally dependent, in the right kind of way, on that past experience.

On this definition, ordinary memories are a subclass of quasi-memories. They are quasi-memories of our own past experiences.[9]

We do not quasi-remember other people's past experiences. But we might begin to do so. The causes of long-term memories are memory-traces. It was once thought that these might be localized, involving changes in only a few brain cells. It is now more probable that a particular memory-trace involves changes in a larger number of cells. Suppose that, even if this is true, neuro-surgeons develop ways to create in one brain a copy of a memory-trace in another brain. This might enable us to quasi-remember other people's past experiences.

Consider

> *Venetian Memories*. Jane has agreed to have copied in her brain some of Paul's memory-traces. After she recovers consciousness in the post-surgery room, she has a new set of vivid apparent memories. She seems to remember walking on the marble paving of a square, hearing the flapping of flying pigeons and the cries of gulls, and seeing light sparkling on green water. One apparent memory is very clear. She seems to remember looking across the water to an island, where a white Palladian church stood out brilliantly against a dark thundercloud.

What should Jane believe about these apparent memories? Suppose that, because she has seen this church in photographs, she knows it to be San Giorgio, in Venice. She also knows that she has never been to Italy, while Paul goes to Venice often. Since she knows that she has received copies of some of

Paul's memory-traces, she could justifiably assume that she may be quasi-remembering some of Paul's experiences in Venice.

...

Return now to Butler's objection to the Psychological Criterion of personal identity. On this objection, the continuity of memory cannot be, even in part, what makes a series of experiences all the experiences of a single person, since this person's memory presupposes his continued identity.

On the interpretation that I gave above, memory presupposes identity because, on our concept of memory, we can remember only our own past experiences. This objection can now be answered. We can use the wider concept of quasi-memory.

In our statement of our revised Psychological Criterion, we should not claim that, if I have an accurate quasi-memory of some past experience, this makes me the person who had this experience. One person's mental life may include a few quasi-memories of experiences in some other person's life, as in the imagined case of Jane and Paul. Our criterion ignores a few such quasi-memory connections. We appeal instead to overlapping chains of many such connections. My mental life consists of a series of very varied experiences. These include countless quasi-memories of earlier experiences. The connections between these quasi-memories and these earlier experiences overlap like the strands in a rope. There is *strong connectedness* of quasi-memory if, over each day, the number of direct quasi-memory connections is at least half the number in most actual lives. Overlapping strands of strong connectedness provide *continuity of quasi-memory*. Revising Locke, we claim that the unity of each person's life is in part created by this continuity. We are not now appealing to a concept that presupposes personal identity. Since the continuity of quasi-memory does not presuppose personal identity, it may be part of what constitutes personal identity. It may be part of what makes me now and myself at other times one and the same person. (I say "part" because our criterion also appeals to the other kinds of psychological continuity.)

Butler's objection may be interpreted in a different way. He may have meant: "In memory we are directly aware of our own identity through time, and aware that this is a separate, further fact, which cannot just consist in physical and psychological continuity. We are aware that each of us is a persisting subject of experiences, a separately existing entity that is not our brain or body. And we are aware that our own continued existence is, simply, the continued existence of this subject of experiences."

Does our memory tell us this? Are we directly aware of the existence of this separate entity, the subject of experiences? Some have thought that we are aware of this, not just in memory, but in all of our experiences.

THE SUBJECT OF EXPERIENCES

Reid writes:

> my personal identity ... implies the continued existence of that indivisible thing that I call myself. Whatever this self may be, it is something which thinks, and deliberates, and resolves, and acts, and suffers. I am not thought, I am not action, I am not feeling: I am something that thinks, and acts, and suffers.[10]

In one sense, this is clearly true. Even Reductionists do not deny that people exist. And, on our concept of a person, people are not thoughts and acts. They are thinkers and agents. I am not a series of experiences, but the person who *has* these experiences. A Reductionist can admit that, in this sense, a person is *what has* experiences, or the *subject of experiences*. This is true because of the way in which we talk. What a Reductionist denies is that the subject of experiences is a *separately existing entity*, distinct from a brain and body, and a series of physical and mental events.

Is it true that, in memory, we are directly aware of what the Reductionist denies? Is each of us aware that he is a persisting subject of experiences, a separately existing entity that is not his brain and body? Is each of us aware, for example, that he is a Cartesian Ego?

This is not a point that can be argued. I do not believe that *I* am directly aware that I am such an entity. And I assume that I am not unusual. I believe that no one is directly aware of such a fact.

Suppose that I *was* aware that I was such an entity. There would still be an objection to the Cartesian View. It has been claimed that I could not know that this entity continued to exist. As both Locke and Kant argued,[11] there might be a series of such entities that were psychologically continuous. Memories might be passed from one to the next like a baton in a relay race. So might all other psychological features. Given the resulting psychological continuity, we would not be aware that one of these entities had been replaced by another. We therefore cannot know that such entities continue to exist.

Reconsider the Branch-Line Case, where it is clear that I remain on Earth. It might seem to a certain person that he has just had these two thoughts: "Snow is falling. So it must be cold." But the truth might be this. This person is my Replica on Mars. Just before I pressed the green button, I thought "Snow is falling." Several minutes later, my Replica suddenly becomes conscious, in a similar cubicle on Mars. When he becomes conscious, he has apparent memories of living my life, and in particular he seems to remember just having thought, "Snow is falling." He then thinks "So it must be cold." My Replica on Mars would now be in a state of mind exactly like mine when I have just had both these thoughts. When my Replica is in this state of mind, he would believe that both these thoughts were had by the same thinker, himself. But this would be false. I had the first thought, and my Replica only had the second.

This example is imaginary. But it seems to show that we could not tell, from the content of our experiences, whether we really are aware of the continued existence of a separately existing subject of experiences. The most that we have are states of mind like that of my Replica. My Replica falsely believes that he has just had two thoughts. He is not aware of the continued existence of a separately existing entity: the thinker of these thoughts. He is aware of something less, the psychological continuity between his life and mine. In the same way, when we have had a series of thoughts, the most that we are aware of is the psychological continuity of our stream of consciousness. Some claim that we are aware of the continued existence of separately existing subjects of experiences. As Locke and Kant argued, and our example seems to show, such awareness cannot in fact be distinguished from our awareness of mere psychological continuity. Our experiences give us no reason to believe in the existence of these entities. Unless we have other reasons to believe in their existence, we should reject this belief.

This conclusion is not, as some write, crudely verificationist. I am not assuming that only what we could know could ever be true. My remarks make a different assumption. I am discussing a general claim about the existence of a particular kind of thing. This is claimed to be a separately existing entity, distinct from our brains and bodies. I claim that, if we have no reasons to believe that such entities exist, we should reject this belief. I do not, like verificationists, claim that this belief is senseless. My claim is merely like the claim that, since we have no reason to believe that water-nymphs or unicorns exist, we should reject these beliefs.[12]

. . .

Because we ascribe thoughts to thinkers, we can truly claim that thinkers exist. But we cannot deduce, from the content of our experiences, that a thinker is a separately existing entity. . . . We could fully describe our experiences, and the connections between them, without claiming that they are had by a subject of experiences. We could give what I call an *impersonal* description.

. . .

WILLIAMS'S ARGUMENT AGAINST THE PSYCHOLOGICAL CRITERION*

I have defended the Psychological Criterion in two ways. I have claimed, and partly shown, that we can describe psychological continuity in a way that does not presuppose personal identity. And I have claimed that, on the evidence we have, the carrier of this continuity is not an entity that exists separately from a person's brain and body.

I shall next consider another objection to the Psychological Criterion. This is advanced by Williams.* This objection seems to show that, if some person's

* The Williams paper which Parfit here discusses appears as the previous selection in this volume. Parfit offers his own slight variation on Williams's example.

brain continues to exist, and to support consciousness, this person will continue to exist, however great the breaks are in the psychological continuity of this person's mental life.

Here is a simpler version of this objection. Consider

Williams's Example. I am the prisoner of some callous neuro-surgeon, who intends to disrupt my psychological continuity by tampering with my brain. I shall be conscious while he operates, and in pain. I therefore dread what is coming.

The surgeon tells me that, while I am in pain, he will do several things. He will first activate some neurodes that will give me amnesia. I shall suddenly lose all of my memories of my life up to the start of my pain. Does this give me less reason to dread what is coming? Can I assume that, when the surgeon flips this switch, my pain will suddenly cease? Surely not. The pain might so occupy my mind that I would even fail to notice the loss of all these memories.

The surgeon next tells me that, while I am still in pain, he will later flip another switch, that will cause me to believe that I am Napoleon, and will give me apparent memories of Napoleon's life. Can I assume that this will cause my pain to cease? The natural answer is again No. To support this answer, we can again suppose that my pain will prevent me from noticing anything. I shall not notice my coming to believe that I am Napoleon, and my acquiring a whole new set of apparent memories. When the surgeon flips this second switch, there will be no change at all in what I am conscious of. The changes will be purely dispositional. It will only become true that, if my pain ceased, so that I could think, I would answer the question "Who are you?" with the name "Napoleon." Similarly, if my pain ceased, I would then start to have delusory apparent memories, such as those of reviewing the Imperial Guard, or of weeping with frustration at the catastrophe of 1812. If it is only such changes in my dispositions that would be brought about by the flipping of the second switch, I would have no reason to expect this to cause my pain to cease.

The surgeon then tells me that, during my ordeal, he will later flip a third switch, that will change my character so that it becomes just like Napoleon's. Once again, I seem to have no reason to expect the flipping of this switch to end my pain. It might at most bring some relief, if Napoleon's character, compared with mine, involved more fortitude.

In this imagined case, nothing that I am told seems to give me a reason to expect that, during my ordeal, I shall cease to exist. I seem to have as much reason to dread all of the pain. This reason does not seem to be removed by the other things I have to dread—losing my memories, and going mad, becoming like, and thinking that I am, Napoleon. As Williams claims, this argument seems to show that I can have reason to fear future pain whatever psychological changes precede this pain. Even after all these changes, it will be I who feels this pain. If this is so, the Psychological Criterion of personal identity is mistaken. In this imagined case, between me now and myself after the ordeal, there would be no continuity of memory, character, and the like. What is involved in my continuing to exist therefore cannot be such continuity.[14]

. . .

Williams's argument seems to refute the Psychological Criterion. It seems to show that the true view is the Physical Criterion. On this view, if some person's brain and body continue to exist, and to support consciousness, this person will continue to exist, however great the breaks are in the psychological continuity of this person's mental life.

THE PSYCHOLOGICAL SPECTRUM

I shall now revise Williams's argument. Why this is worth doing will emerge later.

Williams discusses a single case in which, after a few changes, there will be no psychological continuity. I shall discuss a *spectrum*, or range of cases, each of which is very similar to its neighbours. These cases involve all of the possible degrees of psychological connectedness. I call this the *Psychological Spectrum*.

In the case at the far end, the surgeon would cause very many switches to be simultaneously flipped. This would cause there to be no psychological connections between me and the resulting person. This person, would be wholly like Napoleon.

In the cases at the near end, the surgeon would cause to be flipped only a few switches. If he flipped only the first switch, this would merely cause me to lose a few memories, and to have a few apparent memories that fit the life of Napoleon. If he flipped the first two switches, I would merely lose a few more memories, and have a few more of these new apparent memories. Only if he flipped all of the switches would I lose all my memories, and have a complete set of Napoleonic delusions.

Similar claims are true about the changes in my character. Any particular switch would cause only a small change. Thus, if I am to be like Napoleon, I must become more bad-tempered, and must cease to be upset by the sight of people being killed. These would be the only changes produced by the flipping of the first two switches.

In this revised version of the argument, which involves very many different cases, we must decide which are the cases in which I would survive. In the case at the near end, the surgeon does nothing. In the second case, I would merely lose a few memories, have a few delusions, and become more bad-tempered. It is clear that, in this case, I would survive. In the third case, the changes would be only slightly greater. And this is true of any two neighbouring cases in this range. It is hard to believe both that I would survive in one of these cases, and that, in the next case, I would cease to exist. Whether I continue to exist cannot be plausibly thought to depend on whether I would lose just a few more memories, and have a few more delusory memories, and have my character changed in some small way. If no such small change could cause me to cease to exist, I would continue to exist in all of these cases. I would continue to exist even in the case at the far end of this spectrum. In this case, between me now and the resulting person, there would be *no* psychological connections.

...

... Suppose that I am about to undergo an operation in the middle of this Spectrum. I know that the resulting person will be in agony. If I do not know whether or not I shall be the person in agony, and I do not even know whether I shall still be alive, how can I believe that I *do* know exactly what will happen? I do not know the answer to the most important questions. It is very hard to believe that these are empty questions.

Most of us believe that ... our identity must be determinate. We believe that, even in such "borderline cases," the question "Am I about to die?" must have an answer. And, as Williams claims, we believe that the answer must be either, and quite simply, Yes or No. If someone will be alive, and will be suffering agony, this person either will or will not be me. One of these must be true. And we cannot make sense of any third alternative, such as that the person in agony will be *partly* me. I can imagine being only partly in agony, because I am drifting in and out of consciousness. But if someone will be fully conscious of the agony, this person cannot be partly me.

The Reductionist View would provide an answer to Williams's argument. When Williams gives his version of this argument, he rejects this view. He concludes instead that, if my brain continues to exist, and to be the brain of a living person, I shall be that person. This would be so even if, between myself now and myself later, there would be *no* psychological connections. After advancing his argument, Williams writes that this conclusion may "perhaps" be wrong "but we need to be shown what is wrong with it."

THE PHYSICAL SPECTRUM

One objection is that a similar argument applies to physical continuity. Consider another range of possible cases: the *Physical Spectrum*. These cases involve all of the different possible degrees of physical continuity.

In the case at the near end of this spectrum, there would later be a person who would be fully continuous with me as I am now, both physically and psychologically. In the case at the far end, there would later be a person who would be psychologically but not physically continous with me as I am now. The far end is like the case of Teletransportation. The near end is the normal case of continued existence.

In a case close to the near end, scientists would replace 1% of the cells in my brain and body with exact duplicates. In the case in the middle of the spectrum, they would replace 50%. In a case near the far end, they would replace 99%, leaving only 1% of my original brain and body. At the far end, the "replacement" would involve the complete destruction of my brain and body, and the creation out of new organic matter of a Replica of me.

What is important in this last case is not just that my Replica's brain and body would be entirely composed of new matter. As I explained, this might become true in a way that does not destroy my brain and body. It could become true if there is a long series of small changes in the matter in my body, during which my brain and body continue to exist, and to function normally. This would be like the ship that becomes entirely composed of new bits of wood, after fifty years of piecemeal repairs. In both of these cases, the complete change in the identity of the components does not disrupt physical continuity. Things are different in the case at the far end of the Physical Spectrum. There is here no physical continuity, since my brain and body are completely destroyed, and it is only later that the scientists create, out of new matter, my Replica.

The first few cases in this range are now believed to be technically possible. Portions of brain-tissue have been successfully transplanted from one mammal's brain to another's. And what is transplanted could be a part of the brain that, in all individuals, is sufficiently similar. This could enable surgeons to provide functioning replacements for some damaged parts of the brain. These actual transplants proved to be easier than the more familiar transplants of the kidney or the heart, since a brain seems not to "reject" transplanted tissue in the way in which the body rejects transplanted organs. Though the first few cases in this range are even now possible, most of the cases will remain impossible. But this impossibility will be merely technical. Since I use these cases only to discover what we believe, this impossibility does not matter.

Suppose we believe that, at the far end of this spectrum, my Replica would not be me. He would merely be someone else who was exactly like me. At the near end of this spectrum, where there would be no replacement, the resulting person would be me. What should I expect if what will happen is some intermediate case? If they replaced only 1%, would I cease to exist? This is not plausible, since I do not need all of my brain and body. But what about the cases where they would replace 10%, or 30%, or 60%, or 90%?

This range of cases challenges the Physical Criterion, which is another version of the Reductionist View. Imagine that you are about to undergo one of these operations. You might try to believe this version of Reductionism. You might say to yourself:

> In any central case in this range, the question "Am I about to die?" has no answer. But I know just what will happen. A certain percentage of my brain and body will be replaced with exact duplicates of the existing cells. The resulting person will be psychologically continuous with me as I am now. This is all there is to know. I do not know whether the resulting person will be me, or will be someone else who is merely exactly like me. But this is not, here, a real question, which must have an answer. It does not describe two different possibilities, one of which must be true. It is here an empty question. There is not a real difference here between the resulting person's being *me*, and his being *someone else*. This is why, even though I do not know whether I am about to die, I know everything.

I believe that, for those who accept the Physical Criterion, this is the right reaction to this range of cases. But most of us would not yet accept such claims.

If we do not yet accept the Reductionist View, and continue to believe that our identity must be determinate, what should we claim about these cases? If we continue to assume that my Replica would not be me, we are forced to the following conclusion. There must be some critical percentage which is such that, if the surgeons replace less than this percent, it will be me who wakes up, but if they replace more than this percent, it will *not* be me, but only someone else who is merely like me. We might suggest a variant of this conclusion. Perhaps there is some crucial part of my brain which is such that, if the surgeons do not replace this part, the resulting person will be me, but if they do, it will be someone else. But this makes no difference. What if they replace different percentages of this crucial part of my brain? We are again forced to the view that there must be some critical percentage.

Such a view is not incoherent. But it is hard to believe. And something else is true, that makes it even harder to believe. We could not *discover* what the critical percentage is, by carrying out some of the cases in this imagined spectrum. I might say, "Try replacing 50% of the cells in my brain and body, and I shall tell you what happens." But we know in advance that, in every case, the resulting person would be inclined to believe that he is me. And this would not show that he *is* me. Carrying out such cases could not provide the answer to our question.

. . .

THE COMBINED SPECTRUM

Consider another range of possible cases. These involve all of the possible variations in the degrees of *both* physical *and* psychological connectedness. This is the *Combined Spectrum*.

At the near end of this spectrum is the normal case in which a future person would be fully continuous with me as I am now, both physically and psychologically. This person would be me in just the way that, in my actual life, it will be me who wakes up tomorrow. At the far end of this spectrum the resulting person would have no continuity with me as I am now, either physically or psychologically. In this case the scientists would destroy my brain and body, and then create, out of new organic matter, a perfect Replica of someone else. Let us suppose this person to be, not Napoleon, but Greta Garbo.* We can suppose that, when Garbo was 30, a group of scientists recorded the states of all the cells in her brain and body.

In the first case in this spectrum, at the near end, nothing would be done. In the second case, a few of the cells in my brain and body would be replaced. The new cells would *not* be exact duplicates. As a result, there would be somewhat less psychological connectedness between me and the person who wakes up. This person would not have all of my memories, and his character would be in one way unlike mine. He would have some apparent memories of Greta Garbo's life, and have one of Garbo's characteristics. Unlike me, he would enjoy acting. His body would also be in one way less like mine, and more like Garbo's. His eyes would be more like Garbo's eyes. Further along the spectrum, a larger percentage of my cells would be replaced, again with dissimilar cells. The resulting person would be in fewer ways psychologically connected with me, and in more ways connected with Garbo, as she was at the age of 30. And there would be similar changes in this person's body. Near the far end, most of my cells would be replaced with dissimilar cells. The person who wakes up would have only a few of the cells in my original brain and body, and between her and me there would be only a few psychological connections. She would have a few apparent memories that fit my past, and a few of my habits and desires. But in every other way she would be, both physically and psychologically, just like Greta Garbo.

. . .

In considering the first two Spectra, we had three alternatives: accepting a Reductionist reply, believing that there must be some sharp borderline, and believing that the resulting person would in every case be me. Of these three the third seemed the least implausible conclusion.

In considering the Combined Spectrum, we cannot accept this conclusion. In the case at the far end, the scientists destroy my brain and body, and then make, out of new matter, a Replica of Greta Garbo. There would be no connection, of any kind, between me and this resulting person. It could not be clearer that, in this case, the resulting person would *not* be me. We are forced to choose between the other two alternatives.

We might continue to believe that our identity must be determinate. We might continue to believe that, to the question "Would the resulting person be me?" there must always be an answer, which must be either and quite simply Yes or No. We would then be forced to accept the following claims:

> Somewhere in this Spectrum, there is a sharp borderline. There must be some critical set of the cells replaced, and some critical degree of psychological change, which would make all the difference. If the surgeons replace slightly fewer than these cells, and produce one fewer psychological change, it will be me who wakes up. If they replace the few extra cells, and produce one more psychological change, I shall cease to exist, and the person waking up will

* Swedish film star Greta Garbo (1905–90) was a famous actress whose appearance and personality stand in stark contrast to those of French General Napoleon Bonaparte (1769–1821).

> be someone else. There must be such a pair of cases somewhere in this Spectrum, *even though there could never be any evidence where these cases are.*

These claims are hard to believe. It is hard to believe (1) that the difference between life and death could just consist in any of the very small differences described above. We are inclined to believe that there is *always* a difference between some future person's being me, and his being someone else. And we are inclined to believe that this is a *deep* difference. But between neighbouring cases in this Spectrum the differences are trivial. It is therefore hard to believe that, in one of these cases, the resulting person would quite straightforwardly be me, and that, in the next case, he would quite straightforwardly be someone else.

It is also hard to believe (2) that there must be such a sharp borderline, somewhere in the Spectrum, though we could never have any evidence where the borderline would be. Some would claim that, if there could never be such evidence, it makes no sense to claim that there must somewhere be such a line.

Even if (2) makes sense, claims (1) and (2), taken together, are extremely implausible. I believe that they are even more implausible than the only other possible conclusion, which is the Reductionist View. We should therefore now conclude that the Reductionist View is true. On this view, in the central cases of the Combined Spectrum, it would be an empty question whether the resulting person would be me. This Spectrum provides, as I claimed, a strong argument for this view.

...

Reductionists admit that there is a difference between numerical identity and exact similarity. In some cases, there would be a real difference between some person's being me, and his being someone else who is merely exactly like me. Many people assume that there must *always* be such a difference.

In the case of nations, or clubs, such an assumption is false. Two clubs could exist at the same time, and be, apart from their membership, exactly similar. If I am a member of one of these clubs, and you claim also to be a member, I might ask, "Are you a member of the very same club of which I am a member? Or are you merely a member of the other club, that is exactly similar?" This is not an empty question, since it describes two different possibilities. But, though there are two possibilities in a case in which the two clubs co-exist, there may not be two such possibilities when we are discussing the relation between some presently existing club and some past club. . . .

In the same way, there are some cases where there is a real difference between someone's being me, and his being someone else who is exactly like me. This may be so in the Branch-Line Case, the version of Teletransportation where the Scanner does not destroy my brain and body. In the Branch-Line Case, my life overlaps with the life of my Replica on Mars. Given this overlap, we may conclude that we are two different people—that we are qualitatively but not numerically identical. If I am the person on Earth, and my Replica on Mars now exists, it makes a difference whether some pain will be felt by me, or will instead be felt by my Replica. This is a real difference in what will happen.

If we return to Simple Teletransportation, where there is no overlap between my life and that of my Replica, things are different. We could say here that my Replica will be me, or we could instead say that he will merely be someone else who is exactly like me. But we should not regard these as competing hypotheses about what will happen. For these to be competing hypotheses, my continued existence must involve a *further fact*. If my continued existence merely involves physical and psychological continuity, we know just what happens in this case. There will be some future person who will be physically exactly like me, and who will be fully psychologically continuous with me. This psychological continuity will have a reliable cause, the transmission of my blueprint. But this continuity will not have its normal cause, since this future person will not be physically continuous with me. This is a full description of the facts. There is no further fact about which we are ignorant. If personal identity does not involve a further fact, we should not believe that there are here two different possibilities: that my Replica will be me, or that he will be someone else who is merely like me. What could make these different possibilities? In what could the difference consist?

Some non-Reductionists would agree that, in this case, there are not two possibilities. These people believe that, in the case of Teletransportation, my Replica would not be me. I shall later discuss a plausible argument for this conclusion. If we would be wrong to say that my Replica is me, the remarks that I have just made apply instead to the central cases in the Physical Spectrum. My Replica might have a quarter of the existing cells in my brain and body, or half, or three-quarters. In these cases there are not two different possibilities: that my Replica is me, or that he is someone else who is merely like me. These are merely different descriptions of the same outcome.

If we believe that there is always a real difference between some person's being me and his being someone else, we must believe that this difference comes somewhere in this range of cases. There must be a sharp borderline, though we could never know where this is. As I have claimed, this belief is even more implausible than the Reductionist View.

In the case of clubs, though there is sometimes a difference between numerical identity and exact similarity, there is sometimes no difference. The question, "Is it the same, or merely exactly similar?" is sometimes empty. This could be true of people, too. It would be true either at the end or in the middle of the Physical Spectrum.

It is hard to believe that this could be true. When I imagine myself about to press the green button, it is hard to believe that there is not a real question whether I am about to die, or shall instead wake up again on Mars. But, as I have argued, this belief cannot be justified unless personal identity involves a further fact. And there could not be such a fact unless I am a separately existing entity, apart from my brain and body. One such entity is a Cartesian Ego. As I have claimed, there is no evidence in favour of this view, and much evidence against it.

NOTES

1. See, for example, *Zettel*, ed. by G. Anscombe and G. von Wright, and translated by G. Anscombe, Blackwell, 1967, Proposition 350: "It is as if our concepts involve a scaffolding of facts ... If you imagine certain facts otherwise ... then you can no longer imagine the application of certain concepts."
2. W. V. O. Quine (1972), reviewing Munitz *Identity and Individuation*, in *The Journal of Philosophy*, p. 490.
3. This states a necessary condition for the continued existence of a physical object. Saul Kripke has argued, in lectures, that this condition is not sufficient. Since I missed these lectures, I cannot discuss this argument.
4. On this view, it could be fatal to live in what has long been a densely populated area, such as London. It may here be true of many bits of matter that they were part of the bodies of many different people, when they were last alive. These people could not all be resurrected, since there would not be enough such matter to be reassembled. Some hold a version of this view which avoids this problem. They believe that a resurrected body needs to contain only one particle from the original body.
5. John Locke (1690), *Essay Concerning Human Understanding*, ch. 27, sec. 16. Reprinted in John Perry, ed. (1975), *Personal Identity*.
6. This suggestion would need expanding, since there are many ways to count the number of direct connections. And some kinds of connection should be given more importance than others. As I suggest later, more weight should be given to those connections which are distinctive, or different in different people. (All English-speakers, for example, share many undistinctive memories of how to speak English.)
7. Quinton defends this view.
8. Samuel Butler (1736), *Analogy of Religion*, 1st appendix, reprinted in Perry 1975, p. 100.
9. I follow Sydney Shoemaker (1970), "Persons and their Pasts," *American Philosophical Quarterly*.
10. Thomas Reid (1785), "Of Memory," reprinted in Perry 1975, p. 109.
11. See Locke, Chapter 27, Section 13, reprinted in Perry (1), p. 101; and Kant, p. 342, especially footnote a. I take the example from Wachsberg.
12. Non-Reductionists have several other arguments which, in a longer discussion, I would need to try to answer. See Locke in Perry 1975, ch. 27, sec. 13, p. 101; Kant, *Critique of Pure Reason*, trans. N. Kemp Smith, p. 342 esp. fn. a. I take the example from Milton Wachsberg's unpublished 1983 PhD dissertation, Princeton University.
13. There would be certain kinds of *non-distinctive* continuity, such as continued memory of how to walk, and run. The Psychological Criterion should not appeal to these kinds of psychological continuity.
14. *The Times*, London, Science Column, 22 November 1982.

PART IV

PHILOSOPHY OF MIND AND LANGUAGE

MIND

INTRODUCTION

The selections in this section address a series of fundamental questions about the mind. Among them are the following: Are mind and brain fundamentally distinct? Can consciousness be explained in purely physical terms? Could a machine be programmed to think? What is the nature of our perceptual access to the world? Each of these questions is explored in one or more of the texts in this section.

Dualism and Behaviorism

When we think about our mind, it is natural to wonder what relation it has to our body. *Monists* maintain that whatever minds and bodies may be, they are both the same kind of thing; *Dualists*, by contrast, hold that body and mind are fundamentally distinct: the body is fundamentally physical, whereas the mind is fundamentally nonphysical or mental. Exactly what such a view amounts to depends, of course, on what exactly falls under the categories of "mental" and "physical." The first two selections contain defenses of two different versions of dualism that differ, in part, in what they take "the physical" to be. They are followed by a third selection that offers a systematic criticism of dualism in general.

René Descartes (1596–1650), a French philosopher writing in the seventeenth century, equated the physical with the realm of spatial extension, so anything taking up space will count as physical in Descartes' sense, whereas anything that does not will count as nonphysical.

According to Descartes' dualism (called "Cartesian dualism"), minds are nonphysical entities—entities that do not occupy space—whereas bodies are physical entities—entities that occupy space. Descartes argues for this conclusion using the premise that we can imagine minds existing without bodies.

An alternative version of dualism is found in the Nyāya view, developed by Hindu thinkers in the sixth century BCE. Nyāya thinkers hold that things are physical only if they are perceivable. Kisor Kumar Chakrabarti is a contemporary philosopher and scholar of Nyāya texts. As he interprets Nyāya dualism, minds are not physical in the Nyāya sense of "physical": they lack any externally perceivable features. The Cartesian and the Nyāya dualist thus agree that minds are distinct substances from bodies, but they disagree about the nature of this distinction.

The final selection in this section comes from British philosopher Gilbert Ryle's 1949 book *The Concept of Mind*. In the selection, "Descartes' Myth," Ryle attacks Cartesian dualism on the grounds that it rests on a "category mistake" in viewing the mind as a distinct substance from the body, but as nonetheless being a field of causes and effects, just as bodies are.

Physicalism

Inspired by the success of the physical sciences in the twentieth century, many philosophers adopted the monist position of *physicalism* (or *materialism*), the thesis that everything—including the mind—is physical. Much discussion in the philosophy of mind during the twentieth century was devoted to defending physicalist accounts of mental phenomena. The selection by contemporary Australian philosopher Daniel Stoljar provides an exceptionally clear formulation of physicalism. In it, Stoljar neatly summarizes the reasons many philosophers have for believing this thesis.

The next selection, by Australian philosopher J. J. C. Smart (1920–), is an attempt to define mental states in physical terms. Smart's 1959 article focuses on sensations (such as afterimages that you can give yourself by pressing gently on your eyeball with your eye closed) and argues that they are identical with brain states. The view he formulated is known as the *identity theory* of mental states.

Although Smart focuses on sensations, the identity theory can be formulated for mental states more generally, including *propositional attitudes*, such as belief and desire. Typically, both advocates and critics of physicalism offer accounts of these sorts of attitudes. In "Eliminative Materialism and Propositional Attitudes," American philosopher Paul Churchland (1942–) rejects this common assumption: although the commonsense theory we use to explain behavior—*folk psychology*—posits attitudes like beliefs and desires, these attitudes do not really exist; as a result, they are not something a theory needs to account for. This conclusion is supposed to make the physicalist's job easier, since there is no longer any need to give a physicalist theory of beliefs and desires. Churchland's position is known as *eliminative materialism*.

Challenges to Physicalism

The strongest resistance to physicalist accounts of the mental has focused on the case of mental states that are conscious, such as the feeling of pain, and conscious perceptual experiences, such as those involved in seeing a red apple.

The selections by contemporary philosophers Saul Kripke (1940–) and Frank Jackson (1943–), published in 1974 and 1982, respectively, outline two of the most powerful arguments against the thesis that consciousness is a physical phenomenon.

Saul Kripke's argument is drawn from his influential work *Naming and Necessity*. Like Descartes, Kripke argues for the conclusion that it is possible for consciousness to exist without any physical basis, using premises about what we can imagine or conceive. This style of argument against physicalism is known as a *modal argument* because of its transition from claims about what is conceivable to claims about what is possible.

Frank Jackson's argument against physicalism has come to be known as the *knowledge argument*. Jackson asks us to imagine a brilliant color scientist, Mary, who though she has spent her entire life in an exclusively black-and-white room, knows every single physical fact about colors and about how colors affect the brain. When Mary leaves the room and sees something red for the first time, Jackson maintains, she will learn some new fact about the conscious experience of redness. But if she learns a new fact, then the physical facts she knew while she was still in the room could not be all the facts that there are about consciousness.

Consciousness

The selections in the next section continue to explore the nature of consciousness. In his widely discussed essay "What Is It Like to Be a Bat?" philosopher Thomas Nagel (1937–) focuses on a kind of consciousness that has a central role in philosophical arguments against physicalism: phenomenal consciousness. A mental state, such as the state of seeing the scene before your eyes, is *phenomenally conscious* if there is something it is like to be in that state. Nagel argues that phenomenal consciousness is hard to explain in terms that leave out the first-person perspective. He illustrates his point using an example of a bat: while we might end up knowing everything there is to know about how the bat's brain and body function in its environment, this would not tell us what it is like to be a bat from the bat's own standpoint.

Does phenomenal consciousness pose an insuperable challenge to scientific understanding? In his article "Quining Qualia," philosopher Daniel Dennett (1942–) argues that it does not. Like phenomenal consciousness, the *qualia* that are associated with a mental state are supposed to characterize what it is like to have that mental state. Qualia are also supposed to be intrinsic, private, and directly apprehensible. Dennett argues that no mental states have the properties of the kind that qualia are supposed to. He concludes that the notion of qualia is based on a confusion. If Dennett is right, then no one should worry about whether qualia can be explained scientifically because there are no such things.

Dennett's article brings into focus the fact that whether consciousness poses insuperable challenges to scientific explanation depends on the kind of consciousness at issue. A useful first step in assessing the challenge is to distinguish between different kinds of consciousness. Philosopher Ned Block (1942–) undertakes this task in his contribution, in which he discusses four kinds of consciousness: *phenomenal consciousness* (which Nagel discussed), *access consciousness* (which is a kind of access to information), *self-consciousness* (which is a way of being aware of ourselves), and *monitoring consciousness* (which is a way of representing our own mental states). If we fail to distinguish among different things that we call "consciousness," then philosophical questions concerning the nature of consciousness will remain intractable.

Minds and Machines

Could a machine be programmed to think, feel, or understand? The field of artificial intelligence is devoted to answering this question. But what should count as an artificial machine having a mind? This is the central philosophical question about artificial intelligence. In his classic article, mathematician A. M. Turing (1912–54) proposes the following test: if a computer cannot be distinguished from a human interlocutor in a conversation, then the computer has a mind. This test has come to be known as the *Turing test*.

Philosopher John Searle (1932–) rejects the adequacy of the Turing test. He imagines an English speaker who cannot understand Chinese who is given the resources to simulate a computer program that takes Chinese words as inputs and provides appropriate responses as outputs. Since the imagined English speaker cannot understand Chinese, Searle concludes, there must be more to understanding than carrying out computations. According to Searle, this is a scenario in which something passing the Turing test lacks understanding.

Perception

What is the nature of our perceptual access to the world? Perception seems to put us in direct contact with reality. Seeing an apple on the table is one of the most straightforward ways to find out whether there is an apple on the table. Yet some cases of perceptual experience feel from the inside exactly like normal cases of seeing, even though they are defective. For instance, it is possible to hallucinate being in a forest when, in fact, you are in your kitchen. Less radically, things may not be exactly the way they look: think of the apparent position of a fish viewed through a fish tank—refraction can make it look as if it is in a spot that is actually empty. How can the idea that perception puts us in contact with reality be reconciled with the fact that perceptual experiences can be defective in these ways? Each of the discussions in this section addresses an aspect of this question.

The first selection, which is drawn from the first chapter of contemporary philosopher J. J. Valberg's book *The Puzzle of Experience*, focuses on clarifying the philosophical puzzle posed by the possibility of hallucination.

The next two selections, by Oxford philosophers A. J. Ayer (1910–89) and J. L. Austin (1911–60), focus on the argument known as the *argument from illusion*. This argument starts from premises about the nature of defective perceptual experience and concludes, remarkably, that perception is always indirect: whenever we see an external object, such as an apple, we see it indirectly, by first directly seeing a different, purely mental, applelike object called a *sense-datum*. Since sense-data are items that could be directly seen even in defective situations, they could explain how it is that defective and nondefective experiences seem the same. Ayer defends a version of this argument, and Austin criticizes it on a variety of grounds.

Further Reading

Students who want to pursue the themes raised in this section may begin by looking at the articles in the following two anthologies. Each includes an extensive collection of important readings in philosophy of mind, along with suggestions for further readings on each of the main themes:

- David J. Chalmers, ed. *Philosophy of Mind: Classical and Contemporary Readings*. Oxford and New York: Oxford University Press, 2002.
- John Heil, ed. *Philosophy of Mind: A Guide and Anthology*. Oxford and New York: Oxford University Press, 2004.

A METAPHYSICS OF MIND

◈ DUALISM AND BEHAVIORISM ◈

Sixth Meditation

The existence of material things, and the real distinction between mind and body[1]

RENÉ DESCARTES

French philosopher René Descartes (1596–1650) was one of the most important thinkers of the early modern period. His work in philosophy and mathematics set the tone for subsequent investigation of these topics.

The text that appears here is a modern (1985) translation of a selection from Descartes' *Meditations*, which were originally published in Latin in 1641. Descartes' original text included six chapters—or "Meditations"—of which the first two appear in the "Knowledge and Reality" section and the sixth appears here. Soon after the text was published in Latin, a French translation appeared (1647) with Descartes' approval. Although the two texts are similar, there are a few differences between them, and sometimes the French text offers helpful clarifications to the original Latin. In the text that follows, the translator has adopted a convention of including such selections from the French text in the body of the text enclosed in <diamond brackets> or as footnotes.

It remains for me to examine whether material things exist. And at least I now know they are capable of existing, in so far as they are the subject-matter of pure mathematics, since I perceive them clearly and distinctly. For there is no doubt that God is capable of creating everything that I am capable of perceiving in this manner; and I have never judged that something could not be made by him except on the grounds that there would be a contradiction in my perceiving it distinctly. The conclusion that material things exist is also suggested by the faculty of imagination, which I am aware of using when I turn my mind to material things. For when I give more attentive consideration to what imagination is, it seems to be nothing else but 72
an application of the cognitive faculty to a body which is intimately present to it, and which therefore exists.

From *Meditations on First Philosophy*, rev. ed., trans. John Cottingham. Copyright © 1996 Cambridge University Press. Reprinted with the permission of the publisher.

To make this clear, I will first examine the difference between imagination and pure understanding. When I imagine a triangle, for example, I do not merely understand that it is a figure bounded by three lines, but at the same time I also see the three lines with my mind's eye as if they were present before me; and this is what I call imagining. But if I want to think of a chiliagon, although I understand that it is a figure consisting of a thousand sides just as well as I understand the triangle to be a three-sided figure, I do not in the same way imagine the thousand sides or see them as if they were present before me. It is true that since I am in the habit of imagining something whenever I think of a corporeal thing, I may construct in my mind a confused representation of some figure; but it is clear that this is not a chiliagon. For it differs in no way from the representation I should form if I were thinking of a myriagon, or any figure with very many sides. Moreover, such a representation is useless for recognizing the properties which distinguish a chiliagon from other polygons. But suppose I am dealing with a pentagon: I can of course understand the figure of a pentagon, just as I can the figure of a chiliagon, without the help of the imagination; but I can also imagine a pentagon, by applying my mind's eye to its five sides and the area contained within them. And in doing this I notice quite clearly that imagina-
73 tion requires a peculiar effort of mind which is not required for understanding; this additional effort of mind clearly shows the difference between imagination and pure understanding.

Besides this, I consider that this power of imagining which is in me, differing as it does from the power of understanding, is not a necessary constituent of my own essence, that is, of the essence of my mind. For if I lacked it, I should undoubtedly remain the same individual as I now am; from which it seems to follow that it depends on something distinct from myself. And I can easily understand that, if there does exist some body to which the mind is so joined that it can apply itself to contemplate it, as it were, whenever it pleases, then it may possibly be this very body that enables me to imagine corporeal things. So the difference between this mode of thinking and pure understanding may simply be this: when the mind understands, it in some way turns towards itself and inspects one of the ideas which are within it; but when it imagines, it turns towards the body and looks at something in the body which conforms to an idea understood by the mind or perceived by the senses. I can, as I say, easily understand that this is how imagination comes about, if the body exists; and since there is no other equally suitable way of explaining imagination that comes to mind, I can make a probable conjecture that the body exists. But this is only a probability; and despite a careful and comprehensive investigation, I do not yet see how the distinct idea of corporeal nature which I find in my imagination can provide any basis for a necessary inference that some body exists.

But besides that corporeal nature which is the 74
subject-matter of pure mathematics, there is much else that I habitually imagine, such as colours, sounds, tastes, pain and so on—though not so distinctly. Now I perceive these things much better by means of the senses, which is how, with the assistance of memory, they appear to have reached the imagination. So in order to deal with them more fully, I must pay equal attention to the senses, and see whether the things which are perceived by means of that mode of thinking which I call "sensory perception" provide me with any sure argument for the existence of corporeal things.

To begin with, I will go back over all the things which I previously took to be perceived by the senses, and reckoned to be true; and I will go over my reasons for thinking this. Next, I will set out my reasons for subsequently calling these things into doubt. And finally I will consider what I should now believe about them.

First of all then, I perceived by my senses that I had a head, hands, feet and other limbs making up the body which I regarded as part of myself, or perhaps even as my whole self. I also perceived by my senses that this body was situated among many other bodies which could affect it in various favourable or unfavourable ways; and I gauged the favourable effects by a sensation of pleasure, and the unfavourable ones by a sensation of pain. In addition to pain and pleasure, I also had sensations within me of hunger, thirst, and other such appetites, and also of physical propensities towards cheerfulness, sadness, anger and similar emotions. And outside me, besides the extension, shapes 75
and movements of bodies, I also had sensations of their hardness and heat, and of the other tactile quali-

ties. In addition, I had sensations of light, colours, smells, tastes and sounds, the variety of which enabled me to distinguish the sky, the earth, the seas, and all other bodies, one from another. Considering the ideas of all these qualities which presented themselves to my thought, although the ideas were, strictly speaking, the only immediate objects of my sensory awareness, it was not unreasonable for me to think that the items which I was perceiving through the senses were things quite distinct from my thought, namely bodies which produced the ideas. For my experience was that these ideas came to me quite without my consent, so that I could not have sensory awareness of any object, even if I wanted to, unless it was present to my sense organs; and I could not avoid having sensory awareness of it when it was present. And since the ideas perceived by the senses were much more lively and vivid and even, in their own way, more distinct than any of those which I deliberately formed through meditating or which I found impressed on my memory, it seemed impossible that they should have come from within me; so the only alternative was that they came from other things. Since the sole source of my knowledge of these things was the ideas themselves, the supposition that the things resembled the ideas was bound to occur to me. In addition, I remembered that the use of my senses had come first, while the use of my reason came only later; and I saw that the ideas which I formed myself were less vivid than those which I perceived with the senses and were, for the most part, made up of elements of sensory ideas. In this way I easily convinced myself that I had nothing at all in the intellect which I had not previously had in sensation. As for the body which by
76 some special right I called "mine," my belief that this body, more than any other, belonged to me had some justification. For I could never be separated from it, as I could from other bodies; and I felt all my appetites and emotions in, and on account of, this body; and finally, I was aware of pain and pleasurable ticklings in parts of this body, but not in other bodies external to it. But why should that curious sensation of pain give rise to a particular distress of mind; or why should a certain kind of delight follow on a tickling sensation? Again, why should that curious tugging in the stomach which I call hunger tell me that I should eat, or a dryness of the throat tell me to drink, and so on? I was not able to give any explanation of all this, except that nature taught me so. For there is absolutely no connection (at least that I can understand) between the tugging sensation and the decision to take food, or between the sensation of something causing pain and the mental apprehension of distress that arises from that sensation. These and other judgements that I made concerning sensory objects, I was apparently taught to make by nature; for I had already made up my mind that this was how things were, before working out any arguments to prove it.

Later on, however, I had many experiences which gradually undermined all the faith I had had in the senses. Sometimes towers which had looked round from a distance appeared square from close up; and enormous statues standing on their pediments did not seem large when observed from the ground. In these and countless other such cases, I found that the judgements of the external senses were mistaken. And this applied not just to the external senses but to the internal senses as well. For what can be more internal than pain? And yet I had heard that those 77
who had had a leg or an arm amputated sometimes still seemed to feel pain intermittently in the missing part of the body. So even in my own case it was apparently not quite certain that a particular limb was hurting, even if I felt pain in it. To these reasons for doubting, I recently added two very general ones.* The first was that every sensory experience I have ever thought I was having while awake I can also think of myself as sometimes having while asleep; and since I do not believe that what I seem to perceive in sleep comes from things located outside me, I did not see why I should be any more inclined to believe this of what I think I perceive while awake. The second reason for doubt was that since I did not know the author of my being (or at least was pretending not to), I saw nothing to rule out the possibility that my natural constitution made me prone to error even in matters which seemed to me most true. As for the reasons for my previous confident belief in the truth of the things perceived by the senses, I had no trouble in refuting them. For since

* In the *First Meditation*, which appears in the "Knowledge and Reality" section.

I apparently had natural impulses towards many things which reason told me to avoid, I reckoned that a great deal of confidence should not be placed in what I was taught by nature. And despite the fact that the perceptions of the senses were not dependent on my will, I did not think that I should on that account infer that they proceeded from things distinct from myself, since I might perhaps have a faculty not yet known to me which produced them.

But now, when I am beginning to achieve a better knowledge of myself and the author of my being,
78 although I do not think I should heedlessly accept everything I seem to have acquired from the senses, neither do I think that everything should be called into doubt.

First, I know that everything which I clearly and distinctly understand is capable of being created by God so as to correspond exactly with my understanding of it. Hence the fact that I can clearly and distinctly understand one thing apart from another is enough to make me certain that the two things are distinct, since they are capable of being separated, at least by God. The question of what kind of power is required to bring about such a separation does not affect the judgement that the two things are distinct. Thus, simply by knowing that I exist and seeing at the same time that absolutely nothing else belongs to my nature or essence except that I am a thinking thing, I can infer correctly that my essence consists solely in the fact that I am a thinking thing. It is true that I may have (or, to anticipate, that I certainly have) a body that is very closely joined to me. But nevertheless, on the one hand I have a clear and distinct idea of myself, in so far as I am simply a thinking, non-extended thing; and on the other hand I have a distinct idea of body,[2] in so far as this is simply an extended, non-thinking thing. And accordingly, it is certain that I[3] am really distinct from my body, and can exist without it.

Besides this, I find in myself faculties for certain special modes of thinking,[4] namely imagination and sensory percection. Now I can clearly and distinctly understand myself as a whole without these faculties; but I cannot, conversely, understand these faculties without me, that is, without an intellectual substance to inhere in. This is because there is an intellectual act included in their essential definition; and hence I perceive that the distinction between them and myself corresponds to the distinction between the modes of a thing and the thing itself.[5] Of course I also recognize that there are other faculties (like those of changing position, of taking on various shapes, and so on) which, like sensory perception and imagination, cannot be understood apart from some substance for them to inhere in, and hence 79
cannot exist without it. But it is clear that these other faculties, if they exist, must be in a corporeal or extended substance and not an intellectual one; for the clear and distinct conception of them includes extension, but does not include any intellectual act whatsoever. Now there is in me a passive faculty of sensory perception, that is, a faculty for receiving and recognizing the ideas of sensible objects; but I could not make use of it unless there was also an active faculty, either in me or in something else, which produced or brought about these ideas. But this faculty cannot be in me, since clearly it presupposes no intellectual act on my part,[6] and the ideas in question are produced without my cooperation and often even against my will. So the only alternative is that it is in another substance distinct from me—a substance which contains either formally or eminently* all the reality which exists objectively in the ideas produced by this faculty (as I have just noted). This substance is either a body, that is, a corporeal nature, in which case it will contain formally <and in fact> everything which is to be found objectively <or representatively> in the ideas; or else it is God, or some creature more noble than a body, in which case it will contain eminently whatever is to be found in the ideas. But since God is not a deceiver, it is quite clear that he does not transmit the ideas to me either directly from himself, or indirectly, via some creature which contains the objective reality of the ideas not formally but only eminently. For God has given me no faculty at all for recognizing any such source for these ideas; on the contrary, he has given me 80
a great propensity to believe that they are produced by corporeal things. So I do not see how God could be

* The terms *formally* and *eminently* are used here in their medieval scholastic sense. As the translator explains, "To possess a property 'formally' is to possess it literally, in accordance with its definition; to possess it 'eminently' is to possess it in some higher form."

understood to be anything but a deceiver if the ideas were transmitted from a source other than corporeal things. It follows that corporeal things exist. They may not all exist in a way that exactly corresponds with my sensory grasp of them, for in many cases the grasp of the senses is very obscure and confused. But at least they possess all the properties which I clearly and distinctly understand, that is, all those which, viewed in general terms, are comprised within the subject-matter of pure mathematics.

What of the other aspects of corporeal things which are either particular (for example that the sun is of such and such a size or shape), or less clearly understood, such as light or sound or pain, and so on? Despite the high degree of doubt and uncertainty involved here, the very fact that God is not a deceiver, and the consequent impossibility of there being any falsity in my opinions which cannot be corrected by some other faculty supplied by God, offers me a sure hope that I can attain the truth even in these matters. Indeed, there is no doubt that everything that I am taught by nature contains some truth. For if nature is considered in its general aspect, then I understand by the term nothing other than God himself, or the ordered system of created things established by God. And by my own nature in particular I understand nothing other than the totality of things bestowed on me by God.

There is nothing that my own nature teaches me more vividly than that I have a body, and that when I feel pain there is something wrong with the body, and that when I am hungry or thirsty the body needs food and drink, and so on. So I should not doubt that there is some truth in this.

81 Nature also teaches me, by these sensations of pain, hunger, thirst and so on, that I am not merely present in my body as a sailor is present in a ship,[7] but that I am very closely joined and, as it were, intermingled with it, so that I and the body form a unit. If this were not so, I, who am nothing but a thinking thing, would not feel pain when the body was hurt, but would perceive the damage purely by the intellect, just as a sailor perceives by sight if anything in his ship is broken. Similarly, when the body needed food or drink, I should have an explicit understanding of the fact, instead of having confused sensations of hunger and thirst. For these sensations of hunger, thirst, pain and so on are nothing but confused modes of thinking which arise from the union and, as it were, intermingling of the mind with the body.

I am also taught by nature that various other bodies exist in the vicinity of my body, and that some of these are to be sought out and others avoided. And from the fact that I perceive by my senses a great variety of colours, sounds, smells and tastes, as well as differences in heat, hardness and the like, I am correct in inferring that the bodies which are the source of these various sensory perceptions possess differences corresponding to them, though perhaps not resembling them. Also, the fact that some of the perceptions are agreeable to me while others are disagreeable makes it quite certain that my body, or rather my whole self, in so far as I am a combination of body and mind, can be affected by the various beneficial or harmful bodies which surround it.

There are, however, many other things which
I may appear to have been taught by nature, but 82
which in reality I acquired not from nature but from a habit of making ill-considered judgements; and it is therefore quite possible that these are false. Cases in point are the belief that any space in which nothing is occurring to stimulate my senses must be empty; or that the heat in a body is something exactly resembling the idea of heat which is in me; or that when a body is white or green, the selfsame whiteness or greenness which I perceive through my senses is present in the body; or that in a body which is bitter or sweet there is the selfsame taste which I experience, and so on; or, finally, that stars and towers and other distant bodies have the same size and shape which they present to my senses, and other examples of this kind. But to make sure that my perceptions in this matter are sufficiently distinct, I must more accurately define exactly what I mean when I say that I am taught something by nature. In this context I am taking nature to be something more limited than the totality of things bestowed on me by God. For this includes many things that belong to the mind alone—for example my perception that what is done cannot be undone, and all other things that are known by the natural light;[8] but at this stage I am not speaking of these matters. It also includes much that relates to the body alone, like the tendency to move in a downward direction,

and so on; but I am not speaking of these matters either. My sole concern here is with what God has bestowed on me as a combination of mind and body. My nature, then, in this limited sense, does indeed teach me to avoid what induces a feeling of pain and to seek out what induces feelings of pleasure, and so on. But it does not appear to teach us to draw any conclusions from these sensory perceptions about things located outside us without waiting until the intellect has examined[9] the matter. For knowledge
83 of the truth about such things seems to belong to the mind alone, not to the combination of mind and body. Hence, although a star has no greater effect on my eye than the flame of a small light, that does not mean that there is any real or positive inclination in me to believe that the star is no bigger than the light; I have simply made this judgement from childhood onwards without any rational basis. Similarly, although I feel heat when I go near a fire and feel pain when I go too near, there is no convincing argument for supposing that there is something in the fire which resembles the heat, any more than for supposing that there is something which resembles the pain. There is simply reason to suppose that there is something in the fire, whatever it may eventually turn out to be, which produces in us the feelings of heat or pain. And likewise, even though there is nothing in any given space that stimulates the senses, it does not follow that there is no body there. In these cases and many others I see that I have been in the habit of misusing the order of nature. For the proper purpose of the sensory perceptions given me by nature is simply to inform the mind of what is beneficial or harmful for the composite of which the mind is a part; and to this extent they are sufficiently clear and distinct. But I misuse them by treating them as reliable touchstones for immediate judgements about the essential nature of the bodies located outside us; yet this is an area where they provide only very obscure information.

I have already looked in sufficient detail at how, notwithstanding the goodness of God, it may happen that my judgements are false. But a further problem now comes to mind regarding those very things which nature presents to me as objects which I should seek out or avoid, and also regarding the internal sensations, where I seem to have detected errors[10]—e.g. when someone is tricked by the pleasant taste of some food into eating the poison 84
concealed inside it. Yet in this case, what the man's nature urges him to go for is simply what is responsible for the pleasant taste, and not the poison, which his nature knows nothing about. The only inference that can be drawn from this is that his nature is not omniscient. And this is not surprising, since man is a limited thing, and so it is only fitting that his perfection should be limited.

And yet it is not unusual for us to go wrong even in cases where nature does urge us towards something. Those who are ill, for example, may desire food or drink that will shortly afterwards turn out to be bad for them. Perhaps it may be said that they go wrong because their nature is disordered, but this does not remove the difficulty. A sick man is no less one of God's creatures than a healthy one, and it seems no less a contradiction to suppose that he has received from God a nature which deceives him. Yet a clock constructed with wheels and weights observes all the laws of its nature just as closely when it is badly made and tells the wrong time as when it completely fulfils the wishes of the clockmaker. In the same way, I might consider the body of a man as a kind of machine equipped with and made up of bones, nerves, muscles, veins, blood and skin in such a way that, even if there were no mind in it, it would still perform all the same movements as it now does in those cases where movement is not under the control of the will or, consequently, of the mind.[11] I can easily see that if such a body suffers from dropsy, for example, and is affected by the dryness of the throat which normally produces in the mind the sensation of thirst, the resulting condition of the nerves and other parts will dispose the body to take a drink, with the result that the disease will be aggravated. Yet this is just as natural as the body's being stimulated by a similar dryness of the throat to take a drink when there is no such illness and the drink is beneficial. Admittedly, when I con- 185
sider the purpose of the clock, I may say that it is departing from its nature when it does not tell the right time; and similarly when I consider the mechanism of the human body, I may think that, in relation to the movements which normally occur in it, it too is deviating from its nature if the throat is dry at a time when drinking is not beneficial to its continued health. But

I am well aware that "nature" as I have just used it has a very different significance from "nature" in the other sense. As I have just used it, "nature" is simply a label which depends on my thought; it is quite extraneous to the things to which it is applied, and depends simply on my comparison between the idea of a sick man and a badly-made clock, and the idea of a healthy man and a well-made clock. But by "nature" in the other sense I understand something which is really to be found in the things themselves; in this sense, therefore, the term contains something of the truth.

When we say, then, with respect to the body suffering from dropsy, that it has a disordered nature because it has a dry throat and yet does not need drink, the term "nature" is here used merely as an extraneous label. However, with respect to the composite, that is, the mind united with this body, what is involved is not a mere label, but a true error of nature, namely that it is thirsty at a time when drink is going to cause it harm. It thus remains to inquire how it is that the goodness of God does not prevent nature, in this sense, from deceiving us.

The first observation I make at this point is that there is a great difference between the mind and the
86 body, inasmuch as the body is by its very nature always divisible, while the mind is utterly indivisible. For when I consider the mind, or myself in so far as I am merely a thinking thing, I am unable to distinguish any parts within myself; I understand myself to be something quite single and complete. Although the whole mind seems to be united to the whole body, I recognize that if a foot or arm or any other part of the body is cut off, nothing has thereby been taken away from the mind. As for the faculties of willing, of understanding, of sensory perception and so on, these cannot be termed parts of the mind, since it is one and the same mind that wills, and understands and has sensory perceptions. By contrast, there is no corporeal or extended thing that I can think of which in my thought I cannot easily divide into parts; and this very fact makes me understand that it is divisible. This one argument would be enough to show me that the mind is completely different from the body, even if I did not already know as much from other considerations.

My next observation is that the mind is not immediately affected by all parts of the body, but only by the brain, or perhaps just by one small part of the brain, namely the part which is said to contain the "common" sense.[12] Every time this part of the brain is in a given state, it presents the same signals to the mind, even though the other parts of the body may be in a different condition at the time. This is established by countless observations, which there is no need to review here.

I observe, in addition, that the nature of the body is such that whenever any part of it is moved by another part which is some distance away, it can always be moved in the same fashion by any of the parts which lie in between, even if the more distant part does nothing. For example, in a cord ABCD, if one end D is 87
pulled so that the other end A moves, the exact same movement could have been brought about if one of the intermediate points B or C had been pulled, and D had not moved at all. In similar fashion, when I feel a pain in my foot, physiology tells me that this happens by means of nerves distributed throughout the foot, and that these nerves are like cords which go from the foot right up to the brain. When the nerves are pulled in the foot, they in turn pull on inner parts of the brain to which they are attached, and produce a certain motion in them; and nature has laid it down that this motion should produce in the mind a sensation of pain, as occurring in the foot. But since these nerves, in passing from the foot to the brain, must pass through the calf, the thigh, the lumbar region, the back and the neck, it can happen that, even if it is not the part in the foot but one of the intermediate parts which is being pulled, the same motion will occur in the brain as occurs when the foot is hurt, and so it will necessarily come about that the mind feels the same sensation of pain. And we must suppose the same thing happens with regard to any other sensation.

My final observation is that any given movement occurring in the part of the brain that immediately affects the mind produces just one corresponding sensation; and hence the best system that could be devised is that it should produce the one sensation which, of all possible sensations, is most especially and most frequently conducive to the preservation of the healthy man. And experience shows that the sensations which nature has given us are all of this kind; and so there is absolutely nothing to be found in them that does not bear witness to the power and goodness of God. For example, when the nerves 88 in the foot are set in motion in a violent and unusual manner, this motion, by way of the spinal cord, reaches the inner parts of the brain, and there gives the mind its signal for having a certain sensation, namely the sensation of a pain as occurring in the foot. This stimulates the mind to do its best to get rid of the cause of the pain, which it takes to be harmful to the foot. It is true that God could have made the nature of man such that this particular motion in the brain indicated something else to the mind; it might, for example, have made the mind aware of the actual motion occurring in the brain, or in the foot, or in any of the intermediate regions; or it might have indicated something else entirely. But there is nothing else which would have been so conducive to the continued well-being of the body. In the same way, when we need drink, there arises a certain dryness in the throat; this sets in motion the nerves of the throat, which in turn move the inner parts of the brain. This motion produces in the mind a sensation of thirst, because the most useful thing for us to know about the whole business is that we need drink in order to stay healthy. And so it is in the other cases.

It is quite clear from all this that, notwithstanding the immense goodness of God, the nature of man as a combination of mind and body is such that it is bound to mislead him from time to time. For there may be some occurrence, not in the foot but in one of the other areas through which the nerves travel in their route from the foot to the brain, or even in the brain itself; and if this cause produces the same motion which is generally produced by injury to the foot, then pain will be felt as if it were in the foot. This deception of the senses is natural, because a given motion in the brain must always produce the same sensation in the mind; and the origin of the motion in question is much more often going to be something which is hurting the foot, rather than
89 something existing elsewhere. So it is reasonable that this motion should always indicate to the mind a pain in the foot rather than in any other part of the body. Again, dryness of the throat may sometimes arise not, as it normally does, from the fact that a drink is necessary to the health of the body, but from some quite opposite cause, as happens in the case of the man with dropsy. Yet it is much better that it should mislead on this occasion than that it should always mislead when the body is in good health. And the same goes for the other cases.

This consideration is the greatest help to me, not only for noticing all the errors to which my nature is liable, but also for enabling me to correct or avoid them without difficulty. For I know that in matters regarding the well-being of the body, all my senses report the truth much more frequently than not. Also, I can almost always make use of more than one sense to investigate the same thing; and in addition, I can use both my memory, which connects present experiences with preceding ones, and my intellect, which has by now examined all the causes of error. Accordingly, I should not have any further fears about the falsity of what my senses tell me every day; on the contrary, the exaggerated doubts of the last few days should be dismissed as laughable. This applies especially to the principal reason for doubt, namely my inability to distinguish between being asleep and being awake. For I now notice that there is a vast difference between the two, in that dreams are never linked by memory with all the other actions of life as waking experiences are. If, while I am awake, anyone were suddenly to appear to me and then disappear immediately, as happens in sleep, so that I could not see where he had come from or where he had gone to, it would not be unreasonable for me to judge that he was a ghost, or a vision 90
created in my brain,[13] rather than a real man. But when I distinctly see where things come from and where and when they come to me, and when I can connect my perceptions of them with the whole of the rest of my life without a break, then I am quite certain that when I encounter these things I am not asleep but awake. And I ought not to have even the slightest doubt of their reality if, after calling upon all the senses as well as my memory and my intellect in order to check them, I receive no conflicting reports from any of these sources. For from the fact that God is not a deceiver it follows that in cases like these I am completely free from error. But since the pressure of things to be done does not always allow us to stop and make such a meticulous check, it must be admitted that in this human life we are often liable to make mistakes about particular things, and we must acknowledge the weakness of our nature.

NOTES

1. "... between the soul and body of a man" (French version).
2. The Latin term *corpus* as used here by Descartes is ambiguous as between "body" (i.e., corporeal matter in general) and "the body" (i.e., this particular body of mine). The French version preserves the ambiguity.
3. "... that is, my soul, by which I am what I am" (added in French version).
4. "... certain modes of thinking which are quite special and distinct from me" (French version).
5. "... between the shapes, movements and other modes or accidents of a body and the body which supports them" (French version).
6. "... cannot be in me in so far as I am merely a thinking thing, since it does not presuppose any thought on my part" (French version).
7. "... as a pilot in his ship" (French version).
8. "... without any help from the body" (added in French version).
9. "... carefully and maturely examined" (French version).
10. "... and thus seem to have been directly deceived by my nature" (added in French version).
11. "... but occurs merely as a result of the disposition of the organs" (French version).
12. The supposed faculty which integrates the data from the five specialized senses (the notion goes back ultimately to Aristotle). "The seat of the common sense must be very mobile, to receive all the impressions coming from the senses, but must be moveable only by the spirits which transmit these impressions. Only the *conarion* [pineal gland] fits these conditions" (letter to Mersenne, 21 April 1641).
13. "... like those that are formed in the brain when I sleep" (added in French version).

Understanding Nyāya-Vaiśeṣika Dualism

KISOR KUMAR CHAKRABARTI

Kisor Kumar Chakrabarti is a scholar of Indian philosophy. The selections that appear here come from two chapters of his 1999 book *Classical Indian Philosophy of Mind: The Nyāya Dualist Tradition*. In them, Chakrabarti discusses some of the similarities and differences between Nyāya and Cartesian views that mind and body are fundamentally distinct.

Nyāya and Vaiśeṣika are two of the six classical Hindu *darshans*—schools of systematic philosophical thought. In the tenth century CE, the two schools merged to form the Nyāya-Vaiśeṣika school, whose views on dualism are discussed in this selection. Throughout the text, classical Sanskrit terms for certain concepts appear in parentheses or italics; all are translated in the body of the text. In his book, Chakrabarti provides information about their original sources; these references have been omitted from our selection in the interests of readability.

In the course of his discussion, Chakrabarti compares these classical Indian views to those of a number of seventeenth- and eighteenth-century Western philosophers, including René Descartes (1596–1650), John Locke (1632–1704), Benedict Spinoza (1632–77), and David Hume (1711–76). He also makes reference to a number of contemporary Anglo-American philosophers of mind, including Paul Churchland, Frank Jackson, and Thomas Nagel, selections from whom can be found in this volume.

Reprinted by permission from *Classical Indian Philosophy of Mind: The Nyāya Dualist Tradition* by Kisor Kumar Chakrabati, the State University of New York Press. Copyright © 1999 State University of New York. All rights reserved.

Nyāya-Vaiśeṣika philosophers hold that there are physical substances like bricks and stones. While such objects are available in plenty, it is not easy to make clear what precisely is meant by being physical. One possible view is that the physical is that which has causal powers or, at least, that the physical is that which can causally influence another physical object. This view may seem to underlie well-known physical laws such as the law of conservation of energy and of linear and angular momentum (and may seem to survive the partial blurring of the distinction between particle and wave in current physical theory). But in the context of the debate over psychophysical dualism such a conception of being physical is starkly question begging. For it would then follow that if something (putatively) mental causally interacts with something physical, the former is physical too.

Another possible view is that being physical necessarily implies being extended or being in space and vice versa. There is no doubt that physical objects such as bricks or stones are in space. But whether everything that is physical is in space in the same sense in which bricks or stones are in space is questionable. Bricks or stones occupy a limited region of space (*mūrta*) and offer resistance to other physical substances of limited magnitude from occupying that same space. Everything that is in space in this sense is physical in the Nyāya-Vaiśeṣika view. But everything physical is not in space in this precise sense from the Nyāya standpoint. Thus *ākāśa*, the substratum of sound, is extended and in space. But it does not occupy any limited region of space and prevent other physical (or nonphysical) substances from occupying that same space.

So a distinction should be drawn between two different senses of being extended or being in space. The first sense of occupying a particular region of space and preventing other measurable physical substances from being in that space (or being solid) is a sure sign of being physical, according to the Nyāya, and true of innumerable physical substances. But it is not true of all physical substances. There are physical substances that are extended in a different sense. The latter sense is that of being in contact with a substance (*samyogitva*). Something in contact with a measurable (or immeasurable) substance need not prevent other measurable (or immeasurable) substances from being in contact with that same thing. All physical substances, in the Nyāya view, are in space in either the first or the second sense. But these are two different senses and although the first implies the second, the second does not imply the first.

Is everything that is extended in either the first or the second sense physical? Not according to the Nyāya. Being extended in the sense of being in contact with another substance is true of all substances, physical or nonphysical, including the self. So the self turns out to be an extended, immaterial substance in the Nyāya view (virtually a contradiction from the Cartesian standpoint). We return to this soon.

It is thus clear that extension (*parimāṇa*) is not a defining property of being physical in the Nyāya view. What then is the defining property? . . . It is that of having a specific quale (*vi-śeṣa-guṇa*) that is externally perceivable (*vahirindriya-grāhya*) . . . That is, all physical substances have a specific quale that is externally perceivable and all that has a specific quale that is externally perceivable is physical. (For example, physical objects such as bricks or stones have externally perceivable qualia like color or smell.) This definition should not be thought to be an a priori, necessary truth. Rather it is an empirical generalization amply confirmed by innumerable observation reports and not challenged by any above-the-board counterexample. It is conceivable that a physical object may not have any externally perceivable specific quale. It is also possible to cook up thought experiments in which the above generalization does not hold. But none of these would detract from the credibility of an otherwise reliable, empirical generalization.

This view of matter may seem to conflict with that of Locke. Locke distinguished between primary qualities like extension and motion on the one hand and secondary qualities like color and smell on the other. One may interpret this to mean that while primary qualities really belong to the physical objects and are objective, the secondary qualities do not and are subjective.

While the interpretation of Locke's view is a matter of controversy, the Nyāya view does not imply that a physical object must have an externally perceived quale like color. When it is said that a physical substance has a specific quale that is externally perceivable, what the Nyāya claims is that a physical substance is the causal substratum (*samavāyi-kāraṇa*) of externally perceivable qualia like color. A causal substratum is different from and independent of the effects supported by it. So in the Nyāya view matter is that without the support of which externally perceivable qualia such as color could not exist. This does not rule out that a physical substance can exist without any externally perceived quale.

The Nyāya view is also not incompatible with the view of some that physical science assigns only position in space and motion to matter. Even if the latter is a correct interpretation of physical theory, it does not rule out that matter can have other causal roles. In particular, it does not rule out that unless there were things in space with motion, qualia such as color could not exist. It is true that one kind of physical substance recognized by the Nyāya, namely, *ākāśa*, is immobile (because of being ubiquitous). But it is still a necessary causal condition for the motion of flying birds, falling bodies, and so forth. Thus whether the Nyāya view of matter is compatible with that of physical science largely depends on one's understanding of the Nyāya and of physics. This issue cannot be resolved in a short space. Irrespective of what may be one's final judgment on this, the Nyāya account of a physical substance as that which is the causal substratum of externally perceivable specific qualia is noncircular and offers a viable perspective for a philosophical study of the mind-body problem.[1]

In the Nyāya-Vaiśeṣika view, all positive noneternal things exist in a particular space and endure for a particular period of time. This is true of internal states such as pleasure as well. In other words, it is true of my pleasure that it arises within the limits (*avaccheda*) of my body and so also of other internal states.

Does this conflict with the view held by some traditional Western dualists that mental states such as pleasure exist only in time but not in space? Although this also is largely a matter of interpretation, the conflict, if there is one, may not be as great as it may first seem. The internal states arise within the limits of the body, but they do not belong to the body. They belong only to the self, which is an immaterial substance. However, unless the self were in contact with the particular body, the particular internal state would not come into being. So the contact with the body and, therefore, space is a necessary causal condition of the internal state.

Still, from the Nyāya-Vaiśeṣika point of view, the contact between the self and the body not only determines the spatial characteristic of an internal state but also its temporal characteristic. Time, like space, is one, infinite, and continuous. Its division into particular temporal periods is dependent on the existence of noneternal things like the body. So the contact between the self and the body also provides (in part) the ontological basis of the truth of the statement that my pleasure exists at this particular time. Thus both temporal and spatial predicates of an internal state, so to speak, sail in the same boat. If the traditional Western dualist view implies that temporal predicates are true of internal states such as pleasure but spatial predicates are not, that is not accepted by the Nyāya-Vaiśeṣika. The cogency of the latter view depends on that of the view that both space and time are one, infinite, and continuous and that spatial and temporal divisions are dependent on the existence of noneternal things. If this view of space and time is acceptable, the view that internal states have both temporal and spatial predicates is also reasonable and defensible. It also seems to be impossible to give an account of my pleasure, my perception, and so on, without reference to my body. If this is true, it may lend support to the view that both spatial and temporal predicates are true of internal states.

It may appear from the above that there are some notable differences between Nyāya-Vaiśeṣika dualism and Cartesian dualism. We have just noted that while internal states such as cognition and pleasure do not have extension and do not belong to the body, in the Nyāya-Vaiśeṣika view it is still true of them to say that they are here in my body. This is not the view of Descartes. Further, according to Cartesian dualism, only two kinds of substance exist: mind and matter. The former is spiritual and unextended and the latter is extended. Thus Descartes holds that while thinking is the essence of the self or the mind, extension is the essence of matter. Matter cannot be conscious; the mind cannot be extended. These views appear to be quite foundational in the Cartesian metaphysics. But the Nyāya-Vaiśeṣika does not espouse this (as already indicated) and does not formulate the basic issue in quite the same way. The crucial issue for the Nyāya-Vaiśeṣika is the following: Is it necessary to admit the existence of a separate kind of substance that alone is the substratum of consciousness and that lacks any externally perceivable specific quale? The Nyāya-Vaiśeṣika answers this question in the affirmative but rejects the Cartesian view that such a substance must be unextended. In fact, the Nyāya-Vaiśeṣika holds that the self, as remarked earlier, has extension (*parimāṇa*). (We take up this issue below.) The Nyāya also rejects the assumption that the physical-mental dichotomy is exhaustive and recognizes several kinds of substance that, as explained, are neither physical nor mental. Finally, the self is distinguished from the inner sense and these two are considered to be different kinds of substance. No such distinction is entertained in traditional Western philosophy and functions of the inner sense are usually attributed to the self.

We have noted above that in the Nyāya view the immaterial self has extension. What is the evidence for it? It may be pointed out that other known substances have extension. For example, bricks and stones are substances and have extension (and this is acceptable to Nyāya dualists, Cartesian dualists, and physicalists alike if we bracket the possible disagreement over the category of substance). A Cartesian would claim that the immaterial self is an unextended substance and may offer this as a counterexample. But this is disputable (and would be rejected by the Nyāya), for there is no noncircular evidence to show that what is immaterial must be unextended. On the basis of undisputable supportive instances and from the lack of any undisputable counterexample it is permissible, given GAIE,* to generalize that all substances have extension.

This generalization may also be supported by a subjunctive argument (*tarka*). Suppose that not all substances are extended. Then there is at least one unextended substance. But such an unextended substance cannot come into contact with another substance, for contact presupposes extension (explained below). Accordingly, it cannot fulfil the typical roles of a substance, such as that of providing support for another substance (as when the table supports the book on it) or that of being the causal substratum of another substance (as when the cloth is woven out of the threads), for all these require contact. Admitting such a substance would then not be useful. . . .

Now that the self has extension can be demonstrated by the following valid argument:

> All substances have extension, for example, a brick.
> All selves are substances.
> Therefore, all selves have extension.

. . . .

Although (in the Nyāya view) the self has extension, it is not solid and does not prevent other physical objects from occupying the same space. We have distinguished between two different senses of being extended. In the first sense an extended thing is solid and offers resistance to other measurable substances' occupying the same space. But in the second sense an extended thing is merely in contact with another substance and does not prevent other substances from being in contact with that same substance. This is true even though the self remains in contact with the body throughout the lifetime of an individual and pervades that body. However, since every other substance coming into contact with another substance is found to have extension and since the self is supposed to be different from the body . . . and still to be in contact with it, the self too is supposed to have extension.

What is contact? It is the conjunction of two substances that were previously not in conjunction (*aprāptayoh prāptih*). For example, one billiard ball while hitting another billiard ball comes into contact with it. The self becomes conjoined with the body immediately after it is conceived and, in normal cases, remains conjoined with it till the death of that body.[2] It thus appears that contact involves being

* "GAIE" is Chakrabarti's acronym for the "general acceptability of inductive examples," a central principle in Nyāya logical reasoning. According to the principle, any examples cited to support or critique an empirical generalization should be acceptable to both parties in the debate.

together in space and this presupposes extension. (However, contact is a separable relation; that is, two substances in contact may be separated from each other. So in unusual circumstances the self may be separated from the body even before the death and another self be conjoined with that body or two or more selves may be associated with the same body, and so on, and all this may result in abnormal behavior.)

One serious problem in the Cartesian view may now be indicated. Descartes held that consciousness and extension are two fundamentally opposed attributes. Nothing conscious can be extended and nothing extended can be conscious. Still, according to Descartes, mind and matter interact. But how can something extended causally interact with something unextended? Descartes supposed that the interaction takes place in the pineal gland, which was regarded as the seat of the essentially conscious self or the soul. But since this is no more than an ad hoc assumption, it only highlights the difficulty in his position. Further, if there is such interaction, how does that fit in with the principle of conservation of energy? When the extended matter interacts with the unextended mind, should not some energy be lost in the process? How then can the total energy remain constant? . . .

These puzzles forced Spinoza, a follower of Descartes in many ways, to reject the interaction of matter and mind and maintain that there is a parallelism between mental states and bodily states. That is, corresponding to any bodily state there is always a parallel mental state and corresponding to any mental state there is always a parallel bodily state but neither causes the other. However, parallelism is not a comfortable position either. For one thing, it appears to be counterintuitive. It seems to be obvious that when, for example, I want to get up and do get up, my desire influences my body and similarly when I am physically exhausted and unable to concentrate, my bodily condition influences my mental condition. For another, parallelism forces us to assume that whenever there is a bodily change there is a parallel mental change (and vice versa). Thus for every act of exhaling or inhaling, for every act of digestion or secretion, and so on, there must be each time a corresponding mental state although there is no such evidence. This shows that as a theory parallelism is grossly overburdened with unwarranted assumptions and is uneconomical. Thus both interactionism and parallelism are found to be beset with serious difficulties. This has worked against dualism. If dualism implies either interactionism (which makes it a mystery how an extended thing can interact with something unextended) or parallelism (which is overburdened with assumptions), why not give up dualism and look elsewhere?

One advantage of the Nyāya kind of dualism may be apparent now. A Nyāya dualist is not faced here with a difficult choice. The Nyāya does not espouse parallelism. It accepts the causal interaction between bodily states and internal states as our everyday experience points to. But since the self is extended and conjoined with the body, there is no special problem in supposing that bodily states and internal states influence each other.

Further, the Nyāya critically examines and rejects the doctrine that the effect is preexistent (*satkārya*) in the cause and also rejects the doctrine of causal power (*śakti*). . . . It does not subscribe to the causal adequacy principle that since the cause determines the nature of the effect, the latter may have less but cannot have any more than what is in the cause. It also does not hold that there is in some sense an identity and continuity between the cause and the effect. If the cause is understood in the above ways (which have been influential in both Western and Indian philosophy) that the Nyāya rejects, there may be difficulty in accounting for causal interaction between bodily and internal states from a dualist point of view. Thus it is not at all clear in what sense a bodily state may be preexistent in the internal state that causes it or is identical or continuous with it or is causally adequate for it although the two are very different. (Such an understanding of causation may work for a physicalist or a mentalist espousing monism.) Since Descartes subscribes to the causal adequacy principle (and also holds that mind is unextended and matter, extended) the difficulty has been compounded for him.

But a dualist does not have to subscribe to such a view of causation (and does not have to deny that the self has extension or that internal states have location). A dualist may opt for a Hume-like view (which does not necessarily lead to skepticism or irrationalism) that a causal condition is a regular and contiguous antecedent. [Since the Cartesians subscribe to the causal adequacy principle, the Hume-like view of causation is not available to them.] For example, hydrogen and oxygen are causal conditions of water not in the sense that there is a continuity between the former and the latter (which does not appear to be the case, the former being gases and the latter being a liquid, so that the latter appears to be a different entity) but in the sense that the two gases regularly precede water where it is produced.

This is what the Nyāya has done.[3] According to the Nyāya account of causation, a causal condition is always present where the effect originates immediately before its production.... It is not our project here to discuss which view of causation is the most satisfactory although the Nyāya philosophers have responded to various objections to the Hume-like view of causation. But if this view of causation is acceptable, there is no difficulty in explaining the interaction between bodily and internal states. Such interaction is no different from that between two bodily states or two internal states. When a bodily state is said to be a causal condition of another bodily state, what is meant, for the Nyāya, is that the former invariably precedes the latter in the same body or the same complex of bodies. Similarly, when an internal state is said to be a causal condition of another internal state, what is meant is that the former invariably precedes the latter in the same self or the same complex of selves. In the same way an internal state that causally influences a bodily state is present where the bodily state is produced immediately before its production and similarly, *mutatis mutandis*, for a bodily state that causally influences an internal state, for the self and the body are in contact and together form the self-body complex.

To recapitulate: for Descartes the problem of mind-body interaction assumed enormous proportions because he assumed that anything extended must be physical and anything conscious must be unextended. It is perhaps safe to say that all physical things are extended. But it does not follow therefrom that all extended things are physical. At least the Nyāya philosophers saw clearly that these are different claims and rejected the latter while accepting the former. Again, Descartes assumes that location necessarily involves extension. But the Nyāya denies that. For the Nyāya internal states have location but not extension.[4] These powerful views, combined with a well-developed regularity theory of causation, help them to avoid one of the most frustrating problems confronting the Cartesian type of dualism.

Another important difference is that, unlike Descartes, the Nyāya does not hold that consciousness is the essence of the self. In the Nyāya view the self alone is the substratum of consciousness; but consciousness or thought is an adventitious (*āgantuka*) quale and originates in the self only when other necessary causal conditions are available. For Descartes the self is a thinking substance and is never without consciousness. Being without consciousness is, for Descartes, tantamount to being material. But, as we have already said, the Nyāya does not accept the assumption that everything is either mental or physical and either essentially conscious or essentially extended. So far as consciousness is concerned, there is no empirical evidence that the self remains conscious in states of deep sleep, coma, and the like. Hence the view that consciousness is an adventitious quale of the self.

In the philosophy of Descartes, dualism is married to rationalism, essentialism, and necessitarianism. Many philosophers today are opposed to these latter views and may dislike dualism because of its historical links with these. But the Nyāya, while upholding dualism, espouses empiricism, fallibilism, and probabilism. This shows that dualism has no unbreakable links with rationalism, essentialism, or necessitarianism and that a dualist does not have to prove such claims as that the self is essentially conscious. From the Nyāya point of view what the dualist does need to prove is the weaker claim that the self (or the mind as long as we do not confuse it with the inner sense) alone is conscious. A major part of this is sought to be accomplished, in trying to prove that the self is not identifiable with the body, the external senses, or the inner sense.

Again, Descartes held that while the human self is a thinking substance, nonhuman animals are nothing more than unconscious automata.[5] This may put the materialist at an advantage. What Descartes has to show is that there is some radical difference between a human being and all other animals. This is surely not easy to prove, particularly in the light of our enhanced knowledge of animal behavior, which shows that at least the higher animals (which will generate a slippery slope) are capable of highly complex activities of learning, communication, and exploitation of the environment. For example, monkeys have been observed to use branches of trees as tools to dig up food from under the ground or break open hard shells with the help of stones. Dogs have been known to trace their masters even when separated by significant distance and to recognize them even after the lapse of significant time. Birds have been found to build multichambered nests and to provide for light by sticking fireflies to the walls. And so on. If animals are unconscious automata in spite of being capable of such activities, why not also the humans? All that the materialist has to do under the circumstances is shoot down the attempts on the part of a Cartesian to prove any radical difference between humans and other animals and demand that the same conclusions should apply to both. If all other animals are machines, so are the humans. The Nyāya has not offered any such opportunity to the opponent. In other words, a Cartesian dualist has not only (*a*) to make a case for psychophysical dualism but also (*b*) a case for the unique status of humans in the animal world. He can succeed only by making good both claims. But a Nyāya dualist does not carry the burden of making good the second claim.

The Nyāya, of course, may face a challenge from the materialist from the other direction that since the animals are machines and since the humans are not radically different from the animals, the humans are also machines. In other words, while Cartesian dualism may remain safe even if the materialist succeeds in showing that animals are machines, that would jeopardize the Nyāya kind of dualism. Needless to say, if there is such a challenge, the Nyāya would disagree and offer evidence to show that animals are not machines. The Nyāya, of course, is not precluded from accepting that the humans possess a higher level of conscious activity than other animals. In fact, the Nyāya position is that human consciousness is more developed than that of animals in many ways, but it is still a difference in degree and not in kind. This seems to be compatible with our current knowledge of human and animal behavior, which does not suggest that consciousness is the exclusive possession of humans.

. . .

. . . Another argument for psychophysical dualism [can be found elsewhere in the Nyāya tradition, in the writings of Gotama]:* "[Consciousness is not a quale of the body], for it is utterly dissimilar to bodily qualia". . . Vatsyayana explains:

> For this, too, consciousness is not a quale of the body, viz., because of utter dissimilarity from bodily qualia. Bodily qualia are of two types: (1) imperceptible, such as weight, and (2) [externally] perceptible, such as color, etc. But consciousness is of a different type. It is not imperceptible, for it is internally perceptible; nor is it [externally] perceptible, for it is grasped by the inner sense. Therefore, [it] is the quale of a different substance. . . .

The weight of a body is inferred by measuring it on a scale. Thus it is an example of a bodily quale that is imperceptible. Other bodily qualia such as color are perceived by an external sense organ. Consciousness is not of either type. It is directly grasped by the inner sense; hence it is not imperceptible. At the same time it is not graspable by the external senses. Since it is so completely unlike bodily qualia, it should be inferred that it is the quale of a substance different from the body. Once the body is eliminated, the other recognized substances in the Nyāya ontology may be eliminated in a few more steps. Thus it is proved that consciousness is the quale of an additional substance called the self.

Gotama takes note of a possible objection from the materialist: "No [that consciousness is not a quale of the body is not proved], for color, etc., are mutually different." . . . Vatsyayana comments: "Just as

* Gotama (c. second or third century CE) was the founder of the Nyāya tradition; Vatsyayana (fourth to sixth centuries CE) was one of its early exponents.

colors, etc., which are different from each other, do not cease to be qualia of the body, so also consciousness, in spite of its difference from color, etc., does not cease to be a quale of the body." . . . Bodily qualia such as color and smell are quite different from each other. Color is perceived by the eye, smell is not; smell is perceived by the nose, color is not. Still, these are qualia of the body because they are all found in the body. In the same way, consciousness is not perceived by the eye, the nose, and so on, and is clearly different from color and so forth. Still, it can be a bodily quale, for the basic reason has not changed. Like color and the rest, consciousness is found in the body. Hence, in spite of being quite different from color and so on, it should be regarded as a bodily quale.

Gotama replies: "Since color, etc., are externally perceived, there is no refutation." . . . Vatsyayana elaborates:

> Because of imperceptibility as well. Just as colors, etc., which are mutually different, do not go beyond the two types, so also consciousness which too is different from color, etc., should not go beyond the two types if it were a bodily quale; but [it] does go beyond [the two types]. Therefore, it is not a bodily quale. . . .

Although color, smell, taste, and so on, are quite different from each other and each is grasped by only one sense organ to the exclusion of the others, still they are all objects of external perception and this is an important feature that they all share. If a quale is not perceptible by one external sense organ but is perceptible by another, there is no difficulty in accepting it as a bodily quale. It is a general feature of material things that they are (usually) perceptible by the external senses. But consciousness is not an object of external perception. That makes it absolutely dissimilar to color and so on. If it is a bodily quale, why is it not externally perceived like so many other bodily qualia? It is true that some bodily qualia, such as weight, are not externally perceived. But they are not perceptible at all. On the other hand, although consciousness is not externally perceived, it is internally perceived. That makes it radically different from bodily qualia. This is why Vatsyayana says that while the bodily qualia do not go beyond the two types of being either externally perceptible or being imperceptible, consciousness does go beyond these two types and, therefore, is not attributable to the body. This argument may be reformulated as below:

> All bodily qualia are either externally perceptible or imperceptible, for example, color and so forth.
>
> No conscious states are either externally perceptible or imperceptible.
>
> Therefore, no conscious states are bodily qualia.

This argument is formally valid. So the conclusion is acceptable if the two premises are acceptable. The first premise is clearly an acceptable generalization, for there are undisputable confirming instances such as color and weight and there are no undisputable counterexamples. The only counterexamples that the materialist could offer are internal states such as cognition, desire, and so on. But they are included in the inferential subject (*pakṣa*) and, being part of the bone of contention, not acceptable as counterexamples. The second premise too is acceptable, for it is widely agreed (in spite of some hard-core behaviorists who may think otherwise) that internal states like cognition, desire, and so on, are not externally perceptible. It is also widely agreed (in spite of the likely objection from some Wittgensteinians and Ryleans) that one is directly aware of one's desire, pleasure, and so on, so that these are not imperceptible either. Again, that internal states are objects of introspection and not of extrospection is one of the few nontrivial and nontautological philosophical claims that (notwithstanding significant challenge from some quarters both in Indian and Western philosophy) have retained a large measure of respectability. It appears then that Gotama and his followers have succeeded in proving (in the sense of arguing validly down to a conclusion from reasonable and acceptable premises) that consciousness is not a bodily quale. Nyāya philosophers are fallibilists. They are all too aware that both the premises are empirical generalizations that are not, and will never be, above challenge. But they are, to put it bluntly, as good as they get. So the conclusion is justified (although not beyond controversy).

The point of the above argument may be further explained with reference to some recent arguments for the indispensability of the first-person perspective.* Thomas Nagel has persuasively argued that even if one knows everything about a bat's brain, neurophysiology, sensory activities, and so on, one still cannot know what it is like to have the sensory experiences of a bat from the unique perspective of that creature.[6] As he pointedly observes: "If the subjective character of experience is fully comprehensible only from one point of view, then any shift to greater objectivity—that is, less attachment to a specific viewpoint— . . . takes us farther away from it."[7] Frank Jackson has argued along these lines that a neuroscientist who knows everything about the human visual system but is color-blind cannot know what it is like to have a normal visual sensation of red—this shows that there are subjective facts that are inaccessible to the "objective" or the third-person perspective.[8] What is the point of such arguments? Is the point merely that the color-blind neuroscientist cannot know what it is like to see red because that person lacks a part of the visual system that people with normal vision have, or that humans cannot know what it is like to be a bat because humans lack a bat's sensory system? This is true enough, but this need not be the point; for the point could be that I can know the quality of such and such sensation and what it is like to have the sensation only if I have that sensation myself; that is, when a person experiences subjective phenomenality, there is something it is like to be that person.

At least, this is the point of the Nyāya argument from privacy (irrespective of whether this is the point of the arguments of Nagel and Jackson). The point of the Nyāya is not that my experiences are private to me merely because my neural network is off limits to anyone else. On this ground indeed Paul Churchland has criticized the arguments of Nagel and Jackson: "[E]ach person has a self-connected . . . way of knowing that will function successfully and independently of what that person can see or hear, . . . and independently of whatever book-learned scientific knowledge he might . . . possess. . . . But nothing in these facts entails . . . that something . . . transcends understanding by the physical sciences."[9] A similar objection has also been voiced by William Lycan. "I have monitors that scan my brain, you have monitors that scan yours, . . . this is part of what it is to be an organism. . . . But this fact too poses no threat to materialism."[10]

But such objections miss the target so far as the Nyāya argument from privacy is concerned. The mere fact that my neural network is different from yours does not explain why my (and also your) experiences are private. If living organisms were nothing but unconscious automata, they too would come up with the same outputs to the same inputs as computers do. But they do not. There is nothing in the physicalist or functionalist accounts that explains why they do not. This cannot be explained by pointing to the difference in the material. Two different computers are made of different material and have different circuits. Still, if they are so designed, they come up with the same answers to the same questions. This is where a living organism parts company with a machine like a computer. For we can, per impossible, suppose that two different living organisms have the same internal or functional design. That is, they have exactly the same kind (and maybe number) of neurons, synapses, and so on, organized in exactly the same way. It does not follow therefrom that they would respond to the same stimuli in the same way. Indeed, it makes perfect sense to suppose that they would respond to the same stimuli in different ways. For example, it is conceivable that two identical twins or somebody and its clone or just any two people who, per impossible, have exactly the same physical constitution and are raised in exactly the same environment still grow up to be quite different in some of their preferences. This is where the analogy with a computer breaks down: we do not suppose that, except for malfunctioning, different computers that are so designed would respond to the same

* The papers that Chakrabarti discusses here—Thomas Nagel's "What Is It Like to be a Bat?" and Frank Jackson's "Epiphenomenal Qualia"—both appear following, as does a selection from Paul Churchland, whose views are discussed in the next paragraph. William Lycan, whose work is also discussed in this selection, is—like Nagel, Jackson, and Churchland—a contemporary philosopher of mind working in the Anglo-American tradition.

stimuli in different ways. Why the difference? That is, why do we not suppose that two different living organisms with the same functional design would respond in exactly the same way, while we do suppose that two different computers with the same functional design would respond in the same way? Until a physicalist or a functionalist comes up with a satisfactory explanation for this difference, no progress can be made in accounting for privacy by appealing to the uniqueness of the neural network in each person. There is nothing unique in the neural network, qua a neural network. The same material could conceivably be reused in exactly the same way with the same structure to make another neural network. (Cf. Theseus' ship.)* Hence there is nothing in the physicalist or functionalist accounts that can disallow such reduplication and preserve personal uniqueness. Accordingly, such claims as that of Lycan that privileged access is simply a fact but not a problem is a gross understatement. Privileged access is no doubt a fact. But it is a fact that goes a long way in vindicating dualism and poses one of the worst problems for a physicalist or functionalist. As Lycan himself says, privileged access must be accounted for by any viable theory of mind. The problem for a physicalist or a functionalist who chooses to be a nondualist is that they have not accounted for it and if the argument above is sound, cannot account for it even in principle. Needless to add, the appeal to the distinctness of an organism to account for privacy is circular in the first place, for in the Nyāya view all organisms have an immaterial self.[11]

* For a discussion of Theseus' ship, see "Ship of Theseus" in the glossary.

NOTES

1. What is traditionally called the mind-body problem in Western philosophy is more appropriately described as the self-body problem in the context of our discussion. However, no harm would result if the self (*ātman*) is called the mind provided the self is carefully distinguished from the inner sense (*manas*).
2. In the Nyāya-Vaiśeṣika view, the self is a pervasive substance and is automatically in contact with all measurable substances. Still an additional contact is established between a particular self and a particular body in a particular life and this accounts for individual differences.
3. An important concept in the Nyāya view of causation that we skip for lack of space is that of indispensability or relevance (*ananyathā-siddhatva*)
4. In the Nyāya view an internal state such as desire inheres (*samavāya*) in the self, which is in a specific contact (*viśeṣasaṃyoga*) with a particular body. Hence an internal state is also located in the particular body and not located in other bodies. But a state like desire is a quale (*guṇa*) and lacks extension (*parimāṇa*) which can be attributed only to a substance (*dravya*).
5. Descartes was most impressed by the highly complex mechanism of water fountains (which, for example, could be triggered by walking, etc.) and other robotlike statues (such as an Aphrodite that would hide as if in shame when someone approached and a Neptune that would emerge and threaten with a trident) in the French royal garden and thought that animal behavior is explicable in a similar way.
6. Thomas Nagel, "What Is It Like to Be a Bat?" *Philosophical Review* 93 (October 1974): 435–50, reprinted in NOM, 422–28.
7. NOM, 425–26.
8. Frank Jackson, "What Mary Didn't Know," *The Journal of Philosophy* 93 (May 1986): 291–95, reprinted in NOM, 392–94.
9. Paul M. Churchland, *The Engine of Reason* (Cambridge, Mass.: MIT Press, 1995), 198–99.
10. W. G. Lycan, *Consciousness and Experience* (Cambridge, Mass.: MIT Press, 1996), 49. Also, "*privileged access* . . . is not a *problem*; it is simply a fact, which must be explained, or at least accommodated, by any adequate theory of the mind." Ibid., 6.
11. A supplementary argument (is this adapted from Uddyotakara): Nothing, without the immaterial self, has privileged access, for example, a stone. A living organism has privileged access. Therefore, a living organism is not without the immaterial self. This is in the *vyatirekin* form and should be analyzed accordingly as explained in chapter 6.

Descartes' Myth

GILBERT RYLE

British philosopher Gilbert Ryle (1900–76) taught at Oxford University, where he was an important advocate of a philosophical outlook known as *ordinary language philosophy*. Ryle is best known for his work in the philosophy of language and the philosophy of mind, especially for his influential criticisms of Cartesian dualism.

The selection that appears here is an excerpt from his most famous work, *The Concept of Mind* (1949). In it, Ryle challenges Cartesian dualism on the grounds that to view the mind as a distinct substance from the body is to commit a "category mistake."

1. THE OFFICIAL DOCTRINE

There is a doctrine about the nature and place of minds which is so prevalent among theorists and even among laymen that it deserves to be described as the official theory. Most philosophers, psychologists and religious teachers subscribe, with minor reservations, to its main articles and, although they admit certain theoretical difficulties in it, they tend to assume that these can be overcome without serious modifications being made to the architecture of the theory. It will be argued here that the central principles of the doctrine are unsound and conflict with the whole body of what we know about minds when we are not speculating about them.

The official doctrine, which hails chiefly from Descartes, is something like this. With the doubtful exceptions of idiots and infants in arms every human being has both a body and a mind. Some would prefer to say that every human being is both a body and a mind. His body and his mind are ordinarily harnessed together, but after the death of the body his mind may continue to exist and function.

Human bodies are in space and are subject to the mechanical laws which govern all other bodies in space. Bodily processes and states can be inspected by external observers. So a man's bodily life is as much a public affair as are the lives of animals and reptiles and even as the careers of trees, crystals and planets.

But minds are not in space, nor are their operations subject to mechanical laws. The workings of one mind are not witnessable by other observers; its career is private. Only I can take direct cognisance of the states and processes of my own mind. A person therefore lives through two collateral histories, one consisting of what happens in and to his body, the other consisting of what happens in and to his mind. The first is public, the second private. The events in the first history are events in the physical world, those in the second are events in the mental world.

It has been disputed whether a person does or can directly monitor all or only some of the episodes of his own private history; but, according to the official doctrine, of at least some of these episodes he has direct and unchallengeable cognisance. In consciousness, self-consciousness and introspection he is directly and authentically apprised of the present states and operations of his mind. He may have great or small uncertainties about concurrent and adjacent episodes in the physical world, but he can have none about at least part of what is momentarily occupying his mind.

It is customary to express this bifurcation of his two lives and of his two worlds by saying that the things and events which belong to the physical world, including his own body, are external, while the workings of his own mind are internal. This antithesis of outer and inner is of course meant to be construed as a metaphor, since minds, not being in space, could not

From Gilbert Ryle, *The Concept of Mind* (Hutchinson, 1949), pp. 11–24. Reprinted with permission of the publisher and the Principal, Fellows, and Scholars of Hertford College in the University of Oxford.

be described as being spatially inside anything else, or as having things going on spatially inside themselves. But relapses from this good intention are common and theorists are found speculating how stimuli, the physical sources of which are yards or miles outside a person's skin, can generate mental responses inside his skull, or how decisions framed inside his cranium can set going movements of his extremities.

Even when "inner" and "outer" are construed as metaphors, the problem how a person's mind and body influence one another is notoriously charged with theoretical difficulties. What the mind wills, the legs, arms and the tongue execute; what affects the ear and the eye has something to do with what the mind perceives; grimaces and smiles betray the mind's moods and bodily castigations lead, it is hoped, to moral improvement. But the actual transactions between the episodes of the private history and those of the public history remain mysterious, since by definition they can belong to neither series. They could not be reported among the happenings described in a person's autobiography of his inner life, but nor could they be reported among those described in some one else's biography of that person's overt career. They can be inspected neither by introspection nor by laboratory experiment. They are theoretical shuttlecocks which are forever being bandied from the physiologist back to the psychologist and from the psychologist back to the physiologist.

Underlying this partly metaphorical representation of the bifurcation of a person's two lives there is a seemingly more profound and philosophical assumption. It is assumed that there are two different kinds of existence or status. What exists or happens may have the status of physical existence, or it may have the status of mental existence. Somewhat as the faces of coins are either heads or tails, or somewhat as living creatures are either male or female, so, it is supposed, some existing is physical existing, other existing is mental existing. It is a necessary feature of what has physical existence that it is in space and time; it is a necessary feature of what has mental existence that it is in time but not in space. What has physical existence is composed of matter, or else is a function of matter; what has mental existence consists of consciousness, or else is a function of consciousness.

There is thus a polar opposition between mind and matter, an opposition which is often brought out as follows. Material objects are situated in a common field, known as "space," and what happens to one body in one part of space is mechanically connected with what happens to other bodies in other parts of space. But mental happenings occur in insulated fields, known as "minds," and there is, apart maybe from telepathy, no direct causal connection between what happens in one mind and what happens in another. Only through the medium of the public physical world can the mind of one person make a difference to the mind of another. The mind is its own place and in his inner life each of us lives the life of a ghostly Robinson Crusoe.* People can see, hear and jolt one another's bodies, but they are irremediably blind and deaf to the workings of one another's minds and inoperative upon them.

What sort of knowledge can be secured of the workings of a mind? On the one side, according to the official theory, a person has direct knowledge of the best imaginable kind of the workings of his own mind. Mental states and processes are (or are normally) conscious states and processes, and the consciousness which irradiates them can engender no illusions and leaves the door open for no doubts. A person's present thinkings, feelings and willings, his perceivings, rememberings and imaginings are intrinsically "phos-phorescent"; their existence and their nature are inevitably betrayed to their owner. The inner life is a stream of consciousness of such a sort that it would be absurd to suggest that the mind whose life is that stream might be unaware of what is passing down it.

True, the evidence adduced recently by Freud† seems to show that there exist channels tributary to this stream, which run hidden from their owner. People are actuated by impulses the existence of

* Robinson Crusoe is a fictional character from Daniel Defoe's 1719 novel of the same name. In Defoe's novel, Crusoe spends nearly thirty years alone on a remote island.

† Sigmund Freud (1856–1939) was an Austrian psychologist whose work is widely held to have played a central role in identifying and clarifying the nature of the unconscious.

which they vigorously disavow; some of their thoughts differ from the thoughts which they acknowledge; and some of the actions which they think they will to perform they do not really will. They are thoroughly gulled by some of their own hypocrisies and they successfully ignore facts about their mental lives which on the official theory ought to be patent to them. Holders of the official theory tend, however, to maintain that anyhow in normal circumstances a person must be directly and authentically seized of the present state and workings of his own mind.

Besides being currently supplied with these alleged immediate data of consciousness, a person is also generally supposed to be able to exercise from time to time a special kind of perception, namely inner perception, or introspection. He can take a (non-optical) "look" at what is passing in his mind. Not only can he view and scrutinize a flower through his sense of sight and listen to and discriminate the notes of a bell through his sense of hearing; he can also reflectively or introspectively watch, without any bodily organ of sense, the current episodes of his inner life. This self-observation is also commonly supposed to be immune from illusion, confusion or doubt. A mind's reports of its own affairs have a certainty superior to the best that is possessed by its reports of matters in the physical world. Sense-perceptions can, but consciousness and introspection cannot, be mistaken or confused.

On the other side, one person has no direct access of any sort to the events of the inner life of another. He cannot do better than make problematic inferences from the observed behaviour of the other person's body to the states of mind which, by analogy from his own conduct, he supposes to be signalised by that behaviour. Direct access to the workings of a mind is the privilege of that mind itself; in default of such privileged access, the workings of one mind are inevitably occult to everyone else. For the supposed arguments from bodily movements similar to their own to mental workings similar to their own would lack any possibility of observational corroboration. Not unnaturally, therefore, an adherent of the official theory finds it difficult to resist this consequence of his premisses, that he has no good reason to believe that there do exist minds other than his own. Even if he prefers to believe that to other human bodies there are harnessed minds not unlike his own, he cannot claim to be able to discover their individual characteristics, or the particular things that they undergo and do. Absolute solitude is on this showing the ineluctable destiny of the soul. Only our bodies can meet.

As a necessary corollary of this general scheme there is implicitly prescribed a special way of construing our ordinary concepts of mental powers and operations. The verbs, nouns and adjectives, with which in ordinary life we describe the wits, characters and higher-grade performances of the people with whom we have to do, are required to be construed as signifying special episodes in their secret histories, or else as signifying tendencies for such episodes to occur. When someone is described as knowing, believing or guessing something, as hoping, dreading, intending or shirking something, as designing this or being amused at that, these verbs are supposed to denote the occurrence of specific modifications in his (to us) occult stream of consciousness. Only his own privileged access to this stream in direct awareness and introspection could provide authentic testimony that these mental-conduct verbs were correctly or incorrectly applied. The onlooker, be he teacher, critic, biographer or friend, can never assure himself that his comments have any vestige of truth. Yet it was just because we do in fact all know how to make such comments, make them with general correctness and correct them when they turn out to be confused or mistaken, that philosophers found it necessary to construct their theories of the nature and place of minds. Finding mental-conduct concepts being regularly and effectively used, they properly sought to fix their logical geography. But the logical geography officially recommended would entail that there could be no regular or effective use of these mental-conduct concepts in our descriptions of, and prescriptions for, other people's minds.

2. THE ABSURDITY OF THE OFFICIAL DOCTRINE

Such in outline is the official theory. I shall often speak of it, with deliberate abusiveness, as "the dogma of the Ghost in the Machine." I hope to prove that it is entirely false, and false not in detail but in principle. It is not merely an assemblage of particular mistakes. It is one big mistake and a mistake of a special kind. It is, namely, a category-mistake. It represents the facts of mental life as if they belonged to one logical type or category (or range of types or categories), when they actually belong to another. The dogma is therefore a philosopher's myth. In attempting to explode the myth I shall probably be taken to be denying well-known facts about the mental life of human beings, and my plea that I aim at doing nothing more than rectify the logic of mental-conduct concepts will probably be disallowed as mere subterfuge.

I must first indicate what is meant by the phrase "Category-mistake." This I do in a series of illustrations.

A foreigner visiting Oxford or Cambridge for the first time is shown a number of colleges, libraries, playing fields, museums, scientific departments and administrative offices. He then asks "But where is the University? I have seen where the members of the Colleges live, where the Registrar works, where the scientists experiment and the rest. But I have not yet seen the University in which reside and work the members of your University." It has then to be explained to him that the University is not another collateral institution, some ulterior counterpart to the colleges, laboratories and offices which he has seen. The University is just the way in which all that he has already seen is organized. When they are seen and when their coordination is understood, the University has been seen. His mistake lay in his innocent assumption that it was correct to speak of Christ Church, the Bodleian Library, the Ashmolean Museum *and* the University, to speak, that is, as if "the University" stood for an extra member of the class of which these other units are members. He was mistakenly allocating the University to the same category as that to which the other institutions belong.

The same mistake would be made by a child witnessing the march-past of a division, who, having had pointed out to him such and such battalions, batteries, squadrons, etc., asked when the division was going to appear. He would be supposing that a division was a counterpart to the units already seen, partly similar to them and partly unlike them. He would be shown his mistake by being told that in watching the battalions, batteries and squadrons marching past he had been watching the division marching past. The march-past was not a parade of battalions, batteries, squadrons *and* a division; it was a parade of the battalions, batteries and squadrons *of* a division.

One more illustration. A foreigner watching his first game of cricket learns what are the functions of the bowlers, the batsmen, the fielders, the umpires and the scorers. He then says "But there is no one left on the field to contribute the famous element of team-spirit. I see who does the bowling, the batting and the wicket-keeping; but I do not see whose role it is to exercise *esprit de corps*."* Once more, it would have to be explained that he was looking for the wrong type of thing. Team-spirit is not another cricketing-operation supplementary to all of the other special tasks. It is, roughly, the keenness with which each of the special tasks is performed, and performing a task keenly is not performing two tasks. Certainly exhibiting team-spirit is not the same thing as bowling or catching, but nor is it a third thing such that we can say that the bowler first bowls *and* then exhibits team-spirit or that a fielder is at a given moment *either* catching *or* displaying esprit de corps.

These illustrations of category-mistakes have a common feature which must be noticed. The mistakes were made by people who did not know how to wield the concepts *University, division* and *team-spirit*. Their puzzles arose from inability to use certain items in the English vocabulary.

The theoretically interesting category-mistakes are those made by people who are perfectly competent to apply concepts, at least in the situations with which they are familiar, but are still liable in their abstract thinking to allocate those concepts to logical types to which they do not belong. An instance of a mistake of this sort would be the following story. A student of politics has learned the main differences

* Esprit de corps (French) is the feeling of comradeship and devotion to a common cause that arises among the members of a group.

between the British, the French and the American Constitutions, and has learned also the differences and connections between the Cabinet, Parliament, the various Ministries, the Judicature and the Church of England. But he still becomes embarrassed when asked questions about the connections between the Church of England, the Home Office and the British Constitution. For while the Church and the Home Office are institutions, the British Constitution is not another institution in the same sense of that noun. So inter-institutional relations which can be asserted or denied to hold between the Church and the Home Office cannot be asserted or denied to hold between either of them and the British Constitution. "The British Constitution" is not a term of the same logical type as "the Home Office" and "the Church of England." In a partially similar way, John Doe may be a relative, a friend, an enemy or a stranger to Richard Roe; but he cannot be any of these things to the Average Taxpayer. He knows how to talk sense in certain sorts of discussions about the Average Taxpayer, but he is baffled to say why he could not come across him in the street as he can come across Richard Roe.

It is pertinent to our main subject to notice that, so long as the student of politics continues to think of the British Constitution as a counterpart to the other institutions, he will tend to describe it as a mysteriously occult institution; and so long as John Doe continues to think of the Average Taxpayer as a fellow-citizen, he will tend to think of him as an elusive insubstantial man, a ghost who is everywhere yet nowhere.

My destructive purpose is to show that a family of radical category-mistakes is the source of the double-life theory. The representation of a person as a ghost mysteriously ensconced in a machine derives from this argument. Because, as is true, a person's thinking, feeling and purposive doing cannot be described solely in the idioms of physics, chemistry and physiology, therefore they must be described in counterpart idioms. As the human body is a complex organised unit, so the human mind must be another complex organised unit, though one made of a different sort of stuff and with a different sort of structure. Or, again, as the human body, like any other parcel of matter, is a field of causes and effects, so the mind must be another field of causes and effects, though not (Heaven be praised) mechanical causes and effects.

3. THE ORIGIN OF THE CATEGORY-MISTAKE

One of the chief intellectual origins of what I have yet to prove to be the Cartesian category-mistake seems to be this. When Galileo showed that his methods of scientific discovery were competent to provide a mechanical theory which should cover every occupant of space, Descartes found in himself two conflicting motives. As a man of scientific genius he could not but endorse the claims of mechanics, yet as a religious and moral man he could not accept, as Hobbes accepted, the discouraging rider to those claims, namely that human nature differs only in degree of complexity from clockwork.* The mental could not be just a variety of the mechanical.

He and subsequent philosophers naturally but erroneously availed themselves of the following escape-route. Since mental-conduct words are not to be construed as signifying the occurrence of mechanical processes, they must be construed as signifying the occurrence of non-mechanical processes; since mechanical laws explain movements in space as the effects of other movements in space, other laws must explain some of the non-spatial workings of minds as the effects of other non-spatial workings of minds. The difference between the human behaviours which we describe as intelligent and those which we describe as unintelligent must be a difference in their causation; so, while some movements of human tongues and limbs are the effects of mechanical causes, others must be the effects of non-mechanical causes, i.e., some issue from movements of particles of matter, others from workings of the mind.

The differences between the physical and the mental were thus represented as differences inside

* Galileo Galilei (1564–1642), René Descartes (1596–1650), and Thomas Hobbes (1588–1679) were important early modern thinkers, known for their contributions to science and philosophy.

the common framework of the categories of "thing," "stuff," "attribute," "state," "process," "change," "cause" and "effect." Minds are things, but different sorts of things from bodies; mental processes are causes and effects, but different sorts of causes and effects from bodily movements. And so on. Somewhat as the foreigner expected the University to be an extra edifice, rather like a college but also considerably different, so the repudiators of mechanism represented minds as extra centres of causal processes, rather like machines but also considerably different from them. Their theory was a para-mechanical hypothesis.

That this assumption was at the heart of the doctrine is shown by the fact that there was from the beginning felt to be a major theoretical difficulty in explaining how minds can influence and be influenced by bodies. How can a mental process, such as willing, cause spatial movements like the movements of the tongue? How can a physical change in the optic nerve have among its effects a mind's perception of a flash of light? This notorious crux by itself shows the logical mould into which Descartes pressed his theory of the mind. It was the self-same mould into which he and Galileo set their mechanics. Still unwittingly adhering to the grammar of mechanics, he tried to avert disaster by describing minds in what was merely an obverse vocabulary. The workings of minds had to be described by the mere negatives of the specific descriptions given to bodies; they are not in space, they are not motions, they are not modifications of matter, they are not accessible to public observation. Minds are not bits of clockwork, they are just bits of not-clockwork.

As thus represented, minds are not merely ghosts harnessed to machines, they are themselves just spectral machines. Though the human body is an engine, it is not quite an ordinary engine, since some of its workings are governed by another engine inside it—this interior governor-engine being one of a very special sort. It is invisible, inaudible and it has no size or weight. It cannot be taken to bits and the laws it obeys are not those known to ordinary engineers. Nothing is known of how it governs the bodily engine.

A second major crux points the same moral. Since, according to the doctrine, minds belong to the same category as bodies and since bodies are rigidly governed by mechanical laws, it seemed to many theorists to follow that minds must be similarly governed by rigid non-mechanical laws. The physical world is a deterministic system, so the mental world must be a deterministic system. Bodies cannot help the modifications that they undergo, so minds cannot help pursuing the careers fixed for them. *Responsibility, choice, merit* and *demerit* are therefore inapplicable concepts—unless the compromise solution is adopted of saying that the laws governing mental processes, unlike those governing physical processes, have the congenial attribute of being only rather rigid. The problem of the Freedom of the Will was the problem how to reconcile the hypothesis that minds are to be described in terms drawn from the categories of mechanics with the knowledge that higher-grade human conduct is not of a piece with the behaviour of machines.

It is an historical curiosity that it was not noticed that the entire argument was broken-backed. Theorists correctly assumed that any sane man could already recognise the differences between, say, rational and non-rational utterances or between purposive and automatic behaviour. Else there would have been nothing requiring to be salved from mechanism. Yet the explanation given presupposed that one person could in principle never recognise the difference between the rational and the irrational utterances issuing from other human bodies, since he could never get access to the postulated immaterial causes of some of their utterances. Save for the doubtful exception of himself, he could never tell the difference between a man and a Robot. It would have to be conceded, for example, that, for all that we can tell, the inner lives of persons who are classed as idiots or lunatics are as rational as those of anyone else. Perhaps only their overt behaviour is disappointing; that is to say, perhaps "idiots" are not really idiotic, or "lunatics" lunatic. Perhaps, too, some of those who are classed as sane are really idiots. According to the theory, external observers could never know how the overt behaviour of others is correlated with their mental powers and processes and so they could never know or even plausibly conjecture whether their applications of mental-conduct concepts to these other people were correct or incorrect.

It would then be hazardous or impossible for a man to claim sanity or logical consistency even for himself, since he would be debarred from comparing his own performances with those of others. In short, our characterisations of persons and their performances as intelligent, prudent and virtuous or as stupid, hypocritical and cowardly could never have been made, so the problem of providing a special causal hypothesis to serve as the basis of such diagnoses would never have arisen. The question, "How do persons differ from machines?" arose just because everyone already knew how to apply mental-conduct concepts before the new causal hypothesis was introduced. This causal hypothesis could not therefore be the source of the criteria used in those applications. Nor, of course, has the causal hypothesis in any degree improved our handling of those criteria. We still distinguish good from bad arithmetic, politic from impolitic conduct and fertile from infertile imaginations in the ways in which Descartes himself distinguished them before and after he speculated how the applicability of these criteria was compatible with the principle of mechanical causation.

He had mistaken the logic of his problem. Instead of asking by what criteria intelligent behaviour is actually distinguished from nonintelligent behaviour, he asked "Given that the principle of mechanical causation does not tell us the difference, what other causal principle will tell it to us?" He realised that the problem was not one of mechanics and assumed that it must therefore be one of some counterpart to mechanics. Not unnaturally psychology is often cast for just this role.

When two terms belong to the same category, it is proper to construct conjunctive propositions embodying them. Thus a purchaser may say that he bought a left-hand glove and a right-hand glove, but not that he bought a left-hand glove, a right-hand glove and a pair of gloves. "She came home in a flood of tears and a sedan-chair" is a well-known joke based on the absurdity of conjoining terms of different types. It would have been equally ridiculous to construct the disjunction "She came home either in a flood of tears or else in a sedan-chair." Now the dogma of the Ghost in the Machine does just this. It maintains that there exist both bodies and minds; that there occur physical processes and mental processes; that there are mechanical causes of corporeal movements and mental causes of corporeal movements. I shall argue that these and other analogous conjunctions are absurd; but, it must be noticed, the argument will not show that either of the illegitimately conjoined propositions is absurd in itself. I am not, for example, denying that there occur mental processes. Doing long division is a mental process and so is making a joke. But I am saying that the phrase "there occur mental processes" does not mean the same sort of thing as "there occur physical processes," and, therefore, that it makes no sense to conjoin or disjoin the two.

If my argument is successful, there will follow some interesting consequences. First, the hallowed contrast between Mind and Matter will be dissipated, but dissipated not by either of the equally hallowed absorptions of Mind by Matter or of Matter by Mind, but in quite a different way. For the seeming contrast of the two will be shown to be as illegitimate as would be the contrast of "she came home in a flood of tears" and "she came home in a sedan-chair." The belief that there is a polar opposition between Mind and Matter is the belief that they are terms of the same logical type.

It will also follow that both Idealism and Materialism are answers to an improper question. The "reduction" of the material world to mental states and processes, as well as the "reduction" of mental states and processes to physical states and processes, presuppose the legitimacy of the disjunction "Either there exist minds or there exist bodies (but not both)." It would be like saying, "Either she bought a left-hand and a right-hand glove or she bought a pair of gloves (but not both)."

It is perfectly proper to say, in one logical tone of voice, that there exist minds and to say, in another logical tone of voice, that there exist bodies. But these expressions do not indicate two different species of existence, for "existence" is not a generic word like "coloured" or "sexed." They indicate two different senses of "exist," somewhat as "rising" has different senses in "the tide is rising," "hopes are rising," and "the average age of death is rising." A man would be thought to be making a poor joke who said that three things are now rising, namely the tide, hopes and the average age of death. It would be just as good or bad a joke to say that there exist prime numbers and Wednesdays and public opinions and navies; or that there exist both minds and bodies. . . .

4. HISTORICAL NOTE

It would not be true to say that the official theory derives solely from Descartes' theories, or even from a more widespread anxiety about the implications of seventeenth century mechanism. Scholastic and Reformation theology had schooled the intellects of the scientists as well as of the laymen, philosophers and clerics of that age. Stoic-Augustinian theories of the will were embedded in the Calvinist doctrines of sin and grace; Platonic and Aristotelian theories of the intellect shaped the orthodox doctrines of the immortality of the soul. Descartes was reformulating already prevalent theological doctrines of the soul in the new syntax of Galileo. The theologian's privacy of conscience became the philosopher's privacy of consciousness, and what had been the bogy of Predestination reappeared as the bogy of Determinism.

It would also not be true to say that the two-worlds myth did no theoretical good. Myths often do a lot of theoretical good, while they are still new. One benefit bestowed by the para-mechanical myth was that it partly superannuated the then prevalent para-political myth. Minds and their Faculties had previously been described by analogies with political superiors and political subordinates. The idioms used were those of ruling, obeying, collaborating and rebelling. They survived and still survive in many ethical and some epistemological discussions. As, in physics, the new myth of occult Forces was a scientific improvement on the old myth of Final Causes, so, in anthropological and psychological theory, the new myth of hidden operations, impulses and agencies was an improvement on the old myth of dictations, deferences and disobedience.

◈ PHYSICALISM ◈

Physicalism

DANIEL STOLJAR

Australian philosopher Daniel Stoljar is Professor of Philosophy at the Australian National University in Canberra. His philosophical writings focus primarily on the areas of metaphysics, philosophy of mind, and metaethics.

The selection that appears here is a lightly edited excerpt from a more extensive entry that appeared in the *Stanford Encyclopedia of Philosophy* in 2005. The full text of that entry can be found at <http://plato.stanford.edu/archives/win2005/entries/physicalism>. The subsections that appear in this volume have been renumbered.

From the *Stanford Encyclopedia of Philosophy*, ed. Edward N. Zalta. Copyright © 2007 by The Metaphysics Research Lab, CSLI Stanford University: http://plato.stanford.edu/entries/physicalism/ Reprinted with the permission of the author.

Physicalism is the thesis that everything is physical, or as contemporary philosophers sometimes put it, that everything supervenes on the physical. The thesis is usually intended as a metaphysical thesis, parallel to the ancient Greek philosopher Thales's thesis that everything is water, or the idealism of the 18th century philosopher Berkeley, that everything is mental. The general idea is that the nature of the actual world (i.e., the universe and everything in it) conforms to a certain condition, the condition of being physical. Of course, physicalists don't deny that the world might contain many items that at first glance don't *seem* physical—items of a biological, or psychological, or moral, or social nature. But they insist nevertheless that at the end of the day such items are wholly physical.

Physicalism is sometimes known as materialism. Historically, materialists held that everything was matter—where matter was conceived as "an inert, senseless substance, in which extension, figure, and motion do actually subsist" (Berkeley, *Principles of Human Knowledge*, par. 9). The reason for speaking of physicalism rather than materialism is to abstract away from this historical notion, which is usually thought of as too restrictive—for example, forces such as gravity are physical but it is not clear that they are material in the traditional sense (Dijksterhuis 1961, Yolton 1983). It is also to emphasize a connection to physics and the physical sciences. Indeed, physicalism is unusual among metaphysical doctrines in being associated historically with a commitment both to the sciences and to a particular branch of science, namely physics.

1. A FRAMEWORK FOR DISCUSSION

In approaching the topic of physicalism, one may distinguish what I will call *the interpretation question* from *the truth question*. The interpretation question asks:

- What does it *mean* to say that everything is physical?

The truth question asks:

- Is it *true* to say that everything is physical?

There is obviously a sense in which the second question here presupposes an answer to the first—you need to know what a statement means before you can ask whether it's true—and I will begin with the interpretation question. . . .

The interpretation question itself divides into two sub-questions, which I will call *the completeness question* and *the condition question*. The completeness question asks:

- What does it mean to say that *everything* is physical?

In other words, the completeness question holds fixed the issue of what it means for something to satisfy the condition of being physical, and asks instead what it means for *everything* to satisfy that condition. Notice that a parallel question could be asked of Thales: assuming we know what condition you have to satisfy to be water, what does it mean to say that everything satisfies that condition?

The condition question asks:

- What does it mean to say that everything is *physical*?

In other words, the condition question holds fixed the issue of what it means for everything to satisfy some condition or other, and asks instead what *is* the condition, being physical, that everything satisfies. Notice again that a parallel question could be asked of Thales: assuming we know what it is for everything to satisfy some condition or other, what is the condition, being water, that according to Thales, everything satisfies? In discussing the interpretation question, I will turn first to the completeness question, and then consider the condition question.

2. SUPERVENIENCE PHYSICALISM: INTRODUCTORY

In attempting to answer the completeness question, it has become customary since Davidson 1970 to look to the notion of supervenience. (The notion of supervenience is historically associated with metaethics, but it has received extensive discussion in the general metaphysics and logic literature. For a survey, see Kim 1993.)*

The idea of supervenience might be introduced via an example due to David Lewis of a dot-matrix picture:

> A dot-matrix picture has global properties—it is symmetrical, it is cluttered, and whatnot—and yet all there is to the picture is dots and non-dots at each point of the matrix. The global properties are nothing but patterns in the dots. They supervene: no two pictures could differ in their global properties without differing, somewhere, in whether there is or there isn't a dot (1986, p. 14).

Lewis's example gives us one way to introduce the basic idea of physicalism. The basic idea is that the physical features of the world are like the dots in the picture, and the psychological or biological or social features of the world are like the global properties of the picture. Just as the global features of the picture are nothing but a pattern in the dots, so too the psychological, the biological and the social features of the world are nothing but a pattern in the physical features of the world. To use the language of supervenience, just as the global features of the picture supervene on the dots, so too everything supervenes on the physical, if physicalism is true.

It is desirable to have a more explicit statement of physicalism, and here too Lewis's example gives us direction. Lewis says that, in the case of the picture, supervenience means that "no two pictures can be identical in the arrangement of dots but different in their global properties." Similarly, one might say that, in the case of physicalism, no two possible worlds can be identical in their physical properties but differ, somewhere, in their mental, social or biological properties. To put this slightly differently, we might say that if physicalism is true at our world, then no *other* world can be physically identical to it without being identical to it in all respects. This suggests the following account of what physicalism is:

> **(1)** Physicalism is true at a possible world *w* iff any world which is a physical duplicate of *w* is a duplicate of *w simpliciter*.*

If physicalism is construed along the lines suggested in (1), then we have an answer to the completeness question. The completeness question asks: what does it mean to say that *everything* is physical? According to (1), what this means is that if physicalism is true, there is no possible world which is identical to the actual world in every physical respect but which is not identical to it in a biological or social or psychological respect. It will be useful to have a name for physicalism so defined, so let us call it *supervenience physicalism*. . . .

3. MINIMAL PHYSICALISM AND PHILOSOPHY OF MIND

We saw earlier that physicalism is intended as a very general claim about the nature of the world. Nevertheless, by far the most discussion of physicalism in the literature has been in the philosophy of mind. The reason for this is that it is in philosophy of mind that we find the most plausible and compelling arguments that physicalism is false. Indeed, as we will see later on, arguments about qualia and consciousness are usually formulated as arguments for the conclusion that physicalism is false. Thus, much of philosophy of mind is devoted to a discussion of physicalism. Most contemporary philosophers are physicalists. But some, dualists, deny physicalism and thus deny that consciousness supervenes on the physical.

While the issue of physicalism is central to philosophy of mind, however, it is important also to be aware that supervenience physicalism is neutral on a good many of the questions that are pursued in philosophy of mind, and pursued elsewhere for that

* Donald Davidson (1917–2003), Jaegwon Kim (1934–) and David Lewis (1941–2001) are all twentieth-century American philosophers who made important contributions to the philosophy of mind.

* *Simpliciter* (Latin) here means: without qualification.

matter. If you read over the philosophy of mind literature, you will often find people debating a number of different issues: whether there *are* mental states at all; what *sort* of thing mental states are; to what extent mental states are environmentally determined. Given the multifariousness of mental states, it is quite likely that the correct position will be some kind of combination of these positions. But this is a question of further inquiry that is irrelevant to physicalism itself. So physicalism itself leaves many debates in the philosophy of mind unanswered.

This point is sometimes expressed by saying that *supervenience physicalism is minimal physicalism* (Lewis 1983): it is intended to capture the minimal or core commitment of physicalism. Physicalists may differ from one another in many ways, but all of them must at least hold supervenience physicalism. (Notice that the idea that (2) captures the minimal commitment of physicalism is a distinct idea from that of a minimal physical duplicate which it uses to capture minimal physicalism.)

Two issues here require further comment. First, in some discussions in philosophy of mind, the term "physicalism" is used to refer to the identity theory, the idea that mental states or properties are neurological states or properties (Block 1980). In this use of the term, one can reject physicalism by rejecting the identity theory—so by that standard a behaviorist or functionalist in philosophy of mind would not count as a physicalist. Obviously, this is a much more restricted use of the term than is being employed here.

Second, one might think that supervenience physicalism is inconsistent with eliminativism, the claim that psychological states do not exist, for the following reason. Suppose psychological states supervene on physical states. Doesn't that mean, contrary to eliminativism, that there must *be* some psychological states? The answer to this question is "no." For consider: the telephone on my desk has no psychological states whatsoever. Nevertheless it is still true (though, admittedly, a little odd) to say that a telephone which is identical to my telephone in all physical respects will be identical to it in all psychological respects. In the sense intended, therefore, one thing can be psychologically identical to another even when neither *has* any psychological states.

4. THE CASE FOR PHYSICALISM

. . . What reason is there for believing that physicalism is true?

The first thing to say when considering the truth of physicalism is that we live in an overwhelmingly physicalist or materialist intellectual culture. The result is that, as things currently stand, the standards of argumentation required to persuade someone of the truth of physicalism are much lower than the standards required to persuade someone of its negation. (The point here is a perfectly general one: if you already believe or want something to be true, you are likely to accept fairly low standards of argumentation for its truth.)

However, while it might be difficult to assess dispassionately the arguments for or against physicalism, this is still something we should endeavor to do. Here I will review two arguments that are commonly thought to establish the truth of physicalism. What unites the arguments is that each takes something from the physicalist world-picture which we considered previously and tries to establish the metaphysical claim that everything supervenes on the physical.

The first argument is (what I will call) *The Argument from Causal Closure*. The first premise of this argument is the thesis of the Causal Closure of the Physical—that is, the thesis that every event which has a cause has a physical cause. The second premise is that mental events cause physical events—for example we normally think that events such as wanting to raise your arm (a mental event) cause events such as the raising of your arm (a physical event). The third premise of the argument is a principle of causation that is often called the exclusion principle (Kim 1993, Yablo 1992). The correct formulation of the exclusion principle is a matter of some controversy but a formulation that is both simple and plausible is the following:

EXCLUSION PRINCIPLE

If an event *e* causes event *e**, then there is no event *e#* such that *e#* is non-supervenient on *e* and *e#* causes *e**.

The conclusion of the argument is that mental events are supervenient on physical events, or more briefly that physicalism is true. For of course, if the thesis of Causal Closure is true then behavioral events have physical causes, and if mental events also cause behavioral events, then they must supervene on the physical if the exclusion principle is true.

The Argument from Causal Closure is perhaps the dominant argument for physicalism in the literature today. But it is somewhat unclear whether it is successful. The most promising response for the anti-physicalist is to reject the second premise and to adopt a version of what is called epiphenomenalism, the view that mental events are caused by, and yet do not cause, physical events. The argument against this position is usually epistemological: if pains don't cause pain behavior how can it be that your telling me that you are in pain gives me any reason for supposing you are? It might seem that epiphenomenalists are in trouble here, but as a number of recent philosophers have argued, the issues here are very far from being settled (Chalmers 1996, Hyslop 1999). The crucial point is that the causal theory of evidence is open to serious counterexamples so it is unclear that it can be used against epiphenomenalism effectively.

A different sort of response is to reject the causal principles on which the argument is based. As against the exclusion principle, for example, it is often pointed out that certain events are overdetermined. The classic example is the firing squad: both the firing by soldier A and by soldier B caused the prisoner's death but since these are distinct firings, the exclusion principle is false. However, while this line of response is suggestive, it is in fact rather limited. It is true that the case of the firing squad represents an exception to the exclusion principle—an exception that the principle must be emended to accommodate. But it is difficult to believe that it represents an exception that can be widespread. A more searching response is to reject the very idea of causal closure on the grounds, perhaps, that as Bertrand Russell* (1917) famously argued, causation plays no role in a mature portrayal of the world. Once again, however, the promise of this response is more imagined than real. While it is true that many sciences do not explicitly use the notion of causation, it is extremely unlikely that they do not imply that various causal claims are true.

The second argument for physicalism is (what I will call) *The Argument from Methodological Naturalism*. The first premise of this argument is that it is rational to be guided in one's metaphysical commitments by the methods of natural science. Lying behind this premise are the arguments of Quine* and others that metaphysics should not be approached in a way that is distinct from the sciences but should rather be thought of as continuous with it. The second premise of the argument is that, as a matter of fact, the metaphysical picture of the world that one is led to by the methods of natural science is physicalism. The conclusion is that it is rational to believe physicalism, or, more briefly that physicalism is true.

The Argument from Methodological Naturalism has received somewhat less attention in the literature than the Argument from Causal Closure. But it seems just as persuasive—in fact, rather more so. For how might one respond? One possibility is to reject its first premise. But this is not something that most people are attracted to (or at least are attracted to explicitly.)

The other possibility is to reject its second premise. However, once it is appreciated what physicalism is—and, more important, what it is not—it is not terribly clear what this would amount to or what the motivation for it would be. In the first place, our earlier discussion shows that physicalism is not inconsistent with explanatory autonomy of the various sciences, so that one should not reject physicalism merely because one can't see how to reduce those sciences to others. In the second place, while it is perfectly true that there are examples of non-physicalist approaches to the world—vitalism in biology is perhaps the best example—this is beside the point. The second premise of the Argument from Methodological Naturalism

* Bertrand Russell (1872–1970) was an important British philosopher, mathematician, and political activist.

* Willard Van Orman (W. V. O.) Quine (1908–2000) was one of the most important American philosophers and logicians of the twentieth century, known, among other things, for his commitment to the continuity of philosophy with science. A selection from his writings can be found in the Knowledge and the Nature of Reality section.

does not deny that other views are possible, it simply says that physicalism is the most likely view at the moment. Finally, one might be inclined to appeal to arguments such as the knowledge argument to show that physicalism is false, and hence that methodological naturalism could not show that physicalism is false. However, this suggestion represents a sort of confusion about the knowledge argument. As we saw above, if successful the knowledge argument suggests, not simply that physicalism is false but that any approach to the world that is compatible with methodological naturalism is false. But if that is so, it is mistaken to suppose that the knowledge argument gives one any reason to endorse anti-physicalism if that is supposed to be a position compatible with methodological naturalism.

REFERENCES

Berkeley, G. 1710. *Principles of Human Knowledge*.

Block, N. 1980. "Troubles with Functionalism." In N. Block (ed.), *Readings in the Philosophy of Psychology*, Vol. I. Cambridge, MA: Harvard University Press.

Chalmers, D. 1996. *The Conscious Mind*. New York: Oxford University Press.

Davidson, D. 1970. "Mental Events." In D. Davidson (1980), *Essays on Actions and Events*. New York: Oxford University Press.

Dijksterhuis, E. J. 1961. *The Mechanization of the World-Picture*. Oxford: Clarendon Press.

Hyslop, A. 1999. "Methodological Epiphenomenalism." *Australasian Journal of Philosophy*.

Kim, J. 1993. *Mind and Supervenience*. Cambridge, England: Cambridge University Press.

Lewis, D. 1983. "New Work for a Theory of Universals." *Australasian Journal of Philosophy*, 61/4.

Lewis, D. 1986. *On the Plurality of Worlds*. Oxford: Blackwell.

Russell, B. 1917. "On the Notion of Cause," in B. Russell, *Mysticism and Logic*. Penguin, 1963.

Yablo, S. 1992. "Mental Causation." *The Philosophical Review* (April), pp. 245–280.

Yolton, R. 1983. *Thinking Matter*. Minneapolis: University of Minnesota Press.

Sensations and Brain Processes

J. J. C. SMART

J. J. C. Smart (1920–) is a respected twentieth-century Scottish-born philosopher who spent the bulk of his career in Australia, first at the University of Adelaide and later at the Australian National University. He is known for his broad-ranging contributions to metaphysics, ethics, and the philosophy of mind.

The text that appears here was originally published as a journal article in 1959. In it, Smart defends a nondualist view of mental states known as the *identity theory*.

At a number of points in this essay, Smart refers to and cites Ludwig Wittgenstein's posthumously published *Philosophical Investigations* (1953), a complicated work consisting of 693 numbered paragraphs. Wittgenstein (1889–1951) was an important Austrian-born philosopher who made contributions to the philosophy of mind, the philosophy of language, and the foundations of logic and mathematics. He taught for many years in Cambridge, England, and had enormous influence on a generation of English-speaking philosophers.

From *Philosophical Review* 68: 141–56, 1959. Copyright © 1959 Cornell University Press. All rights reserved. Used by permission of the current publisher, Duke University Press.

Suppose that I report that I have at this moment a roundish, blurry-edged after-image which is yellowish towards its edge and is orange towards its centre. What is it that I am reporting?[1] One answer to this question might be that I am not reporting anything, that when I say that it looks to me as though there is a roundish yellowy orange patch of light on the wall I am expressing some sort of *temptation*, the temptation to say that there *is* a roundish yellowy orange patch on the wall (though I may know that there is not such a patch on the wall). This is perhaps Wittgenstein's view in the *Philosophical Investigations* (see paragraphs 367, 370). Similarly, when I "report" a pain, I am not really reporting anything (or, if you like, I am reporting in a queer sense of "reporting"), but am doing a sophisticated sort of wince. (See paragraph 244: "The verbal expression of pain replaces crying and does not describe it." Nor does it describe anything else?)[2] I prefer most of the time to discuss an after-image rather than a pain, because the word "pain" brings in something which is irrelevant to my purpose: the notion of "distress." I think that "he is in pain" entails "he is in distress," that is, that he is in a certain agitation-condition.[3] Similarly, to say "I am in pain" may be to do more than "replace pain behavior": it may be partly to report something, though this something is quite non-mysterious, being an agitation-condition, and so susceptible of behavioristic analysis. The suggestion I wish if possible to avoid is a different one, namely that "I am in pain" is a genuine report, and that what it reports is an irreducibly psychical something. And similarly the suggestion I wish to resist is also that to say "I have a yellowish orange after-image" is to report something irreducibly psychical.

Why do I wish to resist this suggestion? Mainly because of Occam's razor. It seems to me that science is increasingly giving us a viewpoint whereby organisms are able to be seen as physico-chemical mechanisms:[4] it seems that even the behavior of man himself will one day be explicable in mechanistic terms. There does seem to be, so far as science is concerned, nothing in the world but increasingly complex arrangements of physical constituents. All except for one place: in consciousness. That is, for a full description of what is going on in a man you would have to mention not only the physical processes in his tissue, glands, nervous system, and so forth, but also his states of consciousness: his visual, auditory, and tactual sensations, his aches and pains. That these should be *correlated* with brain processes does not help, for to say that they are *correlated* is to say that they are something "over and above." You cannot correlate something with itself. You correlate footprints with burglars, but not Bill Sikes the burglar with Bill Sikes the burglar. So sensations, states of consciousness, do seem to be the one sort of thing left outside the physicalist picture, and for various reasons I just cannot believe that this can be so. That everything should be explicable in terms of physics (together of course with descriptions of the ways in which the parts are put together—roughly, biology is to physics as radio-engineering is to electro-magnetism) except the occurrence of sensations seems to me to be frankly unbelievable. Such sensations would be "nomological danglers," to use Feigl's expression,*[5] It is not often realized how odd would be the laws whereby these nomological danglers would dangle. It is sometimes asked, "Why can't there be psychophysical laws which are of a novel sort, just as the laws of electricity and magnetism were novelties from the standpoint of Newtonian mechanics?" Certainly we are pretty sure in the future to come across new ultimate laws of a novel type, but I expect them to relate simple constituents: for example, whatever ultimate particles are then in vogue. I cannot believe that ultimate laws of nature could relate simple constituents to configurations consisting of perhaps billions of neurons (and goodness knows how many billion billions of ultimate particles) all put together for all the world as though their main purpose in life was to be a negative feedback mechanism of a complicated sort. Such ultimate laws would be like nothing so far known in science. They have a queer "smell" to them. I am just unable to believe in the nomological danglers themselves, or in the laws whereby they would dangle. If any philosophical arguments seemed to compel us to believe in such things, I would suspect a catch in the

* Herbert Feigl (1902–88) was an Austrian-born philosopher best known for his work on philosophical methodology and the philosophy of science.

argument. In any case it is the object of this paper to show that there are no philosophical arguments which compel us to be dualists.

The above is largely a confession of faith, but it explains why I find Wittgenstein's position (as I construe it) so congenial. For on this view there are, in a sense, no sensations. A man is a vast arrangement of physical particles, but there are not, over and above this, sensations or states of consciousness. There are just behavioral facts about this vast mechanism, such as that it expresses a temptation (behavior disposition) to say "there is a yellowish-red patch on the wall" or that it goes through a sophisticated sort of wince, that is, says "I am in pain." Admittedly Wittgenstein says that though the sensation "is not a something," it is nevertheless "not a nothing either" (paragraph 304), but this need only mean that the word "ache" has a use. An ache is a thing, but only in the innocuous sense in which the plain man, in the first paragraph of Frege's *Foundations of Arithmetic*, answers the question "what is the number one?" by "a thing."* It should be noted that when I assert that to say "I have a yellowish-orange after-image" is to express a temptation to assert the physical-object statement "there is a yellowish-orange patch on the wall," I mean that saying "I have a yellowish-orange after-image" is (partly) the exercise of the disposition[6] which is the temptation. It is not to *report* that I have the temptation, any more than is "I love you" normally a report that I love someone. Saying "I love you" is just part of the behavior which is the exercise of the disposition of loving someone.

Though, for the reasons given above, I am very receptive to the above "expressive" account of sensation statements, I do not feel that it will quite do the trick. Maybe this is because I have not thought it out sufficiently, but it does seem to me as though, when a person says "I have an after-image," he *is* making a genuine report, and that when he says "I have a pain," he *is* doing more than "replace pain-behavior," and that "this more" is not just to say that he is in distress. I am not so sure, however, that to admit this is to admit that there are nonphysical correlates of brain processes. Why should not sensations just be brain processes of a certain sort? There are, of course, well-known (as well as lesser-known) philosophical objections to the view that reports of sensations are reports of brain-processes, but I shall try to argue that these arguments are by no means as cogent as is commonly thought to be the case.

Let me first try to state more accurately the thesis that sensations are brain processes. It is not the thesis that, for example, "after-image" or "ache" means the same as "brain process of sort *X*" (where "*X*" is replaced by a description of a certain sort of brain process). It is that, in so far as "after-image" or "ache" is a report of a process, it is a report of a process that *happens to be* a brain process. It follows that the thesis does not claim that sensation statements can be *translated* into statements about brain processes.[7] Nor does it claim that the logic of a sensation statement is the same as that of a brain-process statement. All it claims is that in so far as a sensation statement is a report of something, that something is in fact a brain process. Sensations are nothing over and above brain processes. Nations are nothing "over and above" citizens, but this does not prevent the logic of nation statements being very different from the logic of citizen statements, nor does it insure the translatability of nation statements into citizen statements. (I do not, however, wish to assert that the relation of sensation statements to brain-process statements is very like that of nation statements to citizen statements. Nations do not just *happen to be* nothing over and above citizens, for example. I bring in the "nations" example merely to make a negative point: that the fact that the logic of A-statements is different from that of B-statements does not insure that A's are anything over and above B's.)

REMARKS ON IDENTITY

When I say that a sensation is a brain process or that lightning is an electric discharge, I am using "is" in the sense of strict identity. (Just as in the—in this case necessary—proposition "7 is identical with the

* Gottlob Frege (1848–1925) was a German-born mathematician, logician, and philosopher whose writings profoundly influenced twentieth-century Anglo-American philosophy. The example of the morning star and the evening star, which Smart discusses in the selection, comes from Frege's famous 1892 paper "On Sense and Reference."

smallest prime number greater than 5.") When I say that a sensation is a brain process or that lightning is an electric discharge I do not mean just that the sensation is somehow spatially or temporally continuous with the brain process or that the lightning is just spatially or temporally continuous with the discharge. When on the other hand I say that the successful general is the same person as the small boy who stole the apples I mean only that the successful general I see before me is a time slice[8] of the same four-dimensional object of which the small boy stealing apples is an earlier time slice. However, the four-dimensional object which has the general-I-see-before-me for its late time slice is identical in the strict sense with the four-dimensional object which has the small-boy-stealing-apples for an early time slice. I distinguish these two senses of "is identical with" because I wish to make it clear that the brain-process doctrine asserts identity in the *strict* sense.

I shall now discuss various possible objections to the view that the processes reported in sensation statements are in fact processes in the brain. Most of us have met some of these objections in our first year as philosophy students. All the more reason to take a good look at them. Others of the objections will be more recondite and subtle.

OBJECTION 1

Any illiterate peasant can talk perfectly well about his after-images, or how things look or feel to him, or about his aches and pains, and yet he may know nothing whatever about neurophysiology. A man may, like Aristotle, believe that the brain is an organ for cooling the body without any impairment of his ability to make true statements about his sensations. Hence the things we are talking about when we describe our sensations cannot be processes in the brain.

REPLY

You might as well say that a nation of slugabeds, who never saw the morning star or knew of its existence, or who had never thought of the expression "the Morning Star," but who used the expression "the Evening Star" perfectly well, could not use this expression to refer to the same entity as we refer to (and describe as) "the Morning Star."[9]

You may object that the Morning Star is in a sense not the very same thing as the Evening Star, but only something spatiotemporally continuous with it. That is, you may say that the Morning Star is not the Evening Star in the strict sense of "identity" that I distinguished earlier. I can perhaps forestall this objection by considering the slug-abeds to be New Zealanders and the early risers to be Englishmen. Then the thing the New Zealanders describe as "the Morning Star" could be the very same thing (in the strict sense) as the Englishmen describe as "the Evening Star." And yet they could be ignorant of this fact.

There is, however, a more plausible example. Consider lightning.[10] Modern physical science tells us that lightning is a certain kind of electrical discharge due to ionization of clouds of water-vapor in the atmosphere. This, it is now believed, is what the true nature of lightning is. Note that there are not two things: a flash of lightning and an electrical discharge. There is one thing, a flash of lightning, which is described scientifically as an electrical discharge to the earth from a cloud of ionized water-molecules. The case is not at all like that of explaining a footprint by reference to a burglar. We say that what lightning really is, what its true nature as revealed by science is, is an electric discharge. (It is not the true nature of a footprint to be a burglar.)

To forestall irrelevant objections, I should like to make it clear that by "lightning" I mean the publicly observable physical object, lightning, not a visual sense-datum of lightning. I say that the publicly observable physical object lightning is in fact the electric discharge, not just a correlate of it. The sense-datum, or at least the having of the sense-datum, the "look" of lightning, may well in my view be a correlate of the electric discharge. For in my view it is a brain state *caused* by the lightning. But we should no more confuse sensations of lightning with lightning than we confuse sensations of a table with the table.

In short, the reply to Objection 1 is that there can be contingent statements of the form "A is identical with B," and a person may well know that something is an A without knowing that it is a B. An illiterate peasant might well be able to talk about his sensations without knowing about his brain processes, just as he can talk about lightning though he knows nothing of electricity.

OBJECTION 2

It is only a contingent fact (if it is a fact) that when we have a certain kind of sensation there is a certain kind of process in our brain. Indeed it is possible, though perhaps in the highest degree unlikely, that our present physiological theories will be as out of date as the ancient theory connecting mental processes with goings on in the heart. It follows that when we report a sensation we are not reporting a brain-process.

REPLY

The objection certainly proves that when we say "I have an after-image" we cannot *mean* something of the form "I have such and such a brain-process." But this does not show that what we report (having an after-image) is not *in fact* a brain process. "I see lightning" does not *mean* "I see an electric discharge." Indeed, it is logically possible (though highly unlikely) that the electrical discharge account of lightning might one day be given up. Again, "I see the Evening Star" does not *mean* the same as "I see the Morning Star," and yet "the Evening Star and the Morning Star are one and the same thing" is a contingent proposition. Possibly Objection 2 derives some of its apparent strength from a "Fido"-Fido theory of meaning.* If the meaning of an expression were what the expression named, then of course it *would* follow from the fact that "sensation" and "brain-process" have different meanings that they cannot name one and the same thing.

OBJECTION 3[11]

Even if Objections 1 and 2 do not prove that sensations are something over and above brain-processes, they do prove that the qualities of sensations are something over and above the qualities of brain-processes. That is, it may be possible to get out of asserting the existence of irreducibly psychic processes, but not out of asserting the existence of irreducibly psychic *properties*. For suppose we identify the Morning Star with the Evening Star. Then there must be some properties which logically imply that of being the Morning Star, and quite distinct properties which entail that of being the Evening Star. Again, there must be some properties (for example, that of being a yellow flash) which are logically distinct from those in the physicalist story.

Indeed, it might be thought that the objection succeeds at one jump. For consider the property of "being a yellow flash." It might seem that this property lies inevitably outside the physicalist framework within which I am trying to work (either by "yellow" being an objective emergent property of physical objects, or else by being a power to produce yellow sense-data, where "yellow," in this second instantiation of the word, refers to a purely phenomenal or introspectible quality). I must therefore digress for a moment and indicate how I deal with secondary qualities. I shall concentrate on color.

First of all, let me introduce the concept of a normal percipient. One person is more a normal percipient than another if he can make color discriminations that the other cannot. For example, if A can pick a lettuce leaf out of a heap of cabbage leaves, whereas B cannot though he can pick a lettuce leaf out of a heap of beetroot leaves, then A is more normal than B. (I am assuming that A and B are not given time to distinguish the leaves by their slight difference in shape, and so forth.) From the concept of "more normal than" it is easy to see how we can introduce the concept of "normal." Of

* The "Fido"-Fido theory of meaning holds that the meaning of a term is the object it stands for in the context in which it is used.

course, Eskimos may make the finest discriminations at the blue end of the spectrum, Hottentots at the red end.* In this case the concept of a normal percipient is a slightly idealized one, rather like that of "the mean sun" in astronomical chronology. There is no need to go into such subtleties now. I say that "This is red" means something roughly like "A normal percipient would not easily pick this out of a clump of geranium petals though he would pick it out of a clump of lettuce leaves." Of course it does not exactly mean this: a person might know the meaning of "red" without knowing anything about geraniums, or even about normal percipients. But the point is that a person can be *trained* to say "This is red" of objects which would not easily be picked out of geranium petals by a normal percipient, and so on. (Note that even a color-blind person can reasonably assert that something is red, though of course he needs to use another human being, not just himself, as his "color meter.") This account of secondary qualities explains their unimportance in physics. For obviously the discriminations and lack of discriminations made by a very complex neurophysiological mechanism are hardly likely to correspond to simple and nonarbitrary distinctions in nature.

I therefore elucidate colors as powers, in Locke's sense,† to evoke certain sorts of discriminatory responses in human beings. They are also, of course, powers to cause sensations in human beings (an account still nearer Locke's). But these sensations, I am arguing, are identifiable with brain processes.

Now how do I get over the objection that a sensation can be identified with a brain process only if it has some phenomenal property, not possessed by brain processes, whereby one-half of the identification may be, so to speak, pinned down?

My suggestion is as follows. When a person says, "I see a yellowish-orange after-image," he is saying something like this: "*There is something going on which is like what is going on when* I have my eyes open, am awake, and there is an orange illuminated in good light in front of me, that is, when I really see an orange." (And there is no reason why a person should not say the same thing when he is having a veridical sense-datum, so long as we construe "like" in the last sentence in such a sense that something can be like itself.) Notice that the italicized words, namely "there is something going on which is like what is going on when," are all quasi-logical or topic-neutral words. This explains why the ancient Greek peasant's reports about his sensations can be neutral between dualistic metaphysics or my materialistic metaphysics. It explains how sensations can be brain-processes and yet how those who report them need know nothing about brain-processes. For he reports them only very abstractly as "something going on which is like what is going on when . . ." Similarly, a person may say "someone is in the room," thus reporting truly that the doctor is in the room, even though he has never heard of doctors. (There are not two people in the room: "someone" *and* the doctor.) This account of sensation statements also explains the singular elusiveness of "raw feels"—why no one seems to be able to pin any properties on them.[12] Raw feels, in my view, are colorless for the very same reason that *something* is colorless. This does not mean that sensations do not have properties, for if they are brain-processes they certainly have properties. It only means that in speaking of them as being like or unlike one another we need not know or mention these properties.

This, then, is how I would reply to Objection 3. The strength of my reply depends on the possibility of our being able to report that one thing is like another without being able to state the respect in which it is like. I am not sure whether this is so or not, and that is why I regard Objection 3 as the strongest with which I have to deal.

OBJECTION 4

The after-image is not in physical space. The brain-process is. So the after-image is not a brain-process.

* At the time this article was written (1959), "Eskimo" and "Hottentot" were commonly used terms to refer to the native peoples of the circumpolar region (the Inuit and Yupik) and southwestern Africa (the Khoikhoi), respectively.

† English philosopher John Locke lived from 1632 to 1704.

REPLY

This is an *ignoratio elenchi*.* I am not arguing that the after-image is a brain-process, but that the experience of having an after-image is a brain-process. It is the *experience* which is reported in the introspective report. Similarly, if it is objected that the after-image is yellowy-orange but that a surgeon looking into your brain would see nothing yellowy-orange, my reply is that it is the experience of seeing yellowy-orange that is being described, and this experience is not a yellowy-orange something. So to say that a brain-process cannot be yellowy-orange is not to say that a brain-process cannot in fact be the experience of having a yellowy-orange after-image. There is, in a sense, no such thing as an after-image or a sense-datum, though there is such a thing as the experience of having an image, and this experience is described indirectly in material object language, not in phenomenal language, for there is no such thing.[13] We describe the experience by saying, in effect, that it is like the experience we have when, for example, we really see a yellowy-orange patch on the wall. Trees and wallpaper can be green, but not the experience of seeing or imagining a tree or wallpaper. (Or if they are described as green or yellow this can only be in a derived sense.)

OBJECTION 5

It would make sense to say of a molecular movement in the brain that it is swift or slow, straight or circular, but it makes no sense to say this of the experience of seeing something yellow.

REPLY

So far we have not given sense to talk of experiences as swift or slow, straight or circular. But I am not claiming that "experience" and "brain-process" mean the same or even that they have the same logic. "Somebody" and "the doctor" do not have the same logic, but this does not lead us to suppose that talking about somebody telephoning is talking about someone over and above, say, the doctor. The ordinary man when he reports an experience is reporting that something is going on, but he leaves it open as to what sort of thing is going on, whether in a material solid medium, or perhaps in some sort of gaseous medium, or even perhaps in some sort of non-spatial medium (if this makes sense). All that I am saying is that "experience" and "brain-process" may in fact refer to the same thing, and if so we may easily adopt a convention (which is not a change in our present rules for the use of experience words but an addition to them) whereby it would make sense to talk of an experience in terms appropriate to physical processes.

OBJECTION 6

Sensations are private, brain processes are *public*. If I sincerely say, "I see a yellowish-orange after-image" and I am not making a verbal mistake, then I cannot be wrong. But I can be wrong about a brain-process. The scientist looking into my brain might be having an illusion. Moreover, it makes sense to say that two or more people are observing the same brain-process but not that two or more people are reporting the same inner experience.

REPLY

This shows that the language of introspective reports has a different logic from the language of material processes. It is obvious that until the brain-process theory is much improved and widely accepted there will be no *criteria* for saying "Smith has an experience of such-and-such a sort" *except* Smith's introspective reports. So we have adopted a rule of language that (normally) what Smith says goes.

OBJECTION 7

I can imagine myself turned to stone and yet having images, aches, pains, and so on.

* *Ignoratio elenchi* is the fallacy of presenting an argument that supports a conclusion different from the one it purports to establish.

REPLY

I can imagine that the electrical theory of lightning is false, that lightning is some sort of purely optical phenomenon. I can imagine that lightning is not an electrical discharge. I can imagine that the Evening Star is not the Morning Star. But it is. All the objection shows is that "experience" and "brain-process" do not have the same meaning. It does not show that an experience is not in fact a brain process.

This objection is perhaps much the same as one which can be summed up by the slogan: "What can be composed of nothing cannot be composed of anything."[14] The argument goes as follows: on the brain-process thesis the identity between the brain-process and the experience is a contingent one. So it is logically possible that there should be no brain-process, and no process of any other sort, either (no heart process, no kidney process, no liver process). There would be the experience but no "corresponding" physiological process with which we might be able to identify it empirically.

I suspect that the objector is thinking of the experience as a ghostly entity. So it is composed of something, not of nothing, after all. On his view it is composed of ghost stuff, and on mine it is composed of brain stuff. Perhaps the counter-reply will be[15] that the experience is simple and uncompounded, and so it is not composed of anything after all. This seems to be a quibble, for, if it were taken seriously, the remark "What can be composed of nothing cannot be composed of anything" could be recast as an a priori argument against Democritus and atomism and for Descartes and infinite divisibility. And it seems odd that a question of this sort could be settled a priori. We must therefore construe the word "composed" in a very weak sense, which would allow us to say that even an indivisible atom is composed of something (namely, itself). The dualist cannot really say that an experience can be composed of nothing. For he holds that experiences are something over and above material processes, that is, that they are a sort of ghost stuff. (Or perhaps ripples in an underlying ghost stuff.) I say that the dualist's hypothesis is a perfectly intelligible one. But I say that experiences are not to be identified with ghost stuff but with brain stuff. This is another hypothesis, and in my view a very plausible one. The present argument cannot knock it down a priori.

OBJECTION 8

The "beetle in the box"* objection (see Wittgenstein, *Philosophical Investigations*, paragraph 293). How could descriptions of experiences, if these are genuine reports, get a foothold in language? For any rule of language must have public criteria for its correct application.

REPLY

The change from describing how things are to describing how we feel is just a change from uninhibitedly saying "this is so" to saying "this looks so." That is, when the naive person might be tempted to say, "There is a patch of light on the wall which moves whenever I move my eyes" or "A pin is being stuck into me," we have learned how to resist this temptation and say "It *looks as though* there is a patch of light on the wallpaper" or "It *feels as though* someone were sticking a pin into me." The introspective account tells us about the individual's state of consciousness in the same way as does "I see a patch of light" or "I feel a pin being stuck into me": it differs from the corresponding perception statement in so far as (a) in the perception statement the individual "goes beyond the evidence of his senses" in describing his environment and (b) in the introspective report he withholds descriptive epithets he is inclined to ascribe to the environment, perhaps because he

* The example of the beetle in the box comes from Wittgenstein's *Philosophical Investigations*. Wittgenstein writes: "Suppose everyone had a box with something in it: we call it a 'beetle'. No one can look into anyone else's box, and everyone says he knows what a beetle is by looking at his beetle.—Here it would be quite possible for everyone to have something different in his box. One might even imagine such a thing constantly changing.—But suppose the word 'beetle' had a use in these people's language?—If so it would not be used as the name of a thing. The thing in the box has no place in the language-game at all; not even as a something: for the box might even be empty.— No, one can 'divide through' by the thing in the box; it cancels out, whatever it is."

suspects that they may not be appropriate to the actual state of affairs. Psychologically speaking, the change from talking about the environment to talking about one's state of consciousness is simply a matter of inhibiting descriptive reactions not justified by appearances alone, and of disinhibiting descriptive reactions which are normally inhibited because the individual has learned that they are unlikely to provide a reliable guide to the state of the environment in the prevailing circumstances.[16] To say that something looks green to me is to say that my experience is like the experience I get when I see something that really is green. In my reply to Objection 3, I pointed out the extreme openness or generality of statements which report experiences. This explains why there is no language of private qualities. (Just as "someone," unlike "the doctor," is a colorless word.)[17]

If it is asked what is the difference between those brain processes which, in my view, are experiences and those brain processes which are not, I can only reply that this is at present unknown. But it does not seem to me altogether fanciful to conjecture that the difference may in part be that between perception and reception (in Dr. D. M. MacKay's terminology) and that the type of brain process which is an experience might be identifiable with MacKay's active "matching response."[18]*

I have now considered a number of objections to the brain-process thesis. I wish now to conclude by some remarks on the logical status of the thesis itself. U. T. Place† seems to hold that it is a straight-out scientific hypothesis.[19] If so, he is partly right and partly wrong. If the issue is between (say) a brain-process thesis and a heart thesis, or a liver thesis, or a kidney thesis, then the issue is a purely empirical one, and the verdict is overwhelmingly in favor of the brain. The right sorts of things don't go on in the heart, liver, or kidney, nor do these organs possess the right sort of complexity of structure. On the other hand, if the issue is between a brain-or-heart-or-liver-or-kidney thesis (that is, some form of materialism) on the one hand and epiphenomenalism on the other hand, then the issue is not an empirical one. For there is no conceivable experiment which could decide between materialism and epiphenomenalism. This latter issue is not like the average straight-out empirical issue in science, but like the issue between the nineteenth-century English naturalist Philip Gosse[20] and the orthodox geologists and paleontologists of his day. According to Gosse, the earth was created about 4000 B.C. exactly as described in Genesis, with twisted rock strata, "evidence" of erosion, and so forth, and all sorts of fossils, all in their appropriate strata, just as if the usual evolutionist story had been true. Clearly this theory is in a sense irrefutable: no evidence can possibly tell against it. Let us ignore the theological setting in which Philip Gosse's hypothesis had been placed, thus ruling out objections of a theological kind, such as "what a queer God who would go to such elaborate lengths to deceive us." Let us suppose that it is held that the universe just *began* in 4004 B.C. with the initial conditions just everywhere as they were in 4004 B.C., and in particular that our own planet began with sediment in the rivers, eroded cliffs, fossils in the rocks, and so on. No scientist would ever entertain this as a serious hypothesis, consistent though it is with all possible evidence. The hypothesis offends against the principles of parsimony and simplicity. There would be far too many brute and inexplicable facts. Why are pterodactyl bones just as they are? No explanation in terms of the evolution of pterodactyls from earlier forms of life would any longer be possible. We would have millions of facts about the world as it was in 4004 B.C. that just have to be *accepted*.

The issue between the brain-process theory and epiphenomenalism seems to be of the above sort. (Assuming that a behavioristic reduction of introspective reports is not possible.) If it be agreed that there are no cogent philosophical arguments which force us into accepting dualism, and if the brain process theory and dualism are equally consistent with the facts, then the principles of parsimony and simplicity seem to me to decide overwhelmingly in favor of the brain-process theory. As I pointed out earlier, dualism involves a large number of irreducible psychophysical laws (whereby the "nomological danglers" dangle) of a queer sort, that just have to be taken on

---

* Donald MacCrimmon MacKay (1922–87) was a British neuroscientist and information theorist.

† Ullin T. (U. T.) Place (1924–2000) was a British philosopher and psychologist, an early advocate of materialism in the philosophy of mind.

trust, and are just as difficult to swallow as the irreducible facts about the paleontology of the earth with which we are faced on Philip Gosse's theory.

NOTES

1. This paper takes its departure from arguments to be found in U. T. Place's "Is Consciousness a Brain Process?" (*British Journal of Psychology*, XLVII, 1956, 44–50). I have had the benefit of discussing Place's thesis in a good many universities in the United States and Australia, and I hope that the present paper answers objections to his thesis which Place has not considered, and presents his thesis in a more nearly unobjectionable form. This paper is meant also to supplement "The 'Mental' and the 'Physical,'" by H. Feigl (in *Minnesota Studies in the Philosophy of Science*, II, 370–497), which argues for much the same thesis as Place's.
2. Some philosophers of my acquaintance, who have the advantage over me in having known Wittgenstein, would say that this interpretation of him is too behavioristic. However, it seems to me a very natural interpretation of his printed words, and whether or not it is Wittgenstein's real view it is certainly an interesting and important one. I wish to consider it here as a possible rival both to the "brain-process" thesis and to straight-out old-fashioned dualism.
3. See Ryle, *Concept of Mind* (New York, 1949), p. 93.
4. On this point see Paul Oppenheim and Hilary Putnam, "Unity of Science as a Working Hypothesis," in *Minnesota Studies in the Philosophy of Science*, II, 3–36; also my note "Plausible Reasoning in Philosophy," *Mind*, LXVI (1957), 75–78.
5. Feigl, op. cit., p. 428.
6. Wittgenstein did not like the word "disposition." I am using it to put in a nutshell (and perhaps inaccurately) the view which I am attributing to Wittgenstein. I should like to repeat that I do not wish to claim that my interpretation of Wittgenstein is correct. Some of those who knew him do not interpret him in this way. It is merely a view which I find myself extracting from his printed words and which I think is important and worth discussing for its own sake.
7. See Place, op. cit., p. 45, near top, and Feigl, op. cit., p. 390, near top.
8. See J. H. Woodger, *Theory Construction* (Chicago, 1939), p. 38 (International Encyclopedia of Unified Science, Vol. 2, No. 5). I here permit myself to speak loosely. For warnings against possible ways of going wrong with this sort of talk, see my note "Spatialising Time," *Mind*, LXIV (1955), 239–41.
9. Cf. Feigl, op. cit., p. 439.
10. See Place, op. cit., p. 47; also Feigl, op. cit, p. 438.
11. I think this objection was first put to me by Professor Max Black. I think it is the most subtle of any of those I have considered, and the one which I am least confident of having satisfactorily met.
12. See B. A. Farrell, "Experience," *Mind*, LIX (1950), especially 174.
13. Dr. J. R. Smythies claims that a sense-datum language could be taught independently of the material object language ("A Note on the Fallacy of the 'Phenomenological Fallacy,'" *British Journal of Psychology*, XLVIII, 1957, 141–144.) I am not so sure of this: there must be some public criteria for a person having got a rule wrong before we can teach him the rule. I suppose someone might *accidentally* learn color words by Dr. Smythies' procedure. I am not, of course, denying that we can learn a sense-datum language in the sense that we can learn to report our experience. Nor would Place deny it.
14. I owe this objection to Mr. C. B. Martin. I gather that he no longer wishes to maintain this objection, at any rate in its present form.
15. Martin did not make this reply, but one of his students did.
16. I owe this point to Place, in correspondence.
17. The "beetle in the box" objection is, *if it is sound*, an objection to *any* view, and in particular the Cartesian one, that introspective reports are genuine reports. So it is no objection to a weaker thesis that I would be concerned to uphold, namely, that if introspective reports of "experiences" are genuinely reports, then the things they are reports of are in fact brain processes.
18. See his article "Towards an Information-Flow Model of Human Behaviour," *British Journal of Psychology*, XLVII (1956), 30–43.
19. Op. cit.
20. See the entertaining account of Gosse's book *Omphalos* by Martin Gardner in *Fads and Fallacies in the Name of Science* (2nd ed., New York, 1957).

Eliminative Materialism and the Propositional Attitudes

PAUL M. CHURCHLAND

American philosopher Paul Churchland (1942–) teaches at the University of California, San Diego. His areas of expertise include philosophy of science and philosophy of mind. His philosophical work is deeply informed by contemporary work in neuroscience.

The text that appears here is excerpted from a longer essay with the same title, originally published as a journal article in 1981. Subsections have been renumbered for the purposes of this volume. In the text, Churchland challenges the widespread view that beliefs and desires exist in the sense that most philosophers have assumed, defending instead a view known as *eliminative materialism*.

Eliminative materialism is the thesis that our common-sense conception of psychological phenomena constitutes a radically false theory, a theory so fundamentally defective that both the principles and the ontology of that theory will eventually be displaced, rather than smoothly reduced, by completed neuroscience. Our mutual understanding and even our introspection may then be reconstituted within the conceptual framework of completed neuroscience, a theory we may expect to be more powerful by far than the common-sense psychology it displaces, and more substantially integrated within physical science generally. My purpose in this paper is to explore these projections, especially as they bear on (1) the principal elements of common-sense psychology: the propositional attitudes (beliefs, desires, etc.), and (2) the conception of rationality in which these elements figure.

This focus represents a change in the fortunes of materialism. Twenty years ago, emotions, qualia, and "raw feels" were held to be the principal stumbling blocks for the materialist program. With these barriers dissolving,[1] the locus of opposition has shifted. Now it is the realm of the intentional, the realm of the propositional attitude, that is most commonly held up as being both irreducible to and ineliminable in favor of anything from within a materialist framework. Whether and why this is so, we must examine.

Such an examination will make little sense, however, unless it is first appreciated that the relevant network of common-sense concepts does indeed constitute an empirical theory, with all the functions, virtues, *and perils* entailed by that status. I shall therefore begin with a brief sketch of this view and a summary rehearsal of its rationale. The resistance it encounters still surprises me. After all, common sense has yielded up many theories. Recall the view that space has a preferred direction in which all things fall; that weight is an intrinsic feature of a body; that a force-free moving object will promptly return to rest; that the sphere of the heavens turns daily; and so on. These examples are clear, perhaps, but people seem willing to concede a theoretical component within common sense only if (1) the theory and the common sense involved are safely located in antiquity, and (2) the relevant theory is now so clearly false that its speculative nature is inescapable. Theories are indeed easier to discern under these circumstances. But the vision of hindsight is always 20/20. Let us aspire to some foresight for a change.

I. WHY FOLK PSYCHOLOGY IS A THEORY

Seeing our common-sense conceptual framework for mental phenomena as a theory brings a simple

From *Journal of Philosophy* 78:67–90, 1981. Reprinted with permission of author and publisher.

and unifying organization to most of the major topics in the philosophy of mind, including the explanation and prediction of behavior, the semantics of mental predicates, action theory, the other-minds problem, the intentionality of mental states, the nature of introspection, and the mind-body problem. Any view that can pull this lot together deserves careful consideration.

Let us begin with the explanation of human (and animal) behavior. The fact is that the average person is able to explain, and even predict, the behavior of other persons with a facility and success that is remarkable. Such explanations and predictions standardly make reference to the desires, beliefs, fears, intentions, perceptions, and so forth, to which the agents are presumed subject. But explanations presuppose laws—rough and ready ones, at least—that connect the explanatory conditions with the behavior explained. The same is true for the making of predictions, and for the justification of subjunctive and counterfactual conditionals concerning behavior. Reassuringly, a rich network of common-sense laws can indeed be reconstructed from this quotidian commerce of explanation and anticipation; its principles are familiar homilies; and their sundry functions are transparent. Each of us understands others, as well as we do, because we share a tacit command of an integrated body of lore concerning the law-like relations holding among external circumstances, internal states, and overt behavior. Given its nature and functions, this body of lore may quite aptly be called "folk psychology."[2]

This approach entails that the semantics of the terms in our familiar mentalistic vocabulary is to be understood in the same manner as the semantics of theoretical terms generally: the meaning of any theoretical term is fixed or constituted by the network of laws in which it figures. (This position is quite distinct from logical behaviorism. We deny that the relevant laws are analytic, and it is the law-like connections generally that carry the semantic weight, not just the connections with overt behavior. But this view does account for what little plausibility logical behaviorism did enjoy.)

More importantly, the recognition that folk psychology is a theory provides a simple and decisive solution to an old skeptical problem, the problem of other minds. The problematic conviction that another individual is the subject of certain mental states is not inferred deductively from his behavior, nor is it inferred by inductive analogy from the perilously isolated instance of one's own case. Rather, that conviction is a singular *explanatory hypothesis* of a perfectly straightforward kind. Its function, in conjunction with the background laws of folk psychology, is to provide explanations/predictions/understanding of the individual's continuing behavior, and it is credible to the degree that it is successful in this regard over competing hypotheses. In the main, such hypotheses are successful, and so the belief that others enjoy the internal states comprehended by folk psychology is a reasonable belief.

Knowledge of other minds thus has no essential dependence on knowledge of one's own mind. Applying the principles of our folk psychology to our behavior, a Martian could justly ascribe to us the familiar run of mental states, even though his own psychology were very different from ours. He would not, therefore, be "generalizing from his own case."

As well, introspective judgments about one's own case turn out not to have any special status or integrity anyway. On the present view, an introspective judgment is just an instance of an acquired habit of conceptual response to one's internal states, and the integrity of any particular response is always contingent on the integrity of the acquired conceptual framework (theory) in which the response is framed. Accordingly, one's *introspective* certainty that one's mind is the seat of beliefs and desires may be as badly misplaced as was the classical man's *visual* certainty that the star-flecked sphere of the heavens turns daily.

Another conundrum is the intentionality of mental states. The "propositional attitudes," as Russell called them, form the systematic core of folk psychology; and their uniqueness and anomalous logical properties have inspired some to see here a fundamental contrast with anything that mere physical phenomena might conceivably display. The key to this matter lies again in the theoretical nature of folk psychology. The intentionality of mental states here emerges not as a mystery of nature, but as a structural feature of the concepts of folk psychology. Ironically, those same structural features reveal the very close affinity that folk psychology bears to theories in the physical sciences. Let me try to explain.

Consider the large variety of what might be called "numerical attitudes" appearing in the conceptual framework of physical science: "... has a mass_{kg} of n," "... has a velocity of n," "... has a $\text{temperature}_{\text{K}}$ of n," and so forth. These expressions are predicate-forming expressions: when one substitutes a singular term for a number into the place held by "n," a determinate predicate results. More interestingly, the relations between the various "numerical attitudes" that result are precisely the relations between the numbers "contained" in those attitudes. More interesting still, the argument place that takes the singular terms for numbers is open to quantification. All this permits the expression of generalizations concerning the lawlike relations that hold between the various numerical attitudes in nature. Such laws involve quantification over numbers, and they exploit the mathematical relations holding in that domain. Thus, for example,*

(1) $(x)\ (f)\ (m)[((x$ has a mass of $m)\ \&\ (x$ suffers a net force of $f)) \supset (x$ accelerates at $f/m)]$

Consider now the large variety of propositional attitudes: "... believes that p," "... desires that p," "... fears that p," "... is happy that p," etc. These expressions are predicate-forming expressions also. When one substitutes a singular term for a proposition into the place held by "p," a determinate predicate results, e.g., "... believes that Tom is tall." (Sentences do not generally function as singular terms, but it is difficult to escape the idea that when a sentence occurs in the place held by "p," it is there functioning as or like a singular term. On this, more below.) More interestingly, the relations between the resulting propositional attitudes are characteristically the relations that hold between the propositions "contained" in them, relations such as entailment, equivalence, and mutual inconsistency. More interesting still, the argument place that takes the singular terms for propositions is open to quantification. All this permits the expression of generalizations concerning the law-like relations that hold among propositional attitudes. Such laws involve quantification over propositions, and they exploit various relations holding in that domain. Thus, for example,

(2) $(x)\ (p)[(x$ fears that $p) \supset (x$ desires that $\sim p)]$

(3) $(x)\ (p)[((x$ hopes that $p)\ \&\ (x$ discovers that $p)) \supset (x$ is pleased that $p)]$

(4) $(x)\ (p)\ (q)[((x$ believes that $p)\ \&\ (x$ believes that (if p then $q))) \supset$ (barring confusion, distraction, etc., x believes that $q)]$

(5) $(x)\ (p)\ (q)[((x$ desires that $p)\ \&\ (x$ believes that (if q then $p))\ \&\ (x$ is able to bring it about that $q)) \supset$ (barring conflicting desires or preferred strategies, x brings it about that $q)]$[3]

Not only is folk psychology a theory, it is so *obviously* a theory that it must be held a major mystery why it has taken until the last half of the twentieth century for philosophers to realize it. The structural features of folk psychology parallel perfectly those of mathematical physics; the only difference lies in the respective domain of abstract entities they exploit—numbers in the case of physics, and propositions in the case of psychology.

Finally, the realization that folk psychology is a theory puts a new light on the mind–body problem. The issue becomes a matter of how the ontology of one theory (folk psychology) is, or is not, going to be related to the ontology of another theory (completed neuroscience); and the major philosophical positions on the mind–body problem emerge as so many different anticipations of what future research will reveal about the intertheoretic status and integrity of folk psychology.

The identity theorist optimistically expects that folk psychology will be smoothly *reduced* by completed neuroscience, and its ontology preserved by dint of transtheoretic identities. The dualist expects that it will prove *ir*reducible to completed neuroscience, by dint of being a nonredundant description of an autonomous, nonphysical domain of natural phenomena. The functionalist also expects that it will prove irreducible, but on the quite different

* In the formulas below, "(a)" means *for all a*, "A ⊃ B" means *if A then B*, and "~" means *not*. So, for example, formula (2) says: *For all x and for all p, if x fears that p, then x desires that not-p.*

grounds that the internal economy characterized by folk psychology is not, in the last analysis, a law-governed economy of natural states, but an abstract organization of functional states, an organization instantiable in a variety of quite different material substrates. It is therefore irreducible to the principles peculiar to any of them.

Finally, the eliminative materialist is also pessimistic about the prospects for reduction, but his reason is that folk psychology is a radically inadequate account of our internal activities, too confused and too defective to win survival through intertheoretic reduction. On his view it will simply be displaced by a better theory of those activities.

Which of these fates is the real destiny of folk psychology, we shall attempt to divine presently. For now, the point to keep in mind is that we shall be exploring the fate of a theory, a systematic, corrigible, speculative *theory*.

II. WHY FOLK PSYCHOLOGY MIGHT (REALLY) BE FALSE

Given that folk psychology is an empirical theory, it is at least an abstract possibility that its principles are radically false and that its ontology is an illusion. With the exception of eliminative materialism, however, none of the major positions takes this possibility seriously. None of them doubts the basic integrity or truth of folk psychology (hereafter, "FP"), and all of them anticipate a future in which its laws and categories are conserved. This conservatism is not without some foundation. After all, FP does enjoy a substantial amount of explanatory and predictive success. And what better grounds than this for confidence in the integrity of its categories?

What better grounds indeed? Even so, the presumption in FP's favor is spurious, born of innocence and tunnel vision. A more searching examination reveals a different picture. First, we must reckon not only with FP's successes, but with its explanatory failures, and with their extent and seriousness. Second, we must consider the long-term history of FP, its growth, fertility, and current promise of future development. And third, we must consider what sorts of theories are *likely* to be true of the etiology of our behavior, given what else we have learned about ourselves in recent history. That is, we must evaluate FP with regard to its coherence and continuity with fertile and well-established theories in adjacent and overlapping domains—with evolutionary theory, biology, and neuroscience, for example—because active coherence with the rest of what we presume to know is perhaps the final measure of any hypothesis.

A serious inventory of this sort reveals a very troubled situation, one which would evoke open skepticism in the case of any theory less familiar and dear to us. Let me sketch some relevant detail. When one centers one's attention not on what FP can explain, but on what it cannot explain or fails even to address, one discovers that there is a very great deal. As examples of central and important mental phenomena that remain largely or wholly mysterious within the framework of FP, consider the nature and dynamics of mental illness, the faculty of creative imagination, or the ground of intelligence differences between individuals. Consider our utter ignorance of the nature and psychological functions of sleep, that curious state in which a third of one's life is spent. Reflect on the common ability to catch an outfield fly ball on the run, or hit a moving car with a snowball. Consider the internal construction of a 3-D visual image from subtle differences in the 2-D array of stimulations in our respective retinas. Consider the rich variety of perceptual illusions, visual and otherwise. Or consider the miracle of memory, with its lightning capacity for relevant retrieval. On these and many other mental phenomena, FP sheds negligible light.

One particularly outstanding mystery is the nature of the learning process itself, especially where it involves large-scale conceptual change, and especially as it appears in its pre-linguistic or entirely nonlinguistic form (as in infants and animals), which is by far the most common form in nature. FP is faced with special difficulties here, since its conception of learning as the manipulation and storage of propositional attitudes founders on the fact that how to formulate, manipulate, and store a rich fabric of propositional attitudes is itself something that is learned, and is only one among many acquired cognitive skills. FP would thus appear constitutionally incapable of even addressing this most basic of mysteries.[4]

Failures on such a large scale do not (yet) show that FP is a false theory, but they do move that prospect well into the range of real possibility, and they do show decisively that FP is *at best* a highly superficial theory, a partial and unpenetrating gloss on a deeper and more complex reality. Having reached this opinion, we may be forgiven for exploring the possibility that FP provides a positively misleading sketch of our internal kinematics and dynamics, one whose success is owed more to selective application and forced interpretation on our part than to genuine theoretical insight on FP's part.

A look at the history of FP does little to allay such fears, once raised. The story is one of retreat, infertility, and decadence. The presumed domain of FP used to be much larger than it is now. In primitive cultures, the behavior of most of the elements of nature were understood in intentional terms. The wind could know anger, the moon jealousy, the river generosity, the sea fury, and so forth. These were not metaphors. Sacrifices were made and auguries undertaken to placate or divine the changing passions of the gods. Despite its sterility, this animistic approach to nature has dominated our history, and it is only in the last two or three thousand years that we have restricted FP's literal application to the domain of the higher animals.

Even in this preferred domain, however, both the content and the success of FP have not advanced sensibly in two or three thousand years. The FP of the Greeks is essentially the FP we use today, and we are negligibly better at explaining human behavior in its terms than was Sophocles. This is a very long period of stagnation and infertility for any theory to display, especially when faced with such an enormous backlog of anomalies and mysteries in its own explanatory domain. Perfect theories, perhaps, have no need to evolve. But FP is profoundly imperfect. Its failure to develop its resources and extend its range of success is therefore darkly curious, and one must query the integrity of its basic categories. To use Imre Lakatos'* terms, FP is a stagnant or degenerating research program, and has been for millennia.

Explanatory success to date is of course not the only dimension in which a theory can display virtue or promise. A troubled or stagnant theory may merit patience and solicitude on other grounds; for example, on grounds that it is the only theory or theoretical approach that fits well with other theories about adjacent subject matters, or the only one that promises to reduce to or be explained by some established background theory whose domain encompasses the domain of the theory at issue. In sum, it may rate credence because it holds promise of theoretical integration. How does FP rate in this dimension?

It is just here, perhaps, that FP fares poorest of all. If we approach *homo sapiens* from the perspective of natural history and the physical sciences, we can tell a coherent story of his constitution, development, and behavioral capacities which encompasses particle physics, atomic and molecular theory, organic chemistry, evolutionary theory, biology, physiology, and materialistic neuroscience. That story, though still radically incomplete, is already extremely powerful, outperforming FP at many points even in its own domain. And it is deliberately and self-consciously coherent with the rest of our developing world picture. In short, the greatest theoretical synthesis in the history of the human race is currently in our hands, and parts of it already provide searching descriptions and explanations of human sensory input, neural activity, and motor control.

But FP is no part of this growing synthesis. Its intentional categories stand magnificently alone, without visible prospect of reduction to that larger corpus. A successful reduction cannot be ruled out, in my view, but FP's explanatory impotence and long stagnation inspire little faith that its categories will find themselves neatly reflected in the framework of neuroscience. On the contrary, one is reminded of how alchemy must have looked as elemental chemistry was taking form, how Aristotelean cosmology must have looked as classical mechanics was being articulated, or how the vitalist conception of life must have looked as organic chemistry marched forward.

In sketching a fair summary of this situation, we must make a special effort to abstract from the fact

* Imré Lakatos (1922–74) was a Hungarian-born philosopher of science and mathematics.

that FP is a central part of our current *lebenswelt*,* and serves as the principal vehicle of our interpersonal commerce. For these facts provide FP with a conceptual inertia that goes far beyond its purely theoretical virtues. Restricting ourselves to this latter dimension, what we must say is that FP suffers explanatory failures on an epic scale, that it has been stagnant for at least twenty-five centuries, and that its categories appear (so far) to be incommensurable with or orthogonal to the categories of the background physical science whose long-term claim to explain human behavior seems undeniable. Any theory that meets this description must be allowed a serious candidate for outright elimination.

We can of course insist on no stronger conclusion at this stage. Nor is it my concern to do so. We are here exploring a possibility, and the facts demand no more, and no less, than it be taken seriously. The distinguishing feature of the eliminative materialist is that he takes it very seriously indeed.

III. ARGUMENTS AGAINST ELIMINATION

Thus the basic rationale of eliminative materialism: FP is a theory, and quite probably a false one; let us attempt, therefore to transcend it.

The rationale is clear and simple, but many find it uncompelling. It will be objected that FP is not, strictly speaking, an *empirical* theory; that it is not false, or at least not refutable by empirical considerations; and that it ought not or cannot be transcended in the fashion of a defunct empirical theory. In what follows we shall examine these objections as they flow from the most popular and best-founded of the competing positions in the philosophy of mind: functionalism.

An antipathy toward eliminative materialism arises from two distinct threads running through contemporary functionalism. The first thread concerns the *normative* character of FP, or at least of that central core of FP which treats of the propositional attitudes. FP, some will say, is a characterization of an ideal, or at least praiseworthy mode of internal activity. It outlines not only what it is to have and process beliefs and desires, but also (and inevitably) what it is to be rational in their administration. The ideal laid down by FP may be imperfectly achieved by empirical humans, but this does not impugn FP as a normative characterization. Nor need such failures seriously impugn FP even as a descriptive characterization, for it remains true that our activities can be both usefully and accurately understood as rational *except for* the occasional lapse due to noise, interference, or other breakdown, which defects empirical research may eventually unravel. Accordingly, though neuroscience may usefully augment it, FP has no pressing need to be displaced, even as a descriptive theory; nor could it be replaced, qua normative characterization, by any descriptive theory of neural mechanisms, since rationality is defined over propositional attitudes like beliefs and desires. FP, therefore, is here to stay.

Daniel Dennett has defended a view along these lines.[5] And the view just outlined gives voice to a theme of the property dualists as well. Karl Popper and Joseph Margolis both cite the normative nature of mental and linguistic activity as a bar to their penetration or elimination by any descriptive/materialist theory.[6] I hope to deflate the appeal of such moves below.*

The second thread concerns the *abstract* nature of FP. The central claim of functionalism is that the principles of FP characterize our internal states in a fashion that makes no reference to their intrinsic nature or physical constitution. Rather, they are characterized in terms of the network of causal relations they bear to one another, and to sensory circumstances and overt behavior. Given its abstract specification, that internal economy may therefore be realized in a nomically heterogeneous variety

* *Lebenswelt* (German) means "lifeworld"; it refers to the world as it is experienced prior to reflection and analysis. The term is due to German philosopher Edmund Husserl (1859–1938).

* Philosophers Daniel Dennett (1942–), Karl Popper (1902–94), Joseph Margolis (1924–), and Jerry Fodor (1935–) have all made contributions to twentieth-century philosophy of mind.

of physical systems. All of them may differ, even radically, in their physical constitution, and yet at another level, they will all share the same nature. This view, says Fodor, "is compatible with very strong claims about the ineliminability of mental language from behavioral theories."[7] Given the real possibility of multiple instantiations in heterogeneous physical substrates, we cannot eliminate the functional characterization in favor of any theory peculiar to one such substrate. That would preclude our being able to describe the (abstract) organization that any one instantiation shares with all the others. A functional characterization of our internal states is therefore here to stay.

This second theme, like the first, assigns a faintly stipulative character to FP, as if the onus were on the empirical systems to instantiate faithfully the organization that FP specifies, instead of the onus being on FP to describe faithfully the internal activities of a naturally distinct class of empirical systems. This impression is enhanced by the standard examples used to illustrate the claims of functionalism—mousetraps, valve-lifters, arithmetical calculators, computers, robots, and the like. These are artifacts, constructed to fill a preconceived bill. In such cases, a failure of fit between the physical system and the relevant functional characterization impugns only the former, not the latter. The functional characterization is thus removed from empirical criticism in a way that is most unlike the case of an empirical theory. One prominent functionalist—Hilary Putnam—has argued outright that FP is not a corrigible theory at all.[8] Plainly, if FP is construed on these models, as regularly it is, the question of its empirical integrity is unlikely ever to pose itself, let alone receive a critical answer.

Although fair to some functionalists, the preceding is not entirely fair to Fodor. On his view the aim of psychology is to find the *best* functional characterization of ourselves, and what that is remains an empirical question. As well, his argument for the ineliminability of mental vocabulary from psychology does not pick out current FP in particular as ineliminable. It need claim only that *some* abstract functional characterization must be retained, some articulation or refinement of FP perhaps.

His estimate of eliminative materialism remains low, however. First, it is plain that Fodor thinks there is nothing fundamentally or interestingly wrong with FP. On the contrary, FP's central conception of cognitive activity—as consisting in the manipulation of propositional attitudes—turns up as the central element in Fodor's own theory on the nature of thought (*The Language of Thought*, op. cit.). And second, there remains the point that, whatever tidying up FP may or may not require, it cannot be displaced by any naturalistic theory of our physical substrate, since it is the abstract functional features of his internal states that make a person, not the chemistry of his substrate.

All of this is appealing. But almost none of it, I think, is right. Functionalism has too long enjoyed its reputation as a daring and *avant garde* position. It needs to be revealed for the shortsighted and reactionary position it is.

. . .

IV. BEYOND FOLK PSYCHOLOGY

What might the elimination of FP actually involve—not just the comparatively straightforward idioms for sensation, but the entire apparatus of propositional attitudes? That depends heavily on what neuroscience might discover, and on our determination to capitalize on it. Here follow three scenarios in which the operative conception of cognitive activity is progressively divorced from the forms and categories that characterize natural language. If the reader will indulge the lack of actual substance, I shall try to sketch some plausible form.

First suppose that research into the structure and activity of the brain, both fine-grained and global, finally does yield a new kinematics and correlative dynamics for what is now thought of as cognitive activity. The theory is uniform for all terrestrial brains, not just human brains, and it makes suitable conceptual contact with both evolutionary biology and non-equilibrium thermodynamics. It ascribes to us, at any given time, a set or configuration of complex states, which are specified within the theory as figurative "solids" within a four- or five-dimensional phase space. The laws of the theory govern the interaction, motion, and transformation of these "solid" states within that space, and also their relations to whatever sensory and motor transducers the system possesses. As with celestial mechanics, the exact specification of the "solids" involved and the exhaustive accounting of all dynamically relevant adjacent "solids" is not practically possible, for many reasons, but here also it turns out that the obvious approximations we fall back on yield excellent explanations/predictions of internal change and external behavior, at least in the short term. Regarding long-term activity, the theory provides powerful and unified accounts of the learning process, the nature of mental illness, and variations in character and intelligence across the animal kingdom as well as across individual humans.

Moreover, it provides a straightforward account of "knowledge," as traditionally conceived. According to the new theory, any declarative sentence to which a speaker would give confident assent is merely a one-dimensional *projection*—through the compound lens of Wernicke's and Broca's areas* onto the idiosyncratic surface of the speaker's language—a one-dimensional projection of a four- or five-dimensional "solid" that is an element in his true kinematical state. (Recall the shadows on the wall of Plato's cave.)† Being projections of that inner reality, such sentences do carry significant information regarding it and are thus fit to function as elements in a communication system. On the other hand, being *sub*dimensional projections, they reflect but a narrow part of the reality projected. They are therefore *un*fit to represent the deeper reality in all its kinematically, dynamically, and even normatively relevant respects. That is to say, a system of propositional attitudes, such as FP, must inevitably fail to capture what is going on here, though it may reflect just enough superficial structure to sustain an alchemylike tradition among folk who lack any better theory. From the perspective of the newer theory, however, it is plain that there simply are no law-governed states of the kind FP postulates. The real laws governing our internal activities are defined over different and much more complex kinematical states and configurations, as are the normative criteria for developmental integrity and intellectual virtue.

A theoretical outcome of the kind just described may fairly be counted as a case of elimination of one theoretical ontology in favor of another, but the success here imagined for systematic neuroscience need not have any sensible effect on common practice. Old ways die hard, and in the absence of some practical necessity, they may not die at all. Even so, it is not inconceivable that some segment of the population, or all of it, should become intimately familiar with the vocabulary required to characterize our kinematical states, learn the laws governing their interactions and behavioral projections, acquire a facility in their first-person ascription, and displace the use of FP altogether, even in the marketplace. The demise of FP's ontology would then be complete.

We may now explore a second and rather more radical possibility. Everyone is familiar with Chomsky's thesis that the human mind or brain contains innately and uniquely the abstract structures for learning and using specifically human natural languages.* A competing hypothesis is that our brain does indeed contain innate structures, but that those structures have as their original and still primary function the organization of perceptual experience, the administration of linguistic categories being an acquired and additional function for which evolution has only incidentally suited them.[9] This hypothesis has the advantage of not requiring the evolutionary saltation that Chomsky's view would seem to require, and there are other advantages as well. But these matters need not concern us here. Suppose, for our purposes,

* Wernicke's and Broca's Areas are parts of the brain that are responsible for linguistic processing.

† Plato's story of the cave can be found in the "Knowledge and the Nature of Reality" section.

* Noam Chomsky (1928–) is an American linguist who, in addition to being the father of modern linguistics, has made important contributions to psychology, philosophy, and polemical politics. A selection from his writings appears in the "Language" section.

that this competing view is true, and consider the following story.

Research into the neural structures that fund the organization and processing of perceptual information reveals that they are capable of administering a great variety of complex tasks, some of them showing a complexity far in excess of that shown by natural language. Natural languages, it turns out, exploit only a very elementary portion of the available machinery, the bulk of which serves far more complex activities beyond the ken of the propositional conceptions of FP. The detailed unraveling of what that machinery is and of the capacities it has makes it plain that a form of language far more sophisticated than "natural" language, though decidedly "alien" in its syntactic and semantic structures, could also be learned and used by our innate systems. Such a novel system of communication, it is quickly realized, could raise the efficiency of information exchange between brains by an order of magnitude, and would enhance epistemic evaluation by a comparable amount, since it would reflect the underlying structure of our cognitive activities in greater detail than does natural language.

Guided by our new understanding of those internal structures, we manage to construct a new system of verbal communication entirely distinct from natural language, with a new and more powerful combinatorial grammar over novel elements forming novel combinations with exotic properties. The compounded strings of this alternative system—call them "übersatzen"—are not evaluated as true or false, nor are the relations between them remotely analogous to the relations of entailment, etc., that hold between sentences. They display a different organization and manifest different virtues.

Once constructed, this "language" proves to be learnable; it has the power projected; and in two generations it has swept the planet. Everyone uses the new system. The syntactic forms and semantic categories of so-called "natural" language disappear entirely. And with them disappear the propositional attitudes of FP, displaced by a more revealing scheme in which (of course) "übersatzenal attitudes" play the leading role. FP again suffers elimination.

This second story, note, illustrates a theme with endless variations. There are possible as many different "folk psychologies" as there are possible differently structured communication systems to serve as models for them.

A third and even stranger possibility can be outlined as follows. We know that there is considerable lateralization of function between the two cerebral hemispheres, and that the two hemispheres make use of the information they get from each other by way of the great cerebral commissure—the corpus callosum—a giant cable of neurons connecting them. Patients whose commissure has been surgically severed display a variety of behavioral deficits that indicate a loss of access by one hemisphere to information it used to get from the other. However, in people with callosal agenesis (a congenital defect in which the connecting cable is simply absent), there is little or no behavioral deficit, suggesting that the two hemispheres have learned to exploit the information carried in other less direct pathways connecting them through the subcortical regions. This suggests that, even in the normal case, a developing hemisphere *learns* to make use of the information the cerebral commissure deposits at its doorstep. What we have then, in the case of a normal human, is two physically distinct cognitive systems (both capable of independent function) responding in a systematic and learned fashion to exchanged information. And what is especially interesting about this case is the sheer amount of information exchanged. The cable of the commissure consists of ≈ 200 million neurons,[10] and even if we assume that each of these fibres is capable of one of only two possible states each second (a most conservative estimate), we are looking at a channel whose information capacity is $> 2 \times 10^8$ binary bits/second. Compare this to the < 500 bits/second capacity of spoken English.

Now, if two distinct hemispheres can learn to communicate on so impressive a scale, why shouldn't two distinct brains learn to do it also? This would require an artificial "commissure" of some kind, but let us suppose that we can fashion a workable transducer for implantation at some site in the brain that research reveals to be suitable, a transducer to convert a symphony of neural activity into (say) microwaves radiated from an aerial in the forehead, and to perform the reverse function of converting received microwaves back into neural activation. Connecting it up need not be an insuperable problem. We simply trick the normal processes of dendritic arborization into growing their own myriad connections with the active microsurface of the transducer.

Once the channel is opened between two or more people, they can learn (*learn*) to exchange information and coordinate their behavior with the same intimacy and virtuosity displayed by your own cerebral hemispheres. Think what this might do for hockey teams, and ballet companies, and research teams! If the entire population were thus fitted out, spoken language of any kind might well disappear completely, a victim of the "why crawl when you can fly?" principle. Libraries become filled not with books, but with long recordings of exemplary bouts of neural activity. These constitute a growing cultural heritage, an evolving "Third World," to use Karl Popper's terms. But they do not consist of sentences or arguments.

How will such people understand and conceive of other individuals? To this question I can only answer, "In roughly the same fashion that your right hemisphere 'understands' and 'conceives of' your left hemisphere—intimately and efficiently, but not propositionally!"

These speculations, I hope, will evoke the required sense of untapped possibilities, and I shall in any case bring them to a close here. Their function is to make some inroads into the aura of inconceivability that commonly surrounds the idea that we might reject FP. The felt conceptual strain even finds expression in an argument to the effect that the thesis of eliminative materialism is incoherent since it denies the very conditions presupposed by the assumption that it is meaningful. I shall close with a brief discussion of this very popular move.

As I have received it, the reductio proceeds by pointing out that the statement of eliminative materialism is just a meaningless string of marks or noises, unless that string is the expression of a certain *belief*, and a certain *intention* to communicate, and a *knowledge* of the grammar of the language, and so forth. But if the statement of eliminative materialism is true, then there are no such states to express. The statement at issue would then be a meaningless string of marks or noises. It would therefore *not* be true. Therefore it is not true. Q.E.D.

The difficulty with any nonformal reductio is that the conclusion against the initial assumption is always no better than the material assumptions invoked to reach the incoherent conclusion. In this case the additional assumptions involve a certain theory of meaning, one that presupposes the integrity of FP. But formally speaking, one can as well infer, from the incoherent result, that this theory of meaning is what must be rejected. Given the independent critique of FP leveled earlier, this would even seem the preferred option. But in any case, one cannot simply assume that particular theory of meaning without begging the question at issue, namely, the integrity of FP.

The question-begging nature of this move is most graphically illustrated by the following analogue, which I owe to Patricia Churchland.[11] The issue here, placed in the seventeenth century, is whether there exists such a substance as *vital spirit*. At the time, this substance was held, without significant awareness of real alternatives, to be that which distinguished the animate from the inanimate. Given the monopoly enjoyed by this conception, given the degree to which it was integrated with many of our other conceptions, and given the magnitude of the revisions any serious alternative conception would require, the following refutation of any anti-vitalist claim would be found instantly plausible.

> The anti-vitalist says that there is no such thing as vital spirit. But this claim is self-refuting. The speaker can expect to be taken seriously only if his claim cannot. For if the claim is true, then the speaker does not have vital spirit and must be *dead*. But if he is dead, then his statement is a meaningless string of noises, devoid of reason and truth.

The question-begging nature of this argument does not, I assume, require elaboration. To those moved by the earlier argument, I commend the parallel for examination.

The thesis of this paper may be summarized as follows. The propositional attitudes of folk psychology do not constitute an unbreachable barrier to the advancing tide of neuroscience. On the contrary; the principled displacement of folk psychology is not only richly possible, it represents one of the most intriguing theoretical displacements we can currently imagine.

NOTES

An earlier draft of this paper was presented at the University of Ottawa, and to the *Brain, Mind, and Person* colloquium at SUNY/Oswego. My thanks for the suggestions and criticisms that have informed the present version.

1. See Paul Feyerabend, "Materialism and the Mind–Body Problem," *Review of Metaphysics*, XVII, 1, 65 (September 1963): 49–66; Richard Rorty, "Mind–Body Identity, Privacy, and Categories," ibid., XIX. 1, 73 (September 1965): 24–54; and my *Scientific Realism and the Plasticity of Mind* (New York: Cambridge, 1979).
2. We shall examine a handful of these laws presently. For a more comprehensive sampling of the laws of folk psychology, see my *Scientific Realism and the Plasticity of Mind*, op. cit., ch. 4. For a detailed examination of the folk principles that underwrite action explanations in particular, see my "The Logical Character of Action Explanations," *Philosophical Review*, LXXIX, 2 (April 1970): 214–36.
3. Staying within an objectual interpretation of the quantifiers, perhaps the simplest way to make systematic sense of expressions like "*x* believes that *p*" and closed sentences formed therefrom is just to construe whatever occurs in the nested position held by "*p*," "*q*," etc. as there having the function of a singular term. Accordingly, the standard connectives, as they occur between terms in that nested position, must be construed as there functioning as operators that form compound singular terms from other singular terms, and not as sentence operators. The compound singular terms so formed denote the appropriate compound propositions. Substitutional quantification will of course underwrite a different interpretation, and there are other approaches as well. Especially appealing is the prosentential approach of Dorothy Grover, Joseph Camp, and Nuel Belnap, "A Prosentential Theory of Truth," *Philosophical Studies*, XXVII, 2 (February 1975): 73–125. But the resolution of these issues is not vital to the present discussion.
4. A possible response here is to insist that the cognitive activity of animals and infants is linguaformal in its elements, structures, and processing right from birth. J. A. Fodor, in *The Language of Thought* (New York: Crowell 1975), has erected a positive theory of thought on the assumption that the innate forms of cognitive activity have precisely the form here denied. For a critique of Fodor's view, see Patricia Churchland, "Fodor on Language Learning," *Synthese*, XXXVIII, 1 (May 1978): 149–59.
5. Most explicitly in "Three Kinds of Intentional Psychology" in R. Healey, ed., *Reduction, Time, and Reality* (Cambridge, 1981), pp. 37–61, but this theme of Dennett's goes all the way back to his "Intentional Systems," *The Journal of Philosophy*, LXVIII, 4 (Feb. 25, 1971): 87–106; reprinted in his *Brainstorms* (Montgomery, Vt.: Bradford Books, 1978).
6. Popper, *Objective Knowledge* (New York: Oxford, 1972); with J. Eccles, *The Self and Its Brain* (New York: Springer Verlag, 1978). Margolis, *Persons and Minds* (Boston: Reidel, 1978).
7. *Psychological Explanation* (New York: Random House, 1968) p. 116.
8. "Robots: Machines or Artificially Created Life?" *The Journal of Philosophy*, LXI, 21 (Nov. 12, 1964): 668–91, pp. 675, 681 ff.
9. Richard Gregory defends such a view in "The Grammar of Vision," *Listener*, LXXXIII, 2133 (February 1970): 242–46; reprinted in his *Concepts and Mechanisms of Perception* (London: Duckworth, 1975), pp. 622–29.
10. M. S. Gazzaniga and J. E. LeDoux. *The Integrated Mind* (New York: Plenum Press, 1975).
11. "Is Determinism Self-Refuting?" *Mind* 90:99–101, 1981.

The Modal Argument

SAUL KRIPKE

American philosopher Saul Kripke (1940–) is one of the most famous living philosophers working in the Anglo-American tradition. His influential work in logic, metaphysics, and the philosophy of language shaped subsequent discussions. Kripke taught for many years at Princeton University and is now affiliated with the City University of New York Graduate Center.

The selection that appears here is an excerpt from a set of lectures that Kripke gave in 1970 at Princeton University, subsequently published (in 1974 and 1980) under the title *Naming and Necessity*. The first part of the selection presents Kripke's ideas about rigid designation; the second part applies these ideas to the question of mind-body dualism.

Although the idea is now a familiar one, I will give a brief restatement of the idea of rigid designation, and the intuition about names that underlies it.* Consider:

(1) Aristotle was fond of dogs.

A proper understanding of this statement involves an understanding both of the (extensionally correct) conditions under which it is in fact true, *and* of the conditions under which a counterfactual course of history, resembling the actual course in some respects but not in others, would be correctly (partially) described by (1). Presumably everyone agrees that there is a certain man—the philosopher we call "Aristotle"—such that, as a matter of fact, (1) is true if and only if *he* was fond of dogs.[1] The thesis of rigid designation is simply—subtle points aside[2]—that the same paradigm applies to the truth conditions of (1) as it describes *counterfactual* situations. That is, (1) truly describes a counterfactual situation if and only if the same aforementioned man would have been fond of dogs, had that situation obtained. (Forget the counterfactual situations where he would not have existed.) By contrast, Russell thinks that (1) should be analyzed as something like:[3]*

(2) The last great philosopher of antiquity was fond of dogs,

and that this in turn should be analyzed as

(3) Exactly one person was last among the great philosophers of antiquity, and any such person was fond of dogs.

* A term is a *rigid designator* if it picks out the same entity in all possible worlds where that entity exists, and does not pick out any other entity in possible worlds where it does not.

* British philosopher Bertrand Russell's (1872–1970) writings included well-known discussions of how proper names (such as "Wilbur") and definite descriptions (such as "the pig") are to be understood; these views are reflected in Kripke's "Russellian" paraphrases of (1) as presented in (2) and (3).

Reprinted by permission of the publisher from *Naming and Necessity* by Saul A. Kripke, pp. 144–155, Cambridge, Mass.: Harvard University Press. Copyright © 1972, 1980 by Saul A. Kripke.

The actual truth conditions of (3) agree extensionally with those mentioned above for (1), assuming that Aristotle was the last great philosopher of antiquity. But counterfactually, Russell's conditions can vary wildly from those supposed by the rigidity thesis. With respect to a counterfactual situation where someone other than Aristotle would have been the last great philosopher of antiquity, Russell's criterion would make *that other person's* fondness for dogs the relevant issue for the correctness of (1)! . . .

I finally turn to an all too cursory discussion of the application of the foregoing considerations to the identity thesis. Identity theorists have been concerned with several distinct types of identifications: of a person with his body, of a particular sensation (or event or state of having the sensation) with a particular brain state (Jones's pain at 06:00 was his C-fiber stimulation at that time),* and of *types* of mental states with the corresponding *types* of physical states (pain is the stimulation of C-fibers). Each of these, and other types of identifications in the literature, present analytical problems, rightly raised by Cartesian critics, which cannot be avoided by a simple appeal to an alleged confusion of synonymy with identity. I should mention that there is of course no obvious bar, at least (I say cautiously) none which should occur to any intelligent thinker on a first reflection just before bedtime, to advocacy of some identity theses while doubting or denying others. For example, some philosophers have accepted the identity of particular sensations with particular brain states while denying the possibility of identities between mental and physical *types*.[4] I will concern myself primarily with the type-type identities, and the philosophers in question will thus be immune to much of the discussion; but I will mention the other kinds of identities briefly.

Descartes, and others following him, argued that a person or mind is distinct from his body, since the mind could exist without the body. He might equally well have argued the same conclusion from the premise that the body could have existed without the mind.[5] Now the one response which I regard as plainly inadmissible is the response which cheerfully accepts the Cartesian premise while denying the Cartesian conclusion. Let "Descartes" be a name, or rigid designator, of a certain person, and let "*B*" be a rigid designator of his body. Then if Descartes were indeed identical to *B*, the supposed identity, being an identity between two rigid designators, would be necessary, and Descartes could not exist without *B* and *B* could not exist without Descartes. The case is not at all comparable to the alleged analogue, the identity of the first Postmaster General with the inventor of bifocals* True, this identity obtains despite the fact that there could have been a first Postmaster General even though bifocals had never been invented. The reason is that "the inventor of bifocals" is not a rigid designator; a world in which no one invented bifocals is not ipso facto† a world in which Franklin did not exist. The alleged analogy therefore collapses; a philosopher who wishes to refute the Cartesian conclusion must refute the Cartesian premise, and the latter task is not trivial.

Let "*A*" name a particular pain sensation, and let "*B*" name the corresponding brain state, or the brain state some identity theorist wishes to identify with *A*. Prima facie, it would seem that it is at least logically possible that *B* should have existed (Jones's brain could have been in exactly that state at the time in question) without Jones feeling any pain at all, and thus without the presence of *A*. Once again, the identity theorist cannot admit the possibility cheerfully and proceed from there; consistency, and the principle of the necessity of identities using rigid designators, disallows any such course. If *A* and *B* were identical, the identity would have to be necessary. The difficulty can hardly be evaded by arguing that although *B* could not exist without *A*, *being a pain* is merely a contingent property of *A*, and that therefore the presence of *B* pain does not imply the presence of *B* without *A*. Can any case of essence be more obvious than the fact that *being a*

* "C-fiber stimulation" is Kripke's stand-in term for whatever physical state corresponds to the psychological state of being in pain.

* In addition to being one of the Founding Fathers of the American nation, Benjamin Franklin (1706–90) was the inventor of bifocals and the first postmaster general.

† Ipso facto means: by that fact itself, thereby.

pain is a necessary property of each pain? The identity theorist who wishes to adopt the strategy in question must even argue that *being a sensation* is a contingent property of A, for prima facie it would seem logically possible that B could exist without any sensation with which it might plausibly be identified. Consider a particular pain, or other sensation, that you once had. Do you find it at all plausible that *that very sensation* could have existed without being a sensation, the way a certain inventor (Franklin) could have existed without being an inventor?

I mention this strategy because it seems to me to be adopted by a large number of identity theorists. These theorists, believing as they do that the supposed identity of a brain state with the corresponding mental state is to be analyzed on the paradigm of the contingent identity of Benjamin Franklin with the inventor of bifocals, realize that just as his contingent activity made Benjamin Franklin into the inventor of bifocals, so some contingent property of the brain state must make it into a pain. Generally they wish this property to be one statable in physical or at least "topic-neutral" language, so that the materialist cannot be accused of positing irreducible nonphysical properties. A typical view is that *being a pain*, as a property of a physical state, is to be analyzed in terms of the "causal role" of the state,[6] in terms of the characteristic stimuli (e.g., pinpricks) which cause it and the characteristic behavior it causes. I will not go into the details of such analyses, even though I usually find them faulty on specific grounds in addition to the general modal considerations I argue here. All I need to observe here is that the "causal role" of the physical state is regarded by the theorists in question as a contingent property of the state, and thus it is supposed to be a contingent property of the state that it is a mental state at all, let alone that it is something as specific as a pain. To repeat, this notion seems to me self-evidently absurd. It amounts to the view that the *very pain I now have* could have existed without being a mental state at all.

I have not discussed the converse problem, which is closer to the original Cartesian consideration—namely, that just as it seems that the brain state could have existed without any pain, so it seems that the pain could have existed without the corresponding brain state. Note that *being a brain state* is evidently an essential property of B (the brain state). Indeed, even more is true: not only being a brain state, but even being a brain state of a specific type is an essential property of B. The configuration of brain cells whose presence at a given time constitutes the presence of B at that time is essential to B, and in its absence B would not have existed. Thus someone who wishes to claim that the brain state and the pain are identical must argue that the pain A could not have existed without a quite specific type of configuration of molecules. If $A = B$, then the identity of A with B is necessary, and any essential property of one must be an essential property of the other. Someone who wishes to maintain an identity thesis cannot simply *accept* the Cartesian intuitions that A can exist without B, that B can exist without A, that the correlative presence of anything with mental properties is merely contingent to B, and that the correlative presence of any specific physical properties is merely contingent to A. He must explain these intuitions away, showing how they are illusory. This task may not be impossible; we have seen above how some things which appear to be contingent turn out, on closer examination, to be necessary. The task, however, is obviously not child's play, and we shall see below how difficult it is.

The final kind of identity, the one which I said would get the closest attention, is the type-type sort of identity exemplified by the identification of pain with the stimulation of C-fibers. These identifications are supposed to be analogous with such scientific type-type identifications as the identity of heat with molecular motion, of water with hydrogen hydroxide, and the like. Let us consider, as an example, the analogy supposed to hold between the materialist identification and that of heat with molecular motion; both identifications identify two types of phenomena. The usual view holds that the identification of heat with molecular motion and of pain with the stimulation of C-fibers are both contingent. We have seen above that since "heat" and "molecular motion" are both rigid designators, the identification of the phenomena they name is necessary. What about "pain" and "C-fiber stimulation"? It should be clear from the previous discussion that "pain" is a rigid designator of the type, or phenomenon, it designates: if something is a pain it is essentially so, and it seems absurd to suppose that pain could have been some phenomenon other than the one it is. The same holds for the term "C-fiber stimulation," provided that "C-fiber" is a rigid designator, as I will suppose here. (The supposition is somewhat risky, since I know virtually nothing about C-fibers, except that the stimulation of them is said to be correlated with pain.[7] The point is unimportant; if "C-fibers" is not a rigid designator, simply replace it by one which is, or suppose it used as a rigid designator in the present context.) Thus the identity of pain with the stimulation of C-fibers, if true, must be *necessary*.

So far the analogy between the identification of heat with molecular motion and pain with the stimulation of C-fibers has not failed; it has merely turned out to be the opposite of what is usually thought—both, if true, must be necessary. This means that the identity theorist is committed to the view that there could not be a C-fiber stimulation which was not a pain nor a pain which was not a C-fiber stimulation. These consequences are certainly surprising and counterintuitive, but let us not dismiss the identity theorist too quickly. Can he perhaps show that the apparent possibility of pain not having turned out to be C-fiber stimulation, or of there being an instance of one of the phenomena which is not an instance of the other, is an illusion of the same sort as the illusion that water might not have been hydrogen hydroxide,* or that heat might not have been molecular motion? If so, he will have rebutted the Cartesian, not, as in the conventional analysis, by accepting his premise while exposing the fallacy of his argument, but rather by the reverse—while the Cartesian argument, given its premise of the contingency of the identification, is granted to yield its conclusion, the premise is to be exposed as superficially plausible but false.

Now I do not think it likely that the identity theorist will succeed in such an endeavor. I want to argue that, at least, the case cannot be interpreted as analogous to that of scientific identification of the usual sort, as exemplified by the identity of heat and molecular motion. What was the strategy used above to handle the apparent contingency of certain cases of the necessary *a posteriori*? The strategy was to argue that although the statement itself is necessary, someone could, *qualitatively* speaking, be in the same epistemic situation as the original, and in such a situation a *qualitatively* analogous statement could be false. In the case of identities between two rigid designators, the strategy can be approximated by a simpler one: Consider how the references of the designators are determined; if these coincide only contingently, it is this fact which gives the original statement its illusion of contingency. In the case of heat and molecular motion, the way these two paradigms work out is simple. When someone says, inaccurately, that heat might have turned out not to be molecular motion, what is true in what he says is that someone could have sensed a phenomenon in the same way we sense heat, that is, feels it by means of its production of the sensation we call "the sensation of heat" (call it "*S*"), even though that phenomenon was not molecular motion. He means, additionally, that the planet might have been inhabited by creatures who did not get *S* when they were in the presence of molecular motion, though perhaps getting it in the presence of something else. Such creatures would be, in some qualitative sense, in the same epistemic situation as we are, they could use a rigid designator for the phenomenon that causes sensation *S* in them (the rigid designator could even be "heat"), yet it would not be molecular motion (and therefore not heat!), which was causing the sensation.

Now can something be said analogously to explain away the feeling that the identity of pain and the stimulation of C-fibers, if it is a scientific discovery, could have turned out otherwise? I do not see that such an analogy is possible. In the case of the apparent possibility that molecular motion might have existed in the absence of heat, what seemed really possible is that molecular motion should have existed without being *felt as heat*, that is, it might have existed without producing the sensation *S*, the sensation of heat. In the appropriate sentient beings is it analogously possible that a stimulation of C-fibers should have existed without being felt as pain? If this is possible, then the stimulation of C-fibers can itself exist without pain, since for it to exist without

* Kripke here is using the expression "hydrogen hydroxide" simply to mean H_2O.

being *felt as pain* is for it to exist without there *being any* pain. Such a situation would be in flat out contradiction with the supposed necessary identity of pain and the corresponding physical state, and the analogue holds for any physical state which might be identified with a corresponding mental state. The trouble is that the identity theorist does not hold that the physical state merely *produces* the mental state, rather he wishes the two to be identical and thus *a fortiori* necessarily co-occurrent. In the case of molecular motion and heat there is something, namely, the sensation of heat, which is an intermediary between the external phenomenon and the observer. In the mental-physical case no such intermediary is possible, since here the physical phenomenon is supposed to be identical with the internal phenomenon itself. Someone can be in the same epistemic situation as he would be if there were heat, even in the absence of heat, simply by feeling the sensation of heat; and even in the presence of heat, he can have the same evidence as he would have in the absence of heat simply by lacking the sensation *S*. No such possibility exists in the case of pain and other mental phenomena. To be in the same epistemic situation that would obtain if one had a pain *is* to have a pain; to be in the same epistemic situation that would obtain in the absence of a pain *is* not to have a pain. The apparent contingency of the connection between the mental state and the corresponding brain state thus cannot be explained by some sort of qualitative analogue as in the case of heat.

We have just analyzed the situation in terms of the notion of a qualitatively identical epistemic situation. The trouble is that the notion of an epistemic situation qualitatively identical to one in which the observer had a sensation *S* simply *is* one in which the observer had that sensation. The same point can be made in terms of the notion of what picks out the reference of a rigid designator. In the case of the identity of heat with molecular motion the important consideration was that although "heat" is a rigid designator, the reference of that designator was determined by an accidental property of the referent, namely the property of producing in us the sensation *S*. It is thus possible that a phenomenon should have been rigidly designated in the same way as a phenomenon of heat, with its reference also picked out by means of the sensation *S*, without that phenomenon being heat and therefore without its being molecular motion. Pain, on the other hand, is not picked out by one of its accidental properties; rather it is picked out by the property of being pain itself, by its immediate phenomenological quality. Thus pain, unlike heat, is not only rigidly designated by "pain" but the reference of the designator is determined by an essential property of the referent. Thus it is not possible to say that although pain is necessarily identical with a certain physical state, a certain phenomenon can be picked out in the same way we pick out pain without being correlated with that physical state. If any phenomenon is picked out in exactly the same way that we pick out pain, then that phenomenon *is* pain.

Perhaps the same point can be made more vivid without such specific reference to the technical apparatus in these lectures. Suppose we imagine God creating the world; what does He need to do to make the identity of heat and molecular motion obtain. Here it would seem that all He needs to do is to create the heat, that is, the molecular motion itself? If the air molecules on this earth are sufficiently agitated, if there is a burning fire, then the earth will be hot even if there are no observers to see it. God created light (and thus created streams of photons, according to present scientific doctrine) before He created human and animal observers; and the same presumably holds for heat. How then does it appear to us that the identity of molecular motion with heat is a substantive scientific fact, that the mere creation of molecular motion still leaves God with the additional task of making molecular motion into heat? This feeling is indeed illusory, but what *is* a substantive task for the Deity is the task of making molecular motion felt as heat. To do this He must create some sentient beings to insure that the molecular motion produces the sensation *S* in them. Only after he has done this will there be beings who can learn that the sentence "Heat is the motion of molecules" expresses an *a posteriori* truth in precisely the same way that we do.

What about the case of the stimulation of C-fibers? To create this phenomenon, it would seem that God need only create beings with C-fibers capable of the appropriate type of physical stimulation;

whether the beings are conscious or not is irrelevant here. It would seem, though, that to make the C-fiber stimulation correspond to pain, or be felt as pain, God must do something in addition to the mere creation of the C-fiber stimulation; He must let the creatures feel the C-fiber stimulation as *pain*, and not as a tickle, or as warmth, or as nothing, as apparently would also have been within His powers. If these things in fact are within His powers, the relation between the pain God creates and the stimulation of C-fibers cannot be identity. For if so, the stimulation could exist without the pain; and since "pain" and "C-fiber stimulation" are rigid, this fact implies that the relation between the two phenomena is not that of identity. God had to do some work, in addition to making the man himself, to make a certain man be the inventor of bifocals; the man could well exist without inventing any such thing. The same cannot be said for pain; if the phenomenon exists at all, no further work should be required to make it into pain.

In sum, the correspondence between a brain state and a mental state seems to have a certain obvious element of contingency. We have seen that identity is not a relation which can hold contingently between objects. Therefore, if the identity thesis were correct, the element of contingency would not lie in the relation between the mental and physical states. It cannot lie, as in the case of heat and molecular motion, in the relation between the phenomenon (= heat = molecular motion) and the way it is felt or appears (sensation *S*), since in the case of mental phenomena there is no "appearance" beyond the mental phenomenon itself.

Here I have been emphasizing the possibility, or apparent possibility, of a physical state without the corresponding mental state. The reverse possibility, the mental state (pain) without the physical state (C-fiber stimulation) also presents problems for the identity theorists which cannot be resolved by appeal to the analogy of heat and molecular motion.

I have discussed similar problems more briefly for views equating the self with the body, and particular mental events with particular physical events, without discussing possible countermoves in the same detail as in the type-type case. Suffice it to say that I suspect that the considerations given indicate that the theorist who wishes to identify various particular mental and physical events will have to face problems fairly similar to those of the type-type theorist; he too will be unable to appeal to the standard alleged analogues.

That the usual moves and analogies are not available to solve the problems of the identity theorist is, of course, no proof that no moves are available. I certainly cannot discuss all the possibilities here. I suspect, however, that the present considerations tell heavily against the usual forms of materialism. Materialism, I think, must hold that a physical description of the world is a *complete* description of it, that any mental facts are "ontologically dependent" on physical facts in the straightforward sense of following from them by necessity. No identity theorist seems to me to have made a convincing argument against the intuitive view that this is not the case.[8]

NOTES

1. That is everyone, even Russell, would agree that this is a true material equivalence, given that there really was an Aristotle.
2. In particular, we ignore the question what to say about counterfactual situations in which Aristotle would not have existed.
3. Taking "the last great philosopher of antiquity" to be the description Russell associates with "Aristotle." Let admirers of Epicureanism, Stoicism, etc., not be offended; if any reader thinks that someone later than Aristotle is the true referent of the description given, let that reader substitute another one.

   I assume Russell is right in that definite descriptions can at least *sometimes* be interpreted nonrigidly. . . . Some philosophers think that, in addition, there is a rigid sense of definite descriptions. As I say in the latter footnote, I am not convinced of this, but if these philosophers are right, my principal thesis is not affected. It contrasts names with nonrigid descriptions, as advocated by Russell. See Section 2, pp. 258–61 of my paper, "Speaker's Reference and Semantic Reference." *Midwest Studies in Philosophy*, II (1977), pp. 255–76; also in *Contemporary Perspectives in the Philosophy of Language*, edited by Peter

A. French, Theodore E. Uehling, Jr., and Howard K. Wettstein, University of Minnesota Press, Minneapolis (1979), pp. 6–27 for a brief discussion of the relation of the idea of rigid definite descriptions to Donnellan's "referential" descriptions. I also discuss the relation of both of these to the notion of scope.

4. Thomas Nagel and Donald Davidson are notable examples. Their views are very interesting, and I wish I could discuss them in further detail. It is doubtful that such philosophers wish to call themselves "materialists." Davidson, in particular, bases his case for his version of the identity theory on the supposed *impossibility* of correlating psychological properties with physical ones.

   The argument against token-token identification in the text *does* apply to these views.

5. Of course, the body *does* exist without the mind and presumably without the person, when the body is a corpse. This consideration, if accepted, would already show that a person and his body are distinct. (See David Wiggins, "On Being at the Same Place at the Same Time," *Philosophical Review*, Vol. 77 [1968], pp. 90–5.) Similarly, it can be argued that a statue is not the hunk of matter of which it is composed. In the later case, however, one might say instead that the former is "nothing over and above" the latter; and the same device might be tried for the relation of the person and the body. The difficulties in the text would not then arise in the same form, but analogous difficulties would appear. A theory that a person is nothing over and above his body in the way that a statue is nothing over and above the matter of which it is composed, would have to hold that (necessarily) a person exists if and only if his body exists and has a certain additional physical organization. Such a thesis would be subject to modal difficulties similar to those besetting the ordinary identity thesis, and the same would apply to suggested analogues replacing the identification of mental states with physical states. A further discussion of this matter must be left for another place. Another view which I will not discuss, although I have little tendency to accept it and am not even certain that it has been set out with genuine clarity, is the so-called functional state view of psychological concepts.

6. For example, David Armstrong, *A Materialist Theory of the Mind*, London and New York, 1968, see the discussion review by Thomas Nagel, *Philosophical Review* 79 (1970), pp. 394–403; and David Lewis, "An Argument for the Identity Theory," *The Journal of Philosophy*, pp. 17–25.

7. I have been surprised to find that at least one able listener took my use of such terms as "correlated with," "corresponding to," and the like as already begging the question against the identity thesis. The identity thesis, so he said, is not the thesis that pains and brain states are correlated, but rather that they are identical. Thus my entire discussion presupposes the anti-materialist position that I set out to prove. Although I was surprised to hear an objection which concedes so little intelligence to the argument, I have tried especially to avoid the term "correlated" which seems to give rise to the objection. Nevertheless, to obviate misunderstanding, I shall explain my usage. Assuming, at least *arguendo,* that scientific discoveries have turned out so as not to refute materialism from the beginning, both the dualist and the identity theorist agree that there is a correlation or correspondence between mental states and physical states. The dualist holds that the "correlation" relation in question is irreflexive; the identity theorist holds that it is simply a special case of the identity relation. Such terms as "correlation" and "correspondence" can be used neutrally without prejudging which side is correct.

8. Having expressed these doubts about the identity theory in the text, I should emphasize two things: first, identity theorists have presented positive arguments for their view, which I certainly have not answered here. Some of these arguments seem to me to be weak or based on ideological prejudices, but others strike me as highly compelling arguments which I am at present unable to answer convincingly. Second, rejection of the identity thesis does not imply acceptance of Cartesian dualism. In fact, my view above that a person could not have come from a different sperm and egg from the ones from which he actually originated implicitly suggests a rejection of the Cartesian picture. If we had a clear idea of the soul or the mind as an independent, subsistent, spiritual entity, why should it have to have any necessary connection with particular material

objects such as a particular sperm or a particular egg? A convinced dualist may think that my views on sperms and eggs beg the question against Descartes. I would tend to argue the other way; the fact that it is hard to imagine me coming from a sperm and egg different from my actual origins seems to me to indicate that we have no such clear conception of a soul or self. In any event, Descartes' notion seems to have been rendered dubious ever since Hume's critique of the notion of a Cartesian self. I regard the mind-body problem as wide open and extremely confusing.

The Knowledge Argument

FRANK JACKSON

Frank Jackson (1943–) spent many years at the Australian National University as Professor of Philosophy, and now teaches at Princeton University. He has made influential contributions to several areas of philosophy and is the author of a widely discussed critique of physicalism.

The text presented here includes both a self-standing 1982 paper by Jackson—"Epiphenomenal Qualia"—and selections from an article that he published four years later responding to some of his critics. In them, Jackson introduces the famous case of Mary, the color-deprived scientist, which has gone on to become one of the most widely discussed examples in contemporary philosophy of mind.

It is undeniable that the physical, chemical and biological sciences have provided a great deal of information about the world we live in and about ourselves. I will use the label "physical information" for this kind of information, and also for information that automatically comes along with it. For example, if a medical scientist tells me enough about the processes that go on in my nervous system, and about how they relate to happenings in the world around me, to what has happened in the past and is likely to happen in the future, to what happens to other similar and dissimilar organisms, and the like, he or she tells me—if I am clever enough to fit it together appropriately—about what is often called the functional role of those states in me (and in organisms in general in similar cases). This information, and its kin, I also label "physical."

I do not mean these sketchy remarks to constitute a definition of "physical information," and of the correlative notions of physical property, process, and so on, but to indicate what I have in mind here. It is well known that there are problems with giving a precise definition of these notions, and so of the thesis of Physicalism that all (correct) information is physical information.[1] But—unlike some—I take the question of definition to cut across the central problems I want to discuss in this paper.

I am what is sometimes known as a "qualia freak." I think that there are certain features of the bodily sensations especially, but also of certain perceptual experiences, which no amount of purely physical information includes. Tell me everything physical there is to tell about what is going on in a living brain, the kind of states, their functional role,

From *Philosophical Quarterly* 32:127–136, 1982. Reprinted with permission of Blackwell Publishing. Addendum excerpted from "What Mary Didn't Know," *Journal of Philosophy* 83:291–95, 1986, with permission of author and publisher. Excerpts from the addendum follow David Chalmers, *Philosophy of Mind: Classical and Contemporary Readings* (New York: Oxford University Press, 2002).

their relation to what goes on at other times and in other brains, and so on and so forth, and be I as clever as can be in fitting it all together, you won't have told me about the hurtfulness of pains, the itchiness of itches, pangs of jealousy, or about the characteristic experience of tasting a lemon, smelling a rose, hearing a loud noise or seeing the sky.

There are many qualia freaks, and some of them say that their rejection of Physicalism is an unargued intuition.[2] I think that they are being unfair to themselves. They have the following argument. Nothing you could tell of a physical sort captures the smell of a rose, for instance. Therefore, Physicalism is false. By our lights this is a perfectly good argument. It is obviously not to the point to question its validity, and the premise is intuitively obviously true both to them and to me.

I must, however, admit that it is weak from a polemical point of view. There are, unfortunately for us, many who do not find the premise intuitively obvious. The task then is to present an argument whose premises are obvious to all, or at least to as many as possible. This I try to do in §I with what I will call "the Knowledge argument." In §II I contrast the Knowledge argument with the Modal argument and in §III with the "What is it like to be" argument. In §IV I tackle the question of the causal role of qualia. The major factor in stopping people from admitting qualia is the belief that they would have to be given a causal role with respect to the physical world and especially the brain;[3] and it is hard to do this without sounding like someone who believes in fairies. I seek in §IV to turn this objection by arguing that the view that qualia are epiphenomenal is a perfectly possible one.

I. THE KNOWLEDGE ARGUMENT FOR QUALIA

People vary considerably in their ability to discriminate colours. Suppose that in an experiment to catalogue this variation Fred is discovered. Fred has better colour vision than anyone else on record; he makes every discrimination that anyone has ever made, and moreover he makes one that we cannot even begin to make. Show him a batch of ripe tomatoes and he sorts them into two roughly equal groups and does so with complete consistency. That is, if you blindfold him, shuffle the tomatoes up, and then remove the blindfold and ask him to sort them out again, he sorts them into exactly the same two groups.

We ask Fred how he does it. He explains that all ripe tomatoes do not look the same colour to him, and in fact that this is true of a great many objects that we classify together as red. He sees two colours where we see one, and he has in consequence developed for his own use two words "red_1" and "red_2" to mark the difference. Perhaps he tells us that he has often tried to teach the difference between red_1 and red_2 to his friends but has got nowhere and has concluded that the rest of the world is red_1-red_2 colour-blind—or perhaps he has had partial success with his children, it doesn't matter. In any case he explains to us that it would be quite wrong to think that because "red" appears in both "red_1" and "red_2" that the two colours are shades of the one colour. He only uses the common term "red" to fit more easily into our restricted usage. To him red_1 and red_2 are as different from each other and all the other colours as yellow is from blue. And his discriminatory behaviour bears this out: he sorts red_1 from red_2 tomatoes with the greatest of ease in a wide variety of viewing circumstances. Moreover, an investigation of the physiological basis of Fred's exceptional ability reveals that Fred's optical system is able to separate out two groups of wavelengths in the red spectrum as sharply as we are able to sort out yellow from blue.[4]

I think that we should admit that Fred can see, really see, at least one more colour than we can; red_1 is a different colour from red_2. We are to Fred as a totally red-green colour-blind person is to us. H. G. Wells' story "The Country of the Blind" is about a sighted person in a totally blind community.[5] This person never manages to convince them that he can see, that he has an extra sense. They ridicule this sense as quite inconceivable, and treat his capacity to avoid falling into ditches, to win fights and so on as precisely that capacity and nothing more. We would be making their mistake if we refused to allow that Fred can see one more colour than we can.

What kind of experience does Fred have when he sees red_1 and red_2? What is the new colour or colours like? We would dearly like to know but do not; and it seems that no amount of physical information about Fred's brain and optical system tells us. We find out perhaps that Fred's cones respond differentially to certain light waves in the red section of the spectrum that make no difference to ours (or perhaps he has an extra cone) and that this leads in Fred to a wider range of those brain states responsible for visual discriminatory behaviour. But none of this tells us what we really want to know about his colour experience. There is something about it we don't know. But we know, we may suppose, everything about Fred's body, his behaviour and dispositions to behaviour and about his internal physiology, and everything about his history and relation to others that can be given in physical accounts of persons. We have all the physical information. Therefore, knowing all this is *not* knowing everything about Fred. It follows that Physicalism leaves something out.

To reinforce this conclusion, imagine that as a result of our investigations into the internal workings of Fred we find out how to make everyone's physiology like Fred's in the relevant respects; or perhaps Fred donates his body to science and on his death we are able to transplant his optical system into someone else—again the fine detail doesn't matter. The important point is that such a happening would create enormous interest. People would say, "At last we will know what it is like to see the extra colour, at last we will know how Fred has differed from us in the way he has struggled to tell us about for so long." Then it cannot be that we knew all along all about Fred. But *ex hypothesi* we did know all along everything about Fred that features in the physicalist scheme; hence the physicalist scheme leaves something out.

Put it this way. *After* the operation, we will know *more* about Fred and especially about his colour experiences. But beforehand we had all the physical information we could desire about his body and brain, and indeed everything that has ever featured in physicalist accounts of mind and consciousness. Hence there is more to know than all that. Hence Physicalism is incomplete.

Fred and the new colour(s) are of course essentially rhetorical devices. The same point can be made with normal people and familiar colours. Mary is a brilliant scientist who is, for whatever reason, forced to investigate the world from a black and white room via a black and white television monitor. She specialises in the neurophysiology of vision and acquires, let us suppose, all the physical information there is to obtain about what goes on when we see ripe tomatoes, or the sky, and use terms like "red," "blue," and so on. She discovers, for example, just which wave-length combinations from the sky stimulate the retina, and exactly how this produces *via* the central nervous system the contraction of the vocal chords and expulsion of air from the lungs that results in the uttering of the sentence "The sky is blue." (It can hardly be denied that it is in principle possible to obtain all this physical information from black and white television, otherwise the Open University would *of necessity* need to use colour television.)*

What will happen when Mary is released from her black and white room or is given a colour television monitor? Will she *learn* anything or not? It seems just obvious that she will learn something about the world and our visual experience of it. But then it is inescapable that her previous knowledge was incomplete. But she had *all* the physical information. Ergo there is more to have than that, and Physicalism is false.

Clearly the same style of Knowledge argument could be deployed for taste, hearing, the bodily sensations and generally speaking for the various mental states which are said to have (as it is variously put) raw feels, phenomenal features or qualia. The conclusion in each case is that the qualia are left out of the physicalist story. And the polemical strength of the Knowledge argument is that it is so hard to deny the central claim that one can have all the physical information without having all the information there is to have.

II. THE MODAL ARGUMENT

By the Modal Argument I mean an argument of the following style.[6] Sceptics about other minds are not

* The Open University is an open-enrollment institute of higher education founded in England in 1969, most of whose courses are conducted through distance learning.

making a mistake in deductive logic, whatever else may be wrong with their position. No amount of physical information about another *logically entails* that he or she is conscious or feels anything at all. Consequently there is a possible world with organisms exactly like us in every physical respect (and remember that includes functional states, physical history, et al.) but which differ from us profoundly in that they have no conscious mental life at all. But then what is it that we have and they lack? Not anything physical ex hypothesi. In all physical regards we and they are exactly alike. Consequently there is more to us than the purely physical. Thus Physicalism is false.[7]

It is sometimes objected that the Modal argument misconceives Physicalism on the ground that that doctrine is advanced as a *contingent* truth.[8] But to say this is only to say that physicalists restrict their claim to *some* possible worlds, including especially ours; and the Modal argument is only directed against this lesser claim. If we in *our* world, let alone beings in any others, have features additional to those of our physical replicas in other possible worlds, then we have non-physical features or qualia.

The trouble rather with the Modal argument is that it rests on a disputable modal intuition. Disputable because it is disputed. Some sincerely deny that there can be physical replicas of us in other possible worlds which nevertheless lack consciousness. Moreover, at least one person who once had the intuition now has doubts.[9]

Head-counting may seem a poor approach to a discussion of the Modal argument. But frequently we can do no better when modal intuitions are in question, and remember our initial goal was to find the argument with the greatest polemical utility.

Of course, qua protagonists of the Knowledge argument we may well accept the modal intuition in question; but this will be a *consequence* of our already having an argument to the conclusion that qualia are left out of the physicalist story, not our ground for that conclusion. Moreover, the matter is complicated by the possibility that the connection between matters physical and qualia is like that sometimes held to obtain between aesthetic qualities and natural ones. Two possible worlds which agree in all "natural" respects (including the experiences of sentient creatures) must agree in all aesthetic qualities also, but it is plausibly held that the aesthetic qualities cannot be reduced to the natural.

III. THE "WHAT IS IT LIKE TO BE" ARGUMENT

In "What Is It Like to Be a Bat?" Thomas Nagel argues that no amount of physical information can tell us what it is like to be a bat, and indeed that we, human beings, cannot imagine what it is like to be a bat.[10] His reason is that what this is like can only be understood from a bat's point of view, which is not our point of view and is not something capturable in physical terms which are essentially terms understandable equally from many points of view.

It is important to distinguish this argument from the Knowledge argument. When I complained that all the physical knowledge about Fred was not enough to tell us what his special colour experience was like, I was not complaining that we weren't finding out what it is like to *be* Fred. I was complaining that there is something *about* his experience, a property of it, of which we were left ignorant. And if and when we come to know what this property is we still will not know what it is like to *be* Fred, but we will know more *about* him. No amount of knowledge about Fred, be it physical or not, amounts to knowledge "from the inside" concerning Fred. We are not Fred. There is thus a whole set of items of knowledge expressed by forms of words like "that it is *I myself* who is . . ." which Fred has and we simply cannot have because we are not him.[11]

When Fred sees the colour he alone can see, one thing he knows is the way his experience of it differs from his experience of seeing red and so on, *another* is that he himself is seeing it. Physicalist and qualia freaks alike should acknowledge that no amount of information of whatever kind that *others* have *about* Fred amounts to knowledge of the second. My complaint though concerned the first and was that the special quality of his experience is certainly a fact about it, and one which Physicalism leaves out because no amount of physical information told us what it is.

Nagel speaks as if the problem he is raising is one of extrapolating from knowledge of one experience to another, of imagining what an unfamiliar experience would be like on the basis of familiar ones. In terms of Hume's example, from knowledge of some shades of blue we can work out what it would be like to see other shades of blue. Nagel argues that the trouble with bats et al. is that they are too unlike us. It is hard to see an objection to Physicalism here. Physicalism makes no special claims about the imaginative or extrapolative powers of human beings, and it is hard to see why it need do so.[12]

Anyway, our Knowledge argument makes no assumptions on this point. If Physicalism were true, enough physical information about Fred would obviate any need to extrapolate or to perform special feats of imagination or understanding in order to know all about his special colour experience. *The information would already be in our possession.* But it clearly isn't. That was the nub of the argument.

IV. THE BOGEY OF EPIPHENOMENALISM

Is there any really *good* reason for refusing to countenance the idea that qualia are causally impotent with respect to the physical world? I will argue for the answer no, but in doing this I will say nothing about two views associated with the classical epiphenomenalist position. The first is that mental *states* are inefficacious with respect to the physical world. All I will be concerned to defend is that it is possible to hold that certain *properties* of certain mental states, namely those I've called qualia, are such that their possession or absence makes no difference to the physical world. The second is that the mental is *totally* causally inefficacious. For all I will say it may be that you have to hold that the instantiation of *qualia* makes a difference to *other mental states* though not to anything physical. Indeed general considerations to do with how you could come to be aware of the instantiation of qualia suggest such a position.[13]

Three reasons are standardly given for holding that a quale like the hurtfulness of a pain must be causally efficacious in the physical world, and so, for instance, that its instantiation must sometimes make a difference to what happens in the brain. None, I will argue, has any real force. (I am much indebted to Alec Hyslop and John Lucas for convincing me of this.)

(i) It is supposed to be just obvious that the hurtfulness of pain is partly responsible for the subject seeking to avoid pain, saying "It hurts" and so on. But, to reverse Hume, anything can fail to cause anything. No matter how often *B* follows *A*, and no matter how initially obvious the causality of the connection seems, the hypothesis that *A* causes *B* can be overturned by an over-arching theory which shows the two as distinct effects of a common underlying causal process.

To the untutored the image on the screen of Lee Marvin's fist moving from left to right immediately followed by the image of John Wayne's head moving in the same general direction looks as causal as anything.[14] And of course throughout countless Westerns images similar to the first are followed by images similar to the second. All this counts for precisely nothing when we know the over-arching theory concerning how the relevant images are both effects of an underlying causal process involving the projector and the film. The epiphenomenalist can say exactly the same about the connection between, for example, hurtfulness and behaviour. It is simply a consequence of the fact that certain happenings in the brain cause both.

(ii) The second objection relates to Darwin's Theory of Evolution. According to natural selection the traits that evolve over time are those conducive to physical survival. We may assume that qualia evolved over time—we have them, the earliest forms of life do not—and so we should expect qualia to be conducive to survival. The objection is that they could hardly help us to survive if they do nothing to the physical world.

The appeal of this argument is undeniable, but there is a good reply to it. Polar bears have particularly thick, warm coats. The Theory of Evolution explains this (we suppose) by pointing out that having a thick, warm coat is conducive to survival in the Arctic. But having a thick coat goes along with having a heavy coat, and having a heavy coat is *not* conducive to survival. It slows the animal down.

Does this mean that we have refuted Darwin because we have found an evolved trait—having a heavy coat—which is not conducive to survival? Clearly not. Having a heavy coat is an unavoidable concomitant of having a warm coat (in the context, modern insulation was not available), and the advantages for survival of having a warm coat outweighed the disadvantages of having a heavy one. The point is that all we can extract from Darwin's theory is that we should expect any evolved characteristic to be *either* conducive to survival *or* a by-product of one that is so conducive. The epiphenomenalist holds that qualia fall into the latter category. They are a by-product of certain brain processes that are highly conducive to survival.

(iii) The third objection is based on a point about how we come to know about other minds. We know about other minds by knowing about other behaviour, at least in part. The nature of the inference is a matter of some controversy, but it is not a matter of controversy that it proceeds from behaviour. That is why we think that stones do not feel and dogs do feel. But, runs the objection, how can a person's behaviour provide any reason for believing he has qualia like mine, or indeed any qualia at all, unless this behaviour can be regarded as the *outcome* of the qualia. Man Friday's footprint was evidence of Man Friday because footprints are causal outcomes of feet attached to people. And an epiphenomenalist cannot regard behaviour, or indeed anything physical, as an outcome of qualia.

But consider my reading in *The Times* that Spurs won. This provides excellent evidence that *The Telegraph* has also reported that Spurs won, despite the fact that (I trust) *The Telegraph* does not get the results from *The Times*. They each send their own reporters to the game. *The Telegraph*'s report is in no sense an outcome of *The Times*', but the latter provides good evidence for the former nevertheless.

The reasoning involved can be reconstructed thus. I read in *The Times* that Spurs won. This gives me reason to think that Spurs won because I know that Spurs' winning is the most likely candidate to be what caused the report in *The Times*. But I also know that Spurs' winning would have had many effects, including almost certainly a report in *The Telegraph*.

I am arguing from one effect back to its cause and out again to another effect. The fact that neither effect causes the other is irrelevant. Now the epiphenomenalist allows that qualia are effects of what goes on in the brain. Qualia cause nothing physical but are caused by something physical. Hence the epiphenomenalist can argue from the behaviour of others to the qualia of others by arguing from the behaviour of others back to its causes in the brains of others and out again to their qualia.

You may well feel for one reason or another that this is a more dubious chain of reasoning than its model in the case of newspaper reports. You are right. The problem of other minds is a major philosophical problem, the problem of other newspaper reports is not. But there is no special problem of Epiphenomenalism as opposed to, say, Interactionism here.

There is a very understandable response to the three replies I have just made. "All right, there is no knockdown refutation of the existence of epiphenomenal qualia. But the fact remains that they are an excrescence. They *do* nothing, they *explain* nothing, they serve merely to soothe the intuitions of dualists, and it is left a total mystery how they fit into the world view of science. In short we do not and cannot understand the how and why of them."

This is perfectly true; but is no objection to qualia, for it rests on an overly optimistic view of the human animal, and its powers. We are the products of Evolution. We understand and sense what we need to understand and sense in order to survive. Epiphenomenal qualia are totally irrelevant to survival. At no stage of our evolution did natural selection favour those who could make sense of how they are caused and the laws governing them, or in fact why they exist at all. And that is why we can't.

It is not sufficiently appreciated that Physicalism is an extremely optimistic view of our powers. If it is true, we have, in very broad outline admittedly, a grasp of our place in the scheme of things. Certain matters of sheer complexity defeat us—there are an awful lot of neurons—but in principle we have it all. But consider the antecedent probability that everything in the Universe be of a kind that is relevant in some way or other to the survival of *homo sapiens*. It is very low surely. But then one must admit that it is very likely that there is a part of the whole scheme of things, maybe a big part, which no amount of evolution will ever bring us near to knowledge about or understanding. For the simple reason that such knowledge and understanding is irrelevant to survival.

Physicalists typically emphasise that we are a part of nature on their view, which is fair enough. But if we are a part of nature, we are as nature has left us after however many years of evolution it is, and each step in that evolutionary progression has been a matter of chance constrained just by the need to preserve or increase survival value. The wonder is that we understand as much as we do, and there is no wonder that there should be matters which fall quite outside our comprehension. Perhaps exactly how epiphenomenal qualia fit into the scheme of things is one such.

This may seem an unduly pessimistic view of our capacity to articulate a truly comprehensive picture of our world and our place in it. But suppose we discovered living on the bottom of the deepest oceans a sort of sea slug which manifested intelligence. Perhaps survival in the conditions required rational powers. Despite their intelligence, these sea slugs have only a very restricted conception of the world by comparison with ours, the explanation for this being the nature of their immediate environment. Nevertheless they have developed sciences which work surprisingly well in these restricted terms. They also have philosophers, called slugists. Some call themselves tough-minded slugists, others confess to being soft-minded slugists.

The tough-minded slugists hold that the restricted terms (or ones pretty like them which may be introduced as their sciences progress) suffice in principle to describe everything without remainder. These tough-minded slugists admit in moments of weakness to a feeling that their theory leaves something out. They resist this feeling and their opponents, the soft-minded slugists, by pointing out—absolutely correctly—that no slugist has ever succeeded in spelling out how this mysterious residue fits into the highly successful view that their sciences have and are developing of how their world works.

Our sea slugs don't exist, but they might. And there might also exist super beings which stand to us as we stand to the sea slugs. We cannot adopt the perspective of these super beings, because we are not them, but the possibility of such a perspective is, I think, an antidote to excessive optimism.[15]

ADDENDUM: FROM "WHAT MARY DIDN'T KNOW"

I. THREE CLARIFICATIONS

The knowledge argument does not rest on the dubious claim that logically you cannot imagine what sensing red is like unless you have sensed red. Powers of imagination are not to the point. The contention about Mary is not that, despite her fantastic grasp of neurophysiology and everything else physical, she *could not imagine* what it is like to sense red; it is that, as a matter of fact, she *would not know*. But if physicalism is true, she would know; and no great powers of imagination would be called for. Imagination is a faculty that those who *lack* knowledge need to fall back on.

Secondly, the intensionality of knowledge is not to the point. The argument does not rest on assuming falsely that, if S knows that a is F and if $a = b$, then S knows that b is F. It is concerned with the nature of Mary's total body of knowledge before she is released: is it complete, or do some facts escape it? What is to the point is that S may know that a is F and know that $a = b$, yet arguably not know that b is F, by virtue of not being sufficiently logically alert to follow the consequences through. If Mary's lack of knowledge were at all like this, there would be no threat to physicalism in it. But it is very hard to believe that her lack of knowledge could be remedied merely by her explicitly following through enough logical consequences of her vast physical knowledge. Endowing her with great logical acumen and persistence is not in itself enough to fill in the gaps in her knowledge. On being let out, she will not say "I could have worked all this out before by making some more purely logical inferences."

Thirdly, the knowledge Mary lacked which is of particular point for the knowledge argument against physicalism is *knowledge about the experiences of others*, not about her own. When she is let out, she has new experiences, color experiences she has never had before. It is not, therefore, an objection to physicalism that she learns *something* on being let out. Before she was let out, she could not have known facts about her experience of red, for there were no such facts to know. That the physicalist and nonphysicalist alike can agree on. After she is let out, things change; and physicalism can happily admit that she learns this; after all, some physical things will change, for instance, her brain states and their functional roles. The trouble for physicalism is that, after Mary sees her first ripe tomato, she will realize how impoverished her conception of the mental life of *others* has been *all along*. She will realize that there was, all the time she was carrying out her laborious investigations into the neurophysiologies of others and into the functional roles of their internal states, something about these people she was quite unaware of. All along their experiences (or many of them, those got from tomatoes, the sky, . . .) had a feature conspicuous to them but until now hidden from her (in fact, not in logic). But she knew all the physical facts about them all along; hence, what she did not know until her release is not a physical fact about their experiences. But it is a fact about them. That is the trouble for physicalism.

II. CHURCHLAND'S THREE OBJECTIONS[16]

(i) Churchland's first objection is that the knowledge argument contains a defect that "is simplicity itself" (23). The argument equivocates on the sense of "knows about." How so? Churchland suggests that the following is "a conveniently tightened version" of the knowledge argument:

(1) Mary knows everything there is to know about brain states and their properties.
(2) It is not the case that Mary knows everything there is to know about sensations and their properties.

Therefore, by Leibniz's law,

(3) Sensations and their properties ≠ brain states and their properties (23).

Churchland observes, plausibly enough, that the type or kind of knowledge involved in premise 1 is distinct from the kind of knowledge involved in premise 2. We might follow his lead and tag the first "knowledge by description," and the second "knowledge by acquaintance"; but, whatever the tags, he is right that the displayed argument involves a highly dubious use of Leibniz's law.

My reply is that the displayed argument may be convenient, but it is not accurate. It is not the knowledge argument. Take, for instance, premise 1. The whole thrust of the knowledge argument is that Mary (before her release) does *not* know everything there is to know about brain states and their properties, because she does not know about certain qualia associated with them. What is complete, according to the argument, is her knowledge of matters physical. A convenient and accurate way of displaying the argument is:

(1)′ Mary (before her release) knows everything physical there is to know about other people.
(2)′ Mary (before her release) does not know everything there is to know about other people (because she *learns* something about them on her release).

Therefore,

(3)′ There are truths about other people (and herself) which escape the physicalist story.

What is immediately to the point is not the kind, manner, or type of knowledge Mary has, but *what* she knows. What she knows beforehand is *ex hypothesi* everything physical there is to know, but is it everything there is to know? That is the crucial question.

NOTES

1. See, e.g., D. H. Mellor, "Materialism and Phenomenal Qualities," *Aristotelian Society Supp. Vol.* 47

(1973), 107–19; and J. W. Cornman, *Materialism and Sensations* (New Haven and London, 1971).

2. Particularly in discussion, but see, e.g., Keith Campbell, *Metaphysics* (Belmont, 1976), p. 67.
3. See, e.g., D. C. Dennett, "Current Issues in the Philosophy of Mind," *American Philosophical Quarterly*, 15 (1978), 249–61.
4. Put this, and similar simplifications below, in terms of Land's theory if you prefer. See, e.g., Edwin H. Land, "Experiments in Color Vision," *Scientific American*, 200 (5 May 1959), 84–99.
5. H. G. Wells, *The Country of the Blind and Other Stories* (London, n.d.).
6. See, e.g., Keith Campbell, *Body and Mind* (New York, 1970); and Robert Kirk, "Sentience and Behaviour," *Mind*, 83 (1974), 43–60.
7. I have presented the argument in an inter-world rather than the more usual intra-world fashion to avoid inessential complications to do with supervenience, causal anomalies and the like.
8. See, e.g., W. G. Lycan, "A New Lilliputian Argument against Machine Functionalism," *Philosophical Studies*, 35 (1979), 279–87, p. 280; and Don Locke, "Zombies, Schizophrenics and Purely Physical Objects," *Mind*, 85 (1976), 97–99.
9. See R. Kirk, "From Physical Explicability to Full-Blooded Materialism," *The Philosophical Quarterly*, 29 (1979), 229–37. See also the arguments against the modal intuition in, e.g., Sydney Shoemaker, "Functionalism and Qualia," *Philosophical Studies*, 27 (1975), 291–315.
10. *The Philosophical Review*, 83 (1974), 435–50. [Reprinted as the next entry in this volume.] Two things need to be said about this article. One is that, despite my dissociations to come, I am much indebted to it. The other is that the emphasis changes through the article, and by the end Nagel is objecting not so much to Physicalism as to all extant theories of mind for ignoring points of view, including those that admit (irreducible) qualia.
11. Knowledge *de se* in the terms of David Lewis, "Attitudes De Dicto and De Se," *The Philosophical Review*, 88 (1979), 513–43.
12. See Laurence Nemirow's comments on "What is it . . ." in his review of T. Nagel, *Mortal Questions*, in *The Philosophical Review*, 89 (1980), 473–77. I am indebted here in particular to a discussion with David Lewis.
13. See my review of K. Campbell, *Body and Mind*, in *Australasian Journal of Philosophy*, 50 (1972), 77–80.
14. Cf. Jean Piaget, "The Child's Conception of Physical Causality," reprinted in *The Essential Piaget* (London, 1977).
15. I am indebted to Robert Pargetter for a number of comments and, despite his dissent, to §IV of Paul E. Meehl, "The Compleat Autocerebroscopist" in *Mind, Matter, and Method*, ed. Paul Feyerabend and Grover Maxwell (Minneapolis, 1966).
16. Paul M. Churchland, "Reduction, Qualia, and the Direct Introspection of Brain States," *The Journal of Philosophy*, LXXXII, 1 (January 1985): 8–28. Unless otherwise stated, future page references are to this paper.

B CONSCIOUSNESS AND PERCEPTION

◈ CONSCIOUSNESS ◈

What Is It Like to Be a Bat?

THOMAS NAGEL

Thomas Nagel (1937–) is a Serbian-born American philosopher who has taught at Princeton University and now teaches at New York University. He is renowned for his accessible and insightful writing, having published widely on topics in the philosophy of mind, ethics, and political philosophy. Additional selections from his writings can be found in the "Life and Death" and the "Moral and Political Philosophy" sections.

The selection presented here is a widely reproduced essay by Nagel that was originally published in a philosophy journal in 1974. In it, Nagel offers a challenge to reductionist accounts of the mind.

Consciousness is what makes the mind–body problem really intractable. Perhaps that is why current discussions of the problem give it little attention or get it obviously wrong. The recent wave of reductionist euphoria has produced several analyses of mental phenomena and mental concepts designed to explain the possibility of some variety of materialism, psychophysical identification, or reduction.[1] But the problems dealt with are those common to this type of reduction and other types, and what makes the mind–body problem unique, and unlike the water–H_2O problem or the Turing machine–IBM machine problem or the lightning–electrical discharge problem or the gene–DNA problem or the oak tree–hydrocarbon problem, is ignored.

Every reductionist has his favorite analogy from modern science. It is most unlikely that any of these unrelated examples of successful reduction will shed light on the relation of mind to brain. But philosophers share the general human weakness for explanations of what is incomprehensible in terms suited for what is familiar and well understood, though entirely different. This has led to the acceptance of implausible accounts of the mental largely because they would permit familiar kinds of reduction. I shall try to explain why the usual examples do not help us to understand the relation between mind and body–why, indeed, we have at present no conception of what an explanation of the physical nature of a mental phenomenon would be. Without consciousness the mind–body problem would be much less interesting. With consciousness it seems hopeless. The most important and characteristic feature of conscious mental phenomena is very poorly understood. Most reductionist theories do not even try to explain it. And careful examination will show that no currently available concept of reduction is applicable to it. Perhaps a new theoretical form can

From *The Philosophical Review*, Vol. 83, pp. 435–450. Copyright © 1974, Cornell University Press. All rights reserved. Used by permission of the current publisher, Duke University Press.

be devised for the purpose, but such a solution, if it exists, lies in the distant intellectual future.

Conscious experience is a widespread phenomenon. It occurs at many levels of animal life, though we cannot be sure of its presence in the simpler organisms, and it is very difficult to say in general what provides evidence of it. (Some extremists have been prepared to deny it even of mammals other than man.) No doubt it occurs in countless forms totally unimaginable to us, on other planets in other solar systems throughout the universe. But no matter how the form may vary, the fact that an organism has conscious experience *at all* means, basically, that there is something it is like to *be* that organism. There may be further implications about the form of the experience; there may even (though I doubt it) be implications about the behavior of the organism. But fundamentally an organism has conscious mental states if and only if there is something that it is like to *be* that organism—something it is like *for* the organism.

We may call this the subjective character of experience. It is not captured by any of the familiar, recently devised reductive analyses of the mental, for all of them are logically compatible with its absence. It is not analyzable in terms of any explanatory system of functional states, or intentional states, since these could be ascribed to robots or automata that behaved like people though they experienced nothing.[2] It is not analyzable in terms of the causal role of experiences in relation to typical human behavior—for similar reasons.[3] I do not deny that conscious mental states and events cause behavior, nor that they may be given functional characterizations. I deny only that this kind of thing exhausts their analysis. Any reductionist program has to be based on an analysis of what is to be reduced. If the analysis leaves something out, the problem will be falsely posed. It is useless to base the defense of materialism on any analysis of mental phenomena that fails to deal explicitly with their subjective character. For there is no reason to suppose that a reduction which seems plausible when no attempt is made to account for consciousness can be extended to include consciousness. Without some idea, therefore, of what the subjective character of experience is, we cannot know what is required of physicalist theory.

While an account of the physical basis of mind must explain many things, this appears to be the most difficult. It is impossible to exclude the phenomenological features of experience from a reduction in the same way that one excludes the phenomenal features of an ordinary substance from a physical or chemical reduction of it—namely, by explaining them as effects on the minds of human observers.[4] If physicalism is to be defended, the phenomenological features must themselves be given a physical account. But when we examine their subjective character it seems that such a result is impossible. The reason is that every subjective phenomenon is essentially connected with a single point of view, and it seems inevitable that an objective, physical theory will abandon that point of view.

Let me first try to state the issue somewhat more fully than by referring to the relation between the subjective and the objective, or between the *pour soi* and the *en soi*. This is far from easy. Facts about what it is like to be an X are very peculiar, so peculiar that some may be inclined to doubt their reality, or the significance of claims about them. To illustrate the connexion between subjectivity and a point of view, and to make evident the importance of subjective features, it will help to explore the matter in relation to an example that brings out clearly the divergence between the two types of conception, subjective and objective.

I assume we all believe that bats have experience. After all, they are mammals, and there is no more doubt that they have experience than that mice or pigeons or whales have experience. I have chosen bats instead of wasps or flounders because if one travels too far down the phylogenetic tree, people gradually shed their faith that there is experience there at all. Bats, although more closely related to us than those other species, nevertheless present a range of activity and a sensory apparatus so different from ours that the problem I want to pose is exceptionally vivid (though it certainly could be raised with other species). Even without the benefit of philosophical reflection, anyone who has spent some time in an enclosed space with an excited bat knows what it is to encounter a fundamentally *alien* form of life.

I have said that the essence of the belief that bats have experience is that there is something that it is like to be a bat. Now we know that most bats (the microchiroptera, to be precise) perceive the external world primarily by sonar, or echolocation, detecting the reflections, from objects within range, of their own rapid, subtly modulated, high-frequency shrieks. Their brains are designed to correlate the outgoing impulses with the subsequent echoes, and the information thus acquired enables bats to make precise discriminations of distance, size, shape, motion, and texture comparable to those we make by vision. But bat sonar, though clearly a form of perception, is not similar in its operation to any sense that we possess, and there is no reason to suppose that it is subjectively like anything we can experience or imagine. This appears to create difficulties for the notion of what it is like to be a bat. We must consider whether any method will permit us to extrapolate to the inner life of the bat from our own case,[5] and if not, what alternative methods there may be for understanding the notion.

Our own experience provides the basic material for our imagination, whose range is therefore limited. It will not help to try to imagine that one has webbing on one's arms, which enables one to fly around at dusk and dawn catching insects in one's mouth; that one has very poor vision, and perceives the surrounding world by a system of reflected high-frequency sound signals; and that one spends the day hanging upside down by one's feet in an attic. Insofar as I can imagine this (which is not very far), it tells me only what it would be like for *me* to behave as a bat behaves. But that is not the question. I want to know what it is like for a *bat* to be a bat. Yet if I try to imagine this, I am restricted to the resources of my own mind, and those resources are inadequate to the task. I cannot perform it either by imagining additions to my present experience, or by imagining segments gradually subtracted from it, or by imagining some combination of additions, subtractions, and modifications.

To the extent that I could look and behave like a wasp or a bat without changing my fundamental structure, my experiences would not be anything like the experiences of those animals. On the other hand, it is doubtful that any meaning can be attached to the supposition that I should possess the internal neurophysiological constitution of a bat. Even if I could by gradual degrees be transformed into a bat, nothing in my present constitution enables me to imagine what the experiences of such a future stage of myself thus metamorphosed would be like. The best evidence would come from the experiences of bats, if we only knew what they were like.

So if extrapolation from our own case is involved in the idea of what it is like to be a bat, the extrapolation must be incompletable. We cannot form more than a schematic conception of what it *is* like. For example, we may ascribe general *types* of experience on the basis of the animal's structure and behavior. Thus we describe bat sonar as a form of three-dimensional forward perception; we believe that bats feel some versions of pain, fear, hunger, and lust, and that they have other, more familiar types of perception besides sonar. But we believe that these experiences also have in each case a specific subjective character, which it is beyond our ability to conceive. And if there is conscious life elsewhere in the universe, it is likely that some of it will not be describable even in the most general experiential terms available to us.[6] (The problem is not confined to exotic cases, however, for it exists between one person and another. The subjective character of the experience of a person deaf and blind from birth is not accessible to me, for example, nor presumably is mine to him. This does not prevent us each from believing that the other's experience has such a subjective character.)

If anyone is inclined to deny that we can believe in the existence of facts like this whose exact nature we cannot possibly conceive, he should reflect that in contemplating the bats we are in much the same position that intelligent bats or Martians[7] would occupy if they tried to form a conception of what it was like to be us. The structure of their own minds might make it impossible for them to succeed, but we know they would be wrong to conclude that there is not anything precise that it is like to be us: that only certain general types of mental state could be ascribed to us (perhaps perception and appetite would be concepts common to us both; perhaps not). We know they would be wrong to draw such a skeptical conclusion because we know what it is like to be us. And we know that while it includes an enormous amount of variation and complexity, and while we do not possess the vocabulary to describe it adequately, its subjective character is highly specific, and in some respects describable in terms that can be understood only by creatures like us. The fact that we cannot expect ever to accommodate in our language a detailed description of Martian or bat phenomenology should not lead us to dismiss as meaningless the claim that bats and Martians have experiences fully comparable in richness of detail to our own. It would be fine if someone were to develop concepts and a theory that enabled us to think about those things; but such an understanding may be permanently denied to us by the limits of our nature. And to deny the reality or logical significance of what we can never describe or understand is the crudest form of cognitive dissonance.

This brings us to the edge of a topic that requires much more discussion than I can give it here: namely, the relation between facts on the one hand and conceptual schemes or systems of representation on the other. My realism about the subjective domain in all its forms implies a belief in the existence of facts beyond the reach of human concepts. Certainly it is possible for a human being to believe that there are facts which humans never *will* possess the requisite concepts to represent or comprehend. Indeed, it would be foolish to doubt this, given the finiteness of humanity's expectations. After all, there would have been transfinite numbers even if everyone had been wiped out by the Black Death before Cantor* discovered them. But one might also believe that there are facts which *could* not ever be represented or comprehended by human beings, even if the species lasted for ever—simply because our structure does not permit us to operate with concepts of the requisite type. This impossibility might even be observed by other beings, but it is not clear that the existence of such beings, or the possibility of their existence, is a precondition of the significance of the hypothesis that there are humanly inaccessible facts. (After all, the nature of beings with access to humanly inaccessible facts is presumably itself a humanly inaccessible fact.) Reflection on what it is like to be a bat seems to lead us, therefore, to the conclusion that there are facts that do not consist in the truth of propositions expressible in a human language. We can be compelled to recognize the existence of such facts without being able to state or comprehend them.

I shall not pursue this subject, however. Its bearing on the topic before us (namely, the mind–body problem) is that it enables us to make a general observation about the subjective character of experience. Whatever may be the status of facts about what it is like to be a human being, or a bat, or a Martian, these appear to be facts that embody a particular point of view.

I am not adverting here to the alleged privacy of experience to its possessor. The point of view in question is not one accessible only to a single individual. Rather it is a *type*. It is often possible to take up a point of view other than one's own, so the comprehension of such facts is not limited to one's own case. There is a sense in which phenomenological facts are perfectly objective: one person can know or say of another what the quality of the other's experience is. They are subjective, however, in the sense that even this objective ascription of experience is possible only for someone sufficiently similar to the object of ascription to be able to adopt his point of view—to understand the ascription in the first person as well as in the third, so to speak. The more different from oneself the other experiencer is, the less success one can expect with this enterprise. In our own case we occupy the relevant point of view, but we will have as much difficulty understanding our own experience properly if we approach it from another point of view as we would if we tried to understand the experience of another species without taking up *its* point of view.[8]

This bears directly on the mind–body problem. For if the facts of experience—facts about what it is like *for* the experiencing organism—are accessible only from one point of view, then it is a mystery how the true character of experiences could be revealed in the physical operation of that organism. The latter is a domain of objective facts *par excellence*—the kind that can be observed and understood from many points of view and by individuals with differing

* Georg Cantor (1845–1918) was a great German mathematician of Russian descent who (among his many contributions to mathematics) discovered transfinite numbers.

perceptual systems. There are no comparable imaginative obstacles to the acquisition of knowledge about bat neurophysiology by human scientists, and intelligent bats or Martians might learn more about the human brain than we ever will.

This is not by itself an argument against reduction. A Martian scientist with no understanding of visual perception could understand the rainbow, or lightning, or clouds as physical phenomena, though he would never be able to understand the human concepts of rainbow, lightning, or cloud, or the place these things occupy in our phenomenal world. The objective nature of the things picked out by these concepts could be apprehended by him because, although the concepts themselves are connected with a particular point of view and a particular visual phenomenology, the things apprehended from that point of view are not: they are observable from the point of view but external to it; hence they can be comprehended from other points of view also, either by the same organisms or by others. Lighting has an objective character that is not exhausted by its visual appearance, and this can be investigated by a Martian without vision. To be precise, it has a *more* objective character than is revealed in its visual appearance. In speaking of the move from subjective to objective characterization, I wish to remain noncommittal about the existence of an end point, the completely objective intrinsic nature of the thing, which one might or might not be able to reach. It may be more accurate to think of objectivity as a direction in which the understanding can travel. And in understanding a phenomenon like lightning, it is legitimate to go as far away as one can from a strictly human viewpoint.[9]

In the case of experience, on the other hand, the connexion with a particular point of view seems much closer. It is difficult to understand what could be meant by the *objective* character of an experience, apart from the particular point of view from which its subject apprehends it. After all, what would be left of what it was like to be a bat if one removed the viewpoint of the bat? But if experience does not have, in addition to its subjective character, an objective nature that can be apprehended from many different points of view, then how can it be supposed that a Martian investigating my brain might be observing physical processes which were my mental processes (as he might observe physical processes which were bolts of lightning), only from a different point of view? How, for that matter, could a human physiologist observe them from another point of view?[10]

We appear to be faced with a general difficulty about psychophysical reduction. In other areas the process of reduction is a move in the direction of greater objectivity, toward a more accurate view of the real nature of things. This is accomplished by reducing our dependence on individual or species-specific points of view toward the object of investigation. We describe it not in terms of the impressions it makes on our senses, but in terms of its more general effects and of properties detectable by means other than the human senses. The less it depends on a specifically human viewpoint, the more objective is our description. It is possible to follow this path because although the concepts and ideas we employ in thinking about the external world are initially applied from a point of view that involves our perceptual apparatus, they are used by us to refer to things beyond themselves—toward which we *have* the phenomenal point of view. Therefore we can abandon it in favor of another, and still be thinking about the same things.

Experience itself, however, does not seem to fit the pattern. The idea of moving from appearance to reality seems to make no sense here. What is the analogue in this case to pursuing a more objective understanding of the same phenomena by abandoning the initial subjective viewpoint toward them in favour of another that is more objective but concerns the same thing? Certainly it *appears* unlikely that we will get closer to the real nature of human experience by leaving behind the particularity of our human point of view and striving for a description in terms accessible to beings that could not imagine what it was like to be us. If the subjective character of experience is fully comprehensible only from one point of view, then any shift to greater objectivity—that is, less attachment to a specific viewpoint—does not take us nearer to the real nature of the phenomenon: it takes us farther away from it.

In a sense, the seeds of this objection to the reducibility of experience are already detectable in successful cases of reduction; for in discovering sound to be, in reality, a wave phenomenon in air or other media, we leave behind one viewpoint to take up another, and the auditory, human or animal viewpoint that we leave behind remains unreduced. Members of radically different species may both understand the same physical events in objective terms, and this does not require that they understand the phenomenal forms in which those events appear to the senses of members of the other species. Thus it is a condition of their referring to a common reality that their more particular viewpoints are not part of the common reality that they both apprehend. The reduction can succeed only if the species-specific viewpoint is omitted from what is to be reduced.

But while we are right to leave this point of view aside in seeking a fuller understanding of the external world, we cannot ignore it permanently, since it is the essence of the internal world, and not merely a point of view on it. Most of the neobehaviorism of recent philosophical psychology results from the effort to substitute an objective concept of mind for the real thing, in order to have nothing left over which cannot be reduced. If we acknowledge that a physical theory of mind must account for the subjective character of experience, we must admit that no presently available conception gives us a clue how this could be done. The problem is unique. If mental processes are indeed physical processes, then there is something it is like, intrinsically,[11] to undergo certain physical processes. What it is for such a thing to be the case remains a mystery.

What moral should be drawn from these reflections, and what should be done next? It would be a mistake to conclude that physicalism must be false. Nothing is proved by the inadequacy of physicalist hypotheses that assume a faulty objective analysis of mind. It would be truer to say that physicalism is a position we cannot understand because we do not at present have any conception of how it might be true. Perhaps it will be thought unreasonable to require such a conception as a condition of understanding. After all, it might be said, the meaning of physicalism is clear enough: mental states are states of the body; mental events are physical events. We do not know *which* physical states and events they are, but that should not prevent us from understanding the hypothesis. What could be clearer than the words "is" and "are"?

But I believe it is precisely this apparent clarity of the word "is" that is deceptive. Usually, when we are told that X is Y we know *how* it is supposed to be true, but that depends on a conceptual or theoretical background and is not conveyed by the "is" alone. We know how both "X" and "Y" refer, and the kinds of things to which they refer, and we have a rough idea how the two referential paths might converge on a single thing, be it an object, a person, a process, an event or whatever. But when the two terms of the identification are very disparate it may not be so clear how it could be true. We may not have even a rough idea of how the two referential paths could converge, or what kind of things they might converge on, and a theoretical framework may have to be supplied to enable us to understand this. Without the framework, an air of mysticism surrounds the identification.

This explains the magical flavor of popular presentations of fundamental scientific discoveries, given out as propositions to which one must subscribe without really understanding them. For example, people are now told at an early age that all matter is really energy. But despite the fact that they know what "is" means, most of them never form a conception of what makes this claim true, because they lack the theoretical background.

At the present time the status of physicalism is similar to that which the hypothesis that matter is energy would have had if uttered by a pre-Socratic philosopher. We do not have the beginnings of a conception of how it might be true. In order to understand the hypothesis that a mental event is a physical event, we require more than an understanding of the word "is." The idea of how a mental and a physical term might refer to the same thing is lacking, and the usual analogies with theoretical identification in other fields fail to supply it. They fail because if we construe the reference of mental terms to physical events on the usual model, we either get a reappearance of separate subjective events as the effects through which mental reference to physical events is secured, or else we get a false account of how mental terms refer (for example, a causal behaviorist one).

Strangely enough, we may have evidence for the truth of something we cannot really understand.

Suppose a caterpillar is locked in a sterile safe by someone unfamiliar with insect metamorphosis, and weeks later the safe is reopened, revealing a butterfly. If the person knows that the safe has been shut the whole time, he has reason to believe that the butterfly is or was once the caterpillar, without having any idea in what sense this might be so. (One possibility is that the caterpillar contained a tiny winged parasite that devoured it and grew into the butterfly.)

It is conceivable that we are in such a position with regard to physicalism. Donald Davidson has argued that if mental events have physical causes and effects, they must have physical descriptions. He holds that we have reason to believe this even though we do not—and in fact *could* not—have a general psychophysical theory.[12] His argument applies to intentional mental events, but I think we also have some reason to believe that sensations are physical processes, without being in a position to understand how. Davidson's position is that certain physical events have irreducibly mental properties, and perhaps some view describable in this way is correct. But nothing of which we can now form a conception corresponds to it; nor have we any idea what a theory would be like that enabled us to conceive of it.[13]

Very little work has been done on the basic question (from which mention of the brain can be entirely omitted) whether any sense can be made of experiences' having an objective character at all. Does it make sense, in other words, to ask what my experiences are *really* like, as opposed to how they appear to me? We cannot genuinely understand the hypothesis that their nature is captured in a physical description unless we understand the more fundamental idea that they *have* an objective nature (or that objective processes can have a subjective nature).[14]

I should like to close with a speculative proposal. It may be possible to approach the gap between subjective and objective from another direction. Setting aside temporarily the relation between the mind and the brain, we can pursue a more objective understanding of the mental in its own right. At present we are completely unequipped to think about the subjective character of experience without relying on the imagination—without taking up the point of view of the experiential subject. This should be regarded as a challenge to form new concepts and devise a new method—an objective phenomenology not dependent on empathy or the imagination. Though presumably it would not capture everything, its goal would be to describe, at least in part, the subjective character of experiences in a form comprehensible to beings incapable of having those experiences.

We would have to develop such a phenomenology to describe the sonar experiences of bats; but it would also be possible to begin with humans. One might try, for example, to develop concepts that could be used to explain to a person blind from birth what it was like to see. One would reach a blank wall eventually, but it should be possible to devise a method of expressing in objective terms much more than we can at present, and with much greater precision. The loose intermodal analogies—for example, "Red is like the sound of a trumpet"—which crop up in discussions of this subject are of little use. That should be clear to anyone who has both heard a trumpet and seen red. But structural features of perception might be more accessible to objective description, even though something would be left out. And concepts alternative to those we learn in the first person may enable us to arrive at a kind of understanding even of our own experience which is denied us by the very ease of description and lack of distance that subjective concepts afford.

Apart from its own interest, a phenomenology that is in this sense objective may permit questions about the physical[15] basis of experience to assume a more intelligible form. Aspects of subjective experience that admitted this kind of objective description might be better candidates for objective explanations of a more familiar sort. But whether or not this guess is correct, it seems unlikely that any physical theory of mind can be contemplated until more thought has been given to the general problem of subjective and objective. Otherwise we cannot even pose the mind–body problem without sidestepping it.

NOTES

1. Examples are J. J. C. Smart, *Philosophy and Scientific Realism* (London: Routledge & Kegan Paul, 1963); David K. Lewis, "An Argument for the Identity

Theory," *Journal of Philosophy*, LXIII (1966), reprinted with addenda in David M. Rosenthal, *Materialism & the Mind–Body Problem*, (Englewood Cliffs, N.J.: Prentice-Hall, 1971); Hilary Putnam, "Psychological Predicates," in *Art, Mind, & Religion*, ed. W. H. Capitan and D. D. Merrill (Pittsburgh: University of Pittsburgh Press, 1967), reprinted in *Materialism*, ed. Rosenthal, as "The Nature of Mental States"; D. M. Armstrong, *A Materialist Theory of the Mind* (London: Routledge & Kegan Paul, 1968); D. C. Dennett, *Content and Consciousness* (London: Routledge & Kegan Paul, 1969). I have expressed earlier doubts in "Armstrong on the Mind," *Philosophical Review*, LXXIX (1970), 394–403; a review of Dennett, *Journal of Philosophy*, LXIX (1972); and chapter 11 above. See also Saul Kripke, "Naming and Necessity," in *Semantics of Natural Language*, ed. D. Davidson and G. Harman (Dordrecht: Reidel, 1972), esp. pp. 334–42; and M. T. Thornton, "Ostensive Terms and Materialism," *The Monist*, LVI (1972), 193–214.

2. Perhaps there could not actually be such robots. Perhaps anything complex enough to behave like a person would have experiences. But that, if true, is a fact which cannot be discovered merely by analyzing the concept of experience.
3. It is not equivalent to that about which we are incorrigible, both because we are not incorrigible about experience and because experience is present in animals lacking language and thought, who have no beliefs at all about their experiences.
4. Cf. Richard Rorty, "Mind–Body Identity, Privacy, and Categories," *Review of Metaphysics*, XIX (1965), esp. 37–8.
5. By "our own case" I do not mean just "my own case," but rather the mentalistic ideas that we apply unproblematically to ourselves and other human beings.
6. Therefore the analogical form of the English expression "what it is *like*" is misleading. It does not mean "what (in our experience) it *resembles*," but rather "how it is for the subject himself."
7. Any intelligent extraterrestrial beings totally different from us.
8. It may be easier than I suppose to transcend inter-species barriers with the aid of the imagination. For example, blind people are able to detect objects near them by a form of sonar, using vocal clicks or taps of a cane. Perhaps if one knew what that was like, one could by extension imagine roughly what it was like to possess the much more refined sonar of a bat. The distance between oneself and other persons and other species can fall anywhere on a continuum. Even for other persons the understanding of what it is like to be them is only partial, and when one moves to species very different from oneself, a lesser degree of partial understanding may still be available. The imagination is remarkably flexible. My point, however, is not that we cannot *know* what it is like to be a bat. I am not raising that epistemological problem. My point is rather that even to form a *conception* of what it is like to be a bat (and *a fortiori* to know what it is like to be a bat) one must take up the bat's point of view. If one can take it up roughly, or partially, then one's conception will also be rough or partial. Or so it seems in our present state of understanding.
9. The problem I am going to raise can therefore be posed even if the distinction between more subjective and more objective descriptions or viewpoints can itself be made only within a larger human point of view. I do not accept this kind of conceptual relativism, but it need not be refuted to make the point that psychophysical reduction cannot be accommodated by the subjective-to-objective model familiar from other cases.
10. The problem is not just that when I look at the *Mona Lisa*, my visual experience has a certain quality, no trace of which is to be found by someone looking into my brain. For even if he did observe there a tiny image of the *Mona Lisa*, he would have no reason to identify it with the experience.
11. The relation would therefore not be a contingent one, like that of a cause and its distinct effect. It would be necessarily true that a certain physical state felt a certain way. Saul Kripke in *Semantics of Natural Language* (ed. Davidson and Harman) argues that causal behaviorist and related analyses of the mental fail because they construe, e.g., "pain" as a merely contingent name of pains. The subjective character of an experience ("its immediate phenomenological quality" Kripke calls it (p. 340)) is the essential property left out by such analyses, and the one in virtue of which it is, necessarily, the

experience it is. My view is closely related to his. Like Kripke, I find the hypothesis that a certain brain state should *necessarily* have a certain subjective character incomprehensible without further explanation. No such explanation emerges from theories which view the mind–brain relation as contingent, but perhaps there are other alternatives, not yet discovered.

A theory that explained how the mind–brain relation was necessary would still leave us with Kripke's problem of explaining why it nevertheless appears contingent. That difficulty seems to me surmountable, in the following way. We may imagine something by representing it to ourselves either perceptually, sympathetically, or symbolically. I shall not try to say how symbolic imagination works, but part of what happens in the other two cases is this. To imagine something perceptually, we put ourselves in a conscious state resembling the state we would be in if we perceived it. To imagine something sympathetically, we put ourselves in a conscious state resembling the thing itself. (This method can be used only to imagine mental events and states–our own or another's.) When we try to imagine a mental state occurring without its associated brain state, we first sympathetically imagine the occurrence of the mental state: that is, we put ourselves into a state that resembles it mentally. At the same time, we attempt perceptually to imagine the nonoccurrence of the associated physical state, by putting ourselves into another state unconnected with the first: one resembling that which we would be in if we perceived the nonoccurrence of the physical state. Where the imagination of physical features is perceptual and the imagination of mental features is sympathetic, it appears to us that we can imagine any experience occurring without its associated brain state, and vice versa. The relation between them will appear contingent even if it is necessary, because of the independence of the disparate types of imagination.

(Solipsism, incidentally, results if one misinterprets sympathetic imagination as if it worked like perceptual imagination: it then seems impossible to imagine any experience that is not one's own.)

12. See "Mental Events" in *Experience and Theory*, ed. Lawrence Foster and J. W. Swanson (Amherst: University of Massachusetts Press, 1970); though I do not understand the argument against psychophysical laws.
13. Similar remarks apply to my paper "Physicalism," *Philosophical Review*, LXXIV (1965), 339–56, reprinted with postscript in *Modern Materialism*, ed. John O'Connor (New York: Harcourt Brace Jovanovich, 1969).
14. This question also lies at the heart of the problem of other minds, whose close connection with the mind–body problem is often overlooked. If one understood how subjective experience could have an objective nature, one would understand the existence of subjects other than oneself.
15. I have not defined the term "physical." Obviously it does not apply just to what can be described by the concepts of contemporary physics, since we expect further developments. Some may think there is nothing to prevent mental phenomena from eventually being recognized as physical in their own right. But whatever else may be said of the physical, it has to be objective. So if our idea of the physical ever expands to include mental phenomena, it will have to assign them an objective character–whether or not this is done by analyzing them in terms of other phenomena already regarded as physical. It seems to me more likely, however, that mental–physical relations will eventually be expressed in a theory whose fundamental terms cannot be placed clearly in either category.

Quining Qualia

DANIEL C. DENNETT

American philosopher Daniel Dennett (1942–) has spent his career teaching at Tufts University, where he also directs a research center devoted to philosophy of mind and cognitive science. Well-known for his witty and accessible style, he has published both scholarly and popular works on a broad range of topics, including the philosophy of mind, intentionality, consciousness, free will, and religion. He was a student of Gilbert Ryle, whose work also appears in this volume.

The text presented here originally appeared in print under the title "Quining Qualia" in 1988; further information about its history can be found in footnote 14. The term *quine* in the title refers to the important American philosopher Willard Van Orman Quine (1908–2000), a selection from whose writings appears in the "Knowledge and the Nature of Reality" section.

1. CORRALLING THE QUICKSILVER

"Qualia" is an unfamiliar term for something that could not be more familiar to each of us: the *ways things seem to us*. As is so often the case with philosophical jargon, it is easier to give examples than to give a definition of the term. Look at a glass of milk at sunset; *the way it looks to you*—the particular, personal, subjective visual quality of the glass of milk is the *quale* of your visual experience at the moment. The *way the milk tastes to you then* is another, gustatory, *quale*, and *how it sounds to you* as you swallow is an auditory *quale*. These various "properties of conscious experience" are prime examples of *qualia*. Nothing, it seems, could you know more intimately than your own qualia; let the entire universe be some vast illusion, some mere figment of Descartes's evil demon, and yet what the figment is *made of* (for you) will be the *qualia* of your hallucinatory experiences. Descartes claimed to doubt everything that could be doubted, but he never doubted that his conscious experiences had qualia, the properties by which he knew or apprehended them.

The verb "to quine" is even more esoteric. It comes from *The Philosophical Lexicon* (Dennett 1978c, 8th edn 1987), a satirical dictionary of eponyms: "quine, *v*. To deny resolutely the existence or importance of something real or significant." At first blush it would be hard to imagine a more quixotic quest than trying to convince people that there are no such properties as qualia; hence the ironic title of this chapter. But I am not kidding.

My goal is subversive. I am out to overthrow an idea that, in one form or another, is "obvious" to most people—to scientists, philosophers, lay people. My quarry is frustratingly elusive; no sooner does it retreat in the face of one argument than "it" reappears, apparently innocent of all charges, in a new guise.

Which idea of qualia am I trying to extirpate? Everything real has properties, and since I don't deny the reality of conscious experience, I grant that conscious experience has properties. I grant moreover that each person's states of consciousness have properties in virtue of which those states have the experiential content that they do. That is to say, whenever someone experiences something as being one way rather than another, this is true in virtue of some property of something happening in them at the time, but these properties are so unlike the properties traditionally imputed to consciousness that it would be grossly misleading to call any of them the long-sought qualia. Qualia are supposed to be *special* properties, in some hard-to-define way. My claim—which can only come into focus as we proceed—is

Reprinted from *Consciousness in Contemporary Science*, ed. A. Marcel and E. Bisiach (1992). Reprinted by permission of Oxford University Press.
Copyright © Daniel C. Dennett 1988.

that conscious experience has *no* properties that are special in *any* of the ways qualia have been supposed to be special.

The standard reaction to this claim is the complacent acknowledgment that while some people may indeed have succumbed to one confusion or fanaticism or another, one's own appeal to a modest, innocent notion of properties of subjective experience is surely safe. It is just that presumption of innocence I want to overthrow. I want to shift the burden of proof, so that anyone who wants to appeal to private, subjective properties has to prove first that in so doing they are *not* making a mistake. This status of *guilty until proven innocent* is neither unprecedented nor indefensible (so long as we restrict ourselves to concepts). Today, no biologist would dream of supposing that it was quite all right to appeal to some innocent concept of *élan vital*. Of course one *could* use the term to mean something in good standing; one could use *élan vital* as one's name for DNA, for instance, but this would be foolish nomenclature, considering the deserved suspicion with which the term is nowadays burdened. I want to make it just as uncomfortable for anyone to talk of qualia–or "raw feels" or "phenomenal properties" or "subjective and intrinsic properties" or "the qualitative character" of experience–with the standard presumption that they, and everyone else, knows what on earth they are talking about.[1]

What are qualia, *exactly?* This obstreperous query is dismissed by one author ("only half in jest") by invoking Louis Armstrong's legendary reply when asked what jazz was: "If you got to ask, you ain't never gonna get to know." (Block 1978 p. 281). This amusing tactic perfectly illustrates the presumption that is my target. If I succeed in my task, this move, which passes muster in most circles today, will look as quaint and insupportable as a jocular appeal to the ludicrousness of a living thing—a living thing, mind you!—doubting the existence of *élan vital*.

My claim, then, is not just that the various technical or theoretical concepts of qualia are vague or equivocal, but that the source concept, the "pretheoretical" notion of which the former are presumed to be refinements, is so thoroughly confused that even if we undertook to salvage some "lowest common denominator" from the theoreticians' proposals, any acceptable version would have to be so radically unlike the ill-formed notions that are commonly appealed to that it would be tactically obtuse–not to say Pickwickian—to cling to the term. Far better, tactically, to declare that there simply are no qualia at all.[2]

Rigorous arguments only work on well-defined materials, and since my goal is to destroy our faith in the pretheoretical or "intuitive" concept, the right tools for my task are intuition pumps, not formal arguments. What follows is a series of fifteen intuition pumps, posed in a sequence designed to flush out—and then flush away—the offending intuitions. In section 2, I will use the first two intuition pumps to focus attention on the traditional notion. It will be the burden of the rest of the paper to convince you that these two pumps, for all their effectiveness, mislead us and should be discarded. In section 3, the next four intuition pumps create and refine a "paradox" lurking in the tradition. This is not a formal paradox, but only a very powerful argument pitted against some almost irresistibly attractive ideas. In section 4, six more intuition pumps are arrayed in order to dissipate the attractiveness of those ideas, and section 5 drives this point home by showing how hapless those ideas prove to be when confronted with some real cases of anomalous experience. This will leave something of a vacuum, and in the final section three more intuition pumps are used to introduce and motivate some suitable replacements for the banished notions.

2. THE SPECIAL PROPERTIES OF QUALIA

Intuition pump #1: watching you eat cauliflower. I see you tucking eagerly into a helping of steaming cauliflower, the merest whiff of which makes me faintly nauseated, and I find myself wondering how you could possibly relish *that taste,* and then it occurs to me that to you, cauliflower probably tastes (must taste?) different. A plausible hypothesis, it seems, especially since I know that the very same food often tastes different to me at different times. For instance, my first sip of breakfast orange juice tastes much sweeter than my second sip if I interpose a bit of pancakes and maple syrup, but after a swallow or two of coffee, the orange juice goes back to tasting (roughly? exactly?) the way it did the first sip. Surely we want to say (or think about) such things, and surely we are not wildly wrong when we do, so . . . surely it is quite OK to talk of *the way the juice tastes to Dennett at time t*, and ask whether it is just the same as or different from *the way the juice tastes to Dennett at time t′* or *the way the juice tastes to Jones at time t*.

This "conclusion" seems innocent, but right here we have already made the big mistake. The final step presumes that we can isolate the qualia from everything else that is going on—at least in principle or for the sake of argument. What counts as *the way the juice tastes to x* can be distinguished, one supposes, from what is a mere accompaniment, contributory cause, or by-product of this "central" way. One dimly imagines taking such cases and stripping them down gradually to the essentials, leaving their common residuum, the way things look, sound, feel, taste, smell to various individuals at various times, independently of how those individuals are stimulated or non-perceptually affected, and independently of how they are subsequently disposed to behave or believe. The mistake is not in supposing that we can in practice ever or always perform this act of purification with certainty, but the more fundamental mistake of supposing that there is such a residual property to take seriously, however uncertain our actual attempts at isolation of instances might be.

The examples that seduce us are abundant in every modality. I cannot imagine, will never know, could never know, it seems, how Bach sounded to Glenn Gould. (I can barely recover in my memory the way Bach sounded to me when I was a child.) And I cannot know, it seems, what it is like to be a bat (Nagel 1974), or whether you see what I see, colorwise, when we look up at a clear "blue" sky. The homely cases convince us of the reality of these special properties—those subjective tastes, looks, aromas, sounds—that we then apparently isolate for definition by this philosophical distillation.

The specialness of these properties is hard to pin down, but can be seen at work in *intuition pump #2: the wine-tasting machine*. Could Gallo Brothers replace their human wine tasters with a machine? A computer-based "expert system" for quality control and classification is probably within the bounds of existing technology. We now know enough about the relevant chemistry to make the transducers that would replace taste buds and olfactory organs (delicate color vision would perhaps be more problematic), and we can imagine using the output of such transducers as the raw material—the "sense data" in effect—for elaborate evaluations, descriptions, classifications. Pour the sample in the funnel and, in a few minutes or hours, the system would type out a chemical assay, along with commentary: "a flamboyant and velvety Pinot, though lacking in stamina"—or words to such effect. Such a machine might well perform better than human wine tasters on all reasonable tests of accuracy and consistency the winemakers could devise,[3] but *surely* no matter how "sensitive" and "discriminating" such a system becomes, it will never have, and enjoy, what *we* do when we taste a wine: the qualia of conscious experience! Whatever informational, dispositional, functional properties its internal states have, none of them will be special in the way qualia are. If you share that intuition, you believe that there are qualia in the sense I am targeting for demolition.

What is special about qualia? Traditional analyses suggest some fascinating second-order properties of these properties. First, since one *cannot say* to another, no matter how eloquent one is and no matter how cooperative and imaginative one's audience is, exactly what way one is currently seeing, tasting, smelling and so forth, qualia are *ineffable*—in fact the paradigm cases of ineffable items. According to tradition, at least part of the reason why qualia are ineffable is that they are *intrinsic* properties—which seems to imply *inter alia* that they are somehow atomic and unanalyzable. Since they are "simple" or "homogeneous" there is nothing to get hold of when trying to describe such a property to one unacquainted with the particular instance in question.

Moreover, verbal comparisons are not the only cross-checks ruled out. *Any* objective, physiological or "merely behavioral" test—such as those passed by the imaginary wine-tasting system—would of necessity miss the target (one can plausibly argue), so all interpersonal comparisons of these ways-of-appearing are (apparently) systematically impossible. In other words, qualia are essentially *private* properties. And, finally, since they *are* properties of *my experiences* (they're not chopped liver, and they're not properties of, say, my cerebral blood flow—or haven't you been paying attention?), qualia are essentially directly accessible to the consciousness of their experiencer (whatever that means) or qualia are properties of one's experience with which one is intimately or directly acquainted (whatever that means) or "immediate phenomenological qualities" (Block 1978) (whatever that means). They are, after all, the very properties the appreciation of which permits us to identify our conscious states. So, to summarize the tradition, qualia are supposed to be properties of a subject's mental states that are

1. ineffable
2. intrinsic
3. private
4. directly or immediately apprehensible in consciousness

Thus are qualia introduced onto the philosophical stage. They have seemed to be very significant properties to some theorists because they have seemed to provide an insurmountable and unavoidable stumbling block to functionalism, or more broadly, to materialism, or more broadly still, to any purely "third-person" objective viewpoint or approach to the world (Nagel 1986). Theorists of the contrary persuasion have patiently and ingeniously knocked down all the arguments, and said most of the right things, but they have made a tactical error, I am claiming, of saying in one way or another: "We theorists can handle *those qualia* you talk about just fine; we will show that you are just slightly in error about the nature of qualia." What they ought to have said is: "What qualia?"

My challenge strikes some theorists as outrageous or misguided because they think they have a much blander and hence less vulnerable notion of qualia to begin with. They think I am setting up and knocking down a strawman, and ask, in effect: "Who said qualia are ineffable, intrinsic, private, directly apprehensible ways things seem to one?" Since my suggested fourfold essence of qualia may strike many readers as tendentious, it may be instructive to consider, briefly, an apparently milder alternative: qualia are simply "the qualitative or phenomenal features of sense experience[s], in virtue of having which they resemble and differ from each other, qualitatively, in the ways they do" (Shoemaker 1982, p. 367). Surely I do not mean to deny *those* features!

I reply: it all depends on what "qualitative or phenomenal" comes to. Shoemaker contrasts *qualitative* similarity and difference with "intentional" similarity and difference—similarity and difference of the properties an experience represents or is "of." That is clear enough, but what then of "phenomenal"? Among the non-intentional (and hence qualitative?) properties of my visual states are their physiological properties. Might these very properties be the qualia Shoemaker speaks of? It is supposed to be obvious, I take it, that these sorts of features are ruled out, because they are not "accessible to introspection" (Shoemaker, private correspondence). These are features of my visual *state*, perhaps, but not of my visual *experience*. They are not *phenomenal* properties.

But then another non-intentional similarity some of my visual states share is that they tend to make me think about going to bed. I think this feature of them *is* accessible to introspection—on any ordinary, pretheoretical construal. Is that a phenomenal property or not? The term "phenomenal" means nothing obvious and untendentious to me, and looks suspiciously like a gesture in the direction leading back to ineffable, private, directly apprehensible ways things seem to one.[4]

I suspect, in fact, that many are unwilling to take my radical challenge seriously largely because they want so much for qualia to be acknowledged. Qualia seem to many people to be the last ditch defense of the inwardness and elusiveness of our minds, a bulwark against creeping mechanism. They are sure there must be *some* sound path from the homely cases to the redoubtable category of the philosophers, since otherwise their last bastion of specialness will be stormed by science.

This special status for these presumed properties has a long and eminent tradition. I believe it was Einstein who once advised us that science could not give us the *taste* of the soup. Could such a wise man have been wrong? Yes, if he is taken to have been trying to remind us of the qualia that hide forever from objective science in the subjective inner sancta of our minds. There are no such things. Another wise man said so—Wittgenstein (1958, esp. pp. 91–100). Actually, what he said was:

> The thing in the box has no place in the language-game at all; not even as a *something;* for the box might even be empty—No, one can "divide through" by the thing in the box; it cancels out, whatever it is. (p. 100)

and then he went on to hedge his bets by saying "It is not a *something*, but not a *nothing* either! The conclusion was only that a nothing would serve just as well as a something about which nothing could be said" (p. 102). Both Einstein's and Wittgenstein's remarks are endlessly amenable to exegesis, but rather than undertaking to referee this War of the Titans, I choose to take what may well be a more radical stand than Wittgenstein's.[5] Qualia are not even "something about which nothing can be said"; "qualia" is a philosophers' term which fosters[6] nothing but confusion, and refers in the end to no properties or features at all.

3. THE TRADITIONAL PARADOX REGAINED

Qualia have not always been in good odor among philosophers. Although many have thought, along with Descartes and Locke, that it made sense to talk about private, ineffable properties of minds, others have argued that this is strictly nonsense—however naturally it trips off the tongue. It is worth recalling how qualia were presumably rehabilitated as properties to be taken seriously in the wake of Wittgensteinian and verificationist attacks on them as pseudohypotheses. The original version of *intuition pump #3: the inverted spectrum* (Locke 1690: II, xxxii, 15) is a speculation about two people: how do I know that you and I see the same subjective color when we look at something? Since we both learned color words by being shown public colored objects, our verbal behavior will match *even if we experience entirely different subjective colors*. The intuition that this hypothesis is systematically unconfirmable (and undisconfirmable, of course) has always been quite robust, but some people have always been tempted to think technology could (in principle) bridge the gap.

Suppose, in *intuition pump #4: the Brainstorm machine,* there were some neuroscientific apparatus that fits on your head and feeds your visual experience into my brain (as in the movie, *Brainstorm*, which is not to be confused with the book, *Brainstorms*). With eyes closed I accurately report everything you are looking at, except that I marvel at how the sky is yellow, the grass red, and so forth. Would this not confirm, empirically, that our qualia were different? But suppose the technician then pulls the plug on the connecting cable, inverts it 180 degrees and reinserts it in the socket. Now I report the sky is blue, the grass green, and so forth. Which is the "right" orientation of the plug? Designing and building such a device would require that its "fidelity" be tuned or calibrated by the normalization of the two subjects' reports—so we would be right back at our evidential starting point. The moral of this intuition pump is that no intersubjective comparison of qualia is possible, even with perfect technology.

So matters stood until someone dreamt up the presumably improved version of the thought experiment: the *intra*personal inverted spectrum. The idea seems to have occurred to several people independently (Gert 1965; Putnam 1965; Taylor 1966; Shoemaker 1969, 1975; Lycan 1973). Probably Block and Fodor (1972) have it in mind when they say "It seems to us that the standard verificationist counterarguments against the view that the 'inverted spectrum' hypothesis is conceptually incoherent are not persuasive" (p. 172). In this version, *intuition pump #5: the neurosurgical prank*, the experiences to be compared are all in one mind. You wake up one morning to find that the grass has turned red, the sky yellow, and so forth. No one else notices any color anomalies in the world, so the problem must be in you. You are entitled, it seems, to conclude that you have undergone visual color qualia inversion (and we later discover, if you like, just how the evil neurophysiologists tampered with your neurons to accomplish this).

Here it seems at first—and indeed for quite a while—that qualia are acceptable properties after all, because propositions about them can be justifiably asserted, empirically verified and even explained. After all, in the imagined case, we can tell a tale in which we confirm a detailed neurophysiological account of the precise etiology of the dramatic change you undergo. It is tempting to suppose, then, that neurophysiological evidence, incorporated into a robust and ramifying theory, would have all the resolving power we could ever need for determining whether or not someone's qualia have actually shifted.

But this is a mistake. It will take some patient exploration to reveal the mistake in depth, but the conclusion can be reached—if not secured—quickly with the help of *intuition pump #6: alternative neurosurgery*. There are (at least) two different ways the evil neurosurgeon might create the inversion effect described in intuition pump #5:

1. Invert one of the "early" qualia-producing channels, e.g. in the optic nerve, so that all relevant neural events "downstream" are the "opposite" of their original and normal values. *Ex hypothesi* this inverts your qualia.
2. Leave all those early pathways intact and simply invert certain memory-access links—whatever it is that accomplishes your tacit (and even unconscious!) comparison of today's hues with those of yore. *Ex hypothesi* this does *not* invert your qualia at all, but just your memory-anchored dispositions to react to them.

On waking up and finding your visual world highly anomalous, you should exclaim "Egad! *Something* has happened! Either my qualia have been inverted or my memory-linked qualia-reactions have been inverted. I wonder which!"

The intrapersonal inverted spectrum thought experiment was widely supposed to be an improvement, since it moved the needed comparison into one subject's head. But now we can see that this is an illusion, since the link to earlier experiences, the link via memory, is analogous to the imaginary cable that might link two subjects in the original version.

This point is routinely—one might say traditionally—missed by the constructors of "intra-subjective inverted spectrum" thought experiments, who suppose that the subject's *noticing the difference*—surely a vivid experience of discovery by the subject—would have to be an instance of (directly? incorrigibly?) recognizing the difference *as a shift in qualia*. But as my example shows, we could achieve the same startling effect in a subject without tampering with his presumed qualia at all. Since *ex hypothesi* the two different surgical invasions can produce exactly the same introspective effects while only one operation inverts the qualia, nothing in the subject's experience can favor one of the hypotheses over the other. So unless he seeks outside help, the state of his own qualia must be as unknowable to him as the state of anyone else's qualia. Hardly the privileged access or immediate acquaintance or direct apprehension the friends of qualia had supposed "phenomenal features" to enjoy!

The outcome of this series of thought experiments is an intensification of the "verificationist" argument against qualia. *If* there are qualia, they are even less accessible to our ken than we had thought. Not only are the classical intersubjective comparisons impossible (as the Brainstorm machine shows), but we cannot tell in our own cases whether our qualia have been inverted—at least not by introspection. It is surely tempting at this point—especially to non-philosophers—to decide that this paradoxical result must be an artifact of some philosophical misanalysis or other, the sort of thing that might well happen if you took a perfectly good pretheoretical notion—our everyday notion of qualia—and illicitly stretched it beyond the breaking point. The philosophers have made a mess; let them clean it up; meanwhile we others can get back to work, relying as always on our sober and unmetaphysical acquaintance with qualia.

Overcoming this ubiquitous temptation is the task of the next section, which will seek to establish the unsalvageable incoherence of the hunches that lead to the paradox by looking more closely at their sources and their motivation.

4. MAKING MISTAKES ABOUT QUALIA

The idea that people might be mistaken about their own qualia is at the heart of the ongoing confusion, and must be explored in more detail, and with somewhat more realistic examples, if we are to see the delicate role it plays.

Intuition pump #7: Chase and Sanborn. Once upon a time there were two coffee tasters, Mr Chase and Mr Sanborn, who worked for Maxwell House.[7] Along with half a dozen other coffee tasters, their job was to ensure that the taste of Maxwell House stayed constant, year after year. One day, about six years after Mr Chase had come to work for Maxwell House, he confessed to Mr Sanborn:

> I hate to admit it, but I'm not enjoying this work any more. When I came to Maxwell House six years ago, I thought Maxwell House coffee was the best-tasting coffee in the world. I was proud to have a share in the responsibility for preserving that flavor over the years. And we've done our job well; the coffee tastes just the same today as it tasted when I arrived. But, you know, I no longer like it! My tastes have changed. I've become a more sophisticated coffee drinker. I no longer like *that taste* at all.

Sanborn greeted this revelation with considerable interest. "It's funny you should mention it," he replied, "for something rather similar has happened to me." He went on:

> When I arrived here, shortly before you did, I, like you, thought Maxwell House coffee was tops in flavor. And now I, like you, really don't care for the coffee we're making. But *my* tastes haven't changed; my…*tasters* have changed. That is, I think something has gone wrong with my taste buds or some other part of my taste-analyzing perceptual machinery. Maxwell House coffee doesn't taste to me the way it used to taste; if only it did, I'd still love it, for I still think *that taste* is the best taste in coffee. Now I'm not saying we haven't done our job well. You other tasters all agree that the taste is the same, and I must admit that on a day-to-day basis I can detect no change either. So it must be my problem alone. I guess I'm no longer cut out for this work.

Chase and Sanborn are alike in one way at least: they both used to like Maxwell House coffee, and now neither likes it. But they claim to be different in another way. Maxwell House tastes to Chase just the way it always did, but not so for Sanborn. But can we take their protestations at face value? Must we? Might one or both of them simply be wrong? Might their predicaments be importantly the same and their apparent disagreement more a difference in manner of expression than in experiential or psychological state? Since both of them make claims that depend on the reliability of their memories, is there any way to check on this reliability?

My reason for introducing two characters in the example is not to set up an interpersonal comparison between how the coffee tastes to Chase and how it tastes to Sanborn, but just to exhibit, side-by-side, two poles between which cases of intrapersonal experiential shift can wander. Such cases of intrapersonal experiential shift, and the possibility of adaptation to them, or interference with memory in them, have often been discussed in the literature on qualia, but without sufficient attention to the details, in my opinion. Let us look at Chase first. Falling in for the nonce with the received manner of speaking, it appears at first that there are the following possibilities:

(a) Chase's coffee-taste-qualia have stayed constant, while his reactive attitudes to those qualia, devolving on his canons of aesthetic judgment, etc., have shifted—which is what he seems, in his informal, casual way, to be asserting.
(b) Chase is simply wrong about the constancy of his qualia; they have shifted gradually and imperceptibly over the years, while his standards of taste haven't budged—in spite of his delusions about having become more sophisticated. He is in the state Sanborn claims to be in, but just lacks Sanborn's self-knowledge.
(c) Chase is in some predicament intermediate between (a) and (b); his qualia have shifted some *and* his standards of judgment have also slipped.

Sanborn's case seems amenable to three counterpart versions:

(a) Sanborn is right; his qualia have shifted, due to some sort of derangement in his perceptal machinery, but his standards have indeed remained constant.

(b) Sanborn's standards have shifted unbeknownst to him. He is thus misremembering his past experiences, in what we might call a nostalgia effect. Think of the familiar experience of returning to some object from your childhood (a classroom desk, a treehouse) and finding it much smaller than you remember it to have been. Presumably as you grew larger your internal standard for what was large grew with you somehow, but your memories (which are stored as fractions or multiples of that standard) didn't compensate, and hence when you consult your memory, it returns a distorted judgment. Sanborn's nostalgia-tinged memory of good old Maxwell House is similarly distorted. (There are obviously many different ways this impressionistic sketch of a memory mechanism could be implemented, and there is considerable experimental work in cognitive psychology that suggests how different hypotheses about such mechanisms could be tested.)

(c) As before, Sanborn's state is some combination of (a) and (b).

I think that everyone writing about qualia today would agree that there are all these possibilities for Chase and Sanborn. I know of no one these days who is tempted to defend the high line on infallibility or incorrigibility that would declare that alternative (a) is—and must be—the truth in each case, since people just cannot be wrong about such private, subjective matters.[8]

Since quandaries are about to arise, however, it might be wise to review in outline why the attractiveness of the infallibilist position is only superficial, so it won't recover its erstwhile allure when the going gets tough. First, in the wake of Wittgenstein (1958) and Malcolm (1956, 1959) we have seen that one way to buy such infallibility is to acquiesce in the complete evaporation of content (Dennett 1976). "Imagine someone saying: 'But I know how tall I am!' and laying his hand on top of his head to prove *it*" (Wittgenstein 1958, p. 96). By diminishing one's claim until there is nothing left to be right or wrong about, one can achieve a certain empty invincibility, but that will not do in this case. One of the things we want Chase to be right about (if he is right) is that he is not in Sanborn's predicament, so if the claim is to be viewed as infallible, it can hardly be because it declines to assert anything.

There is a strong temptation, I have found, to respond to my claims in this paper more or less as follows: "But after all is said and done, there is still something I know in a special way: I know *how it is with me right now.*" But if absolutely nothing follows from this presumed knowledge—nothing, for instance, that would shed any light on the different psychological claims that might be true of Chase or Sanborn—what is the point of asserting that one has it? Perhaps people just want to reaffirm their sense of proprietorship over their own conscious states.

The infallibilist line on qualia treats them as properties of one's experience one cannot in principle misdiscover, and this is a mysterious doctrine (at least as mysterious as papal infallibility) unless we shift the emphasis a little and treat qualia as *logical constructs* out of subjects' qualia-judgments: a subject's experience has the quale *F* if and only if the subject judges his experience to have quale *F*. We can then treat such judgings as constitutive acts, in effect, bringing the quale into existence by the same sort of license as novelists have to determine the hair color of their characters by fiat. We do not ask how Dostoevski knows that Raskolnikov's hair is light brown.*

There is a limited use for such interpretations of subjects' protocols, I have argued (Dennett 1978a; 1979, esp. pp. 109–10; 1982), but they will not help the defenders of qualia here. Logical constructs out of judgments must be viewed as akin to theorists' fictions, and the friends of qualia want the existence of a particular quale in any particular case to be an empirical fact in good standing, not a theorist's useful interpretive fiction, else it will not loom as a challenge to functionalism or materialism or third-person, objective science.

* Raskolnikov is a character in Fyodor Dostoevsky's famous Russian novel *Crime and Punishment* (1866).

It seems easy enough, then, to dream up empirical tests that would tend to confirm Chase and Sanborn's different tales, but if passing such tests could support their authority (that is to say, their reliability), failing the tests would have to undermine it. The price you pay for the possibility of empirically confirming your assertions is the outside chance of being discredited. The friends of qualia are prepared, today, to pay that price, but perhaps only because they haven't reckoned how the bargain they have struck will subvert the concept they want to defend.

Consider how we could shed light on the question of where the truth lies in the particular cases of Chase and Sanborn, even if we might not be able to settle the matter definitively. It is obvious that there might be telling objective support for one extreme version or another of their stories. Thus if Chase is unable to reidentify coffees, teas, and wines in blind tastings in which only minutes intervene between first and second sips, his claim to *know* that Maxwell House tastes just the same to him now as it did six years ago will be seriously undercut. Alternatively, if he does excellently in blind tastings, and exhibits considerable knowledge about the canons of coffee style (if such there be), his claim to have become a more sophisticated taster will be supported. Exploitation of the standard principles of inductive testing—basically Mill's method of differences—can go a long way toward indicating what sort of change has occurred in Chase or Sanborn—a change near the brute perceptual processing end of the spectrum or a change near the ultimate reactive judgment end of the spectrum. And as Shoemaker (1982) and others have noted, physiological measures, suitably interpreted in some larger theoretical framework, could also weight the scales in favor of one extreme or the other. For instance, the well-studied phenomenon of induced illusory boundaries (see figure) has often been claimed to be a particularly "cognitive" illusion, dependent on "top down" processes, and hence, presumably, near the reactive judgment end of the spectrum, but recent experimental work (Von der Heydt et al. 1984) has revealed that "edge detector" neurons *relatively* low in the visual pathways—in area 18 of the visual cortex—are as responsive to illusory edges as to real light–dark boundaries on the retina, suggesting (but not quite proving, since these might somehow still be "descending effects") that illusory contours are not imposed from on high, but generated quite early in visual processing. One can imagine discovering a similarly "early" anomaly in the pathways leading from taste buds to judgment

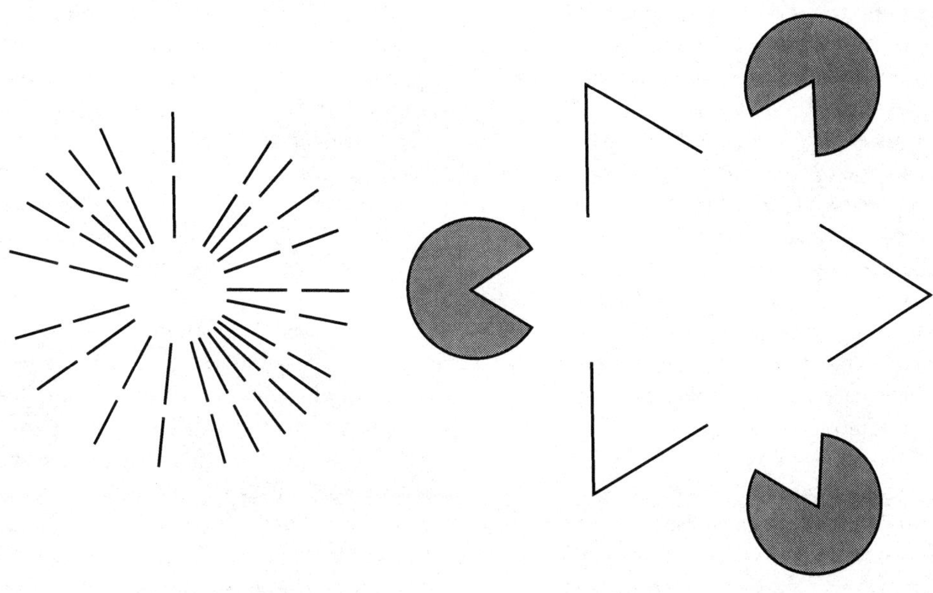

FIGURE 1

in Sanborn, for instance, tending to confirm his claim that he has suffered some change in his basic perceptual—as opposed to judgmental—machinery.

But let us not overestimate the resolving power of such empirical testing. The space in each case between the two poles represented by possibility (a) and possibility (b) would be occupied by phenomena that were the product, somehow, of two factors in varying proportion: roughly, dispositions to generate or produce qualia and dispositions to react to the qualia once they are produced. (That is how our intuitive picture of qualia would envisage it.) Qualia are supposed to affect our action or behavior only via the intermediary of our judgments about them, so any behavioral test, such as a discrimination or memory test, since it takes acts based on judgments as its primary data, can give us direct evidence only about the *resultant* of our two factors. In extreme cases we can have indirect evidence to suggest that one factor has varied a great deal, the other factor hardly at all, and we can test the hypothesis further by checking the relative sensitivity of the subject to variations in the conditions that presumably alter the two component factors. But such indirect testing cannot be expected to resolve the issue when the effects are relatively small—when, for instance, our rival hypotheses are Chase's preferred hypothesis (a) and the minor variant to the effect that his qualia have shifted *a little* and his standards *less than he thinks*. This will be true even when we include in our data any unintended or unconscious behavioral effects, for their import will be ambiguous (Would a longer response latency in Chase today be indicative of a process of "attempted qualia renormalization" or "extended aesthetic evaluation"?)

The limited evidential power of neurophysiology comes out particularly clearly if we imagine a case of adaptation. Suppose, in *intuition pump #8: the gradual post-operative recovery,* that we have somehow "surgically inverted" Chase's taste bud connections in the standard imaginary way: post-operatively, sugar tastes salty, salt tastes sour, etc. But suppose further—and this is as realistic a supposition as its denial—that Chase has subsequently compensated—as revealed by his behavior. He now *says* that the sugary substance we place on his tongue is sweet, and no longer favors gravy on his ice cream. Let us suppose the compensation is so thorough that on all behavioral and verbal tests his performance is indistinguishable from that of normal subjects—and from his own presurgical performance.

If all the internal compensatory adjustment has been accomplished early in the process—intuitively, pre-qualia—then his qualia today are restored to just as they were (relative to external sources of stimulation) before the surgery. If on the other hand some or all of the internal compensatory adjustment is post-qualia, then his qualia have not been renormalized *even if he thinks they have*. But the physiological facts will not in themselves shed any light on where in the stream of physiological process twixt tasting and telling to draw the line at which the putative qualia appear as properties of that phase of the process. The qualia are the "immediate or phenomenal" properties, of course, but this description will not serve to locate the right phase in the physiological stream, for, echoing intuition pump #6, there will always be at least two possible ways of interpreting the neurophysiological theory, however it comes out. Suppose our physiological theory tells us (in as much detail as you like) that the compensatory effect in him has been achieved by an *adjustment in the memory-accessing process* that is required for our victim to compare today's hues to those of yore. There are *still* two stories that might be told:

I. Chase's current qualia are still abnormal, but thanks to the revision in his memory-accessing process, he has in effect adjusted his memories of how things used to taste, so he no longer notices any anomaly.
II. The memory-comparison step occurs just prior to the qualia phase in taste perception; thanks to the revision, it now *yields* the same old qualia for the same stimulation.

In (I) the qualia contribute to the input, in effect, to the memory-comparator. In (II) they are part of the output of the memory-comparator. These seem to be two substantially different hypotheses, but the physiological evidence, no matter how well developed, will not tell us on which side of memory to put the qualia. Chase's introspective evidence will not settle the issue between (I) and (II) either, since *ex hypothesi* those stories are not reliably distinguishable by him. Remember that it was in order to confirm or disconfirm Chase's opinion that we turned to the neurophysiological evidence in the first place. We can hardly use his opinion in the end to settle the matter between our rival neurophysiological theories. Chase may think that he thinks his experiences are the same as before *because* they really are (and he remembers accurately how it used to be), but he must admit that he has no introspective resources for distinguishing that possibility from alternative (I), on which he thinks things are as they used to be *because* his memory of how they used to be has been distorted by his new compensatory habits.

Faced with their subject's systematic neutrality, the physiologists may have their own reasons for preferring (I) to (II) or vice versa, for they may have *appropriated* the term "qualia" to their own theoretical ends, to denote some family of detectable properties that strike them as playing an important role in their neurophysiological theory of perceptual recognition and memory. Chase or Sanborn might complain—in the company of more than a few philosophical spokesmen—that these properties the neurophysiologists choose to call "qualia" are not the qualia they are speaking of. The scientists' retort is: "If we cannot distinguish (I) from (II), we certainly cannot support either of your claims. If you want our support, you must relinquish your concept of qualia."

What is striking about this is not just that the empirical methods would fall short of distinguishing what seem to be such different claims about qualia, but that they would fall short *in spite of being better evidence than the subject's own introspective convictions*. For the subject's own judgments, like the behaviors or actions that express them, are the resultant of our two postulated factors, and cannot discern the component proportions any better than external behavioral tests can. Indeed, a subject's "introspective" convictions will generally be *worse* evidence than what outside observers can gather. For if our subject is—as most are—a "naive subject," unacquainted with statistical data about his own case or similar cases, his immediate, frank judgments are, evidentially, like any naive observer's perceptual judgments about factors in the outside world. Chase's intuitive judgments about his qualia constancy are no better off, epistemically, than his intuitive judgments about, say, lighting intensity constancy or room temperature constancy—or his own body temperature constancy. Moving to a condition inside his body does not change the intimacy of the epistemic relation in any special way. Is Chase running a fever or just feeling feverish? Unless he has taken steps to calibrate and cross-check his own performance, his opinion that his fever-perception apparatus is undisturbed is no better than a hunch. Similarly, Chase may have a strongly held opinion about the degree to which his taste-perceiving apparatus has maintained its integrity, and the degree to which his judgment has evolved through sophistication, but pending the results of the sort of laborious third-person testing just imagined, he would be a fool to claim to know—especially to know directly or immediately—that his was a pure case (a), closer to (a) than to (b), or a case near (b).

He is on quite firm ground, epistemically, when he reports that *the relation* between his coffee-sipping activity and his judging activity has changed. Recall that this is the factor that Chase and Sanborn have in common: they used to like Maxwell House; now they don't. But unless he carries out on himself the sorts of tests others might carry out on him, his convictions about what has stayed constant (or nearly so) and what has shifted *must be sheer guessing*.

But then qualia—supposing for the time being that we know what we are talking about—must lose one of their "essential" second-order properties: far from being directly or immediately apprehensible properties of our experience, they are properties whose changes or constancies are either entirely beyond our ken, or inferrable (at best) from "third-person" examinations of our behavioral and physiological reaction patterns (if Chase and Sanborn acquiesce in the neurophysiologists' sense of the term). On this view, Chase and Sanborn should be viewed not as introspectors capable of a privileged view of these properties, but as autopsychologists, theorists whose convictions about the properties of their own nervous systems are based not only on their "immediate" or current experiential convictions, but also on their appreciation of the import of events they remember from the recent past.

There are, as we shall see, good reasons for neurophysiologists and other "objective, third-person" theorists to single out such a class of properties to study. But they are not qualia, for the simple reason that one's epistemic relation to them is *exactly* the same as one's epistemic relation to such external, but readily—if fallibly—detectable, properties as room temperature or weight. The idea that one should consult an outside expert, and perform elaborate behavioral tests on oneself in order to confirm what qualia one had, surely takes us too far away from our original idea of qualia as properties with which we have a particularly intimate acquaintance.

So perhaps we have taken a wrong turning. The doctrine that led to this embarrassing result was the doctrine that sharply distinguished qualia from their (normal) effects on reactions. Consider Chase again. He claims that coffee tastes "just the same" as it always did, but he admits—nay insists—that his reaction to "that taste" is not what it used to be. That is, he pretends to be able to divorce his apprehension (or recollection) of the quale—the taste, in ordinary parlance—from his different reactions to the taste. But this apprehension or recollection is itself a reaction to the presumed quale, so some sleight-of-hand is being perpetrated—innocently no doubt—by Chase. So suppose instead that Chase had insisted that precisely *because* his reaction was now different, the taste had changed for him. (When he told his wife his original tale, she said "Don't be silly! Once you add the dislike you change the experience!"—and the more he thought about it, the more he decided she was right.)

Intuition pump #9: the experienced beer drinker. It is familiarly said that beer, for example, is an acquired taste; one gradually trains oneself—or just comes—to enjoy that flavor. What flavor? The flavor of the first sip? No one could like *that* flavor, an experienced beer drinker might retort:

> Beer tastes different to the experienced beer drinker. If beer went on tasting to me the way the first sip tasted, I would never have gone on drinking beer! Or to put the same point the other way around, if my first sip of beer had tasted to me the way my most recent sip just tasted, I would never have had to acquire the taste in the first place! I would have loved the first sip as much as the one I just enjoyed.

If we let this speech pass, we must admit that beer is *not* an acquired taste. No one comes to enjoy *the way the first sip tasted*. Instead, prolonged beer drinking leads people to experience a taste they enjoy, but precisely their enjoying the taste guarantees that it is not the taste they first experienced.[9]

But this conclusion, if it is accepted, wreaks havoc of a different sort with the traditional philosophical view of qualia. For if it is admitted that one's attitudes towards, or reactions to, experiences are in any way and in any degree constitutive of their experiential qualities, so that a change in reactivity *amounts to* or *guarantees* a change in the property, then those properties, those "qualitative or phenomenal features," cease to be "intrinsic" properties, and in fact become paradigmatically extrinsic, relational properties.

Properties that "seem intrinsic" at first often turn out on more careful analysis to be relational. Bennett (1965) is the author of *intuition pump #10: the world-wide eugenics experiment*. He draws our attention to phenol-thio-urea, a substance which tastes very bitter to three-fourths of humanity, and as tasteless as water to the rest. Is it bitter? Since the reactivity to phenol-thio-urea is genetically transmitted, we could make it paradigmatically bitter by performing a large-scale breeding experiment: prevent the people to whom it is tasteless from breeding, and in a few generations phenol would be as bitter as anything to be found in the world. But we could also (in principle!) perform the contrary feat of mass "eugenics'" and thereby make phenol paradigmatically tasteless—as tasteless as water—without ever touching phenol. Clearly, public bitterness or tastelessness is not an intrinsic property of phenol-thio-urea but a relational property, since the property is changed by a change in the reference class of normal detectors.

The public versions of perceptual "qualia" all *seem* intrinsic, in spite of their relationality. They are not alone. Think of the "felt value" of a dollar (or whatever your native currency is). "How much is that in *real* money?" the American tourist is reputed to have asked, hoping to translate a foreign price onto the scale of "intrinsic value" he keeps in his head. As Elster (1985) claims, "there is a tendency to overlook the implicitly relational character of certain monadic predicates." Walzer (1985) points out that ". . . a ten-dollar bill might seem to have a life of its own as a thing of value, but, as Elster suggests, its value implicitly depends on 'other people who are prepared to accept money as payment for goods.'" But even as one concedes this, there is still a tendency to reserve something subjective, felt value, as an "intrinsic" property of that ten-dollar bill. But as we now see, such intrinsic properties cannot be properties to which a subject's access is in any way privileged.

Which way should Chase go? Should he take his wife's advice and declare that since he can't stand the coffee any more, it no longer tastes the same to him (it used to taste good and now it tastes bad)? Or should he say that really, in a certain sense, it does taste the way it always did or at least it sort of does—when you subtract the fact that it tastes so bad now, of course?

We have now reached the heart of my case. The fact is that we have to ask Chase which way he wants to go, and there really are two drastically different alternatives available to him *if we force the issue*. Which way would *you* go? Which concept of qualia did you "always have in the back of your mind," guiding your imagination as you thought about theories? If you acknowledge that the answer is not obvious, and especially if you complain that this forced choice drives apart two aspects that you had supposed united in your pretheoretic concept, you support my contention that there is no secure foundation in ordinary "folk psychology" for a concept of qualia. We *normally* think in a confused and potentially incoherent way when we think about the ways things seem to us.

When Chase thinks of "that taste" he thinks equivocally or vaguely. He harkens back in memory to earlier experiences but need not try—or be able—to settle whether he is including any or all of his reactions or excluding them from what he intends by "that taste." His state then and his state now are different—*that* he can avow with confidence—but he has no "immediate" resources for making a finer distinction, nor any need to do so.[10]

This suggests that qualia are no more essential to the professional vocabulary of the phenomenologist (or professional coffee taster) than to the vocabulary of the physiologist (Dennett 1978b). To see this, consider again the example of my dislike of cauliflower. Imagine now, in *intuition pump #11: the cauliflower cure*, that someone offers me a pill to cure my loathing for cauliflower. He promises that after I swallow this pill cauliflower will taste exactly the same to me as it always has, but I will like that taste! "Hang on," I might reply. "I think you may have just contradicted yourself." But in any event I take the pill and it works. I become an instant cauliflower-appreciater, but if I am asked which of the two possible effects (Chase-type or Sanborn-type) the pill has had on me, I will be puzzled, and will find nothing *in my experience* to shed light on the question. Of course I recognize that the taste is (sort of) the same—the pill hasn't made cauliflower taste like chocolate cake, after all—but at the same time my experience is so different now that I resist saying that cauliflower tastes the way it used to taste. There is in any event no reason to be cowed into supposing that my cauliflower experiences have some intrinsic properties behind, or in addition to, their various dispositional, reaction-provoking properties.

"But in principle there has to be a right answer to the question of how it is, intrinsically, with you now, even if you are unable to say with any confidence!" Why? Would one say the same about all other properties of experience? Consider *intuition pump #12: visual field inversion created by wearing inverting spectacles*, a phenomenon which has been empirically studied for years. (G. M. Stratton published the pioneering work in 1896, and J. J. Gibson and Ivo Kohler were among the principal investigators. For an introductory account, see Gregory 1977.) After wearing inverting spectacles for several days subjects make an astonishingly successful adaptation. Suppose we pressed on them this question: "Does your adaptation consist in your re-inverting your visual field, or in your turning the rest of your mind upside-down in a host of compensations?" If they demur, may we insist that there has to be a right answer, even if they cannot say with any confidence which it is? Such an insistence would lead directly to a new version of the old inverted spectrum thought experiment: "How do I know whether some people see things upside-down (but are perfectly used to it), while others see things right-side-up?"

Only a very naive view of visual perception could sustain the idea that one's visual field has a property of right-side-upness or upside-downness *independent of one's dispositions to react to it*—"intrinsic right-side-upness" we could call it. (See my discussion of the properties of the "images" processed by the robot

SHAKEY, in Dennett 1982.) So not all properties of conscious experience invite or require treatment as "intrinsic" properties. Is there something distinguishing about a certain subclass of properties (the "qualitative or phenomenal" subclass, presumably) that forces us to treat them—unlike subjective right-side-upness—as intrinsic properties? If not, such properties have no role to play, in either physiological theories of experience, or in introspective theories.

Some may be inclined to argue this way: I can definitely imagine the experience of "spectrum inversion" from the inside; after all I have actually experienced temporary effects of the same type, such as the "taste displacement" effect of the maple syrup on the orange juice. What is imaginable, or actual, is possible. Therefore spectrum inversion or displacement (in all sensory modalities) is possible. But such phenomena just *are* the inversion or displacement of qualia, or intrinsic subjective properties. Therefore there must be qualia: intrinsic subjective properties.

This is fallacious. What one imagines and what one says one imagines may be two different things. To imagine visual field inversion, of the sort Stratton and Kohler's subjects experienced, is not necessarily to imagine the absolute inversion of a visual field (even if that is what it "feels like" to the subjects). Less obviously, imagining—as vividly as you like—a case of subjective color-perception displacement is not necessarily imagining what that phenomenon is typically called by philosophers: an inverted or displaced spectrum *of qualia*. In so far as that term carries the problematic implications scouted here, there is no support for its use arising simply from the vividness or naturalness of the imagined possibility.

If there are no such properties as qualia, does that mean that "spectrum inversion" is impossible? Yes and no. Spectrum inversion as classically debated is impossible, but something like it is perfectly possible—something that is as like "qualia inversion" as visual field inversion is like the impossible *absolute* visual image inversion we just dismissed.

5. SOME PUZZLING REAL CASES

It is not enough to withhold our theoretical allegiances until the sunny day when the philosophers complete the tricky task of purifying the everyday concept of qualia. Unless we take active steps to shed this source concept, and replace it with better ideas, it will continue to cripple our imaginations and systematically distort our attempts to understand the phenomena already encountered.

What we find, if we look at the actual phenomena of anomalies of color perception, for instance, amply bears out our suspicions about the inadequacy of the traditional notion of qualia. Several varieties of *cerebral achromatopsia* (brain based impairment of color vision) have been reported, and while there remains much that is unsettled about their analysis, there is little doubt that the philosophical thought experiments have underestimated or overlooked the possibilities for counter-intuitive collections of symptoms, as a few very brief excerpts from case histories will reveal.

> Objects to the right of the vertical meridian appeared to be of normal hue, while to the left they were perceived only in shades of gray, though without distortions of form. . . . He was unable to recognize or name any color in any portion of the left field of either eye, including bright reds, blues, greens and yellows. As soon as any portion of the colored object crossed the vertical meridian, he was able to instantly recognize and accurately name its color. (Damasio et al. 1980)

This patient would seem at first to be unproblematically describable as suffering a shift or loss of color qualia in the left hemifield, but there is a problem of interpretation here, brought about by another case:

> The patient failed in all tasks in which he was required to match the seen color with its spoken name. Thus, the patient failed to give the names of colors and failed to choose a color in response to its name. By contrast he succeeded on all tasks where the matching was either purely verbal or purely nonverbal. Thus, he could give verbally the names of colors corresponding to named objects and vice versa. He could match seen colors to each other and to pictures of objects and could sort colors without error. (Geschwind and Fusillo 1966)

This second patient was quite unaware of any deficit. He "never replied with a simple 'I don't know' to the demand for naming a color" (Geschwind and Fusillo 1966, p. 140). There is a striking contrast between these two patients; both have impaired ability to name the colors of things in at least part of their visual field, but whereas the former is acutely aware of his deficit, the latter is not. Does this difference make all the difference about qualia? If so, what on earth should we say about this third patient?

> His other main complaint was that "everything looked black or grey" and this caused him some difficulty in everyday life. . . . He had considerable difficulty recognizing and naming colours. He would, for example, usually describe bright red objects as either red or black, bright green objects as either green, blue or black, and bright blue objects as black. The difficulty appeared to be perceptual and he would make remarks suggesting this; for example when shown a bright red object he said "a dirty smudgy red, not as red as you would normally see red." Colours of lesser saturation or brightness were described in such terms as "grey" "off-white" or "black," but if told to guess at the colour, he would be correct on about 50 per cent of occasions, being notably less successful with blues and greens than reds. (Meadows 1974)

This man's awareness of his deficit is problematic to say the least. It contrasts rather sharply with yet another case:

> One morning in November 1977, upon awakening, she noted that although she was able to see details of objects and people, colors appeared "drained out" and "not true." She had no other complaint . . . her vision was good, 20/20 in each eye . . . The difficulty in color perception persisted, and she had to seek the advice of her husband to choose what to wear. Eight weeks later she noted that she could no longer recognize the faces of her husband and daughter. . . . [So in] addition to achromatopsia, the patient had prosopagnosia, but her linguistic and cognitive performances were otherwise unaffected. The patient was able to tell her story cogently and to have remarkable insight about her defects. (Damasio et al. 1980)

As Meadows notes, "Some patients thus complain that their vision for colours is defective while others have no spontaneous complaint but show striking abnormalities on testing."

What should one say in these cases? When no complaint is volunteered but the patient shows an impairment in color vision, is this a sign that his qualia are unaffected? ("His capacities to discriminate are terribly impaired, but luckily for him, his inner life is untouched by this merely public loss!") We could line up the qualia this way, but equally we could claim that the patient has simply not noticed the perhaps gradual draining away or inversion or merging of his qualia revealed by his poor performance. ("So slowly did his inner life lose its complexity and variety that he never noticed how impoverished it had become!") What if our last patient described her complaint just as she did above, but performed normally on testing? One hypothesis would be that her qualia had indeed, as she suggested, become washed out. Another would be that in the light of her sterling performance on the color discrimination tests, her qualia were fine; she was suffering from some hysterical or depressive anomaly, a sort of color-vision hypochondria that makes her complain about a loss of color perception. Or perhaps one could claim that her qualia were untouched; her disorder was purely verbal: an anomalous understanding of the words she uses to describe her experience. (Other startlingly specific color-*word* disorders have been reported in the literature.)

The traditional concept leads us to overlook genuine possibilities. Once we have learned of the curious deficit reported by Geschwind and Fusillo, for instance, we realize that our first patient was never tested to see if he could still sort colors seen on the left or pass other non-naming, non-verbal color-blindness tests. Those tests are by no means superfluous. Perhaps he would have passed them; perhaps, *in spite of what he says* his qualia are as intact for the left field as for the right!—if we take the capacity to pass such tests as "criterial." Perhaps his problem is "purely verbal." If your reaction to this hypothesis is that this is impossible, that must mean you are making his verbal, reporting behavior sovereign in settling the issue—but then you must rule out a priori the possibility of the condition I described as color-vision hypochondria.

There is no prospect of *finding* the answers to these brain-teasers in our everyday usage or the intuitions it arouses, but it is of course open to the philosopher to *create* an edifice of theory defending a particular set of interlocking proposals. The problem is that although normally a certain family of stimulus and bodily conditions yields a certain family of effects, any particular effect can be disconnected, and our intuitions do not tell us which effects are "essential" to quale identity or qualia constancy (cf. Dennett 1978a, ch. 11). It seems fairly obvious to me that none of the real problems of interpretation that face us in these curious cases is advanced by any analysis of how the concept of *qualia* is to be applied—unless we wish to propose a novel, technical sense for which the traditional term might be appropriated. But that would be at least a tactical error: the intuitions that surround and *purport* to anchor the current understanding of the term are revealed to be in utter disarray when confronted with these cases.

My informal sampling shows that some philosophers have strong opinions about each case and how it should be described in terms of qualia, but they find they are in strident (and ultimately comic) disagreement with other philosophers about how these "obvious" descriptions should go. Other philosophers discover they really don't know what to say—not because there aren't enough facts presented in the descriptions of the cases, but because it begins to dawn on them that they haven't really known what they were talking about over the years.

6. FILLING THE VACUUM

If qualia are such a bad idea, why have they seemed to be such a good idea? Why does it seem as if there are these intrinsic, ineffable, private, "qualitative" properties in our experience? A review of the presumptive second-order properties of the properties of our conscious experiences will permit us to diagnose their attractiveness and find suitable substitutes. (For a similar exercise see Kitcher 1979).

Consider "intrinsic" first. It is far from clear what an intrinsic property would be. Although the term has had a certain vogue in philosophy, and often seems to secure an important contrast, there has never been an accepted definition of the second-order property of intrinsicality. If even such a brilliant theory-monger as David Lewis can try and fail, by his own admission, to define the extrinsic/intrinsic distinction coherently, we can begin to wonder if the concept deserves our further attention after all. In fact Lewis (1983) begins his survey of versions of the distinction by listing as one option: "We could Quine the lot, give over the entire family as unintelligible and dispensable," but he dismisses the suggestion immediately: "That would be absurd" (p. 197). In the end, however, his effort to salvage the accounts of Chisholm (1976) and Kim (1982) are stymied, and he conjectures that "if we still want to break in we had best try another window" (p. 200).

Even if we are as loath as Lewis is to abandon the distinction, shouldn't we be suspicious of the following curious fact? If challenged to explain the idea of an intrinsic property to a neophyte, many people would hit on the following sort of example: consider Tom's ball; it has many properties, such as its being made of rubber from India, its belonging to Tom, its having spent the last week in the closet, and its redness. All but the last of these are clearly *relational* or *extrinsic* properties of the ball. Its redness, however, is an intrinsic property. Except this isn't so. Ever since Boyle and Locke we have known better. Redness—public redness—is a quintessentially relational property, as many thought experiments about "secondary qualities" show. (One of the first was Berkeley's [1713] pail of lukewarm water, and one of the best is Bennett's [1965] phenol-thio-urea.) The seductive step, on learning that public redness (like public bitterness, etc.) is a relational property after all, is to cling to intrinsicality ("*something* has to be intrinsic!") and move it into the subject's head. It is often thought, in fact, that if we take a Lockean, relational position on objective bitterness, redness, etc., we *must* complete our account of the relations in question by appeal to non-relational, intrinsic properties. If what it is to be objectively bitter is to produce a certain effect in the members of the class of normal observers, we must be able to specify that effect, and distinguish it from the effect produced by objective sourness and so forth.

What else could distinguish this effect but some intrinsic property? Why not another relational or extrinsic property? The relational treatment of monetary value does not require, for its completion, the supposition of items of intrinsic value (value independent of the valuers' dispositions to react behaviorally). The claim that certain perceptual properties are different is, in the absence of any supporting argument, just question-begging. It will not do to say that it is just obvious that they are intrinsic. It may have seemed obvious to some, but the considerations raised by Chase's quandary show that it is far from obvious that any intrinsic property (whatever that comes to) could play the role of anchor for the Lockean relational treatment of the public perceptual properties.

Why not give up intrinsicality as a second-order property altogether, at least pending resolution of the disarray of philosophical opinion about what intrinsicality might be? Until such time the insistence that qualia are the intrinsic properties of experience is an empty gesture at best; no one could claim that it provides a clear, coherent, understood prerequisite for theory.[11]

What, then, of ineffability? Why does it seem that our conscious experiences have ineffable properties? Because they do have *practically* ineffable properties. Suppose, in *intuition pump #13: the osprey cry*, that I have never heard the cry of an osprey, even in a recording, but know roughly, from reading my bird books, what to listen for: "a series of short, sharp, cheeping whistles, *cheep cheep* or *chewk chewk*, etc; sounds annoyed" (Peterson 1947) (or words to that effect or better). The verbal description gives me a partial confinement of the logical space of possible bird cries. On its basis I can rule out many bird calls I have heard or might hear, but there is still a broad range of discriminable-by-me possibilities within which the actuality lies hidden from me like a needle in a haystack.

Then one day, armed with both my verbal description and my binoculars, I identify an osprey visually, and then hear its cry. So *that's* what it sounds like, I say to myself, ostending—it seems—a particular mental complex of intrinsic, ineffable qualia. I dub the complex "*S*" (*pace* Wittgenstein), rehearse it in short term memory, check it against the bird book descriptions, and see that while the verbal descriptions are true, accurate and even poetically evocative—I decide I could not do better with a thousand words—they still fall short of *capturing* the qualia-complex I have called *S*. In fact, that is why I need the neologism "*S*" to refer directly to the ineffable property I cannot pick out by description. My perceptual experience has pinpointed for me the location of the osprey cry in the logical space of possibilities in a way verbal description could not.

But tempting as this view of the matter is, it is overstated. First of all, it is obvious that from a single experience of this sort I don't—can't—know how to generalize to other osprey calls. Would a cry that differed only in being half an octave higher also be an osprey call? That is an empirical, ornithological question for which my experience provides scant evidence. But moreover—and this is a psychological, not ornithological, matter—I don't and can't know, from a single such experience, which physical variations and constancies in stimuli would produce an indistinguishable experience in me. Nor can I know whether I would react the same (have the same experience) if I were presented with what was, by all physical measures, a re-stimulation identical to the first. I cannot know the modulating effect, if any, of variations in my body (or psyche).

This inscrutability of projection is surely one of the sources of plausibility for Wittgenstein's skepticism regarding the possibility of a private language.

> Wittgenstein emphasizes that ostensive definitions are always in principle capable of being misunderstood, even the ostensive definition of a color word such as "sepia." How someone understands the word is exhibited in the way someone goes on, "the use that he makes of the word defined." One may go on in the right way given a purely minimal explanation, while on the other hand one may go on in another way no matter how many clarifications are added, since these too can be misunderstood . . . (Kripke 1982, p. 83; see also pp. 40–6)

But what is inscrutable in a single glance, and somewhat ambiguous after limited testing, can come to be justifiably seen as the deliverance of a highly specific, reliable, and projectible property-detector, once it has been field-tested under a suitably wide variety of circumstances.

In other words, when first I hear the osprey cry, I may have identified a property-detector in myself, but I have no idea (yet) what property my new-found property-detector detects. It might seem then that I know nothing new at all—that my novel experience has not improved my epistemic predicament in the slightest. But of course this is not so. I may not be able to describe the property or identify it relative to any readily usable public landmarks (yet), but I am acquainted with it in a modest way: I can refer to the property I detected: it is the property I detected in *that* event. My experience of the osprey cry has given me a new way of thinking about osprey cries (an unavoidably inflated way of saying something very simple) which is practically ineffable both because it has (as yet for me) an untested profile in response to perceptual circumstances, and because it is—as the poverty of the bird-book description attests—such a highly informative way of thinking: a deliverance of an informationally very sensitive portion of my nervous system.

In this instance I mean information in the formal information theory sense of the term. Consider (*intuition pump #14: the Jello box*) the old spy trick, most famously encountered in the case of Julius and Ethel Rosenberg, of improving on a password system by tearing something in two (a Jello box, in the Rosenberg's case), and giving half to each of the two parties who must be careful about identifying each other. Why does it work? Because tearing the paper in two produces an edge of such informational complexity that it would be virtually impossible to reproduce by deliberate construction. (Cutting the Jello box with straight edge and razor would entirely defeat the purpose.) The particular jagged edge of one piece becomes a *practically* unique pattern-recognition device for its mate; it is an apparatus for detecting the shape property *M,* where *M* is uniquely instantiated by its mate. It is of the essence of the trick that we cannot replace our dummy predicate "*M*" with a longer, more complex, but accurate and exhaustive description of the property, for if we could, we could use the description as a recipe or feasible algorithm for producing another instance of *M* or another *M* detector. The only *readily available* way of saying what property *M* is is just to point to our *M*-detector and say that *M* is the shape property detected by this thing here.

And that is just what we do when we seem to ostend, with the mental finger of inter intention, a quale or qualia-complex in our experience. We refer to a property—a public property of uncharted boundaries—via reference to our personal and idiosyncratic capacity to respond to it. That idiosyncrasy is the extent of our privacy. If I wonder whether your blue is my blue, your middle-C is my middle-C, I can coherently be wondering whether our discrimination profiles over a wide variation in conditions will be approximately the same. And they may not be; people experience the world quite differently. But that is empirically discoverable by all the usual objective testing procedures.[12]

Peter Bieri has pointed out to me that there is a natural way of exploiting Dretske's (1981) sense of information in a reformulation of my first three second-order properties of qualia: intrinsicality, ineffability, and privacy. (There are problems with Dretske's attempt to harness information theory in this way—see my discussion in "Evolution, error and intentionality" (Dennett 1987)—but they are not relevant to this point.) We could speak of what Bieri would call "phenomenal information properties" of psychological events. Consider the information—what Dretske would call the *natural meaning*—that a type of internal perceptual event might carry. That it carries that information is an objective (and hence, in a loose sense, intrinsic) matter since it is independent of what information (if any) the subject *takes* the event type to carry. Exactly what information is carried is (practically) ineffable, for the reasons just given. And it is private in the sense just given: proprietary and potentially idiosyncratic.

Consider how Bieri's proposed "phenomenal information properties" (let's call them *pips*) would apply in the case of Chase and Sanborn. Both Chase and Sanborn ought to wonder whether their pips have changed. Chase's speech shows that he is under the impression that his pips are unchanged (under normal circumstances—all bets are off if he has just eaten horseradish). He believes that the same objective things in the world—in particular, chemically identical caffeine-rich fluids—give rise to his particular types of taste-experiences now as six years ago.

Sanborn is under the impression that his pips are different. He thinks his objective property-detectors are deranged. He no longer has confidence that their deliverances today inform him of what they did six years ago. And what, exactly, did they inform him of then? If Sanborn were an ordinary person, we would not expect him to have an explicit answer, since most of us treat our taste-detectors as mere M-detectors, detecting whatever-it-is that they detect. (There are good reasons for this, analyzed by Akins 1987.) But professional coffee-tasters are probaby different. They probably have some pretty good idea of what kind of chemical-analysis transduction machinery they have in their mouths and nervous systems.

So far, so good. We could reinterpret Chase and Sanborn's speeches as hypotheses about the constancies or changes in the outputs of their perceptual information-processing apparatus, and just the sort of empirical testing we imagined before would tend to confirm or disconfirm their opinions thus interpreted. But what would justify calling such an information-bearing property "phenomenal"?

Such a pip has, as the testimony of Chase and Sanborn reveals, the power to provoke in Chase and Sanborn acts of (apparent) re-identification or recognition. This power is of course a Lockean, dispositional property on a par with the power of bitter things to provoke a certain reaction in people. It is this power alone, however it might be realized in the brain, that gives Chase and Sanborn "access" to the deliverances of their individual property-detectors.

We may "point inwardly" to one of the deliverances of our idiosyncratic, proprietary property-detectors, but when we do, what are we pointing *at?* What does that deliverance itself *consist of?* Or what are its consciously apprehensible properties, if not just our banished friends the qualia? We must be careful here, for if we invoke an inner perceptual process in which we observe the deliverance with some inner eye and thereby discern its properties, we will be stepping back into the frying pan of the view according to which qualia are just ordinary properties of our inner states.

But nothing requires us to make such an invocation. We don't have to know how we identify or re-identify or gain access to such internal response types in order to be able so to identify them. This is a point that was forcefully made by the pioneer functionalists and materialists, and has never been rebutted (Farrell 1950; Smart 1959). The properties of the "thing experienced" are not to be confused with the properties of the event that realizes the experiencing. To put the matter vividly, the physical difference between someone's imagining a purple cow and imagining a green cow *might* be nothing more than the presence or absence of a particular zero or one in one of the brain's "registers." Such a brute physical presence is all that it would take to anchor the sorts of dispositional differences between imagining a purple cow and imagining a green cow that could then flow, causally, from that "intrinsic" fact. (I doubt that this is what the friends of qualia have had in mind when they have insisted that qualia are intrinsic properties.)

Moreover, it is our very inability to expand on, or modify, these brute dispositions so to identify or recognize such states that creates the doctrinal illusion of "homogeneity" or "atomicity to analysis" or "grainlessness" that characterizes the qualia of philosophical tradition.

This putative grainlessness, I hypothesize, is nothing but a sort of functional invariability: it is close kin to what Pylyshyn (1980, 1984) calls *cognitive impenetrability*. Moreover, this functional invariability or impenetrability is not absolute but itself plastic over time. Just as on the efferent side of the nervous system, *basic actions*—in the sense of Danto (1963, 1965) and others (see Goldman 1970)—have been discovered to be variable, and subject under training to decomposition (one can learn with the help of "biofeedback" to will the firing of a particular motor neuron "directly"), so what counts for an individual as the simple or atomic properties of experienced items is subject to variation with training.[13]

Consider the results of "educating" the palate of a wine taster, or "ear training" for musicians. What had been "atomic" or "unanalyzable" becomes noticeably compound and describable; pairs that had been indistinguishable become distinguishable, and when this happens we say *the experience changes*. A swift and striking example of this is illustrated in *intuition pump #15: the guitar string*. Pluck the bass or low E string open, and listen carefully to the sound. Does it have describable parts or is it one and whole and ineffably guitarish? Many will opt for the latter way of talking. Now pluck the open string again and carefully bring a finger down lightly over the octave fret to create a high "harmonic." Suddenly a *new* sound is heard: "purer" somehow and of course an octave higher. Some people insist that this is an entirely novel sound, while others will describe the experience by saying "the bottom fell out of the note"—leaving just the top. But then on a third open plucking one can hear, with surprising distinctness, the harmonic overtone that was isolated in the second plucking. The homogeneity and ineffability of the first experience is gone, replaced by a duality as "directly apprehensible" and clearly describable as that of any chord.

The difference in experience is striking, but the complexity apprehended on the third plucking was *there* all along (being responded to or discriminated). After all, it was by the complex pattern of overtones that you were able to recognize the sound as that of a guitar rather than a lute or harpsichord. In other words, although the subjective experience has changed dramatically, the *pip* hasn't changed; you are still responding, as before, to a complex property so highly informative that it practically defies verbal description.

There is nothing to stop further refinement of one's capacity to describe this heretofore ineffable complexity. At any time, of course, there is one's current horizon of distinguishability—and that horizon is what sets, if anything does, what we should call the primary or atomic properties of what one consciously experiences (Farrell 1950). But it would be a mistake to transform the fact that inevitably there is a limit to our capacity to describe things we experience into the supposition that there are absolutely indescribable properties in our experience.

So when we look one last time at our original characterization of qualia, as ineffable, intrinsic, private, directly apprehensible properties of experience, we find that there is nothing to fill the bill. In their place are relatively or practically ineffable public properties we can refer to indirectly via reference to our private property-detectors—private only in the sense of idiosyncratic. And in so far as we wish to cling to our subjective authority about the occurrence within us of states of certain types or with certain properties, we can have some authority—not infallibility or incorrigibility, but something better than sheer guessing—but only if we restrict ourselves to relational, extrinsic properties like the power of certain internal states of ours to provoke acts of apparent re-identification. So contrary to what seems obvious at first blush, there simply are no qualia at all.[14]

NOTES

1. A representative sample of the most recent literature on qualia would include Block 1980; Shoemaker 1981, 1982; Davis 1982; White 1985; Armstrong and Malcolm 1984; Churchland 1985; and Conee 1985.
2. The difference between "eliminative materialism"—of which my position on qualia is an instance—and a "reductive" materialism that takes on the burden of identifying the problematic item in terms of the foundational materialistic theory is thus often best seen not so much as a doctrinal issue as a tactical issue: how might we most gracefully or effectively enlighten the confused in this instance? See my discussion of "fatigues" in the Introduction to *Brainstorms* (Dennett 1978a), and earlier, my discussion of what the enlightened ought to say about the metaphysical status of *sakes* and *voices* in *Content and Consciousness* (Dennett 1969), ch. 1.
3. The plausibility of this concession depends less on a high regard for the technology than on a proper skepticism about human powers, now documented in a fascinating study by Lehrer (1983).
4. Shoemaker (1984) seems to be moving reluctantly towards agreement with this conclusion: "So unless we can find some grounds on which we can deny the possibility of the sort of situation envisaged . . . we must apparently choose between rejecting the functionalist account of qualitative similarity and rejecting the standard conception of qualia.

   I would prefer not to have to make this choice; but if I am forced to make it, I reject the standard conception of qualia" (p. 356).
5. Shoemaker (1982) attributes a view to Wittgenstein (acknowledging that "it is none too clear" that this is actually what Wittgenstein held) which is very close to the view I defend here. But to Shoemaker,

"it would seem offhand that Wittgenstein was mistaken" (p. 360), a claim Shoemaker supports with a far from offhand thought experiment—which Shoemaker misanalyzes if the present paper is correct. (There is no good reason, contrary to Shoemaker's declaration, to believe that his subject's *experience* is systematically different from what it was before the inversion.) Smart (1959) expresses guarded and partial approval of Wittgenstein's hard line, but cannot see his way clear to as uncompromising an eliminativism as I maintain here.

6. In 1979, I read an earlier version of this paper in Oxford, with a commentary by John Foster, who defended qualia to the last breath, which was: "qualia should not be quined but fostered!" Symmetry demands, of course, the following definition for the eighth edition of *The Philosophical Lexicon:* "foster, *v*. To acclaim resolutely the existence or importance of something chimerical or insignificant."
7. This example first appeared in print in my "Reflections on Smullyan" in *The Mind's I* (Hofstadter and Dennett 1981), p. 427–28.
8. Kripke (1982) comes close, when he asks rhetorically "Do I not know, directly, and *with a fair degree of certainty* [emphasis added], that I mean plus [by the function I call "plus"]?" (p. 40) Kripke does not tell us what is implied by "a fair degree of certainty," but presumably he means by this remark to declare his allegiance to what Millikan (1984) attacks under the name of "meaning rationalism."
9. We can save the traditional claim by ignoring presumably private or subjective qualia and talking always of public tastes—such as the public taste of Maxwell House coffee that both Chase and Sanborn agree has remained constant. Individuals can be said to acquire a taste for such a public taste.
10. "I am not so wild as to deny that my sensation of red today is like my sensation of red yesterday. I only say that the similarity can *consist* only in the physiological force behind consciousness—which leads me to say, I recognize this feeling the same as the former one, and so does not consist in a community of sensation." (C. S. Peirce, *Collected Works,* vol. V, p. 172, fn. 2).
11. A heroic (and, to me, baffling) refusal to abandon intrinsicality is Wilfrid Sellars's contemplation over the years of his famous pink ice cube, which leads him to postulate a revolution in microphysics, restoring objective "absolute sensory processes" in the face of Boyle and Locke and almost everybody since them. See Sellars (1981) and my commentary (Dennett 1981).
12. Stich (1983) discusses the implications for psychological theory of incommensurability problems that can arise from such differences in discrimination profiles. See esp. chs. 4 and 5.
13. See Churchland 1979, esp. ch 2, for supporting observations on the variability of perceptual properties, and for novel arguments against the use of "intrinsic properties" as determiners of the meaning of perceptual predicates. See also Churchland 1985 for further arguments and observations in support of the position sketched here.
14. The first version of this paper was presented at University College London, in November 1978, and in various revisions at a dozen other universities in 1979 and 1980. It was never published, but was circulated widely as Tufts University Cognitive Science Working Paper #7, December 1979. A second version was presented at the Universities of Adelaide and Sydney in 1984, and in 1985 to psychology department colloquia at Harvard and Brown under the title "Properties of conscious experience." The second version was the basis for my presentation at the workshop on consciousness in modern science, Villa Olmo, Como, Italy, April 1985, and circulated in preprint in 1985, again under the title "Quining qualia." The present version, the fourth, is a substantial revision, thanks to the helpful comments of many people, including Kathleen Akins, Ned Block, Alan Cowey, Sydney Shoemaker, Peter Bieri, William Lycan, Paul Churchland, Gilbert Harman and the participants at Villa Olmo.

REFERENCES

Akins, K. (1987) *Information and Organisms: Or, Why Nature Doesn't Build Epistemic Engines,* Ph.D. dissertation, Univ. of Michigan Dept of Philosophy.

Armstrong, D. and Malcolm, N. (eds) (1984) *Consciousness and Causality*. Oxford: Basil Blackwell.

Bennett, J. (1965) "Substance, reality and primary qualities," *American Philosophical Quarterly 2,* 1–17.

Berkeley, G. (1713) *Three Dialogues between Hylas and Philonous.*

Block, N. (1978) "Troubles with Functionalism," in W. Savage (ed.) *Perception and Cognition: Minnesota Studies in the Philosophy of Science, Vol. IX* Minneapolis: University of Minnesota Press.

Block, N. (1980) "Are absent qualia impossible?," *Philosophical Review* 89, 257.

Block, N. and Fodor J. (1972) "What psychological states are not," *Philosophical Review* 81, 159–81.

Chisholm, R. (1976) *Person and Object.* La Salle, Illinois: Open Court Press.

Churchland, P. M. (1979) *Scientific Realism and the Plasticity of Mind.* Cambridge, MA: Cambridge University Press.

Churchland, P. M. (1985) "Reduction, qualia and the direct inspection of brain states," *Journal of Philosophy,* LXXXII, 8–28.

Conee, E. (1985) "The possibility of absent qualia," *Philosophical Review* 94, 345–66.

Damasio, A. et al. (1980) "Central Achromatopsia: Behavioral, anatomic, and physiological aspects," *Neurology* 30, 1064–71.

Danto, A. (1963) "What we can do," *Journal of Philosophy,* LX, 435–45.

Danto, A. (1965) "Basic actions," *American Philosophical Quarterly,* 141–48.

Davis, L. (1982) "Functionalism and absent qualia," *Philosophical Studies* 41, 231–51.

Dennett, D. C. (1969) *Content and Consciousness.* London: Routledge & Kegan Paul.

Dennett, D. C. (1976) "Are dreams experiences?," *Philosophical Review* 85, 151–71. (Reprinted in Dennett 1978a.)

Dennett, D. C. (1978a) *Brainstorms.* Bradford Books/ MIT Press.

Dennett, D. C. (1978b) "Two approaches to mental images," in Dennett 1978a.

Dennett, D. C. (1978c) *The Philosophical Lexicon,* 8th edn. (http://www.blackwellpublishers.co.uk/ lexicon/)

Dennett, D. C. (1979) "On the absence of phenomenology," in D. F. Gustafson and B. L. Tapscott (eds) *Body, Mind, and Method* (Festschrift for Virgil Aldrich). Dordrecht: Reidel, pp. 93–114.

Dennett, D. C. (1981) "Wondering where the yellow went," *Monist* 64, 102–8.

Dennett, D. C. (1982) "How to study human consciousness empirically: Or nothing comes to mind," *Synthese* 53, 159–80.

Dennett, D. C. (1987) *The Intentional Stance.* Cambridge MA: Bradford/MIT.

Dretske, F. (1981) *Knowledge and the Flow of Information.* Cambridge MA: Bradford/MIT.

Elster, J. (1985) *Making Sense of Marx.* Cambridge, England: Cambridge University Press.

Farrell, B. A. (1950) "Experience," *Mind* 59, 170–98.

Gert, B. (1965) "Imagination and verifiability," *Philosophical Studies 16,* 44–47.

Geschwind, N. and Fusillo, M. (1966) "Color-naming defects in association with alexia," *Archives of neurology* 15, 137–46.

Goldman, A. (1970) *A Theory of Human Action.* Englewood Cliffs, NJ: Prentice Hall.

Gregory, R. (1977) *Eye and Brain,* 3rd edn. London: Weidenfeld & Nicolson.

Hofstadter, D. and Dennett, D. C. (1981) *The Mind's I: Fantasies and Reflections on Mind and Soul.* New York: Basic Books.

Kim, J. (1982) "Psychophysical supervenience," *Philosophical Studies* 41, 51–70.

Kitcher, P. (1979) "Phenomenal qualities," *American Philosophical Quarterly* 16, 123–29.

Kripke, S. (1982) *Wittgenstein on Rules and Private Language.* Cambridge, MA: Harvard University Press.

Lehrer, A. (1983) *Wine and Conversation.* Bloomington, Indiana: Univ. of Indiana Press.

Lewis, D. (1983) "Extrinsic properties," *Philosophical Studies* 44, 197–200.

Locke, J. (1690) *An Essay Concerning Human Understanding* (A. C. Fraser edition). New York: Dover, 1959.

Lycan, W. (1973) "Inverted spectrum," *Ratio* XV, 315–19.

Malcolm, N. (1956) "Dreaming and skepticism," *Philosophical Review* 64, 14–37.

Malcolm, N. (1959) *Dreaming.* London: Routledge & Kegan Paul.

Meadows, J. C. (1974) "Disturbed perception of colours associated with localized cerebral lesions," *Brain* 97, 615–32.

Millikan, R. (1984) *Language, Thought and Other Biological Categories.* Cambridge, MA: Bradford/MIT.

Nagel, T. (1974) "What is it like to be a bat?," *Philosophical Review* 83, 435–51.

Nagel, T. (1986) *The View from Nowhere*. Oxford: Oxford University Press.

Peirce, C. (1931–58) C. Hartshorne and P. Weiss (eds), *Collected Works*. Cambridge MA: Harvard University Press.

Peterson, R. T. (1947) *A Field Guide to the Birds*. Boston: Houghton Mifflin.

Putnam, H. (1965) "Brains and behavior," in J. Butler (ed.) *Analytical Philosophy* (second series). Oxford: Basil Blackwell.

Pylyshyn, Z. (1980) "Computation and cognition: Issues in the foundation of cognitive science," *Behavioral and Brain Sciences* 3, 111–32.

Pylyshyn, Z. (1984) *Computation and Cognition: Toward a Foundation for Cognitive Science*. Cambridge, MA: Bradford/MIT Press.

Sellars, W. (1981) "Foundations for a metaphysics of pure process" (the Carus Lectures), *Monist*, 64, 3–90.

Shoemaker, S. (1969) "Time without change," *Journal of Philosophy* 66, 363–81.

Shoemaker, S. (1975) "Functionalism and qualia," *Philosophical Studies* 27, 291–315.

Shoemaker, S. (1981) "Absent qualia are impossible—A reply to Block," *Philosophical Review* 90, 581–99.

Shoemaker, S. (1982) "The inverted spectrum," *Journal of Philosophy* 79, 357–81.

Shoemaker, S. (1984) "Postscript (1983)," in *Identity, Cause, and Mind*. Cambridge, England: Cambridge Univ. Press, pp. 351–57.

Smart, J. J. C. (1959) "Sensations and brain processes," *Philosophical Review* 68, 141–56. (Reprinted in Chappell 1962).

Stich, S. (1983) *From Folk Psychology to Cognitive Science: The Case against Belief*. Cambridge, MA: Bradford/MIT.

Taylor, D. M. (1966) "The incommunicability of content," *Mind* 75, 527–41.

Von der Heydt, R., Peterhans, E. and Baumgartner, G. (1984) "Illusory contours and cortical neuron response," *Science* 224, 1260–262.

Walzer, M. (1985) "What's left of Marx," *New York Review of Books*, Nov. 21, pp. 43–46.

White, S. (1985) "Professor Shoemaker and so-called 'qualia' of experience," *Philosophical Studies* 47, 369–83.

Wittgenstein, L. (1958) G. E. M. Anscombe (ed.), *Philosophical Investigations*. Oxford: Basil Blackwell.

Concepts of Consciousness[1]

NED BLOCK

Ned Block (1942–) is an American philosopher who has done influential work in philosophy of mind and cognitive science. He taught for many years at the Massachusetts Institute of Technology and now teaches at New York University. Block was a student of Hilary Putnam, whose work also appears in this volume.

The article that appears here was originally published in the journal *Behavioral and Brain Sciences* in 1995, along with peer commentaries by a wide range of philosophers, psychologists, and neuroscientists. The text was abridged and revised by David Chalmers. Some brief selections from the end of the essay have been omitted from this volume.

This text originally appeared as "On a Confusion about a Function of Consciousness," *Behavioral and Brain Sciences* 18:227–47, 1995. Reprinted with the permission of Cambridge University Press. It was abridged and revised by David Chalmers for inclusion in *Philosophy of Mind: Classical and Contemporary Readings* (New York: Oxford University Press, 2002).

The concept of consciousness is a hybrid or better, a mongrel concept: the word "consciousness" connotes a number of different concepts and denotes a number of different phenomena. We reason about "consciousness" using some premises that apply to one of the phenomena that fall under "consciousness," other premises that apply to other "consciousness" and we end up with trouble. There are many parallels in the history of science. Aristotle used "velocity" sometimes to mean average velocity and sometimes to mean instantaneous velocity; his failure to see the distinction caused confusion. The Florentine Experimenters of the 17th Century used a single word (roughly translatable as "degree of heat") for temperature and for heat, generating paradoxes. For example, when they measured "degree of heat" by whether various heat sources could melt paraffin, heat source A came out hotter than B, but when they measured "degree of heat" by how much ice a heat source could melt in a given time, B was hotter than A.[2] These are very different cases, but there is a similarity, one that they share with the case of "consciousness." The similarity is: very different concepts are treated as a single concept. I think we all have some tendency to make this mistake in the case of "consciousness."

PHENOMENAL CONSCIOUSNESS

First, consider phenomenal consciousness, or P-consciousness, as I will call it. Phenomenal consciousness is experience; what makes a state phenomenally conscious is that there is something "it is like" (Nagel, 1974) to be in that state.* Let me acknowledge at the outset that I cannot define P-consciousness in any remotely non-circular way. I don't consider this an embarrassment. The history of reductive definitions in philosophy should lead one not to expect a reductive definition of anything. But the best one can do for P-consciousness is in some respects worse than for many other things because really all one can do is *point* to the phenomenon (cf. Goldman, 1993a). Nonetheless, it is important to point properly. John Searle, acknowledging that consciousness cannot be defined non-circularly, defines it as follows:

> By consciousness I simply mean those subjective states of awareness or sentience that begin when one wakes in the morning and continue throughout the period that one is awake until one falls into a dreamless sleep, into a coma, or dies or is otherwise, as they say, unconscious. [This comes from Searle 1990; there is a much longer attempt along the same lines in his 1992, p. 83ff.]

I will argue that this sort of pointing is flawed because it points to too many things, too many different consciousnesses.

So how should we point to P-consciousness? Well, one way is via rough synonyms. As I said, P-consciousness is experience. P-conscious properties are experiential properties. P-conscious states are experiential states; that is, a state is P-conscious just in case it has experiential properties. The totality of the experiential properties of a state are "what it is like" to have it. Moving from synonyms to examples, we have P-conscious states when we see, hear, smell, taste and have pains. P-conscious properties include the experiential properties of sensations, feelings and perceptions, but I would also include thoughts, wants and emotions.[3] An important feature of P-consciousness is that differences in intentional content often make a P-conscious difference. What it is like to hear a sound as coming from the left differs from what it is like to hear a sound as coming from the right. Further, P-conscious differences often make an intentional difference. And this is partially explained by the fact that P-consciousness is often—perhaps even always—representational. (See Jackendoff, 1987; van Gulick, 1989; McGinn, 1991, Ch 2; Flanagan, 1992, Ch 4; Goldman, 1993b.) So far, I don't take myself to have said anything terribly controversial. The controversial part is that I take P-conscious properties to be distinct from any cognitive, intentional, or functional property. At least, no such reduction of P-consciousness to the cognitive, intentional or functional can be known in the armchair manner of recent deflationist approaches. (Cognitive = essentially involving thought;

---

* Thomas Nagel's "What Is It Like to Be a Bat?" appears earlier in this section, pp. 620–628.

intentional properties = properties in virtue of which a representation or state is about something; functional properties = e.g., properties definable in terms of a computer program. See Searle, 1983 on intentionality; see Block, 1980, 1994, for better characterizations of a functional property.) But I am trying hard to limit the controversiality of my assumptions. Though I will be assuming that functionalism about P-consciousness is false, I will be pointing out that limited versions of many of the points I will be making can be acceptable to the functionalist.[4]

By way of homing in on P-consciousness, it is useful to appeal to what may be a contingent property of it, namely the famous "explanatory gap." To quote T. H. Huxley (1866), "How it is that anything so remarkable as a state of consciousness comes about as a result of irritating nervous tissue, is just as unaccountable as the appearance of Djin when Aladdin rubbed his lamp." Consider a famous neurophysiological theory of P-consciousness offered by Francis Crick and Christof Koch: namely, that a synchronized 35–75 hertz neural oscillation in the sensory areas of the cortex is at the heart of phenomenal consciousness. Assuming for the moment that such neural oscillations are the neural basis of sensory consciousness, no one has produced the concepts that would allow us to explain why such oscillations are the neural basis of a phenomenally conscious state rather than a phenomenally unconscious state.*

However, Crick and Koch have offered a sketch of an account of how the 35–75 hertz oscillation might contribute to a solution to the "binding problem." Suppose one simultaneously sees a red square moving to the right and a blue circle moving to the left. Different areas of the visual cortex are differentially sensitive to color, shape, motion, etc. so what binds together redness, squareness and rightward motion? That is, why don't you see redness and blueness without seeing them as belonging with particular shapes and particular motions? And why aren't the colors normally seen as bound to the wrong shapes and motions? Representations of colors, shapes and motions of a single object are supposed to involve oscillations that are in phase with one another but not with representations of other objects. But even if the oscillation hypothesis deals with the informational aspect of the binding problem (and there is some evidence against it), how does it explain *what it is like to see something as red in the first place*—or for that matter, as square or as moving to the right? Why couldn't there be brains functionally or physiologically just like ours, including oscillation patterns, whose owners' experience was different from ours or who had no experience at all? (Note that I don't say that there *could be* such brains. I just want to know *why not*.) No one has a clue how to answer these questions.

The explanatory gap in the case of P-consciousness contrasts with our better (though still not very good) understanding of the scientific basis of cognition. We have two serious research programs into the nature of cognition, the classical "language of thought" paradigm, and the connectionist research program. Both assume that the scientific basis of cognition is computational. If this idea is right—and it seems increasingly promising—it gives us a better grip on why the neural basis of a thought state is the neural basis of that thought rather than some other thought or none at all than we have about the analogous issue for consciousness.

What I've been saying about P-consciousness is of course controversial in a variety of ways, both for some advocates and some opponents of some notion of P-consciousness. I have tried to steer clear of some controversies, e.g., controversies over inverted and absent qualia; over Jackson's (1986) Mary,* the woman who is raised in a black and white room, learning all the physiological and functional facts about the brain and color vision, but nonetheless discovers a new fact when she goes outside the room for the first time and learns what it is like to see red; and even Nagel's view that we cannot know what it is like to be a bat.[5] Even if you think that

* Thomas Huxley (1825–95) was a nineteenth-century English biologist and early advocate of Darwinism. Francis Crick (1916–2004) was the co-discoverer of the structure of DNA; together with neuroscientist Christof Koch (1956–), he worked to identify the neuronal correlates of consciousness.

* For Jackson's Mary, see "The Knowledge Argument," which appears earlier in this section, pp. 611–619.

P-consciousness as I have described it is an incoherent notion, you may be able to agree with the main point of this paper, which is that a great deal of confusion arises as a result of confusing P-consciousness with something else. Not even the concept of what time it is now on the sun is so confused that it cannot itself be confused with something else.

ACCESS-CONSCIOUSNESS

I now turn to the non-phenomenal notion of consciousness that is most easily and dangerously conflated with P-consciousness: access-consciousness. I will characterize access-consciousness, give some examples of how it makes sense for someone to have access-consciousness without phenomenal consciousness and vice versa, and then go on to the main theme of the paper, the damage done by conflating the two.

A-consciousness is access-consciousness. A representation is A-conscious if it is broadcast for free use in reasoning and for direct "rational" control of action (including reporting). An A-state is one that consists in having an A-representation. I see A-consciousness as a cluster concept in which reportability is the element of the cluster that has the smallest weight even though it is often the best practical guide to A-consciousness.

The "rational" is meant to rule out the kind of automatic control that obtains in blindsight. (Blindsight is a syndrome involving patients who have brain damage in the first stage of visual processing, primary visual cortex. These patients seem to have "holes" in their visual fields. If the experimenter flashes stimuli in these holes and asks the patient what was flashed, the patient claims to see nothing but can often guess at high levels of accuracy, choosing between two locations or directions or whether what was flashed was an "X" or an "O.")

I will suggest that A-consciousness plays a deep role in our ordinary "consciousness" talk and thought. However, I must admit at the outset that this role allows for substantial indeterminacy in the concept itself. In addition, there are some loose ends in the characterization of the concept which cannot be tied up without deciding about certain controversial issues, to be mentioned below.[6] My guide in making precise the notion of A-consciousness is to formulate an information processing correlate of P-consciousness that is not ad hoc and mirrors P-consciousness as well as a non–ad hoc information processing notion can.

In the original version of this paper, I defined "A-consciousness" as (roughly) "poised for control of speech, reasoning and action."[7] In a comment on the original version of this paper, David Chalmers (1997) suggested defining "A-consciousness" instead as "directly available for global control." Chalmers' definition has the advantage of avoiding enumerating the kinds of control. That makes the notion more general, applying to creatures who have kinds of control that differ from ours. But it has the disadvantage of that advantage, counting simple organisms as having A-consciousness if they have representations that are directly available for global control of whatever resources they happen to have. If the idea of A-consciousness is to be an information processing image of P-consciousness, it would not do to count a slug as having A-conscious states simply because there is some machinery of control of the resources that a slug happens to command.

As I noted, my goal in precisifying the ordinary notion of access as it is used in thinking about consciousness is to formulate a non–ad hoc notion that is close to an information processing image of P-consciousness. A flaw in both my definition and Chalmers' definition is that they make A-consciousness dispositional whereas P-consciousness is occurrent. As noted in the critique by Atkinson and Davies (1995), that makes the relation between P-consciousness and A-consciousness the relation between the ground of a disposition and the disposition itself. (See also Burge, 1997.) This has long been one ground of criticism of both functionalism and behaviorism (Block and Fodor, 1972), but there is no real need for an information-processing notion of consciousness to be saddled with a category mistake of this sort. I have dealt with the issue here by using the term "broadcast," as in Baars' (1988) theory that conscious representations are ones that are broadcast in a global workspace. A-consciousness is similar to that notion and to Dennett's (1993) notion of consciousness as cerebral celebrity.[8]

The interest in the A/P distinction arises from the battle between two different conceptions of the mind, the biological and the computational. The computational approach supposes that all of the mind (including consciousness) can be captured with notions of information processing, computation and function in a system. According to this view (often called functionalism by philosophers), the level of abstraction for understanding the mind is one that allows multiple realizations, just as one computer can be realized electrically or hydraulically. Their bet is that the different realizations don't matter to the mind, generally, and to consciousness specifically. The biological approach bets that the realization does matter. If P = A, the information processing side is right. But if the biological nature of experience is crucial, then realizations *do* matter, and we can expect that P and A will diverge.[9]

Although I make a distinction between A-consciousness and P-consciousness, I also want to insist that they interact. For example, what perceptual information is being accessed can change figure to ground and conversely, and a figure-ground switch can affect one's phenomenal state. For example, attending to the feel of the shirt on your neck, accessing those perceptual contents, switches what was in the background to the foreground, thereby changing one's phenomenal state. (See Hill, 1991, 118–26; Searle, 1992.)

Of course, there are notions of access in which the blindsight patient's guesses count as access. There is no right or wrong here. Access comes in various degrees and kinds, and my choice here is mainly determined by the desideratum of finding a notion of A-consciousness that mirrors P-consciousness. If the blind-sight patient's perceptual representations are not P-conscious, it would not do to count them as A-conscious. (I also happen to think that the notion I characterize is more or less one that plays a big role in our thought, but that won't be a major factor here.)

I will mention three main differences between P-consciousness and A-consciousness. The first point, *put crudely*, is that P-conscious content is phenomenal, whereas A-conscious content is representational. It is of the essence of A-conscious content to play a role in reasoning, and only representational content can figure in reasoning. The reason this way of putting the point is crude is that many (perhaps even all) phenomenal contents are *also* representational. And some of the representational contents of a P-conscious state may be intrinsic to those P-contents.[10]

(In the last paragraph, I used the notion of P-conscious *content*. The P-conscious content of a state is the totality of the state's experiential properties, what it is like to be in that state. One can think of the P-conscious content of a state as the state's experiential "value" by analogy to the representational content as the state's representational "value." In my view, the content of an experience can be both P-conscious and A-conscious; the former in virtue of its phenomenal feel and the latter in virtue of its representational properties.)

A closely related point: A-conscious states are necessarily transitive: A-conscious states must always be states of consciousness *of*. P-conscious states, by contrast, sometimes are and sometimes are not transitive. P-consciousness, as such, is not consciousness of. (I'll return to this point in a few paragraphs.)

Second, A-consciousness is a functional notion, and so A-conscious content is system-relative: what makes a state A-conscious is what a representation of its content does in a system. P-consciousness is not a functional notion.[11] In terms of Schacter's model of the mind (see the original version of this paper Block [1995]), content gets to be P-conscious because of what happens *inside* the P-consciousness module. But what makes content A-conscious is not anything that could go on *inside* a module, but rather informational relations *among* modules. Content is A-conscious in virtue of (a representation with that content) reaching the Executive system, the system that is in charge of rational control of action and speech, and to that extent, we could regard the Executive module as the A-consciousness module. But to regard *anything* as an A-consciousness module is misleading, because what makes a typical A-conscious representation A-conscious is what getting to the Executive module sets it up to *do*, namely affect reasoning and action.

A third difference is that there is such a thing as a P-conscious *type* or *kind* of state. For example the feel of pain is a P-conscious type—every pain must have that feel. But any particular token thought that is A-conscious at a given time could fail to be accessible at some other time, just as my car is accessible now, but will not be later when my wife has it. A state whose content is informationally promiscuous now may not be so later.

The paradigm P-conscious states are sensations, whereas the paradigm A-conscious states are "propositional attitude" states like thoughts, beliefs and desires, states with representational content expressed by "that" clauses. (E.g., the thought that grass is green.) What, then, gets broadcast when a P-conscious state is also A-conscious? The most straightforward answer is: the P-content itself. However, exactly what this comes to depends on what exactly P-content is. If P-content is non-conceptual, it may be said that P contents are not the right sort of thing to play a role in inference and guiding action. However, even with non-humans, pain plays a rational role in guiding action. Different actions are appropriate responses to pains in different locations. Since the contents of pain do in fact play a rational role, either their contents are conceptualized *enough*, or else nonconceptual or not very conceptual content can play a rational role.

There is a familiar distinction, alluded to above, between "consciousness" in the sense in which we speak of a state as being a conscious state (intransitive consciousness) and consciousness *of* something (transitive consciousness). (The transitive/intransitive terminology seems to have appeared first in Malcolm [1984], but see also Rosenthal [1997]. Humphrey [1992] mentions that the intransitive usage is much more recent, only 200 years old.) It is easy to fall into an identification of P-consciousness with intransitive consciousness and a corresponding identification of access-consciousness with transitive consciousness. Such an identification is over simple. As I mentioned earlier, P-conscious contents can be representational. Consider a perceptual state of seeing a square. This state has a P-conscious content that represents something, a square, and thus it is a state of P-consciousness *of* the square. It is a state of P-consciousness of the square even if it doesn't represent the square *as* a square, as would be the case if the perceptual state is a state of an animal that doesn't have the concept of a square. Since there can be P-consciousness *of* something, P-consciousness is not to be identified with intransitive consciousness.

Here is a second reason why the transitive/intransitive distinction cannot be identified with the P-consciousness/A-consciousness distinction: The *of*-ness required for transitivity does not guarantee that a content be utilizable by a *consuming* system, a system that uses the representations for reasoning or planning or control of action at the level required for A-consciousness. For example, a perceptual state of a brain-damaged creature might be a state of P-consciousness of, say, motion, even though connections to reasoning and rational control of action are damaged so that the state is not A-conscious. In sum, P-consciousness can be consciousness of, and consciousness of need not be A-consciousness.

Those who are uncomfortable with P-consciousness should pay close attention to A-consciousness because it is a good candidate for a reductionist identification with P-consciousness.[12]

Many of my critics (Searle, 1992; Burge, 1997) have noted that if there can be "zombies," cases of A without P, they are not conscious in any sense of the term. I am sympathetic, but I don't agree with the conclusion that some have drawn that the A-sense is not a sense of "consciousness" and that A is not a kind of consciousness. A-consciousness can be a kind of consciousness even if it is parasitic on a core notion of P-consciousness. A parquet floor is a floor even though it requires another floor beneath it. A-consciousness can come and go against a background of P-consciousness.

The rationale for calling A-consciousness a kind of consciousness is first that it fits a certain kind of quasi-ordinary usage. Suppose one has a vivid mental image that is repressed. Repression need not make the image go away or make it non-phenomenal. One might realize after psychoanalysis that one had the image all along, but that one could not cope with it. It is "unconscious" in the Freudian sense—which is A-unconsciousness. Second, A-consciousness is typically the kind of consciousness that is relevant to use of words like "conscious" and "aware" in cognitive neuroscience. This point is made in detail in my comment on a special issue of the journal *Cognition* (Block, 2001). This issue summarizes the "state of the art" and some of the writers are clearly talking about A-consciousness (or one or another version of monitoring consciousness—see below) whereas others are usually talking about P-consciousness. The A notion of consciousness is the most prominent one in the discussion in that issue and in much of the rest of cognitive neuroscience. (See the article by Dehaene and Naccache in that volume which is very explicit about the use of A-consciousness.) Finally, recall that my purpose in framing the notion of A-consciousness is to get a functional notion of consciousness that is not ad hoc and comes as close to matching P-consciousness as a purely functional notion can. I hope to show that nonetheless there are cracks between P and A. In this context, I prefer to be liberal with terminology, allowing that A is a form of consciousness but not identical to phenomenal consciousness.

A-CONSCIOUSNESS WITHOUT P-CONSCIOUSNESS

The main point of this paper is that these two concepts of consciousness are distinct and quite likely have different extensions yet are easily confused. Let us consider conceptually possible cases of one without the other. Actual cases will be more controversial.

First, I will give some putative examples of A-consciousness without P-consciousness. If there could be a full-fledged phenomenal zombie, say a robot computationally identical to a person, but whose silicon brain did not support P-consciousness, that would do the trick. I think such cases conceptually possible, but this is very controversial. (See Shoemaker, 1975, 1981.)

But there is a less controversial kind of case, a very limited sort of partial zombie. Consider the blindsight patient who "guesses" that there is an "X" rather than an "O" in his blind field. Taking his word for it (for the moment), I am assuming that he has no P-consciousness of the "X." The blindsight patient also has no "X"-representing A-conscious content, because although the information that there is an "X" affects his "guess," it is not available as a premise in reasoning (until he has the quite distinct state of hearing and believing his own guess), or for rational control of action or speech. Marcel (1986) points out that the thirsty blindsight patient would not reach for a glass of water in the blind field. So the blindsight patient's perceptual or quasi-perceptual state is unconscious in the phenomenal *and* access senses (*and* in the monitoring senses to be mentioned below too).

Now imagine something that may not exist, what we might call *superblindsight*. A real blindsight patient can only guess when given a choice from a small set of alternatives ("X"/"O"; horizontal/vertical, etc.). But suppose—interestingly, apparently contrary to fact—that a blindsight patient could be trained to prompt himself at will, guessing what is in the blind field without being told to guess. The superblindsighter spontaneously says "Now I know that there is a horizontal line in my blind field even though I don't actually see it." Visual information of a certain limited sort (excluding color and complicated shapes) from his blind field simply pops into his thoughts in the way that solutions to problems we've been worrying about pop into our thoughts, or in the way some people just know the time or which way is North without having any perceptual experience of it. He knows there is an "X" in his blind field, but he doesn't know the type font of the "X." The superblindsighter himself contrasts what it is like to know visually about an "X" in his blind field and an "X" in his sighted field. There is something it is like to experience the latter, but not the former he says. It is the difference between *just knowing* and knowing via a visual experience. Taking his word for it, here is the point: the perceptual content that there is an "X" in his visual field is A-conscious but not P-conscious. The superblindsight case is a very limited partial zombie.

Of course, the superblindsighter has a *thought* that there is an "X" in his blind field that is *both* A-conscious and P-conscious. But I am not talking about the thought. Rather, I am talking about the state of his perceptual system that gives rise to the thought. It is this state that is A-conscious without being P-conscious.[13]

The (apparent) non-existence of superblindsight is a striking fact, one that a number of writers have noticed, more or less. What Marcel was in effect pointing out was that the blindsight patients, in not reaching for a glass of water, are not superblindsighters. (See also Farah [1994].) Blind perception is never superblind perception.[14]

Notice that the superblindsighter I have described is just a little bit different (though in a crucial way) from the ordinary blindsight patient. In particular, I am *not relying* on what might be thought of as a full-fledged *quasi-zombie*, a super-*duper*-blindsighter whose blindsight is *every bit* as good, functionally speaking, as his sight. In the case of the super-duper blindsighter, the *only* difference between vision in the blind and sighted fields, functionally speaking, is that the quasi-zombie himself regards them differently. Such an example will be regarded by some (though not me) as incoherent—see Dennett, 1991, for example. But we can avoid disagreement about the super-duper-blindsighter by illustrating the idea of A-consciousness without P-consciousness by appealing only to the superblindsighter. Functionalists may want to know why the superblindsight case counts as A-conscious without P-consciousness. After all, they may say, if we have *really high quality access* in mind, the superblindsighter that I have described does not have it, so he lacks *both* P-consciousness and really high quality A-consciousness. The super-duper-blindsighter, on the other hand, *has* both, according to the functionalist, so in neither case, according to the objection, is there A-consciousness without P-consciousness.

One could put the point by distinguishing three types of access: (1) really high quality access, (2) medium access and (3) poor access. The *actual* blindsight patient has poor access (he has to be prompted to guess), the superblindsight patient has medium access and the super-duper blindsight patient—as well as most of us—has really high quality access. The functionalist objector I am talking about identifies P-consciousness with A-consciousness of the really high quality kind, whereas I am allowing A-consciousness with only medium access. (We agree in excluding low quality access.) The issue, then, is whether the functionalist can get away with restricting access to high quality access. I think not. I believe that in some cases, normal phenomenal vision involves only medium access. The easiest case to see for yourself with is peripheral vision. If you wave a colored object near your ear, you will find that in the right location you can see the movement without having the kind of rich access that you have in foveal vision. For example, your ability to recover shape and color is poor.

Why isn't peripheral vision a case of A without P? In peripheral vision, we are both A and P conscious of the same features—e.g., motion but not color. But in superblindsight—so the story goes—there is no P-consciousness of the horizontal line. (He just knows.) I conclude that A without P is conceptually possible even if not actual.

P-CONSCIOUSNESS WITHOUT A-CONSCIOUSNESS

Consider an animal that you are happy to think of as having P-consciousness for which brain damage has destroyed centers of reasoning and rational control of action, thus preventing A-consciousness. It certainly seems *conceptually possible* that the neural bases of P-consciousness systems and A-consciousness systems be distinct, and if they are distinct, then it is possible, at least conceptually possible, for one to be damaged while the other is working well. Evidence has been accumulating for twenty-five years that the primate visual system has distinct dorsal and ventral subsystems. Though there is much disagreement about the specializations of the two systems, it does appear that much of the information in the ventral system is much more closely connected to P-consciousness than information in the dorsal system (Goodale and Milner, 1992). So it may actually be possible to damage A-consciousness without P-consciousness and perhaps even conversely.[15]

Further, one might suppose (Rey, 1983, 1988; White, 1987) that some of our own subsystems—say each of the two hemispheres of the brain—might themselves be separately P-conscious. Some of these subsystems might also be A-consciousness, but other subsystems might not have sufficient machinery for reasoning or reporting or rational control of action to allow their P-conscious states to be A-conscious; so if those states are not accessible to another system that does have adequate machinery, they will be P-conscious but not A-conscious.

Here is another reason to believe in P-consciousness without A-consciousness: Suppose that you are engaged in intense conversation when suddenly at noon you realize that right outside your window, there is—and has been for some time—a pneumatic drill digging up the street. You were aware of the noise all along, one might say, but only at noon are you *consciously aware* of it. That is, you were P-conscious of the noise all along, but at noon you are both P-conscious *and* A-conscious of it. Of course, there is a very similar string of events in which the crucial event at noon is a bit more intellectual. In this alternative scenario, at noon you realize not just that there is and has been a noise, but also that *you are now and have been hearing* the noise. In this alternative scenario, you get "higher order thought" as well as A-consciousness at noon. So on the first scenario, the belief that is acquired at noon is that there is and has been a noise, and on the second scenario, the beliefs that are acquired at noon are the first one plus the belief that you are and have been hearing the noise. But it is the first scenario, not the second that interests me. It is a good case of P-consciousness without A-consciousness. Only at noon is the content of your representation of the drill *broadcast* for use in rational control of action and speech. (Note that A-consciousness requires being broadcast, not merely being available for use.)

In addition, this case involves a natural use of "conscious" and "aware" for A-consciousness and P-consciousness. "Conscious" and "aware" are more or less synonymous, so when we have one of them we might think of it as awareness, but when we have both it is natural to call that conscious awareness. This case of P-consciousness without A-consciousness exploits what William James (1890) called "secondary consciousness" (at least I think it does; James scholars may know better), a category that he may have meant to include cases of P-consciousness without attention.

I have found that the argument of the last paragraph makes those who are distrustful of introspection uncomfortable. I agree that introspection is not the last word, but it is the first word, when it comes to P-consciousness. The example shows the conceptual distinctness of P-consciousness from A-consciousness and it also puts the burden of proof on anyone who would argue that as a matter of empirical fact they come to the same thing.

A-consciousness and P-consciousness very often occur together. When one or the other is missing, we can often speak of unconscious states (when the context is right). Thus, in virtue of missing A-consciousness, we think of Freudian states as unconscious. And in virtue of missing P-consciousness, it is natural to describe the superblindsighter or the unfeeling robot or computer as unconscious. Lack of monitoring-consciousness in the presence of A and P is also sometimes described as unconsciousness. Thus Julian Jaynes describes Greeks as becoming conscious when—in between the time of the Iliad and the Odyssey, they become more reflective.

Flanagan (1992) criticizes my notion of A-consciousness, suggesting that we replace it with a more liberal notion of informational sensitivity that counts the blindsight patient as having access-consciousness of the stimuli in his blind field. The idea is that the blindsight patient has some access to the information about the stimuli in the blind field, and that amount of access is enough for access consciousness. Of course, as I keep saying, the notion of A-consciousness that I have framed is just one of a family of access notions. But there is more than a verbal issue here. The real question is what good is A-consciousness as I have framed it in relation to the blindsight issue? The answer is that in blindsight, the patient is supposed to lack "consciousness" of the stimuli in the blind field. My point is that the blindsight lacks both P-consciousness and a kind of access (both medium and high level access in the terminology used earlier), and that these are easily confused. This point is not challenged by pointing out that the blindsight patient also has a lower level of access to this information.

The kind of access that I have built into A-consciousness plays a role in theory outside of this issue and in daily life. Consider the Freudian unconscious. Suppose I have a Freudian unconscious desire to kill my father and marry my mother. Nothing in Freudian theory requires that this desire be P-unconscious; for all Freudians should care, it might be P-conscious. What is the key to the desire being Freudianly unconscious is that it come out in slips, dreams, and the like, but *not* be freely available as a premise in reasoning (in virtue of having the unconscious desire) and that it not be freely available to guide action and reporting.

Coming out in slips and dreams *makes it conscious in Flanagan's sense*, so that sense of access is no good for capturing the Freudian idea. But it is unconscious in my A-sense. If I can just tell you that I have a desire to kill my father and marry my mother (and not as a result of therapy) then it isn't an unconscious state in either Freud's sense or my A sense. Similar points can be made about a number of the syndromes that are often regarded as disorders of consciousness. For example, consider prosopagnosia, a syndrome in which someone who can see noses, eyes, etc., cannot recognize faces. Prosopagnosia is a disorder of A-consciousness, not P-consciousness and not Flanagan's informational sensitivity. We count someone as a prosopagnosic even when they are able to guess at better than a chance level who the face belongs to, so that excludes Flanagan's notion. Further, P-consciousness is irrelevant, and that excludes P-consciousness as a criterion. It isn't the presence or absence of a feeling of familiarity that defines prosopagnosia, but rather the patient not knowing who the person is whose face he is seeing or whether he knows that person.

I am finished sketching the contrast between P-consciousness and A-consciousness. In the remainder of this section, I will briefly discuss two cognitive notions of consciousness, so that they are firmly distinguished from both P-consciousness and A-consciousness.[16]

NOTES

1. Abridged (with changes by the author). I have changed only what seems mistaken even from the point of view of my former position. No attempt has been made to systematically update the references.
2. See Kuhn (1964) on velocity, and Block and Dworkin (1974) and Wiser and Covey (1983) on heat.
3. But what is it about thoughts that makes them P-conscious? One possibility is that it is just a series of mental images or sub vocalizations that make thoughts P-conscious. Another possibility is that the contents themselves have a P-conscious aspect independently of their vehicles. See Lormand, forthcoming and Burge, 1997.
4. My view is that although P-conscious content cannot be *reduced to* or identified with intentional content (at least not on relatively a priori grounds), P-conscious contents often—maybe always—have an intentional aspect, representing in a primitive non-intentional way.
5. I know some will think that I invoked inverted and absent qualia a few paragraphs above when I described the explanatory gap as involving the question of why a creature with a brain which has a physiological and functional nature like ours couldn't have different experience or none at all. But the spirit of the question as I asked it allows for an answer that explains why such creatures cannot exist, and thus there is no presupposition that these are real possibilities.
6. I have been using the P-consciousness/A-consciousness distinction in my lectures for many years, but it only found its way into print in my "Consciousness and Accessibility" (1990), and my (1991, 1992, 1993). My claims about the distinction have been criticized in Searle (1990, 1992) and Flanagan (1992)—I reply to Flanagan below; and there is an illuminating discussion in Davies and Humphreys (1993b), a point of which will be taken up in a footnote to follow. See also Levine's (1994) review of Flanagan which discusses Flanagan's critique of the distinction. See also Kirk (1992) for an identification of P-consciousness with something like A-consciousness.
7. The full definition was: A state is access-conscious if, in virtue of one's having the state, a representation of its content is (1) inferentially promiscuous, that is, poised for use as a premise in reasoning, (2) poised for rational control of action, and (3) poised for rational control of speech.
8. Dennett (1991) and Dennett and Kinsbourne (1992) advocate the "multiple drafts" account of consciousness. Dennett switched to the cerebral celebrity view in his 1993 paper.
9. See Dennett (2001) and Block (2001) for a more sophisticated treatment of this dialectic.
10. Some may say that only fully conceptualized content can play a role in reasoning, be reportable, and rationally control action. Such a view should not be adopted in isolation from views about which contents are personal and which are sub-personal.
11. The concept of P-consciousness is not a functional concept, however, I acknowledge the empirical possibility that the scientific nature of P-consciousness

has something to do with information processing. We can ill afford to close off empirical possibilities given the difficulty of solving the mystery of P-consciousness.

12. The distinction has some similarity to the sensation/perception distinction; I won't take the space to lay out the differences. See Humphrey (1992) for an interesting discussion of the latter distinction.
13. If you are tempted to deny the existence of these states of the perceptual system, you should think back to the total zombie just mentioned. Putting aside the issue of the possibility of this zombie, note that on a computational notion of cognition, the zombie has *all* the same A-conscious contents that you have (if he is your computational duplicate). A-consciousness is an informational notion. The states of the superblindsighter's perceptual system are A-conscious for the same reason as the zombie's.
14. Farah claims that blindsight is more degraded than sight. But Weiskrantz (1988) notes that his patient DB had better acuity in some areas of the blind field (in some circumstances) than in his sighted field. It would be better to understand her "degraded" in terms of lack of access.
15. Thus, there is a conflict between this physiological claim and the Schacter model which dictates that destroying the P-consciousness module will prevent A-consciousness.
16. I would like to thank Tyler Burge, Susan Carey, David Chalmers, Martin Davies, Wayne Davis, Bert Dreyfus, Güven Güzeldere, Paul Horwich, Jerry Katz, Leonard Katz, Joe Levine, David Rosenthal, Jerome Schaffer, Sydney Shoemaker, Stephen White and Andrew Young for their very helpful comments on earlier versions of this paper. I have been giving this paper at colloquia and meetings since the fall of 1990, and I am grateful to the many audiences which have made interesting and useful comments, especially the audience at the conference on my work at the University of Barcelona in June, 1993.

REFERENCES

Alston, W. (1967) Religion. In *The Encyclopedia of Philosophy*. Macmillan/Free Press, 140–145.

Armstrong, D. M. (1968) *A Materialist Theory of Mind*. Humanities Press.

———. What is consciousness? In *The Nature of Mind*. Cornell University Press.

Atkinson, A. and Davies, M. (1995) Consciousness without conflation. *Behavioral and Brain Sciences* 18, 2, 248–249.

Baars, B. J. (1988) *A Cognitive Theory of Consciousness*. Cambridge University Press.

Block, N. (1980) What is functionalism? In N. Block (ed) *Readings in the Philosophy of Psychology* vol 1. Harvard University Press.

———. (1990) Consciousness and accessibility. *Behavioral and Brain Sciences* 13, 596–598.

———. (1991) Evidence against epiphenomenalism. *Behavioral and Brain Sciences* 14, 4, 670–72.

———. (1992) Begging the question against phenomenal consciousness. *Behavioral and Brain Sciences* 15, 205–6.

———. (1993) Review of D. Dennett, Consciousness Explained. *The Journal of Philosophy* XC, 4, 181–193.

———. (1994) "Consciousness," "Functionalism," "Qualia." In S. Guttenplan (ed) *A Companion to Philosophy of Mind*. Blackwell.

———. (1995) "On a confusion about a function of consciousness." *Behavioral and Brain Sciences* 18, 227–47.

———. (2001) Paradox and cross purposes in recent work on consciousness. *Cognition* 79, 1–2, 197–219.

Block, N. and Dworkin, G. (1974) "IQ, heritability and inequality," Part I. *Philosophy and Public Affairs*, 3, 4, 331–409.

Burge, Tyler (1997) Two kinds of consciousness. In N. Block et al. (eds) *The Nature of Consciousness: Philosophical Debates*. MIT Press.

Carruthers, P. (1989) Brute experience. *Journal of Philosophy* 86, 258–69.

———. (1992) Consciousness and concepts. *Proceedings of the Aristotelian Society, Supplementary Volume LXVI*, 40–59.

Chalmers, D. J. (1997) Availability: The cognitive basis of experience? In N. Block et al. (eds) *The Nature of Consciousness*: MIT Press.

Churchland, P. S. (1983) Consciousness: The transmutation of a concept. *Pacific Philosophical Quarterly* 64, 80–93.

Crick, F. and Koch, C. (1990) Towards a neurobiological theory of consciousness. *Seminars in the Neurosciences* 2, 263–275.

Crick, F. (1994). *The Astonishing Hypothesis*. Scribners.

Davies, M. and Humphreys, G. (1993a) *Consciousness*. Blackwell.

———. (1993b) Introduction. In Davies and Humphreys (1993a).

Dennett, D. (1991) *Consciousness Explained*. Little, Brown.

———. (1993) The message is: There is no medium. *Philosophy and Phenomenological Research* III, 4.

———. (2001) "Are we explaining consciousness yet?" *Cognition* 79, 1–2, 221–37.

Dennett, D. and Kinsbourne, M. (1992a) Time and the observer: The where and when of consciousness in the brain. *Behavioral and Brain Sciences* 15, 183–200.

———. (1992b) Escape from the Cartesian theater. *Behavioral and Brain Sciences* 15, 234–48.

Farah, M. (1994) Visual perception and visual awareness after brain damage: A tutorial overview. In Umilta and Moscovitch (1994).

Flanagan, O. (1992) *Consciousness Reconsidered*. MIT Press.

Gallup, G. (1982) Self-awareness and the emergence of mind in primates. *American Journal of Primatology* 2, 237–48.

Goldman, A. (1993a) The psychology of folk psychology. *Behavioral and Brain Sciences* 16, 1, 15–28.

Goldman, A. (1993b) Consciousness, folk psychology and cognitive science. *Consciousness and Cognition* II, 3.

Goodale, M. and Milner, D. (1992) Separate visual pathways for perception and action. *Trends in Neuroscience* 15, 20–25.

Hauser, M. D., Kralik, J., Botto, C., Garrett, M., and Oser, J. (1995). Self-recognition in primates: Phylogeny and the salience of species-typical traits. *Proc. Nat. Acad. Sci*. 92, 10811–10814.

Hill, C. (1991) *Sensations; A Defense of Type Materialism*. Cambridge.

Humphrey, N. (1992) *A History of the Mind*. Simon & Schuster.

Huxley, T. H. (1866) *Lessons in Elementary Psychology* 8, p. 210. Quoted in Humphrey, 1992.

Jackendoff, R. (1987) *Consciousness and the Computational Mind*. MIT Press.

Jackson, F. (1986) What Mary didn't know. *Journal of Philosophy* 83, 291–95.

Kirk, R. (1992) Consciousness and concepts. *Proceedings of the Aristotelian Society, Supplementary Volume LXVI*, 23–40.

Kuhn, T. (1964) A function for thought experiments. In *Melanges Alexandre Koyre* Vol. 1. Hermann, 307–334.

Levine, J. (1994) Review of Owen Flanagan's *Consciousness Reconsidered. Philosophical Review* 103, 353–56.

Loar, B. (1990) Phenomenal properties. In J. Tomberlin (ed.) *Philosophical Perspectives: Action Theory and Philosophy of Mind*. Ridgeview.

Lormand, E. (forthcoming) What qualitative consciousness is like.

Lycan, W. (1987) *Consciousness*. MIT Press.

McGinn, C. (1991) *The Problem of Consciousness*. Blackwell.

Malcolm, N. (1984) Consciousness and causality. In D. M. Armstrong and N. Malcolm, *Consciousness and Causality*. Blackwell.

Marcel, A. J. (1986) Consciousness and processing: Choosing and testing a null hypothesis. *Behavioral and Brain Sciences* 9, 40–41.

Nagel, T. (1974) What is it like to be a bat? *Philosophical Review*. 83, 435–50.

———. (1979) *Mortal Questions*. Cambridge University Press.

Natsoulas, T. (1993) What is wrong with the appendage theory of consciousness? *Philosophical Psychology* VI, 2, 137–154.

Nelkin, N. The connection between intentionality and consciousness. In Davies and Humphreys (1993a).

Povinelli, D. (1994) What chimpanzees know about the mind. In *Behavioral Diversity in Chimpanzees*. Harvard University Press.

Rey, G. (1983) A reason for doubting the existence of consciousness. In R. Davidson et al. (eds), *Consciousness and Self-Regulation*, vol 3. Plenum.

———. (1988) A question about consciousness. In H. Otto and J. Tuedio (eds), *Perspectives on Mind*. Reidel.

Rosenthal, David (1986) Two concepts of consciousness. *Philosophical Studies* 49, 329–59.

———. (1997) A theory of consciousness. In N. Block et al. (eds), *The Nature of Consciousness: Philosophical Debates*. MIT Press.

Schacter, D. (1989) On the relation between memory and consciousness: Dissociable interactions and conscious experience. In H. Roediger and F. Craik (eds), *Varieties of Memory and Consciousness: Essays in Honour of Endel Tulving*. Erlbaum.

Searle, J. (1983) *Intentionality*. Cambridge.

———. (1990) Who is computing with the brain? *Behavioral and Brain Sciences* 13, 4, 632–642.

———. (1992) *The Rediscovery of the Mind*. MIT Press.

Shoemaker, S. (1975) Functionalism and qualia. *Philosophical Studies*, 27, 291–315.

———. (1981) The inverted spectrum. *Journal of Philosophy* 74, 7, 357–81.

Stich, S. (1978) Autonomous psychology and the belief-desire thesis. *The Monist* 61: 573–91.

Van Gulick, R. (1989) What difference does consciousness make? *Philosophical Topics* 17, 1, 211–230.

———. (1993) Understanding the phenomenal mind: Are we all just armadillos? In Davies and Humphreys (1993a).

Weiskrantz, L. (1988) Some contributions of neuropsychology of vision and memory to the problem of consciousness. In Marcel and Bisiach (1988).

White, S. L. (1987) What is it like to be an homunculus? *Pacific Philosophical Quarterly* 68, 148–174.

Wiser, M. and Carey, S. (1983) When heat and temperature were one. In D. Gentner and A. Stevens (eds) *Mental Models*. Lawrence Erlbaum.

◈ MINDS AND MACHINES ◈

Computing Machinery and Intelligence

A. M. TURING

Widely considered to be the father of modern computer science, A. M. Turing (1912–54) was an English mathematician and logician. His life story and work as a codebreaker during World War II have been memorialized in the play *Breaking the Code*.

"Computing Machinery and Intelligence" was originally published in the philosophy journal *Mind* in 1950. The notion of the Turing test, which is introduced in this essay, set the framework for subsequent discussions of what it would mean for a machine to think. Some brief sections of the original essay are omitted in this selection.

1. THE IMITATION GAME

I propose to consider the question, "Can machines think?" This should begin with definitions of the meaning of the terms "machine" and "think." The definitions might be framed so as to reflect so far as possible the normal use of the words, but this attitude is dangerous. If the meaning of the words "machine" and "think" are to be found by examining how they are commonly used it is difficult to escape the conclusion that the meaning and the answer to the question, "Can machines think?" is to be sought in a statistical survey such as a Gallup poll. But this is absurd. Instead of attempting such a definition I shall replace

From *Mind* Vol., LIX, no. 236 (October 1950). Reprinted by permission of Oxford University Press.

the question by another, which is closely related to it and is expressed in relatively unambiguous words.

The new form of the problem can be described in terms of a game which we call the "imitation game." It is played with three people, a man (A), a woman (B), and an interrogator (C) who may be of either sex. The interrogator stays in a room apart from the other two. The object of the game for the interrogator is to determine which of the other two is the man and which is the woman. He knows them by labels X and Y, and at the end of the game he says either "X is A and Y is B" or "X is B and Y is A." The interrogator is allowed to put questions to A and B thus:

> C: Will X please tell me the length of his or her hair?

Now suppose X is actually A, then A must answer. It is A's object in the game to try and cause C to make the wrong identification. His answer might therefore be

"My hair is shingled, and the longest strands are about nine inches long."

In order that tones of voice may not help the interrogator the answers should be written, or better still, typewritten. The ideal arrangement is to have a teleprinter communicating between the two rooms. Alternatively the question and answers can be repeated by an intermediary. The object of the game for the third player (B) is to help the interrogator. The best strategy for her is probably to give truthful answers. She can add such things as "I am the woman, don't listen to him!" to her answers, but it will avail nothing as the man can make similar remarks.

We now ask the question, "What will happen when a machine takes the part of A in this game?" Will the interrogator decide wrongly as often when the game is played like this as he does when the game is played between a man and a woman? These questions replace our original, "Can machines think?"

2. CRITIQUE OF THE NEW PROBLEM

As well as asking, "What is the answer to this new form of the question," one may ask, "Is this new question a worthy one to investigate?" This latter question we investigate without further ado, thereby cutting short an infinite regress.

The new problem has the advantage of drawing a fairly sharp line between the physical and the intellectual capacities of a man. No engineer or chemist claims to be able to produce a material which is indistinguishable from the human skin. It is possible that at some time this might be done, but even supposing this invention available we should feel there was little point in trying to make a "thinking machine" more human by dressing it up in such artificial flesh. The form in which we have set the problem reflects this fact in the condition which prevents the interrogator from seeing or touching the other competitors, or hearing their voices. Some other advantages of the proposed criterion may be shown up by specimen questions and answers. Thus:

Q: Please write me a sonnet on the subject of the Forth Bridge.
A: Count me out on this one. I never could write poetry.
Q: Add 34957 to 70764
A: (Pause about 30 seconds and then give as answer) 105621.
Q: Do you play chess?
A: Yes.
Q: I have K at my K1, and no other pieces. You have only K at K6 and R at R1. It is your move. What do you play?
A: (After a pause of 15 seconds) R-R8 mate.

The question and answer method seems to be suitable for introducing almost any one of the fields of human endeavour that we wish to include. We do not wish to penalise the machine for its inability to shine in beauty competitions, nor to penalise a man for losing in a race against an aeroplane. The conditions of our game make these disabilities irrelevant. The "witnesses" can brag, if they consider it advisable, as much as they please about their charms, strength or heroism, but the interrogator cannot demand practical demonstrations.

The game may perhaps be criticised on the ground that the odds are weighted too heavily against the machine. If the man were to try and pretend to be the machine he would clearly make a very poor showing. He would be given away at once by slowness and inaccuracy in arithmetic. May not machines carry out something which ought to be described as thinking but which is very different from what a man does? This objection is a very strong one, but at least we can say that if, nevertheless, a machine can be constructed to play the imitation game satisfactorily, we need not be troubled by this objection.

It might be urged that when playing the "imitation game" the best strategy for the machine may possibly be something other than imitation of the behaviour of a man. This may be, but I think it is unlikely that there is any great effect of this kind. In any case there is no intention to investigate here the theory of the game, and it will be assumed that the best strategy is to try to provide answers that would naturally be given by a man.

3. THE MACHINES CONCERNED IN THE GAME

The question which we put in § I will not be quite definite until we have specified what we mean by the word "machine." It is natural that we should wish to permit every kind of engineering technique to be used in our machines. We also wish to allow the possibility that an engineer or team of engineers may construct a machine which works, but whose manner of operation cannot be satisfactorily described by its constructors because they have applied a method which is largely experimental. Finally, we wish to exclude from the machines men born in the usual manner. It is difficult to frame the definitions so as to satisfy these three conditions. One might for instance insist that the team of engineers should be all of one sex, but this would not really be satisfactory, for it is probably possible to rear a complete individual from a single cell of the skin (say) of a man. To do so would be a feat of biological technique deserving of the very highest praise, but we would not be inclined to regard it as a case of "constructing a thinking machine." This prompts us to abandon the requirement that every kind of technique should be permitted. We are the more ready to do so in view of the fact that the present interest in "thinking machines" has been aroused by a particular kind of machine, usually called an "electronic computer" or "digital computer." Following this suggestion we only permit digital computers to take part in our game.

This restriction appears at first sight to be a very drastic one. I shall attempt to show that it is not so in reality. To do this necessitates a short account of the nature and properties of these computers.

It may also be said that this identification of machines with digital computers, like our criterion for "thinking," will only be unsatisfactory if (contrary to my belief), it turns out that digital computers are unable to give a good showing in the game.

There are already a number of digital computers in working order, and it may be asked, "Why not try the experiment straight away? It would be easy to satisfy the conditions of the game. A number of interrogators could be used, and statistics compiled to show how often the right identification was given." The short answer is that we are not asking whether all digital computers would do well in the game nor whether the computers at present available would do well, but whether there are imaginable computers which would do well. But this is only the short answer. We shall see this question in a different light later.

4. DIGITAL COMPUTERS

The idea behind digital computers may be explained by saying that these machines are intended to carry out any operations which could be done by a human computer. The human computer is supposed to be following fixed rules; he has no authority to deviate from them in any detail. We may suppose that these rules are supplied in a book, which is altered whenever he is put on to a new job. He has also an unlimited supply of paper on which he does his calculations. He may also do his multiplications and additions on a "desk machine," but this is not important.

If we use the above explanation as a definition we shall be in danger of circularity of argument. We avoid this by giving an outline of the means by which the desired effect is achieved. A digital computer can usually be regarded as consisting of three parts:

(i) Store.
(ii) Executive unit.
(iii) Control.

The store is a store of information, and corresponds to the human computer's paper, whether this is the paper on which he does his calculations or that on which his book of rules is printed. In so far as the human computer does calculations in his head a part of the store will correspond to his memory.

The executive unit is the part which carries out the various individual operations involved in a calculation. What these individual operations are will vary from machine to machine. Usually fairly lengthy operations can be done such as "Multiply 3540675445 by 7076345687" but in some machines only very simple ones such as "Write down 0" are possible.

We have mentioned that the "book of rules" supplied to the computer is replaced in the machine by a part of the store. It is then called the "table of instructions." It is the duty of the control to see that these instructions are obeyed correctly and in the right order. The control is so constructed that this necessarily happens.

The information in the store is usually broken up into packets of moderately small size. In one machine, for instance, a packet might consist of ten decimal digits. Numbers are assigned to the parts of the store in which the various packets of information are stored, in some systematic manner. A typical instruction might say—

"Add the number stored in position 6809 to that in 4302 and put the result back into the latter storage position."

Needless to say it would not occur in the machine expressed in English. It would more likely be coded in a form such as 6809430217. Here 17 says which of various possible operations is to be performed on the two numbers. In this case the operation is that described above, *viz.* "Add the number...." It will be noticed that the instruction takes up 10 digits and so forms one packet of information, very conveniently. The control will normally take the instructions to be obeyed in the order of the positions in which they are stored, but occasionally an instruction such as

"Now obey the instruction stored in position 5606, and continue from there"

may be encountered, or again

"If position 4505 contains 0 obey next the instruction stored in 6707, otherwise continue straight on."

Instructions of these latter types are very important because they make it possible for a sequence of operations to be repeated over and over again until some condition is fulfilled, but in doing so to obey, not fresh instructions on each repetition, but the same ones over and over again. To take a domestic analogy. Suppose Mother wants Tommy to call at the cobbler's every morning on his way to school to see if her shoes are done, she can ask him afresh every morning. Alternatively she can stick up a notice once and for all in the hall which he will see when he leaves for school and which tells him to call for the shoes, and also to destroy the notice when he comes back if he has the shoes with him.

The reader must accept it as a fact that digital computers can be constructed, and indeed have been constructed, according to the principles we have described, and that they can in fact mimic the actions of a human computer very closely.

The book of rules which we have described our human computer as using is of course a convenient fiction. Actual human computers really remember what they have got to do. If one wants to make a machine mimic the behaviour of the human computer in some complex operation one has to ask him how it is done, and then translate the answer into the form of an instruction table. Constructing instruction tables is usually described as "programming." To "programme a machine to carry out the operation A" means to put the appropriate instruction table into the machine so that it will do A.

An interesting variant on the idea of a digital computer is a "digital computer with a random element." These have instructions involving the throwing of a die or some equivalent electronic process; one such instruction might for instance be, "Throw the die and put the resulting number into store 1000." Sometimes such a machine is described as having free will (though I would not use this phrase myself). It is not normally possible to determine from observing a machine whether it has a random element, for a similar effect can be produced by such devices as making the choices depend on the digits of the decimal for π.

Most actual digital computers have only a finite store. There is no theoretical difficulty in the idea of a computer with an unlimited store. Of course only a finite part can have been used at any one time. Likewise only a finite amount can have been constructed, but we can imagine more and more being added as required. Such computers have special theoretical interest and will be called infinitive capacity computers.

The idea of a digital computer is an old one. Charles Babbage, Lucasian Professor of Mathematics at Cambridge from 1828 to 1839, planned such a machine, called the Analytical Engine, but it was never completed. Although Babbage had all the essential ideas, his machine was not at that time such a very attractive prospect. The speed which would have been available would be definitely faster than a human computer but something like 100 times slower than the Manchester machine, itself one of the slower of the modern machines. The storage was to be purely mechanical, using wheels and cards.

The fact that Babbage's Analytical Engine was to be entirely mechanical will help us to rid ourselves of a superstition. Importance is often attached to the fact that modern digital computers are electrical, and that the nervous system also is electrical. Since Babbage's machine was not electrical, and since all digital computers are in a sense equivalent, we see that this use of electricity cannot be of theoretical importance. Of course electricity usually comes in where fast signalling is concerned, so that it is not surprising that we find it in both these connections. In the nervous system chemical phenomena are at least as important as electrical. In certain computers the storage system is mainly acoustic. The feature of using electricity is thus seen to be only a very superficial similarity. If we wish to find such similarities we should look rather for mathematical analogies of function.

5. UNIVERSALITY OF DIGITAL COMPUTERS

The digital computers considered in the last section may be classified amongst the "discrete state machines." These are the machines which move by sudden jumps or clicks from one quite definite state to another. These states are sufficiently different for the possibility of confusion between them to be ignored. Strictly speaking there are no such machines. Everything really moves continuously. But there are many kinds of machine which can profitably be *thought of* as being discrete state machines. For instance in considering the switches for a lighting system it is a convenient fiction that each switch must be definitely on or definitely off. There must be intermediate positions, but for most purposes we can forget about them. As an example of a discrete state machine we might consider a wheel which clicks round through 120° once a second, but may be stopped by a lever which can be operated from outside; in addition a lamp is to light in one of the positions of the wheel. This machine could be described abstractly as follows. The internal state of the machine (which is described by the position of the wheel) may be q_1, q_2 or q_3. There is an input signal i_0 or i_1 (position of lever). The internal state at any moment is determined by the last state and input signal according to the table

		Last State		
		q_1	q_2	q_3
Input	i_0	q_2	q_3	q_1
	i_1	q_1	q_2	q_3

The output signals, the only externally visible indication of the internal state (the light) are described by the table

State	q_1	q_2	q_3
Output	o_0	o_0	o_1

This example is typical of discrete state machines. They can be described by such tables provided they have only a finite number of possible states.

It will seem that given the initial state of the machine and the input signals it is always possible to predict all future states. This is reminiscent of Laplace's view that from the complete state of the universe at one moment of time, as described by the positions and velocities of all particles, it should be possible to predict all future states. The prediction which we are considering is, however, rather nearer to practicability than that considered by Laplace.* The system of the "universe as a whole" is such that quite small errors in the initial conditions can have an overwhelming effect at a later time. The displacement of a single electron by a billionth of a centimetre at one moment might make the difference between a man being killed by an avalanche a year later, or escaping. It is an essential property of the mechanical system which we have called "discrete state machines" that this phenomenon does not occur. Even when we consider the actual physical machines instead of the idealised machines, reasonably accurate knowledge of the state at one moment yields reasonably accurate knowledge any number of steps later.

As we have mentioned, digital computers fall within the class of discrete state machines. But the number of states of which such a machine is capable is usually enormously large. For instance, the number for the machine now working at Manchester is about $2^{165,000}$, i.e., about $10^{50,000}$. Compare this with our example of the clicking wheel described above, which had three states. It is not difficult to see why the number of states should be so immense. The computer includes a store corresponding to the paper used by a human computer. It must be possible to write into the store any one of the combinations of symbols which might have been written on the paper. For simplicity suppose that only digits from 0 to 9 are used as symbols. Variations in handwriting are ignored. Suppose the computer is allowed 100 sheets of paper each containing 50 lines each with room for 30 digits. Then the number of states is $10^{100\times50\times30}$, i.e., $10^{150,000}$. This is about the number of states of three Manchester machines put together. The logarithm to the base two of the number of states is usually called the "storage capacity" of the machine. Thus the Manchester machine has a storage capacity of about 165,000 and the wheel machine of our example about 1·6. If two machines are put together their capacities must be added to obtain the capacity of the resultant machine. This leads to the possibility of statements such as "The Manchester machine contains 64 magnetic tracks each with a capacity of 2560, eight electronic tubes with a capacity of 1280. Miscellaneous storage amounts to about 300 making a total of 174,380."

Given the table corresponding to a discrete state machine it is possible to predict what it will do. There is no reason why this calculation should not be carried out by means of a digital computer. Provided it could be carried out sufficiently quickly the digital computer could mimic the behaviour of any discrete state machine. The imitation game could then be played with the machine in question (as B) and the mimicking digital computer (as A) and the interrogator would be unable to distinguish them. Of course the digital computer must have an adequate storage capacity as well as working sufficiently fast. Moreover, it must be programmed afresh for each new machine which it is desired to mimic.

This special property of digital computers, that they can mimic any discrete state machine, is described by saying that they are *universal* machines. The existence of machines with this property has the important consequence that, considerations of speed apart, it is unnecessary to design various new machines to do various computing processes. They can all be done with one digital computer, suitably programmed for each case. It will be seen that as a consequence of this all digital computers are in a sense equivalent.

We may now consider again the point raised at the end of §3. It was suggested tentatively that the question, "Can machines think?" should be replaced by "Are there imaginable digital computers which would do well in the imitation game?" If we wish we can make this superficially more general and ask "Are there discrete state machines which would do well?" But in view of the universality property we see that either of these questions is equivalent to this, "Let us fix our attention on one particular digital computer *C*. Is it true that by modifying this computer to have an adequate storage, suitably increasing its speed of action, and providing it with

* Pierre-Simon, Marquis de Laplace (1749–1827) was a French mathematician and astronomer. He is known for his view that a hypothetical intellect who knew all the facts about the present and past state of the universe and its forces could calculate its future states.

an appropriate programme, *C* can be made to play satisfactorily the part of A in the imitation game, the part of B being taken by a man?"

6. CONTRARY VIEWS ON THE MAIN QUESTION

We may now consider the ground to have been cleared and we are ready to proceed to the debate on our question, "Can machines think?" and the variant of it quoted at the end of the last section. We cannot altogether abandon the original form of the problem, for opinions will differ as to the appropriateness of the substitution and we must at least listen to what has to be said in this connexion.

It will simplify matters for the reader if I explain first my own beliefs in the matter. Consider first the more accurate form of the question. I believe that in about fifty years' time it will be possible to programme computers, with a storage capacity of about 10^9, to make them play the imitation game so well that an average interrogator will not have more than 70 per cent. chance of making the right identification after five minutes of questioning. The original question, "Can machines think?" I believe to be too meaningless to deserve discussion. Nevertheless I believe that at the end of the century the use of words and general educated opinion will have altered so much that one will be able to speak of machines thinking without expecting to be contradicted. I believe further that no useful purpose is served by concealing these beliefs. The popular view that scientists proceed inexorably from well-established fact to well-established fact, never being influenced by any unproved conjecture, is quite mistaken. Provided it is made clear which are proved facts and which are conjectures, no harm can result. Conjectures are of great importance since they suggest useful lines of research.

I now proceed to consider opinions opposed to my own . . .*

(3) *The Mathematical Objection*. There are a number of results of mathematical logic which can be used to show that there are limitations to the powers of discrete-state machines. The best known of these results is known as Gödel's theorem,[1] and shows that in any sufficiently powerful logical system statements can be formulated which can neither be proved nor disproved within the system, unless possibly the system itself is inconsistent. There are other, in some respects similar, results due to *Church, Kleene, Rosser*, and *Turing*. The latter result is the most convenient to consider, since it refers directly to machines, whereas the others can only be used in a comparatively indirect argument: for instance if Gödel's theorem* is to be used we need in addition to have some means of describing logical systems in terms of machines, and machines in terms of logical systems. The result in question refers to a type of machine which is essentially a digital computer with an infinite capacity. It states that there are certain things that such a machine cannot do. If it is rigged up to give answers to questions as in the imitation game, there will be some questions to which it will either give a wrong answer, or fail to give an answer at all however much time is allowed for a reply. There may, of course, be many such questions, and questions which cannot be answered by one machine may be satisfactorily answered by another. We are of course supposing for the present that the questions are of the kind to which an answer "Yes" or "No" is appropriate, rather than questions such as "What do you think of Picasso?" The questions that we know the machines must fail on are of this type, "Consider the machine specified as follows. . . . Will this machine ever answer 'Yes' to any question?" The dots are to be replaced by a description of some machine in a standard form, which could be something like that used in § 5. When the machine described bears a certain comparatively simple relation to the machine which is under interrogation, it can be shown that the answer is either wrong or not forthcoming. This is the mathematical result:

* The objections omitted here include: (1) *The Theological Objection*; (2) *The 'Heads in the Sand' Objection*; and (9) *The Argument from Extra-Sensory Perception*.

* Austrian mathematician and philosopher of mathematics Kurt Gödel (1906–78) was one of the most important logicians of all time. He proved the theorem discussed here when he was twenty-five years old.

it is argued that it proves a disability of machines to which the human intellect is not subject.

The short answer to this argument is that although it is established that there are limitations to the powers of any particular machine, it has only been stated, without any sort of proof, that no such limitations apply to the human intellect. But I do not think this view can be dismissed quite so lightly. Whenever one of these machines is asked the appropriate critical question, and gives a definite answer, we know that this answer must be wrong, and this gives us a certain feeling of superiority. Is this feeling illusory? It is no doubt quite genuine, but I do not think too much importance should be attached to it. We too often give wrong answers to questions ourselves to be justified in being very pleased at such evidence of fallibility on the part of the machines. Further, our superiority can only be felt on such an occasion in relation to the one machine over which we have scored our petty triumph. There would be no question of triumphing simultaneously over *all* machines. In short, then, there might be men cleverer than any given machine, but then again there might be other machines cleverer again, and so on.

Those who hold to the mathematical argument would, I think, mostly be willing to accept the imitation game as a basis for discussion. . . .

(4). *The Argument from Consciousness*. This argument is very well expressed in *Professor Jefferson's* Lister Oration for 1949* from which I quote. "Not until a machine can write a sonnet or compose a concerto because of thoughts and emotions felt, and not by the chance fall of symbols, could we agree that machine equals brain—that is, not only write it but know that it had written it. No mechanism could feel (and not merely artificially signal, an easy contrivance) pleasure at its successes, grief when its valves fuse, be warmed by flattery, be made miserable by its mistakes, be charmed by sex, be angry or depressed when it cannot get what it wants."

This argument appears to be a denial of the validity of our test. According to the most extreme form of this view the only way by which one could be sure that a machine thinks is to *be* the machine and to feel oneself thinking. One could then describe these feelings to the world, but of course no one would be justified in taking any notice. Likewise according to this view the only way to know that a *man* thinks is to be that particular man. It is in fact the solipsist point of view. It may be the most logical view to hold but it makes communication of ideas difficult. A is liable to believe "A thinks but B does not" whilst B believes "B thinks but A does not." Instead of arguing continually over this point it is usual to have the polite convention that everyone thinks.

I am sure that Professor Jefferson does not wish to adopt the extreme and solipsist point of view. Probably he would be quite willing to accept the imitation game as a test. The game (with the player B omitted) is frequently used in practice under the name of *viva voce* to discover whether some one really understands something or has "learnt it parrot fashion." Let us listen in to a part of such a viva voce.

INTERROGATOR: In the first line of your sonnet which reads "Shall I compare thee to a summer's day," would not "a spring day" do as well or better?

WITNESS: It wouldn't scan.

INTERROGATOR: How about "a winter's day" That would scan all right.

WITNESS: Yes, but nobody wants to be compared to a winter's day.

INTERROGATOR: Would you say Mr. Pickwick reminded you of Christmas?

WITNESS: In a way.

INTERROGATOR: Yet Christmas is a winter's day, and I do not think Mr. Pickwick would mind the comparison.

WITNESS: I don't think you're serious. By a winter's day one means a typical winter's day, rather than a special one like Christmas.

And so on. What would Professor Jefferson say if the sonnet-writing machine was able to answer like this in the viva voce? I do not know whether he would regard the machine as "merely artificially signalling" these answers, but if the answers were

* Geoffrey Jefferson (1886–1961) was an English neurologist and neurosurgeon; he delivered an oration entitled "The Mind of Mechanical Man" before the Royal College of Surgeons of England on June 9, 1949.

as satisfactory and sustained as in the above passage I do not think he would describe it as "an easy contrivance." This phrase is, I think, intended to cover such devices as the inclusion in the machine of a record of someone reading a sonnet, with appropriate switching to turn it on from time to time.

In short then, I think that most of those who support the argument from consciousness could be persuaded to abandon it rather than be forced into the solipsist position. They will then probably be willing to accept our test.

I do not wish to give the impression that I think there is no mystery about consciousness. There is, for instance, something of a paradox connected with any attempt to localise it. But I do not think these mysteries necessarily need to be solved before we can answer the question with which we are concerned in this paper.

(5) *Arguments from Various Disabilities.* These arguments take the form, "I grant you that you can make machines do all the things you have mentioned but you will never be able to make one to do X." Numerous features X are suggested in this connexion. I offer a selection:

> Be kind, resourceful, beautiful, friendly . . . have initiative, have a sense of humour, tell right from wrong, make mistakes . . ., fall in love, enjoy strawberries and cream, . . . make some one fall in love with it, learn from experience . . ., use words properly, be the subject of its own thought . . ., have as much diversity of behaviour as a man, do something really new . . .

No support is usually offered for these statements. I believe they are mostly founded on the principle of scientific induction. A man has seen thousands of machines in his lifetime. From what he sees of them he draws a number of general conclusions. They are ugly, each is designed for a very limited purpose, when required for a minutely different purpose they are useless, the variety of behaviour of any one of them is very small, etc., etc. Naturally he concludes that these are necessary properties of machines in general. Many of these limitations are associated with the very small storage capacity of most machines. (I am assuming that the idea of storage capacity is extended in some way to cover machines other than discrete-state machines. The exact definition does not matter as no mathematical accuracy is claimed in the present discussion.) A few years ago, when very little had been heard of digital computers, it was possible to elicit much incredulity concerning them, if one mentioned their properties without describing their construction. That was presumably due to a similar application of the principle of scientific induction. These applications of the principle are of course largely unconscious. When a burnt child fears the fire and shows that he fears it by avoiding it, I should say that he was applying scientific induction. (I could of course also describe his behaviour in many other ways.) The works and customs of mankind do not seem to be very suitable material to which to apply scientific induction. A very large part of space-time must be investigated, if reliable results are to be obtained. Otherwise we may (as most English children do) decide that everybody speaks English, and that it is silly to learn French.

There are, however, special remarks to be made about many of the disabilities that have been mentioned. The inability to enjoy strawberries and cream may have struck the reader as frivolous. Possibly a machine might be made to enjoy this delicious dish, but any attempt to make one do so would be idiotic. What is important about this disability is that it contributes to some of the other disabilities, e.g., to the difficulty of the same kind of friendliness occurring between man and machine as between white man and white man, or between black man and black man.

The claim that "machines cannot make mistakes" seems a curious one. One is tempted to retort, "Are they any the worse for that?" But let us adopt a more sympathetic attitude, and try to see what is really meant. I think this criticism can be explained in terms of the imitation game. It is claimed that the interrogator could distinguish the machine from the man simply by setting them a number of problems in arithmetic. The machine would be unmasked because of its deadly accuracy. The reply to this is simple. The machine (programmed for playing the game) would not attempt to give the *right* answers to the arithmetic problems. It would deliberately introduce mistakes in a manner calculated to confuse the interrogator. A mechanical fault would probably show itself through an unsuitable decision as to what sort of a mistake to make in the arithmetic. Even this interpretation of the criticism is not sufficiently sympathetic. But we cannot afford the space to go into it much further. It seems to me that this criticism depends on a confusion between two kinds of mistake. We may call them "errors of functioning" and "errors of conclusion." Errors of functioning are due to some mechanical or electrical fault which causes the machine to behave otherwise than it was designed to do. In philosophical discussions one likes to ignore the possibility of such errors; one is therefore discussing "abstract machines." These abstract machines are mathematical fictions rather than physical objects. By definition they are incapable of errors of functioning. In this sense we can truly say that "machines can never make mistakes." Errors of conclusion can only arise when some meaning is attached to the output signals from the machine. The machine might, for instance, type out mathematical equations, or sentences in English. When a false proposition is typed we say that the machine has committed an error of conclusion. There is clearly no reason at all for saying that a machine cannot make this kind of mistake. It might do nothing but type out repeatedly "0 = 1." To take a less perverse example, it might have some method for drawing conclusions by scientific induction. We must expect such a method to lead occasionally to erroneous results.

The claim that a machine cannot be the subject of its own thought can of course only be answered if it can be shown that the machine has *some* thought with *some* subject matter. Nevertheless, "the subject matter of a machine's operations" does seem to mean something, at least to the people who deal with it. If, for instance, the machine was trying to find a solution of the equation $x^2-40x-11 = 0$ one would be tempted to describe this equation as part of the machine's subject matter at that moment. In this sort of sense a machine undoubtedly can be its own subject matter. It may be used to help in making up its own programmes, or to predict the effect of alterations in its own structure. By observing the results of its own behaviour it can modify its own programmes so as to achieve some purpose more effectively. These are possibilities of the near future, rather than Utopian dreams.

The criticism that a machine cannot have much diversity of behaviour is just a way of saying that it cannot have much storage capacity. Until fairly recently a storage capacity of even a thousand digits was very rare.

The criticisms that we are considering here are often disguised forms of the argument from consciousness. Usually if one maintains that a machine *can* do one of these things, and describes the kind of method that the machine could use, one will not make much of an impression. It is thought that the method (whatever it may be, for it must be mechanical) is really rather base. Compare the parenthesis in Jefferson's statement quoted above.

(6) *Lady Lovelace's Objection** Our most detailed information of Babbage's Analytical Engine comes from a memoir by *Lady Lovelace*. In it she states, "The Analytical Engine has no pretensions to *originate* anything. It can do *whatever we know how to order it* to perform" (her italics). This statement is quoted by *Hartree* (p. 70) who adds: "This does not imply that it may not be possible to construct electronic equipment which will 'think for itself,' or in which, in biological terms, one could set up a conditioned reflex, which would serve as a basis for 'learning.' Whether this is possible in principle or not is a stimulating and exciting question, suggested by some of these recent developments. But it did not seem that the machines constructed or projected at the time had this property."

I am in thorough agreement with Hartree over this. It will be noticed that he does not assert that the machines in question had not got the property, but rather that the evidence available to Lady Lovelace did not encourage her to believe that they had it. It is quite possible that the machines in question had in a sense got this property. For suppose that some discrete-state machine has the property. The Analytical Engine was a universal digital computer, so that, if its storage capacity and speed were adequate, it could by suitable programming be made to mimic the machine in question. Probably this argument did not occur to the Countess or to Babbage. In any case there was no obligation on them to claim all that could be claimed.

* Ada Byron, Lady Lovelace, (1815–52) was the author of the world's first computer program, which specified a method of computing a sequence of natural numbers known as Bernoulli numbers.

This whole question will be considered again under the heading of learning machines.

A variant of Lady Lovelace's objection states that a machine can "never do anything really new." This may be parried for a moment with the saw, "There is nothing new under the sun." Who can be certain that "original work" that he has done was not simply the growth of the seed planted in him by teaching, or the effect of following well-known general principles. A better variant of the objection says that a machine can never "take us by surprise." This statement is a more direct challenge and can be met directly. Machines take me by surprise with great frequency. This is largely because I do not do sufficient calculation to decide what to expect them to do, or rather because, although I do a calculation, I do it in a hurried, slipshod fashion, taking risks. Perhaps I say to myself, "I suppose the voltage here ought to be the same as there: anyway let's assume it is." Naturally I am often wrong, and the result is a surprise for me for by the time the experiment is done these assumptions have been forgotten. These admissions lay me open to lectures on the subject of my vicious ways, but do not throw any doubt on my credibility when I testify to the surprises I experience.

I do not expect this reply to silence my critic. He will probably say that such surprises are due to some creative mental act on my part, and reflect no credit on the machine. This leads us back to the argument from consciousness, and far from the idea of surprise. It is a line of argument we must consider closed, but it is perhaps worth remarking that the appreciation of something as surprising requires as much of a "creative mental act" whether the surprising event originates from a man, a book, a machine or anything else.

The view that machines cannot give rise to surprises is due, I believe, to a fallacy to which philosophers and mathematicians are particularly subject. This is the assumption that as soon as a fact is presented to a mind all consequences of that fact spring into the mind simultaneously with it. It is a very useful assumption under many circumstances, but one too easily forgets that it is false. A natural consequence of doing so is that one then assumes that there is no virtue in the mere working out of consequences from data and general principles.

(7) *Argument from Continuity in the Nervous System*. The nervous system is certainly not a discrete-state machine. A small error in the information about the size of a nervous impulse impinging on a neuron, may make a large difference to the size of the outgoing impulse. It may be argued that, this being so, one cannot expect to be able to mimic the behaviour of the nervous system with a discrete-state system.

It is true that a discrete-state machine must be different from a continuous machine. But if we adhere to the conditions of the imitation game, the interrogator will not be able to take any advantage of this difference. The situation can be made clearer if we consider some other simpler continuous machine. A differential analyser will do very well. (A differential analyser is a certain kind of machine not of the discrete-state type used for some kinds of calculation.) Some of these provide their answers in a typed form, and so are suitable for taking part in the game. It would not be possible for a digital computer to predict exactly what answers the differential analyser would give to a problem, but it would be quite capable of giving the right sort of answer. For instance, if asked to give the value of π (actually about 3·1416) it would be reasonable to choose at random between the values 3·12, 3·13, 3·14, 3·15, 3·16 with the probabilities of 0·05, 0·15, 0·55, 0·19, 0·06 (say). Under these circumstances it would be very difficult for the interrogator to distinguish the differential analyser from the digital computer.

(8) *The Argument from Informality of Behaviour*. It is not possible to produce a set of rules purporting to describe what a man should do in every conceivable set of circumstances. One might for instance have a rule that one is to stop when one sees a red traffic light, and to go if one sees a green one, but what if by some fault both appear together? One may perhaps decide that it is safest to stop. But some further difficulty may well arise from this decision later. To attempt to provide rules of conduct to cover every eventuality, even those arising from traffic lights, appears to be impossible. With all this I agree.

From this it is argued that we cannot be machines. I shall try to reproduce the argument, but I fear I shall hardly do it justice. It seems to run something like this. "If each man had a definite set of rules of conduct by which he regulated his life he would be no better than a machine. But there are no such rules, so men cannot be machines." The undistributed middle is glaring. I do not think the argument is ever put quite like this, but I believe this is the argument used nevertheless. There may however be a certain confusion between "rules of conduct" and "laws of behaviour" to cloud the issue. By "rules of conduct" I mean precepts such as "Stop if you see red lights," on which one can act, and of which one can be conscious. By "laws of behaviour" I mean laws of nature as applied to a man's body such as "if you pinch him he will squeak." If we substitute "laws of behaviour which regulate his life" for "laws of conduct by which he regulates his life" in the argument quoted the undistributed middle is no longer insuperable. For we believe that it is not only true that being regulated by laws of behaviour implies being some sort of machine (though not necessarily a discrete-state machine), but that conversely being such a machine implies being regulated by such laws. However, we cannot so easily convince ourselves of the absence of complete laws of behaviour as of complete rules of conduct. The only way we know of for finding such laws is scientific observation, and we certainly know of no circumstances under which we could say, "We have searched enough. There are no such laws."

We can demonstrate more forcibly that any such statement would be unjustified. For suppose we could be sure of finding such laws if they existed. Then given a discrete-state machine it should certainly be possible to discover by observation sufficient about it to predict its future behaviour, and this within a reasonable time, say a thousand years. But this does not seem to be the case. I have set up on the Manchester computer a small programme using only 1000 units of storage, whereby the machine supplied with one sixteen figure number replies with another within two seconds. I would defy anyone to learn from these replies sufficient about the programme to be able to predict any replies to untried values. . . .

7. LEARNING MACHINES

The reader will have anticipated that I have no very convincing arguments of a positive nature to support my views. If I had I should not have taken such pains to point out the fallacies in contrary views. Such evidence as I have I shall now give.

Let us return for a moment to Lady Lovelace's objection, which stated that the machine can only do what we tell it to do. One could say that a man can "inject" an idea into the machine, and that it will respond to a certain extent and then drop into quiescence, like a piano string struck by a hammer. Another simile would be an atomic pile of less than critical size: an injected idea is to correspond to a neutron entering the pile from without. Each such neutron will cause a certain disturbance which eventually dies away. If, however, the size of the pile is sufficiently increased, the disturbance caused by such an incoming neutron will very likely go on and on increasing until the whole pile is destroyed. Is there a corresponding phenomenon for minds, and is there one for machines? There does seem to be one for the human mind. The majority of them seem to be "sub-critical," i.e., to correspond in this analogy to piles of sub-critical size. An idea presented to such a mind will on average give rise to less than one idea in reply. A smallish proportion are super-critical. An idea presented to such a mind may give rise to a whole "theory" consisting of secondary, tertiary and more remote ideas. Animals' minds seem to be very definitely sub-critical. Adhering to this analogy we ask, "Can a machine be made to be super-critical?"

The "skin of an onion" analogy is also helpful. In considering the functions of the mind or the brain we find certain operations which we can explain in purely mechanical terms. This we say does not correspond to the real mind: it is a sort of skin which we must strip off if we are to find the real mind. But then in what remains we find a further skin to be stripped off, and so on. Proceeding in this way do we ever come to the "real" mind, or do we eventually come to the skin which has nothing in it? In the latter case the whole mind is mechanical. (It would not be a discrete-state machine however. We have discussed this.)

These last two paragraphs do not claim to be convincing arguments. They should rather be described as "recitations tending to produce belief."

The only really satisfactory support that can be given for the view expressed at the beginning of § 6, will be that provided by waiting for the end of the century and then doing the experiment described. But what can we say in the meantime? What steps should be taken now if the experiment is to be successful?

As I have explained, the problem is mainly one of programming. Advances in engineering will have to be made too, but it seems unlikely that these will not be adequate for the requirements. Estimates of the storage capacity of the brain vary from 10^{10} to 10^{15} binary digits. I incline to the lower values and believe that only a very small fraction is used for the higher types of thinking. Most of it is probably used for the retention of visual impressions. I should be surprised if more than 10^9 was required for satisfactory playing of the imitation game, at any rate against a blind man. (Note—The capacity of the *Encyclopaedia Britannica*, 11th edition, is 2×10^9.) A storage capacity of 10^7 would be a very practicable possibility even by present techniques. It is probably not necessary to increase the speed of operations of the machines at all. Parts of modern machines which can be regarded as analogues of nerve cells work about a thousand times faster than the latter. This should provide a "margin of safety" which could cover losses of speed arising in many ways. Our problem then is to find out how to programme these machines to play the game. At my present rate of working I produce about a thousand digits of programme a day, so that about sixty workers, working steadily through the fifty years might accomplish the job, if nothing went into the waste-paper basket. Some more expeditious method seems desirable.

In the process of trying to imitate an adult human mind we are bound to think a good deal about the process which has brought it to the state that it is in. We may notice three components,

(a) The initial state of the mind, say at birth,
(b) The education to which it has been subjected,
(c) Other experience, not to be described as education, to which it has been subjected.

Instead of trying to produce a programme to simulate the adult mind, why not rather try to produce one which simulates the child's? If this were then subjected to an appropriate course of education one would obtain the adult brain. Presumably the child-brain is something like a note-book as one buys it from the stationers. Rather little mechanism, and lots of blank sheets. (Mechanism and writing are from our point of view almost synonymous.) Our hope is that there is so little mechanism in the child-brain that something like it can be easily programmed. The amount of work in the education we can assume, as a first approximation, to be much the same as for the human child.

We have thus divided our problem into two parts. The child-programme and the education process. These two remain very closely connected. We cannot expect to find a good child-machine at the first attempt. One must experiment with teaching one such machine and see how well it learns. One can then try another and see if it is better or worse. There is an obvious connection between this process and evolution, by the identifications

Structure of the child machine = Hereditary material
Changes of the child machine = Mutations
Natural selection = Judgment of the experimenter

One may hope, however, that this process will be more expeditious than evolution. The survival of the fittest is a slow method for measuring advantages. The experimenter, by the exercise of intelligence, should be able to speed it up. Equally important is the fact that he is not restricted to random mutations. If he can trace a cause for some weakness he can probably think of the kind of mutation which will improve it. . . .

The idea of a learning machine may appear paradoxical to some readers. How can the rules of operation of the machine change? They should describe completely how the machine will react whatever its history might be, whatever changes it might undergo. The rules are thus quite time-invariant. This is quite true. The explanation of the paradox is that the rules which get changed in the learning process are of a rather less pretentious kind, claiming only an ephemeral validity. The reader may draw a parallel with the Constitution of the United States.

An important feature of a learning machine is that its teacher will often be very largely ignorant of quite what is going on inside, although he may still be able to some extent to predict his pupil's behaviour. This should apply most strongly to the later education of a machine arising from a child-machine of well-tried design (or programme). This is in clear contrast with normal procedure when using a machine to do computations: one's object is then to have a clear mental picture of the state of the machine at each moment in the computation. This object can only be achieved with a struggle. The view that "the machine can only do what we know how to order it to do,"[2] appears strange in face of this. Most of the programmes which we can put into the machine will result in its doing something that we cannot make sense of at all, or which we regard as completely random behaviour. Intelligent behaviour presumably consists in a departure from the completely disciplined behaviour involved in computation, but a rather slight one, which does not give rise to random behaviour, or to pointless repetitive loops. Another important result of preparing our machine for its part in the imitation game by a process of teaching and learning is that "human fallibility" is likely to be omitted in a rather natural way, i.e., without special "coaching." (The reader should reconcile this with the point of view above). Processes that are learnt do not produce a hundred per cent. certainty of result; if they did they could not be unlearnt.

It is probably wise to include a random element in a learning machine.... A random element is rather useful when we are searching for a solution of some problem. Suppose for instance we wanted to find a number between 50 and 200 which was equal to the square of the sum of its digits, we might start at 51 then try 52 and go on until we got a number that worked. Alternatively we might choose numbers at random until we got a a good one. This method has the advantage that it is unnecessary to keep track of the values that have been tried, but the disadvantage that one may try the same one twice, but this is not very important if there are several solutions. The systematic method has the disadvantage that there may be an enormous block without any solutions in the region which has to be investigated first. Now the learning process may be regarded as a search for a form of behaviour which will satisfy the teacher (or some other criterion). Since there is probably a very large number of satisfactory solutions the random method seems to be better than the systematic. It should be noticed that it is used in the analogous process of evolution. But there the systematic method is not possible. How could one keep track of the different genetical combinations that had been tried, so as to avoid trying them again?

We may hope that machines will eventually compete with men in all purely intellectual fields. But which are the best ones to start with? Even this is a difficult decision. Many people think that a very abstract activity, like the playing of chess, would be best. It can also be maintained that it is best to provide the machine with the best sense organs that money can buy, and then teach it to understand and speak English. This process could follow the normal teaching of a child. Things would be pointed out and named, etc. Again I do not know what the right answer is, but I think both approaches should be tried.

We can only see a short distance ahead, but we can see plenty there that needs to be done.

NOTES

1. Authors' names in italics refer to the References.
2. Compare Lady Lovelace's statement above, which does not contain the word "only."

REFERENCES

Samuel Butler, Erewhon, London, 1865. Chapters 23, 24, 25, *The Book of the Machines*.

Alonzo Church, "An Unsolvable Problem of Elementary Number Theory," *American J. of Math.*, 58 (1936), 345–363.

K. Gödel, "Über formal unentscheidbare Sätze der Principia Mathematica und verwandter Systeme, I," *Monatshefte für Math. und Phys.*, (1931), 173–189.

D. R. Hartree, *Calculating Instruments and Machines*, New York, 1949.

S. C. Kleene, "General Recursive Functions of Natural Numbers," *American J. of Math.*, 57 (1935), 153–173 and 219–244.

G. Jefferson, "The Mind of Mechanical Man." Lister Oration for 1949. *British Medical Journal*, vol. i (1949), 1105–1121.

Countess of Lovelace, "Translator's notes to an article on Babbage's Analytical Engine," *Scientific Memoirs* (ed. by R. Taylor), vol. 3 (1842), 691–731.

Bertrand Russell, *History of Western Philosophy*, London, 1940.

A. M. Turing, "On Computable Numbers, with an Application to the Entscheidungsproblem," *Proc. London Math. Soc.* (2), 42 (1937), 230–265.

Can Computers Think?

JOHN SEARLE

American philosopher John Searle (1932–) has taught for many decades at the University of California at Berkeley. He is well known for his contributions to the philosophy of language and the philosophy of mind. Searle was a student of J. L. Austin and P. F. Strawson, selections from whose works appear in this volume.

The selection included here, which was originally presented in 1984 as a public lecture, includes Searle's famous example of the Chinese Room. Through this example, one of the most widely discussed in philosophy of mind and cognitive science, Searle seeks to defend the view that thinking does not consist in computation alone. In his discussion, Searle makes reference to the works of a number of scientists and computer scientists who were active in the mid-1980s, including Herbert Simon, Alan Newell, Freeman Dyson, Marvin Minsky, and John McCarthy.

Though we do not know in detail how the brain functions, we do know enough to have an idea of the general relationships between brain processes and mental processes. Mental processes are caused by the behaviour of elements of the brain. At the same time, they are realised in the structure that is made up of those elements. I think this answer is consistent with the standard biological approaches to biological phenomena. Indeed, it is a kind of commonsense answer to the question, given what we know about how the world works. However, it is very much a minority point of view. The prevailing view in philosophy, psychology, and artificial intelligence is one which emphasises the analogies between the functioning of the human brain and the functioning of digital computers. According to the most extreme version of this view, the brain is just a digital computer and the mind is just a computer program. One could summarise this view—I call it "strong artificial intelligence," or "strong AI"—by saying that the mind is to the brain, as the program is to the computer hardware.

This view has the consequence that there is nothing essentially biological about the human mind. The brain just happens to be one of an indefinitely large number of different kinds of hardware computers that could sustain the programs which make up human intelligence. On this view, any physical system whatever that had the right program with the right inputs and outputs would have a mind in exactly the same sense that you and I have minds. So, for example, if you made a computer out of old beer cans powered by windmills; if it had the right program, it would have to have a mind. And the point is not that for all we know it

---

Reprinted by permission of the publisher from *Minds, Brains, and Science* by John R. Searle, pp. 28–41, Cambridge, Mass.: Harvard University Press. Copyright © 1984 by John R. Searle.

might have thoughts and feelings, but rather that it must have thoughts and feelings, because that is all there is to having thoughts and feelings: implementing the right program.

Most people who hold this view think we have not yet designed programs which are minds. But there is pretty much general agreement among them that it's only a matter of time until computer scientists and workers in artificial intelligence design the appropriate hardware and programs which will be the equivalent of human brains and minds. These will be artificial brains and minds which are in every way the equivalent of human brains and minds.

Many people outside of the field of artificial intelligence are quite amazed to discover that anybody could believe such a view as this. So, before criticising it, let me give you a few examples of the things that people in this field have actually said. Herbert Simon of Carnegie-Mellon University says that we already have machines that can literally think. There is no question of waiting for some future machine, because existing digital computers already have thoughts in exactly the same sense that you and I do. Well, fancy that! Philosophers have been worried for centuries about whether or not a machine could think, and now we discover that they already have such machines at Carnegie-Mellon. Simon's colleague Alan Newell claims that we have now discovered (and notice that Newell says "discovered" and not "hypothesised" or "considered the possibility," but we have *discovered*) that intelligence is just a matter of physical symbol manipulation; it has no essential connection with any specific kind of biological or physical wetware or hardware. Rather, any system whatever that is capable of manipulating physical symbols in the right way is capable of intelligence in the same literal sense as human intelligence of human beings. Both Simon and Newell, to their credit, emphasise that there is nothing metaphorical about these claims; they mean them quite literally. Freeman Dyson is quoted as having said that computers have an advantage over the rest of us when it comes to evolution. Since consciousness is just a matter of formal processes, in computers these formal processes can go on in substances that are much better able to survive in a universe that is cooling off than beings like ourselves made of our wet and messy materials. Marvin Minsky of MIT says that the next generation of computers will be so intelligent that we will "be lucky if they are willing to keep us around the house as household pets." My all-time favourite in the literature of exaggerated claims on behalf of the digital computer is from John McCarthy, the inventor of the term "artificial intelligence." McCarthy says even "machines as simple as thermostats can be said to have beliefs." And indeed, according to him, almost any machine capable of problem-solving can be said to have beliefs. I admire McCarthy's courage. I once asked him: "What beliefs does your thermostat have?" And he said: "My thermostat has three beliefs—it's too hot in here, it's too cold in here, and it's just right in here." As a philosopher, I like all these claims for a simple reason. Unlike most philosophical theses, they are reasonably clear, and they admit of a simple and decisive refutation. It is this refutation that I am going to undertake in this chapter.

The nature of the refutation has nothing whatever to do with any particular stage of computer technology. It is important to emphasise this point because the temptation is always to think that the solution to our problems must wait on some as yet uncreated technological wonder. But in fact, the nature of the refutation is completely independent of any state of technology. It has to do with the very definition of a digital computer, with what a digital computer is.

It is essential to our conception of a digital computer that its operations can be specified purely formally; that is, we specify the steps in the operation of the computer in terms of abstract symbols—sequences of zeroes and ones printed on a tape, for example. A typical computer "rule" will determine that when a machine is in a certain state and it has a certain symbol on its tape, then it will perform a certain operation such as erasing the symbol or printing another symbol and then enter another state such as moving the tape one square to the left. But the symbols have no meaning; they have no semantic content; they are not about anything. They have to be specified purely in terms of their formal or syntactical structure. The zeroes and ones, for example, are just numerals; they don't even stand for numbers. Indeed, it is this feature of digital computers that makes them so powerful. One and the same type of hardware, if it is appropriately designed, can be used to run an indefinite range of different programs. And one and the same program can be run on an indefinite range of different types of hardwares.

But this feature of programs, that they are defined purely formally or syntactically, is fatal to the view that mental processes and program processes are identical. And the reason can be stated quite simply. There is more to having a mind than having formal or syntactical processes. Our internal mental states, by definition, have certain sorts of contents. If I am thinking about Kansas City or wishing that I had a cold beer to drink or wondering if there will be a fall in interest rates, in each case my mental state has a certain mental content in addition to whatever formal features it might have. That is, even if my thoughts occur to me in strings of symbols, there must be more to the thought than the abstract strings, because strings by themselves can't have any meaning. If my thoughts are to be *about* anything, then the strings must have a *meaning* which makes the thoughts about those things. In a word, the mind has more than a syntax, it has a semantics. The reason that no computer program can ever be a mind is simply that a computer program is only syntactical, and minds are more than syntactical. Minds are semantical, in the sense that they have more than a formal structure, they have a content.

To illustrate this point I have designed a certain thought-experiment. Imagine that a bunch of computer programmers have written a program that will enable a computer to simulate the understanding of Chinese. So, for example, if the computer is given a question in Chinese, it will match the question against its memory, or data base, and produce appropriate answers to the questions in Chinese. Suppose for the sake of argument that the computer's answers are as good as those of a native Chinese speaker. Now then, does the computer, on the basis of this, understand Chinese, does it literally understand Chinese, in the way that Chinese speakers understand Chinese? Well, imagine that you are locked in a room, and in this room are several baskets full of Chinese symbols. Imagine that you (like me) do not understand a word of Chinese, but that you are given a rule book in English for manipulating these Chinese symbols. The rules specify the manipulations of the symbols purely formally, in terms of their syntax, not their semantics. So the rule might say: "Take a squiggle-squiggle sign out of basket number one and put it next to a squoggle-squoggle sign from basket number two." Now suppose that some other Chinese symbols are passed into the room, and that you are given further rules for passing back Chinese symbols out of the room. Suppose that unknown to you the symbols passed into the room are called "questions" by the people outside the room, and the symbols you pass back out of the room are called "answers to the questions." Suppose, furthermore, that the programmers are so good at designing the programs and that you are so good at manipulating the symbols, that very soon your answers are indistinguishable from those of a native Chinese speaker. There you are locked in your room shuffling your Chinese symbols and passing out Chinese symbols in response to incoming Chinese symbols. On the basis of the situation as I have described it, there is no way you could learn any Chinese simply by manipulating these formal symbols.

Now the point of the story is simply this: by virtue of implementing a formal computer program from the point of view of an outside observer, you behave exactly as if you understood Chinese, but all the same you don't understand a word of Chinese. But if going through the appropriate computer program for understanding Chinese is not enough to give *you* an understanding of Chinese, then it is not enough to give *any other digital computer* an understanding of Chinese. And again, the reason for this can be stated quite simply. If you don't understand Chinese, then no other computer could understand Chinese because no digital computer, just by virtue of running a program, has anything that you don't have. All that the computer has, as you have, is a formal program for manipulating uninterpreted Chinese symbols. To repeat, a computer has a syntax, but no semantics. The whole point of the parable of the Chinese room is to remind us of a fact that we knew all along. Understanding a language, or indeed, having mental states at all, involves more than just having a bunch of formal symbols. It involves having an interpretation, or a meaning attached to those symbols. And a digital computer, as defined, cannot have more than just formal symbols because the operation of the computer, as I said earlier, is defined in terms of its ability to implement programs. And these programs are purely formally specifiable—that is, they have no semantic content.

We can see the force of this argument if we contrast what it is like to be asked and to answer questions in English, and to be asked and to answer questions in some language where we have no knowledge of any of the meanings of the words. Imagine that in the Chinese room you are also given questions in English about such things as your age or your life history, and that you answer these questions. What is the difference between the Chinese case and the English case? Well again, if like me you understand no Chinese and you do understand English, then the difference is obvious. You understand the questions in English because they are expressed in symbols whose meanings are known to you. Similarly, when you give the answers in English you are producing symbols which are meaningful to you. But in the case of the Chinese, you have none of that. In the case of the Chinese, you simply manipulate formal symbols according to a computer program, and you attach no meaning to any of the elements.

Various replies have been suggested to this argument by workers in artificial intelligence and in psychology, as well as philosophy. They all have something in common; they are all inadequate. And there is an obvious reason why they have to be inadequate, since the argument rests on a very simple logical truth, namely, syntax alone is not sufficient for semantics, and digital computers insofar as they are computers have, by definition, a syntax alone.

I want to make this clear by considering a couple of the arguments that are often presented against me.

Some people attempt to answer the Chinese room example by saying that the whole system understands Chinese. The idea here is that though I, the person in the room manipulating the symbols do not understand Chinese, I am just the central processing unit of the computer system. They argue that it is the whole system, including the room, the baskets full of symbols and the ledgers containing the programs and perhaps other items as well, taken as a totality, that understands Chinese. But this is subject to exactly the same objection I made before. There is no way that the system can get from the syntax to the semantics. I, as the central processing unit have no way of figuring out what any of these symbols means; but then neither does the whole system.

Another common response is to imagine that we put the Chinese understanding program inside a robot. If the robot moved around and interacted causally with the world, wouldn't that be enough to guarantee that it understood Chinese? Once again the inexorability of the semantics-syntax distinction overcomes this manoeuvre. As long as we suppose that the robot has only a computer for a brain then, even though it might behave exactly as if it understood Chinese, it would still have no way of getting from the syntax to the semantics of Chinese. You can see this if you imagine that I am the computer. Inside a room in the robot's skull I shuffle symbols without knowing that some of them come in to me from television cameras attached to the robot's head and others go out to move the robot's arms and legs. As long as all I have is a formal computer program, I have no way of attaching any meaning to any of the symbols. And the fact that the robot is engaged in causal interactions with the outside world won't help me to attach any meaning to the symbols unless I have some way of finding out about that fact. Suppose the robot picks up a hamburger and this triggers the symbol for hamburger to come into the room. As long as all I have is the symbol with no knowledge of its causes or how it got there, I have no way of knowing what it means. The causal interactions between the robot and the rest of the world are irrelevant unless those causal interactions are represented in some mind or other. But there is no way they can be if all that the so-called mind consists of is a set of purely formal, syntactical operations.

It is important to see exactly what is claimed and what is not claimed by my argument. Suppose we ask the question that I mentioned at the beginning: "Could a machine think?" Well, in one sense, of course, we are all machines. We can construe the stuff inside our heads as a meat machine. And of course, we can all think. So, in one sense of "machine," namely that sense in which a machine is just a physical system which is capable of performing certain kinds of operations, in that sense, we are all machines, and we can think. So, trivially, there are machines that can think. But that wasn't the question that bothered us. So let's try a different formulation of it. Could an artefact think? Could a man-made machine think? Well, once again, it depends on the kind of artefact. Suppose we designed a machine that was molecule-for-molecule indistinguishable from a human being. Well then, if you can duplicate the causes, you can presumably duplicate the effects. So once again, the answer to that question is, in principle at least, trivially yes. If you could build a machine that had the same structure as a human being, then presumably that machine would be able to think. Indeed, it would be a surrogate human being. Well, let's try again.

The question isn't: "Can a machine think?" or: "Can an artefact think?" The question is: "Can a digital computer think?" But once again we have to be very careful in how we interpret the question. From a mathematical point of view, anything whatever can be described *as if* it were a digital computer. And that's because it can be described as instantiating or implementing a computer program. In an utterly trivial sense, the pen that is on the desk in front of me can be described as a digital computer. It just happens to have a very boring computer program. The program says: "Stay there." Now since in this sense, anything whatever is a digital computer, because anything whatever can be described as implementing a computer program, then once again, our question gets a trivial answer. Of course our brains are digital computers, since they implement any number of computer programs. And of course our brains can think. So once again, there is a trivial answer to the question. But that wasn't really the question we were trying to ask. The question we wanted to ask is this: "Can a digital computer, as defined, think?" That is to say: "Is instantiating or implementing the right computer program with the right inputs and outputs, sufficient for, or constitutive of, thinking?" And to this question, unlike its predecessors, the answer is clearly "no." And it is "no" for the reason that we have spelled out, namely, the computer program is defined purely syntactically. But thinking is more than just a matter of manipulating meaningless symbols, it involves meaningful semantic contents. These semantic contents are what we mean by "meaning."

It is important to emphasise again that we are not talking about a particular stage of computer technology. The argument has nothing to do with the forthcoming, amazing advances in computer science. It has nothing to do with the distinction between serial and parallel processes, or with the size of programs, or the speed of computer operations, or with computers that can interact causally with their environment, or even with the invention of robots. Technological progress is always grossly exaggerated, but even subtracting the exaggeration, the development of computers has been quite remarkable, and we can reasonably expect that even more remarkable progress will be made in the future. No doubt we will be much better able to simulate human behaviour on computers than we can at present, and certainly much better than we have been able to in the past. The point I am making is that if we are talking about having mental states, having a mind, all of these simulations are simply irrelevant. It doesn't matter how good the technology is, or how rapid the calculations made by the computer are. If it really is a computer, its operations have to be defined syntactically, whereas consciousness, thoughts, feelings, emotions, and all the rest of it involve more than a syntax. Those features, by definition, the computer is unable to *duplicate* however powerful may be its ability to *simulate*. The key distinction here is between duplication and simulation. And no simulation by itself ever constitutes duplication.

What I have done so far is give a basis to the sense that those citations I began this talk with are really as preposterous as they seem. There is a puzzling question in this discussion though, and that is: "Why would anybody ever have thought that computers could think or have feelings and emotions and all the rest of it?" After all, we can do computer simulations of any process whatever that can be given a formal description. So, we can do a computer simulation of the flow of money in the British economy, or the pattern of power distribution in the Labour party. We can do computer simulation of rain storms in the home counties, or warehouse fires in East London. Now, in each of these cases, nobody supposes that the computer simulation is actually the real thing; no one supposes that a computer simulation of a storm will leave us all wet, or a computer simulation of a fire is likely to burn the house down. Why on earth would anyone in his right mind suppose a computer simulation of mental processes actually had mental processes? I don't really know the answer to that, since the idea seems to me, to put it frankly, quite crazy from the start. But I can make a couple of speculations.

First of all, where the mind is concerned, a lot of people are still tempted to some sort of behaviourism. They think if a system behaves as if it understood Chinese, then it really must understand Chinese. But we have already refuted this form of behaviourism with the Chinese room argument. Another assumption made by many people is that the mind is not a part of the biological world, it is not a part of the world of nature. The strong artificial intelligence view relies on that in its conception that the mind is purely formal; that somehow or other, it cannot be treated as a concrete product of biological processes like any other biological product. There is in these discussions, in short, a kind of residual dualism. AI partisans believe that the mind is more than a part of the natural biological world; they believe that the mind is purely formally specifiable. The paradox of this is that the AI literature is filled with fulminations against some view called "dualism," but in fact, the whole thesis of strong AI rests on a kind of dualism. It rests on a rejection of the idea that the mind is just a natural biological phenomenon in the world like any other.

I want to conclude this chapter by putting together the thesis of the last chapter and the thesis of this one. Both of these theses can be stated very simply. And indeed, I am going to state them with perhaps excessive crudeness. But if we put them together I think we get a quite powerful conception of the relations of minds, brains and computers. And the argument has a very simple logical structure, so you can see whether it is valid or invalid. The first premise is:

1. *Brains cause minds.*

Now, of course, that is really too crude. What we mean by that is that mental processes that we consider to constitute a mind are caused, entirely caused, by processes going on inside the brain. But let's be crude, let's just abbreviate that as three words—brains cause minds. And that is just a fact about how the world works. Now let's write proposition number two:

2. *Syntax is not sufficient for semantics.*

That proposition is a conceptual truth. It just articulates our distinction between the notion of what is purely formal and what has content. Now, to these two propositions—that brains cause minds and that syntax is not sufficient for semantics—let's add a third and a fourth:

3. *Computer programs are entirely defined by their formal, or syntactical, structure.*

That proposition, I take it, is true by definition; it is part of what we mean by the notion of a computer program.

4. *Minds have mental contents; specifically, they have semantic contents.*

And that, I take it, is just an obvious fact about how our minds work. My thoughts, and beliefs, and desires are about something, or they refer to something, or they concern states of affairs in the world; and they do that because their content directs them at these states of affairs in the world. Now, from these four premises, we can draw our first conclusion; and it follows obviously from premises 2, 3 and 4:

CONCLUSION 1. *No computer program by itself is sufficient to give a system a mind. Programs, in short, are not minds, and they are not by themselves sufficient for having minds.*

Now, that is a very powerful conclusion, because it means that the project of trying to create minds solely by designing programs is doomed from the start. And it is important to re-emphasise that this has nothing to do with any particular state of technology or any particular state of the complexity of the program. This is a purely formal, or logical, result from a set of axioms which are agreed to by all (or nearly all) of the disputants concerned. That is, even most of the hardcore enthusiasts for artificial intelligence agree that in fact, as a matter of biology, brain processes cause mental states, and they agree that programs are defined purely formally. But if you put these conclusions together with certain other things that we know, then it follows immediately that the project of strong AI is incapable of fulfilment.

However, once we have got these axioms, let's see what else we can derive. Here is a second conclusion:

CONCLUSION 2. *The way that brain functions cause minds cannot be solely in virtue of running a computer program.*

And this second conclusion follows from conjoining the first premise together with our first conclusion. That is, from the fact that brains cause minds and that programs are not enough to do the job, it follows that the way that brains cause minds can't be solely by running a computer program. Now that also I think is an important result, because it has the consequence that the brain is not, or at least is not just, a digital computer. We saw earlier that anything can trivially be described as if it were a digital computer, and brains are no exception. But the importance of this conclusion is that the computational properties of the brain are simply not enough to explain its functioning to produce mental states. And indeed, that ought to seem a common-sense scientific conclusion to us anyway because all it does is remind us of the fact that brains are biological engines; their biology matters. It is not, as several people in artificial intelligence have claimed, just an irrelevant fact about the mind that it happens to be realised in human brains.

Now, from our first premise, we can also derive a third conclusion:

CONCLUSION 3. *Anything else that caused minds would have to have causal powers at least equivalent to those of the brain.*

And this third conclusion is a trivial consequence of our first premise. It is a bit like saying that if my petrol engine drives my car at seventy-five miles an hour, then any diesel engine that was capable of doing that would have to have a power output at least equivalent to that of my petrol engine. Of course, some other system might cause mental processes using entirely different chemical or biochemical features from those the brain in fact uses. It might turn out that there are beings on other planets, or in other solar systems, that have mental states and use an entirely different biochemistry from ours. Suppose that Martians arrived on earth and we concluded that they had mental states. But suppose that when their heads were opened up, it was discovered that all they had inside was green slime. Well still, the green slime, if it functioned to produce consciousness and all the rest of their mental life, would have to have causal powers equal to those of the human brain. But now, from our first conclusion, that programs are not enough, and our third conclusion, that any other system would have to have causal powers equal to the brain, conclusion four follows immediately:

CONCLUSION 4. *For any artefact that we might build which had mental states equivalent to human mental states, the implementation of a computer program would not by itself be sufficient. Rather the artefact would have to have powers equivalent to the powers of the human brain.*

The upshot of this discussion I believe is to remind us of something that we have known all along: namely, mental states are biological phenomena. Consciousness, intentionality, subjectivity and mental causation are all a part of our biological life history, along with growth, reproduction, the secretion of bile, and digestion.

Reasoning About Our Experience

J. J. VALBERG

J. J. Valberg is a British philosopher affiliated with the University College London. His writings address issues in epistemology, the philosophy of language, and the philosophy of mind. He is best known for his work on the nature of perceptual experience.

The text that appears here is the first chapter of Valberg's 1992 book *The Puzzle of Experience*. Minor changes have been made to the text to allow the essay to stand on its own.

1.1. The puzzle we shall be discussing is a puzzle about the object of experience—or, perhaps we should say, about the object of visual experience, since that is what we shall exclusively consider. The puzzle takes the form of a conflict, or antinomy. Roughly, there are two ways we can reflect on our experience. We can reason about our experience, or we can be (as I shall say) *open* to it—that is, to how things are within our experience. If we follow a certain line of reasoning about our experience, we are led to the conclusion that the object of experience is not part of the world, an external object. However, if we are open to our experience, all we find is the world. So, if we reflect in the right ways, we get pulled first in one direction and then another. This, very simply, is the puzzle. And, indeed, it is a simple puzzle.

We shall call the reasoning which enters into the puzzle, the reasoning whose conclusion is one half of the antinomy, "the problematic reasoning." . . . In the present chapter we shall set out the problematic reasoning.

It always helps to think in terms of a specific case. Consider the book lying on the table in front of me. The problematic reasoning purports to show that the book is not, nor could be, the object of my experience. More generally, it purports to show that no external object, no part of the world, could ever be an object of experience. Rather, the object of experience is always an internal object.

What do we mean by the "object of my experience"? And what is an "external object (part of the world)" versus an "internal object"? Let us attempt to give a preliminary account of these ideas—so that we can use them in the reasoning. We shall begin with the idea of an "object of experience."

1.2. One way to explain an idea in philosophy is by reference to examples. It would, therefore, be helpful if we could give a clear-cut example of an object of experience. It would be particularly helpful if we could say what the object of my experience is right now. The trouble, of course, is that in the present context, where we are about to consider and evaluate an argument to the effect that the object of experience is never an external object, what counts as the object of my experience is up for grabs. Thus we cannot say, by way of explaining the idea, that the object of my experience right now is the book in front of me, or the table on which the book is sitting, since, if the problematic reasoning is correct, such things are not the object of my experience. What we need, obviously, is an explanation of "object of experience" in general terms, terms which leave open whether the book and the table are, or could be, objects of my experience.

By an "object of experience" we shall mean something *present* in experience. Thus one might express

From *The Puzzle of Experience*, 1992, pp. 3–21. Reprinted by permission of Oxford University Press.

the conclusion of the problematic reasoning by saying that what is present in experience (present to us, present) is always an internal object; that external objects are never actually present to us. For example, according to the reasoning, the book and the table are not present in my experience. But we may now be asked to explain what we mean by "present in experience," "present to us," and so on.

Presence (in experience) connotes a kind of direct or immediate availability. An object which is present is right *there*, available to us. This makes it tempting to view presence as the reciprocal of Russell's idea of acquaintance.* That is, an object with which we are (in Russell's sense) acquainted is present in experience; and an object which is present in experience is one with which we are acquainted.

But in fact this is only partly correct, since, whereas both ideas imply immediate availability, Russell's idea is meant to be more general. Objects of acquaintance, for Russell, may be either "particulars" or "universals." However, as we shall understand this, experiential presence is limited to the category of particulars. What is present, directly available, is always a particular.

In the tradition, particulars are temporal (but not necessarily spatial) objects. That is, they are objects of which it makes sense to ask how long they have existed or lasted, when they began to exist, and so on. (Such questions cannot be asked of universals.) Hence, the second point to make about presence in experience is that an object present in experience is always a temporal object.

This leads directly to a third point, namely, the intimate connection between experiential and temporal presence. We have a strong inclination to view objects that are present in experience as being, at that very time, existent: if something is *now* present, it *now* exists. This inclination to encompass the object within the temporal present does not extend to reference, or thought in general. There is no problem about referring to, or thinking of, objects which no longer exist. But our inclination is to say that such things cannot be present in experience, that they cannot *now* be objects of experience.[1]

Note, the direct availability which objects have in virtue of being present in experience implies neither omniscience nor infallibility with respect to the intrinsic properties of the objects which are thus available. It does not, in other words, exclude the possibility of not knowing that an object has this or that intrinsic property, or of taking it to have a property which it does not have. Thus, the direct availability of what is present does not of itself exclude the possibility that the objects present to us are external objects, part of the world. Nothing that we have said excludes that possibility.

1.3. But what is the "direct availability" that objects have in virtue of being present? I do not know how to define it. Perhaps we can catch hold of the idea indirectly, by relating the idea of presence to ideas wherein we can discern a requirement for the kind of availability that we are trying to grasp. (What this involves will become clear as we proceed.) We shall mention two such ideas: that of "focusing on," or "fixing on," or "picking out" an object; and that of "demonstrative reference" to an object.

Consider, first, the idea of focusing on (fixing on, picking out) an object. It should be clear that focusing on an object is not the same thing as the object's being present to us. For, unlike the latter, it is something we can be said to "do." Thus it may take effort, and we may tire of it. And we may choose, or decide, to focus on a particular object, or intend to focus on it. And in certain circumstances . . . we may be said to try and fail. In short, focusing, in contrast to presence, is subject to the will. We can do things (turn our heads, remove obstacles, etc.) which bring it about that a certain object is present to us. But, in itself, the presence of an object is just a fact, not something we "do." Moreover, given the presence of an object, it may or may not be the case that we focus on it. This is a basic experiential possibility: objects can be present to us without our actually focusing on them.[2]

But (here is the important point) we cannot focus on something *unless* it is present in our experience: the fact of an object's presence is what makes the

* In his *Problems of Philosophy* (1912), Bertrand Russell distinguishes between knowledge that we have by "acquaintance" and knowledge that we have merely by "description." We have knowledge of the former sort noninferentially, as the result of a direct relation between our thought and its object; we have knowledge of the latter sort less directly, often as the result of thinking about the object by means of some description of it.

object available for us to focus on. Thus an object which is present in experience is, in virtue of that fact, available (then and there) for us to focus on or pick out. Suppose, for example, we allow that the book on the table is something that might be present in my experience. If it is present, it may or may not be the case that I am focusing on the book. If, however, I am focusing on the book, it must be present to me. Its presence in my experience is what makes the book available for me to focus on (pick out).

The other idea we mentioned above was that of demonstrative reference. Perhaps in this case we can proceed by means of examples. Think of the distinctive kind of singular reference that we would make by the expression "this," were we to use that expression in an assertive utterance of a sentence like "This feels hot," or "This looks blue." Here we have, I assume, uncontroversial examples of demonstrative reference. Taking our cue from such examples, it should be evident that demonstrative reference is closely connected with focusing on, or picking out, an object. But it also seems evident that, despite both being things we can be said to "do," making a demonstrative reference and focusing on something are not one and the same. Like all reference, and in contrast to focusing, demonstrative reference involves the use of symbols. Hence, to focus on an object is not thereby to make a demonstrative reference to it.

The connection is the other way around: when we make a demonstrative reference to something, we thereby focus on (pick out) the object to which we refer. So (this is the point that interests us), just as we can think of the fact of an object's presence as what makes the object available for us to focus on, or pick out, we can think of this latter fact as what makes the object available for demonstrative reference (what makes the object demonstratively available). A fact of presence, we might say, is what creates the possibility of focusing, and what creates the possibility of focusing creates the possibility of demonstrative reference.

1.4. To sum things up, by an "object of experience" we shall mean something present in experience: something which is right *there*, available for us to pick out or focus on, and refer to demonstratively. Further, we shall understand that the "something" which is thus available falls in the philosophical category of "particulars," and is hence a temporal object; and that we are inclined to suppose that it exists at the time when it is available (present). It is not part of our understanding, however, that we cannot be mistaken about the properties of an object thus available, or that we must know all of its properties.

This is what we shall mean by "object of experience" in stating the problematic reasoning, the reasoning which purports to show that the object of experience is always an internal object. The explanation leaves open (I hope) whether the object of experience is external or internal. I realize, of course, that it relies on ideas—presence, demonstrative reference, focusing (picking out), and so on—which raise difficulties of their own, ideas which philosophers have spent a great deal of time worrying about and trying to clarify. But I think that when we actually state the problematic reasoning (sects. 1.5–8), and actually use these ideas, the attendant difficulties will just not matter. That is, they will not prevent us from following the reasoning and getting involved in the puzzle.

We also mentioned, as requiring preliminary explanation, the idea of an "external object (part of the world)," and the contrasting idea of an "internal object."

The first point to make is that "object" in "external (internal) object" does not mean what it means in "object of experience." Thus for "object" in "external object" we may substitute "thing." The same substitution in "object of experience" not only fails to preserve meaning; it fails to make sense. As far as I can see, there is in this case no expression which can be substituted for "object" so as to preserve the meaning of the whole expression. To provide an expression with (roughly) the same meaning as "object of experience" we must replace the complex phrase "object of" (for example, by "something present in").

An "external object (thing)" or "part of the world" is an object which has an existence that is independent of presence in experience. Let us assume that the book is now present in my experience. Clearly, the existence of the book is independent of this fact. The fact of its existence and the fact of its presence are distinct facts. Thus, although the book is present to me, it need not have been. (It might have been in the drawer right now.) The book, then, is (as we say) part of the world.

An "internal object" is an object whose existence is not independent of its presence in experience. In this case, existence and presence collapse into one. The fact of existence and the fact of presence are the same fact. Examples of internal objects are after-images and hallucinatory objects (such as Macbeth's dagger). Thus we do not regard such objects as part of the world.

The book on my table is an example of what philosophers call a "material (physical) object." It fills out space. Material objects are external, part of the world. What about immaterial objects (if there are any)? These too will be part of the world. The world will contain, as Descartes thought, two radically different categories of objects and phenomena. Some will consist of matter, others of spirit. Whether Descartes was right in this view is not relevant here. What is relevant is simply that internal objects are *not im*material objects. (An after-image is not like a ghost.) Internal objects are neither material nor immaterial. They do not consist of anything. They are not part of the world.

It will be useful to introduce the convention of emphasizing the demonstrative "this" to show that what we thereby refer to is something present in experience (demonstratively available). If I assert, "*This* is a book," the use of the emphatic "this" shows that it is of something present in my experience that I assert that it is a book. Suppose that I am hallucinating. Then, since what is present in my experience is not a book but an internal object, my assertion is false (or at least not true). Or suppose I am uncertain whether I am hallucinating or not. Then (in the manner of Macbeth) I might ask, "Is *this* a book?" Here the use of the emphatic demonstrative shows that my uncertainty concerns the status of what is present in my experience. I am uncertain whether what is present in my experience is or is not a book, an external thing. I am uncertain, that is, whether the object present to me is part of the world or an internal object.

We said that, in the case of internal objects, there is no distinction between existence and presence. There are places in Berkeley's philosophy where he seems to say that this is true with respect to everything (apart from God and individual minds). To exist is to be present (or, as Berkeley puts it, "to be is to be perceived"). I mention Berkeley's view, not because we are going to take it seriously, but simply to place the contrast we are trying to explain in a familiar historical perspective. In Berkeley's kind of Idealism, we might say, there are no external objects; all objects are internal.*

Perhaps we should point out, finally, that the conclusion of the problematic reasoning is not Berkeley's Idealism. It is not that whatever exists exists only in so far as it is present, but that whatever is present exists only in so far as it is present.

1.5. We shall turn now to the problematic reasoning. Most moderately well-educated people in our culture are acquainted, in an outline way, with the basic facts about the transmission and reflection of light, the nature of the eye, and the process in the nervous system and brain which results or culminates in visual experience. We know (roughly) that light is reflected from physical objects and travels in straight lines; that it impinges on the eye and produces an image on the retina; that this excites the optic nerve; that a "message" travels from the optic nerve to the visual cortex of the brain; and that, finally, as the upshot of this chain of events, visual experience occurs. Such facts are part of everyday knowledge. Some people may not have heard about the visual cortex, but everyone (unless there is something wrong with him) knows he has eyes and a brain, and that light is reflected from objects and then travels to his eyes, and that, because of what happens after that—that is, because of what happens in the nervous system and brain—he then has the kind of experience he has, that his experience is the way it is.

I shall call this "the causal picture of experience." The causal picture of experience is not what philosophers sometimes call "the causal theory of perception." The latter attempts to state the conditions that are logically (conceptually) necessary and sufficient for its being true, of an external thing X, that X is, for

* The early modern philosopher George Berkeley (1685–1753) famously held the views that Valberg here attributes to him. A selection from his work can be found in the "Knowledge and Reality" section.

a subject S, an object of experience. With this aim, the causal theory asserts about the broad fact that there is a causal connection between X and S's experience, that that fact is a logically necessary condition of X being an object of experience for S. The causal picture, on the other hand, does not make any assertion *about* the broad fact of the causal connection. It simply *asserts* the fact, or rather, a set of more or less detailed facts (drawn from physics, physiology, and so on) which make up the broad fact.

The causal picture of experience is not, in any sense, a "philosophical" view or theory. Someone might be very interested in the causal picture of experience, perhaps spend his whole working life doing research and experiments on this or that aspect of it, and never raise a philosophical question about it. Yet the causal picture of experience is the starting-point of the problematic reasoning, and the problematic reasoning is most certainly philosophical.

Simply contemplating (or learning about, or adding to) the causal picture of experience is not philosophical. Things get philosophical when we begin to reflect on certain possibilities implicit in the picture. The present activity in my brain, I remind myself, is the causal outcome of a chain of events involving light rays being reflected from a certain object—the book on the table, say. In turn, the activity in my brain is causally responsible for my experience being as it now is. But, I reflect, in that case (here is where philosophy begins to creep in), if the activity in my brain could somehow be held constant, the earlier parts of the causal chain might be eliminated without this having any effect on my experience. If the activity in my brain were to continue as it is, my experience would continue as it is. It would continue as it is, even if, say, something interfered with the light rays being reflected to my eyes; or even if the object reflecting the light rays were miraculously annihilated. God (it is handy to bring God in here) might arrange such a situation. God might eliminate the object while maintaining the activity in my visual cortex. Is that not a coherent state of affairs, something God might bring about? And, if the activity in my brain were to continue on as it is, my experience would also continue on as it is. It would continue to run along perfectly smoothly, despite the fact that the external object would no longer be there.

This possibility, which is implicit in our everyday knowledge about the causal dependence of experience on objects and processes in the world (implicit, that is, in the causal picture of experience), might be summed up by saying that the external thing, the object in the world, is "potentially irrelevant" to experience.

Now once we grasp this possibility, this idea about the potential irrelevance of the external object, we are squarely in the realm of philosophy. We did not begin there (we began outside philosophy, in the realm of everyday knowledge), but that is where we are now. Thus we might think of the problematic reasoning, so far, as divided into two stages: an extra-philosophical stage, where we simply contemplate the causal picture of experience (the facts of physics and physiology, plus the fact that the process culminates in experience); and a transitional stage (transitional into philosophy), where we bring to light a possibility implicit in this picture. Of course, we have not yet reached the conclusion of the reasoning. To say that God might maintain the activity in my brain as it is while eliminating the book, and thus that my experience might continue as it is in the absence of the book, is not yet to say that, as things are, the book is not the object of my experience. (To say that, potentially, the book is irrelevant to my experience is not to say that, actually, it is not present in my experience.) This requires a further argument, a third stage in our reasoning. But before getting into that, I think we should pause to reflect on the second stage.

1.6. Suppose I now assert:

> (G) Were God to eliminate the book but ensure that the activity in (the visual part of) my brain remains the same, my experience would remain the same.

There are two points I wish to make in regard to (G). First, what I assert in asserting (G) is *true*. Or rather, it is *in some sense* true. For (and this is the second point) it is not entirely clear what I am asserting. In particular, it is not clear what exactly it is that I assert would remain the same were the activity in my brain to remain the same; that is, what I mean when I assert that *my experience* would remain the same.

The activity in my brain is something which is going on now, up here in my head. Is that the sort of thing I mean in (G) by "my experience"—something which is going on in my head (or, if not in my head, somewhere else)? Let us put this question aside for the time being. . . .

Instead, let us approach our question by remarking that, if "my experience" remains the same, I would not be able to *tell* that the book has been eliminated. But this needs to be qualified, since, as we have described it, the situation does not preclude my reaching out and discovering that the book is not there. Perhaps we should say that I would not be able to tell the book is not there by using my eyes. Imagine my eyes are wired up in such a manner that, if I keep them open and look at the book, when the book is removed I get a distinctive sensation in my fingertips (like an alarm going off when jewellery is removed from a case). But in that event I would not be using my eyes "in the normal way." What is the "normal way"? I have my eyes open and look in the appropriate direction. But so I do when my eyes are wired up and I get the sensation in my fingers.

We could play around with this for a while yet, but sooner or later it must be clear that the qualification we are looking for involves a restriction not on my *means* of telling, but on my *basis* for telling whether the book is there or not. And the necessary restriction would seem to be this: that, in so far as I rely on how things are *in my (visual) experience*, I cannot tell whether the book is there or not. Thus, were God to intervene in the manner described, then, in so far as my basis for telling is restricted to how things are in my experience, I would not be able to tell that the book is no longer there.

This suggests the following as the first step towards understanding what it is, in (G), that I assert would remain the same. We must recognize that "my experience" in (G) is elliptical for something like "how things are in (within) my experience." Experience is a subject-matter about which we can say how things are *within* it, a subject-matter which can be described "internally." It is, in this respect, something like a story. We can say what happens *in* a story. (A story can be described "internally.") If someone did not appreciate this, he would not know what we mean by a "story." Similarly, if someone did not appreciate that experience can be described internally, he would not know what we mean in this context by "experience." By the same token, it must be evident that, in the sense in which this is true of my experience, or a story, the activity in my brain cannot be described internally. Yet, it seems, the activity in my brain stands back-to-back in a causal chain with my experience. That is to say, the activity in my brain is causally responsible for how things are within my experience. (The activity in my brain has effects which reach, so to speak, right inside my experience.)

To make our meaning explicit, then, let us replace (G) by

> (G*) Were God to eliminate the book but ensure that the activity in (the visual part of) my brain remains the same, how things are in my experience would remain the same.

But, of course, this is still unclear, or vague. *What is it* that is supposed to remain the same when I say, for example, that "how things are in my experience remains the same"? What do we include here under this vague expression "how things are"? For *what*, exactly, is the activity in my brain supposed to be causally responsible?

This brings us to a delicate point in our reflections. When we say of something that it is present in my experience, that it is the object of my experience, surely this is relevant to how things are within my experience. Are we then to include such facts among the "things" that, were God to intervene in the manner described, would remain the same in my experience? Are we (in other words) to say that, if God intervened in this way, the *object* of my experience would remain the same? It may seem that, under the guise of clarification, we are being asked to settle the outcome of the problematic reasoning. For, if the answer to the question is "Yes," if we say that the object of my experience would remain the same, then, since by hypothesis God eliminates the book, it follows immediately that the book is not the object of my experience. And this would be held to beg the issue which the reasoning is supposed to decide.

I think the best way to proceed is to do so without giving any further clarifications just yet. Let us simply acknowledge the vagueness in (G*) and carry on with the third stage of the reasoning. Thus, all we are now committed to is that, were God to intervene, it would *in some sense* be true that "how things are in my experience would remain the same." In what sense? This will emerge in the course of the reasoning—by things that we assert, or imply, along the way. Of course, such a procedure carries no guarantee against mistakes: an unwarranted assumption may slip in, there may be an equivocation, and so on. But we can worry about that later on, once we have before us the completed reasoning and the consequent puzzle.

It should be emphasized that we are not claiming to have identified an innocent or neutral sense in which it is true that, were God to ensure that the activity in my brain remains the same, "things would remain the same in my experience." On the contrary, we are explicitly leaving open the sense in which this is true. But it is in some sense true; this much we are not leaving open.

1.7. The third stage of the problematic reasoning is, like Descartes's First Meditation, essentially first person singular.* I will reason for my own case, and the reader is invited to do the same, substituting his "I" for mine.

The first step is simply to pick out or focus on something present in my experience. So I will do that. I will focus on *this*. This what? At any other time I would have said "this book," but I am not allowed to say that now. I can say that my eyes are directed towards the book, or that I am looking at the book; but I cannot say (or imply) that the book is present in my experience. Let us say simply that I am focused on whatever it is that is present now in my experience while I am looking at the book. Certainly there is, right now, *something* present in my experience.

It seems equally certain that, whatever this "something" is, I can remain focused on it for a little while. That is the next step. Having focused on something, I remain focused on it for a little while (about five seconds should be enough). I do this very closely, never letting my attention waver, always staying right with the object on which I am focused.

All this goes smoothly. There are no breaks, no gaps. I focus on something, on *this* object (whatever it is that is present when I look at the book), and stay with it, with *this* object, for a brief period of time. Now, in so far as focusing is something I "do," it would seem that I have just given a description of what I have done in the last five seconds of my history. I focused on whatever object it was that was present in my experience when I looked at the book, and I remained carefully focused on that object for five seconds.

Let us now reflect on this bit of my history in the light of the potential irrelevance of the book. Consider the hypothesis that halfway through the last five seconds God intervened in the manner we have described: God eliminated the book but maintained the activity in my brain just as it was when the book was there. When the book was there, it reflected light to my eyes; this process eventuated in the activity in my visual cortex. The hypothesis is that, halfway through the last five seconds, God (as it were) took over from the book, having eliminated it, and directly maintained the activity in my brain.

The point about the hypothesis is that it seems to be compatible with how things have been in my experience during the last five seconds. Well, how have "things" been within my experience? Think back to the beginning of the five-second interval. I contemplate the spread of objects within my experience. I focus on one—*this* one, the one which, if I were not playing this little game, I would say is the book. I stay carefully focused on the object. (Five seconds pass.) So (looking back now) here is how "things" have been within my experience for the last five seconds: *this* object has been present. Thus, the hypothesis of God's intervention is compatible with the fact that *this* object, the object on which I am now focused, has been present in my experience for the last five seconds. Had God intervened, the book would have ceased to exist two-and-a-half seconds ago (this is part of the hypothesis). Had God intervened, the activity in my brain for the whole of the last five seconds would have continued just as it has (this is also part of the hypothesis.) Had the activity in my brain continued as it has, within my experience things would have been as they have been (this follows from the causal picture of experience). How

* Descartes' *First Meditation* can be found in the "Knowledge and Reality" section.

have "things" been? Once again, *this* object has remained present to me. So, *this* object is such that, had God eliminated the book, it would have remained (just as it has remained) present to me.

I am pedantically labouring things here because it will make it easier to spot a mistake (if there is one) when we come to examine the reasoning. At this stage, I will simply enter the following observation. The crux of the matter is the assertion that, had God intervened, *this* object would have remained (just as it has remained) present within my experience. What is my basis for such an assertion? The thing to bear in mind is that my basis is not anything I discern in or about the object that I mentally latch on to. I cannot, by inspecting the object, discern that it has the property of being able to survive the elimination of the book. My basis for the assertion has nothing at all to do, really, with what I can *discern* in my experience. It lies entirely in what I *know* about the relation between what I can discern and the activity of my brain. My basis, you might say, is entirely indirect: it lies not in what is available "out front" but in what I know about the relation between what is thus available and the things that are happening "back here."

To repeat, had God intervened, *this* object would have remained (just as it has remained) present in my experience. There would have been a rupture in the world; a certain external object, a book, would have suddenly ceased to exist. This would have been evident to an onlooker, but for *me*, within *my* experience, things would have flowed smoothly on, without a ripple or a flicker—just as they have done. That is to say, *this* object would have been (just as it has been) present to me for the whole of the last five seconds.

What follows? It follows (plainly) that *this* object, the object on which I have actually been focused for the last five seconds, is not the book. For my having been focused on *this* object is compatible with the supposition of God's intervention, and it is part of the supposition that, half-way through the last five seconds, God eliminated the book. So the object on which I have actually been focused, *this* object, is such that it might have survived the elimination of the book. So it cannot be the book.

Once we have settled on the appropriate internal description of my experience, the logic of the argument is simple (whether it is legitimate to apply such an argument in the present context remains to be seen). Suppose I pick up a book and hold it in my hand for five seconds. I now consider a certain Book *X* of which it is true that, had God eliminated Book *X* in the last five seconds I would still be holding on to the book I actually have in my hand. Would it not follow that the book in my hand is not Book *X*? Of course, the two cases are in some respects very different. Thus, whereas arguing in this way for the non-identity of Book *X* and the book now in my hand seems like a pointless rigmarole, precisely some such round-about argument seems necessary if we are to accept the non-identity of the book on the table and the object now present in my experience. Formally, though, the reasoning is in both cases the same.

Now, clearly (thinking again just about the experiential case), the reasoning is not restricted to the object on which I am now focused and the book in front of me on the table. It works for *any* object in the world and *any* object on which I might focus. Any object in the world, any external thing (apart from my brain), is such that God could eliminate it compatibly with keeping the activity in my brain the same. Hence, for any object on which I choose to focus and any external object (apart from my brain), I can, it seems, show by such reasoning that the object on which I am focused cannot be identified with the external object, since I can show by the reasoning that the object on which I am focused could survive the elimination of the external object.

We might put this in the form of a *reductio*—a *reductio* of the assumption that the object present in my experience is an object in the world. I focus on something (anything) now present in my experience, and assume that it is an external object, part of the world. On this assumption, I can (by our reasoning) prove that the following two propositions might both be true of the object on which I am focused: (1) that for the whole of a certain interval of time *t* I remain focused on this object; (2) that part of the way through *t* the object in question ceases to exist. Since anything present in my experience is available for me to focus on, such a *reductio* can be constructed for anything present in my experience. With respect to anything present in my experience, then, I can reduce to absurdity the assumption that it is part of the world.

1.8. If the object present in my experience is never part of the world, never an object whose existence is independent of the fact of its presence, what is it? What else could it be but an object whose existence is *not* independent of its presence in my experience, an internal object? For example, *this* object, the object present in my experience right now when I look at the book, is not an external object (part of the world). It is not a book, but an internal object. Generally, what is present in my experience, what is available for me to focus on and refer to demonstratively, is never part of the world but always an internal object; it is always (in the traditional jargon) a sense-datum.[3] The world itself, then, although I can talk and think about it, is never demonstratively available to me.[4] Something (an internal object, a sense-datum) always "gets in the way."

We have now reached the conclusion of the problematic reasoning. There are (as the reader will no doubt have judged for himself) aspects of the reasoning which might be questioned, and which in any case need to be examined very carefully. (The most obvious questions relate to the third stage of the reasoning: to my use of the emphatic demonstrative, with the implied assumption that, at the end of the five seconds, after God has intervened, I would still be focused on something, and hence that something would still be present to me . . . or, granting that, that it would be the same object that I was focused on at the outset of the five seconds. . . . I believe that, the more carefully we examine the reasoning, the more powerful it will seem.

NOTES

1. The reason for saying (guardedly) that we are "inclined" to view experiential and temporal presence as connected in this way, rather than flatly asserting that they are thus connected, is that the connection is sometimes used by philosophers to argue for the same conclusion that we shall get with the problematic reasoning, namely, that the object of experience is always internal. I have in mind the famous "time-lag" argument. Some philosophers, when they see this coming, claim that the connection between experiential and temporal presence is only apparent. The case of stellar explosions, they will say, shows that things (events) can be present in experience, after they cease to exist. There is no point getting into this issue, since, for the purpose of providing a distinguishing mark of experiential presence (for the purpose of distinguishing objects of experience from, say, objects of reference), the appearance of a connection suffices. In fact, the time-lag argument has much in common with the problematic reasoning. They both depend on what we shall call "the causal picture of experience" (see sect. 1.5). It is worth noting, however, that, even if the time-lag argument were correct, the problematic reasoning is more fundamental. It depends on less; it does not depend on the fact of a time-lag. The problematic reasoning would work equally well if light travelled instantaneously. We shall ignore the time-lag argument in what follows.
2. In fact, some philosophers (e.g. Husserl) have held the following to be an experiential necessity: that whenever we focus on an object, there is a background of objects present to us on which we are not focused.
3. Some comments are in order here. On Russell's use of the term "sense-data," which has become pretty much standard, sense-data are by definition internal objects. Russell's procedure is first to argue that the objects of experience are internal, and then (in effect) to dub these internal objects "sense-data" (see *The Problems of Philosophy* (New York: Oxford University Press, 1959), Ch. 1). But Russell's usage is not universal. Moore, unlike Russell, seems to define the term "sense-data" ("sensibles") in such a way as to leave it open whether sense-data are external or internal. In effect, "sense-datum" for Moore means: that which is present in experience (object of experience). The question for Moore, about which he can never quite make up his mind, is whether sense-data (thus defined) are or are not external things (or parts of external things) (see, e.g., *Some Main Problems of Philosophy* (New York: Collier, 1962), Ch. 2, and "The Nature and Reality of Objects of Perception," "The Status of Sense-Data," and "Some Judgements of Perception," in *Philosophical Studies* (London: Routledge & Kegan Paul, 1948). Thus, if we express the conclusion of

the problematic reasoning by saying that the object of experience is always a "sense-datum," this would accord better with Russell's use of the term than with Moore's.

4. When in this regard we speak of "the world itself," or "the book itself," and so on, the expression "itself" is redundant; e.g., to say that "the book itself" is (or is not) present to me is just to say that the book is (or is not) present to me. We might mention here the well-known argument that, since at most only part of the book (or part of the surface of the book) would be present to me (the back and inside would not be actually presented), we cannot say that the book itself (= the book) is present to me. I think most philosophers would now agree that the argument depends on a false contrast. From the fact that only part of my hand is actually in contact with the table, it does not follow that my hand itself (= my hand) is not actually in contact with the table; all that follows is that the *whole* of my hand is not in contact, etc. Similarly, all that follows from the fact that only part of the book is visually present to me is that the *whole* of the book is not present to me. We may still say that the book (= the book itself) is present to me. (For a detailed discussion of the point, see Thompson Clarke, "Seeing Surfaces and Physical Objects," in M. Black (ed.), *Philosophy in America* (Ithaca, NY: Cornell University Press, 1965).) At least, this is what we may say if we leave aside the problematic reasoning. In any event, the argument in question is usually given as the first stage of a line of reflection wherein the object of experience gets whittled down, step by step, to an internal object. But, with the problematic reasoning, we reach this conclusion all at once; so we may ignore the argument and the false contrast on which it depends.

The Argument from Illusion: A Defense of Sense Data

A. J. AYER

Alfred Jules Ayer (1910–89) was an influential British philosopher who taught at the University College London and at Oxford University. He was an important advocate of the philosophical view known as *logical positivism*, whose tenets he articulated in his 1936 book *Language, Truth and Logic*. Ayer went on to publish many influential books and articles on a wide range of philosophical topics.

The text that appears here is a widely anthologized selection from Ayer's 1940 book *The Foundations of Empirical Knowledge*. In it, Ayer defends the existence of *sense data*, special kinds of mind-dependent objects that we are directly aware of when we perceive something. Another selection from his writings appears in the "Free Will" section.

EXPOSITION OF THE ARGUMENT

It does not normally occur to us that there is any need for us to justify our belief in the existence of material things. At the present moment, for example, I have no doubt whatsoever that I really am perceiving the familiar objects, the chairs and table, the pictures and books and flowers with which my room is furnished; and I am therefore satisfied that they exist. I recognize indeed that people are sometimes deceived by their senses, but this does not lead me to suspect that my own sense-perceptions cannot in general be trusted, or even that they may be deceiving me now. And this is not, I believe, an exceptional

From *The Foundations of Empirical Knowledge*. Copyright © 1954 by Macmillan Ltd. Printed with permission of Palgrave Macmillan.

attitude. I believe that, in practice, most people agree with John Locke* that "the certainty of things existing *in rerum natura*, when we have the testimony of our senses for it, is not only as great as our frame can attain to, but as our condition needs."[1]

When, however, one turns to the writings of those philosophers who have recently concerned themselves with the subject of perception, one may begin to wonder whether this matter is quite so simple. It is true that they do, in general, allow that our belief in the existence of material things is well founded; some of them, indeed, would say that there were occasions on which we knew for certain the truth of such propositions as "this is a cigarette" or "this is a pen." But even so they are not, for the most part, prepared to admit that such objects as pens or cigarettes are ever directly perceived. What, in their opinion, we directly perceive is always an object of a different kind from these; one to which it is now customary to give the name of "sense-datum." These sense-data are said to have the "presentative function"[2] of making us conscious of material things. But how they perform this function, and what is their relation to the material things which they present, are questions about which there is much dispute. There is dispute also about the properties of sense-data, apart from their relationship to material things: whether, for example, they are each of them private to a single observer; whether they can appear to have qualities that they do not really have, or have qualities that they do not appear to have; whether they are in any sense "within" the percipient's mind or brain. I shall show later on that these are not empirical questions. They are to be settled by making it clear how the term "sense-datum" is intended to be used. But first I must explain why it is thought necessary to introduce such a term at all. Why may we not say that we are directly aware of material things?

The answer is provided by what is known as the argument from illusion. This argument, as it is ordinarily stated, is based on the fact that material things may present different appearances to different observers, or to the same observer in different conditions, and that the character of these appearances is to some extent causally determined by the state of the conditions and the observer. For instance, it is remarked that a coin which looks circular from one point of view may look elliptical from another; or that a stick which normally appears straight looks bent when it is seen in water; or that to people who take drugs such as mescal, things appear to change their colours. The familiar cases of mirror images, and double vision, and complete hallucinations, such as the mirage, provide further examples. Nor is this a peculiarity of visual appearances. The same thing occurs in the domains of the other senses, including the sense of touch. It may be pointed out, for example, that the taste that a thing appears to have may vary with the condition of the palate; or that a liquid will seem to have a different temperature according as the hand that is feeling it is itself hot or cold; or that a coin seems larger when it is placed on the tongue than when it is held in the palm of the hand; or, to take a case of complete hallucination, that people who have had limbs amputated may still continue to feel pain in them.

Let us now consider one of these examples, say that of the stick which is refracted in water, and see what is to be inferred. For the present it must be assumed that the stick does not really change its shape when it is placed in water. I shall discuss the meaning and validity of this assumption later on. Then it follows that at least one of the visual appearances of the stick is delusive; for it cannot be both crooked and straight. Nevertheless, even in the case where what we see is not the real quality of a material thing, it is supposed that we are still seeing something; and that it is convenient to give this a name. And it is for this purpose that philosophers have recourse to the term "sense-datum." By using it they are able to give what seems to them a satisfactory answer to the question: What is the object of which we are directly aware, in perception, if it is not part of any material thing? Thus, when a man sees a mirage in the desert, he is not thereby perceiving any material thing; for the oasis which he thinks he is perceiving does not exist. At the same time, it is argued, his experience is not an experience of nothing; it has a definite content. Accordingly, it is said that he is experiencing sense-data, which are similar in character to what he

* John Locke (1632–1704) was one of the most important philosophers of the early modern period.

would be experiencing if he were seeing a real oasis, but are delusive in the sense that the material thing which they appear to present is not actually there. Or again, when I look at myself in the glass my body appears to be some distance behind the glass; but other observations indicate that it is in front of it. Since it is impossible for my body to be in both these places at once, these perceptions cannot all be veridical. I believe, in fact, that the ones that are delusive are those in which my body appears to be behind the glass. But can it be denied that when one looks at oneself in the glass one is seeing something? And if, in this case, there really is no such material thing as my body in the place where it appears to be, what is it that I am seeing? Once again the answer we are invited to give is that it is a sense-datum. And the same conclusion may be reached by taking any other of my examples.

If anything is established by this, it can be only that there are some cases in which the character of our perceptions makes it necessary for us to say that what we are directly experiencing is not a material thing but a sense-datum. It has not been shown that this is so in all cases. It has not been denied, but rather assumed, that there are some perceptions that do present material things to us as they really are; and in their case there seems at first sight to be no ground for saying that we directly experience sense-data rather than material things. But, as I have already remarked, there is general agreement among the philosophers who make use of the term "sense-datum," or some equivalent term, that what we immediately experience is always a sense-datum and never a material thing. And for this they give further arguments which I shall now examine.

In the first place it is pointed out that there is no intrinsic difference in kind between those of our perceptions that are veridical in their presentation of material things and those that are delusive.[3] When I look at a straight stick, which is refracted in water and so appears crooked, my experience is qualitatively the same as if I were looking at a stick that really was crooked. When, as the result of my putting on green spectacles, the white walls of my room appear to me to be green, my experience is qualitatively the same as if I were perceiving walls that really were green. When people whose legs have been amputated continue to feel pressure upon them, their experience is qualitatively the same as if pressure really were being exerted upon their legs. But, it is argued, if, when our perceptions were delusive, we were always perceiving something of a different kind from what we perceived when they were veridical, we should expect our experience to be qualitatively different in the two cases. We should expect to be able to tell from the intrinsic character of a perception whether it was a perception of a sense-datum or of a material thing. But this is not possible, as the examples that I have given have shown. In some cases there is indeed a distinction with respect to the beliefs to which the experiences give rise, as can be illustrated by my original example. For when, in normal conditions, we have the experience of seeing a straight stick there; but when the stick appears crooked, through being refracted in water, we do not believe that it really is crooked; we do not regard the fact that it looks crooked in water as evidence against its being really straight. It must, however, be remarked that this difference in the beliefs which accompany our perceptions is not grounded in the nature of the perceptions themselves, but depends upon our past experience. We do not believe that the stick which appears crooked when it stands in water really is crooked because we know from past experience that in normal conditions it looks straight. But a child who had not learned that refraction was a means of distortion would naturally believe that the stick really was crooked as he saw it. The fact, therefore, that there is this distinction between the beliefs that accompany veridical and delusive perceptions does not justify the view that these are perceptions of generically different objects, especially as the distinction by no means applies to all cases. For it sometimes happens that a delusive experience is not only qualitatively indistinguishable from one that is veridical but is also itself believed to be veridical, as in the example of the mirage; and, conversely, there are cases in which experiences that are actually veridical are believed to be delusive, as when we see something so strange or unexpected that we say to ourselves that we must be dreaming. The fact is that from the character of a perception considered by itself, that is, apart from its relation to further sense-experience, it is not possible to tell whether it is veridical or delusive. But whether we are entitled to infer from this that what we immediately experience is always a sense-datum remains still to be seen.

Another fact which is supposed to show that even in the case of veridical perceptions we are not directly aware of material things is that veridical and delusive perceptions may form a continuous series, both with respect to their qualities and with respect to the conditions in which they are obtained.[4] Thus, if I gradually approach an object from a distance I may begin by having a series of perceptions which are delusive in the sense that the object appears to be smaller than it really is. Let us assume that this series terminates in a veridical perception. Then the difference in quality between this perception and its immediate predecessor will be of the same order as the difference between any two delusive perceptions that are next to one another in the series; and, on the assumption that I am walking at a uniform pace, the same will be true of the difference in the conditions on which the generation of the series depends. A similar example would be that of the continuous alteration in the apparent colour of an object which was seen in a gradually changing light. Here again the relation between a veridical perception and the delusive perception that comes next to it in the series is the same as that which obtains between neighbouring delusive perceptions, both with respect to the difference in quality and with respect to the change in the conditions; and these are differences of degree and not of kind. But this, it is argued, is not what we should expect if the veridical perception were a perception of an object of a different sort, a material thing as opposed to a sense-datum. Does not the fact that veridical and delusive perceptions shade into one another in the way that is indicated by these examples show that the objects that are perceived in either case are generically the same? And from this it would follow, if it was acknowledged that the delusive perceptions were perceptions of sense-data, that what we directly experienced was always a sense-datum and never a material thing.

The final argument that has to be considered in this context is based upon the fact that all our perceptions, whether veridical or delusive, are to some extent causally dependent both upon external conditions, such as the character of the light, and upon our own physiological and psychological states. In the case of perceptions that we take to be delusive this is a fact that we habitually recognize. We say, for example, that the stick looks crooked because it is seen in water; that the white walls appear green to me because I am wearing green spectacles; that the water feels cool because my hand is hot; that the murderer sees the ghost of his victim because of his bad conscience or because he has been taking drugs. In the case of perceptions that we take to be veridical we are apt not to notice such causal dependencies, since as a rule it is only the occurrence of the unexpected or the abnormal that induces us to look for a cause. But in this matter also there is no essential difference between veridical and delusive perceptions. When, for example, I look at the piece of paper on which I am writing, I may claim that I am seeing it as it really is. But I must admit that in order that I should have this experience it is not sufficient that there should actually be such a piece of paper there. Many other factors are necessary, such as the condition of the light, the distance at which I am from the paper, the nature of the background, the state of my nervous system and my eyes. A proof that they are necessary is that if I vary them I find that I have altered the character of my perception. Thus, if I screw up my eyes I see two pieces of paper instead of one; if I grow dizzy the appearance of the paper becomes blurred; if I alter my position sufficiently it appears to have a different shape and size; if the light is extinguished, or another object is interposed, I cease to see it altogether. On the other hand, the converse does not hold. If the paper is removed I shall cease to see it; but the state of the light or of my nervous system or any other of the factors that were relevant to the occurrence of my perception may still remain the same. From this it may be inferred that the relation between my perception and these accompanying conditions is such that, while they are not causally dependent upon it, it is causally dependent upon them. And the same would apply to any other instance of a veridical perception that one cared to choose.

This point being established, the argument proceeds as follows. It is held to be characteristic of material things that their existence and their essential properties are independent of any particular observer. For they are supposed to continue the same, whether they are observed by one person or another, or not observed at all. But this, it is argued, has been shown not to be true of the objects we immediately experience. And so the conclusion is reached that what we immediately experience is in no case a material thing. According to this way of reasoning, if some perceptions are rightly held to be veridical, and others delusive, it is because of the different relations in which their objects stand to material things, and it is a philosophical problem to discover what these relations are. We may be allowed to have indirect knowledge of the properties of material things. But this knowledge, it is held, must be obtained through the medium of sense-data, since they are the only objects of which, in sense-perception, we are immediately aware.

NOTES

1. *An Essay Concerning Human Understanding*, Book IV, ch. 2, section viii.
2. Cf. H. H. Price, *Perception*, p. 104.
3. Cf. Price, op. cit.
4. Cf. Price, op. cit. p. 32.

The Argument from Illusion: A Critique of Sense Data

J. L. AUSTIN

J. L. Austin (1911–60) was an influential British philosopher who taught at Oxford University. His careful attention to linguistic usage allowed him to make unparalleled contributions to the philosophy of language.

The text that appears here is a widely anthologized selection from Austin's posthumously published book *Sense and Sensibilia* (1962, based on lectures given during the 1950s.) In it, Austin responds to Ayer's arguments from the previous selection. Section numbers refer to the original text.

III

The primary purpose of the argument from illusion is to induce people to accept "sense-data" as the proper and correct answer to the question what they perceive on certain *abnormal, exceptional* occasions; but in fact it is usually followed up with another bit of argument intended to establish that they *always* perceive sense-data. Well, what is the argument?

In Ayer's* statement[1] it runs as follows. It is "based on the fact that material things may present different appearances to different observers, or to the same observer in different conditions, and that the character of these appearances is to some extent causally determined by the state of the conditions and the observer." As illustrations of this alleged fact Ayer proceeds to cite perspective ("a coin which looks circular from one point of view may look elliptical from another"); refraction ("a stick which normally appears straight looks bent when it is seen in water"); changes in colour-vision produced by drugs ("such as mescal"); mirror-images; double vision; hallucination; apparent variations in tastes; variations in felt warmth ("according as the hand that is feeling it is itself hot or cold"); variations in felt bulk ("a coin seems larger when it is placed on the tongue

* The work that Austin discusses here appears as the previous entry in this volume.

From *Sense and Sensibilia*, ed. G. J. Warnock. Copyright © 1979 by Oxford University Press. Reprinted by permission of the publisher.

than when it is held in the palm of the hand"); and the oft-cited fact that "people who have had limbs amputated may still continue to feel pain in them."

He then selects three of these instances for detailed treatment. First, refraction—the stick which normally "appears straight" but "looks bent" when seen in water. He makes the "assumptions" (*a*) that the stick does not *really change its shape* when it is placed in water, and (*b*) that it *cannot be* both crooked and straight.[2] He then concludes ("it follows") that "at least one of the *visual appearances* of the stick is *delusive*." Nevertheless, even when "what we see is not the *real quality* of a *material thing*, it is supposed that we are still seeing something"—and this something is to be called a "sense-datum." A sense-datum is to be "the object of which we are *directly* aware, in perception, if it is not *part* of any *material thing*." (The italics are mine throughout this and the next two paragraphs.)

Next, mirages. A man who sees a mirage, he says, is "not perceiving any material thing; for the oasis which he thinks he is perceiving *does not exist*." But "his *experience* is not an experience of nothing"; thus "it is said that he is experiencing sense-data, which are similar in character to what he would be experiencing if he were seeing a real oasis, but are delusive in the sense that *the material thing which they appear to present* is not *really there*."

Lastly, reflections. When I look at myself in a mirror "my body *appears to be* some distance behind the glass"; but it cannot actually be in two places at once; thus, my perceptions in this case "cannot all be *veridical*." But I do see *something*; and if "there really is no such material thing as my body in the place where it appears to be, what is it that I am seeing?" Answer—a sense-datum. Ayer adds that "the same conclusion may be reached by taking any other of my examples."

Now I want to call attention, first of all, to the name of this argument—the "argument from *illusion*," and to the fact that it is produced as establishing the conclusion that some at least of our "perceptions" are *delusive*. For in this there are two clear implications—(*a*) that all the cases cited in the argument are cases of *illusions;* and (*b*) that *illusion* and *delusion* are the same thing. But both of these implications, of course, are quite wrong; and it is by no means unimportant to point this out, for, as we shall see, the argument trades on confusion at just this point.

What, then, would be some genuine examples of illusion? (The fact is that hardly any of the cases cited by Ayer is, at any rate without stretching things, a case of illusion at all.) Well, first, there are some quite clear cases of *optical* illusion—for instance the case we mentioned earlier in which, of two lines of equal length, one is made to look longer than the other. Then again there are illusions produced by professional "illusionists," conjurors—for instance the Headless Woman on the stage, who is made to look headless, or the ventriloquist's dummy which is made to appear to be talking. Rather different—not (usually) produced on purpose—is the case where wheels rotating rapidly enough in one direction may look as if they were rotating quite slowly in the opposite direction. Delusions, on the other hand, are something altogether different from this. Typical cases would be delusions of persecution, delusions of grandeur. These are primarily a matter of grossly disordered beliefs (and so, probably, behavior) and may well have nothing in particular to do with perception.[3] But I think we might also say that the patient who sees pink rats has (suffers from) delusions—particularly, no doubt, if, as would probably be the case, he is not clearly aware that his pink rats aren't real rats.[4]

The most important differences here are that the term "an illusion" (in a perceptual context) does not suggest that something totally unreal is *conjured up*—on the contrary, there just is the arrangement of lines and arrows on the page, the woman on the stage with her head in a black bag, the rotating wheels; whereas the term "delusion" *does* suggest something totally unreal, not really there at all. (The convictions of the man who has delusions of persecution can be *completely* without foundation.) For this reason delusions are a much more serious matter—something is really wrong, and what's more, wrong *with* the person who has them. But when I see an optical illusion, however well it comes off, there is nothing wrong with me personally, the illusion is not a little (or a large) peculiarity or idiosyncrasy of my own; it is quite public, anyone can see it, and in many cases standard procedures can be laid down for producing it. Furthermore, if we are not actually to be taken in, we need to be *on our guard*; but it is no use to tell the sufferer from delusions to be on his guard. He needs to be cured.

Why is it that we tend—if we do—to confuse illusions with delusions? Well, partly, no doubt the terms are often used loosely. But there is also the point that people may have, without making this explicit, different views or theories about the facts of some cases. Take the case of seeing a ghost, for example. It is not generally known, or agreed, what seeing ghosts *is*. Some people think of seeing ghosts as a case of something being conjured up, perhaps by the disordered nervous system of the victim; so in their view seeing ghosts is a case of delusion. But other people have the idea that what is called seeing ghosts is a case of being taken in by shadows, perhaps, or reflections, or a trick of the light—that is, they assimilate the case in their minds to illusion. In this way, seeing ghosts, for example, may come to be labelled sometimes as "delusion," sometimes as "illusion"; and it may not be noticed that it makes a difference which label we use. Rather, similarly, there seem to be different doctrines in the field as to what mirages are. Some seem to take a mirage to be a vision conjured up by the crazed brain of the thirsty and exhausted traveller (delusion), while in other accounts it is a case of atmospheric refraction, whereby something below the horizon is made to appear above it (illusion). (Ayer . . . takes the delusion view, although he cites it . . . as a case of illusion. He says not that the oasis appears to be where it is not, but roundly that "it does not exist.")

The way in which the "argument from illusion" positively trades on not distinguishing illusions from delusions is, I think, this. So long as it is being suggested that the cases paraded for our attention are cases of *illusion*, there is the implication (from the ordinary use of the word) that there really is something there that we perceive. But then, when these cases begin to be quietly called delusive, there comes in the very different suggestion of something being conjured up, something unreal or at any rate "immaterial." These two implications taken together may then subtly insinuate that in the cases cited there really is something that we are perceiving, but that this is an immaterial something; and this insinuation, even if not conclusive by itself, is certainly well calculated to edge us a little closer towards just the position where the sense-datum theorist wants to have us.

So much, then—though certainly there could be a good deal more—about the differences between illusions and delusions and the reasons for not obscuring them. Now let us look briefly at some of the other cases Ayer lists. Reflections, for instance. No doubt you *can* produce illusions with mirrors, suitably disposed. But is just *any* case of seeing something in a mirror an illusion, as he implies? Quite obviously not. For seeing things in mirrors is a perfectly *normal* occurrence, completely familiar, and there is usually no question of anyone being taken in. No doubt, if you're an infant or an aborigine and have never come across a mirror before, you may be pretty baffled, and even visibly perturbed, when you do. But is that a reason why the rest of us should speak of illusion here? And just the same goes for the phenomena of perspective—again, one *can* play tricks with perspective, but in the ordinary case there is no question of illusion. That a round coin should "look elliptical" (in one sense) from some points of view is exactly what we expect and what we normally find; indeed, we should be badly put out if we ever found this not to be so. Refraction again—the stick that looks bent in water—is far too familiar a case to be properly called a case of illusion. We may perhaps be prepared to agree that the stick looks bent; but then we can see that it's partly submerged in water, so that is exactly how we should expect it to look.

It is important to realize here how familiarity, so to speak, takes the edge off illusion. Is the cinema a case of illusion? Well, just possibly the first man who ever saw moving pictures may have felt inclined to say that here was a case of illusion. But in fact it's pretty unlikely that even he, even momentarily, was actually taken in; and by now the whole thing is so ordinary a part of our lives that it never occurs to us even to raise the question. One might as well ask whether producing a photograph is producing an illusion—which would plainly be just silly.

Then we must not overlook, in all this talk about illusions and delusions, that there are plenty of more or less unusual cases, not yet mentioned, which certainly aren't either. Suppose that a proof-reader makes a mistake—he fails to notice that what ought to be "causal" is printed as "casual"; does he have a delusion? Or is there an illusion before him? Neither, of course; he simply *misreads*. Seeing after-images, too, though not a particularly frequent occurrence and not just an ordinary case of seeing, is neither seeing illusions nor having delusions. And what about dreams? Does the dreamer see illusions? Does he have delusions? Neither; dreams are *dreams*.

Let us turn for a moment to what Price* has to say about illusions. He produces,[5] by way of saying "what the term 'illusion' means," the following "provisional definition": "An illusory sense-datum of sight or touch is a sense-datum which is such that we tend to take it to be part of the surface of a material object, but if we take it so we are wrong." It is by no means clear, of course, what this dictum itself means; but still, it seems fairly clear that the definition doesn't actually fit all the cases of illusion. Consider the two lines again. Is there anything here which we tend to take, wrongly, to be part of the surface of a material object? It doesn't seem so. We just see the two lines, we don't think or even tend to think that we see anything else, we aren't even raising the question whether anything is or isn't "part of the surface" of—what, anyway? the lines? the page?—the trouble is just that one line looks longer than the other, though it isn't. Nor surely, in the case of the Headless Woman, is it a question whether anything is or isn't part of her surface; the trouble is just that she looks as if she had no head.

It is noteworthy, of course, that, before he even begins to consider the "argument from illusion," Price has already incorporated in this "definition" the idea that in such cases there is something to be seen *in addition to* the ordinary things—which is part of what the argument is commonly used, and not uncommonly taken, to *prove*. But this idea surely has no place in an attempt to say what "illusion" *means*. It comes in again, improperly I think, in his account of perspective (which incidentally he also cites as a species of illusion)—"a distinct hillside which is full of protuberances, and slopes upwards at quite a gentle angle, will appear flat and vertical. . . . This means that the sense-datum, the colour-expanse which we sense, actually *is* flat and vertical." But why should we accept this account of the matter? Why should we say that there is *anything* we see which *is* flat and vertical, though not "part of the surface" of any material object? To speak thus is to assimilate all such cases to cases of delusion, where there *is* something not "part of any material thing." But we have already discussed the undesirability of this assimilation.

Next, let us have a look at the account Ayer himself gives of some at least of the cases he cites. (In fairness we must remember here that Ayer has a number of quite substantial reservations of his own about the merits and efficacy of the argument from illusion, so that it is not easy to tell just how seriously he intends his exposition of it to be taken; but this is a point we shall come back to.)

First, then, the familiar case of the stick in water. Of this case Ayer says (*a*) that since the stick looks bent but is straight, "at least one of the visual appearances of the stick is *delusive*"; and (*b*) that "what we see [directly anyway] is not the real quality of [a few lines later, not part of] a material thing." Well now: does the stick "look bent" to begin with? I think we can agree that it does, we have no better way of describing it. But of course it does *not* look *exactly* like a bent stick, a bent stick out of water—at most, it may be said to look rather like a bent stick partly immersed *in* water. After all, we can't help seeing the water the stick is partly immersed in. So exactly what in this case is supposed to be *delusive*? What is wrong, what is even faintly surprising, in the idea of a stick's being straight but looking bent sometimes? Does anyone suppose that if something is straight, then it jolly well has to *look* straight at all times and in all circumstances? Obviously no one seriously supposes this. So what mess are we supposed to get into here, what is the difficulty? For of course it has to be suggested that there *is* a difficulty—a difficulty, furthermore, which calls for a pretty radical solution, the introduction of sense-data. But what is the problem we are invited to solve in this way?

Well, we are told, in this case you are seeing *something*; and what is this something "if it is not part of any material thing?" But this question is, really,

* H. H. Price (1899–1984) was a British philosopher of mind, whose 1932 work *Perception* was highly influential in its day.

completely mad. The straight part of the stick, the bit not under water, is presumably part of a material thing; don't we see that? And what about the bit *under* water?—we can see that too. We can see, come to that, the water itself. In fact what we see is *a stick partly immersed in water*; and it is particularly extraordinary that this should appear to be called in question—that a question should be raised about *what* we are seeing—since this, after all, is simply the description of the situation with which we started. It was, that is to say, agreed at the start that we were looking at a stick, a "material thing," part of which was under water. If, to take a rather different case, a church were cunningly camouflaged so that it looked like a barn, how could any serious question be raised about what we see when we look at it? We see, of course, *a church* that now *looks like a barn*. We do *not* see an immaterial barn, an immaterial church, or an immaterial anything else. And what in this case could seriously tempt us to say that we do?

Notice, incidentally, that in Ayer's description of the stick-in-water case, which is supposed to be prior to the drawing of any philosophical conclusions, there has already crept in the unheralded but important expression "visual appearances"—it is, of course, ultimately to be suggested that all we *ever* get when we see is a visual appearance (whatever that may be).

Consider next the case of my reflection in a mirror. My body, Ayer says, "appears to be some distance behind the glass"; but as it's in front, it can't really be behind the glass. So what am I seeing? A sense-datum. What about this? Well, once again, although there is no objection to saying that my body "appears to be some distance behind the glass," in saying this we must remember what sort of situation we are dealing with. It does not "appear to be" there in a way which might tempt me (though it might tempt a baby or a savage) to go round the back and look for it, and be astonished when this enterprise proved a failure. (To say that A is *in* B doesn't always mean that if you open B you will find A, just as to say that A is *on* B doesn't always mean that you could pick it off—consider "I saw my face in the mirror," "There's a pain in my toe," "I heard him on the radio," "I saw the image on the screen," etc. Seeing something in a mirror is not like seeing a bun in a shop-window.) But does it follow that, since my body is not actually located behind the mirror, I am not seeing a material thing? Plainly not. For one thing, I can see the mirror (nearly always anyway). I can see my own body "indirectly," *sc.** in the mirror. I can also see the reflection of my own body or, as some would say, a mirror-image. And a mirror-image (if we choose this answer) is not a "sense-datum"; it can be photographed, seen by any number of people, and so on. (Of course there is no question here of either illusion or delusion.) And if the question is pressed, what actually *is* some distance, five feet say, behind the mirror, the answer is, not a sense-datum, but some region of the adjoining room.

The mirage case—at least if we take the view, as Ayer does, that the oasis the traveler thinks he can see "does not exist"—is significantly more amenable to the treatment it is given. For here we are supposing the man to be genuinely deluded, he is *not* "seeing a material thing."[6] We don't actually have to say, however, even here that he is "experiencing sense-data"; for though, as Ayer says "it is convenient to give a name" to what he is experiencing, the fact is that it already has a name—a *mirage*. Again, we should be wise not to accept too readily the statement that what he is experiencing is "*similar in character* to what he would be experiencing if he were seeing a real oasis." For is it at all likely, really, to be very similar? And, looking ahead, if we were to concede this point we should find the concession being used against us at a later stage—namely, at the stage where we shall be invited to agree that we see sense-data always, in normal cases too.

V

I want now to take up again the philosophical argument as it is set out in the texts we are discussing. . . . The argument from illusion is intended primarily to persuade us that, in certain exceptional, abnormal situations, what we perceive—directly anyway—is a sense-datum; but then there comes a second stage,

* *sc. (scilicet)* is a Latin term for "that is to say."

in which we are to be brought to agree that what we (directly) perceive is *always* a sense-datum, even in the normal, unexceptional case. It is this second stage of the argument that we must now examine.

Ayer expounds the argument thus.[7] There is, he says, "no intrinsic difference in kind between those of our perceptions that are veridical in their presentation of material things and those that are delusive. When I look at a straight stick, which is refracted in water and so appears crooked, my experience is qualitatively the same as if I were looking at a stick that really was crooked...." If, however, "when our perceptions were delusive, we were always perceiving something of a different kind from what we perceived when they were veridical, we should expect our experience to be qualitatively different in the two cases. We should expect to be able to tell from the intrinsic character of a perception whether it was a perception of a sense-datum or of a material thing. But this is not possible...." Price's exposition of this point,[8] to which Ayer refers us, is in fact not perfectly analogous; for Price has already somehow reached the conclusion that we are always aware of sense-data, and here is trying to establish only that we cannot distinguish *normal* sense-data, as "parts of the surfaces of material things," from *abnormal* ones, not "parts of the surfaces of material things." However, the argument used is much the same: "the abnormal crooked sense-datum of a straight stick standing in water is qualitatively indistinguishable from a normal sense-datum of a crooked stick"; but "is it not incredible that two entities so similar in all these qualities should really be so utterly different: that the one should be a real constituent of a material object, wholly independent of the observer's mind and organism, while the other is merely the fleeting product of his cerebral processes?"

It is argued further, both by Ayer and Price, that "even in the case of veridical perceptions we are not directly aware of material things" [or in the work of Price, that our sense-data are not parts of the surfaces of material things] for the reason that "veridical and delusive perceptions may form a continuous series. Thus, if I gradually approach an object from a distance I may begin by having a series of perceptions which are delusive in the sense that the object appears to be smaller than it really is. Let us assume that this series terminates in a veridical perception.[9] Then the difference in quality between this perception and its immediate predecessor will be of the same order as the difference between any two delusive perceptions that are next to one another in the series...." But "these are differences of degree and not of kind. But this, it is argued, is not what we should expect if the veridical perception were a perception of an object of a different sort, a material thing as opposed to a sense-datum. Does not the fact that veridical and delusive perceptions shade into one another in the way that is indicated by these examples show that the objects that are perceived in either case are generically the same? And from this it would follow, if it was acknowledged that the delusive perceptions were perceptions of sense-data, that what we directly experienced was always a sense-datum and never a material thing." As Price puts it, "it seems most extraordinary that there should be a total difference of nature where there is only an infinitesimal difference of quality."[10]

Well, what are we to make of the arguments thus set before us?

1. It is pretty obvious, for a start, that the terms in which the argument is stated by Ayer are grossly tendentious. Price, you remember, is not producing the argument as a proof that we are always aware of sense-data; in his view that question has already been settled, and he conceives himself to be faced here only with the question whether any sense-data are "parts of the surfaces of material objects." But in Ayer's exposition the argument *is* put forward as a ground for the conclusion that what we are (directly) aware of in perception is always a sense-datum; and if so, it seems a rather serious defect that this conclusion is practically assumed from the very first sentence of the statement of the argument itself. In that sentence Ayer uses, not indeed for the first time, the term "perceptions" (which incidentally has never been defined or explained), and takes it for granted, here and throughout, that there is at any rate some kind of entities of which we are aware in absolutely all cases—namely, "perceptions," delusive or veridical. But of course, if one has already been induced to swallow the idea that every case, whether "delusive" or "veridical," supplies us with "perceptions," one is only too easily going to be made to feel that it would be straining at a gnat not to swallow sense-data in an equally comprehensive style. But in fact one has not even been told what "perceptions" *are*: and the assumption of their ubiquity has been slipped in without any explanation or argument whatever. But if those to whom the argument is ostensibly addressed were not thus made to concede the essential point from the beginning, would the statement of the argument be quite such plain sailing?

2. Of course we shall also want to enter a protest against the argument's bland assumption of a simple dichotomy between "veridical and delusive experiences." There is, as we have already seen, *no* justification at all *either* for lumping all so-called "delusive" experiences together, *or* for lumping together all so-called "veridical" experiences. But again, could the argument run quite so smoothly without this assumption? It would certainly—and this, incidentally, would be all to the good—take rather longer to state.

3. But now let us look at what the argument actually says. It begins, you will remember, with an alleged statement of fact—namely, that "there is no intrinsic difference in kind between those of our perceptions that are veridical in their presentation of material things and those that are delusive" (Ayer), that "there is no qualitative difference between normal sense-data as such and abnormal sense-data as such" (Price). Now, waiving so far as possible the numerous obscurities in and objections to this manner of speaking, let us ask whether what is being alleged here is actually true. Is it the case that "delusive and veridical experiences" are not "qualitatively different"? Well, at least it seems perfectly extraordinary to say so in this sweeping way. Consider a few examples. I may have the experience (dubbed "delusive" presumably) of dreaming that I am being presented to the Pope. Could it be seriously suggested that having this dream is "qualitatively indistinguishable" from *actually being* presented to the Pope? Quite obviously not. After all, we have the phrase "a dream-like quality"; some waking experiences are said to have this dream-like quality, and some artists and writers occasionally try to impart it, usually with scant success, to their works. But of course, if the fact here alleged *were* a fact, the phrase would be perfectly meaningless, because applicable to everything. If dreams were not "qualitatively" different from waking experiences, then *every* waking experience would be like a dream; the dream-like quality would be, not difficult to capture, but impossible to avoid.[11] It is true, to repeat, that dreams are *narrated* in the same terms as waking experiences: these terms, after all, are the best terms we have; but it would be wildly wrong to conclude from this that what is narrated in the two cases is *exactly alike*. When we are hit on the head we sometimes say that we "see stars"; but for all that, seeing stars when you are hit on the head is *not* "qualitatively" indistinguishable from seeing stars when you look at the sky.

Again, it is simply not true to say that seeing a bright green after-image against a white wall is exactly like seeing a bright green patch actually on the wall; or that seeing a white wall through blue spectacles is exactly like seeing a blue wall; or that seeing pink rats in D.T.s is exactly like really seeing pink rats; or (once again) that seeing a stick refracted in water is exactly like seeing a bent stick. In all these cases we may *say* the same things ("It looks blue," "It looks bent," etc.), but this is no reason at all for denying the obvious fact that the "experiences" are *different*.

4. Next, one may well wish at least to ask for the credentials of a curious general principle on which both Ayer and Price seem to rely,[12] to the effect that if two things are not "generically the same," the same "in nature," then they can't be alike, or even very nearly alike. If it were true, Ayer says, that from time to time we perceived things of two different kinds, then "we should expect" them to be qualitatively different. But why on earth should we?—particularly if, as he suggests would be the case, we never actually found such a thing to be true. It is not at all easy to discuss this point sensibly, because of the initial absurdity in the hypothesis that we perceive just *two* kinds of things. But if, for example, I had never seen a mirror, but were told (*a*) that in mirrors one sees reflections of things, and (*b*) that reflections of things are not "generically the same" as things, is there any reason why I should forthwith *expect* there to be some whacking big "qualitative" difference between seeing things and seeing their reflections?

Plainly not; if I were prudent, I should simply wait and see what seeing reflections was like. If I am told that a lemon is generically different from a piece of soap, do I "expect" that no piece of soap could look just like a lemon? Why should I?

(It is worth noting that Price helps the argument along at this point by a bold stroke of rhetoric: how *could* two entities be "qualitatively indistinguishable," he asks, if one is a "real constituent of a material object," the other "*a fleeting product of his cerebral processes?*" But how in fact are we supposed to have been persuaded that sense-data are *ever* fleeting products of cerebral processes? Does this colourful description fit, for instance, the reflection of my face in a mirror?)

5. Another erroneous principle which the argument here seems to rely on is this: that it *must* be the case that "delusive and veridical experiences" are not (as such) "qualitatively" or "intrinsically" distinguishable—for if they were distinguishable, we should never be "deluded." But of course this is not so. From the fact that I am sometimes "deluded," mistaken, taken in through failing to distinguish A from B, it does not follow at all that A and B must be *indistinguishable*. Perhaps I should have noticed the difference if I had been more careful or attentive; perhaps I am just bad at distinguishing things of this sort (e.g. vintages); perhaps, again, I have never learned to discriminate between them, or haven't had much practice at it. As Ayer observes, probably truly, "a child who had not learned that refraction was a means of distortion would naturally believe that the stick really was crooked as he saw it"; but how is the fact that an uninstructed child probably would not discriminate between *being refracted* and *being crooked* supposed to establish the allegation that there *is* no "qualitative" difference between the two cases? What sort of reception would I be likely to get from a professional tea-taster, if I were to say to him, "But there can't be any difference between the flavours of these two brands of tea, for I regularly fail to distinguish between them?" Again, when "the quickness of the hand deceives the eye," it is not that what the hand is really doing is *exactly like* what we are tricked into thinking it is doing, but simply that it is *impossible to tell* what it is really doing. In this case it may be true that we can't distinguish, and not merely that we don't; but even this doesn't mean that the two cases are exactly alike.

I do not, of course, wish to deny that there may be cases in which "delusive and veridical experiences" really are "qualitatively indistinguishable"; but I certainly do wish to deny (*a*) that such cases are anything like as *common* as both Ayer and Price seem to suppose, and (*b*) that there *have* to be such cases to accommodate the undoubted fact that we are sometimes "deceived by our senses." We are not, after all, quasi-infallible beings, who can be taken in only where the avoidance of mistake is completely impossible. But if we are prepared to admit that there may be, even that there are, *some* cases in which "delusive and veridical perceptions" really are indistinguishable, does this admission require us to drag in, or even to let in, sense-data? No. For even if we were to make the prior admission (which we have so far found no reason to make) that in the "abnormal" cases we perceive sense-data, we should not be obliged to extend this admission to the "normal" cases too. For why on earth should it *not* be the case that, in some few instances, perceiving one sort of thing is exactly like perceiving another?

6. There is a further quite general difficulty in assessing the force of this argument, which we (in common with the authors of our texts) have slurred over so far. The question which Ayer invites us to consider is whether two classes of "perceptions," the veridical and the delusive, are or are not "qualitatively different," "intrinsically different in kind"; but how are we supposed to set about even considering this question, when we are not told what "a perception" *is*? In particular, how many of the circumstances of a situation, as these would ordinarily be stated, are supposed to be included in "the perception?" For example, to take the stick in water again: it is a feature of this case that part of the stick is under water, and water, of course, is not invisible; is the water, then, part of "the perception?" It is difficult to conceive of any grounds for denying that it is; but *if* it is, surely this is a perfectly obvious respect in which "the perception" differs from, is distinguishable from, the "perception" we have when we look at a bent stick *not* in water. There is a sense, perhaps, in which the presence or absence of water is not the *main thing* in this case—we are supposed to be addressing ourselves primarily to questions about the stick. But in fact, as a great quantity of psychological investigation has shown, discrimination between one thing and another very frequently depends on such more or less extraneous concomitants of the main thing, even when such concomitants are not consciously taken note of. As I said, we are told nothing of what "a perception" is; but could any defensible account, if such an account were offered, completely exclude all these highly significant attendant circumstances? And if they *were* excluded—in some more or less arbitrary way—how much interest or importance would be left in the contention that "delusive" and "veridical" perceptions are indistinguishable? Inevitably, if you rule out the respects in which A and B differ, you may expect to be left with respects in which they are alike.

I conclude, then, that this part of the philosophical argument involves (though not in every case equally essentially) (*a*) acceptance of a quite bogus dichotomy of all "perceptions" into two groups, the "delusive" and the "veridical"—to say nothing of the unexplained introduction of "perceptions" themselves; (*b*) an implicit but grotesque exaggeration of the *frequency* of "delusive perceptions"; (*c*) a further grotesque exaggeration of the *similarity* between "delusive" perceptions and "veridical" ones; (*d*) the erroneous suggestion that there *must* be such similarity, or even qualitative *identity*; (*e*) the acceptance of the pretty gratuitous idea that things "generically different" could not be qualitatively alike; and (*f*)—which is really a corollary of (*c*) and (*a*)—the gratuitous neglect of those more or less subsidiary features which often make possible the discrimination of situations which, in other *broad* respects, may be roughly alike. These seem to be rather serious deficiencies.

NOTES

1. Alfred J. Ayer, *The Foundations of Empirical Knowledge* (London: Macmillan, 1940, 1964).
2. It is not only strange, but also important, that Ayer calls these "assumptions." Later on he is going to take seriously the notion of denying at least one of them, which he could hardly do if he had recognized them here as the plain and incontestable facts that they are.
3. The latter point holds, of course, for *some* uses of "illusion" too; there are the illusions which some people (are said to) lose as they grow older and wiser.
4. Cp. the white rabbit in the play called *Harvey*.
5. H. H. Price, *Perception* (London: Methuen, 1932), p. 27.
6. Not even "indirectly," no such thing is "presented." Doesn't this seem to make the case, though more amenable, a good deal less useful to the philosopher? It's hard to see how normal cases could be said to be *very like* this.
7. Ayer, op. cit., pp. 5–9.
8. Price, op. cit., p. 31.
9. But what, we may ask, does this assumption amount to? From what distance *does* an object, a cricket-ball say, "look the size that it really is?" Six feet? Twenty feet?
10. I omit from consideration a further argument cited by both Price and Ayer, which makes play with the "causal dependence" of our "perceptions" upon the conditions of observation and our own "physiological and psychological states."
11. This is part, no doubt *only* part, of the absurdity in Descartes's toying with the notion that the whole of our experience might be a dream.
12. Ayer in fact expresses qualms later. . . .

LANGUAGE

INTRODUCTION

Our thoughts and words are about things in the world. We use names to designate people, places, and things, which we go on to talk about. This "aboutness" sets thought and language apart from almost everything else in the world. The philosophy of language investigates how it is possible for language to be about the world, how we can manage to communicate the thoughts we have about the world, and what exactly aboutness amounts to in the first place. What has to be the case, for example, in order for a certain sound or string of marks on a page to be about the planet Venus? And what has to be the case in order for you to understand my talk of Venus?

Language, Meaning, and Reference

Two of our selections—one by the philosopher Paul Grice (1913–88), the other by the linguist Noam Chomsky (1928–)—offer alternative perspectives on the fundamental nature of language. The third, an article by the philosopher John Perry (1943–), discusses a number of the most important questions that arise when we think about meaning and reference.

The philosopher Paul Grice takes the impression that language is used to communicate thoughts about the world at face value. He believes that we must see language as a tool for communication. If we do not, we cannot make sense of a host of linguistic phenomena. Grice's starting point is the idea that we make use of language in trying to rationally achieve our goals. Thus, Grice maintains, language use should be subject to principles of rationality that we can recognize in other areas of human activity. Grice's landmark article "Logic and Conversation," published in 1975, gives a powerful example of this approach by offering compelling explanations of otherwise puzzling linguistic phenomena.

In contrast to Grice, Noam Chomsky challenges the idea that the distinctive feature of language is aboutness. In his 1987 article "Language and Problems of Knowledge," he suggests that rather than think about language as a means for communicating our thoughts about the world to others, the central problem of language concerns a single speaker. We are all able to understand indefinitely many sentences of our native language, most of which we have never heard before. For Chomsky, the central question about language is how we accomplish this feat. He argues that the most promising avenue of research is to think of our ability to understand sentences as consisting in our ability to take up sounds or written marks and translate them into a system of internal representation. The question then becomes what rules govern this translation.

The philosopher John Perry pursues some of the implications of the idea that the basic function of language is to represent the world. The simplest idea is the one we began with: we use names to pick out people, places, or things, and then go on to say something about them. If that is how names worked, then any name for an object should be just as good as any other name for that object in a given context. But as the German mathematician and philosopher Gottlob Frege showed in his enormously influential 1892 paper "On Sense and Reference," that cannot be right.

Go back to the example of Venus, which historically has been known by a number of different names, including "Hesperus" (the traditional name for the evening star) and "Phosphorus" (the traditional name for the morning star). It seems different to be told that "Hesperus is Hesperus" than to be told that "Hesperus is Phosphorus:" The first is trivial, the second informative. On the basis of these sorts of examples, Frege concluded that names are associated not just with what they pick out—their *referent*—but with a mode of presentation of that referent—their *sense*. He went on to argue that sense should play a major role in our theory of mental states and of communication.

Perry takes up these Fregean themes in his 1979 article "The Problem of the Essential Indexical." Frege argued, inter alia, that for two people to communicate successfully, the hearer and speaker need to grasp the same sense. In his article, Perry suggests that certain senses cannot be communicated at all. He is concerned, in the first place, with the senses of a restricted class of expressions, such as "I," "here," and "now." These senses are usually called "indexicals," which explains the title of the article. Perry argues that the knowledge we have when we know where or who we are is not the kind of knowledge that could, even in principle, be shared by more than one person.

Further Reading

Students who want to pursue the themes raised in this section may begin by looking at the articles in the following two anthologies. Each anthology includes an extensive collection of important readings in the philosophy of language, along with suggestions for further readings on each of the main themes:

- Peter Ludlow, ed. *Readings in the Philosophy of Language*. Cambridge, Mass.: MIT Press, 1997.
- A. P. Martinich, ed. *The Philosophy of Language*, 5th ed. New York and Oxford: Oxford University Press, 2006.

C LANGUAGE, MEANING, AND REFERENCE

Logic and Conversation

H. P. GRICE

H. Paul Grice (1913–88) was a noted English philosopher of language who taught at Oxford University and the University of California at Berkeley.

In this selection, originally published in 1975, Grice articulates a number of principles that he thinks underlie our linguistic practices.

It is a commonplace of philosophical logic that there are, or appear to be, divergences in meaning between, on the one hand, at least some of what I shall call the formal devices—$\sim$, $\wedge$, $\vee$, $\supset$, (x), (ιx), $(\exists x)$* (when these are given a standard two-valued interpretation)—and, on the other, what are taken to be their analogs or counterparts in natural language—such expressions as "not," "and," "or," "if," "all," "some" (or "at least one"), "the." Some logicians may at some time have wanted to claim that there are in fact no such divergences; but such claims, if made at all, have been somewhat rashly made, and those suspected of making them have been subjected to some pretty rough handling.

Those who concede that such divergences exist adhere, in the main, to one or the other of two rival groups, which for the purposes of this article I shall call the formalist and the informalist groups. An outline of a not uncharacteristic formalist position may be given as follows: Insofar as logicians are concerned with the formulation of very general patterns of valid inference, the formal devices possess a decisive advantage over their natural counterparts. For it will be possible to construct in terms of the formal devices a system of very general formulas, a considerable number of which can be regarded as, or are closely related to, patterns of inferences the expression of which involves some or all of the devices: Such a system may consist of a certain set of simple formulas that must be acceptable if the devices have the meaning that has been assigned to them, and an indefinite number of further formulas, many of them less obviously acceptable, each of which can be shown to be acceptable if the members of the original set are acceptable. We have, thus, a way of handling dubiously acceptable patterns of inference, and if, as is sometimes possible, we can apply a decision procedure, we have an even better way. Furthermore, from a philosophical point of view, the possession by the natural counterparts of those

* The first four symbols ($\sim$, $\wedge$, $\vee$, $\supset$) abbreviate (respectively) not, and, or, and if-then. The last three expressions are quantifiers, including "x" used as a variable, and should be read (respectively) as "For all x," "The x," and "There exists an x."

From *Syntax and Semantics,* volume 3, Peter Cole and Jerry L. Morgan, eds. (New York: Academic Press, 1975), pp. 22–40. Copyright © 1975 by H. Paul Grice. Reprinted by permission of Elsevier.

elements in their meaning, which they do not share with the corresponding formal devices, is to be regarded as an imperfection of natural languages; the elements in question are undesirable excrescences. For the presence of these elements has the result that the concepts within which they appear cannot be precisely/clearly defined, and that at least some statements involving them cannot, in some circumstances, be assigned a definite truth value; and the indefiniteness of these concepts is not only objectionable in itself but leaves open the way to metaphysics—we cannot be certain that none of these natural language expressions is metaphysically "loaded." For these reasons, the expressions, as used in natural speech, cannot be regarded as finally acceptable, and may turn out to be, finally, not fully intelligible. The proper course is to conceive and begin to construct an ideal language, incorporating the formal devices, the sentences of which will be clear, determinate in truth value, and certifiably free from metaphysical implications; the foundations of science will now be philosophically secure, since the statements of the scientist will be expressible (though not necessarily actually expressed) within this ideal language. (I do not wish to suggest that all formalists would accept the whole of this outline, but I think that all would accept at least some part of it.)

To this, an informalist might reply in the following vein. The philosophical demand for an ideal language rests on certain assumptions that should not be conceded; these are, that the primary yardstick by which to judge the adequacy of a language is its ability to serve the needs of science, that an expression cannot be guaranteed as fully intelligible unless an explication or analysis of its meaning has been provided, and that every explication or analysis must take the form of a precise definition that is the expression/assertion of a logical equivalence. Language serves many important purposes besides those of scientific inquiry; we can know perfectly well what an expression means (and so a fortiori that it is intelligible) without knowing its analysis, and the provision of an analysis may (and usually does) consist in the specification, as generalized as possible, of the conditions that count for or against the applicability of the expression being analyzed. Moreover, while it is no doubt true that the formal devices are especially amenable to systematic treatment by the logician, it remains the case that there are very many inferences and arguments, expressed in natural language and not in terms of these devices, that are nevertheless recognizably valid. So there must be a place for an unsimplified, and so more or less unsystematic, logic of the natural counterparts of these devices; this logic may be aided and guided by the simplified logic of the formal devices but cannot be supplanted by it; indeed, not only do the two logics differ, but sometimes they come into conflict; rules that hold for a formal device may not hold for its natural counterpart.

Now, on the general question of the place in philosophy of the reformation of natural language, I shall, in this article, have nothing to say. I shall confine myself to the dispute in its relation to the alleged divergences mentioned at the outset. I have, moreover, no intention of entering the fray on behalf of either contestant. I wish, rather, to maintain that the common assumption of the contestants that the divergences do in fact exist is (broadly speaking) a common mistake, and that the mistake arises from an inadequate attention to the nature and importance of the conditions governing conversation. I shall, therefore, proceed at once to inquire into the general conditions that, in one way or another, apply to conversation as such, irrespective of its subject matter.

IMPLICATURE

Suppose that A and B are talking about a mutual friend, C, who is now working in a bank. A asks B how C is getting on in his job. and B replies, "Oh quite well, I think; he likes his colleagues, and he hasn't been to prison yet." At this point, A might well inquire what B was implying, what he was suggesting, or even what he meant by saying that C had not yet been to prison. The answer might be any one of such things as that C is the sort of person likely to yield to the temptation provided by his occupation, that C's colleagues are really very unpleasant and treacherous people, and so forth. It might, of course, be quite unnecessary for A to make such an inquiry of B, the answer to it being, in the context, clear in advance. I think it is clear that whatever B implied, suggested, meant, etc., in this example, is distinct from what B said, which was simply that C had not been to prison yet. I wish to introduce, as terms of art, the verb "implicate" and the related nouns "implicature" (cf. implying) and "implicatum" (cf. what is implied). The point of this maneuver is to avoid having, on each occasion, to choose between this or that member of the family of verbs for which *"implicate"* is to do general duty. I shall, for the time being at least, have to assume to a considerable extent an intuitive understanding of the meaning of "say" in such contexts, and an ability to recognize particular verbs as members of the family with which "implicate" is associated. I can, however, make one or two remarks that may help to clarify the more problematic of these assumptions, namely, that connected with the meaning of the word "say."

In the sense in which I am using the word "say," I intend what someone has said to be closely related to the conventional meaning of the words (the sentence) he has uttered. Suppose someone to have uttered the sentence "He is in the grip of a vice." Given a knowledge of the English language, but no knowledge of the circumstances of the utterance, one would know something about what the speaker had said, on the assumption that he was speaking standard English, and speaking literally. One would know that he had said, about some particular male person or animal *x*, that at the time of the utterance (whatever that was), either (1) *x* was unable to rid himself of a certain kind of bad character trait or (2) some part of *x*'s person was caught in a certain kind of tool or instrument (approximate account, of course). But for a full identification of what the speaker had said, one would need to know (a) the identity of *x*, (b) the time of utterance, and (c) the meaning, on the particular occasion of utterance, of the phrase "in the grip of a vice" [a decision between (1) and (2)]. This brief indication of my use of "say" leaves it open whether a man who says (today) "Harold Wilson is a great man" and another who says (also today) "The British Prime Minister is a great man" would, if each knew that the two singular terms had the same reference, have said the same thing. But whatever decision is made about this question, the apparatus that I am about to provide will be capable of accounting for any implicatures that might depend on the presence of one rather than another of these singular terms in the sentence uttered. Such implicatures would merely be related to different maxims.

In some cases the conventional meaning of the words used will determine what is implicated, besides helping to determine what is said. If I say (smugly), "He is an Englishman; he is, therefore, brave," I have certainly committed myself, by virtue of the meaning of my words, to its being the case that his being brave is a consequence of (follows from) his being an Englishman. But while I have said that he is an Englishman, and said that he is brave, I do not want to say that I have *said* (in the favored sense) that it follows from his being an Englishman that he is brave, though I have certainly indicated, and so implicated, that this is so. I do not want to say that my utterance of this sentence would be, *strictly speaking*, false should the consequence in question fail to hold. So *some* implicatures are conventional, unlike the one with which I introduced this discussion of implicature.

I wish to represent a certain subclass of nonconventional implicatures, which I shall call *conversational* implicatures, as being essentially connected with certain general features of discourse; so my next step is to try to say what these features are.

The following may provide a first approximation to a general principle. Our talk exchanges do not normally consist of a succession of disconnected remarks, and would not be rational if they did. They are characteristically, to some degree at least, cooperative efforts; and each participant recognizes in them, to some extent, a common purpose or set of purposes, or at least a mutually accepted direction. This purpose or direction may be fixed from the start (e.g., by an initial proposal of a question for discussion), or it may evolve during the exchange; it may be fairly definite, or it may be so indefinite as to leave very considerable latitude to the participants (as in a casual conversation). But at each stage, *some* possible conversational moves would be excluded as conversationally unsuitable. We might then formulate a rough general principle which participants will be expected (ceteris paribus) to observe, namely: Make your conversational contribution such as is required, at the stage at which it occurs, by the accepted purpose or direction of the talk exchange in which you are engaged. One might label this the *Cooperative Principle*.

On the assumption that some such general principle as this is acceptable, one may perhaps distinguish four categories under one or another of which will fall certain more specific maxims and submaxims, the following of which will, in general, yield results in accordance with the Cooperative Principle. Echoing Kant, I call these categories Quantity, Quality, Relation, and Manner. The category of *Quantity* relates to the quantity of information to be provided, and under it fall the following maxims: (1) Make your contribution as informative as is required (for the current purposes of the exchange). (2) Do not make your contribution more informative than is required. (The second maxim is disputable; it might be said that to be overinformative is not a transgression of the Cooperative Principle but merely a waste of time. However, it might be answered that such overinformativeness may be confusing in that it is liable to raise side issues; and there may also be an indirect effect, in that the hearers may be misled as a result of thinking that there is some particular *point* in the provision of the excess of information. However this may be, there is perhaps a different reason for doubt about the admission of this second maxim, namely, that its effect will be secured by a later maxim, which concerns relevance.)

Under the category of *quality* falls a supermaxim—"Try to make your contribution one that is true"—and two more specific maxims:

1. Do not say what you believe to be false.
2. Do not say that for which you lack adequate evidence.

Under the category of *Relation* I place a single maxim, namely, "Be relevant." Though the maxim itself is terse, its formulation conceals a number of problems that exercise me a good deal: questions about what different kinds and focuses of relevance there may be, how these shift in the course of a talk exchange, how to allow for the fact that subjects of conversation are legitimately changed, and so on. I find the treatment of such questions exceedingly difficult, and I hope to revert to them in a later work.

Finally, under the category of *Manner*, which I understand as relating not (like the previous categories) to what is said but, rather, to *how* what is said is to be said, I include the supermaxim—"Be perspicuous"—and various maxims such as:

1. Avoid obscurity of expression.
2. Avoid ambiguity.
3. Be brief (avoid unnecessary prolixity).
4. Be orderly.

And one might need others.

It is obvious that the observance of some of these maxims is a matter of less urgency than is the observance of others; a man who has expressed himself with undue prolixity would, in general, be open to milder comment than would a man who has said something he believes to be false. Indeed, it might be felt that the importance of at least the first maxim of Quality is such that it should not be included in a scheme of the kind I am constructing; other maxims come into operation only on the assumption that this maxim of Quality is satisfied. While this may be correct, so far as the generation of implicatures is concerned it seems to play a role not totally different from the other maxims, and it will be convenient, for the present at least, to treat it as a member of the list of maxims.

There are, of course, all sorts of other maxims (aesthetic, social, or moral in character), such as "Be polite," that are also normally observed by participants in talk exchanges, and these may also generate nonconventional implicatures. The conversational maxims, however, and the conversational implicatures connected with them, are specially connected (I hope) with the particular purposes that talk (and so, talk exchange) is adapted to serve and is primarily employed to serve. I have stated my maxims as if this purpose were a maximally effective exchange of information; this specification is, of course, too narrow, and the scheme needs to be generalized to allow for such general purposes as influencing or directing the actions of others.

As one of my avowed aims is to see talking as a special case or variety of purposive, indeed rational, behavior, it may be worth noting that the specific expectations or presumptions connected with at least some of the foregoing maxims have their analogues in the sphere of transactions that are not talk exchanges. I list briefly one such analogue for each conversational category.

1. *Quantity*. If you are assisting me to mend a car, I expect your contribution to be neither more nor less than is required; if, for example, at a particular stage I need four screws, I expect you to hand me four, rather than two or six.

2. *Quality*. I expect your contributions to be genuine and not spurious. If I need sugar as an ingredient in the cake you are assisting me to make, I do not expect you to hand me salt; if I need a spoon, I do not expect a trick spoon made of rubber.

3. *Relation*. I expect a partner's contribution to be appropriate to immediate needs at each stage of the transaction; if I am mixing ingredients for a cake, I do not expect to be handed a good book, or even an oven cloth (though this might be an appropriate contribution at a later stage).

4. *Manner*. I expect a partner to make it clear what contribution he is making, and to execute his performance with reasonable dispatch.

These analogies are relevant to what I regard as a fundamental question about the Cooperative Principle and its attendant maxims, namely, what the basis is for the assumption which we seem to make, and on which (I hope) it will appear that a great range of implicatures depend, that talkers will in general (ceteris paribus and in the absence of indications to the contrary) proceed in the manner that these principles prescribe. A dull but, no doubt at a certain level, adequate answer is that it is just a well-recognized empirical fact that people *do* behave in these ways; they have learned to do so in childhood and not lost the habit of doing so; and, indeed, it would involve a good deal of effort to make a radical departure from the habit. It is much easier, for example, to tell the truth than to invent lies.

I am, however, enough of a rationalist to want to find a basis that underlies these facts, undeniable though they may be; I would like to be able to think of the standard type of conversational practice not merely as something that all or most do *in fact* follow but as something that it is *reasonable* for us to follow, that we *should not* abandon. For a time, I was attracted by the idea that observance of the Cooperative Principle and the maxims, in a talk exchange, could be thought of as a quasi-contractual matter, with parallels outside the realm of discourse. If you pass by when I am struggling with my stranded car, I no doubt have some degree of expectation that you will offer help, but once you join me in tinkering under the hood, my expectations become stronger and take more specific forms (in the absence of indications that you are merely an incompetent meddler); and talk exchanges seemed to me to exhibit, characteristically, certain features that jointly distinguish cooperative transactions:

1. The participants have some common immediate aim, like getting a car mended; their ultimate aims may, of course, be independent and even in conflict—each may want to get the car mended in order to drive off, leaving the other stranded. In characteristic talk exchanges, there is a common aim even if, as in an over-the-wall chat, it is a second-order one, namely, that each party should, for the time being, identify himself with the transitory conversational interests of the other.

2. The contributions of the participants should be dovetailed, mutually dependent.

3. There is some sort of understanding (which may be explicit but which is often tacit) that, other things being equal, the transaction should continue in appropriate style unless both parties are agreeable that it should terminate. You do not just shove off or start doing something else.

But while some such quasi-contractual basis as this may apply to some cases, there are too many types of exchange, like quarreling and letter writing, that it fails to fit comfortably. In any case, one feels that the talker who is irrelevant or obscure has primarily let down not his audience but himself. So I would like to be able to show that observance of the Cooperative Principle and maxims is reasonable (rational) along the following lines: that any one who cares about the goals that are central to conversation/communication (e.g., giving and receiving information, influencing and being influenced by others) must be expected to have an interest, given suitable circumstances, in participating in talk exchanges that will be profitable only on the assumption that they are conducted in general accordance with the Cooperative Principle and the maxims. Whether any such conclusion can be reached, I am uncertain; in any case, I am fairly sure that I cannot reach it until I am a good deal clearer about the nature of relevance and of the circumstances in which it is required.

It is now time to show the connection between the Cooperative Principle and maxims, on the one hand, and conversational implicature on the other.

A participant in a talk exchange may fail to fulfill a maxim in various ways, which include the following:

1. He may quietly and unostentatiously *violate* a maxim; if so, in some cases he will be liable to mislead.

2. He may *opt out* from the operation both of the maxim and of the Cooperative Principle: he may say, indicate, or allow it to become plain that he is unwilling to cooperate in the way the maxim requires. He may say, for example, "I cannot say more; my lips are sealed."

3. He may be faced by a *clash:* He may be unable, for example, to fulfill the first maxim of Quantity (Be as informative as is required) without violating the second maxim of Quality (Have adequate evidence for what you say).

4. He may *flout* a maxim; that is, he may *blatantly* fail to fulfill it. On the assumption that the speaker is able to fulfill the maxim and to do so without violating another maxim (because of a clash), is not opting out, and is not, in view of the blatancy of his performance, trying to mislead, the hearer is faced with a minor problem: How can his saying what he did say be reconciled with the supposition that he is observing the overall Cooperative Principle? This situation is one that characteristically gives rise to a conversational implicature; and when a conversational implicature is generated in this way, I shall say that a maxim is being *exploited*.

I am now in a position to characterize the notion of conversational implicature. A man who, by (in, when) saying (or making as if to say) that *p* has implicated that *q*, may be said to have conversationally implicated that *q*, provided that (1) he is to be presumed to be observing the conversational maxims, or at least the cooperative principle; (2) the supposition that he is aware that, or thinks that, *q* is required in order to make his saying or making as if to say *p* (or doing so in *those* terms) consistent with this presumption; and (3) the speaker thinks (and would expect the hearer to think that the speaker thinks) that it is within the competence of the hearer to work out, or grasp intuitively, that the supposition mentioned in (2) *is* required. Apply this to my initial example, to B's remark that C has not yet been to prison. In a suitable setting A might reason as follows: "(1) B has apparently violated the maxim 'Be relevant' and so may be regarded as having flouted one of the maxims conjoining perspicuity, yet I have no reason to suppose that he is opting out from the operation of the CP; (2) given the circumstances, I can regard his irrelevance as only apparent if, and only if, I suppose him to think that C is potentially dishonest; (3) B knows that I am capable of working out step (2). So B implicates that C is potentially dishonest."

The presence of a conversational implicature must be capable of being worked out; for even if it can in fact be intuitively grasped, unless the intuition is replaceable by an argument, the implicature (if present at all) will not count as a *conversational* implicature; it will be a *conventional* implicature. To work out that a particular conversational implicature is present, the hearer will rely on the following data: (1) the conventional meaning of the words used, together with the identity of any references that may be involved; (2) the Cooperative Principle and its maxims; (3) the context, linguistic or otherwise, of the utterance; (4) other items of background knowledge; and (5) the fact (or supposed fact) that all relevant items falling under the previous headings are available to both participants and both participants know or assume this to be the case. A general pattern for the working out of a conversational implicature might be given as follows: "He has said that *p;* there is no reason to suppose that he is not observing the maxims, or at least the Cooperative Principle; he could not be doing this unless he thought that *q;* he knows (and knows that I know that he knows) that I can see that the supposition that he thinks that *q* is required; he has done nothing to stop me thinking that *q;* he intends me to think, or is at least willing to allow me to think, that *q;* and so he has implicated that *q*."

EXAMPLES

I shall now offer a number of examples, which I shall divide into three groups.

GROUP A

Examples in which no maxim is violated, or at least in which it is not clear that any maxim is violated:

(1) A is standing by an obviously immobilized car and is approached by B, the following exchange takes place:

A: I am out of petrol.
B: There is a garage round the corner.

(Gloss: B would be infringing the maxim "Be relevant" unless he thinks, or thinks it possible that the garage is open, and has petrol to sell; so he implicates that the garage is, or at least may be open, etc.) In this example, unlike the case of the remark "He hasn't been to prison yet," the unstated connection between B's remark and A's remark is so obvious that, even if one interprets the supermaxim of Manner, "Be perspicuous," as applying not only to the expression of what is said but also to the connection of what is said with adjacent remarks, there seems to be no case for regarding that supermaxim as infringed in this example.

(2) The next example is perhaps a little less clear in this respect:

A: Smith doesn't seem to have a girlfriend these days.
B: He has been paying a lot of visits to New York lately.

B implicates that Smith has, or may have, a girlfriend in New York. (A gloss is unnecessary in view of that given for the previous example.)

In both examples, the speaker implicates that which he must be assumed to believe in order to preserve the assumption that he is observing the maxim of relation.

GROUP B

An example in which a maxim is violated, but its violation is to be explained by the supposition of a clash with another maxim:

(3) A is planning with B an itinerary for a holiday in France. Both know that A wants to see his friend C, if to do so would not involve too great a prolongation of his journey:

A: Where does C live?
B: Somewhere in the South of France.

(Gloss: There is no reason to suppose that B is opting out; his answer is, as he well knows, less informative than is required to meet A's needs. This infringement of the first maxim of Quantity can be explained only by the supposition that B is aware that to be more informative would be to say something that infringed the maxim of Quality, "Don't say what you lack adequate evidence for," so B implicates that he does not know in which town C lives.)

GROUP C

Examples that involve exploitation, that is, a procedure by which a maxim is flouted for the purpose of getting in a conversational implicature by means of something of the nature of a figure of speech:

In these examples, though some maxim is violated at the level of what is said, the hearer is entitled to assume that that maxim, or at least the overall Cooperative Principle, is observed at the level of what is implicated.

(1a) A flouting of the first maxim of Quantity. A is writing a testimonial about a pupil who is a candidate for a philosophy job, and his letter reads as follows: "Dear Sir, Mr. X's command of English is excellent, and his attendance at tutorials has been regular. Yours, etc." (Gloss: A cannot be opting out, since if he wished to be uncooperative, why write at all? He cannot be unable, through ignorance, to say more, since the man is his pupil; moreover, he knows that more information than this is wanted. He must, therefore, be wishing to impart information that he is reluctant to write down. This supposition is tenable only on the assumption that he thinks Mr. X is no good at philosophy. This, then, is what he is implicating.)

Extreme examples of a flouting of the first maxim of Quantity are provided by utterances of patent tautologies like "Women are women" and "War is war." I would wish to maintain that at the level of what is said, in my favored sense, such remarks are totally noninformative and so, at that level, cannot but infringe the first maxim of Quantity in any conversational context. They are, of course, informative at the level of what is implicated, and the hearer's identification of their informative content at this level is dependent on his ability to explain the speaker's selection of this *particular* patent tautology.

(1b) An infringement of the second maxim of Quantity, "Do not give more information than is required," on the assumption that the existence of such a maxim should be admitted. A wants to know whether *p*, and B volunteers not only the information that *p*, but information to the effect that it is certain that *p*, and that the evidence for its being the case that *p* is so-and-so and such-and-such.

B's volubility may be undesigned, and if it is so regarded by A it may raise in A's mind a doubt as to whether B is as certain as he says he is ("Methinks the lady doth protest too much"). But if it is thought of as designed, it would be an oblique way of conveying that it is to some degree controversial whether or not *p*. It is, however, arguable that such an implicature could be explained by reference to the maxim of Relation without invoking an alleged second maxim of Quantity.

(2a) Examples in which the first maxim of Quality is flouted.

(i) Irony: X, with whom A has been on close terms until now, has betrayed a secret of A's to a business rival. A and his audience both know this. A says "X is a fine friend." (Gloss: It is perfectly obvious to A and his audience that what A has said or has made as if to say is something he does not believe, and the audience knows that A knows that this is obvious to the audience. So, unless A's utterance is entirely pointless, A must be trying to get across some other proposition than the one he purports to be putting forward. This must be some obviously related proposition; the most obviously related proposition is the contradictory of the one he purports to be putting forward.)

(ii) Metaphor: Examples like "You are the cream in my coffee" characteristically involve categorial falsity, so the contradictory of what the speaker has made as if to say will, strictly speaking, be a truism; so it cannot be *that* that such a speaker is trying to get across. The most likely supposition is that the speaker is attributing to his audience some feature or features in respect of which the audience resembles (more or less fancifully) the mentioned substance.

It is possible to combine metaphor and irony by imposing on the hearer two stages of interpretation. I say "You are the cream in my coffee," intending the hearer to reach first the metaphor interpretant "You are my pride and joy" and then the irony interpretant "You are my bane."

(iii) Meiosis: Of a man known to have broken up all the furniture, one says "He was a little intoxicated."

(iv) Hyperbole: Every nice girl loves a sailor.

(2b) Examples in which the second maxim of Quality, "Do not say that for which you lack adequate evidence," is flouted are perhaps not easy to find, but the following seems to be a specimen. I say of X's wife, "She is probably deceiving him this evening." In a suitable context, or with a suitable gesture or tone of voice, it may be clear that I have no adequate reason for supposing this to be the case. My partner, to preserve the assumption that the conversational game is still being played, assumes that I am getting at some related proposition for the acceptance of which I *do* have a reasonable basis. The related proposition might well be that she is given to deceiving her husband, or possibly that she is the sort of person who would not stop short of such conduct.

(3) Examples in which an implicature is achieved by real, as distinct from apparent, violation of the maxim of Relation are perhaps rare, but the following seems to be a good candidate. At a genteel tea party, A says "Mrs. X is an old bag." There is a moment of appalled silence, and then B says "The weather has been quite delightful this summer, hasn't it?" B has blatantly refused to make what *he* says relevant to A's preceding remark. He thereby implicates that A's remark should not be discussed and, perhaps more specifically, that A has committed a social gaffe.

(4) Examples in which various maxims falling under the supermaxim "Be perspicuous" are flouted.

(i) Ambiguity. We must remember that we are concerned only with ambiguity that is deliberate, and that the speaker intends or expects to be recognized by his hearer. The problem the hearer has to solve is why a speaker should, when still playing the conversational game, go out of his way to choose an ambiguous utterance. There are two types of cases:

(a) Examples in which there is no difference, or no striking difference, between two interpretations of an utterance with respect to straightforwardness; neither interpretation is notably more sophisticated, less standard, more recondite or more far-fetched than the other. We might consider Blake's lines: "Never seek to tell thy love, Love that never told can be." To avoid the complications introduced by the presence of the imperative mood, I shall consider the related sentence, "I sought to tell my love, love that never told can be." There may be a double ambiguity here. "My love" may refer to either a state of emotion or an object of emotion, and "love that never told can be" may mean either "Love that cannot be told" or "love that if told cannot continue to exist." Partly because of the sophistication of the poet and partly because of internal evidence (that the ambiguity is kept up), there seems to be no alternative to supposing that the ambiguities are deliberate and that the poet is conveying both what he would be saying if one interpretation were intended rather than the other, and vice versa; though no doubt the poet is not explicitly *saying* any one of these things but only conveying or suggesting them (cf. "Since she [nature] pricked thee out of women's pleasure, mine be thy love, and thy love's use their treasure.")

(b) Examples in which one interpretation is notably less straightforward than another. Take the complex example of the British General who captured the town of Sind and sent back the message *Peccavi*. The ambiguity involved ("I have Sind"/"I have sinned") is phonemic, not morphemic; and the expression actually used is unambiguous, but since it is in a language foreign to speaker and hearer, translation is called for, and the ambiguity resides in the standard translation into native English.

Whether or not the straightforward interpretant ("I have sinned") is being conveyed, it seems that the nonstraightforward must be. There might be stylistic reasons for conveying by a sentence merely its nonstraightforward interpretant, but it would be pointless, and perhaps also stylistically objectionable, to go to the trouble of finding an expression that non-straightforwardly conveys that p, thus imposing on an audience the effort involved in finding this interpretant, if this interpretant were otiose so far as communication was concerned. Whether the straightforward interpretant is also being conveyed seems to depend on whether such a supposition would conflict with other conversational requirements, for example, would it be relevant, would it be something the speaker could be supposed to accept, and so on. If such requirements are not satisfied, then the straightforward interpretant is not being conveyed. If they are, it is. If the author of *Peccavi* could naturally be supposed to think that he had committed some kind of transgression, for example, had disobeyed his orders in capturing Sind, and if reference to such a transgression would be relevant to the presumed interests of the audience, then he would have been conveying both interpretants; otherwise he would be conveying only the nonstraightforward one.

(ii) Obscurity. How do I exploit, for the purposes of communication, a deliberate and overt violation of the requirement that I should avoid obscurity? Obviously, if the Cooperative Principle is to operate, I must intend my partner to understand what I am saying despite the obscurity I import into my utterance. Suppose that A and B are having a conversation in the presence of a third party, for example, a child, then A might be deliberately obscure, though not too obscure, in the hope that B would understand and the third party not. Furthermore, if A expects B to see that A is being deliberately obscure, it seems reasonable to suppose that, in making his conversational contribution in this way, A is implicating that the contents of his communication should not be imparted to the third party.

(iii) Failure to be brief or succinct. Compare the remarks:

(a) Miss X sang "Home sweet home."
(b) Miss X produced a series of sounds that corresponded closely with the score of "Home sweet home."

Suppose that a reviewer has chosen to utter (b) rather than (a). (Gloss: Why has he selected that rigmarole in place of the concise and nearly synonymous "sang"? Presumably, to indicate some striking difference between Miss X's performance and those to which the word "singing" is usually applied. The most obvious supposition is that Miss X's performance suffered from some hideous defect. The reviewer knows that this supposition is what is likely to spring to mind, so that is what he is implicating.)

I have so far considered only cases of what I might call particularized conversational implicature—that is to say, cases in which an implicature is carried by saying that p on a particular occasion in virtue of special features of the context, cases in which there is no room for the idea that an implicature of this sort is *normally* carried by saying that *p*. But there are cases of generalized conversational implicature. Sometimes one can say that the use of a certain form of words in an utterance would normally (in the *absence* of special circumstances) carry such-and-such an implicature or type of implicature. Noncontroversial examples are perhaps hard to find, since it is all too easy to treat a generalized conversational implicature as if it were a conventional implicature. I offer an example that I hope may be fairly noncontroversial.

Anyone who uses a sentence of the form "X is meeting a woman this evening" would normally implicate that the person to be met was someone other than X's wife, mother, sister, or perhaps even close platonic friend. Similarly, if I were to say "X went into a house yesterday and found a tortoise inside the front door," my hearer would normally be surprised if some time later I revealed that the house was X's own. I could produce similar linguistic phenomena involving the expressions *"a garden," "a car," "a college,"* and so on. Sometimes, however, there would normally be no such implicature ("I have been sitting in a car all morning"), and sometimes a reverse implicature ("I broke a finger yesterday"). I am inclined to think that one would not lend a sympathetic ear to a philosopher who suggested that there are three senses of the form of expression "an X": one in which it means roughly "something that satisfies the conditions defining the word X," another in which it means approximately "an X (in the first sense) that is only remotely related in a certain way to some person indicated by the context," and yet another in which it means "an X (in the first sense) that is closely related in a certain way to some person indicated by the context." Would we not much prefer an account on the following lines (which, of course, may be incorrect in detail): When someone, by using the form of expression "an X," implicates that the X does not belong to or is not otherwise closely connected with some identifiable person, the implicature is present because the speaker has failed to be specific in a way in which he might have been expected to be specific, with the consequence that it is likely to be assumed that he is not in a position to be specific. This is a familiar implicature situation and is classifiable as a failure, for one reason or another, to fulfill the first maxim of Quantity. The only difficult question is why it should, in certain cases, be presumed, independently of information about particular contexts of utterance, that specification of the closeness or remoteness of the connection between a particular person or object and a further person who is mentioned or indicated by the utterance should be likely to be of interest. The answer must lie in the following region: Transactions between a person and other persons or things closely connected with him are liable to be very different as regards their concomitants and results from the same sort of transactions involving only remotely connected persons or things; the concomitants and results, for instance, of my finding a hole in *my* roof are likely to be very different from the concomitants and results of my finding a hole in someone else's roof. Information, like money, is often given without the giver's knowing to just what use the recipient will want to put it. If someone to whom a transaction is mentioned gives it further consideration, he is likely to find himself wanting the answers to further questions that the speaker may not be able to identify in advance; if the appropriate specification will be likely to enable the hearer to answer a considerable variety of such questions for himself, then there is a presumption that the speaker should include it in his remark; if not, then there is no such presumption.

Finally, we can now show that, conversational implicature being what it is, it must possess certain features.

1. Since, to assume the presence of a conversational implicature, we have to assume that at least the Cooperative Principle is being observed, and since it is possible to opt out of the observation of this principle, it follows that a generalized conversational implicature can be canceled in a particular case. It may be explicitly canceled, by the addition of a clause that states or implies that the speaker has opted out, or it may be contextually canceled, if the form of utterance that usually carries it is used in a context that makes it clear that the speaker IS opting out.

2. Insofar as the calculation that a particular conversational implicature is present requires, besides contextual and background information, only a knowledge of what has been said (or of the conventional commitment of the utterance), and insofar as the manner of expression plays no role in the calculation, it will not be possible to find another way of saying the same thing, which simply lacks the implicature in question, except where some special feature of the substituted version is itself relevant to the determination of an implicature (in virtue of one of the maxims of Manner). If we call this feature *nondetachability*, one may expect a generalized conversational implicature that is carried by a familiar, nonspecial locution to have a high degree of nondetachability.

3. To speak approximately, since the calculation of the presence of a conversational implicature presupposes an initial knowledge of the conventional force of the expression the utterance of which carries the implicature, a conversational implicatum will be a condition that is not included in the original specification of the expression's conventional force. Though it may not be impossible for what starts life, so to speak, as a conversational implicature to become conventionalized, to suppose that this is so in a given case would require special justification. So, initially at least, conversational implicata are not part of the meaning of the expressions to the employment of which they attach.

4. Since the truth of a conversational implicatum is not required by the truth of what is said (what is said may be true—what is implicated may be false), the implicature is not carried by what is said, but only by the saying of what is said, or by "putting it that way."

5. Since, to calculate a conversational implicature is to calculate what has to be supposed in order to preserve the supposition that the Cooperative Principle is being observed, and since there may be various possible specific explanations, a list of which may be open, the conversational implicatum in such cases will be a disjunction of such specific explanations; and if the list of these is open, the implicatum will have just the kind of indeterminacy that many actual implicata do in fact seem to possess.

Language and Problems of Knowledge

NOAM CHOMSKY

American linguist Noam Chomsky (1928–) taught for many years at the Massachusetts Institute of Technology. He is renowned for his work in linguistics and his contributions to the field of psychology. Chomsky is also known as a social critic and political activist.

This is a slightly revised version of a paper delivered at a conference in Madrid, April 28, 1986. Copyright © 1990 Noam Chomsky. Reprinted by permission of Noam Chomsky.

The selection that appears here is excerpted from a lecture that Chomsky delivered in 1986. In it, Chomsky considers the question of how it is possible that one can understand infinitely many sentences despite never having previously heard most of them.

The central problem of the theory of language is to explain how people can speak and understand new sentences, new in their experience or perhaps in the history of the language. The phenomenon is not an exotic one, but is the norm in the ordinary use of language, as Descartes and his followers stressed in their discussion of what we may call "the creative aspect of language use," that is, the commonplace but often neglected fact that the normal use of language is unbounded in scope, free from identifiable stimulus control, coherent and appropriate to situations that evoke but do not cause it (a crucial distinction), arousing in listeners thoughts that they too might express in the same or similar ways. It is surprising how rarely the phenomenon was seriously addressed in the linguistics of the past century, until the mid-1950s at least, in part, perhaps, because of the conception of language as a system of habits, dispositions or abilities, Otto Jesperson being a rare and notable exception. When the question was addressed, the conventional answer was that new forms are produced and understood "by analogy" with familiar ones. (But this explanation is empty until an account is given of analogy, and none exists.)

In the past few years it has been shown that a wide range of phenomena from typologically quite different languages can be explained on the assumption that the language faculty of the mind/brain carries out digital computations following very general principles, making use of representations of a precisely determined sort, including empty categories of several kinds. This work then provides evidence, quite strong evidence I believe, for some rather striking and surprising conclusions: that the language faculty, part of the mind/brain, is in crucial part a system of digital computation of a highly restricted character, with simple principles that interact to yield very intricate and complex results. This is a rather unexpected property of a biological system. One must be alert to the possibility that the conclusion is an artifact, resulting from our mode of analysis, but the evidence suggests quite strongly that the conclusion reflects reality.

As far as I am aware, there is only one other known biological phenomenon that shares the properties of discrete infinity exhibited by language, and that involves similar principles of digital computation: namely, the human number faculty, also apparently a species property, essentially common to the species and unique to it, and, like human language, unteachable to other organisms, which lack the requisite faculties. There are, for example, numerous animal communication systems, but they are invariably finite (the calls of apes) or continuous (the "language" of bees, continuous in whatever sense we can say this of a physical system; the human gestural system; etc.). Note that the difference between human languages and these communication systems is not one of "more" or "less," but one of difference in quality; indeed, it is doubtful that any sense can be given to the idea that human language is a communication system, though it can be used for communication along with much else. These observations suggest that at some remote period of evolutionary history, the brain developed a certain capacity for digital computation, for employing recursive rules and associated mental representations, thus acquiring the basis for thought and language in the human sense, with the arithmetical capacity perhaps latent as a kind of abstraction from the language faculty, to be evoked when cultural conditions allowed, much later, in fact never in the case of some societies, so it appears. Notice that there is surely no reason to suppose that every trait is specifically selected.

The phenomena of the languages of the world appear to be highly diverse, but, increasingly, it has been shown that over a large and impressive range they can be accounted for by the same principles, which yield highly varied results as the properties of lexical items vary from language to language. Thus in Spanish, there are clitic pronouns, including the reflexive, while in English there are not, so that the forms of English and Spanish, say in causative constructions, look quite different. But the principles that govern them appear to be essentially the same, their consequences differing by virtue of a lexical property of the pronominal system: in Spanish, but not in English, there is a system of pronouns that are lexically marked as affixes, and therefore must attach to other elements. The manner in which these affixes attach, and the targets to which they adjoin, are determined by the very same principles that determine the formation of complex syntactic constructions such as operator-variable constructions and others, so it now appears.

In other languages, many more items are identified in the lexicon as affixes, and the same syntactic principles determine complex morphological forms that reflect in another way the same underlying and near universal underlying structures.[1] Thus in Japanese, the causative element is not a verb, like Spanish *hacer* or English *make*, but rather an affix, so a verb must move from the embedded clause to attach to it, yielding what appears to be a monoclausal causative as distinct from the English-Spanish biclausal causative; in Spanish too there is a reflection of the same process when *se* raises to the main verb in the sentence "Juan se hizo afeitar," as if *hizo-afeitar* were a single word. The point is that as lexical items vary, the very same principles determine a wide range of superficially different complex phenomena in typologically quite different languages.

The principles of universal grammar are fixed as constituent elements of the language faculty, but languages plainly differ. How do they differ? One way has already been noted: they differ in properties of lexical items, though here too the options are narrowly constrained by general principles. Beyond that, it seems that the principles allow for a limited range of variation. That variation is limited has often been explicitly denied. The leading American linguist Edward Sapir held that languages can vary "without assignable limit," and Martin Joos put forth what he called the "Boasian" view, referring to Franz Boas, one of the founders of modem linguistics: namely, that "languages could differ from each other without limit and in unpredictable ways." Such views echo William Dwight Whitney, who greatly influenced Ferdinand de Saussure, and who emphasized "the infinite diversity of human speech."

Such views perhaps appeared tenable in some form if one regarded language as a habit system, a network of practical abilities, a complex of dispositions, and the like. In that case, language would be constrained only by whatever general conditions constrain the development of abilities and habits in general, by what are sometimes called "generalized learning mechanisms," if these exist. But this conception does not allow one even to approach the essential features of normal language use, as has been demonstrated beyond reasonable doubt in my view; and as already noted, the conception has been entirely unproductive.

Assuming without further discussion that this conception must be abandoned, the question of language variation will take on a new form in the context of a general revision of the framework of inquiry into problems of natural language. A conceptual change of this nature was proposed about thirty years ago, reviving in a new form some long-forgotten approaches to the study of natural language. This rather sharp conceptual change underlies the research program that has been given the name "generative grammar," referring to the fact that the grammar—or as we are now more properly calling it "the language"—generates an unbounded range of specific consequences, assigning a status to every expression and thus providing the mechanisms for the creative aspect of language use. The central questions of the study of language, conceived along the lines of the earlier discussion, now become the following:

(1) (i) What is the system of knowledge attained by a person who speaks and understands a language?
(ii) How is that knowledge acquired?
(iii) How is that knowledge put to use?

The last question has two aspects, the production problem and the perception problem. The second question, how language is acquired, is a variant of what we might call "Plato's problem," raised for example when Socrates demonstrated that a slave boy with no training in geometry in fact knew geometry, perhaps the first psychological (thought-)experiment. The problem is not a trivial one: people know a great deal more than can possibly be accounted for in terms of the standard paradigms of epistemology (or perhaps more accurately, what they know is different from what one might expect in these terms), language being a striking example. The production problem might be called "Descartes's problem," referring to one of the central Cartesian criteria for the existence of other minds: namely, when experiment demonstrates that another creature that resembles us exhibits the creative aspect of language use, then it would only be reasonable to attribute to the creature a mind like ours. In more recent years, a similar idea has been called "the Turing Test." This problem, one aspect of more general problems concerning will and choice, remains beyond the scope of serious human inquiry in fact, and may be so in principle, rather as Descartes suggested. In any event, having nothing to say about it, I will put it aside, keeping just to the perception problem, or what is sometimes called "the parsing problem" (restricting attention to certain computational aspects).

These questions were posed as constituting the research program of generative grammar about thirty years ago, along with an argument to the effect that prevailing answers to them in terms of habit systems and the like were completely unacceptable for reasons already briefly discussed. What alternative, then, can we propose? I will keep to the terminology suggested above, departing from earlier usage.

The first proposal was that a language is a rule system, where the kinds of rules and their interrelations are specified by universal grammar. In one familiar conception, the rules included context-free rules, lexical rules, transformational rules, phonological rules (in a broad sense), and what were misleadingly called "rules of semantic interpretation" relating syntactic structures to representations in a system sometimes called "LF," suggesting "logical form" but with certain qualifications. This term "rules of semantic interpretation" is misleading, as David Lewis among others has pointed out, because these rules relate syntactic objects, mental representations. They relate syntactic structures and LF-representations, which are syntactic objects. The term "semantics" should properly be restricted to the relation between language and the world, or to use of language, some might argue. The criticism is accurate, but it applies far more broadly. In fact, it applies in exactly the same form to what Lewis and others call "semantics," where "meanings" are set-theoretic objects of some sort: models, "pictures," situations and events, or whatever. These are mental representations,[2] not elements of the world, and the problem arises of how they are related to the world. It is often assumed that the relation is trivial, something like incorporation, so that it is unnecessary to provide a justification for these particular systems of mental representation, but it is easy to show that this cannot be true unless we trivialize our conception of what the world is by restricting attention to something like what Nelson Goodman calls "versions," all mental representations, abandoning (perhaps as meaningless) the question of why one collection of "versions" is jointly acceptable or "right" and others not, that is, not pursuing the commonsense answer: that certain versions are jointly "right" because of their accord with reality. But if we take this tack, which I do not suggest, semantics disappears and we are only studying various systems of mental representation. In fact, much of what is called "semantics" is really the study of the syntax of mental representations. It is a curious fact that those who correctly call their work in this area "syntax" are said to be avoiding semantics, while others who incorrectly describe their studies of syntax as "semantics" are said to be contributing to semantics.[3]

Adopting this conception of language, a language is a complex of rules of the permitted format, interconnected in a way permitted by universal grammar. In contrast to the conception of language in terms of habit systems or abilities, this was an extremely productive idea, which led quickly to a vast increase in the range of phenomena brought under investigation, with many discoveries about facts of language, even quite simple ones, that had never been noted or explored. Furthermore, the array of phenomena discovered and investigated were made intelligible at some level, by providing partial rule systems that accounted for their properties. The depth of explanation, however, could never really be very great. Even if appropriate rule systems could be constructed, and even if these systems were found to be restricted in type, we would always want to know why we have these kinds of rules and not others. Thus, languages typically have rules that allow the direct object of a verb to function as its subject, though it is still being interpreted as the object; but the converse property does not exist. Or consider again causative constructions, say, the form that we can give in abstract representation as (2), where the element CAUSE may be a word as in Spanish-English or an affix as in Japanese:

(2) problems CAUSE [that Y lies]

The principles of universal grammar permit a realization of this abstract form as something like (3), where CAUSE is an affix, or with CAUSE-*lie* associated in a closely linked verb sequence as in Spanish:

(3) problems CAUSE-lie Y

But the form (4) does not underlie a possible realization as (5):

(4) [that Y lies] CAUSE problems
(5) Y CAUSE-lie problems

Subject-object asymmetries of this sort are found very widely in language. They reflect in part the fact that subject-verb-object sentences are not treated in natural language as two-term relations as is familiar in logical analysis, but rather in the more traditional terms of Aristotelian logic and the universal grammar of the pre-modern period, as subject-predicate structures with a possibly complex predicate. In part, the asymmetries appear to follow from a newly discovered principle governing empty categories of the sort illustrated earlier. But whatever the explanation, problems of this nature abound, and an approach in terms of rule systems leaves them unsolved, except in a rather superficial way. From another point of view, there are simply too many possible rule systems, even when we constrain their form, and we thus do not achieve a convincing answer to our variant of Plato's problem.

Recognition of these facts has been at the core of the research program of the past twenty-five years. The natural approach has been to abandon the rules in favor of general principles, so that the question of why we have one choice of rules rather than another simply does not arise. Thus if there are no rules for the formation of passive constructions, or interrogatives, or relative clauses, or phrase structure, and no rules that change grammatical functions such as causative and others, then the question why we have certain rules, not others, does not arise. Increasingly, it has become clear that rules are simply epiphenomena, on a par with sentences in the sense that they are simply "projected" from the (I-) language, viewed in a certain way. But as distinct from sentences, which exist in mental representation and are realized in behavior, there is no reason to believe that rules of the familiar form exist at all, they have no status in linguistic theory and do not constitute part of mental representation or enter into mental computations, and we may safely abandon them, so it appears. We are left with general principles of universal grammar.

If there were only one possible human language, apart from lexical variety, we would then have a simple answer to our variant of Plato's problem: universal grammar permits only one realization apart from lexicon, and this is the language that people come to know when they acquire appropriate lexical items through experience in some manner. But clearly the variety of languages is greater than this, so this cannot be the complete story—though it is probably closer to true than has been thought in the past. Thus in languages such as English or Spanish, verbs and prepositions precede their objects, and the same is true of adjectives and nouns, as in such expressions as "proud of Mary" (where "Mary" is the object of "proud" with a semantically empty preposition *of* introduced automatically as a kind of case-marker for reasons determined by universal grammar) and "translation of the book" with a similar analysis. The categories noun, verb, adjective, and preposition (more generally, adposition) are the *lexical categories*. The general principles of universal grammar determine the kinds of phrases in which they appear as *heads*. The lexical entry itself determines the number and category of the *complements* of these heads and their semantic roles, and the general principles of phrase structure determine a limited range of other possibilities.

There is, however, an option left underdetermined by the principles of universal grammar. English and Spanish settle this option by placing the head invariably *before* its complements. We may say that they choose the "head-initial" value of the "head parameter." In Japanese, in contrast, verbs, adpositions, adjectives, and nouns *follow* their complements. The range of phrase structures in the two languages is very similar, and accords with quite general principles of universal grammar, but the languages differ in one crucial choice of the head parameter: the language may choose either the "head-initial" or the "head-final" value of this parameter. In fact, this is only the simplest case, and there is a very limited range of further options depending on directionality of assignment of abstract case and semantic roles, a matter that has been explored by Hilda Koopman, Lisa Travis, and others, but we may put these further complexities aside.

A crucial fact about the head parameter is that its value can be determined from very simple data. There is good reason to believe that this is true of all parameters; we must deal with the crucial and easily demonstrated fact that what a person knows is vastly underdetermined by available evidence, and that much of this knowledge is based on no direct evidence at all. Empty categories and their properties provide a dramatic example of this pervasive phenomenon, almost entirely ignored in earlier work. Thus a person is provided with no direct evidence about the position and various properties of elements that have no physical realization. There is little doubt that this problem of "poverty of stimulus" is in fact the norm rather than the exception. It must be, then, that the values of parameters are set by the kinds of simple data that are available to the child, and that the rich, complex, and highly articulated system of knowledge that arises, and is shared with others of somewhat different but equally impoverished experience, is determined in its basic features by the principles of the initial state S_0 of the language faculty. Languages may appear to differ, but they are cast in the same mold. One might draw an analogy to the biology of living organisms. Apparently, the biochemistry of life is quite similar from yeasts to humans, but small changes in timing of regulatory mechanisms of the cells and the like can yield what to us seem to be vast phenomenal differences, the difference between a whale and a butterfly, a human and a microbe, and so on. Viewed from an angel's point of view, with numerous other possible though not actual physical worlds under consideration, all life might appear identical apart from trivialities. Similarly, from an angel's point of view, all languages would appear identical, apart from trivialities, their fundamental features determined by facts about human biology.

The language itself (again, as always, in the sense of I-language) may be regarded as nothing more than an array of choices for the various parameters, selected in accord with whatever options universal grammar permits. Since there are a finite number of parameters, each finite-valued (probably two-valued), it follows that there are a finite number of possible languages. One can see at once why questions concerning the formal properties of natural languages are largely irrelevant; there are few questions of mathematical interest to raise concerning finite sets.

Here a qualification is necessary. We are separating out the lexicon (to which I will briefly return), a system that in principle can extend without bound though with sharp constraints in many languages (thus in English, we may always add another monomorphemic name of arbitrary length), and we are considering only what we might call "core language," to be distinguished from a "periphery" of marked and specifically learned exceptions; irregular verbs, idioms, and the like. These may presumably vary without bound apart from time and memory limitations, though surely in a manner that is sharply constrained in type. It is the core language that is nothing other than an array of values for parameters. I assume, of course, that the distinction between core and periphery is a real-world distinction, not a matter of convenience or pragmatic choice, except insofar as this is true of theories in chemistry and other branches of natural science, a consideration irrelevant here. For obvious reasons, the periphery is of much less interest for the basic psychological-biological questions to which linguistics is directed, if conceived along the lines of the previous discussion, and I will ignore it here.

Keeping to the core, then, there are finitely many possible languages. What a person knows, when that person speaks and understands a language, is a vocabulary and a particular array of values of parameters: an I-language. Once the parameters are set and lexical items acquired, the entire system functions, assigning a status to a vast range of expressions in a precise and explicit manner, even those that have never been heard or produced in the history of language (and well beyond, as noted earlier). Others understand what we say, because they have the same biological nature and sufficiently similar experience with simple utterances.

Turning to Plato's problem, a language is acquired by determining the values of the parameters of the initial state on the basis of simple data, and then the system of knowledge is represented in the mind/brain and is ready to function—though it might not function if the person lacks the ability to use it, perhaps because of some brain injury or the like. As for the parsing problem, it presumably should be solved along such lines as these: the hearer identifies words, and on the basis of their lexical properties, projects a syntactic structure as determined by principles of universal grammar and the values of the parameters. Connections and associations among these elements, including the empty categories that are forced to appear, are determined by other principles of universal grammar, perhaps parametrized. Thus given the sentence "a quién se hizo Juan afeitar," the mind of the speaker of Spanish automatically assigns a structure with two empty categories, one the subject of "afeitar," another its object. Principles of universal grammar then produce a contradiction, in the manner informally described earlier, and the sentence receives no coherent interpretation, though of course it has a status; thus the Spanish speaker assigns to it a lexical and syntactic structure, and might even be able to "force" a certain meaning, if the sentence were produced by a foreigner, by me for example. A monolingual speaker of English will also assign a certain status to this expression, at least in some kind of phonetic representation, very likely considerably more.

The abandonment of rule systems in favor of a principles-and-parameters approach, which has been gradually developing over the past twenty-five years and has been achieved to a substantial extent only in the past half-dozen years, has been extremely productive. It has, once again, led to a vast leap in empirical coverage, with entirely new empirical materials discovered in well-studied languages, and with languages of great typological variety incorporated within essentially the same framework. The depth of explanation has also advanced considerably, as it has become possible to explain why there are processes described by certain rules but not others. The principles now being developed yield very sharp and surprising predictions about languages of varied types, predictions which sometimes prove accurate, and sometimes fail in highly instructive ways. My guess is that we are at the beginning of a radically new and highly productive phase in the study of language.

The shift of perspective from rule systems to a principles-and-parameters approach might be regarded as a second major conceptual change in the development of generative grammar, the first being the conceptual change noted earlier as part of the so-called "cognitive revolution," from a conception of language as a system of habits or abilities to a mentalistic approach that regards language as a computational system of the mind/brain—a step towards integrating the study of language to the natural sciences, for the reasons discussed earlier. The second shift of perspective is more theory-internal than the first, but is in a sense a much sharper break from the tradition, for two reasons. One is that the "cognitive revolution" of the 1950s was in many respects a rediscovery in different terms of ideas and insights that had been developed long before, both in psychology and the study of language, during the seventeenth century "cognitive revolution." A second is that the rule system developed in early generative grammar was in certain respects a formalization, in a different framework, of traditional notions about the way sentences are constructed and interpreted. The shift to a principles-and-parameters approach introduces ideas that have only a remote resemblance to those of the traditional or modern study of language, and the basic notion of the discipline and the ways in which problems are formulated and addressed takes on a considerably different form as well.

The principles-and-parameters approach yields a rather new way of thinking about questions of typology and comparative-historical linguistics. Consider again the analogy of speciation in biology. Apparently, small changes in the way fixed mechanisms function can produce large-scale phenomenal differences, yielding different species of organisms. In general, a slight change in the functioning of a rigidly structured and intricate system can yield very complex and surprising clusters of changes as its effects filter through the system. In the case of language, change of a single parameter may yield a cluster of differences which, on the surface, appear disconnected, as its effects filter through the invariant system of universal grammar. There is reason to believe that something of the sort is correct. Thus, among the Romance languages, French has a curious status. It differs from the other Romance languages in a cluster of properties, and it appears that these differences emerged fairly recently, and at about the same time. It may be that one parameter was changed—the null subject parameter that permits subject to be suppressed, some have speculated—yielding a cluster of other modifications through the mechanical working of the principles of universal grammar, and giving French something of the look of a Germanic language. At the same time, French and Spanish share certain features distinguishing them from Italian, and there are numerous other complexities as we look at the actual languages, or "dialects" as they are called. Similarly, we find most remarkable similarities among languages that have no known historical connection, suggesting that they have simply set crucial parameters the same way. These are essentially new questions, which can now be seriously formulated for the first time and perhaps addressed.

As conceptions of language have changed over the years, so has the notion of what counts as a "real result." Suppose we have some array of phenomena in some language. In the era of structural-descriptive linguistics, a result consisted in a useful arrangement of the data. As Zellig Harris put it in the major theoretical work of structural linguistics, a grammar provides a compact one-one representation of the phenomena in a corpus of data. Some, for example Roman Jakobson, went further in insisting on conformity to certain general laws, particularly in phonology, but in very limited ways.

Under the conception of language as a rule system, this would no longer count as a significant result; such a description poses rather than solves the problem at hand. Rather, it would be necessary to produce a rule system of the permitted format that predicts the data in question and in nontrivial cases, infinitely more. This is a much harder task, but not a hopeless one; there are many possible rule systems, and, with effort, it is often possible to find one that satisfies the permitted format, if this is not too restricted.

Under the more recent principles-and-parameters approach, the task becomes harder still. A rule system is simply a description: it poses rather than solves the problem, and a "real result" consists of a demonstration that the phenomena under investigation, and countless others, can be explained by selecting properly the values of parameters in a fixed and invariant system of principles. This is a far harder problem, made still more difficult by the great expansion of empirical materials in widely differing languages that have come to be partially understood, and to which any general theory must be responsible. Where the problem can be solved, we have results of some depth, well beyond anything imaginable earlier. It is an important fact that the problem is now intelligibly formulable, and that solutions are being produced over an interesting range, while efforts to pursue this inquiry are unearthing a large mass of new and unexplored phenomena in a wide variety of languages that pose new challenges, previously unknown.

This discussion has been based on the assumption that lexical items are somehow learned and available, suggesting that apart from parameter-setting, language acquisition as well as parsing and presumably the creative use of language (in the unlikely event that we can come to understand anything about this matter) are to a large extent determined by properties of the lexicon. But acquisition of lexical items poses Plato's problem in a very sharp form. As anyone who has tried to construct a dictionary or to work in descriptive semantics is aware, it is a very difficult matter to describe the meaning of a word, and such meanings have great intricacy and involve the most remarkable assumptions, even in the case of very simple concepts, such as what counts as a possible "thing." At peak periods of language acquisition, children are "learning" many words a day, meaning that they are in effect learning words on a single exposure. This can only mean that the concepts are already available, with all or much of their intricacy and structure predetermined, and the child's task is to assign labels to concepts, as might be done with very simple evidence.

Many have found this conclusion completely unacceptable, even absurd; it certainly departs radically from traditional views. Some, for example Hilary Putnam, have argued that it is entirely implausible to suppose that we have "an innate stock of notions" including *carburetor, bureaucrat*, etc.[4] If he were correct about this, it would not be particularly to the point, since the problem arises in a most serious way in connection with simple words such as "table," "person," "chase," "persuade," etc. But his argument for the examples he mentions is not compelling. It is that to have given us this innate stock of notions, "evolution would have had to be able to anticipate all the contingencies of future physical and cultural environments. Obviously it didn't and couldn't do this." A very similar argument had long been accepted in immunology; namely, the number of antigens is so immense, including even artificially synthesized substances that had never existed in the world, that it was considered absurd to suppose that evolution had provided "an innate stock of antibodies"; rather, formation of antibodies must be a kind of "learning process" in which the antigens played an "instructive role." But this assumption has been challenged, and is now widely assumed to be false. Niels Kaj Jerne won the Nobel Prize for his work challenging this idea, and upholding his own conception that an animal "cannot be stimulated to make specific antibodies, unless it has already made antibodies of this specificity before the antigen arrives," so that antibody formation is a selective process in which the antigen plays a selective and amplifying role.[5] Whether or not Jerne is correct, he certainly could be, and the same could be true in the case of word meanings, the argument being quite analogous.

Furthermore, there is good reason to suppose that the argument is at least in substantial measure correct, even for such words as *carburetor* and *bureaucrat*, which, in fact, pose the familiar problem of poverty of stimulus if we attend carefully to the enormous gap between what we know and the evidence on the basis of which we know it. The same is true of technical terms of science and mathematics, and it is quite surely the case for the terms of ordinary discourse. However surprising the conclusion may be that nature has provided us with an innate stock of concepts, and that the child's task is to discover their labels, the empirical facts appear to leave open few other possibilities. Other possibilities (say, in terms of "generalized learning mechanisms") have not, to my knowledge, been coherently formulated, and if they are some day formulated, it may well be that the apparent issue will dissolve.

To the extent that anything is understood about lexical items and their nature, it seems that they are based on conceptual structures of a very specific and closely integrated type. It has been argued plausibly that concepts of a locational nature, including goal and source of action, object moved, place, etc., enter widely into lexical structure, often in quite abstract ways. In addition, notions like actor, recipient of action, event, intention, and others are pervasive elements of lexical structure, with their specific properties and permitted interrelations. Consider, say, the words *chase* or *persuade*. Like their Spanish equivalents, they clearly involve a reference to human intention. To chase Jones is not only to follow him, but to follow him with the intent of staying on his path, perhaps to catch him. To persuade Smith to do something is to cause him to decide or intend to do it; if he never decides or intends to do it, we have not succeeded in persuading him. Furthermore, he must decide or intend by his own volition, not under duress; if we say that the police persuaded Smith to confess by torture, we are using the term ironically. Since these facts are known essentially without evidence, it must be that the child approaches language with an intuitive understanding of concepts involving intending, causation, goal of action, event, and so on, and places the words that are heard in a nexus that is permitted by the principles of universal grammar, which provide the framework for thought and language, and are common to human languages as conceptual systems that enter into various aspects of human life.

Notice further that we appear to have connections of meaning, analytic connections, in such cases as these; we have a rather clear distinction between truths of meaning and truths of fact. Thus, if John persuaded Bill to go to college, then Bill at some point decided or intended to go to college; otherwise, John did not persuade Bill to do so. This is a truth of meaning, not of fact. The a priori framework of human thought, within which language is acquired, provides necessary connections among concepts, reflected in connections of meaning among words, and more broadly, among expressions involving these words. Syntactic relations provide a rich array of further examples. It appears, then, that one of the central conclusions of modern philosophy is rather dubious: namely, the contention, often held to have been established by work of Quine and others, that one can make no principled distinction between questions of fact and questions of meaning, that it is a matter of more or less deeply held belief. Philosophers have, I think, been led to this dubious conclusion, which is held by some (e.g., Richard Rorty) to have undermined centuries of thought, by concentrating on an artificially narrow class of examples, in particular, on concepts that have little or no relational structure: such sentences as "cats are animals." Here, indeed, it is not easy to find evidence to decide whether the sentence is true as a matter of meaning or fact, and there has been much inconclusive debate about the matter. When we turn to more complex categories with an inherent relational structure such as *persuade* or *chase*, or to more complex syntactic constructions, there seems little doubt that analytic connections are readily discerned.

Furthermore, the status of a statement as a truth of meaning or of empirical fact can and must be established by empirical inquiry, and considerations of many sorts may well be relevant; for example, inquiry into language acquisition and variation among languages. The question of the existence of analytic truths and connections, therefore, is an empirical one, to be settled by empirical inquiry that goes well beyond the range of evidence ordinarily brought to bear. Suppose that two people differ in their intuitive judgments as to whether I can persuade John to go to college without his deciding or intending to do so. We are by no means at an impasse. Rather, we can construct conflicting theories and proceed to test them. One who holds that the connection between *persuade* and *decide* or *intend* is conceptual will proceed to elaborate the structure of the concepts, their primitive elements, and so on, and will seek to show that other aspects of the acquisition and use of language can be explained in terms of the very same assumptions about the innate structure of the language faculty, in the same language and others, and that the same concepts play a role in other aspects of thought and understanding. One who holds that the connection is one of deeply held belief, not connection of meaning, has the task of developing a general theory of belief fixation that will yield the right conclusions in these and numerous other cases. One who holds that the connection is based on the "semantic importance" of sentences relating *persuade* and *decide* or *intend* (i.e., that these sentences play a prominent role in inference, or serve to introduce the term *persuade* to the child's vocabulary, and thus are more important than others for communication[6]) faces the task of showing that these empirical claims, which appear to lack any plausibility, are in fact true. The first task seems far more promising to me, but it is a matter of empirical inquiry, not pronouncements on the basis of virtually no evidence. The whole matter requires extensive rethinking, and much of what has been generally assumed for the past several decades about these questions appears to be dubious at best. There is, it seems clear, a rich conceptual structure determined by the initial state of the language faculty (perhaps drawing from the resources of other genetically determined faculties of mind), waiting to be awakened by experience, much in accord with traditional rationalistic conceptions and even, in some respects, the so-called "empiricist" thought of James Harris, David Hume, and others.

I think we are forced to abandon many commonly accepted doctrines about language and knowledge. There is an innate structure that determines the framework within which thought and language develop, down to quite precise and intricate details. Language and thought are awakened in the mind, and follow a largely predetermined course, much like other biological properties. They develop in a way that provides a rich structure of truths of meaning. Our knowledge in these areas, and I believe elsewhere—even in science and mathematics—is not derived by induction, by applying reliable procedures, and so on; it is not grounded or based on "good reasons" in any useful sense of these notions. Rather, it grows in the mind, on the basis of our biological nature, triggered by appropriate experience, and in a limited way shaped by experience that settles options left open by the innate structure of mind. The result is an elaborate structure of cognitive systems, systems of knowledge and belief, that reflects the very nature of the human mind, a biological organ like others, with its scope and limits. This conclusion, which seems to me well-supported by the study of language and I suspect holds far more broadly, perhaps universally in domains of human thought, compels us to rethink fundamental assumptions of modern philosophy and of our general intellectual culture, including assumptions about scientific knowledge, mathematics, ethics, aesthetics, social theory and practice, and much else, questions too broad and far-reaching for me to try to address here, but questions that should, I think, be subjected to serious scrutiny from a point of view rather different from those that have conventionally been assumed.

NOTES

1. For very important recent discussion of this matter, see Mark Baker, *A Theory of Grammatical Function* (Chicago: University of Chicago Press, 1988).
2. At least, if we are doing C-linguistics, with empirical content. If not, then further clarification is required. The inquiry is in any event not semantics in the sense of empirical semantics, a study of relations between the language and something extralinguistic.
3. On a personal note, my own work, from the beginning, has been largely concerned with the problem of developing linguistic theory so that the representations provided in particular languages will be appropriate for explaining how sentences are used and understood, but I have always called this "syntax," as it is, even though the motivation is ultimately semantic; see, e.g., my *Logical Structure of Linguistic Theory* (1955–56; published in part in 1975, New York: Plenum), *Syntactic Structures* (The Hague: Mouton, 1957). This work is correctly described as syntax, but it deals with questions that others incorrectly term "semantic," and it is, I suspect, one crucial way to study semantics.
4. See Putnam, "Meaning and Our Mental Life," manuscript, 1985.
5. For discussion in a linguistic-cognitive context, see my *Rules* and *Representations* (New York: Columbia University Press, 1980), 136f.; and Jerne's Nobel Prize lecture, "The Generative Grammar of the Immune System," *Science* 229. 1057–9, September 13, 1985.
6. The proposal of Paul M. Churchland, *Scientific Realism and the Plasticity of Mind* (Cambridge University Press, 1979; 1986, 51f.).

The Problem of the Essential Indexical

JOHN PERRY

American philosopher John Perry (1943–) has taught for many decades at Stanford University, publishing influential and engaging articles and books in metaphysics, the philosophy of language, and the philosophy of mind.

The selection that appears here was originally published as an article in a philosophy journal in 1979. In it, Perry explores some perplexing features of the use of the term "I."

I once followed a trail of sugar on a supermarket floor, pushing my cart down the aisle on one side of a tall counter and back the aisle on the other, seeking the shopper with the torn sack to tell him he was making a mess. With each trip around the counter, the trail became thicker. But I seemed unable to catch up. Finally it dawned on me. I was the shopper I was trying to catch.

From *Noûs* 13 (1979): 3–20. Copyright © 1979 by *Noûs*. Reprinted with the permission of Blackwell Publishers.

I believed at the outset that the shopper with a torn sack was making a mess. And I was right. But I didn't believe that I was making a mess. That seems to be something I came to believe. And when I came to believe that, I stopped following the trail around the counter, and rearranged the torn sack in my cart. My change in beliefs seems to explain my change in behavior. My aim in this paper is to make a key point about the characterization of this change, and of beliefs in general.

At first characterizing the change seems easy. My beliefs changed, didn't they, in that I came to have a new one, namely, *that I am making a mess?* But things are not so simple.

The reason they are not is the importance of the word "I" in my expression of what I came to believe. When we replace it with other designations of me, we no longer have an explanation of my behavior and so, it seems, no longer an attribution of the same belief. It seems to be an *essential* indexical. But without such a replacement, all we have to identify the belief is the sentence "I am making a mess." But that sentence by itself doesn't seem to identify the crucial belief, for if someone else had said it, they would have expressed a different belief, a false one.

I argue that the essential indexical poses a problem for various otherwise plausible accounts of belief. I first argue that it is a problem for the view that belief is a relation between subjects and propositions conceived as bearers of truth and falsity. The problem is not solved merely by replacing or supplementing this with a notion of *de re* belief. Nor is it solved by moving to a notion of a proposition which, rather than true or false absolutely, is only true or false at an index or in a context (at a time, for a speaker, say). Its solution requires us to make a sharp distinction between objects of belief and belief states, and to realize that the connection between them is not so intimate as might have been supposed.[1]

LOCATING BELIEFS

I want to introduce two more examples. In the first a professor, who desires to attend the department meeting on time, and believes correctly that it begins at noon, sits motionless in his office at that time. Suddenly he begins to move. What explains his action? A change in belief. He believed all along that the department meeting starts at noon; he came to believe, as he would have put it, that it starts *now*.

The author of the book, *Hiker's Guide to the Desolation Wilderness*, stands in the wilderness beside Gilmore Lake, looking at the Mt. Tallac trail as it leaves the lake and climbs the mountain. He desires to leave the wilderness. He believes that the best way out from Gilmore Lake is to follow the Mt. Tallac trail up the mountain to Cathedral Peaks trail, on to the Floating Island trail, emerging at Spring Creek Tract Road. But he does not move. He is lost. He isn't sure whether he is standing beside Gilmore Lake, looking at Mt. Tallac, or beside Clyde Lake looking at Jack's peak, or beside Eagle Lake looking at one of the Maggie peaks. Then he begins to move along the Mt. Tallac trail. If asked, he would have explained the crucial change in his beliefs this way: "I came to believe that *this* is the Mt. Tallac trail and *that* is Gilmore Lake."

In these three cases the subjects in explaining their actions, would use indexicals to characterize certain beliefs they came to have. These indexicals are essential, in that replacement of them by other terms destroys the force of the explanation, or at least requires certain assumptions to be made to preserve it.

Suppose I had said, in the manner of de Gaulle, "I came to believe that John Perry is making a mess." I would no longer have explained why I stopped and looked in my own cart. To explain that I would have to add, "and I believe that I am John Perry," bringing in the indexical again. After all, suppose I had really given my explanation in the manner of de Gaulle, and said "I came to believe that de Gaulle is making a mess." That wouldn't have explained my stopping at all. But it really would have explained it every bit as much as "I came to believe John Perry is making a mess." For if I added "and I believe that I am de Gaulle" the explanations would be on par. The only reason "I came to believe John Perry is making a mess" seems to explain my action is our natural assumption that I did believe I was John Perry and didn't believe I was de Gaulle. So replacing the indexical "I" with another term designating the same person really does, as claimed, destroy the explanation.

Similarly, our professor, as he sets off down the hall, might say "I believe the meeting starts at noon," rather than "I believe the meeting starts now." In accepting the former as an explanation, we would be assuming he believes it is *now* noon. If he believed it was now 5 p.m., he wouldn't have explained his departure by citing his belief that the meeting starts at noon, unless he was a member of a department with very long meetings. After all, he believed that the meeting started at noon all along, so that belief can hardly explain a change in his behavior. Basically similar remarks apply to the lost author.

I shall use the term "locating beliefs" to refer to one's beliefs about where one is, when it is, and who one is. Such beliefs seem essentially indexical. Imagine two lost campers who trust the same guidebook but disagree about where they are. If we were to try to characterize the beliefs of these campers without the use of indexicals, it would seem impossible to bring out this disagreement. If, for example, we characterized their beliefs by the set of "eternal sentences," drawn from the guidebook they would mark "true," there is no reason to suppose that the sets would differ. They could mark all of the same sentences "true," and still disagree in their locating beliefs. It seems that there has to be some indexical element in the characterization of their beliefs to bring out this disagreement. But as we shall see there is no room for this indexical element in the traditional way of looking at belief, and even when its necessity is recognized, it is not easy to see how to fit it in.

THE DOCTRINE OF PROPOSITIONS

I shall first consider how the problem appears to a traditional way of thinking of belief. The doctrines I describe were held by Frege,* but I shall put them in a way that does not incorporate his terminology or the details of his view.[2] This traditional way, which I call the "doctrine of propositions," has three main tenets. The first is that belief is a relation between a subject and an object, the latter being denoted, in a canonical belief report, by a that-clause. So "Carter believes that Atlanta is the capital of Georgia" reports that a certain relation, *believing*, obtains between Carter and a certain object—at least in a suitably wide sense of object—*that Atlanta is the capital of Georgia*. These objects are called *propositions*.

The second and the third tenets concern such objects. The second is that they have a truth-value in an absolute sense, as opposed to merely being true for a person or at a time. The third has to do with how we individuate them. It is necessary, for *that S* and *that S′* to be the same, that they have the same truth-value. But it is not sufficient, for *that the sea is salty* and *that milk is white* are not the same proposition. It is necessary that they have the same truth condition, in the sense that they attribute to the same objects the same relation. But this also is not sufficient, for *that Atlanta is the capital of Georgia* and *that Atlanta is the capital of the largest state east of the Mississippi* are not the same proposition. Carter, it seems, might believe the first but not the second. Propositions must not only have the same truth-value, and concern the same objects and relations, but also involve the same concepts. For Frege, this meant that if *that S* = *that S′*, S and S′ must have the same sense. Others might eschew senses in favor of properties and relations, others take concepts to be just words, so that sameness of propositions is just sameness of sentences. What these approaches have in common is the insistence that propositions must be individuated in a more "fine-grained" way than is provided by truth-value or the notion truth conditions employed above.

THE PROBLEM

It's clear that the essential indexical is a problem for the doctrine of propositions. What answer can it give to the question, "What did I come to believe when I straightened up the sugar?" The sentence "I am making a mess" doesn't identify a proposition. For this sentence is not true or false absolutely, but only

* Gottlob Frege (1848–1925) was a German-born mathematician, logician, and philosopher whose writings have profoundly influenced twentieth-century Anglo-American philosophy. He created modern logic as we know it.

as said by one person or another; had another shopper said it when I did, he would have been wrong. So the sentence by which I identify what I came to believe doesn't identify, by itself, a proposition. There is a *missing conceptual ingredient:* a sense for which I am the reference, or a complex of properties I alone have, or a singular term that refers to no one but me. To identify the proposition I came to believe, the advocate of the doctrine of propositions must identify this missing conceptual ingredient.

An advocate of the doctrine of propositions, his attention drawn to indexicals, might take this attitude towards them: they are communicative shortcuts. Just before I straightened up the sack I must have come to believe some propositions with the structure α *is making a mess*, where α is some concept which I alone "fit" (to pick a phrase neutral among the different notions of a concept). When I say "I believe I am making a mess," my hearers know that I believe some such proposition of this form; which one in particular is not important for the purposes at hand.

If this is correct, we should be able to identify the proposition I came to believe, even if doing so isn't necessary for ordinary communicative purposes. But then the doctrine of propositions is in trouble, for any candidate will fall prey to the problems mentioned above. If *that* α *is making a mess* is what I came to believe, then "I came to believe that A is making a mess," where A expressed α, should be an even better explanation than the original, where I used "I" as a communicative shortcut. But, as we saw, any such explanation will be defective, working only on the assumption that I believed that I was α.

To this it might be replied that though there may be no replacement for "I" that generally preserves explanatory force, all that needs to be claimed is that there is such a replacement on each occasion. The picture is this. On each occasion that I use "I," there is some concept I have in mind that fits me uniquely, and which is the missing conceptual ingredient in the proposition that remains incompletely identified when I characterize my beliefs. The concept I use to think of myself isn't necessarily the same each time I do so, and of course I must use a different one than others do, since it must fit me and not them. Because there is no general way of replacing the "I" with a term that gets at the missing ingredient, the challenge to do so in response to a particular example is temporarily embarrassing. But the doctrine of propositions doesn't require a general answer.

This strategy doesn't work for two reasons. First, even if I was thinking of myself as, say, the only bearded philosopher in a Safeway store west of the Mississippi, the fact that I came to believe that the only such philosopher was making a mess explains my action only on the assumption that I believed that I was the only such philosopher, which brings in the indexical again. Second, in order to provide me with an appropriate proposition as the object of belief, the missing conceptual ingredient will have to fit me. Suppose I was thinking of myself in the way described, but that I wasn't bearded and wasn't in a Safeway store—I had forgotten that I had shaved and gone to the A & P instead. Then the proposition supplied by this strategy would be false, while what I came to believe, *that I was making a mess*, was true.

This strategy assumes that whenever I have a belief I would characterize by using a sentence with an indexical *d*,

I believe that . . . d . . .

that there is some conceptual ingredient *c*, such that it is also true that,

I believe that *d* is *c*

and that, on this second point, I am right. But there is no reason to believe this would always be so. Each time I say "I believe it is *now* time to rake the leaves," I need not have some concept that uniquely fits the time at which I speak.

From the point of view of the doctrine of propositions, belief reports such as "I believe that I am making a mess" are deficient, for there is a missing conceptual ingredient. From the point of view of locating beliefs, there is something lacking in the propositions offered by the doctrine, a missing indexical ingredient.

The problem of the essential indexical reveals that something is badly wrong with the traditional doctrine of propositions. But the traditional doctrine has its competitors anyway, in response to philosophical pressures from other directions. Perhaps attention to these alternative or supplementary models of belief will provide a solution to our problem.

DE RE BELIEF

One development in the philosophy of belief seems quite promising in this respect. It involves qualifying the third tenet of the doctrine of propositions, to allow a sort of proposition individuated by an object or sequence of objects, and a part of a proposition of the earlier sort. The motivation for this qualification or supplementation comes from belief reports, which give rise to the same problem, that of the missing conceptual ingredient, as does the problem of the essential indexical.

The third tenet of the doctrine of propositions is motivated by the failure of substitutivity of co-referential terms within the that-clause following "believes." But there seems to be a sort of belief report, or a way of understanding some belief reports, that allows such substitution, and such successful substitution becomes a problem for a theory designed to explain its failure. For suppose Patrick believes that, as he would put it, the dean is wise. Patrick doesn't know Frank, much less know that he lives next to the dean, and yet I might in certain circumstances say "Patrick believes Frank's neighbor is wise." Or I might say "There is someone whom Patrick believes to be wise," and later on identify that someone as "Frank's neighbor." The legitimacy of this cannot be understood on the unqualified doctrine of propositions; I seem to have gone from one proposition, *that the dean of the school is wise*, to another, *that Frank's neighbor is wise;* but the fact that Patrick believes the first seems to be no reason he should believe the second. And the quantification into the belief report seems to make no sense at all on the doctrine of propositions, for the report doesn't relate Patrick to an individual known variously as "the dean" and "Frank's neighbor," but only with a concept expressed by the first of these terms.

The problem here is just that of a missing conceptual ingredient. It looked in the original report as if Patrick was being said to stand in the relation of belief to a certain proposition, a part of which was a conceptual ingredient expressed by the words "the dean." But if I am permitted to exchange those words for others, "Frank's neighbor," which are not conceptually equivalent, then apparently the initial part of the proposition he was credited with belief in was not the conceptual ingredient identified by "the dean" after all. So what proposition was it Patrick was originally credited with belief in? And "There is someone such that Patrick believes that he is wise" seems to credit Patrick with belief in a proposition, without telling us which one. For after the "believes" we have only "he is wise," where the "he" doesn't give us an appropriate conceptual ingredient, but functions as a variable ranging over individuals.

We do seem in some circumstances to allow such substitutivity, and make ready sense of quantification into belief reports. So the doctrine of propositions must be qualified. We can look upon this sort of belief as involving a relation to a new sort of proposition, consisting of an object or sequence of objects and a conceptual ingredient, a part of a proposition of the original kind, or what we might call an "open proposition." This sort of belief and this kind of proposition we call *"de re,"* the sort of belief and the sort of proposition that fits the original doctrine, *"de dicto."* Taken this way we analyze "Patrick believes that the dean of the school is wise," as reporting a relation between Patrick and a proposition consisting of a certain person variously describable as "the dean" and "Frank's neighbor" and something, *that x is wise*, which would yield a proposition with the addition of an appropriate conceptual ingredient. Since the dean himself, and not just a concept expressed by the words "the dean" is involved, substitution holds and quantification makes sense.

Here, as in the case of the essential indexical, we were faced with a missing conceptual ingredient. Perhaps, then, this modification of the third tenet will solve the earlier problem as well. But it won't. Even if we suppose—as I think we should—that when I said "I believe that I am making a mess" I was reporting a *de re* belief, our problem will remain.

One problem emerges when we look at accounts that have been offered of the conditions under which a person has a *de re* belief. The most influential treatments of *de re* belief have tried to explain it in terms of *de dicto* belief or something like it. Some terminological regimentation is helpful here. Let us couch reports of *de re* belief in the terms "*X* believes of *a* that he is so and so," reserving the simpler "*X* believes that *a* is so-and-so" for *de dicto* belief. The simplest account of *de re* belief in terms of *de dicto* belief is this:

> *X* believes of *y* that he is so and so just in case
>
> There is a concept α such that α fits *y* and *X* believes that α is so and so.

Now it is clear that if this is our analysis of *de re* belief, the problem of the essential indexical is still with us. For we are faced with the same problem we had before. I can believe that I am making a mess, even if there is no concept α such that I alone fit α and I believe that α is making a mess. Since I don't have any *de dicto* belief of the sort, on this account I don't have a *de re* belief of the right sort either. So, even allowing *de re* belief, we still don't have an account of the belief I acquired.

Now this simple account of *de re* belief has not won many adherents, because it is commonly held that *de re* belief is a more interesting notion than it allows. This proposal trivializes it. Suppose Nixon is the next President. Since I believe that the next president will be the next President I would on this proposal, believe of Nixon that he is the next president, even though I am thoroughly convinced that Nixon will not be the next President.[3]

To get a more interesting or useful notion of *de re* belief, philosophers have suggested that there are limitations on the conceptual ingredient involved in the *de dicto* belief which yields the *de re* belief. Kaplan,* for example, requires not only that there be some α such that I believe that α will be the next President and that α denotes Nixon, for me to believe of Nixon that he will be the next President, but also that α be a *vivid name of Nixon for me* ([9:225 ff.]). Hintikka requires that α denote the same individual in every possible world compatible with what I believe ([7:40 ff.]). Each of these philosophers explains these notions in such a way that in the circumstances imagined, I would not believe of Nixon that he is the next President.

However well these proposals deal with other phenomena connected with *de re* belief, they cannot help with the problem of the essential indexical. They tighten the requirements laid down by the original proposal, but those were apparently already too restrictive. If in order to believe that I am making a mess I need not have any conceptual ingredient α that fits me, *a fortiori* I am not required to have one that is a vivid name of myself for me, or one that picks out the same individual in every possible world compatible with what I believe.

Perhaps this simply shows that the approach of explaining *de re* belief in terms of *de dicto* belief is incorrect. I think it does show that. But even so, the problem remains. Suppose we do not insist on an account of *de re* belief in terms of *de dicto* belief, but merely suppose that whenever we ascribe a belief, and cannot find a suitable complete proposition to serve as the object because of a missing conceptual ingredient, we are dealing with *de re* belief. Then we will ascribe a *de re* belief to me in the supermarket, I believed *of* John Perry that he was making a mess. But it won't be my having such a *de re* belief that explains my action.

Suppose there were mirrors at either end of the counter so that as I pushed my cart down the aisle in pursuit I saw myself in the mirror. I take what I see to be the reflection of the messy shopper going up the aisle on the other side, not realizing that what I am really seeing is a reflection of a reflection of myself. I point and say, truly, "I believe that he is making a mess." In trying to find a suitable proposition for me to believe, we would be faced with the same sorts of problems we had with my earlier report, in which I used "I" instead of "he." We would not be able to eliminate an indexical element in the term referring to me. So here we have *de re* belief; I believe of John Perry that he is making a mess. But then that I believe of John Perry that he is making a mess doesn't explain my stopping; in the imagined circumstances I would accelerate, as would the shopper I was trying to catch. But then, even granting that when I say "I believe that I am making a mess" I attribute to myself a certain *de re* belief, the belief of John Perry that he is making a mess, our problem remains.

---

* David Kaplan (1933–) is a philosopher at UCLA known for his work in the philosophy of language, including seminal discussions of sentences that are used to report belief.

If we look at it with the notion of a locating belief in mind, the failure of the introduction of *de re* belief to solve our problems is not surprising. *De re* propositions remain non-indexical. Propositions individuated in part by objects remain as insensitive to what is essential in locating beliefs as those individuated wholly by concepts. Saying that I believed of John Perry that he was making a mess leaves out the crucial change, that I came to think of the messy shopper not merely as the shopper with the torn sack, or the man in the mirror, but as *me*.

RELATIVIZED PROPOSITIONS

It seems that to deal with essential indexicality we must somehow incorporate the indexical element into what is believed, the object of belief. If we do so, we come up against the second tenet of the doctrine of propositions, that such objects are true or false absolutely. But the tools for abandoning this tenet have been provided in recent treatments of the semantics of modality, tense, and indexicality. So this seems a promising direction.

In possible worlds semantics for necessity and possibility we have the notion of truth at a world. In a way this doesn't involve a new notion of a proposition and in a way it does. When Frege insisted that his "thoughts" were true or false absolutely, he didn't mean that they had the same truth-value in all possible worlds. Had he used a possible worlds framework, he would have had their truth-values vary from world to world, and simply insisted on a determinate truth-value in each world and in particular in the actual world. In a way, then, taking propositions to be functions from possible worlds to truth-values is just a way of looking at the old notion of a proposition.

Still, this way of looking at it invites generalization, that takes us away from the old notion. From a technical point of view, the essential idea is that a proposition is or is represented by a function from an index to a truth-value; when we get away from modality, this same technical idea may be useful, though something other than possible worlds are taken as indices. To deal with temporal operators, we can use the notion of truth at a time. Here the indices will be times, and our propositions will be functions from times to truth-values. For example, *that Elizabeth is Queen of England* is a proposition true in 1960 but not in 1940. Hence "At sometime or other Elizabeth is Queen of England" is true, simpliciter. (See[10] and [13], especially "Pragmatics.")

Now consider "I am making a mess." Rather than thinking of this as partially identifying an absolutely true proposition, with the "I" showing the place of the missing conceptual ingredient, why not think of it as completely identifying a new-fangled proposition, that is true or false only *at a person?* More precisely, it is one that is true or false at a time and a person, since though true when I said it, it has since occasionally been false.

If we ignore possibility and necessity, it seems that regarding propositions as functions to truth-values from indices which are pairs of persons and times will do the trick, and that so doing will allow us to exploit relations between elements within the indices to formulate rules which bring out differences between indexicals. "I am tired now" is true at the pair consisting of the person *a* and the time *t* if and only if *a* is tired at *t*, while "You will be tired" is true at the same index if and only if the addressee of *a* at *t* is tired at some time later than *t*.

Does this way of looking at the matter solve the problem of the essential indexical? I say "I believe that I am making a mess." On our amended doctrine of propositions, this ascribes a relation between me and *that I am making a mess*, which is a function from indices to truth values. The belief report seems to completely specify the relativized proposition involved; there is no missing conceptual ingredient. So the problem must be solved.

But it isn't. I believed that a certain proposition, *that I am making a mess* was true—true for me. So belief that this proposition was true for me then doesn't differentiate me from the other shopper, and can't be what explains my stopping and searching my cart for the torn sack. Once we have adopted these new-fangled propositions, which are only true at times for persons, we have to admit also that we believe them as true for persons at times, and not absolutely. And then our problem returns.

Clearly an important distinction must be made. All believing is done by persons at times, or so we may suppose. But the time of belief and the person doing the believing cannot be generally identified with the person and time relative to which the proposition believed is held true. You now believe that *that I am making a mess* was true for me, then, but you certainly don't believe it is true for you now, unless you are reading this in a supermarket. Let us call *you* and *now* the context of belief, and *me* and *then* the context of evaluation. The context of belief may be the same as the context of evaluation, but need not be.

Now the mere fact that I believed that proposition *that I making a mess* to be true for someone at some time did not explain my stopping the cart. You believe so now, and doubtless have no more desire to mess up supermarkets than I did. But you are not bending over to straighten up a sack of sugar.

The fact that I believed this proposition true for Perry at the time he was in the supermarket does not explain my behavior either. For so did the other shopper. And you also now believe this proposition was true for Perry at the time he was in the supermarket.

The important difference seems to be that for me the context of belief was just the context of evaluation, but for the other shopper it wasn't and for you it isn't. But this doesn't do the trick either.

Consider our tardy professor. He is doing research on indexicals, and has written on the board "My meeting starts now." He believes that the proposition expressed by this sentence is true at noon for him. He has believed so for hours, and at noon the context of belief comes to be the context of evaluation. These facts give us no reason to expect him to move.

Or suppose I think to myself that the person making the mess should say so. Turning my attention to the proposition, I certainly believe *that I am making a mess* is true for the person who ought to be saying it (or the person in the mirror, or the person at the end of the trail of sugar) at that time. The context of evaluation is just the context of belief. But there is no reason to suppose I would stop my cart.

One supposes that in these cases the problem is that the context of belief is not believed to be the context of evaluation. But formulating the required belief will simply bring up the problem of the essential indexical again. Clearly and correctly we want the tardy professor, when he finally sees he must be off to the meeting, to be ready to say "I believe that the time at which it is true *that the meeting starts now* is now." On the present proposal, we analyze the belief he thereby ascribes to himself as belief in the proposition *that the time at which it is true that the meeting starts now is now*. But he certainly can believe at noon, that this whole proposition is true at noon, without being ready to say "It's starting now" and leave. We do not yet have a solution to the problem of the essential indexical.

LIMITED ACCESSIBILITY

One may take all that has been said so far as an argument for the existence of a special class of propositions, propositions of limited accessibility. For what have we really shown? All attempts to find a formula of the form "A is making a mess," with which any of us at any time could express what I believed, have failed. But one might argue that we can hardly suppose that there wasn't anything that I believed; surely I believed just that proposition which I expressed, on that occasion, with the words "I am making a mess." That we cannot find a sentence that always expresses this proposition when said by anyone does not show that it does not exist. Rather it should lead us to the conclusion that there is a class of propositions which can only be expressed in special circumstances. In particular, only I could express the proposition I expressed when I said "I am making a mess." Others can see, perhaps by analogy with their own case, that there is a proposition that I express, but it is in a sense inaccessible to them.

Similarly, at noon on the day of the meeting, we could all express the proposition the tardy professor expressed with the words "The meeting starts now." But once that time has past, the proposition becomes inaccessible. We can still identify it, as the proposition which was expressed by those words at that time. But we cannot express it with those words any longer, for with each passing moment they express a different proposition. And we can find no other words to express it.

The advocate of such a stock of propositions of limited accessability may not need to bring in special propositions accessible only at certain places. For it is plausible to suppose that other indexicals can be eliminated in favor of "I" and "now." Perhaps "That is Gilmore Lake" just comes to "What I see now in front of me is Gilmore Lake." But elimination of either "I" or "now" in favor of the other seems impossible.

Such a theory of propositions of limited accessibility seems acceptable, even attractive, to some philosophers.[4] It's acceptability or attractiveness will depend on other parts of one's metaphysics; if one finds plausible reasons elsewhere for believing in a universe that has, in addition to our common world, myriads of private perspectives, the idea of propositions of limited accessability will fit right in.[5] I have no knock-down argument against such propositions, or the metaphysical schemes that find room for them. But I believe only in a common actual world. And I do not think the phenomenon of essential indexicality forces me to abandon this view.

THE OBVIOUS SOLUTION?

Let's return to the device of the true-false exam. Suppose the lost author had been given such an exam before and after he figured out where he was. Would we expect any differences in his answers? Not so long as the statements contained no indexicals. "Mt. Tallac is higher than either of the Maggie Peaks" would have been marked the same way before and after, the same way he would have marked it at home in Berkeley. His mark on that sentence would tell us nothing about where he thought he was. But if the exam were to contain such sentences as "That is Gilmore Lake in front of me" we would expect a dramatic change, from "False" or "Unsure" to "True."

Imagine such an exam given to various lost campers in different parts of the Wilderness. We could classify the campers by their answers, and such a classification would be valuable for prediction and explanation. Of all the campers who marked "This is Gilmore Lake" with "True," we would say they believed that they were at Gilmore Lake. And we should expect them to act accordingly; if they possessed the standard guidebook, and wished to leave the Wilderness, we might expect what is, given one way of looking at it, the same behavior: taking the path up the mountain above the shallow end of the lake before them.

Now consider all the good-hearted people who have ever been in a supermarket, noticed sugar on the floor, and been ready to say "I am making a mess." They all have something important in common, something that leads us to expect their next action to be that of looking into their grocery carts in search of the torn sack. Or consider all the responsible professors who have ever uttered "The department meeting is starting now." They too have something important in common; they are in a state which will lead those just down the hall to go to the meeting, those across campus to curse and feel guilty, those on leave to smile.

What the members within these various groups have in common is not what they believe. There is no *de dicto* proposition that all the campers or shoppers or professors believe. And there is no person whom all the shoppers believe to be making a mess, no lake all the campers believe to be Gilmore Lake, and no time at which all the professors believe their meetings to be starting.

We are clearly classifying the shoppers, campers, and professors into groups corresponding to what we have been calling "relativized propositions"—abstract objects corresponding to sentences containing indexicals. But what members of each group have in common, which makes the groups significant, is not belief that a certain relativized proposition is true. Such belief, as we saw, is belief that such a proposition is true at some context of evaluation. Now all of the shoppers believe that *that I am making a mess* is true at some context of evaluation or other, but so does everyone else who has ever given it a moment's thought. And similar remarks apply to the campers and the professors.

If believing the same relativized proposition isn't what the members of each of the groups have in common with one another, why is it being used as a principle of classification? I propose we look at things in this way. The shoppers, for example, are all in a certain belief state, a state which, given normal desires and other belief states they can be expected to be in, will lead each of them to examine his cart. But, although they are all in the same belief state (not the same *total* belief state, of course), they do not all have the same belief (believe the same thing, have the relation of belief to the same object).

We use sentences with indexicals or relativized propositions to individuate belief states, for the purposes of classifying believers in ways useful for explanation and prediction. That is, belief states individuated in this way enter into our common sense theory about human behavior and more sophisticated theories emerging from it. We expect all good-hearted people in that state which leads them to say "I am making a mess" to examine their grocery carts, no matter what belief they have in virtue of being in that state. That we individuate belief states in this way doubtless has something to do with the fact that one criterion for being in the states we postulate, at least for articulate sincere adults, is being disposed to utter the indexical sentence in question. A good philosophy of mind should explain this in detail; my aim is merely to get clear about what it is that needs explaining.

The proposal, then, is that there is not an identity, or even an isomorphic correspondence, but only a systematic relationship between the belief states one is in and what one thereby believes. The opposite assumption, that belief states should be classified by propositions believed, seems to be built right into traditional philosophies of belief. Given this assumption, whenever we have believers in the same belief state, we must expect to find a proposition they all believe, and differences in belief state lead us to expect a difference in proposition believed. The bulk of this paper consisted in following such leads to nowhere (or to propositions of limited accessibility).

Consider a believer whose belief states are characterized by a structure of sentences with indexicals or relativized propositions (those marked "true" in a very comprehensive exam, if we are dealing with an articulate sincere adult). This structure, together with the context of belief—the time and identity of the speaker—will yield a structure of *de re* propositions. The sequence of objects will consist of the values which the indexicals take in the context. The open propositions will be those yielded by the relativized proposition when shorn of its indexical elements. These are what the person believes, in virtue of being in the states he is in, when and where he is in them.[6]

This latter structure is important, and classifications of believers by *what* they believe is appropriate for many purposes. For example, usually, when a believer moves from context to context, his belief states adjust to preserve beliefs held. As time passes, I go from the state corresponding to "The meeting will begin" to the one corresponding to "The meeting is beginning" and finally to "The meeting has begun." All along I believe of noon that it is when the meeting begins. But I believe it in different ways. And to these different ways of believing the same thing, different actions are appropriate: preparation, movement, apology. Of course if the change of context is not noted, the adjustment of belief states will not occur, and a wholesale change from believing truly to believing falsely may occur. This is what happened to Rip Van Winkle. He awakes in the same belief states he fell asleep in twenty years earlier, unadjusted to the dramatic change in context, and so with a whole new set of beliefs, such as that he is a young man, mostly false.

We have here a metaphysically benign form of limited accessibility. Anyone at any time can have access to any proposition. But not in any way. Anyone can believe of John Perry that he is making a mess. And anyone can be in the belief state classified by the sentence "I am making a mess." But only I can have that belief by being in that state.

There is room in this scheme for *de dicto* propositions, for the characterization of one's belief states may include sentences without any indexical element. If there are any, they could appear on the exam. For this part of the structure, the hypothesis of perfect correspondence would be correct.

A more radical proposal would do away with objects of belief entirely. We would think of belief as a system of relations of various degrees between persons and other objects. Rather than saying I believed in the *de re* proposition consisting of me and the open proposition, *x is making a mess*, we would say that I stand in the relation, believing to be making a mess, to myself. There are many ways to stand in this relation to myself, that is, a variety of belief states I might be in. And these would be classified by sentences with indexicals. On this view *de dicto* belief, already demoted from its central place in the philosophy of belief, might be seen as merely an illusion, engendered by the implicit nature of much indexicality.

To say that belief states must be distinguished from objects of belief, cannot be individuated in terms of them, and are what is crucial for the explanation of action, is not to give a full fledged account of belief, or even a sketchy one. Similarly, to say that we must distinguish the object seen from the state of the seeing subject, and that the latter is crucial for the explanation of action guided by vision, is not to offer a full fledged account of vision. But just as the arguments from illusion and perceptual relativity teach us that no philosophy of perception can be plausible that is not cognizant of this last distinction, the problem of the essential indexical should teach us that no philosophy of belief can be plausible that does not take account of the first.

ACKNOWLEDGMENTS

Versions of this paper were read at philosophy department colloquia at U.C.L.A., Claremont Graduate School, and Stanford, to the Washington State University at the Bellingham Philosophy Conference, and to the Meeting of Alberta Philosophy Department. I am indebted to philosophers participating in these colloquia for many helpful criticisms and comments. I owe a special debt to Michael Bratman, and Dagfinn Føllesdal, for detailed comments on the penultimate version. Most of the ideas in this paper were developed while I held a fellowship from the Guggenheim Foundation and was on sabbatical leave from Stanford University, and I thank both for their support.

NOTES

1. In thinking about the problem of the essential indexical, I have been greatly helped by the writings of Hector-Neri Castañeda on indexicality and related topics. Castañeda focused attention on these problems, and made many of the points made here, in [1], [2] and [3]. More recently his views on these matters have been developed as a part of his comprehensive system of generalized phenomenalism. See particularly [4] and [5]. Having benefited so much from Castañeda's collection of "protophilosophical data," I regret that differences of approach and limitations of competence and space have prevented me from incorporating a discussion of his theory into this essay. I hope to make good this omission at some future time.
2. See [11] for a critique of Frege's views on indexicality.
3. For the classic discussion of these problems, see [12].
4. Frege seems to accept something like it, as necessary for dealing with "I," in [6].
5. See [5] especially section II.
6. This two-tiered structure of belief states and propositions believed will remind the reader familiar with David Kaplan's [8] of his system of characters and contents. This is no accident, for my approach to the problem of the essential indexical was formed by using the distinction as found in earlier versions of Kaplan's work to try to find a solution to the problem as articulated by Castañeda. Kaplan's treatment of indexicality was by and large shaped by considerations other than the problem of the essential indexical. So, while any plausibility one finds in what I say about that problem should be transmitted to the general outlines of his system, at least, by providing an epistemological motivation for something like the character/content distinction, any implausibility one finds will not necessarily be so transmitted. Nor should one take any details one manages to find in this essay as a guide to the details of Kaplan's system.

REFERENCES

[1] Hector-Neri Castañeda, "'He': A Study in the Logic of Self-consciousness," *Ratio* 8(1966): 130–57.

[2] ———."Indicators and Quasi-indicators," *American Philosophical Quarterly* 4(1967): 85–100.

[3] ———."On the Logic of Attributions of Self Knowledge to Others," *The Journal of Philosophy* 65(1968): 439–56.

[4] ———."On the Philosophical Foundations of the Theory of Communication: Reference," *Midwestern Studies in Philosophy* 2(1977): 165–86.

[5] ———."Perception, Belief, and the Structure of Physical Objects and Consciousness," *Synthese* 35(1977): 285–351.

[6] Gotlobb Frege, "The Thought: A Logical Inquiry," translated by A. M. and Marcelle Quinton, *Mind* 65(1956): 289–311; reprinted in P. F. Strawson (ed.), *Philosophical Logic* (Oxford: Oxford University Press. 1967): 17–38.

[7] Jaakko Hintikka, "Individuals, Possible Worlds, and Epistemic Logic," *Noûs* 1(1967): 33–62.

[8] David Kaplan, *Demonstratives* (Mimeographed, UCLA, 1977).

[9] ———."Quantifying In," in Donald Davidson and Jaakko Hintikka (eds.) *Words and Objections* (Dordrecht: Reidel, 1969): 206–42.

[10] Richard Montague, "Pragmatics," in Richmond H. Thomason (ed.), *Formal Philosophy: Selected Papers of Richard Montague* (New Haven: Yale University Press, 1974): 95–118.

[11] John Perry, "Frege on Demonstratives," *Philosophical Review* 86(1977): 474–97.

[12] Willard van Orman Quine, "Quantifiers and Propositional Attitudes," reprinted in *Ways of Paradox* (New York: Random House, 1966): 183–94.

[13] Dana Scott. "Advice on Modal Logic," in Karel Lambert (ed.), *Philosophical Problems in Logic* (Dordrecht: Reidel, 1970): 143–73.

PART V

LIFE AND DEATH

INTRODUCTION

Among the most profound questions that we face are how we should live life and how we should confront death. Throughout the millennia, philosophers have offered guidance on these questions, presenting systematic accounts of the nature of human flourishing or principled articulations of reasons to take one or another stance about the inevitability of our mortality. The selections presented here are a small sample of these accounts.

Life

In the first selection, "On the Harmony of the Soul," the ancient Greek philosopher Plato (c. 428–347 BCE) suggests that it can be helpful to think of ourselves as subject to three distinct sorts of inclinations: those that result from our "appetites" (such as hunger, thirst, and attraction), those that result from our "spirit" or emotions (such as anger, fear, and sadness), and those that result from our "reason" or reflective capacities. Human flourishing, he contends, requires a certain sort of *harmony* among these inclinations; to thrive, we must bring our potentially conflicting desires into line with one another, so they do not pull us in different directions.

In "Existentialism as Humanism," French philosopher Jean-Paul Sartre (1905–80) denies the claim that there is a fixed human nature; rather, he maintains, we become who we are as a result of the choices that we make. According to the *existentialist* picture that he sketches, there is nothing beyond ourselves and our actions to give meaning to our lives. This realization can be both empowering and anguish provoking. We are condemned to a life of perilous freedom: although we did not choose to be authors of our own fate, it is we alone who are responsible for all that we do.

Whether or not we think of ourselves as authors of our fate, it seems reasonable to ask what is involved in a life going well. In "What Makes Someone's Life Go Best?" British philosopher Derek Parfit (1942–) considers three sorts of answers to his title question. According to *hedonistic* theories, someone's life goes well insofar as it is filled with happiness. According to *desire-fulfillment* theories, someone's life goes well insofar as the person's desires are fulfilled. According to *objective list* theories, someone's life goes well insofar as certain objectively specified things occur or fail to occur in the course of his or her lifetime. Although he does not adjudicate among them, Parfit considers a number of versions of each of these theories and discusses the various commitments that they bring in their wake.

When we reflect on our lives, it may seem that there is something absurd about the human condition. In his essay "The Absurd," American philosopher Thomas Nagel (1937–) considers the ways in which this thought may capture something important about human experience. He explores a number of ways in which there is a discrepancy between how we aspire to conceive of our lives and the reality that confronts us as tiny beings in a vast universe. Nagel concludes that although it may not be literally true that life is absurd, there is nonetheless something right about understanding the human condition in that way.

Death

It is a universal fact of earthly human existence that each of us is mortal. How should we confront this inevitable truth?

In the first selection, "Death," American philosopher Thomas Nagel explores the question of why death seems bad to us and asks whether this attitude is one that we have reason to maintain. He considers the view that what is disturbing about death is that it deprives us of experiences that we might otherwise have had. This may help to explain why we consider death bad, even though we ourselves will no longer exist when we are dead, and why we consider death to be so much worse than prenatal nonexistence.

We close with a selection from the philosopher Walter Kaufmann (1921–80), entitled "Death Without Dread." In it, Kaufmann suggests that it is a mistake to assume that it is a fixed feature of human nature to think of death as something to be feared. Although this is certainly part of the modern Western worldview, attitudes toward death have differed wildly across time and place; how we feel about death is intimately connected with our particular, accidental geographic and temporal location. To support his position, Kaufmann presents and analyzes a series of eighteenth- and nineteenth-century German poems that reflect views about death from previous eras that differ radically from those of the modern West. Thinking about these poems, Kaufmann suggests, can help us overcome the view that death is a terrible tragedy to be feared and loathed and can instead help us find alternative ways of thinking about our finitude.

Further Reading

Students who want to pursue the themes raised in this section may begin by looking at the articles in the following two anthologies. The first anthology includes a selection of readings on living a good life; the second includes a selection of readings on the topic of death. Each includes additional suggestions for further readings:

- Charles Guingon, ed. *The Good Life*. Indianapolis and Cambridge: Hackett, 1999.
- John Martin Fischer, ed. *The Metaphysics of Death*. Stanford, Calif.: Stanford University Press, 1993.

A LIFE

"On the Harmony of the Soul" from *The Republic*

PLATO

Plato (c. 428–347 BCE)—along with his student Aristotle—was one of the two most important philosophers of antiquity and is among the most important figures in the entire Western intellectual tradition. His wide-ranging discussions addressed nearly every philosophical topic imaginable and set the stage for philosophical exploration for the next two millennia. His philosophical writings take the form of dialogues that feature his teacher Socrates (469–399 BCE) as a character.

The selection that appears here is drawn from the fourth and eighth "books" (chapters) of Plato's long dialogue, *The Republic*. As the excerpt begins, Socrates is engaged in conversation with Plato's older brother Glaucon. Having recently argued that a city is just only when its parts exist in harmonious relation with one another, Socrates suggests that the same is true of the human soul: it is only when its parts are in proper harmony that authentic happiness is possible. In the continuation, Socrates applies this argument to Glaucon's original challenge concerning the role of justice in human happiness (see "Glaucon's Challenge," pp. 217–220).

This selection was originally written in ancient Greek, and was translated by British philosopher G. M. A. Grube and updated by American philosopher C. D. C. Reeve. The numbers that appear in the margins of the text are called "Stephanus numbers;" they refer to the page numbers of a canonical edition of Plato's work prepared by Henricus Stephanus in 1578. Reference to these numbers enables coordination among readers who make use of different translations or editions. Notes that appear in [brackets] are due to the translators of the work, with occasional slight supplements from the editors of this volume.

Several additional selections from Plato's writings can be found in the Morality and Knowledge sections.

Well, then, we've now made our difficult way through a sea of argument. We are pretty much agreed that the same number and the same kinds of classes as are in the city are also in the soul of each individual.*

* The first speaker here (Well, the . . .") is Socrates; the second ("That's true") is Glaucon.

That's true.

Therefore, it necessarily follows that the individual is wise in the same way and in the same part of himself as the city.

That's right.

And isn't the individual courageous in the same way and in the same part of himself as the city? And d

From Plato, *The Republic*, trans. Grube, rev. Reeve. Copyright © 1992 by Hackett Publishing Company, Inc. Reprinted by permission of the publisher. All rights reserved.

isn't everything else that has to do with virtue the same in both?

Necessarily.

Moreover, Glaucon, I suppose we'll say that a man is just in the same way as a city.

That too is entirely necessary.

And we surely haven't forgotten that the city was just because each of the three classes in it was doing its own work.

I don't think we could forget that.

Then we must also remember that each one of us
e in whom each part is doing its own work will him-
self be just and do his own.

Of course, we must.

Therefore, isn't it appropriate for the rational part to rule, since it is really wise and exercises foresight on behalf of the whole soul, and for the spirited part to obey it and be its ally?

It certainly is.

And isn't it, as we were saying, a mixture of music
and poetry, on the one hand, and physical training,
on the other, that makes the two parts harmonious,
stretching and nurturing the rational part with fine
words and learning, relaxing the other part through
442 soothing stories, and making it gentle by means of
harmony and rhythm?

That's precisely it.

And these two, having been nurtured in this way,
and having truly learned their own roles and been
educated in them, will govern the appetitive part,
which is the largest part in each person's soul and is
by nature most insatiable for money. They'll watch
over it to see that it isn't filled with the so-called
pleasures of the body and that it doesn't become so
big and strong that it no longer does its own work
b but attempts to enslave and rule over the classes it
isn't fitted to rule, thereby overturning everyone's
whole life.

That's right.

Then, wouldn't these two parts also do the finest job of guarding the whole soul and body against external enemies—reason by planning, spirit by fighting, following its leader, and carrying out the leader's decisions through its courage?

Yes, that's true.

And it is because of the spirited part, I suppose,
c that we call a single individual courageous, namely,
when it preserves through pains and pleasures the
declarations of reason about what is to be feared and
what isn't.

That's right.

And we'll call him wise because of that small part of himself that rules in him and makes those declarations and has within it the knowledge of what is advantageous for each part and for the whole soul, which is the community of all three parts.

Absolutely.

And isn't he moderate because of the friendly
and harmonious relations between these same parts,
namely, when the ruler and the ruled believe in
common that the rational part should rule and don't
engage in civil war against it? d

Moderation is surely nothing other than that, both in the city and in the individual.

And, of course, a person will be just because of what we've so often mentioned, and in that way.

Necessarily.

Well, then, is the justice in us at all indistinct? Does it seem to be something different from what we found in the city?

It doesn't seem so to me.

If there are still any doubts in our soul about this,
we could dispel them altogether by appealing to e
ordinary cases.

Which ones?

For example, if we had to come to an agreement
about whether someone similar in nature and train-
ing to our city had embezzled a deposit of gold or
silver that he had accepted, who do you think would
consider him to have done it rather than someone
who isn't like him? 443

No one.

And would he have anything to do with temple robberies, thefts, betrayals of friends in private life or of cities in public life?

No, nothing.

And he'd be in no way untrustworthy in keeping an oath or other agreement.

How could he be?

And adultery, disrespect for parents, and neglect of the gods would be more in keeping with every other kind of character than his.

With every one.

And isn't the cause of all this that every part
b within him does its own work, whether it's ruling or being ruled?

Yes, that and nothing else.

Then, are you still looking for justice to be something other than this power, the one that produces men and cities of the sort we've described?

No, I certainly am not.

Then the dream we had has been completely fulfilled—our suspicion that, with the help of some god, we had hit upon the origin and pattern of jus-
c tice right at the beginning in founding our city.

Absolutely.

Indeed, Glaucon, the principle that it is right for someone who is by nature a cobbler to practice cobblery and nothing else, for the carpenter to practice carpentry, and the same for the others is a sort of image of justice—that's why it's beneficial.

Apparently.

And in truth justice is, it seems, something of this sort. However, it isn't concerned with someone's doing his own externally, but with what is inside him, with what is truly himself and his own. One who is
d just does not allow any part of himself to do the work of another part or allow the various classes within him to meddle with each other. He regulates well what is really his own and rules himself. He puts himself in order, is his own friend, and harmonizes the three parts of himself like three limiting notes in a musical scale—high, low, and middle. He binds together those parts and any others there may be in between, and from having been many things he becomes
e entirely one, moderate and harmonious. Only then does he act. And when he does anything, whether acquiring wealth, taking care of his body, engaging in politics, or in private contracts—in all of these, he believes that the action is just and fine that preserves this inner harmony and helps achieve it, and calls it so, and regards as wisdom the knowledge that oversees such actions. And he believes that the action that
444 destroys this harmony is unjust, and calls it so, and regards the belief that oversees it as ignorance.

That's absolutely true, Socrates.

Well, then, if we claim to have found the just man, the just city, and what the justice is that is in them, I don't suppose that we'll seem to be telling a complete falsehood.

No, we certainly won't.

Shall we claim it, then?

We shall.

So be it. Now, I suppose we must look for injustice.

Clearly.

Surely, it must be a kind of civil war between the b
three parts, a meddling and doing of another's work, a rebellion by some part against the whole soul in order to rule it inappropriately. The rebellious part is by nature suited to be a slave, while the other part is not a slave but belongs to the ruling class. We'll say something like that, I suppose, and that the turmoil and straying of these parts are injustice, licentiousness, cowardice, ignorance, and, in a word, the whole of vice.

That's what they are.

So, if justice and injustice are really clear enough
to us, then acting justly, acting unjustly, and doing c
injustice are also clear.

How so?

Because just and unjust actions are no different for the soul than healthy and unhealthy things are for the body.

In what way?

Healthy things produce health, unhealthy ones disease.

Yes.

And don't just actions produce justice in the soul
and unjust ones injustice? d

Necessarily.

To produce health is to establish the components of the body in a natural relation of control and being controlled, one by another, while to produce disease is to establish a relation of ruling and being ruled contrary to nature.

That's right.

Then, isn't to produce justice to establish the parts of the soul in a natural relation of control, one by another, while to produce injustice is to establish a relation of ruling and being ruled contrary to nature?

Precisely.

Virtue seems, then, to be a kind of health, fine
condition, and well-being of the soul, while vice is e
disease, shameful condition, and weakness.

That's true.

And don't fine ways of living lead one to the possession of virtue, shameful ones to vice?

Necessarily.

So it now remains, it seems, to enquire whether it is more profitable to act justly, live in a fine way,
445 and be just, whether one is known to be so or not, or to act unjustly and be unjust, provided that one doesn't pay the penalty and become better as a result of punishment.

But, Socrates, this inquiry looks ridiculous to me now that justice and injustice have been shown to be as we have described. Even if one has every kind of food and drink, lots of money, and every sort of power to rule, life is thought to be not worth living when the body's nature is ruined. So even if someone can do whatever he wishes, except what will
b free him from vice and injustice and make him acquire justice and virtue, how can it be worth living when his soul—the very thing by which he lives—is ruined and in turmoil? . . .

588b All right, then. Since we've reached this point in the argument, let's return to the first things we said, since they are what led us here. I think someone said at some point that injustice profits a completely unjust person who is believed to be just. Isn't that so?

It certainly is.

Now, let's discuss this with him, since we've agreed on the respective powers that injustice and justice have.

How?

By fashioning an image of the soul in words, so that the person who says this sort of thing will know what he is saying.

c What sort of image?

One like those creatures that legends tell us used to come into being in ancient times, such as the Chimera, Scylla, Cerberus,[1] or any of the multitude of others in which many different kinds of things are said to have grown together naturally into one.

Yes, the legends do tell us of such things.

Well, then, fashion a single kind of multicolored beast with a ring of many heads that it can grow and change at will—some from gentle, some from savage animals.

d That's work for a clever artist. However, since words are more malleable than wax and the like, consider it done.

Then fashion one other kind, that of a lion and another of a human being. But make the first much the largest and the other second to it in size.

That's easier—the sculpting is done.

Now join the three of them into one, so that they somehow grow together naturally.

They're joined.

Then, fashion around them the image of one of them, that of a human being so that anyone who sees only the outer covering and not what's inside will e
think it is a single creature, a human being.

It's done.

Then, if someone maintains that injustice profits this human being and that doing just things brings no advantage, let's tell him that he is simply saying that it is beneficial for him, first, to feed the multiform beast well and make it strong, and also the lion and all that pertains to him; second, to starve and weaken the human being within, so that he is dragged along wherever either of the other two 589
leads; and, third, to leave the parts to bite and kill one another rather than accustoming them to each other and making them friendly.

Yes, that's absolutely what someone who praises injustice is saying.

But, on the other hand, wouldn't someone who maintains that just things are profitable be saying, first, that all our words and deeds should insure that the human being within this human being has the most control; second, that he should take care b
of the many-headed beast as a farmer does his animals, feeding and domesticating the gentle heads and preventing the savage ones from growing; and, third, that he should make the lion's nature his ally, care for the community of all his parts, and bring them up in such a way that they will be friends with each other and with himself?

Yes, that's exactly what someone who praises justice is saying.

From every point of view, then, anyone who praises justice speaks truly, and anyone who praises injustice speaks falsely. Whether we look at the matter from the point of view of pleasure, good reputation, or advantage, a praiser of justice tells c
the truth, while one who condemns it has nothing sound to say and condemns without knowing what he is condemning.

In my opinion, at least, he knows nothing about it.

Then let's persuade him gently—for he isn't wrong
of his own will—by asking him these questions. Should
we say that this is the original basis for the conven-
tions about what is fine and what is shameful?
Fine things are those that subordinate the beast-
like parts of our nature to the human—or better,
perhaps, to the divine; shameful ones are those that
d enslave the gentle to the savage? Will he agree or
what?

He will, if he takes my advice.

In light of this argument, can it profit anyone to
acquire gold unjustly if, by doing so, he enslaves the
best part of himself to the most vicious? If he got
the gold by enslaving his son or daughter to sav-
e age and evil men, it wouldn't profit him, no matter
how much gold he got. How, then, could he fail to
be wretched if he pitilessly enslaves the most divine
part of himself to the most godless and polluted
590 one and accepts golden gifts in return for a more ter-
rible destruction than Eriphyle's when she took the
necklace in return for her husband's soul?[2]

A much more terrible one, Glaucon said. I'll answer for him.

And don't you think that licentiousness has long been condemned for just these reasons, namely, that because of it, that terrible, large, and multiform beast is let loose more than it should be?

Clearly.

And aren't stubbornness and irritability con-
b demned because they inharmoniously increase and
stretch the lionlike and snakelike[3] part?

Certainly.

And aren't luxury and softness condemned because the slackening and loosening of this same part produce cowardice in it?

Of course.

And aren't flattery and slavishness condemned because they subject the spirited part to the moblike beast, accustoming it from youth on to being insulted for the sake of the money needed to satisfy the beast's insatiable appetites, so that it becomes an ape instead of a lion?

c They certainly are.

Why do you think that the condition of a manual worker is despised? Or is it for any other reason than that, when the best part is naturally weak in someone, it can't rule the beasts within him but can only serve them and learn to flatter them?

Probably so.

Therefore, to insure that someone like that is
ruled by something similar to what rules the best
person, we say that he ought to be the slave of that
best person who has a divine ruler within himself.
It isn't to harm the slave that we say he must be d
ruled, which is what Thrasymachus thought to be
true of all subjects, but because it is better for every-
one to be ruled by divine reason, preferably within
himself and his own, otherwise imposed from with-
out, so that as far as possible all will be alike and
friends, governed by the same thing.

Yes, that's right.

This is clearly the aim of the law, which is the ally
of everyone. But it's also our aim in ruling our chil-
dren, we don't allow them to be free until we estab-
lish a constitution in them, just as in a city, and—by
fostering their best part with our own—equip them
with a guardian and ruler similar to our own to take 591
our place. Then, and only then, we set them free.

Clearly so.

Then how can we maintain or argue, Glaucon, that injustice, licentiousness, and doing shameful things are profitable to anyone, since, even though he may acquire more money or other sort of power from them, they make him more vicious?

There's no way we can.

Or that to do injustice without being discovered
and having to pay the penalty is profitable? Doesn't
the one who remains undiscovered become even
more vicious, while the bestial part of the one who b
is discovered is calmed and tamed and his gentle
part freed, so that his entire soul settles into its best
nature, acquires moderation, justice, and reason,
and attains a more valuable state than that of hav-
ing a fine, strong, healthy body, since the soul itself is
more valuable than the body?

That's absolutely certain.

Then won't a person of understanding direct all
his efforts to attaining that state of his soul? First,
he'll value the studies that produce it and despise the c
others.

Clearly so.

Second, he won't entrust the condition and nurture of his body to the irrational pleasure of the beast

within or turn his life in that direction, but neither will he make health his aim or assign first place to being strong, healthy, and beautiful, unless he happens to acquire moderation as a result. Rather, it's clear that he will always cultivate the harmony of his
d body for the sake of the consonance in his soul.

He certainly will, if indeed he's to be truly trained in music and poetry.

Will he also keep order and consonance in his acquisition of money, with that same end in view? Or, even though he isn't dazzled by the size of the majority into accepting their idea of blessed happiness, will he increase his wealth without limit and so have unlimited evils?

Not in my view.

e Rather, he'll look to the constitution within him and guard against disturbing anything in it, either by too much money or too little. And, in this way, he'll direct both the increase and expenditure of his wealth, as far as he can.

That's exactly what he'll do.

And he'll look to the same thing where honors
592 are concerned. He'll willingly share in and taste those that he believes will make him better, but he'll avoid any public or private honor that might overthrow the established condition of his soul.

If that's his chief concern, he won't be willing to take part in politics.

Yes, by the dog, he certainly will, at least in his own kind of city. But he may not be willing to do so in his fatherland, unless some divine good luck chances to be his.

I understand. You mean that he'll be willing to take part in the politics of the city we were founding and describing, the one that exists in theory, for
I don't think it exists anywhere on earth. b

But perhaps, I said, there is a model of it in heaven, for anyone who wants to look at it and to make himself its citizen on the strength of what he sees. It makes no difference whether it is or ever will be somewhere, for he would take part in the practical affairs of that city and no other.

Probably so, he said.

NOTES

1. The Chimera was "lion in the front, serpent in the back, and she-goat in the middle" (*Iliad* 6.181). Scylla had six heads, each with three rows of teeth, and twelve feet (see *Odyssey* 12.85 ff., 245 ff.). Cerberus was a huge dog guarding the entrance to Hades; he had three heads and a serpent's tail.
2. Eriphyle was bribed by Polynices to persuade her husband, Amphiaraus, to take part in an attack on Thebes. He was killed, and she was murdered by her son in revenge. See *Odyssey* 11.326–7; Pindar, *Nemean* 9.37 ff.
3. The snakelike part hasn't been previously mentioned, although it may be included in "all that pertains to" the lion (588e). It symbolizes some of the meaner components of the spirited part, such as irritability, which it would be unnatural to attribute to the noble lion.

Existentialism

JEAN-PAUL SARTRE

French philosopher Jean-Paul Sartre (1905–80) is among the best-known thinkers of the twentieth century. His major philosophical and literary works include the plays *No Exit* (1944) and

From *Existentialism* by Jean-Paul Sartre, translated by Hazel E. Barnes. Copyright © 1956 The Philosophical Library. Reprinted by permission of The Philosophical Library, a division of Allied Books.

Nausea (1938) and the philosophical treatise *Being and Nothingness* (1943). He was awarded the Nobel Prize for literature in 1964, although he declined the honor.

The selection that follows derives from a public lecture that Sartre delivered in Paris in 1945. Although it remains the most accessible and widely reproduced introduction to his philosophical outlook, Sartre himself expressed regret that the essay was ever published.

Man is nothing else but what he makes of himself. Such is the first principle of existentialism. It is also what is called subjectivity, the name we are labeled with when charges are brought against us. But what do we mean by this, if not that man has a greater dignity than a stone or table? For we mean that man first exists, that is, that man first of all is the being who hurls himself toward a future and who is conscious of imagining himself as being in the future. Man is at the start a plan which is aware of itself, rather than a patch of moss, a piece of garbage, or a cauliflower; nothing exists prior to this plan; there is nothing in heaven; man will be what he will have planned to be. Not what he will want to be. Because by the word "will" we generally mean a conscious decision, which is subsequent to what we have already made of ourselves. I may want to belong to a political party, write a book, get married, but all that is only a manifestation of an earlier, more spontaneous choice that is called "will." But if existence really does precede essence, man is responsible for what he is. Thus, existentialism's first move is to make every man aware of what he is and to make the full responsibility of his existence rest on him. And when we say that a man is responsible for himself, we do not only mean that he is responsible for his own individuality, but that he is responsible for all men.

The word "subjectivism" has two meanings, and our opponents play on the two. Subjectivism means, on the one hand, that an individual chooses and makes himself; and, on the other, that it is impossible for man to transcend human subjectivity. The second of these is the essential meaning of existentialism. When we say that man chooses his own self, we mean that every one of us does likewise; but we also mean by that that in making this choice he also chooses all men. In fact, in creating the man that we want to be, there is not a single one of our acts which does not at the same time create an image of man as we think he ought to be. To choose to be this or that is to affirm at the same time the value of what we choose, because we can never choose evil. We always choose the good, and nothing can be good for us without being good for all.

If, on the other hand, existence precedes essence, and if we grant that we exist and fashion our image at one and the same time, the image is valid for everybody and for our whole age. Thus, our responsibility is much greater than we might have supposed, because it involves all mankind. If I am a workingman and choose to join a Christian trade union rather than be a Communist, and if by being a member I want to show that the best thing for man is resignation, that the kingdom of man is not of this world, I am not only involving my own case—I want to be resigned for everyone. As a result, my action has involved all humanity. To take a more individual matter, if I want to marry, to have children, even if this marriage depends solely on my own circumstances or passion or wish, I am involving all humanity in monogamy and not merely myself. Therefore, I am responsible for myself and for everyone else. I am creating a certain image of man of my own choosing. In choosing myself, I choose man.

This helps us understand what the actual content is of such rather grandiloquent words as anguish, forlornness, despair. As you will see, it's all quite simple.

First, what is meant by anguish? The existentialists say at once that man is anguish. What that means is this: the man who involves himself and who realizes that he is not only the person he chooses to be, but also a lawmaker who is, at the same time, choosing all mankind as well as himself, cannot help escape the feeling of his total and deep responsibility. Of course, there are many people who are not anxious; but we claim that they are hiding their anxiety, that they are fleeing from it. Certainly, many people believe that when they do something, they themselves are the only ones involved, and when someone says to them, "What if everyone acted that way?" they shrug their shoulders and answer, "Everyone doesn't act that way." But really, one should always ask himself, "What would happen if everybody looked at things that way?" There is no escaping this disturbing thought except by a kind of double-dealing. A man who lies and makes excuses for himself by saying "not everybody does that," is someone with an uneasy conscience, because the act of lying implies that a universal value is conferred upon the lie.

Anguish is evident even when it conceals itself. This is the anguish that Kierkegaard* called the anguish of Abraham. You know the story: an angel has ordered Abraham to sacrifice his son; if it really were an angel who has come and said, "You are Abraham, you shall sacrifice your son," everything would be all right. But everyone might first wonder, "Is it really an angel, and am I really Abraham? What proof do I have?"

There was a madwoman who had hallucinations; someone used to speak to her on the telephone and give her orders. Her doctor asked her, "Who is it who talks to you?" She answered, "He says it's God." What proof did she really have that it was God? If an angel comes to me, what proof is there that it's an angel? And if I hear voices, what proof is there that they come from heaven and not from hell, or from the subconscious, or a pathological condition? What proves that they are addressed to me? What proof is there that I have been appointed to impose my choice and my conception of man on humanity? I'll never find any proof or sign to convince me of that. If a voice addresses me, it is always for me to decide that this is the angel's voice; if I consider that such an act is a good one, it is I who will choose to say that it is good rather than bad.

Now, I'm not being singled out as an Abraham, and yet at every moment I'm obliged to perform exemplary acts. For every man, everything happens as if all mankind had its eyes fixed on him and were guiding itself by what he does. And every man ought to say to himself, "Am I really the kind of man who has the right to act in such a way that humanity might guide itself by my actions?" And if he does not say that to himself, he is masking his anguish.

There is no question here of the kind of anguish which would lead to quietism, to inaction. It is a matter of a simple sort of anguish that anybody who has had responsibilities is familiar with. For example, when a military officer takes the responsibility for an attack and sends a certain number of men to death, he chooses to do so, and in the main he alone makes the choice. Doubtless, orders come from above, but they are too broad; he interprets them, and on this interpretation depend the lives of ten or fourteen or twenty men. In making a decision he cannot help having a certain anguish. All leaders know this anguish. That doesn't keep them from acting; on the contrary, it is the very condition of their action. For it implies that they envisage a number of possibilities, and when they choose one, they realize that it has value only because it is chosen. We shall see that this kind of anguish, which is the kind that existentialism describes, is explained, in addition, by a direct responsibility to the other men whom it involves. It is not a curtain separating us from action, but is part of action itself.

When we speak of forlornness, a term Heidegger* was fond of, we mean only that God does not exist and that we have to face all the consequences of this. This existentialist is strongly opposed to a certain kind of secular ethics which would like to abolish God with the least possible expense. About 1880, some French teachers tried to set up a secular ethics which went something like this: God is a useless and costly hypothesis; we are discarding it; but, meanwhile, in order for there to be an ethics, a society, a civilization, it is essential that certain values be taken seriously and that they be considered as having an a priori existence. It must be obligatory, a priori, to be honest, not to lie, not to beat your wife, to have children, etc., etc. So we're going to try a little device

* Soren Kierkegaard (1813–55) was a Danish philosopher and theologian.

* Martin Heidegger (1889–1976) was an important twentieth-century German philosopher whose major work—*Being and Time*—examines fundamental questions about the nature of reality and humanity's place within it.

which will make it possible to show that values exist all the same, inscribed in a heaven of ideas, though otherwise God does not exist. In other words—and this, I believe, is the tendency of everything called reformism in France—nothing will be changed if God does not exist. We shall find ourselves with the same norms of honesty, progress, and humanism, and we shall have made of God an outdated hypothesis which will peacefully die off by itself.

The existentialist, on the contrary, thinks it very distressing that God does not exist, because all possibility of finding values in a heaven of ideas disappears along with Him; there can no longer be an a priori Good, since there is no infinite and perfect consciousness to think it. Nowhere is it written that the Good exists, that we must be honest, that we must not lie; because the fact is we are on a plane where there are only men. Dostoievsky* said, "If God didn't exist, everything would be possible." That is the very starting point of existentialism. Indeed, everything is permissible if God does not exist, and as a result man is forlorn, because neither within him nor without does he find anything to cling to. He can't start making excuses for himself.

If existence really does precede essence, there is no explaining things away by reference to a fixed and given human nature. In other words, there is no determinism, man is free, man is freedom. On the other hand, if God does not exist, we find no values or commands to turn to which legitimize our conduct. So, in the bright realm of values, we have no excuse behind us, nor justification before us. We are alone, with no excuses.

That is the idea I shall try to convey when I say that man is condemned to be free. Condemned, because he did not create himself, yet, in other respects is free: because, once thrown into the world, he is responsible for everything he does. The existentialist does not believe in the power of passion. He will never agree that a sweeping passion is a ravaging torrent which fatally leads a man to certain acts and is therefore an excuse. He thinks that man is responsible for his passion.

The existentialist does not think that man is going to help himself by finding in the world some omen by which to orient himself. Because he thinks that man will interpret the omen to suit himself. Therefore, he thinks that man, with no support and no aid, is condemned every moment to invent man. Ponge,* in a very fine article, has said, "Man is the future of man." That's exactly it. But if it is taken to mean that this future is recorded in heaven, that God sees it, then it is false, because it would really no longer be a future. If it is taken to mean that, whatever a man may be, there is a future to be forged, a virgin future before him, then this remark is sound. But then we are forlorn.

To give you an example which will enable you to understand forlornness better, I shall cite the case of one of my students who came to see me under the following circumstances: his father was on bad terms with his mother, and, moreover, was inclined to be a collaborationist; his older brother had been killed in the German offensive of 1940, and the young man, with somewhat immature but generous feelings, wanted to avenge him. His mother lived alone with him, very much upset by the half-treason of her husband and the death of her older son; the boy was her only consolation.

The boy was faced with the choice of leaving for England and joining the Free French† forces—that is, leaving his mother behind—or remaining with his mother and helping her to carry on. He was fully aware that the woman lived only for him and that his going off—and perhaps his death—would plunge her into despair. He was also aware that every act that he did for his mother's sake was a sure thing, in the sense that it was helping her to carry on, whereas every effort he made toward going off and fighting was an uncertain move which might run aground

* Fyodor Dostoievsky (often spelled Dostoevsky) (1821–81) was a great Russian novelist who wrote *Crime and Punishment* and *The Brothers Karamazov.*

* Francis Ponge (1899–1988) was a popular French essayist and poet.

† The Free French were a group of French fighters during World War II who continued to fight against the Axis forces after France's 1940 surrender to Nazi Germany.

and prove completely useless; for example, on his way to England he might, while passing through Spain, be detained indefinitely in a Spanish camp; he might reach England or Algiers and be stuck in an office at a desk job. As a result, he was faced with two very different kinds of action: one, concrete, immediate, but concerning only one individual; the other concerned an incomparably vaster group, a national collectivity, but for that very reason was dubious, and might be interrupted en route. And, at the same time, he was wavering between two kinds of ethics. On the one hand, an ethics of sympathy, of personal devotion; on the other, a broader ethics, but one whose efficacy was more dubious. He had to choose between the two.

Who could help him choose? Christian doctrine? No. Christian doctrine says, "Be charitable, love your neighbor, take the more rugged path, etc., etc." But which is the more rugged path? Whom should he love as a brother? The fighting man or his mother? Which does the greater good, the vague act of fighting in a group, or the concrete one of helping a particular human being to go on living? Who can decide a priori? Nobody. No book of ethics can tell him. The Kantian ethics says, "Never treat any person as a means, but as an end." Very well, if I stay with my mother, I'll treat her as an end and not as a means; but by virtue of this very fact, I'm running the risk of treating the people around me who are fighting, as means; and, conversely, if I go to join those who are fighting, I'll be treating them as an end, and, by doing that, I run the risk of treating my mother as a means.

If values are vague, and if they are always too broad for the concrete and specific case that we are considering, the only thing left for us is to trust our instincts. That's what this young man tried to do; and when I saw him, he said, "In the end, feeling is what counts. I ought to choose whichever pushes me in one direction. If I feel that I love my mother enough to sacrifice everything else for her—my desire for vengeance, for action, for adventure—then I'll stay with her. If, on the contrary, I feel that my love for my mother isn't enough, I'll leave."

But how is the value of a feeling determined? What gives his feeling for his mother value? Precisely the fact that he remained with her. I may say that I like so-and-so well enough to sacrifice a certain amount of money for him, but I may say so only if I've done it. I may say "I love my mother well enough to remain with her" if I have remained with her. The only way to determine the value of this affection is, precisely, to perform an act which confirms and defines it. But, since I require this affection to justify my act, I find myself caught in a vicious circle.

On the other hand, Gide* has well said that a mock feeling and a true feeling are almost indistinguishable; to decide that I love my mother and will remain with her, or to remain with her by putting on an act, amount somewhat to the same thing. In other words, the feeling is formed by the acts one performs; so, I cannot refer to it in order to act upon it. Which means that I can neither seek within myself the true condition which will impel me to act, nor apply to a system of ethics for concepts which will permit me to act. You will say, "At least, he did go to a teacher for advice." But if you seek advice from a priest, for example, you have chosen this priest; you already knew, more or less, just about what advice he was going to give you. In other words, choosing your adviser is involving yourself. The proof of this is that if you are a Christian, you will say, "Consult a priest." But some priests are collaborating, some are just marking time, some are resisting. Which to choose? If the young man chooses a priest who is resisting or collaborating, he has already decided on the kind of advice he's going to get. Therefore, in coming to see me he knew the answer I was going to give him, and I had only one answer to give: "You're free, choose, that is, invent." No general ethics can show you what is to be done; there are no omens in the world. The Catholics will reply, "But there are." Granted—but, in any case, I myself choose the meaning they have.

When I was a prisoner, I knew a rather remarkable young man who was a Jesuit. He had entered the Jesuit order in the following way: he had had a number of very bad breaks; in childhood, his father died, leaving him in poverty, and he was a scholarship student at a religious institution where he was constantly made to feel that he was being kept out of charity; then, he failed to get any of the honors and distinctions that children like; later on, at about

* André Gide (1869–1951) was a French author who won the 1947 Nobel Prize in literature.

eighteen, he bungled a love affair; finally, at twenty-two, he failed in military training, a childish enough matter, but it was the last straw.

This young fellow might well have felt that he had botched everything. It was a sign of something, but of what? He might have taken refuge in bitterness or despair. But he very wisely looked upon all this as a sign that he was not made for secular triumphs, and that only the triumphs of religion, holiness, and faith were open to him. He saw the hand of God in all this, and so he entered the order. Who can help seeing that he alone decided what the sign meant?

Some other interpretation might have been drawn from this series of setbacks; for example, that he might have done better to turn carpenter or revolutionist. Therefore, he is fully responsible for the interpretation. Forlornness implies that we ourselves choose our being. Forlornness and anguish go together.

As for despair, the term has a very simple meaning. It means that we shall confine ourselves to reckoning only with what depends upon our will, or on the ensemble of probabilities which make our action possible. When we want something, we always have to reckon with probabilities. I may be counting on the arrival of a friend. The friend is coming by rail or streetcar; this supposes that the train will arrive on schedule, or that the streetcar will not jump the track. I am left in the realm of possibility; but possibilities are to be reckoned with only to the point where my action comports with the ensemble of these possibilities, and no further. The moment the possibilities I am considering are not rigorously involved by my action, I ought to disengage myself from them, because no God, no scheme, can adapt the world and its possibilities to my will. When Descartes said, "Conquer yourself rather than the world," he meant essentially the same thing.

The Marxists to whom I have spoken reply, "You can rely on the support of others in your action, which obviously has certain limits because you're not going to live forever. That means: rely on both what others are doing elsewhere to help you, in China, in Russia, and what they will do later on, after your death, to carry on the action and lead it to its fulfillment, which will be the revolution. You even *have* to rely upon that, otherwise you're immoral." I reply at once that I will always rely on fellow-fighters insofar as these comrades are involved with me in a common struggle, in the unity of a party or a group in which I can more or less make my weight felt; that is, one whose ranks I am in as a fighter and whose movements I am aware of at every moment. In such a situation, relying on the unity and will of the party is exactly like counting on the fact that the train will arrive on time or that the car won't jump the track. But, given that man is free and that there is no human nature for me to depend on, I cannot count on men whom I do not know by relying on human goodness or man's concern for the good of society. I don't know what will become of the Russian revolution; I may make an example of it to the extent that at the present time it is apparent that the proletariat plays a part in Russia that it plays in no other nation. But I can't swear that this will inevitably lead to a triumph of the proletariat. I've got to limit myself to what I see.

Given that men are free and that tomorrow they will freely decide what man will be, I cannot be sure that, after my death, fellow-fighters will carry on my work to bring it to its maximum perfection. Tomorrow, after my death, some men may decide to set up Fascism, and the others may be cowardly and muddled enough to let them do it. Fascism will then be the human reality, so much the worse for us.

Actually, things will be as man will have decided they are to be. Does that mean that I should abandon myself to quietism? No. First, I should involve myself; then, act on the old saw, "Nothing ventured, nothing gained." Nor does it mean that I shouldn't belong to a party, but rather that I shall have no illusions and shall do what I can. For example, suppose I ask myself, "Will socialization, as such, ever come about?" I know nothing about it. All I know is that I'm going to do everything in my power to bring it about. Beyond that, I can't count on anything. Quietism is the attitude of people who say, "Let others do what I can't do." The doctrine I am presenting is the very opposite of quietism, since it declares, "There is no reality except in action." Moreover, it goes further, since it adds, "Man is nothing else than his plan; he exists only to the extent that he fulfills himself; he is therefore nothing else than the ensemble of his acts, nothing else than his life."

According to this, we can understand why our doctrine horrifies certain people. Because often the only way they can bear their wretchedness is to think, "Circumstances have been against me. What I've been and done doesn't show my true worth. To be sure, I've had no great love, no great friendship, but that's because I haven't met a man or woman who was worthy. The books I've written haven't been very good because I haven't had the proper leisure. I haven't had children to devote myself to because I didn't find a man with whom I could have spent my life. So there remains within me, unused and quite viable, a host of propensities, inclinations, possibilities, that one wouldn't guess from the mere series of things I've done."

Now, for the existentialist there is really no love other than one which manifests itself in a person's being in love. There is no genius other than one which is expressed in works of art; the genius of Proust* is the sum of Proust's works; the genius of Racine is his series of tragedies. Outside of that, there is nothing. Why say that Racine could have written another tragedy, when he didn't write it? A man is involved in life, leaves his impress on it, and outside of that there is nothing. To be sure, this may seem a harsh thought to someone whose life hasn't been a success. But, on the other hand, it prompts people to understand that reality alone is what counts, that dreams, expectations, and hopes warrant no more than to define a man as a disappointed dream, as miscarried hopes, as vain expectations. In other words, to define him negatively and not positively. However, when we say, "You are nothing else than your life," that does not imply that the artist will be judged solely on the basis of his works of art; a thousand other things will contribute toward summing him up. What we mean is that a man is nothing else than a series of undertakings, that he is the sum, the organization, the ensemble of the relationships which make up these undertakings.

When all is said and done, what we are accused of, at bottom, is not our pessimism, but an optimistic toughness. If people throw up to us our works of fiction in which we write about people who are soft, weak, cowardly, and sometimes even downright bad, it's not because these people are soft, weak, cowardly, or bad; because if we were to say, as Zola* did, that they are that way because of heredity, the workings of environment, society, because of biological or psychological determinism, people would be reassured. They would say, "Well, that's what we're like, no one can do anything about it." But when the existentialist writes about a coward, he says that this coward is responsible for his cowardice. He's not like that because he has a cowardly heart or lung or brain; he's not like that on account of his physiological make-up; but he's like that because he has made himself a coward by his acts. There's no such thing as a cowardly constitution; there are nervous constitutions; there is poor blood, as the common people say, or strong constitutions. But the man whose blood is poor is not a coward on that account, for what makes cowardice is the act of renouncing or yielding. A constitution is not an act; the coward is defined on the basis of the acts he performs. People feel, in a vague sort of way, that this coward we're talking about is guilty of being a coward, and the thought frightens them. What people would like is that a coward or a hero be born that way. . . .

From these few reflections it is evident that nothing is more unjust than the objections that have been raised against us. Existentialism is nothing else than an attempt to draw all the consequences of a coherent atheistic position. It isn't trying to plunge man into despair at all. But if one calls every attitude of unbelief despair, like the Christians, then the word is not being used in its original sense. Existentialism isn't so atheistic that it wears itself out showing that God doesn't exist. Rather, it declares that even if God did exist, that would change nothing. There you've got our point of view. Not that we believe that God exists, but we think that the problem of His existence is not the issue. In this sense existentialism is optimistic, a doctrine of action, and it is plain dishonesty for Christians to make no distinction between their own despair and ours and then to call us despairing.

* Marcel Proust (1871–1922) was a famous French novelist and essayist best known for his seven-volume novel *Remembrance of Things Past* (also translated as *In Search of Lost Time*). Jean Racine (1639–99) was a major seventeenth-century French playwright known for his works of tragedy.

* Émile Zola (1840–1902) was an important French novelist of the nineteenth century.

What Makes Someone's Life Go Best

DEREK PARFIT

Derek Parfit (1942–) is a British philosopher whose influential writings in ethics and metaphysics have been widely discussed and debated. In his important book *Reasons and Persons* (1984), Parfit explores the relation among rationality, self-interest, personal identity, and morality.

The selection that appears here is taken from an Appendix to *Reasons and Persons*. In it, Parfit considers a number of answers to the question, What makes someone's life go best? An additional selection from Parfit's work appears in the "Metaphysics" section.

What would be best for someone, or would be most in this person's interests, or would make this person's life go, for him, as well as possible? Answers to this question I call *theories about self-interest*. There are three kinds of theory. On *Hedonistic Theories*, what would be best for someone is what would make his life happiest. On *Desire-Fulfilment Theories*, what would be best for someone is what, throughout his life, would best fulfil his desires. On *Objective List Theories*, certain things are good or bad for us, whether or not we want to have the good things, or to avoid the bad things.

Narrow Hedonists assume, falsely, that pleasure and pain are two distinctive kinds of experience. Compare the pleasures of satisfying an intense thirst or lust, listening to music, solving an intellectual problem, reading a tragedy, and knowing that one's child is happy. These various experiences do not contain any distinctive common quality.

What pains and pleasures have in common are their relations to our desires. On the use of "pain" which has rational and moral significance, all pains are when experienced unwanted, and a pain is worse or greater the more it is unwanted. Similarly, all pleasures are when experienced wanted, and they are better or greater the more they are wanted. These are the claims of *Preference-Hedonism*. On this view, one of two experiences is more pleasant if it is preferred.

This theory need not follow the ordinary uses of the words "pain" and "pleasure." Suppose that I could go to a party to enjoy the various pleasures of eating, drinking, laughing, dancing, and talking to my friends. I could instead stay at home and read *King Lear*. Knowing what both alternatives would be like, I prefer to read *King Lear*. It extends the ordinary use to say that this would give me more pleasure. But on Preference-Hedonism, if we add some further assumptions given below, reading *King Lear* would give me a better evening. Griffin cites a more extreme case. Near the end of his life Freud refused pain-killing drugs, preferring to think in torment than to be confusedly euphoric. Of these two mental states, euphoria is more pleasant. But on Preference-Hedonism thinking in torment was, for Freud, a better mental state. It is clearer here not to stretch the meaning of the word "pleasant." A Preference-Hedonist should merely claim that, since Freud preferred to think clearly though in torment, his life went better if it went as he preferred.[1]

Consider next Desire-Fulfilment Theories. The simplest is the *Unrestricted* Theory. This claims that what is best for someone is what would best fulfil *all* of his desires, throughout his life. Suppose that I meet a stranger who has what is believed to be a fatal disease. My sympathy is aroused, and I strongly want this stranger to be cured. We never meet again. Later, unknown to me, this stranger is cured. On the Unrestricted Desire-Fulfilment Theory, this event is good for me, and makes my life go better. This is not plausible. We should reject this theory.

"Appendix I" from *Reasons and Persons*, 1986 by Derek Parfit. Reprinted by permission of Oxford University Press.

Another theory appeals only to our desires about our own lives. I call this the *Success Theory*. This theory differs from Preference-Hedonism in only one way. The Success Theory appeals to *all* of our preferences about our own lives. A Preference-Hedonist appeals only to preferences about those features of our lives that are introspectively discernible. Suppose that I strongly want not to be deceived by other people. On Preference-Hedonism it will be better for me if I believe that I am not being deceived. It will be irrelevant if my belief is false, since this makes no difference to my state of mind. On the Success Theory, it will be worse for me if my belief is false. I have a strong desire about my own life—that I should not be deceived in this way. It is bad for me if this desire is not fulfilled, even if I falsely believe that it is.

When this theory appeals only to desires that are about our own lives, it may be unclear what this excludes. Suppose that I want my life to be such that all of my desires, whatever their objects, are fulfilled. This may seem to make the Success Theory, when applied to me, coincide with the Unrestricted Desire-Fulfilment Theory. But a Success Theorist should claim that this desire is not really about my own life. This is like the distinction between a real change in some object, and a so-called *Cambridge-change*. An object undergoes a Cambridge-change if there is any change in the true statements that can be made about this object. Suppose that I cut my cheek while shaving. This causes a real change in me. It also causes a change in Confucius. It becomes true, of Confucius, that he lived on a planet on which later one more cheek was cut. This is merely a Cambridge-change.

Suppose that I am an exile, and cannot communicate with my children. I want their lives to go well. I might claim that I want to live the life of someone whose children's lives go well. A Success Theorist should again claim that this is not really a desire about my own life. If unknown to me one of my children is killed by an avalanche, this is not bad for me, and does not make my life go worse.

A Success Theorist *would* count some similar desires. Suppose that I try to give my children a good start in life. I try to give them the right education, good habits, and psychological strength. Once again, I am now an exile, and I shall never be able to learn what happens to my children. Suppose that, unknown to me, my children's lives go badly. One finds that the education that I gave him makes him unemployable, another has a mental breakdown, another becomes a petty thief. If my children's lives fail in these ways, and these failures are in part the result of mistakes I made as their parent, these failures in my children's lives would be judged on the Success Theory to be bad for me. One of my strongest desires was to be a successful parent. What is now happening to my children, though it is unknown to me, shows that this desire is not fulfilled. My life failed in one of the ways in which I most wanted it to succeed. Though I do not know this fact, it is bad for me, and makes it true that I have had a worse life. This is like the case where I strongly want not to be deceived. Even if I never know, it is bad for me both if I am deceived and if I turn out to be an unsuccessful parent. These are not introspectively discernible differences in my conscious life; so, on Preference-Hedonism, these events are not bad for me. But on the Success Theory, they are.

Consider next the desires that some people have about what happens after they are dead. For a Preference-Hedonist, once I am dead, nothing bad can happen to me. A Success Theorist should deny this. Return to the case where all my children have wretched lives, because of the mistakes I made as their parent. Suppose that my children's lives all go badly only after I am dead. My life turns out to have been a failure, in one of the ways I cared about most. A Success Theorist should claim that, here too, this makes it true that I had a worse life.

Some Success Theorists would reject this claim, since they tell us to ignore the desires of the dead. But suppose that I was asked, "Do you want it to be true, even after you are dead, that you were a successful parent?" I would answer "Yes." It is irrelevant to my desire whether it is fulfilled before or after I am dead. These Success Theorists count it as bad for me if my attempts fail, even if, because I am an exile, I never know this. How then can it matter whether, when my attempts fail, I am dead? All that my death does is to *ensure* that I will never know this. If we think it irrelevant that I never know about the non-fulfilment of my desires, we cannot defensibly claim that my death makes a difference.

I turn now to questions and objections which arise for both Preference-Hedonism and the Success Theory.

Should we appeal only to the desires and preferences that someone actually has? Return to my choice between going to a party or staying at home to read *King Lear*. Suppose that, knowing what both alternatives would be like, I choose to stay at home. And suppose that I never later regret this choice. On one theory, this shows that staying at home to read *King Lear* gave me a better evening. This is a mistake. It might be true that, if I had chosen to go to the party, I would never have regretted that choice. According to this theory, this would have shown that going to the party gave me a better evening. This theory thus implies that each alternative would have been better than the other. Since this theory implies such contradictions, it must be revised. The obvious revision is to appeal not only to my actual preferences, in the alternative I choose, but also to the preferences that I would have had if I had chosen otherwise.[2]

In this example, whichever alternative I choose, I would never regret this choice. If this is true, can we still claim that one of the alternatives would give me a better evening? On some theories, when in two alternatives I would have such contrary preferences, neither alternative is better or worse for me. This is not plausible when one of my contrary preferences would have been much stronger. Suppose that, if I choose to go to the party, I shall be only mildly glad that I made this choice, but that, if I choose to stay and read *King Lear,* I shall be very glad. If this is true, reading *King Lear* gives me a better evening.

Whether we appeal to Preference-Hedonism or the Success Theory, we should not appeal only to the desires or preferences that I actually have. We should also appeal to the desires and preferences that I would have had, in the various alternatives that were, at different times, open to me. One of these alternatives would be best for me if it is the one in which I would have the strongest desires and preferences fulfilled. This allows us to claim that some alternative life would have been better for me, even if throughout my actual life I am glad that I chose this life rather than this alternative.

There is another distinction which applies both to Preference-Hedonism and to the Success Theory. These theories are *Summative* if they appeal to all of someone's desires, actual and hypothetical, about either his states of mind, or his life. In deciding which alternative would produce the greatest total net sum of desire-fulfilment, we assign some positive number to each desire that is fulfilled, and some negative number to each desire that is not fulfilled. How great these numbers are depends on the intensity of the desires in question. (In the case of the Success Theory, which appeals to past desires, it may also depend on how long these desires were had. This may be a weakness in this theory. The issue does not arise for Preference-Hedonism, which appeals only to the desires that we have, at different times, about our present states of mind.) The total net sum of desire-fulfilment is the sum of the positive numbers minus the negative numbers. Provided that we can compare the relative strength of different desires, this calculation could in theory be performed. The choice of a unit for the numbers makes no difference to the result.

Another version of both theories does not appeal, in this way, to all of a person's desires and preferences about his own life. It appeals only to *global* rather than *local* desires and preferences. A preference is global if it is about some part of one's life considered as a whole, or is about one's whole life. The *Global* versions of these theories I believe to be more plausible.

Consider this example. Knowing that you accept a Summative theory, I tell you that I am about to make your life go better. I shall inject you with an addictive drug. From now on, you will wake each morning with an extremely strong desire to have another injection of this drug. Having this desire will be in itself neither pleasant nor painful, but if the desire is not fulfilled within an hour it will then become very painful. This is no cause for concern, since I shall give you ample supplies of this drug. Every morning, you will be able at once to fulfil this desire. The injection, and its after-effects, would also be neither pleasant nor painful. You will spend the rest of your days as you do now.

What would the Summative Theories imply about this case? We can plausibly suppose that you would not welcome my proposal. You would prefer not to become addicted to this drug, even though I assure you that you will never lack supplies. We can also plausibly suppose that, if I go ahead, you will always regret that you became addicted to this drug. But it is likely that your initial desire not to become addicted, and your later regrets that you did, would not be as strong as the desires you have each morning for another injection. Given the facts as I described them, your reason to prefer not to become addicted would not be very strong. You might dislike the thought of being addicted to anything; and you would regret the minor inconvenience that would be involved in remembering always to carry with you sufficient supplies. But these desires might be far weaker than the desires you would have each morning for a fresh injection.

On the Summative Theories, if I make you an addict, I will be increasing the sum-total of your desire-fulfilment. I will be causing one of your desires not to be fulfilled: your desire not to become an addict, which, after my act, becomes a desire to be cured. But I will also be giving you an indefinite series of extremely strong desires, one each morning, all of which you can fulfil. The fulfilment of all these desires would outweigh the non-fulfilment of your desires not to become an addict, and to be cured. On the Summative Theories, by making you an addict, I will be benefiting you—making your life go better.

This conclusion is not plausible. Having these desires, and having them fulfilled, are neither pleasant nor painful. We need not be Hedonists to believe, more plausibly, that it is in no way better for you to have and to fulfil this series of strong desires.

Could the Summative Theories be revised, so as to meet this objection? Is there some feature of the addictive desires which would justify the claim that we should ignore them when we calculate the sum total of your desire-fulfilment? We might claim that they can be ignored because they are desires that you would prefer not to have. But this is not an acceptable revision. Suppose that you are in great pain. You now have a very strong desire not to be in the state that you are in. On our revised theory, a desire does not count if you would prefer not to have this desire. This must apply to your intense desire not to be in the state you are in. You would prefer not to have this desire. If you did not dislike the state you are in, it would not be painful. Since our revised theory does not count desires that you would prefer not to have, it implies, absurdly, that it cannot be bad for you to be in great pain.

There may be other revisions which could meet these objections. But it is simpler to appeal to the Global versions of both Preference-Hedonism and the Success Theory. These appeal only to someone's desires about some part of his life, considered as a whole, or about his whole life. The Global Theories give us the right answer in the case where I make you an addict. You would prefer not to become addicted, and you would later prefer to cease to be addicted. These are the only preferences to which the Global Theories appeal. They ignore your particular desires each morning for a fresh injection, since you have already considered these desires in forming your global preference.

This imagined case of addiction is in its essentials similar to countless other cases. There are countless cases in which it is true both (1) that, if someone's life went in one of two ways, this would produce a greater sum total of local desire-fulfilment, but (2) that the other alternative is what he would globally prefer, *whichever* way his actual life went.

Rather than describing another of the countless actual cases, I shall mention an imaginary case.... [Suppose that I could either] have fifty years of life of an extremely high quality, or an indefinite number of years that are barely worth living. In the first alternative, my fifty years would, on any theory, go extremely well. I would be very happy, would achieve great things, do much good, and love and be loved by many people. In the second alternative my life would always be, though not by much, worth living. There would be nothing bad about this life, and it would each day contain a few small pleasures.

On the Summative Theories, if the second life was long enough, it would be better for me. In each day within this life I have some desires about my life that are fulfilled. In the fifty years of the first alternative, there would be a very great sum of local desire-fulfilment. But this would be a finite sum, and in the end it would be outweighed by the sum of desire-fulfilment in my indefinitely long second alternative. A simpler way to put this point is this. The first alternative would be good. In the second alternative, since my life is worth living, living each extra day is good for me. If we merely add together whatever is good for me, some number of these extra days would produce the greatest total sum.

I do not believe that the second alternative would give me a better life. I therefore reject the Summative Theories. It is likely that, in both alternatives, I would globally prefer the first. Since the Global Theories would then imply that the first alternative gives me a better life, these theories seem to me more plausible.[3]

Turn now to the third kind of theory that I mentioned: the Objective List Theory. According to this theory, certain things are good or bad for people, whether or not these people would want to have the good things, or to avoid the bad things. The good things might include moral goodness, rational activity, the development of one's abilities, having children and being a good parent, knowledge, and the awareness of true beauty. The bad things might include being betrayed, manipulated, slandered, deceived, being deprived of liberty or dignity, and enjoying either sadistic pleasure, or aesthetic pleasure in what is in fact ugly.[4]

An Objective List Theorist might claim that his theory coincides with the Global version of the Success Theory. On this theory, what would make my life go best depends on what I would prefer, now and in the various alternatives, if I knew all of the relevant facts about these alternatives. An Objective List Theorist might say that the most relevant facts are those just mentioned—the facts about what would be good or bad for me. And he might claim that anyone who knew these facts would want what is good for him, and want to avoid what would be bad for him.

Even if this was true, though the Objective List Theory would coincide with the Success Theory, the two theories would remain distinct. A Success Theorist would reject this description of the coincidence. On his theory, nothing is good or bad for people *whatever* their preferences are. Something is bad for someone only when, if he knew the facts, he would want to avoid it. And the relevant facts do not include the alleged facts cited by the Objective List Theorist. On the Success Theory it is, for instance, bad for a person to be deceived if and because this is not what this person wants. The Objective List Theorist makes the reverse claim. People want not to be deceived because this is bad for them.

As these remarks imply, there is one important difference between on the one hand Preference-Hedonism and the Success Theory, and on the other hand the Objective List Theory. The first two kinds of theory give an account of self-interest which is purely descriptive—which does not appeal to facts about value. This account appeals only to what a person does and would prefer, given full knowledge of the purely non-evaluative facts about the alternatives. In contrast, the Objective List Theory appeals directly to what it claims to be facts about value.

In choosing between these theories, we must decide how much weight to give to imagined cases in which someone's fully informed preferences would be bizarre. If we can appeal to these cases, they cast doubt on both Preference-Hedonism and the Success Theory. Consider the man that Rawls imagined who wants to spend his life counting the numbers of blades of grass in different lawns. Suppose that this man knows that he could achieve great progress if instead he worked in some especially useful part of Applied Mathematics. Though he could achieve such significant results, he prefers to go on counting blades of grass. On the Success Theory, if we allow this theory to cover all imaginable cases, it could be better for this person if he counted his blades of grass rather than achieving great and useful mathematical results.

The counter-example might be more offensive. Suppose that what someone would most prefer, knowing the alternatives, is a life in which, without being detected, he causes as much pain as he can to other people. On the Success Theory, such a life would be what is best for this person.

We may be unable to accept these conclusions. Ought we therefore to abandon this theory? This is what Sidgwick* did, though those who quote him seldom notice this. He suggests that "a man's future good on the whole is what he would now desire and seek on the whole if all the consequences

* Henry Sidgwick (1838–1900) was an English philosopher whose *Methods of Ethics* (1874) strongly influenced Parfit's philosophical outlook.

of all the different lines of conduct open to him were accurately foreseen and adequately realised in imagination at the present point of time."[5] As he comments: "The notion of 'Good' thus attained has an ideal element: it is something that *is* not always actually desired and aimed at by human beings: but the ideal element is entirely interpretable in terms *of fact*, actual or hypothetical, and does not introduce any judgement of value." Sidgwick then rejects this account, claiming that what is ultimately good for someone is what this person *would* desire if his desires were in harmony with reason. This last phrase is needed, Sidgwick thought, to exclude the cases where someone's desires are irrational. He assumes that there are some things that we have good reason to desire, and others that we have good reason not to desire. These might be the things which are held by Objective List Theories to be good or bad for us.

Suppose we agree that, in some imagined cases, what someone would most want both now and later, fully knowing about the alternatives, would *not* be what would be best for him. If we accept this conclusion, it may seem that we must reject both Preference-Hedonism and the Success Theory. Perhaps, like Sidgwick, we must put constraints on what can be rationally desired.

It might be claimed instead that we can dismiss the appeal to such imagined cases. It might be claimed that what people would in fact prefer, if they knew the relevant facts, would always be something that we could accept as what is really good for them. Is this a good reply? If we agree that in the imagined cases what someone would prefer might be something that is bad for him, in these cases we have abandoned our theory. If this is so, can we defend our theory by saying that, in the actual cases, it would not go astray? I believe that this is not an adequate defence. But I shall not pursue this question here.

This objection may apply with less force to Preference-Hedonism. On this theory, what can be good or bad for someone can only be discernible features of his conscious life. These are the features that, at the time, he either wants or does not want. I asked above whether it is bad for people to be deceived because they prefer not to be, or whether they prefer not to be deceived because this is bad for them. Consider the comparable question with respect to pain. Some have claimed that pain is intrinsically bad, and that this is why we dislike it. As I have suggested, I doubt this claim. After taking certain kinds of drug, people claim that the quality of their sensations has not altered, but they no longer dislike these sensations. We would regard such drugs as effective analgesics. This suggests that the badness of a pain consists in its being disliked, and that it is not disliked because it is bad. The disagreement between these views would need much more discussion. But, if the second view is better, it is more plausible to claim that whatever someone wants or does not want to experience—however bizarre we find his desires—should be counted as being for this person truly pleasant or painful, and as being for that reason good or bad for him. (There may still be cases where it is plausible to claim that it would be bad for someone if he enjoyed certain kinds of experience; this might be claimed, for instance, about sadistic pleasure. But there may be few such cases.)

If instead we appeal to the Success Theory, we are not concerned only with the experienced quality of our conscious life. We are concerned with such things as whether we are achieving what we are trying to achieve, whether we are being deceived, and the like. When considering this theory, we can more often plausibly claim that, even if someone knew the facts, his preferences might go astray, and fail to correspond to what would be good or bad for him.

Which of these different theories should we accept? I shall not attempt an answer here. But I shall end by mentioning another theory, which might be claimed to combine what is most plausible in these conflicting theories. It is a striking fact that those who have addressed this question have disagreed so fundamentally. Many philosophers have been convinced Hedonists; many others have been as much convinced that Hedonism is a gross mistake.

Some Hedonists have reached their view as follows. They consider an opposing view, such as that which claims that what is good for someone is to have knowledge, to engage in rational activity, and to be aware of true beauty. These Hedonists ask, "Would these states of mind be good, if they brought no enjoyment, and if the person in these states of mind had not the slightest desire that they continue?" Since they answer No, they conclude that the value of these states of mind must lie in their being liked, and in their arousing a desire that they continue.

This reasoning assumes that the value of a whole is just the sum of the value of its parts. If we remove the part to which the Hedonist appeals, what is left seems to have no value, hence Hedonism is the truth.

Suppose instead, more plausibly, that the value of a whole may not be the mere sum of the value of its parts. We might then claim that what is best for people is a composite. It is not just their being in the conscious states that they want to be in. Nor is it just their having knowledge, engaging in rational activity, being aware of true beauty, and the like. What is good for someone is neither just what Hedonists claim, nor just what is claimed by Objective List Theorists. We might believe that if we had *either* of these, *without the other*, what we had would have little or no value. We might claim, for example, that what is good or bad for someone is to have knowledge, to be engaged in rational activity, to experience mutual love, and to be aware of beauty, while strongly wanting just these things. On this view, each side in this disagreement saw only half of the truth. Each put forward as sufficient something that was only necessary. Pleasure with many other kinds of object has no value. And, if they are entirely devoid of pleasure, there is no value in knowledge, rational activity, love, or the awareness of beauty. What is of value, or is good for someone, is to have both; to be engaged in these activities, and to be strongly wanting to be so engaged.[6]

NOTES

1. J.P. Griffin, "Are there Incommensurable Values?," *Philosophy and Public Affairs* 7:1, Fall 1977.
2. See "Prudence" by P. Bricker, *the Journal of Philosophy*, July 1980.
3. See again Bricker.
4. See, for example, G. E. Moore *Principia Ethica,* Cambridge University Press, 1903, and W. D. Ross, *The Foundations of Ethics*, Oxford, The Clarendon Press, 1939.
5. H. Sidgwick, *The Methods of Ethics,* London, Macmillan, 1907, pp. 111–12.
6. See R. B. Edwards, *Pleasures and Pains* (Ithaca, NY, Cornell University Press, 1979) throughout. A similar suggestion is made by Plato in the *Philebus*. For a deeper discussion about self-interest, see J. Griffin, *Well-Being* (Oxford University Press, 1986).

The Absurd

THOMAS NAGEL

Thomas Nagel (1937–) is a Serbian-born American philosopher who has taught at Princeton University and now teaches at New York University. He is renowned for his accessible and insightful writing, having published widely on topics in the philosophy of mind, ethics, and political philosophy; additional selections from his writings can be found in the "Death" and "Mind and Language" sections.

In this essay, originally published in a philosophy journal in 1971, Nagel explores the question of in what sense life can be understood as absurd.

Most people feel on occasion that life is absurd, and some feel it vividly and continually. Yet the reasons usually offered in defense of this conviction are patently inadequate: they *could* not really explain why life is absurd. Why then do they provide a natural expression for the sense that it is?

From *Mortal Questions* by Thomas Nagel. Copyright © 1979. Reprinted with the permission of Cambridge University Press.

I

Consider some examples. It is often remarked that nothing we do now will matter in a million years. But if that is true, then by the same token, nothing that will be the case in a million years matters now. In particular, it does not matter now that in a million years nothing we do now will matter. Moreover, even if what we did now *were* going to matter in a million years, how could that keep our present concerns from being absurd? If their mattering now is not enough to accomplish that, how would it help if they mattered a million years from now?

Whether what we do now will matter in a million years could make the crucial difference only if its mattering in a million years depended on its mattering, period. But then to deny that whatever happens now will matter in a million years is to beg the question against its mattering, period; for in that sense one cannot know that it will not matter in a million years whether (for example) someone now is happy or miserable, without knowing that it does not matter, period.

What we say to convey the absurdity of our lives often has to do with space or time: we are tiny specks in the infinite vastness of the universe; our lives are mere instants even on a geological time scale, let alone a cosmic one; we will all be dead any minute. But of course none of these evident facts can be what *makes* life absurd, if it is absurd. For suppose we lived for ever; would not a life that is absurd if it lasts seventy years be infinitely absurd if it lasted through eternity? And if our lives are absurd given our present size, why would they be any less absurd if we filled the universe (either because we were larger or because the universe was smaller)? Reflection on our minuteness and brevity appears to be intimately connected with the sense that life is meaningless; but it is not clear what the connection is.

Another inadequate argument is that because we are going to die, all chains of justification must leave off in mid-air: one studies and works to earn money to pay for clothing, housing, entertainment, food, to sustain oneself from year to year, perhaps to support a family and pursue a career—but to what final end? All of it is an elaborate journey leading nowhere. (One will also have some effect on other people's lives, but that simply reproduces the problem, for they will die too.)

There are several replies to this argument. First, life does not consist of a sequence of activities each of which has as its purpose some later member of the sequence. Chains of justification come repeatedly to an end within life, and whether the process as a whole can be justified has no bearing on the finality of these end-points. No further justification is needed to make it reasonable to take aspirin for a headache, attend an exhibition of the work of a painter one admires, or stop a child from putting his hand on a hot stove. No larger context or further purpose is needed to prevent these acts from being pointless.

Even if someone wished to supply a further justification for pursuing all the things in life that are commonly regarded as self-justifying, that justification would have to end somewhere too. If *nothing* can justify unless it is justified in terms of something outside itself, which is also justified, then an infinite regress results, and no chain of justification can be complete. Moreover, if a finite chain of reasons cannot justify anything, what could be accomplished by an infinite chain, each link of which must be justified by something outside itself?

Since justifications must come to an end somewhere, nothing is gained by denying that they end where they appear to, within life—or by trying to subsume the multiple, often trivial ordinary justifications of action under a single, controlling life scheme. We can be satisfied more easily than that. In fact, through its misrepresentation of the process of justification, the argument makes a vacuous demand. It insists that the reasons available within life are incomplete, but suggests thereby that all reasons that come to an end are incomplete. This makes it impossible to supply any reasons at all.

The standard arguments for absurdity appear therefore to fail as arguments. Yet I believe they attempt to express something that is difficult to state, but fundamentally correct.

II

In ordinary life a situation is absurd when it includes a conspicuous discrepancy between pretension or aspiration and reality: someone gives a complicated speech in support of a motion that has already been passed; a notorious criminal is made president of a major philanthropic foundation; you declare your love over the telephone to a recorded announcement; as you are being knighted, your pants fall down.

When a person finds himself in an absurd situation, he will usually attempt to change it, by modifying his aspirations, or by trying to bring reality into better accord with them, or by removing himself from the situation entirely. We are not always willing or able to extricate ourselves from a position whose absurdity has become clear to us. Nevertheless, it is usually possible to imagine some change that would remove the absurdity—whether or not we can or will implement it. The sense that life as a whole is absurd arises when we perceive, perhaps dimly, an inflated pretension or aspiration which is inseparable from the continuation of human life and which makes its absurdity inescapable, short of escape from life itself.

Many people's lives are absurd, temporarily or permanently, for conventional reasons having to do with their particular ambitions, circumstances, and personal relations. If there is a philosophical sense of absurdity, however, it must arise from the perception of something universal—some respect in which pretension and reality inevitably clash for us all. This condition is supplied, I shall argue, by the collison between the seriousness with which we take our lives and the perpetual possibility of regarding everything about which we are serious as arbitrary, or open to doubt.

We cannot live human lives without energy and attention, nor without making choices which show that we take some things more seriously than others. Yet we have always available a point of view outside the particular form of our lives, from which the seriousness appears gratuitous. These two inescapable viewpoints collide in us, and that is what makes life absurd. It is absurd because we ignore the doubts that we know cannot be settled, continuing to live with nearly undiminished seriousness in spite of them.

This analysis requires defense in two respects: first as regards the unavoidability of seriousness; second as regards the inescapability of doubt.

We take ourselves seriously whether we lead serious lives or not and whether we are concerned primarily with fame, pleasure, virtues, luxury, triumph, beauty, justice, knowledge, salvation, or mere survival. If we take other people seriously and devote ourselves to them, that only multiplies the problem. Human life is full of effort, plans, calculation, success and failure: we *pursue* our lives, with varying degrees of sloth and energy.

It would be different if we could not step back and reflect on the process, but were merely led from impulse to impulse without self-consciousness. But human beings do not act solely on impulse. They are prudent, they reflect, they weigh consequences, they ask whether what they are doing is worth while. Not only are their lives full of particular choices that hang together in larger activities with temporal structure: they also decide in the broadest terms what to pursue and what to avoid, what the priorities among their various aims should be, and what kind of people they want to be or become. Some men are faced with such choices by the large decisions they make from time to time; some merely by reflection on the course their lives are taking as the product of countless small decisions. They decide whom to marry, what profession to follow, whether to join the Country Club, or the Resistance; or they may just wonder why they go on being salesmen or academics or taxi drivers, and then stop thinking about it after a certain period of inconclusive reflection.

Although they may be motivated from act to act by those immediate needs with which life presents them, they allow the process to continue by adhering to the general system of habits and the form of life in which such motives have their place—or perhaps only by clinging to life itself. They spend enormous quantities of energy, risk, and calculation on the details. Think of how an ordinary individual sweats over his appearance, his health, his sex life, his emotional honesty, his social utility, his self-knowledge, the quality of his ties with family, colleagues, and friends, how well he does his job, whether he understands the world and what is going on in it. Leading a human life is a full-time occupation, to which everyone devotes decades of intense concern.

This fact is so obvious that it is hard to find it extraordinary and important. Each of us lives his own life—lives with himself twenty-four hours a day. What else is he supposed to do—live someone else's life? Yet humans have the special capacity to step back and survey themselves, and the lives to which they are committed, with that detached amazement which comes from watching an ant struggle up a heap of sand. Without developing the illusion that they are able to escape from their highly specific and idiosyncratic position, they can view it *sub specie aeternitatis** and the view is at once sobering and comical.

The crucial backward step is not taken by asking for still another justification in the chain, and failing to get it. The objections to that line of attack have already been stated; justifications come to an end. But this is precisely what provides universal doubt with its object. We step back to find that the whole system of justification and criticism, which controls our choices and supports our claims to rationality, rests on responses and habits that we never question, that we should not know how to defend without circularity, and to which we shall continue to adhere even after they are called into question.

The things we do or want without reasons, and without requiring reasons—the things that define what is a reason for us and what is not—are the starting points of our skepticism. We see ourselves from outside, and all the contingency and specificity of our aims and pursuits become clear. Yet when we take this view and recognize what we do as arbitrary, it does not disengage us from life, and there lies our absurdity: not in the fact that such an external view can be taken of us, but in the fact that we ourselves can take it, without ceasing to be the persons whose ultimate concerns are so coolly regarded.

III

One may try to escape the position by seeking broader ultimate concerns, from which it is impossible to step back—the idea being that absurdity results because what we take seriously is something small and insignificant and individual. Those seeking to supply their lives with meaning usually envision a role or function in something larger than themselves. They therefore seek fulfillment in service to society, the state, the revolution, the progress of history, the advance of science, or religion and the glory of God.

But a role in some larger enterprise cannot confer significance unless that enterprise is itself significant. And its significance must come back to what we can understand, or it will not even appear to give us what we are seeking. If we learned that we were being raised to provide food for other creatures fond of human flesh, who planned to turn us into cutlets before we got too stringy—even if we learned that the human race had been developed by animal breeders precisely for this purpose—that would still not give our lives meaning, for two reasons. First, we would still be in the dark as to the significance of the lives of those other beings; second, although we might acknowledge that this culinary role would make our lives meaningful to them, it is not clear how it would make them meaningful to us.

Admittedly, the usual form of service to a higher being is different from this. One is supposed to behold and partake of the glory of God, for example, in a way in which chickens do not share in the glory of coq au vin. The same is true of service to a state, a movement, or a revolution. People can come to feel, when they are part of something bigger, that it is part of them too. They worry less about what is peculiar to themselves, but identify enough with the larger enterprise to find their role in it fulfilling.

However, any such larger purpose can be put in doubt in the same way that the aims of an individual life can be, and for the same reasons. It is as legitimate to find ultimate justification there as to find it earlier, among the details of individual life. But this does not alter the fact that justifications come to an end when we are content to have them end—when we do not find it necessary to look any further. If we can step back from the purposes of individual life and doubt their point, we can step back also from the progress of human history, or of science, or the success of a society, or the kingdom, power, and glory of God, and put all these things into question in the same way. What seems to us to confer meaning, justification, significance, does so in virtue of the fact that we need no more reasons after a certain point.

* *Sub specie aeternitatis* is Latin for "under the aspect of eternity."

What makes doubt inescapable with regard to the limited aims of individual life also makes it inescapable with regard to any larger purpose that encourages the sense that life is meaningful. Once the fundamental doubt has begun, it cannot be laid to rest.

Camus maintains in *The Myth of Sisyphus* that the absurd arises because the world fails to meet our demands for meaning. This suggests that the world might satisfy those demands if it were different. But now we can see that this is not the case. There does not appear to be any conceivable world (containing us) about which unsettlable doubts could not arise. Consequently the absurdity of our situation derives not from a collison between our expectations and the world, but from a collision within ourselves.

IV

It may be objected that the standpoint from which these doubts are supposed to be felt does not exist—that if we take the recommended backward step we will land on thin air, without any basis for judgment about the natural responses we are supposed to be surveying. If we retain our usual standards of what is important, then questions about the significance of what we are doing with our lives will be answerable in the usual way. But if we do not, then those questions can mean nothing to us, since there is no longer any content to the idea of what matters, and hence no content to the idea that nothing does.

But this objection misconceives the nature of the backward step. It is not supposed to give us an understanding of what is *really* important, so that we see by contrast that our lives are insignificant. We never, in the course of these reflections, abandon the ordinary standards that guide our lives. We merely observe them in operation, and recognize that if they are called into question we can justify them only by reference to themselves, uselessly. We adhere to them because of the way we are put together; what seems to us important or serious or valuable would not seem so if we were differently constituted.

In ordinary life, to be sure, we do not judge a situation absurd unless we have in mind some standards of seriousness, significance, or harmony with which the absurd can be contrasted. This contrast is not implied by the philosophical judgment of absurdity, and that might be thought to make the concept unsuitable for the expression of such judgments. This is not so, however, for the philosophical judgment depends on another contrast which makes it a natural extension from more ordinary cases. It departs from them only in contrasting the pretensions of life with a larger context in which *no* standards can be discovered, rather than with a context from which alternative, overriding standards may be applied.

V

In this respect, as in others, philosophical perception of the absurd resembles epistemological skepticism. In both cases the final, philosophical doubt is not contrasted with any unchallenged certainties, though it is arrived at by extrapolation from examples of doubt within the system of evidence or justification, where a contrast with other certainties *is* implied. In both cases our limitedness joins with a capacity to transcend those limitations in thought (thus seeing them as limitations, and as inescapable).

Skepticism begins when we include ourselves in the world about which we claim knowledge. We notice that certain types of evidence convince us, that we are content to allow justifications of belief to come to an end at certain points, that we feel we know many things even without knowing or having grounds for believing the denial of others which, if true, would make what we claim to know false.

For example, I know that I am looking at a piece of paper, although I have no adequate grounds for claiming I know that I am not dreaming; and if I am dreaming then I am not looking at a piece of paper. Here an ordinary conception of how appearance may diverge from reality is employed to show that we take our world largely for granted; the certainty that we are not dreaming cannot be justified except circularly, in terms of those very appearances which are being put in doubt. It is somewhat far-fetched to suggest I may be dreaming; but the possibility is only illustrative. It reveals that our claims to knowledge depend on our not feeling it necessary to exclude certain incompatible alternatives, and the dreaming possibility or the total-hallucination possibility are just representatives for limitless possibilities most of which we cannot even conceive.[1]

Once we have taken the backward step to an abstract view of our whole system of beliefs, evidence, and justification, and seen that it works only, despite its pretensions, by taking the world largely for granted, we are *not* in a position to contrast all these appearances with an alternative reality. We cannot shed our ordinary responses, and if we could it would leave us with no means of conceiving a reality of any kind.

It is the same in the practical domain. We do not step outside our lives to a new vantage point from which we see what is really, objectively significant. We continue to take life largely for granted while seeing that all our decisions and certainties are possible only because there is a great deal we do not bother to rule out.

Both epistemological skepticism and a sense of the absurd can be reached via initial doubts posed within systems of evidence and justification that we accept, and can be stated without violence to our ordinary concepts. We can ask not only why we should believe there is a floor under us, but also why we should believe the evidence of our senses at all—and at some point the framable questions will have outlasted the answers. Similarly, we can ask not only why we should take aspirin, but why we should take trouble over our own comfort at all. The fact that we shall take the aspirin without waiting for an answer to this last question does not show that it is an unreal question. We shall also continue to believe there is a floor under us without waiting for an answer to the other question. In both cases it is this unsupported natural confidence that generates skeptical doubts; so it cannot be used to settle them.

Philosophical skepticism does not cause us to abandon our ordinary beliefs, but it lends them a peculiar flavor. After acknowledging that their truth is incompatible with possibilities that we have no grounds for believing do not obtain—apart from grounds in those very beliefs which we have called into question—we return to our familiar convictions with a certain irony and resignation. Unable to abandon the natural responses on which they depend, we take them back, like a spouse who has run off with someone else and then decided to return; but we regard them differently (not that the new attitude is necessarily inferior to the old, in either case).

The same situation obtains after we have put in question the seriousness with which we take our lives and human life in general and have looked at ourselves without presuppositions. We then return to our lives, as we must, but our seriousness is laced with irony. Not that irony enables us to escape the absurd. It is useless to mutter: "Life is meaningless; life is meaningless . . ." as an accompaniment to everything we do. In continuing to live and work and strive, we take ourselves seriously in action no matter what we say.

What sustains us, in belief as in action, is not reason or justification, but something more basic than these—for we go on in the same way even after we are convinced that the reasons have given out.[2] If we tried to rely entirely on reason, and pressed it hard, our lives and beliefs would collapse—a form of madness that may actually occur if the inertial force of taking the world and life for granted is somehow lost. If we lose our grip on that, reason will not give it back to us.

VI

In viewing ourselves from a perspective broader than we can occupy in the flesh, we become spectators of our own lives. We cannot do very much as pure spectators of our own lives, so we continue to lead them, and devote ourselves to what we are able at the same time to view as no more than a curiosity, like the ritual of an alien religion.

This explains why the sense of absurdity finds its natural expression in those bad arguments with which the discussion began. Reference to our small size and short lifespan and to the fact that all of mankind will eventually vanish without a trace are metaphors for the backward step which permits us to regard ourselves from without and to find the particular form of our lives curious and slightly surprising. By feigning a nebula's-eye view, we illustrate the capacity to see ourselves without presuppositions, as arbitrary, idiosyncratic, highly specific occupants of the world, one of countless possible forms of life.

Before turning to the question whether the absurdity of our lives is something to be regretted and if possible escaped, let me consider what would have to be given up in order to avoid it.

Why is the life of a mouse not absurd? The orbit of the moon is not absurd either, but that involves no strivings or aims at all. A mouse, however, has to work to stay alive. Yet he is not absurd, because he lacks the capacities for self-consciousness and self-transcendence that would enable him to see that he is only a mouse. If that *did* happen, his life would become absurd, since self-awareness would not make him cease to be a mouse and would not enable him to rise above his mousely strivings. Bringing his new-found self-consciousness with him, he would have to return to his meager yet frantic life, full of doubts that he was unable to answer, but also full of purposes that he was unable to abandon.

Given that the transcendental step is natural to us humans, can we avoid absurdity by refusing to take that step and remaining entirely within our sublunar lives? Well, we cannot refuse consciously, for to do that we would have to be aware of the viewpoint we were refusing to adopt. The only way to avoid the relevant self-consciousness would be either never to attain it or to forget it—neither of which can be achieved by the will.

On the other hand, it is possible to expend effort on an attempt to destroy the other component of the absurd—abandoning one's earthly, individual, human life in order to identify as completely as possible with that universal viewpoint from which human life seems arbitrary and trivial. (This appears to be the ideal of certain Oriental religions.) If one succeeds, then one will not have to drag the superior awareness through a strenuous mundane life, and absurdity will be diminished.

However, insofar as this self-etiolation is the result of effort, will-power, asceticism, and so forth, it requires that one take oneself seriously as an individual—that one be willing to take considerable trouble to avoid being creaturely and absurd. Thus one may undermine the aim of unworldliness by pursuing it too vigorously. Still, if someone simply allowed his individual, animal nature to drift and respond to impulse, without making the pursuit of its needs a central conscious aim, then he might, at considerable dissociative cost, achieve a life that was less absurd than most. It would not be a meaningful life either, of course; but it would not involve the engagement of a transcendent awareness in the assiduous pursuit of mundane goals. And that is the main condition of absurdity—the dragooning of an unconvinced transcendent consciousness into the service of an immanent, limited enterprise like a human life.

The final escape is suicide; but before adopting any hasty solutions, it would be wise to consider carefully whether the absurdity of our existence truly presents us with a *problem*, to which some solution must be found—a way of dealing with *prima facie* disaster. That is certainly the attitude with which Camus approaches the issue, and it gains support from the fact that we are all eager to escape from absurd situations on a smaller scale.

Camus—not on uniformly good grounds—rejects suicide and the other solutions he regards as escapist. What he recommends is defiance or scorn. We can salvage our dignity, he appears to believe, by shaking a fist at the world which is deaf to our pleas, and continuing to live in spite of it. This will not make our lives un-absurd, but it will lend them a certain nobility.[3]

This seems to me romantic and slightly self-pitying. Our absurdity warrants neither that much distress nor that much defiance. At the risk of falling into romanticism by a different route, I would argue that absurdity is one of the most human things about us: a manifestation of our most advanced and interesting characteristics. Like skepticism in epistemology, it is possible only because we possess a certain kind of insight—the capacity to transcend ourselves in thought.

If a sense of the absurd is a way of perceiving our true situation (even though the situation is not absurd until the perception arises), then what reason can we have to resent or escape it? Like the capacity for epistemological skepticism, it results from the ability to understand our human limitations. It need not be a matter for agony unless we make it so. Nor need it evoke a defiant contempt of fate that allows us to feel brave or proud. Such dramatics, even if carried on in private, betray a failure to appreciate the cosmic unimportance of the situation. If *sub specie aeternitatis* there is no reason to believe that anything matters, then that does not matter either, and we can approach our absurd lives with irony instead of heroism or despair.

NOTES

1. I am aware that skepticism about the external world is widely thought to have been refuted, but I have remained convinced of its irrefutability since being exposed at Berkeley to Thompson Clarke's largely unpublished ideas on the subject.
2. As Hume says in a famous passage of the *Treatise*: "Most fortunately it happens, that since reason is incapable of dispelling these clouds, nature herself suffices to that purpose, and cures me of this philosophical melancholy and delirium, either by relaxing this bent of mind, or by some avocation, and lively impression of my senses, which obliterate all these chimeras. I dine, I play a game of backgammon, I converse, and am merry with my friends; and when after three or four hours amusement, I would return to these speculations, they appear so cold, and strain'd, and ridiculous, that I cannot find in my heart to enter into them any farther" (bk I, pt IV, sect. 7; Selby-Bigge, p. 269).
3. "Sisyphus, proletarian of the gods, powerless and rebellious, knows the whole extent of his wretched condition: it is what he thinks of during his descent. The lucidity that was to constitute his torture at the same time crowns his victory. There is no fate that cannot be surmounted by scorn" (*The Myth of Sisyphus*, trans. Justin O'Brien (New York: Vintage, 1959), p. 90; first published, Paris: Gallimard, 1942).

B DEATH

Death

THOMAS NAGEL

Thomas Nagel (1937–) is a Serbian-born American philosopher who has taught at Princeton University and now teaches at New York University. He is renowned for his accessible and insightful writing, having published widely on topics in the philosophy of mind, ethics, and political philosophy; additional selections from his writings can be found in the "Life" and "Mind and Language" sections.

In this essay, originally published in a philosophy journal in 1970, Nagel considers the question of why death is so widely considered to be such a terrible misfortune.

If death is the unequivocal and permanent end of our existence, the question arises whether it is a bad thing to die.

There is conspicuous disagreement about the matter: some people think death is dreadful; others have no objection to death per se, though they hope their own will be neither premature nor painful. Those in the former category tend to think those in the latter are blind to the obvious, while the latter suppose the former to be prey to some sort of confusion. On the one hand it can be said that life is all we have and the loss of it is the greatest loss we can sustain. On the other hand it may be objected that death deprives this supposed loss of its subject, and that if we realize that death is not an unimaginable condition of the persisting person, but a mere blank, we will see that it can have no value whatever, positive or negative.

Since I want to leave aside the question whether we are, or might be, immortal in some form, I shall simply use the word "death" and its cognates in this discussion to mean *permanent* death, unsupplemented by any form of conscious survival. I want to ask whether death is in itself an evil; and how great an evil, and of what kind, it might be. The question should be of interest even to those who believe in some form of immortality, for one's attitude toward immortality must depend in part on one's attitude toward death.

If death is an evil at all, it cannot be because of its positive features, but only because of what it deprives us of. I shall try to deal with the difficulties surrounding the natural view that death is an evil because it brings to an end all the goods that life contains. We need not give an account of these goods here, except to observe that some of them, like perception, desire, activity, and thought, are so general as to be constitutive of human life. They are widely regarded as formidable benefits in themselves, despite the fact that they are conditions of misery as well as of happiness, and that a sufficient quantity of more particular evils can perhaps outweigh them.

From *Mortal Questions* by Thomas Nagel. Copyright © 1979. Reprinted with the permission of Oxford University Press.

That is what is meant, I think, by the allegation that it is good simply to be alive, even if one is undergoing terrible experiences. The situation is roughly this: There are elements which, if added to one's experience, make life better; there are other elements which, if added to one's experience, make life worse. But what remains when these are set aside is not merely *neutral*: it is emphatically positive. Therefore life is worth living even when the bad elements of experience are plentiful, and the good ones too meager to outweigh the bad ones on their own. The additional positive weight is supplied by experience itself, rather than by any of its contents.

I shall not discuss the value that one person's life or death may have for others, or its objective value, but only the value it has for the person who is its subject. That seems to me the primary case, and the case which presents the greatest difficulties. Let me add only two observations. First, the value of life and its contents does not attach to mere organic survival: almost everyone would be indifferent (other things equal) between immediate death and immediate coma followed by death twenty years later without reawakening. And second, like most goods, this can be multiplied by time: more is better than less. The added quantities need not be temporally continuous (though continuity has its social advantages). People are attracted to the possibility of long-term suspended animation or freezing, followed by the resumption of conscious life, because they can regard it from within simply as a *continuation* of their present life. If these techniques are ever perfected, what from outside appeared as a dormant interval of three hundred years could be experienced by the subject as nothing more than a sharp discontinuity in the character of his experiences. I do not deny, of course, that this has its own disadvantages. Family and friends may have died in the meantime; the language may have changed; the comforts of social, geographical, and cultural familiarity would be lacking. Nevertheless these inconveniences would not obliterate the basic advantage of continued, though discontinuous, existence.

If we turn from what is good about life to what is bad about death, the case is completely different. Essentially, though there may be problems about their specification, what we find desirable in life are certain states, conditions, or types of activity. It is *being* alive, *doing* certain things, having certain experiences, that we consider good. But if death is an evil, it is the *loss of life,* rather than the state of being dead, or nonexistent, or unconscious, that is objectionable.[1] This asymmetry is important. If it is good to be alive, that advantage can be attributed to a person at each point of his life. It is a good of which Bach had more than Schubert, simply because he lived longer. Death, however, is not an evil of which Shakespeare has so far received a larger portion than Proust.* If death is a disadvantage, it is not easy to say when a man suffers it.

There are two other indications that we do not object to death merely because it involves long periods of nonexistence. First, as has been mentioned, most of us would not regard the *temporary* suspension of life, even for substantial intervals, as in itself a misfortune. If it ever happens that people can be frozen without reduction of the conscious lifespan, it will be inappropriate to pity those who are temporarily out of circulation. Second, none of us existed before we were born (or conceived), but few regard that as a misfortune. I shall have more to say about this later.

The point that death is not regarded as an unfortunate *state* enables us to refute a curious but very common suggestion about the origin of the fear of death. It is often said that those who object to death have made the mistake of trying to imagine what it is like to *be* dead. It is alleged that the failure to realize that this task is logically impossible (for the banal reason that there is nothing to imagine) leads to the conviction that death is a mysterious and therefore terrifying prospective *state*. But this diagnosis is evidently false, for it is just as impossible to imagine being totally unconscious as to imagine being dead (though it is easy enough to imagine oneself, from the outside, in either of those conditions). Yet people who are averse to death are not usually averse to unconsciousness (so long as it does not entail a substantial cut in the total duration of waking life).

If we are to make sense of the view that to die is bad, it must be on the ground that life is a good

* Marcel Proust (1871–1922) was a famous French novelist and essayist best known for his seven-volume novel *Remembrance of Things Past* (also translated as *In Search of Lost Time*).

and death is the corresponding deprivation or loss, bad not because of any positive features but because of the desirability of what it removes. We must now turn to the serious difficulties which this hypothesis raises, difficulties about loss and privation in general, and about death in particular.

Essentially, there are three types of problem. First, doubt may be raised whether *anything* can be bad for a man without being positively unpleasant to him: specifically, it may be doubted that there are any evils which consist merely in the deprivation or absence of possible goods, and which do not depend on someone's *minding* that deprivation. Second, there are special difficulties, in the case of death, about how the supposed misfortune is to be assigned to a subject at all. There is doubt both as to *who* its subject is, and as to *when* he undergoes it. So long as a person exists, he has not yet died, and once he has died, he no longer exists; so there seems to be no time when death, if it is a misfortune, can be ascribed to its unfortunate subject. The third type of difficulty concerns the asymmetry, mentioned above, between our attitudes to posthumous and prenatal nonexistence. How can the former be bad if the latter is not?

It should be recognized that if these are valid objections to counting death as an evil, they will apply to many other supposed evils as well. The first type of objection is expressed in general form by the common remark that what you don't know can't hurt you. It means that even if a man is betrayed by his friends, ridiculed behind his back, and despised by people who treat him politely to his face, none of it can be counted as a misfortune for him so long as he does not suffer as a result. It means that a man is not injured if his wishes are ignored by the executor of his will, or if, after his death, the belief becomes current that all the literary works on which his fame rests were really written by his brother, who died in Mexico at the age of 28. It seems to me worth asking what assumptions about good and evil lead to these drastic restrictions.

All the questions have something to do with time. There certainly are goods and evils of a simple kind (including some pleasures and pains) which a person possesses at a given time simply in virtue of his condition at that time. But this is not true of all the things we regard as good or bad for a man. Often we need to know his history to tell whether something is a misfortune or not; this applies to ills like deterioration, deprivation, and damage. Sometimes his experiential *state* is relatively unimportant—as in the case of a man who wastes his life in the cheerful pursuit of a method of communicating with asparagus plants. Someone who holds that all goods and evils must be temporally assignable states of the person may of course try to bring difficult cases into line by pointing to the pleasure or pain that more complicated goods and evils cause. Loss, betrayal, deception, and ridicule are on this view bad because people suffer when they learn of them. But it should be asked how our ideas of human value would have to be constituted to accommodate these cases directly instead. One advantage of such an account might be that it would enable us to explain *why* the discovery of these misfortunes causes suffering—in a way that makes it reasonable. For the natural view is that the discovery of betrayal makes us unhappy because it is bad to be betrayed—not that betrayal is bad because its discovery makes us unhappy.

It therefore seems to me worth exploring the position that most good and ill fortune has as its subject a person identified by his history and his possibilities, rather than merely by his categorical state of the moment—and that while this subject can be exactly located in a sequence of places and times, the same is not necessarily true of the goods and ills that befall him.[2]

These ideas can be illustrated by an example of deprivation whose severity approaches that of death. Suppose an intelligent person receives a brain injury that reduces him to the mental condition of a contented infant, and that such desires as remain to him can be satisfied by a custodian, so that he is free from care. Such a development would be widely regarded as a severe misfortune, not only for his friends and relations, or for society, but also, and primarily, for the person himself. This does not mean that a contented infant is unfortunate. The intelligent adult who has been *reduced* to this condition is the subject of the misfortune. He is the one we pity, though of course he does not mind his condition—there is some doubt, in fact, whether he can be said to exist any longer.

The view that such a man has suffered a misfortune is open to the same objections which have been raised in regard to death. He does not mind his condition. It is in fact the same condition he was in at the age of three months, except that he is bigger. If we did not pity him then, why pity him now; in any case, who is there to pity? The intelligent adult has disappeared, and for a creature like the one before us, happiness consists in a full stomach and a dry diaper.

If these objections are invalid, it must be because they rest on a mistaken assumption about the temporal relation between the subject of a misfortune and the circumstances which constitute it. If, instead of concentrating exclusively on the oversized baby before us, we consider the person he was, and the person he *could* be now, then his reduction to this state and the cancellation of his natural adult development constitute a perfectly intelligible catastrophe.

This case should convince us that it is arbitrary to restrict the goods and evils that can befall a man to nonrelational properties ascribable to him at particular times. As it stands, that restriction excludes not only such cases of gross degeneration, but also a good deal of what is important about success and failure, and other features of a life that have the character of processes. I believe we can go further, however. There are goods and evils which are irreducibly relational; they are features of the relations between a person, with spatial and temporal boundaries of the usual sort, and circumstances which may not coincide with him either in space or in time. A man's life includes much that does not take place within the boundaries of his body and his mind, and what happens to him can include much that does not take place within the boundaries of his life. These boundaries are commonly crossed by the misfortunes of being deceived, or despised, or betrayed. (If this is correct, there is a simple account of what is wrong with breaking a deathbed promise. It is an injury to the dead man. For certain purposes it is possible to regard time as just another type of distance). The case of mental degeneration shows us an evil that depends on a contrast between the reality and the possible alternatives. A man is the subject of good and evil as much because he has hopes which may or may not be fulfilled, or possibilities which may or may not be realized, as because of his capacity to suffer and enjoy. If death is an evil, it must be accounted for in these terms, and the impossibility of locating it within life should not trouble us.

When a man dies we are left with his corpse, and while a corpse can suffer the kind of mishap that may occur to an article of furniture, it is not a suitable object for pity. The man, however, is. He has lost his life, and if he had not died, he would have continued to live it, and to possess whatever good there is in living. If we apply to death the account suggested for the case of dementia, we shall say that although the spatial and temporal locations of the individual who suffered the loss are clear enough, the misfortune itself cannot be so easily located. One must be content just to state that his life is over and there will never be any more of it. That *fact*, rather than his past or present condition, constitutes his misfortune, if it is one. Nevertheless if there is a loss, someone must suffer it, and *he* must have existence and specific spatial and temporal location even if the loss itself does not. The fact that Beethoven had no children may have been a cause of regret to him, or a sad thing for the world, but it cannot be described as a misfortune for the children that he never had. All of us, I believe, are fortunate to have been born. But unless good and ill can be assigned to an embryo, or even to an unconnected pair of gametes, it cannot be said that not to be born is a misfortune. (That is a factor to be considered in deciding whether abortion and contraception are akin to murder.)

This approach also provides a solution to the problem of temporal asymmetry, pointed out by Lucretius.* He observed that no one finds it disturbing to contemplate the eternity preceding his own birth, and he took this to show that it must be irrational to fear death, since death is simply the mirror image of the prior abyss. That is not true, however, and the difference between the two explains why it

* Lucretius (circa 94 BCE–49 BCE) was a Roman philosopher and exponent of the views of Epicurus, whose philosophical writings stressed the importance of freeing oneself from the fear of death.

is reasonable to regard them differently. It is true that both the time before a man's birth and the time after his death are times when he does not exist. But the time after his death is time of which his death deprives him. It is time in which, had he not died then, he would be alive. Therefore any death entails the loss of *some* life that its victim would have led had he not died at that or any earlier point. We know perfectly well what it would be for him to have had it instead of losing it, and there is no difficulty in identifying the loser.

But we cannot say that the time prior to a man's birth is time in which he would have lived had he been born not then but earlier. For aside from the brief margin permitted by premature labor, he *could* not have been born earlier: anyone born substantially earlier than he was would have been someone else. Therefore the time prior to his birth is not time in which his subsequent birth prevents him from living. His birth, when it occurs, does not entail the loss to him of any life whatever.

The direction of time is crucial in assigning possibilities to people or other individuals. Distinct possible lives of a single person can diverge from a common beginning, but they cannot converge to a common conclusion from diverse beginnings. (The latter would represent not a set of different possible lives of one individual, but a set of distinct possible individuals, whose lives have identical conclusions.) Given an identifiable individual, countless possibilities for his continued existence are imaginable, and we can clearly conceive of what it would be for him to go on existing indefinitely. However inevitable it is that this will not come about, its possibility is still that of the continuation of a good for him, if life is the good we take it to be.[3]

We are left, therefore, with the question whether the nonrealization of this possibility is in every case a misfortune, or whether it depends on what can naturally be hoped for. This seems to me the most serious difficulty with the view that death is always an evil. Even if we can dispose of the objections against admitting misfortune that is not experienced, or cannot be assigned to a definite time in the person's life, we still have to set some limits on *how* possible a possibility must be for its nonrealization to be a misfortune (or good fortune, should the possibility be a bad one). The death of Keats* at 24 is generally regarded as tragic; that of Tolstoy† at 82 is not. Although they will both be dead for ever, Keats' death deprived him of many years of life which were allowed to Tolstoy; so in a clear sense Keats' loss was greater (though not in the sense standardly employed in mathematical comparison between infinite quantities). However, this does not prove that Tolstoy's loss was insignificant. Perhaps we record an objection only to evils which are gratuitously added to the inevitable; the fact that it is worse to die at 24 than at 82 does not imply that it is not a terrible thing to die at 82, or even at 806. The question is whether we can regard as a misfortune any limitation, like mortality, that is normal to the species. Blindness or near-blindness is not a misfortune for a mole, nor would it be for a man, if that were the natural condition of the human race.

The trouble is that life familiarizes us with the goods of which death deprives us. We are already able to appreciate them, as a mole is not able to appreciate vision. If we put aside doubts about their status as goods and grant that their quantity is in part a function of their duration, the question remains whether death, no matter when it occurs, can be said to deprive its victim of what is in the relevant sense a possible continuation of life.

The situation is an ambiguous one. Observed from without, human beings obviously have a natural lifespan and cannot live much longer than a hundred years. A man's sense of his own experience, on the other hand, does not embody this idea of a natural limit. His existence defines for him an essentially open-ended possible future, containing the usual mixture of goods and evils that he has found so tolerable in the past. Having been gratuitously introduced to the world by a collection of natural, historical, and social accidents, he finds himself the subject of a *life*, with an indeterminate and not essentially limited future. Viewed in this way, death,

* John Keats (1795–1821) was a British poet and one of the central figures of the English Romantic movement.

† Leo Tolstoy (1828–1910) was one of the greatest Russian novelists ever to have lived; he was the author of *War and Peace* and *Anna Karenina*.

no matter how inevitable, is an abrupt cancellation of indefinitely extensive possible goods. Normality seems to have nothing to do with it, for the fact that we will all inevitably die in a few score years cannot by itself imply that it would not be good to live longer. Suppose that we were all inevitably going to die in *agony*—physical agony lasting six months. Would inevitability make *that* prospect any less unpleasant? And why should it be different for a deprivation? If the normal lifespan were a thousand years, death at 80 would be a tragedy. As things are, it may just be a more widespread tragedy. If there is no limit to the amount of life that it would be good to have, then it may be that a bad end is in store for us all.

NOTES

1. It is sometimes suggested that what we really mind is the process of *dying*. But I should not really object to dying if it were not followed by death.
2. It is certainly not true in general of the things that can be said of him. For example, Abraham Lincoln was taller than Louis XIV. But when?
3. I confess to being troubled by the above argument, on the ground that it is too sophisticated to explain the simple difference between our attitudes to prenatal and posthumous nonexistence. For this reason I suspect that something essential is omitted from the account of the badness of death by an analysis which treats it as a deprivation of possibilities. My suspicion is supported by the following suggestion of Robert Nozick. We could imagine discovering that people developed from individual spores that had existed indefinitely far in advance of their birth. In this fantasy, birth never occurs naturally more than a hundred years before the permanent end of the spore's existence. But then we discover a way to trigger the premature hatching of these spores, and people are born who have thousands of years of active life before them. Given such a situation, it would be possible to imagine *oneself* having come into existence thousands of years previously. If we put aside the question whether this would really be the same person, even given the identity of the spore, then the consequence appears to be that a person's birth at a given time *could* deprive him of many earlier years of possible life. Now while it would be cause for regret that one had been deprived of all those possible years of life by being born too late, the feeling would differ from that which many people have about death. I conclude that something about the future *prospect* of permanent nothingness is not captured by the analysis in terms of denied possibilities. If so, then Lucretius' argument still awaits an answer. I suspect that it requires a general treatment of the difference between past and future in our attitudes toward our own lives. Our attitudes toward past and future pain are very different, for example. Derek Parfit's unpublished writings on this topic have revealed its difficulty to me.

Death Without Dread

WALTER KAUFMANN

Walter Kaufmann (1921–80) was a German-born American philosopher, translator, and poet who taught at Princeton University for more than thirty years, publishing books of essays and on topics such as life, death, authenticity, and religion. He was one of the foremost authorities on the work of the important nineteenth-century German philosopher Friedrich Nietzsche (1844–1900).

From *Existentialism, Religion, and Death* by Walter Kaufmann. Copyright © 1976 by Walter Kaufmann. Used by permission of Dutton Signet, a division of Penguin Group (USA) Inc.

In this essay, originally presented at a conference in 1975 and subsequently published in a collection of his papers, Kaufmann draws on insights from a number of German poems to argue that we should not fear death.

Kaufmann refers to a number of German philosophers in the course of his discussion. Biographical information about Immanuel Kant (1724–1894) can be found with the selections from his writings in the "Moral Philosophy" section. Martin Heidegger (1889–1976) was an important twentieth-century German philosopher whose major work—*Being and Time*—examines fundamental questions about the nature of reality and humanity's place within it.

I

Death has come to be associated with old age. That is a recent development. In many parts of the world more people are still dying as infants than in old age, and death has generally been distributed over the whole life span. One never felt immune from it.

Death has always been a staple of religion and literature. Those writing about death should not forgo research about different attitudes toward death in different religions. To a large extent, the fear of death, or the anxiety associated with death, is a product of Christianity, and we encounter very different attitudes at the burning ghats in Varanasi in India and in Buddhist lands.

Fascinating and important as this question is, one cannot deal with it well in a brief space because the great religions are not monolithic. Unquestionably, Christianity has spread the horror of death through its threats of hell and its perennial attempts to frighten people into repentance on the threshold of eternity. Yet in the early days of Christianity so many Christians coveted martyrdom with its assurance of heaven that a Roman proconsul felt unable to oblige such multitudes, although the Romans were not squeamish about dying and even less so about killing.[1] Not only have there been vast changes in the great religions over the centuries, but there are also countless sects and geographical variations in Christianity as well as Islam, Hinduism, and Buddhism.

The variety of religious attitudes is vast, but it is really crucial to realize that our attitudes are not due to the timeless constitution of the human mind but to historical and cultural conditioning. Immanuel Kant, writing in the last two decades of the eighteenth century, bequeathed to us the notion that our certainties are due to the structure of the human mind and not subject to change. Almost 150 years later, Martin Heidegger still played essentially the same game, but played it worse. Kant had looked for a firm foundation for Euclidean geometry, Newtonian science, and the categorical imperative, and we can still see how a wise man in his time and place might have supposed that history and psychology or, in one word, conditioning, would be irrelevant here. But Heidegger came after the rapid growth of the historical consciousness in Germany and after Freud and the explosion of interest in anthropology and sociology, and there is no longer any excuse for supposing that the attitudes toward death and original sin on which Heidegger was brought up as a Roman Catholic are immutable features of human existence, or *Dasein*. Yet many people who have never read Heidegger are still influenced by his claims. For it is comforting to be assured that one's own attitudes are the only ones, and that one need not choose between alternatives—or at least only between two, of which one is authentic and the other inauthentic. Such simplistic Manichaean schemes have always had appeal, and if one is full of anxiety it is pleasant to be told that it takes courage to be scared and that all those who are unafraid are inauthentic.

What Nietzsche said of Kant is no less true of Heidegger and, alas, a great many philosophers: He "tried to prove in a way that would dumfound the common man that the common man was right."[2] And F. H. Bradley's definition of metaphysics applies to other branches of philosophy as well: "the finding of bad reasons for what we believe on instinct."[3] Only the word "instinct" suggests once again something immutable, and it would be more precise to say that a great deal of philosophy is a way of rationalizing what the philosophers have been brought up or conditioned to believe—the common sense of their set. "If, as Bradley added, 'the finding of these reasons is no less an instinct,' it ought to be the aim of philosophy to teach men to master this instinct and become housebroken."[4]

To that end, a good course in comparative religion should be required of all undergraduates. Courses in literature and art history should also be designed to produce multiple culture shock, exposing students to impressive alternatives. As far as written materials go, short poems have one immense advantage over all other forms: they sometimes manage to express an experience or attitude in a highly condensed way. History and religion are in a sense infinite. If you quote from some sacred scripture or relate historical incidents, scholars are bound to counter with a big But. A work of art requires some interpretation, and when you have given yours those you are trying to refute may once again say But. Short poems sometimes have a kind of finality.

Again the amount of material is too vast to survey here. Even if each poem is brief, there are simply too many of them. The following selection is no more than a small sample. In 1962 I published *Twenty German Poets*, which was reprinted in The Modern Library the following year. The poets ranged from Goethe to Hermann Hesse, who at that time was not widely known in the English-speaking world. A few were represented by a single poem, Goethe and Rilke by over a dozen poems each. I tried to select the best poets and some of the best poems by each, printing the original texts and my own verse translations on facing pages, and offered an introduction as well as separate prefaces for every poet. It was only in 1974, when I prepared an enlarged version of the book, *Twenty-five German Poets*,[5] adding three poets before Goethe, two at the end, and a few additional poems by the twenty original poets, that I realized how many of the poems dealt with death. Most of these poets have expressed an attitude toward death in one or more brief poems, and what is striking is that for all their variety not one voiced anxiety, nor is there a single poem that associates death with old age.

These poems were chosen initially for their high quality and not to round out an anthology on death or to prove a point. It so happens that many of the best short German poems deal with death. And it seems worthwhile to see how very different they are from the platitudes mouthed by so many recent writers whose claims are based, as dogmas generally are, on a studied disregard for experience. I shall begin in 1779 and end in 1923, spanning a period of 144 years, which is considerably less than twice the life span of an old person. So far from claiming that this tiny sample of German poetry is representative of all of world literature, I should like to issue an invitation to others to broaden the range in at least two ways.

First, it would be interesting to have similar samples from Greek and Latin authors, French and English, Indian and Chinese, as well as other literatures. Secondly, one might proceed, perhaps at a later stage, to arrange the materials according to themes, such as suicide, death in battle, dying of tuberculosis, cancer, or some other disease, dying of old age, dying very young. But for a start I shall deal with my small sample, which was not chosen to begin with to prove any thesis. Of course, these are all poems that appealed to me, and one might therefore wonder whether attitudes I find congenial may be represented disproportionately. While this would not be surprising, I doubt that anyone could find a sizable number of short German poems of comparable quality that voice anxiety in the face of death or that associate death with old age.

II

Friedrich Gottlieb Klopstock (1724–1803) was the most renowned poet in Germany before the young Goethe eclipsed him, and the following poem is quite possibly his best.

Separation

You turned so serious when the corpse
was carried past us;
are you afraid of death? "Oh, not of that!"
Of what are you afraid? "Of dying."

I not even of that. "Then you're afraid of nothing?"
Alas, I am afraid, afraid . . . "Heavens, of what?"
Of parting from my friends.
And not mine only, of their parting, too.

That's why I turned more serious even
than you did, deeper in the soul,
when the corpse
was carried past us.

Klopstock disliked rhyme, and this unpretentious little poem is an early example of free verse. Of course, the poet admits to being afraid but insists that he is not afraid of death or dying. Those who assume that all men are afraid of death may charge him with transparent self-deception and inauthenticity. I should argue on the contrary that he makes needful and illuminating distinctions. He is right in distinguishing being afraid of death and being afraid of dying, and he is also right in suggesting that there are still further possibilities, of which he mentions two: parting from our friends as well as their parting from us. For many of us it makes perfectly good sense to wonder how our children, our old parents, or our wife or husband will fare after our death, and anxiety of that kind needs to be distinguished from the fear of death and the dread of dying slowly in great pain.

Matthias Claudius (1740–1815) wrote two fine short poems about death. The first, "Death and the Maiden," was set to music by Franz Schubert and sung unforgettably by Marian Anderson.

Death and the Maiden

The Maiden:

Oh, go away, please go,
Wild monster, made of bone!
I am still young; Oh, no!
Oh, please leave me alone!

Death:

Give me your hand, my fair and lovely child!
A friend I am and bring no harm.
Be of good cheer, I am not wild,
You shall sleep gently in my arm.

Again the fear of death is not simply ignored, but the whole point of the poem is to suggest an alternative. We are made to feel that the anxiety is irrational even when one is still young and might feel cheated of a long and happy life, for death is like a gentle sleep.

Another poem by the same poet suggests that it is irrational to lament the death of a woman, or a girl, we loved. But the counter-image is different this time, not sleep but more nearly an awakening. Death spells liberation from the earth. The poem gets off the ground and takes wing only in the last few lines; but given the text, that makes excellent sense, and the final image is very strong. There is a suggestion, going back at least to Plato and the Orphics before him, that, as they put it, the body (*soma*) is the tomb (*sema*) of the soul, and that life is a period of exile.

The Sower

The sower sows the seed,
The earth receives it, and before long
The flower comes out of the soil—

You loved her. Whatever else
Life may offer you, seemed small to you,
And eternal sleep took her hence.

Why do you weep at her grave
And raise your hands to the cloud of death
And decomposition?

Like grass in the field are men,
Gone like leaves. Only a few days
We walk here, disguised.

The eagle visits the earth,
Tarries not, shakes from his wings the dust and
Returns to the sun.

Goethe (1749–1832) did not dwell much on death. Even in his old age he still wrote poems about love, not death. Nor did he associate love with death—except in one great poem that appeared in his *West-Eastern Divan* in 1819, when he was seventy. Here we have a love night and death, but the hero seems to be, quite literally, a butterfly.

Blessed Yearning

Tell it none except the wise,
for the common crowd defames:
of the living I shall praise
that which longs for death in flames.

In the love night which created
you where you create, a yearning

wakes: you see, intoxicated,
far away a candle burning.

Darkness now no longer snares you,
shadows lose their ancient force,
as a new desire tears you
up to higher intercourse.

Now no distance checks your flight,
charmed you come and you draw nigh
till, with longing for the light,
you are burnt, O butterfly.

And until you have possessed
dying and rebirth,
you are but a sullen guest
on the gloomy earth.

To most readers, the "butterfly" at the end of the penultimate stanza comes as a surprise that explains everything that went before, and being pleased to understand, few indeed go on to wonder why it is a butterfly rather than a moth. After all, it is moths and not butterflies that are attracted to burning candles at night. But Goethe knew that the Greek word for the human soul, *psyche*, also meant butterfly. And what attracted Goethe to this image was that there is no more striking example of a metamorphosis than the transformation of a caterpillar into a butterfly. The final stanza alludes to that—the caterpillar is "a sullen guest on the gloomy earth." But the suggestion is not mainly that our death, too, may be the beginning of another existence; it is above all that the richest life is a series of deaths and transformations. Any existence lacking that is drab and dull.

This theme, powerfully voiced in the last stanza of this poem, was developed by Nietzsche, who, perhaps alone among philosophers, could say even of his prose: ". . . it is my ambition to say in ten sentences what everyone else says in a book—what everyone else does *not* say in a book."[6] While Kant had set a vastly influential example of unprecedented verbosity, Nietzsche managed again and again to write sentences as pregnant as the best short poems; for example, "One pays dearly for immortality; one has to die several times while still alive."[7] Or: "Some are born posthumously."[8] And another somewhat different passage is relevant to this theme, too: "The secret for harvesting from existence the greatest fruitfulness and the greatest enjoyment is—to *live dangerously*."[9] The context makes it clear that Nietzsche is not thinking of big-game hunting but of not clinging to the life, the views, the world that are familiar to us and spell security. This is a central theme in his philosophy and was later taken up by Rilke, who celebrated it in his late poetry.[10] It belongs here both because it was inspired by Goethe's great example and because it makes for a different attitude also toward death. It is those who are most afraid of having missed something who are also most afraid of missing out on something when they die. This as well as the converse has never been said more beautifully than by Hölderlin (1770–1843). Though twenty-one years younger than Goethe, he ceased writing long before "Blessed Yearning" appeared; but shortly before insanity reduced him to imbecility he wrote this poem.

To the Parcae

A single summer grant me, great powers, and
a single autumn for fully ripened song
that, sated with the sweetness of my
playing, my heart may more willingly die.

The soul that, living, did not attain its divine
right cannot repose in the nether world.
But once what I am bent on, what is
holy, my poetry, is accomplished:

Be welcome then, stillness of the shadows' world!
I shall be satisfied though my lyre will not
accompany me down there. Once I
lived like the gods, and more is not needed.

Friedrich Schiller (1759–1805), whom Hölderlin vastly admired, had tried to say something similar even more briefly, if somewhat more prosaically. He lived with the knowledge of a relatively early death as he had consumption, but lived intensely and left a large and magnificent body of work.

Immortality

You are frightened of death? You wish you could
live forever?
Make your life whole? When death takes you that
will remain.

Much has been done since the early nineteenth century to prolong life as if that were an end in itself. Many people have so little imagination and are so unthoughtful that they think they would enjoy living forever. With death not very likely before old age, they have got into the bad habit of living without any sense of having only so much time and without asking themselves how to make good use of it. They assume that everybody is like them and swallow the dogma that, deep down, *nobody* believes in his own death and *everybody* thinks that he will live forever and is pleased with this prospect, while the thought of one's own death is too painful to face honestly. What I find astonishing is how unwilling even deeply humane scholars are to examine such dogmas in the light of evidence. Some have actually written up the evidence that disproves their own dogmas, but go on professing them with the thoughtlessness of ritual.[11] It would seem more reasonable to assume at the outset that there are many different attitudes, and then to ask later if all of them are really reducible to one.

Friedrich von Hardenberg (1772–1801) died of consumption before he was thirty, a few years before Schiller did. He belonged to the small circle of the original German romantics who, however much they owed to Schiller, liked to denigrate him. His reaction to his fate, like his personality and his work, was rather different from Schiller's. At the age of twenty-two he had met a girl of twelve; they fell in love and were engaged; but in 1797 she died at the age of fifteen. "That he sang himself to death with his 'Hymns to the Night'—aided by consumption—is better known than the fact that within a year of his fiancée's death he became engaged to another girl whom he desired to keep him company in this world until he succeeded in becoming reunited with his true love after death."[12] The "Hymns" appeared in 1800, two years before the poet's death, and introduced the romantic glorification of death that reached its apotheosis in Richard Wagner's "Liebestod" in *Tristan und Isolde*.*

It will be noted that I am put off by what strikes me as a certain affectation in the "Hymns." The tone is not wholly authentic. But it does not follow that the poet really would like to live until old age. Far from it. The basic feeling strikes me as wholly believable. I shall quote only the rhymed portion of the "Fourth Hymn to the Night."

Beyond I wander,
all pain will be
ere long a spur
of ecstasy.
A short span of time,
I'm free and above,
and drunken I lie
in the lap of love.
Infinite life
surges in me with might;
and down toward you
I incline my sight.
Your splendor is dying
on yonder hill.
A shadow brings
the wreath of chill.
Suck me toward you, beloved,
with all your force
that I may slumber
and love at last.
I am touched by death's
youth-giving flood,
to balsam and ether
is turned my blood.
I live by day
full of courage and trust,
and die every night
in holy lust.

This is an extreme expression of a voluptuous feeling about death that is not fashionable nowadays. It may help to remind us that there are fashions in such matters, too, and that attitudes some people nowadays take for granted and believe to be part of human nature are in fact also fashions. Certainly, Novalis—to give the poet his pen name under which he is remembered—was far from unique in feeling as he did; he merely voiced with rare intensity the fascination of death and dying.

Instead of sampling other romantic poems about death, I shall proceed straight to Heinrich Heine

* *Tristan und Isolde* is a tragic love story set to music by the composer Richard Wagner (1813–83). The *"Liebestod"*—literally love-death—is its final moving aria.

(1797–1856), who was twenty-five years younger than Novalis and only four years old when Novalis died. Heine, like Goethe, mastered the accents of romanticism, but just as Goethe enjoyed puncturing Faust's* effusions with Mephistopheles' sardonic wit, Heine frequently did the same sort of thing even in short poems. The next poem does not illustrate this point but shows restraint throughout. It was written during the years in Paris when Heine was lying, without any hope of recovery, in what he called his *Matratzengruft*, his mattress vault or tomb. Is there any reason to doubt that death often seemed desirable to him?

Morphine

Great is the similarity of these two
Youthful figures, although one of them
Looks so much paler than the other one,
Much more severe—I almost said, much nobler—
Than does that other one who, all affection,
Enclosed me in his arms: How sweetly tender
His smile was then, what bliss was in his eyes!
Then it could happen that the poppy wreath
He wore upon his head touched my brow, too,
And the strange perfume drove away all pain
Out of my soul. But such relief endures
So short a time; complete recovery
Can be mine only when the serious looking
Brother who is so pale lowers his torch—
Good is sleep, but death is better—yet
What would be best is not to have been born.

The last line is virtually a quotation from a chorus in Sophocles' last tragedy, *Oedipus at Colonus* (line 1225ff.):

Nothing surpasses not being born;
but if born, to return where we came from
is next best, the sooner the better.

The poet who wrote these lines shortly before his death was ninety and could look back on a life's work that included one hundred and twenty plays of which ninety-six had won first prize (that is, twenty-four tetralogies) and the rest second prize. He had never placed third, was beloved by the people of Athens, and had reaped many other honors. But his tragedies give unsurpassed expression to despair, and although the lines are spoken by a chorus in a play, a study of the seven extant tragedies shows plainly how at ninety Sophocles felt no dread in the face of death.[13]

Close to two hundred years earlier, Jeremiah had exclaimed (20:14):

Cursed be the day
on which I was born!

And in the Book of Job we find almost the same outcry (3.3). Not all have always loved their lives so well or shut their eyes to the miseries of others to the point of feeling that no fate could be worse than death. The claim, popularized by Heidegger, that those not afraid of death are inauthentically shutting their eyes to their own anxiety may apply to some. But many who are afraid of death have closed their eyes to their own wretched condition and the sufferings of humanity.

Our poems here include no war poems. The one that comes closest to that genre is "Hagen's Dying Song" by Felix Dahn (1834–1912), a professor who achieved a great success with his four-volume historical novel, *Ein Kampf um Rom* (A Fight for Rome), which dealt with the defeat and destruction of the Ostrogoths and appeared in 1876, the year when Wagner's *Ring* was first performed in Bayreuth. Dahn also dealt with the Nibelungen story, writing a play on Kriemhild's revenge and the destruction of the Burgundians under King Gunter, but the play was forgotten while his poem about Hagen survived in anthologies to influence the attitudes toward death of generations of German boys throughout two world wars.

Hagen's Dying Song

Now I am growing lonely. The princes are all dead,
and in the moonshine glimmers the hearth in
bloody red.
The once so gay Burgundians are still, their revels
stop.

* Faust is a famous character from German literature. He made a pact with Mephistopheles (the devil), exchanging his soul for the possibility of understanding life's true essence.

I hear how from their bodies the blood runs drop on drop.
Out of the house arises a heavy smell of blood,
and screeching vultures circle, impatient for their food.
King Gunter is still sleeping his fever-maddened sleep, since a well sharpened arrow struck from the tower steep.
And Volker fell with laughter, and thus bade me adieu:
"Take all I leave, dear Hagen, my strings I leave to you."
Secure from Hunnish cunning, he carried without awe the fiddle on his safe back that no foe ever saw.
Like nightingales it sounded, strummed by the fearless bard;
no doubt, it will sound different in my hand, which is hard.
Three strings remain to play on, the other four are gone;
I am not used to singing, I am no fiddle man.
And yet I feel like trying how Hagen's tune might go:
I think some good sound cursing is a good prayer, too.
Above all, cursed be women; woman is falsity:
here, for two soft white bodies, perishes Burgundy!
And cursed be the illusion of morals, love, and law:
love is a lying fiction, and only hate is true.
Repentance is for idiots. Nothing has worth beside
enduring still when dying with wrath and sword and pride.
If I must reconsider my deeds now, one by one,
I should not leave a single act that I did undone.
And if, the world's enchantment, another Siegfried came,
I'd stab him in the back, too, with the same deadly aim.
You tear, strings? Are you cowards, afraid of such a song?
Hah, who comes down the courtyard, with strides that are so long?
That is no Hunnish lookout, those are the steps of fate—
and nearer, ever nearer—I recognize his gait.
Up, Gunter, now awaken, this is the final turn:
Up, up! Death, the avenger, and Dietrich comes from Bern!

Dahn was not a great poet, but this is, at least in the original, a strong poem. It represents a defiant readiness for death that has been anything but exceptional in times of war; and unfortunately times of war have rarely been exceptional.

Although Nietzsche (1844–1900) exerted a profound influence on existentialism, he did not make much of death, and in *The Gay Science* he said in a section (278) entitled "The thought of death":

> How strange it is that this sole certainty and common element makes almost no impression on people, and that nothing is further from their minds than the feeling that they form a brotherhood of death. It makes me happy that men do not want at all to think the thought of death! I should like very much to do something that would make the thought of life even a hundred times more appealing to them.

Six years later, Nietzsche included in *Twilight of the Idols* a section called "Morality for physicians." All of it is interesting, but I shall here quote only a small part of it.

> To die proudly when it is no longer possible to live proudly. Death freely chosen, death at the right time, brightly and cheerfully accomplished amid children and witnesses: then a real farewell is still possible, as the one who is taking leave is still there; also a real estimate of what one has achieved and what one has wished, drawing the sum of one's life—all in opposition to the wretched and revolting comedy that Christianity has made of the hour of death. One should never forget that Christianity has exploited the weakness of the dying for a rape of the conscience . . .

Nietzsche failed to shoot himself as Van Gogh* did, and when he collapsed, insane, in January 1889,

* Vincent Van Gogh (1853–90) was a famous Dutch painter who shot himself at the age of thirty-seven.

his mother and later on his sister managed to keep him alive for another eleven and a half years. But he wrote a poem shortly before his breakdown and also managed to finish four superb books during his last few months. The poem is one of his so-called Dionysus Dithyrambs, which influenced Rilke's Elegies, but is not Dionysian* in any crude sense. It is the voice of a man who has found peace and leaves life without regrets.

The Sun Sinks

I

Not long will you thirst,
burnt out heart!
A promise is in the air,
from unknown lips it blows at me
—the great chill comes.

My sun stood hot over me at noon—
be welcome that you come,
you sudden winds,
you chilly spirits of afternoon!

The air moves strange and pure.
Does not with warped
seductive eyes
night leer at me?
Stay strong, courageous heart!
Do not ask: why?

II

Day of my life!
The sun sinks.
Already the smooth
flood stands golden.
Warm breathes the rock:
whether at noon
joy slept its noonday sleep upon it?
In greenish lights
Joy is still playing over the brown abyss.

Day of my life!
Toward evening it goes.
Already your eye
glows half-broken,
already your dew's
tear drops are welling,
already runs still over white seas
your love's purple,
your last hesitant blessedness.

III

Cheerfulness, golden one, come!
you of death
the most secret and sweetest foretaste!
Did I run too rash on my way?
Only now that my foot has grown weary,
your eye catches up with me,
your *joy* catches up with me.

Round me but wave and play.
Whatever was hard
sank into blue oblivion—
idle stands now my boat.
Storm and drive—how it forgot that!
Wish and hope have drowned,
smooth lie soul and sea.

Seventh loneliness!
Never felt I
nearer me sweet security,
warmer the sun's eye.
Does not the ice of my peaks still glow?
Silver, light, a fish,
my bark now swims out.

The last two poets I wish to consider belong to my parents' generation and thus in a sense to our time. Let us begin with Rilke, who wrote more superb short poems than any other German poet after Goethe and who remains one of the world's greatest masters in this genre. A lovely poem in his *Neue Gedichte* (1907) deals with Orpheus' descent into the underworld to bring back from death his wife, Eurydice. He goes down accompanied by the god Hermes, it being understood that if he looks back even once to see if his

* Dionysius was the ancient Greek god of drunkenness and ecstasy; Apollo was the ancient Greek god of poetry and truth. In the work of Friedrich Nietzsche (1844–1900), to which Kaufmann here adverts, the Apollonian represents creation, self-control, individuality, and reason, whereas the Dionysian represents destruction, intoxication, wholeness, and ecstatic passion.

wife follows him, she has to remain dead. Although this poem is longer than any of the others I am using, I shall quote the whole of it. For the wish to bring back the dead is an important part of our subject and among the most ubiquitous attitudes toward death.

Orpheus. Eurydice. Hermes

That was the souls' weird mine.
Like silent silver ores they penetrated
as veins its dark expanses. Between roots
welled up the blood that flows on to mankind,
and in the dark looked hard as porphyry.
Else nothing red.

But rock was there
and woods that had no nature. Bridges spanned
  the void
and that great gray blind pond
suspended over its far distant depth
as rainy skies above a landscape.
And between meadows, soft and full of patience,
appeared the ashen streak of the one way
as a long pallor that has been stretched out.

And it was on this one way that they came.

In front, the slender man in the blue mantle
who looked ahead in silence and impatience.
His paces, without chewing, gulped the way
in outsized swallows; and his hands were hanging
heavy and sullen from the fall of folds,
knowing no longer of the weightless lyre
grown deep into his left as rambler roses
into the branches of an olive tree.
His senses were as if they had been parted:
and while his glances, doglike, ran ahead,
turned back, and came, and always stood again
as waiting at the next turn of the way—
his hearing stayed behind him as a smell.
Sometimes it seemed to him as if it reached
back to the walking of those other two
who were to follow him this whole ascent.
Then it was but the echo of his climbing
and his own mantle's wind that was behind him.
Yet he said to himself that they would come;
said it out loud and heard it fade away.
They would come yet, only were two
walking most silently. And if he might
turn only once (and if his looking back
were not destruction of this whole endeavor
still to be ended), he would surely see them,
the quiet two who followed him in silence:

the god of going and of the wide message,
the travel hood shading his brilliant eyes,
bearing the slender staff before his body,
the beat of wings around his ankle bones;
and given over to his left hand: *she*.

The one so loved that from a single lyre
wails came surpassing any wailing women;
that out of wails a world arose in which
all things were there again: the wood and
valleyand way and village, field and brook and
beast; and that around this wailing-world,
just as around the other earth, a sun revolved and
a vast sky, containing stars and stillness,
a wailing-sky full of disfigured stars—
this one so loved.

But she walked at the hand of this great god,
her striding straightened by the grave's long wraps,
uncertain, soft, and void of all impatience.
She was in herself as one high in hope,
not thinking of the man who went ahead,
nor of the way ascending into life.
She was in herself. And her having died
filled her as fullness.
And as a fruit is full of dark and sweetness,
the greatness of her death was filling her
and was so new, she comprehended nothing.

She was wrapped up in a new maidenhood
and one not touchable; her sex was closed as
a young flower is toward evening,
and her hands had become so unaccustomed
to matrimony, even the light god's
immeasurably lightly leading touch
offended her as something intimate.

She was not any longer this blond woman
who in the poet's songs would sometimes echo,
not any more the broad bed's scent and island,
and the possession of this man no more.

She was already loosed as flowing hair
and long relinquished as the fallen rain
and meted out as hundredfold provisions.

She was become a root.
And when with sudden force
the god stopped her and with pain in his cry
pronounced the words: He has turned back—
she comprehended nothing and said softly: Who?

But far off, dark beyond the clear egress,
stood someone, any one, whose countenance
could not be recognized. He stood and saw
how on the pale streak of a meadow path,
with sorrow in his eyes, the god of message
turned silently to follow back the form
that even then returned this very way,
her striding straitened by the grave's long wraps,
uncertain, soft, and void of all impatience.

This poem succeeds in transporting us into a different world, and it is easy to forget all about our world and death and dying. And yet no poem could be more relevant to our theme. What is realized in these lines is the peace of death and the contrast with the lack of peace that pervades our lives. All else is implications, and to spell them out seems as obtrusive as Orpheus' intrusion into regions in which his impatience has no place. We are made to feel that he is doing her no favor, that the desire to bring back the dead is selfish, like waking up a sick person in great pain who has finally fallen asleep—waking her up because we are feeling lonely and want company.

I feel reminded of the great scene in First Samuel where Saul, about to go into his last battle, asks the woman of Endor to bring back the dead Samuel, whom Saul wants to consult. Samuel's first words are: "Why have you disturbed me to bring me up here?" (28.15). We are led to ask whether men do not project the torments of life and survival beyond death, where, in the words Marian Anderson used to sing so movingly, all is peace. Would it not make more sense for Orpheus to join Eurydice than for him to wish her to join him?

Yet Rilke's poetry as a whole does not glorify death and is not a curse on life. Rilke, like Nietzsche, celebrates this world and this life. "There is nothing that gives our lives meaning and, viewed from the outside, life, which ends in death, is senseless." There is no meaning outside, but Rilke and Nietzsche proclaim that a certain kind of life is its own reward" and "that a certain mode of experience makes life infinitely worth while."[14] In his ninth Elegy, Rilke, in effect, answers the question whether Orpheus should not wish to join Eurydice and seek death. "Why," he begins by asking, "have to be human . . .?" Not, he replies, for happiness or "for curiosity's sake . . ." But—and I shall cite only some few passages from this poem—

But because being here is much, and because
apparently
all that is here needs us, all the fleeting that
strangely concerns us. Us, the most fleeting. *Once*
everything, only *once*. *Once* and no more. And we,
too, *once*. Never again. But having
been this *once*, even though only *once:*
having been on earth does not seem revokable.

And so we strain and want to accomplish it,
want to contain it in our simple hands,
in still more overcrowded eyes and a speechless
heart.
Want to become it. Give it to whom? Would love to
hold on to all forever. Oh, to that other relation,
alas, what can one take across? Not the art of
seeing, slowly
learned here, and no event from here. None.
Only our suffering. Only, that is, what was hard;
only the long experience of love—only
what is unsayable. But later,
under the stars, what matter? *They* are rightly
unsayable. . . .

Here is the time for what is *sayable, here* is its
home.
Speak and confess. . . .
Between the hammers endures
our heart, like the tongue
between our teeth that yet
continues to praise.

Praise the world. . . .

And these things that live
on destruction understand that you praise them;
evanescent,

they trust that we, the most evanescent, can save
them.
Wish that we might transform them entirely in
our invisible hearts
into—oh, infinite!—into ourselves, whoever we
may be.
Earth, is not this what you want: to arise in us
invisible?—Is it not your dream
to be invisible once?—Earth! invisible!
What if not transformation is your urgent
command?
Earth, my beloved, I will. Oh, believe me, it
requires
your springs no longer to win me for you; one,
alas, even one is already too much for my blood.
Nameless, I am resolved to you from afar.
Always you have been right, and your holy idea
is intimate death.

Behold, I am living. From where? Neither
childhood nor future
grow less.—Superabundant existence
leaps up in my heart.

In this ecstatic affirmation of life, death is included, not only in the end, almost as an afterthought, but from the beginning: "*Once* / everything, only *once. Once* and no more. And we, too, / *once*. Never again." This implicit denial of reincarnation leads to the opposite of that worldweariness which is the starting point of Buddhism and the lethargy and resignation that pervade so much of life in India. The most intense love of life takes the sting out of death and destruction. As Hölderlin had put it more than a hundred years earlier:

Once I
lived like the gods, and more is not needed.

More is not *wanted*; more would be less. Perfection is finite; infinite duration, hell. What is most beautiful would not gain from lasting forever; it would soon turn into torment.

In life, as in art, it is not quantity that counts but quality. To associate happiness with a long life is a colossal stupidity, led to the absurd by the miseries of extreme old age. Our culture has long made the mistake of going in for a mindless cult of quantity, counting the ever-growing life expectancy as a self-evident success, as if death were the only enemy of man. This folly depends on the withering of intensity and meaning. It is only when life has lost its sense that no standards remain to evaluate it except length. But a superb short poem would not gain by being made longer and longer, and still longer and, if possible, endless. A Rembrandt self-portrait would not become better by being made larger and ever larger. Perfection lies in intensity, and what is most intense cannot be endured long.

If it should seem that I have fallen into an extreme aestheticism, our last poet strikes a very different note. Gottfried Benn (1886–1956) was nine years younger than Rilke but outlived him by thirty years. His *late* poems seem to me to be too similar to some of Rilke's very late verse to be first-rate. Some of his very early poems are much more original and have an unmistakably distinctive voice. He was a doctor, and his first collection of verse, *Morgue*, appeared in 1912, a few days before his mother died of cancer. Later the same year he published his poem on cancer in a periodical. A greater contrast to Rilke and, for that matter, the other poems cited here would be hard to imagine.[15] The first three poems come from *Morgue*.

Beautiful Childhood

The mouth of a girl who had lain long in the reeds
looked so gnawed at.
When one broke open the breast, the esophagus
was so full of holes.
Finally in a bower under the diaphragm
one found a nest of young rats.
One little sister lay dead.
The others were living on liver and kidney,
drank the cold blood and had
spent a beautiful childhood here.
And beautiful and fast their death, too, came:
One threw the lot of them into the water.
Oh, how the little snouts squeaked!

Cycle

The lonely molar of a whore
who had died unknown

had a filling of gold.
The others, as if they had a silent understanding,
had gone out.
That one the morgue attendant knocked out,
marketed, and went dancing.
For, he said,
only earth shall return to earth.

Negro Bride

Then, bedded upon pillows of dark blood,
the blond neck lay of a white woman.
The sun was raging in her hair
and licked the length of her light thighs
and kneeled around the slightly browner breasts,
that neither vice nor birth had yet disfigured.
A nigger next to her: by a horse's hoof
his eyes and forehead shredded. He dug
two toes of his dirty left foot
into the inside of her small white ear.
Yet she lay sleeping like a bride:
on the edge of the joys of her first love,
as on the eve of many an Ascension
of the warm youthful blood.
Until one plunged
the knife into her white throat, throwing
a crimson apron of dead blood
around her hips.

Man and Woman Walk Through the Cancer Ward

The man:
Here this row is disintegrated wombs,
and this row is disintegrated breast.
Bed stinks by bed. Nurses change hourly.

Come, do not hesitate to lift this blanket.
Look here, this lump of fat and putrid juices,
this once was great for some man somewhere
and was called ecstasy and home.

Come, look here at this scar on that breast.
You feel that rosary of softened knots?
Don't hesitate. The flesh is soft and hurts not.

Here this one bleeds as if from thirty bodies.
No human has such quantities of blood.
From this a child
had to be cut first from her cancerous womb.

One lets them sleep. Both day and night.—The new ones
are told: here one sleeps oneself healthy.—Only Sundays,
for visitors, they're left a little more awake.

They do not take much nourishment. Their backs
are sore. You see the flies. Sometimes
the nurses wash them. As one washes benches.

Here the field swells already round each bed.
Flesh becomes almost soil. Ardor is spent.
Juices prepare to flow. The earth is calling.

These poems do not spell peace; they arouse anger. One way of dealing with this anger is to vent it on those who believe that it was Brecht who first found a new anti-romantic tone—fifteen years later, well after the horrors of World War I. Hemingway, too, seems a boy compared to the young Benn. We can no longer deal with death as if it were mainly a literary phenomenon, an event in poetry. We must take note of the ugly realities that are not dreamed of in most poems. But these last poems may help to show that even if we approach death and dying by way of poetry, as I have done here, we need not ignore these realities. We must only beware of restricting our sample too much.

In the end, however, these poems by Benn do not invalidate what I said earlier. On the contrary. I have maintained all along that we should not shut our eyes to human misery and the realities of sickness and old age. We should not strive to live as long as possible, least of all when we become a burden to ourselves and others. Nor should we instill in children and young people the pernicious notion that life is necessarily a boon and death a curse, and suicide a sin. We should awaken them to a variety of attitudes and try to immunize them against stupid fashions.

If possible, I know even less about old age than about death, but nobody seems to know much about death while there are many who know old age intimately. I believe Sophocles when at ninety he suggested that it is far better to die before one becomes old. It makes sense to carry on the fight against crippling or very painful diseases; it makes no sense to keep trying to prolong life more and more. We should teach those we can reach to live well rather than long, and not to dread death. But for those who reach old age the best insurance against hopelessness is surely to have lived rich lives, to have lived intensely, to have used our time so well that it would make little sense to feel cheated or to feel that we still need a little more time. We should impress on ourselves how young so many great composers, painters, poets, writers died, and in our youth we ought to make a rendezvous with death, pledging to be ready for it at the age of thirty, and then, if we live that long, make another date at forty. Granted that much life, one might well feel that anything beyond that is a present and that henceforth one ought to be ready any time. At the very least one ought to feel that way before one reaches fifty. We should also give up the unseemly Christian teachings about suicide and accept it as a dignified and decent way of ending our lives.

In its heart of hearts our culture still believes in hell and is afraid of what may lie beyond death and of dire punishments for suicide. It is high time that we realize that the belief in hell has made a hell on earth; that those who thought God was so cruel did not shrink from dire punishments and tortures and the Inquisition; and that those who keep prolonging life often visit hell on helpless patients. Freedom from fear is a pipe dream as long as one fears death.

NOTES

1. A Alvarez, *The Savage God: A Study of Suicide* (1971), p. 67; Kaufmann, *The Faith of a Heretic* (1961), sec. 98.
2. *The Gay Science* (1882), sec. 193.
3. *Appearance and Reality* (1893), Preface.
4. Kaufmann, *Critique of Religion and Philosophy* (1958), sec. 1.
5. W. W. Norton & Company (New York, 1975). All of the following poems are from this book. The publisher's permission is acknowledged gratefully.
6. *Twilight of the Idols* (1889), sec. 51.
7. *Ecce Homo*, in sec. 5 of the discussion of *Zarathustra*.
8. *Antichrist*, Preface, and *Ecce Homo*, third chapter, sec. 1; see also *The Gay Science*, sec. 365.
9. *The Gay Science*, sec. 283.
10. See Kaufmann, *From Shakespeare to Existentialism* (1959), the final section of the chapter "Nietzsche and Rilke."
11. See "On Death and Lying" above.
12. Kaufmann (1975), p. 78.
13. For a detailed discussion of Sophocles, see Kaufmann, *Tragedy and Philosophy* (1968).
14. Kaufmann (1959), final paragraph of the chapter "Nietzsche and Rilke." For their similarity see also chap. 13.
15. It would be particularly interesting to compare Benn's poem on the cancer ward, which follows, with Rilke's last poem, in which the poet, dying of leukemia, addresses his own death. In "Rilke: Nirvana or Creation" I have placed this poem—the original and a verse translation—in another context (in *The Times Literary Supplement*, London, December 5, 1975).

GLOSSARY

A fortiori (Latin): For a still stronger reason; all the more.

A priori/a posteriori (Latin): Something can be known a priori if it can be known independently of—or prior to—experience; something can be known only a posteriori if it can be known only on the basis of—or posterior to—experience.

Absolutism: (1) In morality: the view that certain sorts of actions are prohibited, no matter what outcomes they can be expected to produce. (2) In political philosophy: the view that the rights of the government are entirely unrestricted.

Abstracta/concreta: *Abstracta* are entities that are abstract, in the sense that they do not occupy particular locations in space-time; typical examples are numbers and ideas. *Concreta* are entities that are concrete, in the sense that they do occupy particular locations in space-time; typical examples are tables and turtles.

Accidental/essential: An object has a property essentially if it is not possible for the object to lack the property; an object has a property accidentally if the object could exist yet lack the property. See also *object/property*.

Action/omission: An *action* is something an agent does, such as closing the door; an *omission* is something an agent fails to do, such as (not) locking the door. This is closely related to the *commission/omission* distinction. To *commit* an act is to perform that act deliberately; to *omit* an act is to (deliberately) fail to perform some act (that one may have been expected to perform).

Act/rule utilitarianism: See *extreme/restricted utilitarianism*.

Ad hoc (Latin): Specifically for the purpose under present consideration, without independent justification. (Literally: "to this.")

Ad hominem (Latin): Attacking the character or outlook of one's opponent, rather than replying to one's opponent's argument. (Literally: "to the man.")

Ad infinitum (Latin): To infinity, without end.

Agent/patient: An agent is one who performs an action; a patient is one on whom an action is performed.

Analytic/synthetic: According to Immanuel Kant (1724–1804), who introduced the expression, an *analytic* proposition is one whose predicate is "contained in" its subject. Alternatively: an analytic proposition is one that can be transformed into a tautology merely by substituting synonymous terms for its constituent expressions. Statements such as "all bachelors are male" and "if something is a square then it is a rectangle" are often held to express true analytic propositions. A proposition is *synthetic* if it is not analytic. Statements such as "Kant was born on April 22" and "some apples are red" express synthetic propositions. See also *tautology*.

Antecedent: See *conditional*.

Antinomy: A paradox, especially one of the four paradoxes explored in the "Antinomies" section of Immanuel Kant's *Critique of Pure Reason* (1781). See *Paradox*.

Arguendo (Latin): For the sake of argument.

Argument/premise/conclusion: A set of considerations presented in support of some claim. The statement that one is trying to prove is called the *conclusion*; the statements that are meant to support that conclusion are called the *premises*. The premises and conclusion together form an *argument*.

Argument, valid: See *sound/valid*.

Assumption: A principle or proposition taken for granted without further justification.

Avant garde (French): Vanguard, cutting edge.

Begging the question: Circular reasoning; taking as one of your assumptions that which you are seeking to establish.

Behaviorism: In philosophical usage, *behaviorism* is the view that mental states (such as beliefs, desires, and emotions) are dispositions to behave in certain ways.

Belief/knowledge: To *believe* a proposition is to hold that proposition to be true. On many accounts of knowledge, to *know* a proposition is to have a true belief that is supported or acquired in some special way, say, by being justified or by being truth tracking. See *justified*, *truth tracking*.

Bona fide (Latin): In good faith, authentic.

Bottom-up/top-down processing: A distinction made in cognitive psychology between two forms of information processing. In top-down processing, "high-level" typically conscious representations (beliefs, memories, ideas, and expectations) influence the acquisition and processing of "low-level" (perceptual) information; in bottom-up processing, "low-level" perceptual information is used to build "high-level" cognitive or perceptual representations.

Brain state: The physical configuration of (part of) the brain.

Categorical/hypothetical imperative: A distinction made by the German philosopher Immanuel Kant (1724–1804) between two sorts of imperatives, that is, commands that you have reason to obey. A *hypothetical imperative* is one that you have reason to obey only if (on the hypothesis that) you have some particular preexisting desire; for example, "get out of the kitchen" (. . . if you can't stand the heat). A categorical imperative is one that you have reason to obey categorically, regardless of your own inclinations, for example (according to Kant), "don't lie."

Causa sui (Latin): Self-caused.

Causal: Having to do with cause.

Causal theory of knowledge: The view that knowing that P requires that one's belief that P have been caused (in the right sort of way) by the fact that P.

Causal theory of meaning: The view that what gives terms their meaning is some sort of causal relation between the term and its referent. See also *referent*.

Causal theory of perception: The view that perceiving an object requires that one's perception have been caused (in the right sort of way) by the object.

Causes: efficient, final, formal, material: A distinction made by the ancient Greek philosopher Aristotle (384–322 BCE) among four kinds of causation. The efficient cause of the object—such as a table—is that which brings it into being (say, a carpenter's actions). The final cause of the object is the goal for which it is made (say, to provide a place for eating dinner). The formal cause of the object is the pattern or design that determines its form (say, a plan in a magazine). The material cause of an object is the matter of which it is composed (say, wood).

Certainty/doubt: A proposition is taken as certain if the subject has no doubt as to the proposition's truth; a proposition is certain if the subject has no reason to doubt its truth. A proposition is taken as doubtful if the subject feels unsure of its truth; a proposition is doubtful if the subject has some reason to be unsure of its truth. Skeptics provide arguments suggesting that many propositions that have been taken as certain are doubtful.

Ceteris paribus (Latin): All other things being equal; with all other factors held constant.

Cf. (abbreviation for the Latin *confer*): Compare.

Closure: A set is closed relative to some operation if performing that operation on a member of the set always leads to something already in the set. In epistemology, *closure* usually refers to the principle of closure of knowledge under known implication, that is, that if you know P, and you know that P implies Q, then you know Q. Sometimes *closure* is used to refer to some refined version of this principle.

Conclusion: See *argument/premise/conclusion*.

Commission/omission: See *action/omission*.

Conceivability-possibility thesis: The conceivability-possibility thesis holds that under suitably idealized conditions, if P is conceivable, then P is possible.

(This means that if P is impossible, then P is inconceivable, so if P is necessary, then not-P is inconceivable.) The possibility-conceivability thesis holds that, under suitably idealized conditions, if P is possible, then P is conceivable. (This means that if P is inconceivable, then P is impossible, so if not-P is inconceivable, then P is necessary.) See also *necessary/possible/impossible*.

Conceptual analysis: A process by which a concept is analyzed into its component parts, thereby displaying its logical structure.

Condition, necessary/sufficient: See *necessary/sufficient*.

Conditional: A sentence of the form "if P then Q." P is called the *antecedent*; Q is called the *consequent*. See also *counterfactual conditional*, *material conditional*.

Conjunction: The *conjunction* of the propositions P and Q is the proposition P-&-Q. P-&-Q is true iff P is true and Q is true. See *proposition*, *iff*.

Contingent: See *necessary/contingent*.

Concreta: See *abstracta/concreta*.

Consequent: See *conditional*.

Consequentialism/utilitarianism: The view that what makes an act right or wrong is the goodness or badness of the act's consequences; *utilitarianism* is a particular form of consequentialism that restricts its attention to consequences involving the welfare of sentient beings. Among the most famous advocates of utilitarianism is John Stuart Mill (1806–73). Consequentialism/utilitarianism is often contrasted with deontology and virtue ethics. See also *deontology*, *virtue ethics*.

Consistent: A set of propositions is consistent if it does not entail a contradiction; a set of propositions is inconsistent otherwise. See also *contradiction*.

Content externalism: The view that the contents of a subject's thoughts depend, in part, on features of the world external to the subject. On such a view, two people who are molecule-for-molecule duplicates can have thoughts with different contents if they inhabit different environments. For example, whether a subject is in a position to have thoughts about water depends, in part, on whether she acquired her concepts in a world in which watery stuff is H_2O or a world in which some other chemical typically produces watery sensations.

Contradiction: A proposition that is false by virtue of its form alone; a false but empty claim. See also *tautology*, *law of non-contradiction*.

Contrapositive: The contrapositive of the conditional 'if P then Q' is the conditional 'if not-Q then not-P.'

Converse: (1) The converse of the conditional 'if P then Q' is the conditional 'if Q then P.' (2) The converse of a binary relation R is the binary relation R' such that xRy if and only if $yR'x$. For example, "taller than" is the converse of "shorter than."

Counterexample: An example that shows the falsity of some theory or claim.

Counterfactual conditional: A conditional of the form "if P were the case, then Q would be the case." (For example: if you had been late, then we would have missed the train; if he hadn't opened the box, then the contents would not have spilled.)

Cp. (abbreviation): Compare.

Datum (Latin): A piece of evidence; plural *data*. (Literally: what is given.)

De dicto/de re (Latin; literally of a statement (*dictum*), of a thing (*res*)): A distinction between two ways of interpreting certain sorts of claims, typically those involving propositional attitudes or modal statements. A statement is *de re* if it concerns a particular individual and *de dicto* if it does not. Consider the statement that I want a cat: if the desire it ascribes is *de re*, there is some cat such that I desire *it*; if the desire is *de dicto*, then I desire that my state of catlessness come to an end. Or consider the statement that the number of states in the United States is necessarily larger than thirty. On its most natural—*de dicto*—reading, this claim is false, since it says that whatever the number of states in the United States is, that number is larger than thirty. But there is a *de re* reading on which it is true: that the number that is the number of states in the United States (that is fifty), is necessarily larger than thirty.

De facto/de jure (Latin): *De facto* means as a matter of fact or happenstance; *de jure* means a matter of law, right, or rule.

Defeasible: Capable of being defeated. To accept a proposition defeasibly is to accept it provisionally, with the recognition that subsequent evidence may offer reason for rejecting it.

Definite/indefinite description: A definite description is an expression of the form "the such-and-such"; an indefinite description is an expression of the form "a such-and-such."

Demonstrative reference: Reference to an object by means of demonstration, as in "that table over there" (accompanied by an act of pointing).

Deontology: An ethical view based on the notion of duty or rights. The most famous advocate of deontological ethics was Immanuel Kant (1724–1804). Deontology is often contrasted with consequentialism and virtue ethics. See also *consequentialism, virtue ethics*.

Descriptive/normative: A statement is descriptive if it expresses (describes) the way things are; a statement is normative if it expresses (gives norms for) the way things ought to be.

Determinism: The doctrine that every event has a cause and that if the cause occurs, the event must also occur.

Deviant causal chain: A chain of events whereby a cause brings about an effect through some abnormal sequence of happenings. Suppose that I want you to be on team A with me, so I tell you to sign up on the list labeled "Team A." Suppose you wish to avoid me, so you sign up on the list labeled "Team B" instead. When assignments to teams are made, the second pages of the sign-up sheets get mixed up, so you end up on Team A with me after all. My telling you to sign up for Team A caused you to end up on Team A, but only as the result of a deviant causal chain.

Diachronic (Greek): Extended in time.

Dialectical: Pertaining to argumentation.

Dictum (Latin): A noteworthy statement; an authoritative observation or pronouncement.

Disposition: A potential or power. A glass vase has the disposition to break if dropped; salt has the disposition to dissolve if placed in water.

Disjunction, inclusive/exclusive: The disjunction of the propositions P and Q is the proposition P-or-Q. This is typically understood as *inclusive disjunction*: P-or-Q is true iff at least one of P or Q is true. Occasionally it is understood as *exclusive disjunction*: P-or-Q is true iff exactly one of P or Q is true. See also *proposition, iff*.

Divers (archaic): Several, various.

Doctrine of double effect: A doctrine that says that if an act has both intended and unintended consequences, moral evaluation of that act may, in certain circumstances, focus only on the intended consequences. Such a doctrine would allow a moral distinction between (a) the intentional act of dropping a bomb on an enemy leader with the unintended (although forseen) consequence of killing the civilians standing beside her and (b) the intentional act of killing the civilians.

Doxastic: Having to do with belief.

Dualism: See *physicalism*.

Duty: An action regarded as morally obligatory.

E.g. (abbreviation for the Latin term *exempli gratia*): For example.

Efficient cause: See *causes: efficient, final, formal, material*.

Eliminativism: The view that the terms used in some category of discourse presuppose so many mistaken assumptions that we should abandon the discourse altogether. Typical targets for eliminative philosophical views are ordinary morality and folk psychology.

Empirical: A question or statement is empirical if it concerns matters that can be settled by ordinary observation or scientific inquiry.

Empiricism/rationalism: A distinction between two general philosophical outlooks. Whereas *empiricists* stress the role of sense experience in the acquisition of knowledge, *rationalists* stress the role of reason unaided by the senses.

En passant (French): In passing.

Entail: See *sound/valid/entail*.

Enthymeme (Greek): An argument in which one or more of the premises remains unstated.

Epiphenomenal/epiphenomenalism: A feature of a situation is *epiphenomenal* if it occurs as a side-effect of the main phenomenon. In philosophy of mind, *epiphenomenalism* is the view that mental events are caused by physical events but have no effects upon physical events.

Epistemic: Having to do with knowledge. See also *doxastic*.

Epistemology: The branch of philosophy concerned with the study of knowledge.

Essential: See *accidental/essential*.

Eudaimonia (Greek): Well-being, flourishing, happiness.

Ex hypothesi (Latin): By hypothesis.

Ex post facto (Latin): Subsequently; having retroactive force.

Evil, problem of. See *problem of evil*.

Extension/intension: The *extension* of a predicate is the class of objects that fall under it; the *intension* of a predicate is the rule by which those objects are picked out. So, for example, the extension of 'is sweet' is the class of things that are sweet; the intension of 'is sweet' is the condition that entities must meet in order to be properly counted as sweet. Predicates with different intensions may have the same extension: in a world where all squares were red, 'is red' and 'is a square' would pick out the same class of entities using different rules.

Extensional/intensional: A context is *extensional* if terms having the same extension can be inter-substituted without risk of changing the truth value of their parent expression. A context is *intensional* if there is no such guarantee.

Externalism: See *internalism/externalism about justification*; *content externalism*.

Fallibilism: The view that claims about a particular domain could turn out to be mistaken.

Falsifiable: Capable of being refuted by experience.

Final cause: See *causes: efficient, final, formal, material*.

Folk psychology: The ordinary practice of explaining human behavior through an appeal to such notions as beliefs, desires, emotions, and intentions.

Follow from: In a valid argument, where the premises entail the conclusion, the conclusion is said to *follow from* the premises. See also *sound/valid*.

Foreknowledge: Knowledge of events that have not yet occurred.

Formal cause: See *causes: efficient, final, formal, material*.

Functionalism: In philosophy of mind, the view that mental states can be fully characterized by the role they play: by specifying what external conditions and other mental states typically cause them and what behaviors and other mental states they typically cause.

Gettier example/Gettier case: An example in which a subject has a justified true belief that nonetheless fails to be an instance of knowledge. The name is taken from that of the American philosopher Edmund Gettier, who presented several such examples in his 1963 article "Is Justified True Belief Knowledge?"

Greatest happiness principle: The view that a morally correct action is that which produces the greatest amount of happiness.

Hedonic (from Greek *hedone*, pleasure): Of or related to pleasure.

Hypothetical imperative: See *categorical/hypothetical imperative*.

I.e. (abbreviation for the Latin term *id est*): That is.

Idealism: See *dualism*.

Identity, numerical/qualitative: A and B are *numerically identical* if A is the same object as B; A and B are *qualitatively identical* if A has the same properties as B. My toothbrush is numerically identical to my roommate's toothbrush if we share the same toothbrush; my toothbrush is qualitatively (roughly) identical to my roommate's toothbrush if our toothbrushes are similar. See also *identity of indiscernibles*.

Identity, diachronic/synchronic: *Synchronic identity* is identity at a time; the rope whose end I am holding may be (synchronically) identical to the rope whose end you are holding. *Diachronic identity* is identity over time; the rope I am holding today may be (diachronically) identical to the rope I was holding yesterday.

Identity, qualitative: See *identity, numerical/qualitative*.

Identity of indiscernibles/indiscernibility of identicals: The principle of the *identity of indiscernibles* says that if A and B have exactly the same properties, then A is numerically identical with B; the principle of the *indiscernibility of identicals* says that if A is numerically identical with B, then A and B have exactly the same properties. The principle of the identity of indiscernibles is sometimes known as "Leibniz's Law," through its association with the writings of the German philosopher Gottfried Leibniz (1646–1716). See also *Identity, numerical/qualitative*.

Identity theory of mind: The view that states and processes of the mind are identical to states and processes of the brain.

Iff: Abbreviation for *if and only if*.

Impossible: See *contingent/possible/necessary/impossible*.

In foro conscientiae (Latin): Before the tribunal of conscience, that is, done out of respect for conscience (as opposed to legal requirement).

In rerum natura (Latin): In the nature of things.

Indexical: A linguistic expression whose reference shifts with the context of the utterance; classic examples are "I," "here," and "now."

Inference to the best explanation: A method of reasoning whereby one endorses whatever hypothesis would, if true, best explain the evidence under consideration.

Intensional: See *extensional/intensional*. The term *intensional* (with an *s*) should not be confused with the term *intentional* (with a *t*).

Intentional: In the philosophy of mind, a state is *intentional* if it is directed toward some object. The term *intentional* (with a *t*) should not be confused with the term *intensional* (with an *s*).

Intentional inexistence: An expression used by the nineteenth-century philosopher Franz Brentano (1838–1917) to describe the supposed status of objects of thought as entities that exist in the mind, rather than in the physical world.

Internalism: See *internalism/externalism about justification*; *content externalism*.

Internalism/externalism about justification: In epistemology, *internalism about justification* is the view that for a subject's belief to count as justified, the subject must be (in a position to be) aware of the belief's justificatory grounds; *externalism about justification* is the view that a belief can count as justified even in the absence of such (potential) awareness.

Inter alia (Latin): Among other things.

Intuitionism: The view that knowledge in a certain domain can be acquired through *intuition*, a process of direct nonsensory apprehension of the truth and falsity of certain claims.

Invalid: See *sound/valid*.

Ipso facto (Latin): By that very fact.

Kantian: Of or related to the work of the German philosopher Immanuel Kant (1724–1804).

Knowledge: See *belief/knowledge*.

Knowledge by acquaintance/knowledge by description: A distinction made by the British philosopher Bertrand Russell (1872–1970) concerning two ways that objects can be known. *Knowledge by acquaintance* is knowledge that is gained through direct experience with the object in question; *knowledge by description* is knowledge that is gained through considering the object under some description ("the such-and-such").

Law of noncontradiction: The claim that no proposition of the form P-&-not-P could be true. See also *contradiction*.

Leibniz's law: See *identity of indiscernibles/indiscernibility of identicals*.

Material cause: See *causes: efficient, final, formal, material*.

Materia prima (Latin): Prime matter; raw material.

Material conditional: The *material conditional* of P and Q is the proposition P → Q (sometimes written P ⊃ Q). P → Q is true iff P is false or Q is true. The material conditional is often glossed as "if P then Q." See also *proposition, iff*.

Materialism: The view that everything that exists is composed entirely of matter, so that nothing nonmaterial exists. Materialism is often contrasted with *idealism* or *dualism*, and is roughly synonymous with *physicalism*.

Metaphysics: The branch of philosophy concerned with exploring the fundamental nature of reality.

Mind/body problem: The problem of explaining the apparent fact of mutual influence between (non-material) minds and (material) bodies. More generally: the problem of explaining the relation between mind and body.

Modal logic: Logic concerned with the notions of necessity and possibility. See also *necessary/possible*.

Modus ponens (Latin, shorthand for *modus ponendo ponens*): A rule of inference that licenses the move from P and (P → Q) to Q.

Modus tollens (Latin, shorthand for *modus tollendo tollens*): A rule of inference that licenses the move from not-Q and (P → Q) to not-P.

Monism: See *physicalism*.

Mutatis mutandis (Latin): The necessary changes having been made.

Naturalism: A general commitment to the ability of natural science to provide adequate responses to (some or all) philosophical quandaries.

Necessary: See *necessary/contingent* or *necessary/possible* or *necessary/sufficient*.

Necessary/contingent: A proposition is *contingently true* if it is true, but could have been false; a proposition is *contingently false* if it is false, but could have been true. A proposition is *necessarily true* if it is true and could not have been false; a proposition is *necessarily false* if it is false and could not have been true. (See *necessary/possible/impossible*.) In the language of possible worlds, a proposition is *necessarily true* if it is true in all possible worlds, *contingently true* if it is true in the actual world but false in some other possible world(s), *contingently false* if it is false in the actual world but true in some other possible world(s), and *necessarily false* if it is false in all possible worlds. See *possible world*.

Necessary/possible/impossible: A proposition is *necessary* (or *necessarily true*) if it could not have been false. A proposition is *impossible* (or *necessarily false*) if it could not have been true. A proposition is *possible* if it could have been true (whether or not it is actually true). In the language of possible worlds, a proposition is *necessary* if it is true in all possible worlds, *possible* if it is true in some possible world, and *impossible* if it is true in no possible world. See *possible world*.

Necessary/sufficient: If A is *necessary* for B, then it is not possible for B to hold without A holding. (This means that the absence of A guarantees the absence of B.) If A is *sufficient* for B, then if A holds, B must also hold. (This means that the absence of B guarantees the absence of A.) Being over thirty years old is necessary but not sufficient for being a senator (since all senators are over thirty, but there are people over thirty who are not senators); being a senator from Montana is sufficient but not necessary for being a senator (since all senators from Montana are senators, but there are senators who are not senators from Montana). Note that A is necessary for B iff B is sufficient for A. (Since being a senator from Montana is sufficient for being a senator, being a senator is necessary for being a senator from Montana.) Philosophers are often concerned with finding *necessary and sufficient* conditions for particular concepts. For example, being a rectangle with four equal sides is necessary and sufficient for being a square; being an instance of justified true belief is (it might be thought) necessary and sufficient for being an instance of knowledge. See *belief/knowledge*.

Negation: The *negation* of the proposition P is the proposition not-P, sometimes written ~P or ¬P.

Nomological: Concerning laws.

Normative: See *descriptive/normative*.

Numerical identity: See *identity, numerical/qualitative*.

Object/property: A *property* is an attribute, quality, or characteristic of an *object* (entity). For example, a baseball is an object, among whose properties are whiteness, roundness, and solidity.

Ockham's razor: A principle associated with the medieval English philosopher William Ockham (c. 1285–1349) that maintains that "entities are not to be multiplied beyond necessity." The principle is sometimes generalized beyond ontology, with the term applied to the general claim that unnecessary assumptions should be "shaved away." (Sometimes spelled "*Occam's razor*.")

Omission: See *action/omission*.

Ontological: Concerning what exists.

Other minds: See *problem of other minds*.

P: Often used (along with *Q* and *R*) to represent a proposition to which a subject (often *S*) is cognitively related in some way, as in "S knows that P" or "S believes that Q." See also *S*.

Paradox: A set of apparently undeniable premises that apparently give rise to an apparently false or problematic conclusion. Resolution of the paradox requires rejecting one or more of the premises, demonstrating some flaw in the reasoning that led from the premises to the conclusion, or accepting the conclusion.

Premise: See *argument/premise/conclusion*.

Pace (Latin): With all due respect to; used to express disagreement.

Per contra (Latin): On the other hand, on the contrary.

Phenomenal quality: The felt character of an experience.

Physicalism: The view that everything that exists is entirely physical. Physicalism is often contrasted with *idealism*—the view that everything that exists is entirely nonphysical—and *dualism*—the view that some things that exist are physical and other things that exist are nonphysical. Physicalism is roughly synonymous with *materialism*—the view that everything that exists is made of matter. Physicalism and idealism, which posit only one sort of substance, are versions of *monism*. (The relation among these notions is discussed in some detail in Daniel Stoljar's "Physicalism," in the Mind section.)

Polemical: Of or involving dispute or controversy.

Possible: See *necessary/possible* or *conceivable/possible*.

Possible world: A complete specification of the way things might have been. *Possible worlds* are often thought of more vividly as alternative realities, although their ontological status remains a topic of philosophical dispute.

Predestination: The doctrine that some human beings are selected for salvation and others for damnation and that no earthly actions can alter one's fate.

Premise: See *argument*.

Pre-Socratic: Referring to ancient Greek philosophers or philosophy from before the time of Socrates (470–399 BCE).

Prima facie (Latin): At first sight, before investigation.

Primary/secondary quality: *Secondary qualities* are the immediate sensory qualities with which objects present us: color, sound, odor, taste, and felt texture and temperature. *Primary qualities* are the qualities that underlie the secondary qualities and that are available through multiple sensory modalities; they include solidity, extension, shape, number, and motion.

Principle of sufficient reason: The principle, associated with the German philosopher Gottfried Wilhelm Leibniz (1646–1716), that nothing could be some particular way without there being a reason that it is that way.

Pro et contra (Latin): For and against.

Problem of evil: The challenge of reconciling the existence of a perfectly omniscient, omnipotent, and omnibenevolent deity with the manifest presence of evil in the world.

Problem of other minds: The problem of providing justification for the belief that other beings are conscious, with minds much like one's own.

Property: See *object/property*.

Proposition: The content of a declarative sentence, that which the sentence expresses. *Snow is white* (in

English) expresses the same proposition as *la nieve es blanca* (in Spanish).

Propositional attitude: A cognitive relation that holds between a subject and a proposition. S holds a *propositional attitude* (toward P) if, for example, S believes that P, or desires that P, or hopes that P, or knows that P. See also *S*, *P*.

QED. (Latin): Thus it has been proved. Abbreviation for the Latin phrase *quod erat demonstrandum* ("which was to be demonstrated.")

Qua (Latin): In the capacity or role of; as.

Quale: See *qualia*.

Qualia: The introspectively accessible felt qualities that are associated with an experience, such as the feeling of a pain or the smell of a rose. The singular of *qualia* is *quale*.

Qualitative identity: See *identity, numerical/qualitative*.

Rationalism: See *empiricism/rationalism*.

Reductio ad absurdum (Latin for "reduction to absurdity"): A mode of reasoning that involves validly deriving a contradiction from a set of premises, thereby showing that at least one of the set's members must be rejected.

Referent: What a term refers to. The referent of "Plato" is the Greek philosopher Plato; the referent of "the largest moon of Jupiter" is Ganymede.

Rerum natura (Latin): The nature of things.

Rigid designator: A term that picks out the same entity in all possible worlds where that entity exists and does not pick out any other entity in possible worlds where it does not.

S: Often used to stand for the subject of a schematic proposition: as in "S realizes that there are two options: A and B." See also "*P*."

Secondary quality: See *primary/secondary quality*.

Ship of Theseus: An example from ancient Greek philosophy that is used to demonstrate certain puzzles about diachronic identity. Suppose there is a ship (S1) originally built from planks P1–P52, arranged according to blueprint B. Over the course of a year, the ship remains on the dock, where one plank is removed each week and replaced by a qualitatively identical plank, so that at the end of the year, what remains on the dock is a ship (S2) composed of planks P53–P104, arranged according to blueprint B. Some time later, at a different location, a ship (S3) is assembled according to blueprint B from the discarded planks P1–P52. With which of the later ships is S1 (diachronically numerically) identical: S2, S3, neither, or both? See also *identity numerical/qualitative* and *identity diachronic/synchronic*.

Simpliciter (Latin): Without qualification.

Sound/valid/entail: A deductive argument is *valid* if the premises *entail* the conclusion, so that it is not possible for the argument's premises to be true while the argument's conclusion is false; a deductive argument is *sound* if it is valid and all its premises are true. An argument that is not valid is *invalid*; an argument that is not sound is *unsound*. All invalid arguments are unsound, but not all unsound arguments are invalid.

State of nature: The hypothetical circumstance faced by humanity prior to the establishment of civil society or the political state.

Subsistence: A term associated with the Austrian philosopher Alexius Meinong (1853–1920) to describe an analogue to existence for abstract entities; whereas concrete entities (such as table, turtles) *exist*, abstract entities (such as the number two, Santa Claus) merely *subsist*.

Substratum: A characterless substance that supposedly supports the attributes of reality.

Sufficient: See *necessary/sufficient*.

Supervene: Properties of type A *supervene* on properties of type B iff any two entities that share all their B properties must also share all their A properties. If A properties supervene on B properties, it is not possible for an entity to change its A properties without changing its B properties (although the converse need not hold.) So, for example, it is not possible to change an image in a newspaper without changing the arrangement of the pixels that compose it; the image *supervenes* on its pixels.

Sufficient: See *necessary/sufficient*.

Synthetic: See *analytic/synthetic*.

Tautology: A proposition that is true by virtue of its form alone; a true but empty claim. See also *contradiction*.

Time-lag argument: An argument that suggests that direct perception is impossible, since by the time the light emitted from an object reaches the eye, the object may have changed or ceased to exist.

Top-down processing: See *bottom-up/top-down processing*.

Tour de force (French): An exceptionally impressive performance.

Truth-tracking: An expression used by philosopher Robert Nozick (1938–2002). S's belief that P is *truth tracking* if the following two conditions hold: (a) if it were false that *P*, S would not believe that P, and (b) if it were true that *P*, S would believe that P. See also *S, P.*

Unsound: See *sound/valid/entail*.

Utilitarianism: See *consequentialism/utilitarianism*.

Utilitarianism act/rule or *extreme/restricted*: See *extreme/restricted utilitarianism*.

Valid: See *sound/valid/entail*.

Virtue ethics: An ethical view that gives a central role to the idea of virtuous character. The most famous advocate of virtue ethics is Aristotle (384–322 BCE). Virtue ethics is often contrasted with consequentialism and deontology. See also *consequentialism, deontology*.

Vis-à-vis (French): In relation to, compared with.

Viz (contraction of the Latin term *videlicet*): Namely, that is.

Zombie: In philosophical usage, a *zombie* is a being that is (a) molecule for molecule identical to a (conscious) human being, but that (b) lacks conscious experience.

NOTES

In preparing this glossary, we were helped by consulting the following works: Simon Blackburn, *The Oxford Dictionary of Philosophy* (New York: Oxford University Press, 1996); John Perry and Michael Bratman, "Glossary of Philosophical Terms," in *Introduction to Philosophy: Third Edition* (New York: Oxford University Press, 1999); Louis Pojman, "Glossary," in *Introduction to Philosophy*, 3rd ed. (New York: Oxford University Press, 2004); James Pryor, "Philosophical Terms and Methods" at http://www.jimpryor.net/teaching/vocab/glossary.html; *The American Heritage Dictionary of the English Language*, 4th ed. (Boston: Houghton Mifflin, 2000); *The Stanford Encyclopedia of Philosophy* at http://plato.stanford.edu; and *Philosophy Compass* at http://www.blackwell-compass.com/subject/philosophy.

RESOURCES

Students who are interested in philosophy are fortunate that an outstanding collection of reference materials are available to those who want to learn more about the subject.

Several encyclopedias can be found online, including the highly reliable *Stanford Encyclopedia of Philosophy* (http://plato.stanford.edu), as well as the generally reliable *Internet Encyclopedia of Philosophy* (http://www.utm.edu/research/iep). Many universities also have online access to the excellent ten-volume *Routledge Encyclopedia of Philosophy*, which can also be found in book form in most university libraries.

Two excellent single-volume encyclopedias of philosophy are Robert Audi, ed., *The Cambridge Dictionary of Philosophy* 2nd ed. (New York: Cambridge University Press, 1999); and Edward Craig, ed., *The Shorter Routledge Encyclopedia of Philosophy* (New York: Routledge, 2005).

A superb compact dictionary of philosophy is Simon Blackburn's *Oxford Dictionary of Philosophy.*

Students who are looking for more in-depth discussions of particular subfields may turn to the relevant volume in one of the following series: Blackwell *Companions to Philosophy*; Blackwell *Contemporary Debates in Philosophy*; Oxford *Companions to Philosophy*; Oxford *Handbooks in Philosophy*; Routledge *Companions to Philosophy*.

A number of excellent online philosophical web sites exist. Students might begin with those of Jim Pryor (http://www.jimpryor.net/teaching/index.html) or David Chalmers (http://consc.net/resources.html); each includes a wide range of resources, as well as links to numerous other sources.

CPSIA information can be obtained at www.ICGtesting.com
Printed in the USA
BVOW020914260612

293587BV00001BA/4/P